# SOCIAL CHANGE: ,

## Explorations, Diagnoses, and Conjectures

*Edited by*

# George K. Zollschan and Walter Hirsch

*With an Introduction by*
## DON MARTINDALE

Schenkman Publishing Company

A Halsted Press Book

JOHN WILEY & SONS
New York — London — Sidney — Toronto

LIBRARY OF CONGRESS CATALOGING IN PUBLICATION DATA
MAIN ENTRY UNDER TITLE:

SOCIAL CHANGE.

INCLUDES INDEX.
1. SOCIAL CHANGE — ADDRESSES, ESSAYS, LECTURES.
I. ZOLLSCHAN, GEORGE K.   II. HIRSCH, WALTER, 1919–
HM101.S6917          301.24          75-8736
ISBN 0-470-98408-2
ISBN 0-470-98409-0 pbk.

# SOCIAL CHANGE:

## Explorations, Diagnoses, and Conjectures

# Contents

v

*Don Martindale*

# INTRODUCTION

Like all special sciences, Sociology has for its distinctive subject matter a limited set of empirical events between which, it assumes, are closer relations than between these events and others outside the set. The distinctive subject matter of Sociology is comprised of interhuman behavior. The object of sociological theory is to explain how the various forms in which it is distributed arise in the first place and, thereafter, are either maintained or transformed. Though one of the oldest divisions of sociological study is between social structure, the characteristics of social systems when maintained at a more or less steady state, and social change, the formation and destruction of social systems, in the long run the problems of structure and change are inseparable.

In view of this, it was surely an astonishing phenomenon in the period following World War II, when American Sociology had attained a position of unparalleled authority in the world and at a time when everyone was staggered by the dizzy accelerating pace of change, to learn that sociology's theory of change was in trouble.

Units of government and the foundations have poured millions into sociological research. A generation of sociological entrepreneurs had grown up, adept at soliciting funds, establishing institutes for research, organizing little bureaucracies of secretaries and assistants and distributing patronage. New professional recognition had been forthcoming as government, industry, and a variety of other organizations, including large hospitals, had added sociologists to their staffs. Virtually new areas had developed in sociology itself as it sent out colonizing movements into neighboring disciplines (educational sociology, the sociology of health, the sociology of mental health, industrial sociology, and political sociology). And from the midst of all these dramatic transformations in sociology has come the admission that *its theory of social change is the weakest branch of sociological theory.*

This confession by some of the most highly placed persons in American sociology has usually been accompanied by the assurance that sociology's lack of an adequate theory of change is either of no great importance or merely a temporary state of affairs. One cannot but wonder whether this confession and smug reassurance proceed from breath-taking *naiveté* or from an unctuous philistinism.

For man is a bird of passage. To be sure, at times he rides with his head tucked under his wing, asleep on the lifting waves, and on occasion he feeds along the eroding shores of time, stopping to rest on a gray rock or a marine-worm-weakened, weathered piling. But surely he is most fully himself when he lifts his wings and speeds along the buffeting winds of change between the revolving seasons of his spinning-top world as it whirls about its dying star.

To confess that sociology — which was born as a science of interhuman behavior — can account for structure but not for change is like saying that one can account for a bird at rest, but not for a bird in flight. A review of the major substantive issues of contemporary sociology and the major theories may help to clarify some of the reasons why sociology, which arose as a science of social motion, had largely failed in its original intent. It may also assist in evaluating some of the attempts in the present symposium to restore it once more to the status of a science of motion.

## The Major Substantive Issues of Contemporary Sociology

As a science, sociology attempts to discover the laws of interhuman behavior. The explanations that compose its theories may be distinguished in terms of the aspect or phase of interhuman behavior to which they are addressed. The most elementary units into which interhuman behavior can be analyzed are single social acts. Since every social act necessarily involves more than a single person, one can observe the arrangement that obtains between the persons involved and carry out an analysis of social action in terms of social relations. One can, to be sure, analyze social actions into their component parts, but when one does, his analysis has moved outside the proper field of sociology into psychology or physiology or biology. This may be valuable, and one may return with new tools to the analysis of social actions and their formation into patterns of varying complexity — re-entering the field of sociology once more.

Social actions are always the behavior of individuals. A human individual entering interaction with others must be calculable and predictable within limits by others, or the interaction becomes impossible. If an individual desires values which he can only obtain in interaction, he must meet the expectations of others. Whether or not they wish it, thus, the parties to human interaction are implicated in a process of reconstructing themselves. It is not possible to create a special system of social life without also creating the personalities that make it possible. A special branch of social theory is concerned with social persons.

At times, considerable advantage may accrue to the parties in a social arrangement if the social actions of a limited number of individuals are stabilized into a reciprocal pattern of some permanence. They then form groups. The members of a group usually symbolize the pattern in which they are participants, sufficiently apart from themselves to permit individuals to leave or join without changing the pattern in any essentials. Conceived in abstraction from any particular group, the pattern is a group institution. The theory of groups and institutions is also one of the basic branches of sociological theory.

Individuals act in numerous groups. The personalities they develop for one may not be completely adequate for another. Moreover, the actions engaged in may partially conflict from group to group. The formation of social persons and social groups thus undergoes a secondary process of reconstruction which adapts them to the requirements of a more or less consistent total way of life. Systems of social behavior sufficiently comprehensive to carry a given plurality of persons through a normal year and a normal lifetime of any given member become a community. The theory of communities is also a basic subject matter of sociology.

Finally, learned modes (cultural forms) play a major role in every aspect of interhuman behavior. Moreover, over and beyond the cultural forms directly instrumental to social arrangements of all types, the creation and synthesis of cultural forms may go on. There is considerable value in the examination of culture in its own right and not simply incidentally to the study of various aspects of social behavior.

From the standpoint of the substantial matters that it attempts to explain, the various branches of sociological theory are:

### The Branches of Sociological Theory

| Branch | Character |
| --- | --- |
| Theory of social action and social relations | Analysis of the nature, elements, types, and operations of social actions |
| Theory of social persons | Analysis of the nature, component parts, types, and operations of social persons |

| Theory of social groups and institutions | Analysis of the formation and destruction of groups and institutions from social actions and social relations |
|---|---|
| Theory of communities | Analysis of the reorganization of groups and institutions into total ways of life |
| Theory of culture | Analysis of the development of cultural forms within and apart from social structures. Study of the formation of styles and civilizations |

Social change can have no other subject matter than the formation and destruction of interhuman arrangements of these various kinds. The individual chapters in the symposium here presented are usually confined to one or a few of the branches of theory outlined above. Together they provide, as I shall attempt to show, a rather complete conspectus of these various theoretical branches.

### Major Points of View in Contemporary Sociology

In addition to the branches of subject matter with which it is concerned, sociology offers a number of points of view (theories) of its subject matter. These theoretical orientations differ according to the aspects of social life taken to be fundamental and the kinds of regularities hypothesized among the various aspects of social life.

It is possible to construct a general paradigm of current theoretical orientations on the basis of the aspect of social interaction thought to be most fundamental. From this standpoint the current schools of theory break down into two broad types: holistic and elementaristic. Holistic theories assume that the primary human social reality is some more or less comprehensive, organically unified system. There are some differences among holistic theories, depending on their special conceptions of this organic whole. However, the earmark of theories of sociological "holism" is that some type of equilibrium theory is central to their explanations of social life.

By contrast to types of sociological *holism, elementaristic* theories of social life take the various complex patterns of social life to be secondary and derivative. The essential social reality is traced to social actions or social persons or some properties of either. Equilibrium states in the complex byproducts of individual behavior are, from this perspective, "freaks" of social life. At the same time, depending upon the conception of the ultimate unit or atom of social life, different kinds of sociological elementarism are possible.

From the standpoint of their basic suppositions about the character of social life, the major contemporary types of sociological theory are as follows:

### Major Types of Sociological Theory

| General Type | Major Examples | Unit of Social Life Assumed to be Basic |
|---|---|---|
| Holistic Theories | Positivistic and pure organicism | Society and/or culture conceived as an organismic unity |
| | Functionalism and neo-functionalism | Total social systems conceived as organismic units |
| | Catholic or neo-Thomist sociology | The Church conceived as a spiritual unity |
| | Marxian and neo-Marxian conflict theory | Society composed of classes or conflict groups |
| Elementaristic Theories | Social behaviorism, symbolic interactionism, pluralism, existentialism | Social action or some aspects of it |
| | Formalism | Social forms |
| | Individualistic forms of conflict theory | Interests |
| | Phenomenology, existentialism | Essences and types |

Since social and cultural change is concerned with the formation and destruction of interhuman arrangements, any given approach is inevitably affected by the theoretical perspective (be it consciously or unconsciously held) of the writer. Our outline of the various types of sociological theory can serve to identify the theoretical perspectives of the particular writer. These theoretical perspectives can help to account both for what he assumes to be the basic subject matter for a study of social change and how he handles it.

### Some Notes on the Contemporary Crisis in the Theory of Social Change

The two paradigms sketched above on the branches and types of sociological theory and a few historical observations make it possible to locate the source of the crisis in the theory of social change which provided the basic rationale for the present symposium.

The special sociological theories did not emerge all at once. Throughout the nineteenth century sociology was dominated by forms of *positivistic organicism*, considering society as an organic unity and proposing to apply to the analysis of society the positive methods of empirical science. The sub-parts of society were considered in terms of the organs of biological forms. The smallest sub-part, the family, was not analyzed by the positivistic organicists as either social actions or social persons.

Both social structure and social change were analyzed in terms of the predominance of the whole over the parts and the functional relation of parts within the whole. Social structure consisted of the interrelation of parts and whole.

The positivistic organicists were willing to admit that human society was affected by biological factors on the one hand, and environmental factors on the other. However, in its most fundamental nature society was considered an organism which maintained itself in the face of such external factors. The fundamental reasons for what happened to society arose from within it. Evolution was the one notion which permitted positivistic organicism to budget the concept of change in its scheme. If the whole of society was seen as evolving toward ever higher ends, the notion of organicity was preserved while accounting for change in terms of society itself.

Once the positivistic organicists had arrived at this comforting view of social change, they felt free to tear historical and ethnographic materials out of their various contexts and fit them to prefabricated conceptions of progress-evolution. However, such arbitrary procedure permitted so many different and contradictory constructions that the entire enterprise was called into question.

The only major theoretical competitor to positivistic organicism in the nineteenth century was the collectivistic form of conflict theory. As illustrated by Marxism, the idea of a large-scale organic unit moving toward a state of equilibrium also dominated its notion of society. The primary units of social life, however, were not institutions but militantly organized classes. The mechanism of social change was found in class struggle. Class conflicts were resolved by the establishment of ever more comprehensive equilibrium states. The concepts of organicity, equilibrium, and progress-evolutionism were retained by Marxism, which dreamed of a classless society as the utopian fulfillment of history.

However, the multiplication of alternative versions of social evolutionism by the conflict theorists only made the babble of voices more confusing. When exacting standards were applied to social data, the arbitrary procedure of tearing social facts out of context and arranging them into prefabricated patterns became untenable. The failure to establish a mechanism that could adequately account for social evolution (comparable to the genetic changes in biological organisms) destroyed the last vestige of plausibility in the social evolutionary schemes. The entire theory began to collapse, and with it many of sociology's ties with history and ethnology.

Into the vacuum created by the decline of the progress-evolution theory of social change moved the culture lag theory of social change on the one hand, and various cyclical theories of culture on the other. The culture lag theory reconstructed the progress-evolution formula in a disguised and limited form by drawing a distinction between material and non-material culture. Material culture, in turn, was largely identified with technology and viewed as progressive, though usually prevented from bringing about the rapid evolution of society as a whole only by the lag between it and non-material culture.

Upon analysis, the distinction between material and non-material culture broke down. However, so strong was the felt need for the progress-evolution formula that this conception of social change persisted despite the many unanswered criticisms repeatedly made against it.

For the rest, in the period following World War I a series of holistic and cyclical theories of culture appeared. The most famous of these were advanced by Oswald Spengler, Arnold Toynbee, and Pitirim Sorokin. Unfortunately, the evidence for the organicity of culture and for the particular cultural integrations and sequences (cycles) was often as arbitrary as the evidence for the various progress-evolution theories. (The chapter by Schneider and the answer by Sorokin bring this discussion up to date.)

Contemporary functionalist theory in modified manner habilitated the same basic suppositions as positivistic organicism. Step by step these theoretical suppositions have led functionalism down the same road once traveled by its great predecessor. As functionalism runs its triumphant course in the post-World War II period, reconstructing by degrees the same general theory of social structure as its predecessor, difficulty has begun to appear.

What at first was reported as a minor and temporary flaw began increasingly to assume the properties of a major change. Functionalism was having trouble with its theory of social change. Functionalist suppositions were, in short, driving their adherents toward a progress-evolution formula such as had ended so disastrously earlier. Understandably, there was much reluctance to take this step. Nevertheless, so powerful is the impetus in this direction that a minor revival of social evolutionary theory in sociology has been occurring in the 1960's. (The chapter by Boskoff in this volume is the latest stage in this development.)

If one applies the paradigm of theory types above to the crisis in the theory of social change, it immediately becomes evident that this crisis is bound up with the fate of a limited number of the types of sociological theories, primarily with holistic types, and especially positivistic organicism in the past and functionalism in the present. It is also evident that the analysis of social change from the standpoint of the various atomistic theories is relatively unexplored.

The present symposium vigorously carries forward the exploration of the problems of social and cultural change from a number of holistic and elementaristic positions. From the point of view of holistic theories, the crux of change lies in the larger social configurations: communities, societies, and civilizations. From the point of view of elementaristic theories, change is a problem for social arrangements of every level of complexity. In opening its doors to discussion by theorists of both types, this symposium treats social forms of every level of complexity from social actions to high-order socio-cultural syntheses.

## Some Notes on the Organization and Content of the Present Volume

The editors have divided the volume into sections containing related materials and have written insightful introductions to each section. Nevertheless there is some value in reviewing the volume as a whole from the standpoint of the two paradigms sketched above as a way of isolating a number of integrating themes.

### Section One

Aptly titled "General Perspectives on Social Change," Section One contains three essays of very different character and quality, but which share the property of supplying points of view from which the problems of social and cultural change can be approached.

The delightful essay by Kenneth Boulding which opens the symposium with its dancing metaphors and flashing wit identifies what he believes to be the elements of social interaction essential for the study of social change (or for that matter, social structure). These are images, thresholds, and systems. Boulding's *images* (meanings, ideas, symbols) are the counterpart of what Max Weber describes as the "meaningful components of social action," Robert MacIver as "the dynamic assessments of social situations," and Znaniecki as "the humanistic component" of society. In making images a kind of fundamental unit in explaining inter-human behavior, Boulding joins the ranks of the social behaviorists. However, he quickly places alongside images "thresholds" and "systems" organismically conceived as basic elements which must be taken into account — ideas which are domesticated in functionalist theory. Boulding's essay thus proposes to bridge the social behaviorist and functionalist perspectives.

Like Boulding's essay, Sosensky's has potential general relevance for sociology and does not apply alone to its theory of change. Sosensky carries out an epistemological critique of concept formation in sociology on the basis of a distinction between metaphorical and analogical statements. In his view, metaphorical statements are qualitative assertions of the existence of an identity where a relation cannot yet be specified. Sosensky's critique leads to the melancholy conclusion that nearly all of the most important theories of society are metaphorical and as such not only pre-scientific but pre-logical. While Sosensky applies his critique to the change theories of Talcott Parsons and Ralf Dahrendorf, his analysis presumably applies generally to sociology as a whole.

The third essay on "The Structure of Societal Revolutions" by C. P. Wolf is a global approach to the entire development of human society, conceiving of "what happened in history" as a series of revolutionary reorderings of social relations in all areas followed by structural differentiation and reintegration after each revolutionary upset. The essay has affinities with the works of the founders of sociology and with their counterparts (such as Talcott Parsons) in the present.

### Sections Two and Three

Section Two, "Further Steps in the Theory of Institutionalization" and Three, "Metamorphoses in the Theory of Institutionalization" by Zollschan and his associates constitute much more than an examination of institutions proper (that is the stabilization of the solutions to interpersonal problems); they constitute the outline of *an entirely new system of sociology*. These two sections comprise, in effect, a book within the book.

Zollschan and his associates have developed a distinctive form of elementaristic social theory (drawing upon, but transforming, various components of symbolic interactionism, Weber's form of social behaviorism, Freud's theory of individual psychology and aspects of ethnomethodology, existentialism, and phenomenology). In a manner reminiscent of the role of problematic situations in John Dewey's form of pragmatism, exigencies are made central to this system of theory. It is not inappropriate to label it *Exigentialism*.

Exigencies, it is argued, provide the occasions for all innovations in interpersonal relations. The human response to an exigency is a two-phase process: Articulation and Activation. Conceived as the development of ideas in response to exigencies, Articulation is identified with Boulding's concept of the Image. It is said to possess three coordinates: Salience, Justifiability and Specificity. Activation is conceived as the implementation of the ideas cast up in the course of the Articulating phase of the response to an exigency. Institutionalization is the resultant crystallization of interpersonal processes into social relations and social structure, together with the establishment of mutually understood systems of meaning or culture.

In the chapter, "Goal Formation as the Key for Explaining Conduct and Society: A Discussion of Some Old 'Suggestions' for a Theory of Institutionalization," Michael A. Overington and George K. Zollschan present the basic framework of Exigential theory together with an interesting account of the manner in which various of its ingredients were brought together in Zollschan's biography. The chapter by T.

Dunbar Moodie, "Social Order as Social Change: Towards a Dynamic Conception of Social Order," explores with unusual lucidity some of the limitations in Parsons's theory of social action during the first phase of his theoretical development and indicates the manner in which they can be corrected by Exigential theory. Also Moodie indicates some of the lines along which Exigentialism can be generalized into a total system of theory.

The Chapter by George Zollschan and Walter Friedman, "Leadership and Social Change: An Intelligent Child's Garden of Raspberries, with a Bestiary, and a Zoo, and an Expulsion" moves beyond the problems of institutionalization to an important division of the theory of social persons, the problem of leadership. An interesting typology of leadership is advanced in terms of the various subdimensions of the two-phase response to exigencies: Articulation and Activation.

| Response | Pure type of Leader |
|---|---|
| Articulation | |
| Salience | The Martyr, Idol, Sensitizer |
| Justification | The Inhibitor, Seducer |
| Specification | The Formulator |
| Activation | |
| Valience | The Resource Supplier, Strategist |
| Application | The Expert, Innovator, Magician |
| Legitimation | The Lawgiver, Ideologue, Apologist, Propagandist |

The chapter by George Zollschan and Robert Brym, "A Transconceptualization of Concepts in Sociology of Knowledge and Sociology of Science," is a general review of the sociology of knowledge together with proposals for a new attack on its problems from the standpoint of Exigential theory. The chapter by James Dow "The Potential of a Mathematical Model of Social Change" is an attempt to translate Exigential theory into formal mathematical language.

While the chapters in Section Two move far outside the theory of institutionalization (at least as this is narrowly conceived), those of Section Three move even further afield. The chapter by George Zollschan, "Concerning the Fourfold Root of the 'Principle of Sufficient Reason' in Sociological Explanation," is a new attack on the division of sociological theories. In terms of the nature of the social agent (the individual or the collective) and the voluntarism of the agent (active or passive) a fourfold classification is arrived at.

| | | Nature of Social Agent | |
|---|---|---|---|
| | | Individual | Collective |
| Voluntarism of Social Agent | Pro-active | Proactive Individualism | Proactive Collectivism |
| | Reactive | Reactive Individualism | Reactive Collectivism |

Exigentialism is identified as a form of Proactive Individualism. The chapter by George Zollschan and Michael A. Overington on "Reasons for Conduct and the Conduct of Reason: The Eightfold Route to Motivational Ascription" is a general review of the problem of motivation in recent sociology and psychology together with an attempt to pull whatever the authors find valuable in it into the framework of Exigential theory. The chapter, "A Lexicon of Motive, Action, and Society: Prototractatus Teleosociologicus," by George Zollschan outlines, in a logically systematic manner, the major concepts and propositions of Exigential theory as they exist at the present time.

### Section Four

In contrast to the previous sections, Section Four of the symposium approaches the problems of change from a holistic point of view. The two recent dominant forms of holism, Structure-Functionalism and Conflict Theory (of which Marxism is the most vigorous subform) are ably represented in the essays by Alvin Boskoff, "Functional Analysis as a Source of a Theoretical Repertory and Research Tasks in the Study of Social Change," and David Lockwood, "Social Integration and System Integration." Neither thinker, however, presents a doctrinaire version of the position he develops. Boskoff undertakes to modify the prevailing functionalist position in a manner which would strengthen its ability to account for change, and Lockwood calls attention to some basic similarities between functionalism and Marxism, raises critical objections in current change theories of each and develops ways in which he feels the Conflict point of view can be made more adequate.

H. David Kirk in, "Toward a Taxonomy of Social Discontinuities," modifies the systems approach to change in quite a different manner from either Boskoff or Lockwood. Noting that disturbances of various sorts are universal to social systems, he proposes that strain and conflict are better viewed as normal rather than abnormal. Kirk advances the notion of "role handicap" as a critical point were the effect of past changes become manifest in interpersonal relations and which, in turn, represent tension points where new changes may be initiated. Then moving beyond the problem of role handicap to the problem of individual identity on the one hand and to the system on the other, Kirk develops a general typology of social discontinuities of either a symbolic or instrumental type which may be manifest at the level of the self (identity), the role, or the system.

In the concluding essay in Section Four, "Mathematical Models of Social Change" James M. Beshers explores some of the possibilities of formalizing the underlying assumptions of the various classical theories of change and formulating them mathematically, with the ultimate objective of achieving full theoretical clarity with respect to the ideas involved and ascertaining the empirical steps necessary for their verification. At the present stage of analysis, his mathematical models are based on simplifying assumptions that give them primarily illustrative significance.

## Section Five

In contrast to the essays in Section Four, those in Section Five are elementaristic. In one way or other all assign primacy to the individual, his ideas and actions — treating social structure as a crude euphemism for interpersonal strategies. The essays in this section have a family resemblance to those in Sections Two and Three.

In "Idea systems in the Individual and in Society," Donald J. Levinson takes up the problem posed by Boulding in his concept of the image and by Zollschan in his concept of Activation, of exploring the role of ideas and ideologies in the dynamics of those interpersonal strategies we describe as social systems. Levinson proposes to bring together the concepts of ideology, personality and social structure to explain the interrelated components of autocracy and democracy.

Benjamin Zablocki's "The Use of Crisis as a Mechanism of Social Control" looks at the situations which Zollschan described as exigencies as representing ratios of risk and hope which may not only have the function of consolidating interpersonal strategies, but which may be systematically exploited by persons in positions of authority for consolidating their expropriation of power.

Operating within a symbolic interactionist framework Leon Warshay, in "Breadth of Perspective, Social Type and Dialectics of Change," explores some of the relationships between social circumstances which create persons of broad or narrow perspective and which place individuals in strategic positions to influence the course of events. He calls attention to the ironic fact that the very conditions which create broad perspectives often isolate the individual from positions to exercise direct influence on events. Only in severe crises do persons with broad perspective tend to be called to leadership roles, when it is often too late.

In "The Acceptance and Rejection of Change," H. G. Barnett treats the process by which an innovation is accepted as moving through contact and assimilation to projection and in which a special role is played by values. Barnett's essay illustrates the Pluralistic Behavioral point of view which was particularly well adapted to study of the problems of diffusion.

In the essay that concludes the section "The Experience of Change: Tempo and Stress," Robert and Jeanette Lauer, like Warshay, take a symbolic interactionist perspective. Change, the Lauers urge, inevitably brings stress, undermining a sense of well being and forcing the individual to respond by adaptation, escapism or activism. Armed with this typology of possible responses, the Lauers utilize the Jacksonian era of American history as a case in point of a period characterized by a high level of stress and hence as displaying social manifestations of all three sorts.

## Section Six

The section "Broad Historical Perspectives" raises the question of change in a context of specific historical developments in the manner of the classical sociologists. The early 19th century sociologists were socio-cultural holists who saw their mission as the establishment of the laws of history. Toward the end of the century dissident elementaristic positions were elaborated which rested on the assumption that though human social life manifests law-like regularities, the drift and thrust of history are unique. However, as illustrated by Max Weber, they retained an interest in history.

Sorokin was a classical type socio-cultural holist who conceived human history as the dialectical unfolding of man's vision of meaning and value. Sorokin differed from his classical counterparts primarily in dropping an evolutionary for a cyclical theory of change, characterized by three major civilizational forms — Ideate, Idealistic, and Sensate — which follow one another inevitably and without end. Sorokin brought the abundant recourses of his rhetoric to the denunciation of the Sensate sewers of contemporary civilization. While Louis Schneider brings various features of Sorokin's method and theory under critical review and while Sorokin replied, there seems little doubt that both men shared the same general perspective.

The other two essays in this section are elementaristic in point of view though they are directed to particular historical developments. My essay on "The Roles of Humanism and Scientism in the Evolution of Sociology" rests on the assumption that the development of early sociology was unique to Western man's efforts at self understanding. The forms assumed by sociology were determined by (1) the tools for understanding (which arose and were perfected in special social contexts) and (2) the nature of the communities which provided both the context for and subject matter of sociological understanding. It is useful to compare this essay with Zollschan's, chapter 9.

The essay on "Economic Development and Change in Social Values and Thought Patterns," by Bert F. Hoselitz, resumes a type of analysis of historical societies similar to that initiated by Max Weber. In his studies of the influence of the economic ethic of the world religions on economic conduct in the various world areas, Weber had attempted to assess the role of religion in the unique appearance of intact capitalism in the West. Hoselitz proposes to reopen the inquiry into the relation between everyday ethics and economic development on the basis of a revision of Weber's typology of traditionalistic and rational action by the addition of F. S. C. Northrop's distinction between aesthetic mentality, thought to be typical of the Orient, and analytic mentality, thought to be typical of the Occident.

## Section Seven

In "Cultural Change, Cultural Contact and Social Movements," an interesting variety of less comprehensive (than in the previous section) social changes are reviewed and analyzed: a social movement; the evolution of a utopian community type; the response of officials in an underdeveloped country trapped in the ambiguous area of overlap between nativist and British colonial administrations; the development of transnational institutions which may potentially be building the foundations for a world community.

In "Feminism and Social Change; A Case Study of a Social Movement," J. A. Banks and Olive Banks studied the English feminist movement, seeking to identify both social and extrasocial (i.e. demographic) factors which placed strains on women's traditional situation, laying the foundation for movements to resolve their tensions. Neither Marxist nor functionalistic theories were found adequate to the explanation of peculiarities of the feminist movement, a finding which suggests that the theory of social movements is in need of serious review.

In his study of structural transformations that have been occurring in the kibbutz, Erik Cohen (in part on the basis of theories of Yonina Talmon-Garber) had recourse to Ferdinand Toennies's typology of Gemeinschaft-Gesellschaft, modified somewhat by the addition of Schmalenbach's concept of the Bund. With some possible variations along the way, it was found that utopian kibbutzim began their lives as Bunds (small ideologically intense, personalized communities) tending to traditionalize into Communes (similar to Toennies's Gemeinschaften) and eventually to rationalize and industrialize into Associations (similar to Toennies's Gesellschaften).

In "Conflict and Change in a Northern Nigerian Emirate," Ronald Cohen tested a series of hypotheses originally advanced by A. B. Frank to account for responses to conflicting standards on the part of Russian industrial workers to the behavior of native officials in Nigeria. These officials found themselves in ambiguous conflict situations between the nativist and British Colonial administrations; these situations were also characterized by an inconsistent enforcement of the rules. Such conflict situations were found to elict an opportunistic flexibility, with individuals exploiting their personal resources to develop a variety of expedients to circumvent predicaments arising from conflicting requirements. Such individuals, it is suggested, have the potential for evolving into effective agents of change.

In "Transnational Mechanisms for Social Change," William Evan examines the possibility that international professional associations and international corporations may be quietly creating the social foundation for the eventual appearance of an international community.

### Section Eight

The section on "The Dynamics of Organizations, Professions, and Foundations" is devoted to the formation and transformation of types of groups and institutions that are of especial significance for complex societies: large-scale organizations, professions, and philanthropic foundations. Though these types of institutions have ancient counterparts, their variety, quantity and increasing predominance in the affairs of some nations of the West are relatively recent.

In "Organizational Change: A Review and Synthesis of the Literature," Philip M. Marcus breaks down the literature on change in large-scale organizations into evolutionary theories, interventionist or planned-phase theories, environmentalist theories (which locate the sources of change in organizations in their surrounding milieus), and competition and conflict theories of change in organization. He proposes a synthesis of organizational theory in which other approaches will be primarily accommodated within the framework of economic models (competition and conflict theories).

In "The Dynamics of Professionalization: The Case of Urban Planning" Harry Gold explores the forces for and obstacles to professionalization in the relatively new category-type (characterized by a fairly broad spectrum of occupational skills, rather than a narrow technical specialization) of occupation represented by urban planning. Urban planners find their professional aspirations circumscribed by the power of older, established professions on the one hand and by the extensive growth of large-scale organizations on the other. The essay opens new perspectives on the problem of professionalization.

In "Risk Capital Philanthropy: The Ideological Defense," Richard Colvard examines the attempts to legitimize and increase the autonomy of philanthropic foundations which have developed in rich profusion in the twentieth century. Established as tax shelters for the super-rich and as self-perpetuating bodies for the conduct of scientific research and educational and social reform, the foundations have tried to walk the narrow line between non-controversial and genuinely innovating activities (with potentially revolutionary implications). In the process, Colvard suggests, they are tending to carry out the type of "creative destruction" on which the progress of both capitalism and science have depended.

### Section Nine

In the final section, "Diagnoses of our Time," attention is directed to the countercultural revolt of the late 1960s, to the tensions in contemporary nationalism, and to the role of science and scientists in contemporary affairs.

In "Sorokin's Theories of Cultural Change; Implications for the Future of the Counterculture," Janet Poppendieck summarizes Sorokin's theory of socio-cultural supersystems and applies its resources to the countercultural movement. She explores the possibility that the counter-cultural revolts mark the close of the Sensate phase of Western Civilization and the opening of what Sorokin in his later works increasingly described as an Integralist Society and Culture.

The essay on "The Crisis of Nationalism" is based on the assumption that the nation is the dominant type of community of contemporary man and, as such, central to his problems and his hopes. As a community the nation is an open strategy of collective life, not a closed system. It is subject to transformation both from inner- and extra-community forces. The essay undertakes to identify a number of tensions which appear to be responsible for deep going transformations in the nation-state.

The final essay by Walter Hirsch, "Knowledge, Power and Social Change: The Rule of American Scientists," accepts the proposition that science is the single most potent force for change in the contemporary world. It explores the extent to which the scientist, by virtue of the importance of his activity, is in a position to exercise decisive control over the direction of contemporary affairs. Without in any way detracting from the significance of science, Hirsch details reason for skepticism about the possibility of a hegemony of scientists. Of the three primary spheres of scientific activity, government, business and the university, in two (government and business) scientists have always been forced to respond to extra-scientific pressures. In the third, the universities, which have been the traditional sphere of pure science and most fully under the control of the scientist, new forces have tended to penetrate which weaken the autonomy of the scientist even here. Meanwhile a differentiation and fragmentation of scientific roles has been occurring which creates new divisions in the scientific community. In the ten years since the essay was first written confirming evidence has accumulated of the correctness of Hirsch's prognostications. Meanwhile new evidence of pressures on the scientist's autonomy have emerged which are summarized in a postscript.

### Alternative Uses of the Present Volume

The primary purpose of the present volume is to chart the dimensions of social change. However, since social change, in its most comprehensive sense, covers the formation and destruction of all social and cultural forms, the essays inevitably range over the entire field of sociology. Moreover, since one cannot sensibly talk about something changing without at least a minimum description of the thing changed, the volume contains an inventory of the more or less stabilized interhuman arrangements that are euphemistically called "social structures."

By a simple reordering of the chapters, the present volume can be employed as a primary or supplementary text in courses in social organization or social structure. By social organization is meant the stabilized order that obtains in the day to day operations of a social system; by social structures one means the nuclei of relations that together make up a social organization. For convenience one can divide social structures into: social relations, social persons, institutions (political, economic, domestic, religious, etc.), communities, and cultures. In tabular form the following are various categories of social structure and the chapters in which the particular structure is treated or illustrated in whole or in part.

*Social Structures Treated in the Volume*

| Category | Chapters Where Treated |
|---|---|
| Social Relations | 1, 4, 5, 10, 14, 17, 19 |
| Institutions | |
|    Theory of | 4, 5, 10, 29 |
|    Political | 27 |
|    Economic | 13, 14, 28 |
|    Philanthropic | 31 |
|    Professional | 28, 30, 34 |
|    Domestic | 25 |
| Community | 3, 12, 14, 26, 33 |
| Culture | 3, 7, 9, 23, 32, 34 |

While the present volume offers a spirited set of essays touching every category of social structure and while it offers original contributions to most theoretical perspectives, its most fundamental value lies in its confrontations of the many-sided problems of social change. In the background of its discussions broods the realization that all human arrangements are provisional. In contrast to the confident mood expressed in the concept of the deathless system that dominated so much of sociology in the immediate post-war years, the volume is informed by a sense of transience that has been increasingly characteristic of the field as a whole in the decade since *Explorations in Social Change,* the forerunner of this symposium, appeared. This is quite in accord with the trend in the mood of scientists as a whole for which even the stars are no longer images of immutability, but are perceived as being blasted away from one another at enormous speeds by the giant explosion that created the present universe. From this perspective the events of human society are but evanescent incidents on a ball of cosmic dust that spins around a dying star.

# SECTION ONE

## general perspectives on social change

# Introduction

Conceptions of social change have been of crucial importance in social thought for quite as long as conceptions of social order, which, until very recently, appeared to dominate the field. The decline of social change in sociological discussion was, in a sense, well deserved. "Social dynamics" of the classical type (irrespective of whether it was dominated by Comtean ideas of evolution or by Marxist ideas of conflict) was haunted by the *Laplacean demon*. This endearing sprite, conjured into existence by the incredible success of Newtonian mechanics, personified the seeming omnipotence of the principle of determinancy. His demonic qualities depended in essence upon only one skill, ostensibly quite reasonable and modest — he knew the nature and disposition of all things present. However, since determinancy implied that the future as well as the past were contained in the present, the Laplacean demon was able to predict (and post-dict) the nature and disposition of all things future and past. The world was a four-dimensional clockwork, governed by reversible time and Newtonian mechanics. Given this picture of the world, science strove for omniscience — omniscience attainable through possession by (or of) the Laplacean demon. As most readers of this volume will surely agree, anything the physicists could do, our forebears in the social sciences could do at least as well.

As the principle of determinancy was abandoned by the physicist for better things, however, its parallel abandonment by the imitative sociologists left the latter with only a clockwork mechanism. Sociological theory, particularly in America (the fellows in Europe were still chasing unfashionable demons), became practically synonymous with an emphasis upon the regular and the repetitive — the *normative* and the *functional*. The pendulum was left ticking monotonously and soullessly, but the Laplacean demon had been exorcised from the clock. It is not our intention to bring the demon back into sociological theory. His existence, like that of other demons, was predicated upon unrealistic hopes, fears, and assumptions. He could exist only in a world conceived of as a closed system, and such a world has never existed. Microcosmic simulacra of such closed worlds (as, for example, the solar system viewed exclusively from the point of view of mechanics) are freaks of nature. Except in such freak cases in which prediction (say, of eclipses) and prophecy overlap, the future cannot be prophesied — not even by "scientists".

But we may take comfort. As Sir Karl Popper rightly points out: "The main usefulness of the physical sciences does not lie in the prediction of eclipses; and, similarly, the practical usefulness of the social sciences does not depend on the power to prophesy historical or political developments." Neither, we should like to add, does the theoretical illumination shed by either group of sciences depend upon their prophetic powers. Scientific advances depend upon the formulation and testing of *conditional* predictions. Clarification and elucidation of conditions under which predictions are sensibly made are among the primary tasks of scientific endeavour. If we go about this business with energy, imagination, and with a modicum of success, the nostalgia for closed systems will be given up without any feeling of loss.

Boulding's discussion begins by examining how much a hypothetical Laplacean demon in the social sciences would have to know in order to reduce the complex flow of historical processes to predictability. "The state of affairs on Wednesday," he suggests, "depends not only on the state on Tuesday, but also on the state on Monday." Therefore, the requirement for the demon to know "all" about the state of affairs on Wednesday would not be sufficient in itself. The differential equations governing the real socio-historical system would acquire an entirely new order of complexity — Boulding's demon would be faced by "difference equations of an infinite degree." But these are not the only obstacles in the way of a reduction of human history to something like the celestial mechanics of Newton or Laplace. Undoubtedly, Professor Boulding would agree that some branches of modern physics also have to deal with much more complicated systems. Social systems also have "threshold" characteristics in which outputs are triggered only when inputs of a certain value are achieved. Additionally, social systems differ from mechanical systems in that what Boulding calls "images" produce effects upon the dynamics of society. His concept of "self-justifying images" has found many parallel expressions among social scientists and others. Zollschan and his collaborators in Sections Two and Three put image-building ("articulation," as they call it) in an even more central place in relation to social change. Boulding's requirement for the social sciences, in the light of these difficulties, may appear quite modest by comparison with the aim of general historical dynamics. He wants a "guide to present action and certain reasonably secure expectations . . . a reasonably accurate measure of possible futures that we can choose among." Those of us who are working with him in seeking these ends know that their achievement is a far from trivial task.

A measure of the magnitude of the tasks that lie before the social sciences is given by Sosensky in his highly technical, philosophical examination of the problem of "quality" in relation to certain sociological concepts. Quality, as Sosensky uses the term, is a measure of incompleteness or "primitiveness" of a concept. A term is qualitative "when the necessary and sufficient conditions for the same attribute of different subjects (or items) cannot be specified." If he is correct in his analysis, then the area of inchoate quality, as distinct from formal *specificity*, in sociological theory is appallingly large. Sosensky applies his logical tools to the dissection of Talcott Parsons's and Ralf Dahrendorf's theories. Whereas the editors, themselves sociologists, must confess to a sneaking hope that things are not quite as bad as Sosensky depicts them, a challenge has been issued which no serious social scientist can afford to ignore. This is particularly welcome at a time when *most* outside criticisms of theory in the behavioral sciences have degenerated into ignorant and frivolous attacks by persons who have not given it careful consideration. Certainly, no accusation of carelessness or superficiality could fairly be leveled at Sosensky. The field is ripe for a new *Methodenstreit,* and the issue of *metaphoric* versus *analogic* reasoning Sosensky presents sounds far more promising than the tired old battle between protagonists of *erklären* and *verstehen.*

Boulding and Sosensky are concerned with the methodological issues which need to be faced in dealing with the subject of social change. Wolf's chapter, while also sensitive to methodological issues, provides a panoramic view of "societal revolutions" which he defines as "marked changes in the quantity *and* quality of social relations." This is done from the viewpoint of macro-functional evolutionary theory. Whether his truly heroic effort to subsume the entirety of social changes which have occurred in human history within the framework of a specifiable set of structural parameters is convincing must be left to the reader to decide. Certainly, Wolf goes further towards meeting methodological criticism head-on than any of the other efforts in this *genre* we have encountered in our reading. The macro-functional evolutionist approach constitutes one contemporary attempt to lay the Laplacean demon to rest without relinquishing the assumptions of structural-functionalism in sociological theory.

In the subsequently following two sections of this volume, Zollschan attacks structural-functionalism from a radically individualistic perspective. The tension between these two approaches will probably serve as one of the major points of sociological debate for years to come.

# 1

*Kenneth E. Boulding*

# The Place of the Image in the

# Dynamics of Society*

"The dynamics of society" may seem like merely a pretentious way of talking about history. It is, however, history with a difference; history conceived not as narrative or chronicle, not even as a connected story or tale, but history conceived as a system, that is, as a social system with emphasis on regularities and patterns as well as discontinuities and gaps.

Social systems are, of course, very different from physical systems. The difference is so great that some people have denied that social systems exist at all. This would be a confession of intellectual defeat, however, which I am not prepared to make. The patterns of history may be almost infinitely complex but they are patterns. To deny any pattern to history is to deny any possibility of influencing the future, for influence can only come by following the pattern. In this matter of the interpretation of history, we indeed go between Scylla and Charybdis, the one being the council of despair that refuses to find any pattern or system in the ongoing flux of man and society; the other being the self-assured cockiness that sees patterns where they do not in fact exist. Perhaps the latter is in fact the greater danger. The human mind has a craving for patterns. Anarchy and randomness are abhorrent to us and we have a profound tendency to organize the unorganized, whether this is in sense data, in historical sequences, or in the labor market. We must constantly be on our guard, therefore, against

---

* An earlier form of this chapter was given as an address before the Public Relations Institute, Cornell University, August 10, 1961.

inadequate, incomplete, and premature patternings of history. Nevertheless, without patterns, we cannot live and without some interpretation of history, we cannot guide our actions intelligently. Perhaps even a false guide is better than none at all.

The great difference between social and physical systems is that social systems contain information, images, and symbols as essential elements, whereas physical systems can generally be described completely without these variables and aspects. The basic concept of any dynamic system is that of a succession of "states." A state of the system is a complete abstract description of the relevant variables of a system as they exist at a moment in time. It is like a frame on a reel of film. The dynamics of a system consist, in the first place, of the succession of states, as frames succeed one another in a movie. The system can be dynamically described, that is, reduced to "law," if any one state can be deduced in its entirety from a finite number of preceding states. The simplest case, of course, is where the state on any one day bears a constant relation to the state of the previous day — the "day" here being, of course, any arbitrary unit of time. This is what we mean by a difference equation of the first degree. If there is a constant relation between the state of the world on Monday and the state of the world on Tuesday, and if we are given the state of the world on Monday, we can proceed to deduce the state of the world on Tuesday. Then, given the state of the world on Tuesday, we can deduce the state on Wednesday. Thus we can go on indefinitely and project the whole system indefinitely into the future, or for that matter, back into the past.

In difference equations of the second degree, the state of affairs on, let us say, Wednesday, depends not only on the state on Tuesday, but also on the state on Monday. Systems as simple as this are adequate to describe the whole glorious counterpoint of celestial dynamics. It is little wonder that the success of astronomers in predicting celestial events is the envy of all other sciences. When we are looking for systems and patterns in history, therefore, we are looking for something like difference equations, that is, stable relationships between the past and the present. The economist, for instance, looks for a stable relationship between the household expenditure of today and the income of yesterday. This in one form is the consumption function. In social systems, however, we must reckon with the fact that simple dynamic relationships of this kind do not exist in a truly stable form. There may be temporary stabilities which are helpful in short-run predictions; there are, however, virtually no long-run stabilities of a simple order.

We can, indeed, think of human history as determined by difference equations of an infinite degree. Today depends not only on yesterday or even on the day before yesterday, but on all previous yesterdays. A relationship of this complexity is not only too complex to handle but is theoretically incapable of giving prediction. A dynamic system of an infinite order is one which we are incapable of discovering because the discovery of stable dynamic relationships can only take place if there is experience over a period of time longer than the order of the relationship. We could never hope to discover, for instance, whether the relationship between Monday and Tuesday was stable if our whole experience was limited to these two days. We never, indeed, obtain certainty in our knowledge of these relationships. There is a small probability, as the philosophers have pointed out, that the sun will not rise tomorrow. The probability of the truth of a dynamic relationship, however, increases very rapidly with an increase in the number of cases. If from our observance of the relation between Monday and Tuesday, we venture to predict on Tuesday on the basis of this relationship what will happen on Wednesday, and our prediction is fulfilled, we will be justified in thinking that this might have been an accident. If, however, our prediction is fulfilled also on Thursday, Friday, Saturday, and on a number of succeeding days, confidence in the original law relating yesterday to today will be strongly fortified.

A single disappointment, however, can shatter a law, and in history (that is, in social systems), these disappointments are extremely frequent. To give but a single example, in the United States and indeed in the Western world generally, it was observed that a peak in the price level came roughly in 1815, in 1865, and in 1919. A long cycle of from 50 to 60 years, called the Kondratiev, was postulated on this experience. On the basis of this observation in the *Encyclopedia of the Social Sciences* about 1934, the very distinguished economist, John R. Commons, predicted that prices would continue to fall until 1952, after which they would rise again. Needless to say, this prediction was very far from the truth and it is apparent today that the Kondratiev was largely an accident. To give another example, Mr. Sewell Avery of Montgomery Ward, on the basis of the experience of 1919-1920, expected a sharp depression after the end of the second World War. In this expectation he was disappointed, at considerable cost to the corporation which he directed.

The difference between social and physical systems is not confined to the complexity and order of the difference or differential equations which govern them. Social systems are characterized by at least two other peculiarities which differentiate them very sharply from simple physical systems, such as celestial mechanics. The first characteristic is the predominance of "threshold" systems in which small causes can sometimes produce very large consequences. The second characteristic is that social systems are what I call "image-directed," that is, there are systems in which the knowledge of the systems themselves is a significant part of the system's own dynamics and in which, therefore, knowledge about the system changes the system.

In view of the fact that social systems are the creation of the human organism, and especially of the human nervous system, it is not surprising to find that the closest analogue to the threshold quality of social systems is to be found in the neural networks of the human nervous system. The essential element of a threshold system is something like a neuron — an element which has inputs and outputs but in which the output depends upon the sum of the inputs reaching a certain threshold. It would be more accurate to say that some function of the inputs must reach a certain threshold, as the function does not have to be simply additive. As long as the threshold is not reached an addition to input produces no output whatever. The moment the threshold is reached, there is an output. In the case of the neuron, as far as we know, this output is fairly standardized. We can, however, postulate elements of as great complexity as we wish. A system of this kind is represented in Figure 1 where the square boxes represent "neurons" or threshold elements. The number in each box is the "height" of its threshold elements. Thus, suppose we assume that each of the threshold elements of Row 1 receive 20 units of input. Only Element A will "fire." It will produce an output of 20 which it will pass along the lines marked by the arrows to the next row of threshold elements. As will be seen from the figure, only Element C in Row 2 will fire, and the process will again pass along the lines marked by the arrows to the third row of elements. In this row, both Elements B and D will fire,

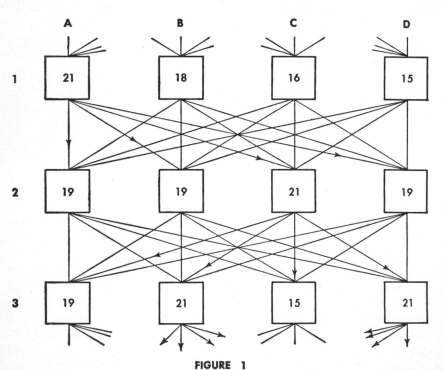

**FIGURE 1**

which may mean, of course, that still more elements will fire in Row 4 when this is reached.

It is obvious that systems of this kind are very complex, although some of their properties have been explored by the mathematical biologists. These are systems in which, if I dare quote Browning,

> Oh, the little more and how much it is
> And the little less, and what worlds away!

It was for the loss of a nail, we remember in the nursery rhyme, that the kingdom was lost. There are times in history when a very small change in output can cause one threshold unit to fire which otherwise would not have fired and the whole course of history is changed. It is this among other things which makes prediction so difficult in the social sciences. If we are to be able to predict in social systems, we must know a good deal about the thresholds of the threshold units involved. Unfortunately, this information is often very hard to come by. The higher the threshold, the harder it is to find out where it is. The elements that correspond to neurons in the neural network are, of course, persons in the social system; the firing of a neuron corresponds to the decision of a person — a decision, that is to say, is output of some kind, usually of communication or of information, which follows from the cumulative result of a number of past inputs. These outputs result only, however, when the past inputs accumulate over some threshold. Where the thresholds are low, the behavior is repetitive and easy to find out about. Every morning, for instance, men stagger into the bathroom and shave. This is a very low-level decision. In fact, some people deny the name of decision to these habitual reactions. However, there is input in the shape of the alarm clock and the information which reaches us from our physical surroundings and this is sufficient to carry us over the threshold of behavior. It may be, indeed, that on Saturday morning, the threshold is not reached and we do not shave.

The situation is further complicated in social systems by the fact that the decisions of different persons have different weights. In Figure 1, I have supposed all the threshold elements to be equal in the sense that each one is connected with the next set by an equal number of lines of communication. In social systems, this is not true. There are some elements which are connected to very many others, other elements connected to only a few. The decisions of a sharecropper in Mississippi or a shoeshine boy in New York are communicated to a very small circle of other persons. The decisions of a President or a Pope are communicated to hundreds of millions of people and may affect the lives of all of them. This is because communication in social systems is neither a uniform nor a random effort but is organized into role structures and organizations. An organization, in fact, has been defined as a set of roles linked by lines of communication.

At this point there are two extreme views of the nature of social systems between which we have to pick our way. On the one hand, there is the purely mechanical view that the nature of a role occupant is quite unimportant and that the decision is determined by the role structure itself. The course of history in this view is determined by great impersonal social forces and the actual decisions of the decision-maker, no matter how exalted, are relatively unimportant. At the other extreme, we have the "great man" theory of history in which the decision of those placed in powerful roles is regarded as all-important and history is written largely in terms of the character and peculiarity of kings, dictators, generals, and prophets. Karl Marx may be regarded as representative of the one extreme and perhaps Thomas Carlyle of the other.

The truth clearly lies somewhere between these two extreme positions. Exactly where it lies, however, is hard to say. We can certainly distinguish large and apparently impersonal forces which operate on the dynamics of social systems. Such things as changes in climate, the discovery of new lands, the accumulation of knowledge and skill, and the growth of population seem at times to be almost independent of the human will. In what Baumol has called "the magnificent dynamics" of the classical economics there is little place for individual decision. In the Malthusian system, for instance, if we once accept the initial premise that the only effective check on the growth of population is starvation and misery, then no matter how grandiose our images or how reasonable our decisions the end is the same. We may illustrate this perhaps in Figure 2. If the system of decision points is triangular in the sense that the number of decision points continually declines in the course of time, then no matter what the path of the system, it all follows down to the same end. It cannot be doubted that systems of this kind exist. It is also clear, however, that the social system of mankind as a whole, up to the present rate, has not been a system of this kind. If anything, indeed, it is a reverse triangle; that is, the number of decision points continually increases with time so that the system becomes less and less determinate in a mechanical sense, hence, the path becomes more and more important.

We now come to the second great peculiarity of social systems, which is that they are to a considerable extent determined by the images we have of them and the knowledge we have about them. They are, that is to say, in part image-determined. It is very important to say "in part" image-determined because there are mechanical elements, independent of the image, of great importance in any social system and we neglect these at our peril. I recall an old Peter Arno cartoon of a very jolly party in an airplane which is about to crash into a cliff, the caption being "My God, we're out of gin!" The future of that small social system could be deduced from its physical environment quite independently of any images of its own future which it might possess. Social systems, therefore, are always mixed systems in the sense that they combine both the

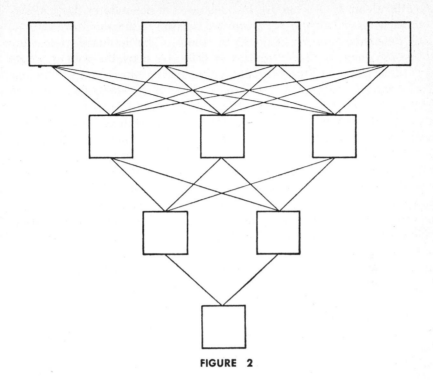

**FIGURE 2**

mechanical and image-determined elements. One may venture a guess that as the knowledge of society increases, the image-determined elements in social systems becomes more important. That is, as I said in my book, *The Image* (1), there is a strong tendency for the latent to become manifest. Man begins with an image of a world which has really very little to do with his actual environment or the actual system in which he lives. To some extent, these images may be self-reinforcing, and where this is the case, he does not change them easily. It occasionally happens, however, that he is disappointed and is aware of his disappointments and, under these circumstances, there may be a change in the image towards "reality." I would rather leave the question of what is meant by reality to another time, or even to another person. Our common sense notions, however, that some images may be truer than others, are probably not wholly illusory.

Even images which are in some sense false, however, produce marked effects upon the dynamics of society. Dr. Fred Polak in his great book, *The Image of the Future* (2), has brought together an impressive array of historical evidence to indicate that one of the major elements, perhaps indeed the most important single element, which governs the dynamics of particular societies is the nature of the image of the future which prevails in them. One might even extend this concept to the behavior of the individual. If we contrast, for instance, the behavior of the graduate student with that of the bum, we will see pretty clearly that the principal difference is in the image of the future. The graduate student has a long-run image of the future in which he sees himself enjoying certain rewards as a result of the pains and efforts he is now enduring. The bum has hardly any image of the future beyond that of the immediate moment, or if he has any image, it is so depressing that it is repressed. Polak's major point is that in the dynamics of a society, the principal factor is not so much the particular content of the image of the future as its quality of optimism or pessimism. A society which has a negative or pessimistic image of the future is likely to be disorganized and its image of the future is all too likely to be fulfilled. On the other hand, the society which has an optimistic image of the future, even though this image may be quite unrealistic, will be well organized and will go forward into some future, although not necessarily the future of its image. An excellent illustration of this principle is to be found in the remarkable degree of coherence and organization present among the millenialist and chiliastic sects like Jehovah's Witnesses or the Seventh Day Adventists. Here we have a group of people with a highly positive image of their own future of a strictly metaphysical or trans-empirical kind. It is an image not shared by most of the population and a great many people would regard it as unrealistic or even ludicrous. The fact, however, that it is positive and full of hope means that in this world, these subcultures are well organized and, in fact, move toward a positive and desirable future even in this world, in spite of the fact that their basic image of the future is otherworldly. The strength of the Communists likewise depends upon their having a highly positive image of the future. This does not differ so much from that of the millenialist as we might think. Even though the golden future of the Communist image is ostensibly in this world, it is so remote that it might just as well be in another.

Examples of self-justifying images of the future are very common in economic life. It is a commonplace of economics that if everybody expects a rise in prices, everybody will act so as to bring the rise in prices about, and the same goes for the expectation of falling prices. If most businessmen expect a depression, they are likely to behave in such a way as to bring it about. If there is a general expectation of economic development, this is also an important element in bringing it about. And, by contrast, if people have a strong impression that any attempt to better their own position will fail, they are likely to be apathetic and unwilling to exert themselves in new enterprises. The general level of aspiration of the people, as many writers have pointed out, is perhaps the largest single element in the psychological substratum of economic development. In a slightly different area, the expectations of war and peace, likewise, are frequently self-justified. Where we have two countries such as the United States and Canada which are genuinely at peace in the sense that not even the threat of war is used as an instrument in their relationship, the total absence of the expectation of war justifies itself. There are no preparations for war and virtually no possibility of war. On the other hand, the strong expectation of war almost invariably produces it, for this leads to an arms race, which eventually leads to an intolerable situation in which one side or the other precipitates overt conflict.

A question of great importance is the extent to which men's images can be deliberately manipulated and hence, insofar as images determine the future, the future itself can be manipulated. The "cause" of our images is to be found in our total experience. The growth of the image follows a process which is related to biological growth. It is, however, very different from biological growth in the sense that it is peculiarly subject to symbolic changes. This is the prime difference between man and the lower animals. The lower animals undoubtedly have images and they may even have dreams. These images, however, are derived from direct experience and are not derived from symbols about experience. A dog can have an image of chasing a rabbit after he has once chased one; he can never derive an image of chasing a rabbit from hearing someone talk about it or reading about it in a book. A human being, by contrast, can derive images of things of which he has no direct personal experience. I have never been to Antarctica but I have read about it and as a result I have a fairly clear image of what it is like. If I went to Antarctica I am sure there are some things which would surprise me, for the image derived from symbols is never quite as vivid or as accurate as the image derived from direct experience. I would, however, be very surprised if I was very surprised. It is the essentially symbolic nature of the human image which dominates the social system. It is this which makes human history so profoundly different from any other record of events or any other temporal system. Because of this, the image-makers are a profoundly significant element in society when it comes to the interpretation of social dynamics. These are the writers, the preachers, the teachers, the politicians, the orators — and even the advertising and public relations men!

It is easy to acknowledge the importance of the role of the image-maker in society; it is not so easy to understand or to assess it. The difficulty here is that we are dealing with symbolic systems and these are systems we understand very little. We are unquestionably dealing with threshold systems of a kind, but we do not really know what the inputs and outputs are and we know even less about what determines and constitutes the thresholds themselves. What is it for instance, that gives a symbol power? Duns Scotus "fired France for Mary without spot" and the Virgin, as Henry Adams saw so clearly, built some of the greatest monuments of the human spirit. A middle-western Protestant today is not similarly fired. Under the sign of the crescent, the Arabs almost conquered the world, and shifted the center of civilization from the

Mediterranean toward the Persian Gulf. I must confess that the Koran, which moved so many, moves me very little, and I find it hard to enter even by the gates of empathy into an experience that is at the same time so profound and so remote. Now it is nationalism and communism that seem to fire men to devotion and action. Tomorrow, these, too, may seem hollow and unrewarding.

The problem is that the image is not merely an aggregate of information, it is a structure — a structure, moreover, of great complexity and many dimensions. Its complexity is so great that there is a powerful urge to simplify it, and the symbol is the simplification of the image. A symbol, that is, is something which stands for or evokes an image of much greater complexity than its literal self. At a commonplace, statistical level, we see it in such concepts as the price level, which reduces a massive list of individual prices to a single number. Similarly the flag invokes a complex and emotionally rich image of national history and the cross invokes a similar rich image of Christian experience, martyrdom, and doctrine. Our image is as frequently clarified and made more powerful as a spring of action by the loss of information as it is by the gain. We have, for instance, a profound tendency to try to reduce a multi-dimensional reality to a single linear dimension. We have a strong urge, for instance, to reduce the almost infinitely dimensioned variety of the human character to a single dimension of good and bad. Even worse, we set up a point on this continuum and divide all mankind into two boxes — the good guys and the bad guys, the right people and the wrong people, the ins and the outs, the good families and the riff-raff, the free world and the Communists, the whites and the blacks. The stereotyping of the image inevitably leads to a loss which can sometimes even be measured in economic terms. The trouble with discrimination is that it is undiscriminating — that is, it discriminates according to an unreal and false set of criteria.

We must, however, at least be moderately humble at this point. There is no litmus paper of truth. There is no simple way of identifying the truth of the image. In theory, indeed, there is no way at all, for images can only be compared with images; they can never be compared with reality. In practice, I think there is a certain skill at truth, and the least we can say is that a demand for it produces a certain supply. One suspects, perhaps, that the main difficulty with the provision of truth is the absence of demand, rather than any basic inelasticity in the supply.

When one thinks of the image-makers, one thinks also, unfortunately, of lies. And the question arises, therefore, what is the power of a lie in determining a course of the dynamics of a society? Goebbels believed, of course, that the bigger the lie, the more often and the more loudly it was shouted, the better chance it had of being believed. There is, unfortunately, a certain amount of evidence to justify this hypothesis. On the other hand, truth has a certain advantage which the lie does not. The lie may be found out, whereas the truth cannot. That is, the lie cannot be found to be a truth and the truth cannot be found to be a lie. The lie, that is to say, can only be justified within the symbolic system — it cannot be justified outside it in the cold school of hard experience. I think, therefore, that we are justified in assuming a certain "outability" of truth and that Lincoln's favorite aphorism that you can't fool all of the people all of the time is ultimately truer than Goebbel's belief.

One circumstance, however, must require withdrawal at least in part of the optimism of the previous paragraph. When the image is self-justifying, what does it mean to say that it is true or false? In a world of fairy wishing-caps what would happen to the truth? This is a real problem and one stands, indeed, on the edge of an abyss — the abyss of fairyland — a horror where all dreams are true and in which, therefore, there is no truth. The only escape from this nightmare, I think, is the faith that images are self-justified only in the short run. The belief that prices are going to rise may cause prices to rise for a while, but not forever. Eventually, the underlying reality of the world must impose itself on the self-justifying realities of the image. It is a very real problem in social organization, however, as to how we defend ourselves against self-justifying images. These may only be justified in the short run, but the short run can be a desperately long space of time. To paraphrase Lincoln again, we can fool too many of the people too much of the time. The record of history is full of great expectations that were self-justified for a while but which eventually were disappointments.

I may seem at this point almost to be arguing for the mechanical interpretations of social systems which are so attractive in their seeming objectivity, and so free from the corruption of dreams. The image of the social system as mechanical, however, is itself a retreat from reality, for social reality is more complex than any mechanical system can possibly describe. Mechanical views of history, like those of Marx, are therefore likely to lead to results that are as perverse and dangerous as those which stem from the efforts of the liar, the propagandist, and the deliberate perverter of the truth. The Communists are certainly better intentioned than the Nazis, but they may have caused just as great a sum of human misery, and even the most selfless efforts of Christian missionaries have occasionally accomplished disintegration and disaster for the societies which they have influenced. What I am pleading for, therefore, is not a return to clear — and therefore false — mechanical views of history, it is rather that we should dedicate ourselves to a long, slow task, the task of developing true images of social systems, true in the sense that they conform to the nature of man himself and to his potentialities — which I believe are greater than any that we have yet brought to light. They should be true also in the sense of giving us skill in the handling of our society. I do not believe that I have ever asked of the image of a social system that it would enable us to foretell the future. It is not too much to ask of such an image, however, that it give us a guide to present action and certain reasonably secure conditional expectations.

What we ask from the image is a reasonably accurate measure of possible futures that we can choose among. I do not believe either that we are a helpless pawn of destiny or that we are the masters of our fate. The truth lies somewhere in between. We have real choices, but the choices are within a limited menu. The menu perhaps grows longer all the time, but it is always limited. It should be the great business of the science of society to learn the limits of this menu — to learn what we cannot have as well as what we can have, and hence, to guide our choice into those areas which are not only desirable, but realizable.

The most important property of man's image, however, is his ability to change it. Without this, we may be trapped in images which are self-reinforcing even though they are not self-justifying. The image, that is to say, is reinforced in defiance of experience. It is the skill of learning which is the greatest hope of the human race. It is the will to learn which is its greatest question mark. If the image-maker conceives his role as that of the printer, printing his image upon the plastic minds of mankind, then he betrays his function as a teacher. For the teacher is not an imprinter; he is one who cooperates with the inward teacher, the will to learn, the mysterious inner forces of growth and development of the image within the personality of the individual. Unless there is a basic respect for the individual image, the image-maker, whether preacher, politician, writer, ad-man, or even professor, becomes the mere propagandist who may actually destroy the tender buds of true knowledge and so help to imprison mankind behind the terrible walls of false images. It may be true that man has mostly lived in these prisons — prisons of superstition, magic, ideology, priest-craft, party lines, and thought control. But I believe he was not made to be so imprisoned; it is for this hope that man can and must break out of his image prisons into that "free world" of the future for which we think he was made and toward which his potentialities impel him. In this world there is only one loyalty, loyalty to the truth. It is a difficult and painful loyalty to possess, especially in a world that recognizes it so little. In this loyalty, however, there lies, it seems to me, the only image of the future which is truly creative, and it is a future which we do not wholly have to wait to enjoy. No man, I think, in this world can live wholly free from lies but he can love the truth and direct the current of his mind and life towards it. If this sounds like moralizing, I will not deny it; I would only point out that values are an essential part of the image and constitute, indeed, that aspect of it which is most influential in affecting behavior and the dynamic course of society.

## BIBLIOGRAPHY

1. Boulding, Kenneth E. *The Image*. Ann Arbor: University of Michigan Press, 1956.
2. Polak, Fred L. *The Image of the Future*, translated and abridged by Elise Boulding. San Francisco: Jossey Bass/Elsevier, 1973.

# 2

*Irving Sosensky*

# The Problem of Quality in Relation

# to Some Issues in Social Change[1]

## PART 1

The problem of social change, referred to in the title of this volume and the proposed titles of its chapters, is reminiscent of the earliest formulations of philosophic problems; the titles suggest not merely "change," but what does not change while change goes on, i.e., what is referred to as the "problem of permanence and change." There are various senses in which "permanence" and "change" can — and have, in the history of thought — been taken. Aristotle's notions of Substance and Being with their attendant notions of Actuality and Potentiality represent one kind of conceptual structuring; Galileo's formulation of the law of free fall as a proportion between the units of time and the squares of the units of distance (the units of distance change while the units of time are permanent) represents another. Other formulations may be indicated but they all entail the question of identity and difference, a distinction whose vintage is about the same as those of "permanence" and "change," which will provide us with our conception of quality.

[1] I gratefully acknowledge help from the following: Professor A. C. Benjamin of the University of Missouri and Professor R. F. Grabau of Purdue University both criticized an earlier draft of Part 1 and provided invaluable suggestions; Professor W. L. Rowe of Purdue University read the present version of Part 1 and was extremely helpful; Professors George Zollschan and Walter Hirsch of Purdue University were uncommonly stimulating and generous with their time; the Purdue Research Foundation awarded me a grant for the summer of 1959 to pursue my interest in "quality." All instances of error and obscurity are my sole responsibility.

"Quality," if anything, has had more philosophic senses than "permanance" and "change." For Aristotle, quality was "That in virtue of which" something was classified in a certain way; for Locke it meant "power"; for Russell it meant sense-data; for Dewey it was the ineffable and unique; and so on. The non-philosophic occurrences of "quality" are more ubiquitous: it bears on value, standards of workmanship, the *je ne sais quoi* of women, paintings, scenes in the theatre and natural scenery, property (in the sense of "property of a thing"), feelings, and so on. Nevertheless, a certain substratum of sense seems to perdure through all of them. We want to clarify that first.

We shall want to say that logic is irrelevant to quality. To the extent that an issue is determinable by logic, it is non-qualitative; and conversely, to the extent that one is purely in the realm of "quality," it is a realm to which "logic" is unfitted. No logical rule or law can decide issues we shall refer to as "qualitative," although, quality once having been decided, "logic" has to do with sentences about it.

## A

Aristotle's law of non-contradiction stated that "the same attribute cannot at the same time belong and not belong to the same subject in the same respect." He held that it is a necessary truth about everything that is. Recently (17, pp. 57–58) it was argued that it does not formulate factual descriptions, empirically or ontologically. In the following way, an objector to the law argues:

A penny can be said to be sensibly both circular and non-circular; therefore the law of non-contradiction is not a necessary truth about that fact, since this is a violation of the law.

A defender of the law then replies:

True, but that is in different respects; in the same respect, that is, when the penny is perpendicular at its center to the eye's line of sight, the penny is not sensibly both circular and non-circular. The law is therefore not violated.

The objector, however, may press:

But within that respect, we may say that a line drawn from the surface of the eye at the point where the line of sight meets it to a point on the edge of the penny both subtends and does not subtend an angle of 30 degrees. The law is therefore violated.

The defender again replies:

True, but not in the same respect; at a given distance, in that respect, the angle subtended is not both 30 degrees and not 30 degrees.

Two things are noteworthy. First, if the law of non-contradiction is a factual truth, then appeal to the same fact should suffice for its defense. Thus, if anyone were to question the law of gravity by citing a case in which a body attracted to another did not move according to the law of inverse squares, a defender of the law of gravity would point to extraneous changing forces being exerted on the body in the course of its movement, citing the principle of the composition of forces as a reason why the movement of the body in question constitutes merely an apparent violation of the law. The only recourse of the objector would be to show that the defender's evidence is wrong, i.e., that the facts appealed to are really not facts at all. If the objector is wrong, then the defender's appeal suffices, unless the objector cites other facts. But this argument cannot go on indefinitely, for at some point there must be agreement as to what constitutes the relevant facts. But in the argument over the law of non-contradiction, no such agreement can ever be reached, for as soon as a defender cites a respect, the objector can find another apparent violation, and there is no "fact" which will hold as a criterion in the face of all objections.

Second, since there is no fact to which the protagonists can appeal, and there is no other principle analogous to the principle of the composition of forces, it follows that the only place we may look for that to which the defender of the law of non-contradiction may appeal is the principle itself, and this turns out to be the case.

For in order to say whether the penny is either sensibly circular or non-circular, one must first decide what is either sensible or non-sensible; that is, the law of non-contradiction is implicit before applying it to the case; had it not been so, it would not have been applicable. At each challenge the defender must proceed the same way: to decide the penny's sensible circularity, he must decide what is line and non-line, perpendicular and non-perpendicular, center of the eye and non-center of the eye, and so on. The "respect" constitutes the formulation of the total set of conditions which provide for the distinction between the sensibly circular and non-circular. It is implied in the use of "respect" by the defender as a criterion in order to establish itself.

Analogous comments may be made about relations, for which attributes may be regarded as a special case. Of two posts placed on a north-south line, we may say that each is both to the right and left of the other; to which it may be replied that this is not so in the same respect, i.e., not from the same side of the line. Each is both darker and lighter than the other but not in the same respect, i.e., if the light intensity remains constant, and so on. Being on a side or non-side, being on the left or non-left, and being x light intensity or non-x intensity depend on the prior use of the law of non-contradiction.

The foregoing argument is used to demonstrate that the law of non-contradiction is a rule relevant to the formation of sentences about things but does not describe things. The point here is not what the argument is directed for or against, but that it illustrates the meaning of "respect," "attribute," and "subject."

Which of these is crucial to our point may be discovered by changing the strategy of the encounter.

> Objector: A penny is sensibly both circular and non-circular.
> Defender: It is not both in the same respect.
> Objector: In what respect?
> Defender: In the respect that the penny is perpendicular at its center to the line of sight.
> Objector: But a line drawn from the surface of the eye at the point at which the line of sight meets it to the edge of the penny both subtends and does not subtend an angle of 30 degrees with the line of sight.
> Defender: Not in the same respect.
> Objector: In what respect?

And so on. The key term is "respect." An analysis of its usage reveals two distinct relevant definitions:

1) $P_i$ is a respect if it is the only member of a class $K$ of attributes $P_1$, $P_2$, . . . , $P_n$, that is an attribute of the subject $S$, and $A$ is an attribute of $S$ if $P_i$ is.

For example: in the discussion of the penny, the class $K$ of attributes $P_1$, $P_2$, . . . , $P_n$, is the class of angles at which the line of sight intersects the center of the surface of the penny; the respect $P_i$ is a member of the class $K$, i.e., the perpendicularity of the line of sight to the surface of the penny at the center; $A$ is the circularity; $S$ is the penny. If the penny is perpendicular to the line of sight at the center ($P_i$), then the penny ($S$) appears sensibly circular ($A$).

Again, "A man is healthy in respect of the functioning of his organs": $S$ is the man: $A$ is "healthy": $K$ is the class $P_1$, $P_2$, . . . , $P_n$: of possible ways in which the organs can function; if they function in a certain way ($P_i$), then the man ($S$) is healthy ($A$).

2) $A$ is a respect if it is an attribute of a subject $S$, and $S$ is a member of a class of subjects $C$ which $A$ partly specifies.

For example: "A person is a man in respect of courage." The person, $S$, is a member of the class $C$ of men in respect of the attribute $A$ of courage. The attribute "courage" partly specifies the class of men in this sense (i.e., the moral sense). To specify the class completely, we have to add a number of other respects, such as maturity, judgment, etc. Then we have a number of respects, i.e., a person is a man in respect of maturity, in respect of judgment, etc.: the person is a member of the class of men in *these* respects.

Again, "A person is psychiatrically normal." A person, $S$, is a member of the class $C$ of normal people, in respect of psychiatric considerations, $A$. "Psychiatric considerations" partly specifies the class $C$ of normal people, which would be comprised of all those who are medically normal, socially normal, psychiatrically normal, etc. Finally, "A man is intelligent entrepreneurially." A man, S, is a member of the class C of intelligent people in respect of entrepreneurial activities, A. "Entrepreneurial" partly specifies the class of intelligent people, which is comprised of those who are intellectually intelligent, socially intelligent, etc.

We shall refer to definition (1) as the P-respect and definition (2) as the A-respect. The P-respect formulates the necessary and sufficient conditions for the attribute A. For example, we may say that if the penny is perpendicular at its center to the line of sight, then it is sensibly circular, but we can also say that if the penny is sensibly circular, it is perpendicular at its center to the line of sight.

Moreover, an examination of the relations between "subject," "attribute," and "respect" indicates that other employment than that made in the law of non-contradiction, i.e., the *same* subject, the *same* attribute, and the *same* respect, may be considered. We talk about two attributes of the same respect, or one attribute of the same subject in different respects, and so on. Under such circumstances comparison is introduced. Thus, to say that the two subjects S and S' are different in a certain respect is to say one of two things: (1) they have different attributes A and A' if $P_i$ is the only member of a class K of attributes that is an attribute of S and S' (e.g., two coins, S and S', may have the attributes "sensible circularity" (A) and "sensible ellipticity" (A') in respect of their surfaces being perpendicular at the center of the line of sight, $P_i$, an attribute which is the only member of the class K of angles at which the line of sight may intersect the surface of the coins at the center, $P_1, P_2, \ldots P_n$.); (2) S has a different attribute than S' and both attributes (A and A' respectively) partly define the class C (e.g., S may be a person who has judgment (A) and S' a person who has courage (A'); both attributes partly define the class C of being a "man" in the "moral" sense). But a further discussion of these considerations must be postponed until we discuss sameness and likeness.

B

There are domains where sameness and likeness overlap, and there are domains in which one is applicable and the other is not.

That "sameness" is used under varying circumstances is most firmly attested to by various formulations. Thus,

1) Identity: If Gerald Ford is identical with the present President of the United States, then Gerald Ford and the present president of the United States are the same.

2) Class: If unmarried mature women are spinsters and vice versa, then the classes are the same.

3) Attribute: If James and Michael are both six feet tall, they both have the same attribute.

4) Class of attributes: If the attributes defining "material object" are the same as the attributes defining "body," then the classes of attributes are the same.

5) Relations: If $a$ is to the right of $b$, and $c$ is to the right of $d$, then $a$ bears the same relation to $b$ that $c$ does to $d$.

6) Classes of relations: If the class of comparative sizes is the class of greater than, less than, and equal to, and vice versa, then each of the two classes is the same.

7) "Sameness" occurs where neither class nor attribute is specified. An example is G. E. Moore's "good," which is "simple" and "unanalyzable," and of which two cases would be said to be the "same," though one could not immediately specify a class of attributes by which they could be said to be "the same."

"Likeness" must be distinguished from "sameness."

1) $a$ is like $b$ if $a$ and $b$ are members of the same class.

2) "Likeness" has to do with including two classes in the same class. The class of cats and the class of dogs are included in the class of animals and are said to be "alike."

3) If two subjects have the same attribute they are said to be alike.

4) "Likeness" is used when two subject-matters have some attributes in common, but not others. Thus, Torricelli introduced the "sea of air" concept, calling attention to the common attributes of water and air. Both have pressure or weight, both are relatively homogeneous, and so on. Nevertheless, they are not the same, for all their attributes are not the same. In this case, we use "likeness" or "similarity" as one does in the case of the dog and cat.

5) There is a sense of likeness which involves neither class nor attribute, e.g., when we speak of "bottling up our emotions": where the likeness suggested is between a bottle containing a liquid and a person "confining" his emotions.

Likeness (4) is the point at which "likeness" and "sameness" overlap. It is often argued that if two subjects are members of the same class, or have the same attribute, they are "the same." But, because in certain respects the subjects are members of the same class and in others they are not, it is clear that the locution "same" is out of place, and "likeness" or "similarity" is apropos. We shall use "same in a given respect" or "same in given respects" as equivalent to "like" or "similar" when it is understood that more than one attribute is relevant to a subject.

# C

If $a$ is to the right of $b$, and $c$ is to the right of $d$, we speak of $a$ having the same relation to $b$ that $c$ does to $d$. We speak of "being to the right of" and "being to the left of" as being relations that are "alike" or "similar," i.e., they are "the same in given respects": they may be described as "directional relations," in the same class of relations. If we speak of the "higher" and "lower" notes of the musical scale, we also say that these are "similar" to "directional" relations; but "right" and "left" are alike in a way that "higher" and "lower" notes and "directional" relations are not. The former are analogous and the latter are metaphorical.

An analogy can be spoken of with clarity if we specify the respect in which the analogy holds. A telephone relay system is analogous to a traffic system: electrical impulses enter and leave the telephone system, autos enter and leave the traffic system; a switch holds up the current, the traffic officer holds up the traffic. In each case we may speak of the same relations. But the traffic system has certain relations that the telephone system hasn't: a driver may be arrested.

Or, consider the analogy:

The kidney is the filter of the body.

That it is an analogy implies that there is a comparison; therefore the attributes of each kind must be listed:

The kidney has the following attributes: it is composed of biochemical matter; blood moves through it; it is connected to a system of blood vessels; it has chemicals which eliminate the impurities from the blood; it is a permanent fixture of its system and is never replaced; it is located in a certain place; it has a certain shape.

The filter of a mechanical system has the following attributes: it is metallic in composition; oil or some other fluid necessary to the operation of the mechanical system flows through it; it is connected to a system of pipes or tubes; it has a wire mesh which eliminates the impurities in the oil or other fluid; though it performs a permanent function within the system it must be replaced intermittently; it has a certain shape; it is in a certain place.

We began with an analogy, and "analogy" means "proportion," so the original proposition may be formulated:

The kidney is to the body as the filter is to the mechanical system.

Or,

The relation the kidney bears to the body is like the relation the filter bears to the mechanical system.

We may ask:

In what respect?

That this question is permissible shows that the preceding indicative sentence may be formulated:

> The relation the kidney bears to the body is the same as the relation the filter bears to the mechanical system *in given respects.*

The same question may be repeated, and the reply is:

> The kidney bears the same relation to the body that the filter does to a mechanical system in the respects that: both the kidney and the filter trap impurities; fluids move through them; both are connected to a system comprised of tubes, and so on.

"Two things are the same in given respects," then, is the same as "two things have some of the same attributes." In a comparison, "same attribute" has the force that it has in the law of non-contradiction. Therefore, to list the attributes in respect of which the kidney and the filter of a mechanical system is a filter is to list the A-respects.

But there are respects in which they are different. Thus:

> The relation a kidney bears to an animal is unlike the relation a filter bears to a mechanical system.

The same question is permissible; and the reply:

> The relation the kidney bears to the animal body is unlike the relation the filter bears to the mechanical system in the respects that: the kidney gets rid of its impurities and the filter of the mechanical system does not; the filter of the mechanical system must be replaced, and the kidney need not; and so on.

The statement of an analogy requires the formulation of both likenesses and unlikenesses.

But a different strategy may be employed. Instead of listing the A-respects in which the subjects are alike, we select the A-respect in which both subjects are alike and then proceed to ask in which respect the A-respects are alike. The result is a P-respect, thus:

> In what respects is the attribute "trapping impurities" of the kidney the same as the attribute "trapping impurities" of the filter of the mechanical system?

To which the reply is:

> They are the same in the respect that both separate those objects which, if allowed to continue through the system, would render it inefficient.

In what respect would each of the systems be rendered inefficient?

Each system would be rendered less efficient in the respects that their expected tasks would be performed less rapidly or less precisely, and that more energy would be required for the performance of the tasks.

And so on.

"Trapping impurities" is an A-respect of the filter; it is also an A-respect of the kidney. But asking for the respect in which the A-respect "trapping impurities" of the kidney is like the A-respect "trapping impurities" of the filter is to try to provide a respect in which they are alike, that is, a P-respect. The respect in which "trapping impurities" of the kidney and "trapping impurities" of the mechanical filter are alike is that both the kidney and the filter separate those objects which, if allowed to continue through the system, would render it inefficient. But "separating those objects which, if allowed to continue through the system would render it inefficient" specifies the necessary and sufficient conditions for "trapping impurities." Therefore, we may state:

If the kidney traps impurities, then it separates those objects which, if allowed to continue through the system, would render the system inefficient.

and

If the kidney separates those objects which, if allowed to continue through the system, would render the system inefficient, then it traps impurities.

also

If the filter traps impurities, then it separates those objects which, if allowed to continue through the system, would render the system inefficient.

and

If the filter separates those objects which, if allowed to continue through the system, would render the system inefficient, then it traps impurities.

Since the same attributes bear the same relations to each other in both cases, it would follow that:

If the kidney and the filter of the mechanical system trap impurities, then both separate those objects which, if allowed to continue through the system, would render it inefficient.

and

If both the kidney and the filter of the mechanical system separate those objects which, if allowed to continue through the system would render it inefficient, they both trap impurities.

What is referred to in the first sentence is the necessary and sufficient condition of that which is referred to in the second.

Nevertheless, each time another respect is asked for, a factual answer can be given. This is not always true of different senses of a word; it is never true of genuine metaphors.

## D

Words in a language sometimes mean the same thing and sometimes mean different things. *Prima facie*, it would appear that when the same word "has different meanings," those meanings are analogous in the sense that "kidney" and "filter of a mechanical system" are analogous; but this is not always true.

"Touchstone" originally referred to a piece or block of quartz (named "basanite") easily kept fairly smooth and used to determine how much gold was present in a gold alloy. The following method was used: a piece of alloy whose proportions of gold and other metals was unknown was scratched against a surface of basanite, leaving a streak. The color of this streak was compared to the color of a streak produced by an alloy of known composition, and the expert could tell how much gold was in the unknown alloy. For example, a yellow streak meant more gold; a reddish streak meant more copper.

"Touchstone" is used in other ways, as may be seen from the following quotes from Clive Bell and William Hazlitt: ". . . an original work is the touchstone that exposes educated taste masquerading as sensibility"; and ". . . well digested schemes will stand the touchstone of experience." Another use occurs in a proverb: "Men have a touchstone whereby to try gold, but gold is the touchstone whereby to try men." If we consider the original use and this last use of "touchstone," we would be tempted to say, I think, that the two uses entail different meanings, like "cat" and "concept," but we don't really want to say this, so we use the locution "having different senses," and suggest that there is some connection, unlike "cat" and "concept." We want to say:

Sense *A* (the basanite) is like sense *B* (the gold). But how are they alike? *Prima facie*, the comparison urges that this is an analogy, so, stating the matter as a proportion:

The touchstone is to gold as gold is to men.

Which may then be re-stated:

Touchstone bears the same relation to gold that gold does to men.

And again the question:

In what respect?

The answer:

The touchstone tries gold and gold tries men.

And we ask:

In what respect is the trying of gold by the touchstone like the trying of men by gold?

We propose, in answer:

In the respect that the touchstone tests gold and gold tests men.

But we are puzzled by "tests"; in what respects are *they* alike? The answer:

The touchstone "determines the value" of gold, and gold "determines the value" of men.

Yet there is something wrong, for the touchstone does not determine the value of the gold, but of the gold alloy; and presumably it determines its value by determining the proportion of the gold in the alloy. The proverb is confusing. But suppose that the intended phrase is not "gold" but "gold alloy." Then the last comparison reads:

The touchstone determines the value of the gold alloy, and gold determines the value of men.

Then we ask:

In what respect?

The answer does not provide us with an unequivocal "sameness of respect." For if we ask in what respect the touchstone determines the value of the gold alloy, and in what respect gold determines the value of men, we don't get the same respect:

The touchstone determines the value of the gold alloy as an exchange commodity; gold determines the value of men as moral creatures.

The sameness of respect has seemingly eluded us, but let's make another attempt. Is there buried in this last statement a possible sameness of respect?

The touchstone determines the dependability of the gold alloy; gold determines the dependability of man.

But the dependability of the gold in the gold alloy is conditioned by the market and the sharpness of the trader; the dependability of a man's moral qualities may not be conditioned by the milieu in which the moral quality is exhibited. Thus, though a man might not be able to prevent his company from charging exorbitant prices, he himself might be scrupulously honest; he may be persistent in trying to accomplish his purposes though he may fail; he may be dutiful in the performance of tasks for his superiors though those around him are not and he accomplishes nothing: moral dependability is in no specifiable respect like the "dependability" of a gold alloy. On analysis, the "common meaning" of the two "senses" of "touchstone" seem to disappear. Putting the matter in our terminology, on selecting an apparent A-respect in which the different "touchstones" are alike, we can discover no P-respect which enables us to clearly specify what is constituted by the A-respect in which we feel that they are like. But there is a *prima facie* plausibility in the expectation that they are; and that distinguishes this case from the case of "cat" and "concept."[2]

## E

This difference makes us look elsewhere, namely, in metaphor, because there neither the sameness nor the similarity is discoverable.

Consider the following rather commonplace metaphor:

The mother is the heart of the family.

Consider it an analogy:

The mother is to the family as the heart is to the body.

And:

The mother bears the relation to the family that the heart does to the body.

To which we may ask:

In what respect?

The answer is difficult to find, so we try an A-respect:

[2] The reader may find the following example more convincing: "stretching the truth is like stretching a rubber band" (from 7, pp. 57–58).

The mother provides the force for the family's spirit and the heart provides the force for the blood's movement through the body.

Again, something is wrong, and it centers on "force." We know clearly enough what is intended by the heart's force: the heart pumps — it compresses, it pushes. But the mother doesn't pump — compress and push; she stimulates, she organizes, she encourages, she prepares. Apparently, we have the "P-respect."

The mother's activities bear the same relation to the family that the heart's activities do to the body.

But again:

In what respect?

And a possible answer:

The mother's activities are responsible for the family being what it is *qua* family, and the heart's activities are responsible for the body's being what it is *qua* body.

But strictly speaking, this is not true. If the mother died or deserted the family, the father or the eldest child would perform the functions that the mother had previously performed, even though not in exactly the same way; but if the heart were destroyed, nothing could replace it. Moreover, while the mother does not maintain herself with the same indispensability as the heart, the functions she performs do often seem all pervading, at least in stereotype; whereas the heart, necessary though it is to the maintenance of life, is not all pervasive. And if we pursue the matter with, "In what respect are they alike?" the "P-respect" we seek will not be found. Nevertheless we are quite willing to argue that the likeness and the sameness do exist.

We cannot specify the attributes by which we have compared the relations, yet we would want to say that they are alike or the same: we would want to say that the mother's relation to the family and the heart's relation to the body are alike, or the same, though we cannot see how. The definitive test has been met: the likeness or the sameness has been communicated. What is said about the metaphor may be said about the likeness — and the sameness too — of the different senses of "touchstone." Why, after all, the same word?

F

We may speak of quality whenever there are subjects that are the same or alike, but where no P-respect in which they are alike may be

specified; more explicitly, we may speak of quality when the same necessary and sufficient conditions for the same attributes of different subjects
cannot be specified.

This definition excludes, and is specifically intended to exclude, two
things, namely, the identity of an individual subject-matter on the one
hand, and purely logical properties on the other. Thus, though the
previous example of identity, namely, "JFK is the present President of the
United States," was in terms of a property, we may wish to say that
there is an identity because of the fact that what is referred to by both
designations is the same individual. But the "same" individual is not
"like" the same individual, because the same individual is identical with
the same individual, and to use "like" is to assert or suppose not one, but
at least two.

It should be clear also that quality has no dependence on logical issues.
That a given instance may be said to be the same sort of thing as another
is not a logical rule, though propositions may logically follow from the
assertion of sameness. As shown in the discussion about the penny, logical rules cannot determine the selection of subjects or attributes, and
therefore respects, unless terms are implicitly defined to include them.
Since no respect can be specified, the rules of logic have even less relevance in this context to quality.

## PART 2

We began this chapter by juxtaposing "permanence and change" and
"quality," then tried to show that quality has to do with "sameness" and
"likeness." "Permanence" and "change" also entail "sameness": to be
permanent is to remain the same; to change is not to remain the same.
We stated then that we are concerned with "what does not change while
change goes on"; hence we are concerned with what remains the same
while something does not. But, for instance, Aristotle's "substance" and
"being" (what "remains the same") and "potentiality" and "actuality"
(what does not), and Galileo's units of time (which "remain the same" or
are "permanent") and units of distance (which do not), leading to a proportion (which is also "permanent"), exhibit conceptual differences.

Moreover, the sense in which Galileo's units of time "remain the
same" and that in which his proportion "remains the same" are distinct.
Reflection on the history of, for example, the science of mechanics exhibits the fact that at every conceptual advance the various senses given
"permanence" and "change" are altered. In dealing with "social change"
it is wise to follow this lead.

But a word of caution is in order. Despite widespread admission that
"science" is often a sophomoric encomium for the more formalized empirical disciplines, some "natural scientists" display a contempt for disciplines less formalized than theirs, to which many "social scientists"

exhibit sensitivity. Formally, sociological investigation of social change falls short of what sociologists want, but a like condition is true of physics and logic. Sociology falls shorter in this regard, but affirming or denying that it is "science" is irrelevant to honest discussion. Our thesis is that the definition of "quality" we propose is exhibited in sociology by the fact that it is incomplete, as is readily admitted, in a sense or even in various senses that those disciplines more closely allied with classical mechanics are not; but this comparison is not intended to be invidious, for in various ways physics and logic are themselves incomplete.

Our thesis is derived from the fact that the investigators in the field suppose that there is some other way in which sociology can be made a more effective instrument to analyze the phenomena it presently does. It is this point which gives us our interpretation of sociology as to some extent qualitative: there is some presently unknown respect in which it can be said that the data of social change presently under investigation are the same or alike.

What will emerge from our analysis may seem paradoxical: though purely qualitative or metaphorical comparisons do not provide us with clear suggestions as to a line of investigation, nevertheless logically structured, analogical comparisons lead us to claim an unspecifiable respect, however tentatively it may be regarded as unspecifiable; therefore the search for a new respect entails a qualitative sameness or likeness. In many ways this is the permanence that bears on social change.

It may be advisable to indicate what the application of the mode of analysis we have been suggesting is by providing two examples of it before discussing sociological theories themselves. In the first we shall discuss an issue in the history of science. In the second we shall specifically devise a culture hypothesis in order to indicate the bearing of "quality" on theories of social change. After that, the theories of Talcott Parsons and Ralf Dahrendorf will be considered in analogous ways.

## A

The discernment of quality by distinguishing metaphor and analogy may be shown in the "plenist-vacuist" controversy about space. This controversy between Torricelli (24, p. 165), Otto von Guericke, Hooke (30, p. 101), and Boyle (2, pp. 26–27) on the one hand, and many Cartesians and those in the Tradition (13, chapter 4), on the other. The seventeenth- and eighteenth-century "principle of plenitude" was that God created a complete world in every respect, which was a *plenum formarum*, or a full scale of forms or beings, admitting no omission. Thus, there was a scale of biological species (or beings) which admitted every possible variation of species or beings and omitted none; a scale for non-living beings, divine beings, etc.; likewise with respect to space

(13, p. 52). No omissions were possible, and Descartes' material substance, defined as extension, was identified with space (10, p. 41). Cartesians in general fused this with an older doctrine, that "nature abhors a vacuum," *horror vacui*, therefore it is constantly "full" (11, pp. 103–104); Boyle referred to these men as "plenists," and to himself and others of like mind who opposed this part of the broader plenist doctrine as "vacuists"; they argued for the existence of a vacuum (2, pp. 26–27).

The plenists argued on the basis of comparisons which were metaphorical, while the vacuists argued on the basis of comparisons which were analogical. The plenists tended to support their conception of a non-vacuous space by direct comparison with the plenitude of the world in other respects. I know of no specific argument to the effect that space had to be conceived of as a plenum because, for instance, the scale of biological forms was a plenum; nevertheless, it is clear from the literature (13, chapter 4) that the conception of both as "filled" was meant to support the general doctrine of plenitude; which means that both were conceived of as being "the Same" or "alike." This sameness or likeness is seen to be metaphorical.

The comparison might be formulated in this way:

Position in space is like position in the scale of living things.

If conceived of as an analogue,

Position of a body is to space as place of a species is to the scale of living things.

And reformulated:

Position of a body bears the relation to space that the place of a species bears to the scale of living things.

And we ask:

In what respect?

In answer, we try:

In the respect that the body is immediately adjacent to other bodies and the species is immediately adjacent to other species.

But this is suspicious; it makes no sense to suggest that one species is next to another in the sense that a body is next to another body; a given species is "next to" another species because of the way in which we order our knowledge, and this hardly amounts to the same sense. We may try other A-respects, but the likeness or the similarity will be discovered to be metaphorical: there is no specifiable respect in which they are alike.

The vacuists argued, quite differently, that there can be a vacuum because air is like water, and volumes devoid of water can be obtained beneath the surface of the sea. Torricelli advanced the hypothesis that there was a "sea of air" surrounding the earth. The implicit comparison was analogical:

1) The sea is a fluid and so is the air.
   In what respect?
2) The sea moves in currents and so does the air.
   In what respect?
3) Portions of a volume of water may move, pushing aside other portions; portions of a volume of air may move, pushing aside other portions.

An A-respect is specified in (1); the P-respect of that A-respect is in (2); and (3) provides a P-respect of (2). In (1) and (2), $S$ and $S'$ are "volume of water" and "volume of air," respectively; both have the attribute of $A$, i.e., of being a fluid. $P_i$ is "moving in currents," an attribute which is a member of $K$, the class of various ways of moving, one other of which may be moving in a collection of distinct particles. $A$ is, of course, an attribute of $S$ because $P_i$ is.

There are, of course, various respects in which water and air are not alike, e.g., that the surface of a volume of water is observable and the surface of a volume of air is not, water is virtually incompressible and air (as Boyle discovered) has a "spring."

The likenesses between water and air, then, were not qualitative but could be made explicit in terms of P-respects, and it is this factor which enables the investigator explicitly to formulate, hypothetically, comparisons in other respects, seeking sameness of A-respect formulable in terms of P-respect. In the case of a metaphor, we cannot specify A-respects and P-respects.

And it shows: Torricelli was led to construct a barometer as a result of his speculations about air weight; Boyle demonstrated the existence of a vacuum and formulated Boyle's Law.

The plenist doctrine, on the contrary, provided few consistent or clear explanations of other phenomena. For example, they said that the reason water does not flow out of a narrow-necked bottle held upside down was that the space surrounding it was already occupied, so it had nowhere to go (24, pp. 163–170). But the same would have to be true about a container of water with a broad opening, and it isn't. Or consider another case. If a container with an opening is emptied of air, the opening plugged, and the container plunged into water, then, if the opening is unplugged, the water will rush in. Otto von Guerike had done this, and some plenists might have argued that this demonstrated that nature abhorred a vacuum. What could have been understood by this? That nature will destroy a vacuum? Such an interpretation is contrary to what is suggested in the plenist's interpretation of the above experiment, for it supposes the existence of a vacuum to be destroyed. The principle at this point becomes incapable of application, and does not suggest further ways out.


## B

Recently (26) the Pygmies of the great Congo Rain Forest were ascribed the following attributes: they were driven into the forests about a thousand years ago by "the great Bantu invasion"; that now they come out of the forests occasionally to obtain various articles (e.g., knives, clothes) they recognize or suppose to be superior to the articles they might manufacture; that in order to obtain these articles, they hire themselves out occasionally to the Bantu "villagers" who currently live at the edge of the forest; that the "villagers" regard them as inferior; that in order to control the Pygmies, the villagers use various methods: they "adopt" Pygmy families and provide for their initiation, engagement, marriage and death fêtes, i.e., these are the means by which the villagers hope to manage the Pygmies and to keep on good terms with the spirits of the forest. These people of the forest, moreover, are fleet of foot, deft, agile, and camouflage themselves well; they are dangerous to outsiders they consider inimical and therefore the villagers rarely venture there; they have their own forest communities with their own distinctive organization; that in the forest their sustenance comes from hunting, and gathering honey and fruits.

Margaret Murray (16) investigated the witch-phenomenon of the later medieval-early modern period, and discovered, from the literature (e.g., trial reports, personal reports, court records, autobiographies) of the period that those pleasant, relatively harmless creatures referred to as elves, fairies, sprites, pixies, bogies, etc., after the sixteenth century (beginning approximately with Spenser's *Faerie Queen* and Shakespeare's *Midsummer Night's Dream*) were, prior to that period, described in much stronger terms, and indeed were dealt with harshly. Her theory is that these creatures were actually the survivors of a Stone Age culture who had been driven into the forest by invaders who followed and themselves occupied the more fertile agricultural areas, and, of course, built the cities. They were described by the dominant inhabitants of England as being shorter than themselves, fleet of foot, agile, and capable of excellent camouflage. They were hunters, and were regarded as extremely dangerous, especially if met in the forest. They had their own religion (according to Professor Murray, they were worshipers of "the Horned God"), and ecclesiastical authorities violently opposed them, though lay authorities opposed them with considerably less vigor. Hence the violence of the sixteenth- and seventeenth-century witch hunts against fairies or "witches" who had "infiltrated" the dominant society; for, in fact, many of them attained positions of prominence.

Finally, consider the following statement.

> In Greek mythology, Satyrs are sprites of the woodland, in the train of Dionysus, with puck noses, bristling hair, goat-like ears, and short tails. They are depicted as wanton, cunning, and cowardly creatures, and always fond of wine and women. They dwell in woods and on mountains, where they hunt, and tend cattle, dance and frolic with the Nymphs (for whom they lie in ambush), make music pipe and flute, and revel with Dionysus . . . . They were considered as foes to mankind, because they played people all kinds of roguish pranks, and frightened them by impish tricks. . . . In art and poetry they gained a higher significance, owing to the festivals of Dionysus. . . . In early art they are represented for the most part as bearded and old, and often very indecorous. As time went on they were represented ever younger and more graceful, and with an expression of amiable roguishness . . . (25, pp. 559–560).

Given these ideas, a man might be tempted to formulate a culture hypothesis to the effect that if an invading group drives the group from its area into forests and mountains nearby, the relations between the groups proceed from a stage of violent opposition with limited points of contact, through a period wherein the victorious group ascribes supernatural powers to the displaced group, to a period of gradual albeit contemptuous acceptance. Could this hypothesis apply to, say, a given wave of invasion in India where original inhabitants were displaced into the forests, or similar circumstances in Southeast Asia, or to the Slavic displacement of the Finno-Ugrians in the north of Russia? Are the satyrs of Greek art the consequence of a displaced culture?[3] Probably not. Nevertheless, because of the similarities, a clear line of investigation may be formulated in cases of ignorance of the presence or absence of a given attribute. For example;

> The fairies of sixteenth-century England were like the Pygmies of the present-day Congo Rain Forests.
> In what (A-) respect?
> In the respect that their sustenance and dwellings were in the forests.
> In what respect are these alike?
> In the respect that the materials of their sustenance and for their dwellings are obtained within the forests.
> In what respect are these alike?
> In the respect that food was obtained primarily by hunting and the dwellings were constructed primarily out of the soil and vegetation obtainable in the forest.

[3] An alternative theory: Jane Harrison thought that "satyrs" originated in initiation rites, with men dancing in animal skins (8, pp. 341–346).

To ask for the respect in which two subjects have the same A-respect is to ask, of course, for a P-respect. In this sequence each specified respect is the necessary and sufficient condition of the preceding respect.

Since apparently the conditions are analogous, that is, they are the same in certain respects, a clear line of investigation is suggested by the simple question as to whether they are alike in other respects.

Suppose, however, that one were to try to formulate an analogy between the kinds of circumstances just referred to and the relations between minority groups and dominant groups within communities. Merton speaks of the resentment which members of the "in-group" feel toward members of the "out-group"; they are resentful of them, attribute unpleasant characteristics to them, particularly inferior intelligence (for example, Negroes), and where this thesis obviously conflicts with the facts (in the case of Jews), a kind of immorality (15, pp. 182–188).

Could such a theory be maintained on the basis of factual similarity? The facts are, in this case, of different classifications. For example: the Pygmies are not members of the Bantu society, they have no desire to supplant them in terms of leadership in the Bantu society, nor to advance in any way in it; indeed, the contrary phenomenon occurs: the villagers try as much as possible to incorporate the Pygmies into their community practices for their own material benefit, while the Pygmies wish to avoid as much as possible involvement in the activities of the villagers, except those activities which provide them with what they want.

But certain likenesses may be urged. While the Bantus wish to incorporate the Pygmies into their cultural activities, they have no desire that they physically occupy the land that they, the villagers, occupy. It could be urged that the exclusion of the minority-groupers by the dominant-groupers from the status benefits of the society is "like" the exclusion of the Pygmies by the villagers from the occupation of their land. If one asks in what respect the exclusions are alike, the common "respect" is hard to find. To be sure, there would be certain concomitants of the status of power which would render it "like" the exclusion of the Pygmies. For example, the exclusions of minority-groupers from certain neighborhoods in more "civilized" societies is like the exclusion of Pygmies from various villages, but this is not essential to the issue since dropping the bars in one neighborhood results in property depreciation there and raising the bars in a new one. "Social" exclusion is in no respect "like" the physical exclusion of groups of people from the ownership and control of land. Such a suggestion, then, would be a purely metaphorical attempt to render two disparate sets of phenomena the same, hence subject to the same generalization.

For example, what would be the respect in which they would be alike? Consider a factor of more obvious pertinence, namely, the benefits that would accrue if one were to ask in what respect benefits would accrue to the minority-grouper who managed to become accepted by the dominant-groupers. The benefit would be an improvement in status: he would have access to groups to which he had little or none before; he would enjoy the regard of the dominant-groupers, he would be permitted to enjoy their leisure. "Benefit" in this sense is *toto coelo* different from "benefit" in the sense of an increase of necessities. The senses of "benefit" are metaphorically alike. That every man acts to benefit himself is a recognized truism. We recognize it to be so because those who use it intend the statement as something more than a truism: that the expected consequence of an act is always a benefit. But this would apply to cases of masochism, self-sacrifice, and so on, which would mean that "benefit" in this context is badly defined. To say that "status-benefits" are as different from "necessity-benefits" as I claim, we would have to ask: in what respect are they alike? There is none specifiable, though human talent may perceive "likeness," or "sameness."

My point is that there would (assuming a greater amount of data than presented here) be some justification to seek some of the characteristics of the Pygmy-villager situation in, say, the situation produced by the Indian invasions, or the Slavic displacement of the Finno-Ugrians in the North of Russia. But, on the basis of the similarities presented, there would be no grounds for asserting a similarity between, say, the relations between Negroes and Whites in present-day America on the one hand, and between the pygmies and the villagers on the other. There the similarity would be metaphoric. Since there is no respect in which they are specifically alike, there is no clear line of investigation suggested.

## C

In this section and the following ones we shall deal with theories specifically formulated to handle sociological data, concerned with social change. The examples we have already dealt with have been of different sorts: "ordinary" or "common-sense" language was used in the kidney-filter analogy, archaic theoretical language in connection with the plenist-vacuist controversy, and a primitive sort of conceptual jargon ("displacement") in connection with our "culture hypothesis." This section and the ones that succeed will deal with relatively sophisticated concepts deliberately devised and structured to deal with events to which the attention of investigators had already been attracted. But even so, our claim remains the same: that such conceptual structures provide us with analogies and P-respects suggesting possible lines of endeavor; that where there are no P-respects claimed, samenesses or likenesses are purely qualitative; and that the attempt to formulate a general theory provides us with "quality." The theories with which we shall be concerned will be those of Talcott Parsons and Ralf Dahrendorf.

Much of Parsons' theory can be viewed from the vantage point of his use of the terms "system" (what does not change) and "concrete" (what does). We shall begin with "system." As is well known, Parsons' approach to sociology is "systematic," as evidenced by the frequency with which such terms as "system," "structure," "frame of reference," "organization," "relation," and others appear in his titles and discussions. But the "system" of which he speaks must be thought of in terms of "unit acts" (21, p. 43) or "action" (that is, change) (23, p. 53). In the course of his writings Parsons' definition of these terms differs; in one of his latest works he has defined it as behavior which is (1) oriented toward a goal, (2) in a situation, (3) regulated by norms, and (4) motivated, or involves the expenditure of effort or energy (23, p. 51). Action requires an "actor" in a situation composed of objects (physical, cultural, or other actors). To these he bears "relations," which are "organized" into a "system" of "orientations" (viewpoints, goals, plans of action).

Actions themselves are organized into systems, which Parsons holds are, fundamentally, three: *Personality* systems, which are those actions of an actor which are interconnected and organized by "the structure of need-dispositions," and compatible with the actions and goals of other individual actors; *Social* systems, which are interactions of actors, engaging the focus of their attention, where other actors are the objects of a given actor's cathexis, cognition, and evaluation (in terms of the other's, or "alter's," goals and means thereunto) and engaging in "concerted action" with a common value and "a consensus of normative and cognitive expectations"; and *Cultural* systems, which involve the organization of values, norms, and symbols "abstracted" from the "elements" of the personality and social systems which have a degree of "consistency" with one another, and are "transmissible" from one personality or social system to another (23, pp. 54–55).

All these are involved in the "frame of reference" of the theory of action involving actors which, whether individuals or "collectivities," are "empirical systems of action" — a situation which consists of those objects by which the actor orients himself, and the orientation of the actor to the situation, which involves cathexes, standards, plans by which the actor orients himself. Of these orientations, there are two. The first is *Motivational,* which has to do with the actor's gratifications and deprivations; of these there are three "modes": "cognitive," which has to do with the various ways in which the actor views the objects in connection with his need dispositions; "cathectic," in which the actor attributes significance to objects in terms of his needs and drives; and "evaluative," which is the means by which the actor "allocates" his activity and energy among the various "cathected" objects (23, pp. 61–63).

The second kind of orientation is the *Value Orientation,* which has to do with norms and criteria of selection relevant to choice. This also has three modes: the "cognitive," which has to do with criteria of the validity of cognitive judgments; the "appreciative," which has to do with the consistency of the various standards by which cathectic objects are judged; and the "moral" mode, which has to do with the standards by which various types of action and their consequences are judged with respect to their effects on various systems of action (23, pp. 67–76).

Parsons speaks of the "dilemmas" of orientation, and conceives of them in terms of "dichotomies." There are five dichotomies, or "pattern variables," so called because "any specific orientation is characterized by a pattern of the five choices" (23, p. 76). That is, they are the choices an actor must make with respect to a situation before that situation can become determinate and meaningful to him. They are: 1) Affectivity-Affective neutrality; 2) Self-orientation-Collectivity orientation; 3) Universalism-Particularism; 4) Ascription-Achievement; 5) Specificity-Diffuseness. In connection with the situation, these enable a concrete choice of specific action to be made. In connection with the personality system, they enable a choice to be made between habits. In connection with the collectivity, they define a person's rights and duties, i.e., his role. And in connection with the cultural system, the variables enter as a choice between standards of value (23, p. 78). In various ways, the pattern variables are defined with respect to the personality, the social, and the cultural systems.

With these in the background, we shall discuss the personality system first, then the social and cultural systems.

The central notion of the personality system, apart from the idea that it is a system of actions, is motivation. Parsons distinguishes two different meanings of "motivation": "energy" or "drive," and "a set of tendencies on the part of the organism to acquire certain goal objects . . ." (23, p. 111). In this latter sense, it refers to the system of orientations, plans for means and goal reaching with respect to cathected objects. Drives are "innate"; "need-dispositions" are those tendencies which are acquired in the process of drive activity. The latter term has two meanings: (1) the tendency to achieve a certain end; and (2) the disposition to do something with an object designed for the purpose. These may be had with respect to attitudes and relationships to objects (which may, the reader will recall, be other persons as well as oneself), with respect to cultural standards (or "internalized social values"), and with respect to role expectations (e.g., esteem if one has high social status; love, if one is a parent, etc.). With these characteristics in mind, we must conceive of the personality as a system which has a "persistent tendency toward an optimum (as distinguished from maximum) level of gratification" (23, p. 121). This is done by correctly resolving "problems of allocation" and "problems of integration." The former have to do with time and energy, and the latter with drives and need dispositions, i.e., avoiding "conflict" between them.

Parsons, of course, develops his personality system theory in much greater detail than is possible in a short statement of his position.

The difference between the personality system and the social system lies in what Parsons calls the differences of the "foci" of organization. The focus of the personality system is the act and its standards, while the focus of the social system is the role, and the complex of roles in which individuals engage. Most important to roles (undefined, by the way), are the "role expectations," which "organize . . . the reciprocities, expectations, and responses to those expectations in the specific inter-action systems of ego and one or more alters" (23, p. 190). It is the reciprocal of the "sanction," which is what the relevant alters expect of the egos, that is, that of the individual in question. Each ego, then, has an orientation role and an object-role; the former has to do with ego's orientation toward alter, and the latter has to do with the fact that alter regards ego as a social object.

In a social system, the roles vary with the institutionalization, i.e., the integration of the role expectations and sanction patterns in accordance with a value system which is common to members of the collectivity. In a collectivity, under these circumstances, action is in concert toward various objects and various sorts of objects. Two other types of "social aggregates" are "categories" of persons (mere classifications) and "pluralities" of people who are ecologically interdependent (as is supposed to happen in the market in perfect competition). The collectivity differs from the category in that the category involves no "action in concert"; it differs from both the social system and the social aggregate in that it has "solidarity," wherein there are tendencies toward shared gratifications.

Inherent, therefore, in Parsons' approach to "the social system" is "the *inter*-action of the individual actors, that it takes place under such circumstances that it is possible to treat such a process of inter-action as a 'system'" (22, p. 1). It is conceived in terms of "the action frame of reference" which has to do with "one or more actors" in a situation that includes other actors. Hence, it is a "relational scheme," requiring situations. Parsons holds that, at some point, "the most elementary components of any action system may be reduced to the actor and his situation" (22, p. 7). For purposes relevant to the social system Parsons describes the situation in the following way:

> The situation is described as consisting of objects of orientation so that the orientation of a given actor is differentiated relative to the different objects and classes of objects, namely, social, physical and cultural objects. The social object is an "actor" which may in turn be another individual actor (alter), the actor who is taken as a point of reference himself (ego) or a collectivity which is treated as a unit for purposes of the analysis of orientation. Physical objects are empirical entities which do not "interact" or "respond" to ego. They are means and conditions of his action. Cultural objects are symbolic elements of the cultural tradition, ideas or beliefs, expressive symbols or value patterns so far as they are treated as situational

objects by ego and are not "internalized" as constitutive elements of the structure of his personality (22, p. 4).

"The most elementary components of action in general" are formulated in the context of the social system. "Need-disposition system" is the most elementary, of which "the two most primary or elementary aspects" are the "gratificational" and the "orientational." The first concerns the "content" and what the "cost" of the actor's interaction with the world is; the second concerns the how," i.e., patterns of organization with respect to the actions toward the world. The first therefore is cathectic (". . . the significance of the ego's relation to the object or objects in question for the gratification-deprivation balance of his personality."). The most fundamental "orientational" category is the "cognitive" orientation or "mapping," which is most generally treated as the "definition" of the aspects of the situation relevant to the actor's interests . Finally, these entail "an evaluative aspect of all concrete action orientation," which means "an ordered selection among . . . alternatives." The last three are, of course, the modes of motivational orientation, and along with the object-system categorize the elements of action "on the broadest level" (22, pp. 7–8).

These elements are involved in the structure of an "expectation" which has to do with action. Since the reference is to the future, expectation has a time element. That is, it implies a temporal dimension of the actor's concern with the development of the situation. From the point of view of the pattern variables, expectation may be differentiated "along an activity-passivity co-ordinate." The future state which the actor acts to bring about, and hence "expects" is called the "goal." Expecting, then, has to do with activity; "merely waiting," having to do with passivity, is referred to as "anticipation" (22, p. 8).

Further conceptual development runs along similar lines. Parsons goes on to discuss "cognitive," "appreciative," and "moral" standards along with "relational," "regulative," and "cultural" institutions. These merge into the social structure, which he discusses in terms of "relations," "status," and "role" (i.e., the "structure" of relations within which the actor finds himself, the specific "place" he has and the norms according to which he must act). But again, an exhaustive treatment of Parsons is impossible in these pages, and we have discussed enough of the "social system" for our purposes.

Parsons' discussion of the cultural system has not, to date, been extensive. By and large, the cultural system has to do with the "meanings," "signs," or "symbols" which become relevant to the actor's expectations system. When these "serve as media of communication between actors," we have the beginnings of "culture." A cultural system, then, includes "systems of interaction of a plurality of actors oriented to a situation and where the system includes a commonly understood system of cultural symbols" (22, p. 5). The elements of a cultural system are constituted by "symbol systems" of which there are the usual three sorts: cognitive, having a connection with beliefs or ideas; cathectic, having a connection with "expressive symbols," in which the orientation brought about by the object of cathexis is "inward toward the affective state" (23, p. 163), and evaluative, in which "regulatory symbols" or "normative ideas" have the primacy. Each of these provides a corresponding pattern or type of standard of value orientation (referred to also as "normative ideas" and "evaluative symbols"): cognitive, e.g., veridical and non-veridical standards; appreciative, which have to do with standards in connection with art, persons (i.e., personal responses), and collectivities; and moral, e.g., good and bad.

With respect to action-orientations, i.e, actions in which the foci of orientation are standards, ideas, and symbols, the same triad turns up in another guise. They are "instrumental" where the foci are on cognitive problems to be solved by reference to cognitive standards; "expressive," where the foci are on cathectic problems to be solved by reference to appreciative standards; and "moral," where the foci are on evaluative problems to be solved by reference to moral standards (23, pp. 157–159).

Each of these three systems (personality, social, and cultural) is indispensable to the other, though not "derivable" from the other (22, p. 6). There are, however, certain "transformations" (undefined) between one and the other, though on this "theoretical level" they are not a "single system." Finally "it is a fundamental property of action thus defined that it does not consist of ad hoc 'responses' to particular 'stimuli' but that the actor develops a *system* of 'expectations' relative to the various objects of the situation" (22, p. 6). The latter is particularly indicated by the fact that the five pattern variables are applicable in all three systems.

It has been pointed out that Parsons has not developed a "unified deductive system" but that what "derivations" there are are "connotative" (28, p. 93). That is true. Nevertheless, he has worked out a set of terms and statements the nature of which can provide us with a setting for the formulation of analogies. For example:

A) A university is a social system whose members have roles, and a street gang is a social system whose members have roles.

In what respect are these alike?

B) In the respect that the members each have role expectations within their respective social systems.

In what respect are these alike?

C) In the respect that in each social system the role expectations are of love, esteem, and so on.

In this case $S$ and $S'$ are the university and the street gang, $A$ is "a social system whose members have roles," $P_i$ is "having role expectations within the social system," which is a member of the class (of attributes $K$ with members $P_1, P_2, \ldots, P_n$.) of expectations. (A) and (B) are equivalent.

Few people have used the conceptual structure Parsons has proposed as a guide to inquiry, though there are some cases (6, pp. 419–427). Possibly the most successful application of his theory is executed by himself, in Chapter 10 of *The Social System*, which analyzes the medical profession in the light of his concepts. Would casting Parsons' conceptual structure in the above analogical pattern provide a suggestion for a direction of investigation (12, p. 44)?[4] My point is that the pattern suggests further points of comparison between the above social systems; e.g., are role expectations of the same sort in both the university and the street gang?

Likeness sought for may not, of course, obtain in fact. There remains the possibility of a perceived likeness in one A-respect, where no P-respect can be specified. For example:

The child "loves" his father and the gang member "loves" his gang leader.

In what respect are these alike?

The child obeys his father and the street gang member obeys his leader.

This is too often false — in what other respect, then?

And so on with respect to other claimed likenesses. If all of them are discovered to be false and there is yet perceived a likeness or sameness, then the claimed likeness or sameness may be judged to be "qualitative."

There is a legitimate claim to be made for Parsons' "systematic" organization of concepts and statements. Though he does not always distinguish clearly between "action system" and "system of statements and concepts about the action system," there is nevertheless a system of concepts and statements which must be regarded as maintaining a permanent status, in the sense that any kind of social change (action) is ultimately capable of being described by them. A specific actor and action may be described by statements about goals, norms, motivations, and situations as well as by statements about features of the "action system," constituted by the personality, social, and cultural systems. They are or may be persistently used to describe any social change. In order to describe any social change or action, the entire system must be brought to bear.

---

[4] "The use of formalism in sociological data is not yet likely to lead to new findings. But it can disclose unnoticed implications or clarify the relations among propositions" (12, p. 44).

But, first, we want to specify change relative to what does not change; the kind of job for which such concepts as "variable," "constant," and "function" are suited. Parsons does use "variable" and "function." Yet the sense which attends his use of "variable" (in connection with "pattern variables") is only slightly analogous to its use in mathematics and mathematical physics. As for "function," its use in sociology (particularly Parsons' sociology) is merely parallel rather than identical with its use in mathematical physics. Its use in sociology, as distinct from its use in mathematics or formalized physical theory, is to refer to a process which varies on the condition that a number of others do, but the variation is either of a non-formalized sort (i.e., no definite proportion can be formulated between the process in question and those which constitute its conditions), or it is one which cannot be traced in detail.

Second, we want to preclude reference to certain kinds of change. In classical mechanics, for example, a given prediction must be formulated in terms of the fundamental concepts defined in the definitions and the axioms. But if a body is moving because of gravitational attraction, we are not compelled to add that it is moving because of centrifugal force; centrifugal force may be added to the gravitational force but each force may be separately estimated, given certain initial conditions. In Parsons' system the description of an action does not preclude the social system or the cultural system when the personality system is involved; nor, for example, can it be said that when the cognitive elements are present, the cathectic and appreciative elements are precluded. All such elements are involved in every action; we must take into consideration the entire "action system" and recognize that all the concepts and statements constituting Parsons' system are entailed, logically or otherwise. Individuals (or "actors") may be described as changing, but the systematic structure may not; and the system of concepts and statements formulates the respects in which the individuals change. Still, we want, it would appear, other ways of speaking of change than by using "change" or a synonym, as Parsons does with "action."

Parsons is trying to provide a conceptual apparatus in terms of which a theory of "social action" (or change) may be interpreted. Is the specification of "sameness" of any mode of behavior interpretable in these terms? It is instructive to compare Parsons' position with that of physical theorists prior to the formalization of physical theory; as an example, William of Heytesbury (c. 1313–1372).[5] Consider the change in the theory of motion (change of position) between Heytesbury and Galileo, in particular, free fall. Heytesbury believed that motion should be conceived of in terms of a proportion between spaces and times (29, p. 119; 4, pp. 93–95). What distinguishes Heytesbury's theory from Galileo's is the Heytesbury formulation that the spaces traversed were directly

---

[5] The comparison with pre-Galilean physics is not invidious; it is merely that the examples are simpler.

proportional to the times, rather than the squares of the times. Hindsight guarantees us the falsity of this formulation. Nevertheless, analysis and criticism continued after Heytesbury, so we may presume that the investigators of the time were convinced of the incompleteness of their investigations into local motion. That is, they felt that the correct formula had not been achieved (29, pp. 143–147). On the other hand, they did feel that the phenomena Heytesbury described were alike, but in some other respect than he specified. The respect, was, of course, formulated by Galileo. But since Heytesbury's formulation did not succeed, certainly Galileo and others felt that there must be some other respect in terms of which the instances of "local motion" were alike. Prior to Galileo's formulation this respect was unknown, although sought. And for this reason, it is justifiable to say that, from this standpoint, their physics was "qualitative."

Parsons' position is analogous. He says that if any person is to be described as performing a "unit act," he must conform to all the prerequisites he specifies, otherwise he is not. The assertion of sameness or likeness of the subjects is assumed to be incomplete precisely because the formula in terms of which the sameness and likeness is to be asserted has not yet been found. It is more than possible that the Parsons' concept will not figure in what may turn out to be the successful formulation, but that is what makes his formulations of the various aspects of sociological concepts qualitative: what is being sought is some other respect in terms of which the subjects may be said to be the same; and what is claimed is that they are the same in an unspecified, unknown respect.

This is what strikes us so forcefully about "system." There are few more difficult words in the history of intellectual endeavor than "system." Its extension ranges from purely formal systems of logic to mechanical systems. When we consider the many "systems" we encounter in proceeding from one end to the other (geometrical systems, physical systems, biological systems, organizational systems, personality systems, astronomical systems, and so forth) for which there is no common definition, we may begin to understand the care we must exercise in using the word, and why, ultimately, we can define the word, if at all, ostensively: we may indicate this system or that system by appropriate means and state what properties each has which are responsible for its being a system. That is as far as we can go.

Parsons, at least sometimes, seems to confuse one kind of "system" with another. On the one hand, he talks about the "system" of human actions, each of which conditions and is conditioned by others; on the other, he seems to be talking about a theoretical "system" of propositions (or other symbolic expressions), each of which bears logical relations to the others. Whatever conditions may cause the behavior of certain actions, they do not, except by reference, or the rule-making capacity of propositions, "cause" logical relations to occur.

But, even when *prima facie* consideration of passages he has written suggests that he is dealing with the system of actions (when he writes that the "actor develops a *system* of 'expectations' relative to the various objects of the situation") he is confusing. Does he mean that expectations, anticipations, and preferences can be ordered in terms of their probabilities, and the desired can be ordered in terms of preference, so that some sort of answer can be given to "What is preferred?" by combining the expected and the anticipated? But of course, "needs" must be brought in. To be sure, there is a sense in which Parsons considers this when he says that the system of expectations "*may* be structured only relative to his own need-dispositions and the probabilities of gratifications are deprivations contingent on the various alterations of action which he may undertake" (22, p. 53). Two comments are relevant:

First, Parsons has limited his discussion to situations in which the actor perceives possible gratifications and deprivations (22, p. 4). Why Parsons insists on setting up his system this way is puzzling. Samuel Lubell once suggested that people often conceive their present problems in terms of past problems or conflicts which may have nothing to do with them (14, p. 162). Most people are often positively mistaken or not clear about their need dispositions, i.e., what they need to fulfill certain conditions of their psyche, to eliminate destructive factors in their psyche, or to create circumstances that provide gratification. These are facts of which Parsons must be aware.

Second, respondents to questionnaires provide information in ways other than by explicit replies to questions. More than their explicit answers may be properly inferred, much of which may contradict the explicit answers to explicit questions. The respondent may be lying, but he may also believe what is false.

If the causes perceived by an investigator are different from what a respondent says they are, two possibilities emerge. (1) The interpretation may be made relative to a frame of reference containing factors of which the respondent is not conscious, but which have to do with his behavior. For example, a man may be in a severe state of depression without knowing that the immediate cause of it was the fact that someone he admired was just rude to him; he might even protest that this is not the reason and honestly believe it. (2) The interpretation may be made relative to a frame of reference which has to do with the individual, but only insofar as he is a member of a given kind or class. For example, a dominant-group member may suppose his dislike of a minority-group member stems from the minority group's "infraction" of certain "rules," e.g., working late at night or on Sundays. An investigator might recognize from the pattern of the dominant-group member's attributes and replies that his attitude is typical of dominant group-minority group relations. These suggest that "beginning" with the individual's own perception of his cathexes, rather than with a theoretical structure, is not always the best way.

It is too early to tell which kinds of clues and evidence are less reliable than others, and to preclude still others. If the theoretical structure says one thing and the experimental or investigative techniques another, either the theoretical system must be so defined as not to preclude the techniques (in which case the terms of the system mean something different) or the theoretical system itself has to be replaced or modified. Parsons, by insisting that this "action system" have to do only with perceived gratifications and deprivations, would eliminate much investigation.

It is hard to say with complete conviction what apparently misleads Parsons, but this writer is reasonably sure that one of the most basic reasons is his commitment to what he conceives of as the "concrete." Unfortunately, the word is used in many senses. For our purposes, three may be isolated:

1) The empirical sense — "A concrete name is a name which stands for a thing; an abstract name is a name which stands for an attribute of a thing."[6] Thus, in the sentence, "This paper is white," *this paper* is concrete and *whiteness* is abstract.

2) The poetic sense, involving an evoked image of an object as though directly present to perception, where the image is particularly vivid; in this context, "concrete" is synonymous with "vivid." For example, in "Beauty is but a flower which wrinkles will devour," the image evoked is of a flower losing its firmness in the process of decay. But which flower, in what sort of circumstances, Thomas Nash does not say. To be sure "wrinkling" does occur in individual flowers, but it is the "wrinkling," i.e., the attribute, that one must imagine as well as the flower to which it happens.

3) The Hegelian sense, in which the concrete is that which is immersed in its relations; one must consider the individual in its milieu of relations and connections. In Hegel's philosophy, "concrete" is the opposite of "abstract"; to "abstract" is to consider an object apart from its circumstances, connections, and relations. Perceiving a man, one notes many characteristics displayed in varying circumstances; many men display even more characteristics in even more varying circumstances. To select two, as Aristotle did, and define "man" in terms of the characteristics "rational" and "animal" is to ignore the others, and to abstract "rational" and "animal" from the circumstances, relations, and connections in which they are displayed. In this way Hegel arrives at the "abstract universal," since "rational animal" is an "abstraction" conceived of and attributable to all men. This is the sort of thing to which Hegel was opposed. "Man" must be known in terms of the concrete circumstances in which he develops — in terms of the entire history of circumstances, involving man's trials, victories, hardships, triumphs, and so on. In this case man is known in terms of all the connections and relations in which each circumstance of his development occurs. It is under

[6] J. S. Mill, *System of Logic*, Bk. 1, ch. 2, par. 4. Mill's definition has been a standard one since the nineteenth century.

this condition that Hegel can talk about "man" being a "concrete universal." It is in this context of discussion that Hegel conceived of "concrete" as having to do with that which was not abstracted from its circumstances, connections, and relations.

It would appear, *prima facie*, that Parsons is using the Hegelian sense of "concrete." For he does try to discuss the "unit action" as an act which is exercised only in the "system" he provides. What he apparently is saying is that the "act" takes place only within the "personality," "social," and "cultural" systems. The unit act and the individual actor, then, have to be conceived in these terms.

Two points are relevant. One is that, though Parsons seems to suggest that the unit act can only be understood within the circumstances in which it occurs, he is more interested in "blocking off" the unit act so that any act by a given actor may be completely described. The description of the act is provided by highly abstract terms, e.g., when the motivational orientation is described by the triad of cognitive, cathectic, and evaluative, none of these terms can be said to be "concrete" in any of the current senses. Secondly, if one objects to the above by pointing out that Hegel's classification of knowledge is done this way, it may be replied that this is so only to a limited extent, for Hegel's system had to do with the dialectical ordering — the "unity" of the "thesis" and "antithesis" in a higher "synthesis." Parson's ordering, though often triadic, is not dialectical. Parsons' use of "concrete" seems to be a mixture of the senses we specified; that is what may lead to some of his difficulties. Take, for example, his apparent confusion between the senses of "system." He feels, apparently, that it is necessary to talk about "system" in order to talk about the "concrete," but in doing so, he does not differentiate between the formal requirement of a system of knowledge, and requirements of a system of actions.

Thus, Parsons talks about individuals who conform only to abstract characteristics which he speaks of as being "in the concrete." This is further compounded when he defines "social" and "cultural" in abstract terms different from those in which one is accustomed to hearing them defined. Presumably he would want to argue that these are the characteristics that they do in fact display, and for this reason he can sensibly talk about their being "concrete." But to this there are two obvious answers. For one thing, the terms for characteristics we attribute to individuals on the common-sense level "in the concrete," are not likely to mean the same thing when interpreted in a theoretical context. Thus, "force" was once interpreted in terms of human exertion, but that is far from the meaning the term eventually acquired in classical mechanics (19, p. 118).[7] In this case, the concrete, though it may have enabled the early mechanicians to arrive at a concept of force employable in a theoretical framework, was *toto coelo* different from what its theoretical

---

[7] An excellent source of similar examples is (27, chapter 3).

requirements demanded — if anything, they demanded a withdrawal from the concrete. For another thing, many central factors used in many classical sciences are not discoverable "in the concrete," e.g., mass.

The previous points about "system" and the "concrete" enable us, I think, to pinpoint one other way in which we can say that the sociology of Parsons is "qualitative." He wishes to argue that what he is providing is a "system." But he always believes his "system" to be incomplete, as is evidenced by the fact that he is continually adding to it. But it is not only from this standpoint that we may regard Parsons' work as incomplete, for if we ask what the criteria for the system of sociology are which would enable us to accept it as valid and composed of true statements, the criteria would be only partly specified. For example, two criteria for the acceptability of a logical system are consistency and completeness; these criteria would apply to the formal system constructed in Newton's *Principia;* but other criteria would have to apply, for one needs "co-ordinating definitions" or "correspondence rules" to relate the terms used in the system and the experimental phenomena. In the case of Galileo's law of free fall, $S = \frac{1}{2}at^2$, we would have to provide a set of rules which would correspond the various computed positions with, say, the various distances a freely falling body moves, starting with 0 velocity along with the positions of the hands on a clock. Undoubtedly correspondence rules would be present in the various areas of a formalized system of sociology. But it is precisely such rules that we do not know, rules which enable us to provide a "definition" of a sociological "system."

We previously pointed out that there is no common definition of "system" applicable to all those entities to which the word refers; we also pointed out that cases into which some rigor has been introduced do provide some criteria, and the criteria of what a system constitutes differ from case to case. Parsons uses "system" in an anticipatory way, for the presumption of his investigation is that there are criteria other than those presently available by which we may decide that the statements which describe the phenomena in question belong to a "system."

If therefore we ask:

In what respect is sociology a system?

the answer that Parsons and many others would give is:

There are many but we don't know some.

That is, there is some respect, presently incapable of being specified, in which the phenomena referred to in sociological statements can be said to be "the same" or "alike"; but a system of statements and concepts, "permanent" and "remaining the same" in the sense of persistent (or possible) reference to objects of social change, cannot be formulated.

D

Dahrendorf tries to approach sociology on a less ambitious basis, for his terms are fewer and more restricted in scope and he combines with this moderate application of Occam's Razor a persistent attempt to state empirical "conditions" for the theoretical terms he proposes. He tries to explain social change in terms of class, and he defines class in terms of "conflict": a "class" is any group of persons whose activities are directed against another person or group of persons. This formulation grows out of Dahrendorf's conception of the opposition between "coercion theory" and "integration theory" respectively, the theory that an ubiquitous social change is to be explained in terms of social conflicts and that social integration is to be explained in terms of the coercion of some members of society by others (5, p. 162), and the theory that social change is to be explained in terms of "functional relations" and the repetition of process patterns (5, p. 159). Each of these is invalid for various purposes, and Professor Dahrendorf wishes to provide a theory in terms of which social change may be conceived as both. That is, patterned group processes do occur, within a functional unity, but the mechanics of this process is conflict.

Individuals have "interests" or "values" impressed upon them by their social milieu; they are exhibited in "associations" where each individual has a "role," i.e., performs a function necessary to the operation of that association. In any society each individual belongs to more than one association and in each he performs no more than one role. His role in the association brings out two kinds of interests: latent and manifest. Latent interests are unconscious but dependent upon his role, and manifest interests are those which are made explicit through the individual's performance in and articulation of his role (5, pp. 172–189).

Dahrendorf then distinguishes between "interest groups," based upon manifest interests which he describes as "psychologically real," in which the association has an explicit and manifest organization of roles ordered in relation of authority and subjection or "imperative co-ordination," and secondary or "quasi-groups," which cannot be said to be groups in any "real" (organized) sense, but which have various latent interests in common, e.g., those occupying correlative positions in different organizations. Inasmuch as latent conflict arises out of authority-subjection, quasi-groups are the area of recruitment for interest groups. To the extent that quasi-groups take on any structure of organization, they become interest groups, e.g., labor unions and employer associations. Classes emerge when an association has groups which develop out of the respective authority-imperative orders of the associations (5, p. 206). By "authority" we are to understand a person's capacity to command someone else, where that capacity depends solely on what the protagonists do in the association.

"Permanence" and "change" have to be understood in this context. What possesses "permanence" here is the "imperatively coordinated association," which Dahrendorf thinks of as "structure." The latter does not have permanence in the sense that, say, an ontologist's conception of "being" may have, but Dahrendorf's conception of "structure" does provide us with a relatively formalized sketch of the permanent elements in a social organization. Yet "structure" is ambiguous; on the one hand, we are required to view the association as a web of interlocking commanding-commanded relationships; on the other hand, "structure" is to be understood as the conflicting groups which compose a given society. "There are, within social structures, certain elements or forces which are at the same time their constituent parts (and therefore 'function' within them) and impulses operating toward their supersedence and change . . . social classes are elements of this kind" (5, p. 123). Dahrendorf is opposed to the biological analogy to be found in "structural-functional" analysis; he finds it too constricting. "Society is process"; and this does not mean that it is a process of specific organs performing various functions, though the constitution of the organs is continually changing. Process in society must be so conceived that we may speak of change, but also so that we may speak of elements which change (i.e., classes, themselves being replaced by others); the mechanism is "conflict." We can understand what Dahrendorf is thinking about; a class conflict between landowners and entrepreneurs was historically succeeded by a class conflict between entrepreneurs and proletarians; and yet the societies within which these occurred remained "the same," e.g., in Germany.

There are three "empirical" (as opposed to "formal") conditions for the formation of interest groups out of quasi-groups: "technical" (those embracing the normative and procedural conditions, e.g., constitution, rules of procedure, norms, etc.); "political" conditions (specifically, political parties); and "social" conditions (communication between the members of a society) (5, pp. 182–189). Since they are the conditions for the formation of interest groups, they are the conditions for conflict. The intensity or violence of conflict varies according to many factors, of which Dahrendorf selects four: the extent to which the many possible conflict-fronts (due to the many imperatively ordered associations in a society) reduce to a few; the capacity of those higher in authority to distribute rewards and facilities; the degree to which associations are "open" or "closed" (and hence the extent to which mobility is possible); and the extent to which conflict is regulated by (not "suppressed," a word Dahrendorf considers "meaningless") the existing associations (5, pp. 210–231). The intensity, so measured, is (Dahrendorf theorizes) directly proportional to the "radicalness of structure change" and the "suddenness of structure change," that is, the extent to which norms are changed, and the extent to which the original occupants of various positions in the imperatively coordinated association are replaced.

What is important here is not society, but the features by means of which Dahrendorf wishes to describe as "the same" society or association. Galileo formulated $S = \frac{1}{2}at^2$ to describe the motion (change) of a freely falling body. The features he isolated were distance and time. Dahrendorf wants to select the features of the replacement of imperative order participants, and the number which are replaced as well as the value change they represent, and to make these the key to social change. For Galileo there was a direct proportion between the distance traversed by the falling body and the squares of the units of the times. Dahrendorf has not formulated a proportion in terms of which the various features of social change may be computed; nor does he claim to, though he does suggest a scale for the intensity and violence of social conflict, from 0 to 1, (5, p. 230), and hence claims to be developing concepts in terms of which various features of social changes might be formulated. Dahrendorf contrives, then, to formulate a conceptual structure in terms of which A-respects and P-respects may be formulated.

A) A strike in the auto industry is a social conflict about wages and working conditions and a strike in the newspaper industry is about wages and working conditions.

In what respect?

B) In the respect that both emerge out of manifest interests about wages and working conditions in imperatively coordinated associations.

In what respect?

C) In the respect that both emerge out of latent interests about wages and working conditions and proceed to manifest interests about wages and working conditions.

$S$ and $S'$ are the strikes in the respective industries, $A$ is the social conflict, $P_i$ is "about wages and working conditions," and $K$ is the class of attributes "issues about which there are social conflicts." (C) is the necessary and sufficient condition of (B), (B) is the necessary and sufficient condition of (A). There is a clear analogy between a strike in the automobile industry and a strike in the newspaper industry, and we may claim the similarities specified on an analogical basis. In this case, no reference to quality is required.

Nevertheless for the purposes of a "science" which will enable us to predict relevant differences between times and places, this is less than fully adequate. The discipline may become more adequate in this way when the concepts are more effectively quantized. But part of the trouble is that the concepts are not precise enough.

What does "precise" mean? Aristotle stated that no greater precision should be provided than is required by the subject. As it stands, the statement is merely good advice. Its relevance can be clarified only when "precision" has effects or consequences in a given discipline. Precision affects a given discipline if the refinements introduced by "making precise" are capable of producing refinements in the consequences. If the refinements are such that they either do not show up in the consequences or that the consequences are capable of being formulated in other terms equally well, then the "making precise" is not very good, and might better have been left out.

"Making precise" is the introduction of discriminations which had not previously been an explicit part of the concept in question. The greater the number of refinements, the greater the precision. Obvious examples of this have to do with the divisions that are marked off in an inch on a ruler and the calibrations marked off on a thermometer. But these are not the only kinds of "making precise" that can be attempted; there are others. Torricelli, by insisting that air had "weight," rendered it capable of calibrations it had not been capable of before.

But "making precise" requires caution. William Heytesbury, attempting to discover how the motion of a freely falling body should be determined, discussed, as an example, a freely falling wheel turning as it fell (29, p. 119). Which part of the wheel, he asked, should be regarded as the criterion of its velocity? His answer was that part of the wheel which was moving the most rapidly. It turned out that this refinement was unnecessary for many purposes. If we want to find out where a wheel that is freely falling will be, we simply calculate the time it has been falling; it is unnecessary to raise the question as to which part of the wheel is going fastest at a given moment. On the other hand, if we wish to know how the wheel will bounce, such a determination would have to be made. Heytesbury's attempt was a refinement, but unnecessary.

Medieval physicists distinguished between uniform and diform motion. The distinction, was, essentially, between the motion of an object which is the same distance per unit of time, and motion which is not. Diform motion had not yet been further made precise so as to have something to do with acceleration or deceleration. Yet we would have to argue that it constituted another class of kinds of motion, more precise than those theories which did not make the distinction. The lesson, of course, is that we can't always tell when to apply Aristotle's dictum and when not: the point in introducing a distinction is usually a hope that it will eventuate in an observable or manipulable differentiation in things. But if it doesn't immediately do so, there is no guarantee that it is pointless.

Or consider another case. A seventeenth-century chemist named Stahl distinguished what he thought of as a "fiery substance" in the air, which he referred to as phlogiston (3). Phlogiston was of such a nature that, when a metallic ore was heated, it united with certain substances in the oxide, caused them to leave the ore, and produce the pure metal. But phlogiston was never observed. What later came to be known as "reduction" was explained by it and it explained the occurrence of (relatively) pure metals. The point is that it was a discrimination, a conceptual refinement which had to do with observable phenomena, and in its way it was successful. To this extent it could be said to be more "precise" than the alchemical theories which preceded it.

Other examples may be adduced. But my point is that the establishment of precision is a way of classifying certain subjects as "the same" or "different." To make precise is to add refinements and to eliminate reference to attributes. In the history of the attempts to formulate the laws of motion, weight and impetus were eliminated as primitive concepts, while the remaining primitives were reduced to distance and time, and calibrated into finer subdivisions. New discrimination must be able to select various phenomena or subjects and make them "the same," which is where "quality" comes in. For, apart from the explanatory (and hence, logical) structure which have been imposed upon them, there is no way of discussing things as "non-qualitative."

The medieval physicists correctly (as it later turned out) believed that local motion had to be described in terms of a proportion. They were not clear about what the proportion was between, i.e., what specific criteria to select. Dahrendorf's attempt is to analyze social conflict in terms of "intensity" and "radicalness." But apart from the theoretical attributes he formulates in their connection, specific criteria to show the proportion between them are imprecise. Doubtless an industrial strike is a *prima facie* example of social conflict. Nevertheless we get lost in an endeavor to discover the criteria by which we are to decide that there is a strike. Is it a criterion that there is a work stoppage on a workday? But maybe they are going on their vacations. Is it that the laborers dislike their employers? Often they don't, and in certain cases may dislike their union officers more. Is the criterion of the conflict, then, the discussion of the union officers with the officers of management over the demands of the specific local? But if it is a discussion, why is it necessarily a conflict? Very well, then, it is a discussion of a certain sort, i.e., bargaining. But is bargaining conflict? Two men who sit down to bargain over the price of a commodity would not necessarily be regarded as being in conflict: each, after all, may have decided on the same price without argument, and to use the occasion for bargaining as an excuse to have a pleasant conversation. Why, then, insist upon this in the case of industrial and social phenomena? If the management wants to avoid a long, costly strike and the union officers want to avoid putting their comrades on a starvation basis, and if the management wants to please its stockholders but yet wants to lay off its men for a time because demand is slack, management and labor may agree on a short "strike" because it is advantageous to all to do so.

It is possible to dissolve every suggested criterion in a morass of analysis, unless we know where we are going — unless we already have an idea of what units of analysis will produce clear and dependable knowledge. "Quality" enters because there is no known respect in terms of which we may provide the analysis.

In terms of our example of the auto strike and the newspaper strike:

The auto strike is like the newspaper strike.

In what respect (where "respect" is restricted to an attribute that is a criterion)?

In the respect that in both cases the strikers left their jobs.

But that's no criterion: one group may have left for a vacation and the other may have left over wages and working conditions.

And so on, following the sequence of the previous paragraph. If no common, logically ordered, specifiable criteria (i.e., A-respects with P-respects) may be discovered for calling a given occurrence a "strike," then the only condition for saying that one is "like" another is "quality."

It is true that conflict may be determined by various "indicators" and indices, as Lazarsfeld shows. But the kind of indicators he discusses are not of the sort referred to above. They are such terms as "cohesiveness," "relevant disruptive forces," "location in society," etc. There is no obvious connection between these sets of attributes. We may be tempted to argue that the less the "cohesiveness," the greater the probability that one of the above-mentioned occurrences would indicate a strike. Nevertheless, if we were to seek a relevant respect in which they were alike apart from their connection with a strike, but which would be an indicator of a strike, the likeness would be hard to find, e.g.,

Mr. S and Mr. S′ had common grievances (one "variate" of "cohesiveness") and left the plant.

In what respect are their departures alike?

Apart from certain obvious biological traits common to both occasions but which are irrelevant, we would be hard put to it to state a likeness or sameness, or to formulate a conceptual structure persistently (or "permanently") capable of dealing with the above and other social changes effectively. Nevertheless, there is a claimed likeness or sameness, and this is qualitative.

## E

A common concern with many theoretical sociologists, among whom Parsons and Dahrendorf must be numbered, is the concept of "equilibrium."

Both these writers suppose that it is the task of sociological theory to provide a concept of equilibrium for the social order, so that it is possible for us to say under what conditions the community or society maintains itself. That is, they are asking what elements must remain unvarying (or permanent), or what group of elements must remain in an unvarying (or permanent) proportion, in order that the society or community merit some such description as "stable." That is, "equilibrium" is advanced as a means of formulating statements about the permanent features of social change.

Parsons' conception is "functional"; unit acts take place in the personality, social, and cultural systems, hence the "structure" is maintained. In *The Social System,* Parsons distinguishes between "static" and "moving" equilibria; he is concerned with moving equilibria. The concept of the moving equilibrium revolves around notions of two processes: that by which the actor orients himself to his role; and that by which orientations generating deviant behavior are "counterbalanced" by the "mechanisms of social control" (22, p. 482). In *Values, Motives and Systems of Action,* if I understand him correctly, he refers to the first as "allocation," which he defines more generally in the following way: ". . . processes which maintain a distribution of the components or parts of the system which is compatible with a given state of equilibrium." The second he refers to as "integration," which he defines again more generally as ". . . processes by which relations to the environment are mediated in such a way that the distinctive internal properties and boundaries of the system as an entity are maintained in the face of variability in the external situation" (23, p. 108). Though the descriptions of both processes in the different volumes do not seem to me to be strictly consistent, this may be accounted for in terms of a change of mind, or further development of thought. And in any case it is not to our purpose to criticize this aspect of Parsons' theory.

For Dahrendorf, the conception of equilibrium has to do with interlocking imperatively coordinated associations while the participants do or do not shift "places" in the different orders.

In Parsons' terms, this is also a "moving equilibrium," though a more simply conceived one. In order to see what is happening here, it is best to see what meanings are capable of being attributed to "equilibrium." I think five kinds of equilibrium can be distinguished:

1) Simple mechanical, where the balance of equal forces is conceived of in terms of levers, pulleys, screws, inclined planes, winches, and solids immersed in liquids.

2) Equilibrium in a system of moving bodies, where the movements of the individual bodies may be traced in paths that remain the same, as in the solar system.

3) Thermodynamical, where the equilibrium exists when the mean velocity of the molecules in various portions of a volume are the same.

4) Biological, where a given state (often referred to as the "G state") exists in a way such that if some of a number of conditions vary, the G state will vary, and vice versa.

5) The economic, where equilibrium describes the maintenance of supply, demand, and price of a given commodity in a competitive market.[8]

The attempt to discuss sociology in terms of "equilibrium" is not analogical but metaphorical. If one attempts to say that sociological equilibrium is analogous to simple mechanical equilibrium, one may ask in what respect the balance of weights on a lever is the same as or like the "allocation" of roles in society, or the regulation of conflict and coercion. If the claim is that it is like the equilibrium of the solar system, the respect is impossible to find. Parsons tries to "analogize" between the action system and the solar system in terms of "allocation" (23, pp.107–108), and this writer finds it puzzling. In what respect do we say that the distribution of "forces" is "like" the distribution of social roles or factors in a personality? I find the respect impossible to specify, just as some years ago certain sociologists were opposed to the supposed analogy in the term "social forces." There is no explicit respect in which it can be said that social forces and physical forces are the same, or alike. A similar objection occurs to use of the thermo-dynamical conception of equilibrium: society is not conceived of as "homogeneous" in all of its "sectors"; rather it is conceived of as being different in all of its sectors. As to the biological analogy, it has received enough criticism; but as an example it must be pointed out that "the flow of blood" is in no P-respect the same as "the flow of social change." Finally, one wonders indeed just what is being exchanged for what on the sociological scene, since exchange of commodities is central to the notion of equilibrium in the economic sense. To this it may be replied that they are alike because each person does perform an act on the condition that another perform an act, and this, it may be claimed, is "like" exchange of commodities: one person gives another a commodity if the other person gives him another commodity. But this is merely an analogy by courtesy, so to speak, for what is really alike is not the relations which are specified in each of the contexts, but the purely formal structure of the sentence specifying the acts in question, i.e., the propositional form "if . . . , then. . . ."

The attempt to describe society as a whole in terms of a broad concept like "equilibrium" results in the attempt to state the likeness or sameness of all sociological objects of change in terms of an unspecifiable though permanent respect, so that this supports the contention of sociological theorists that their objects are alike in some unspecifiable respect.

[8] Following Pareto's suggestion: sociology ceases to be similar to economics "when we come to the question of correspondences with reality" (20, p. 1291).

F

Considerations of this sort lead us to reflect upon the work of Robert K. Merton. He explicitly attacks the kind of generalizations attempted by Parsons and Dahrendorf, those which are applicable to societies as a whole; he rejects the present or near-future possibility of theories of the broadest range, and advocates "theories of the middle range" to avoid on the one hand, empty formulations, and on the other hand, "raw empiricism." That is to say, here one finds the most explicit statement that sociology is a discipline in which the formulations of general statements are recognized to be subject to immanent change.

In his discussion of the codification of laws (15, p. 49) Professor Merton makes reference to the work of B. L. Whorf who, in examining the reasons for various accidents in his capacity as a fire insurance inspector, noted that people reacted to their conceptions of states of affairs rather than to what the states of affairs in fact were. For example, in the presence of gasoline drums people are careful with matches, cigarettes, and other things likely to cause a fire; whereas in the presence of empty gasoline drums people behave carelessly, lighting cigarettes, freely tossing about lighted stubs, and so on, though in fact the "empty" drums are at least as hazardous as the filled ones because they contain highly explosive vapor. "Empty" is ambiguous: it means null and void, and it means devoid of gasoline. To the uninitiate it means the former; to the technical staff it means the latter. Hence conceptualization is different for each, and is responsible for different kinds of behavior. Merton's point is that sociological conceptualization determines an investigator's response to data in a similar way.

There are, then, different respects in which the data of social change may be rendered "the same" or "alike," depending on how the investigator conceptualizes them. But he cannot know antecedently which of many conceptualizations will be successful, if any. If a "theory of the middle range" is proposed, one class of data may be rendered "the same" as another, and formulations are to this extent "the same" relevant to social changes, though, as noted, themselves subject to change. If a theory of Parsonian scope is proposed, formulations are to be regarded as "permanent" relevant to social change. In either case, what is asserted to be the same or alike in given respects is admittedly alike in other respects, presently unknown.

BIBLIOGRAPHY

1. Burtt, E. A. *The Metaphysical Foundations of Physics*. New York: Harcourt, Brace, 1932.

2. Conant, J. B. "Robert Boyle's Experiments in Pneumatics," Case I,

*Harvard Case Studies in Experimental Science,* Vol. 1. Cambridge: Harvard University Press, 1957.

3. Conant, J. B. "The Overthrow of the Phlogiston Theory," Case II, *Harvard Case Studies in Experimental Science,* Vol. 1. Cambridge: Harvard University Press, 1957.

4. Crombie, A. C. *Medieval and Early Modern Science,* Vol. 2. New York: Doubleday-Anchor Books, 1959.

5. Dahrendorf, Ralf. *Class and Class Conflict in Industrial Society.* Stanford. Stanford University Press, 1959.

6. Gouldner, Alvin W. "Organizational Analysis," in Robert K. Merton, Leonard K. Broom, and Leonard S. Cottrell (eds.), *Sociology Today.* New York: Basic Books, 1959.

7. Hanson, Norbert R. *Patterns of Discovery.* London: Cambridge University Press, 1958.

8. Harrison, Jane. *Themis,* 2nd ed. London: Cambridge University Press, 1927.

9. Hempel, Carl. "The Logic of Functional Analysis," in Llewelyn Gross (ed.), *Symposium on Sociological Theory.* Evanston, Ill.: Row, Peterson and Co., 1959.

10. Jammer, Max. *Concepts of Space.* Cambridge: Harvard University Press, 1957.

11. Koyre, Alexander. *From the Closed World to the Infinite Universe.* New York: Harper Torchbook, 1958.

12. Lazarsfeld, Paul F. "Problems in Methodology," in Robert K. Merton, Leonard K. Broom, and Leonard S. Cottrell (eds.), *Sociology Today.* New York: Basic Books, 1959.

13. Lovejoy, A. O. *The Great Chain of Being.* Cambridge: Harvard University Press, 1936.

14. Lubell, Samuel. *The Future of American Politics,* 2nd ed., rev. New York: Harper Torchbook, 1956.

15. Merton, Robert K. *Social Structure and Social Theory.* Glencoe, Ill.: The Free Press, 1949.

16. Murray, Margaret. *The God of the Witches.* New York: Doubleday-Anchor Books, 1960.

17. Nagel, Ernest. "Logic Without Ontology," in Krikorian (ed.), *Naturalism and the Human Spirit.* New York: Columbia University Press, 1944.

18. Nagel, Ernest. "A Formalization of Functionalism," in *Logic Without Metaphysics.* Glencoe, Ill.: The Free Press, 1956.

19. Nagel, Ernest. *The Structure of Science.* New York: Harcourt, Brace and World, 1962.

20. Pareto, Vilfredo. "On the Equilibrium of the Social System," a selection from *The Mind and Society,* in Talcott Parsons, Edward Shils, Kaspar D. Naegele, and Jesse R. Pitts (eds.), *Theories of Society.* Glencoe, Ill.: The Free Press, 1961, Vol. 2.

21. Parsons, Talcott. *The Structure of Social Action*, 2nd ed. Glencoe, Ill.: The Free Press, 1949.

22. Parsons, Talcott. *The Social System*. Glencoe, Ill.: The Free Press, 1951.

23. Parsons, Talcott, and Edward Shils, eds. "Values, Motives and Systems of Action," Part 2 of *Toward a General Theory of Action*. New York: Harper Torchbook, 1962.

24. Pascal, Blaise. *The Physical Treatises of Pascal. The Equilibrium of Liquids, The Weight of the Mass of the Air*, translated by I.H.B. and A.G.H. Spiers. New York: Columbia University Press, 1937.

25. Seyffert, Oskar. *Dictionary of Classical Antiquities*, revised and edited by Henry Nettleship and J. E. Sandys. New York: Meridian Library, 1956.

26. Turnbull, Colin M. "The Lesson of the Pygmies," *Scientific American*, January 1962.

27. Watson, W. H. *On Understanding Physics*. New York: Harper Torchbook, 1959.

28. Williams, Robin M. Jr. "The Sociological Theory of Talcott Parsons," in Max Black (ed.), *The Social Theories of Talcott Parsons*. Ithaca, N.Y.: Cornell University Press, 1961.

29. Wilson, Curtis M. *William Heytesbury, Medieval Logic and the Rise of Mathematical Physics*. Madison: University of Wisconsin Press, 1956.

30. Wolf, A. *A History of Science, Technology and Philosophy in the Sixteenth and Seventeenth Centuries*, 2nd ed. New York: Harper Torchbook, 1959, Vol. 1.

# 3

*C. P. Wolf*

# The Structure of Societal Revolutions[1]

Ours is often called an "age of revolution." The revolutionary phenomenon of our revolutionary age is commonly addressed in political terms, as *political* revolution. I want to argue that this is a case of partly mistaken identity — that revolution is fundamentally a *societal* phenomenon, that revolutionary change is *societal* change, and that an accurate estimate of the revolutionary situation must involve *societal* analysis. Insistence upon full societal context as the context of sociological meaning is a tenet of functionalism more professed than practiced. I shall argue, however, that such understanding can be achieved through the structural-functional theory of macro-social change: the theory of structural differentiation.

My argument is organized into three main parts, taken for purposes of theory construction as a problem-solving process (Fig. 1). Part I places the revolutionary phenomenon in societal perspective and explores some analytic problems connected with treating revolutionary change as change in the structure of society. Part II presents several defining criteria for societal revolutions and proposes a historical series based on their application. Part III compares three macro-change models — the "economic," "religious" and "sociological" — to account for these revolutionary eras. The "sociological model" includes a "power model" consisting

[1] I wish to thank George K. Zollschan for his encouragement and criticism of an earlier draft. Martin U. Martel performed editorial heroics beyond the call of colleagueship. The argument of this chapter was presented in a talk given at the New School for Social Research in April, 1972.

of part-theories of political revolution and a macro-model, the "theory of structural differentiation." Parsons' "evolutionary universals" schema is cited as exemplifying the latter construction. The discussion closes with a reformulation and deployment of the differentiation model.

### Fig. 1.  The Structure of Societal Revolutions: Analytic Outline

| I. THE PROBLEM | II. THE PROCEDURE | III. THE SOLUTION |
|---|---|---|
| "What happened in history" — the history of society — and why? | Definition<br>  Conceptual<br>    Irreversibility<br>    Suddenness<br>    Acceleration<br>    Discontinuity<br>    Violence | Technology and the<br>  Moral Order<br><br>The "Economic Model"<br><br>The "Religious Model" |
| Specification: The "Revolutionary Theme" Institutional Revolutions | Empirical<br>  Population Index<br>  Index of Revolutionary Potential | The "Sociological Model"<br>  Sociological Theories<br>    of Revolution<br>  Theory of Structural<br>    Differentiation |
| Societal Revolutions<br>  The Structure of<br>    Society<br>"Engel's Problem"<br>"Evolution" and<br>  "Revolution"<br>"Normal" and "Revolutionary Change" | Enumeration<br>Classification<br>Dating<br>Duration<br>Distribution | Evolutionary Universals<br><br>"What is Revolutionary<br>about Societal Revolutions?" |

## I. The Problem

The problem this chapter addresses can be stated, broadly and baldly, in the question "What happened in history — the history of society — and *why?*" It concentrates on the "revolutionary theme" and its variations, the events and epochs in the history of society which have been called "revolutionary."[2]

The rhetoric of "Revolution" is currently in fashion.[3] Applied to all manner of conditions and causes, the word has been flagrantly abused and

---

[2] Another phrasing of the question is Hobsbawm's (29, p. 28): "how humanity got from the caveman to modern industrialism or post-industrialism, and what changes in society were associated with the progress, or necessary for it to take place, or consequential upon it."

[3] According to Brogan (5, p. 1), the idea of revolution has its origin in the reality of political life as experienced from classical times onward: "As a concept, as a reality, revolution is one of the oldest political institutions of our western civilization. The overthrow of an established practical order, not merely to replace one Amurath by another, but to replace one social, religious, political system by another, is no new thing. The problem of revolution, of the class war, of the instability of political institutions, was pondered as deeply by Plato and Aristotle as by any writer or thinker of this or the last age."

This intellectual pedigree is challenged by Dahrendorf (11, p. 156n4), who contends that ". . . Aristotle (to say nothing of Plato) and all others down to the frequently debased. Too often it signifies not an economy of thought but a substitute for thought.[4] The revolutionary idea is conceived here as an organizing principle spanning vast stretches of societal evolution with at least a semblance of intellectual structure, even if it is not yet a scientific system. By highlighting the human record it provides an ordered set of answers to Childe's question. This long historical view may help to put current "revolutions" and rumors of revolution into a better perspective. As Condorcet wrote at the height of the French Revolution, "Everything now tells us that we are close upon one of the great revolutions of the human race. If we wish to learn what to expect from it and to procure a certain guide to lead us in the midst of its vicissitudes, what could be more suitable than to have some picture of the revolutions that have gone before it and prepared its way?"[5]

Questions of this order of magnitude should require no apology before an audience of sociologists. At its best, the sociological tradition is a tradition of wholeness which, taking "society" as our object of inquiry, must imply historical synthesis. The topic as construed lies squarely within this tradition of historical macro-sociology or, to give it a modern name, "evolutionary functionalism." Recovery and redirection of this tradition after an extended period of "analytic sociology" has been called the "macro-analytic revolution" (101, p. iii). Apart from the Cold War polemics in which Wittfogel couched his phrase — the need for "big-structured concepts" to wage ideological competition against Marxism — what seems distinctive of recent developments is a demand for empirical precision as well as intellectual substance. "Holistic *and* quantitative" might be our manifesto, and that is the present aim if not yet its achievement.

### The Revolutionary Theme

The sociological tradition is itself a revolutionary tradition, although some, like Salomon and Nisbet, would say rather "counterrevolutionary." Sociology as an intellectual tradition arises from Enlightenment rationalism, and that is its true radicalism — the appeal to rational authority

---

eighteenth century lacked what one might call pervasive 'sociological thinking,' i.e., an unwavering sense of the autonomously social (and thus historical) level of reality. Such thinking required a radical break with the undisputed constants of earlier epochs, a break that first became general in the age of the great revolutions. For this reason one may well derive the birth of sociology from the spirit of revolution."

[4] Referring to the agricultural, commercial, industrial, scientific, technological, and vital (demographic) revolutions, Hauser (26, p. 2) observes, "Each of these revolutions is obviously the invention of scholars seeking a short and snappy chapter or book title to connote complex and highly significant patterns of events." Whereupon, feeling the sociologist unfairly excluded from this naming process, he proceeds to christen one of his own: the "social morphological revolution."

[5] Quoted in Horowitz (32, p. 1). As well as instructive, the comment is unwittingly ironic. Short months later Condorcet himself fell victim to the Terror.

for the analysis, and moral basis, of social arrangements. Though forged in that intellectual revolution, our tradition has been tempered in response to the forces it prophesied and unleashed in the "age of revolutions," particularly by the French democratic revolution and the British industrial revolution.[6] The "revolutionary theme" thus not only represents a convenient summarization of large-scale changes in the structures of society, but also forms part of the structure of consciousness by which such change is perceived and understood.

Alternative formulations of the central tendencies in societal change find expression in global terms such as "modernization" and "secularization"; in Stein's (83) trio of "industrialization," "urbanization" and "bureaucratization," in a word — Weber's "rationalization" of society. All translate freely to revolutionary change of various descriptions; composing them to the revolutionary theme suggests a kind of comparability among members of an ordered set and continuity along an historical continuum. But whereas the revolutionary idea has brought forth much comment, its thematic unity as a *series*, rather than disconnected events, is rarely sounded. What would seem a natural extension to the full range of societal evolution is attempted only in Ribeiro's *The Civilizational Process* (74), and there he employs what are essentially technological criteria in demarcating revolutionary eras, while I detect greater tension and interaction between "technology and the moral order."

*Institutional revolutions.* Further specification of the revolutionary theme is achieved by isolating types of revolution, mainly on the institutional level of analysis — political, economic, "social" and religious especially, and their respective subtypes.[7] As a counterpart each faces a distinctive object and mode of analysis — revolutionary parties and elites,

[6] For example, "The positivism of Saint-Simon and Comte is the expression of the new society born in the French Revolution and the English industrial revolution" (89, p. 319). Salomon (77, p. 67) asserts that sociology came into existence as a philosophy of total revolution, a rationalization of the political, social and industrial revolutions then underway. Its revolutionary message is a denunciation of radical politics, however; "Saint-Simon and Comte held that political revolution dealt merely with superficialities, ignoring the real tasks which confronted the modern age, and that only total social revolution could bring about the perfection of mankind." Not political revolution but the evolution of industrial society was destined to achieve this result, they believed (77, p. 104). Nisbet (63, pp. 76–88) has drawn attention to the coincidence, and convergence, of conservatism as a social philosophy and of sociology, arising in direct response to the French Revolution. Features they are said to share in common are the priority and superiority of society over the individual and the organic relatedness of things social, the latter allegedly carrying over into modern sociological functionalism.

[7] E.g. democratic, industrial, bourgeois, charismatic. Johnson distinguishes five subtypes of political revolution alone, the Jacquerie, the Anarchist Rebellion, the Jacobin Communist, the Conspiratorial *coup d'etat*, and the Militarized Mass Insurrection. Meisel (53, pp. 211–12) adds a sixth, what might be termed the Bonapartist, "the revolution staged by professional army leaders, acting in lieu of absent or still insufficiently developed social forces and civilian parties. . . ."

technological innovations and shifts in the mode of production, class formations and class relations, charismatic leaders and movements. Each is associated with characteristic institutions and crisis mechanisms — industrial capitalism and "relative deprivation," for example. The list can be lengthened to encompass other institutional areas as well, "family revolutions" and "educational revolutions" as well as institutional organizations such as governments, corporations and churches. Two variant types, cultural and psychological revolutions (or "revolutions of consciousness") may be viewed as "correlates" of the revolutionary process on supra- and sub-institutional levels.

In reality, these institutional revolutions are not free-standing "pure types." They exist in varying degrees of "morphological correlation," as leading or lagging parts of a total institutional system. It is tempting to entertain the causal primacy of one or another, conspicuously the economic, as in historical materialism, over and against the others. But exceptions occur; for instance, it is by no means apparent that the industrial revolution preceded the demographic, or that both might not be traced to a common ancestory, say the religious revolution of ascetic Protestantism or, far earlier still, radical monotheism. Again, it might be assumed that there is a certain equivalence between revolutionary types which permits substitution of one for another. Thus we might ask, "When does a social revolution take a religious form and when does it manifest a political one?" or "What predisposed the British to 'choose' the industrial revolution and the French the democratic?" From yet another perspective we might predict the emergence of a particular revolutionary type at a particular revolutionary stage, as in the succession of political, social, economic and "balanced" revolutions Wilkie (97) documents for the Mexican case.[8]

## Societal Revolutions

Whatever the relationship considered, it is necessary to conceive institutional revolutions in the relation of parts (or aspects) of a larger whole — the structural system of a total society. As Hill (28, p. 31) urges, "we must widen our view so as to embrace the total activity of society. Any event so complex as a revolution must be seen as a whole." Similarly, Tiryakian (88, p. 126) observes, "If societal change is to be a distinct phenomenon for sociological analysis, it cannot be mere change

[8] As a species of social movements generally, revolutionary movements might be expected to pass through a sequence of phases such as the one Brinton describes, ". . . involving first economic and political weakness of the old regime in the midst of general prosperity; disaffection of specific groups, especially the intellectuals; transfer of power; rule of the moderates; accession of the extremists and the reign of terror and virtue; and finally, a period of relaxation of some of the revolution's excesses, institutionalization of some elements of its program, and a return to many of society's old ways" (quoted in 80, p. 18).

in the content of institutional life but rather a change in the societal structure within which institutions are organized."[9]

On this reckoning, revolutions are *societal* productions and revolutionary change entails "significant" change in the structures of society. Hence we define as "revolutionary" those transformations which result in a structural change and corresponding to every such revolution is a decisive alteration in the pattern of society — the urban revolution and urban society, the industrial revolution and industrial society, the democratic revolution and democratic society, and so on.[10] Having identified revolutionary change with "significant structural change," we are now forced to examine what that implies. The emphasis on "societalization" provides a criterion of significance — changes in the structure of *society* — only to plunge us into the usual difficulties of deciding what precisely that structure might comprise and when revolutionary change has actually occurred.

*The structure of society.* Perhaps the most rigorous attempt to anatomize the structure of society is Levy's (43) logic of structural-functional requisite analysis. On this procedure "significant" structures are those whose operation satisfies the conditions of societal existence, minimally survival. In turn these conditions are established by the nature of the unit (human society) in its setting—that is, by its functional requirements—and structures are adduced as "requisite" relative to such functional requisites. The structures of role differentiation, solidarity, economic and political allocation, integration and expression are thus designated; the current listing of functional imperatives follows Parson's "system problems" or AGIL schema. Despite persistent dif-

---

[9] "This general societal structure (which structures and orders the more differentiated structures of institutions) is a moral/religious frame of reference. . . ." On the "religious model" of societal change see below. Kuhn's (39, pp. 92–93) stress on *extra*institutional factors in revolutionary change is likewise notable: "Political revolutions aim to change political institutions in ways that those institutions themselves prohibit. Their success therefore necessitates the partial relinquishment of one set of institutions in favor of another, and in the interim, society is not fully governed by institutions at all." Political recourse fails in revolutionary crises because antagonists "differ about the institutional matrix within which political change is to be achieved and evaluated, because they acknowledge no supra-institutional framework for the adjudication of revolutionary difference. . . ." Consequently, "Though revolutions have had a vital role in the evolution of political institutions, that role depends upon their being partially extrapolitical or extrainstitutional events."

[10] This formula applies less well to the scientific revolution as a movement of thought — that is, as an intellectual or cultural revolution. Nevertheless we can readily conceive of the rise of science in relation to society as a shifting balance of interinstitutional relations. This would satisfy Ginsberg's (19, p. 140) definition of "structural change" as "changes in the parts of a structure due to changes in other parts or to a change in the balance of forces." Similarly, the demographic revolution assumes a distinctly social character when viewed in institutional context, as Hauser (26) does, and not simply as numerical expansion in population size and density. In either case, mentalistic or materialistic, social mediation is decisive.

ficulty in applying very exact or even approximate quantitative measures, we nevertheless receive at least the impression of structural significance from the criterion of functional importance.

So specified, structural requisites are analogous to what Ashby (1, pp. 42-43) terms "essential variables," those whose values cannot exceed a critical limit or ratio if the biological organism is to survive. Inasmuch as survival-related variables "are closely linked dynamically so that marked changes in any one leads sooner or later to marked changes in the others" (1, p. 42), the magnitude of readjustive change furnishes a secondary criterion of significant system change. Now in biological organisms such change normally takes the form of behavioral adaptation, but, as Radcliffe-Brown (72, p. 83) recognized, *structural* change is distinctive of social organisms; meeting altered conditions of existence may well depend upon a change of structural type. In this sense we could say that all societal revolutions are "conservative" revolutions.[11] The analytic problem then becomes one of deciding when

> One of Rommer's examples concerns the evolution of Devonian lungfishes into the earliest amphibians. . . . The invasion of the land was feasible only with strong fins (which in due time became legs). But strong fins were not developed "in order to" invade the land. The climate of the epoch was tempestuous; the water level of the pools in which the lungfishes lived was subject to sudden recessions. There was thus selection for those strains of lungfishes which, when stranded by such a recession, had strong enough fins to *get back to the water*. Only much later did some of their descendants come to stay ashore most of the time (30, p. 137).

a society is "the same" as before significant structural change has occurred. Besides a criterion of significance we require a criterion of sameness. This perplexity is well illustrated by Radcliffe-Brown himself:

> There is no break in continuity from type to type of society. If you consider the United States from the earliest days to the present — it is still, in one sense, the same society. You call them both — the society of one hundred years ago and that of today – the United States. In what sense? In the sense that there has been a structural continuity involving certain other kinds of continuities, that go along with it, and upon which that primary continuity depends. Yet, on the other hand, I would say that there are certain differences between the *kind* of system which you had in 1837 and the kind you have in 1937. If you are going to compare them, I will say that you have got to treat them, not as societies of one type, but as societies of two types. Where does the change come? I would say it does not come precisely anywhere. Where you draw the line is more or less arbitrary. You are facing the same problem always in all history of social development (72, pp. 74-75).

[11] Here too organic analogy may be found, in "Rommer's Rule," which reads: "The initial survival value of a favorable innovation is conservative, in that it renders possible the maintenance of a traditional way of life in the face of changed circumstances."

Parsons (66, p. 237) for instance maintains that despite marked structural change, the underlying value pattern of United States society—"instrumental activism"—has remained substantially intact.[12]

*"Engel's Problem."* Granting now a tentative if vague answer to the question of *what* is "significant" structural change, we are entitled to ask *when* such change can be said to have occurred. The distinction between "detail" and "structural change," or between "within system change" and "change of the system," is commonplace, but without definitely fixing the point at which one passes into the other. The classic statement of this dilemma was put in Engel's assertion (following Marx and Hegel) that, at some indeterminate point, quantitative change is transformed into qualitative change. Since revolutionary change would culminate in the latter, predicting discontinuity becomes a matter of supreme importance to revolutionists in their anxiety to catch the revolutionary moment. Thus did Trotsky inquire, "Through what stage are we passing?"

*"Evolution" and "revolution."* Not only in dialectical materialism do "Qualitative and quantitative changes condition two essentially different kinds of development, *evolution* and *revolution* . . ." (95, p. 324). In general evolutionary perspective, White (95, p. 281) considers, "when the changes are quantitative we call the . . . process evolution; when they are qualitative we call it revolution." More particularly, "Evolution is change within the framework and limits of a system. Revolution is a *radical* transformation of a system, the substitution of one principle, or basis, of organization for another." By way of illustration, "no amount of change or growth within primitive society based upon kinship could ever have produced civil society based upon property relations" (96, p. 282). Reflecting on mid-nineteenth-century Belgian experience, Kittell (36, p. 119) likewise distinguishes between "industrial evolution" and "industrial revolution," the latter marked by innovations creating social dislocations and tensions "which disposed a large number of people to alter conditions radically rather than to adapt to them. . . ." Although he adds (36, p. 120), "Long-range adaptations, to the extent that they relieved social tension, might better be called 'evolutionary,' " it was to a *changed* societal situation that adjustment was made, and adjustment was made by societal change. Belgian society was not "the same" as it had been before industrialization.

On this score also, Tiryakian (67, p. 73) speaks of "social change"

---

[12] Elsewhere Parsons (68, p. 21) affirms that "At the most general theoretical levels, there is no difference between processes which serve to maintain a system and those which serve to change it. The difference lies in the intensity, distribution, and organization of the 'elementary' components of particular processes relative to the status of the structures they affect." Attention shifts then to determining "threshold" values of system variables as predictors of structural change. On Parsons's reading of the revolutionary situation see below.

as "a quantitative elaboration of structural differentiation," and "societal change" as "a discontinuous process of structural innovation. . . ." Parsons (65, pp. 28-29) declines the distinction, however, stating that "differentiation is not a 'linear' process of continuous increase in the value of a variable which might be called 'differentiatedness.'" Instead, "the process seems to occur by relatively *discontinuous* stages . . ."[13] Indeed, the notion of revolutionary change as a discontinuity in rates of "normal change" provides a operational meaning for, and possible solution of, Engel's Problem.

*"Normal"* and *"revolutionary change."* The title of this chapter is self-consciously adapted to parallel that of Kuhn's celebrated work, *The Structure of Scientific Revolutions* (39). It is therefore natural to assay the "paradigm" of "normal" and "revolutionary change" in scientific knowledge which forms his central argument. For Kuhn (39, pp. x, 91), "paradigms" are "universally recognized scientific achievements that for a time provide model problems and solutions to a community of practitioners," and "scientific revolutions" are "those non-cumulative developmental episodes in which an older paradigm is replaced in whole or in part by an incompatible new one" — the Ptolemaic cosmology by the Copernican, for example. Kuhn himself makes an analogy between scientific and political revolutions; in both, the revolutionary process follows a similar course, moving from a pre-paradigmatic stage through paradigm crystallization, crisis and, finally, paradigm change. Unfortunately, his thesis is quite rudimentary and can scarcely bear the analytic weight pressed upon it. Its principal benefit is instead more sociological: that "each scientific revolution alters the historical perspective of the community that experiences it . . ." (39, p. xi), and that along with such change in world view, "revolution" involves "a certain sort of reconstruction of group commitments" (40, p. 180).

## II. The Procedure

We now come to the procedure by which alternative solutions may be posed and compared. The method of procedure is "logico-empirical," following a logical progression from definition through enumeration and classification to, in the final section of the chapter, interpretation and causal explanation.

### Definition

What "counts" as a societal revolution? The revolutionary idea has been used to section off large chunks of history: where the lines are

---

[13] ". . . which we interpret provisionally to mean that the 'integrative' processes must have a chance to 'catch up' with the consequences of a given step in differentiation before the latter process can go farther without destroying the system." Gouldner (23, p. 361) has accused Parsons of transforming "the Marxist mechanism of *revolution* — the conflict between the forces and relations of production — into a mechanism of *evolution*" by means of the process of structural differentiation.

drawn and which the cutting points chosen varies, of course. A number of defining characteristics have been employed: irreversibility, suddenness, acceleration, discontinuity, and violence. These dimensions of conceptual definition will be reviewed briefly in turn.

*Irreversibility.* The idea of revolution as the irreversibility of events finds expression in Hockett and Ascher's (30, p. 135) definition, "A revolution is a relatively sudden set of changes that yield a state of affairs from which a return to the situation just before the revolution is virtually impossible." This seems to be the sense of the word intended by V. Gordon Childe when he speaks of the 'Neolithic Revolution' and of the 'Urban Revolution.' The notion *of cumulative* structural change fits here as well. In political revolutions, counterrevolutionary strains are also set in motion and "safeguarding the revolution" becomes an obsession of the revolutionary elite.[14] This susceptibility to reversion and recurrence is sometimes held to disqualify radical politics as a form of revolutionary change, although the political aspect is always present in any structural transformation. An example of the kind of irreversibility the authors intend would be the industrial revolution; as Levy remarks, no society that has become industrialized has ever reverted to a preindustrial state. Gareau's account of the failure of the Morgenthau Plan for the forced "pastoralization" of postwar Germany (17) is a case in point.[15]

*Suddenness.* The suddenness of revolutionary change, Hockett and Ascher suggest, must be viewed in relation to some historical time perspective. The "drastic changes" which culminate in what they call the "human revolution" — the organic evolution to man — "may have required a good many millions of years; yet they can validly be regarded as 'sudden' in view of the tens of millions of years of mammalian history that preceded them." As Mathias suggests, when "judged against a perspective of the whole sweep of history, the adjective 'revolutionary' is surely appropriate" in reference to the industrial revolution as well

[14] Meisel (53, p. 20) contends that "a counterrevolution, to be successful, must itself be another revolution; . . . distinct from a mere turning back of the historic clock, it partakes of the revolutionary current. Although counterrevolution moves in a different direction, it is fed by the identical hopes and frustrations as the revolution." Borkenau (3, p. 240) anticipates the "structural imbalance" theory of revolutions when he writes, "Every revolution attempts to carry through one monistic principle of society to its logical end. But in fact no human society can ever be ruled by one monistic principle. Counterrevolutions are the enhancement of those principles which have been systematically suppressed by revolution. They restore the balance. . . ." What is to be considered "revolution" and what "counterrevolution" has often provoked lively debate. In the case of the "Napoleonic Revolution," for instance, Elton (16, p. 175) argues that "The Empire . . . was nothing more nor less than the final stage of the Revolution," while to others "Bonapartist" has become a standard epithet for reactionaries of the military-adventurist type.

[15] Tilly (86, p. 457) however cites "pastoralization" as a frequent *local* response to industrialism.

(49, p. ix). Societal revolutions, especially the earlier ones, may appear glacial in their movement, and, partly for this reason, Redfield (73, pp. ix-x) prefers the word "transformation" to "revolution." Mingay (56, p. 11) reminds us however that "revolutionary changes need only be radical and need not be sudden."[16]

*Acceleration.* If suddenness of change does not necessarily stamp a revolutionary character, some writers believe it is the change in the *rate* of change that can be so considered. Boulding (4, p. 98) is one who views terms such as "industrial revolution," "managerial revolution," even the "Copernican" and "Keynesian" revolutions, as "descriptions of what mathematicians might call the second differentials of history, that is, they are changes in the rate of change. If we want to invent a new word to describe them, perhaps the term *accelerations* is the best word, for a period of acceleration is one in which the rate of change increases."

*Discontinuity.* Acceleration must be viewed against a field of relatively constant change, hence a refinement on the preceding is to stress, as Wilbur argues, "large-scale discontinuous changes in the social fabric of society, that is revolution" (57, p. 337). Cipolla (7, p. 31) applies this criterion of discontinuity when he states, "The Agricultural Revolution of the eighth millennium B.C. and the Industrial Revolution of the eighteenth century A.D. . . . created deep breaches in the continuity of the historical process. With each one of these two Revolutions, a 'new story' begins: a new story dramatically and completely alien to the previous one."

*Violence.* According to Maguire (45, p. 1), the "classical" concept of revolution entails "the violent or extra-legal transfer of political power." Ryan (76, p. 123) takes the former to epitomize "true revolution":

> Revolution is a condition in which an existing order of society is rejected through violence by its members. In this context, the term excludes social changes which simply because of their massiveness have frequently been called "revolutionary." Accordingly the great transformation of England associated with the "industrial revolution" is not included within the bounds of the concept.

This is a highly restrictive definition, connoting strictly political revolution. Even within that limited sphere, force and fraud as mechanisms of revolutionary change are seriously in question. McAlister (51, p. 16) characterizes political revolution as bringing about qualitative changes in the structure of mobilizing and sharing power by whatever means.[17]

[16] Dahrendorf (10, p. 234n26) reverses the equation, preferring suddenness to radicalness as the criterion of revolutionary change. The latter was treated above as the problem of "qualitative" change.

[17] Tiryakian's (87, p. 74) "refusal to consider large-scale physical violence to be the hallmark of revolutions" stems from his view that "The structural conditions that in one instance may favor violent political revolution may elsewhere suggest quite different solutions. Essentially, the 'leap' in structural organization involved in

A more fundamental objection to the classical concept is that "such a definition fails to express the complete scope of the modern revolution. Today we are no longer able to think of revolution in terms of 'purely political' transfer of power" (45, p. 2). Thus Meusel (54, p. 367) holds that "a recasting of the social order is, at least in modern times, a far more important characteristic of revolutions, than a change of political constitution or the use of violence in the attainment of this end." For, as Tiryakian (88, p. 126) remarks, "To localize revolution in the political or even the economic sector is to mistake the part for the whole, in the sense that a social revolution is a 'total social phenomenon,' of which political or economic transformations are only parts."

The definition we will adopt for present purposes draws on this "tendency toward total transformation of societal structure" (87, pp. 75-76). Accordingly, we may think of changes in society as being more revolutionary the more sectors of institutional organization they encompass. The structural size of society increases in evolutionary complexity, however, and the structural location of revolutionary change may be expected to alter as well. It follows that no institutional sector, or theory, is sovereign in directing the course of revolutionary change. Although "totalization" of the revolutionary phenomenon may be a recent development, this conception opens too the widest historical perspective.

*Empirical definition.* Having now established some conceptual dimensions of the term we are in a position to request its empirical referents. One measure frequently invoked is that of population increase. For example,

> Arnold Toynbee spoke of the "far greater rapidity which marks the growth of population" as "the first thing that strikes us about the Industrial Revolution — a decennial increase of round 10 per cent at the close of the eighteenth century and of 14 per cent in the first decade of the nineteenth century, as against 3 per cent as the largest decennial increase before 1751" (14, p. 257nl).

The growth of world population does roughly follow an exponential curve that may fairly describe revolutionary changes in the structure of human society. Sheer population increase as a gauge of ecological dominance does signalize the "human revolution" and its cultural elaborations. Expanded numerical size of "peoples" within the species does imply enhanced adaptive capacity resulting from or leading to societal change. Nonetheless, this single measure cannot be relied on to make the needed distinctions within the overall revolutionary process.

The agricultural revolution is marked by the *de*population of hunters

---

societal change may, in public life, become externalized in either the political *or* the economic sphere." Thus, Borkenau (3, p. 10) finds, "History is full of examples of the most tremendous changes in the way of life being carried out without any break in the continuity of law, and without any violent upheaval."

throughout the world, from close to 100 percent to less than 50 percent, and under 1 percent presently. A better indication would be the lessened distribution of wild as against domesticated strains of maize that Mangelsdorf and MacNeish have plotted for the Valley of Mexico (8, p. 32). Again, the lethal range of weaponery has enlarged in approximate geometrical ratio since 1750 (25, p. 37), suggesting a revolution in military technology. Returning to the industrial revolution, valid measures of phases such as the "price revolution" are better stated in time series of wage-price differentials, although rural depopulation might provide an indirect measure. In general, decoding societal structures and structural change by a population index appears an uncertain procedure.

If we find numerical increase in population size too gross a measure, refinements are present in Tiryakian's (87, p. 84) composite "Index of Revolutionary Potential." He asks, "If we formulate societal change as one involving a qualitative 'leap' in the basic societal ground of meaning that transforms institutional structure within a short period of time, how are sociological predictions of such discontinuities possible?" As an answer, he gives three lead indicators whose performance symbolizes deep-seated uncertainty and incipient change in the "grounds of meaning": (i) significant increases in rates of urbanization, (ii) significant increases in the distribution and public acceptance of sexual promiscuities, and (iii) significant increases in the outbreak of non-institutional religious phenomena.

With regard to urbanization, Tiryakian's (87, p. 92) rationale is that beyond some hypothetical demographic and ecological limits the efficiency of social institutions will be impaired. In addition to social dislocation and pathology, urban concentration serves to intensify the class struggle Marx conceived, the "common conditions" of urban interaction among the industrial proletariat heightening class consciousness and promoting class formation. The revolutionary character of sexual deregulation is most closely associated with Marcuse (46, p. 33), who considers this rejection of dominant morality "a disintegrative factor." The ferment of non-institutional religion is glimpsed in McFarland's study of religious movements in postwar Japan, *The Rush Hour of the Gods* (52). Empirical applications of such an index might range across community, class or national boundaries, as in urban riot prediction models, "the revolutionary potential of the working class" or the ill-fated Project Camelot.

### Enumeration: "Two, Three, . . . Many Revolutions"

Assuming at least a minimum definition of what counts as a societal revolution, we turn now to the task of enumerating actual cases falling under that rubric. Specifications vary widely between authors but — as if it were a mystical number — most finally settle on three, as in "Childe's three great revolutions — the food-producing, the urban, and the industrial . . ." (73, p. x);[18] as to *which* three, opinions diverge. "Taking history as a single career," Nash (59, p. 225) offers a slightly different set, beginning with the earliest human revolution — a "culturological" revolution in his view — telescoping the agricultural and urban, and concluding with the industrial.

Besides taking a single department of culture such as technology, or the human record as a whole, another way of cataloguing societal revolutions is to consider a single period of culture history. Some periods selected will naturally appear more "revolutionary" than others, and in any given period certain institutional developments will command greater attention. For example, the eighteenth century has often been called an "age of revolution," emphasizing political and economic developments, while these tend to be suppressed in viewing the supposedly quiescent sixteenth century — quiescent, that is, if one is willing to overlook or discount the Protestant Reformation and its aftermath, the "Tudor revolution" in government and the early rise of the nation state, the "age of exploration" as an outgrowth of the commercial revolution and its effect in the "price revolution," the "early" English industrial revolution, and other such occurrences. Nisbet (62, p. 317) remarks, "No doubt there is some degree of applicability of 'revolution' to every aspect of culture in every age."

Continuing into the nineteenth century, Nisbet (p. 23) reduces the number from three to two — "the Industrial Revolution . . . as distinctively English as the political revolution beginning in 1789 is French. . . ." Threeness is shortly restored, for later on (pp. 42–44) he extracts three "fundamental and widespread processes" common to both which together "convey a great deal of what revolutionary change meant to philosophers and social scientists of the nineteenth century": individualization, abstraction, and generalization.[19]

Coming down to the twentieth century, Parsons (69, p. 854) recognizes three revolutions — industrial, democratic, and educational — and a tendency central to all that subsumes Nisbet's processes — structural differentiation. All three revolutions were "major agencies of upgrading through the immense increase of generalized and mobile resources.

---

[18] Contrary to Redfield, Childe's third revolution is not the industrial but the "revolution of human knowledge" precipitated by settled urban life. The rise of great religions coordinate with the rise of great cities — what Jaspers (33) calls the "Axial Period" — is a prime example.

[19] "Abstraction" is "the tendency of historic values to become ever more secular, ever more utilitarian, but increasingly separated from the concrete and particular roots which for many centuries had given them both symbolic distinctness and means of realization," while "generalization" is the process of universalizing identities and loyalties (62, pp. 43, 44).

All three also clearly posed major problems of integration for the societies in which they have appeared[20] and have necessitated major shifts of what we call value-generalization." Finally, all three presupposed a common base of structural development.

Bringing us to the present is the well-known "triple revolution" of technological militarism, cybernation and human rights discussed by Perrucci and Pilisuk (70, pp. xiii-iv). Perversely enough, Ward (94, pp. 16-17) identifies *four* "revolutions of modernization": equality, secularity, fertility, and technology, which combine to produce "the mutation of a quite new kind of society. . . ." Though universal in scope, their workings are by no means uniform in effect, and the resulting incongruity generates yet a fifth revolution, called the "revolution of rising expectations" by Adlai Stevenson, and by others the "revolution of rising frustrations."

Even five revolutions is a gross underenumeration for, as Ward (p. 13) observes, "we live in the most catastrophically revolutionary age that men have ever faced. Usually one thinks of a revolution as one event or at least as one interconnected series of events. But we are in fact living with ten or twenty such revolutions. . . ." What distinguishes the revolutions of our time, forcing a universal approach to human problems, is that "these changes have occurred simultaneously during a very narrow historical span, and are still acting and reacting upon the whole of humanity. Their effect thus becomes cumulative . . ." (75, p. 12). The tempo of revolutionary change has quickened and readjustive change is faced with a compounding of effects.

With this cursory glance at a sample of enumerations and enumerators, I will now venture to inventory the broad spectrum of societal revolutions and suggest a crude chronology for the series.[21]

### Dating, Duration and Distribution

We come now upon a plague of problems, of dating, duration, and distribution. *When* does a revolution occur? Does it commence from a datable event, and can its preconditions be separated from its participants? Shall we select the initial point of occurrence, the time at which the trend is definitely established, or its termination? Elton (16, p. 3) attests to the elusiveness of revolutionary phenomena; the more deeply a revo-

[20] The problem of integration may be viewed as the counterpart, and consequence, of differentiation. Parsons (69, p. 861) interprets the educational revolution as "the most salient manifestation of a new phase in the development of modern society where integrative problems rather than economic or . . . political problems are paramount." On the "integrative revolution" in new nations see Geertz (18).

[21] Each of these main revolutionary (or societal) types is dealt with at length in a forthcoming monograph, *Societal Revolutions,* to which the present chapter serves as introduction.

lution is studied "the further its roots will be found reaching into the past, the less possible will it seem to select a particular date for its origination." Conversely, can the point at which revolutions become general be separated from their continuing effects? The inclusion of postdated secondary recurrences — the "second agricultural revolution" of pre-industrial England (or the "green revolution" of present-day Asia), testifies to their potent influence.

Societal revolutions are mass events, not point events. While it may be possible to discern some "event structure" in the revolutionary process — a succession of pivotal scientific discoveries, for instance — the metric of societal change must record not clock or calendar time but *structural* time. Gluckman (20, p. 219) suggests that institutional structures have a built-in time scale or "structural duration": "Thus the structure of a family system can only be analyzed in four generations, and in subsistence systems perhaps only in five to six generations." On social psychological ground (for example, acculturation) it may require no less than three generations to register appreciable change, and what a "generation" amounts to in elapsed time is itself variable — e.g., the compression of rising "political generations."

The question of assessing the duration of change has also to deal with the discontinuities revealed by the investigation. The gap between the urban and commercial revolutions is most conspicuous, spanning upwards of two millenia within which is contained the rise of great cultural traditions in classical antiquity, the fall of the Roman Empire in the West, as well as the so-called "Dark Ages." Are we to suppose nothing of great moment transpired in this long interval? Surely it was the era of religious revolutions *par excellence*—Jasper's "Axial Period" (33). Even the "Dark Ages" have been partially rehabilitated through the recent efforts of historians of technology, the works of Lynn White, Jr., for instance, and Christopher Dawson's writings on religion. Is there, then, any justification for continuing to assert its unrevolutionary character?

The full account of revolutionary changes is enormously complicated in historical detail, but in essentials the argument runs as follows. The structural innovation of the urban revolution was an emergent societal formation — the ancient city — where there arose new situations and relationships whose normative regulation forced an expansion of the moral order (37). The Axial Period represents a consolidation of the urban revolution which, by removing its structural limitations and by a rationalization of its internal contradictions, allowed the stabilization, indeed stagnation, of this social type.[22] Breaking out of urban involution required the dismantling of hierarchic structures which were then

---

[22] "In the Axial Period the same processes that represent a kind of solution to the problems of the time are seen in retrospect to signal the decline of creative thought" (47, p. 76).

## Fig. 2. A Roster of Societal Revolutions

| | | |
|---|---|---|
| 2 million? | | Human Revolution |
| | |   Biological Revolution |
| | |   Cultural Revolution |
| | |   Hunting Revolution |
| 10-8th mil. | | Agricultural (Neolithic) Revolution |
| | 8900 |   Herding Revolution |
| | 5500-5000 |   Hydraulic Revolution |
| 6-3000 | | Urban Revolution |
| | 32-2800 |   Revolution of Human Knowledge |
| | |     The "Axial Period" |
| | |   Metallurgical Revolution |
| 13-15th A.D. | | Commercial Revolution |
| | 16th |   Gunpowder Revolution |
| | |   Price Revolution |
| 15-16th | | Communications Revolution |
| | c. 1450 |   Printing Revolution |
| 16-17th | | Scientific Revolution |
| | 1543 |   Copernican Revolution |
| | 1642 |   Galilean Revolution |
| | 1687 |   Newtonian Revolution |
| | 1859 |   Darwinian Revolution |
| | 1905 |   Einsteinian Revolution |
| | 1920s |   Freudian Revolution |
| | 1930s |   Keynesian Revolution |
| 18-19th | | Industrial Revolution |
| | 16-17th |   Early Industrial Revolution |
| | 16-18th |   Second Agricultural Revolution |
| 18-20th | | Demographic Revolution |
| 18-20th | | Democratic Revolution |
| | 1640 |   Puritan Revolution |
| | 1775 |   American Revolution |
| | 1789 |   French Revolution |
| | 1917 |   Communist Revolution |
| | 1933 |   Totalitarian Revolution |
| | 1945- |   Revolutions of National Liberation |
| 1890- | | Organizational Revolution |
| | 1100 |   Papal Revolution |
| | 16th |   Tudor Revolution |
| | 1890 |   Corporate Revolution |
| | |   Managerial Revolution |
| | |   Capitalist Revolution |
| 1945- | | Cybercultural Revolution |
| ? | | Humanistic Revolution? |
| | 1960s |   Environmental Revolution |

replaced by quasi-autonomous orders, first in feudal societies and subsequently, through economic mechanisms such as the shift in the terms of trade from countryside to town (61), in the medieval city. Detection of discontinuity between urban and commercial revolutions points, then, to a crucial transition in the social function of cities, from religio-political to commercial centers.

Discontinuity in spatial distribution also marks these revolutionary developments. Since the urban revolution, all are distinctively if not exclusively "Western" in character. Both Parsons and Ward locate the world revolutionary epicenter in the North Atlantic area, Parsons (69, p. 854) quaintly combining spatio-temporal reference in the "northwest corner of the seventeenth century European system: England, France, and Holland." At the same time, there appears a growing tendency towards "globalization" of the revolutionary phenomenon. The intellectual career of the "French Revolution" is illuminating in this regard, as it broadens in scope to what Tocqueville called the "European Revolution" and Godechot (21, p. vii), the "Atlantic Revolution." Yet, even worldwide democratic revolution manifested in revolutionary wars of "national liberation" and other forms, retains the flavor of what von Laue (92, pp. 81-82) considers a general "revolution of structural Westernization."

If it is true that Europe has been, in Heer's words, the "mother of revolutions" (27) and global revolution in Kuman's opinion is "the theory and practice of a European idea" (41), the "Eurocentric" view proves disserviceable in assessing contemporary revolutionary movements. As Mazlish, Kaledin and Ralston (50, p. 225) state,

> Revolution has generally been considered as a phenomenon peculiar to the European, or at least Europeanized, world. That is to say, the conventional ideas as to what constitutes a revolution and the conventional theories used to analyze the dynamics of the revolutionary process have been drawn from the European experience. As a result, the great upheavals that have taken place in Asia, embodying a different constellation of social and political forces, have until recently been difficult to place within a familiar intellectual context. They have been, therefore, unclassifiable and little noticed.

More than a "failure of revolutionary nerve" (78, p. 386) or "counterrevolutionary reflex" (64), perhaps it is this conceptual blindness — the absence of a vocabulary for revolution expressed in a non-western idiom — that explains why "we have proved so incapable of dealing in revolutionary terms with a revolutionary situation" (78, p. 387) like Vietnam.

### III. The Solution

"What gave rise to the Russian revolution?" asked Woodrow Wilson (99, p. 145). "The answer can only be that it was the product of a whole

social system. . . ." Wilson went on to say, "It was due to a systematic
denial of the rights and privileges which all normal men desire and
must have if they are to be contented and within reach of happiness."
But this doctrine of the (natural) "rights of man" fails utterly to explain
why at this time and under these conditions such rights were violently
and successfully asserted — if indeed the event can be so ascribed.
What we seek is some awareness of the weights and impacts of various
elements in the revolutionary situation, their interdependencies and
interconnections — in short, the *structure* of societal revolutions.

In response to the demand for structure we have assembled here
some ingredients for a theory of societal revolutions, but at present they
are far from composing an integrated theory. The ordering of revolutions given above (Fig. 2) is roughly chronological, but is there logical
order in their unfolding as well? Ideally, we would uphold each successive revolution as a natural and logical outgrowth of its predecessors,
just as Hockett and Ascher (30, p. 135) assert that the urban revolution could not have occurred had it not been for the agricultural revolution, and that in turn without the human revolution.[23] Meisel (53,
pp. xi, 18-19) contrasts two schools of what he proposes calling "revo-
lutionology," an older historical school concerned with telling the *story*
of a revolution and a newer sociological school whose purpose is "to
understand the fundamental nature of *laws* assumed to underlie all revolutions" and their causal mechanisms. Adopting this latter perspective,
"the elucidation of the social structure of revolutionary situations" lies
at the core of the Theory of Revolutions (Dahrendorf, quoted in 98, p.
125). In the effort to penetrate that core, I will review three main interpretive traditions or "models" of societal change bound in the
context of "technology and the moral order."

### Technology and the Moral Order

The great transformations of humanity are only in part reported in terms
of the revolutions in technology with resulting increases in the number of
people living together. There have also occurred changes in the thinking
and valuing of men which may also be called "radical and indeed revolutionary innovations." Like changes in the technical order, these changes
in the intellectual and moral habits of men become themselves generative
of far-reaching changes in the nature of human living (73, pp. 22-23).

Redfield goes on to say that such changes in the moral order

. . . do not reveal themselves in events as visible and particular as do
material inventions, or even always as increasing complexity in the systems

---

[23] This is a logic of "value-added" analysis, that "earlier stages must combine
*according to a certain pattern* before the next stage can contribute its particular
value . . ." (80, p. 14).

of social relationships. Nor is it perhaps possible to associate the moral transformations with limited periods of time as we can associate technological revolutions with particular spans of years. (73, p. 23)

Nef (60, p. 5) too, acknowledges a difference in the rates of social metabolism between the two orders: "A revolution in the ways human minds work seems to manifest itself differently from a revolution in the economic life of human societies." Technological change moves with startling rapidity and "such changes are revolutionary, one may say, only if they affect a large proportion of the population, and alter radically their habits of work, of transportation, of consumption and of communication." On the other hand, "The revolutionary stage in intellectual history is . . . generally the stage in which a few powerful minds emphasize certain hitherto neglected values and methods, and relate them potentially in novel ways to the life of action which individuals and societies have to lead in order to inhabit the earth."

These differences, in rates of change and mass effects, are familiarly addressed in terms of Ogburn's "cultural lag hypothesis." Though it is widely assumed that the contrast has sharpened greatly in recent times, Redfield (73, pp. 23, 18) traces the course of societal change generally as one of shifting proportions in technology and the moral order. "In the folk society the moral order is great and the technical order is small." Whereas "every precivilized society of the past fifty or seventy-five millenniums had a moral order to which the technical order was subordinate," with the rise of civilized societies the technical order assumes a dominant role in shaping further development.

Redfield is careful to disclaim a total inversion of their relations, however; "It is not enough to say that the technical order is destroyer of the moral order. It is not enough to identify civilization with development in the technical order alone. It is also to be recognized that the effects of the technical order include the creation of new moral orders" (73, p. 77). Whereas in folk societies "the moral order begins as something preeminent but incapable of changing itself," in civilized societies it becomes less eminent but more creative. "While the technical order continues to expand, and to have profound influence on the moral communities of mankind, these communities now have a new power to create values that in turn demand . . . the control and limitation of the development of the technical order" (73, p. 76). The logically possible interrelations between technology and the moral order can be schematized as follows, inserting a third (social) order between them:[24] White (96, pp. 18-28), a technological determinist, directs the causal flow from bottom ("substructure" in Marxist terminology) to top ("superstructure") (a). Parsons reverses direction, arguing instead for the primacy of normative culture as the highest level in his "cybernetic

[24] Compare also Lenski (42, p. 102).

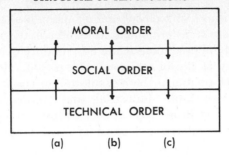

Fig. 3. Technical, Social and Moral Orders

hierarchy" (c). A third position is that of social determinism, some-times identified with Emile Durkheim. From this standpoint (b), both technical and moral orders are located in reference to social relations, and changes in either are referred to changes in their structure. Hence neither the history of technology nor the history of morals — nor both apart from the mediation of social relations — is adequate for under-standing societal change. Before us now are three major accounts of revolutionary change. For simplicity's sake they can be labeled the "eco-nomic model," the "religious model" and the "sociological model." Each warrants further discussion before we can hope to arbitrate, or decide, among them.[25]

### The "Economic Model"

Kaplan (34, p. 91) upholds the primacy of technology as giving rise to "an appropriate social system and ideology." Similarly, the prime movers

[25] While this analysis centers on the empirical structure of societal revolutions, it must be realized that there is another, *normative* structure to be conceived and con-sidered as well — the necessity of revolution. Do we need a revolution? Citing "the failure of the political and economic system to begin to solve the problems of our society," Griffith (24, p. 385) warns that "our present institutions and ways of pro-ceeding are heading us more and more towards greater injustice and inhumanity and that only by radical change can we hope to avoid catastrophe." Revolutionism for him is more than a question of political possibility; it is a moral imperative. So also said Proudhon (71, p. 42):

> A revolution is an act of sovereign justice, in the order of moral facts, springing out of the necessity of things, and in consequence carrying with it its own justification.
> *Is there today sufficient reason in society for revolution?*
> In a word, is the occasion for revolution presented at the moment, by the nature of things, by the connection of acts, by the working of institutions, by the advance in needs, by the order of Providence?
> . . . *Is there sufficient reason for a revolution in the nineteenth century?* [This ques-tion] . . . resolves itself into the following: *What is the tendency of society in our day?*

Grasping the complex interplay between factual and moral orders of existence con-tinues to exercise the sociological imagination in societies of our own day.

in Ribeiro's sequences of sociocultural evolution are "technological revolutions" . . . "those transformations in man's ability to exploit nature or to make war that are prodigious enough to produce qualitative alterations in the whole way of life of societies" (74, p. 13). He recognizes eight such major transformations: the agricultural, urban, irrigation, metallurgical, pastoral, mercantile, industrial, and thermonuclear revolutions. Corresponding to each are typical sociocultural formations, undifferentiated horticultural villages and nomadic pastoral hordes in the case of the agricultural revolution, for instance. Ribeiro concedes (74, p. 16) that "this series of technological revolutions is not sufficient to explain the whole evolutionary process. The reason for this is that it is not the invention itself that produces consequences, but rather its dissemination into various sociocultural contexts. . . ." The technological criterion as a gauge of revolutionary change is itself suspect, as in Wittfogel's (100, p. 115) contention that the hydraulic revolution was an "organizational revolution," not a technological one.

Unquestionably the leading exponent of the "economic model" is Marx himself and it goes without saying that the Marxist revolutionary idea has been subjected to endless interpretation, revision, deviation and contention. One major criticism of Marxist theory is its failure as a predictive model; for example, "To see weakness in the 'pure' Marxist materialistic model, we need only consider how badly Marx misjudged the revolutionary situation of post-1848 Europe (where objective conditions would have led one to predict a revolution in England and other industrial countries)" (87, p. 86). Although Tiryakian does not indicate what "objective conditions" he has in mind — presumably the debate over the standard of living — he assigns predictive failure to the circumstance that "socioeconomic or 'objective' conditions are insufficient to determine the stability or instability of any given society." More "subjective" factors such as public trust and elite self-legitimation also play a leading part.

### The "Religious Model"

An alternative to the "economic model" lays overwhelming stress on the moral order as source and sanction for revolutionary change. Two factors have seemed to weigh against this interpretation, the view of religion as sublimating or etherealizing inner-worldly concern and revolutionary consciousness, and the innate conservatism of institutional religion itself. Countering these views of religion as antithetical to revolution, others have argued that revolution is fundamentally a religious phenomenon and a powerful impetus to revolutionary action. Although Proudhon (71, p. 294) declared, "Revolution takes the place of Revelation," the irrationalist tendencies of revolutionary ideologies and their sovereign claims to fanatical adherence vitiate this displacement. Moreover, if religion constitutes a challenge to a revolutionary movement's "immanentism" (45, p. 73), it does so by issuing a *competing* claim to transcendental authority. Finally, if revolutionary regimes have instituted new moralities these too partake of the sacred, with "political religion" occupying the center of value.

If, as Durkheim conceived it, religion is a societal phenomenon, the reverse is equally true: society is a religious phenomenon, resting on a "sacred order."[26] "Religion" can then be defined as the basic orientation to "the *grounds of meaning* of the total society, including the basic value premises that articulate society's perception of reality, and that underlie the organization of major social institutions" (87, p. 80).

> In our model of total societies, we assume that the basic foundation of the social order is essentially a moral (religious-normative) one. That is, the general "way of life" or "world-view" of a society is an all-encompassing structure of structures (*societal* structure) that by virtue of its fundamentality is and must be considered "sacred."

> Therefore, societal change involves a fundamental redefinition of the situation, a negation of the moral validity of the existent social order and a new basic religious/sacred reorientation that simultaneously is a desacralization of the *status quo.* (87, p. 82)[27]

From this it follows that "The religious sphere has a double societal function: to provide the major basis of legitimation for a social order, and to be the major source of inspiration for illegitimizing it. *Religion is a major vehicle both for the status quo and societal change*" (87, pp. 82-83). On this understanding, revolutionary change is both the culmination of a process of structural dissolution and a radical restructuring of the societal situation (87, p. 77). A classification of these effects implies a further distinction, that between institutional and non institutional religion.

> . . . If we accept the notion that social revolutions essentially involve a fundamental reordering of the social structure, and if we accept the supposition that the social order is essentially viewed as a moral phenomenon by the members of the collectivity, then there must be a new source of morality involved in societal change, one that both desacralizes the present system and paves the way for the acceptance of a new order.

---

[26] Shils (79, p. 117) describes the "sacred order of society" as its center of value; "The center, or the central zone, is a phenomenon of the realm of values and beliefs. It is the center of the order of symbols, of values and beliefs, which govern the society. It is the center because it is the ultimate and irreducible; and it is felt to be such by many who cannot give explicit articulation to its irreducibility. The central zone partakes of the nature of the sacred. In this sense, every society has an 'official' religion. . . ."

[27] Moore (57, p. 37) concurs in this judgment, reserving the term "revolution" to fundamental changes in "the normative order, including notably the forms of legality and, crucially, the basis of legitimacy for the state itself."

Since established religion represents a compromise with the on-going secular institutions, the only other possible host of revolutionary thought, however unwittingly, is the non-institutional religious sector. (87, p. 95)

Hence it is outside the sphere of institutional religion that "we find a
radical denial of the legitimacy of previous institutions" and in "the
covert, non-institutional sphere of society that new basic meanings, innovations or radical renovations of cultural definitions of the situation are
generated as responses to societal strains" (87, pp. 89, 83). Moreover,
"The non-institutional religious sphere provides the grounds for *mass*
(not elite) rejection of the constitutive structure of society" (87, p. 82).

### The "Sociological Model"

Both models previously presented share equally the difficulty of par-
celling out the material from the non-material elements of culture and, by
implication, of separating cause from effect. To illustrate:

> . . . industrialization cannot be defined as the *impact* upon the "social
> structure" of the factory system, rapid communication and transportation,
> a high level of scientific training, and so on. These are all part of the
> same complex. The former set of phenomena cannot come into being unless
> the social structure is being transformed somewhat. They are not, strictly
> speaking, to be viewed as a set of *causal* variables working on a static and
> passive set of social patterns. Rather, they *are* the changes to be ex-
> plained. (22, p. 374)

The "sociological model" is properly viewed as a complement, not an
alternate, to the preceding two. It presents the level of intersection
and interaction of technical and moral orders inseparable from — yet
irreducible to — either. The example of the industrial revolution, the
technological revolution *par excellence* (not however lacking in intellectual or even spiritual components), will make this clearer. "About
1760 a wave of gadgets swept over England," began a schoolboy's essay
(2, p. 42). We hope to see something more by inspection of the
tables below.[28]

What makes these tables intelligible and interesting is due not so
much to the gadgetry as to the "impact" of factory organization on
family structure and the societal reaction which attended it. The decisive turning point is seen to occur between 1820-30, not with the shift
in workplace from cottage to factory but with the incorporation of non-
family members into work groups. What this represents is the final loss
of family control over members engaged in industrial production. The
family's "loss of function" is most apparent in one anomalous figure, the
desired hours of work for children rising from 8 in 1833 to 12 in 1835

---

[28] These tables are extracted from Smelser (81) and interpreted in general accord
with his analysis.

### Table 1.  Social Change in the Industrial Revolution

1. Technical-Organizational Means of Production.

| Year | Technical Process | Work Organization | Work Group |
|---|---|---|---|
| -1770 | Cottage Weaving | Domestic Industry | Family Group |
| 1770-90 | Spinning Jenny | Domestic Industry | Family Group |
|  | Water Frame | Factory Production | Family Members, Parish Wards, "Assistants" |
| 1790-1820 | Steam Mule | Factory Production | 2–3 (Family) |
| 1820-1830 | Power Loom | Factory Production | 4–9 (Non-Family) |

2. Hours of Work.

| Year | Actual | | Desired | |
|---|---|---|---|---|
|  | Children | Adults | Children | Adults |
| 1831-33 | 10 | 10 | 10 | 10 |
| 1833 | $8^2$ | $(10)$* | 8 | $8^3$ |
| 1835 | 8* | $(10)$* | 12 | 12 |
| 1837 | 8 | $(10)$* | 10 | 10 |

1. Labor demands.
2. Factory Act of 1833.
3. Society for National Regeneration.
* = estimated

— much to the embarrassment of social legislators and factory reformers. What is taking place here is not the greedy exploitation of child labor but the last attempt to keep the family group intact within the industrial workplace. Its eventual failure signalled the advent of massive industrial unrest — the Chartist Movement. Also, it signifies the separation of home and work, of family and economy, and the further stripping of family-centered functions of socialization later displaced on the public schools. These separations are illustrative of some main features of societal change on the macro-structural level, considered below in terms of the "theory of structural differentiation."

Elaborations on the macro-sociological model occur at points connected with hypotheses explaining the phenomena of political revolution in particular, among them (i) the marginality hypothesis, (ii) the contiguity hypothesis, (iii) the polarization hypothesis, (iv) the class rise hypothesis, and (v) the interrupted progress hypothesis. Together these can be said to comprise a "power model" of revolutionary change. As previously noted, however, they furnish only partial accounts since radical politics must ultimately be referred to extra-political and extra-institutional — that is, to societal — conditions. A sixth hypothesis, (vi) that of structural imbalance, effects this transition.[29]

(i). The *marginality hypothesis* is stated in Coleman's (9, p. 625)

---

[29] All six hypotheses derive from the Marxist revolutionary idea, testifying to both its fertility and ambiguity (cf. 90). For recent and competent analyses of these and related theories see Kramnick (38) and Stone (85).

view that "revolutionary activity will be carried out only by groups with control of resources that lie outside the system of collective decisions (that is, the government), such as actors with newly gained economic power, or those with military force but little governmental power, or those with access to resources supplied by another social system." An extension of this argument towards the "class rise" position is that rapid structural differentiation of societies creates instability in the stratification system by the social promotion of "powerful people who are little committed to norms restricting organizational competition to peaceful means" (84, p. 178).

(ii) The *contiguity hypothesis,* somewhat contradictorily, asserts that "a revolution is always a function of a struggle between the group in power and a challenging group located just below it in the power hierarchy. Both groups are in the minority with reference to the total population . . ." (31, p. 324). This deviates from the Marxist position by construing the class struggle historically as elite competition — not "conflicts between the exploiters and the exploited, but the strife between rival groups for the control of the exploited" (91, p. 1315).

(iii) The *polarization hypothesis* to nineteenth century political economist Lorenz von Stein meant the *breakdown* of a separation between an ideal state and the political society. Hegel had postulated a state "above politics" and class antagonisms within the society at large; von Stein argued that far from constituting the realm of freedom the actual state was a captive of the ruling class and was perverted to its class interest (35, p. 306). Revolutionary forces were generated by this *de*polarization of state and society. The more accustomed version of polarization sees the "vital center" eclipsed by class alignments and class antagonisms sharply dividing societal groups, the structured strains all running in the same direction and mutually reinforcing one another instead of crosscutting class lines to cancel out or moderate conflict. "This is precisely the situation which Marxists call revolutionary, and which . . . occurred in Germany before 1933 and in Moscow and Petrograd in 1917" (44, p. 15).

(iv) The *class rise hypothesis* is succinctly put in Elton's (16, pp. 10-11) words, "*In any society the revolutionaries will come from the class which is already acquiring power.*" Although *which* rising class aspires to and achieves dominance is often in doubt, this "social interpretation" has been widely applied, especially to the "model revolution" of modern times, the French ("bourgeois").[30] The "triumph of the middle classes" (58) continues throughout the 19th century, only to falter — as

---

[30] Meisel complains, "Sometimes the historians are not certain which way the rebellious class is moving, up or down." The "storm over the gentry" and its class position in Stuart England is another issue in this controversy.

the Marxists would have it — before a rising proletariat. Thus,

> . . . on the whole, the success of the proletarian revolution in Russia was no historical vagary; the pointer of power finally came to rest in accordance with the real balance of social forces; the industrial proletariat was, in the circumstances, the strongest of the various classes which might have ruled. It had already risen to potential dominance before it seized the state. It seized the state not by a bloody rebellion against a master class, but simply by exercising power which it already had gained. (82, pp. 63-64)

Counterpart to the rising expectations of an ascending class is a "class fall" or "status anxiety" hypothesis whereby revolutionary action is instigated by a class descending the social scale but striving to retain or recapture its former eminence (53, p. 212).

(v) The *interrupted progress hypothesis* combines features of both "class rise" and "class fall" *within* strata, rather than as opposed forces between different class formations. On this account, "Revolutions are most likely to occur when a prolonged period of objective economic and social development is followed by a short period of sharp reversal. People then subjectively fear that ground gained with great effort will be quite lost; their mood becomes revolutionary" (12, p. 5). In particular, "revolutions are probable wherever structural changes in the legally sanctioned distribution of power and social rewards have been slight or retrogressive" (57, p. 338).

(vi) The *structural imbalance hypothesis* focuses not so much on power or class structures and the status congruence of groups within them; instead, its structural pose rests on a proportionality between institutional sectors. On this view, "Any prolonged and exaggerated imbalances between the social and technical sectors lead to stagnation. And the pressures for development are such that stagnation is intolerable over a long period. This is what revolutions are all about" (32, p. 72). This sort of structural imbalance forms "a causative base for revolution-making" (32, p. 354), and fomenting revolution means essentially the removal of such "flagrant inconsistencies between the political and the economic and social orders . . ." (5, p. 7). The abstract formulation of this "institutional equilibrium" hypothesis is given in analytic categories of the "theory of structural differentiation."

*The theory of structural differentiation.* According to Dahrendorf (quoted in 98, p. 125), constructing the Theory of Revolutions involves "a contribution to the discovery of elements constituting a general theory of social change." Elsewhere (102), I have argued that the theory of structural differentiation constitutes *the* structural-functional theory of macro-social change, including revolutionary change as here defined. On this reckoning, societal change is a process of differentiation and crystallization in major institutional spheres. The resulting transformations and conformations indicate salient evolutionary sequences and stages and denominate revolutionary change in the structures of society.

In the tradition of evolutionary functionalism, they are most fully identified and specified in Parsons' "evolutionary universals in society." His schema outlines which structures undergo successively the process of differentiation and what the functional consequences are for the institutional system as a whole.

"*Evolutionary universals*" are defined by Parsons (67, pp. 340-41) as "a complex of structures and associated processes the development of which so increases the long-run adaptive capacity . . . that only systems that develop the complex can attain certain higher levels of general adaptive capacity." He cites ten such "institutional complexes" — communication, religion, kinship, technology, stratification, cultural legitimation, bureaucracy, money and markets, generalized universalistic norms and democratic association. Breaks in this series represent three main evolutionary stages, the "primitive," "archaic" and "modern." Transition from primitive to archaic occurs through a process of differentiation of political and religious functions from kinship, while bureaucratic organization, money and markets, a universalistic legal system and democratic association "are fundamental to the modern type of society."[31] Where is the correspondence between this series and the one for societal revolutions sketched above (Fig. 2)?

The first four of Parsons' evolutionary universals form the base from which all societal development takes its departure: they are universals of culture without which human society could not have come into existence or long persisted. As such — excepting religion — they are virtually synonymous with the "human revolution" or at least its social consequences. The agricultural revolution still represents a pre-revolutionary stage in Parsons' schema, but its consequence in surplus accumulation gives rise to the process of stratification (or vice versa). The urban revolution depicts not only a drastic change in settlement pattern but also in social organization; as Miner (55, p. 304) notes, "The first appearance of cities in every part of the world has been associated with the development of economic and politico-religious differentiation in the society at large."

"Urban involution" of the Oriental city is subsequently broken through by the "escape" of money and markets from bureaucratic control in the rise of western medieval cities, precipitating the commercial revolution (13). The rise of economic society and its culmination in the industrial revolution creates pressures for "generalized universalistic norms," of occupational recruitment and labor commitment as well

---

[31] (67, p. 339). Bureaucratization may be considered a "modern" development in contrast with the "patrimonial" character of historical bureaucratic societies. Only with the "Tudor revolution in government," Elton (15, p. 12) contends, does the distinction between service to the state through a national bureaucracy and service on the king's person through a royal household become institutionalized.

as economic "rationality." Further generalization from this industrial base to the *political* economy results then in forms of "democratic association," the extension and equalization of citizenship rights and statuses which are the essence of "democratic revolution." Parsons belatedly speculates that "science" may come to comprise a future institutional complex on a par with the other ten. While his schedule of evolutionary universals does not directly coincide with our roster of societal revolutions, the resemblances are strong. More serious is the criticism that Parsons' "change model" does not incorporate a "process model" as its micro-structure. The reformulation of differentiation theory which follows is a tentative step towards remedying that condition.

### What Is Revolutionary about Societal Revolutions?

Finally, how shall we assess those changes in the structure of society that can be called revolutionary — that is, as setting in motion a process of cumulative change whose outcome is the emergence of a distinctive type of society? In structural terms, what is revolutionary about societal revolutions? I would say we are in the presence of an authentic societal revolution when marked changes occur in the quantity *and* quality of social relations. To describe such change I will employ four structural categories: (i) "conditions of existence," (ii) "societal scale," (iii) "bases of association," and (iv) "carrying capacity." By "conditions of existence" I refer to the mechanisms of cultural adjustment and cultural control pertaining to the non-human environment, particularly the Marxian "mode of production." By "societal scale" I mean the quantity of social relations as determined by population size and density. By "bases of association" I indicate the quality of social relations: the rules for bringing social actors and collectivities into association with one another and maintaining them in interaction. Lastly, by "carrying capacity" I infer the prospects for societal stability or instability — "revolutionary potential" — resulting from the combined values of the preceding three.

Each of these diagnostic categories can be illustrated briefly. White (96, p. 301) connects the first and last when he writes, "The institutions of primitive society broke down and gave way because they could not contain and accommodate the new technological forces introduced by the cultivation of plants and the domestication of animals." Childe conveys the idea of "societal scale" when he supposes that revolutions manifest themselves "in an upward kink in the population curve" (6, p. 19). In terms of "bases of association," Walzer (93, p. 3) perceives a radical change in political affiliation during the Puritan Revolution. Because the work of the Calvinist saints required cooperation,

. . . they organized to carry it through successfully and they joined forces with any man who might help them without regard to the older bonds of family and neighborhood. They sought "brethren" and turned away if necessary from their relatives; they sought zeal and not affection. Thus there arose the leagues and covenants, the conferences and congregations which are the prototypes of revolutionary discipline.

Whatever the plausibility these concepts and cases may claim, only when brought together in a conceptual system do they acquire real utility. Their systematic power can be illustrated by more intensive analysis of a single episode of the urban revolution: the social organization of Mecca and the origins of Islam.

*A case in point.*   We are now in a position to answer the question, "What is revolutionary about societal revolutions?"

1. Societal revolutions are revolutionary in terms of a change in the conditions of existence.

In the case of 7th century Mecca (103), the mode of production had shifted from nomadic pastoralism to settled agriculture and, subsequently, to long-distance caravan trade as a preindustrial urban mode of production.

2. Societal revolutions are revolutionary in terms of expansion in societal scale.

The rapid increase in population size accommodated by economic expansion became concentrated in the oasis village of Mecca.

3. Societal revolutions are revolutionary in terms of changes in the bases of association.

With urbanization and commercialization the quality of social relations altered from kinship-based (consanguinity) to locality-based (territoriality).

4. Societal revolutions are revolutionary in terms of carrying capacity.

The limits of adaptive capacity under pre-existing bases of association, expanding societal scale and a changing mode of production were transcended in a religious revolution and extended on a new level by the Islamic state. The revolutionary situation was produced by the ultimately futile effort to perpetuate the old social order in a drastically changed situation; it was resolved by a charismatic movement that created and legitimated what Durkheim termed "the system of rules actually needed."

*A Marxist metaphor.*   Not only can the transformations of society be described in terms such as these, we may also refer them to the formulations of leading commentators on the revolutionary theme. Chief among these, of course, is Marx himself. In his and Engels' *Communist Manifesto* (48), we read:

> The essential condition for the existence, and for the sway of the bourgeois class, is the formation and augmentation of capital. . . . (p. 16)

The bourgeoisie cannot exist without constantly revolutionizing the instruments of production, and thereby the relations of production, and with them the whole relations of society. (p. 7)

The bourgeoisie keeps more and more doing away with the scattered state of the population, of the means of production, and of property. It has agglomerated population, centralized means of production, and has concentrated property in a few hands. The necessary consequence of this was political centralization. (pp. 9-10)

But with the development of industry the proletariat not only increases in number, it becomes concentrated in greater masses, its strength grows, and it feels that strength more. The various interests and conditions of life within the ranks of the proletariat are more and more equalized, in proportion as machinery obliterates all distinctions of labor, and nearly everywhere reduces wages to the same low level. (p. 17)

The productive forces at the disposal of society no longer tend to further the development of the conditions of bourgeois property; on the contrary, they have become too powerful for these conditions, by which they are fettered, and so soon as they overcome these fetters, they bring disorder into the whole of bourgeois property. The conditions of bourgeois society are too narrow to comprise the wealth created by them. (p. 12)

Throughout these passages Marx can be understood as imputing values for our terms in a particular stage of societal development, values which threaten to exceed the permissible limits of tolerance for the system as a whole. In a nutshell, this was Marx's "great analytic insight": that capitalist property relations (bases of association) cannot contain (carrying capacity) the social relations of production (societal scale) within an industrial mode of production (conditions of existence).

In this chapter I have tried to establish some parameters for analyzing the structure of societal revolutions. It has been my contention that this structure can be expressed most cogently in terms of the theory of structural differentiation. Making sensible these structural problems and solutions, in full historical content and societal context, remains unfinished business scarcely begun. We are some years (but not light-years) distant from achieving a societal theory of revolutions and, beyond that, a theory of societal revolutions. I hope to have advanced one strategic approach towards that end.

# BIBLIOGRAPHY

1. Ashby, W. Ross. *Design for a Brain*. 2nd ed. New York: John Wiley, 1960.

2. Ashton, Thomas S. *The Industrial Revolution, 1760–1830*. New York: Oxford University Press, 1964.

3. Borkenau, Franz. *The Totalitarian Enemy*. London: Faber and Faber, 1940.

4. Boulding, Kenneth E. *A Primer on Social Dynamics: History as Dialectics and Development*. New York: Free Press, 1970.

5. Brogan, D. W. *The Price of Revolution*. New York: Harper and Brothers, 1951.

6. Childe, V. Gordon. *Man Makes Himself*. New York: Mentor, 1951.

7. Cipolla, Carlo M. *The Economic History of World Population*. 4th ed. Baltimore, Md.: Penguin, 1967.

8. Clark, Grahame. *Aspects of Prehistory*. Berkeley: University of California Press, 1970.

9. Coleman, James S. "Foundations for a Theory of Collective Decisions," *American Journal of Sociology*, 71, 6 (May 1966): 615-27.

10. Dahrendorf, Ralf. *Class and Class Conflict in Industrial Society*. Stanford, Calif.: Stanford University Press, 1959.

11. Dahrendorf, Ralf. *Essays in the Theory of Society*. Stanford, Calif.: Stanford University Press, 1968.

12. Davies, James C. "Toward a Theory of Revolution," *American Sociological Review* 27, 1 (February 1962): 5-19.

13. de Roover, Raymond. "The Commercial Revolution of the Thirteenth Century," pp. 80-85 in Frederic C. Lane and Jelle C. Riemersma (eds.), *Enterprise and Secular Change*, London: Allen and Unwin, 1953.

14. Dobb, Maurice H. *Studies in the Development of Capitalism*. New York: International, 1947.

15. Elton, G. R. *The Tudor Revolution in Government: Administrative Changes in the Reign of Henry VIII*. Cambridge: Cambridge University Press, 1953.

16. Elton, Godfrey. *The Revolutionary Idea in France, 1789–1871*. New York: Longmans, Green, 1923.

17. Gareau, Frederick H. "Morgenthau's Plan for Industrial Disarmament in Germany," *Western Political Quarterly* 14, 2 (June 1961): 517–34.

18. Geertz, Clifford. "The Integrative Revolution: Primordial Sentiments and Civil Politics in the New States," pp. 105-57 in Clifford Geertz (ed.), *Old Societies and New States: The Quest for Modernity in Asia and Africa*. New York: Free Press, 1963.

19. Ginsberg, Morris. *Essays in Sociology and Social Philosophy*. Baltimore, Md.: Penguin, 1968.

20. Gluckman, Max. "The Utility of the Equilibrium Model in the Study of Social Change," *American Anthropologist* 70, 2 (April 1968): 219-37.

21. Godechot, Jacques. *The Counter-Revolution: Doctrine and Action, 1789–1804.* Translated by Salvator Attanasio. New York: Howard Fertig, 1971.

22. Goode, William J. *World Revolution and Family Patterns.* New York: Free Press of Glencoe, 1963.

23. Gouldner, Alvin W. *The Coming Crisis of Western Sociology.* New York: Basic Books, 1970.

24. Griffith, J. A. G. "Why We Need a Revolution," *Political Quarterly* 40, 4 (October-December 1969): 383-93.

25. Hart, Hornell. "Acceleration in Social Change," pp. 27-55 in Francis R. Allen et al., *Technology and Social Change.* New York: Appleton-Century-Crofts, 1957.

26. Hauser, Philip M. "The Chaotic Society: Product of the Social Morphological Revolution," *American Sociological Review* 34, 1 (February 1969): 1-19.

27. Heer, Friedrich. *Europe, Mother of Revolutions,* translated by Charles Kessler and Jennetta Adcock. New York: Frederick A. Praeger, 1972.

28. Hill, Christopher. *Puritanism and Revolution: Studies in Interpretation of the 17th Century.* New York: Schocken, 1964.

29. Hobsbawm, E. J. "From Social History to the History of Society," *Daedalus* 100, 1 (Winter 1971): 20-45.

30. Hockett, Charles F., and Robert Ascher. "The Human Revolution," *Current Anthropology* 5, 3 (June 1964): 135-47.

31. Hopper, Rex D. "Cybernation, Marginality, and Revolution," pp. 313-30 in Irving Louis Horowitz (ed.), *The New Sociology: Essays in Social Science and Social Theory in Honor of C. Wright Mills.* New York: Oxford University Press, 1964.

32. Horowitz, Irving Louis. *Three Worlds of Development: The Theory and Practice of International Stratification.* New York: Oxford University Press, 1966.

33. Jaspers, Karl. "The Axial Age of Human History," pp. 597-605 in Maurice R. Stein, Arthur J. Vidich, and David Manning White (eds.), *Identity and Anxiety: Survival of the Person in Mass Society.* Glencoe, Ill.: Free Press, 1960.

34. Kaplan, David. "The Law of Cultural Dominance," pp. 69-92 in Marshall D. Sahlins and Elman R. Service (eds.), *Evolution and Culture.* Ann Arbor: University of Michigan Press, 1960.

35. Kelly, George Armstrong, and Clifford W. Brown, Jr. (eds.), *Struggles in the State: Sources and Patterns of World Revolution.* New York: John Wiley, 1970.

36. Kittell, Allan H. "The Revolutionary Period of the Industrial Revolution: Industrial Innovation and Population Displacement in Belgium, 1830–1880," *Journal of Social History* 1, 2 (Winter 1967): 119-48.

37. Kluckhohn, Clyde. "The Moral Order in the Expanding Society," pp. 391-404 in Carl H. Kraeling and Robert M. Adams (eds.), *City Invincible: A Symposium on Urbanization and Cultural Development in the Ancient Near East.* Chicago: University of Chicago Press, 1960.

38. Kramnick, Isaac. "Reflections on Revolution: Definition and Explanation in Recent Scholarship," *History and Theory* 11, 1 (1972): 26-63.

39. Kuhn, Thomas S. *The Structure of Scientific Revolutions.* Chicago: University of Chicago Press, 1962.

40. Kuhn, Thomas S. *The Structure of Scientific Revolutions.* 2nd ed., enl. Chicago: University of Chicago Press, 1970.

41. Kuman, Krishan (ed.), *Revolution — The Theory and Practice of a European Idea.* London: Weidenfeld and Nicolson, 1971.

42. Lenski, Gerhard. *Human Societies: A Macrolevel Introduction to Sociology.* New York: McGraw-Hill, 1970.

43. Levy, Marion J., Jr. *The Structure of Society.* Princeton, N.J.: Princeton University Press, 1952.

44. Lipset, Seymour Martin. *Political Man: The Social Bases of Politics.* Garden City, N.Y.: Doubleday, 1963.

45. Maguire, James Joseph. *The Philosophy of Modern Revolution.* Washington, D.C.: Catholic University of America Press, 1943.

46. Marcuse, Herbert. "The End of Utopia," *Ramparts* 18, 10 (April 1970): 28-34.

47. Martindale, Don. *Social Life and Cultural Change.* Princeton, N.J.: D. Van Nostrand, 1962.

48. Marx, Karl, and Friedrich Engels. *The Communist Manifesto,* translated by Paul M. Sweezy and Leo Huberman. New York: Monthly Review Press, 1964.

49. Mathias, Peter. "Preface," pp. vii-ix, in R. M. Hartwell (ed.), *The Causes of the Industrial Revolution in England.* London: Methuen, 1967.

50. Mazlish, Bruce, Arthur D. Kaledin, and David B. Ralston. "The Chinese Revolution," pp. 225-30 in Bruce Mazlish, Arthur D. Kaledin and David B. Ralston (eds.), *Revolution: A Reader.* New York: Macmillan, 1971.

51. McAlister, Jr., John T. "The War We Didn't Understand," *University* 43 (Winter, 1969-70): 13-21.

52. McFarland, H. Neill. *The Rush Hour of the Gods: A Study of New Religious Movements in Japan.* New York: Macmillan, 1967.

53. Meisel, James H. *Counterrevolution: How Revolutions Die.* New York: Atherton, 1966.

54. Meusel, Alfred. "Revolution and Counter-Revolution," pp. 367-76, Vol. 13, in Edwin R. A. Seligman (ed.), *Encyclopedia of the Social Sciences.* New York: Macmillan, 1934.

55. Miner, Horace. *The Primitive City of Timbuctoo.* rev. ed. Garden City, N.Y.: Doubleday, 1965.

56. Mingay, G. E. "The Agricultural Revolution in English History: A Reconsideration," pp. 11-28 in W. E. Minchinton (ed.), *Essays in Agrarian History: Vol. II.* New York: Augustus M. Kelley, 1968.

57. Moore, Wilbert E. "Predicting Discontinuities in Social Change," *American Sociological Review* 29, 3 (June 1964): 331-38.

58. Morazé, Charles. *The Triumph of the Middle Classes: A Study of European Values in the Nineteenth Century*, translated by George Weidenfeld. New York: World, 1966.

59. Nash, Manning. "Social Prerequisites to Economic Growth in Latin America and Southeast Asia," *Economic Development and Cultural Change* 12, 3 (April 1964): 225-42.

60. Nef, John U. *Cultural Foundations of Industrial Civilization.* New York: Harper and Brothers, 1960.

61. Nell, Edward J. "Economic Relationships in the Decline of Feudalism: An Examination of Economic Interdependence and Social Change," *History and Theory* 6, 3 (1967): 313-50.

62. Nisbet, Robert A. *The Sociological Tradition.* New York: Basic Books, 1966.

63. Nisbet, Robert A. *Tradition and Revolt: Historical and Sociological Essays.* New York: Random House, 1968.

64. O'Brien, Conor Cruise. "The Counterrevolutionary Reflex," pp. 136-41 In Robert Perrucci and Marc Pilisuk (eds.), *The Triple Revolution: Social Problems in Depth.* Boston: Little, Brown, 1968.

65. Parsons, Talcott. "The American Family: Its Relations to Personality and to the Social Structure," pp. 3-33 in Talcott Parsons and Robert F. Bales (eds.), *Family, Socialization and Interaction Process.* Glencoe, Ill.: Free Press, 1955.

66. Parsons, Talcott. "Some Considerations on the Theory of Social Change," *Rural Sociology* 26, 3 (September 1961): 219-39.

67. Parsons, Talcott. "Evolutionary Universals in Society," *American Sociological Review* 29, 3 (June 1964): 339-57.

68. Parsons, Talcott. *Societies: Evolutionary and Comparative Perspectives.* Englewood Cliffs, N.J.: Prentice-Hall, 1966.

69. Parsons, Talcott. "On Building Social System Theory: A Personal History," *Daedalus* 99, 4 (Fall 1970), 826-81.

70. Perrucci, Robert and Marc Pilisuk. "Introduction: Social Problems and the Triple Revolution," pp. vii-xiv in Robert Perrucci and Marc Pilisuk (eds.), *The Triple Revolution: Social Problems in Depth.* Boston: Little, Brown, 1968.

71. Proudhon, Pierre Joseph. *General Idea of the Revolution in the Nineteenth Century*, translated by John Beverly Robinson. London: Freedom Press, 1923.

72. Radcliffe-Brown, A. R. *A Natural Science of Society.* Glencoe, Ill.: Free Press, 1957.

73. Redfield, Robert. *The Primitive World and Its Transformations.* Ithaca, N.Y.: Cornell University Press, 1953.

74. Ribeiro, Darcy. *The Civilizational Process*, translated by Betty J. Meggers. Washington, D.C.: Smithsonian Institution Press, 1968.

75. Rossi, Mario. *The Third World: The Unaligned Countries and the World Revolution.* New York: Funk and Wagnalls, 1963.

76. Ryan, Bryce F. *Social and Cultural Change.* New York: Ronald, 1969.

77. Salomon, Albert. *The Tyranny of Progress: Reflections on the Origins of Sociology.* New York: Noonday Press, 1955.

78. Shaplen, Robert. *The Lost Revolution: The U.S. in Vietnam, 1946–1966.* rev. ed. New York: Harper and Row, 1966.

79. Shils, Edward A. "Center and Periphery," pp. 117-30 in Edward A. Shils (ed.), *The Logic of Personal Knowledge.* Glencoe, Ill.: Free Press, 1961.

80. Smelser, Neil J. *Theory of Collective Behavior.* New York: Free Press of Glencoe, 1963.

81. Smelser, Neil J. "Sociological History: The Industrial Revolution and the British Working-Class Family," *Journal of Social History* 1, 1 (Fall 1967): 17-35.

82. Soule, George. *The Coming American Revolution.* New York: Macmillan, 1934.

83. Stein, Maurice R. *The Eclipse of Community: An Interpretation of American Studies.* New York: Harper and Row, 1964.

84. Stinchcombe, Arthur L. "Social Structure and Organizations," pp. 142-93 in James G. March (ed.), *Handbook of Organizations.* Chicago: Rand McNally, 1965.

85. Stone, Lawrence. "Theories of Revolution," *World Politics* 18, 2 (January 1966): 159-76.

86. Tilly, Charles. "Clio and Minerva," pp. 433-66 in John C. McKinney and Edward A. Tiryakian (eds.). *Theoretical Sociology: Perspectives and Development.* New York: Appleton-Century-Crofts, 1970.

87. Tiryakian, Edward A. "A Model of Societal Change and Its Lead Indicators," pp. 69-97 in Samuel Z. Klausner (ed.), *The Study of Total Societies.* Garden City, N.Y.: Doubleday, 1967.

88. Tiryakian, Edward A. "Structural Sociology," pp. 111-35 in John C. McKinney and Edward A. Tiryakian (eds.), *Theoretical Sociology: Perspectives and Development.* New York: Appleton-Century-Crofts, 1970.

89. Touraine, Alain. (Review of 23), *American Journal of Sociology* 77, 2 (September 1971): 317-23.

90. Tucker, Robert C. *The Marxian Revolutionary Idea.* New York: W. W. Norton, 1969.

91. Turner, Ralph E. *The Great Cultural Traditions: II. The Classical Empires.* New York: McGraw-Hill, 1941.

92. Von Laue, Theodore H. *The Global City: Freedom, Power, and Necessity in the Age of World Revolutions.* Philadelphia: J. B. Lippincott, 1969.

93. Walzer, Michael. *The Revolution of the Saints: A Study in the Origins of Radical Politics.* New York: Atheneum, 1968.

94. Ward, Barbara. *The Rich Nations and the Poor Nations.* New York: W. W. Norton, 1962.

95. Wetter, Gustav A. *Dialectical Materialism: A Historical and Systematic*

*Survey of Philosophy in the Soviet Union,* translated by Peter Heath. New York: Frederick A. Praeger, 1963.

96. White, Leslie A. *The Evolution of Culture: The Development of Civilization to the Fall of Rome.* New York: McGraw-Hill, 1959.

97. Wilkie, James W. *The Mexican Revolution: Federal Expenditure and Social Change since 1910.* Berkeley: University of California Press, 1967.

98. Willer, David, and George K. Zollschan. "Prolegomenon to a Theory of Revolutions," pp. 125-51 in George K. Zollschan and Walter Hirsch (eds.), *Explorations in Social Change.* Boston: Houghton Mifflin, 1964,

99. Wilson, Woodrow. "The Road away from Revolution," *Atlantic Monthly,* 132, 2 (August 1923): 145-46.

100. Wittfogel, Karl A. "The Hydraulic Civilizations," pp. 152-64 in William L. Thomas, Jr. (ed.), *Man's Role in Changing the Face of the Earth.* Chicago: University of Chicago Press, 1956.

101. Wittfogel, Karl A. *Oriental Despotism: A Comparative Study of Total Power.* New Haven, Conn.: Yale University Press, 1963.

102. Wolf, C. P. "The Theory of Structural Differentiation," paper presented at the 65th Annual Meeting of the American Sociological Association, Washington, D.C.: 1 September 1970.

103. Wolf, Eric R. "The Social Organization of Mecca and the Origins of Islam," *Southwestern Journal of Anthropology* 7, 4 (Winter 1951): 329-56.

# SECTION TWO

further steps in the theory
of institutionalization

# Introduction

When the first formal exposition of Zollschan's framework for an individualistic, motivationally oriented, theory of institutionalization appeared in 1964 (2, pp. 89-207) it was not anticipated that the sociological community would take to it with great enthusiasm. Our anticipations have been borne out. Reviewers were mildly favourable (but extremely vague) about it and the field reacted with deafening silence. Then (around ten years ago) sociology in North America appeared to be the proprietary domain of structural functionalist theory, with the tattered proletarians of the *Chicago School* — true to form — "accommodating" themselves to their peripheral locations in "social space."

Sorokin alone (may his puckish soul forever quaff great drafts of *Tokayi Essenz* in the Finno-Ugrian Valhalla!) gave star billing to the theoretical model in his compendious *Sociological Theories of To-day*. He admitted without reluctance, that it was reminiscent of "medieval scholasticism at its decadent phase" (1, p. 598n). It is quite inconceivable, of course, that Pitirim Aleksandrovitch could have been entirely unaware of the flowers that sprang out of the decay of scholasticism in the great, creative (guaranteed "non-sensate") period of pre-classical cosmography and mechanics. His attack (if, indeed, it was meant as an attack) was an ambivalent one. It alone would have made the effort worthwhile.

Meanwhile, if the field of sociology was not showing interest in the new work, the world of social processes was providing a degree of corroboration exceeded by our fondest expectations. Revolutionary movements gathered momentum which, despite many of their participants' paying lip-service to Marxist rhetoric, were entirely inexplicable within Marx's theoretical frame of reference. A generalized theory of exigencies such as the one enunciated by Zollschan and his associates was uniquely fitted for explaining the organized discontent of minority groups, women, students, adolescents in general, and homosexuals. A single-exigency framework (or, more properly regarded, a crypto-double-exigency framework) postulating political subjection, generated by dialectical peculiarities allegedly immanent in economic relations of production, is hardly fitted to carry the burden of social reality on its hunched and distorted shoulders.

One consequence of this social unrest in recent years has been the increasing frequency of citations of one particular old chapter, the title of which contained the word "revolution," in journals marginal to "mainstream" sociology such as *Theory and History* and a variety of Marxist periodicals. It is abundantly clear that most of these citations refer to this single word in the title rather than to the theoretical contents of the piece itself.

It was only around the time when this new volume was conceived that straws in the wind could be detected, indicating that the exigency-action-articulation model was beginning to exert an influence. Dunbar Moodie had found the ideas useful for his study on the rise of Afrikaner nationalism and consented to rewrite the methodological appendix as a chapter for the volume. Jim Dow, a mathematician-anthropologist, became intrigued with formalizing possibilities. Robert Brym, a promising student of surprising youth had discovered the theory while visiting Israel; from an English lecturer. Walter Friedman became interested in the course of a discussion on followership and charisma. Michael Overington, whose formidable critical talents are inadequately acknowledged by mere co-authorship of a couple of chapters in this volume, forced a re-appraisal of some basic aspects of the entire model. It began to appear at last as though all that was needed to see sound ideas come to fruition was Methusalemian longevity.

The first chapter in this section, by Overington and Zollschan, is meant to provide a panoramic overview of the model as initially presented in 1964 as well as of its origins in Zollschan's intellectual biography. Thus, it enacts one aspect of an empirical sociology of science as well as presenting a reference point in this volume for fundamental notions of the Theory of Institutionalization.

Moodie's splendid piece is the second in the section. A born anglophone, he contrives to get the central ideas of the model across with admirable simplicity and vigor and adds many interesting angles of his own. His generous remarks are gratefully acknowledged.

An earlier version of Zollschan and Friedman's chapter, written by the senior author in 1961, was to have been published in the abortive second edition of Gouldner's *Studies in Leadership*. Since the paper had been officially accepted by the editor it was cited in *Explorations in Social Change* (pp. 97, 118, 124). The present publication serves, among other things, to give a referent to a previously disembodied reference. Friedman's enthusiasm for old wine on the point of going sour led to the present distillation. Lovers of acerbic brews will find it suited to their palate; philistine devotees of the conventional leadership literature are in for some shocks.

Two approaches are potentially available for testing a theoretical framework such as Zollschan presents. One of these is an attempt to specify the social contexts within which parameters of the framework can be embedded in particular times and at particular places. A less conventional but, perhaps, more promising avenue for the empirical examination of highly complex recursive and interactive models of social processes, such as the one presented by Zollschan, is by formal modelling techniques. Both approaches are featured in the following section. The chapter by Zollschan and Brym provides an attempt at the former. Dow's chapter is an initial step towards a workable computer model.

Zollschan and Brym's "Transconceptualization of Sociology of Knowledge and Sociology of Science" is a frolic on phenomenology and epistemology and sociology of knowledge. It contrives to come out with an affirmative answer to the question whether scientific sociology is possible, entirely without the slightest taint of positivism. To be believed, it has to be read!

Alfred Schütz writes somewhere that phenomenology finds its starting place in a radicalization of Cartesian doubt. If this is indeed the case, Jim Dow returns the compliment by transforming the phenomenological characterization of an exigency as "the gap between what is and what ought to be" into a dimension of Cartesian vector space. This exercise may prove to be but the first step in an extended series of successively nearer formal approximations to the model in its full complex simplicity. Perhaps a twist of the verbal "lattice" there presented, can produce an entire society of Moebius men, wildly interacting in their algebraic topological paradox-world.

## BIBLIOGRAPHY

1. Sorokin, Pitirim A. *Sociological Theories of To-day*. New York: Harper & Row, 1966.
2. Zollschan, George K. *et al.*, "Section Two: Working Papers in the Theory of Institutionalization" in George K. Zollschan, *Explorations in Social Change*, Boston: Houghton Mifflin and Co., 1964 and London: Routledge and Kegan Paul, 1964, pp. 89-207.

# 4

*Michael A. Overington*
*and George K. Zollschan*

# Goal Formation as the Key for Explaining Conduct and Society: A Discussion of Some Old "Suggestions" for a Theory of Institutionalization

*Music is the hidden metaphysical activity of a mind that does not know it is philosophizing.*[1]

— Schopenhauer

This chapter, in a very real sense, is the joint effort of the co-authors. The old suggestions were first put forward by Zollschan at the Meetings of the American Association for the Advancement of Science in Philadelphia in 1962. Later, a slightly reworded version appeared as the introduction to a series of chapters published in *Explorations in Social Change* in 1964 under the caption heading: "Working Papers in the Theory of Institutionalization" (10).

This current chapter can be seen, in first approximation, as Zollschan's effort to respond to Overington's request for the intellectual context in which the original statement was made and, therefore, to be understood.

[1] This is our translation of the original Latin used by Schopenhauer (in *Welt als Wille und Vorstellung*, Book III, Section 52) when mimicking another characterization of music proposed by Leibnitz who saw it as an unconscious form of numerical counting! Schopenhauer's Latin goes as follows: *Musica est exercitium metaphysices occultum nescientis se philosophari animi.*

The context in question was essentially composed of the problems raised by the confrontation between Zollschan's own training and predilections and the state of sociological theory in North America at that time. But, over and above such contextual emplacement, this chapter means to solidify the fluid character of the originally stated theory so that it may provide a stable background against which the current revisions and extensions of the theory in this volume may be viewed.

It is proper to ask whether the contrapuntal complexities of the above mentioned Section Introduction and of the four chapters that followed it, clearly reveal their programatic character to any but the most expert practitioners in the art of the fugue. Our present effort presents a brief and, we trust, painless course in sociological harmony and counterpoint that should reveal the architectonic themes of Zollschan's earlier work stripped of their baroque complexities.

Like any compositions, the earlier works retain whatever vitality they may possess without further gloss. But it should not be forgotten that these chapters were strictly what their collective title claimed for them; namely, "working papers." As such, their utility has been to provide a place from which to continue the exercise which they initiated. Returning to them ten or more years later constitutes an effort to provide a contemporary and authoritative, if not definitive, reading.

In these papers of 1962–1963, there was a programme that may best be understood, in retrospect, as a contribution to the effort to resolve the many conceptual problems rooted in the Kantian understanding of freedom under universal determinism which had been meant to solve the problem of moral action in a Newtonian world. This "solution" so bedeviled the nineteenth century that Max Weber was driven to distraction in his attempt to demonstrate the possibility of scientific enquiry concerning free persons. Nor has there been a general scheme for such enquiry more adequate than Weber's, despite its serious flaws. This programme, then, recommends a return to Weber's handling of Kantian dualism as the starting point for the establishment of a sociological framework of ideas which would allow for achievement of the Weberian goal of a "science of free persons" without the defects of Weber's own theory or those of sociology in the modern period.

Central to any understanding of Zollschan's model is the notion that goal construction or goal formation is the key for unlocking the problems both of social systems and of the human personality. In turn, the variables involved in processes leading to goal construction are themselves seen as the basic primitive concepts out of which all analysis of social action may profitably be formed. This contrasts with Weber's conception of goals as inert, lying around like so much dust on a carpet waiting to be vacuumed up by Parsons' social systems model where (continuing to exist in encapsulated condition) they are safe from genuinely "voluntaristic" action, let alone human contact! What Weber had simply assumed — the formation of goals — becomes *the* problematic of action for Zollschan.

In shifting stress from the mere existence of goals as termini for intelligible action to their formation, Zollschan turns to Freud for inspiration. It is precisely by his effort to subsume Freud together with Weber into a theoretical framework that would do justice to both of their viewpoints, especially their conceptions of terms like "rationality," "sense," and "meaning," that Zollschan hopes to handle the Kantian problem of *cause* versus *reason*. In effect, Zollschan decomposes the development of any reason or goal into an open system of variegated *determinate* part processes in which the values of parameters of the model may be treated as independent variables in the analysis *without* making the model deny the self-caused character of human action.

Nevertheless, this is not merely an attempt to solve the problems of the long departed Max Weber — grateful, no doubt, as he would be! We can still find today the "Kantian Problem" in contemporary sociology in the distinction between *cause* and *reason,* and the claimed radical disjunction between explanations that appeal to one *or* the other. People like to say that humans are either determined or free, or that it is conceptually improper to give accounts that draw both on the concept of cause and the concept of reason in the same analysis. Yet many sociologists are unconcerned, perhaps even unaware, of the "problem" and blithely provide "causal" accounts of aggregate behaviour that are informed by social psychological discussions of what, on close examination, turn out to be nothing else than individual "reasons." Is this "solution by disregard" of the problem sufficient to handle it in the long run, or will it succeed merely in postponing the inevitable difficulties that such procedures entail? Zollschan's model proclaims his belief that only a firm conceptual resolution can be successful in the long run. Only such a resolution will root sociological praxis and eliminate the increasing profusion of accounting schemes that are established to give expression to the desires of sociologists to offer "scientific" (narrowly viewed as "causal") explanations at the same time as the notion of humans as self-constituting elements in the social process is retained.

Yet *cause* and *reason* accounts are disjunct only under a particular set of assumptions, the most significant of which is the absolute alternative character of these accounts as predicates of human existence; an assumption which eliminates the conception of human "being" as *self-caused*. Zollschan's program, in essence, formulates reasons *as* causes. It takes its beginning in the belief that a major part of the contemporary confusion and disagreement among sociologists concerned with the explanation of social action is located in the terminological influences, the connotational restrictions, that "cause" and "reason" place upon their thinking. Thus, while the programme was intended as a unifying conceptual model of social action that sought to establish a vocabulary of primitive terms and state their major conceptual dimensions and relations, it operates meta-linguistically. It proposes a theoretical scheme that avoids "cause" and "reason," thus dissolving the barriers between sociologists who will only use one or the other of these terms in explanations of action, while at the same time dealing with the issues raised by the concepts of *cause* and *reason*. The program aims, in brief, to provide an abstract set of concepts that in their relationships describe the process of human action and give scientists studying such action an internally consistent and exhaustive array of testable parameters.

Before discussing this programme, however, it may be best to reconstruct the major intellectual influences that worked on Zollschan in the formulation of his position. By doing so it becomes possible both to locate the influence of individual thinkers on the model and to suggest the historical and personal circumstances that made these influences salient in its development. One may point to four individuals in particular — Weber, Freud, Marx, and Popper — as the proximate intellectual influences on Zollschan and his model of social action. Each of these persons' ideas evoked a response in the model, not only in terms of producing specific aspects of it, but also in giving Zollschan an intellectual audience with which to speak, argue and collaborate. It is fair to add, however, that the early formulation of the model occurred when sociological theory in North America was still dominated by the work of Parsons and his disciples. To the extent that there was an explicit contemporary audience for this first presentation of the model, it was an audience of Parsonians; but Parsonians who had become aware of the neo-Marxist critiques levelled against them by Lockwood and Dahrendorf. Moreover, it is hard for sociologists to spend even part of their working lives in North America without inhaling the spirit of symbolic interactionism that permeates the very atmosphere of sociology. Much as Parsons assumed some of the basic elements of symbolic interactionism in *The Structure of Social Action* without benefit of citation (one does not cite the air one breathes any more than one pays for it in the market place), so also did Zollschan assume them in 1963.

Weber comes first in this little catalogue as the implicit context for a choice of primitives in the model. Thus, concepts like "society," "person," "action," and "goal" are taken for granted and neologisms like "exigency," "salience," "justifiability," and so on, are taken as primitives. One must look to Weber in order to find what is intended as the meaning of these broader, unstated concepts that act as a framework for Zollschan's model of social action. To present a pared-down version of his notions: *acts* are goal-directed (or goal-oriented) behaviour; *persons* are human organisms who act (i.e. have goals) as well as merely "behave"; persons interact, that is to say they take each other's action into account and are directed thereby; *society* consists of more or less patterned interactions of persons, of the *ensemble* of such patterns.

However, Weber is not given pride of place simply because his fundamental concepts provide an implicit background to Zollschan's model, but also because he is taken as the authoritative theorist of social action. Thus, this model attempts to improve on Weber's efforts, without ignoring the Kantian context of his work. The explanation of social action in particular is organized around the concept of *goal*, rather than "meaning" or "*verstehen*." But rather than regard goals as "given," as just lying around in the social world to be "taken up" by individuals, the actual creation of goals itself becomes the central process of concern for sociology and personality psychology, insofar as the latter enters the model. Although already existing goals may be "accepted" by persons, such acceptance is viewed as but a special case of goal creation.

Now, while Weber's notion of meaningful action implies intentionality and consciousness, save possibly in the cases of traditional and affective behaviour, Zollschan's reorientation of the explanation of social action around the concept of goal makes it both possible and desirable to understand the concept as applicable to both conscious and unconscious goals, and, therefore, to place Freud (particularly the Freud that sociologists have been unwilling, or unable, to handle — the discoverer of the unconscious and the dynamic structures of symbol formation and symbol transformation) in a *sociological* account of action. Yet, Freud does not go unchanged into the model; the notion of goals ranging along directionalities that are determined by "drives" is abandoned in favour of an account of unconscious aims, including but not limited to, "dreams," "symptoms," and "parapraxes," that treats them as directed intentionally toward goals, where the rationality of the action is available to a trained and sensitized observer. In so doing, Zollschan elects Freud's "as if" description of unconscious motives; their goal-directed character that is hidden from the actor, rather than their ostensive determination by drives, as more appropriate to the Weberian thrust of his model.[2] Indeed, Freud's account of *repression* — why the goal-intended character of individual action appears clear to the interpretive vision of the analyst, but alien and unintended to the patient — iconically represented by concepts like "inhibition," "prohibition," and "dreamcensor," is clearly related to Weber's much more limited theory of legitimate orders and the legitimation of authority.

Zollschan's model at its abstract level may be seen as an expansion of Marx's schema: Praxis → Existence → Consciousness. It is hardly

---

[2] Neither does this reworking of Freud's concepts of *drives* take Zollschan out of the main line of Freudian metapsychology. On the contrary, he anticipates later developments as exemplified, for instance, by various contributions in (5). We shall return briefly to this point in our discussion.

possible to formulate a theory of social action without taking a position on the priority of consciousness or action. One selects one or the other, or denies the distinction as do the symbolic interactionists, but one takes a position. Here, Zollschan finds it necessary to collapse Praxis and Existence into a single category — the exigential realm. Thus, human *being*, for both Marx and Zollschan, is produced by action, but the dynamic thrust of Zollschan's model makes History and Being simply the context in which appears the exigency — the "prime mover" of this theory of social action. For the analysis of any action episode, the individual's past as organism or person, the *ensemble* of prior individual actions and behaviours, and the history of that resistant externality that is not contained by the individual or the society, form a context in which there emerges some exigency, some resistance or state requiring change that is seen as the "start" of the episode. Yet, this primordial level is of little interest to Zollschan; he extends the Marxian schema to $Praxis_1 \rightarrow Existence \rightarrow Consciousness \rightarrow Praxis_2$ in order to deal with the changed praxis, Revolutionary Praxis ($Praxis_2$), that emerges from the articulation of interests (read Consciousness) and concentrates in his model on the last two elements, Consciousness and $Praxis_2$.

He does not, however, equate Consciousness with the articulation of interests as Marx does; rather, he views interests as one of two varieties of goals: namely, goals that are opposed to the goals of others, to which he adds goals that are not in opposition, that are either coherent with, or irrelevant to, others' goals. To summarize the relation of Zollschan's model to Marx, perhaps resort to a conceptual schematic will be helpful:

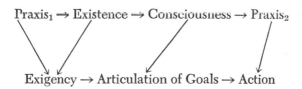

$$Praxis_1 \rightarrow Existence \rightarrow Consciousness \rightarrow Praxis_2$$

$$Exigency \rightarrow Articulation\ of\ Goals \rightarrow Action$$

The last of the four major influences on this model of social action is Karl Popper, the British philosopher. Zollschan responds both negatively and positively to his work. Firstly, he rejects the parody of sociology that Popper offers with his conception of unintended consequences as the beginning and end of the substantive *matter* of sociology. Secondly, he accepts Popper's methodological programme of "methodological individualism" for the social sciences as well as the general prescription for natural science as the construction of a parsimonious and testable set of interrelated concepts. This is to say that Zollschan takes up an interesting challenge, the attempt to provide a theoretical model of social action, to address a range of problems that Popper excludes from the field of sociological enquiry, that yet meets the scientific criteria established by Popper for the natural sciences. Thus, the model offers a number of theoretical parameters that seek to decompose and to exhaust the conceptual dimensions of social action. At the same time, the discussion of the parameters indicates the character of the epistemic rules that Zollschan accepts as appropriate for providing empirical estimates of the parameters, as well as some sense of the conditions that will limit the generality of the model. In brief, the model is a deliberate effort to construct a *testable* scheme for the analysis of human action, that at the same time serves as a meta-linguistic solution to the problem of giving both "cause" and "reason" accounts of human action. It suggests a conceptual language that aims to be more than simply a typology of action, which is stated so as to permit analysts to interpret the parameters as independent variables in the construction of social conduct. Self-causation through goal orientation becomes the "reason" for action.[3]

Yet, this account gives only a feeling for the intellectual influences that root Zollschan's model; we still have no sense of the historical and personal circumstances in which they became salient. Of course, for those captivated by the abstract, impersonal rhetoric that sociologists use for presenting introspection, retrospection, and speculation on the data that their lives dredge up for review in more or less systematic collections, it may well be improper to talk about the rather personal character of that "dredging" procedure. However, for persons interested in the processes that operate in what positivists mistakenly term "the context of discovery" (what might better be thought of as the context of the sociologist's personal knowledge) such attempts to speak about that context, whether biographical, autobiographical, or observed, are so rare as to deserve every encouragement.[4] What follows is Zollschan's response to such determined encouragement.

---

[3] In the meta-linguistic solution one finds echoes of Ronald Dore's "meta-SP language" (4).

[4] The burden of modern positivism's reconstruction of the process of science weighs heavily upon many sociologists. With eyes fixed determinedly on some "context of justification" — on journals and monographs in which we reconstruct our personal experience as sociologists into a discourse whose aim is the production of agreement in one's audience — it has been hard to take that same personal experience seriously as part of the scientific process. Given the obsession of positivism with logical form as a criterion for scientific acceptability, it is not surprising that "logic of discovery" has become a sort of "dirty" phrase which covers formally non-logical realms of research all the way from dreams, through bathroom inspiration, to every aspect of the collection and analysis of data, however accomplished. What is most surprising is that such a peculiarly limited philosophy of science has been allowed to possess the meta-theoretical accounts of sociology at the same time as theory and research are happy in a praxis and rhetoric that pay it little attention. Overington's encouragement of Zollschan's autobiographical efforts stems from the conviction that sociological meta-theory needs a fresh start through an injection of some sociology

Any attempt to respond to the request for an account of a personal context of this model of social action requires some consideration of a fundamental metaphysical conviction inherent in the establishment of the model: namely, that the act of creation is paradigmatic for action in general. In a sense, then, the act of creation becomes what Kenneth Burke has called a "representative anecdote"; the notion of Creation becomes a source for the conception of all acts. Thus, novelty, change, emergence, self-causation, rationality, and so on, become aspects of action in general, and routine and stasis become particular cases of action that are noticeable precisely because they violate the conceptual logic of "creation." Nor, as Burke argues, is it important to profess allegiance to a particular theological account of Creation (3, pp. 59-72); it is sufficient to note that Zollschan first encountered the conception in a Jewish mystical tradition that has been intertwined with philosophical and scientific thought in the West from the earliest times in such a fashion as to make it part of the tacit knowledge of intellectuals in any contemporary scientific or humanistic field.[5] What is critical, however, is that such a literally primordial rooting for a theory of social action may confront many social scientists with a *Schreckensbildniss,* a picture of horror that poses a fearful challenge both to their credulity and courage. If, quite unlike Goethe's Faust who recognized the Spirit of Earth (that *Schreckensbildniss*) as his counterpart in nature, such readers fail to recognize their own conception of social action in an account of Creation, it will not be surprising. There is after all little encouragement and less reward for social scientists who wish to examine the roots of their traditions, but it is precisely such examinations that require the most intellectual nerve as they often reduce the high-flown pretensions of our theorizing to nothing more than a cloacal miasma. Yet, for those social scientists capable of shock at the "creative imagery," perhaps some of that will recede if it is recognized that it is exactly this imagery of creative thought and action that underlies Kantian constructivism as well as the manifold varieties of philosophical voluntarism and methodological hypothetico-deductivism that have issued from it. In Kant's view, the human being did not merely construct his conceptions of phenomena but effected even their very perceptual presentation by active impression of the forms of his thought

---

into its "mindless philosophizing." In particular, this meta-theory requires recasting as the empirical study of the process of constructing sociological knowledge, where that process is visualized as having two major parts: the personal experience of sociologists in their research, and the reconstruction of that experience in a rhetoric that — through courting disagreement by "publication" — seeks to produce agreement on the scientific facticity of that experience.

  [5] For an engrossing account of kabbalistic influences on the development of a different scientific field — pre-classical and classical physics in this instance — see Jammer (6, especially pp. 25 52).

upon a whimsical, undescribed and indescribable, shadow-realm of vapid inertia. Thus, at least the notion of *thoughts* as acts of creation may demonstrably be located in a tradition that has impeccable, if often unrecognized, credentials.

This "formative" conception of the model is early featured in Zollschan's work, where, as the opening sentence of an address to the 1961 A.A.A.S. Meetings and the closing sentence of a paper with Robert Perrucci, it appears as "states of equilibrium are special cases of dynamics at all levels of scientific analysis (9, p. 122)." This statement was intended to convey the idea that Zollschan's account of institutionalization sought to supply what Max Black had called "independent mechanical principles" to supplement the shortcomings of Parsons' equilibrium theory of social systems. Taken in the context of the Zollschan and Perrucci essay the statement meant that social stability was to be explained by the same principles as had been adduced for the explanation of social change. Moreover, at the individual level an even more radical formulation of the same notion was possible and necessary. The general model, therefore, portrays all action, even automatized states of routine habituation, as special cases of innovative action, thereby covering both change and stability, innovation and routine.

In the ideal case, the selection of problems to which a model such as this applies would be based on strategic scientific considerations related to the construction of an overall map of the realm to which it is theoretically applicable. In this less than ideal case, however, strategic considerations necessarily became conjoined with opportunistic ones. This is, of course, part of the nature of the situation in all large-scale projects. Indeed, though the demands of opportunity may often be galling, the necessity of applying the model to specific problems has frequently provided hints for better overall strategies than might have been yielded by more abstract speculations on analytic priorities, uninterrupted by such necessities.

The first occasion for airing what might be regarded as the "Ur-model" came in Kansas City where Zollschan was engaged in the study of the relationship between committee structures and urban processes while working at the Institute of Community Studies. Arnold Rose, who was then putting together his "Chicago Tradition" volume (7), invited Warren Peterson, also working at the Institute, to contribute a chapter. Deadline pressures led to a "crash" collaboration in which Zollschan contributed a set of variables that connected an urban population aggregate, ecologically viewed as Park does, with the institutional system of community organizations and associations. These connecting variables were conceptualized as the "institutionalization of needs," and organizations and associations were seen as crystallizing in relation to those needs. Yet, the needs were not seen as inert and given but gestated in a "substratum of exigencies" and were "typically delivered into public consciousness by opinion leaders." Moreover, Park's ecological principle of *accommodation* could be related to such needs. If viewed from the "action perspective" as "accommodation of interests," interests simply become special kinds of needs which clashed with the needs of others, and are similar to "demand" in economics and "motive" in psychology.

This collaboration with Peterson resulted in an invitation to present a paper in an urban planning session at the Midwest Meetings in 1961, where Zollschan presented a five factor theory of planning processes in metropolitan communities. The five factors were Salience, Articulation, State of Technology, Costs, and Ideology. Ideology, that is, regarding appropriate needs and appropriate levels for their satisfaction. Here, the model of social action is essentially complete, lacking only a distinction of two phases in the construction of action, the articulation and action components, and the division of the Ideology factor into "justification" and "legitimation" corresponding to the two phases. The same five factor theory was again used in the development of a paper on leadership that was to appear in the abortive second edition of Gouldner's *Studies of Leadership*. But here, the factors which had previously been taken as components of planning processes were transmuted into occasions for the exercise of leadership. The curious may find an elaboration of this never published step in the development of the later model in chapter six of this present volume.

The model in the 1964 form of *Explorations in Social Change* emerged in a lunch time conversation with Robert Perrucci on the convenient paper napkin. At the time, Perrucci was a pre-doctoral Instructor at Purdue University working on a dissertation that concerned itself with relations in a mental hospital ward. This interest tied in with Zollschan's earlier observational research on the effects of various therapeutic milieux at Topeka State Hospital and provided a common concern for the integration of psychiatric and sociological concepts which was the proximate stimulus for Zollschan's production of the basic two phase model. Yet, to understand the meaning of this step one must return to the London School of Economics, where Zollschan spent his undergraduate and immediate postgraduate years.

In those years, Zollschan encountered three strong but inconsistent intellectual influences that have operated on him ever since. As the contemporary of the immediate post-war student generation, although younger than his peers, he was part of a group, many of whom went on to become pillars of the British sociological establishment. Together with David Lockwood and some others, Zollschan founded the Thursday Evening Club, devoted to discussion of fundamental issues in sociology. The dominant point of view of that Club, represented by such individuals as Lockwood, Dahrendorf, Dore, Joe and Olive Banks, Tropp, and so on, was neo-Marxist opposition to Talcott Parsons. Yet, while the oppositional stance "took" with Zollschan, the neo-Marxism remained no more than a marginal influence.

Strongly attracted to the views and personality of Karl Popper, Zollschan began to attend Popper's graduate seminar (as legendary in its own way as the Thursday Evening Club and a principal breeding ground for many leading contemporary methodologists) in his second undergraduate year, and after graduation became Sir Karl's assistant for a year. Additionally, he had a course of analysis at the London Institute of Psychoanalysis. The simultaneous impression of these diverse yet highly stimulating influences had a price: the difficulty of attending to three inconsistent yet authoritative traditions whenever attempting to speak sociologically.

This, however, returns us to the paper napkin and the lunch with Perrucci; quite a few of the tensions that had built up in that London high noon were resolved in a moment of ball point on fluffy paper. The Weber-Popper postulate of "methodological individualism" could provide a legitimate bridge between sociological and psychiatric concepts. Social structures, as much as personality structures, were to be seen as configurations composed of elements involved in goal (or perhaps "need") creation. The three dimensions of both phases of the model corresponded to the rationale underlying Freud's structural distinction of Id, Ego, and Superego. Of course, not all of Freud's substantive assumptions were upheld, but the model was "structurally isomorphic" with Freud's. Finally, social structure was rendered as the synthesis of individual goals in some way implicating other individuals and their goals. Unlike Weber's monstrously overgrown ideal type of social structures, which added new ad hoc elements as the account moved from the primordial social act to the overarching structure of the State and Church, Zollschan's model contained all the dynamic terms necessary for such a range of accounts without the adduction of new elements other than merely descriptive or ideographic ones. It is an orderly and internal development of the model on the paper napkin that is the programme of the *Explorations* volume and is our focus here.

What then is this programme? It is certainly not offered as a competitor to other conceptual frameworks that are in current use. Rather it seeks to provide a more general model of human action that would allow for the conceptual reinterpretation and subsumption of previous theoretical work in social action theory. Thus, Zollschan exhibits the model's capacity to handle issues of conflict and consensus, eliminating that pernicious dichotomy through a rendering of these two processes as aspects of a general pattern of social action, rather than by the more common strategy of *asserting* that both are important to any full theory of societal processes. It is not, however, our intention to repeat the analyses offered in the four chapters of *Explorations*; we seek only to elucidate the programme that underlies these and to give it, the model of 1964, a contemporary authoritative reading. Theories and theorists change; the energies of sociologists are better spent in the empirical assay of the worth of attempts to explain the empirical social world than they are in the conceptual exegesis of the various states of such work. This reading hopes to save much energy.

Zollschan's model of social action is, in outline, deliberately parsimonious. He wants to give an account of the grounds for action with as few concepts as possible, and to account for all kinds of action with the same set of primitives *without* the addition of ad hoc concepts for each special case. He achieves this aim with a two phase model of action that takes its start in an *exigency*, some existential condition that makes problematic whatever the individual is doing, or not doing. The first phase of the model describes a process in which conscious or unconscious images form and are constructed so as to locate needs corresponding to the exigency. The formation of these images is not merely cognitive but channels affect and incorporates limitations imposed by inhibitions. Associated with these needs and the images in which they are revealed are arrays of possibilities for handling the needs. Goals are "preferable" possibilities.

The second phase involves an assessment of the possible and appropriate needs–goals relationship in terms of the exigency which then operates as the "motive" of action. One could say that in this model all human action is motivated by goals; all accounts of human action are rendered in terms of goals; all accounts of human action in terms of goals are accounts of the causes of action; human motives, therefore, are goals as causes. The conflict between *reason* and *cause* analyses is resolved by finding causes in reasons, where the reason in question is a statement of the individual's goal.

Of course, with respect to any account of human action it must be asked, "Whose account, whose statement of a goal, is to take precedence in any given situation?" Should one assign priority to the actor's or to the observer's account, to the subject or to the sociologist, to the privileged "insider" or to the omniscient "outsider"? Such a question is central to any model of social action that accounts for such action by means of motivational framework; thus the issue is raised for the work of Freud, Marx, Pareto, and Weber as well as Zollschan. In all these cases the theorist elects a similar solution, he assumes the authority for the "correct" or "proper" attribution of causality in some particular event and thereby demonstrates his belief in the validity of his account over the "rationalization" of the actor. "Whose account, whose goal?" The answer is clear, the sociologist's account and goal. Zollschan, then, in taking the individual's goal as the reason for his action is not insisting that we reduce sociological explanation to the process of asking persons for their own rationales but is following a tradition amongst

theorists of social action in taking the identification of individuals'
goals as the sociologist's responsibility.

It is now time to give the expression "goal" a more careful examination. As the term is used in Zollschan's programme it is far from a
simple concept. In its employment it corresponds to a variety of expressions in common usage. Means and ends are not distinguished but
are viewed as gaining their character as "means" or "ends" in relationship to relative positions they hold in chains or pathways of goals. Needs
are treated as automatically implying goals, so that one finds the expression "need-goal" being used. Interests, complementarity, and cooperation are treated as goals in interaction. In its original understanding,
"goal" was viewed as a concept akin to "gravity" in mechanics; as a
sort of "eidetic mass" that exercises attraction at a distance. Yet, that
particular metaphor hardly appears on the surface of the account that
is offered; it is quite sufficient just to recognize that "causation" by goals
provides a "pull" rather than a "push" notion of motivation. While
Zollschan's conceptual labours with the term "goal" may best be viewed
as part of his struggle to show the subsumptive power of his model, at
the more simple level that we are seeking in this chapter, a goal might
be seen as the individual's construction (not necessarily conscious or
deliberative) of a possible future that will release him from an exigency
in his life.

Yet there is more to the idea than this. Goals that concern a model
of social action are those that appear in social situations; in interactions.
One may think of three kinds of interactional goals that occur in face-
to-face settings: interest, complementarity, and cooperation. The first
of these, *interest*, is a goal situation where the actor's goal is opposed
by the goals of others; the second, *complementarity*, refers to responses
of others as the goal; and the final one, *cooperation*, requires joint action
for the achievement of the goal (and, therefore, makes that joint action
itself a subsidiary goal). In any of these three interactional situations
the goal may be characterized as focused or diffuse and as variably
*elastic* (or replaceable by other goals). Under no circumstances are
social systems viewed as having goals, though the concerted goals
of individual actors fundamentally structure such systems.

There is, furthermore, a neat circularity in the relation to the kind of
exigency that "starts" the whole process. Thus, exigencies may be cognitive, affective, or evaluative. In other words, they may be a condition
calling for change that is the result of a failed hypothesis (or less
specific expectation); the inaccessibility of some desired object or objective; or discrepancies between a value and an actually existing situation. Since goals may be seen as the answers to "questions" posed by
exigencies, one may speak of cognitive, affective, and evaluative *goals*
as a further dimension to the notion of interactional goals.

Yet we have still to attend to the conception of the *exigency* that Zollschan uses as a sort of "prime mover" in the model of social action. Although it must be said that the important parts of the model deal with the translation of this exigency into a "need-goal," Zollschan tries to strike the right balance in his discussion, saying enough to convey the essential characteristics of the exigency without saying so much that the model demands some theoretical construct that is prior to the exigency and provides it, in turn wtih a context. The exigency is in conception a necessary theoretical element in the model that gives completeness to the analysis of the conditions of individual action. Where the individual in question is an *organism* the exigency can be conceptualized either as an excitation or as some resistance to spontaneous behaviour. Where the individual is a *person,* on the other hand, the exigency can be viewed as some existential condition calling for change. At the ontogenetic level, "exigency" is treated as closely linked with Freudian notions of personality development. In the general model of social action the notion is given much less attention. Here, the processes of need articulation, goal formation, and action take central positions.

One may think of three variable dimensions that might be used to understand the character of exigencies. As originally formulated they appeared in a typological presentation, but the thrust of Zollschan's work is such as to make them more consistent as variable constructs; his Popperian concern for testing is better served by treating them so than as types. One may state, therefore, the three "types of discrepancy" as exigencies presented to individuals by a failure, or problem, in the sphere of action that may be located on affective, evaluative and cognitive dimensions. Any problem in the sphere of action, therefore, will involve a failure to reach some more or less desired, legitimated or expected goal; where that "failure" registers with the individual as a tension or problematic situation. In general, one would expect that most exigencies will fall somewhere on an affective dimension, few actions involve objects about which one cares nothing; but the degree to which these tensions and problems involve a violation of legitimated expectations will fluctuate considerably. Many men would *care* very much that a beautiful woman, so receptive to their overtures in the bar, proved unwilling to leave with them; but while desire and expectation would create an affective and cognitive exigency for most, only for Casanova would experience have made the expectation *legitimized* and thus have placed the exigency noticeably on an evaluative dimension.

What kind of individual is it that is set into "motion" by the exigency? So far, at least, we have presented the human being as both an *organism* and a *person,* using these terms as primitives. It will suffice for this brief account if we merely suggest the relationship between these concepts in the setting of the individual social actor, rather than try to restate the dynamics of organism and person that Zollschan has outlined elsewhere (8). Thus in infancy, the individual may be viewed as merely an organism with the potentiality of an emergent personhood. Past infancy, however, the human individual co-exists as organism and person. The extent to which organism is enacted in personhood or personhood embodies organismic process varies from individual to individual and from situation to situation. Therefore, the degree to which the two phases of the model involve conscious processes is also variable; the tendency, indeed the temptation, to understand the phases of the model and their six coordinates as conscious, unnecessarily restricts the generality of Zollschan's programme and should be resisted.

We turn to the two phase model itself after these prefatory remarks. Readers who expect that it will prove as complex as some of the talk about "exigencies," (indeed, how could it fail to be more involved than discussion of what was admittedly but a theoretical convenience) will surely be surprised by the brevity of the account. One of the major virtues of Zollschan's work is the parsimonious character of the basic model, and the two phase, six dimensional model of social action is exactly that. Treated generally, the six dimensions are *each* seen as necessary conditions; *tout ensemble* they are a sufficient condition for action toward a goal. Which is to say that the model offers necessary and sufficient conditions, in modern formulations, causal conditions for the production of individual's goals, where that same goal is the *reason* for action. It is here that Zollschan offers the solution to the disjunction between "cause" and "reason" analysis that plagues theories of social action and does it without changing the meaning of either cause or reason. (2, p. 101 ft. 9)

The first phase of this model of social action is one of "articulation," the transformation of some excitation or problem, some exigency, into a need. In a gravitational metaphor, it is the fusion of energies into a mass, or at least the first step in such a process of fusion. But as presented in the model the three coordinate dimensions of this phase, "salience," "justifiability," and "specifiability" measure theoretical variables in a cognitive process. Each of these variables may, in principle, be connected to empirical indicators, as may the other three dimensions of phase two, but Zollschan deliberately avoids the statement of epistemic rules that might prematurely foreclose the generality of the program, preferring to suggest their character through his discussion of these six theoretical parameters and his "indebtedness" to the operationalization of them that *Explorations* contains. (1) In brief, "salience" is a measure of the importance or consequence of an exigency to an individual and there is some feeling that this is temporally prior to the other two dimensions of articulation. However, "justifiability" and "specifiability" are treated as *fully* coordinate, addressing respectively the degree to which the exigency "may" and "can" be articulated, "may" and "can" be transformed into a need. Given that some exigency is of sufficient importance, it may be translated into a need through the individual's willingness and capacity to do so. For the primipara in her ninth month, every abdominal cramp is of importance and she is more than willing to "recognize" her symptoms as the onset of labour. She simply does not know, however, whether it is or not — the situation is one of chronic misspecification. Husbands and obstetricians find themselves bombarded with fruitless articulation. On the other hand, for the mother of several children, busy with her family and job, the ninth month arrives with far less anticipation, abdominal cramps are less important, and though more than capable she is often unwilling to "recognize" her sensations at the onset of labour. Husbands and obstetricians are often "notified" quite late about such "unjustifiable" conditions. Moreover, it should be recognized that justifiability can become viewed as a component of articulation only from the perspective of an observer with the capacity to infer the range of inhibitions on the individual's expectancy set. In essence, such inference implies that the observer has knowledge of what the individual "can" but "may not" think.

The second phase of the model, like the first, has three coordinate dimensions, "valence," "application," and "legitimation" which operate as variables in shaping an articulated need into actions directed toward a particular goal. Like salience, however, valence appears to have a temporal priority in this phase, so that the issue of the place a particular need might have in a hierarchy of values becomes resolved before matters of ability and willingness become pertinent. Thus, valence is seen as a measure of opportunity–cost, with respect to a particular need so that a modified exigency, an articulated need, will take on importance *relative* to other need-goals. Indeed, the whole second phase of this model may be viewed as a shaping process in which a need is translated into action toward a particular goal by an assessment of its relative importance, in a value hierarchy of need-goals that the individual is capable and willing to entertain as reasons for acting. This process may be conceived of as a set of questions addressed to this range of need-goals in relation to the modified exigency: "What are the costs of taking this goal and foregoing others?" "Can it be done?" and "May it be done?" If we return to our very pregnant women, it is clear that the articulation of an abdominal sensation as the onset of labour is a necessary condition for their attending to this rather than other needs that will be foregone. Nonetheless, one would expect that the beginning of labour will be of greater importance relative to other need-goals for the primipara; likewise the multipara will be less willing though more capable than the new mother in matching the need created by her recognition of the start of labour to some goal, like getting off to the hospital.

What follows these two phases of the model is the emergence of action directed toward goals, some examples of which Zollschan examined in three of the four 1964 chapters; but neither these papers nor their substance concern our reconstruction of the general model. It remains to remind the reader, first, the intention of this chapter was to provide an authoritative reading of the 1964 programme so as to yield a baseline against which to take the work collected in Sections Two and Three of this volume. Second, the original chapters address a variety of specific issues: institutionalization, conflict, change, order, revolution, alienation, a developmental model of personality, all of which are organized by the programme we have here restated, and all of which retain their substantive interest. No forceful peroration is needed. The whole thrust of this chapter has been to point to the future, to the chapters that follow. And so we may call a halt to the exposition of Zollschan's previous thematic developments and let the orchestra tune up. If music be the stuff of motive, something may be gained by lending what follows an attentive ear.

## BIBLIOGRAPHY

1. Andersen, Ronald M., and Robert L. Eichorn. "Application of a Theory of Social Change to Heart Disease and its Consequences," in George K. Zollschan and Walter Hirsch (eds.), *Explorations in Social Change*. Boston: Houghton Mifflin and Co., 1964, pp. 201-207.

2. Blum, Alan, and Peter McHugh. The Social Ascription of Motives," *American Sociological Review*, Vol. 36 (February, 1971).

3. Burke, Kenneth. *A Grammar of Motives*. Berkeley: University of California Press, 1969.

4. Dore, Ronald. "Function and Cause," *American Sociological Review*, Vol. 26 (December, 1961), pp. 843-853.

5. Holt, Robert R. (ed.), *Motives and Thought: Psychoanalytic Essays in Honor of David Rapaport*, (Psychological Issues, Monograph 18-19), 1967.

6. Jammer, Max. *Concepts of Space: The History of Theories of Space in Physics*. Cambridge, Massachusetts: Harvard University Press, 1969.

7. Rose, Arnold. ed., *Human Behavior and Social Process*. Boston: Houghton Mifflin, 1962.

8. Zollschan, George K. "Beyond the Reality Principle," in *Explorations in Social Change*. Boston: Houghton Mifflin and Co., 1964. pp. 175-200.

9. Zollschan, George K., and Robert Perrucci. "Social Stability and Social Process," in *Explorations in Social Change*. Boston: Houghton Mifflin and Co., 1964. pp. 93-124.

10. Zollschan, George K., and Walter Hirsch (eds.). *Explorations in Social Change*. Boston: Houghton Mifflin and Co., 1964.

# 5

T. Dunbar Moodie

## Social Order as Social Change: Towards a Dynamic Conception of Social Order*

*The reflection of nature [and of values] in man's thought must be understood not "lifelessly," not "abstractly," not devoid of movement, not without contradictions, but in the eternal process of movement, the arising of contradictions and their solution.*

—Lenin

This chapter is an attempt to diagnose the source of some of the dead-ends which bedevil current sociological theory. It stems from metatheoretical uncertainties" which arose in the course of several years detailed research on the rise of Afrikaner nationalism in South Africa (17). The arguments herein are thus best seen in a series of tentative metatheoretical reflections upon research recently completed.

I start with a critique of Talcott Parsons because his influence continues to dominate sociological theory. Furthermore, the *Structure of Social Action* (19) remains a classical text. I shall argue in this paper however that the basic metatheoretical assumptions of his theory are not

* An earlier version of this paper was read at the Third Conference of the Association for Sociology in Southern Africa in June 1972. That effort grew out of certain questions raised in the 1972 Honours Seminar at Natal University and especially from frequent dialogue with Geoff. Waters. Since then I have rewritten it completely at the Institute for Advanced Study in Princeton after severe criticism from Robert Bellah. But my greatest debt is to Meredith, my wife, whose editorial assistance has improved not only the style but also the substance of my argument.

so much wrong as simply inadequate because he has assumed an insufficiently dynamic and voluntarist conception of the unit act. He thus arrives at an analytic frame of reference for social order which is systematically misleading in empirical analysis. I proceed to suggest an alternative conception of the unit act and to reconsider certain sociological terms in the light of this alternative. I conclude with a statement of the status of theory in sociological research.

In *The Structure of Social Action,* Talcott Parsons rightly perceives that the adequate sociological theory presupposes a metatheoretical frame of reference whose basic assumptions are rooted in the understanding of social action. To this end, he develops the concept of the "unit act," whose major constituents, he says, serve as *a priori* categories of social scientific thought in much the same way that mass and energy are non-reducible assumptions of modern physics.

These basic categories for the study of human action, Parsons argues, are that human conduct takes place in a temporal and subjective context, and hence, is purposive, and that such action is made up of certain structural components which have to be present for human social action to take place. These structural elements in action he calls ends, means, norms and conditions.

An "act" for Parsons thus involves a purposive actor pursuing ends within a situation made up of conditions which become means insofar as they are used by the actor to attain his ends. In selecting from the conditions of his situation in pursuit of ends, however, the actor is not guided by reason alone, but rather tends to "try to conform action to patterns which are, by the actor and other members of the same collectivity, deemed desirable" (19, p. 76). In other words, the actor is not concerned with efficiency alone, but pursues his ends in conformity with normative patterns. "Action," says Parsons, "must always be thought of as involving a state of tension between two different orders of elements, the normative and the conditional. As process, action is, in fact, the process of alteration of the conditional element in the direction of conformity with norms" (19, p. 732).

An analyst who ignores norms, says Parsons, ends up in radical positivism, whereas one who ignores conditions becomes an idealist. The error of utilitarianism, on the other hand, is to treat reason as the only norm. In this case the normative aspect of action is reduced to insistence on rationality, ignorance, or error in the actor's selection of means. Insistence on the randomness of ends in utilitarianism tends to overlook or at least de-emphasize the systematic integration of the ends of a plurality of actions (19, p. 56).

In Parsons' "voluntarism," on the other hand, the normative elements retain their analytic independence and interdependence. They "become integral with the analytic system itself, positively interdependent with the other elements in specifically determinate ways." The role of conditional elements is not denied, but they are considered as "interdependent with the normative" (19, p. 82). The purpose of *The Structure of Social Action* was to demonstrate that the theories of Pareto, Durkheim and Weber, converged from very different directions upon an action frame of reference which was "voluntaristic" in Parsons' sense.

It is perhaps worth stating again that this action frame of reference is for Parsons purely metatheoretical. It may be said to have, he says, "what many, following Husserl, have called a 'phenomenological' status. It involves no concrete data that can be 'thought away,' that are subject to change. It is not a phenomenon in the empirical sense. It is the indispensable logical framework in which we describe and think about the phenomena of action" (19, p. 733).

I believe that it is precisely at the level of this "indispensable logical framework" that we must reconsider Parsons' contribution. For the major difficulty with his approach to social analysis stems, I argue, from his definition of the unit act. If action is "the process of alteration of the conditional elements in the direction of conformity with norms," what is the role of the actor in the situation? Is he more than a passive vessel for the action of norms on conditions? Does the actor play any active role in the action frame of reference? In stressing the importance of the normative, Parsons seems to overlook the creative role of the actor, not only in selecting means but also in interpreting norms. The role of the actor in action cannot be dismissed under the general rubric of "subjectivity." Furthermore, ends cannot be assumed to be "givens" in the unit act but rather arise from the direction of the actor's interpretation of the situation.

In his later writings Parsons himself recognizes that "the actor is the unit of systems of action . . . Hence in some sense a 'psychology' is an essential *part of* . . . a theory of social action" (30, p. 26; cf. 19, p. 738). He proposes psychoanalysis as the most adequate psychology. In his treatment of Freud, however, Parsons deals largely with processes of internalization, with the superego as bridge between personality and social systems. He thus neglects the tension between the individual and his "reality" which is so crucial to Freud.[2] In his earliest treatment of socialization, Parsons seems aware of his bias (20, p. 448, n. 60), but argues that it is admissible since he is concerned with the theoretical integration of psychological and sociological systems of analysis. This orientation, however, desensitizes him to the dialectical reciprocity of the individual and the social.

[1] Metatheory defines the basic categories of an intellectual enquiry; theory, on the other hand, consists of generalizations which are subject to empirical proof or falsification.

[2] Zollschan (34, pp. 177–188) is a useful summary of Freud's theory of socialization which takes more adequate account of this tension.

In fact, despite the stress on voluntarism in Parsons' early writing, it is still subordinated to his emphasis on norms. Indeed, in his later work Parsons is able to construct an entire analytic social system whose hierarchy of control is rooted in values, descending in specificity through norms to role definitions (21, pp. 38ff.). Conditions have become exogenous sources of "strain," means are now resources, and ends or goals have become situation-specific values. The norms of the original action unit have become the overarching values of an essentially static social system, and the only route to change lies in structural differentiation in accordance with the logic of the value-system, or evolutionary value-changes, the origins of which are not explained. Such a theory of the social system is avowedly analytic and not empirical. Its application in analysis, however, leads almost inevitably to a normative bias, even as Marx's model of man as primarily a producer leads to an economic bias.

What is needed is a model of the unit act which retains Parsons' insistence upon the interdependence of norms and conditions, but which also shows how the tension between them is mediated by an actor, who formulates and pursues goals within a situation. Both norms and conditions become relevant in social action when they have been perceived and interpreted by an actor who is able, within limits, to mediate the tension between them. Such a metatheory, I believe, has been suggested by George Zollschan.[3]

Zollschan proposes that the basic unit act be defined in terms of an actor's response to exigencies. The exigential source of motivation he defines as "a discrepancy (for a person) between a consciously or unconsciously desired or expected state of affairs and an actual situation" (34, p. 89). Exigencies may stem from discrepancies experienced in the normative (cognitive or evaluative), conditional (organic or situational), or intentional (means-ends) aspects of the actor's situation. Interaction between persons is of course in itself a rich source of exigencies, as are the unintended consequences of one's own or others' acts.

When an actor experiences an exigency which is sufficiently salient not to be ignored, he will react. In its simplest form, his response may be purely emotive, for example, a temper tantrum.[4] In most instances, however, the individual will articulate or interpret the situation and formulate a goal which then guides his course of action. It is possible,

[3] The most complete statement of Zollschan's "theory of institutionalization" is (34, pp. 89–200). He summarizes his conception of the unit act on (34, pp. 89–97). While I make full and free use of Zollschan's argument, there are changes in emphasis and terminology. He thus can not be held responsible for my formulation.

[4] I choose for the purpose of this paper to leave emotive response as a residual category. I am, however, well aware that Freud proposed a theory of unconscious articulation which would enable me to integrate emotive action more closely to the metatheory proposed here.

in certain cases, that the articulation and interpretation alone will suffice to alleviate the perceived discrepancy. It is this process of articulation which is peculiarly human. In Cassirer's words, "Man has, as it were, discovered a new method of adapting himself to his environment. Between the receptor system and the effector system, which are to be found in all animal species, we find in man a third link which we may describe as the *symbolic system*. This new acquisition transforms the whole of human life" (4, pp. 42-43).

Human action is thus, characteristically, a response to exigencies in the context of one or more symbolic universes which are available to the consciousness of the individual as a result of socialization. The symbolic universe is never imposed as a blueprint, of course, but, as we shall see, is itself susceptible to modification and reinterpretation. Reference to symbolic universes and socialization, however, raises two further immediate considerations. Firstly, the threshold of salience for an exigency depends not only on the relative intensity of the discrepancy experienced but also upon the expectations which the individual brings to the situation. Such expectations will derive in turn from the individual's symbolic universe. Secondly, effective purposive action in response to an exigency may be immediate and without prior conscious articulation. This we shall call "habitual" action, which depends upon stock interpretations available to an individual as a result of social learning or previous experience. Although exigencies, by their very nature, are always "phenomena touching individual persons," similar exigencies may be experienced by persons in similar situations. Furthermore, patterns of symbols may be shared by a number of actors and a pool of *ad hoc* articulations which cover a wide range of typical exigencies are commonly available to individuals. Social interaction is thus patterned in terms of common goals and typical expectations. Zollschan speaks of a principle of conservation in the process of institutionalization.

When such "habitual" action proves ineffective in meeting the exigency, a new process of articulation, goal-formation and action may take place. The existence of "established patterns of interaction" or processes of institutionalization are obviously crucial to sociology. However, if we overlook the exigential origin of institutional patterns and the fact that reciprocity of expectations is often problematic, we attribute to "institutions" an unchanging existence which they simply do not have. It is not enough to insist that institutions always have a history (3, p. 72), because the question immediately arises as to where history stops and the institution begins. Institutionalization never stands still; social patterns are constantly shifting. This is as important to sociological analysis as the equally true statement that complex patterns of institutionalization are always dependent on prior typifications.

Thus, common acceptance of typical articulations in response to shared problems (as with factory laborers, for instance) provides the basis of class consciousness. As Marx (16, pp. 334-338) well knew, and E. P. Thompson (29) has recently brilliantly shown for the English working class, working class consciousness, far from being inevitable, in fact grows up in a context in which exigencies are articulated by leaders and then accepted and modified by their fellows in the course of a long history of struggle. A "class" characterized by common consciousness is therefore not a static entity but a dynamic pattern of interaction between individuals facing common exigencies. If we fail to acknowledge that most of the key terms used in sociological discourse are shorthand for patterns of action which are fluid in the above sense, we distort and falsify the constantly changing social reality.

To recapitulate, I have argued that Parsons' notion of the unit act, in which the actor pursues his ends within a situation fraught with tension between norms and conditions, is insufficiently voluntarist. Unless one can conceive of the actor as actively mediating within and between norms and conditions, either one arrives at a notion of impersonal dialectic, or one is forced into idealism, which overstresses norms (highly generalized values) or positivism, which overstresses conditions. I argue, following Zollschan, that both norms and conditions are important in action, but as mediated by the interpretive activity of a subject.

Such an avowedly voluntarist view of the unit act does not deny the possibility of a systematic relation between unit acts. However, it does suggest that interaction (of what Parsons calls "systems of action") whether cooperative or in conflict, cannot be assumed to be functionally structured like an organism and may, in fact, not constitute a "system" at all. The extent to which institutionalization is systematic must be treated as an empirical question, rather than assumed in every case.

## II

A reconsideration of the action frame of reference such as I propose above will, I think, have wide implications for sociological analysis. This can perhaps best be made clear by discussion of some key sociological concepts. In this section, I will discuss "role," "organization," "community," "culture," and "power."

For most sociologists, social structure has very concrete "objectivity." This is believed to consist of an organized system of roles (as positions), delimited by specific norms (as rules). Such rule-determined sets of positions are often referred to as institutions. In this sense, the family, the church, the market, the state, the school, and so on, are all institutions, which can be clearly depicted on a blueprint or flow-chart. They stand against the individual as objective realities to which he must adjust. Socialization then, becomes a process of fitting the individual to his roles which are provided by the institutions of the society. The individual must "internalize" the society in order to act at all.

Now, if our basic metatheoretical assumptions about human action are valid, this notion of institutions as static "givens" needs radical revision. If the process of institutionalization grows out of problem-solving interactions in response to perceived exigencies, then unless one could conceive of interaction in which every individual sees himself in a perfect state of equilibrium with his situation, institutionalization is a never-ending process.

Interesting support for this contention on the level of *roles* comes from the work of Aaron Cicourel (5, cf. 7, pp. viii-45). He shows clearly that in American society at least, roles cannot be conceived as having existence which transcends individual actors, neither are they "slots" in a fixed and given social structure to which the individual is somehow moulded willy-nilly.

Parsons himself has long argued that role comprehends no more than how an individual's conception of the expectations of others inclines him to act in a particular way. The term is valid for human conduct, he says, only if it is always taken to include the expectations of others and the actor's own conception of these expectations. Hence, a distinction must be made between role-expectations and role-performances (22, p. 154).

Parsons believes that in a social system role expectations are, of course, fixed in terms of the common values of the system. This assertion will be discussed more fully when I deal with "culture." However, for the moment it is sufficient to state that Cicourel has shown that role performances in certain American instances are negotiated in the process of interaction, rather than fixed beforehand by common meanings.[5] To be sure, common symbolic patterns are not irrelevant in the negotiation of role performances, but they are not simply prescriptive for action; furthermore the availability of several alternative patterns of meaning for the actors makes prediction even more tenuous. Goffman's (14, pp. 85-152) concept of role-distance, in which the actor retains his own interpretations of the situation but acts in accordance with the perceived expectations of others, is particularly useful in understanding such situations.

The "existence" of formal *organizations* with stated purposes and constitutionally situated hierarchies of positions might be considered to negate the experiential conception of role proposed here. Although formal organizations do have clearly stated purposes and are systematically structured in terms of these formal goals, this in no way justifies one's hypostatizing them or using them as models for wider social systems. A bureaucratic organization, with its formal goals and constituted structure, may have for its clients and employees a "meaning" which makes

[5] Taylor (28, p. 23) argues, I think questionably, that "negotiation" is absent in some traditional societies. However, it suffices for my argument if Cicourel's findings are valid at least in American society.

it seem an independent social person. It may even be treated in law as a person. However, as Barker points out, "the essence of the unity of a group is its expressed purpose; and legal personality belongs to that essence. With the individual it is different: the essence of his life-unity is a continuing spring or power of purpose; and that is the essence to which his legal personality belongs" (12, p. lxxvi).

A corporation is thus indeed an institution, precipitated out of the process of institutionalization, frozen, as it were, to meet certain specific goals which have been articulated by its founders and/or by its controlling staff. But the survival of a formal organization does not necessarily imply that all members of the organization share its purposes or behave according to its constitution. They could, but this remains an empirical question which must be asked anew for each organization. In fact, numerous empirical studies have shown quite clearly that formal organizations fulfill for their members many goals which are quite extraneous to the formal purpose of the organization. Furthermore, although the formal systematic structure of an organization may be constitutionally laid down, it is seldom rigorously applied.[6] If, however, an organization is perceived as no longer being able to meet the exigency for which it has been set up it becomes redundant and must either change, like the "March of Dimes," or eventually collapse, like coal-mining in West Virginia.[7]

Simple statements about the redundancy of organizations, however, must be regarded with caution, because organizations tend to adapt to changing exigencies. Furthermore, earlier established patterns of institutionalization may preclude an organization's ever achieving its stated purpose; the organization may continue simply because it meets goals of other individuals or groups in the situation.[8] In fact, the very continuance of the organization often seems more important to the members and leaders than the realization of its formally stated purpose. In this respect the organization may be said to have become a community.

A *community* differs from an organization in that it is believed by its members to exist for its own sake, rather than for any formal purpose. Zollschan (34, pp. 112-120) defends at some length, the compatibility of his formulation of the unit act and the notion of community. According to his argument, patterns of interaction which are tightly interdependent tend to resist change because change usually creates even more salient exigencies for individuals than the original discrepancy(ies). For

---

[6] See Crozier (6), Gouldner (15) and Selznick (24) for numerous empirical instances.

[7] Saint-Simon's belief in the redundancy of the French aristocracy and Marx's prediction that commodity-capitalism would collapse, use of an organization analogy for society — as of course do all social contract theorists.

[8] Selznick's (24) study of the T.V.A. is a classical example of this.

this reason, articulation and independent action may seem to be inversely related to interdependence. This observation might help to explain the lack of a revolutionary class consciousness in highly indistrialized societies. At the same time, since perfect social interdependence is essentially impossible, even communities will be subject to gradual change.

Two further points seem relevant in this context. Firstly, too rapid social change may destroy a tightly integrated community. The case of steel axes for aboriginal Australians provides the classical example here. (26, chapter 5). Secondly, the existence of communities may pose exigencies for outsiders, who will therefore attempt to change them. An example would be the manner in which the head-tax was introduced into native communities under colonial rule in order to obtain labor.[9]

To argue that the continuance of a community can best be understood in terms of the individual's perception of the exigential consequences of articulation and action independent of communal constraints may seem to many both rationalist and utilitarian. However, the argument that we ought to act "for the sake of the community" is surely common in all communal groups, whether it be expressed in terms of the wrath of the ancestors, the comforts of American suburbia, the bonhomie of a play group, victory for a team, and so on. Important to stress in this context is that the discrepancies which create exigencies are experienced by individuals in terms of their symbolic universes. Those *cultures* (or symbolic universes) in which life is perceived to be a "one-possibility thing" (cf. 27) will clearly prevent perception of many fundamental exigencies which would be highly salient in other cultural contexts. On the other hand, even in such extreme cases, situational exigencies will lead individuals to articulate and formulate goals which may give rise to a process of gradual change in the very "one-possibility thing" which life is perceived to be.

Furthermore, in all but such extreme cases, the individual will have a number of different cultural meanings from which to select when he interprets a situation. For example, the appearance of an unidentified flying object may be interpreted in modern society as a visitor from outer space, a portent of Christ's second coming, an enemy spy machine, or simply a natural phenomenon. Depending on the interpretation the appearance may be welcomed, ignored, feared, or, as happened recently in a small South African town, fired upon by the local policeman.

Equally, a single individual may use several different universes of

---

[9] In fact the existence of tightly-knit primitive communities seems to have aroused in Western imperial breasts fears of social regression similar to those described by Slater (25) with regard to honeymooners in middle-class America. Communal isolation is regarded by the modern industrialist as a peril similar to dyadic withdrawal in the marital context. Thus forced labor requires no moral justification.

meaning in interpretation. For example, a particular possible goal may be seen simultaneously as immoral, aesthetic, demonic, erotic, and contrary to the material interests of the individual. This seems to be what Schutz (23, pp. 209-59) means by multiple realities."[10] Whether or not an individual will choose to act in pursuit of such a particularized goal will depend on his personal hierarchy of values.

Thus any discussion of culture must distinguish between public and personal patterns of meaning, that is symbolic universes. In addition, one cannot assume simple congruence between symbolic universes and individual articulations in response to salient exigencies in particular situations.

Public meanings are those symbolic patterns which others make available to an actor. Personal meanings are the symbolic universes which are internalized by the individual as a result of his own particular biography; they correspond to the Meadian "me," precipitated in the individual, as it were, from the processes of articulation, action and institutionalization. Such private meanings change, of course, as the individual articulates exigencies, formulates goals, and acts in particular situations.

It is this sensitivity to changing meanings which makes Zollschan's model of the unit act so enormously fruitful in empirical analysis. It also, of course, makes empirical analysis much more difficult. For individuals and "typical" groups act in terms of articulations in actual situations. These articulations will be shaped by universes of meaning, both personal and public, as well as by the actor's perception and experience of conditions.

It is necessary to add here that certain exigencies may be perceived as in some sense "ultimate," that is, they may be related to fundamental human questions of identity and destiny. This human predicament, including apparently fortuitous suffering, may be given meaning (coherence) and hence explained in terms of a systematic articulation which we call religious. If the ultimate exigency is highly salient, and the religious articulation acceptable, the latter may take on an all-pervasive importance in processes of articulation in response to other exigencies (cf. 10). However, we may not assume that this is always the case. The salience of the religious articulation differs from situation to situation and from individual to individual. Peter Worsley's discussion of "religion as a category" is very relevant here. He says:

> It is necessary always to distinguish who "they" are, who says what in what situation, and what the "task orientation" of the various actors in the situation is, for "religion" — in the form of esoteric lore and theology — is differentially distributed throughout a society, or elements of it will be

---

[10] One of Weber's deepest fears seems to have been that in the process of "rationalization" the rational development of one of the many possible multiple realities would deny reality to the others (11, pp. 327–357).

differentially distributed, or occur only in specific situations, contexts, and "niches," or be available differentially to different actors. I studied an Australian aboriginal tribe where the knowledge of the beliefs and rituals of "their" culture on the part of most members was abysmal: as elementary and confused as that of the average Church of England congregation member. Only the ritual specialists and leaders (and a few sceptics) possessed esoteric lore or thought about its meaning . . . A spurious unity is projected on to other people's belief systems by outside observers — sociologists and anthropologists . . . This over-systematization of belief is commonly accompanied by a spurious ontological "priority" or hierarchy: the assumption that general cosmological, philosophical, etc., beliefs are somehow "primary" or "higher" . . . This is a natural disease of academics . . . (33, pp. 300-301).

Presumably, however, such religious lore is readily available to members of a group who experience ultimate exigencies; who are suddenly faced with fundamental questions, like death or disaster, mental anguish or physical suffering.

The major argument of this paper, then, is that exigencies are individual and situational, and that one cannot hope to understand social change without getting back to the basic unit act. Social order is thus dynamic. On the other hand, one may speak sensibly of social order and in some, but few, situations it may be possible to speak simply of roles and norms without concerning oneself with individuals. One may certainly speak of common *types* of situations in which individuals may arrive at a similar *range* of articulations — or more likely, where followers will accept the articulations of leaders. This raises the question of power.

*Power* implies the likelihood that an interpretation of a common situation will be accepted by others as having relevance for their action. The extent to which such acceptance is based on coercion, common interests, or subjective commitment will depend on the situation itself. Weber's distinctions between "the chief," his "subjects" and his "administrative staff" are useful here (31, 1:12). The chief's power over his staff will more likely involve their subjective commitment than his power over his subjects. This is not to deny that subjects may be committed, but rather to imply that loyalty is differentially distributed in any sphere where power is effectively exercised. Loyalty may involve commitment to the leader's person or to some conception of order which the leader is believed to represent and articulate authoritatively. (Notice that such a distinction is analytic, for commitment to the leader's person may stem from commitment to the order he represents, and vice-versa). In either case, the leader may offer radically new reinterpretations of existing public meanings.

In distinguishing between a chief and his staff, Weber stressed the enforcement function of the staff. This overlooks the importance of the staff as a source of articulations for the leader. In fact it is often possible to distinguish between an advisory and an enforcement staff. To the extent that the advisory staff do their job properly, the enforcement staff should presumably be kept less busy. In situations where the leader has power but little or no legitimacy, the activities of the enforcement staff will become crucial. On the other hand, Goffman (13, pp. 173–320) shows convincingly that even in a "total institution" secondary adjustment by "inmates" both makes coercive power more tolerable for the dominated and also makes enforcement easier for the "staff."

Legitimate power is clearly related both to effectiveness and to commitment. A leader's articulations are more likely to be acceptable to his followers if they meet common exigencies. Erikson's *Young Man Luther* (9) is a splendid study of effectiveness in this sense. Luther's power depended on his ability to articulate a new interpretation of Christian symbols for sixteenth-century man. Erikson does not note the important fact that once Luther's articulation had become a public meaning-system it was open to reinterpretation by Anabaptists and German peasants in a manner which he bitterly rejected but could not control. In an effort to do so, he appealed to the German princes to use their coercive power.[11]

It is essentially the fact of power as here defined which enables sociologists to speak sensibly of "group action," "role allocation," "class interests," and so on. The temptation to hypostasize such terms is almost irresistible. However, to do so is to ignore two crucial factors: the extent to which leader's are constantly rearticulating in response to exigencies and the extent to which power is based on a dialectical reciprocity between the leaders and the led. In itself, this reciprocity is a major source of exigencies for both the "chief," his "staff," and his "subjects."

### III

This paper has attempted to follow the early Parsons in his formulation of a frame of reference which will have a phenomenological status in social theory similar to the space-time framework of classical physics. I believe that the position taken here moves beyond Parsons, however, in developing a conception of the unit act which is genuinely voluntarist. The discussion of key sociological concepts in the second part of the paper is a tentative, and certainly brief, effort to demonstrate the usefulness of Zollschan's metatheoretical stance in understanding the inherently dynamic nature of social order. Analysis of social order with this perspective must by definition be analysis of social change.

Sociological theory has tended to treat *social change* as a process of

[11] Even in more representative freer society, innovative action in sensitive areas will be slowed to the extent that the majority and/or the elected leaders refuse to accept the articulations of creative minorities, thus denying them the power to act effectively. Voluntary associations are important channels of expression for such minority opinion.

variation which is measured against some stable limiting factor, whether this be values, social structure, or man's productive capacities. If there is any internal logic in social change, however, I reiterate that this logic be sought rather in the manner in which individuals constantly change their articulations and actions in response to exigencies. At the root of new institutionalization lie exigencies which may be experienced at a variety of levels. Discrepancies may be felt in accepted patterns of meaning, in clusters of expectation and interaction, in the individual's handling of his own libidinal energy, or on the simple material level. The process of articulation and goal-formation in itself gives rise to further exigencies which, if sufficiently salient, must be reckoned with if the actor is to resolve the original dissonance. Successful resolution involving interaction may ultimately lead to new institutionalization.

Delineation of the sources of social change must hence be discovered in empirical investigation — not assumed *a priori*. The frequently argued distinction between consensus and conflict models of society as basic metatheoretical stances, or even ideal types, is false and misleading. Patterns of interaction in response to exigencies invariably involve elements of both conflict and consensus. The degree to which each of the latter is present in any situation represents an empirical rather than a theoretical problem — at most a theoretical rather than a metatheoretical one.

Thus, the distinction between "institutions" and "events," as typified in the argument that history deals with events, whereas sociology deals with institutions, fails close scrutiny. Institutions, on examination, are seen to consist of myriad series of events, patterned on the basis of common goals, and the intended or unintended consequences of extraneous goals. Events, defined as action responses to articulated exigencies, make up the substance of all human conduct. Hence any "analytical" distinction between social statics and social dynamics will lead to false deductions for sociological explanation.

As it is here conceived, the metatheory of action stands in very close relation to empirical analysis. The above described model of the unit act in social relations does not present an "analytical" closed system, but rather a series of assumptions which allow an open frame of reference within which analysis and perhaps theory-building can take place.

With regard to theory, I agree with Max Weber that "theory-construction can never be decided *a priori*. Here too, there is only one criterion, namely, that of success in revealing concrete cultural phenomena in their interdependence, their causal conditions and their *significance*" (30, p. 92). Theory implies generalizations which have cross-cultural and historical validity. Such generalizations, while they may be useful in understanding particular phenomena, miss the individual significance of such phenomena. And yet it is surely this "individual significance" which social science attempts to understand. As Weber rightly perceived:

Laws are important and valuable in the exact natural sciences, in the measure that those sciences are *universally valid*. For the knowledge of historical phenomena in their concreteness, the most general laws, because they are most devoid of content, are also the least valuable . . . An "objective" analysis of cultural events . . . is meaningless . . . Firstly, because the knowledge of social laws is not knowledge of social reality, but is rather one of the various aids used by our minds for attaining this end; secondly, because knowledge of *cultural* events is inconceivable except on the basis of the *significance* which the concrete constellations of reality have for us in certain *individual* concrete situations . . . (30, p. 80).

For these reasons I wished to attempt an explanation of the Afrikaner rise to power and the development of apartheid theory (17). Not only do I believe these events to have a particular significance for understanding current developments in South Africa, but they have personal significance for me and my compatriots, whether black, white, coloured, or asiatic. My work may also contribute another "case" in the analysis of modernization or nationalism but its primary importance is in understanding South Africa, and its meaning for South Africans and, perhaps, the world. Compendia of generalizations like those of Akzin (1) and Duverger (8) proved most useful, but more as guides to insight than as sources of testable propositions.

I argue, then, that the sociologist must try to liberate his discipline from the distortions imposed by rigid theoretical categorizations. His view should be to examine the extent to which a particular significant pattern of action or symbolic universe is changing, and to discover the causes of such change in the interpretations and expectations of actors in situations. Having done this, he may suggest the implications of a particular new pattern of institutionalization for the actions and expectations of other actors. Eventually, therefore, he may "predict," but his predictions can be no more than a statement of the alternatives open to actors in key positions and their consequences for others (cf. 32, pp. 91–94). Any such apparent understanding of alternatives and consequences depends upon sensitive examination of the way in which other actors in similar situations have acted in the past. Sociology must thus be firmly rooted in historical enquiry.

## BIBLIOGRAPHY

1. Akzin, Benjamin. *State and Nation*. London: Hutchinson University Library, 1964.
2. Avineri, Shlomo. *The Social and Political Thought of Karl Marx*. Cambridge: Cambridge University Press, 1971.
3. Berger, Peter L., and Thomas Luckman. *The Social Construction of Reality*. Harmondsworth: Penguin Books, 1971.

4. Cassirer, Ernst. *An Essay on Man.* Garden City: Doubleday Anchor, n.d. (first published by Yale University Press, 1944).

5. Cicourel, Aaron V. *The Social Organization of Juvenile Justice.* New York: John Wiley, 1967.

6. Crozier, Michel. *The Bureaucratic Phenomenon.* Chicago: University of Chicago Press, 1964.

7. Dreitzel, Hans Peter (ed.). *Recent Sociology No. 2.* New York: Macmillan, 1970.

8. Duverger, Maurice. *Political Parties.* New York: John Wiley, 1955.

9. Erikson, Erik. *Young Man Luther.* New York: Norton, 1962.

10. Geertz, Clifford. "Religion as a Cultural System," in Michael Banton (ed.), *Anthropological Approaches to the Study of Religion.* London: Tavistock Press, 1966.

11. Gerth, Hans, and Mills, C. W. (eds.). *From Max Weber.* London: Routledge & Kegan Paul, 1948.

12. Gierke, Otto. *Natural Law and the Theory of Society.* Translated with an introduction by Ernest Barker. Boston: Beacon Press, 1957.

13. Goffman, Erving. *Asylums.* Garden City: Doubleday Anchor Books, 1961.

14. Goffman, Erving. *Encounters.* Indianapolis: Bobbs-Merrill Company, 1961.

15. Gouldner, Alvin. *Patterns of Industrial Bureaucracy.* Glencoe: The Free Press, 1954.

16. Marx, Karl. "The Eighteenth Brumaire of Louis Bonaparte," in Karl Marx & Frederick Engels. *Selected Works, Volume I.* Moscow: Foreign Languages Publishing House, 1962.

17. Moodie, T. Dunbar. *The Rise of Afrikanerdam.* Berkeley: University of California Press, in press.

18. Parsons, Talcott, Robert F. Bales. *Family, Socialization and Interaction Process.* New York: Free Press, 1955.

19. Parsons, Talcott. *The Structure of Social Action.* New York: Free Press, 1949.

20. Parsons, Talcott. "The Superego and the Theory of Social Systems," in Rose Laub Coser (ed.), *The Family: Its Structure and Functions.* New York: Saint Martin's Press, 1964.

21. Parsons, Talcott, Shils, Edward, Naegele, Kaspar D., and Pitts, Jesse R. (eds.). *Theories of Society.* New York: Free Press, 1961.

22. Parsons, Talcott, and Shils, Edward A. (eds.) *Toward a General Theory of Action.* Cambridge, Mass.: Harvard University Press, 1951.

23. Schutz, Alfred. *Collected Papers I: The Problem of Social Reality.* The Hague: Nijhoff, 1962.

24. Selznick, Philip. *TVA and the Grass Roots.* Berkeley: University of California Press, 1949.

25. Slater, Philip. "Social Limitations on Libidinal Withdrawal," in Rose Laub Coser (ed.), *The Family: Its Structure and Functions.* New York: Saint Martin's Press, 1964.

26. Spicer, Edward (ed.) *Human Problems and Technological Change.* New York: John Wiley, 1965.

27. Stanner, W. E. H. "The Dreaming," in T.A.G. Hungerford (ed.), *Astralian Signpost,* Melbourne: Cheshire, 1956.

28. Taylor, Charles. "Interpretation and the Sciences of Man," in *The Review of Metaphysics,* Vol. 25, No. 1, September 1971.

29. Thompson, E. P. *The Making of the English Working Class.* Harmondsworth: Penguin Books, 1969.

30. Weber, Max. *The Methodology of the Social Sciences.* Glencoe: The Free Press, 1949.

31. Weber, Max. *The Theory of Social and Economic Organization.* Edited with an introduction by Talcott Parsons. Glencoe: Free Press, 1964.

32. Winch, Peter. *The Idea of a Social Science.* London: Routledge & Kegan Paul, 1963.

33. Worsley, Peter. *The Trumpet Shall Sound.* 2nd Edition. London: Granada Publishing (Paladin Books), 1970.

34. Zollschan, George K., Walter Hirsch. *Explorations in Social Change.* Boston: Houghton Mifflin and Co., 1964.

# 6

*George K. Zollschan*
*and Walter Friedman*

# Leadership and Social Change:

# An Intelligent Child's Garden of

# Raspberries, with a Bestiary, and a Zoo,

# and an Expulsion

### Preliminary Remarks

In this chapter we shall be concerned with the conditions or circumstances in which leadership arises, linking such conditions with the original model of motive and institutionalization proposed by Zollschan. It is our intention to show that some form of leadership is present in many, if not all, instances of institutionalization and collective behaviour. What is more, Zollschan's theoretical model contains a number of elements which may be used to construct a typology of occasions for leadership; occasions which, if they were not taken, would condemn processes of institutionalization and social change to latency. In a special sense, therefore, leadership can be viewed as the logical and necessary accompaniment of processes transforming exigencies affecting individuals or classes of individuals into changes in established patterns of social interaction. Notions concerning the manner in which such processes of transformation occur must be restated and expanded to provide an initial characterization of the way in which the problem of leadership will be handled.

Firstly, an exigency is a subjective discrepancy between "what is" and what, in any one of a number of senses, "ought to be." Consequently, an exigency arises either as result of an indigenous change in the existence of a person or, alternatively, because of exposure to alternatives capable of being articulated as "preferable." Secondly, articulated ideas, communicated by others, can be seized upon by the person experiencing an exigency to provide articulation for it. Thirdly, different persons are differentially exposed to various kinds of exigencies; differentially equipped to articulate needs and goals; and differentially situated with respect to their capacity to attain goals.

In first approximation, then, leadership in social change processes may be characterized as consisting of a number of activities. The actual exercise of leadership in a particular situation can, of course, consist of any single one of these activities or of a combination of them. The activities may be listed as follows: Provision of articulated goals, or ideologies, or even merely specification of problems for persons experiencing exigencies. Presentation to potential followers of preferable alternatives to some currently prevailing condition of existence or type of activity. Finally, mobilization of persons for the attainment of goals and provision of various requisites for such goal attainment. Each of these activities or "leadership functions" is capable of finer analytic reduction. A larger part of the argument we intend to present in this chapter will consist, precisely, in the presentation of typologies of articulation leadership and action leadership.

Differential exposure to exigencies, differential equipment to articulate needs and goals, and differential capacities and opportunities with respect to goals; all of the foregoing determine the selection of individuals to whom the term "leader" in some sense or another can be applied. Given the variety of exigencies which fall to the human lot, the diversity of articulations that can occur to some person or another, the numberless combinations of chance and of skill which provide access to goals, it becomes apparent that leadership phenomena are more widespread and pervasive than is commonly recognized in the language of common usage.

What person is there, after all, who has not under certain circumstances at some time provided an articulation, suggested an alternative, or given direction in the attainment of a goal to someone else? We may take comfort (at least, if we are inclined to take comfort) in the knowledge that virtually all of us — under the general definitions provided by the model of motive and institutionalization — correspond in some sense to the definition of a "leader." Or, perhaps, we should feel dismay that our very general system of definitions blurs the distinction between leadership and non-leadership, thereby rendering the term redundant.

Both comfort and dismay should be tempered with caution, however. Our very special way of viewing leadership, at the same time as conferring the title on activities not usually so described, deprives other activities commonly described as "leadership" of that title. Like any theoretically grounded special model, we suppose, the model of leadership presented here leads to surprising, perhaps even to counter-intuitive, results. No apology at all is necessary, in our view, for results which differ from established habits of thinking and routines of language usage. For the sake of clarity, however, an additional word is necessary to provide the reader with some guidelines to ease the task of understanding the type of argument we intend to present.

As was intimated right at the outset of this discussion, leadership is viewed here as being evoked by "occasions" necessitating, or calling for, or inherently involving its exercise. We shall try to show that such occasions for leadership can usefully be conceptualized as corresponding to the coordinates of articulation and action in Zollschan's model. No implication follows that every such occasion potentially calling for leadership will be met; for, while every "leader" (by our definition) necessarily grasps an occasion, not every "occasion" finds its leader.

The foregoing point is rather important since it makes clear that neither the *trait* nor the *situational* approach is being applied in our discussion. To be sure, occasions for leadership as we conceive of them can be viewed as particular kinds of "situations" arising out of systematic processes involved in all social changes (or involved in all such processes, at any rate, if the fundamental postulates of the model are accepted). But only in special cases where leadership is viewed as an involuntary predicament inherently involved in an occasion (as it has to be in one of the types which will be discussed below) is it unambiguously "situational" in character — even in the narrowly particular sense that the term "situational" can be said to apply in this analysis. We are, therefore, entirely in agreement with Hollander and Julian (6, p. 388) who see both the trait and situational approaches as being glib and distortive of reality.

It has been mentioned that the occasions for leadership to which reference will be made are analytically separated elements of a model of institutionalization. This may raise the question (at least, in some minds) of whether the following discussion is not narrowly concerned with the exercise of leadership in social change processes alone and ignores routine occasions in which leadership exists. To such a question we reply that the entire thrust of Zollschan's theoretical orientation is to emphasize social change processes rather than some real or imagined condition of social stability. Indeed "social stability" — so far as it makes sense to speak of such a state — is necessarily and always considered as a special case of social dynamics. The implication of such an orientation for the study of leadership is crystal clear. Leadership, like any social process, must be considered as a phenomenon in *statu nascendi* rather than in solidified, or ossified, or frozen form.

Instead of being viewed as a facility for the performance of functions upholding social structures, leadership becomes the set of occasions in which ideas and goals are formulated in a way that is meaningful for followers, and in which efforts to attain these goals are mobilized. Indeed, we go so far as to declare that, if leadership is necessary for the maintenance of any particular *status quo* this is only because there are forces in operation that militate toward its dissolution or overthrow. In other words, leadership exists in a situation of social stability only because its absence would *pose* an exigency for persons implicated in the social structure under consideration.

The prime concern of this discussion is with the presentation of a typology of leadership related to the theoretical co-ordinates of articulation and action in Zollschan's model of motive and institutionalization. We recognize that typologies are not everybody's "cup of tea" and that this holds particularly true of instances, such as this, where types are presented which rarely (if ever) are encountered in pure form. If such a typology will be found useful in future discussions and research on questions of leadership it is because the typology grows out of a general theoretical framework, a framework in which interconnections between diverse ranges of hitherto apparently unrelated phenomena become evident.

The issue of surplus meanings attaching to the term leadership will be briefly examined prior to the exposition of the typology. Weber's notion of charismatic leadership will receive especial attention. The chapter concludes with a theoretical distinction between the notions of leadership and followership and a discussion of the conceptual clarification to be attained by accepting such an asymmetry of terms.

### Leadership and Libido: "Gratuitous" Surplus Meanings

We have hinted at the conception of leadership involving the production of ideas adopted by others, as well as mobilization of co-ordinated efforts for the achievement of goals. This conception will be expanded in our subsequent discussion. No amount of expansion, however, can hope to encompass all of the uses and misuses to which the term "leadership" is put, both in common parlance and in the relevant learned literatures. Even when we limit the topic to the Lasswellian question: "who leads whom, when and how"; (10) or to Rustow's emendation of it: "who leads whom from where to where," ("whence" to "whither"?) (15, p. 20) we hardly begin to grasp the slippery encrustations of meanings that have accumulated round this term.

Fritz Redl, in a now classical typology of "central persons" based on psychoanalytic notions (13) was even moved to fight shy of "leadership" as a generic term altogether, and reserved the expression "leader" for but one of his ten types.[1] Redl's own discussion of types of central persons classifies these into three groups: 1) objects of identification on various grounds (love, fear); 2) objects of various drives (love, aggression); and 3) "ego supports" (sic) (13, p. 583). Our own initial characterization comes closest to Redl's third group. The types of focal persons discussed by Redl under this heading provide for "drive satisfaction" for "ego defence" and for the resolution of inner conflicts. If the terminology of drives, ego defences, and conflicts is substituted by our language using terms such as "exigency," "articulation" and "goal," it is clear that Redl's group of "ego supporting" types can be subsumed under our discussion without undue problems.[2]

The idea that leaders can be objects of identification or that the very fact of having a leader may constitute a goal state for followers (which is one possible way of interpreting Redl's discussion of leaders as "drive objects") cannot be lightly dismissed. Our discussion treats these "surplus meanings" as subsidiary, or additional, to the central theme under consideration: namely, the propulsion (or prevention) of social change.

Redl's discussion, tied as it is to routine events in school classrooms, does not particularly emphasize leadership in the context of social transformation. The special association of leadership with social change, however, is by no means original to this presentation. Max Weber's notion that legitimate orders (that is, shared or common expectations and value suppositions providing legitimation for structures of social relationships) are, so to speak, the "invention" of charismatic leaders is still a subject of lively debate in the contemporary sociological literature.[3] Weber applied the term *charisma* to persons to whom exceptional powers or qualities are ascribed by their followers[4] (19, p. 48). It is interesting to note, in this connection, that the expression "exceptional" or "extraordinary" (*"ausseralltäglich"*) is used by Weber to characterize both

---

[1] Redl uses the term "leader" for the type he feels corresponds most closely to Freud's description (3); namely, as an object of incorporation into the ego-ideal (13, pp. 573–574).

[2] Tolman's distinction between drives and needs (17, pp. 288–290) corresponds quite closely to our distinction between exigencies and needs. Drives, however, are normally envisaged as organismic imperatives. Exigencies, by contrast, can be situational as well as somatic; indeed they are viewed as a combination of the two. Consequently drives are a sub-class of the more inclusive class of exigencies. Use of the term "exigency," moreover, requires fewer assumptions concerning the state of the organism.

[3] Various scattered statements by Max Weber on the subject of charismatic leadership and available in English translation have been collected by Eisenstadt (18). Some of the uses to which Weber's ideas in this area have been put are discussed below.

[4] The original German for routinization — *"veralltäglichung"* — literally translates (and the reader should pardon the expression!) as "everyday-ization." The other cornerstone of Weber's theory of institutionalization is his depiction of the secular trend towards rationality.

charisma and the category of affective behaviour. In his typology of social structures (18, pp. 31, 215) the category of affective behaviour is virtually inert except as related to instances of "emotional surrender" either to a charismatic leader or to a legitimate order. Thus Weber, as much as Redl, finds it necessary to portray leaders as the objects of affect.

Weber's conjunction of charismatic leadership with "non-everyday" events may be traced to the influence of Friedrich Gottl (5). The latter had suggested that economics, like other social sciences (*Aktionswissenschaften*) had the task of unravelling the meaning of everyday experience (5, p. 76). In relation to Gottl's legacy of ideas, Weber's notion of charismatic leadership did double duty. Firstly, it provided a theoretical bridging concept for the transition from one state of "everyday experience" to another (or, perhaps rather from one painfully constructed ideal type of everyday experience to another). Secondly, it made systematic provision for the release of affect during the course of such transition: affect which otherwise appears pretty much bottled up in Weber's description of social processes.

It is popularly known that Weber's theory concerning routinization of charisma constitutes one of the cornerstones of his theory of institutionalization.[5] The Etzionis overshot the mark in describing him as a cyclical change theorist (2, p. 5). Still, it is undeniable that an uncanny aroma of successive cycles of routinization and charismatic deroutinisation does cling to Weber's writings. The notion of routine and its disturbance can be applied to Zollschan's theoretical model. Doing so helps to illuminate a significant difference between the theory of institutionalization proposed here and Weber's rather spasmodic depiction of the establishment of legitimate orders.

All persons are regularly subject to excitations and tensions inherent in the conditions of their existence. The very maintenance of continuity and coherence in experience is itself a source of tension. To substantiate the latter statement one need merely point out that where what we may call "coherence tension," becomes excessive for the person in question, psychosis ensues. Normally, people cope with established levels of tension and recurrent excitation by habitual behavioural routines and ideational orientations. Such routines and orientations may be the precipitate of previous ideation, action, and institutionalization, or may arise on a

[5] It has become something of a parlour-game to trace Weber's use of the term "charisma." Nietzsche, Rudolf Sohm, and Pauline Epistles (*Corinthians* 12:8-11, for instance) are all candidates for the privilege of semantic transmission. The matter is of such shattering irrelevance as to exercise a virtually fatal attraction for men of "learning." We are content with the touristic observation that "charisma" means "gratuity" in modern Greek. It meant much the same sort of thing ("present," "gift") in classical Greek. The Apostle Paul used the expression to refer to divers handouts by the *Spiritus Sanctus*. True to form, the German classicist revival took up this meaning of "baksheesh from beyond," and this *jenerweltliche* aspect of the baksheesh stuck to it in Weber's writings.

pre-articulate level. In either case, coping occurs pre-consciously as much as consciously. Where coping is more or less adequate, we may join Gottl and Weber in speaking of an "everyday realm."

Viewed from this perspective, an exigency can be described as a state in which routine coping is inadequate, or becomes inadequate. Additionally, disturbances of routine coping and tacit ideation (from whatever source) also constitute exigencies. Finally, the adequacy of such coping may be put to question when the person is exposed to "preferable" routines or ideas. Such exposure can, of course, occur as the result of influence or example presented by another.

In comparing this point of view with Weber's, two differences should be noted. Each of these differences corresponds to one of the unnecessarily dual meaning Weber attaches to the concept "charismatic leadership."

Firstly, articulation and action in response to a "deroutinizing" exigency do not necessarily require leadership at all; at least, leadership in the sense of a central person who is instrumental in the creation of new routines or to whom such instrumentality is widely ascribed. For one thing, articulation and re-routinized action may be confined to one person. For another, even if the new routines are widely adopted, their adoption may lend itself more suitably to interpretation as an aggregate rather than as a centralized social process. To the extent, therefore, that charisma is involved in any episode of deroutinization, Zollschan's theoretical model may be regarded as a radical generalization of the Weberian theory of charisma. Charisma, so regarded, flows from an upturned horn of plenty!

Secondly, leadership — even leadership that manifestly creates new "legitimate orders" — can occur without occasioning abreaction of affect in followers (whether through the elicitation of "emotional surrender" or in whatever other form). This is not meant to assert that leadership in Weber's sense never exists. Examples of persons who are foci of emotional cathexis for their followers are easy enough to find. The statement merely declares that cathexis to some persons characterized as leader is not a theoretically inevitable accompaniment of followership. It demotes leadership of this particular kind in historical importance and renders it subject to finer analysis.

The foregoing remarks suggest that cathexis to a leader is not an unconditional accompaniment of all leader-follower phenomena but that its occurrence should be treated as a problem separate from that of the emergence of leadership. More generally, they underline the problem of *conditions* under which abreaction of affect accompanies articulation and action. Our present discussion cannot go into the special problems of cathexis and abreaction in any depth. It is quite sufficient, for our purposes, to point out that these problems are *analytically* separable from any discussion of institutionalization and of the role of leadership in institutionalization.

The issue of analytical separability will loom large in the pages that follow. The procedure adopted corresponds to Galilean rather than to Weberian methods of procedure. Pure types of occasions for leadership are isolated, corresponding not, as in Weberian methods, to particular historical instances or classes of historical instances (suitably simplified and distorted to fit theoretical needs) but to general parameters drawn from Zollschan's theory of institutionalization.

Whether leadership itself constitutes a goal-state for given persons who rise to such occasions or, for that matter, whether followership itself constitutes a goal-state for those who are influenced by such persons, is left open. Moreover, as we use the expression here, "leadership" may refer either to a single person or to a leadership corps.

### Occasions for Leadership and Pure Types of Leader 1: An Heraldic Bestiary

The coordinates of articulation and action identified in Zollschan's basic model of motive and institutionalization may be viewed as occasions for the exercise of leadership. In referring to these institutionalization co-ordinates as occasions for leadership we avoid the one-sidedness of either the 'trait' or 'situational' approaches. We shall show that leadership can be as much a predicament as a personal characteristic; that it can depend as much on privileged access to some occasion for its performance as on any active desire to exercise it. The basis of differentiation of leaders from others shifts kaleidoscopically according to the occasion for leadership being examined. Theoretical pure types of leadership can be fitted to each of these occasions. In so doing, a classification is obtained which cuts across traditional boundaries; a classification no less illuminating, we trust, for being new.

*1) Salience: The Martyr, Idol, Sensitizer:* The first factor, salience, when viewed in isolation, occupies a marginal position in the model. Salience is a measure of exigency; a measure of the distance between actually present and desired states. Free-floating tension, excitation without conceptual location, does not lend itself readily to analysis of processes of institutionalization. In first approximation, therefore, one may conceive a salience leader as a person stricken by an exigency more intensely or directly than others. This kind of priority, standing at the frontline of the exigency, so to speak, is not normally termed leadership in common parlance unless the greater vulnerability to the exigency is accompanied by relevant specification and justification. Yet, it is undeniable that high vulnerability to a given exigency can have group-integrative effects, giving rise to sympathizers or curious onlookers (as in an automobile crash . . . or a crucifixion) rather than to followers in the narrow sense of the word. Still, an influence process of sorts is at work, with the "victim" of the exigency influencing the actions of others less by his own actions than by his predicament. Thus the *martyr* provides a fitting type for the occasion of salience.

Another type who influences others by what may be called his predicament rather than by any active influence-attempts is the *idol*; a type who presents a preferable alternative to persons not otherwise experiencing an exigency (perhaps through his appearance, or comportment, or style). In this typology, therefore, "martyr" and "idol" are equivalent. It is hardly necessary to stress that such equivalence exists purely in relation to the type of leadership in question. No moral or theological equivalence between martyrs and idols in general need be assumed because of the above.

It is, moreover, possible to extend the notion of salience leadership to persons not directly experiencing an exigency but calling the attention of others to it. Such persons may, perhaps, empathize with those experiencing the exigency and sensitize others to it without, necessarily, being vulnerable themselves. Alternatively, they may draw attention to an exigency for purely opportunistic reasons. To the martyr, therefore, we may add the *sensitizer* as another type of salience leader.

Martyrdom and the active sensitization of others may, of course, be combined in one person. One variant of the case in which martyrdom and sensitization overlap, a highly significant case, is the leader who willingly places himself in a situation of high risk. Here, the leader influences others by his or her own "suffering" or "heroism" or both. Indeed, leadership can occur through the creation of feelings of "solidarity in martyrdom" among a group of followers. Such feelings of solidarity, clearly, can extend beyond the circle of those directly exposed to the exigency.

2) *Specification: The Formulator:* Priority in the specification of needs and goals conforms more readily to currently fashionable usages of the term "leadership" than does martyrdom. The person who decides that something must be done about an exigency and specifies it to the satisfaction of followers conforms to this type. Idiosyncratic formulations of need by potential specification leaders, however precise, or ingenious, or apposite they may be in principle, do not in themselves guarantee a following. When formulators are too far "ahead" of potential followers in the capacity of grasping the meaning and consequences of an exigency, for example, their leadership remains unrealised (1, p. 594). Of course, the would-be formulator may be outside acceptable bounds in other directions than "ahead."

In actual instances of priority in specification, vagueness rather than precision may help to establish the formulator of needs or of ideas as a leader. This is particularly true of instances where appeal is made to a heterogeneous followership, differentially exposed to the exigency and bringing to the situation widely divergent ideational presuppositions. The development of a common ideology among a substantial number of followers does not necessarily call for very high levels of ingenuity and perceptiveness with respect to the precise nature of the originating exigency on the part of a successful leader.

Persons intent on assuming the mantle of leadership through formulating needs may even do so by proposing false specifications for the exigencies besetting their potential followers. Racialist myths, sham theories of social stratification, verbalized phantasies of all kinds of "liberation" or "salvation"; all of these lend themselves well for canalizing generalized tensions whose origins remain effectively obscure. It matters little, in such cases, whether the lie is deliberate or the object of sincere belief on part of the leader.

Apart from persons deliberately intent on acquiring influence through the formulation of needs, specification leadership is likely to be exercised by those who, by virtue of their footing in an existing institutional structure, are in a favorable position to become aware of new exigencies as these arise within their general areas of competence. The specification of what might be termed "aggregate needs" in particular, is likely to be made by officials or others with an overview of the area in which particular exigencies occur. The formulation of a need for more maternity hospital facilities in a given city, for instance, is more likely to be made by an official of a municipal hospital board or a hospital administrator than by this or that pregnant woman who happens to experience the exigency of lying in a hospital corridor during parturition.

3) *Justification: The Inhibiter, Seducer:* The horizon of justifications contains deep layers of personality formation. In first approximation, in any event, it appears useful to refer to this horizon from a negative point of view; as that of "counter-justifications." Counter-justifications are prohibitions, inhibitions, and repressions which militate against the articulation of a need, even where a salient exigency ("corresponding" to the need) is experienced and the cognitive means for specification are present. One must, therefore, speak of two types of leader under this heading: the *inhibiter* who establishes counter-justifications, and the *seducer* who releases them.

Leadership is discussed in this typology as arising in response to occasions for leadership. The inhibiter, here, takes up a strictly tangential position. Such leadership requires the power to punish or otherwise extinguish previously prevalent activities and their associated ideas. It is, therefore, often proper to speak of "subjects" rather than "followers." Typically, such power exists prior to, or independently of, the occasion for leadership. The source of power, however, may spring from identification or attraction as well as from coercion.

The possibility must be entertained that a sufficiently salient exigency may lend a leader with a suitable "solution" (or better still, in a position of monopoly with respect to the supply of suitable articulations) the necessary power to suppress certain kinds of activities. In such a case, justification and specification leadership are, of course, combined in the same person or group. Alternatively, a person who acts to re-establish inhibitions weakened by special circumstances (as in a riot, or a mob) also qualifies for classification under the heading here discussed.

The establishment of counter-justifications normally occurs in situations in which it is usual to speak of "socialization" or "re-socialization" ("brain-washing" or Skinnerian "behavior modification" provide examples but by no means, exhaust resocialization possibilities). Changing patterns of socialization may occur in response to new legitimations. The legitimation leader to be discussed below may thus have an indirect effect on actions by followers which serve to establish (whether intentionally or unintentionally) counter-justifications in newly born generations or in new cohorts of recruits to some collectivity.

The other type of justification leader under contemporary conditions — the person who "liberates" inhibitions rather than inculcates them — is a more easily recognizable figure. We agree with the Freudians that some types of inhibition and repression are universal concomitants of childhood socialization. Counter-justifications thus acquired in most cases have to do with authority relations, sexual behavior, control of aggression and, more general, aesthetic and ethical standards. The seducer is able to annul counter-justifications, usually in combination with specification or legitimation calling for the overthrow of authority, the expression of aggression or sexuality (in whatever form and with whatever object) or changes in aesthetic and ethical standards.

Seduction leadership which annuls counter-justifications selectively with respect to a particular scapegoat is a highly prevalent variety of this type. Opportunistic seduction leaders can use a scapegoat (or a scapegoat population, however designated or defined) as a means for lowering tension levels occasioned in their followers by the presence of counter-justifications. The tensions are lowered, of course, by making the scapegoat the target of released aggressions, sexual perversions, and so forth. It is worth noting, however, that the elicitation of active resistance or the exercise of violence against entrenched tyrannical powers (existing in reality, not necessarily only in phantasy) may also call for a kind of "seduction": seduction which rids the subjected persons of their "slave mentality" by lifting certain counter-justifications.

## Occasions for Leadership and Pure Types of Leaders 2: A Magico-political Zoo

The foregoing typology has classified occasions for leadership associated with articulation and pure types of leaders who rise to such occasions. In shifting attention to action, and mobilization for action, some supplementary remarks are necessary.

The exercise of leadership (unless it be simply through passive martyrdom which happens to be visible to others) implies activity on part of the leader. At the very least, specifications and justifications, and even just expressions of alarm or sympathy at an exigency, are communicated to followers — and communication is a species of activity. Clearly, therefore, when applied to phenomena of leadership the distinction between the phases of articulation and action refers to followers rather than to leaders. Leadership of the types discussed above gives rise to changes in orientation or "consciousness" in followers but not necessarily to organized activity.

All this does not mean, of course, that changes in orientation on the part of followers cannot result in unorganized or uncoordinated changes in the latters' activity. An active homosexual, for instance, exposed to the justification leadership provided by "gay liberation," may lose the shame or guilt he or she may have previously felt in pursuit of sexual aims. It is even possible (assuming that the justification is sufficiently potent) that a previously inactive homosexual might be moved to seek a partner congenial to this sexual orientation, thereby translating the new-found justification into personal activity.[6] Articulation leadership may thus instigate or encourage aggregate or common changes in activity. Organized changes, requiring conjoint activity towards goals, on the other hand, call for the additional types of leadership to be discussed below.

4) *Valence: The Resource Supplier, Strategist:* In Zollschan's theoretical model the term "valence" is used to refer to the opportunity-cost of a goal in terms of other goals foregone in its pursuit. It thus requires the priority ordering of a particular articulated goal in relation to other existing goals which compete for the expenditure of time and effort. When viewed as an occasion for leadership, therefore, it calls for one of the following types of leader: i) the person who can supply resources necessary for goal attainment; or ii) the person who makes strategic decisions regarding goals and action priorities.

The *resource supplier* is one who by virtue of ownership or privileged access to resources (money, tools, weapons, committed or indentured personnel) can change the priority of a goal of conjoint activity by

---

[6] The difficulty of providing examples for pure types is illustrated by this instance. Granting the status of leadership to "gay liberation" (here viewed as a leadership corps) it is clear that the leadership involved — like leadership in nearly all actual cases — represents a mixed rather than pure type. It is fair to assume (without having engaged in any deep study of this movement) that the elements of justification and legitimation are probably most prominent in this empirical mix. The example used here stresses the justification element only since it refers to the lifting of inhibitions on emotional states and on activity.

affecting its attainment chances. Needless to say, the availability of necessary resources can be a crucial factor in the determination of priorities. Mobilization of potential resources is a function which applies to all occasions for leadership. Any aspect of social structure can readily be viewed on the analogy with capital in economics. Institutionalization, the continuous creation of social structures, *ipso facto* creates resources. All coordinates of institutionalization are involved in this generalized kind of resource formation. To the extent that these coordinates constitute occasions for leadership, and to the extent that such occasions are taken, resources are being produced.

The supply of resources, on the other hand, (as distinct from their production, or creation, or mobilization) implies the capacity to transfer already existing resources to other "uses" or to activate available resources which lie idle.[7]

Prestige provides a fine illustration of an idle resource. When a person who enjoys prestige among a relevant given population "lends" his prestige to the pursuit of a goal, he acts as a resource supplier for its legitimation. Such a person may, of course, sully the purity of his type by actively engaging in legitimizing activities in addition to merely lending his prestige.

Supply of resources is "subsidiary" to application and/or legitimation, from the perspective of actual goal attainment. Conversely, application and legitimation are subsidiary to resource supply from the perspective of goal selection. Powers of persuasion and know-how are also kinds of resources but these are properly dealt with under different headings.

The *strategist* as a type overlaps to some degree with the formulator. The latter, as has been seen, specifies a need which may or may not be immediately associated with goals of action. Where the need is highly salient, closely associated with a goal, and calls for relatively uncomplicated activity, a specification may itself determine valence. The conditions of close association of a specified need with fitting goals and of uncomplicated activity for reaching goals are not always present. In their absence, and also where conjoint activity calls for division of labor, the strategist, as a pure type, comes into his own. Empirically, he may often be found sitting at the top of some "imperatively coordinated association."

5) *Application: The Expert, Innovator Magician:* Where attainment of a goal requires some measure of technical competence, if only competence in the organization of co-operative or conjoint activities, an occa-

---

[7] Gamson's discussion of what he calls "slack" resources (4, pp. 97–99) blurs over the distinction we are making between "potential" and "idle" resources. Potential resources have to be created by mobilization or production. Idle resources are in existence and available: they are just not being used at a given moment. The above distinction is perfectly familiar in economic theory, (see, for example, 7). It is rather surprising that the distinction has not penetrated into the better-advertised published models of political and social processes based on economic analogies.

sion for leadership arises for persons with the necessary skills. Where these skills are specialized or "scarce" they are properly called *expertise* and constitute a basis for the exercise of leadership.

Of particular interest from the point of view of social and technical change is the situation in which no previously existing techniques for meeting a specified need are available. The *innovator* who creates such techniques demonstrates expertise in its most concentrated and sublimated form.

An interesting variant of the expert is the *magician*. Magicians, though they do not supply the necessary techniques for bridging the gap between an articulated need and goals that might mitigate the need, provide ritual substitutes for goal attainment — substitutes often as good, if not better, than merely the real thing.[8]

Innovations, whether of the magical or "straight" variety, translate unsatisfied needs into new techniques. In some ways, therefore, they occupy a position intermediate between specification leadership and application leadership proper. With respect to the originating exigency, and the occasion for leadership presented by it, innovators are articulation leaders in pure form. The element of specification is involved with respect to a second-order exigency, requiring the development of new techniques. Clearly, in special settings where innovativeness becomes institutionalized (research organizations, for instance) the development of innovative techniques becomes relegated to the status of mere expertise.

Innovativeness is not exclusively confined to the application leader. Possibilities for invention and novelty exist in connection with almost all pure types of leadership. The special importance of innovativeness in connection with application, however (particularly where a new need arises for which no routine solutions are available), merits reservation of the term *innovator* under this heading.

6) *Legitimation: The Lawgiver, Ideologue, Apologist, Propagandist:* Up to this point in our presentation of the typology only the leader and followers, or potential followers, have been considered. Legitimation offers a more complex occasion for leadership since several "publics" may be involved besides the followers themselves to whom the goal must be legitimized. Additionally, one faces the question, when considering legitimation, to what extent the new goal encompasses the lives of followers. Both the question of a multiplicity of target publics for legitimation and the question of the extent to which routines of followers have to be changed, affect the degree to which the goal has to be

---

[8] The tension between perceived needs and desirable goals, where technical means are not available (or, at any rate, are not reliable) was clearly noted by Malinowski and forms the core of his theory of magic (11, p. 18). Jarvie has very properly stressed that new magic, much as any other new technique, depends upon innovative leadership (8, pp. 123–124).

compatible (or be made compatible) with values previously held by members of the relevant target publics.

Where the goal constitutes an "interest" (see Chapter 11) and non-followers fall into competing or opposing groups, legitimation to members of such groups may be a matter of little or no importance. This also holds where the followership constitute a sect with an ideology that asserts something like "if you are not for me, you are against me."

The luxury of ignoring non-followers as targets for legitimation is not always available, however. Often it is necessary, or advisable, to make attempts to recruit persons whose potential for followership has not been heightened by personal experience of the originating exigency. Here, the legitimation leader acts as *propagandist*. In other cases, permission, facilitation, or perhaps merely tolerance and good will for activities supporting the goal must be sought from others. Here, the legitimation leader acts as *apologist*. In both of these instances, legitimation will be effective only if it presents the goal in such a light as to make it appear compatible with previously established value systems known or assumed to hold sway over members of the relevant target publics. One can conceive of situations where a given goal cannot be so legitimized, thus forcing those who espouse the goal into covert or secret activity.[9]

In cases where a goal does not encompass the lives of the followers, the aim of legitimation also is to harmonize the new goal with values already held by the followers (or assumed to be held by them). Any new partial (that is to say, non-encompassing) pattern of activity is most smoothly and expeditiously legitimized where consistency with previously established values and ideologies can be optimized. Where a potential new goal is not capable of being harmonized in this way, it may abort.[10]

The above considerations affecting legitimation as an occasion for leadership refer equally to the solitary legitimation of any idiosyncratic goal. Where a new goal is relatively encompassing, however, and requires

---

[9] Secrecy is not necessarily regarded as a defect by members who practice it. On the contrary, occasionally it may be sought for its own sake. Differences of legitimation corresponding to different target publics lend themselves to arrangements in a hierarchy of prestige, thereby giving certain legitimations a kind of "chic" lacked by others. For an amusing, if theoretically rather cloudy, discussion of this matter see Simmel (16, pp. 345–376).

[10] The degree of value consistency found necessary by a group of followers may vary according to the situation or according to the personalities of the followers. A highly valent need for which only one goal is fitting may necessitate tolerance of value incongruity among those who have the need. In our terms, this constitutes a second-order evaluative exigency for them. Additionally, what we may call "needs for value consistency" vary between different persons or populations. The latter point deserves more, and better, empirical investigation than it has received (See 10; 12, pp. 82–108).

fundamental and far-reaching changes of routine, the occasion for leadership is heightened. Here the complete reorganization of value systems is required; a kind of reorganization for which many persons may not be equipped. The legitimation leader undoubtedly makes his most dramatic entrance on the social stage when he successfully effects such a "transvaluation of values" among relevant followers.[11] It is in this guise he earns the designation of "lawgiver."

In view of the different kinds of legitimation a given goal may require vis-à-vis different publics, legitimation leadership is the type where a leadership corps and some division of labor is most to be expected.

### Ab-"Führ": The Notion of "Followership" and the Elimination of Some Theoretical Confusions

*Adventavit Asinus, Pulcher et Fortissimus.*

— anon.

The coordinates of action and articulation have been treated as a sort of perspective from which every occasion for leadership may be regarded. Leadership, viewed as an aspect of the institutionalization process, becomes significant wherever interpersonal influence is present, or necessary, or relevant. In first approximation, therefore, leadership as we consider it in this discussion is a "natural" and spontaneous accompaniment of the transformation of exigencies into institutionalization of novel social structures and cultural patterns. In many cases, additionally, leadership must be regarded as a prerequisite of stages in such a transformation as much as an accompaniment of it. Indeed, it is precisely where leadership is not merely entailed by the institutionalization process but exhibits itself as demonstrably necessary for its continued operation, that our theoretical analysis may be expected to find its readiest applicability to the study of empirical cases.

Our special treatment of leadership as a facility for, or at least accompaniment of, the part-processes analytically implicated in institutionalization brings into relief a state of asymmetry between leadership and followership. Further discussion of this asymmetry will provide some clarification in the understanding of leadership-followership phenomena. Essentially, what we are claiming is that it is proper to speak of followership occurring in circumstances where leadership, in the restricted

---

[11] Even massive transvaluations build upon previous systems of legitimacy and "acceptability" for purposes of reassuring followers and obtaining recruits. To cite but one example, Mary Baker Eddy's Christian Science movement was directed against the pretensions of nineteenth century "scientism" — particularly as exhibited by the medical profession. Use of the word "science" in the name given to the movement served to neutralize its opposition to "legitimate" science. Generally, the emergence of entirely original legitimations — springing, like Pallas Athene, fully-formed from the brow of Jove — is as rare as the wisdom Athene is supposed to represent.

sense the term has been used here, is absent. In other words, follower-ship turns out to be a more inclusive category than does leadership so long as the definition of leadership is restricted to the types enumerated and discussed above. As a result, a number of conventionally accepted connotations of "leadership" can be shown to refer to followership only. Elimination of the gratuitous intellectual ballast clinging to the notion of leadership will free our hands for necessary advances in theory and research hitherto blocked by a plethora of value-laden and obscurantist implications.

The full-scale development of a distinct typology for followership is a task which will not concern us here. Such a typology, in any case, would necessarily be less closely bound to questions of institutionalization and social change than the foregoing typology of leadership. Some of the reasons for this have been alluded to above. Where the very fact of being led constitutes a goal state for potential followers (or, better put, where not being led poses an exigency for these) satisfaction of the goal in and of itself may be of little consequence for social change. What is more, achievement of "follower goals" may occur in such a direct and automatic fashion as virtually to obviate the analytic machinery of Zollschan's institutionalization model. As previously indicated, a person or group of persons satisfying such a need on the part of followers do not necessarily qualify for the appelation of "leader" in the special terminology here presented. An adequate typology of followership, there-fore, would have to take into account elements other than those directly symmetrical with the foregoing leadership typology; namely, (i) ex-igencies which call for leadership by some person for their articulation; and (ii) goals whose effectance calls for leadership. Some of these addi-tional elements are listed below.

The following three classes of instances correspond to a rough break-down of elements that may constitute, singly or in combination, a need for being led without necessarily providing occasions for leadership. Firstly, needs for coordination and guidance in routine interpersonal situations, whether of the *task* or *communal* varieties. Secondly, senti-ments of adulation or aversion. The objects of these sentiments exert influence over followers by inviting approach and, perhaps, imitation in the former case and avoidance or flight in the latter. Thirdly, there is a mixed and varied assortment of personal needs which can only be satisfied in situations where influence or power is exercised by others. Most suitable for illustrative purposes are self-abasing needs for sub-ordination, obedience, and perhaps even punishment. Such needs, though properly described as "personal" may, of course, be widely shared in certain types of societies. We shall try to show how consid-eration of these types of followership can help to purge the subject of some of those gratuitous surplus meanings which have hitherto mired down scientific progress.

(1) *Spheres of Leadership Activity:* For the sake of simplicity we shall apply the generic term "ruler" to all persons who coordinate interpersonal transactions and exchanges whether in associational or communal settings. It is hardly necessary to point out that rulers are not necessarily and always leaders. To be sure, when rulership combines with power or some equally relevant resource, opportunities exist for rulers to take occasions for leadership not easily available to others. For that matter, rulers with power are in a position to thwart the leadership of others. On the other hand, it must be kept in mind that concentration of political power itself creates exigencies and thereby multiplies potential occasions for leadership.

It is obvious that leadership occurs in spheres of thought and action quite distinct from the political sphere and, also, that this can happen even in totalitarian structures of tyranny so long as the sphere in question is insulated from concerns associated with anything resembling political power. The pure type of occasion as combined and emphasized in the person of a particular leader varies — fairly systematically, we believe — with the sphere in which the leadership occurs. The reader is invited to try his or her own hand in the construction of models which fit the effective exercise of leadership in different spheres of thought and action.

(2) *Adulation and Aversion:* In a highly engaging study Orrin Klapp relates sentiments of praise, condemnation and ridicule to general "typing models" existing in a society (9, p. 18) and guiding people positively by imitation or negatively by avoidance. It is difficult to resist the temptation of regarding persons who correspond at least to Klapp's *Hero* (and possibly also *Villain* and even *Fool*) models as being, in some sense at least, leaders. Such usage, however, would debase the heuristic utility of the term. It is only fair to point out that the expressions "leadership" or "leader" appear very rarely in Klapp's book.

Under specifiable conditions, being the subject of adulation (or aversion) can itself give a person a sort of power over others. There are followers who will attempt to make physical contact with "celebrities" or who will run away at the approach of lepers. This alone is insufficient, in our opinion, to justify the characterization of celebrities (or of lepers) as "leaders." Of course, to the extent that a person defines a new type model (or variant of a type model) — either by the example of passive salience leadership or with active intent — he fits perfectly into our foregoing typology of leadership. The same applies to the person who fosters the general acceptance and use of the novel type model or, if you will, its "institutionalization."

(3) *Socio-Cultural "Personal Quirks" and the Abreaction of Affect:* In cleansing the analysis of leadership of its gratuitous charismatic connotations certain matters must be emphasized. On the one hand, leadership often occurs in practice without being recognized as such by fol-

lowers. We suspect that this fact lies at the base of much of the theoretical hocus-pocus perpetrated by the proponents of various forms of sociological holism which talk of impersonal social processes shaping individual fates. Clearly, where leadership occurs without being recognized as such by followers, it is unlikely to elicit abreaction of affect or acquire any charismatic quality.

Conversely, non-leaders may become the object of strong affect by followers for reasons quite extraneous to the analysis presented in this chapter. It is clear that visibly advertised objects of adulation (or even of ambivalent aversion) lend themselves particularly well to such purposes. When, in addition, there exist followers who seek to find (or invest) certain persons with alleged qualities calling for obedience or even worship, conditions for Weberian grand-opera outbursts of charismatic affect are in existence. The personal quirks which characterize such followers we would like to group together under the term *tyrannotropism*. An examination of the types and conditions of tyrannotropism falls beyond the boundaries of this discussion. One would look for its causation in systems of child-rearing prevalent in those social settings in which the characteristic occurs. Here, it suffices to repeat that the adjective "charismatic" is more suitably accompanied by the term "followership" than it is by the term "leadership." Again, it is proper to caution that the institutionalization of systems which foster tyrannotropism in persons, as well as the development of counteracting measures which dissolve such systems of authoritarian or romanticist socialization, call for leadership proper in the precise sense in which the term has been used in our foregoing analysis.

(4) *A Final Backward Look:* The harsh remarks addressed at Max Weber in these pages are not meant to denigrate our indebtedness to him for opening an intellectual cauldron to sociological inspection, the strict analysis of whose contents has defied scholarship for so many decades. We are happy to accept description as Weberian *epigoni* but reluctant to join so many of our colleagues in the guise of Weberian *Nachschlepper!* Our efforts in this chapter have been to provide a recipe for the contents of the Weberian charismatic cauldron. Alternatively viewed, the typology of leadership presented in these pages and the comments on followership which follow them may be called the Leadership Garden of Eden. Here, the elemental forces of symbol formation and societalization have gyred and gambolled for us in unimpeded theoretical purity. If the foregoing theoretical depiction of paradise is kept sharply in mind, expulsion of further examinations of the subject assayed into the cruel and messy world of social reality can be made at least "theoretically" endurable.

## BIBLIOGRAPHY

1. Dexter, Lewis A. "Some Strategic Considerations of Innovating Leadership," in Alvin W. Gouldner (ed.), *Studies in Leadership*. New York: Harper, 1950.

2. Etzioni, Amitai, and Eva Etzioni (eds.), *Social Change*. New York: Basic Books, 1964.

3. Freud, Sigmund. "Group Psychology and the Analysis of the Ego," in *Complete Works*, Vol. 18 (pp. 67-143). London: Hogarth Press, 1955.

4. Gamson, William A. *Power and Discontent*. Homewood: Dorsey Press, 1968.

5. Gottl, Friedrich (later, Friedrich von Gottl-Ottlilienfeld). *Die Herrschaft des Wortes*. Jena, Gustav Fischer, 1901.

6. Hollander, Edwin P. and James W. Julian. "Contemporary Trends in the Analysis of Leadership Processes," *Psychological Bulletin*, Vol. 71 (1969), pp. 387-397.

7. Hutt, William H. *The Theory of Idle Resources*. London: Jonathan Cape, 1939.

8. Jarvie, Ian C. *The Revolution in Anthropology*. Chicago: Henry Regnery (Gateway), 1967.

9. Klapp, Orrin E. *Heroes, Villains, and Fools*. Englewood Cliffs, N.J.: Prentice-Hall (Spectrum), 1962.

10. Lasswell, Harold D. *Politics: Who gets What, When and How*. New York: McGraw-Hill, 1937.

11. Malinowski, Bronislaw. *Magic, Science, and Religion*. Boston: Beacon Press, 1948.

12. Osgood, C. E., and P. H. Tannenbaum. "The Principle of Congruity in the Prediction of Attitude Change," *Psychological Review*, Vol. 62 (1955), pp. 42-44.

13. Redl, Fritz. "Group Emotion and Leadership." *Psychiatry*, Vol. 5 (1942), pp. 573-596.

14. Rokeach, Milton. *Beliefs, Attitudes and Values*. San Francisco: Jossey-Bass, 1969.

15. Rustow, Dankwert A. "The Study of Leadership," in *Philosophers and Kings: Studies in Leadership*. New York: Braziller, 1970.

16. Simmel, Georg. "Secret Societies," in *The Sociology of Georg Simmel*, translated and edited by Kurt H. Wolff. New York: Free Press, 1950.

17. Tolman, Edward C. "A Psychological Model," in Talcott Parsons and Edward A. Shils (eds.), *Toward a General Theory of Action*. New York: Harper (Torchbooks), 1961.

18. Weber, Max. *Economy and Society*, 3 vols. Edited by G. Roth and C. Wittich. New York: Bedminster, 1968.

19. Weber, Max. *On Charisma and Institution Building*, edited by S. N. Eisenstadt. Chicago: University of Chicago Press, 1968.

# 7

*George K. Zollschan*
*and Robert J. Brym*

# A Transconceptualization of Concepts in Sociology of Knowledge and Sociology of Science

Knowledge itself, the beliefs and values that people hold, forms the central theme of sociology, a fact that has prompted Winch to refer to it as "misbegotten epistemology" (54, p. 43). Without engaging in profitless disputes concerning the legitimacy of sociology's conception, it is still useful to ask whether the subject inherently lends itself to scientific investigation in any non-trivial sense. This question gains in importance from the substantial current of opinion in contemporary sociology which denies even pre-scientific status to the field, claiming, instead, that sociology is a special form of *gnosis* or even of *praxis* (16, p. 512). One assumes that the possession of accredited diplomas (or perhaps even of other sociological entrance vouchers) lends to their possessors the right of privileged access to such cerebral activity! When philosophers carp from the sidelines, they merit polite (if not always respectful) attention. A massive loss of scientific nerve in the field itself calls for emergency measures of conceptual clarification. This chapter constitutes such a measure.

Contemporary "radical" and "reflexive" sociology trace their intellectual origin to the work of Karl Mannheim or, more strictly, from Mannheim's generalization of the Marxian-Hegelian anticipation of existentialism. Consequently, Mannheim's sociology must become a serious matter of concern in this discussion. In order to lead up to Mannheim's views it is necessary, first, to discuss the breakdown of traditional epistemology and its supercession by two rival orientations: sociology of knowledge and scientific methodology. Secondly, the transformation of Mannheim's sociology of knowledge in empirical sociological studies, particularly under Robert K. Merton's influence, must receive attention.

Only after clearing the ground and removing the rubbish — "underlabourer" work which Locke attributed to philosophy, will it be possible to propose a new system of categories to investigate sociology of knowledge. In so doing, a distinction will be made between factors determining the authentication of belief and conditions for the production of belief in general, or of any particular belief. Finally, we shall examine the question whether scientific authentication of belief is possible in sociology. A critique of Merton's characterization of sociology of knowledge serves well as a starting point for this investigation.

Merton describes sociology of science as a "subdivision of the sociology of knowledge" and goes on to refer to "that particular kind of knowledge which springs from and returns to controlled experiment or controlled observation." (32, p. 531) Traditional *Wissensoziologie*, he maintains, in common with "interpretations of man and culture which share similar presuppositions,"[1] views "verbalization and ideas . . . as expressive, or derivative, or deceptive . . . [and] functionally related to some substratum." It is thus one of a number of methodologies for unmasking or debunking myths, errors, and rationalizations. Merton attaches great importance to the inclusion of sociology of science under the general rubric of sociology of knowledge, and the corresponding cessation of the latter's "debunking" attitude. "The 'Copernican Revolution' in this area of inquiry", he writes, "consisted in the hypothesis that not only error or illusion or unauthenticated belief but also the discovery of truth was socially (historically) conditioned." Thereby, he feels, reference to factors outside sociology (such as economic, or biological, or emotional substrates of belief) can be avoided.

Merton's claims regarding the recency and revolutionary nature of theories concerning conditions for the emergence or production of both "true" and erroneous belief find little support by the evidence. Only Pareto, on Merton's list of sociologies of knowledge, specifically

---

[1] The quotation, and those immediately following it, are from (32, pp. 458-459). The list of interpretations includes: Ideological analysis, *Wissenssoziologie*, psychoanalysis, Marxism, semanticism, propaganda analysis, and "to some extent" functional analysis. Our argument here is not directly concerned with what Merton calls semanticism and propaganda analysis.

reserves his motivational substratum of *residues* exclusively for the explanation of non-logical conduct, leaving logical conduct in a *sui generis* position requiring no causal explanation.[2] All the other orientations are vitally concerned with social factors conducive to the discovery or establishment of "truth," though, to be sure, all of them also share severe difficulties in pinning down this concept. If, indeed, any revolution of thinking has taken place in this area,[3] then, quite contrary to Merton's argument, it is the transformation of traditional epistemology into theoretical orientations postulating the causal dependence of a given belief on conditions exogenous to this belief and its direct object.[4] For the purposes of this discussion, we shall lump all of these orientations together under the common heading of "sociology of knowledge."[5]

It is not at all clear from Merton's statements why a more inclusive characterization of sociology of knowledge as being concerned also with "authenticated" belief should have any bearing on restricting causes of belief to the sphere of sociology. Nor, for that matter, is it clear why such a restriction should constitute a "Copernican Revolution." But there is a more fundamental criticism of Merton's assertion which will comprise one of the central themes of this discussion: namely, that he places analyses of the causation of authenticated belief squarely within the province of sociology of knowledge. We shall take up a position contrary to the last assertion and argue that analytic clarity can only be attained when sociology of knowledge and sociology of science are treated as distinct areas of investigation. Paradoxically, in emphasizing such a distinction, we hope to reconcile scientific method and sociology of knowledge. Much more important than this, however, is our aim to give a stimulus to the rediscovery of sociology as a scientific adventure.

[2] Actually, when it suits him, Pareto can contradict himself on that score, as for example in proposition 1768 of the *Trattato* (35, p. 1229). Our description, however, corresponds to his avowed theoretical intentions. We are indebted to Anthony Piepe for this information. See also (37).

[3] Alfred Schutz is said to have directed Kurt Wolff's attention to Xenophanes of Colophon and Sextus Empiricus as precursors of sociology of knowledge (55, pp. 577 and 598). Like Merton, however, we confine our discussion to post-Kantian varieties of sociology of knowledge.

[4] The position of ambiguity taken in this discussion on whether the objects of beliefs are signs or denotata is deliberate. For an exposition of some of the special problems associated with different types of objects of belief see (33).

[5] Although astrological theories have been put forward to account for people's "fate" and sunspot theories to explain trade cycles, we are not familiar with explanations of extra-epistemological causation of belief or opinion emanating from fields other than those covered by the behavioural and social sciences. This discussion is limited to historical materialism and psychoanalysis besides sociology proper.

## A Digression on 'Truth': [6]

We have shown that sociology of knowledge, in the broad sense we are using the expression here, is concerned with the causation of belief or opinion by factors extraneous to the "real" or ontological characteristics of the object of belief. It is an historical offshoot of epistemology — the philosophical field concerned with the direct relationship between knowledge and the objects of this knowledge — which it seeks either to supplement or to supplant. Its development is closely connected with changing conceptions regarding the constitution of truth. Indeed, we shall argue that sociology of knowledge appears in the history of ideas precisely at those points where direct access to the objects of knowledge is either regarded as unproblematic or where the very existence of true objects of knowledge, independent of the knower, is denied. A hasty overview of some major themes in the history of Western epistemology is consequently unavoidable, to set the stage for a discussion of the advent of sociology of knowledge.

Every schoolboy knows that Plato attributed to *ideas* a higher reality, of which the actual objects of belief are corrupted or degenerated forms. The true forms are inborn or *anamnesic* in humans, but accessible only indirectly through the practice of philosophy. The difficulty of access to the Platonic heaven of truth was vividly portrayed in the allegory of the cave. Early modern empiricism, culminating in the writings of David Hume, went beyond concern with difficulties of grasping the truth to a measure of doubt in its existence apart from sense impressions. A radical statement of this position might convey an image of the world as an inherently meaningless (or, at least, not necessarily meaningful) bombardment of sense impressions. Truth, if there was such a thing as truth, arose out of the human proclivity to organize and systematize sense impressions; a proclivity greatly facilitated by their apparent tendency to repeat themselves in sequences of definite order.

The Kantian philosophy arose out of the attempt to rescue a transcendental realm of truth from this empiricist onslaught. Truth was transferred by Kant from the Platonic heaven to a noumenal realm "out there," upon which the human understanding impressed the categories of perception and conception, thereby transforming the true forms, or

---

[6] The term "digression" in this context contains a *double entendre*. One of its meanings is that exposition of the history of epistemology is a very subsidiary (though not unnecessary) part of the following discussion. Consequently we are not concerned with exhaustive documentation or with elaborate justification of emphases and interpretations presented under this heading. The work from which the following thumbnail sketches are drawn has been done by Zollschan in connection with research on philosophical traditions influencing Max Weber's thought. The other meaning of the *double entendre* we can safely leave to the reader to divine.

*noumena,* into the empirical phenomena of knowledge. Only in the sphere of morality (and, more generally, of rational human conduct) did Kant allow direct, unmediated, access to the truth; namely, that special kind of truth associated with man's "intelligible" as distinct from "empirical" character.

Karl Popper attaches great importance to what he calls Kant's "activist" — as distinct from the empiricists' "passivist" — theory of knowledge (39, p. 214). In Kant's epistemology, knowledge did not stream into the mind through the senses but was the result of mental activity. The idea of knowledge as a human product, or artifact, or creation, Popper suggests, provided the soil out of which the luxuriant variety of modern sociologies of knowledge could grow. Be that as it may, three members of the post-Kantian generation of epistemologists can legitimately be described as the intellectual parents or grandparents of all currently influential sociologies of knowledge: Schopenhauer, Hegel, and Comte.

From the point of view represented here, Schopenhauer makes perhaps the most radical departure from previous conceptualizations of the truth. While accepting the Kantian distinction between noumena and phenomena, he rejects the idea that noumena lie inertly around us. Instead, he places them in the *Wille.* Wille imbues all of nature; but human actions, in particular, have meaning only if they are understood as willed. The image of truth in Schopenhauer's conception thus becomes transformed from one of forms or stable relations into one of forces and motives. Knowledge is seen as the precipitate of such forces and motives. Hegel, on the other hand, reabsorbs both phenomena and noumena into a unitary realm of *Geist* — an amalgam of reason and reality which unfolds itself in history. Human knowledge is itself but one of the manifestations of Geist. Here also, the traditional image of truth is transformed. It loses its stability and becomes fluid over time, being governed in its evolution by the operation of the dialectic triad. Both of these views may be characterized as "moving staircase" conceptions, to distinguish them from traditional images of truth as quite immutable *sub specie aeternitatis.*[7]

If older epistemological orientations saw truth as stable and supertemporaneous, most of them also conceived it to be notoriously difficult to attain. Comte's positivism, by contrast, is based on the idea of direct access to the truth by the exercise of observation. Observation is not the passive reception of sense impressions as described by the empiricists, but an active seeking of them which leads to "positive" knowledge.[8] We want to characterize this as the "sitting duck" concep-

[7] Wolff (55, p. 571) cites a letter from Karl Mannheim dated April 15, 1946, in which the "moving staircase" image appears.

[8] The meanings attributed to the term "positive" by Comte include the adjectives "certain" and "indubitable " (19, p. 354).

tion of truth, as distinct from the moving staircase images of Hegel and Schopenhauer. Unproblematic as access to positive knowledge is, in Comte's view, the human understanding must undergo a determinate process of evolution before it chooses the proper route to such knowledge. In each area of knowledge the understanding proceeds first through a theological and later through a metaphysical stage before untrammelled positivistic observation comes to hold sway. The pace of evolution in each area of knowledge varies according to specified criteria. This generalization, widely known as the "law of three stages," is the central principle of Comte's social dynamics. Thus, by declaring epistemology to be inherently unproblematical, Comtean positivism transfers the whole problem of knowledge in the arena of "science." It maps the path to positive knowledge of the truth by means of an evolutionist generalization.

While Comte qualifies as an immediate forerunner of sociology of knowledge in his own intellectual tradition,[9] the Schopenhauer-Hegel onslaught on older conceptions of fixed and stable noumenal truth exerted influence on the development of *Wissenssoziologie* primarily through the mediation of Marxist historical materialism (which will concern us later) and Nietzsche's philosophy. Nietzsche extends certain Hegelian and Schopenhauerian ideas in radicalized form and combines them to produce his own theory of knowledge. In Hegelian dialectics contradiction is a manifestation of the "cunning of reason" as it works itself out sequentially over time in the triadic process of thesis, antithesis, and synthesis. Nietzsche synchronizes this process; for him all things are contradictory in themselves. Truth becomes nothing more than error conditioned by existence. At the same time, Schopenhauer's Wille becomes Nietzsche's "Will to Power," of which "Will to Truth" is but a component. Man creates knowledge propelled by his Will to Truth, thus putting meaning into a world which is inherently meaningless. Like God, truth is dead in Nietzsche's philosophy: from the ontological perspective, the objective world is a bottomless abyss of chaos; from the voluntaristic perspective, knowledge is a tissue of lies functional for the expression of the knower's Will to Power.[10] In such a philosophical orientation, classical epistemological questions concerning the relationship between knowledge and its object become quite redundant.

### The Rival Heirs of Epistemology:

For persons active in the rapidly advancing natural sciences in the mid-nineteenth century the job on hand was too rewarding to invite

[9] Since Comte coined the word "sociology" he qualifies, by a head's length at least, for the title of first sociologist of knowledge!

[10] In line with the foregoing characterization of images of truth, a description of Nietzsche's view as the "tightrope" conception of truth may appeal to those familiar with *Also Sprach Zarathustra*.

agonized epistemological speculation. Various adaptations of Comte's naively realistic positivism seemed admirably suited to account for the discoveries being made. Only with the increasing sophistication of explanatory models in later years, and the correspondingly increasing "abstractness" of scientific observation, were non-positivistic formulations regarding scientific knowledge put forward and accepted by the scientific community.[11] But these formulations were "methodological" rather than strictly epistemological in character. That is to say, instead of being concerned with the noumenal or ontological character of objects of knowledge, methodological questions confine themselves to a concern with given items of knowledge themselves, from the point of view of their validity, or authentication, or confirmation.

The transformation of epistemology into modern methodology in the hands of philosophers and practitioners concerned with the natural sciences occurred more or less contemporaneously with the development of sociology of knowledge. Indeed, it may appear something of an historical paradox that sociology of knowledge, seeking the causation of belief extraneously to the ontological nature of the object of belief, should develop just at the time when confidence in the validity of scientific theories appeared increasingly justified. The paradox is recognized as illusory when it is remembered that both methodology and sociology of knowledge reject concern with ontological metaphysics. And it is also worth noting that nearly all sociologies of knowledge are constrained to make some special allowance for the confirmed findings of "exact" science. They do not consider the validity of findings in the natural sciences to be relative to some sociological or psychological perspective, though social and social-psychological factors may be adduced by them for the explanation of conditions under which such findings are made or inhibited. Even Habermas and his followers, who cast contemporary science in the role of mere "technocratic ideology" (48, p. 210) do not deny that standards of "certainty and exactness" (sic.) obtain in the physical sciences; standards attained for reasons, presumably, having to do with methods of testing (or, perhaps, with the nature of the subject matter itself) rather than with the ideology as such. Their critique is aimed at what they consider to be the dire consequences of adopting scientific attitudes rather than at the validity of scientific findings. Nietzsche alone (if we stretch a point and include his views under the heading of sociology of knowledge) found himself able to ignore the triumphant fecundity of the scientific "Will to Truth" and accused scientists of "libidinous eunuchism."[12]

11 Neo-Kantian *construcstivism* (Herman Cohen, Fritz Natorp), *conventionalism* (Mach, Poincaré), as well as Vaihinger's *fictionalism* come to mind. More recently, Bridgeman's *operationism* combines certain positivistic and neo-Kantian features.

12 Actually he uses the phrase to describe asceticism (34, p. 216) but characterizes science as allied with the ascetic ideal a few pages earlier (34, p. 211).

When sociology of knowledge is concerned with extra-scientific knowledge, however, or with knowledge in the social sciences, the situation is quite different. Here, issues of validity and authentication become blurred and acute logical and metaphysical problems arise. Tested facts often give way to self-fulfilling prophecies or to ideational constructions backed up, at best, by circumstantial evidence, and, at worst, by blatantly wish-fulfilling phantasies. In discussing some of these problems, we intend to concentrate our attention first on the theory of Karl Mannheim. We do so in the belief that Mannheim's work portrays, with unusual clarity and candour, most of the difficulties to be found in more recent work in the area. In order to locate Mannheim in his intellectual tradition, it will be useful to give brief illustrations of Marx and Freud, viewed, broadly speaking, as sociologists of knowledge, as well as of the manner in which Max Weber's conceptualization of the subject matter of sociology impinges on sociology of knowledge. Marx and Freud, starting from entirely divergent assumptions, are both specifically concerned with the liberation of a "sense of reality." Truth posed as little of a problem to them as to Comte.[13] They are concerned, instead, with the explanation (and eradication) of historical socio-economic or, respectively, biographical socio-emotional conditions for the existence of obstacles to the attainment of such truth. Weber, on the other hand, saw the issue of truth as so intensely problematical that he found it necessary to develop explanatory models (ideal types) which were deliberately unrealistic.

Mannheim's views are a continuation in the history of ideas, via the mediating influence of the three aforementioned thinkers, of the breakdown of traditional epistemology in the philosophies of Schopenhauer, Hegel, and Nietzsche. The intellectual tradition stemming from Comte has also found resonance; namely, in Durkheim's sociology of knowledge. By way of contrast with the Mannheimian tradition, we will discuss this briefly before proceeding to a discussion of Marx, Freud and Weber.

### Good Intentions on the Road to Mannheim:

The Comtean tradition finds its most distinguished exemplar in the person of Emile Durkheim, who attempted to provide a better methodo-

---

[13] In relation to Marx's views on scientific truth a few additional words seem indicated. Marx's primary notion of scientific truth is, of course, the truth inherent in "scientific socialism" and the emerging proletarian consciousness. This does not, however, negate his acceptance of the validity of findings in the natural sciences. Though he criticizes the natural sciences for their "abstract" orientation and their lack of concern in the human consequences of findings, he does not throw doubt on the findings themselves. See, for example, Bottomore and Rubel's introduction to their selection from his writings (5, p. 73). On the issue of Marx's stand *vis-à-vis* an independently existing realm of nature see footnote 18 below.

logical foundation for a positivist approach to sociology. This was to be achieved by establishing the existence of "social facts" which could truly be equated with material "things" since both were exterior to the person and constraining upon him.[14] But Durkheim goes further than merely attempting to establish the status of social facts as empirical phenomena. The concepts in which we think, he maintains, are part of a vocabulary which we, as individuals, did not create. Consequently, he speaks of a *conscience collective* and, indeed, maintains that "impersonal reason is only another name given to collective thought." (10, p. 494) Durkheim does not intend this position to affect adversely the validity of impersonal reason. On the contrary, the collective experience embodied in the conscience collective is vastly more embracing than any single individual's contact with reality. As someone said later in much the same vein, "forty million Frenchmen cannot be wrong." Durkheim's most radical assertion is that the experience of social life itself actually generates in persons the Kantian categories of thought (10, pp. 488f.). The categories of *time* and *space*, for example, reflect the rhythms and arrangements of social organization.

A corrolary of Durkheim's sociological fundamentalism is that different societies, by virtue of different rhythms and arrangements of their social structures, should generate categorically different types of knowledge. Durkheim, in collaboration with Marcel Mauss, did address himself to this problem as it applies to a variety of simple societies, (12) but the primary emphasis of his orientation is on the cognitive consensus within given societies. From the point of view of the development of a sociology of knowledge concerned with a wider range of problems than those arising from cross-cultural comparisons or the analysis of culture contacts, it can therefore be regarded as a retrogressive step from Marxist historical materialism with which Durkheim was perfectly well acquainted.[15] Marx's theory had related differences in consciousness to differences in the position a person held in the social structure (that is to say, in relation to the means of production) and to interests associated with such differences in social location.

The Marxian point of view is vastly superior for purposes of explaining kinds of intra-societal differences in ideology and belief that sociologists encounter in their observations. What is more, Marx had admitted the category of "false consciousness" into his theory, thereby introducing, however clumsily it was done, an element of sophistication

---

[14] Dunkheim's positivistic approach is announced in (11); his attempts to provide an evidential base for metaphysical organicism are scattered throughout his entire work, but the most explicit statement may be found in (10, pp. 462–496).

[15] Durkheim is at pains to distinguish his position from that of historical materialism on the grounds that *conscience collective* is something more than a "mere epiphenomenon" (10, p. 471).

almost entirely lacking in the Durkheimian conception of a perfect correspondence between conscience collective and "reality." It is hardly surprising, therefore, that Mannheim's sociology of knowledge, intellectually descended as it is from historical materialism, receives greater critical attention today than do Durkheim's views in this area.[16]

Karl Marx accepted from Hegel both the idea of a dialectical flow of history and the conceptual fusion of reality and reason. Instead of characterizing the metaphysical substance of history as Geist, however, Marx wants to found history on a "materialist basis." This phrase has led to a great deal of misunderstanding. We incline to the view that Marx meant by it simply the exclusion of any reference to "forces or agencies beyond those of human beings living and working in society" (5, p. 21). Thus, materialism for Marx is the absence of metaphysics. Metaphysics is to be excluded, moreover, by establishing human praxis or "pro-action" as the prime mover of human existence.[17] In other words, "human reality is totally self-enclosed, having no transcendent domain to which to relate" (45, p. 160). But materialism enters Marx's thinking in another sense as well. The type of pro-action significant in the shaping of human existence is economic activity or "material" production. It is in connection with material production and more particularly, with interests arising out of one's position of domination or subjection in relationships of production, that consciousness arises.

Marx conceives of modes of production, relations of production, and the resulting class structure of society, as the true social reality. All institutional forms not directly involved in the above, as well as ideational productions (forms of consciousness) are superstructures or epiphenomena of this "realm of necessity."[18] At any period in history the ruling ideas are those of the dominant class; members of the subjected class who accept these ideas are afflicted with false consciousness. The converse relationship, however, does not hold true. For example, bourgeois philosophers (like Marx himself) who embrace the ideation springing out of the proletarian predicament do not suffer from false consciousness. In part this may be because Marx appears to attribute an increment of truth to the ideas of the subjected but ascendant class at any time. Certainly, this is especially the case for proletarian con-

---

[16] The ethnological work of Durkheim's school, represented by Granet, Levy-Bruhl, Halbwachs, and others, may be exempted from this stricture.

[17] *Praxis* is usually translated as "social practice." We find it more evocative of Marx's intentions to adopt Allport's felicitous term "pro-action" for this purpose.

[18] Nature also constitutes a realm of necessity. Thus Marx admits that freedom must always remain limited by the necessities of human metabolism (39, p. 103). This lends strength to Rothenstreich's assertion that the "reality" created by *praxis* in Marx's theory is the reality of history and society only, and not natural reality (45, p. 50).

sciousness, since the advent of the realm of freedom and the attendant disappearance of classes is to be brought about by the apocalyptic proletarian revolution. If the realm of freedom is also one of true consciousness, and Marx clearly believes this to be the case, proletarian consciousness is *ipso facto* the matrix of true consciousness.

Marx stresses the predicament of a person with regard to his access to the means of production as fundamentally determinative of that person's interests and, therefore, also of his ideation. Freud, by contrast, sees ideation as the precipitate of delays in the gratification of biological drives (somatic excitations). For purposes of this discussion, he may be placed in the voluntaristic tradition stemming from Schopenhauer and continuing through Nietzsche.[19] The absence of a drive object in "primary process" thinking leads to hallucination of (or, in a later stage of psychic development, phantasy about) the gratifying object; a sequence of events Freud calls "wish-fulfillment." Against this, Freud sets a "secondary process" model of cognition — the "reality principle." Here, the delay in gratification has become "structuralized" in the form of cognition, and "detour activity," in the sense of search for satisfying objects, replaces primitive wish-fulfillment ideation. Reality is therefore viewed by Freud as the realm in which drive objects (potential gratifications) as well as painful excitations and frustrations are located. Cognition obeying the reality principle provides a sort of map for the conceptual location of such gratification and frustration (56; also 43). It is interesting to note that Nietzsche's conception of Will to Truth never gets beyond Freud's primary process model.

Freud stresses emphatically that human ideation contains elements both of primary and secondary process thinking.[20] In any given area of ideation, a person may remain fixated at the primary process level or regress to it. In addition, ideation has three states: conscious, preconscious, and unconscious. Preconscious ideation differs from conscious simply in that the latter involves focused attention. Unconscious ideation also exists, however, and may be inferred from specifiable distortions of affect and behaviour. Much of Freud's work was concerned with the mechanism of "repression" whereby segments of reality, as well as inner emotional states, are either not allowed or able to enter consciousness in the first place (primary repression) or actually expelled from consciousness after having been the subject of secondary process cognition. Psychoanalytic therapy, roughly speaking, is concerned with

[19] Freud did not proclaim himself to be a member of this tradition and it does not really matter for purposes of our argument whether his brand of voluntarism was arrived at independently. There is some circumstantial evidence that Nietzschean influences may have reached him through his contact with Georg Groddeck and Lou Andreas-Salome.

[20] At least, in the case of individuals past infancy who are not severely psychotic. Infants and severe psychotics are limited to primary process cognition.

the maximal extension of the ideational realm available to a person's consciousness, and the consequent extension of rational control over behaviour.

Freud's theory may safely be described as a sociology of knowledge as much as a psychology of cognition since, in his view, the development of the psyche occurs primarily in familial and other social settings. Psycho-analytic therapy, also, cannot be described other than as a social transaction. It operates primarily by the elucidation of "transference" to the therapist of attitudes and affects held by a patient toward significant social objects. It is a matter of doubt, on the other hand, whether the *verstehende* sociology of Max Weber properly qualifies for description as a sociology of knowledge at all, at least in the sense in which we have been using the expression; namely, as a theory explaining beliefs by reference conditions lying outside the objects of these beliefs. Weber's interest does not lie primarily in explanation of the causation of ideologies and belief systems.[21] Rather, he tends to take these as independent variables and to trace their consequences on the constitution of social structures and on the occurrence of social changes. None the less, the role of knowledge or belief is so central to Weber's sociology that his influence on Mannheim, and on the contemporary sociology of knowledge in general, can hardly be overrated.

A central concept in Weber's sociology is "social action." Action he sees as social in as far as it takes the behaviour of others into meaningful account and is directed thereby. The element of orientation to the behaviour of others, which Weber sees as essential in characterizing distinctively *social* action, implies also that actors develop an understanding of the "meaning" of the actions of others with whom they enter into social relations. Society, therefore, constitutes an arena in which a good part of the show consists in the development and exercise of reciprocal understanding of motives or meanings; of ways in which given sequences of behaviour "make sense." Participation in social process is tantamount to an exercise of the understanding of motivated action — one's own and that of others. At the same time,

[21] Weber's work does contain hints interpreted by a number of commentators as foreshadowing sociology of knowledge. The most famous of these (50, p. 249) comments on the "decided propensity of Protestant asceticism for empiricism, rationalized on a mathematical basis . . .". More direct is a statement in which he writes of the exclusive interest in social criticism and social ethics in classical Greece after Socrates as an obstacle to the development of the modern type of natural science. This interest, moreover, he describes as "socially conditioned" (51, p. 147). The thesis of a relationship between asceticism and science has a prior history, as footnote 12 above has already indicated. Merton's later development of this thesis (32, pp. 574–606) is hotly disputed by Feuer (13). Weber's personal reactions to Mannheim's sociology of knowledge would, probably, not have been too different from the comments made by von Schelting in his critique (47, pp. 310-311).

according to Weber, sociological explanation has precisely this understanding of motivated action as one of its principal aims (hence the term *verstehende soziologie*). It is as though the practice of sociological analysis were a heightened form of social participation!

Explanations which make an action intelligible in the normal course of everyday life, Weber considers to be "adequate on the level of meaning." Sociological analysis, however, cannot be satisfied with this kind of commonsense explanation or rationalization of action in terms of generally understood and accepted motives; it must press for "causal adequacy." In a causally adequate explanation, adequacy is measured not only by the explanation's intelligibility at face value but also by the degree to which it correctly apprehends the causal connection between motives and observable action (49, pp. 276-283). Weber quite clearly wishes causal adequacy to refer to the scientist's critical attitude. He is not entirely convincing, however, when he tries to adduce criteria for the "correct" apprehension of such causal connections.

Weber believes that raw social reality presents itself to the sociological observer as a chaotic stream of isolated events of endless variety and inexhaustible number. The only way to handle this overpowering wealth of raw sociological observations is by the exercise of selectivity in what is to be explained; selectivity of problems and of strategic parameters of analysis. Selectivity is made possible by the fact that social scientists approach the buzzing hive of social reality with values of their own. These values lend interest and significance to certain aspects of the whole.[22] Once the problems and parameters have been selected in line with the scientist's value orientation, however, the sociological explanation itself must be value-free; bound only by the norms of logical method (49, pp. 177–183).

### The Resurrection of the 'Geist':

Mannheim's conception of the subject matter of sociology is quite similar to Max Weber's. Briefly put, Mannheim's argument is that the knowledge (and particularly the political and social knowledge) of persons is tied to the special perspectives associated with their social ("existential") locations. Existentially bound perspectives play for Mannheim the role that meaningful actions take in Weber's sociology. Just as Weber attempts to supercede explanations merely adequate on the level of meaning by causally adequate explanations, so sociology of knowledge is to overcome the limitations of social perspectives by the very act of becoming aware of them. Mannheim describes Weber's

[22] There is no real logical or methodological ground why selection should not occur, say, by chance or convenience. There is also a question as to whether evaluations based on heuristic considerations solely would qualify as *wertbeziehung*. Weber's exclusive emphasis on this criterion can be traced to Rickert's influence (44).

proposal concerning the value oriented selection of the subject of investigation followed by value-free attribution of causal adequacy, as an attempt to discover and analyze the "social equation" present in every view of social events (by analogy, presumably, with the "personal equation" found in observations made by the natural sciences). By contrast to the "purely formalizing knowledge" obtainable by taking such social equations into account, Mannheim proposes "dynamic intellectual meditation" as the *via regia* into an understanding of the essentials of historical and political truth. (27, p. 189)

What he means by this can best be elucidated by comparison with Freudian therapy. Mannheim takes issue with what he considers to be the Freudian emphasis on human thoughts as distortions. He does, however, accept the idea of unconscious motivation in thinking. Unlike Freud he sees this as situational rather than drive motivation. Bringing unconscious motives under conscious control is, indeed, the central purpose of his method. Much as successful Freudian therapy changes the patient's behaviour by increasing the range of conscious control, so sociology of knowledge is more than merely a description of how certain views spring from certain milieux. It is a self-correcting critique of one's own special perspective (27, pp. 47 and 258; also 28, p. 218).[23]

Mannheim readily acknowledges Marxism as the *fons et origo* of his central idea, but is critical of what he takes to be its primary concern with revealing "errors" of thinking springing from the interest position of its opponents. The thought process of every group, not just of groups one happens to oppose, Mannheim maintains, is *seinsverbunden* — bound to its special conditions of social existence. Furthermore, social class membership is not necessarily the only existential base for perspectives of knowledge. Perspectives and the actions associated with such perspectives should not, therefore, be viewed as erroneous or distorted. They are not epiphenomena of a more basic reality but are themselves the very phenomena of historical and social process. The practice and propagation of sociology of knowledge, by analyzing special perspectives, widens and therefore changes them (27, p. 285). Since, moreover, these perspectives are themselves the essential substance of history, sociology of knowledge also acts as an instrument of social change. Perspectivism may thus be regarded as a dedogmatized, generalized form of the Marxist conception of class consciousness.

On the face of it, Mannheim's stress on widening perspectives is innocuous enough. Gaining insight into the perspectives of others (or, for that matter, one's own in relation to others) by reference to the social condi-

[23] Actually, Mannheim's views resemble Nietsche's more than they do Freud's. Nietzsche had considered "objectivity to be the state in which one had one's inclinations for or against something under control" (20, p. 157; Zollschan's translation).

tions from which such perspectives spring is, after all, but one step beyond "seeing the other fellow's point of view" and who could object to that? Who, furthermore, would seriously dispute the contention that the acquisition of such insight broadens the personal perspective of anyone who gains it? The problem glossed over by this is that of the correct attribution of a particular existential base to a given perspective. Mannheim constantly assumes that true observation of perspectives and the social (existential) bases from which they allegedly spring — not to speak of the nature of the connection between these two classes of phenomena — is directly given to the observer. If one questions or denies direct observational access to such knowledge, and in the absence of some demonstratedly reliable technique for making such observations correctly, the entire argument bcomes highly problematic. How is one to tell that a person's "awareness" of existentially based perspectives is not simply a phantasy or a Freudian projection? Mannheim's avoidance of this problem is closely related to the general methodological question of the location of referents for any of his assertions. His rejection as "a disruptive and unjustifiable notion" of the view that there is a "sphere of truth in itself" (27, p. 308) does not rally scrve to exempt him from the requirement of specifying realms of some kind of "reality" with respect to which his assertions are made. Four such realms may be discerned in his work.

Firstly, there are the realities associated with the "exact sciences" (as also with the "purely formalizing" types of sociological knowledge such as Weberian ideal types or classical economic thcory). Mannheim does not meddle with scientific findings or formal systems in his sociology of knowledge. He contents himself by saying that the "model of modern mathematical natural science cannot be regarded appropriate for knowledge as a whole," and with this statement dismisses the kinds of knowledge conforming with this model from his consideration.[24] Secondly, there are the empirical conditions of social existence from which the various perspectives of knowledge are supposed to spring. Mannheim shows great virtuosity in developing historical vignettes to illustrate his contention regarding the existential determination of knowledge. He does not, however, examine critically the exact conditions under which specific sets of circumstances will give rise to specifiable beliefs.[25] Mannheim introduces the third sphere of reality in connection with a discussion of false consciousness.

[24] He does try to suggest, however, that scientific observations are subject to the same relativity of perspectives as exist in the social sphere. Thus, he cites with approbation Westphal's primitive operationalism and Heisenberg's indeterminacy principle (27, pp. 166 and 305).

[25] Merton (32, pp. 489-502) presents a painstaking analysis of the various "connectives of knowledge and society" advanced by Mannheim. This reveals a farrago of unintegrated and unexamined assumptions.

Though he rejects this concept as applicable to the perspective of an opponent, he wants to retain it for circumstances in which the perspective prevents "man from adjusting himself at that historical stage" (27, p. 95). One of the examples he gives for this kind of maladjustment is the ecclesiastical prohibition of usury "in the period of rising capitalism." The question arises: is the period of rising capitalism itself a phenomenon composed purely of changing perspectives or does it contain additional elements exterior to (and, perhaps, even constraining upon) the realm of knowledge itself? The same question applies also to the existential conditions under which a perspective arises. Are these conditions themselves entirely composed of previously existing perspectives, and the actions arising from these perspectives? Mannheim never poses these questions frontally and thus maintains a position of ambiguity with respect to their implied answers.

Some clues to his assumptions concerning the existence of a reality outside the varied realm of cognitive perspectives may, however, be gleaned from consideration of his fourth realm of reality. This consists of the "synthesis from the most comprehensive . . . point of view of the partial perspectives;" a reality one may progressively approach by the exercise of dynamic intellectual meditation (27, p. 189). Free floating intellectuals, by virtue of their loose attachment to any particular social position, can overcome the limitations of special perspectives more easily than others and thus, gain privileged access to this sphere of reality. Mannheim considers this fourth sphere of reality — the sphere revealed by his own explorations — as the most vital. The importance he attaches to this trans-perspectival concept of truth makes it likely that he would also prefer the realities of existential location and historical stage to lie within its wider, "synthetic," confines.

It is unnecessary to elaborate on the well-worn criticisms of Mannheim's position: that *ad hominem* argumentation rather than reasoned criticism of the content of assertions should be viewed as the road to the attainment of understanding. Secondly, that the nearest approximation to truth should be a synthesis of partial truths and even of some downright lies as well (as in the case of perspectives maladapted to their historical stage).[26] Also, that contrary to Mannheim's assumptions, many persons occupy several positions (often with wildly varied associated perspectives). Finally, that, the alleged lack of attachment of many intellectuals to specifiable social locations is highly questionable. What we want to stress, despite Mannheim's occasional professions to the

---

[26] The three blind men of fable, confronted by an elephant, who pereceive it from their respective "perspectives" as a tree, a wall, and a suspended rope, will not necessarily arrive at the (elephantine) truth if they attempt to widen their perspective by comparing their observations. The kind of "free floating" that takes the perspectives of the others into account is in no way equivalent to an experimental investigation of the beast's contours.

contrary, is his total lack of interest in empirical confirmation. Sociology of knowledge for him simply is not a research field. It is a method of trans-empirical *gnosis* through which, by laying bare alleged existential preconditions of ideation, users of the method become possessed of a kind of stupefied metaphysical "awareness" of essential political and social truth. Additionally, it is a field of application — an active intervention into historical process — since states of awareness are themselves constitutive of this process. Consequently, the truth of history is mutable. The practice of sociology of knowledge assures not only that one is "tuned in" to this shifting truth, but that one is active in changing it. Perhaps the clearest defining characteristic held in common by various shades of contemporary radical sociologists consists in their emulation of Mannheim's last-mentioned view.

### The Idea of a Sociology of Knowledge:

Merton's paradigm for the sociology of knowledge, developed originally as a framework from the classification of ideas in this area, serves equally well as a set of questions calling for empirical sociological research. In so doing, it departs from the emphasis on intuitive insight and the larger issues of "historical meaning" inherent in Mannheim's approach and stresses, instead, the issue of validation. The questions posed by the paradigm concern the exact location of the existential bases for mental production; the precise specification of the types of mental production to be analyzed; the connecting relationship between existential bases and mental productions; and the "functions" imputed by the researcher to these existentially based mental productions (32, pp. 460-461).

In fact, a vast accumulation of empirical findings at least tangential to the concerns of sociology of knowledge as outlined by Merton's paradigm has become available. "Existential bases" such as rural-urban location, socio-economic status, position in organizations, and even experiences of rearing in childhood, have been statistically correlated with political preferences, racial attitudes, and opinions on virtually every conceivable topic. Enlightening as this mass of research has sometimes been in other respects, its impact upon the development of an empirically based sociology of knowledge along the lines of Merton's implied program has been disappointing. No matter how much information on the social conditions of various specified populations is made available, contemporary social and political events continue to take the sociologist by surprise. Inferences drawn from the reliably established correlations of today are overthrown by the events of tomorrow.

The spectacle of British dockworkers, who normally express left-wing views, demonstrating in favour of a racialist speech by a reactionary right-wing politician may not any more cause bafflement in sociological ranks (25). But the explanations proffered for this kind of event do not rest upon either of the types of causation suggested by Mannheim: namely, changes in the dockworkers' social conditions or, for that matter, a widening of their perspectives through the practice of dynamic intellectual meditation. Similarly, the transmogrification of American college students from the inarticulate philistine sheep of the 1950s into the vanguard (chronologically speaking, at least) of the international adolescent revolution of articulate philistine sheep of the 1960s and early 1970s, is not matched by equally startling changes in the conditions of their social existence. Though many intellectuals would have welcomed student activism in the quiet years, and some actively called for it, none was able to produce anything remotely resembling a prediction of later years. The suggestion that student radicals are "babies who were picked up — they expect their demands to be met quickly,"[27] ingenious as it is, depends upon the questionable assumption that permissive child-rearing (and we see no objection to letting this stand as an "existential base") began just precisely at the time these people were born. Hastily manufactured *post hoc* explanations, such as the above, characterize the typical stance of sociologists of knowledge when confronted with some unanticipated change in ideology or opinion.

Kurt Wolff, contrasting the kind of empirical research here described with Mannheim's orientation, suggests that the former suffers from "social nominalism" as against the "social realism" of the latter's views as expressed in *Ideology and Utopia*.[28] It is adherence to social nominalism which makes work in the area less than "adequate to the subject matter of sociology and to the historical occasion" (55, p. 591), or in other words, a *nicht wissenswerte Wissenschaft*. The point of view represented in this chapter, by contrast, cannot accept the central premise of Hegelian "realism;" namely, its self-assumed privileged access to the "truth." Sociology of knowledge, if it is to be an empirical field of investigation, rather than the machinery of rationalization or intellectual legitimation of some ideology or other, requires a theory providing systematic answers to the questions posed by Merton. Neither Mannheim nor Merton himself present such a theory.

Indeed, it is remarkable how impoverished sociological theory has been concerning the precise connection between existential conditions and the production of beliefs and ideologies. Since the writings of Marx and Nietzsche, emphasis has universally been placed on the *utility*

[27] Attributed to David Riesman in a newspaper article (8, p. 10).
[28] See (55, p. 581). Karl Popper has previously referred to these orientations respectively as "methodological individualism" and "methodological collectivism" (40, pp. 148-149).

of a particular ideology or belief for the believer. Theories which stress *interests,* for example, see these as unambiguously inherent in given social circumstances. On the other hand, theories stressing the *functions* of belief or opinion systematically ignore causation and look instead at the consequences of the belief; especially consequences of the maintenance of a desired (or abstractly "desirable") state of affairs.[29] The time is overripe for going beyond such facile and superficial approaches and developing a theory with some potential, at least, for doing justice to the complexities surrounding the determination of certain kinds of attitude and belief. Zollschan's theoretical model of institutionalization lends itself for use as an instrument for the elucidation of variables useful in the construction of such a theory (57, pp. 89-97 and chapter 4 of this volume). The theoretical model describes the conditions under which action will take place. It begins by postulating an initial state of behavioral inertia or behavioral routine, which is disturbed by the occurrence of an exigency. Since the focus of attention is on what Max Weber calls "meaningful action" rather than on merely reactive behaviour, the first step in the theory concerns the articulation of ideas regarding the nature of the exigency and the goals of action for meeting it. The threshold of articulation is conceptualized as a function of three variables: the salience of the exigency, the justifiability of the potential articulation, and the availability of ideational resources to give it form (that is to say, its "specifiability"). Whether action is triggered as a result of a particular articulation is subjected to a separate, though parallel, analysis. Here the variables are the relative valency of the articulated goal, its legitimacy, and the availability of means for attaining it.

Essentially, the articulation of ideas and of goals of action is described by the theory as a creative act. Ideas and ideologies communicated by others can, however, be seized upon as providing the *mot juste* for one's personal exigency. An interest is conceptualized as an articulated goal which is perceived by the actor as coming into conflict with the goals of others (53, p. 131).

In the light of this theory, the knowledge, or belief, or ideology, of a person consists of his more or less systematic store of articulations. A new articulation must draw on his "horizon of expectations."[30] Equally,

[29] Psychological learning theory must be considered as a continuation of traditional epistemology of the empiricist variety, rather than as a theory concerned with "existential" determinants of knowledge. Since, under the assumptions of learning theory, belief (if its existence is not denied outright) corresponds to a species of "response" and the object of belief to "stimulus," psychological behaviourism may accurately be described as concerned with direct relationships between belief and its objects.

[30] This is a phrase Zollschan owes to Sir Karl Popper's lectures given at the London School of Economics in 1949 or 1950.

inhibitions, avoidances, and generalized preferences of cognitive, or moral, or aesthetic style have been called the "horizon of justifications." Exigencies themselves leave a residue of potential for new articulation. Some require continuous activity over time; others cannot be stilled, since goals articulated to meet them are unachievable or clash with other goals. The resulting chronic state of subliminal irritation is described as an equilibrium of tensions (or excitations, or deprivations). It follows from the postulation of such an equilibrium of tensions that a new articulation may result in new action where no new exigency can easily be demonstrated.

The articulation of ideas and of goals of action has hitherto been referred to as a creative act. This creative act, however, does not proceed *ex nihilo*. If the parameters proposed by Zollschan are to match empirical processes, each of them must, in some sense, be "existentially" located. The innovativeness of any articulation, the creativeness of any act is found in the relationship between the situation in which the exigency is met and the "situation" to which articulation is addressed. An examination of the existential location of exigencies, as well as of the coordinates of articulation and action, brings the problems inherent in the idea of a sociology of knowledge sharply into focus.

### The Transconceptualization of Existential Bases:

The notion that society is an interplay — a sort of "dialectical" process — in which men are both products and agents is by no means a new one. Marx's emphatic statement in the *Theses on Feuerbach* that *praxis* creates existence (31, pp. 107-109) is counterposed by his own stress in other places on the effects of established systems of production on human activity (29). More recently, Berger and Pullberg (3) and Berger and Luckmann (4) have used a similar notion in analyses of structures of meaning stressing that ". . . it is important to emphasize that the relationship between man, the producer, and the social world, his product, is and remains a dialectical one . . . The product acts back on the producer" (4, p. 61). Similarly, Sartre has characterized the use of the "progressive-regressive" method of analysis based on the assumption that man is defined *dans son projet* (46, p. 60). Explanation for the striving that underlies such projection into the world is traced ("regressively") to the human free will. In so far as constraints exist on free will, however, the philosopher must follow the movement of the striving ("progressively") through its possibilities. Sartre's proposal for a method is suggestive; but it remains a mere aspiration "as long as we are not given some instance of how it is done" (24, p. 298).

In reviewing these notions of processes in which man produces society and society produces man, it would seem advisable to differentiate two moments in this interaction process: the moment which views man as agent we shall term the *pro-active moment;* the moment which views man as product may be termed the *determining moment.* Zollschan's theoretical model, originally developed to explain social change and institutionalization, has previously stressed the pro-active moment. Consideration of existential conditions and constraints extend the model's scope to embrace categories pertaining to the determining moment.

This brief glimpse at Zollschan's model suffices to indicate, in broad outline, the various points at which "determination" of ideation and of social action occur. Quite clearly, the expression "existential base," when used in terms of this model, describes a number of highly diverse elements. With respect to specifiable kinds of exigencies, the existential base refers to loci of exposure to the experience of these exigencies. With respect to articulation, it refers to available means for specifying and justifying a need as well as to blockages and constraints which militate against the occurrence of justification and specification. Facilitations and constraints on action (as these present themselves to the persons in question) can equally be construed as existential bases. A commonly held (but not necessarily complete) classification of existential spheres in which exigencies may be experienced might enumerate these as: (1) The Organism; (2) The Material Environment, both natural and constructed; (3) The Age Distribution of the population in the territory under consideration; (4) Social Relations, including patterns of identification with others and with collectivities; (5) Patterns of Symbols, including identifications with (or cathexis to) symbols; (6) Levels and Types of Technology. Thus, in the organismic sphere, factors such as age, sex, health, and other elements of physical constitution both differentiate individuals within a population and determine the chances of experiencing exigencies. In the material environment, geographical location, natural disaster and localised types of environmental pollution play the same part, and so forth. Such a picture of existential spheres in which "exigency chances" are differentially distributed is helpful only in first approximation. For instance, when examining any given person who experiences an exigency, these spheres might be extremely difficult to separate. This is not to say that no exigencies are connected with a particular existential sphere in a direct and uncomplicated way. Some kinds of physical illness or natural disaster provide examples of direct connection. Even in simple cases such as these, however, there might exist complicating elements. Certain types of physical illness are related to occupational activities or even geographical locations.[31] Exposure to regularly recurrent natural disasters also, may have some connection with economic status and edu-

---

[31] Silicosis among coal-miners, duodenal ulcers among industrial executives, and arthritis in temperate, humid climates spring to mind as obvious examples.

cational level. Business executives do not normally build their villas on the slopes of Mount Vesuvius.

When one turns to the social, symbolic and technological spheres, the complication of associating particular exigencies with particular existential bases becomes very much greater. Thus, the experience of being "unemployed" (which is likely to pose an exigency for at least those persons in industrial societies who are accustomed to "gainful employment") may involve the overlap of a number of spheres. Besides economic cycles (a special sub-species of social relations in general) demographic changes or technological changes may increase competition for a given type of employment or render the associated skills obsolete. Similarly, exigencies underlying membership in the Women's Liberation Movement are "organismic" only in the most trivial sense. They have, rather, to do with the nature of the relations between men and women as institutionalized in a particular society, or stratum of society; both, as these are formally experienced in types of legal and occupational discrimination and, informally, in the general quality of typical encounters between individual men and women.

In light of the complexities to which we have referred, it seems advisable to redefine the existential spheres in which exigencies are experienced so as to align them more closely with the phenomenological world of those liable to exposure to exigencies. It is worth noting that such analytically reconstructed existential spheres are not, in any way, less accessible to empirical investigation than the previously enumerated, conventionally adopted ones. Let us characterize those of them which affect exigencies specifically as follows: (1) A state of environmental constancy where "environment" is either external or organic. This includes elements such as standards of material consumption, adjustment to climate, level of physical functioning, and so forth; (2) A sense of identity with specifiable levels of self-respect, guilt, shame, and so forth; (3) A level of sexual, affective, or cooperative response from others in the immediate social circles in which the person of reference moves. This sphere includes also elements such as "adequate privacy" or "social isolation;" (4) The specifiability or determinacy of responses from others outside immediate social circles; (5) Distributive justice — the legitimacy of the distribution of "authority," "rewards," "advantages," from the perspective of the person of reference; (6) The overall coherence or "sense" of life as a system of experience. An exigency may arise as a result of an indigenous (or "immanent") change in any of these spheres or because of exposure to alternatives.

The existence of a discrepancy between "what is" and "what ought to be" in any of these spheres requires articulation if it is to give rise to novel ideation. It is not necessary, of course, for all those exposed to an exigency to be capable of articulating it. Acceptance of another's articulation is a sufficient condition. An alternative view is that the articulation of an exigency by another may be construed as the exposure to an articulation itself constitutive of the exigency. It is heuristically useful, however, to assume that exigencies are experienced in the absence of articulation. Postulating independent experience of such inarticulate exigencies can serve to explain various psychiatric symptoms (58; also 56). For example, in conversion hysteria paralysis of various limbs may be interpreted as a kind of "body language" in which the ideationally inarticulate exigency is "dysfunctionally" articulated.

The salience of the exigency is a measure of the phenomenological distance between "what is" and "what ought to be;" in other words, it is a measure of the discrepancy itself for the individual in a given state which constitutes the exigency. The other elements of articulation — justification and specification — like an exigency itself, can be construed as being dependent on existential spheres. Specification depends upon the existence of a symbolic medium or vehicle for its expression. It thus depends, in an industrial society, on such elements as type and amount of education, restricted or elaborated linguistic code (2, pp. 271-276) current access to relevant information or to practitioners skilled in the articulation of exigencies generated in particular spheres,[32] and even, let it not be entirely forgotten, elements to do with the inventiveness or creativity of the articulator. Educational experience, elaborated linguistic codes, and cognitive inventiveness are, of course, differentially distributed in any population. So, for that matter, are the "means of justification," although these are more subtly difficult to locate in existential spheres. Justification (or counter-justification) is related to repressions and inhibitions, as well as to the deepest personal and collective identifications, acquired during a person's life history. Its principal foci have to do with such elements as authority, tradition, aggression and sex.

Given the occurrence of an exigency and its articulation as a need, the elaboration or selection of goals of action also exists within determining spheres. Application requires knowledge (or access to knowledge) of appropriate actions and technical means for achieving a goal. Paul Revere's ride was "caused," in one sense, by a threatening invasion of British troops. In another sense, it was "determined" by the availability of domesticated horses and the absence of wireless telegraphy. Successful legitimation of a goal, similarly, presupposes that members of the "target population" for legitimations (persons whose permission, co-

[32] Examples of such practioners in a contemporary society roughly corresponding to the spheres enumerated above might be: (1) physicians; (2) psychiatrists; (3) marriage counselors; (4) language teachers for recent immigrants, ombudsmen, social workers; (5) lawyers, politicians; and finally (6) clergy or charismatic prophets.

operation, or adherence is sought) hold values which could support the goal; or that they hold values which can be turned and elaborated in such a way that it is likely that they would support it.

Valence, which measures the priority of a goal, or the "opportunity cost" in relation to other goals, is a derivative from other processes in the schema. With the exception of a special instance to be discussed below, it cannot boast of an existential sphere to call entirely its own. Instead, it reflects both competing goals and the salience of the originating exigency as this becomes refracted through articulation. The clarity and precision of the articulated need as well as subjective possibilities of attaining goals associated with the need, all enter into the determination of valence. The special instance in which valence associates with a particular existential sphere is related to the extent to which a need is experienced as *urgent*. Indeed, urgency can suitably be characterized as a sub-class of valence where a deadline exists for the person. While there are certainly "objective" instances of urgent needs in people's lives (that is to say, needs which are experienced as urgent by the overwhelming majority of adult persons in all societies) people do vary, both individually and "cross-culturally" or "cross-historically," in their "urgency thresholds." Psychologists commonly refer to such thresholds as degrees of "impulse control" or "frustration tolerance." Freud, unerringly, saw the paradigm for urgency thresholds in the universal human problem of sphincter control. Quite clearly, rationality like continence, depends upon the existence of urgency thresholds. Urgent actions are a more direct reflection of the salience of the originating exigency (in this case to be called "emergency") than generally valent actions. Urgent actions may occur where activity is not restrained to await appropriate articulation or to consider "costs".

It is conceivable, though no systematic research exists on the subject as yet, that different urgency thresholds exist in any given person with respect to different types of exigencies. Be that as it may, the distribution of urgency thresholds (and, perhaps, special types of urgency thresholds) in a relevant population at a given time, constitutes yet another existential sphere which ought to be taken into consideration by an adequate sociology of knowledge.[33]

It can readily be seen, therefore, that the bridge connecting an

---

[33] To cite but one example where distribution of urgency thresholds in a population might affect the course of social change, we propose the hypothesis that adolescents have a lower urgency threshold than adults. The special conditions under which such a hypothesis holds or not probably deserve investigation. Granting the hypothesis (for the sake of the argument, without qualification), it could lead to certain predictions regarding "revolutionary potential" in a country. Where a steeply rising birthrate produces a high proportion of adolescents, the chances of radical or revolutionary social movements gaining large numbers of adherents is enhanced.

existential base with a given item of ideation is a structure characterized by a degree of complexity merging upon the arabesque. Separate existential spheres exist for the experience of exigencies, for their specification and justification as needs and, finally, for application, legitimation and the threshold of urgency. If the parameters we have proposed correspond with any degree of faithfulness to empirical processes, any assumption of a simple unilateral relationship between a unitary existential base and associated mental productions has to be abandoned. Yet, relinquishing this fundamentally preposterous notion turns out to be a gain for the sociology of knowledge rather than a loss. What is lost is an illusion; gained is a system of parameters which lend themselves (at least in principle) to empirical investigation.

The central paradox of previous sociology of knowledge is bound up with the issue of ideational and ideological novelty. Quite simply, if an idea is predictable, be it from the existential base or from any other kind of information, then it cannot be a novel idea. This paradox is avoided in our formulation which, since it involves a multivariate, open system, specifies parameters yet raises no false hopes regarding the possibility of predicting the content of ideas. Every historical situation differs from other historical situations, at least in some respects. We contend that every historical situation exhibits a unique "effective blend" of existential factors which shape the eventuating idea system. What our formulation does offer is a program of research and a system of categories for the classification and explanation of existential spheres.

To those who would argue that the program of research implied by the foregoing enumeration of various existential spheres is inappropriate in the light of limitations in the current state of social research technique, we would answer with Kaplan's parable of the *drunkard's search:* "There is a story of a drunkard searching under the street lamp for his house key, which he had dropped some distance away. Asked why he didn't look where he had dropped it, he replied, 'it's lighter here'!"[34] It is the proper task of theory to guide research where to look for keys to its riddles.

## A Touchstone for Experience

Newton wrote the *Principia* while home on the farm during an outbreak of the Plague in Cambridge. Though an intriguing topic for speculation, the exact relationship between Newton's absence from his place of employment and this outburst of scientific creativity remains

[34] Kaplan uses this example to defend "logic in use" against the incomparably more elegant, precise, and powerful "reconstructed logic" of the methodologists. It can be used, with at least equal relevance, to defend speculative theory building beyond the point where techniques of investigation are immediately at hand.

obscure.[35] For while questions concerning the precise etiology and epidemiology of the Plague have yielded to scientific investigation, the problem of the conditions under which scientific advances occur remains a puzzle. This discussion attempts to clear a way toward the solution of, at least, some aspects of this puzzle; specifically, those aspects having to do with *social* conditions of scientific advance.

The foregoing discussion of existential spheres determining or constraining knowledge or belief has deliberately ignored consideration of objects of knowledge or belief. It refers to processes operating in the production of illusion or myth, even to wildly irrational acts and thoughts, as much as it does to the knowledge "grounded" in its object. Yet, some elements of "reality" outside the aforementioned existential spheres in which the belief is incubated do seep into belief. To be sure, the reality in question may be distorted reality or a reality valid only under highly special limiting conditions. To give a rather trivial example, a given item of belief concerning the material world is unlikely to be sustained for very long if manipulations in the material world guided by this belief meet with unambiguous and constant failure. Of course, this statement does not imply that beliefs guiding relatively successful manipulations are in any sense "true," merely that they bear some relationship to reality which is not contradictory in a very obvious way. The rising tide, to refer to Anglo-Saxon mythology, will not recede even at the bidding of kings.

The problem of relating belief to some object of belief in a noncontradictory way is not one that necessarily touches every kind of ideation. Religious beliefs, for instance, contain, among other things, strategies for maintaining personal equilibrium in face of outrages of fortune; strategies whose efficiency depends upon the faith of the believer rather than on some objective condition outside the believer. The very "non-objectivity" of the ubiquitous yet ultimately unknowable deity of Judaism, and religious traditions stemming from Judaism, gives life strategies guided by such a conception a "freshness of experience which experience demands" (1, p. 156). Clearly, Bakan does not have dogmatic religious orthodoxy in mind when he goes on to write: "Mankind

---

[35] That is not to say that the topic has lacked public attention. For example, Feuer (13, pp. 411-419) attributes Newton's creativity when back with his mother at her farm at Woolsthorpe to the latter's previous severe experience of maternal rejection. But this kind of explanation is not really satisfactory. Does it rest, perhaps, on the tacit generalization that maternally deprived children will be "creative" if given an opportunity to return to their mother? If so, has any real attempt been made to test this generalization? Or are there additional elliptic generalizations concerning the types of children and types of conditions for which the aforementioned generalization holds? Our discussion of existential spheres reveals the inadequacy of explanations such as the one cited and provides a classification of the various dimensions that would have to be explored in order to locate a particular outburst of creativity.

has developed a concept of God with whom he forever plays peekaboo and through it learns how to manage his life" (1, p. 157).

There are other items of belief besides religious, or moral, or merely "practical" life strategies which are devoid of an object. Music (and *especially* music which is abstract or non-programatic) can stir at least a musical person's existence to its depths. Even heuristics for pinning down objects in an elusive "real world" (like epistemology or methodology), though they might give relatively successful prescriptions for attaining "objectivity" (or at least, provide warning signals for points when objectivity is not being attained) lack any intrinsic facticity of their own. In discussing science — the systematic search for objectivity — we shall be concerned with one such heuristic strategy. What is special about such a strategy is precisely that it attempts to relate belief to its objects in a far-reaching and systematic manner without in any way denying the origin of such belief in realms (our existential spheres) which are extraneous to such an object.

A sharp delimitation of the term "science" has much to recommend it. There may be some virtue in defining science as being "what scientists do" when engaged in the pleasantries of everyday conversation, but the variety of person who have been called scientists and the variety of roles described as being scientific are so great, so diverse, and finally, so contradictory from the point of view of any coherent unitary conception of science as a human activity, that all virtue is lost if such a loose definition is followed in sociological analysis. Indeed, the current weakness of sociology of science as a field of inquiry can be adduced to the tendency of many of its practitioners to be overly liberal in their interpretation of what science constitutes.

A few examples may serve to indicate the conceptual chaos surrounding the meaning of "science". Isaac Newton (at least, in his early years) is considered by many historians of science to be the ideal scientist — a sort of historical paragon of what it really means to be a scientist. Yet Charles Madge (quoting Keynes) calls him the "last of the magicians", out of place in the rational technical *eidos* of the natural sciences (26, p. 39). Don Martindale contrasts humanism with science, seeing the latter arising out of a "new orientation toward instruments, material things, and the physical world" (29, p. 460). By contrast, Feuer distinguishes the emergence of the "new philosophy" of what he calls "scientific intellectuals" with the current "hegemony of the managerial technicians" in the scientific realm (13, p. 401) and depicts the true scientists as being oriented more toward both erotic and intellectual adventure than towards mere "instruments and material things". Within the sphere of sociology itself, Gouldner (who, when it suits him, follows a Mannheimian type of orientation) contrasts those who conceive of sociology as a natural science "developing cumulatively and continuously" with sociological humanists who seek not information but a change in awareness — in the "quality of mind" (17, p. 269; also 16). Thus, we have science depicted by different commentators as being technical, or materialistic, or intellectually adventurous, and these diverse and incompatible conceptions of the nature of science are bound to color sociological explanations of the area.

We do not intend to burden our discussion of science with any prior substantive conceptions concerning cumulation, materialism, or hedonism. Instead, we propose to arrive at an initial characterization of science by examining the formal characteristics of scientific activity as interpreted in the study of scientific method. In taking this course, we shall let Karl Popper be the guide. Popper of course is not the only methodologist who might be followed in arriving at a definition of science amenable to unambiguous sociological analysis. Certainly, we shall not be concerned here with a defense of the Popperian methodology against alternative and competing views. Popper makes his own case ably enough, and interested readers may be referred to his work.[36] Popper is followed strictly by an act of choice, and we are content to employ a simplified schematic version of his central methodological principles merely as an heuristic instrument for the examination of the nature of distinctively scientific activity.[37]

Science shares with some other forms of rationalistic activity the basic aim of explanation. What is distinctive about scientific explanation is that conjectured explanations of matters to be explained (explicanda) are systematically subjected to testing. Only if such conjectures or theories ·resist all attempts at falsification are they provisionally acceptable as "confirmed" scientific explanations. One corollary of this point of view is that the process of scientific discovery is one in which hypotheses deriving from theory are constantly subjected to testing, to attempted falsification. To qualify as scientific, an attempted explanation must be testable (in principle, at least, if not actually in practice; testable hypotheses occasionally must await the development of adequate methods of testing). An explanation which is posed in such a way as to be impossible to falsify may satisfy curiosity or longing, and even further "awareness", but it is not a scientific explanation.

Two activities go hand in hand in the process of scientific discovery: the testing of existing theories and the invention of new (testable) theories. Popper, as a methodologist, is particularly concerned with the logical properties of the testing process rather than with existential conditions under which scientific ideation takes place. Any situation of testing requires, besides the theory itself, a set of concrete circumstances

<hr>

[36] Interested persons are referred primarily to (38). A short summarizing discussion may be found in (41).

[37] It should be stressed that the following comments are not meant to serve as an exposition of Popper's methodology. Their purpose is merely to help us provide a demarcation between sociology of science and sociology of knowledge.

(initial conditions) in which the theory may be tested. An hypothesis is deduced from the theory to apply to the given or established set of initial conditions.[38]

Whether the hypothesis satisfies what the theory sets out to explain is then a matter for observation; whether what is predicted by the hypothesis "fits" observation or not constitutes the actual test of the theory. Prediction and explanation are logically equivalent. A prediction is simply a hypothesis referring to events in an anticipated given future configuration of initial conditions. Any prediction is dependent upon the anticipated set of initial conditions actually becoming established. Thus, a conditional prediction is distinct from prophecy which claims to foresee events independently of the presence of the required set of initial conditions.

This logical model of explanation and prediction — Popper's hypothetico-deductive system — also extends to applied science and scientific historiography. In applied science the theory is established (confirmed) and so are desired specifications. What has to be created are the appropriate set of initial conditions in which the universal law (or scientific generalization) stated by the theory satisfies the specifications for the desired application.

Any technical advance depends upon something like theory, at least, if the term is extended to include unsystematic, implicit, and perhaps even unconscious expectations concerning the consequences of the technical actions employed. But technology only qualifies as "applied science" when the theory that comes into play is explicit and is logically employed for setting up initial conditions meeting equally explicit specifications.

In scientific historiography also, initial conditions (historical events) rather than the theory are in question. An explanation here, in other words, does not proffer a generalization for testing but tests explanations of what "really happened" given the operation of the appropriate laws governing the events in question. Traditional history has tended to take the generalizations or laws it has employed for granted. As in pre-scientific (or unscientific) technology, such laws, for example, assumptions of rationality on the part of historical characters, or of pleasure-seeking and pain-avoidance, are implicit and often trivial. History only qualifies as scientific historiography when the theories governing relations between the relevant events are explicit. It should be added that these comments regarding historiography apply equally to any particularizing (idio-

[38] The term "theory" in this context, is limited to explanations couched as universal propositions, though historical explanations are also theoretical — as will be shown. Such limited usage has the advantage of providing a sharp demarcation between *ad hoc* hypotheses — applicable to a given set of initial conditions only — and hypotheses logically deriving from a theory which is independently testable in a variety of sets of initial conditions.

graphic) science concerned with spatio-temporally fixed events. Thus geography, cosmography (the "mapping" part of astronomy) or, for that matter, "sociography", are all concerned with the testing of assertions regarding initial conditions in the light of some implicit or explicit theoretical laws. When these laws are explicit, the fields in question qualify as particularizing sciences.

The foregoing discussion of scientific theory, technology, and "idiography" advances the process of testing as the touchstone for distinguishing between scientific and non-scientific activity in these spheres. It lays equal emphasis on the presence of explicit theory; theory to be tested, theory to affect directly the process of testing idiographic assertions, or theory for establishing technological application. In advocating a view of scientific method from the point of view of the logic and philosophy of science, two elements of scientific activity have therefore been distinguished: the production of theories and hypotheses, and their exposure to "systematic doubting" and, wherever possible, to crucial test.

Besides the moving staircase and sitting duck images of truth, a new one has emerged in this discussion: that of physical obstacles in the way of a blind man. He can stumble into them by accident, or actively seek their contours with his stick. There is nothing in the image to imply whether the obstacles themselves are either stationary or mobile, and any such implication is not necessary. Plato's cave is inescapable — what matters is to find one's way around in it, preferably without disaster. Methodology provides the rules for doing this; sociology of science examines conditions under which such rules come to be followed.

## Sociology of Knowledge and Sociology of Science

The proposition that scientific activity develops confirmed or objective knowledge precisely by the deliberate exposure of manipulations and prediction to failure — by *testing,* in other words — presents the notion that knowledge develops in two analytically separable realms: the realm of *existential* spheres in which ideation is incubated and the realm of *experiential* spheres in which ideation becomes subjected to criticism and testing. In a special sense, this formulation mirrors Kant's distinction between a priori and a posteriori knowledge. Ideation developing in the existential sphere is a priori knowledge. Theories subjected to test and tentatively confirmed constitute a posteriori knowledge. Sociology of science, we propose, should be concerned with conditions which facilitate or hinder the institutionalization of systematic doubting and testing.

Popper's hypothetico-deductive prescription for scientific discovery is open to justified criticism, particularly if the prescription is taken as a description of what scientists actually do most of the time while about their business. It emphasizes dramatically the very special circumstances of the "crucial experiment" and implies that crucial experiments are the goals towards which scientific activity should be directed.

Kuhn's discussion of scientific revolutions is probably a more accurate description of fundamental changes in scientific knowledge as they actually occur. Kuhn speaks of a change of the *paradigm* or comprehensive metatheory which guides the day-to-day puzzle-solving of normal science as a scientific revolution. Such revolutions occur because of a "growing sense . . . that our existing paradigm has ceased to function adequately in the explanation of an aspect of nature to which the paradigm had previously led the way" (23, p. 91). In that sense scientific revolutions have common features with political revolutions. The Popperian concept of scientific discovery, seen in the light of this comparison, has the flavour of Mao's "permanent revolution" (22, p. 242). Kuhn himself, however, insists that his position does not depart very greatly from Popper's, either on the question of testability-in-principle or on the asymmetry of falsification and confirmation (22, pp. 247-248). He suggests, on the other hand, that the decision as to whether or not the result of an actual test actually falsifies a particular theory is not as clear-cut as Popperian rhetoric would imply.

We are generally in agreement with Kuhn's point that the actual decision to abandon a paradigm or a particular theory cannot be as precisely outlined as a superficial interpretation of Popper's methodology would suggest. At the same time, we consider the analogy between scientific and political revolutions to be profoundly misleading. To compare crises precipitated by falsification (or systematic failures in Kuhn's "puzzle-solving") with crises preceding political revolutions ignores the demarcated existential and experimental realms which Popper's conception of science has enabled us to delineate so sharply.

Political revolutions, in common with other instances of social change, find their origin in exigencies. The exigencies leading to scientific discovery, however, are of a very distinct type. An established articulation outside the province of science may become modified or discarded upon the experience of new exigencies. In the absence of such exigencies, however, it tends to be maintained unchanged so long as it appears adequate to the originating exigency evoking it. Testing, on the other hand, involves a deliberate search for exigencies (cognitive discrepancies) independently of the apparent and immediate adequacy of an articulation. Kuhn's picture of scientific revolutions gives an entirely inadequate portrayal of the scientist as a deliberate agent provocateur in the field of cognition.

The special task of sociology of science is the development of sociological analysis of the conditions under which people's ideas about the world become subjected to intentional and systematic exposure to falsification. Conversely, of course, sociology of science must interest itself also in conditions inhibiting such a development. Some further clarification of sociology of science as a distinct area within the sociology of knowledge is required before we proceed to our final question; namely, whether sociology is a field inherently suitable for scientific investigation.

The characterization of testing in terms of Zollschan's theory of articulation, when viewed by itself, may give an inadequate picture of scientific activity. Perhaps, it conjures up the image of an individual obsessively doubting his own ideas and goals. Such an image could not even qualify as a convincing caricature of a scientist about his business. The idea of doubt must, of course, be augmented by an unequivocal statement that science is a special set of social relationships in which systematic doubts, and more overtly, doubts about the public articulations of others rather than one's own articulations, become institutionalized. Popper himself has given a felicitous description of this process. He sees science as being differentiated from mythology only in that its tradition of myths is accompanied by a "second-order tradition — that of critically discussing the myth" (42, p. 127). Sociology of science, then, is concerned with conditions under which the seemingly perverse search for negative instances becomes institutionalized in critical and testing traditions. It is further concerned with circumstances conducive to the maintenance or dissolution of such traditions.

The establishment of systematic testing, in a given ideational sphere, as a method for founding the veracity of ideas is yet another process requiring attention by sociology of science. As the history of science amply reveals, this is a separate process from the establishment of a critical tradition. The kind of systematic, theoretically guided experimentation I have described as "testing" does not occur spontaneously even where a vigorous critical tradition is in existence. Herbert Butterfield, for instance, has pointed out that experimentation had for centuries been "an affair of wild and almost pointless fluttering . . . in many respects irrelevant to the true progress of understanding." "It is not until the seventeenth century that the resort to experiments comes to be tamed and harnessed, so to speak, and is brought under direction . . ." (6, p. 91). Part of the explanation for the development of experimentation in certain natural sciences must undoubtedly be sought in the development of critical traditions in these areas to the point of clarity where appeals to observation must have seemed both natural and impelling. But the seemingly inevitable appeal to observation has historically depended upon the separate and prior development of techniques and instruments of observation. Explanation of such separate developments and the social conditions conducive to such developments is also within the preserve of sociology of science.

Differences between the conditions for the institutionalization of experimental theory testing and those for the institutionalized application of tested and confirmed theories, not to speak of conditions for the emergence of scientific historiography, can also be clarified by the suggested demarcation of sociology of science. Much as theoretically guided experimentation depends upon the prior development of observational techniques, so applied science and scientific historiography depend upon the existence of a stock of usable confirmed theories. In practice, however, demands for technological applications and historical explanations are frequently met in cases where scientific criteria of application and historiography cannot be satisfied. The analysis of unscientific and pseudo-scientific technologies is relevant for sociology of science, particularly where the existence of these acts as a barrier to the development of genuine testing in the relevant fields.

Once experimental science is institutionalized, quite definite consequences do, of course, ensue for the production of those kinds of ideas (theories and hypotheses) which are meant to be scientific or, in other words, are meant to refer to an object realm lying outside the existential spheres. Such ideas will undergo continuous elaboration and clarification to the point where they can be conclusively tested. A scientific attitude may even subject the production of some kinds of ideas to "methodological inhibition". But feedbacks, such as this, from empirical science to the production of ideas should not be allowed to obscure the distinction between ideational production and the institutionalization of systematic testing; between processes governing the existential realm and processes governing the experimental realm.

### Sociology of Science and a Scientific Sociology:

We have suggested that scientific activity develops confirmed or objective knowledge precisely through the deliberate exposure of predictions and manipulations to failure; by *testing*, in other words. Quite obviously, some kind of "reality-testing" also occurs in practical everyday activities. People engaged in such reality-testing develop consciously tentative working models of the situation in which they operate. The conditions of everyday life do not normally allow that such *ad hoc* working models be tested at all exhaustively. The working model is retained, so to speak, as long as it "works".

Social participation, equally, implies that persons carry with them working models of the goals and beliefs of others. Max Weber was groping towards this realization in his attempt to characterize the nature of social action. As we have pointed out above, he viewed the purpose of sociology as consisting of the improvement of such models. Causally adequate models (ideal types) consisted of fictitional or imaginary experiments based on deliberately highly selective and unrealistic assumptions. He could find no way, however, of penetrating the boundaries separating the existential from the experiential realm. His entire program for sociology was a prioristic in our sense of the term. The relationships of "causality" imputed by the sociological analyst were entirely impervious to test. In a sense, Mannheim's perspectivism — the idea that existential free floatation could provide more comprehensive models of such fictional relations of causality — provides an example of unconscious irony about the Weberian program. Both must be viewed as dupes of the history of science.

Talcott Parsons' "solution" of the problem of testing working models of goals and beliefs is an interesting (though, indubitably, quite unintentional) attempt to revive the Kantian theory of morals. The latter, it may be remembered, posits that intelligible selves are free (that is to say, not determined or "caused") and, therefore, only predictable to the extent that they are governed by moral order. Parsons' variation on the Kantian theme of moral order is to depict society as a system of normative integration. Indeed, Parsons elevates the problem of shared or coordinated beliefs (what he calls "double contingency") into the overriding exigency of social life. Thereupon, he directly proceeds on the assumption that social systems are integrated with respect to beliefs and norms guiding action (36, pp. 36-45). This intellectual maneuver guarantees interpersonal predictability in any given social system. At the same time, it circumvents the entire problem of testing. Where predictability is predicated, testing becomes unnecessary!

No one can fail to agree with Parsons that the absence of predictable responses from others can pose exigencies for any actor. As a matter of fact, predictability of social responses has been proposed by us as one of the existential spheres in which exigencies originate. Where Parsons strains one's credulity is in the assumption that exigencies in this sphere are automatically met by social organization. The extent of sharing, or overlap, or co-ordination of beliefs and values is not something to be presupposed but a problem to be investigated in any society at any point in time.

In stressing the problematic nature of interpersonal systems of meanings we stand aligned with Goffman, (15) phenomenological sociologists like Peter Berger, (4), and ethnomethodologists such as Cicourel and Garfinkel (7; 14). Like them, we believe that persons build *ad hoc* models (often unconscious ones) of other people and of social contexts and situations; models which are subject, loosely speaking at least, to testing. The initial discussion and investigation of such working models that has taken place to date is highly illuminating and suggestive. Continuing research along these lines, we suspect, will do more than any strictly theoretical discussion can achieve in destroying static models of social processes based on normative consensus, or for that matter, on coercion. Our approach, however, stresses motivational and change processes more emphatically than is done elsewhere. We suspect that people's models of others and of society at large are constructed in close connection with their articulation of needs and attempts to attain goals. When people are investigated for the exigencies they experience, the needs they articulate, and the goals for which they strive, an eventually testable explanation for the human construction of social reality begins to swim into focus.

Our emphasis on change processes and on existential spheres may seem, at first glance, to align us with radical sociologists who echo Marx in the claim that the task of sociology is not to explain society but to change it. We differ markedly from this school of thought in a number of ways. Firstly, radical sociologists, as does Parsons, place exclusive, or near-exclusive emphasis on exigencies emanating from but one of our existential spheres; in their case, the sphere of distributive justice. Given this starting assumption, their principal problem shifts from that of mutual predictability to the acquisition of undistorted knowledge of "objective interests" as these are distributed in society. The implication that any person has unambiguously fixed objective interests has been put severely to question both by our critique of Mannheim and by our discussion of the multiplicity of existential spheres which surround a person's life.

Secondly, we do not believe that it is necessary or proper for sociologists to arrogate the burden of guiding social change to themselves. Social change is ubiquitous and, under contemporary conditions at least, occurs as much (or as little) in the absence of the active intervention of sociologists as when the dubious benefits of such intervention are noisily exercised. Finally, we believe that change processes can only be controlled and guided with wisdom and foresight when tested and reasonably well confirmed explanations of factors involved become available.

None the less, the goal of general human emancipation with which adherents of the radical school tempt their audience arouses amused sympathy. Optimum net overall "liberation" is a fetching alternative to the optimum net overall felicities promised by their equally "radical" utilitarian forebears. The utilitarians, however, assumed that people knew what their real interests were. Their libertarian progeny are not guilty of such gross naiveté. For the latter, "true consciousness" is the preserve of a privileged elite. In Marx's view, the carriers of truth were clearly the class-conscious proletariat (particularly as its consciousness was interpreted by Karl Marx himself). Mannheim replaced the indoctrinated Marxist proletarian with the free-floating intellectual as the type of person who had, at least, the potential for embracing the most comprehensive truth. Now we have the radical sociologists claiming monopoly in the supply of *mots justes* for the exigencies that beset us all. Voting patterns in the early 1970s (in countries with multi-party systems and where secret balloting applies) suggest that the majority of those who bother to vote begged to be excused from accepting the radical sociologists' articulations of their exigencies.[39] We maintain that exigencies, goals, and interests are not directly accessible to any specially "favoured" group. Instead they are objects for scientific investigation.

The sarcasm directed at radical sociology here is not meant to extend to the conception of "false consciousness." We have defended this notion above, in our favourable comparison of Marx's conception of consciousness with Durkheim's. Willer and Zollschan, moreover, have argued for the necessity of notions such as "false articulation" and "pseudo-interests" (53, p. 132). There is an asymmetrical relationship between objective interest and false consciousness much as there is between confirmation and falsification in scientific method.

We do maintain that notions like false consciousness require evidence for the experience of a specified exigency independently of the articulation itself. Additionally, they require a scientific analysis of whether the articulated goals are: (1) suitable to the nature of the exigency; (2) attainable; and (3) unlikely to lead to punishing side-consequences. The rhetoric of anti-scientific sociology shows but dim awareness of the technical problems involved in attempting to make any genuinely objective judgment concerning the question. It may be added that even an objective judgment of the kind described here would ignore moral issues.

With the few exceptions noted above, this broad survey has revealed sociological theorizing to be in a situation where one or another form of self-encapsulated a priorism reigns supreme. The formulation presented here concerning existential spheres, when taken in conjunction with Zollschan's previously published theoretical model of motive and institutionalization (57, pp. 89-97 and Chapter 4, this volume) provides a pointer for treating existential a prioris as objects for empirical investigation. Any proposal for treating social facts (or other elements in the "realm of intelligbles") more or less *comme des choses* is bound to be associated with the tired clarion call of classical positivism. The most cursory examination of the methodology espoused in our argument, however, should reveal its fundamental opposition to the two main dogmata of positivistic thinking; namely, naive observationalism and the claims that scientific knowledge can be "positive" or final.

Two questions remain to be answered in our enquiry. One is methodological, the other belongs to sociology of science. The methodological question refers to problems of investigating exigencies, articulations, and actions as these are hatched in their respective existential spheres. The sociology of science question asks why a program for genuine the-

---

[39] Is it entirely improper to suspect that radical sociologists are reverting to the position of that "arch-positivist" Auguste Comte, who wanted to replace the existing "system of oppression," or "power elite," or "establishment," and so on by a priesthood of sociologists? Without wishing to put undue strain on professional collegiality, we feel that such a shift of power would replace the whips of oppression by scorpions!

ory-testing should have been so long delayed in the development of sociology as an academic discipline.

As regards the methodological question, there are grounds for distinct optimism that the elicitation of ideation and action in existential spheres is subject to systematic enquiry. Disconnected fragments of such enquiry litter the social sciences and the non-behavioristic psychological study of motivation. To revert to Butterfield's language, the theory for taming and harnessing these almost pointless efforts and bringing them under direction is in process of construction.

The alleged "freedom" or "instability" or "fluidity" of intelligibles which has prompted organicist and consensualist-functionalist shortcuts to a theory of social processes — shortcuts which violate the theoretical requirement of testability — has not been conclusively established to be greater than instabilities in natural realms. As simple a compound as $H_2O$ is experientially encountered in liquid, solid, or gaseous states. Water (or steam, or ice), like human conduct and social organization, can be very puzzling to the naive explorer who alternatively sweats, or drowns, or bruises his head on encountering it in its various states. Simple theories concerning variation in temperature and pressure bring this apparently formless monstrosity to heel. Figuratively speaking, the monster can even be trained to bring one's slippers![40] An eventual "Boyle's Law" of sociology will undoubtedly contain more parameters than its namesake in physical chemistry. The notions of articulation, action, and institutionalization are meant to supply sociology with at least some of the necessary strategic parameters. The suggestion concerning existential spheres hastens the day when these parameters can be subjected to fairly rigorous scientific manipulation.

The sociology of science question, which makes anxious enquiry into reasons for the scientific retardedness of theories of human conduct and social structure, can be answered without contradicting the optimism previously declared concerning the possibility for creating a scientific sociology. We want to suggest that one of these reasons lies in the temporal priority of spectacular advances in classical mechanics. Efforts to emulate the natural sciences, in the absence of any adequate understanding of the nature of scientific discovery, led to the preposterous methodological conception of positivism and to its associated "scientism" (18) or "science-faking" as we prefer to call it. This science-faking led to the theoretical shortcuts.

Efforts by sociologists to free themselves of one or another of the constituents of science-faking have given rise to the formation of schools.

---

[40] Quite obviously, the various states of water were, in a sense, "known" before exact theories of variations in temperature and pressure had been proposed. Water also served as a medium of navigation prior to such proposals. In the same way, of course, we "know" society and some even manage to utilize social processes for their own successful propulsion.

The defensive orthodoxies of schools, more intent on the continuation of ideological myths than on scientific advance, constitute yet another reason for retardation in sociology. Even more important is the associated fact that in a climate where there is a dearth of genuinely scientific advances, severe problems are caused concerning the evaluation of intellectual products and the allocation of rewards. The existence of schools assures that work can be evaluated and rewards allocated on criteria which have absolutely nothing to do with scientific originality. Potentially original sociological scientists, therefore, may find themselves operating in isolation and under professional conditions highly unconducive for the fruition of their efforts.

One final word may be in order, to make explicit what has been implied in this essay concerning the nature of an eventual sociological science. The *cosmos* is an open system, and so are societies and their histories and for that matter, the experienced lives of individual persons. Science, which involves uncovering and explaining limited systems within the cosmos (or society) can guide individual choice largely by setting theoretical limits to possibilities of choice. The idea that all choice is determined may be trivially correct, but choice is determined by the interplay of diverse systems and therefore not only determined but also, in a sense, "free." Free, that is, unless we postulate personalities and groups (the sites of choice) as closed systems. There is no need for anxiety that sociological science will reveal (or create) a human ant-heap. It is only sociological scientism, with its improper postulation of closed systems where none exist, which threatens such a Byzantine outcome. "... Artificial abstractions, with their bony hands ..." may not be able to grasp the "... sap of true life ..." in the social sciences any more than in any other science. (52, pp. 134–156). But precisely in this limitation of science lies human freedom. We urge progress toward a sociological science, but only in the belief that the recognition of the necessity of science facilitates freedom.

# BIBLIOGRAPHY

1. Bakan, David. *On Method.* San Francisco: Jossey-Bass, 1969.

2. Bernstein, Basil, B., "Language and Social Class," *British Journal of Sociology,* Vol. 11, 1960, pp. 271–276.

3. Berger, Peter and Stanley Pullberg. "Reification and the Sociological Critique of Consciousness." *History and Theory,* Vol. 4, 1965, pp. 196–211.

4. Berger, Peter, and Thomas Luckman. *The Social Construction of Reality.* New York, Anchor, 1966.

5. Bottomore, T. B., and Maximilien Rubel. "Introduction," *Karl Marx: Selected Writings in Sociology and Social Philosophy.* New York: McGraw-Hill, 1964.

6. Butterfield, Herbert. *The Origins of Modern Science, 1300–1800.* New York: Macmillan and Co., 1957.

7. Cicourel, Aaron. *Method and Measurement in Sociology.* New York: Free Press, 1964.

8. Davy, John. *The Times,* London, May 29, 1968, p. 10.

9. Desan, Wilfrid. *The Marxism of Jean-Paul Sartre.* New York: Anchor, 1965.

10. Durkheim, Emile. *Elementary Forms of the Religious Life,* translated by J. W. Swain. New York: Collier, 1961.

11. Durkheim, Emile. *The Rules of Sociological Method,* translated by Sarah A. Solovay and J. H. Mueller. Glencoe: Free Press, 1964.

12. Durkheim, Emile, and Marcel Mauss. *"De quelques formes primitives de classification,"* L'annee sociologique, Vol. 6, 1901–1902.

13. Feuer, Lewis S. *The Scientific Intellectual.* New York: Basic Books, 1963.

14. Garfinkel, Harold. *Studies in Ethnomethodology.* Englewood Cliffs: Prentice Hall, 1967.

15. Goffman, Erving. *The Presentation of Self in Everyday Life.* New York: Anchor, 1959.

16. Gouldner, Alvin W. *The Coming Crisis of Western Sociology.* London: Heineman, 1970.

17. Gouldner, Alvin W. *Enter Plato.* New York: Basic Books, 1965.

18. Hayek, F. A., "Scientism and the Study of Society," in *The Counter-Revolution of Science.* Part I. New York: Free Press, 1955.

19. Høffding, Harald. *A History of Modern Philosophy,* translated by B. E. Meyer. New York: Macmillan and Co., 1935, Vol. 2.

20. Jaspers, Karl. *Nietzsche: Einführung in das Verständniss seines Philosophierens.* Berlin: de Gruyter, 1947.

21. Kaplan, Abraham. *The Conduct of Inquiry.* San Francisco: Chandler, 1964.

22. Kuhn, Thomas S. "Reflections on my Critics," in Imre Lakatos and Alan Musgrave (eds.), *Criticism and the Growth of Knowledge.* Cambridge: Cambridge University Press, 1970.

23. Kuhn, Thomas S. *The Structure of Scientific Revolutions.* Chicago: University of Chicago Press, 1962.

24. Lichtheim, George. "Sartre, Marxism, and History," in *The Concept of Ideology and Other Essays.* New York: Random House, 1967.

25. Lipset, S. M. *Political Man.* New York: Doubleday, 1960.

26. Madge, Charles. *Society in the Mind: Elements of Social Eidos.* Glencoe: Free Press, 1964.

27. Mannheim, Karl. *Ideology and Utopia.* New York: Harcourt-Brace, 1965.

28. Mannheim, Karl. *Man and Society in an Age of Reconstruction,* translated by E. A. Shils. London: Routledge and Kegan Paul Ltd., 1940.

29. Martindale, Don. "The Roles of Humanism and Scientism in the Evolution of Sociology," in G. K. Zollschan and W. Hirsch (eds.), *Ex-*

*plorations in Social Change.* Boston: Houghton Mifflin, 1964, and London, Routledge, 1964.

30. Marx, Karl. "The German Ideology," in R. C. Tucker (ed.), *The Marx-Engels Reader.* New York: Norton, 1972, pp. 110–164.

31. Marx, Karl. "Theses on Feuerbach," in R. C. Tucker (ed.), *The Marx-Engels Reader.* New York: Norton, 1972, pp. 107–109.

32. Merton, Robert K., *Social Theory and Social Structure.* (Revised Edition), Glencoe: Free Press, 1957.

33. Morris, Charles W. *Foundations of the Theory of Signs.* Chicago: University of Chicago Press, 1938.

34. Nietzsche, Friedrich. *A Genealogy of Morals,* translated by W. A. Haussman and John Gray. London: Unwin, 1899.

35. Pareto, Vilfredo. *The Mind and Society.* New York: Dover, 1963.

36. Parsons, Talcott. *The Social System.* New York: Free Press, 1951.

37. Piepe, Anthony. *Knowledge and Social Order.* London: Heineman, 1972.

38. Popper, Sir Karl R. *The Logic of Scientific Discovery.* New York: Basic Books, 1959.

39. Popper, Sir Karl R. *The Open Society and its Enemies,* Vol. 2. New York: Harper Torchbooks, 1962.

40. Popper, Sir Karl R. *The Poverty of Historicism.* London: Routledge and Kegan Paul, Ltd., 1961.

41. Popper, Sir Karl R. "Three Views Concerning Human Knowledge," in *Conjectures and Refutations.* New York: Basic Books, 1962.

42. Popper, Sir Karl R. "Toward a Theory of Tradition," in *Conjectures and Refutations.* New York: Basic Books, 1962.

43. Rapaport, David. "The Structure of Psychoanalytic Theory: A Systematizing Attempt," in Sigmund Koch, *Psychology: A Study of A Science,* New York: McGraw-Hill, 1959, Vol. 3.

44. Rickert, Heinrich. *Die Grenzen der Naturwissenschaftlichen Begriffsbildung,* 3rd edition. Tübingen: Mohr-Siebeck, 1921.

45. Rothenstreich, Nathan. *Basic Problems of Marx's Philosophy.* Indianapolis: Bobbs-Merrill, 1965.

46. Sartre, Jean-Paul. *Search for a Method,* translated by Hazel Barnes. New York: Knopf, 1963.

47. Schelting, Alexander von. *Max Weber's Wissenschaftslehre.* Tübingen: Mohr-Siebeck, 1934.

48. Shroyer, Trent. "Toward a Critical Theory for Advanced Industrial Society," in Hans P. Dreitzel (ed.), *Recent Sociology,* No. 2. New York: Macmillan and Co., 1970.

49. Weber, Max. *Gesammelte Aufsätze zur Wissenschaftslehre.* Tübingen: Mohr-Siebeck, 1922.

50. Weber, Max. *The Protestant Ethic and the Spirit of Capitalism,* translated by T. Parsons. New York: Scribner, 1958.

51. Weber, Max. *The Religion of India,* translated by H. H. Gerth and Don Martindale. New York: Free Press, 1958.

52. Weber, Max. "Science as a Vocation." In *From Max Weber*, translated by H. H. Gerth and C. Wright Mills. New York: Oxford University Press, 1946.

53. Willer, David, and G. K. Zollschan. "Prolegomenon to a Theory of Revolutions," in G. K. Zollschan and W. Hirsch, eds., *Explorations in Social Change*. Boston: Houghton Mifflin, 1964; London: Routledge and Kegan Paul, 1964.

54. Winch, Peter. *The Idea of a Social Science*. London: Routledge and Kegan Paul, 1958.

55. Wolff, Kurt H. "The Sociology of Knowledge and Sociological Theory," in Llewellyn Gross, *Symposium on Sociological Theory*. New York: Row Peterson, 1959.

56. Zollschan, George K. "Beyond the Reality Principle." In G. K. Zollschan and W. Hirsch (eds.), *Explorations in Social Change*. Boston: Houghton Mifflin, 1964; London: Routledge and Kegan Paul, 1964.

57. Zollschan, George K. *Introduction* to "Working Papers in the Theory of Institutionalization." In G. K. Zollschan and W. Hirsch (eds.), *Explorations in Social Change*. Boston: Houghton Mifflin, 1964; London: Routledge and Kegan Paul, 1964.

58. Zollschan, George K., and Philip Gibeau. "Concerning Alienation: A System of Categories for the Exploration of Rational and Irrational Behavior," in G. K. Zollschan and W. Hirsch (eds.), *Explorations in Social Change*. Boston: Houghton Mifflin and Co., 1964, and London: Routledge and Kegan Paul, 1964.

# 8

*James Dow*

# The Potential of a Mathematical Model of Social Change

The theory of social change that George Zollschan and other contributors developed in the forerunner of the present volume (2) is a coherent theory in which consequences result from specific causes, viz., goal oriented action results from articulated goals which result from individual exigencies. Because all steps in the process are logically interconnected, an exigency arose for Zollschan and myself which led to our articulation of the goal that the model should be formulated in more mathematical terms. This article represents the resulting action. I have attempted with the assistance of Zollschan to formulate the theory in a more mathematical way. It transforms the theory into an operational model that can be used to simulate real societies.

## The Model of the Individual

At the beginning of the chain of processes leading ultimately to social action is the exigency, "a discrepancy (for a person) between a consciously or unconsciously desired or expected state of affairs and an actual situation." (2, p. 89). Two factors go into making up the exigency, the ideal situation and the actual situation of an individual, the difference between which constitutes a "discrepancy." Our first problem is to describe a "situation" mathematically. Often, a number of potentially measurable variables, such as the health of the individual, his financial status, the amount of love he receives, the state of his house,

200

the state of various tools he needs, etc., helps us to do this. Such variables would have to be quite numerous to describe the complete situation of an individual, but they can be reduced to a manageable number of measurable ones in a heuristic model.

If a finite number of variables, $N$, are sufficient to describe the situation of an individual, his ideal situation $\vec{I}$ and his perceived actual situation $\vec{P}$ can be expressed as vectors in an $N$-dimensional Euclidean vector space called the situation space, S, the bases of which are the $N$ dimensions in which the selected variables are measured. A discrepancy $\vec{X}$ can be described as the difference between these two vectors:

$$\vec{X} = \vec{I} - \vec{P}$$

An exigency itself has the character of both he ideal situation and the discrepancy between it and the perceived situation. For instance the exigency of being lower middle class includes not only the ideal of increasing one's wealth but also the ideal of the kind of wealthy upper middle class life that one wants to lead. Therefore an exigency can be described as the vector pair:

$$(\vec{X}, \vec{I})$$

A measure of the force of the exigency is the absolute value of the discrepancy, $|\vec{X}|$. This number is zero when the ideal and perceived situations are the same, and it increases positively as the distance between the ideal and the actual situation increases.

Because "... no simple or direct relationship need exist between the composition of an exigency and the expressed form of the need into which it becomes condensed and in which it becomes expressed," (2, p. 90), there is no simple mapping that translates exigencies into goals. One solution to the problem posed by this indeterminacy is to work with the entire set of goals that are specifiable in the culture of the individuals with whom we are concerned. Let us call this set G and indicate its elements, the goals, by g. The specifiability of a particular goal g for individual i can be indicated by an integer $\tau(g,i)$ which is zero if the goal g cannot be specified by individual i and which is one if g can be specified by him.

The justifiability of a goal can be described as a real number function $v(g,i)$ where $g \in G$ and $i \in I$, the set of all individuals in the society under examination.

Salience is the only requisite for articulation that depends on the exigencies. However, the way in which an exigency contributes saliency to particular goals is not made clear in the theory. Apparently, the same exigency can contribute saliency to a number of goals. Saliency can be described as a real number function of g in I, i in I, and $\vec{X}$, and $\vec{I}$ in S, as follows:

$$\sigma(g,i,\vec{X},\vec{I})$$

One can think of $\sigma$ as a set of continuous functions (one for each combination of g and i) over two vector spaces of $N$ dimensions or over one vector space of *2N* dimensions. Each $\sigma$ for a given $i$ and $g$ is a potential field in a space of *2N* dimensions. A possible simplification of $\sigma$ could be made by making it a function of $|\vec{X}|$ rather than of $\vec{X}$. This would reduce the different $\sigma(g,i)$ to potential fields over a space of *N+1* dimensions. This simplification is reasonable because the magnitude of the saliency is most dependent on the magnitude of the discrepancy and not on its direction and because the particular goals to which the saliency applies are more directly related to the ideal that has contributed to the exigency than to the direction of change required to reach that ideal.

Once one has measures of saliency $\sigma(g,i,\vec{X},\vec{I})$, specifiability $\tau(g,i)$, and justifiability $\upsilon(g,i)$, how can one describe the process of articulation of a particular goal $g$ by a particular individual $i$? One solution is to think of articulation as the crossing of a threshold surface in a three dimensional Euclidean vector space whose coordinates are $\sigma$, $\tau$, and $\upsilon$. This surface can be reduced to a curve in two dimensions, since $\tau$ can have only the values of *0* and *1*. When $\tau$ has the value of *0* the goal is unspecifiable and cannot be articulated; no curve exists in this case. But when $\tau = 1$, a two dimensional curve in a plane whose coordinates are $\sigma$ and $\upsilon$ suffices to define the threshold of articulation. Such a curve and region of articulation is shown in Figure 1. Thus if all the functions $\sigma$, $\tau$, and $\upsilon$ are known, one can specify when a certain goal will be ar-

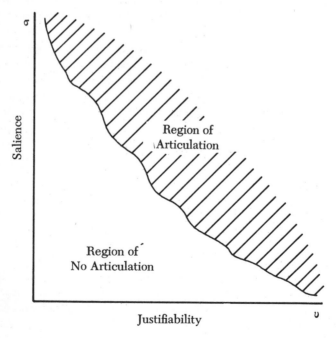

Figure 1. Conditions for articulation of goal **g** by individual **i** when $\tau = 1$.

ticulated by a particular individual. The contribution of several exigencies to the articulation of one goal can be dealt with by summing $\sigma$ for the different $(\vec{X}, \vec{I})$.

Once an individual has articulated a particular set of goals, other factors determine which of any of these goals will be translated into action. Let us call the set of articulated goals $H_i$. The first requisite for action, valence, requires a comparison of the goals in $H_i$. The theory conceives of this, more or less, as an ordering of the goals in $H_i$. The nature of this ordering is not specified, but let us assume for the moment that it is a complete ordering and that an integer $k(g)$ can be assigned to each goal in $H_i$ according to its rank, such that 1 is the highest rank and $n$, the number of elements in $H_i$, is the lowest. Valence can then be described as a positive real number function:

$$\phi(\sigma(g), k(g))$$

Since an individual can entertain only a few highly valent goals at one time, the effect of a low ranking would be to reduce the power of salience. Hence a possible form for $\phi$ would be

$$\phi = \frac{\sigma(g)}{k(g)} \tag{1}$$

Also the original salience of a goal is a measure that might be rationally used by an individual to rank his articulated goals, so another form for $\phi$ might be

$$\phi = (\sigma[g])^2 \tag{2}$$

However the forms (1) and (2) seem likely only if the goals are not related to each other, as studying for an exam and brushing one's teeth. Yet there exist in the plans of men elaborate sets of interrelated goals articulated out of exigencies arising from the pursuit of some primary goal. The valences of the goals of these sets may be particularly dependent on the valence of the primary goal, such as cleaning one's shirt and combing one's hair depend on going out on a date. In these cases the forms (1) and (2) are inappropriate.

When goals are interrelated, valence can be a function of the rational plan of action used by an individual. Consider the case of a primary goal P and a number of intermediate goals related to P which have to be achieved before P can be achieved. Figure 2 shows a possible arrangement of goals that could present themselves to an individual whose situation was at A. He could reach P by a number of different paths passing through different combinations of intermediate goals, for example ABCDP, AGJFP, or AGCEFP. As an example, if P was the goal of buying a new automobile, B might be the goal of looking for one on sale in a showroom, G might be to make an offer to a man down the street who has one for sale, C might be to buy one from the showroom, J might be to buy the one from the man down the street, etc. The valences of these goals depend on how the individual sees the network of intermediate goals at any particular moment. If the individual sees the entire network clearly and if he makes a rational choice of path on the basis of minimizing some quantity such as cost, all the goals on the chosen path take on a high valence dependent on the salience of P; and the plan of action is simplified into a linear one like the one shown in Figure 3. The valence of the goals on a linear path might be given by a formula something like this

$$\phi(g) = (P)\frac{1}{d} \tag{3}$$

where $d$ is the distance following the arrows from the person's present position of achievement to goal $g$. If the individual lacked information or the capacity to form a picture of all the actions required to reach goal P but knew the general direction in which he wanted to proceed, he might conceive of a goal network like the one illustrated in Figure 4.[1] Again equation (3) would be a good measure of the valence of these goals, but nearby goals would have competing valences.[2] The individual would be confronted with difficult choices as he proceeded toward his primary goal P, and the lengths of the arrows in the diagram would shrink or expand as rational thought increased or decreased the valences of the intermediate goals. Arrows would disappear as intermediate goals were achieved or abandoned. Thus in a situation where intermediate goals arise out of the articulations of secondary exigencies, the conception of the interrelationship of the goals by the actor would affect their valences.

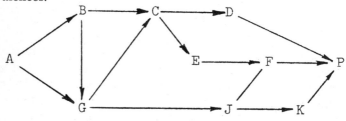

**FIGURE 2**

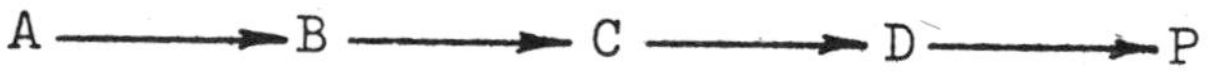

A ——————→ B ——————→ C ——————→ D ——————→ P

**FIGURE 3**

---

[1] The lack of complete rationality in human problem solving has been studied by psychologists for many years. A current approach to this situation is that of Newell and Simon (1, p. 53).

[2] This situation is categorized as "ambivalence" by Zollschan (2, p. 94).

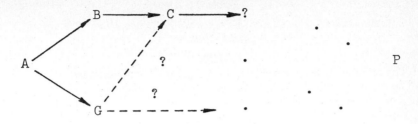

**FIGURE 4**

Legitimation makes reference to a value system set up by the society and therefore might be represented by the same function $v(g,i)$ that represents justification. If not, legitimation can be represented by its own function

$$\psi(g,i).$$

Application, the technology required to achieve a certain goal (2, p. 94), can be represented by a function $\chi(g,i)$ of the goal $g$ and the individual $i$. Application varies with the individual because each person has a different access to the technologies of his society.

The conditions for action like the conditions for articulation can be represented by a threshold surface in a vector space. This time the co-ordinates of the space are $\phi$, $\chi$, *and* $\psi$; and the surface should look something like

$$c = \frac{1}{\phi \chi \psi}.$$

Thus the variables and relationships in Zollschan's theory of social change can be represented by three mathematical sets, three Euclidean vector spaces, three types of vectors, two surfaces, and six numerical functions all of which are summarized in Table 1. Following this, Table 2 which is the analog of Table 1 on page 95 of the first edition of *Explorations in Social Change* (2, p. 95) gives the mathematical expression of an exigency, of the three requisites for articulation, and of the three requisites for action. When the dimensions of the situation space S are specified, when the set of goals G is specified, and when the functions $\sigma$, $\tau$, $v$, $\phi$, $\chi$, $\psi$, $r$, and $a$ are specified, the mathematical model will tell us what goals will be articulated and acted on by an individual. The dimensions, goals, and functions can be specified from empirical studies, or on a purely *ad hoc* basis just to examine their theoretical implications.

### The Model of Society

All the processes that have been discussed so far are internal to a single individual, but a theory of institutionalization requires knowledge of processes that include more than one individual; in other words,

## Table 1.

### *Mathematical Terms Used to Express the Zollschan-Hirsch Theory of Social Change*

#### SETS
$G$: The set of all goals, $g$, specifiable in the culture being examined.

$I$: The set of all individuals, $i$, in the culture being examined.

$H_i$: The set of all goals which have been articulated by individual $i$ at a particular time.

#### EUCLIDEAN VECTOR SPACES
S: The situation space of $N$ dimensions in which the perceived ideal situations and actual situations of an individual are represented as vectors.

AR: The two-dimensional articulation space with co-ordinates $\sigma$, and $v$.

AC: The three-dimensional action space with co-ordinates $\phi$, $\chi$, and $\psi$.

#### VECTORS
$\vec{I}$: in S representing the ideal situation of individual $i$ at a particular time.

$\vec{P}$: in S representing the actual situation of individual $i$ at the same time.

$\vec{X} = \vec{I} - \vec{P}$: The discrepancy between the ideal and actual situations of individual $i$ at this time.

#### SURFACES
$r(\sigma,v) = 0$: The threshold curve in AR separating the region of articulation from the region of no articulation.

$a(\phi,\chi,\psi) = 0$: The threshold surface in AC separating the region of action from the region of no action.

#### NUMERICAL FUNCTIONS
$\sigma(g,i,\vec{X},\vec{I})$: A potential field over 2S measuring the salience of goal $g$ for individual $i$.

$\tau(g,i)$: An indication of the specifiability of goal $g$ for individual $i$. It has the values 0 and 1.

$v(g,i)$: A measure of the justifiability of goal $g$ for individual $i$.

$\phi(g,i)$: A measure of the valence of goal $g$ in H for individual $i$.

$\chi(g,i)$: A measure of the application, the available technology for goal achievement, of goal $g$ in H for individual $i$.

$\psi(g,i)$: A measure of the legitimacy of goal $g$ in H for individual $i$.

## Table 2.

*Mathematical Expressions of the Phases of Articulation–Activation–Institutionalization and Their Co-ordinates Shown in Table 1 of the First Edition of* Explorations in Social Change *(2, p. 95)*

| CO-ORDINATES | EXIGENCIES | REQUISITES FOR ARTICULATION | REQUISITES FOR ACTION |
|---|---|---|---|
| Deprivation Equilibrium | | Salience $\sigma(g,i,\vec{X},\vec{I})$ | Valence $\phi(\sigma(g),k(g),i)$ |
| Knowledge | $(\vec{X},\vec{I})$ | Specification $\tau(g,i)$ | Application $\chi(g,i)$ |
| Ideology | | Justification $v(g,i)$ | Legitimation $\psi(g,i)$ |

knowledge of social processes. To understand institutionalization one needs a societal model which can take into account the interactions of individuals as well as their actions. In the societal model now to be developed each individual is represented by an individual model, and the social processes are represented as the effects of the actions of individuals on the potentials for action of others.

It is possible to portray the articulations and the actions of each individual in a group by a unique individual model in the manner that has just been discussed. What is needed in the societal model, in addition, is a mathematical rendering of how the actions of some individuals affect the parameters for action of others. Figure 5 shows where this societal feedback should occur. In Figure 5 the model of the individual is depicted as a three-step psychological process. The first step is a process called Exigency Experiences in which tensions and excitations are converted into exigencies. The second step is where exigencies and various other parameters cause the articulation of goals. This step has been termed Articulation Process. The third step, in which articulated goals are converted into actions, has been termed Action Generation.

Figure 5 shows five paths by which social processes influence individual processes: (1) by stimulating discrepancies in the individual, (2) by providing dimensions for locating situations in S, (3) by providing a set of specifiable goals, (4) by creating the values which give goals their justifiability and legitimacy, and (5) by providing the technology required to achieve a goal. Operating in the other direction, individual goal oriented actions affect the social processes; so a feedback exists between individual actions and the parameters which determine whether or not actions will take place. For instance an individual who articulates and tries to achieve a goal affects the specifiability, the legitimacy, the justifiability, and the applicability of that goal for others.

Goal oriented action becomes institutionalized when the network of interrelated feedbacks for all the individuals in a group causes their action potentials (the vectors $[\phi, \chi, \psi]$ in AC) to remain above the threshold level (i.e. in the action zone). To analyze with mathematical techniques when and why this occurs one has to specify precisely and quantitatively how individual actions affect the social processes and how these processes in turn affect the individual actions, tasks which are made quite difficult by the complexity of the social processes. For example one might assume that any action by individual $i$ aimed at achieving goal $g$ would result in an increased specifiability, justifiability, and legitimacy of that goal for others. Yet this is an over simplification, because the justifiability and legitimacy of $g$ for another individual $k$ could depend on whether $i$ and $k$ were members of the same group or class. If $i$ and $k$ were members of antagonistic groups, $i$'s action toward $g$ instead might decrease its legitimacy for $k$. Another possibility is that the specifiability of $g$ for $k$ might not be increased by $i$'s action because $k$ does not recog-

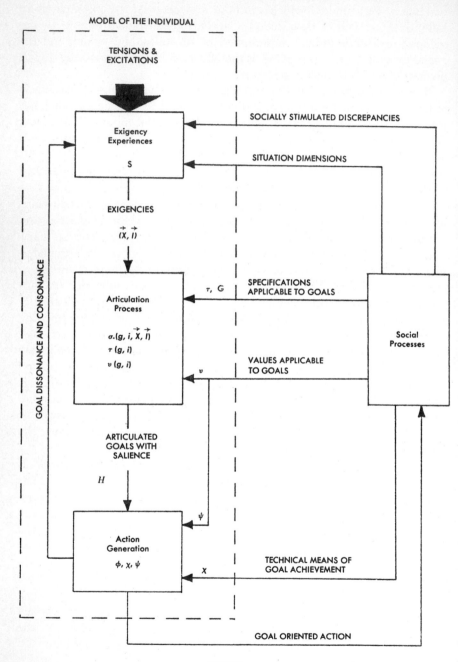

FIGURE 5

nize it as oriented toward achievement of g. To achieve this effect *i* could surround his action with propaganda that would make it appear that his action was directed toward another goal *h* when in fact in *i*'s cognitive model it is directed toward g. Whether or not *i*'s action toward g would increase the technology available to *k* for g's realization might also depend on whether or not *i* and *k* were members of the same group or on what resources *i* commanded in a system of unequal distribution of technological resources. If the president of the United States should decide to send a man to the moon, the means of achieving many goals would more likely increase for others, than if you or I should decide to send someone to the moon.

Whether or not action by *i* toward g stimulates discrepancies in others also depends on a host of factors. If *i* is General Motors and g is selling new automobiles, a rash of deflated masculinity images might result from advertising campaigns. Actions aimed at economic goals often stimulate envy or greed in others, and these discrepancies play their parts in generating more actions that perpetuate economic institutions. In general, goal oriented actions affect how other people experience needs, but the ways in which they do this are complex.

Many such problems exist in developing a societal model out of the model of the individual. Yet progress can be made toward a general model if the modeling of social feedback can be simplified. One way to do this is to condense all paths affecting the valence of goals into one. Such a simplification is shown in Figure 6, which can be compared to the more complex system shown in Figure 5. The following paragraphs will illustrate how it is then possible to represent the societal feed-back process shown in Figure 6 as a system of first-order difference equations.

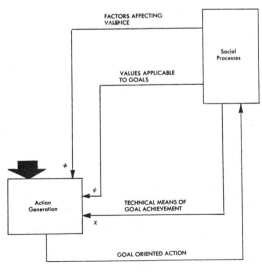

FIGURE 6

The society will be defined in the abstract as $K$ individuals numbered $1, \ldots, K$. These individuals have the potential of articulating $J$ goals numbered $1, \ldots, J$; and for each articulated goal $g$ there are $A_g$ possible goal-oriented actions numbered $1, \ldots, A_g$. Valence $\phi$ for an individual is a function of the goal to which it applies and not of the action contemplated to reach that goal; but on the other hand legitimation $\psi$ and application $\chi$ as they have been described are also functions of the particular action which is taken toward reaching the goal. Certain actions toward achieving a goal may be more legitimate than others, and the technology available for some actions may be greater than that available for other actions aimed at achieving the same goal. Therefore let:

$\phi_{g,i}(t)$   be the valence of goal $g$ for individual $i$ at time $t$,

$\chi_{g,i,j}(t)$   be the application of the $j$-th action taken toward achieving goal $g$ by individual $i$ at time $t$,

and   $\psi_{g,i,j}(t)$   be the legitimation of the $j$-th action taken toward achieving goal $g$ by individual $i$ at time $t$.

Our simplified model proposes that after the initial values of the above quantities have been specified at $t = 0$ they are increased or decreased in increments as a result of goal oriented actions taken by members of the society at later times. The times can be represented by a series of integers from 1 up to whatever number is necessary to understand the behavior of the system. The model assumes that the societal feedbacks do not vary with time or with the current values of the variables $\phi$, $\chi$, or $\psi$. They are assumed to be functions only of the individuals and the actions taken by them. The feedback to valence is given as

$D\phi_{g,i}(k,l,p)$,   the change in the valence of a goal $g$ for individual $i$ caused by individual $k$ taking the $l$-th action aimed at achieving goal $p$ for him.

Similarly the feedback to application is given as

$D\chi_{g,i,j}(k,l,p)$,   the change in application of the $j$-th action aimed at achieving goal $g$ for individual $i$ cause by individual $k$ taking the $l$-th action aimed at achieving goal $p$ for him;

and the feedback to legitimation is given as

$D\psi_{g,i,j}(k,l,p)$,   the change in legitimation of the $j$-th action aimed at achieving goal $g$ for individual $i$ cause by individual $k$ taking the $l$-th action aimed at achieving goal $p$ for him.

The valences, applications, and legitimations at any time $t+1$ are given in terms of the valences, applications, legitimations, and actions at a previous time $t$ by the following difference equations:

$$\phi_{g,i}(t+1) = \phi_{g,i}(t) + \sum_{k=1}^{K} \sum_{p=l}^{J} \sum_{l=1}^{A_p} D\phi_{g,i}(k,l,p)\, b_{k,l,p}(t) \tag{4}$$

$$\chi_{g,i,j}(t+1) = \chi_{g,i,j}(t) + \sum_{k=1}^{K} \sum_{p=l}^{J} \sum_{l=1}^{A_p} D\chi_{g,i,j}(k,l,p)\, b_{k,l,p}(t) \tag{5}$$

$$\psi_{g,i,j}(t+1) = \psi_{g,i,j}(t) + \sum_{k=1}^{K} \sum_{p=l}^{J} \sum_{l=1}^{A_p} D\psi_{g,i,j}(k,l,p)\, b_{k,l,p}(t). \tag{6}$$

The function $b_{k,l,p}$ indicates whether action has or has not been taken. $b_{k,l,p}(t)$ is zero if at time $t$ individual $k$ does not take the $l$-th action aimed at achieving goal $p$ for him,[3] and it is one if he does take this action at

[3] If specific non-actions prove to have an effect on other persons, the non-actions can be incorporated into $b$ as a kind of negative action. If $b_{i,j,g}$ represents an action taken toward $g$ and if $b_{i,j+1,g}$ represents not taking the action, then when $b_{i,j,g} = 0$, $b_{i,j+1,g} = 1$, and when $b_{i,j,g} = 1$, $b_{i,j+1,g} = 0$.

time $t$. The values of the $b_{k,l,p}(t)$ at time $t$ can be calculated from the values of the $\phi_{g,i}(t)$, $\chi_{g,i,j}(t)$, and $\psi_{g,i,j}(t)$ at this time by using the procedure outlined in the discussion of the model of the individual. In other words if the vector

$$(\phi_{g,i}(t)\,,\,\chi_{g,i,j}(t)\,,\,\psi_{g,i,j}(t))$$

does not lie in the region of action, $b_{i,j,g}(t)$ is zero, and if it does lie in the region of action, $b_{i,j,g}(t)$ is one.

The action threshold surface $a(\phi,\chi,\psi) = 0$ in the model of the individual enters into the societal model here. $a(\phi,\chi,\psi)$ might easily depend on the particular individual $i$, goal $g$, or action $j$ contemplated, or it may not be dependent on these factors. It should be written most generally as a function of them as follows:

$$a_{g,i,j}(\phi,\chi,\psi).$$

Thus the societal model has been given as a system of simultaneous difference equations with the forms

$$f(t+1) = f(t) + c\, b(t) \quad \text{or} \quad \Delta f(t) = c\, b(t).$$

The solution of this system of equations gives us the pattern of action over time in terms of the matrix function

$$[b_{k,l,p}(t)] \quad t = 1, \ldots$$

The solution is dependent on the parameters listed in Table 3. It is a difficult solution to analyze because of the non-linearity of $[b(t)]$.

Table 4 lists the large number of parameters that have to be specified before a society can be modeled. If a society consisted of just 10 persons who had five goals they could strive for by means of 3 possible actions for each goal, the model would require 150 surfaces $a(\phi,\chi,\psi)$, 350 initial values of $\phi$, $\chi$, and $\psi$ and 52,500 feedback parameters $D\phi$, $D\chi$, and $D\psi$. The possible combinations of these parameters in this relatively simple model might honestly be said to be astronomical; yet the model is not unrealistic, because living social systems are complex. The problem of complexity is not too serious, because simple sociological considerations quickly lead to great reductions in the number of parameters that have to be specified.

## Table 3.

*Parameters to Be Specified in the Mathematical Model*

1. Parameters in the Model of the Individual. These parameters are described in Table 1:

   $G, S, r(\sigma,\upsilon), a(\phi,\chi,\psi), \sigma(g,i,X,I), \tau(g,i), \upsilon(g,i), \phi(g,i), \chi(g,i), \psi(g,i)$

2. Parameters in the Model of Society:

   $K$: The number of persons in the society

   $J$: The number of goals that can potentially be articulated by members of the society

   $A_g, g = 1, \ldots, J$: The number of actions that are oriented toward achieving goal $g$.

   $a_{g,i,j}(\phi,\chi,\psi), g = 1, \ldots, J, i = 1, \ldots, K, j = 1, \ldots, A_g$:

   The action threshold surfaces in AC that tell when individual $i$ will take action $j$ oriented toward achieving goal $g$ for him.

   $\phi_{g,i}(0) \quad , \quad \chi_{g,i,j}(0) \quad , \quad \psi_{g,i,j}(0) \quad , \quad g = 1, \ldots, J, i = 1, \ldots, K$
   $j = 1, \ldots, A_g$ :

   The initial values of valence, application, and legitimation at time $t = 0$.

   $D\phi_{g,i}(k,l,p), D\chi_{g,i,j}(k,l,p), \quad D\psi_{g,i,j}(k,l,p), g = 1, \ldots, J$
   $i = 1, \ldots, K, j = 1, \ldots, A_g$ :

   The feedback constants for valence, application, and legitimation.

### Table 4.

*The Number of Parameters That Have to Be Specified*

| Parameters | Number |
|---|---|
| $a_{g,i,j}(\phi,\chi,\psi)$ | $K \sum_{g=1}^{J} A_g$ |
| $\chi_{g,i,j}(0)$ | $K \sum_{g=1}^{J} A_g$ |
| $\psi_{g,i,j}(0)$ | $K \sum_{g=1}^{J} A_g$ |
| $\phi_{g,i}(0)$ | $KJ$ |
| $D\chi_{g,i,j}(k,l,p)$ | $\left( K \sum_{g=1}^{J} A_g \right)^2$ |
| $D\psi_{g,i,j}(k,l,p)$ | $\left( K \sum_{g=1}^{J} A_g \right)^2$ |
| $D\phi_{g,i}(k,l,p)$ | $K_2 J \sum_{g=1}^{J} A_g$ |

Many things can be done with the societal model just outlined. In the first place it is hardly worth striving for elegance in the solution of the difference equations (4), (5), and (6), because they may not be in the particularized form that sociologists will want to use, and because the solutions can be calculated by electronic computers. The use of the model can take one, the other, or both of two directions: (1) to search out the parameters that result in special processes such as institutionalization, sporadic but unsuccessful attempts at change, or no successful collective efforts, or (2) to discover what patterns of social action result when the parameters are specified according to social structures that have already been hypothesised.

Although the model has the potential for analyzing social behavior in which no social groups are involved, it also is likely to reveal structures that are presently dealt with in terms of social groups. For example let us examine a few hypothetical situations that might occur if we used the model in the first manner, to search for parameters. A negative case of no social interaction would exist if all the DX (here X is used to indicate either $\phi$, $\chi$, or $\psi$.) were zero; and a case of sustained social interaction would exist if the $DX_{g,i,j}(k,l,p)$ were large when $k$ and $i$ were members of the same group and small when they were not. If they were very, very small when $k$ and $i$ were not members of the same group, a case of pluralism would be simulated.

If the model were used in the second manner, to discover patterns of social action, group structure would help to assign values to the parameters. For example, a common threshold surface $a(\phi,\chi,\psi) = 0$ might be assigned to all individuals who were members of the same group. Another variant might assign common $a_{g,i,i}$ $(\phi,\chi,\psi)$ and common $DX_{g,i,f}(k,l,p)$ to all individuals who are members of the same group. This variant could be improved by giving a few individuals in each group a lower action threshold when it is necessary to allow for innovators.

Because the speed of modern computers permits the rapid analysis of a large number of theoretical cases, it should be possible to use this mathematical model to learn more about the conditions under which institutionalization occurs. Probably the conditions so discovered that will arouse the most interest will be the ones that are not presently revealed by non-mathematical analysis.

## BIBLIOGRAPHY

1. Newell, Allen, and Herbert A. Simon. *Human Problem Solving*. Englewood Cliffs, N.J.: Prentice-Hall, Inc., 1972.
2. Zollschan, George K., and Hirsch, Walter, eds. *Explorations in Social Change*. Boston: Houghton Mifflin, 1964.

# SECTION THREE

metamorphases in the theory
of institutionalization

# Introduction

The *troika* of chapters presented in this section is intended to convey the Theory of Institutionalization, Pegasus-like, to a new plane of conceptualization. Though each chapter can stand alone and lends itself to uses related strictly to the topic with which it deals, a consistent development of ideas underlies the section as a whole.

Viewed initially from the perspective of a unified argument to which each of the chapters contributes, Zollschan's "Fourfold Root" develops compass points for the location of different kinds of metatheoretical approaches in sociology and thus indicates, even if it cannot by itself entirely vindicate, the direction taken by Zollschan's model relative to alternative possibilities that have been explored and exploited in sociology. The alternatives outlined by this chapter are termed pro-active collectivism, reactive collectivism, pro-active individualism, and reactive individualism. Together these orientations form a grid in which both classical and contemporary sociological theories can be organized for purposes of classification and theoretical relations between them sharpened and clarified. Zollschan's option for proactive individualism is openly confessed and, to a limited extent, justified.

Zollschan and Overington's "Reasons for Conduct and the Conduct of Reason" singles out motivation by Goals or Reasons as the element in any social theorist's explanatory model to be subjected to analysis and criticism. In doing so, it appears to veer toward the metatheoretical orientation of pro-active individualism previously outlined in the "Four-

217

fold Root." However, the chapter advances the argument characteristic of that orientation in some astonishing ways. It proposes, in effect, that "reasons" (in some sense or another) are precisely the element held in common by all social scientific theories and that motivation, defined in its broadest sense, applies to all of the metatheoretical orientations discussed in the previous chapter, even if only in an ironic sense.

The "Prototractatus" is the culmination of the section. It provides a statement, rough though it may be, of the overall model as it stands in its present state of development. The prefix "proto" gives unambiguous warning that what is being presented is not regarded in any way as a final statement. What this tentative lexicon of action invites is the attention of critics who share our concern for the development of general theoretical frameworks in sociology and allied fields. In effect, the piece constructs a language — both its terms and some of its elementary syntax — which will provide for explanations of action. The purpose of constructing this language is to spell out in greater detail the range of theoretical terms, as well as some of the more important combinatorial rules, proposed in "Reasons for Conduct" as potentially more adequate and general than currently accepted accounts.

Taken by itself, the "Fourfold Root" embodies such advantages as may be gained from organizing a large body of existing theory along new principles. Such a conceptual rotation is designed to breathe life into the cliché-ridden corpse of theoretical exegesis (without, we hope, making too many of the theorists discussed "turn in their graves"). Our sociological Lazarus can only be raised by inventing a meta-theoretical device which upsets the comfortable cohabitation of "old friends" and joins "old enemies" in unaccustomed warm embrace. If the *Structure of Social Action* brought the benefits of "European Sociology" to North American natives, the "Fourfold Root" liberates their progeny (which now, effectively, comprises all the world's sociologists) from the procrustean bed into which its formulations had been poured.

"Reasons for Conduct and the Conduct of Reason" proposes a unified solution for at least three perennial debates: the debate concerning the relativity of theoretical accounts of motives; the debate concerning the necessity of differentiating between law-like and rule-following explanations of human conduct; and finally, the debate concerning the possibility of an acceptable criterion for evaluating the conceptual adequacy of social explanations. The frequent use of the word "debate" in the foregoing sentence will amply reveal how work in the chapter proceeded! The solutions to these various controversies allow for an integrated presentation of the problem of motivation theory regarded in all of its dimensions. In so doing, it becomes possible to present a general theory of motive potentially encompassing the entire range of social productions of explanations. If persons wish to use the piece for improving the rationality of their conduct they are, of course, most welcome to do so. In any case, we are confident that readers will find that it improves the conduct of their social-scientific rationality!

The first draft of Zollschan's "Prototractatus" was conceived and completed on Mik'laj Kopernik's five-hundredth birthday. Whether Copernicus received the compliment with favour is hard to tell. In many ways this lexicon of action provides antiphonal companionship to the previous chapters: the Mahlerian complexities of the "Fourfold Root," the fugal convolutions of the "Conduct of Reason" both resolve themselves more clearly in a series of declarative statements with a decidedly Mozartian touch. Certainly, the first draft was the first piece Zollschan has ever "shaken out of his sleeve." Most fortunately, it received a second, extremely salutory, "shaking up" by Michael Overington who has supplied the piece with a priorly appended "Metatractatus" in the form of instructions for use. If the lacunae all careful readers will still fill in this work, act merely to attract persons intending to detract, the meshes between the holes are sure to catch quite a few of them. The piece is a blueprint (or better, a partial blueprint) for a full-scale exposition of the theoretical model which will be done in good time.

# 9

*George K. Zollschan*

# Concerning the Fourfold Root of the "Principle of Sufficient Reason" in Sociological Explanation

*Philosophy is a monster with many heads,*
*each speaks with a different tongue.*
                                    *Schopenhauer*

When Schopenhauer presented his doctoral thesis (73) he considered statements about the conjunction of motive and action to be one of the four ways in which ideas can be related so as to yield acceptable explanations.[1] Later in his life (74) he promoted motive — or rather its subtrate, *Wille* — to the rank of primeaval phenomenon, designed to replace the insubstantial realm of *noumena* with which Kant had environed the human apparatus of reasoning and perception. Natural

---

[1] This is, of course, the *principium rationis sufficientis agendi* which refers to the relation between motive and action. The other forms of relationship between ideas according to Schopenhauer are: between ground and consequent; between cause and effect; and space-time relations (73; see also 28, p. 219).

forms, including organisms, Schopenhauer saw as concretions and embodiments of Wille.[2]

Schopenhauer did not systematically extend his conception of Wille as the principle which creates forms in nature and binds them together to consideration of the manner in which social "structures" are constituted. Yet, it is precisely in application to social structures (viewed, perhaps, as complex instrumentalities for goal attainment; 103, p. 94) that the notion of motive as the principle of structural formation and maintenance has direct applicability. For Schopenhauer, motive was the consciousness of Wille and also the matrix of conscious representation. Transdiction of the idea of motive into Kant's noumenal void made for an inspiring metaphor of physical energies and biological vitalities underlying the flux of appearances. It made also for a dangerously literal application of Schiller's dictum: *"Was der Geist verspricht, leistet die Natur"* (approximately: "what mind anticipates, nature yields"). Yet, Schiller's verificationist notion, though hardly applicable to natural manifestations scientifically regarded, has an uncanny ring of truth when applied to the construction of social realities. My theoretical model applies the notion of motive to the realm to which it properly belongs, the realm of social and of psychic structures.

I shall show that various sociological approaches are susceptible to a fourfold classification. I shall argue, moreover, that one of these types (currently the most neglected) is superior to the other three in its explanatory potential. As already intimated, this is a type of explanation based on motive. In connection with the question of motive, an additional preliminary word is in order.

Broadly speaking, two conceptions of motive are extant: motive by "reasons" or "goals," and motivation dependent upon some stimulation or excitation either internal or external to the organism in question. The former of these I refer to as the sociological conception of motive; the latter (where applied to social phenomena) the psychologistic conception of motive. Among other things, the following classification clarifies the demarcation between psychologistic and genuinely sociological explanations of social events.

Two cross-cutting distinctions are suitable for categorizing the various kinds of explanatory models which have been, at various times and in various places, proposed and accepted in sociological analysis. The first of these axes concerns the unit of analysis: whether it is individuals whose activities (aggregated as well as concerted) are viewed as composing the society or whether the culture, or social system, or even *Geist*,

---

[2] It is worth noting that Schopenhauer was the philosophical forerunner of Freudian *libido* theory. He describes the sexual impulse as ". . . the kernel of the will-to-live and, consequently, the concentration of all willing" (74, pp. 513–514). This is not meant to decry Freud's originality, the consummation of which went far beyond mere philosophical *apercús*.

is considered irreducible merely to the actions of individuals composing it or acting as its "carriers."[3] The second of these axes distinguishes the units of analysis selected (whether wholes or individuals) according to whether they are conceptualized as pro-active originators of effects or as entirely reactive to their situations.[4] The resulting four categories we may call, respectively: Pro-active Holism, Pro-active Individualism, Reactive Holism, and Reactive Individualism.[5]

These categories are not proposed as being exhaustive in the sense that other kinds of distinctions between types of explanatory models are considered impossible, or illegitimate, or even unenlightening. The Windelband-Rickert distinction between nomothetic and ideographic explanation (98, pp. 136-160; 70) cuts across them, as do distinctions between explanatory models based on assumptions of consensus versus assumptions of conflict (see, for example, 11, pp. 158-163; 69, pp. 129-131).[6] Parsons's very special use of the terms "positivistic" and "voluntaristic" (56, pp. 81-82) also corresponds, broadly speaking, to the pro-active — reactive dichotomy. Since his avowedly "voluntaristic" theory fits least uncomfortably into the category of reactive holism, and also because of his highly idiosyncratic employment of these terms, they are intentionally avoided. Nagel's fourfold classification of explanatory strategies as *deductive, probabilistic, functional* or *teleological,* and *genetic* refers to logical forms of explanation rather than to the characteristics of explanatory models in the sense discussed here (54, pp. 20-26). In principle, at least, several (though not all) of these explanatory strategies could be employed in any one of the types of explanatory models distinguished here.[7]

Neither is the claim advanced that all sociological theories can be

[3] The distinction between holism (or collectivism) and individualism (or elementism) is well established in the relevant literature. Discussions of it may be found in Hayek (26, pp. 53–63), Martindale (46, pp. 150–151). More recently Jarvie (34, pp. 173–178) has documented the methodological individualism debate in a lengthy, though itself far from complete, discussion.

[4] The expression "pro-active" is suggested by Murray (53, p. 15) and has subsequently been used by Allport (2) and Zollschan and Hansen (102, p. 37).

[5] This categorical system was first developed in conversation with Professor Hansen of the University of California, Berkeley, when working on our joint paper (102). At that time it was not considered sufficiently highly developed to warrant exposition.

[6] Ronald Dore's fourfold classification of *piecemeal, historical, static,* and *issues* approaches depends upon the acceptance of previously stated propositions implying the stance of methodological individualism (14, 1967, pp. 418–419).

[7] Nagel's classification is meant to apply to scientific fields generally. In application to sociology and allied fields it is somewhat misleading. For one thing, teleological explanations in sociology can conform to the deductive model. What is more, lumping together teleological with functional explanations obscures the issue of individualism versus collectivism. Nagel does address himself to this issue later in his book and displays a very shallow understanding of what is involved (54, pp. 535–546).

fitted perfectly into the categorical scheme. Few can, if their full complexity (not to speak of ambiguity) is taken into account. Symbolic interactionism, for instance, is particularly difficult to fit. It seems to straddle the orientations of reactive holism and pro-active individualism, though individualist statements can usually be found in any symbolic, interactionist account.[8] Parsons also draws the earliest comprehensive statement of his own theoretical position (56) from what he takes to be a "convergence" between different theories variously fitting, as I hope to indicate, into the reactive holist, pro-active individualist, and reactive individualist categories. The particular categories chosen here have been developed because they present compass points for mapping theoretical themes which appear repeatedly in sociological writings. It is hoped their elucidation can help to clear up a certain amount of confusion. The fact that the classification of various views into one or another category cannot be entirely neat and tidy need not, necessarily, be seen as a disadvantage. Indeed, one may express the hope that, in the future, it will stimulate theoreticians to commit themselves less ambiguously to their chosen positions.

The proposed set of categories orders types of explanations put forward and accepted in the social sciences regardless of their soundness on some methodological criterion. Instead, it constitutes a classification of types of explanatory models irrespective of whether these have been adopted as metaphysical dogmata concerning the reality in question or "self-evident" sets of axioms, or selected on strictly methodological grounds. My own preference for pro-active individualism will show clearly enough in the following discussion but may as well be stated at the outset. The suggested categories are not "paradigmata" in Kuhn's

---

[8] It is enlightening to compare the papers by Arnold Rose and Herbert Blumer in a symposium designed to consolidate the symbolic interactionist position (71, pp. 3–19; and 7, pp. 179–192). Rose stresses "role" and "socialization" components and the approach. Judging by his account, symbolic interactionism could be fitted into the reactive holism category. Blumer, on the other hand, stresses terms like "self-interpretation," "definition of the situation," and so forth. His account fits unambiguously into the pro-active individualist category.

One may note that Blumer in this particular context, unlike Rose, professes an interest in applying symbolic interactionist theory to problems of social change.

In a study of symbolic interactionists' opinions on the suitability of symbolic interaction theory for handling the topic of social change, Vaughan & Reynolds (101) describe the responses of that group of sociologists who consider symbolic interactionism suitable for analysis of social change in terms strongly suggestive of pro-active individualism.

Oddly enough, members of the group giving this positive reply (which is seen as being relatively unorthodox in the context of American Sociology in the three decades prior to his article) are linked by a "cohesive, multibonded, network of relationships" (101, p. 337). The maintenance of a position of pro-active individualism, since it is unorthodox, paradoxically requires vigorously conducted symbolic interaction with like-minded "significant others!"

sense of the term, since little if anything corresponding to Kuhn's "normal science" as yet exists in sociology.[9]

Popper's discussion of what he calls "essentialist" and "nominalist" explanation probably provides the soundest available demarcation between metaphysics and methodology in scientific argument (66, Vol. 1, pp. 31-33). Put in the briefest possible way, nominalist argument proceeds by developing "if $x$ then $y$" propositions (or the logical co-variants) rather than making statements about the essential nature of the subject matter under consideration. A word on the last point may serve to clarify the meaning of the pro-active-reactive distinction as employed in this discussion. A modern nominalist interpretation requires no assumption that pro-action is inherently "uncaused." Translated into nominalist terms, the freedom versus determinism problem, for instance, ceases to be bothersome in sociological explanation. In a nominalist frame of reference, pro-action means no more than that, for purposes of the analysis under consideration the unit in question is an explanatory terminus; that its motions, or operations, or goals are most suitably viewed as independent variables. The ascription of reactivity to a unit, by the same reasoning, implies that its operations are suitably construed as dependent variables. The decision as to which variable is dependent or independent, in the final analysis, becomes a matter of heuristics.[10]

The above discussion clarifies a distinction I would suggest between psychological and sociological explanations of motive. In psychological explanations motivated activity is viewed as dependent upon events obtruding themselves on the person. In sociological explanations of motive, activity is viewed as depending on goals attracting the person. My earlier characterization of the reactivity of a unit as being relative to the unit's "situation" may also be expanded in the context of this argument. "Situation" can be taken to mean any source of variation upon which the unit's operations are dependent. It may, thus, include some aspects of the structure of the unit itself. For instance, when the reactive system in question is an animal's behavior viewed as responding to stimulation, such responses may be explained by stimuli originating from *within* the

[9] By "normal science" Kuhn means a tradition of research "firmly based upon one or more past scientific achievements" and acknowledged, for a time, as supplying foundation for further practice. A situation prior to the establishment of normal science is characterized by the existence of competing "schools" (38, pp. 10, 16).

Admittedly, it is not always easy to find a clear cut and unambiguous distinguishing mark between what Kuhn calls normal science and this or that competing school; at any rate, so long as the latter contains a cumulative tradition of research rooted in overarching assumptions shared by members of that school. Moreover, what constitutes a firm basis on past scientific achievements is frequently a matter of opinion.

[10] This is not to imply that problems of moral responsibility, or cognate issues, can be settled in a similar manner. Quite clearly, attribution of responsibility is different from (if not more than) a question of heuristics. Kant may have been perfectly right in insisting upon a metaphysical definition of pro-activity on the basis of morality.

animal's organism as well as to stimuli originating in its environment. Both organism and environment as interactive system may be construed as constituting the animal's situation. For exactly analogous reasons, sociological explanations based upon the idea of mutually entailing relationships of variables in some "social system" will be designated as reactive unless these variables are specifically related to activities of individuals (as they emphatically are in the "economic systems" of macro-economic analysis).[11]

Motive as an explanatory principle is central only in individualistic types of explanation. Holistic explanations, if they consider motives at all, view them as subserving, or being totally shaped by, processes which are defined (whether correctly or not) as lying outside the realm of motive. Nevertheless, holistic explanations as much as individualistic ones can be categorized according to whether or not they contain fundamental assumptions of a supra-individual nisus operating through history.

### Pro-active Collectivism: Evolutionary Nisus and the 'Active Society'

Lunovis habet somnium
se culmen rer' ess' ominum
Lunovis.[12]

The term "evolution" has acquired a number of meanings in the history of its use. As rigorously employed in Darwinian biology it refers to

[11] Nagel argues that macroeconomic postulates include "assumptions concerning relations between large-scale statistical aggregates" and are not, therefore, individualistic (54, pp. 543–544). I should like to make it clear that I regard models based on aggregates of this type as individualistic models. Indeed, there is no methodological distinction between macro-economics and marginal utility economics in this particular respect. The supply functions, demand functions, Edgeworth contract curves, and the like of marginal utility economics are all based on reasoning from *aggregates* of individuals making economic decisions (models of monopolistic and monopsonistic exchange and their modifications are, of course, exceptions to this rule). Watkins is more correct on this issue when he relates Keynesian economics to "individualistic variables" such as propensities to consume, propensities to save, liquidity preferences, and so forth (82, p. 35). In calling such variables "psychological," however, Watkins offends against my distinction between psychological and sociological conceptions of motive.

[12] Poetic accompaniment for these Schopenhaurian quartet movements is supplied by his admirer Christian Morgenstern (51; 52). Morgenstern's German is quite untranslatable and should, in any case, be easily enough intelligible to readers inured to Parsonian sociologese. The first of these "German" poems to be featured here, however, is in a sort of Latin and, therefore, translatable. As a service to non-classicists the following free translation is provided by the author:
"A Mooncalf up there had the dream,
It was Creation's act supreme,
A Mooncalf."

a two-step process of *variation* (mutation) and *selection* (differential viability) of species. Selection besides the special case of assortative mating depends upon the differing levels of adaptation of various zoological and botanical forms to their environments; their differential success in the "struggle for existence." In and of itself, Darwin's evolutionary hypothesis can be characterized as an historical statement about the ancestry of plants and animals (66, Vol. 2, p. 322). As applied to explanations of social processes, however, "evolutionism" typically refers to conceptions of social change as being subject to specifiable principles of historical development.[13] Implicit in such principles is the idea of a *nisus*, a force acting in and through history and impelling historical events in a particular direction. Rather than using the broader and possibly confusing term "evolutionism," I therefore use the expression "evolutionary nisus." The idea of an inner spring uncoiling itself in human history justifies the term "pro-active" for evolutionist views of the kind to be considered. The collectivist nature of such views is implicit in the postulate of directionality in historical process which either is inherent in the nature and constitutive of all individuals, or occurs regardless of their incidental purposes or intentions.

Two major varieties of pro-active holism are to be distinguished for our purposes. The first may be described as positivistic evolutionism. It finds its purest statement in Comte's conception of "social dynamics." The other is dialectical evolutionism as exemplified in Hegel's philosophy. Both of these strains have had great influence on social thought; Comte's directly and Hegel's mainly through the mediacy of Marx's views.[14]

---

[13] There is no inherent reason why sociology should not concern itself with intended, or stochastic, or unintended variations in the forms of social relationships or items of culture, and the selection of such differentiated structures or culture items according to some specifiable principle. W. G. Sumner, for example, wrote of the "struggle for existence" and of "societal selection" precisely in the senses indicated above (81, pp. 119–159, and 173–260). Concerns of this type are customarily placed under the rubric of "social Darwinism" rather than of "evolutionism."

[14] The term "evolution" was introduced into scientific discourse by Herbert Spencer after the death of both Comte and Hegel (80). The designation of views based on pro-active collectivism as "evolutionist," however, conforms to what since has become common usage.

Spencer's views are not developed here in any detail because they fit less well into the category of pro-active holism than do those of the thinkers here discussed; namely: Comte, Hegel, and Marx. Though Spencer's sociology does imply a conception of evolutionary social process as being — in some sense — independent of individual persons, he clearly enunciates a moral preference for the emergence of highly individualistic and pro-active persons as one of the possible resultants of societal evolution. (78, p. 569). The resultant in question he designates Industrial Society, as distinct from Military Society which is centralized and dominated by collectivist orientations.

The central principle of Comte's social dynamics is the Law of Three Stages. Each stage of evolution is bound up with a common mode of thought and sentiment. The initial, *theological* type of thought is replaced, via the intermediate *metaphysical* stage, by *positivism*. This Comte sees as an inevitable and determinate pattern of development which, however, proceeds at different rates in different societies, and in different spheres of thought within a given society. When a sphere of thought reaches the positive stage it gains the status of science (see 28, pp. 333-354). Comte's positivism is based on the idea of direct access to the "truth" by the exercise of observational induction. Unproblematic as access to positive knowledge is, in this "sitting duck" conception of truth, the human understanding must undergo a determinate path of evolution before it chooses, and finds, the proper route to such knowledge.

Comte views his Law of Three Stages as one of the first fruits of sociology's assumption of positive status. One may well ask how such a generalization could itself result from the exercise of direct observation. His answer to this question is highly germane to the present discussion. He states that, in the realm of inorganic matter, elements rather than the whole are observable. In the organic realm, by contrast, ". . . the whole of the object is . . . more readily accessible" (26, p. 176). It is clear that social as well as biological phenomena belong to the organic realm. Thus, mankind viewed as an organism becomes the basis of Comte's conception of sociology and the history of mankind displays determinate stages of development much as a given biological organism can be demonstrated to go through phases of growth and maturation. The underlying principle propelling the growth and maturation of this social organism may properly be described as something like a "gravitational pull" of positive knowledge. Many current conceptions of economic development, are infused by similar assumptions of a gravitational pull upon socio-economic systems of expectations of higher material standards of living.

Hegel's central assumption is that history does not simply flow along but that it has a "meaning"; that the world is ruled by reason. To understand this plan or *Geist* of history is the special task of philosophy. Since the nature of the Geist is freedom, and the Geist is free only insofar as it knows itself to be free, Hegel wants to depict the history of the world as a process whereby the Geist comes to know itself and thereby becomes free. Every historical event is related to this process of becoming (freely translated from 70, p. 10.).

Kant's logical problem concerning the antimonies of reason is transmuted in Hegelian dialectics into the dynamic process whereby history progresses towards its metaphysical climax — the realm of freedom

(66, Vol. 1, p. 38).[15] The dialectic motion of history proceeds as follows: each state of history (thesis) is in its measure ". . . a revelation of the Absolute, but each is one-sided, and therefore in the long run leads to contradiction" (27, p. 299). The Geist develops by making contradictions more explicit (antithesis). Thesis and antithesis then become resolved in synthesis, and the synthesis, in turn, becomes a new thesis generating inner contradictions of its own. In this dialectic progression the Geist advances to ever higher degrees of truth and freedom; and in this advance Hegel finds the meaning of history.

Hayek, among others, has noted the basic agreement between Comte and Hegel (see, 26, p. 192). Certainly, Hegel's Geist is a holistic concept much as is Comte's social super-organism and Hegel's *Volksgeister* (national spirits) correspond to Comte's different societies.[16] Individuals for Hegel are mere moments in history and even the activity of major historical figures (his "world historical individuals") constitutes no more than the "cunning of reason" in endowing them with extra-large rations of Geist (see 42, pp. 308-309). Again, in Comte's end-state, mankind guided by positive knowledge of determinate laws, exhibits some startling similarities with Hegel's realm of freedom in which freedom and necessity come to coincide, as do reality and reason. In both conceptions, history is propelled by moving forces in the direction of the end-state described. Such points of similarity between positivistic and dialectical evolutionism, however, must not be allowed to obscure the stark opposition of these two views on the question of determinacy.

The fundamental axiom of positivism is that phenomena are governed by laws. Determinacy is universal. Like other levels of natural existence, society is governed by rational laws operating with natural necessity. Hegelian dialectics, on the other hand, views the world as an indeterminate process of becoming. "Being-as-such is the acting subject becoming conscious of its own existence" (86, pp. 15-16). According to this view, if society were governed by natural laws it would be unfree and, therefore, irrational. To this extent, then, the Hegelian view may be said to hold an increment of pro-activity. Marcuse draws an additional conclusion about the opposition of positivism and dialectics. He sees positivism as essentially biased in favor of social harmony, while the ontological contradictions built into the fundamental assumption of dialectics dispose proponents of the dialectical method to analyse

[15] Dialectics can thus be understood as Hegel's response to the Kantian demonstration of logical problems arising out of the attempt to deduce matters of fact by pure reason alone (98, p. 24). Hegel had no time for Kant's "philosophy of reflection" which separated subject from object. The *Geist* was conceived by him as an amalgam of subject and object evolving dialectically through history toward the "Absolute."

[16] Berlin describes him as viewing human institutions as ". . . great collective quasi-personalities, which possess a life and character of their own and cannot be described purely in terms of the individuals who compose them" (4, p. 53).

social processes in terms of social contradictions and, therefore, of conflict (see 45, pp. 374-388).

The opposition between Hegelian dialectics and positivistic assumptions of determinism becomes somewhat blurred in the work of Karl Marx (Marcuse's disclaimers notwithstanding) whose self-avowed aim is precisely to establish dialectics as the "laws of motion" of societal process (see, for example 66, Vol. 2, pp. 81-88). Marcuse is correct, however, in attributing to dialectical theories a tendency towards emphasising conflict rather than consensus in social relations.

Materialism, Marx's philosophical starting point, consists for him in the replacement of Hegel's Geist by *Praxis* as the "substance" of evolutionary process. Praxis is natural, real, and sensuous. It creates "existence" and existence, in its turn, determines consciousness. Hegel was standing on his head, so to speak. The substitution of Praxis for Geist is meant to plant Hegelianism on its feet. Men begin to distinguish themselves from animals as soon as they *produce* their means of subsistence. For man, therefore, the essential feature of Praxis is production. On the human or social plane of existence, "materialism" thus finds its exemplification in "material" production; and Marx is primarily, perhaps exclusively, concerned with this plane (see 72, especially pp. 30-35 for a brilliant discussion of Marx's philosophical presuppositions).

While pro-action is inherently constitutive of Marx's conception of Praxis creating social existence, sociological holism is professed by him explicitly. "The real nature of man is the totality of social relations . . ." (47, p. 68) and any individual can only be regarded in the context of the particular form of society to which he belongs. What remains individual in this conception is "consciousness," but consciousness is the product of existential conditions created by Praxis which, itself, is social. Dialectical process on the social plane, for Marx, becomes embodied in the idea of class conflict.

Marx has a conception of evolutionary stages in history — primitive communism; oriental despotism; feudalism; capitalism — each of which is characterized by a distinctive mode of production (49, pp. 47-49). Modes of production are associated with relations of production. Such relations of production necessarily entail differentials of access to, and control of, the means of production (at least, in evolutionary phases between primitivism and the post-historical classless society).

Out of these, existentially given, differences in ownership and control arises consciousness of interest. Marx's sociology proper is concerned with the conditions under which consciousness of interest arises and with the formation of classes as organized interest groups. Together with consciousness, non-economic relations (including political power) constitute a superstructure based upon the "objective" reality of production, its modes, means and relations (see 11, pp. 8-27 for a concise and lucid exposition of Marx's sociology).

The law of development governing history is conflict between classes. Revolutionary changes involving the succession of different classes to dominance in the underlying basic structure of relations of production, are the measure of dialectical process in history. Overarching all of these changes is a gigantic dialectic triad in which an original pre-historic state of freedom (thesis) is lost at the price of economic pro-ductivity (antithesis) involving exploitative relations of production and alienation. The post-historical classless society is to provide the synthesis in which both freedom and economic productivity come to a state of mutual entailment. (11, pp. 28-29).

It is unnecessary to elaborate on the reasons why theories of social change based upon conceptions of an evolutionary nisus have become unfashionable in contemporary sociology. For one thing, Popper has given them the coup de grace from the point of view of their scientific respectability (see particularly, 67). Percy Cohen has enumerated some of the considerations influencing the rejection of such theories in favor of orientations more inclined toward reactive holism (10, p. 38).[17] The recent resurgence of interest in social evolution as evinced by Parsons and some of his followers is based on ideas of *differentiation* and *adaptation* (61, 63). Briefly stated, this conception of evolution views social systems as becoming differentiated in response to the functional problems faced by them. The hypothesis proposed is that the more highly differentiated systems are more "adaptive" (58, p. 339).[18] This emphasis in neo-evolutionist sociology on social systems responding to problems

[17] Cohen mentions the assumptions, among others, that "existing primitive societies represented the early stages of human social development" and that societies could be placed on an evolutionary scale relative to fixed criteria of development. Infer-ences from the assumption of unilineal development, through a determinate succession of stages, have proved particularly vulnerable to criticism. Not sufficiently vulnerable, however, to deter Professor Parsons from adopting a terminology of developmental stages in his recent neo-evolutionist treatise (10, pp. 26–27).

[18] There is a striking similarity between the terms "differentiation" and "adapta-tion" and the Darwinian concepts of "variation" and "selection." This aping of Darwinian terminology must not be allowed to obscure the fundamental difference between the Parsonian and Darwinian concepts of evolution. Differentiation, in Parsonian terms, refers to increasing functional specialization, not to random varia-tion. Adaptation, also, does not refer to viability in a given environment but to a system's functioning in relation to its environment. Parsons changes the meaning in his neo-evolutionist writings to refer to the capacity for taking "further developmental steps" (61, p. 339). It is not at all clear from reading Parsons' account in what direction such developmental steps are supposed to lead, that is, unless development itself is taken to mean movement in the direction of ". . . more differentiated social and symbolic systems" (816, p. 386). If the latter interpretation is correct and adaption refers to the capacity to differentiate, the Parsonian hypothesis may be rephrased as follows: the more differentiated a social (or symbolic) system, the greater is its capacity to undergo further differentiation. Though the hypothesis stated in this way is quite plausible, one does wonder if Parsons would not have wanted to say something over and beyond this formulation.

generated in their "environments," though holistic in tone, conveys the image of reactivity rather than of pro-activity. The inner spring, the nisus, is missing. Nevertheless, recourse to the rhetoric of evolutionism suggests dissatisfaction on the part of theorists employing the reactive holist model of explanation with its capacity to do justice to social change.

Neo-evolutionism is not the only current tendency in sociological thought attesting to the continued viability of pro-active holism as an accepted rhetoric of explanation. Dialectical analysis, also, had contemporary proponents, notably, in the English speaking world, Herbert Marcuse (43; 44; 45). In recent years, various versions of this approach have enjoyed great popularity among sociologists. The idea of a fixed directionality in history is rather weak in modern sociological dialectics. Yet, the banner of an evolutionary nisus, though tattered, flaps on bravely against the storm of disappointed prognostications.

The need among many sociologists for explanations based on assumptions of pro-activity, additionally, finds expression, if not satisfaction, in theoretical formulations denuded of the conception of an evolutionary nisus. Etzioni's theory of societal guidance provides a noteworthy case in point (17, 18). Etzioni's imagery of an end-state, conceived of as the "active society, one that is master of itself" and achieves the "fuller realization of its values," is presented merely as a desirable option, not as an inevitable outcome (17, pp. vii, 6). His formulations are not meant to do the relatively modest service of acting as "midwife" to history. Their avowed purpose is to act as a progenitor of future history; a progenitor, however, whose fecundity is subject to prudent scientific doubt. To be sure, a view of history as the unfolding of the *conditions* for collective mastery of fate may be glimpsed in Etzioni's account but such mastery lies latent until the present time. The history of mankind up to the dawn of the "post-modern" period is one of accommodation to "social bonds" or, at best, protest against them.[19] Now ". . . man is reaching a new phase in which ability to obtain freedom, as well as the ability to subjugate others, is greatly extended" (17, p. 5). The eternal "now" is the point in time at which Hegel's history always reaches its climax.[20] For Etzioni, the equally momentous "now" marks the point at which reactivity is no longer necessary and the realm of (collective) pro-activity can come into its own.

Etzioni's sociological holism is propounded with unusually stark candour. Resting his case on a variety of statements ranging all the way from Martin Buber's designation of "I-Thou" mutuality as the primary

[19] The date of publication of Etzioni's book, perhaps, serves to demarcate the merely modern period from the post-modern one. For a deliciously acid account of Etzioni's conception of evolutionary phases, see Nisbet's review (55, pp. 990–991).

[20] Embarrassingly enough for Hegel's admirers today, the "now" of his own time and place was embodied in the Prussian garrison state.

substance of human existence, to Selznick's protestation that even leaders are not free to follow their whims but are "agents of institutionalization" (17, pp. 2, 83), he comes to the conclusion that "the individual is almost completely absorbed in the society . . . and accounted for by it . . ." (17, p. 3). The word "almost" in the preceding quotation is intended to give some leeway for "individual reflection" (shades of Marx's "consciousness") which must be translated into social action before it can be of any consequence, in his view. Proceeding from this position of metaphysical collectivism, Etzioni then goes on to postulate the axiom that ". . . the self which is to be activated . . . (is the) self of a social collectivity (17, p. 2; my parentheses). With such an idea of a non-individual, but acting collective "self" it becomes possible to maintain the position of pro-active holism in pristine purity without much dependence on the conception of an evolutionary nisus.

### Reactive Collectivism: Parsonian Formalism and its Antecedents

> Oh Mensch, gesetzt, du spiegelst dich
> im, sagen wir, — im all!
> Und senkrecht! — wärest du dan nicht
> ganz in demselben Fall? (51, p. 47).

Contemporary reactive collectivism has two major roots in the history of ideas. One of these is cultural determinism, the other is sociological formalism. The influential social theorists associated with each of these tendencies respectively are Durkheim and Simmel. Cultural determinism need not be inherently reactive in character. There are strong elements of cultural determinism in the major theories of pro-active collectivism previously examined. Cultural determinism is mentioned under the present heading merely to attest to its importance as a component of contemporary reactive collectivism. Sociological formalism, on the other hand, provides the classical blueprint for reactive collectivism. I shall argue, indeed, that Parsons' views can best be described as formalistic in character.

It has frequently been argued that Pareto's emphasis on the interdependence of variables in "social systems" qualifies him also as a reactive holist.[21] It should be remembered, however, that the variables Pareto considered important are partly the (hypothesized) characteristics of individual members of society and partly, their power positions in the society in question. Social system equilibria are accounted for by

---

[21] Sidney Hook, for instance, has praised Pareto for abandoning simple cause-effect relations in favor of the notion of systemic interdependence (33, p. 58). For similar reasons Parsons accorded Pareto the privilege of numbering him among the forerunners of his own theory of action.

Pareto entirely by such strictly individualistic factors. Indeed, it is clear that Pareto meant such equilibria to be logically equivalent to general equilibrium in economics.[22] I am, therefore, inclined to classify Pareto as the intellectual fountainhead of reactive individualism in sociological explanation. It cannot be gainsaid, however, that the notion of equilibrium systems which looms so large in reactive collectivism leans heavily on Pareto's influence.

Clifford Geertz, as an advocate of cultural determinism who has interested himself in problems of modernization, stands as a fitting representative of this position in the present discussion.[23] He describes culture patterns as a template "for the organization of social and psychological processes, much as genetic systems provide such a template for the organization of organic processes" (22, p. 62). Like Durkheim, Geetz views religion as the matrix of culture. He even goes so far as to claim that it establishes in its adherents both "moods and motivations." Without cultural patterns, he writes, man would be ". . . a kind of formless monster . . . a chaos of spasmodic impulses and vague emotions" (23, p. 13; see also p. 4).[24] Ideologies first take hold when

22 Pareto was a leading economist of his generation and the successor of M.E.L. Walras in the economics chair at the University of Lausanne. The Lausanne school is associated with general equilibrium theory in economics. (80, pp. 27–28). Walras, along with Menger and Jevons was one of the founders of marginal utility economics.

23 I shall discuss Geertz's formulation of cultural determinism rather than reach back to Durkheim's, by now rather stale and hackneyed, exposition of this point of view.

24 Geertz's eloquent advocacy of the psychologically formative properties of "culture" leads one to suspect that he does not keep a household pet. Can one imagine Herr Professor Rickert's cat Mitzi, for example, as a "formless and chaotic monster" (for a discussion of Mitzi and her owner see pp. 248-9 below)? Would one have to assume, alternatively, that both Mitzi and Rickert were patterned on the identical "cultural template?"

On the subject of culture items establishing moods and motives I decided to engage in a small project of empirical investigation. My hypothesis was that any given culture item would establish different moods and motives in different persons. Geertz's statement must, of course, be taken to be enthymimetic and to mean that a ritual (or whatever) establishes the *same*, or, at least, *similar* moods and motives in those who engage in it or are in some other way related to, or affected by it. As the experimental mood-and-motive-establishing culture item I chose Beethoven's string quartet, op. 131. A recording of this musical item was played to a number of subjects (all of them with apparently unimpaired hearing). The item was selected because it is known for its power to elicit moods, motives, and even physical changes in its hearers. Franz Schubert is said to have developed a feverish temperature on first hearing it and Richard Wagner, in characteristically demented fashion, fulminated giddily about "fiddlers whirling into the abyss."

To establish my hypothesis it will be sufficient to report on but two responses. A newly married couple found the item "sexy" and shortly after hearing it retired to their quarters. A somewhat depressed subject, on the other hand, expatiated at length on what he took to be its "infinite sadness." In like fashion, I hypothesize, a re-

"a political system begins to free itself from the governance of received tradition" (22, pp. 63-64).

The *fons et origo* of legitimate authority Geertz finds in what he calls "primordial attachments." These depend upon congruencies of kinship, speech, and custom; they are independent of factors such as common interest, personal affection, incurred obligation, and so on (21, pp. 108-112). In short, primordial attachments are attachments *an sich*. Though Geertz does not say so, it can be suspected that such attachments must stem from having one's social and psychological processes patterned, as it were, on the selfsame template as the others to whom one is primordially attached. Social integration according to Geertz, consists of the aggregation of primordial groups into larger units (21, p. 153). Indeed, Geertz finds one of the central problems of government in new states as the avoidance of a clash between primordial and civil loyalties.

The metaphor of cultural influences shaping the characteristics of personality much as the "genetic code" forms an organism's physical characteristics is a superficially attractive one. Certainly, it is preferable on every count to Durkheim's infelicitous image of a *conscience collective*. Cultural determinists betray grave naïveté about genetics if they derive from such a metaphor the conclusion that similarities of cultural influence necessarily lead to uniformity of the personalities assumedly formed by such influences. A cursory inspection of fingerprint records at Scotland Yard or the headquarters of the F.B.I. would convince them of the error of such a conclusion. It is surely a reasonable assumption that for every person who is "formed" in a culture, the impingement of the culture is, at the very least, as different as are the fingerprints of the individual culture bearers. Dogmatic assertions concerning primordial attachments, moreover, offer but a poor substitute for reasoned theorists concerning the development of object cathexes.

Simmel's sociological formalism is certainly exempt from the charges of naiveté that can so easily be levelled against the proponents of cultural determinism. Indeed, its very premise was informed by a sophisticated appreciation of human individuality and individual pro-activity. In the seminal essay in which he gave sociological formalism systematic expression, he suggested that a different question was needed for social explanation than Kant's question "how is knowledge of society possible?" It was necessary to ask, instead, "how is society possible?" (75, p. 338.) Society was a person's *Vorstellung* (or constructed representation) in a different and more complicated sense from the manner in which the external world presented itself to his perception. Persons did not merely

---

ligious ritual (even among "primitives") will elicit as many moods and motives as there are persons who participate in it. I warmly recommend this hypothesis to anthropologists as worthy of further investigation. Not even all Alorese, or Azande, or Kwakiutl (let alone "China-men") are alike. My researches establish this generalization also for denizens of what may well be called "Plainville."

*perceive* social phenomena, they *created* them by entering into relationships with others.

Simmel saw the a prioris of society as the categories of *typing* and of *vocation.* By "typing," Simmel had in mind what later came to be called "role theory." He argued, in effect, that we perceive persons in social relationships as role incumbents or members of social categories. In so doing it is possible to relate to them "appropriately" as well as to make generalizations about them in their roles. Yet, Simmel insisted that a person's existence was not entirely pre-empted by his assumption of social roles. The interplay of personality and the various roles assumed by it was an essential characteristic of social life. It was the category of *vocation,* of self-investment in roles, which bridged the hiatus between individual and social existence. Governed by this category, individuals accepted personally "anonymous" roles on the basis of an intensely personal, inner calling. In other words, by accepting social roles individuals, viewed initially as pro-active, became subject to the categories of social determinacy. Starting from these germinal ideas, Simmel wanted to establish sociology as a special field of knowledge concerned with social forms and divorced from consideration of particular motivational or purposive contents.

The Kantian foundation of Simmel's formalism has been discarded in contemporary sociological discussion. Its influence is very much alive, however, and takes the form of what may be called "structural determinism." This approach insists on autonomous principles governing social structures independently of the motives of implicated individuals. Though structural determinism is tacitly accepted by very many sociologists, Peter Blau deserves to be singled out as a structuralist who is fully conscious of his intellectual debt to Simmel's ideas.[25] In a recent published debate with Homans (in which the latter takes his established psychologistic stance) Blau proposes two theoretical generalizations which, he asserts, are totally independent of individualistic considerations. These propositions could well represent Simmelian notions of "forms." They are: 1) the larger the size of a formal organization, the greater its structural differentiation; and 2) the greater the structural differentiation in a formal organization, the greater the "need" for mechanisms of co-ordination (6, p. 333).[26] Blau provides reasonably satisfactory empirical indicators for the expressions "structural differentiation" and "mechanisms of co-ordination."

[25] In the first chapter of his treatise on sociological exchange theory, Blau dissociates himself from Weber's and Parsons's emphasis on social action (5, p. 13). Indeed, the chapter is entitled "the structure of social associations" thus providing both a pastiche of the title of Parsons's early work and what Blau would like to have considered as a free translation of Simmel's expression *Formen der Vergesellschaftung.*

[26] Blau's second proposition could just as well have been phrased: the greater the structural differentiation, the greater the number of (or the more elaborate) mechanisms of coordination. I interpret the slippage of the term "need" into this state-

As hypotheses concerning the effect of size on formal organizations, these statements are open to testing and, perhaps, to further elaboration of conditions under which they would be confirmed or rejected.[27] Taken as categorical rather than hypothetical statements, on the other hand, any consideration of testing or of special conditions under which the statements hold are excluded by definition. Structural differentiation and mechanisms of coordination in response to increasing size would be inexorable properties of social life inherent in the very fact of formal organization, much as Kant had held Euclidian space to be an inexorable property of thought *(Denknotwendigkeit)*. The statements would not be open to test, neither could any human artifice or evolutionary tendency alter them. It follows that sociological formalism, if strictly carried through, necessarily implies an orientation of reactive holism. I should like to emphasize that no such conclusion is mandatory if statements about organizational, or kinship, or other social structures are viewed as hypotheses and not as categorical *Strukturnotwendigkeiten*. Concern with social structures does not, in itself, necessarily have to commit sociologists to reactive collectivism any more than espousal of pro-active individualism requires sociologists to deny or ignore the realities of social structure.[28]

---

ment as a Freudian slip — as the unconscious tribute paid by reactive holism to the principles of pro-active individualism. Blau lays himself wide open in this instance to Homans' reply: "if organizations have needs, they certainly are not met unless men in the organizations themselves feel the need to meet the organizational needs" (30, p. 341). It is only fair to add that Blau's reactive collectivism is not as rigidly or as dogmatically upheld as are similar views of some of his colleagues.

[27] In point of fact, the literature concerning the relationship of organization size with structural differentiation and other parameters is quite substantial. The net result is characteristically inconclusive. It seems to be that ". . . we are without knowledge of any 'causal' effects of size on structural differentiation" (48, p. 632).

[28] Gellner's challenge to methodological individualism by pointing to the existence of tribes with segmentary patrilineal kinship structures which maintain themselves over time, betrays some confusion on this issue (24, p. 268). Gellner thinks that a methodological individualist would have to explain the existence and maintenance of the structure in question by reference to dispositions whose effect is to maintain the system. Such an explanation would, of course, be crudely psychologistic in character. The structure exists and, if Gellner is correct, the tribesmen never give the matter much thought. The very fact that they give the matter little or no thought is an adequate explanation for the maintenance of the structure and, let it be added, an *individualistic* explanation. I would suggest that the development of such a structure, say, out of a matrilineal one, or its transformation into a "Western style" nuclear family structure would be accompanied by quite a lot of "thought" among the tribesmen. What is more, explanation of such changes, or prediction of conditions under which such changes might occur, would suffer from serious weaknesses if they excluded the motives of implicated individuals. This is not to maintain, even by merest implication, that outcomes of motivated conduct always (or, for that matter, ever) correspond to individuals' intentions. Only that they culminate and stabilize in such fashion as to permit individuals to accommodate to them. More on all of these issues follow below.

I have pointed out (in note 25 of this chapter) that Blau is at pains to preserve the purity of his structuralism from contamination by any concern with "action," which he attributes to Parsons as well as to Max Weber. Now, it is perfectly true that Parsons makes what he calls "the structure of social action," the starting point of his intellectual odyssey in sociology. The *fata morgana* pursued by Parsons bears the name of "voluntarism"; but the variety of voluntarism it describes bears little resemblance to Schopenhauer's animated, intensely pro-active, *Wille*. Instead, it is a voluntarism which docilely accommodates itself to "necessities" more properly described as Hegelian in character. The necessities in question Parsons describes as "structural-functional" (62, p. 219; 63, p. 242). Without attempting to trace the peregrinations of Parsons through anything like all of their perilous episodes, I shall try to establish that structural-functionalism amounts, essentially, to a type of formalism. In addition, Parsons' reactive collectivism, which has been widely noted,[29] is intelligible (so far as Parsons can ever be intelligible) only if interpreted as resting on a submerged, formalistic stratum of ideas.

Parsons' aboriginal "unit act" (later to be abandoned by him in favor of notions like "status-role" as the true "atom" of social physics) can suitably be viewed as an enumeration of many, if not all, of the abstract components of any Weberian ideal type (56, pp. 43-51, 77-82).[30] Parsons seeks to provide thereby a solution for the irksome problem of what he calls Weber's "ideal type atomism." As he rightly points out: "the general elements concerned are not always combined in the particular way that one type concept involves; they are independently variable over a wider range" (56, p. 618). If we overlook the uncouth phraseology of "unit acts" (and the hint of a spurious analogy with physical

[29] The compilation of a catalogue of criticisms of Parsons on the score of what I call reactive collectivism would constitute a formidable research task in its own right. Perhaps the most apposite and elegant critique is to be found in Buckley (9, pp. 23-31). My own discussion of Parsons' ideas in this chapter is not primarily meant to add another item to this catalogue but merely to expound the formalistic properties of structural-functionalism and illustrate their affinity with reactive collectivism.

[30] The familiar list comprises, besides an *actor,* the following components — all of them to be interpreted from the subjective point of view of the actor: an *end,* a *situation* consisting of *means* and *conditions;* and *normative standards* for selecting between alternative means. It might possibly be argued that the abstraction of these notions from concrete "contents" of goals, situations, and so forth, itself betokens a formalistic approach. Such arguments would be most likely to issue from a position of radical historical or linguistic particularism which denies the possibility of context-free (or metalinguistic) generalizations in social life. Personally, I see no greater difficulty of speaking, say, of a "goal" *in abstracto* than a physicist has in speaking of "mass" *in abstracto;* irrespective of whether the mass is composed of basalt, or granite, or green cheese. Parsons' emphasis on the actor's subjective point of view certainly separates this particular analysis from his later formalism.

molecules or atoms) Parsons' isolation of the abstracted "general elements" of models of social structure and social process may be considered a distinct contribution. Certainly, it overcomes residual influences of Rickert's historical particularism that tended to persist not consistently, but nevertheless sporadically, in Weber's own thinking. But Parsons is not willing to allow these basic variables of sociological analysis take what path they will. He has to regiment them into "systems" so as to explain the miracle of "order," the mirage of a this-worldly *nirvana* that apparently holds him in intellectual thralldom.

In *The Structure of Social Action,* Parsons brings Durkheimian cultural determinism, *via* the notion of "common-value integration" (56, p. 773) as well as Pareto's idea of general equilibrium systems into play, to aid him in the laborious construction of a program for an all-embracing, if disconcertingly free-floating and abstracted, generalized model of social order: the "action frame of reference." This involves the perilously balanced notion of conduct in society as teleologically determined by ends or reasons while, at the same time, integrated into systems of equilibrium and consensus. In later writings the action frame of reference is retained (at least, as a terminological convention) but the unit act is dropped. Parsons then begins to speak of action as the locus of interpenetration of three systems (separate fields of forces, as it were) cultural, social, and personality (see, for example, 57, p. 6). It seems to be at this point in the development of Parsonian theory that the transformation is initiated from an uneasily poised pro-active individualism into an apparently unconsciously formalistic variety of reactive holism.

The celebrated essay with Shils introduces the *pattern variables* as a set of dichotomous alternatives governing both role expectations and personal habits of choice. The habits, however, are described as being "usually a bit of internalized culture" (65, p. 78). It had previously been stated in the same article that culture did not comprise a "concrete system of action" on account of possessing the unstable property of being liable to be either internalized or, conversely, externalized and objectified (65, p. 67). In practice, then, this leaves only two systems as determinants of action: persons (themselves "usually" culture determined) and social role systems. But, as I shall show, the number of these *opopoeia* varies inconsistently with the vagaries of Parsons' thinking. There is a statement that certain pattern variables have a special affinity with personal need-dispositions while others are particularly important in connection with role expectations. Parsons, however, regularly ignores this nominal concession to personal motivation.[31] The one point where

[31] In the cited paper, *affectivity-neutrality* is described as one of the pattern variables related particularly to need-dispositions. Yet, in this discussion of medical practice, Parsons makes a special point of emphasizing neutrality as an essential characteristic of physicians' roles (57, p. 435). It might be possible to object to this

personal motivation as a determinant of social events is given crucial importance is very revealing about the sociologistically monist tendency in Parsonian thought. The celebrated "double contingency paradigm" elevates any person's interest that others should react "appropriately" into the single dominating motive in Parsonian sociology (65, pp. 105-106). The very elevation to prime place of this "motive for structure," as it were, has the function of absolving Parsons from treating motive as a social determinant except for the creation and maintenance of social structure itself.[32]

The pattern variables isolate elements previously syncretized in overarching distinctions such as Tönnies' between *Gemeinschaft* and *Gesellschaft,* or Durkheim's between *mechanical* and *organic solidarity.* Separated as pattern variables these elements permutate into a variety of types of different, possible, social systems. As Martindale points out: "Parsons . . . seems to have indicated a way to mass produce ideal types on an assembly-line basis" (46, p. 75). Yet, the all-important component of Weberian types — the ends of action — previously recognized by Parsons in his depiction of the unit act, are missing in the constructive typology of pattern variable permutations. Even if used for the analysis of personal dispositions, pattern variable analysis shrinks Parsons's much vaunted voluntarism to the narrow measure of a small and strictly delimited number of paltry orientational choices. Ends (or, as Parsons would prefer to put it, "concrete ends") may still exist for people in this conception. But their effects on social structure, at any rate, are discounted in this type of analysis.

Parsons's disquisition on psychological theory attests to the extent to which he has forsaken Weberian pro-active individualism. A fourth system, the organism, is added to "interpenetrate" with the others in the action frame of reference (59, p 647). Weber had been at pains to distinguish meaningful conduct from "merely reactive" organismic behavior. Parsons, in his early work, adumbrated on the same distinction at quite excessive length (56, especially, pp. 85-88, 115-117, 484-487). By admitting the organism into the charmed circle of systems of action, *motivation by reasons* which, after all, lies at the root of his own definition of "action," implicitly ceases to be a characteristic of it. In the same paper Parsons establishes his sociologistic determinism in an unusually emphatic manner. "The *main* structure of the human personality," he writes, is ". . . organized about internalized social object systems" (59, p. 655, my italics). Made *in vacuo,* a statement such as the above need

---

example since Parsons is concerned, in the place under consideration, with the "social system." I shall adduce further evidence below to show that Parsons increasingly has made motivation subservient to social system properties in any context.

[32] A few pages later, to be sure, one is offered a list of the four personal need-dispositions. Not too surprisingly, in view of what has gone before, these turn out to be needs for: "response," "love," "approval," and "esteem!"

not necessarily lead to the inference that its proposer espouses reactive collectivism. It may be recalled, however, that the "internalized systems" to which Parsons refers, much as the external ones, are structured by the pattern variables and that they develop through sequential phases associated with the system-problems to which our attention must now turn.

Thus far, only the structural elements of Parsons' loose-knit formalism have concerned us. The System Problems complete the edifice of structural-functional analysis. These are conceived of as highly abstract "functional imperatives" governing all action systems: *goal attainment; adaptation; integration,* and *pattern maintenance.* In the *Working Papers* (65) Parsons, following Bales' observations on problem solving in small groups, had viewed these primarily as sequential problems faced by action systems and accounting, so to speak, for their "motions" through time. As I have indicated, he put them to use in tracing the paths of "internalization" of social systems into the personalities of persons impacted in them. It is in the scheme for integrating economic and sociological theory, however, that Parsons' early ambitions for a structural-functional theory finally come to fruition (58). For the present discussion, it is important because it presents Parsonian reactive holism in its fully developed form.

Structural differentiation in this scheme is patterned in relation to the four functional imperatives. In addition, the pattern variables "correspond" to these imperatives (58, p. 36). To put the matter more clearly, and more honestly, specified role expectations and orientational choices are elicited by the particular functional imperative in which the roles (and the "orienters") find themselves. By itself, of course, this consideration does not commit Parsons to any generalization concerning specifiable relationships of "elicitation" (or, as some might call it "explanation"). On the highly abstract level of analysis from which Parsons surveys his world, the functional imperatives are abstractions without content. The particular goals to which a system is supposed to be "oriented," the external exigencies to which it is supposed to *adapt* to, the discords which must be resolved in the *maintenance* of systemic harmony, do not correspond to processes or events which bear a systematic resemblance to each other from one application of the scheme to the next. Parsons's hierarchy of levels of organization and control, though undoubtedly meant to bring order into the confusion referred to here, serves only to compound the logical difficulties of the scheme (60, pp. 7-16).[33] Whether one tries to relate them to hierarchical levels or not, the contents of these purely formalistic *Funktionsnotwendigkeiten* vary

[33] The hierarchical concept itself, with its emphasis on the determination of lower systemic levels by higher ones, underlines even further the collectivist proclivities of Parsonian theory.

vertiginously from one discussion to the next. They seem to be selected ad hoc to illuminate the latest piece of scenery selected by the Parsonian *Geistesblitz*.[34]

What people actually do, what they believe, how they relate to each other, the way that communities or associations are socially structured, these are questions for which most sociologists, perhaps naively, seek to find theoretical explanations. I do not believe that Parsons is seriously interested in discovering the theoretical conditions under which given specifiable actions, or beliefs, or relations, or structures occur. Matters such as these belong, rather, into the voluntaristic Parsonian "realm of freedom." The realm of necessity is mapped by the abstract, functional imperatives. These do not explain the banausic drifts and currents of social and personal flux. Instead, they enshrine, in a manner open neither to question nor to test, that sublime "order" which Parsons has made his life's work to elucidate. His Laocoon-like struggle with the English language suggests that, perhaps, he himself has never been able to face the bleak conclusion to which his own analysis leads. Even when used merely as a taxonomic framework for comparative studies, the Parsonian system seems curiously lifeless and sterile.[35]

The ascent through waste places which leads from Kant's *Denknotwendigkeiten*, through the Simmel-Blau *Strukturnotwendigkeiten*, to the *Funktionsnotwendigkeiten* of Parsons, is sprayed with verbal mire and strewn with logical boulders. After struggling through and past these obstacles certain common characteristics of various topographical features become apparent. Every sort of categorialism or formalism seems to carry a metaphysic of reactive holism. For Kant, nature was a punctual clockwork. For Simmel, in his later guise as a sociological formalist and for his followers, society was a similarly reactive system. For Parsons, the abstract concept of social order in itself is a reactively equilibrated whole. Kant (while remaining personally punctual to the very end) exempted the intelligible self from determination by the world machine. The later Simmel granted pro-activity to individuals so long as they stayed out of the entanglements of *vergesellschaftung* —

---

[34] In a recent contribution, indeed, Parsons seems to have attained the *satori* of cosmic perspective of a "system of action" of which society, culture, personality, and organism, are subsystems obeying, respectively, the imperatives of integration, pattern-maintenance, goal-attainment, and adaptation. (62, p. 6).

[35] Lipset's comparison of several English-speaking Democracies using Parsonian categories provides a case in point (40, p. 285). His discussion of "value differences" in the countries considered (leaving aside its holist connotations) must appear extremely arbitrary to anyone acquainted with the ways of life prevailing in them. Parsons, cited on the cover, rewards Lipset for "reaching a new level of maturity" in this work. Yet, Lipset himself feels constrained to add an additional "pattern variable" — *elitism-equalitarianism* (sic) — to a list which Parsons had insisted was an exhaustive one.

out of social interactions.[36] Parsons, my study suggests, because of his vastly more abstract concerns, is far more "liberal" than his formalist predecessors. He suggests that events in the "concrete" social world can happen entirely as they please. The complexities of his own writing and the consequently widespread diffusion of popularizations of it, unfortunately, have led many of his knowledgeable as well as his un-witting followers to the diametrically opposite conclusion. The Parson-ian rhetoric (rather than any intellectual content it may possess) has implanted in them the belief that sociological theory leads to the dis-covery of "real" self-equilibrating, socio-cultural systems in which human individuality is totally absorbed and explained away.

### Reactive Individualism: Professor Homans and the Pigeons

"redet er nicht im Schlaf? horch!
'Wer ich bin? . . .
Eine lebendige Litfass-Säule
etiquettiert von oben bis unten."
(52, p. 40)

On previous pages I have described Pareto as the fountainhead of reactive individualism in sociological theory. Since his sociological con-tributions have had little direct influence on contemporary theories I shall dismiss him very briefly, here. He saw human actions as fitting into two categories: *logical* and *non-logical*. The first covered scientific activities as well as the exercise of rational, economic choices. The sec-ond — at least, as it was enacted on the stage of historical events — was the subject of sociological analysis. Much as economic choices led to equilibria of price, the analysis of which he himself enormously advanced as an economist, so illogical action could be shown to lead to equilibria of social relations.

The problem was to find an equivalent in the realm of "illogic" to the rational choices of economic men. Pareto thought that he had found this in the personal core dispositions of men, the consistent behavioral manifestations of which were capable of scientific classification. Such behavioral manifestations of motivational dispositions Pareto called *residues*, while the conventional reasons given for the behaviors in ques-tion he called *derivations*. The odd terminology was meant to reflect Pareto's procedures which consisted (or, at least, so he thought) of sifting out *residual* systematic constancies of behavior from the variety of

---

[36] Individuals could even be pro-active as well as reactively determined by the exigencies of the structural whole so long as their chosen vocation or calling blew them enthusiastically through its pre-existing vortices.

their distorting explanatory or justifying statements, "non-logically" *derived* from this or that behavior in ordinary social life. Certain persons were dominated by one or another residue more than others. The interplay of social life was systematically related to the position held in society by persons dominated by particular residues.

Though he brought the notion of equilibrium systems into sociology, Pareto viewed these systems as being composed of the actions and interactions of individuals. It was never the total system that governed personal action (as it tended to become in Parsons' adaptation of it for his own ends). Instead, it was individuals carrying, or being propelled by, certain residues whose interactions and conjoint actions brought about systemic processes in society, in exactly the same way as the rational, economic choices of individuals occasioned equilibria of price. I have argued previously for treating economic theory as individualistic in type. The same considerations support my characterization of Pareto as a sociological individualist. Moreover, since the category of illogical actions is portrayed as entirely reactive to blind underlying residues, it is entirely proper to characterize Pareto as a reactive individualist.

Pareto was in vogue at Harvard when both Parsons and Homans were students there. His influence on Parsons has already been alluded to. Homans was also inspired by Paretean ideas. Indeed, he even collaborated on a little book intended to introduce Pareto's sociological ideas to English readers in simplified form (32). While Parsons was rather selective in his adoption of notions from Pareto and lost little time in fusing them with foreign organicist ideas gleaned from Durkheim, Homans' recent work traces a more direct and cleaner line of development (see, particularly, 29).

Pareto's theory of residues is too similar to outmoded instinct psychologies to render it usable for Homans' contemporary purposes. Instead, Homans has enlisted Skinnerian behaviorism to replace the theory of residues as the proper substrate for his own brand of reactive individualism. Professor Skinner is extremely careful to limit himself to manipulatable variables. He has even raised the question "are theories of learning necessary?" and given it a negative answer (77). Indeed, he hardly concerns himself with stimuli in the classical sense of the term at all, or with any merely hypothetical relationships such stimuli might bear to specifiable responses. He is concerned with responses alone (he calls them *operants*) and confines himself to the experimental study of their reinforcement. In his conception, a reinforcer may be defined as anything that increases the probability of the occurrence ("rate of emission") of an operant. Such a conception may appear tautological to the uninitiated but it must be borne in mind that considerations of logic (since they are, themselves, not open to experimental manipulation) play no part in the Skinnerian world-view. Skinnerian psychology eschews all speculation or conjecture: *hypotheses non fingo* might well serve as its motto.

The basic postulate of Skinner's model of behaviour is that "the great majority of behavior patterns are established and maintained by means of differential reinforcement of activities once performed" (39, pp. 27-28). The cited use of the term "activity" instead of "operant" follows Homans' earlier adaptation of Skinnerian psychology for sociological purposes (29, p. 19) which primarily concerns us here. The starting point, then, are spontaneous activities performed ("emitted") by the organism in question. Under nonexperimental or "free" or "natural" conditions certain activities are reinforced, others are not. Reinforced activities come to predominate in the organism's total activity. So far as one can speak of personality traits or inner states at all, these correspond to "reinforcement histories" (12, p. 13). Predominating patterns of behaviour in an organism under free conditions are conceived as resultants to something akin to natural selection — selection, that is, of forms of behavior in an organism rather than of organismic forms in the evolutionary process. Allegedly, purposive behavior is explained in this way much as Darwin explained "purpose" in evolution (8, p. 370).

It is possible that Homans might reject my depiction of Skinnerian psychology as reactive. As I have shown, it does not rest entirely on a theory of behavioral causation by stimuli. The organism (at least, at the start of experimentation with it) is viewed as emitting operants (Homans's "activities") entirely without the aid of external manipulation. To that limited extent Skinner's organisms could be described as "proactive." But such unelicited activities are interpreted in Skinner's theory as inherently random and meaningless. That this interpretation stems from methodological ambitions for conceptual austerity does not alter the fact. The implied "emptiness" of operants places them, surely, on the same reactive level as the derivations about which Pareto expressed himself with scornful disdain.

One difference between Pareto and Skinner on the question of behavioral causation is worth noting. Skinner's organisms are subject to conditioning. Pareto, on his part, gave little thought to the question of mechanisms whereby illogical actions might be transformed into scientific activity and rational economic choice. One assumes, of course, that illogical action is a rudimentary pattern of behavior in humans, and that scientific activities and economic choices somehow grew out of it. What Homans does, in effect, is to use Skinner's notion of operant conditioning to supply such mechanisms of transformation. He goes one step further, however, and obliterates the Paretean category of illogical action by assimilating the "theory" (if Skinner will pardon the expression) of operant conditioning with a homespun version of exchange economics (see, 29, especially pp. 52-56, 68-70). In so doing, he simultaneously dethrones Pareto's rational choices to the humble status of no more than reinforced activities. The hiatus between logical and illogical action is abolished with a stroke of the pen. Much as Skinner's pigeons can be taught "bowling" (Skinnerians become incapacitated by their indoctrination from distinguishing between far-flung similes and genuine analogies) so humans become conditioned, as it were, to "choose at the margin." Menger's hoary "motive of self interest" is given a new lease on life. It can now be interpreted as a glimmering anticipation of positive reinforcement and "Skinner-box economics." It should, moreover, be added that the kind of activity that had traditionally been called "economics" by people like Menger or Pareto is demonstrated to be only one special variety of that rich assortment of "exchanges" that fill the chocolate box of social life with positive reinforcements.

Detailed description of Homans' exchange theory is unnecessary for the task on hand. Like most of Homans' writing it is done with clarity and grace. Homans believes that a psychologistic approach is necessary because what he calls the "rational theory" is allegedly forced to take men's values or goals as simply given (30, p. 322).[37] It is implied here, that explication of conditions for the formation of particular values or goals is a crucial area of sociological analysis and this is, of course, absolutely correct. I made this point myself in 1964 and will adumbrate it later in this discussion. What is called into question is the contention that psychologism (be it Skinnerian or of any other sort) can provide the proper answers for the conditions of goal formation in a manner, and on a level, suitable for sociological explanation.

Deutsch has pointed out that sociological propositions based on assumptions of operant conditioning have no clear-cut meaning when applied to activities which are not mechanically repetitive (13). A perusal of Homans' work suggests that the latter would readily grant that social processes do not exhibit mechanical repetitiveness, at least, not all the time. Quite beyond this apt but elementary criticism, however, lies a more fundamental question concerning the nature of the subject matter treated in sociology. As shown above, Homans himself has recently come around to the view that sociology has something to do with values and goals. Now, discussions of values and goals (like references to logic and theory and argument) rely precisely on appeals to the kinds of "inner states" which operant conditioning, in common with other varieties of behaviorism, strenuously denies.[38] Twitches and salivations, one grants, may make up part of social life. But whatever is understood by them strikes me to be quite uninteresting. Homans,

---

[37] He seems to mean by this the collectivistic implications of theories stressing rationality. The argument below will show that no such implications are necessary for sociological theories in which rationality is given an explanatory role.

[38] Popper has argued that behaviourism is a self-defeating "philosophy" because its arguments attempt to establish the nonexistence of arguments (66, Vol 2, p. 294).

again, is not primarily concerned with such matters. Instead, he adopts behavioristic rhetoric in apparently blissful unconsciousness that it obscures the subject matter he is trying to explain. Clearly, he wants to eat his pellet and have it too.

In an unpublished paper, read at the annual meetings of the American Sociological Association in Chicago in 1965, I attacked theories which fall short of something like Weber's "level of meaning." I objected to "confining social theory in the pigeon coop and suffusing it with the odour of the doghouse." Homans' vigorous and eloquent prose would seem, on the face of it, to make him an unlikely candidate for such a stricture.

## Pro-active Individualism: Max Weber's Abortive Attempt

Der Rabe Ralf . . . .
Dem niemand half . . . .
half sich allein
am Rabenstein
(51, p. 22)

Individualistic explanations of social events rival pro-active collectivism and the conception of evolutionary nisus both in influence and in antiquity. Generally, such explanations have fallen short of the requirements for an orientation of pro-activity as previously outlined. Some have been based on psychologistic appeals to an assumed fixed, common, "human nature" describable in terms of a limited number of "appetites" or "affections" or "passions." Such explanations, though couched in vigorously individualistic terms, attribute little personal "individuality" to men. Others (like utilitarianism and classical economics), though referring to "wants" or "ends" or "goals," were concerned with some assumed nexus or common denominator like "demand" or "utility" or "ophelimity" (felicity), thereby obscuring the role played by reference to particular goals in sociological explanation.[39] With the exception of money, postulates of a common denominator for diverse goals rest on theoretically flimsy assumptions. What is more, such postulates tend to deflect attention from individual actions — the conditions for their elicitation and their social-structural consequences — to relatively unstructured, aggregative social phenomena.

[39] Parsons has criticized what he calls the "randomization of ends" in the utilitarian approach on the grounds that it eliminates consideration of goals as components of ordered normative systems governing social action (56, pp. 699–700). His grounds, clearly, rest on assumptions of reactive collectivism. A similar critique can be made, however, on grounds of pro-active individualism since consideration of particular goals is a requisite, in this orientation, for the explanation of particular actions or particular structures.

By contrast to earlier attempts at individualistic explanations of social phenomena, Max Weber's choice of pro-active individualism as his preferred explanatory orientation was highly deliberate and justified by him at length on purely methodological grounds (88; 84; 85; 86; 87). Among classical sociologists of major stature Max Weber alone developed a body of sociological theory in which motive plays an integral part.[40] In order to understand the peculiar convolutions of his reasoning it is necessary to go back to Kantian dualism and some of its later ramifications in the heated debate over method (Methodenstreit) which Weber attempted to resolve.

Kant (37) believed that basic reality, the realm of *noumena* (from the Greek *nous;* "breath" or "spirit"), is not directly accessible to the understanding. In his view men impressed upon such raw reality the categories of perception and conception, thereby creating the realm of *phenomena* (or representations in the mind). *Causality* was one of the categories employed in this "transcendental synthesis" of raw sensibility. The "empirical" or phenomenal self was bound by the category of causality. The idea of moral responsibility, however, obliged us to think of ourselves as free agents; that is to say, as having an undetermined, directly noumenal, self. Otherwise, quite clearly, judgments of responsibility for action would be groundless (36, p. 189). This noumenal "self an sich" was "intelligible" without imposition of the categories employed for representing the realm of appearances. It is extremely unclear from Kant's writing whether *rationality* and *morality* were to be viewed as separable guides for the free play of practical reason (or "action") or whether they were inherently compounded. On the one hand, he declared that "appetition" (which we might render as "goal setting" or, perhaps, "goal formation") was the faculty for acting as a prime mover or undetermined effectuator of consequences in the world. On the other hand, true freedom required independence from "inclinations" and, therefore, had to belong to the moral realm (36, pp. 265, 214).

From a contemporary perspective, it is not difficult to see that the rock on which Kant's philosophy foundered was the entirely unnecessary metaphysical postulate of a principle of universal determinacy, a principle Kant believed was embedded in the operation of our understanding of the natural (or "empirical") world (68, pp. 294, 193-200). The converse postulate, that the operation of reason was free in the sense of

---

[40] Some might argue that Pareto's *residues* correspond to "motivational dispositions" and, therefore, that motives play as integral a part in Pareto's sociology as they do in Weber's. Even if this argument were granted (and quite apart from the question of whether Pareto can properly be characterized as a "classical sociologist of major stature") Pareto's residues are not motives in the distinctively sociological sense; namely, goals or "reasons." Rather, as I have shown above, they are akin to alleged or hypothetical psychological traits dominating persons' behavior.

being "uncaused," is, of course, equally unnecessary. Max Weber's methodological writings are concerned, in large part, precisely with the problem of determinacy as applied to the realm of practical reason, the realm of socio-historical studies. Indeed, his attempted solution of the problem became essential for his delineation of the subject matter of sociology. These writings, also, helped to clear the way for the contemporary realization of the needlessness for Kant's above-mentioned postulates.

Prior to Weber's work there had been considerable intellectual discomfort with Kantian dualism. The social-structural formalism of Simmel, to which I have referred, constitutes but one of a number of diverse intellectual gambits designed to circumvent, or evade, or negate Kantian dualism. Not all thinkers, however, were discomfited by dualism in its Kantian expression. Windelband and Rickert, from one point of view, and Dilthey and Gottl from another, found in it the grist for their methodological mills. Weber's sociological epistomology derives from the attempt to mediate in the dispute between these criss-crossing dualisms.

Windelband reconceptualized Kantian dualism as the difference between *nomothetic* laws and *ideographic* descriptions. Nomothetic laws inhabited a world devoid of quality or savour (98, pp. 144-145). Additionally, no overarching universal formula *("Welformel")* could lead from such laws to the deduction of particular states of affairs at a given moment of time (98, p. 159). Particular events were worth describing only if they were unique; they were to be viewed from the perspective not of science but of history. Our sense of individual freedom rested on the already mentioned fact that appeal to universal laws could not lead to the deduction of a particular concrete state of affairs at a given time (except occasionally, when dealing with repetitive closed systems).

Rickert's massive tome (70) developed Windelband's clear and crisp argument only in one important respect. He maintained that any object or creature under the sun (say a "leaf" or a "cat") was uniquely individual. But "any old cat" so to speak, was likely to be of interest as a unique object only by way of serving as an example of a general set of such objects *(Gattungs-exemplar)* (70, p. 175). Our own beloved "Mitzi," however, excites us to the flashpoint of ideographic illumination (very freely translated, one might say *umdichtet.)* (70, p. 269.) Why is this the case? Because Mitzi has value for us. Roughly at this point in the argument Rickert extended the idea of "value" beyond Windelband's depiction of it as the quality attaching to any object or event worth knowing *(wissenswert).* Values — autonomous values, absolute values — were beyond doubt. They belonged to the province of the historian (as "ideographer"). The generalizations of natural science, on the other hand, were concerned with the world of mere appearances; a world subject to doubt. Culture (which Rickert felt was the proper term to use for what Hegel had called *"Geist"*) was both the medium and the ultimate object of value (70, p. 395). For that reason the cultural sciences were essentially value-laden. This, precisely, was what gave them an increment of truth value.[41]

Dilthey's reconceptualization of Kantian dualism took a different form. Though often regarded as a Hegelian, while Windelband and Rickert were credited with being members of the neo-Kantian school of thought, Dilthey's dualistic methodology bears on the surface, greater resemblance to Kant's distinction between phenomenal and intelligible realms. Rickert had struggled to provide a new philosophical foundation for Kant's association of morality with freedom. Dilthey, on the other hand, reworked Kant's epistemological distinction between the allegedly direct intelligibility of mental functioning[42] and the mere "appearance" of natural events mediated by the categories. Dilthey rejected any distinction between "the knowing self and the self we know" (27, p. 30). Thought did not compose order in nature but found it there. Kantian dualism was to be replaced by the distinction between *description* and *explanation*. Descriptive science was concerned with direct, immediate, self-involved, experience *("Erlebniss")*. As such it was, in a sense, "beyond doubt." Explanatory science, by contrast, since it did not deal with lived experience, depended upon merely conjectural hypotheses. The types of mental processes involved in these two types of knowledge he gave different names: respectively, *verstehen* (intuitive understanding or, better, "lived" understanding) and *erklären* (explanation or clarification). The difference with Kant, as is readily apparent, lies mainly in the replacement of phenomena arrived at through "transcendental synthesis" by conjectural hypotheses. Lived experience was not conjectural but self-involving and immediate.

Other persons were directly experienced and, therefore, *verstanden* on the analogy with our own self (27, p. 119). Direct understanding or analogic understanding by itself, however, did not obviate the necessity for inferential reasoning. Such inferences argued to coherent personalities "effectuating" the understood behavior rather than to mechanical "causes" of such behavior. In view of this teleological premise, the intelligibility of human action or of a culture object (symbol or artefact) depended upon its meaning *(Bedeutung)*. Meaning, in other words,

---

[41] Rickert's point of view is far from defunct today. Louch, in a recent work (41) proposes a similar form of "moralistic particularism." The book in question more than equals Rickert's in point of obscurity but is entirely unredeemed by Rickert's concession of a proper function to nomothetic generalizations in *Kulturwissenschaft* ("in their place," of course) or by Rickert's occasional, possibly quite unintended, flashes of hilarious humour. This brief account of Rickert's ideas seems to have emphasized the humour without, I very much hope, detracting from his intended meaning.

[42] Kant's allegation, among other faults, greatly overestimated the capacity of his *epigoni* to "understand" (verstehen) what he himself had in mind or (dare one say it?) his own capacity to render it "intelligible" in his own writings.

involved the apprehension of *effectuation* in human affairs. Analysis of meanings was the task of *Geisteswissenschaft* (roughly corresponding to social science) as distinct from the natural sciences which were concerned not with meanings but with causes.

The dispute between the two divergent offshoots of Kantian dualism described above was not the only debate which formed the intellectual context in which Weber fashioned his *Verstehende Soziologie*. Another dispute he was simultaneously trying to resolve was between Karl Menger and his followers (the so-called "Austrian school of economics") which followed a variant of classical economic theory [43] and members of the German historical school of economics. The latter are mainly remembered today for their advancement of arguments in favour of protectionism (state imposed import tariffs) in the interest of "infant industries." More generally, they were interested in economic development (regarded, usually, from a Hegelian point of view) rather than in economic analysis along lines suggested by Ricardo or Jevons. Gottl had entered the second debate with a set of methodological presuppositions borrowed from Dilthey (25). It was primarily through Gottl's work that Weber received Dilthey's influence.

Gottl's contribution to the debate had been the suggestion that economics was the science of experience of routine or "everyday" *(alltägliche)* events (30, p. 69). It had the task of unravelling or unlocking *(erschliessen)* the meaning of this everyday experience irrespective of the historical stage of economic development at which it occurred. Classical economics was word-bound, attempting to put everyday thinking behind it, while at the same time, becoming enslaved by terms derived from it (25, p. 76). The title of Gottl's book actually translates into English as "domination by words." The sciences of action *(Aktionswissenschaften,* a term by which he meant to replace Dilthey's *Geisteswissenschaft)* were concerned with everyday routine. Their task was to develop disciplines of thinking adequate for undertaking the descriptive analysis of configurations of meaning (25, p. 133). The content of everyday meanings was self-evident to the point of unconsciousness. The task of economics (and, by implication one assumes, of the other sciences of action) was not "discovery" in the natural science sense of the word, but to make everyday thinking both conscious and rigorous (25, p. 81). Only the actions of madmen were unintelligible and thus, to be subjected to the procedures of natural science explanation (25, p. 78). The subject matter of economics, thus, became in his view, the striving of men in the living stream of action. He developed a typology of such "striving" which clearly exercised a profound and far-reaching influence on Weber's chapter "Sociological Categories of Economic Action" (90, pp. 63-211).

---

[43] "Manchester economics" as the Germans insisted on calling it though its origins are clearly traceable to Scotland.

Weber's attempted solution of the *Methodenstreit* was thoroughly nominalistic in spirit. Unfortunately, however, he retained the essentialist terminologies inherited from his friends Rickert and Gottl. He rejected the Dilthey-Gottl distinction between the natural sciences and the social sciences as based on fundamentally different kinds of epistemological processes. Sociology, like any other field of knowledge, had the task of explanation. Yet, Weber retained the terms *verstehen* and *meaning (Bedeutung* or, as he often calls it, "*Sinn*"). Action was meaningful in that it made sense. This implied for Weber that actors were goal-oriented and that their meaningful actions (as distinct from what had to be interpreted as random behavior) were explainable if interpreted as constituting means for the achievement of the goals in question. Action, furthermore, was social to the extent that it needed to be interpreted as taking account of the reactions of others and being influenced thereby.

Persons acting on motives were what sociology was about. In a sense, therefore, scientific sociological explanation was similar to the reciprocal understandings of ordinary social participation. This is the sense in which Weber's description of his theoretical position as *Verstehende Soziologie* must be understood. The interpretative understanding of action was not an ultimate, irreducible, or even self-evident *Erlebniss* but was of the same nature and had exactly the same logical properties as any concept about the natural world (86, p. 126). Of course, the hypotheses concerning motive employed by the participants in the social process (their own and those of others) were often diffuse, contradictory, lacking in rigor, and of a disconcertingly (as well as disconcertedly) *ad hoc* character. For that reason it became crucial for sociology to provide a demarcation between strictly sociological understanding and the kind of understanding adequate for ordinary social participation. This Weber attempted, not very successfully, with the notions of statistical regularities corresponding to intelligible intended meanings and, in the absence of these, of ideal-type constructs (90, p. 9-11).

In response to Rickert's argument that values were the key for unlocking the mysteries of historically unique events, Weber took the position that historical analysis had to be value-free as much as analysis in any other scientific field. In order to qualify for scientific respectability such analysis had to be acceptable as valid by persons holding different values from those espoused by the historian (especially 86, pp. 89-91; also the translated 84; 85, pp. 59-69). To be sure, the selection of problems as also of parameters depended upon the scholar's evaluation of their significance — his "value orientation." Valuations, in addition, much as any other ends or goals, were part of the subject matter of sociological analysis. Scientific statements about such valuations were statements of fact not of value. Thus, values were not inherently constitutive of "historical individuality" but entered analysis as the scientist's interest in the selection of certain problems, in the heuristic delineation of suitable parameters and finally, as "facts" entering the explanation of events.

Meaningful action, viewed as being motivated by goals or purposes or values, was calculable and predictable and, therefore, subject to "causal" analysis. Causal, that is to say, in that "if $x$ then $y$" propositions could be applied in the explanation of social events. In order to apply this form of proposition, clearly, one of its terms had to refer to a goal or purpose or value. As Baumgarten puts it, it was just as possible to speak of a *causa causans* as of a *causa causata* (3, pp. 589-593, 604).[44] In this way, the old Kantian equation of indeterminancy with the initiation of effects in the world could be dissolved with elegance and aplomb. Weber demonstrated, long before the advent of cybernetics that "teleological" explanation was compatible with scientific procedure. In proposing the methodological principle that sociological explanation (explanation of social conduct, and social relations, and social structures) required the postulation of "typical" subjective intentions or goals on the part of individuals, Weber was emphatic in his stress that such goals were not to be explained by psychology. They belonged squarely in the particular realm of activity (communal, organizational, political, economic, religious) they themselves helped to constitute (86, p. 63; also 88). The reciprocal understanding of motivated conduct, equally, was not specifically "psychological" (except where called for, in impu-

---

[44] Weber makes a distinction between "motivationally" adequate (*sinnhaft adequat*) and "causally" adequate explanations. The former can never be more than plausible hypotheses. The latter should be based on empirically determined, statistical regularities corresponding to the goal (his example is Gresham's Law) (91; pp. 97–98). Causal explanation also considered elements affecting the chances of success of an action in attaining its postulated goal. Here, his example concerns arithmetical problems. A motivationally adequate manner of handling a mathematical problem is to obtain a correct solution (here he is clearly thinking of bankers, or schoolboys earnestly desiring to pass examinations, for whom a "correct" solution rather than just any solution may properly be assumed to be the goal). A causally adequate explanation would take into account empirical probabilities of aggregates of persons obtaining correct results, in addition to the empirically determinable frequencies of arithmetical errors, misinterpretations of problems, and so forth (89, pp. 536–537; compare the miserably poor translation 91, pp. 98–100). An example of what Weber has in mind in this context was provided in another place (86, p. 59). Medieval Florentine bankers, who did not know Arabic numerals, regularly made arithmetical errors. These errors, one adds, were not systematically in their own "favour"; they were apparently quite unintentional. Such errors, Weber felt, could not be grasped by motivationally adequate explanation alone.

Parsons, who besides being a very muddled thinker, has his own axe to grind, misinterprets this completely. He suggests that causally adequate explanation refers to the "overt cause of an action which can be described *without reference to the state of mind of the actor*" (89, p. 99; my italics). This contention is belied even by his own execrable translation of Weber's themselves not overly lucid words (89, p. 100).

tations of "affect") but involved consideration of constraints and opportunities existing in the particular realm in which such conduct took place (86, p. 108).

A classification of types of action lent both flexibility and generality to Weber's motivational conception of society. *Zweckrational* action optimized the overall net achievement of ends for the actor. *Wertrational* action was conduct which could be construed as subserving or constituting an absolute value in itself. *Traditional* behavior was only marginally endowed with intention and meaning; ends were fixed by custom. It bordered on the merely "reactive." Weber's discussion of the fourth and final type, *Affective* behavior, is embarrassingly weak. He intended it to refer to behaviour in which the ends of action were emotionally determined and understood empathically rather than rationally.[45] With the notions of motive, reciprocal understanding, and the classification of types of action, Weber constructed a typology of social structures ranging from simple social relationships to State and Church.

It might appear as though the ideas presented thus far would lend themselves unambiguously to the construction of a sociology in which the notion of motive plays a central role. Such a conclusion, however, has to be modified in the light of a fundamental ambiguity of the meaning of "rationality" as Weber employs this term. Rational action (particularly Zweckrational action) depended upon rules of experience. For an observer to understand actions as being related to goals, he also had to assume that the actor followed some experiential maxim such as "if I do *x, y* will follow" (87, p. 325). In the social realm, moreover, in which actions affected other persons, rational activity presupposed the sound estimation of reasonable chances of the occurrence of "suitable" reactions from others. Custom, under certain circumstances, could give some guidelines for the accurate prediction of others' reac-

---

[45] Franz Alexander's notion of "emotional syllogisms" seems to fit what Weber had in mind (see 1; especially pp. 401–403). I have previously referred to the fact that Friedrich Gottl had wanted to establish the sciences of action as "sciences of the everyday." Gottl had also written that unintelligibility was the privilege of madmen. Nine years before 1913 (when Weber's classification of types of action first appeared) Weber had argued against Gottl that psychopathological states — he mentioned hysteria in particular — were open to interpretative understanding and that he would have more to say on the subject (86, p. 102). The "privilege" of unintelligibility, so to speak, was to be removed even from the mad. That he did not return to the subject may, perhaps, be due to the fact that his friend Karl Jaspers had meanwhile published his *Allgemeine Psychopathologie* (35), and that he felt that this expressed all he wanted to say on the subject. Jaspers' psychiatric theory may fairly be described as *Verstehende Psychiatrie*.

Weber's discussion of affect (much like Jasperian psychiatry, which owes so much to Weber) suffers from the fact that he did not resort to the Freudian expedient of attributing unconscious goals to what he calls affective behavior. In consequence, it remains an inert component of his systematic typology of social structures.

tions. It was *rational law,* however, as distinct from judicial (or lordly) whim or from *khadi justice,*[46] which made the consequences of certain acts highly predictable. Rational bureaucratic rules had similar effect.

Thus rational means-end activity, particularly where it involved or in some way affected others, depended upon rules on the basis of which rational evaluations regarding consequences could be undertaken. Statements people made "counted" on having an effect or, at least, being understood more or less as meant. Similarly, workers could count on chances of receiving specifically fashioned bits of metal or pieces of paper in return for muscular exertions over particular periods of time. They could also count on these objects being accepted in exchange for items such as "trousers," "coal," and "bread" ("understood" by Weber as corresponding to their goals). Moreover, should (illegal) attempts be made to deprive them of their precious trousers and so forth, men wearing spiked helmets would intervene and restore these items (87, p. 325).[47]

Zweckrational action thus became linked almost inextricably with legal-rational and bureaucratic social relations. Indeed, the legal-rational and bureaucratic rules constituted, in Weber's view, prerequisites for the exercise of Zweckrational action. Weber noted a trend, particularly in the Protestant world, toward increasing rationalization both of technical and of social conditions for predicting the repercussions of actions (see, for example, 94, p. 139). It is interesting that he saw this not as an increase in the potential facilitation of the satisfaction of motives but as resulting, almost inevitably, in dull and banausic subjection to the social machinery of rationality. When he cited Tolstoi on the subject of "science," Weber clearly had the entire rational-social sphere in mind (94, p. 143).[48] Only the irruption into the social scene of charismatic leaders, inflated with "prophetic pneuma" (and capable,

[46] "Khadi justice" is a phrase Weber uses to refer to the administration of justice on the basis of religious, political, or otherwise expediental considerations rather than on the basis of fixed and formal rules (92, p. 213; also 93, p. 216).

[47] Winch has commented on Weber's Brechtian use of *"Verfremdungseffekt"* in this passage (96, p. 118). Weber, of course, uses derealization to emphasize that the physical behavior of workers and the physical objects representing "money" can only be explained by reference to rules and shared meanings. The use of derealization here suggests something in addition. Freud, in a discussion of derealization *(Entfremdunsgefühl)* linked this to the experience of something "wrong" or "forbidden" (19, p. 311). Weber's descent into the realm of *physis* in this passage, I would suggest, registers his discomfort with the holistic connotations that this example might otherwise imply. Parsons, as I point out above, fell into precisely the trap that Weber was here trying to avoid.

[48] The quotation is: "Science is meaningless because it gives no answer to our question, the only question important for us: 'What shall we do and how shall we live.'" Weber gives no reference but it is from (82). One might well wonder why Weber was not aroused to curiosity concerning the special social conditions under which such a question can become salient.

let it not be forgotten, of eliciting *affect* from their followers!) punctuated the secular drift toward rationalized disenchantment.

The point at issue here is not whether social arrangements can be, under certain conditions, inadequate for satisfying motives. Rather it is that, for Weber, the social machinery of predictable repercussions to action is necessarily and inherently antagonistic to the goals of persons who serve as its cogs. Thus, on the one hand, rationality employed by the individual is the instrument for goal attainment; on the other hand, as existing in a system of rules, it objectifies a sense of alienation. Parsons, who conscripted Weber as one of the sociologists whose work supposedly "converged" in his theory of action, was able to blur over the ambiguity by tacit assimilation of individuals' goals to the conditions of social system functioning. Weber himself had far too realistic a grip on the subject matter to allow himself such a gambit. Instead, he saw the ambiguity of reason as inevitable; as inevitable as a Greek tragedy.

We have seen previously that Rickert's "values" much as Dilthey's "meaning," when stripped by Weber of their essentialist connotations, resolved themselves into no more than prescriptions for pro-active individualism.[49] I have tried to show also, how Weber's soberly nominalistic approach dissolved the old Kantian equation of pro-activity with indeterminacy. At the same time, Weber's typology of social structures was free from any implication that social relations and institutions were simply reflections of individual motives. On the contrary, in his view, action had to be construed as being guided as much by situational constraints as by subjective interest.[50] Neither was Weber interested in tracing the origins of social structures, at least, not in the same sense

---

[49] Watkins has argued that Weber proposed holistic ideal types in his 1904 essay (85) and only later (90) switched to an individualistic orientation. It is perfectly true that Weber was disentangling his own point of view from Rickert's in the 1904 paper and that his discussion in it was by no means clear. Watkins, however, claims that "Weber's earlier conception of an ideal type presupposed that one could detect the traits of some historic 'whole' *while remaining aloof from the detail of personal behavior*" (82, p. 27; my italics). In fact, no statement corresponding to the italicized part of Watkins' assertion is to be found in the paper he cites. On the contrary, in the same paper Weber anticipates some of his later, admittedly clearer, formulations (see, for example, his discussion of the "state" in 85, p. 99).

While disputing Watkins' argument as it refers to sources cited by him, I admit that Weber's substantive (as distinct from methodological) work does occasionally lose sight of the program of pro-active individualism he espoused.

[50] This is one of the meanings one may infer from Weber's unfortunate term "objective possibility." Popper used the expression "logic of the situation" for much the same sort of idea. Of course, the degree to which the logic of a situation assumed by those implicated in it or inferred by an observer is "objective" is subject to serious question. The symbolic interactionist idea of subjective and intersubjective "definitions of the situation" is more subtly in line with the orientation of pro-active individualism in this regard.

as evolutionist or social contract theories. What he did attempt to show was that all social forms can be resolved into the "reasonable likelihood" *(Chanze)* of certain specifiable actions taking place.

Despite these clear advantages, however, Weber's program failed to become established in the practice of sociological theorists. I have drawn attention above to the ambiguity of the concept "rationality" in Weber's use. This surely is one of the reasons why he "left no true descendants" (100, p. 1). Associated with this ambiguity was the tendency to emphasize predictable elements in social situations (or predictable repercussions to actions) and thus to deflect attention from individual actors and their goals to systems of formalized rules or norms viewed as super-individual and constraining. There is an implication here that formalized rules or maxims present the nearest approximation to be found in sociology to the "laws" of the natural sciences. Weber himself strenuously denied any attempt to equate social norms with natural laws. The whole of his Stammler paper (87) is devoted to an attack on such a point of view. None the less, his ambiguity could lead very naturally to the adoption of a position of reactive holism. He kept slipping into the rhetoric of holism in his historical work and my discussion of Parsons's ideas has demonstrated how a transition from Weber's pro-active individualism to a position of reactive holism could be effected without occasioning too many shouts of protest.

There is another difficulty in Weber's conception of sociological method which militates against the widespread adoption of pro-active individualism in the form in which he espoused it. This relates to Weber's insistence that ideal types have no necessary connection with actually existing states of affairs in society; that they "comprise collections of attributes which are logically interrelated but characteristic in their entirety of no existing society" (40, p. 59). The example on which Weber drew was, of course, marginal utility economics. In its classical statements by theorists such as Menger, this was susceptible to being described as a formal logic for the optimization of relative advantages. Menger himself, however, had described economic laws as being analogous to the laws of the natural sciences. What is more, in Menger's view such laws governed the "quantitative effects of the human impulse of self-interest" (50, p. 87). Deviations from effects predictable on the basis of such laws were to be attributed to processes analogous, say, to "friction" or "atmospheric resistance" in the mechanics of free fall. In first approximation, Weber's notion of ideal types can fruitfully be viewed as an alternative attempt to describe the methodological status of "Austrian" economic theory.

What Weber suggested was that the theory did not describe economic choices and decisions as they would "naturally" occur in the absence of frictions. The treatment of conduct as though it was totally under the sway of rational, businesslike, calculation was unrealistic;[51] yet, its very lack of faithfulness to reality gave it heuristic value. What is more, the fact that the idealized rational abstractions of marginal utility economics "fitted" actual events with a reasonably close degree of approximation was due to peculiarities of the historical era of capitalism (88, pp. 394-395). Weber's own training had been in the German historical tradition of economics which leant on Savigny's "organic" conception of jurisprudence as well as on Hegelian ideas of evolution. Weber found himself in the position of wanting to reject the "historicism" of this tradition (as it has since been termed by Hayek, 26, and Popper, 67). Yet he did not accept the natural science pretensions of marginal utility economics or its claim that economic laws were not "bound by conditions of place and time" (50, p. 107). Neither did Weber accept what he himself called the "psychologism" of Menger's school (see, for example, 86, p. 108).

In demoting economic theory to an ideal type with limited application to a particular historical configuration of events, Weber was able to reconcile its claims with what he considered to be the legitimate core of his own tradition of "developmental economics." At the same time, it occurred to him that the heuristic power of marginal utility theory could be harnessed for the social sciences at large.[52] This was to be achieved, in effect, by claiming that marginal utility theory was only a particular form of ideal type, that moreover, the notion of ideal types could be generalized so as to apply to a wider range of historical and social events. In this fashion, ideal types were proposed by him as suitable instruments for purposes of sociological explanation. Weber's insistence that such ideal types did not correspond to models of "real" processes, while consistent with his rejection of historicism and "scientism" in marginal utility theory, was not conducive to the development of a continuous and cumulative tradition of sociological theory.

It is interesting to note that Popper's prescription for the social sciences is very much like Weber's in all significant respects but one. The Popperian rallying cries of "methodological individualism," "logic of the situation," and opposition of "psychologism" all find antecedents in Weber's methodological writings.[53] Popper differs from Weber only in

[51] Or, in the incomparably clearer language of Norbert Wiener: that each player of the market game "at every stage, in view of the information available to him, plays in accordance with a completely intelligent policy, which will in the end assure him of the greatest possible reward" (95, p. 185).

[52] It should not be forgotten that marginal utility theory was the first widely recognized scientific achievement in any area of social studies (see, for instance, 93, p. 35).

[53] That is not to imply that Popper's ideas are directly derived from Weber's work. On the contrary, Popper shows little evidence of having read Weber's writings more than superficially.

his reaffirmation of Menger's equation of the methods of the social and the natural sciences. He also differs in his consequent rejection of ideal types as proposed by Weber, namely, as intrinsically unreal, and therefore untestable, models of rational action (see, 67, especially, pp. 130-143, 152-158).

On the question of the explanatory status of marginal utility economics, I am inclined to agree with Weber rather than with Menger or Popper. The model was clearly unrealistic (or, in Weber's sense, "ideal") at least, in the form taken by its pristine statements by economists such as Jevons, Walras, and Menger. Its unreality did not just consist of the imaginary isolation of the model from "frictions," or better, "imperfections." Rather, such a model of optimizing decisions described a limiting case; a state likely to be realized only under very special conditions.[54] Indeed, Weber's discussion of what he called *formal* and *substantive* rationality laboriously enumerated the limiting conditions necessary for the establishment of formal rationality in various areas in which it applied; namely, a money economy, the labor market, and in capital accounting (91, pp. 211-212, 247-248, 275-278).

If Weber's argument for ideal types was, indeed, that successful models in the social sciences are necessarily unrealistic models of limiting cases, he offended against it in his own practice. Not all of Weber's ideal type analyses were unrealistic in the sense of being tied to limiting assumptions of formal rationality. Furthermore, Weber adduced no prima facie methodological reasons why unrealistic models should be preferable to realistic ones.[55] Besides his special interest in putting marginal utility

[54] I do not know of a major paradigm in the natural sciences based, in the first instance, on the intentional adoption of a model of limiting conditions. Possibly Weber saw this feature as providing a genuine distinction between natural science and social science analysis, though he does not make this explicit other than by indirection.

It is interesting to note that the advance of theoretical physics since Galileo and Kepler has typically demonstrated that discarded theories "held good" under special limiting conditions. Thus Galileo's laws of free fall hold good under the limiting condition that the earth, to all intents and purposes, is infinite in mass relative to the falling object. An engineer concerned, say, with designing a net to catch falling objects would learn more from Galileo's physics than from fancy Newtonian considerations of "mutual attraction" and "inverse square laws of distance." Of course, if the "falling" object were a comet on a possible collision path with earth, Newtonian or perhaps even Einsteinian considerations would become relevant in predicting the "gravity" of the impending disaster.

[55] It is interesting that advances in economics since Weber's day have been in the direction of more "realistic" models. One may single out in particular the work of Herbert Simon in this context. Simon distinguishes between what he called *maximizing* (or "minimaxing") and *satisficing* action and shows that the latter can both be specified and developed into a more realistic model (76, pp. 204–205, 242–252, 272–273). Simon also makes an interesting distinction between subjective and objective rationality (76, pp. 277–278). Distinctions such as Simon's constitute a substantial advance over Weber's distinction between formal and substantive rationality and, particularly, over the latter's very poor discussion of substantive rationality.

economics in its place, so to speak, Weber may have wanted to emphasize the importance of making explicit the special conditions under
which any model of social processes would have explanatory value.
To this one may counter that there is no reason to assume that models
in the natural sciences are, in any sense, less subject to conditions than
sociological models; and Weber himself showed a very clear awareness
of this in his own methodological disquisitions. Neither did Weber's
suggested ideal type methodology propose any strikingly novel way in
which assumptions concerning initial conditions could be clarified.
In sum, while Weber's sociology was based on assumptions of pro-active
individualism, it failed, for reasons previously indicated, to establish a
viable intellectual tradition.

### Principium Rationis Agendi — Sufficientis? Weber and the Paradox of Rationality:

The foregoing review of meta-theoretical orientations in sociology has
attempted to highlight the weaknesses of each of these approaches without, hopefully, doing the protagonists selected for representing them too
great an injustice. In recapitulating the main critical points scattered
throughout this discussion and drawing them together into a coherent
argument, it will be useful to concentrate on one in particular. When
distinguishing these orientations, then, I shall refer especially to the differential location of independent variables (or "causal forces") that are
postulated as accounting for the maintenance of socio-cultural structures
or systems, or for changes in such structures or systems.

In placing emphasis on this point I return, yet again, to the issues
raised by Kantian dualism, though not necessarily in their nineteenth
century guise. In introducing this discussion I pointed out that the
freedom versus determinism problem could be resolved into a decision
as to whether a particular variable was a dependent or an independent
one. I also admitted that, in the final analysis, the ascription of dependence or independence to a given variable becomes a matter of
heuristics. Now, having reviewed the systematic variation of such
ascription of independent variables (or location of "determinants") in
our four orientations, we are in a better position to pass judgment on
various heuristic strategies, bearing in mind the consequences of choosing a particular strategy on the production of different kinds of analysis
or explanations. In other words, a position of *indifferentism* regarding
heuristics must be abandoned for a responsible position of *advocacy*
when considering a particular field of investigation at a particular juncture in its scientific development.

Though, initially, it may appear difficult to grasp, there are parallelisms
between the heuristic decisions to which I have alluded above and certain historically important decisions in classical Physics. Take the char-

acteristics of space, for instance. Einstein (15, pp. xi-xv) stresses the importance of the notion of "absolute space" (that is to say, "container space" in which the box, so to speak, is postulated as having no sides) for the classical Theory of Motion. This is simply another way of making the point that space, thus conceptualized, is selected as the independent variable determining the motion of bodies. Einstein adds, incidentally, that he considers this *heuristic* decision to be "one of Newton's greatest achievements." This is despite the fact that modern four-dimensional field theories depending upon space-time parameters lean much more heavily on rival conceptions of space, such as those put forward by Leibnitz and Huygens, namely, space as a relative positional quality of material objects. What Einstein is saying, essentially, is that Newton's decision was "correct" at that juncture in the development of physics.

I should like to think it is in the same spirit that I urge in favour of pro-active individualism as the heuristic orientation offering the best promise of scientific advance to sociology at this juncture of its development. What is more, that it offers this promise precisely because it postulates the actions of individual persons as the preferred independent variable for sociological explanation. In order to provide a justification for this statement, some remarks are necessary concerning the consequences of adopting alternative orientations on the way in which individual conduct has to be viewed.

In pro-active collectivism individual conduct is either viewed as determined by historically "programmed" sequences of events or as swallowed up in the blind *Behemoth* of a postulated "collective self." Reactive collectivism, instead, singles out equilibrating tendencies or forces for emphasis in its accounts of social determination. Though theories falling into one or another of these classifications may picture the independent forces they postulate as operating *through* individual persons as well as *upon* them — though such forces may be resonated or even refracted by individuals — the personal effectiveness of individuals in "making a difference" to the flow of social events is downgraded to the vanishing point.

Similarly, reactive individualism, by reducing action to mere motion, emplaces individual conduct in a *reinforcement field* which determines it absolutely (at least, if interpreted in terms of a space-time continuum). Ironically, Homans' individualistic protestations assume a hollow ring when one notes that the determining reinforcements in such an explanatory framework, at any rate as applied to sociology, ultimately have to be described primarily, if not exclusively, as social in origin. The case can easily be made for considering reactive individualism as a form of crypto-collectivism!

Well, then, what is the virtue of assigning to individual persons "personal effectiveness in making a difference?" It is easy enough to quote

Goethe to the effect that we think we drive the Fates, but we are really driven by them or, alternatively, to make pious reference to the Nineteenth Proverb of Solomon the King which comments on the multiplicity of goals harboured by men and concludes that it is the plan of the Almighty which will prevail. The initial answer to such an interrogation is a simple one: currently extant collectivistic and/or reactive sociological orientations have abundantly evidenced their impotence either to trace the patterns woven by the Fates or to map the contours of the Divine Plan (whichever theological option they might prefer).

The answer to our question is that orientations other than pro-active individualism not only fail to provide schemata for understanding the character of human action in its historical and social specificity but have encased their failures in deliberately abstract and rigid explanatory models; models devoid of intuitive or existential placement.[56] Few social scientists (not to speak of ordinary social participants) make *sense* of their conduct as clusters of operants under external reinforcement, or of themselves as the puppets of historical processes or of equilibrating tendencies in "social systems." If they do, one finds psychiatric labels to describe their depersonalization. Yet it is precisely such counter-intuitive imagery that these orientations employ.

To justify explanations which are devoid of intuitive or existential meaning, one would have to demonstrate, at the very least, that existentially meaningless explanations such as are generated by these orientations have predictive capacities which justify jettisoning our existential worlds. Physics, to be sure, reached such a stage when Maxwell's Equations proved their power. Then, the familiar environing images of the material world; images like "pull" and "push" and "three-dimensional perspectives" could be given up. Or, better, such images could be given up by specialists concerned with making "electro-magnetic sense," as distinct from intuitive or existential sense, of the world. Before sociologists abandon the intuitive world of motivational ascription (a world they still share with ordinary participants, whether they admit it or not) they would be advised to insist on some equivalent promise of making sense of human conduct in an alternative way. A willingness to give up our pre-Galilean sociology ought surely to depend upon the ultimate advent of something like a Maxwellian model.

The foregoing argument, essentially, provides a contemporary justification of Max Weber's choice of methodological individualism. To complete a rendition of this viewpoint one merely has to add that the intuitive, motive-driven, worlds of social participants themselves deter-

[56] Yet it should be clear that many of the theorists whose work falls within these analyses have succeeded in one thing: they have smuggled in a variety of action images that operate illicitly in their schemes acknowledging no obligation to pay the price that such intuitive notions demand, namely a framework that gives such intuitive notions a theoretical grounding.

mine these participants' actions and must, therefore, remain part and parcel of the subject-matter of sociology even in the eventuality that sociological explanations were, themselves, to become highly abstracted from such intuitive worlds.

It is at this point that Max Weber's theoretical shortcomings, to which I have referred above, become acutely problematic. As I have tried to show, the ambiguity of reason — the simultaneous reference of the term "rationality" both to motives and to rules or "maxims of experience" — blunted the edge of Weber's pro-active individualism. The inexorable advance of ever more inclusive interpersonal networks of meshing and controlling rationality in the social world that Weber depicted, could be interpreted as constituting a continuous narrowing of choice to that bitter limiting point at which any manifestation of personal spontaneity would have to be described as "irrational."

In an early essay after his partial recovery from a crippling depression, when Weber seemed to be on the way of providing a foundation for sociology as a science of motive, while quite incidentally, providing a "solution" for Kantian dualism, he wrote of an "atmospheric change" (81, p. 112). A new day was dawning. Minerva, the owl, could settle down to a well-earned rest. Science was taking over from philosophy the discussion of reason. It did not take very long before Weber recognized this change of climate as the advent of a new Ice Age. Within the frame of rationality as he had constructed it, the much-vaunted Sociological Individualism of Method pointed a forbiddingly bony finger in the direction of a Social Collectivism in Fact.

### Lift-Off: Principium Agendi — Sufficientis Rationis!

Is it necessary to assume that Weber's personal failure to provide an adequate grounding for pro-active individualism places the sociological enterprise into a quadruple bind from which there is no possible escape? In my opinion this question permits an optimistically negative reply. The rock on which Weber's project stumbled consisted of a mistaken conception of the manner in which the components of sociological explanatory models were to be assembled. As Weber conceived of model building, individuals' ends as well as established rules or maxims had to be built into each model, in a completed form. A reinterpretation of the central problem of sociological model building permits us to escape the paradox of rationality posed by his techniques.

The reinterpretation suggested here does not demand any drastic change of perspective from the viewpoint taken by Weber. It consists, quite simply, of the proposal that models of social processes concern themselves with the *formation* of individual ends and the *establishment* of interpersonal rules, rather than with postulated ends and rules in some already established form. Four years before Weber had anticipated a rosy dawn for scientific sociology — a dawn he was later to reinterpret as the harbinger of an icy night — there appeared in Vienna a book with the snappy title: *Traumdeutung* ("dream interpretation") (20). The German, in sharp contrast to Weber's was pellucidly clear. It contained, among other things, some useful suggestions for the construction of models of goal-creation and rule-formation. Weber seems to have had some superficial second-hand acquaintance with its contents, but reacted to its rhetoric with misplaced (and uncharacteristic) moralistic condemnation. This missed opportunity provides my occasion for addressing a sociological audience.

My theoretical model of image or need-articulation and of activation toward goals associated with such images or needs, accepts Weber's methodological individualism but gives it substance previously lacking. This is done by providing the individuals modelled sociologically with the opportunity to create definitions of the ends they seek and of the situations in which they seek such ends. The manner in which this process of creative definition is sociologically constructed is strongly influenced by Freudian notions.

The model of articulation I propose contains three variable coordinates, as does the symmetrical model of activation. Both phases of the model are intended to be generally applicable to all persons in any cultural situation. Individual as well as contextual variations are reflected by the variables of the model. Thus, while Weber's conceptions of artificially postulated "finished" ends or goals leads inexorably to his paradox of rationality, my conception of six independently variable coordinates of articulation and action lend postulated "actors in situations" a range of free play which provides, in principle at least, for continuously creative social change. The fundamental categories of the scheme, and some of the more important relationships amongst them, are presented in chapter 11 of this volume.

## BIBLIOGRAPHY

1. Alexander Franz. "The Logic of Emotions and its Dynamic Background" *International Journal of Psychoanalysis*, 1935, Vol. 16, pp. 399–413.

2. Allport, Gordon. "The Open System in Personality Theory," in *Journal of Abnormal and Social Psychology*, Vol. 61, 1960, pp. 301–310.

3. Baumgarten, Eduard. *Max Weber: Werk and Person*. Tübingen: Mohr (Siebeck), 1964.

4. Berlin, Isaiah. *Karl Marx*. New York: Oxford University Press, 1959.

5. Blau, Peter M. *Exchange and Power in Social Life*. New York: Wiley. 1964.

6. Blau, Peter M. Comment on George C. Homans' paper, "The Relevance of Psychology to the Explanation of Social Phenomena," in Robert Borger

and Frank Cioffi, eds., *Explanation in the Behavioural Sciences,* Cambridge, Cambridge University Press, 1970, pp. 329–339.

7. Blumer, Herbert. "Society as Symbolic Interaction," in Arnold Rose (ed.), *Human Behavior and Social Processes.* Boston: Houghton Mifflin and Co., 1962, pp. 179–192.

8. Boakes, R. A. and M. S. Halliday, "The Skinnerian Analysis of Behaviour," in Robert Borger and Frank Cioffi (eds.), *Explanation in the Behavioural Sciences.* Cambridge: Cambridge University Press, 1970, pp. 345–374.

9. Buckley, Walter. *Sociology and Modern Systems Theory.* Englewood Cliffs: Prentice-Hall, 1967.

10. Cohen, Percy S. *Modern Social Theory.* London: Heinemann, 1968.

11. Dahrendorf, Ralf. *Class and Class Conflict in Industrial Society.* Stanford: Stanford University Press, 1959.

12. deCharms, Richard. *Personal Causation.* New York: Academic Press, 1968.

13. Deutsch, Morton. "Homans in the Skinner Box," in Herman Turk and R. L. Simpson, eds. *Institutions and Social Exchange: The Sociologies of Talcott Parsons and George C. Homans.* Indianapolis: Bobbs-Merrill, 1971, pp. 81–90.

14. Dore, Ronald Philip. "Function and Cause," in N. J. Demerath 3rd. and Richard A. Peterson, eds., *System, Change and Conflict.* New York: Free Press, 1967, pp. 403–419.

15. Einstein, Albert. Introduction to Max Jammer, *Concepts of Space.* Cambridge, Massachusetts: Harvard University Press, 1969, pp. xi-xv.

16. Eisenstadt, S. N. "Social Change, Differentiation and Evolution," *American Sociological Review,* Vol. 29, 1964, pp. 375–386.

17. Etzioni, Amitai. *The Active Society.* New York: Free Press, 1968.

18. Etzioni, Amitai. "Toward a Theory of Societal Guidance," in Sara Jane Heidt and A. Etzioni (eds.), *Societal Guidance.* New York: Crowell, 1969.

19. Freud, Sigmund. "A Disturbance of Memory on the Acropolis," in *Collected Papers,* Vol. 5. London: Hogarth Press, 1950.

20. Freud, Sigmund. "The Interpretation of Dreams," in *The Basic Writings of Sigmund Freud,* translated by A. A. Brill. New York: Random House, 1938, pp. 183–549.

21. Geertz, Clifford. "The Integrative Revolution: Primordial Sentiments and Civil Politics in the New States," in Clifford Geertz (ed.), *Old Societies and New States.* New York: Free Press, 1963, pp. 105–157.

22. Geertz, Clifford. "Ideology as a Cultural System." In David E. Apter (ed.), *Ideology and Discontent.* New York: Free Press, 1964, pp. 46–47.

23. Geertz, Clifford. "Religion as a Cultural System." In Michael Banton (ed.), *Anthropological Approaches to the Study of Religion.* New York: Praeger, 1966, pp. 1–46.

24. Gellner, Ernest. "Explanations in History," in May Brodbeck (ed.),

*Readings in the Philosophy of the Social Sciences.* New York: Macmillan and Co., 1968.

25. Gottl, Friedrich (later Friedrich von Gottl-Ottlilienfeld). *Die Herrschaft des Wortes.* Jena: Gustav Fischer, 1901.

26. Hayek, F. A. v. *The Counter Revolution of Sciences.* Glencoe: Free Press, 1955.

27. Hodges, H. A. *The Philosophy of Wilhelm Dilthey.* London: Routledge and Kegan Paul, 1952.

28. Høffding, Harald. *A History of Modern Philosophy,* translated from the German edition by B. E. Meyer. (2 Vols.), Vol. 2. London: Macmillan and Co., 1900.

29. Homans, George C. *Social Behavior: Its Elementary Forms.* New York: Harcourt, Brace and World, 1961.

30. Homans, George C. Reply to Peter Blau's comment on his paper, "The Relevance of Psychology to the Explanation of Social Phenomena," in Robert Borger and Frank Cioffi (eds.), *Explanation in the Behavioral Sciences.* Cambridge: Cambridge University Press, 1970, pp. 340–343.

31. Homans, George C. "Commentary," in Herman Turk and R. L. Simpson, eds., *Institutions and Social Exchange: The Sociologies of Talcott Parsons and George C. Homans.* Indianapolis: Bobbs-Merrill, 1971, pp. 363–379.

32. Homans, George C., and Charles P. Curtis, Jr. *An Introduction to Pareto.* New York: Knopf, 1934.

33. Hook, Sidney. "Pareto's Sociological System," in James H. Meisel (ed.), *Pareto and Mosca.* Englewood Cliffs: Prentice-Hall (Spectrum), 1965, pp. 57–61.

34. Jarvie, Ian C. *Concepts and Society.* London: Routledge and Kegan Paul, 1972.

35. Jaspers, Karl. *Allgemeine Psychopathologie.* Berlin: Springer, 1913.

36. Kant, Immanuel. *Critique of Practical Reason,* translated by T. K. Abbot. London: Longmans, Green and Company, 1873.

37. Kant, Immanuel. *Critique of Pure Reason,* translated by Norman Kemp Smith. London: Macmillan and Co., 1958.

38. Kuhn, Thomas S. *The Structure of Scientific Revolutions.* Chicago: University of Chicago Press, 1962.

39. Kunkel, John H. *Society and Economic Growth.* New York: Oxford University Press, 1970.

40. Lipset, Seymour Martin. *Political Man.* New York: Doubleday (Anchor), 1963.

41. Louch, A. R. *Explanation and Human Action.* Berkeley: University of California Press, 1966.

42. Löwith, Karl. *From Hegel to Nietzsche.* London: Constable, 1965.

43. Marcuse, Herbert. *Eros and Civilization.* London: Sphere, 1969.

44. Marcuse, Herbert. *One Dimensional Man.* London: Sphere, 1968.

45. Marcuse, Herbert. *Reason and Revolution.* Boston: Beacon Press, 1960.

46. Martindale, Don. "Sociological Theory and the Ideal Type," in Llewellin Gross (ed.), *Symposium on Sociological Theory*. Evanston: Row-Peterson, 1959, pp. 57–91.

47. Marx, Karl. "Theses on Feuerbach," in *Karl Marx: Selected Writings in Sociology and Social Philosophy*, translated by T. B. Bottomore. T. B. Bottomore and Maximillen Rubel (eds.). New York: McGraw-Hill, 1956, pp. 67–69.

48. Mayhew, Bruce H. *et al.*, "System Size and Structural Differentiation in Formal Organizations: A Baseline Generator for Two Major Theoretical Propositions." *American Sociological Review*, Vol. 37 (October 1972), pp. 629–633.

49. Meier, Gerald M. and Robert E. Baldwin, *Economic Development*. New York: Wiley, 1957.

50. Menger, Karl. *Problems of Economics and Sociology*, translated by F. J. Nock. Louis Schneider (ed.) Urbana: University of Illinois Press, 1963.

51. Morgenstern, Christian. *Galgenlieder*. Zürich: Verlag der Arche, 1952.

52. Morgenstern, Christian. *Stilles Reifen (Auswahl)*. München: Piper, (no date).

53. Murray, Henry A. "Preparations for the Scaffold of a Comprehensive System," in Sigmund Koch (ed.), *Psychology: A Study of a Science*. 6 vols. Vol. 3. New York: McGraw-Hill, 1959, pp. 7–54.

54. Nagel, Ernest. *The Structure of Science*. New York: Harcourt, Brace & World, 1951.

55. Nisbet, Robert. "Review of *The Active Society* by Amitai Etzioni," *American Sociological Review*, Vol. 33 (1968), pp. 990–991.

56. Parsons, Talcott. *The Structure of Social Action*. New York: Free Press, 1949.

57. Parsons, Talcott. *The Social System*. New York, Free Press, 1951.

58. Parsons, Talcott, and Neil J. Smelser, *Economy and Society*. New York: Free Press, 1965.

59. Parsons, Talcott. "An Approach to Psychological Theory in Terms of the Theory of Action," in Sigmund Koch, (ed.), *Psychology: A Study of a Science*. 6 vols. Vol. 3, New York: McGraw-Hill, 1959, pp. 612–711.

60. Parsons, Talcott. "General Theory in Sociology," in Robert K. Merton, Leonard Broom and Leonard S. Cottrell, Jr., (eds.), *Sociology Today*. New York: Basic Books, 1959, pp. 3–38.

61. Parsons, Talcott. "Evolutionary Universals in Society" *American Sociological Review*, Vol. 29 (1964), pp. 339–357.

62. Parsons, Talcott. "The Present Position and Prospects of Systematic Theory in Sociology," in *Essays in Sociological Theory*. (Rev. Ed.) New York: The Free Press, 1964, pp. 221–237.

63. Parsons, Talcott. *Societies: Evolutionary and Comparative Perspectives*. Englewood Cliffs: Prentice-Hall, 1966.

64. Parsons, Talcott, and Edward A. Shils (with the assistance of James

Olds). "Values, Motives, and Systems of Action," in Talcott Parsons and Edward A. Shils (eds.), *Toward a General Theory of Action.* New York: Harper (Torchbooks), 1962, pp. 47–275.

65. Parsons, Talcott, Robert F. Bales, and Edward A. Shils. *Working Papers in the Theory of Action.* Glencoe, Illinois: The Free Press, 1953.

66. Popper, Sir Karl Raimund. *The Open Society and its Enemies.* (2 vols.) New York: Harper and Row, 1962.

67. Popper, Sir Karl Raimund. *The Poverty of Historicism.* London: Routledge and Kegan Paul, 1961.

68. Popper, Sir Karl Raimund. *Conjectures and Refutations.* New York: Basic Books, 1962.

69. Rex, John. *Key Problems of Sociological Theory.* London: Routledge and Kegan Paul, 1961.

70. Rickert, Heinrich. *Die Grenzen der Naturwissenschaftlichen Begriffsbildung* (3rd ed.). Tübingen: Mohr (Siebeck), 1921.

71. Rose, Arnold. "A Systematic Summary of Symbolic Interaction Theory," in Arnold Rose (ed.), *Human Behavior and Social Processes.* Boston: Houghton Mifflin and Co., 1962, pp. 3–19. 1962.

72. Rothenstreich, Nathan. *Basic Problems in Marx's Philosophy.* New York: Bobbs-Merrill, 1965.

73. Schopenhauer, Arthur. *Uber die Vierfache Wurzel des Satzes vom Zureichenden Grund.* Rudolstadt: 1813.

74. Schopenhauer, Arthur. *The World as Will and Representation.* (2 vols.) translated by E. F. J. Payne. New York: Dover, 1958, Vol. 2.

75. Simmel, George. "How is Society Possible?" in Kurt H. Wolff, (ed. and translator), *George Simmel 1858–1918.* Columbus: Ohio State University Press, 1959, pp. 337–356.

76. Simon, Herbert A. *Models of Man.* New York: Wiley, 1957.

77. Skinner, B. F. "Are Theories of Learning Necessary?" *Psychological Review,* Vol. 57 (1950), pp. 193–216.

78. Spencer, Herbert. *Principles of Psychology.* London: Williams and Norgate, 1890.

79. Spencer, Herbert. *The Principles of Sociology.* (Vol. 1) New York: Appleton, 1896.

80. Stigler, George J. *The Theory of Price.* New York: Macmillan and Co., 1947.

81. Sumner, William Graham. *Folkways.* Boston: Ginn and Co., 1940.

82. Tolstoy, Leo. *What to Do?* translated by Isabel F. Hapgood. New York: Crowell, 1887.

83. Watkins, J. W. N. "Ideal Types and Historical Explanation," *British Journal for the Philosophy of Science,* Vol. 3 (1952), pp. 22–43.

84. Weber, Max. "The Meaning of 'Ethical Neutrality' in Sociology and Economics," in *The Methodology of the Social Sciences,* translated and edited by E. A. Shils and H. A. Finch. Glencoe: The Free Press, 1949, pp. 1–47.

85. Weber, Max. "Objectivity in Social Science and Social Policy," in *The Methodology of the Social Sciences*, translated and edited by E. A. Shils and H. A. Finch. Glencoe: The Free Press, 1949, pp. 50–112.

86. Weber, Max. "Roscher und Knies und die logischen Probleme der historischen Nationalökonomie," in *Gesammelte Aufsätze zur Wissenschaftslehre* (2nd ed.). Tübingen: Mohr (Siebeck), 1951, pp. 1–145.

87. Weber, Max. "R. Stammlers 'Uberwindung' der materialistischen Geschichtsauffassung," in *Gesammelte Aufsätze zue Wissenschaftslehre*. Tübingen: Mohr (Siebeck), 1951, pp. 291–359.

88. Weber, Max. "Die Grenznutzlehre und das 'psychophysische Grundgesetz," in *Gesammelte Aufsätze zur Wissenschaftslehre*. Tübingen: Mohr (Siebeck), 1951, pp. 384–399.

89. Weber, Max. "Soziologische Grundbegriffe," in *Gesammelte Ausätze zur Wissenschaftslehre*. Tübingen: Mohr (Siebeck), 1951, pp. 527–565.

90. Weber, Max. *Economy and Society*. G. Roth and C. Wittich (eds.). New York: Bedminster Press, 1968.

91. Weber, Max. *The Theory of Social and Economic Organization*, translated by A. M. Henderson and T. Parsons. Glencoe: The Free Press, 1947.

92. Weber, Max. *Law in Economy and Society*, edited by Max Rheinstein, translated by E. A. Shils and Max Rheinstein. Cambridge, Mass.: Harvard University Press, 1954.

93. Weber, Max. "Bureaucracy," in *From Max Weber: Essays in Sociology*, translated and edited by H. H. Gerth and C. Wright Mills. London: Routledge and Kegan Paul, 1948, pp. 196–244.

94. Weber, Max. "Science as a Vocation," in *From Max Weber: Essays in Sociology*, translated and edited by H. H. Gerth and C. Wright Mills. London: Routledge and Kegan Paul, 1948, pp. 129–156.

95. Wiener, Norbert. *Cybernetics*. New York: John Wiley and Sons, 1948.

96. Winch, Peter. *The Idea of a Social Science*. London: Routledge and Kegan Paul, 1958.

97. Winckelman, Johannes. "Max Weber's Verständniss von Mensch und Gesellschaft," in Kurt Engisch, B. Pfister and J. Winckelman (eds.), *Max Weber: Gedächtnisschrift*. Berlin: Dunker & Humblot, 1966, pp. 195–243.

98. Windelband, Wilhelm. "Geschichte und Naturwissenschaft (Strassburger Rektoratsrede, 1894)." Printed in Wilhelm Windelband, Präludien. (Vol. 2.) Tübingen: 1911, pp. 136–160.

99. Wolfson, Murray. *A Reappraisal of Marxian Economics*. New York: Columbia University Press, 1966.

100. Wrong, Dennis (ed.). *Max Weber*. Englewood-Cliffs, N.J.: Prentice-Hall, 1970.

101. Vaughan, Ted R., and Larry T. Reynolds. "The Sociology of Symbolic Interaction," in Larry T. Reynolds and Julia M. Reynolds (eds.), *The Sociology of Sociology*. New York: David McKay, 1970, pp. 324–339.

102. Zollschan, George K., and Donald A. Hensen. "On Motivation: Toward Socially Pertinent Foundations," in Donald A. Hansen (ed.), *Explorations in Sociology and Counselling*. Boston: Houghton Mifflin and Co., 1969, pp. 30–63.

103. Zollschan, George K., and Robert Perrucci. "Social Stability and Social Process: An Initial Presentation of Relevant Categories," in George K. Zollschan and Walter Hirsch (eds.), *Explorations in Social Change*, London: Routledge and Keegan Paul, 1964, pp. 99–124.

# 10

*George K. Zollschan*
*and Michael A. Overington*

# Reasons for Conduct and the Conduct of Reason: The Eightfold Route to Motivational Ascription

*"Every intellect, when it conceives and comprehends . . . any concept, grasps and encompasses this matter . . . and in turn is grasped, enveloped, and clothed within the mind that has comprehended and conceived it. The mind for its part, is also clothed in the concept at the time it comprehends and grasps it with the intellect. This is a wonderful union . . . which has no parallel anywhere in the material world."*

> Rabbi Schneur Zalman of Liadi
> *Likutei Amarim (Tanya)*

### The Eightfold Route to Motivational Ascription:

If one wishes to examine the various accounts of motivation of social action that have been (or might be) offered there are obvious advantages to doing so within a framework that will organize the presentation and also make possible some comparison of their conceptual adequacy. However, before worrying about this framework it is necessary to suggest a general conception which justifies taking "drives," "plans," "rationalizations," and so on as motives. Put otherwise, unless we can specify a general concept which allows for a comparison of theories of motivation we shall be left with little more than a description of theories of meanings of the term "motivation." This is not to argue for an ordinary language analysis of the term (an analysis, that is to say, of what it means to ordinary language philosophers). It is to suggest, rather, that without some explicit definition of "motivation" the appearance of any theory into the discussion will be little more than a single element in a puzzle which the selection, *tout complet*, presents to the reader. While the elucidation of rule following conduct is one important kind of theorizing about motives, forcing readers to articulate the rule we have followed, in order to present theories of motivation, would hardly be consistent with our effort to secure some clarity in the presentation of the conceptual position of theories of motivation in general. This chapter, therefore, presents an explicit understanding of what we mean by "motivation" as well as giving a basis for comparing the theories we have selected. As a result, we hope to exemplify the range of more or less adequate theories of motivation at the same time as we provide the major parameters of a theory that is complete when judged by the standards we have espoused.

How, then, shall we formulate an understanding of our subject? Judging by the often lackluster presentation that results when a narrow definition is accepted, something might well be gained by stretching the notion quite out of its usual shape so as to include needs, drives, plans, rationalizations, goals, and so on, as well as other notions of motive, by identifying a principle common to the whole range. Such a general principle may be found in their character as "explanations." Whatever else these various formulations of motive may have in common, they are at least "explanations" — attempts to respond to "why" questions about human conduct in a social world. In other words, the various conceptions of motives as factors within or outside the individual (or both) that exercise a push or pull towards conduct, are proposals by their authors for an account of the nature of conduct performed by individuals. In establishing the notion of "explanation" as the general character of all theories of motivation we obviously recognize that we have broadened the meaning of "motivation" to include any theory which takes as its *explicandum* the individual's conduct. A strict interpretation of this conception would force the inclusion of a range of theories from the theological to the biological; we have been less inclusive than we might in our discussion in limiting the range of theories considered to psychological and sociological ones. Nonetheless, we do want the broad definition to stand since it provides the basis for a thoroughly reflexive account of motivation, an account only partially rendered by our discussion of theories of motivation. To elaborate this point let us turn to the question of *who* affirms the explanation.

Now it must be clear that, while accounts of conduct are always provided by observers, those keen-eyed reporters need not be social scientists. Theorizing about one's own and others' motives, offering explanations for one's own or others' conduct, is not an enterprise restricted to the social sciences. On the contrary, it is something all persons do merely to get around in their world.[1] In a strong sense, then, theories of motivation offered by social scientists are simply one subset of such theories. The social and social-psychological conditions to which one might point in describing (thereby explaining and perhaps even "motivating") motivational theorizing in general are equally applicable to that special subset of such theories which is the concern of this chapter. Let us pull back from the multiple images that a complete set of social accounts refracts before our eyes and turn to the more simple and immediate issue of the dimensions along which we may catalogue the "theorizing observer" of conduct.

The first dimension must surely treat just *whose* conduct is being observed, that of the observer himself or that of some other. This merely suggests that one may offer explanations for others as well as oneself; self observation and "explanation" has no claim to privilege, it merely is different in giving access to experiences not available to the outside observer and vice versa. The second dimension is the degree to which the observer "shares" the world of the actor. As polar types one may think of these as "member" and "stranger," terms which surely conjure up a multiplicity of notions from the literature on these types.[2] Certainly, the use of these terms is intended to resonate to other discussions of the two types. At this simple level of first approximation we are referring to the capacity of the observer to formulate the actor and his world "in the same way" as does the actor. The third and last dimension along which we might distribute observers and "theorizers" about conduct is with respect to their intended audience. Although many are possible along this dimension, our purposes are best served by distinguishing two categories, the social scientific and the naive. Even this distinction is but a heuristic one, in which the term "social scientific" refers to observer's accounts which are addressed to social scientists and the term "naive" is a residual category for *all* other kinds of accounts.

[1] This, of course, is a position that is associated with Alfred Schutz (44) and many of his followers, both acknowledged and unacknowledged, for example Blum and McHugh (1) and Scott and Lyman (46). It should not be forgotten, however, that there is also such a tradition in social psychology in North America: this has "narrowed" from the work of Fritz Heider (19) and passes under the title "Attribution Theory." A somewhat more expanded version of work under this tradition is that of Richard de Charms (6).

[2] In particular we are thinking of the papers of Schutz (45) and Simmel (51), each of which bears the title "The Stranger."

From these three dimensions it is possible to develop the following typology of "theoretical observers":

| | |
|---|---|
| 1.    Self Observers | 2.    Observers of Others |
| 1.1.  Member | 2.1.  Member |
| 1.1.1. Naive | 2.1.1. Naive |
| 1.1.2. Social Scientific | 2.1.2. Social Scientific |
| 1.2.  Stranger | 2.2.  Stranger |
| 1.2.1. Naive | 2.2.1. Naive |
| 1.2.2. Social Scientific | 2.2.2. Social Scientific |

We have, therefore, eight types of perspectives from which observers can offer accounts of conduct. It may help readers if we provide some sense of what these types might look like in an empirical context.

While it is fair to assume that we are all self observers, providing accounts of our conduct to a variety of audiences, we know quite little in a systematic way about such explanations.[3] Nor do most contemporary social sciences provide much legitimation for introspection; a technique which is the explanation of conduct in general by a self observer addressing a social scientific audience. However, we could expect that persons such as confessors, probation officers, psychiatrists, and others, who are in positions to require explanations of conduct from their "clients" would have some information of a more systematic nature. The distinction between "member" and "stranger" with respect to self observation is an interesting one. The usual expectation that one would have is that the self observer would always be in a "member" position with respect to his own conduct; however, it is possible to conceive of being a "stranger to oneself," of encountering one's own conduct as something performed by an alien self that presents a problem in its explication.

Nonetheless, we are more concerned about the perspective of the observer of others, how we account for the conduct of other people in their relationships. Here, one would expect considerable similarity between the accounts of naive observers of themselves or others. Thus for example, what we know about stereotyping may be expected to apply to self and others. However, the focus of our chapter is on explanations of social scientific intent by "members" or "strangers." This is a distinction which can separate the work of anthropologists, ethnographers, symbolic interactionists among others, from formal modelers, survey researchers and so on. This is not to claim that all those falling in the first group penetrate the "emic" dimension in their explanations; merely that many seek to do so as a methodological principle. The sec-

[3] However, one may find an essayistic beginning to an understanding of this problem in the work of Kenneth Burke, for example (4), and more recently in the paper by Scott and Lyman (46).

ond group whose concern is with the "etic," *the general* character of action, makes the issue of "member" or "stranger" an irrelevant one.[4]

## Scientific Explanation of Motive:

We must now consider further the demarcation of social scientific explanations from the residual category of the naive account. We have made the distinction in terms of the intention of the author of the account to address a social scientific audience. We can hardly allow such a comment to pass without some further amplification, since the notion of the audience to which accounts are presented will serve as our rule for inclusion and exclusion of theories of motivation. Firstly we want to distinguish between "scientific publics," as congeries of individuals who respond to, and judge, the production of social scientists, and "scientific audiences." The latter term refers to the intentional construction of individual social scientists concerning the character of the respondents to and judges of their production. The degree of overlap between public and audience in any particular case is, of course, an empirical question. It results from the individual's capacity and willingness to bring them into coincidence. For example, certain types of schizophrenics separate audience and public in order to enact and protect the character of a particular audience.[5] However, for most of us "socialization" at all stages of our life cycle produces both capacity and desire to correlate "inner" and "outer" worlds; to bring audience and public into correspondence. Indeed, as our example seeks to show, the very unwillingness or incapacity to do this is grounds for a psychiatric label: publics are the authorities (some more authoritative than others) which attest the reality of our audience-addressed speech. In the special case of the social scientist, the individual's training is geared to making it both possible and desirable for the individual to bring together scientific audience and public in such a way as to impose public standards of scientific adequacy on the research of the individual.[6] The scientific community or public is the locus of judgment concerning the "adequacy"

[4] This distinction between "emic" and "etic" kinds of analysis has its origins in modern linguistics and has been applied to the study of social and cultural processes as a way to distinguish between them. The emic approach is involved with developing a first hand contextual understanding of the world of social participants *as it appears to them;* it produces accounts by "social scientific members." The etic approach on the other hand, is concerned with providing a "social scientific" stranger's account of *general* social and cultural patterns.

[5] For a wonderfully sympathetic, semi-autobiographical account of the separation of audience and public in schizophrenia see Hannah Green (17).

[6] Both John Ziman (63) and Michael Polanyi (38) emphasize the apprenticeship served by the scientist as the place where, by following the ostensive enactment of the rules of research that are provided by the "master," the neophyte acquires the standards, values, norms, assumptions, and so on of the scientific public to which the master orientates his work. This enactment of "public address" becomes the base for the apprentice's construction of a scientific audience that will legitimate and watch his work when the years of training are long forgotten.

of research in the sense that it establishes and maintains the criteria which allow the speech of individual scientists *qua* scientists to be attested as scientifically "real." If we continue with our imagery, then, the adequacy of scientific statements has to do with the rhetorical character of such speech in alleging that a statement is not falsified after test. If we extend Sir Karl Popper's falsifiability criterion (39, pp. 33-65) here within our rhetorical imagery we may distinguish between three kinds of statements which have sometimes been said to demarcate scientific from other kinds of statements. Firstly, there are statements which are "non-falsifiable," protected by their argumentative form from being tested. Perhaps they refer to past or future situations, to ideal typical ones, or whatever; nonetheless, they have this character only at some particular time and place and in the context of some particular theoretical framework. At some other time and place, in some other theoretical context, they might become part of the class of statements which we shall call "not falsified." Secondly, therefore, we have those statements which are "not falsified" *in a given situation;* statements which are "pragmatically adequate." Often these are the kinds of statements which suffice for engineering: whether mechanical, electrical, civil, or social. Finally, we have statements that are "not falsified" *after testing by the standards of the scientific public.* This progression is not an implicit claim that the standards of the scientific "test" are necessarily more severe by some absolute criterion, merely that the argumentative form of scientific speech must attend to what is the most convincing rhetoric if it is to secure agreement on the scientific facticity of the statement. The most creative scientists will be precisely those most accomplished in constructing what their publics believe to be plausible and rigorous tests of their statements, thereby providing for plausible and rigorous arguments when they are reported. Creative scientists are precisely those individuals who have been able to locate in their audiences the scientific public's appreciation and recognition of the most plausible arguments. As a consequence they are able to invent the kinds of tests that have the most a priori justification as candidates to falsify the claim made by the theory at issue. Put less formally, this creativity, when presented in the report of a test, should evoke from the public a feeling that "if that did not show it false (or "confirm" it) nothing will." It is this notion of audience as the scientist's intent to address a delimited public that will serve as a base for including the theories that we do in our discussion of *scientific* theories of motivation.

What principles of conceptual adequacy do we intend to use to organize our discussion and assessment of theories of motivation? In the first place we need to account for our particular use of the notions of "law" and "rule" and our refusal to enshrine a distinction between these terms as fundamental to accounts of conduct. In the second, we want to introduce the dramatistic system of Kenneth Burke as a framework for judging the completeness of these theories of motivation.

In the white heat of his advocacy of moral individualism (40) Popper hammers out a discussion of the origins of the distinction between *nature* and *convention* in Greek thought, tracing it back to Protagoras (40, p. 57). This difference between nature and society is not to be found in all societies, he maintains, but emerges only after the "magical closed society of tribalism" has broken down. Popper's innocence of anthropological evidence, quite evidently, is no restraint on the claim that there is something about tribalism that inhibits the development of an understanding of the difference between the norms of everyday life and the regularities of the natural world. But what is this distinction in more modern terms? Does it not amount to the difference between natural and normative laws, between invariant regularities and regularities that can be followed or not, and that even can be changed? Now, for Popper there are laws of the social world that are like natural laws; "natural laws of social life" (40, p. 67). When these are contrasted with the normative regulation we find ourselves with a distinction between laws and rules.

If we continue our consideration of this difference, in a Popperian framework, we are led to ask exactly and in what respects *laws* (in the sense of laws of nature) and *rules,* including, inter alia, juridical laws (in the sense of conventions), are different. Put in other words, we wonder if, indeed, there is quite the difference that Popper as well as Protagoras declare. Thus, with respect to a specifiable item of conduct one is forced to ask whether it be law-determined or rule-governed, or rule-following. It should be plain that breaking a rule is possible only under the assumption that the conduct in question is an example of rule-following action. Obversely, breaking a rule cannot, by definition, be categorized as "deviation" from lawlike invariance.

Popper recognizes that all given laws hold good only under certain conditions which are in principle specifiable. The number of such conditions one might conceivably specify in order to "hedge" any given law is, in principle, limitless. Indeed, the listing of such conditions is a way of indicating in what overlapping intellectual, ideational, temporal and spatial perspective an imaginary observer would be able to locate the phenomena to which the law is applicable. On the other hand, *adequate* rather than *complete* hedging conditions are the concerns of *scientific* observers and will depend on the special perspective and tacit understandings and misunderstandings held by relevant scientific publics. In practice, such tacit assumptions often become revealed in the judgement of scientific communities that a law, after testing in a "new" area, is restricted in its conditional application.

Moreover, these comments about conditions apply equally well to primitive concepts, that is, to those concepts which are not reduced or reduceable to other concepts employed in explanation. Indeed, it may be difficult to draw an exact distinction between what is a "condition" and what is a "primitive." Take the notion that physical space has Euclidian properties. In a sense one can interpret this as a "property" of the primitive concept "Space"; in another sense, one can take it as one of the set of tacit conditions under which the inverse square of distance holds good. One could reasonably maintain that Newtonian laws owed their predictive and explanatory strength to the fact, among other things, that at magnitudes to which Newtonian propositions normally apply, "Space," to all intents and purposes, may be treated as closely approximating Euclidian properties. Perhaps we can push the notion of conditions a little farther now and suggest that the distinction between laws and rules is altogether unnecessary for sociological purposes if one is willing to entertain the rather simple idea that rules are followed and broken *under specific conditions.* This is only to say, after all, that *both* rules and laws are conditional, and further, that there is no a priori ground for denying in principle that one could study the conditions under which rules are followed and broken.[7]

Whether one believes that conduct is law-determined or rule-following in its character, specific conduct is an occasion for examining the generality of the explanatory law or rule. Indeed, there is no empirical way to decide whether one is dealing with lawful conduct or not. Investigation merely turns up the conditions under which there exists invariance. Formulating these instances of conditional invariance as lawful rather than as selective rule-following has to be a meta-theoretical decision. We need to rethink, therefore, the distinction between laws and rules so as to exhibit salutary agnosticism with respect to the difference between them.

Perhaps we can achieve this aim by proposing a dimensional concept of "conditional invariance" as a replacement for both law and rule so that all conduct would be viewed as conforming to some invariant regularity under varying conditions. Thus what was formally called lawful conduct would now amount to any invariance the conditions of which necessarily *excluded* individual choice to conform to or deviate from the invariance. Rule-following conduct, on the other hand, would be seen as any invariance the conditions of which necessarily *included* individual choice to conform to, or deviate from, the invariance. But does not this reformulation work only by packing into "choice" the distinction that was formally exhibited by laws and rules? Would the issue now not be whether or not these "choices" are made lawfully or as a result of rule-following? Of course, we court the dangers of an infinite regress

---

[7] This is emphatically not an attempt to finesse a way through the arguments between contemporary proponents of the unity of science position and partisans of the view that the social sciences have a special quality established by the inherent instability of rule-following action of human persons. Rather, we are suggesting that this debate may be of little use to social scientists concerned to account for *particular* human activity.

by this formulation. The only way of dealing with this danger is to confront it with the idea of "conditional invariance" as an understanding that conduct conforms to invariant regularities under varying and specifiable conditions. The question of what conditions will "adequately" locate the invariance must be seen as given by the appropriate scientific publics; and theories of motivation — "explanations" of conduct — must be seen as statements of the conditions under which conduct will conform to particular invariant regularities.

## A Framework for Classifying Theories of Motivation:

It is here that we need to introduce Kenneth Burke, for in his meta-theoretical scheme of the "Pentad" one finds a framework for organizing theories of motivation in terms of the range and completeness of the conditions that they specify and imply. At the same time, elements of the scheme may be used to make sense of the distinction, *which others have made,* between laws and rules. Briefly, we shall regard accounts of conduct that conceive it as law determined as placing the conditional element in situations and instrumentalities, what Burke calls *Scene* and *Agency,* and accounts of action which view it as rule-following as locating the conditional in goals, persons, and acts, what Burke calls *Purpose, Agent* and *Act.* In doing this we are arguing that a completely "adequate" theory of motivation would take note of these five terms of the Pentad and would therefore collapse the distinction between laws and rules.

The importance of Kenneth Burke's work lies in the utility of his dramatistic system as a meta-theoretical framework for theories of motivation; for "explanations" of conduct. Of course, Burke's work is more than this; it operates as a method for analyzing action (that is essentially as we plan to use it). At the same time, it is also a sociology of knowledge rooted in a very personal reading of Marx and Freud as well as a theory of society based on a conception of language as the fundamental building block of both social order and conflict. What we need to do is sketch the outlines of his dramatistic system so that readers may understand how it is used in the organization and assessment of the varied theories of motivation that we seek to review in the body of this chapter.

In his earlier work Burke was concerned to make sense of the sources and variance in naive observers' explanations of others. Since the Second World War he has devoted himself to working out the idea of a linguistically based and internally "logical" theory of motivational statements. Yet, in both the earlier and later work he has been anxious to make sense of verbal accounts of action, which through a consistent perspectivism has made him dissatisfied with single factor accounts. The understanding of verbally given accounts cannot be less complex than the convoluted character of the symbolic relationships that words bear to each other, and Burke enacts his belief in the fundamental complexity of words and their relations in the way that he argues *with himself* in his work. Looking for some simple statement in his work, in some ways, therefore, violates his purposes as a dialectical thinker, but it is possible to distill some of the essence of his system into a few words.

For this purpose we turn to *A Grammar of Motives* (4) where one may find a codification of the later system in what Burke calls the Pentad. Here, there is an explicit statement of the rules for explaining human action; or perhaps better, a statement of what kind of questions about action have to be asked by the theorist if they are concerned to offer a "complete" account. As Burke has it: "In any rounded statement about motives, you must have some word that names the *act* (names what took place, in thought or deed), and another that names the *scene* (the background of the act, the situation in which it occurred); also you must indicate what person or kind of person *(agent)* performed the act, what means or instruments he used *(agency)*, and the *purpose*" (4, p. xv). The Pentad is the five terms Act, Scene, Agent, Agency, and Purpose and they may be seen most helpfully as a series of questions that the theorist answers; Act becomes equivalent to "What was done?", Scene is the same as "In what situation was it done?" and so on. Thus, a complete explanation of action will contain, either explicitly or implicitly, answers to the five questions that are contained in the terms of the Pentad.

There is, however, a little more to the dramatistic system than the Pentad, even stripped and violated for our use as it is here. We have to pay some minimal attention to the relationships that Burke asserts to exist between the terms of explanations, in particular between the terms of the Pentad. In effect, he wants to argue that there exists a consistency between the various terms which he calls "ratios" such that in an explanation, for example, the nature of the situation and the nature of the agent and his act will all be consistent with each other, if the account is to be viewed as "sensible." An account of the limited range of activity employed by agents in a bank presupposes that the activity takes place in a situation coherent with the limits; thus, the legal-rational action of the teller "makes sense" in the bank seen as a legal-rational situation.

Finally, we have to point out to readers that not only are the terms of the Pentad most sensible in explanations when they are specified consistently with each other, but there is also a real sense in which any one of the terms, at either a conceptual or empirical level, is but an icon for the whole array. In effect, Burke is arguing that the notion of action, as a concept, must contain, if not explicitly, then implicitly, the conceptions of agents, agencies, purposes, situations, and acts. If, therefore, in some account of action there is explicit mention of only one or two of the pentadic terms, the others have to be there packed into those terms which *are* mentioned. Thus, in the action frame, situations necessarily contain *from the meaning of "action,"* agents, agencies, purposes, and acts; and acts necessarily contain the notion of agents performing the act through instrumentalities towards ends and in situations, and so on for each term of the Pentad.

Our purposes with Burke and his Pentad, however, are quite simple; we wish to take his conception of a "rounded statement of motives" to be the equivalent of an "adequately complete explanation of conduct." We utilize the Pentad, as a series of questions, as the basis for evaluating the conceptual generality, and therefore the conceptual adequacy, of theories of motivation. Our first step in making it possible to assess the conceptual adequacy of theories of motivation was taken early on in the chapter when we enunciated a definition of "motivation" broad enough to trap all theories that sought to account for human action, no matter what their particular terminology. We have, thereby, made it possible to compare such theories; the pentadic scheme makes it possible to evaluate them in terms of their relative generality. Naturally, we recognize that there is more to conceptual adequacy than mere generality. Matters of internal consistency, parsimony, and so on could all arise. But if one is interested in *general* theories of action, general theories of motivation, then *conceptual generality* must take pride of place. The most parsimonious account of action benefits nothing if it is not conceptually general. Thus, in our presentation of theories of motivation we shall seek to exhibit the relative generality of the various accounts by referring to the terms of the Pentad; although it must be noted that these theories of action, as Burke remarks, could be shown to make at least implicit reference to all the pentadic terms. Therefore, in exhibiting their generality we shall pay attention to which of the terms are an *explicit* "feature" of the scheme and assign conceptual generality only to those which take trouble to feature no one in preference to any other.

One might well ask, "why Burke?" His system is hardly common currency amongst motivational theorists, indeed he is not even recognized by himself or scientific publics as a social scientist. A legitimate answer to such a question is that it is simply the "analytic election" of the authors. Indeed, any attempt on our part to display the grounds for selecting Burke's scheme makes *those* grounds the actual framework within which conceptual adequacy is to be judged. However, we are making no absolute claims for Burke's scheme. It is a heuristic framework for us and we are clear that we have reasons for choosing it above others. Two reasons stand out: first, this meta-theory of Burke's is intended to be applicable to all and any account of action, whether by the naive or social scientific observer. It provides probably the only effort, at any rate in English, at ordering both vocabularies of motive and the theories of social scientific observers. We, of course, are concerned only with the latter in this chapter; however, the advantages of taking an evaluational framework that is more general than the case in question are not to be minimized. Second, and correlatively, this framework circumvents, as does our own typology of explanations, one of the most pressing problems of theories of motivation; that is, whose motivational account, whose explanation of action, is to be preferred — the actor's or the observer's, (in our terminology, the self observer's or the observer's of others's). For Burke, while it is possible to evaluate them in terms of their generality, all explanations of action have equal status. This is no mean achievement and sufficient grounds to justify the utility of his meta-theoretical framework for our purposes.

To this point we have defined theories of motivation as "explanations," as accounts of conduct addressed to various audiences and judged by a variety of publics. We have restricted our interest to explanations of conduct addressed to social scientific audiences and sought to establish a framework within which to present, compare, and evaluate the motivational theories of a number of psychologists and sociologists. We have also made some effort to avoid a number of the conceptual pitfalls that beset the feet of the wary and unwary alike in this area. However, we still need a few more comments on the issue of laws and rules and the relation that this distinction has to yet one more dichotomous pair, causes and reasons.

In part, the problem here is the result of varying terminological and conceptual usage; causes and laws are often treated as equivalents and rules and reasons suffer a similar fate. While we are aware that the parts of these pairs are not strict equivalents and thus common usage is not correct in making the tie-up, contrasting these two pairs is not so strange. Rather, it has its roots in Kant's effort to understand moral action, action according to reason, action following or breaking rules, in a world fashioned by categories of the mind themselves modelled on Newtonian constructs of space, time, and causality. It is not ignorance on our part, therefore, that leads us to imply (with common usage) that one can pair off laws and causes against reasons and rules, certainly there is a difference between the members of the pairs; nonetheless, we prefer to accord pride of place to the Kantian distinction that underlies the dichotomy. Of course, as readers will recognize, we do not believe that Kant's solution was successful. Indeed, Overington and Zollschan have indicated in chapter 4 the continuing vitality of the problem of doing causal science of voluntaristic action. Using this distinction, however, evidences our concern to highlight what many theorists consider to be *the* crucial distinction between explanations of conduct no matter what terms are used to symbolize it. The distinction between causal and "reason" analysis, between natural science and "cultural" science is a far more important link between these pairs of terms than is any difference in the connotations that pull them apart. We have, therefore, been deliberately cavalier in talking in one breath of laws and causes, calling those who use such an approach "social physicists," and in another breath speaking of rules and reasons, calling users of these accounts "grammarians." The difference between laws and causes and again between rules and reasons is, *for our purposes,* a difference that does not make a difference.

### Psychologistic Theories of Motive:

Attempts to subject human conduct to social physical types of lawlike explanation may be found in both of those miscellaneous bundles of intellectual traditions gathered together under the blanket terms "psychology" and "sociology." Indeed, one finds in both of these patchwork fields instances of intellectual and experimental traditions in which there is an insistence upon the applicability of strictly "causal" explanations of conduct. The common origins of the various strands of sociological and psychological thinking in self-proclaimed "social physical" speculations of various thinkers in the seventeenth century is briefly chronicled in English by Sorokin (52, pp. 4-12) leaning heavily on Spektorskiy's monumental Polish-Russian study of the subject.[8]

There can be little doubt that the emphasis on strict causation to the exclusion of attribution of reasons has met with greater success in experimental psychology than in sociology. For that reason the former takes pride of place in this account. Moreover, because of differences both in focus and in rhetoric, psychological theories will be discussed separately from sociological theories; both being considered on the same continuum ranging from emphasis on strict causation to emphasis on what might be called "effectuation."

In considering psychological theories we shall first discuss behavioristic psychology and move from it to some contemporary critiques of the notion of *stimulus* as cause. Consideration of Freud's dualistic rhetoric of motive will crown our account of "psychological" theories, broadly considered. The parallel discussion of sociological viewpoints on the causation-effectuation continuum will range from positivistic and collectivist sociologies, through Simmel's formalism and Mead's symbolic interactionism, to Weber's dualistic notion of the explanation of motive. Finally, we shall briefly consider some contemporary philosophical discussions of motive.

The basic assumptions of classical behaviorism are very simple. Causal (by which is meant non-teleological) explanation is held to be the only

---

[8] The contemporary convergence of some of these strands in the Social Exchange theory of Homans and his followers Zollschan has called *Reactive Individualism* and discussed in chapter 9. For purposes of the present discussion, focused more specifically on motive than on general types of sociological explanation, it will be helpful to return to some of the issues raised in the above-mentioned chapter.

type of explanation which is scientifically acceptable. Where behavior, be it animal or human, constitutes the *explicandum*, *stimuli* are causes and *responses* are effects. In recent years it has become fashionable to refer to causes as "independent variables" and to effects as "dependent variables." An additional assumption is that behavior (some would even claim "all" conduct) is "caused" in this fashion and thus consists of responses to stimuli. Emphases vary among classical behaviorists on whether stimuli come primarily from within the organism (in which case they are called *drives*, particularly if the stimulation in question is regularly repetitive) or from the organism's environment. Differences of opinion also occur on whether the stimulus-response (or "reflex arc") model requires the interposition of "intervening variables" and whether such intervening variables should be conceptualized as neurological.[9] The stimulus-response model has become such an article of faith for psychologists that Miller, Galanter, and Pribram were moved to write: "you might as well deny the small intestine or the medulla oblongata as doubt the reflex arc" (34, p. 22).

Associated with the notion of the reflex arc is the concept of *conditioning*. Pavlov's conditioning of dogs to salivate at the sound of a tone which had previously been regularly paired with the dispensation of food (itself a natural or "unconditioned" stimulus for canine salivation) became the paradigm for classical learning theory (see, for example, 32, p. 165). Around the term "conditioning" accumulated a plethora of other terms, the most important being "reinforcement" and "extinction." *Reinforcement* was originally seen as strengthening the bond between a stimulus and a conditioned response (6, p. 15). *Extinction*, conversely, removed such a bond — it could be attempted by the withholding of reinforcing stimuli, or by pairing with painful or "aversive" stimulation. Noam Chomsky, in criticizing notions like "stimulus," "response," and "reinforcement," suggests that they are relatively well defined with respect to restricted experiments, such as those involving bar-pressing or other highly specific manipulations. If, however, a psychologist accepts the broad definition of terms, characterizing any physical event impinging on the organism as a stimulus and any item of the organism's behavior as a response, "he must conclude that behavior has not been demonstrated to be lawful" (5, p. 30).

Skinner, whose ideas are more fully discussed in chapter 9, introduces stimuli not so much as causes of responses but as consequences of activity. Hence, they may be called "contingent stimuli." Such contingent

---

[9] When we refer to "intervening variables" in this context, we have in mind ideal models. MacCorquedale and Meehl have proposed a formal distinction between *intervening variables* and *hypothetical constructs*, restricting the first of these terms to quantities obtained by a "specified manipulation of the values of empirical variables (29, p. 103). What they call hypothetical constructs, on the other hand, refers to what we call "ideal models" below.

stimuli may be reinforcing or aversive. The reinforcement or extinction of a given activity depends upon the frequencies of reinforcing or aversive stimulation, as well as upon the absence of stimulation (negative reinforcement) — in other words, they depend upon the contingencies of reinforcement. Skinner's experimental work consists of attempts to arrange these contingencies. In this work, termed *instrumental conditioning* or *operant conditioning* to distinguish it from reflex conditioning in classical behaviorist experimentation, Skinner arrives at operational definitions of what constitute reinforcing or aversive stimuli. "Stray" stimulation is rigorously excluded by means of the use of automatic machinery.

It should be clear from the foregoing account that Skinner is a *virtuoso* in the manipulation of *Occam's razor*, a veritable Sweeney Todd of the pigeon coop. Perhaps it is precisely because of this economy of means that the locus of causality shifts, in Skinner's operations, from stimuli emanating either from inside or outside of the organism to a point of interaction between the organism's activity and the external, physical stimulus. "Emmissions" of activity, treated as random in origin but clearly emanating, as it were, "from inside," are patterned and moulded over time by external contingencies of reinforcement. Skinner's views on motivation, besides dominating contemporary psychological learning theory in North America, are second only to Freud's in the influence they enjoy among American sociologists today (see, for example 21; 28). Perhaps the reasons for this lie in the double attraction of their austere simplicity and their "neatness" for the puritan mind. Indeed, if we may invert the words of a German puritan expression of approbation, the phrase "*reinlich aber ärmlich*" fits Skinnerian psychology with great precision.

The notions of stimulus and response no longer enjoy universal adherence among academic psychologists. In their delightful little book Miller, Gallanter and Pribram opine "it is so reasonable to insert between the stimulus and the response a little wisdom" (34, p. 2). When inserted, admittedly in the somewhat restricted form of the notions of *image* and *plan,* the authors find that the outer trappings of stimulus and response can be allowed to fall away.

The notion of images rather than stimuli guiding persons' activities they derive from Boulding (2). For their purposes, such images assume the characteristics of Bartlett's "schemata" or Tolman's "cognitive maps" (34, pp. 7-9). Their problem thus becomes the description of "how actions are controlled by an organism's internal representation of its universe" (34, p. 12). It is precisely at this point, they feel, that earlier cognitive psychologies had faltered.

The solution of this problem, they believe, is to accept Norbert Wiener's proposal that feedback loops are the fundamental building blocks of the nervous system (62, pp. 131-155). They call such feedback loops "test, operate, test, exit" (TOTE) units. In their conception, incongruities between the state of the organism and the image (or "state being tested for") constitute the proximal stimuli. Activity persists until such stimulation (or incongruity) is removed (34, pp. 25-27). Plans are hierarchical organizations of such TOTE units. *Planning* is envisaged as the construction of a list of tests to perform. *Intention* refers to the "uncompleted parts of a plan whose execution has already begun" (34, p. 61). The sheer execution of plans in itself is seen by them merely as a concomitant of being alive. Images, however, determine which plans, out of the multitude potentially available, are actually executed.

Both classical and operant behaviourism provide explanations of conduct characteristic of similar lawful, or causal accounts, in that they locate motivation in situations and instrumentalities. Classical behaviourism, invented by Pavlov and Watson, makes the stimulus, an element in a situation that is either "inside" or "outside" the agent, the motive for action, such that a lawful explanation becomes the statement of the conditions under which particular stimulus-response patterns would be found. Skinner, of course, reverses this causal order so that responses, "operants" in his vocabulary of motives, become behavioural instrumentalities emitted by organisms and then reinforced by stimuli viewed as scenic rewards or punishments whose effect is to alter rates of operant emission. Thus agencies are reinforced in scenes. Nor, in fact, do Miller, Gallanter and Pribram in their cybernetic reformulation more than change the location of the instrumentality that causes conduct, so that TOTE units become agencies on neurological scenes.

We have to look at another recent critique of theories based on the notion of stimulus which has been attempted by Richard de Charms (6) to find any shift of the location of motivational "force" among theorist's concerned to address an audience of psychologists. It is not a general criticism of "learning" theories that de Charms mounts, rather it is a reconsideration of the meaning of ego involvement, as it is used by academic psychologists, that leads him to a critique of the tradition of research on achievement motivation as well as to some rather basic questioning of the psychological literature on motivation in general.

The phrase "ego involvement" has typically been used in experimental psychology with human subjects in a manner implying some sort of threat to the subject's self-esteem should failure occur in set laboratory tasks. Thus, ego-involving instructions have the effect of curtailing the subject's freedom as compared to actions resulting from the subject's free choice. De Charms mentions an experiment by Green (16) in which two different types of instructions were used: ego-involving and task-orienting instructions. *Inter alia* findings seem to indicate that task-orienting instructions, implying no threat to the subjects' self-esteem, result in better recall of interrupted tasks than do ego-involving instructions. On the basis of these findings, de Charms concludes that so-called ego-involving instructions may actually interfere with the self investment of subjects in certain tasks (6, pp. 340-343).

With these considerations in mind, as well as on the basis of a rather superficial discussion of the philosophical problems of dualism, causation, and hedonism (6, pp. 29-60), de Charms arrives at the conception of *personal causation.* "Personal causation is the initiation by an individual of behavior intended to produce a change in his environment" (6, p. 6). The person himself, in other words, can sometimes be viewed as the causal "origin" of his behavior rather than as the "pawn" of forces operating upon him (6, p. 271). Such forces are envisaged rather inclusively as anything ranging from social pressures (as, for example, psychological laboratory instructions to experimental subjects) to reflexological imperatives. Here de Charms arrives at a conception not at all dissimilar to Max Weber's distinction between rational and merely reactive behavior.[10] What is more, his discussion of self identification with a task in the "origin state" is highly reminiscent of the conception of *calling* brought into sociology by Georg Simmel and Max Weber.[11] With de Charms, it would appear, the psychology of motivation comes full circle to a realignment with a sociology that formulates motives as residing in the purposes of agents.

[10] Max Weber's distinction is not exactly the same as de Charms'. According to de Charms' depiction of the pawn and origin states, it would be quite possible for a person to act rationally in Weber's sense and yet feel himself to be a pawn (6, pp. 323–326, following Koch, 27, pp. 67–68). The crux of being in a pawn state is conceived by de Charms to be "the instrumental quality of behavior that is engaged in only for the sake of obtaining an externally mediated goal (6, p. 325). Compare this statement with the discussion of what Zollschan and Perrucci have called extraneous goals, particularly as these apply to "reluctant prostitutes" and the like (66, pp. 105–106, and 108); also the discussion of the relationship between rationality and alienation (65, pp. 158–160). The trained incapacity of experimental psychologists to grasp some very simple basic characteristics of explaining human behavior is illustrated in the following, rather touching quotation: "We must . . . school ourselves in the discipline of conceiving that certain activities, even some that demand great expenditures of energy, are sought for their own sake" (6, p. 327).

[11] Simmel introduces the notion of *vocation (Beruf)* as one of the a prioris making society "possible" (47, p. 354). Weber first considered the notion of *calling* in *The Protestant Ethic and the Spirit of Capitalism* (59). Here, he sees the notion as providing evidence for the affinity of Calvinism with capitalism and also seeks to show that the contemporary conception of a *profession* (again *Beruf*) is historically founded on religious ideas (57, pp. 554–555). De Charms repeatedly attests to the influence Michael Polanyi (38) has exerted on his thinking. It is interesting to note that Polanyi's discussion of "acceptance of calling" (38, pp. 321–324) is highly reminiscent of Weber's thoughts on the question. Of course, the idea that something like a moral commitment is necessary for a person's actions to be intelligible, not merely phenomenal, goes back to Kant's discussions of the *categorical imperative* (25, pp. 65–84) and, even earlier, to the "ought" as expressing a kind of necessity (26, pp. 469–479).

The final conclusions of de Charms are forcefully reminiscent of Dilthey's psychology! The fact that men conceive of themselves and of others as origins of causality is adduced to differentiate the study of "man as a psychological being" from the study of "anything else in the world" (6, p. 356). In dealing with man as a subject of study anthropomorphism is not something to be avoided. On the contrary, "I am probably in a better position to draw inferences about other people than I am to draw any other kind of inferences" (6, p. 277).[12] Such inferences are not gained by immediate perception but through a process of attribution.

Yet, having painfully rediscovered these hoary ideas, de Charms is still unable to jettison behavioristic metaphysics and the associated naive observationalism which prompts him tacitly to assume that things or events in the world *other* than persons are merely "stimulus objects." He goes on to claim, for example, that "the concept of motivation has no place in a strictly objective science of behavior" (6, p. 355) because there is no phenomenal reality identifiable as a motive. Since he very properly compares the concept "motive" with concepts such as "energy" in physics (6, pp. 257–258), one is left wondering whether energy, by the same token, has no place in a "strictly objective" science of mechanics.

De Charms may be capable of a felicitous discussion of the *n. ach* measure and of rediscovering human persons as sources of "effectuation," as we style it, but his contribution is not a crucial one for our purposes. Although the reading and citational traditions of psychology and sociology are different and contributions within these fields often made independently of each other, he advances (and this may be important for the development of psychology) the treatment of motives only to a proto-Weberian, pre Freudian position. With the work of Weber and Freud as classical statements about motivation *his* general achievement is necessarily a limited one. It is perhaps appropriate, therefore, to conclude this survey of psychological accounts of conduct with a brief examination of Freud's position.

### Freud: A Psychology of Effectuation:

The Freudian theory of motivation occupies a special place in this account. As is well known, psychoanalytic language uses two sets of terminology with reference to motive; a terminology of *drives* (*Triebe*,

---

[12] Dilthey receives no mention in de Charms' book. Neither does Wilhelm Wundt, whose concept of *creative synthesis (Schöpferische Synthese)* is quite similar to some of the elements of what de Charms attributes to personal causation. (On this subject see Weber, 60, pp. 49–63). One is left with the feeling that Sorokin's remarks in a chapter entitled "Amnesia and New Columbuses" (53, pp. 3–20) fits here with embarrassing aptness.

mistranslated by James Strachey and others as "instincts") and a terminology of *wishes* which were depicted by Freud as unconscious reasons or goals. Accordingly, it seems to point toward both a law-governed and a rule-following account of motivation. Psychoanalytic theory may properly be viewed as a swarm of genuinely Galilean idealizations developed, initially, for the purpose of making neurotic symptoms, dreams, and parapraxes equally intelligible as rational or conventional action. Freud himself wrote of his earlier psychoanalytic explorations: "The investigation which lay at the root of Breuer and Freud's studies have led above all . . . (to the result) that hysterical symptoms have *sense* and *meaning* (14, p. 108; our italics). To be sure, the sense and meaning lent to hysterical symptoms (and later to other types of symptoms as well as to dreams and parapraxes) was for particular publics. These publics included, in particular, the (psychoanalytic) scientific public as well as the wider public of analysands willing and able to give up their "frozen" accounts for those proposed by the analyst.

We shall not here be concerned with the linguistic propriety or impropriety of speaking of "unconscious" ends or reasons. Hughes suggests that this usage reflects Hans Vaihinger's fictionalist philosophy (22, p. 110), and Peters implies the same without mentioning Vaihinger by name (37, p. 93). Vaihinger had drawn a distinction between hypotheses and useful fictions. The former were directly testable, that is to say, they could be rejected or confirmed as somehow reflecting or doing justice to the reality they were supposed to explain. The latter were auxiliary constructs, not directly testable or necessarily congruent with reality but useful (or even necessary) for making events intelligible.[13] In unfortunate uses of the term by psychologists, which blur

[13] Vaihinger's own language is verificationist (56, pp. 86–93). We are freely translating him into a language consistent with Popper's conception of hypotheses and of testing. Such a rendition in no way detracts from Vaihinger's meaning. Popper himself (40, vol. 2, pp. 96–97 and pp. 324–325) seems to insist that statements about behavior should be hypothetical in order to qualify as scientific statements and are to be interpreted in terms of the actor's "logic of the situation." The question arises here: does Popper regard the logic of all and any actors' situations to be directly intelligible or are these themselves inferential constructs? If they are inferential constructs, they do not differ from Vaihinger's fictions. No simple or straightforward procedure seems to exist which would enable one to treat such inferred logics of the situation as hypotheses and test them. Simply subjecting them to criticism, though certainly enlightening, would not constitute a genuine test.

The last point brings me to another place where Popper concerns himself with something like fictional constructions; namely, his discussion of imaginary experiments or *idealizations*. Here he suggests the rule that idealizations made must be concessions to the opponent or at least acceptable to the opponent. In view of the chaotically numerous and divergent approaches to explaining behavior that exist today, it is difficult to see how any idealization could be proposed that would be acceptable to all possible opponents. Skinner, for example, finds all idealizations unacceptable.

Vaihinger's distinction between hypotheses and heuristic fictions, such fictions are called "hypothetical constructs." We shall call them "idealizations" or "ideal models" to distinguish them from attempted simulations or "iconic models."[14]

Psychoanalytic theory may properly be viewed as a system of such idealizations and unconscious reasons or ends as the formulation by a social scientific observer of the action of others, of the rules followed by both members and strangers, under the condition that the rule not be articulated by these actors. Freud's interests, naturally enough when one considers the fact that he saw his main task as the development of a psychiatric therapy, were mainly in organizing these unconscious patterns of rule following as personality types. Now Freud saw personality (the "psyche") as a system of motivational structures, as organized collections of rules, that were to be understood by the theorist in the light of genetic or "natural history" considerations. In the course of his long and phenomenally productive life, he changed his views on these considerations several times. Material presented here will not delve into these changes of view but leans on David Rapaport's systematic presentation (42) and follows the conclusions of Zollschan's earlier paper (64). In parts it constitutes a précis of the previous study.

The crucial distinction is between *primary process* and *secondary process* functioning. The former refers to the manner in which activity is energized. The latter refers to the manner in which activity is directed. The primary process model may be depicted as follows (42, pp. 71-73):

a) Restlessness → sucking → subsidence of restlessness (or "gratification") This model describes the *pleasure principle*.

---

[14] Essentially, ideal models are variations of two forms. The first is a simplified model in which complex interactions or effects are rendered intelligible by the imaginary isolation of factors. Galileo's "frictionless inclines" are, of course, the renowned example. Max Weber's insistence that ideal types are not hypotheses as well as his terming them "utopias" indicate that he thought of them as variations of this form of idealization. The second form corresponds to solutions of "black box" problems in engineering, where the machinery or circuitry in the box is not known and a model must be constructed to relate inputs and outputs in a systematic and predictable manner. By definition of the problem there is no way in which the box can be opened — so the solution necessarily must be viewed as a heuristic fiction. The first form of fiction meets Vaihinger's requirement that it be proposed in full realization of its impossibility (56, p. 93). The second form is meant to correspond to the actually existing state of affairs and, therefore, occupies a position between the first form and hypotheses proper for which independent evidence can be adduced.

Braithwaite, when emphasizing a distinction between the theoretical concepts of a theory and the model for this theory, makes the statement: "Thinking of scientific theories by means of models is always as-if thinking" (3, p. 93). A particularly acute problem in the social and behavioral sciences at present is that many models have been developed for often unstated theories in which the theoretical concepts themselves are extremely unclear.

b) Drive → absence of drive object → hallucination of gratifying object. This model describes *wish fulfillment*.

c) Drive → absence of drive object → discharge of affect.

Affect may be discharged in outward behavior ("alloplastically") by acts such as howling or kicking, or inwardly ("autoplastically") through somatization or the establishment of anxiety. This is Freud's model of affect. A combination of models (b) and (c) yields the complete model of primary process motivation (d) below. One notes that Freud's conception of primary process motivation necessarily includes considerations of affect.

d) Drive → absence of drive object → hallucination of gratifying object and/or affect discharge. A "drive object" may be inferred (admittedly by circular reasoning) as any object or event which may be reasonably interpreted as "gratifying" or leads to subsidence of restless activity.

Clearly, the primary process model of conduct is one of drive reduction. Gratification is seen as an affective and behavioral equivalent of inertia in physics. Drives are excitations originating, so to speak, from within. Freud describes these as "continuing pressures" and distinguishes them from external excitations which he thought produced only momentary impact (13, pp. 508-509). To ward off external excitations there develops a *stimulus shield* that serves to reduce their impact. When excitations in the environment breach the stimulus shield Freud speaks of *trauma*. The mastery of traumata is attempted by repetition of motor activity or imagery analogous to that consequent upon the experience of a drive.

When drive tensions mount and the drive object is absent and if, in addition, primary process discharge is insufficient by itself to lead to quiescence, there develop control and defense structures. These structures raise the drive-discharge threshold: they develop into "an experiential connexion system of progressively more differentiated and discrete ideas" (41, p. 696). Delays themselves, as it were, give rise to psychic structures as well as to the peculiar characteristics of these structures in particular individuals. With the development of these structures there arises secondary process behavior and cognition.

The secondary process model differs from the primary process model in several respects. Drive discharge by the shortest path is replaced by detour activities in which satisfaction is searched for and reached in roundabout ways. Rapaport's shift in terminology from "gratification" to "satisfaction" in the secondary process model, is meant to indicate that complete tension discharge is replaced by discharge compatible with the maintenance of tension — tension which is inevitable because of the existence of structure. Primeval drive objects give way to objects and objectives which are invested or charged with affect or, in Freud's term "cathected." The general implications of using the term cathexis is that primary process activity refers to energy discharge (activation of bodily movements, certain kinds of bodily dysfunction, and imagery) while secondary process functioning directs energy to particular objects or goals. There is no assumption that a person's system of congeries of cathected goals or objects is such as to optimise net satisfaction or, in other words, is "fulfilling." Satisfaction or fulfillment, if they are to occur, must in some way "match" the actual gratificatory potential of the goal or object chosen for cathexis (always consistent with the maintenance of structural tension). Mismatches are possible. Indeed, such mismatches constitute the major ground for psychoanalytic therapy.[15]

The general picture of motivation left by the Freud-Rapaport account is a highly complex one. The major psychic structures in this system of descriptive idealizations correspond roughly with separate sources of motive. Libidinal excitations emanate from the *Id*, as do derivatives of repressed wishes (themselves viewed as largely libidinal in origin). The *ego* is seen as the *organon* of secondary process, and also as the source of drives conducive to individual self preservation (for example, "hunger").[16] The *super-ego* is the source of self punishment or guilt. Finally, Freud introduced the virtually unmodifyable, darkly despotic, compulsion to repeat as a distinct primeval *death drive* (11, pp. 36-38). The so-called *mechanisms* whereby drives undergo a variety of specified transformations were adduced to account for the multiplex diversity of human behavior and imagery with which Freud concerned himself. However, the death drive (repetition compulsion) had first been conceptualized as a mechanism for the mastery of traumata, and the superego is the precipitate of another mechanism — *introjection* (12, p. 48).

As a theorist of motivation Freud's greatness is given in his recognition that, although motivation has its primordial roots in drives, these play their part in the lives of persons past early childhood, under a variety of symbolic translations that serve to hide their origins from the self observer. The grammar which actors follow in order to pay homage to the syntactic authorities of their pasts is hidden from them. These primitive psychic energies — these hidden instrumentalities — work their effects in subtle transformations. The grammars of individual actors are *causes* to all but the trained therapist, the psychoanalytic observer of

---

[15] These remarks on cathexis follow the interpretation proposed by Rubinstein (43, p. 47). Rubinstein himself develops an abstract deductive system of hypotheses designed to fit the psychoanalytic theory of motivation. He comes to the conclusion that such a system can be subjected to non-existential interpretation in its theoretical terms. In this way expressions like "energy," "structure," or "cathexis" can be understood as merely descriptive linguistic renditions of such formal theoretical terms, designed to provide them with existential meaning but inadequate for lending them scientific status as genuine explanations (43, pp. 62–63).

[16] Freud did not consider the so-called *ego drives* to have much importance in occasioning the kinds of behavior and imagery problematic from his perspective (that is, symptoms, parapraxes, and dreams).

others. The rigidity of conduct characterizing diagnostically specified types of personalities remains in effect as long as the diagnosed patient is unable to articulate the (unconscious) rule that he or she slavishly follows. The therapist's specification of the conditions of the invariance or statement of the "rule" is intended to transform the invariance (for the actor) from cause to reason.

When successful, the process of "working through" in psychoanalytic therapy consists precisely of the transformation, the release, of such invariances of "fixed" conditions into free choices of the actor. Thus — to supersede the tired terminology of "causes" and "reasons" — therapy becomes, as it were, the place in which motivation is shifted from scenes and agencies to agents and purposes. In our interpretation, Freud makes his entrance as a grammar master of mankind — as the empirical grammarian who, by discovering hidden and forbidden syntaxes "determining" conduct, makes such syntaxes available for guiding free stylistic choice.

### Sociological Social Physics:

Unlike behaviouristic psychology, the various traditions which together can properly be characterized as sociological social physics have remained at the stage of largely programatic formulation. That is not to say there has been no empirical research which can be fitted under this rubric; merely that such research fails to reveal even the fitful continuity or lumpy cumulation of behaviouristic "findings" — particularly findings in areas concerned with the "conduct" of Rattus norvegicus "sapiens."[17]

The first thinker who fully deserves to be discussed under this heading is, of course, Comte. Kantian dualism serves as a useful backdrop for Comte's position though, quite clearly, a jumble of other influences quite distinct from Kant's also operated on the formation of Comte's ideas. Comte admired Kant's "celebre conception de la double réalité, a la fois objective et subjective" (20, pp. 335, 585-586) but refused to accept dualism as suitable for his purposes. Mental and social facts, like any other facts, were to be regarded as phenomena. What is more, Comte's positivistic metaphysics required such phenomena to correspond with perfect exactness to objective reality. The whole thrust of Comte's argument, however, ignores issues of individual conduct and refers instead to collective states of mentation and to social structures corre-

---

[17] In a recent survey of the critical literature, Annette Ehrlich (10) draws attention to the "American obsession with rats" (10, p. 25) in animal studies by psychologists, noting at the same time that the general principles of "learning theories" have been developed from these studies. Moreover, the rat used for experimental work, has through "50 years of selective breeding in the laboratory . . . [become] an organism that is not even typical any longer of the Norway rat." (10, p. 27). Psychologists have bred a sub-species of Rattus norvegicus that functions so well in the environment where it learns and earns that it might well justify the honorific "sapiens."

sponding to these states, both taking determinate patterns of transformation over time.

The Comtean rhetoric refers to a collective agent unerringly (though not necessarily consciously) directed toward the purpose of possessing "positive" knowledge, and avoids the issue of a human psychology, omitting this from his hierarchy of sciences. However, if all this seems strange to contemporary eyes it must be more the result of terminology than content. If we were to translate Comte's language into a more recognizable set of terms, we find that he is proposing systematic attitude change in social aggregates. What separates his work from someone like Arthur Stinchcombe (54) is that the three stages of societal development trace, in effect, the changes in the location of human reasons for action. Stinchcombe, of course, has neither a theory of development nor any particular account of motives separate from the rather simple "causal force" model that attaches to the techniques of aggregate analysis. Comte, on the other hand, makes an effort to understand how the world becomes intelligible for persons. Which is to say that one may formulate the three stages of development as changes in the scenic location of accounts of action. The world is made intelligible, becomes a place within which to act (to act meaningfully), through the attribution of explanations for action to a variety of scenes, to Gods, to Forces, and to "Facts." Although persons individually or in aggregate will account for actions by reference to these three scenes, the final victory of "Facts" will lead to Positivism, the religion of humanity. The ultimate account of action, then, will be located in "Facts" under the interpretive authority of a scientific priesthood. In view of the fact that Comte's own work was not based on anything resembling observation — despite his claim that positive knowledge was supposed to rest upon direct observation — it is easy to see how the charge of "science-faking" can be laid at his door (18).

In point of fact, it is not until the publication of Durkheim's *Regles de la Methode* (8) that positivism receives a systematic methodological statement. Durkheim sees the problem of establishing sociology as a scientific discipline as tantamount to the problem of demonstrating the existence of *social facts;* facts as "substantial" in their own way as he supposed material objects (*"choses"* — "things") to be in their way! Durkheim's tour de force is to postulate that the entity or substantiality, in short — the "facticity" of social facts, as much as of material objects, depends upon their being external to individuals and constraining upon them (8, p. 13).

On close examination, Durkheim's social facts turn out to be cultural norms which ("obviously," he would say) emanate from outside any specifiable given individual yet are coercive on the conduct of many if not all individuals. The rules or norms which Durkheim presents as coercive are, in reality, only *governing rules* under the special conditions where persons allegedly governed by them are viewed in the aggregate.

Translated into terms we have previously proposed, Durkheim sees individual behaviour as "typically rule-following" rather than as "generally rule-governed." The deviation of individual conduct from interpersonal (or better, "extra-personal") norms Durkheim treats as randomly variable. He views such deviance not merely as "normal" (using the term in this instance in something like a statistical sense) but as positively necessary; for how could norms be maintained unless attention were drawn to them sporadically by their infraction?

Durkheim's notion of individual conduct occurs not in relation to deviance under circumstances in which norms are firmly established. Instead, individual conduct as a subject for reflection or analysis crops up in connection with the concept of *anomie* — the deregulation of normative patterns in society. In this context, Durkheim's outright suspicion of individual motives comes clearly to the surface. Unless human appetites are limited by norms, in his view, they become insatiable ". . . the more one has, the more one wants . . ." is the hallmark of any anomic goal (9, p. 248).

His discussion of marriage may serve as a case in point (though economic activity could be used just as well to exemplify his position). Thus, in his terms, it is a married person's ". . . duty to find happiness in his lot . . ." The unmarried person, on the other hand, has a ". . . morbid desire for the infinite . . ." and Durkheim implies that this is apt to lead to the unsatisfiable quest of Don Juan. But even if this does not occur ". . . new hopes constantly awake only to be deceived, leaving a trail of weariness and disillusionment behind them" (9, pp. 270-271).

Leaving aside whatever light these quotations may throw upon Durkheim's Victorian bourgeois philistinism, one may ask whether such comments could not equally well describe an unsuccessful marriage, or, conversely, whether they are really of general applicability to all persons who are not married (even after, unlike Durkheim, one takes the precaution of limiting the age-range under discussion in some suitably relevant manner). One may well conclude that, for Durkheim, sexual goals are intrinsically unachievable and doomed to frustration except when bridled (and saddled) by the protective, normatively regulated, ennui of married life. For that matter, by simple extension of the argument, any goal-seeking activity by an individual seems to be doomed to frustration in the same way. Individuals' goals can be achieved only if they are, so to speak, imbedded in norms.[18] Nevertheless, the notion of individual conduct either conforming to norms or deviating from such norms lies at the center of organicist views of society. The functionalist

18 Merton separates two elements in Durkheim's undifferentiated expression "norms" — "institutionalized means" and "cultural goals." He uses this strategy for an attempted explanation of individual deviance as one of a specifiable number of types of dissociation between means and what one might call their "normatively attached" goals. Individual motivation in his analysis becomes reduced, in first ap-

and structural-functionalist inheritors of this viewpoint have occasionally felt compelled by their subject matter to add individual goals; but such goals are interpreted by them as stemming from social structures rather than from the individuals to whom the goals are attributed.

When it comes to the pentadic location of motives, Durkheim's concern with aggregates provides for an interesting accounting scheme with respect to individual conduct. The rules which govern conduct in the aggregate are instrumentalities lodged in the universal scene provided by the *conscience collective* and individual conduct is theoretically sensible, for Durkheim, insofar as it follows these rules, or deviates in a statistically random fashion from them. Thus, individual action becomes a source of random error that decreases in theoretical interest as the specification of the collective norms increases in accuracy and the aggregate unit of analysis increases in size. However, in providing this accounting scheme Durkheim is able to entertain the possibility of statistical laws of aggregate conduct without losing the conception of rule-following action at the individual level. The price that he, and later his sociologist heirs, have to pay for this solution to Kantian dualism is the exclusion of individual action from the realm of sociological concerns, conceived as it is as mere random error. In modern terms, the explanation of action becomes the error term in a multiple regression equation![19]

---

proximation, to a binary logic of acceptance or rejection of means or goals or both.

That Merton cannot stick with his initial strategy and has to resort to an element foreign to the initial simplicity of his binary logic by introducing an "acceptance and replacement" term is, of course, a weakness that fatally undermines his pseudo-deterministic intentions in the earlier argument. It is hardly necessary to add that "means" and "goals" are such only in relation to tightly specified situations and that the distinction of these terms is highly questionable in itself. But, in this second respect, Max Weber is just as guilty as Merton.

[19] Readers will surely notice that here and elsewhere we have given scant attention to contemporary sociological theories. There are two major reasons for this. Firstly, the range of motivational theories is meant to be exemplified, not exhausted by our discussion. Secondly, and more importantly, there is precious little that contemporary theories contribute, in terms of our concerns here, which is different from the work of the earlier theorists that we *are* treating.

It is no longer original to comment on the dominance of research based on more or less randomly sampled aggregates; even a cursory examination of research trends in North America makes this clear. In the analyses which are so based these collections of individual characteristics and attitudes are combined and recombined by means of a variety of bivariate and multivariate techniques. The statistical aggregates so constructed are then treated as the attributes and attitudes of individual members of quasi-groups through which causal forces stream in Durkheimian fashion to produce mean differences amongst these "groups." Those concerned for the later appearance of those mysterious currents that, pulsing through whole populations, produced increases in the suicide rate should take heart. They may now find these same currents, or some very close hydrological or meteorological counterpart, coursing through path models leaving the sophisticated theorist to analyze the error terms and their relationships, where individuals still produce their perturbations. There is nothing here to bring variety to our discussion.

The Marxian variant of sociological social physics partially accepts the notion of conduct as rule-following. With acutely penetrating insight, however, it assigns the designation of "false consciousness" to the rules in question. Rules are viewed as the deliberate or unintended product of the "means of intellectual production," means which Marx considers as being exclusively owned by the dominant class, at least, at the beginning of any new historical period. The notion of rules as a manufacture is, of course, a great advance over the inert notion of rules as quasi-naturalistic "givens" which initially confront all individuals as alien and gain upon these individuals a coercive grip of iron.

The manufacture of rules in the interest of the dominant class and for the effective ("legitimate") subjugation of the subordinate class is only a by-product of the operation of the Marxian concept-mill, however. The true motives, in Marx's view, are "class interests." The dawn of consciousness in new classes consists of members becoming aware of these interests and beginning to organize so as to become able to act upon them. In a simplified schematic form of the theory, each class may be depicted as a collective agent equipped by the conditions of production with a pre-fabricated purpose. The historical stage itself (together with the system of production which it embodies and exemplifies) is the scene. The ruling class at any stage may be viewed as a sort of collective agent dominating the scene. The awakening of class consciousness in new classes — and particularly in the working class — adds additional collectives to take their places on the "historical stage."[20]

Yet, unlike Durkheim, Marx does not relegate the action of individual members to a statistical error term. Classes may be viewed as collective actors precisely because they are *not* statistical aggregates, however inconvenient this may be for survey researchers. Classes are composed of "real, living" persons and "History (of classes and social relations in general) is *nothing* but the activity of men in pursuit of their ends" (31, p. 63). Insofar as history is the production of human persons in their social relations, the regularities which characterize these relationships are invariant under specifiable historical and class conditions. It is only in the context of historically rooted class interests that both individual and collective action makes sense to Marx. Motives for action, then, are interest based purposes which historical social situations present to individuals as parts of collectivities. Marx, here, bridges the gap between causes and reasons since these concrete historical social situations are themselves the creation of the productive activity of individuals, and the individual's capacity to enact the purpose is given in the conditions under which "class consciousness" and political organization in support of class — that is "objective" — interests develop. These conditions though specifiable (see 30) are not determinate.

[20] Grammarians, linguistic philosophers, and other syntactic compulsives are invited to try and deal with the above sentence "grammatically!"

Pareto's programmatic leanings to a variant of social physics are, perhaps, even more clearly enunciated than are Durkheim's. In the *Trattato* (36) a massively long introductory section is devoted to exposition of the "logico-experimental method" Pareto prescribed for sociological use. Though apparently he was too busy to follow his own methodological fiat in more than a merely perfunctory way, his ambition to construct sociology along lines of a mathematically determinate equilibrium system was proclaimed quite uninhibitedly. A brief exposition of this Italianate social physics may be found in chapter 9.

Yet, oddly enough, despite these physicalist protestations Pareto displays greater sensitivity to the issues raised by us in this chapter than any other sociologist of his period or prior to it with the possible exception of Max Weber. In effect, with his distinction between residues, derivations and sentiments he is proposing a distinction between conduct, linguistic expressions (what we would call "stated reasons") and states of mind (perhaps best rendered as "motivational sets" in the present context) (36, p. 267). Conduct and stated reasons are observables; motivational sets are idealizations. Linguistic expressions as adequate theories are, in themselves, sufficient causes of what Pareto calls "logical" action. Hypothesized motivation must be summoned from the deep, however, to provide causal explanations for "non-logical" conduct; conduct which Pareto designates as the proper subject matter for sociological investigation. Here, three possible causal sequences are proposed: 1) the motive causes both the conduct and the reasons stated for it, though the latter two are actually unrelated; 2) the motive gives rise to particular conduct and both of the aforementioned combine to produce the reason;[21] 3) the motive gives rise to a particular reason which produces the conduct.[22] Pareto's applications of these interesting, highly "modern," distinctions may be disappointing; their almost prophetic character in relation to contemporary discussions of conduct, reasons, and motives is undeniable.

There is yet another way in which Pareto anticipates contemporary concerns regarding attributions of motive. Action, to be logical, requires an identity of objective end and subjective purpose (36, p. 151). It is not difficult to see that "subjective purposes" must refer to outcomes intended by the behaving person. Objective ends, on the other hand, are outcomes attained by adequate and appropriate means as seen from the point of view of "other persons who have more extensive knowledge." The question of who has better knowledge with respect to the appropriateness and adequacy of any given item of conduct (and even the associated question of what the end is supposed to be toward which

[21] This could describe Marx's "reflection," Freud's (or, more properly, Ernest Jones's) "rationalization," or Schutz's "because of" motive (44, Vol. I, pp. 69–72).

[22] This describes what Max Weber has in mind by an "end" or Schutz by an "in order to" motive.

many types of actions are directed) obviously, is one that can give rise
to inconclusive debate. Pareto would have been better advised for his
particular purpose to postulate a hypothetical "all-knowing observer"
as did Leibnitz (or, perhaps, better still, a hypothetical "all-perceiving
observer" as did Berkeley). The general distinction between "actor" and
"observer" which Pareto introduces into sociology, however, opens up
the entire prismatic spectrum of accounts that may be given by different
observers and classes of observers (including self-observers) for a particular item of conduct.

While it would do him an injustice not to recognize the startlingly contemporary methodology that he proposes, the collapse of his system into
the *residues,* and the confusion in his use of residues and *sentiments,*
gives his system no similarly privileged position with respect to the
Pentad. Thus, motivation, as he *uses* it, refers to "sentimental residues"
or perhaps to "residual sentiments," and the relative individual balances
amongst them that serve as scenic impellers for conduct.

### The Sociology of Effectuation:

The sociologists to be discussed under the present heading divorce
their ideas entirely from crudely deterministic notions of social "causation." Three theorists serve to exemplify attempts to replace sociological
social physics with conceptions which give individual motives greater
free play. Each, in his own way, demonstrates the formidable theoretical
difficulties which must be surmounted in establishing effectuation by
motivated conduct as a workable principle of explanation in sociology.
Each also provides some different clues as to how the problem can be
tackled. The thinkers to be discussed are Simmel, Mead, and Max Weber.

Simmel's emphasis varies according to whether he is addressing his
audience in the capacity of psychological or sociological formalist. Psychological formalism is his earlier theoretical position. This may be
understood as Simmel's attempt to cope with problems raised by Kantian
dualism and, particularly, Kant's notion of direct access to the "intelligible self" seen as noumenal. Put in the simplest way, Simmel's position
is that we have no direct access to the behaviour of other individuals
as noumena and more particularly, we have no direct access to historical
actors. This psychological formalism receives its clearest statement in his
little volume on historical method (50), where Simmel suggests, that
there is a separate range of categories or "forms" which we impress upon
the behaviour of historical actors in order to construct their action as
intelligible.

Simmel felt that much as we impress upon nature the categories of
thought, so we bring to bear on human conduct psychological organizing propositions. These were to be regarded as ". . . the a priori of

historical science" (50, p. 33).[23] If psychology were a science with general laws, he maintained, history would be applied psychology much as "astronomy" (by which he must have meant "solar system mechanics") is applied mathematics. A plausible interpretation of what he was trying to get at with the implication that psychology was not a science with general laws would be that psychological categories lacked any effective equivalent of the Kantian category of *causation*. Thus Simmel, as psychological formalist, seems to be proposing something very much akin to a grammar of motives; although he would prefer to call it a "geometry" of motive.

His later views on motive (49) tend to contradict the earlier unitary conception and replace it with a dualistic one in which motive, causally regarded, is initially devoid of purpose but leads to grammatical self-assignment of purposes. The argument goes as follows: "After ends have created the thought of means, means create the idea of an end" (49, p. 207). Obviously, unless one is to indulge in paradoxical word-games along with Simmel, it becomes necessary to distinguish between two ways in which the expression "end" is used by him in the above passage, respectively, as raw volitions and as desired states or goals. The raw ends that create the thought of means are manifestations of the category of volition. Evidently, Simmel intends this to be the nearest possible formal psychological equivalent of the Kantian category of causation. But Simmel goes on to say that the will itself, being nothing more than a psychological category, is without conscious content. Consciousness by itself, on the other hand, cannot lead to the setting of purposes (49, p. 481). Thus, while Kantian *causation* necessarily has attached effects in relation to particular phenomena, Simmelian volition is inherently free-floating. It is the confluence of blind will with the (initially quite aimless) consciousness of means which lead to the creation of purposes. Once means have been found (or established) they give rise to conscious images of "ends" in the second sense in which Simmel used the term. The means, as it were, specify an end or point to it.

The employment of means to ends, according to Simmel, is distinctive of what he calls "intellect." Tools are a tangible expression of means. Money is a generalized means free from specific "content" (meaning, in this context, free from highly circumscribed "occasions for use") (49, p. 206). With money, therefore, the means emerges as a "category" in its own right and the contents of experience come to be organized in an interlocking teleological system (49, p. 482). This argument seems to mark the point of transition to Simmel's sociological formalism in which purposes are demoted to mere "content" and means or agencies take over

[23] There is nothing novel in these psychological categories. They correspond to the long established typology of *cognition, conation* and *affect*. He refers to these as "knowing," "desiring," and "feeling." In a later work (49, p. 481) he added to these the categories of "being," "oughting," and "hoping."

as forms. The sociological as distinct from psychological formalism which Zollschan briefly discusses in chapter 9 thus becomes a sort of grammar or geometry of social structures from which considerations of purpose are intentionally excluded. Certainly, strictly viewed from the point of view of a grammar of motive, these later social forms must be regarded as scenic. Purposes are merely contingent "scenery."[24]

Simmel exercised an enormous influence on all founding members of the Chicago School. This contention is relatively easy to demonstrate with respect to Robert Park and his students. Park is known to have studied under Windelband and is suspected to have attended some of Simmel's own lectures. Certainly, isolated sparks from Simmel's anvil are fanned in Chicago into flaming branches of Sociology. *Die Grosstadt und das Geistesleben* (48) is transformed into the field of urban sociology; the *Exkurs uber den Fremden* (51) becomes transmuted into the basis for a sociology of social marginality and of cultural assimilation.

Simmel's direct influence on Mead is more difficult to establish. Certainly, both Simmel and Mead received a common influence from Wilhelm Wundt (who, incidentally, also exerted a direct influence on Karl Bühler and Ernst Cassirer). Wundt introduced the term *gesture* as one of the pivotal concepts of his notion of psycho-physical parallelism. The importance of this notion for both Mead and Bühler hardly requires adumbration. Where Mead's symbolic interactionism seems to differ from other variants and developments of Wundt's idea (i.e. of transformation of the "physical" gesture into the "psychological" symbol) is in that it makes symbolic interaction the substrate both of individual personalities and of the society in which they are formed and which they form.

If we now make a pentadic articulation of Mead's theory of motives, if we specify the term which is featured in his accounting scheme, we find that as with the other pragmatists (see 4, p. 275-287) Mead may be seen as concerned with Agency. However, unlike Burke, who locates

---

[24] Max Weber himself latches on to Simmel's work in a number of places. He has praise for a distinction made by Simmel, and overlooked in Dilthey's work, between the objective understanding of the sense of a statement or action and the subjective interpretation of the motive of the speaking or acting persons (49, p. 15; 60, p. 93). Yet, later Weber sees himself as departing from Simmel's method in "drawing a sharp distinction between subjectively intended and objectively valid 'meanings'; two different things which Simmel not only fails to distinguish but often deliberately treats as belonging together." (61, p. 88, or 58, Vol. I, p. 4).

Instead of accepting Simmel's motivational formulation of means to which reference has been made above, Weber prefers to follow the ideas of another Diltheyan — Friedrich Gottl. Tenbruck interprets Gottl's argument as suggesting that economic action was not ruled by economic laws, but sprang from intelligible choices and decisions of people; choices and decisions based exclusively on their "logic of the situation" — "*reine Sachlogic der Situation*"; 55, p. 606). Persons engaged in economic activity, in other words, were following rules which were situationally or "scenically" specific.

Mead's conception of agency in "biologic functioning," we prefer to express agency in Mead as the central process of the conscious act. Thus, reflective consciousness, for Mead *the* problematic of social psychology, is conceived as that agency through which blocked Impulses are transformed, by "Perception" and "Manipulation," into action which reaches its "Consummation" in unblocking conduct, thus permitting the person to resume their behavioural or reflective pursuits (33, pp. 3-23). It must be recognized, too, that Mead's formulation of the Act and its four stages is the central analytic concept in his thought. Thus, the formulation of agency as its process places that Pentadic term in the very centre of Mead's framework. In the Act, consciousness operates to organize the individual's attention in such a way as to produce from the impulse an image of the blockage about which action hypotheses are constructed for testing against that block. Put more fully these hypotheses concern *what instrumentality* solves the problem which has created the moment of consciousness. Rather than Mind, Self, and Society it might better be Mind, Self in Agency.

Weber's definition of "motive" *(Motiv)* in *Wirtschaft und Gesellschaft* places his work at the center of the contemporary debate on "reasons" and "causes." The definition introduces his distinction between sociological interpretation and the kind of understanding adequate for ordinary social participation. Weber's initial characterization of "motive" — if we may be permitted to move away from the stilted, "authorized" translations — is an account of a particular item of conduct which appears to the behaving person himself or to some observer as an "adequate" (or, better, "plausible") reason for the behaviour in question. Weber expands the foregoing statement by adding that reasons are plausible to the extent that the relationship of such reasons to the conduct accounted for by them, affirms typical thought processes or conventionally recognized emotions.[25]

The above statement refers to naive understandings which are the "stuff" of social intercourse in Weber's view. Weber goes on to state that a correct sociological inference *also* involves an account for action but, in addition, requires that the reason given in such an account corresponds, in effect, to the "real motive." It corresponds, in other words, to the motive as "cause" of the action. Weber insists, at least, that the sociologists' formulation of the motive should provide an explanation "objectively likely" in the light of comparative experience. It is difficult to tell from examination of Weber's scattered writings on the subject

---

[25] The following may be compared with the translations offered in 58, Vol. 1, pp. 11–12 or 61, pp. 98–100. Though our translation, admittedly, is very much freer than either Henderson and Parsons's or even Rheinstein's, it does have the modest advantage of making sense! To the extent it does that, we have followed Weber's instructions for "adequate" motivational attribution by rendering a plausible account in English of his own intentions.

exactly how a social scientist is supposed to substantiate the "objective likelihood" that a given motive is the cause of a given act. He makes explicit reference to the social scientist's allegedly more inclusive comparative knowledge of more or less analogous action sequences. Though he nowhere says so in as many words, it is quite clear that he also wishes to point to the scientist's *critical attitude* toward a motive — the explicit treatment of the motive as a scholarly conjecture — as distinct from the possibly uncritical acceptance a conventional reason might gain in ordinary social life. While social participation involves acceptance of naive reasons, social analysis requires such reasons to be subjected to questions.

Plainly, Weber had two entirely distinct meanings of the expression "motive" in mind . . . The first referred to any naive reason for conduct found acceptable in a given "speech community."[26] Such reasons might, indeed, correspond to, or otherwise indicate, genuine causes of action, but need not do so. They were to be seen as acceptable accounts only, not as strict explanations. The second meaning of "motive," on the other hand, refers to it as an explanation of the objectively likely cause of the item of conduct or complex of action to be explained. Since, in Weber's view, sociological explanation could not aspire to statements of "strict" causation properly speaking, statements of objective likelihood would make do in their place.

It is embarrassingly obvious that the crucial methodological requirement which would provide a firm demarcation between these two different meanings of "motive" is missing. Weber suggests no clear-cut procedure for subjecting what he calls "causally adequate" accounts to a genuine test, so as to distinguish them from merely "meaningful" attributions of reasons. Indeed, ideal types, which are Weber's principal instrument for the presentation of relationships of determinacy in conduct, are deliberately made impervious to testing.

While Weber was constantly tottering on the brink of taking a first step in the direction of establishing sociology as a field of scientific knowledge in his methodological disquisitions, he consistently became mired down in ostensive historical "facts." Systematic selection and distortion of such facts (which, in essence constitutes the core of ideal-type construction) is, to be sure, preferable to unsystematic and unwitting simplifications, selections, and distortions which litter historical work. It is no substitute for any serious attempt to develop general parameters not tied to any particular time or place. Weber played Galilean games but lacked Galilean gall.

Perhaps Weber's failure to provide a clear demarcation between these two meanings to motive lies at the root of C. Wright Mills's conception of "vocabularies of motive" (35) in which the latter develops Weber's

[26] Speech community is Scott & Lyman's (46) expression for a collectivity sharing very similar (or perhaps identical) criteria for — in their own language — "honouring" accounts.

first definition and totally ignores the second. Mills's original statement (influenced, to be fair about it, as much by Mead and by Kenneth Burke as by his partial reading of Weber) views motives, naive reasons for conduct, as the "naming of consequences" (35, p. 396). To the extent that such "naming" is meant to correspond to the formulation of a goal by an individual (as distinct from individuals being directly "activated" by temporarily prior mental states) such a view of motive simply stresses that explanations of conduct referring to teleological causations by ends require the self observer to specify such ends. But this is not the main point Mills wants to make. The crux of his argument is that ends or goals are named by specific reference to some conventional vocabulary of motives. In social situations vocabularies of motive become agencies of social control. Vocabularies of motive, glossaries of goal statements typical for different social situations are, in his words, "significant determinants of conduct" (35, p. 398).[27]

In a later development of this argument (15, p. 112-129) the notion of vocabularies of motive is expanded to include unverbalized, perhaps even unverbalizable, terms. This startling idea of "vocabularies without words" reflects the influence of Freud, whose ideas are allowed belated ingress into the theory, albeit in "doctored" form.[28] What requires stress as being particularly important in this notion of vocabularies of motive, however, is that it ignores motives as determinants of action emanating from the individual actors themselves and places the source of their "influence" (not "determination," please note) firmly inside typical social situations for which the vocabularies serve as agencies of control. Motive becomes a characteristic of social situations rather than of the individuals who enact them. Even more important, the vocabularies which make the naming of motives possible — and therefore themselves constitute the motives — are viewed as situationally specific perhaps even to the extent of being untranslatable from one situation to the next. One may note that Mills terminates his earlier contribution on this subject with the following "oracular" statement: "To simplify vocabularies of motive into a socially abstracted terminology is to destroy the legitimate use of motive in the explanation of social action" (35, p. 404).

[27] One supposes that the "significant determinants" to which reference is made are something less than just plain determinants. Mills — himself a glorious deviant from typical "situated actions" — must surely have recognized that "social controls" failed to bring, at any rate, all of their victims into line in any genuinely deterministic sense. Or could the young Mills have mistaken correlation for causation and thus introduced the word "significant" to refer to relations of variables not even presumptively deterministic? The foregoing rhetorical question has to be answered affirmatively. Probably all that Mills wanted to say was that vocabularies typical of specified social situations contributed significantly to the activation of typical conduct in these situations in a statistical sense of the word.

[28] We can only hope that "doctored" is a suitably "typical" word for this situation. The wordlessness of this vocabulary dumbly ostentates the Unconscious.

Our previous reading of Weber has indicated that he would have rejected the conception of situationally specific vocabularies of motive with indignation. For one thing, such a conception denies Weber's chosen position of methodological individualism in favour of something, in effect, very much like Schäffle's organicism (functionalism) which he explicitly rejects a couple of pages after his introduction of the definitions of motive. For another, as has already been pointed out, such a conception stresses one of Weber's two meanings to the exclusion of the other, while Mills displays the effrontery of referring to his own preferred half-definition by citing the original German! (35, p. 396). To be sure, the postulation of feedback effects from the imputation of conventional reasons to the actual determination of action were noteworthy. Weber himself had made masterly use of quite similar feedback notions in a number of his studies, notably in a little piece describing modern capitalist activity as an unanticipated consequence of the imputation of "motives" to the Almighty himself! (59)[29]

Yet, despite the authenticity of these objections, an embarrassing residual fact stares one unblinkingly in the face. Ideal types, like Mills's situationally particularistic vocabularies of motive, quite deliberately avoided the kinds of universal terms which Mills called "socially abstracted." Of course, while Mills himself proposed vocabularies of motive as actually existing states of linguistic conduct in "real" social situations, Weber's ideal types did not profess to be more than heuristic models of historical events, social structures, or socio-cultural transformations. However, Weber's deliberate methodological decision to construct ideal types *ad hoc*, as it were, attests to his extreme hesitancy, nay refusal, to obliterate the special characteristics of such modelled events, structures, or change processes. Like Mills, though less consciously so, Weber held a conception of the effectuation of action not as "causal" in any mechanical sense but as what we would now call "grammatical." In every one of Weber's ideal types is impacted a unique rhetoric of motives, explicitly concocted for the explanatory task on hand. Indeed, the very choice of the rather unfortunate expression "objective likelihood" to be the criterion for "causally adequate" explanations, suggests very clearly that Weber was groping for a grammatical as distinct from deterministic conception of motive.

The construction of a distinct rhetoric of motives for every ideal type meant that each of Weber's "occasions for social explanation" had to be equipped with special goals, means, maxims, even vocabularies, suitable for the greatest possible illumination of the stage set. Emphasis could be varied at liberty, from ideal type to ideal type, on scene, agency, agent, or purpose as primary or "representative" element. Actions, in

---

[29] In view of the ideology of predetermination in which these imputations were contained, perhaps it would be more accurate to describe what was imputed as "immotives" in this particular case.

every case, had to be viewed as the *explicandum* so as to conform with Weber's definition of the subject matter of *Verstehende Soziologie*. These actions were not blindly coerced by the operation of invariant universal laws but, as it were, "clear-sightedly" formulated in their causal relations by the design of the theoretical scenery. The very distortion of this scenery was designed to squeeze the optimum of explanatory juice out of the "show."

Before our readers all skip off like bare-arsed Bacchae, drunk by all this heady "explanatory juice," it will be salutary to consider, for a sober moment, the trouble into which Weber got himself by omitting a statement of the universal grammar for construction of the special rhetorics which bedecked each stage. Little wonder that Weber's epigoni have found themselves baffled by the mere effort of interpretation of any consistent principles Weber might have applied, let alone in the application of such principles for the construction of new stage sets. One almost feels that, since the purposes of modelled individual actors were so often overshadowed or even swamped by the "rational" requirements of agencies available for their employ, Weber intended at least to arrogate to himself a kind of Nietzschean untrammelled freedom in the act of ideal type construction. This would be freedom from universal grammatical rules which, even if self-constructed, would be binding. The absence of an explicit account of a universal grammar providing for the specific selectivity of goals, means, maxims, vocabularies, and so forth which bedeck any given ideal type makes it necessary, for those who wish to follow Weber's initiatives in sociological theory to reconstruct Weber's *enactment* of such a universal grammar in the array of ideal types he presented to his public.

### Philosophical Grammarians of Motive:

So we come to the other end of our continuum, to those who insist on a grammatical, or rule-following, account of action, who formulate motives, therefore, as instrumentalities which effectuate the purposes of agents. If we are rather brief with our exemplars here it is not merely because we are mildly out of sympathy with their position, but also because it is a position that is easy to delineate. R. S. Peters in a very lucid and entertaining book (37) distinguishes between four kinds of accounts of human conduct: "his reason" explanations "the reason" explanations, causal explanations, and "end-state" (by which he means *functional* or *homeostatic*) explanations. "His reason" explanations are accounts given by self observers. They differ from "the reason" explanations (given by an observer of others; and, preferably, we might add, by an all-knowing one) in that they may, on occasion, imply prevarication or false consciousness on the part of the subject. In other words, they may be mere *rationalizations* in the psychoanalytic sense of that term (37, pp. 5-6, and p. 59). Both "his reason" and "the reason" accounts are explanations which presume rule following or goal directed action. Causal and end-state explanations, by contrast, refer not to specific goals or reasons but, respectively, to blind drives and the overall reduction of tension or need.[30] The difference between these two classes of explanations leads Peters to postulate that a logical distinction exists between the earlier two and the later two types of explanation.

Peters argues that explanation of human conduct by reference to "reasons" assumes not only ends and norms of efficiency and consistency for attaining such ends but also appeal to social standards and conventions. Explanations of these types presuppose a purposive rule-following model. Consequently, ". . . anthropology or sociology must be the basic sciences of human action in that they exhibit a systematic framework of norms and goals which are necessary to classify actions as being of a certain sort" (37, p. 7). Adoption of such a point of view shifts emphasis from the issue of explaining the motive of a particular individual at a given time (or the motive of some suitably delimited aggregate of individuals) to explanation of principles affecting the development of social norms, their "internalization" or enforcement and, perhaps also, conditions under which such norms cease to apply. What is relatively new here is Peters's insistence that "reason" accounts can be logically ascribed to conduct solely when it is of a conventional sort.

If explanations by "reason" are extended to cover unconventional conduct with novel ends in view, or if, for that matter, "his reason" accounts are seen to include, as they logically do, causal and end-state accounts, then Peters's case for the logical impossibility of general theories of motivation is greatly weakened, if not entirely eliminated. Peters, in effect, is offering us one more attempt to preserve the reasons-causes distinction, arguing that sociological accounts of action are essentially concerned with a rule-following understanding of that action. His effort is worth including as an iconic representative for other linguistic philosophers who have also been working this side of the street. We can see no "reasons," "causes," or "end-states" in his position that lead us to abandon the effort being made here to dissolve this very distinction on behalf of the conception of "conditional invariance."

A recent article by Blum and McHugh (1, pp. 98-109) evinces even more radical insistence upon an unbridgeable gap between motive and physical motions than does Peters's argument. Interestingly enough, here also stress is laid upon conventional rules with respect to explaining behavior. They differ from Peters crucially, however. In their view, rule-following characterizes *the observer* of some item of behavior, not the actor. They are interested in discussing the rules that observers of others

---

[30] Peters makes the distinction between end-states such as "quiescence" or "satisfaction" and particular ends or goals such as "becoming Prime Minister" (see 37, pp. 20–21).

follow when providing accounts of action, and are at great pains to stress that the actual physical behavior in and of itself is unimportant in the attribution of motives. To be sure, they admit in a footnote (1, p. 100) that there *may* exist what they call "concrete states of affairs" corresponding to a motive. These are of no interest to them, however, and they add the charitable comment that they have no wish to run psychologists out of business by concerning themselves with such states of affairs. "Motives," they maintain, "acquire their analytic status as observers rules. They are not forces or events in the world extraneous to an observer." And, ". . . the sociological import of motive resides in its procedural implication for the *treatment* of objects and not in the state of the objects themselves" (1, p. 103).

The reason adduced for taking this position is that motive cannot be separated from a description of the very action it is to explain. In consequence, the quest for a motive calls for an explication of the situation which makes the events that take place "socially possible." True, "the quest for a motive . . . is a request for a theory" (1, p. 101), but the theory they believe to be suitable in such a case concerns itself not with an explanation, but with the *rules* for making explanations! It is difficult to see how these statements differ from the opinion, say, that the concept of gravity cannot be separated from a description of moving (or, in a restricted sense "falling") bodies. That celestial mechanics, therefore, calls for explication of circumstances (or initial conditions) under which motion is "naturally possible." Finally, the explication of what is naturally possible is provided through a "grammar," a set of rules for explication.[31]

[31] The notion that "laws" of gravity are no more than merely "grammatical" is not as startling as may appear at first sight. Thus Einstein, in his introduction of Jammer's history of spatial notions in physics, describes the concept of absolute space very much as a sort of grammatical term used to give the "classical principle of inertia (and therewith the classical laws of motion) an exact meaning" (24, p. xiv). DuBois-Reymond, a century earlier, is even more explicit — writing of the notion of reciprocal forces of attraction that they are no more than a "rhetorical device" (cited in 23, p. 235). Our own equation of scientific primitives with grammatical expressions earlier in this chapter testifies, if testimony is needed, to the depth of our understanding of these points.

Our use of *Verfremdungseffekt* in placing Galilean physics of motion in juxtaposition with imputations of motive is intended, merely, to emphasize the pathetic irrelevance of Blum and McHugh's comments for the development of scientific explanations of motive.

There is a difference between Galilean and conventional rhetorics, whose illustration flows like a subterranean stream through our entire discussion. Bringing this problem to the surface remains a task on our future agenda, but two points where the stream surfaced in this chapter may be brought to the reader's attention. Galileo's experiments were intentionally "naturally impossible" and their objective impossibility, so to speak, was exactly what produced the possibility for establishing "objective knowledge." In the body of this chapter we have criticized Weber's notion of "objective likelihood" as falling short of Galilean criteria in exactly this sense. Similarly, we have praised Freud for meeting such criteria with his formulations.

Nonetheless, we must recognize that our comments here are somewhat beside the point made by Blum and McHugh. Surely they are correct in arguing that there must be conditional invariances which describe (explain?) the provision of observers' accounts, and surely it is helpful to establish how the term "motive" is properly used, from the viewpoint of linguistic analysis. But is it enough to deal with theories of motivation by offering a theory of theories of motivation? Clearly our answer must be that meta-theory is not theory, nor is meta-theory based on linguistic analysis the most fruitful base for such endeavors, other than accounts of the use of terms by linguistic philosophers![32]

In conclusion, one may note an interesting step-like progression in the thinking of those types of sociologists and social philosophers who put rule-following at the centre of their theoretical analyses. Organicists and functionalists like Durkheim and Merton see rule-following conduct itself as the fundamental *materia* or substance of social existence. Ironically, it is not the rule-following individual on whom they concentrate their discussion but the rule-governed aggregate. Linguistic philosophers like Peters or Winch replace reasons for conduct offered by naive observers for the brute conduct itself as the element which is supposed to be governed by rules. Of course, Mills asserts that precisely such reasons at least partially determine the conduct itself. Finally, Blum and McHugh lose all interest in any inherent properties that the conduct itself might have, or any importance that the accounts of naive observers might possess, in order to consider the rules followed by members in attributing motives to others.

### Reasons for Conduct and the Conduct of Reason:

This presentation of a representative collection of theories of motivation finds the various theorists struggling with the dilemma posed by Kantian dualism. Some take their solution in seizing the dilemma by one horn, rejecting one or other of the major premises, thus rejecting a causal science of action or moral agency. Others have sought to escape the dilemma through the horns, claiming that there is another possibility, that action is the causal construction of agents. The first strategy, of course, denies the dilemma by either ignoring the volition of individuals or the necessity for causal explanations. It is essentially uninteresting. The second strategy, on the other hand, denies that the dilemma is exactly as stated, constructing a third possibility which combines causal science and moral agency in the notion of effectuation. In chapter 9

---

[32] We really can do no better than quote Paul Diesing (7, p. 317) on this matter. With regard to the use of conceptual analysis in the social sciences he remarks: "Its practitioners make the basic mistake of supposing that scientific language is the same as ordinary language, and that the culture of social scientists is the same as the culture of those philosophers whose stock in trade is ordinary language." Exactly!

and here, too, the limits of theories of effectuation, especially the most adequate one, Max Weber's, have been explored. What is more, it has been suggested (in this volume, chapters 4 and 9) that Zollschan's model of motivation, as a theory of effectuation, is capable of surmounting the difficulties at which Weber's theoretical mount balked. Yet the logic of our presentation in this chapter, the conceptualization of "conditional invariance" in place of the cause-reason distinction, requires us to discuss briefly the effectiveness of Zollschan's theory in the light of its adequacy as a general theory of motivational invariances and its featuring of pentadic conditions.

Zollschan suggests in his model of social action that individually constructed goals act analogously to a Newtonian gravity construct in "pulling" persons through action in some present toward that image of the future which is the goal. The generality of this model is emphasized by insisting that it apply to both the conscious and non-conscious construction of goals which then serve as proposed solutions to the imbalance of tensions precipitated by an exigency in the individual's life space. The various dimensions of the process through which the exigency is matched to a goal are meant to locate, in their dynamic relations, the complex invariances of the articulation and, at the same time, exhibit the pentadic featuring of conditions. Thus, the coordinate dimensions of the articulation phase of the model, Salience, Specification and Justification, indicate the individual's balance of tension, and relative ability as well as normative capacity (and freedom from inhibitions) to form the inchoate exigency into an image, or need-goal. This image is projected then as an incipient act through the Activation phase of the model that produces concrete goal-oriented action by comparing the image to a valency-weighted range of possible and appropriate goals, indicated by the terms Valence, Application and Legitimation.

On the face of it Zollschan's model, as sketched above, with the strong emphasis on the expression "goal," would appear to make Purpose the featured pentadic element. This would be altogether too superficial a reading. Indeed, we should like to claim that both phases of the model respond to the full range of questions that is proposed by the Pentad to any theory of motivation. With respect to the Articulation phase, or better, to the Exigency that under certain conditions leads to that phase, it is quite clear that we are dealing with the location of the Scene, which is conceived and experienced as something out of the individual's control. The ultimate production of action is the individual's exhibition that the exigency may be brought under control. When it comes to the three dimensions of Articulation, Salience is rendered in terms of Purpose; the purpose of articulating the exigency at all may be seen as the overall nature of the process which is represented by the salience of the exigency. "Specifying" and "Justifying" the exigency amount to processes of locating what it is, to whom it is presented (what "self"), how it appears, and in what kind of situation it occurs, where the production of an image depends on bringing the answers to these questions into some kind of consistency. An individual with a syphilitic chancre could locate the Scene as the bar; the Agency as the infected prostitute; the Act as the sexual intercourse; and the Agent as the "fool" who did it all. All the elements of the Pentad get their due.

When it comes to the Activation phase we again attach purpose to a single coordinate, namely Valence, which is viewed as the Purpose of this projection of the specifiable and justifiable salient exigency, as an incipient act. The capacity and willingness to match up some image with a proposed act follows a procedure very close to the pattern of articulation. To continue our example: "If I don't see a doctor and get some shots I'll probably infect my old lady and our next kid will be born blind." Here, the individual locates the scene as a doctor's office; the agency as the antibiotic injections; the act as appeal for medical help; and the agent as a physician and, more centrally, a responsible and concerned husband. In this example, of course the issue of consistency is raised by the formulation of the agent as a "responsible husband." What kind of scene, act and agency will be consistent with such an agent? Clearly, it would not be appropriate to neglect the chancre (supposing one lacked medical qualifications) or to treat it oneself. When it comes to theories of motivation that formulate agents as causal effectuators of action, the location of the identity of the activating agent is the first step of the process that leads to action. The other terms of the Pentad, insofar as they are featured, are made consistent with such an agent and his audiences; in short, with such an "identity."

This brief account of Zollschan's model of action completes our summary and conceptual evaluation of motivational theories. As we suggested earlier these theories do exhibit limitations in their conceptual generality when viewed in terms of the Pentad. Moreover, these limits are very close to our initial suggestions. The "causal" theories place their conditions in scenes and agencies, the rule-following accounts locate their conditions in agents, purposes, and acts. However, we did find that a third category emerged as we constructed our survey, so that the simple bi-polarity of social physicists and grammarians becomes more like a continuum of "conditional invariance" with the inclusion of those theorists who speak in terms of effectuation. It was this latter group of theorists that came closest to conceptual adequacy judged in the light of Burke's classificatory scheme for statements of motives. Yet, each one of them was less than complete. It is only in the model of social action proposed by Zollschan that we find a conceptually general theory of motivation. One might reasonably ask, would this not also be true of many of the other theories if we had given them the same treatment, would it not be true, at least of the theories of effectuation? Yes, certainly, it would be possible for a Burkean to tease out all of the terms of the Pentad from many of the theories that we have so lightly sifted through it. As we noted earlier, any theory of "action," precisely because it is such a theory contains packed into the pentadic term or terms that it features, all the other terms. The issue, however, where we are using the Pentad for assigning conceptual adequacy to theories, is how *explicit* is the reference to the pentadic terms?

We cannot claim, therefore, that Zollschan's model is necessarily more general, and therefore more adequate, only that it may be *shown* to exhibit an attention to motives which formulates purposes as the end product of a series of answers to the questions of the Pentad. The other theories of effectuation, by contrast, require *us* to ask where each answers these same questions. In using the Pentad as the basis for evaluating the conceptual generality of the conditions under which explanatory invariances operate in motivational theories we are providing ourselves with no more than the minimum criterion for such an evaluation. We can ask, with respect to this theory or that, does it concern itself with the five conditions under which action takes place? And if the answer is "Yes," what then? Is mere completeness with regard to the Pentad not to be supplemented with further criteria that apply to the nature of the usuage of these conditions? If the Pentad is a reasonable criterion for the evaluation of conceptual adequacy, then further assessment of theories might arguably be made with regard to the way in which the Pentad is handled. Thus, the questions raised are (1) are the conditions explicit? (2) internally consistent? (3) available to empirical assessment? If we elect Zollschan's theory of action as an adequate theory of motivation, then, it is not merely because we find that it makes explicit the pentadic conditions, but also because that model appears more capable in its genesis and development than its competitors, notably Weber and Freud, of exhibiting the kind of unified general theory of social action required by the Pentad, *while being available to empirical evaluations*.

This matter of the empirical assessment of theories of motivation brings us back to Burke. Twice before we have drawn readers' attention to the ambiguity of the terms of the Pentad, yet something else needs to be said about them. The ambiguity is not accidental but central to his enterprise; central not only because "action" involves the other terms of the Pentad, but in the sense that his terms are set so as to locate deliberately the places in motivational accounts where transformations amongst motivational "explanatory" terms may and do take place. The terms of the Pentad are ambiguous precisely because accounts of motives, explanations of action, are ambiguous and slippery things. "Scene," in any given account, may be an agent, agency, purpose, or act. In any particular account of action, therefore, any or all of these terms may be taken (given) as the situation of action. Likewise, "agents" may be given as agencies, acts, purposes, and scenes; and so on for all the terms.

Such a wonderful flexibility is useful for naive accounts where "veracity" is simply an issue of obtaining a Public's agreement or acceptance; where all that is necessary is the fabrication of a "good story." It is hardly so helpful for social scientific accounts of action which must also obtain acceptance by a Public — a Public in this case whose agreement is conditioned by a very limited set of decision rules on what is (and more especially, on what is not) a "good story"! In order to harness Burke's insights to our purposes we need a way to pin down the terms of the Pentad so as to give a "pentadically complete" explanation of action yet, at the same time, provide an explanation sufficiently stable for empirical evaluation. It is in this context that a reformulation of the relation between the Pentad and Zollschan's model of the generation of action may be proposed so that the conditions under which action appears invariant are given unambiguous positions within a theoretical model of action. As a first approximation, the two-phase model will tie down purpose, agent, agency within its six coordinates. These will be bracketed, in a genetic sense with respect to some particular action, by the conjunction of Exigency with scene and Action with act.

We should further explicate the precise tie up of the six coordinates with the three remaining pentadic terms. In effect we consider the pentadic terms as restated in both the Articulation and Activation phase of the model. Thus, with regard to Articulation where exigencies are processed into images, the *Salience* of the exigency, its weight in a balance of organismic and externally located tensions that bear on the individual, will be treated as the overall Purpose of the process of Articulation. Construction of this tension disturbance into an image becomes the purpose of this first phase. Now *Specification* is readily seen as an instrumentality dimension, dealing as it does with experiential and situational competencies to grasp the exigency and is a clear candidate for Agency. The last of these three coordinate dimensions, *Justification,* applying as it does to the individual's normative armoury and inhibitory limitations, is associated with Agent.

When we shift our attention to the Activation phase of the model we may conceive the same pattern repeated. In this second phase of Zollschan's model, images, need-goals, are turned into Acts that are organized by these very images through the three dimensions of the phase. *Valence,* the cost of pursuing this image rather than that in action, is viewed as the Purpose of the process of Activation. Similarly, *Application,* as the individual's competency to turn an image into action, is associated with Agency. Finally, Legitimation, dealing with the individual's collection of norms and inhibitions with respect to a range of need-goals, is paired with Agent.

This proposed set of relations between Burke's Pentad and the dimensions of Zollschan's model is but one possible way of pinning down the Burkean grammar of action to variables in a causal effectuation model.

In principle, of course, there are many ways to pin down the Pentad in such a model. Nonetheless, having made this particular option, discussion of alternatives becomes gratuitous. We drop, therefore, the Burkean *terms* in favour of the *parameters* (Zollschan's variables) which are symmetrical with them, in order to scotch the tendency of elements of the Pentad to flow one into another. At the same time, however, it is important to preserve the flexibility associated with Burkean concepts so as to achieve that potential for descriptive exhaustiveness which this flexibility represents.

Within this "fixation" of the Pentad, therefore, where Scene is associated with Exigency, we may still think of exigencies as rooted in agencies, scenes, purposes, or agents without falling into vertiginous ambiguity. For example, the various existential spheres to which reference is made in chapter 7 of this volume could be generated by attending to the pentadic questions with respect to the location of exigencies. Similarly, where Act is associated with Action we may consider action as primarily concerned with agencies, or with scenes, or purposes, or agents; all as "goals." Here we have constructed a theory of motivation, an explanatory scheme for action, which is conceptually adequate in its generality vis-à-vis the pentadic specification of conditions for action and is, at the same time, available for empirical assessment through delineation of parameters individually measurable and collectively testable, at least in principle.

If we state this claim more fully, the importance of melding Burke's poetry of motive with Zollschan's modelling of action becomes more starkly revealed. Firstly, Zollschan's model formulates human motives as self-constructed goals, where the process of goal-formation is conditionally invariant within the pentadic dimensions. Insofar as the dimensions of the Pentad are an exhaustive catalogue of the range of conditions under which action may be seen as invariant, this model is a general social scientific explanation of action. Secondly, since the imputation of motives — "offering of accounts" — is a member of the more general class of "social action," Zollschan's model operates as an explanation for the construction of accounts by the whole gamut of "theoretical observers" presented as a typology at the beginning of this chapter.

It requires but little thought on the reader's part to recognize that in this latter use, Zollschan's model becomes a general framework accounting for the production of explanations themselves. In effect, it provides a single framework within which to organize our understanding as social scientists of the accounts of naive *as well as* social scientific observers of human action. Consequently, it is both a sociology of common sense rhetorics and a sociology of social science. More than this, its application extends to any area where "explanations" are offered. Thus, necessarily, it is a theoretical framework for sociology of science and sociology of knowledge as well. We have, therefore, in a single formulation both a general model of reasons for conduct and an equally general model for the conduct of reason.

## BIBLIOGRAPHY

1. Blum, Alan and Peter McHugh. "The Social Ascription of Motives," *American Sociological Review*, Vol. 36 (February 1971), pp. 98–109.

2. Boulding, Kenneth E. *The Image*. Ann Arbor: University of Michigan Press, 1956.

3. Braithwaite, Richard Beven. *Scientific Explanation*. New York: Harper and Row, 1960.

4. Burke, Kenneth. *A Grammar of Motives*. Berkeley: University of California Press, 1969.

5. Chomsky, Noam. "Review of B. F. Skinner "Verbal Behavior," *Language*, Vol. 35 (1959), pp. 26–58.

6. de Charms, Richard. *Personal Causation*. New York: Academic Press, 1968.

7. Diesing, Paul. *Patterns of Discovery in the Social Sciences*. Chicago: Aldine, 1971.

8. Durkheim, Emile. *The Rules of Sociological Method*. New York: The Free Press, 1964.

9. Durkheim, Emile. *Suicide*. New York: The Free Press, 1951.

10. Ehrlich, Annette. "The Age of the Rat," *Human Behavior*, Vol. 3 (March 1974), pp. 25–28.

11. Freud, Sigmund: "Beyond the Pleasure Principle," *Complete Works*, Vol. 17, London: Hogarth Press, 1955.

12. Freud, Sigmund. "The Ego and the Id," in *Complete Works*, Vol. 19, London: Hogarth Press, 1961.

13. Freud, Sigmund. "The Interpretation of Dreams," in *The Basic Writings of Sigmund Freud*, translated by A. A. Brill. New York: Random House, 1938, pp. 183–549.

14. Freud, Sigmund. "Psychoanalysis," (originally prepared for Max Marcuse (ed.), *Handwörterbuch für Sexualwissenschaft*), in *Collected Papers*, (5 vols.), Vol. 5. London: Hogarth Press, 1950.

15. Gerth, Hans H., and C. Wright Mills. *Character and Social Structure*. New York: Harcourt, Brace & World, 1964.

16. Green, D. R. "Volunteering and the Recall of Interrupted Tasks," *Journal of Abnormal Psychology*, Vol. 66 (1963), pp. 397–401.

17. Green, Hannah. *I Never Promised You a Rose Garden*. New York: Signet, 1964.

18. Hayek, F. A. von. *The Counter Revolution of Science*. Glencoe: The Free Press, 1955.

19. Heider, Fritz. *The Psychology of Interpersonal Relations*. New York: John Wiley and Sons, 1958.

20. Høffding, Harald. *A History of Modern Philosophy.* Vol. 2. Translated from the German edition by B. E. Meyer. London: Macmillan, 1900.

21. Homans, George C. *Social Behavior: Its Elementary Forms.* New York: Harcourt, Brace and World, 1961.

22. Hughes, H. Stuart. *Consciousness and Society.* New York: Knopf, 1958.

23. Jammer, Max. *Concepts of Force.* Cambridge, Massachusetts: Harvard University Press, 1957.

24. Jammer, Max. *Concepts of Space.* Cambridge, Massachusetts: Harvard University Press, 1969.

25. Kant, Immanuel. *Critique of Practical Reason,* translated by T. K. Abbott. London: Longmans, Green & Co., 1873.

26. Kant, Immanuel. *Critique of Pure Reason,* translated by Norman Kemp Smith. London: Macmillan and Co., 1958.

27. Koch, Sigmund. "Behavior as 'Intrinsically' Regulated: Work Notes towards a Pre-Theory of Phenomena Called 'Motivational,'" in M. R. Jones (ed.), *Nebraska Symposium on Motivation.* Lincoln: University of Nebraska Press, 1956, pp. 1–46.

28. Kunkel, John H. *Society and Economic Growth.* New York: Oxford University Press, 1970.

29. MacCorquedale, K., and P. E. Meehl. "On a Distinction between Hypothetical Constructs and Intervening Variables," *Psychological Review,* Vol. 55 (1948), pp. 95–107.

30. Marx, Karl. *The Eighteenth Brumaire of Louis Bonaparte.* New York: International Publishers Co., 1963.

31. Marx, Karl. *Karl Marx: Selected Writings in Sociology and Social Philosophy.* T. B. Bottomore, and M. Rubel (eds.). New York: McGraw-Hill, 1964.

32. Marx, Melvin H. and Tom N. Tombaugh. *Motivation.* San Francisco: Chandler Publishing Co., 1967.

33. Mead, George H. *The Philosophy of the Act.* Chicago: University of Chicago Press, 1938.

34. Miller, George A., Eugene Galanter, and Karl H. Pribram. *Plans and the Structure of Behavior.* New York: Holt Rhinehart and Winston, 1960.

35. Mills, C. Wright. "Situated Actions and Vocabularies of Motive," in *Symbolic Interaction: A Reader in Social Psychology.* Jerome G. Manis and Bernard K. Meltzer (eds.). Boston: Allyn and Bacon, 1972, pp. 393-404.

36. Pareto, Vilfredo. *The Mind and Society.* Translation of *Trattato di Soziologia Generale* by Andrea Bongiorno and Arthur Livingston. New York: Dover Publications, Inc., 1963.

37. Peters, R. S. *The Concept of Motivation.* London: Routledge and Keegan Paul, 1958.

38. Polanyi, Michael. *Personal Knowledge.* New York: Harper and Row, 1964.

39. Popper, Sir Karl Raimund. *Conjectures and Refutations.* New York: Basic Books, 1962.

40. Popper, Sir Karl Raimund. *The Open Society and Its Enemies*. New York: Harper and Row, (2 Vols.), 1962.

41. Rapaport, David. *The Organization and Pathology of Thought*. (Translations and a Commentary on Selected Sources), New York: Columbia University Press, 1951.

42. Rapaport, David. "The Structure of Psychoanalytic Theory: A Systematizing Attempt," in Sigmond Koch, *Psychology: A Study of a Science*. (6 vols.), Vol. 3. New York: McGraw-Hill, 1959.

43. Rubinstein, Benjamin B. "Explanation and Mere Description: A Metascientific Examination of Certain Aspects of the Psychoanalytic Theory of Motivation," in Robert R. Holt, (ed.), *Motives and Thought*. New York: International Universities Press (Monograph 18/19 of *Psychological Issues*), 1967.

44. Schütz, Alfred. *Collected Papers*. (3 Vols.) The Hague: Nijhoff, 1962–1966.

45. Schütz, Alfred. "The Stranger," in *Collected Papers*. The Hague: Nijhoff, 1964, Vol. 2, pp. 91–105.

46. Scott, Marvin B., and Stanford M. Lyman. "Accounts," in *Symbolic Interaction: A Reader in Social Psychology*, Jerome G. Manis and Bernard K. Meltzer (eds.). Boston: Allyn and Bacon, 1972, pp. 404–429.

47. Simmel, Georg. "How is Society Possible?" in Kurt H. Wolff, (editor and translator) *Georg Simmel 1858–1918*. Columbus, Ohio State University Press, 1959, pp. 337–356.

48. Simmel, Georg. "The Metropolis and Mental Life," in Kurt Wolff (ed.), *The Sociology of Georg Simmel*. New York: The Free Press, 1950, pp. 409–424.

49. Simmel, Georg. *Philosophie des Geldes*. Munich: Dunker and Humblot, 1930 (5th ed.).

50. Simmel, Georg. *Die Probleme der Geschichtsphilosophie*. Leipzig: Dunker & Humblot, (1st ed.) 1892.

51. Simmel, Georg. "The Stranger," in Kurt Wolff (ed.), *The Sociology of Georg Simmel*. New York: The Free Press, 1950, pp. 402–408.

52. Sorokin, Pitirim A. *Contemporary Sociological Theories*. New York: Harper and Row, 1928.

53. Sorokin, Pitirim A. *Fads and Foibles in Modern Sociology*. Chicago: Henry Regnery, 1956.

54. Stinchcombe, Arthur. *Constructing Social Theories*. New York: Harcourt, Brace & World, 1968.

55. Tenbruck, Friedrich H. "Die Genesis der Methodologie Max Weber," in *Kölner Zeitschrift für Soziologie und Sozialpsychologie*, Vol. 11, 1959, pp. 573–630.

56. Vaihinger, Hans. *Die Philosophie des Als-Ob*. Leipzig: Felix Meiner, 1923.

57. Weber, Max. "Antikritisches zum 'Geist' des Kapitalismus," in *Archiv fur Sozialwissenschaft und Sozialpolitik*, Vol. 31, 1910, pp. 554–599.

58. Weber, Max. *Economy and Society.* Guenther Roth and Claus Wittich (eds.). New York: Bedminster Press, 1968.

59. Weber, Max. *The Protestant Ethic and the Spirit of Capitalism.* New York: Charles Scribner's Sons, 1958.

60. Weber, Max. "Roscher und Knies und die logischen Problems der Historischen Nationalökonomie," in *Gesammelte Aufsätze zur Wissenschaftslehre.* (2nd ed.) Tübingen: Mohr (Siebeck), 1951, pp. 1–145.

61. Weber, Max. *The Theory of Social and Economic Organization.* Translated by A. M. Henderson and T. Parsons. Glencoe: Free Press, 1947.

62. Wiener, Norbert. *Cybernetics.* New York: Wiley, 1948.

63. Ziman, John. *Public Knowledge.* Cambridge: Cambridge University Press, 1968.

64. Zollschan, George K. "Beyond the 'Reality Principle,' in George K. Zollschan and Walter Hirsch (eds.), *Explorations in Social Change.* Boston: Houghton Mifflin and Co., and London: Routledge & Keegan Paul, 1964, pp. 175–200.

65. Zollschan, George K., and Phillip Gibeau, "Concerning Alienation: A System of Categories for the Explanation of Rational and Irrational Behavior," in George K. Zollschan and Walter Hirsch (eds.), *Explorations in Social Change.* Boston: Houghton Mifflin and Co., 1964, and London: Routledge and Keegan Paul, 1964, pp. 152–174.

66. Zollschan, George K., and Robert Perrucci, "Social Stability and Social Process: An Initial Presentation of Relevant Categories," in George K. Zollschan and Walter Hirsch (eds.), *Explorations in Social Change.* Boston: Houghton Mifflin and Co., and London: Routledge & Keegan Paul, 1964, pp. 99–124.

# 11

*George K. Zollschan*

# A Lexicon of Motive, Action, and Society:

# Prototractatus Teleosociologicus

*We think we hear much, but only genuinely begin to hear when we have let the caccophonous jumble of noise die down and but one voice speaks.*

Meister Ekkehart

### A Preliminary Chuckle*

1. Start at the beginning and read to the end. There are no shortcuts that have not, already, been cut short.

2. Each new term is announced typographically. Readers should take good note of the meaning of these terms since they occur later without further explication.

3. The logic of presentation is a genetic one; beginning with the individual and moving through social relationships to social structures, culture and history.

4. The internal organization of all sections, except the seventh and last one, is logically coherent. Some effort has been given to providing parallelisms between the sections. Complete logical intercorrelation has not been attempted.

5. Despite the format, this is not a propositional calculus rigorously

---

* This part of the chapter was done by Michael A. Overington, alternately hampered and assisted by the author.

318

regarded. There are undefined terms. Most of these primitives, however, may be thought of in Max Weber's or Sigmund Freud's usage — whichever is appropriate in the particular case.

6. There are many places in the number scheme that have no propositions. A test of the reader's comprehension is to fill them.

7. Whatever cannot be read in the lines can be perceived between them!

### Exigency:

1. What is, is that it is. When what is is not as it should be, or has to be, or can be, an *Exigency* is present.

1.1 Only persons experience Exigencies. Organisms experience *Excitations*.[1] The distinction between an Excitation and an Exigency in humans corresponds to Freud's distinction between "primary" and "secondary process" activity, cognition, and affect (4, pp. 699-704; 8).

1.11 The Extent of the *Discrepancy* between what is and what ought to be is measured by *Salience*. See also 2.13.

1.12 Simultaneous exposure to a multiplicity of Exigencies renders Salience relative at any point of time. The summation of Exigencies experienced by a person at any point of time may be termed the *Balance of Tensions*.[2]

1.2 Constancy and regularity in the incidence of Excitations and their removal give rise to an *Horizon of Justifications* in the person through the medium which links primary and secondary process.

1.21 The Horizon of Justifications consists of representations of "good" objects and objectives and "bad" objects and objectives.

1.3 Constancy and regularity in the incidence of Exigencies and their Articulation in the development of a human give rise to an *Horizon of Expectations or Specifications*. Here, objects and objectives can come to be represented in an evaluatively neutral light.

1.4 Exigencies are composed of Discrepancies in Tensions, Justifications, and Specifications (Expectations). Respectively, such Discrepancies are termed *Affective, Evaluative*, and *Cognitive*.

### Articulation:

2. *Articulation* transforms Exigencies into *Ideas* or *Images* or *Needs* with associated *Goals*.

---

[1] An excitation is the relationship between a stimulus and the subject viewed as a system of behavior. This relationship constitutes the irreducible datum of personality psychology (or, at any rate, of a personality psychology usable by sociology); not some abstracted, disembodied, ostensively "objectively measured" physical event.

[2] Elsewhere (6, 8, 9, 10, 11) I have referred to this variously as "equilibrium of excitations" and "equilibrium of tensions." "Balance" is a better term than "equilibrium" since the former relies on fewer tacit assumptions.

2.1 Salience, Justifiability, and Specifiability are the coordinates of Articulation.

2.11 The nature of the Image or Idea or Need-Goal in which an Exigency becomes represented depends upon the abovementioned co-ordinates.

2.12 Articulation minimizes and/or balances net overall Salience (Tension). Consequently, any Idea or Need may represent a condensation of several distinct Exigencies. Freud called an Idea or Image which articulated a number of different exigencies "overdetermined." I speak instead of *Conservation of Articulation* (10, p. 50).

2.13 Salience is the importance of the Exigency relative to all other Tensions at a point of time.

2.131 *Urgency* is a special case of Salience where a "deadline" exists in the short run.

2.14 Specifiability is the capacity to construct and focus an Image.

2.15 Justifiability is the inhibitory limitation set on the Specifiability of a given Exigency.

2.2 The *Personality* of an individual at any point in time consists of the Balance of Tensions, the Horizon of Expectations, and the Horizon of Justifications. Alternatively, individual Personality may be viewed as a generalized propensity to articulate Exigencies in a manner specifiable by the given state of the aforementioned structures.

2.21 Continuity of Personality over time is a function of the *Conservation Of Articulation*. It is expressed in the form of routines of articulation.

2.3 An Exigency incapable of any sort of Articulation gives rise to free-floating affect and strictly reflex behavior.

2.31 Strictly reflex behavior also occurs under specifiable conditions in response to Excitations capable of articulation. Such behavior is of merely peripheral interest to sociology; that is — unless the behavior itself (the "response") is experienced as an Exigency.

2.4 Where a variety of Goals are capable of Articulation in response to an Exigency, the tendency will be to articulate those which lie in the directionality of previously established routines.

2.5 The extent to which an Articulation fails to reflect (or "drain") the Salience of an Exigency increasess overall Tension in the Personality.

2.51 The extent to which an Articulated Image fails to reflect the "objective" nature and location of an Exigency measures "false consciousness."

2.52 Decreases in the levels of Tension may result from false Articulation. In such a case, the Articulation may reflect both the Salience of tensions other than those occasioned by the originating Exigency and an incapacity to Specify or Justify the originating Exigency.

2.53 "Wish-fulfillment" phantasies and dreams are mechanisms for the attainment of Tension Balance.

### Activation:

3. Where *Action* occurs it is toward Goals. Action is a person's strategy for optimising net overall Goal attainment. Consequently, any given act may represent locomotion toward a variety of Goals.

3.1 Activation transforms Images or Need-Goals into Goal-directed Actions. *Valence, Legitimation,* and *Application* are the coordinates of Activation.

3.11 Valence is the opportunity-cost of acting toward a Goal in relation to other Goals foregone.

3.12 Application is Know-how (whether correct or spurious) for acting toward a Goal.

3.13 Legitimation is the normative limitation set upon an Action.

3.2 The *Character* of an individual at any point of time consists of that person's Goals and the balance of their Valencies, his Application skills (technical repertoire), and his fund of Legitimations. Alternatively viewed, individual Character may be described as a general propensity to act toward Goals in a manner consistent with the given state of the aforementioned structures.

3.21 Continuity of Character over time is a function of the *Conservation of Action.* This is expressed in the form of Routines of Action.

3.3 A Goal incapable of achievement may either be resorbed into the Personality structure (and, perhaps, rearticulated), or be substituted for by other Goals, or give rise to *Alienation.* The symptoms of Alienation vary systematically with the nature of the Goal and the existing Character structure of individuals harbouring the Goal. An initial step in explaining the systematics of this variation has been undertaken previously (9). The psychiatric theory of neuroses is concerned with a range (as yet unspecified) of alienative predicaments.

3.31 A property of Goals is their *Elasticity:* the extent to which they are substitutable by other Goals.

3.4 Where incompatible Goals exist for a person, *Ambivalence* is present.

3.5 The extent to which the Valence of a Goal fails to drain the Salience of the originating Exigency increases the overall tension in the Personality.

3.6 *Rationality* is (optimally) effective Action for the attainment of a specific Goal.

3.61 *Rationale* describes activity where a course of effective Action toward the attainment of a specific Goal is unattainable for a person.

3.62 *Artistry* is the optimization of Goal achievement with respect to a cluster of Goals (particularly where the Goals in the cluster are widely dispersed). High Artistry is taking the shortest distance to the attainment of widely dispersed Goals; it exemplifies the limiting case of Conservation of Action on the individual level.

3.7 Action toward a Goal is subject to any of the following outcomes and of their combinations and permutations.

3.71 Action fails to attain the Goal. When this occurs by itself this results either in Alienation after the act or in re-articulation. Successful re-articulation in such a case is *learning*.

3.711 Where Action persists in the face of clear failure "repetition compulsion" exists.

3.712 Action results in second order Exigencies ("punishment").

3.72 Action attains its Goal.

3.721 Where the Goal reflects a recurrent or enduring need, a *Routine* is established.

3.73 Action attains *Satisfaction* other than the Goal. This occurs through: a) drainage of Salience of an unarticulated or falsely articulated Exigency; b) re-alignment of the Balance of Tensions such as to reduce total tension; c) the serendipitous revelation of a "preferred state."

3.731 Where a Satisfaction is recurrent or enduring a Routine is established.

3.74 Where punishment outweighs the combination of Goal attainment and extraneous Satisfaction a condition exists similar to (3.71) above.

3.741 Punishment may have a goal-like character for a person, in such a case *Masochistic* Action is present. Masochistic Goals originate out of Evaluative Discrepancies.

3.8 A Goal is *Distal* when it requires prolonged activity for its initial attainment.

3.81 Persons who act toward Distal goals have *Goal Perseveration*. Goal Perseveration varies inversely with the phenomenological distance of a Goal. Explication of interpersonal variability in Goal Perseveration is the task of the psychological theory of human development.

3.811 *Ceteris paribus,* the Valence of a Goal varies inversely with the square of the phenomenological distance.

3.82 Distal Goals are attained by activity toward more or less systematically aligned sequences of intermediate Goals.

3.821 Intermediate Goals may be satisfying or punishing. Where the punishments along the pathway to a distal Goal outweigh Satisfactions a condition exists similar to (3.71) above.

3.9 *Potency* with respect to a Goal measures the capacity to attain the Goal.

3.91 Potency with respect to a range of relevant and legitimate Goals draws *Esteem* (from those who recognize the Goals and consider them Legitimate). *Self-esteem* is a variant of Esteem.

3.92 Esteem varies positively with the ostensive "difficulty" of attaining a Goal.

3.93 Recognized handicaps increase the ostensive difficulty of attaining a Goal.

3.94 Possession of a characteristic or attribute which itself has the characteristics of a Goal-state may be termed *Endowment*.

3.941 The only sensible way to distinguish between Potency and Endowment (loosely termed "achievement" and "ascription") is with respect to the ostensible "effort" expended.

3.95 Esteem varies positively with the Valence of a (Legitimate) Endowment.

3.951 The Valence of an Endowment is a partial function of its ostensive "rarity."

## Social Relations:

4. A *Social Relationship* exists where: a) the responses of the other(s) is the Goal; b) cooperation of the other(s) is required for attainment of the Goal.

4.01 The Goals sought by participants in a Social Relationship may be the same or different.

4.011 A given Social Relationship may provide the avenue to different Goals for different persons.

4.012 A given Social Relationship may provide the avenue to a diversity of Goals for one person.

4.013 Goals attained through the participation in a Relationship include the avoidance of Exigencies (punishments) consequent upon non-participation or cessation of participation.

4.02 Since a Social Relationship can carry many Goals it may become independent of any particular Goal. This circumstance lies at the base of the structuralist fallacy which seeks to posit a "logic" of structures independent of any Goal.

4.021 A contributory factor in perpetuating the structuralist fallacy rests on the occurrence of second order Exigencies attendant upon the elicitation of cooperation and response. To postulate that such Exigencies are capable of a strictly delimited range of Articulations is absurd.

4.1 Only persons have Goals. Social relationships have Routines, *Rules* and *Policies*.

4.11 Routines may undergo gradual changes not intended (or, perhaps, even noticed) by participants. Such changes are the resultant of aggregate Goal shifts.

4.12 Persons who intentionally establish or change policies and rules are *Rulers*.

4.121 *Rulership* in any given relationship may be concentrated or diffused. Explication of the systematics of Rulership is the task of political theory.

4.122 Rulers remain Rulers so long as the Policies and Rules they promulgate are accepted by participants in the Relationship.

4.13   Specific Policies and sets of Rules may constitute a Goal-state for a person. Policies and Rules may be Articulated as Goals if a threat to their continuation or promulgation poses an Exigency.

4.131   Rulership may constitute a Goal-state for a person.

4.132   Subordination may constitute a Goal-state for a person.[3]

4.133   Where different Rules and Policies affecting a person in a *Structure* are incompatible, they pose an Exigency for that person.

4.2   A *Social Structure* is either a) an aggregate of separate Social Relations governed by approximately similar Routines, Policies, and Rules; and/or b) a complex organization of Social Relations.

4.201   The Valence of a Social Relationship (or Structure) for a participant measures the extent to which the Relationship contributes to the net overall Goal optimization of the participant.

4.202   Where a person has a choice of Relationships (or Structures) these will be selected according to their Valence.

4.21   The durability of a Social Relationship (or Structure) over time is a function of the Conservation of Action.

4.211   Relationships (or Structures) in which a person is implicated become the avenue along which various Goals are Articulated.

4.212   A Social Relationship (or Structure) persists as long as it meets Goals of participants.

4.22   Where participation in a Social Relationship (or Structure) is Valent, the maintenance of the Structure can become a Goal-state for the participant (or, conversely, a threat to the continuation of the Structure poses an Exigency for the participant). This circumstance lies at the base of *Conservation of Structure.*

4.23   Social Relationships (or Structures) persist as long as the Satisfaction attained through them outweighs punishments involved in being implicated in them for a sufficient number of participants to sustain the Relationship (or Structure). The postulate that the maintenance of Structures is itself the principal (if not exclusive) Goal of participants is the functionalist fallacy.

4.3   *Power* is the capacity to facilitate or impede the Goal attainment of other persons (to subject other persons to Exigencies).

4.31   Where Rulers possess Power the Relationship (or Structure) is "imperatively coordinated."

4.311   In any given Relationship (or Structure) Power may be derived from the fiat of Rules or Rulers in a more inclusive structure.

4.32   Power derives from privileged (or monopolistic) access to a) means of violence; b) means of Legitimation; c) relevant information (Specifications, Know-how).

---

[3] Dahrendorf's contention (1, pp. 167–179) that subordination is the principal "class-forming" exigency is an unwarranted generalization.

4.321 The Power of a person is durable so long as privileged (monopolistic) access to the above-mentioned resources is maintained.

4.322 Power in any given Structure may be concentrated or diffuse. Explication of the systematics of Power distribution is the task of political theory.

4.33 *Authority* is Power which a person assumes so as to enjoy general Legitimacy. The term "general" is kept intentionally vague.

4.4 An *Interest* is a Goal which clashes with the Goals of another or of others, (6).

4.41 Clashing Policies become Interests where the Policies in question constitute Goal states for the persons who espouse them.

4.42 Clashing Rules become Interests where the Rules in question constitute Goal-states for the persons who espouse them.

4.43 An Interest in the maintenance of an established Relationship or Structure is a *Vested Interest*.

4.44 An Interest group is a Social Relationship subserving the attainment of an Interest.

4.5 "Division of Labor" occurs where activities directed toward Goals or Interests (and/or activities obeying Policies and Rules) differ systematically for different participants in a Social Structure.

4.501 Division of Labor exists where persons with differentiated characteristics seek responses from each other.

4.502 Division of Labor exists where persons with differentiated characteristics (such as 'skills') cooperate for the attainment of Goals or Interests.

4.503 Division of Labor exists where Goals or Interests to which activities are directed require differentiated and varied Routines. Where such Activities are necessary but not in existence, their absence occasions a second order Exigency for persons for whom the Goals or Interests exist.

4.504 A *Role* is a differentiated Routine in a Social Structure with Division of Labor.

4.51 The *Prestige* of a Role for a person is a measure of that person's evaluation of the contribution of that Role to the attainment of that person's Goals and Interests.

4.511 Prestige depends partially upon visibility of Role performance. Where the performance is highly visible and visibility is itself part of the performance (as in the case of performing artists or entertainers) Prestige verges on Esteem.

4.512 Prestige depends partially upon the ostensive Goal-Potency of Role incumbents.

4.513 Prestige depends partially upon the conferer's evaluation of the abstract Valence of the Goals and Interests which a Role subserves. (The extent to which the Goal or Interest must be Valent for the conferer himself is subject to systematic variation according to person and occasion).

4.514 Prestige depends partially upon the Esteem to which familiar incumbents of a particular Role are held by the conferer.

4.515 Prestige depends partially upon the Legitimacy of a Role.

4.6 Coordination of Roles depends upon the extent to which different Routines related to the attainment of a Goal or Interest must be concerted in order to attain the Goal or Interest.

4.61 Where lack of structural coordination poses a second order Exigency, such coordination becomes the objective of Policies and Rules.

4.62 The existence of coordination poses second order Exigencies for the coordinated.

4.7 Any specified Routine (and this includes all Roles) is a locus of Exigencies specific to persons engaged in the Routine.

4.71 The Exigencies of any role are a combined function of the Role and the Personality of the person engaging in the Role.

4.8 For any person, society is the ensemble of Structures impinging on that person.

4.81 Societies do not exist except for persons.

4.82 Where a similarly demarcated society exists for an aggregate of persons *Social Integration* exists.

4.821 The degree of Integration of society depends upon the extent to which Structures are interdependent and imperatively coordinated.

4.83 The tighter the degree of Structural Integration, the greater the potential resistance to the development of novel Relationships and Structures (11, p. 115).

4.831 The above in no way implies that novel Relationships and Structures are less likely to arise in tightly integrated structural ensembles; merely that their development will pose more Exigencies.

### Culture:

5. *Culture* (insofar as it makes sense to use this term) exists where effective *Symbolic Communication* occurs between persons.

5.01 Popper's extension of Bühler's conception of hierarchical levels of language is used here to establish the meaning of Symbolic Communication in first approximation (3, p. 295).

5.011 Popper speaks of *Descriptive Communication* at four levels of language: a) expressive or symptomatic; b) stimulative or signal; c) descriptive; and d) argumentative.

5.012 Where Communication reaches the descriptive level Symbolic Communication exists. Symbolic Communication is enriched where, additionally, Communication reaches the level of argumentative language.

5.02    *Prescriptive* (hortatory, admonitory) *Communication* is subject to a parallel analysis of language levels, as is Descriptive Communication: a) expressive; b) signal; c) prescriptive; d) moral and aesthetic.

5.021    Where hortatory or warning signals are freely and voluntarily adaptable to varied situations (including bodily feeling states and emotional states) and make distinctions between situations, a prescriptive language is present. Where Communication reaches the prescriptive level Symbolic Communication exists.

5.022    Where Prescriptive Communications are open to comparison and to question, a moral and/or aesthetic language is present. Moral and aesthetic language is on a par with argumentative language.

5.023    A persons' Horizon of Justifications consists of prohibitions and preferences existing at a pre-symbolic level.

5.024    A person's Horizons of Expectations is discussed under 5.1.

5.03    Mathematics and logic occupy a position intermediate between Descriptive and Prescriptive Communication.

5.031    Mathematics and logic aid in the transition from the descriptive/prescriptive level to the argumentative/moral-aesthetic level of language.

5.04    Language at any given level in the hierarchy may contain elements of language from lower levels in the hierarchy.

5.041    The more Symbolic Communication (taken to refer to the descriptive and prescriptive levels and to levels above these in the hierarchy) channels and contains elements of expressive and stimulative language, the more is it *Embodied* language.

5.05    The Freudian "mechanism" of *Isolation* consists of a reduction of Excitations through the use (or construction) of *Disembodied* language. (8, p. 192).

5.051    The failure of psychoanalytic therapy to handle Isolation is related to its exclusive reliance upon symbolic levels of communication.

5.06    Where argumentative language reaches a level of clarity in which arguments are susceptible to testing, the potential for science exists.

5.1    A person's Horizon of Expectations corresponds to that person's repertoire of descriptive and argumentative resources.

5.11    Descriptive and argumentative resources are acquired through articulating *Cognitive Discrepancies.*

5.12    Cognitive Discrepancies in a person originate as second order Exigencies relating to the communication of specific Needs (Exigencies) while in a state of infantile dependency.

5.13    The elicitation of rationally suitable response and cooperation from others through Symbolic Communication remains a source of Cognitive Discrepancies throughout the lifespan of the person.

5.14    The maintenance of existential consistency and continuity through variations of experience over time is a source of Cognitive Discrepancies throughout the life span of the person.

5.15   Every person in every Culture has a unique Horizon of Expectations. The postulate of an identity of Horizons of Expectations in any Culture constitutes the existential version of the group-mind fallacy.

5.16   The *Discursive Integration* of any given society is an inverse function of the multiplicative combination of number and Salience of cognitive discrepancies.

5.2   A person's Horizon of Legitimations corresponds to that person's symbolically elaborated preferences and prohibitions.

5.21   Prescriptive and moral/aesthetic languages are acquired through articulating *Evaluative Discrepancies*.

5.22   Evaluative Discrepancies in a person originate as disturbances of environmental routines as they impinge upon the individual.

5.23   The elicitation of "evaluatively suitable" responses and cooperation from others through Symbolic Communication remains a source of Evaluative Discrepancies throughout the life span of the person.

5.24   The maintenance of evaluative consistency and continuity through variations over time is a source of Evaluative Discrepancies throughout the life span of the person.

5.25   Every person in every Culture has a unique Horizon of Legitimation. The postulate of an identity of Horizons of Legitimation in any Culture constitutes the evaluative version of the group mind fallacy.

5.26   The *Normative Integration* of any given society is an inverse function of the multiplicative combination of number and Salience of Evaluative Discrepancies.

5.3   For purposes of this argument, *Commerce* may be viewed as a form of Symbolic Communication.

5.31   Where use or consumption of a material object constitutes a Goal state for a person, the object in question is a *Commodity*.

5.311   Where cooperation of other persons is required for the attainment of a Goal, this cooperation is describable as a *Service*.

5.312   Personal response, as distinct from cooperation, is never a Service. Personal response lies outside the realm of Commerce.

5.32   Where a Commodity or Service constitutes a Goal-state for an aggregate of persons it is potentially *Marketable* (that is to say, exchangeable for other Goals and Services).

5.321   Involuntary deliverers of services (slaves, domesticated animals) are Marketable Commodities.

5.33   Marketable Commodities which, additionally, are durable can serve as a Goal-attainment potential ("store of value"). The exchange of such Commodities constitutes Commerce on a level parallel with descriptive/prescriptive language.

5.34   Money (coined metals, paper tokens, and finally, credit) is an elaboration of Commerce parallel to the argumentative/moral-aesthetic level of language.[4]

5.35 *Commercial Integration* (a "market economy") exists where money is "generally" acceptable for Commodities and Services.

5.351 Persons vary with respect to their capacity and/or desire to participate in Markets.

5.36 "Classical" and "neo-classical" economics (the "British" and "Austrian" Schools) are concerned with explication of the systematics of market economies under the (unrealistic) limiting assumption of general and complete Market participation.

5.4 *Technology* is symbolically elaborated Action toward Goals.

5.41 A person's Horizon of Applications corresponds to that person's *Technological Repertoire*.

5.411 A person's Technological Repertoire includes access to sources of understandable (usable) technical information.

5.412 A person's Technological Repertoire includes the capacity to elicit cooperation from others with requisite "Know-how."

5.42 *Artefacts* constitute the material embodiment of Technology.

5.421 *Tools* (in a special but broad sense of this term) are material concretizations of Know-how.

5.43 In the final analysis *techné* ("knowing how") and *epistemé* ("knowing that") are inseparable.

5.431 The above consideration does not invalidate the analytical distinction between Specification of Goals and Application of Know-how for their attainment.

5.5 Every Social Structure depends for its existence upon the presence (or establishment) of a modicum of Discursive, Normative, Commercial, and Technical Integration. The structural-functionalist fallacy consists of an entirely unwarranted extreme exaggeration of the requisite modicum of these types of Integration (especially the Normative type).

5.51 The requisite modicum of Discursive, Normative, Commercial and Technical Integration for a Social Structure varies systematically

---

[4] For the foregoing account of the development of money I am greatly indebted to the economist Carl Menger (2, pp. 152–155). He uses this example, among others, to support organicist (or, what would now be called "functionalist") assumptions on the flimsy grounds that money was never intentionally legislated into existence by some central authority. Contrary, to this position, I insist on treating development of money as the result of articulated and goal-oriented (that is to say, "intentional" or "quasi-intentional") actions of aggregates of persons. Menger himself generally espoused the kind of Galilean approach to social phenomena which I am developing here. His acceptance of some organicist ideas in his celebrated "debate" with Gustaf Schmoller rests on a tacit, holistic assumption foreign to his otherwise impeccable individualism.

Oddly enough, as is briefly stated in proposition 5.36 below and argued at greater length in Chapter 9 of this Volume — economics itself (at least, as Menger envisaged the field) does not conform to Galilean procedures but rather to what Max Weber called an *ideal type*.

with territorial dispersion, Division of Labor, differentials of Power and differentials of Prestige. The systematics of this variation constitute a vast, largely unexplored, area of sociological research.

5.52　The *Factual Integration* of a Structure is a complex positive multiplicative function of the previously enumerated types of Integration combined with the aggregate Valence of the Structure.

5.6　A *Tradition* is any type of Integration (or subtype of Integration) which extends in time beyond the term of participation of any given person.

5.61　Durability of Tradition over time is a function of the *Conservation of Symbols*.

## Historicity:

6.　A *Socio-Historical Configuration* is the ensemble of persons, Exigencies, Symbols (including Artefacts), Goals, and Structures existing in a delimited spatio-temporal location.

6.1　A *Socio-historical Depiction* is a more or less deliberate selection of elements from a Socio-Historical Configuration.

6.11　Criteria of selection may be more or less conscious. They are affected by: a) presuppositions of the historian (moral and/or aesthetic and/or heuristic); b) availability of information.

6.2　*Social Change* is any variation in Exigencies, Symbols, Goals, and Structures from one Socio-Historical Configuration to the next.

6.21　*Historicity* is a measure of the systematic dependence of a given Socio-Historical Configuration upon prior ones.

6.211　To the extent that any Socio-Historical Configuration constitutes a set of initial conditions, and to the extent that any scientific explanation (sociological or other) requires sets of initial conditions, the postulate of general historicity of social change is trivially correct.

6.212　In the absence of scientific sociological explanation, claims for Historicity are empty. Every variety of evolutionism or cyclical theory of Social Change thus far enunciated merely serves as a cloak for explanatory-theoretical nakedness.

6.3　The form of sociological explanation employable for Social Change and for Social Stability is identical.

6.4　For every conservation principle mentioned in this lexicon, a parallel principle of entropy can be enunciated.

6.5　Every "new" Structure and/or Symbol System is the result of individual Articulations and Actions. The Articulations and Actions in question can, of course, be by an aggregate of individuals.

6.6　That "outcomes" of action are often unintended and/or unanticipated is trivially the case. This fact alone has absolutely no explanatory value.

**The Last Laugh:**

7. When something that has to be said cannot be said clearly in an existing language[5], a new language must be found or invented for it.

Where independent measures for the parameters proposed are not available they must be invented.[6]

What has to be said cannot be silenced.

## BIBLIOGRAPHY

1. Dahrendorf, Ralf. *Class and Class Conflict in Industrial Society.* Stanford, California: Stanford University Press, 1959.

2. Menger, Carl. *Problems of Economics and Sociology,* Edited by Louis Schneider, translated by F. J. Nock. Urbana, Ill.: University of Illinois Press, 1963.

3. Popper, Sir Karl R. *Conjectures and Refutations.* New York: Basic Books, 1962.

4. Rapaport, David. *The Organization and Pathology of Thought.* (Translations and a Commentary on Selected Sources.) New York: Columbia University Press, 1951.

5. Spinoza, Benedictus de (Baruch d'Espinoza). "Ethica Ordine Geometrico Demonstrata," in *Opera Posthuma.* Amsterdam: J. Rieuwentsz, 1667.

6. Willer, David, and George K. Zollschan. "Prolegomenon to a Theory of Revolutions," in George K. Zollschan and Walter Hirsch (eds.), *Explorations in Social Change.* Boston: Houghton Mufflin and Co., 1964, and London: Routledge, 1964.

7. Wittgenstein, Ludwig. *Tractatus Logio-Philosophicus.* London: Routledge and Keegan Paul, 1922.

8. Zollschan, George K. "Beyond the 'Reality Principle,'" in George K. Zollschan and Walter Hirsch (eds.), *Explorations in Social Change.* Boston: Houghton Mifflin and Co., 1964, and London: Routledge and Keegan Paul, 1964.

9. Zollschan, George K., and Philip Gibeau. "Concerning Alienation: A System of Categories for the Exploration of Rational and Irrational Behavior," in George K. Zollschan and Walter Hirsch (eds.), *Explorations in Social Change.* Boston: Houghton Mifflin and Co., 1964, and London, Routledge and Keegan Paul, 1964.

10. Zollschan, George K., and Donald A. Hansen. "On Motivation: Toward Socially Pertinent Foundations," in Donald A. Hansen (ed.), *Explora-*

[5] Some dialect of Wittgenstein's preference perhaps (7).

[6] Tests and measurement engaged in without genuine theory cannot advance scientific theory directly. They constitute harmless fun for mechanically-minded children. This is not to deny, however, that the development of tests and measures independently of adequate theory may prove useful when such theory is proposed.

*tions in Sociology and Counseling.* Boston: Houghton Mifflin and Co., 1969.

11. Zollschan, George K., and Robert Perucci. "Social Stability and Social Process: An Initial Presentation of Relevant Categories," in George K. Zollschan and Walter Hirsch (eds.), *Explorations in Social Change.* Boston: Houghton Mifflin and Co., 1964 and London: Routledge and Keegan Paul, 1964.

# SECTION FOUR

social system models of change

# Introduction

A major strength of structural-functionalism is its *vue d'ensemble* —
the panoramic view of social events considered so crucial by Durkheim
and before him by Comte, who, if not the initiator of the intellectual en-
deavours here represented, at least concocted their barbaric appellation.
Although this visual strategy of taking in the whole in one glance admittedly avoids the well-known pitfall of "not seeing the woods for the
trees," it is difficult to see how one can "find a way through the woods"
without having an equally acute perception of the individual trees. The
opening skirmishes of the theory of institutionalization, some of which
were presented in the previous section, have deliberately, and we hope
provocatively, eschewed such a *vue d'ensemble*. In Sections Two and
Three we have focused upon the "individual in society," stricken by
exigencies and articulating goals. Social structure is seen as a product
of the interaction of such persons seeking their goals, and also as a system (or, perhaps, a congeries) of loci of exposure of persons to different
exigencies.

Such an approach, Kingsley Davis' claims that functionalism and sociology are equivalent notwithstanding, is truly sociological without being
either functionalist or reductionist in character. It has some similarities,
to be sure, with the so-called micro-reductionism of contemporary mo-
lecular biology (that is, if one allows a somewhat generous analogy
between real organisms and merely conceptual "social systems"), but
it certainly is not reductionism in Davis' sense of reducing the level of
sociological analysis to what he understands to be a "psychological" one.

335

It may be viewed as reductionist in the special sense of reducing both "functional sociology" and "functional psychology," in his terminology, to something akin to what we may call the "rationale of the situational field." These "democratically imperialistic" claims of functionalism are strongly reminiscent of a Viennese working-class jingle of the pre-Hitler era (too simple to translate) which goes: *"Ich bin kein Jud, ich bin kein Christ, ich bin ein Kommunist."* Of course, one adds to this the further benevolent injunction "and so are you." The resulting "universalistic" professions have the potential of becoming rather dangerous. Another Viennese working-class jingle springs to mind, which replaced the aforementioned one after the advent of Hitler: *"Willst du nicht mein Bruder sein, dann schlag ich dir den Schaedel ein,"* ("If you don't want to be my brother, I'll smash your skull.") Over-exuberant members of the functionalist school (and a special school it was, is, and remains) should take this warning to heart, as indication of what can happen to people who do not distinguish between fish, flesh, and fowl.

Boskoff's brand of structural-functionalism is, certainly, far from over-exuberant. Indeed, serious concern with problems of social change appears to bring out the best in members of the structural-functional persuasion (for reasons which are not at all mysterious, at least to their critics). The trouble appears to be that so few of them have allowed themselves concerns of similar gravity. At the risk of indulging in some editorial over-exuberance of our own, we pronounce Boskoff's learned and deeply concerned contribution surely one of the clearest, best, and (not least important) most concise statements of the structural-functional position ever published. After erecting the customary scaffolding of functions, levels, and mechanisms, he adds a time dimension, reducing this to "sources of," "filtering or control of," and "reverberation to" innovative values and behavior. But only then does he take his really major step, and effectively use the ingredients of his system for the systematic production of hypotheses that, in principle at least, have the potential of being put to test. This move, in his own words, "from the comfortable level of *formulation* to the exciting but often disquieting level of demonstration" is cause for congratulation. There are two questions to be asked about Boskoff's amibitious program of research. Firstly, is the structural-functional scaffolding particularly crucial for any of the hypotheses put forward; could they not have been equally well constructed by a conflict theorist, or a formalist, or a social behaviorist, or what have you? Secondly (and independent of the first question), does his scaffolding lead to the production of more and "better" (that is, more readily testable) hypotheses? Boskoff, we know, will be the first to agree that these two independent questions provide the surest touchstones for future judgment of his ambitious, exploratory formulation.

David Lockwood, one of the earliest and boldest critics of structural-functional theory, with a swift and sure grasp comes, *inter alia,* to the conclusion that dialectical materialism is merely one variant of "functional" theory! But Professor Davis should mix his triumph with caution; Lockwood claims dialectical materialism forms a part of a *very* special and purified kind of functional theory. He sets his course with a distinction between two elements of functional theory: *normative integration*, and what he calls *system integration*. The first, which he suggests has drawn the fire of some of the critics of functionalism, emphasizes "common value elements" and insists that the "study of social stability must precede the study of social change." Lockwood rejects this variant of functionalism. The second contains the potentiality of "strain, tension, or contradiction" — it consists of the compatibility or incompatibility "between the dominant institutional order of a social system and its material base." Well — all this may be functionalism, but it certainly is not what Professor Davis means by it. Lockwood takes Marx's theory as the first illustration of his highly original sort of funtionalism and attempts to show that it constitutes a special case of system malintregation (the "production crisis" of capitalism). He then proceeds to compare this with the "embourgeoisement crisis" of the communist state. Translate his somewhat volatile "material base" into a "substratum of exigencies," and you get something very similar to the theory of institutionalization.

Kirk's chapter, by contrast, provides a very explicit link between functional theory and something very much like the theory of institutionalization. Starting with a concept he calls *situational discrepancy* (very much akin to the exigencies of the last section), Kirk moves on to another concept, *role handicap* (interferences with role performance) which he links with the foregoing. He then examines typical means of (attempted) adaptation and asks to what extent, if at all, these means served the desired end. The various phases of this model are illustrated with references to the relocation of Japanese-Americans during World War II, and the case of families with adopted children. His conclusions are applied to yet another case, that of the family with a retarded child. Kirk's chapter is a fundamental revision of an earlier chapter that appeared in the first edition of *Explorations in Social Change*. It constitutes a significant advance both in the elegance and in the applicability of his model. The chapter is included in this section (it might well have gone into the next) because of the model's potential for bridging some of the theoretical gaps between the foregoing chapters in this Section and those contained in the previous section of the volume.

In the Elysian Fields of Pythagorean number mysticism there must surely be an enclave reserved for the followers of Professor Markov. This is a very important area for behavioral scientists, for it is one of the few heavens populated by members of their own kind. Among their number, Beshers, superbly indifferent to the rival claims of functionalism and alternative theoretical formulations, makes his pronouncements in these pages. His remarks defining what he means by social change contain the statement that an effective causal analysis must be able to predict "no change" following the same laws with which we predict "change." Hence, the mechanism governing both social change and social stability operates something like a "balance of forces." All our authors would appear to be in agreement with these statements. Holding out the prospect of future mathematical conquests in such realms as the transmogrification of the "Protestant ethic" into capitalist production and exchange, Beshers confines himself to a somewhat simpler problem, namely, that of inter-generational social mobility. Although (like all mathematical writings) slow reading, the chapter is a model of lucidity and simplicity, and implications for more ambitious kinds of formalized problems of social change are clearly and temptingly spelled out.

# 12

*Alvin Boskoff*

# Functional Analysis as a Source

# of a Theoretical Repertory and

# Research Tasks in the Study

# of Social Change

Among sociologists and other social scientists, there is considerable disquietude about the prevailing inadequacies in analyzing and explaining social change (10; 48; 61, chapter 7; 45, pp. 810–818; 40, chapter 1). The problem of change, both in its theoretical and practical forms, has achieved an urgency for which scholars and administrators have been largely unprepared, except on an intuitive basis. Consequently, in recent years a variety of social scientists have re-focused their efforts on devising appropriate concepts, hypotheses, and related methods of gathering and analyzing crucial data concerning social change as a problem in its own right (74, pp. 18–33; 64; 18; 37; 77; 45; 69).

While it is perhaps too early to evaluate the results of this revivified concern, it may be in order to indicate briefly what seem to be the most disturbing shortcomings in theories of social change in the recent past. In fact, since this paper reflects another attempt to contribute to a theoretical renaissance, perhaps this summary critique can also provide an implicit set of standards for evaluating the discussion to follow. I believe five related points can be made:

1) Theories of social change have traditionally been too grandiose, too general, and therefore too simplified in their attention to the complex variables of social behavior. In trying to explain all social changes in all known societies for all historical periods, theorists have inevitably set forth over-extended and mutually competitive principles of change. Some well-known items would include: diffusion theory; imitation; invention; increasing heterogeneity; evolutionary stages; challenge and response; class conflicts; and inner or immanent tendencies (35, chapters 10, 14; 70; 71, chapter 5; 66). In reaction to such theories, some theorists have transferred their efforts to more restricted empirical levels, such as population change, marriage and family dynamics, social aspects of change in industrial systems, religious organization, and racial and ethnic relations. But often — and understandably — these specialized areas contain important substantive problems that deflect attention from social change per se.

2) Ever since Comte made the analytical distinction between social statics and social dynamics, sociologists have tended to erect a thick and impenetrable wall between analyses of structure and change. In practice, this meant either (a) ignoring one problem for the other, or (b) postponing analyses of change until problems of social organization (socialization, differentiation, stratification, power, and so on) could be defined and properly studied (10, pp. 260–262). Indeed, the textbooks in introductory sociology (even such outstanding ones as Kingsley Davis' *Human Society* or Bennett and Tumin's *Social Life*) generally treat social change as an uncomfortable appendage. As a result, change seems to be epiphenomenal — an accident, intrusion, or catastrophe — and sometimes a mystery (as "the little man upon the stair").

Furthermore, the controversially prominent structural-functional approach in its early development also seemed to emphasize structural problems. Its critics have rashly concluded that such an approach is therefore inherently incapable of analyzing change without horrendous damage to its conceptual structure (48; 61; 20; 34). But I shall later seek to show that the analysis of social change is not only feasible but theoretically and empirically enhanced by a modified structural-functional framework — a sociological equivalent of retaining the engine but shifting into higher gear.

3) A related difficulty of theories of social change is the failure to develop a distinctive (but not isolated) conceptual kit. On the one hand, change is not clearly defined in relation to such kindred concepts as social process, development, cycle, evolution, and adaptation, though MacIver, Znaniecki, and others have provided quite workable distinctions (36, pp. 405–415; 78, pp. 326–328; 10, p. 266). An equally gnawing problem has been an absence of general or specific concepts appropriate to change itself. Until recently, sociologists seemed to work primarily with *synonyms* — "dynamics," "variation," "alteration," "deviation" —

adding little to the *analysis* of change. Now we are beginning to exchange synonyms for such analytically promising concepts as "dynamic assessment" or "definition of the situation," "innovation," "transitional periods," "radical opposition," and "types of deviant behavior" (37; 3; 11). However, a minimal set of concepts for describing social change seems to await a systematic analysis of change, which is a major tenet of this chapter.

4) In view of the preceding criticism, it is not surprising that much confusion exists concerning the proper units of analysis. What should be the focus of study, observation, and measurement? The theoretical literature is all-encompassing; it includes personality types, social relationships, technology, value systems, institutionalized activities, control systems, stratification systems, communities, and politically or culturally organized societies. But what is (or are) the *crucial* unit(s) of analysis, as derived from theory and/or experience?

5) The last difficulty to be considered at this point is slowly receding: the traditional (and sometimes unconscious) concern with examining the *direction* or *trend* in social change, rather than a search for the "mechanics" or basic processes and conditions of change. Certainly, it is desirable to search for evidence of increasing rationality, variations in types of solidarity, processes of secularization, or alternations of Ideational, Idealistic, and Sensate supersystems. But the *conditions* of such changes have often been considered either in an a priori manner or as theoretical afterthoughts of a vague and non-empirical nature. As a result, change has tended to assume an inevitable, irreversible cast that precludes analysis of periods of little significant change or of successful resistance to change.

## Fundamental Problems in Analysis of Social Change

On the basis of the preceding discussion, and given the evolving nature of sociology and related disciplines, the fruitful study of social change appears to require attention to several basic problems. This is not a matter of demonstration, but rather one of probable utility — to be tested and revised through application and further discussion.

1) Analysis of social change is probably inseparable from prior identification of *analytically separable social systems* (54, pp. 3–5, pp. 68–81; 78, pp. 12–13; 79, p. 164; 13, pp. 95–98), preferably communities and national or "cultural" societies. The study of "dynamics" in *specific organizations* (e.g., an industrial firm or a government agency) or in *isolated institutional areas* (e.g., religion, family and kinship, art, education) is almost bound to ignore the operation of some important interrelations with influential groups. Thus, changes in family structure require close attention to the operation of the local status structure, the economic system, the politico-legal system, and perhaps educational and medical trends.

"System" is a concept easily misunderstood or taken with humorless literality. For most sociological purposes, a "system" may be simply conceived as an analytically isolated set of interrelated variables whose "identity" is sufficiently clear to permit a base point from which to study the operation of any implicated variable (6, pp. 125–134; 7, pp. 58–75; 32). Social systems, therefore, refer to socially relevant sets of behavioral variables that can be identified with concrete, relatively continuous interaction networks (groups, communities, societies). Note that living systems are inherently "dynamic" rather than marked by "true" or "stable" equilibrium, since "perfect" equilibrium is incompatible with action, reaction, or work (6, p. 132). Furthermore, it is neither logically nor empirically necessary to exclude or ignore from the concept of system such phenomena as tension, strain, and conflict — or even the presence of semi-autonomous units (53, chapters 12–14; 54, chapter 7; 26, pp. 241–270). But the notion of a "system" does involve the crucial assumption that the operation of these system-challenging phenomena does not interfere with the identifiability of the system over some time interval.

2) Once social change is identified with social systems, the distinctive nature of social change can be clarified — as compared with such concepts as "process," "development," and so on. Whereas "process," "development," and "cycle" deal with predictable variations in the operation of social systems (that is, in terms of the strength of the variables and their demonstrable interactive effects), based on study of *previous* phases of their operation, social change may be defined as significant variations from processual and developmental patterns (37, p. 27, pp. 63–65, p. 176, pp. 326–327; 79, p. 164; 10, pp. 263–266).

For example, a given community may experience growth in population, area, and number of organizations as a consequence of a healthy economic base. With increasing prosperity, congestion develops and the social and economic elites relocate themselves beyond the municipal boundaries. One result may be a diminution of local leadership, expressed in inadequate attention to recurring civic problems. This in turn may be followed by withdrawal of some firms to more "progressive" communities and thus an eventual population decline. While this is a somewhat fictitious illustration, it should be clear that the hypothesized "variations" are (1) highly significant for the entire system, and (2) not easily foreseeable or extrapolable from earlier processes or trends.

3) A third problem to which a theory of social change must give serious attention derives from the nature of change as significant but "unpredictable" variations in social systems. As MacIver and Znaniecki (among others) have persuasively argued, these interruptions in established patterns of social systems require a type of explanation different from that used for the genesis and development of social systems. Such an explanation must deal with social *causation,* that is, those processes that account for the *production* of significant variations and also for the *application*

or *containment* of such variations (37, pp. 63–65, p. 123, p. 176; 79, p. 164, pp. 224–231). Earlier theories of social change had either approached causation from a non-social standpoint (geography, race, destiny, divine will) or had prematurely fixed upon single social or psychological variables (for example, imitation, diffusion, "the great man," technological development [65, chapters 1, 2–7, 10, 11]). A more fruitful approach might redefine the problems of causation as marked by an interdependent series of decision-making processes in component social units of social systems. In this way, causation need not be the stepchild of assertion and vague generalization, but a product of statements faithful to fact about conscious and unconscious, direct and indirect, evaluative actions of identifiable persons, role-clusters, and organizations.

4) Although the two are undeniably interrelated, it is particularly important to distinguish between social change and cultural change (10, pp. 263–264; 74, p. 27; 79, p. 336, pp. 396–398; 23, p. 6; 75). A basic reason for this distinction is that the nature of these interrelations may and does vary and thus presents problems in causal analysis. If we define the cultural aspect as involving values and techniques approved for human adaptation to the socio-physical environment, and the social aspect as comprising the patterns of association and reciprocal influences connected with group formation, persistence, and change, then the complex interdependence-independence of social and cultural dimensions can be explored.

It can be generally accepted that, for a given population, associational patterns and value systems rarely develop at comparable rates or with great logical consistency. Instead of analyzing these differential rates in terms of cultural or social *lag*, perhaps it makes more sense to point to the flexibility of these dimensions. In research terms, both the social and the cultural can operate with respect to each other either as independent or dependent variables. For example, we know that persons in regular association generate "new" values or standards (for instance, work groups and informal quotas, scientific groups and "new" hypotheses). On the other hand, the application of a strongly held set of values can produce important alterations in pre-existing social relationships (for example, the abolition of slavery or the development of representative government). However, it is also evident that social and cultural variables *fail* to achieve significant effects in the other sphere. Reform movements (segmentally organized expressions of value systems) often eventuate in little or no genuine changes in the organization and operation of governmental, educational, and economic groups. And, as industrial sociologists have shown, organizational change may not be followed by desired valuational shifts among group members.

The import of this variety of interrelationships seems reasonably clear: it is unwise to treat social and cultural variables interchangeably or as consistently interdependent. Instead, we must view these dimensions and their operation as an important aspect of the causal analyses of social change, seeking types of variables that help to distinguish the emergence of each of the above-mentioned interconnections between social and cultural variables. Theories of social change will thus be enabled to unite hypotheses, inference, research techniques, and data with greater fidelity to the complexities of the phenomena of change.

## A Structural-Functional Orientation to Social Change

At the present stage of development in the social sciences, the most promising avenue to a comprehensive and workable theory of social change appears to be a suitably modified structural-functional approach (45; 15; 64). The prevailing opinion to the contrary stems, I believe, from a fixation on one or two characteristics of earlier formulations of this approach — characteristics that do not seem basic or inherent in modern structural-functionalism. The remainder of this chapter will therefore be devoted to: (1) a summary of fundamental postulates that define the nature of structural-functionalism; (2) a conceptual framework which provides an initial orientation toward social change; and (3) a set of researchable hypotheses derived from this framework.

### General Orientation

Since statements about structural-functionalism vary with each proponent and critic, a definitive formulation that cites chapter and verse is not possible. The interpretation that follows tries to avoid both the earlier exuberance of its champions and the tangential inadequacies pointed out by its critics. Consequently, my interpretation must in fairness be labeled a *modified structural-functionalism*, which can be sketched in a series of postulates.

1) The first requisite is the notion of conceptually closed systems of variables. Simply stated, this involves two further assumptions drawn from experience and pre-existing theory. First, it is assumed that the most crucial variables can be separated for analysis from the total complex of variables presumed to be relevant to some problem. The crucial variables are taken to represent aspects of *association* among persons — not biological traits, personality characteristics, or most categories of cultural patterns. Second, it is assumed that the crucial variables are sufficiently interrelated with one another to permit the analyst to construct an identifiable and meaningful entity (76, pp. 90–100; 4, chapter 5; 68, chapter 26).

2) Once identified in this manner, the system is presumed to operate in time and space through the working of its component variables. However, these variables over time are conceptualized in terms of patterned clusters or differentiated substructures, whose interdependent operation

is fundamental to the continued viability of the system. Furthermore, and this is a disputed point, the component structures of a system comprise a starting-point both for analysis of relative stability *and* change.

3) These substructures are conceived as specialized (but not necessarily rational or perfect) "solutions" to a repertory of "needs" of the system (31, chapter 4; 1). But it is misleading to refer to "needs" of a system; and it is equally unprofitable to speak of "needs" of individual members without a reductionism that logically precludes the concept of a social system. Instead, I would suggest that these needs have reference to problems of *relating* the performance of individuals to the interactive social networks (groups) in which they must act. It follows that the system is marked by an empirically definable range of adjustments of individuals to social networks, and vice versa. The relative importance of these types of adjustment is a painfully moot question in the annals of social theory.

4) The functional relations postulated as basic to social systems may be defined as (a) the demonstrable effects of one substructure on the operation of one or more other substructures in the same system, or the simple co-variation of two or more "parts" — for example, a change in the allocation of library space in a university and a consequent alteration in the availability of reserve readings for some courses, but with little or no noticeable effect on the university as a social system, and (b) the effect of any combination of substructures on the operation of the system as a whole, particularly with respect to other systems. Plainly, two methodological consequences should be pursued. First, to remove functional analysis from the realm of intuitive judgments, a *causal framework* (14, p. 173; 28; 47) and the investigation of *alternative causal sequences* in system variables and structures seems not only desirable but imperative. Second, the latter type of functional analysis provides a logical and practical justification for a structural-functional analysis of change.

5) Change *in* a system (process, development, differentiation) is equivalent to the first type of functional analysis. But change *of* a system (Type 2) — or social change — is likewise an integral part of the conceptual-theoretical kit of structural-functionalism.

6) The analysis of change (change of systems) follows an explicit bias that is consistent with previous postulates, but may be modified without destroying the fundamental thrust of this orientation. In general, the analyst first seeks for sources and precipitants of eventual change *within* the system (67, chapters 43–46; 54, pp. 201–207). Contrary to recent criticisms, this requires a *diachronic* or *historical* approach to systems, in order to locate (a) temporal points at which substructures may be shown to reflect altered operation or "new" (unpredictable) effects on other substructures, and (b) the *emergence of conditions* that help account for such shifts in operation and/or consequences. Since systems are

conceptually or analytically "closed," "external" variables often must be investigated. However, the analyst must demonstrate the significance of these external variables by investigating their effects upon specific substructures and upon the larger system.

The conceptual ingredients for a structural-functional analysis of social change have been available in various forms for more than a generation; they are basically simple and familiar, requiring no esoteric language or tortuous exposition, as some critics assert.

First, the operation of social systems is conceived as comprising four fundamental and interrelated processes (or system needs and functional problems). These processes can be investigated at the system level and also with reference to component structures or subsystems (55, chapter 4; 56, pp. 13–15). These are:

1) *The Adaptive Function.* The adaptive or instrumental function, through appropriate roles, serves to create and apply technical means through which aspects of the environment (physical and social) can be converted into objects and mechanisms suitable for the satisfaction of goals identified with systems or substructures. Adaptive structures therefore tend to exhibit a high degree of rationality, since judgments of efficiency and effectiveness can be quantitatively made and compared. Economic sectors of societies are largely adaptive, as are the breadwinner role in the family system, the purchasing office of universities, fund-raising committees of churches, and so on.

2) *The Goal-Attainment Function.* Each system (and in varying degrees, each subsystem) possesses a set of declared or implicit objectives which its representatives seek to achieve. These goals may be realizable or illusory; they may be variably beneficial or harmful to the system or to significant components of the system; and the source of these goals may range from rational discussion to charismatic imposition. In any case, the creation and pursuit of this function are major attributes of *political phenomena* in every compartment of human association.

Essentially, *political* aspects of behavior may be identified in those activities which organize or manipulate the behavior of others in order to realize some objectives for a social system. Thus, we may recognize "politics" not only in the maneuverings of public officials, but also in the choice of a desirable family vacation, in the revision of a college curriculum, and in price-fixing among competitive firms. Goal-attainment in each case is inherently "political" because the differential interests and values of the participants are *temporarily aligned* by the mechanisms of *power* (or infallible persuasion) to produce an artificial consensus reflected in behavior directed toward a common goal. In terms of this approach, all political phenomena represent the goal-attainment function. But not all goal-attainment is necessarily political, since a prior consensus (whatever its source) does not require the use of power as a leveler of difference or a dissipator of resistance.

3) *Tension-Management and Pattern-Maintenance.* The preceding two functions deal principally with the system's relation to its environment. "Internal" relations are of course interdependent with "external" relations, but the former may be analytically distinguished from the total operation of social systems with some profit. One extremely important "problem" in this regard is that of proper *motivation* of members to perform roles predictably. This is not merely a matter of learning role specifications; in addition, (a) members must often perform without immediate prospect of reward (that is, gratification must be deferred), and (b) members must retain in *latent* form appropriate attitudes and skills in the intervals between performances. The problem of deferred gratification, which has been called "tension-management," is normally handled by such mechanisms as discipline, graded and predictable sets of rewards (promotion, seniority, career patterns), formal education, and approved forms of tension reduction (sports, recreation, out-group aggression, and so on). The closely related problem of pattern-maintenance has been resolved in varying degrees by rehearsals and practice sessions, interim or "brush-up" training, pep talks, and other organized forms of exhortation.

4) *Integration.* The problem of integration is essentially one of maintaining the identity of a system and the attraction of its over-arching goals, which might otherwise be threatened by the necessary pursuit of adaptive, tension-management, and goal-attainment functions. In short, successful internal specialization may create narrowed and contradictory allegiances. Integrative processes serve to demonstrate or assert the common underlying interests and values of the members in component structures, as well as their collective difference from other systems. Some examples are the broad appeals of certain charismatic leaders, ceremonial occasions (in every cultural sector), and the use of "central" organizations with representation from constituent groups in a community.

## A Structural-Functional Hierarchy of Organizational Levels

We may now turn to a conceptual scheme that defines characteristic substructures for the operation of social systems, as formulated in recent years by Parsons (57, chapter 2). Essentially, Parsons has developed a functionally relevant typology of levels of group organization *within* societies. Each level of organization possesses: (a) a distinctive subsystem of social relationships; (b) some effective radius of responsibility; and (c) a special concern for one (or two) functional problems.

1) *The Primary-Technical Level.* The most basic operational unit is a relatively small group with clearly defined, rather narrow objectives. These objectives normally involve effective adaptation of persons and the physical environment to one another in order to make some predictable contribution to other units and thus to the larger system. In general,

these technical units are dependent on other units for equipment, standards of operation, and controls. Some illustrations are shop or factory crews, primary-school classes, nuclear family units (particularly during child-rearing periods), professional sports teams, symphony orchestras, and actors' companies.

2) *The Managerial Level.* To mediate and control the operations of several specialized but interdependent technical units, a managerial system normally develops. Essentially, managerial roles take as given some set of goals or policies, which guides processes of supervising technical units. Groups with managerial responsibilities therefore are extremely goal-oriented, but serve to achieve significant goals (for example, profit, educated persons, national aggression) by (a) providing tension-management and pattern-maintenance "services" to subordinate technical units, and (b) sustaining a "low-level" routine integration among such units. A bureaucratic system, which we can find in governmental, economic, religious, educational, and recreational spheres, is in these terms an ascending series of managerial units.

3) *The Institutional Level.* The operations of managerial units require support and legitimation in the form of: (a) goal specification; (b) development of some hierarchy or priority of goals; (c) "lending" superior prestige and authority to strengthen managerial decisions when challenged. This "policy-making" role complex is the property of the *institutional level* of organization, which is reflected in such concrete groups as boards of trustees, appellate or superior court systems, professional licensing organizations, independent regulatory commissions, and monocratic political systems. Normally, institutional groups coordinate managerial units within a *single* sector of cultural activities. As far as the four functional problems are concerned, however, institutional groups seem to focus on "internal" issues. A predominant concern is apparently with *integration* on the philosophical-abstract level (leaving its translation into profane operations to managerial units), with secondary emphasis on educational and honorific activities (pattern-maintenance).

4) *The Societal Level.* The most inclusive and complex organizational level is the societal, which provides coordination among specialized units at the institutional level as the latter provide coordination among managerial units. Conceptually, the societal level should be independent of specific institutional units, representing an inter-institutional core of values. In practice, however, societies have always witnessed the ascendancy of one of three types of institutional groups — governmental, economic, or religious — to the societal level. At the same time it should be noted that the assumption of full responsibility on the societal level is immeasurably difficult, as even despotic dictatorships have discovered. This simply means that complex social systems cannot achieve: (a) *parity* among specialized institutional groups; (b) *coherence* in interests and values of institutional groups; or (c) an *autonomous, socially impartial*

body that can long remain above the narrower socio-cultural bases of institutional levels — in short, the ideal of the philosopher-king. Consequently, some institutional groups may be said to achieve the quasi-societal level. This is particularly reflected in responsibility for relations with other systems.

A third important element in this conceptual framework, already strongly implicit in the preceding typology, is the patterns of control and coordination as these affect (a) the maintenance of action systems and the production of innovative behavior, and (b) the relative flow of innovative patterns to various subsystems. But a conceptualization of the *variety* of controls from a structural-functional standpoint has only recently been suggested by Parsons (57, chapter 5) and should be incorporated (on a trial basis, at least) in our framework.

Briefly, the coordinative-control complex is centered in the operation of the institutional level of organization. In practice, institutional controls are translated into *specialized functional mechanisms* that help maintain such key institutional tasks as (a) making binding policy decisions, and (b) implementing these decisions through allocating facilities and responsibilities to subordinate levels. These functional mechanisms are:

1) *Authority.* This concerns the right to make decisions on specific matters that are morally and practically unquestioned by subordinates.

2) *Authorization.* Obviously dependent on the prior existence of a system of authority, authorization refers to the process by which subordinate units are permitted to use authority for application to specifically defined situations or problems included within the radius of the superordinate authority. Thus, a department chairman in an American university may hire a staff member (a delegation of authority vested in the board of trustees and appropriate deans), but he may not in most instances compel the staff member to join a particular religious group.

3) *Regulation.* Unlike authorization, regulation involves a restricted type of control. Essentially, it involves general supervision of subordinate (usually technical) units by setting more or less definite "limits of acceptable action" for such units.

4) *Legitimation.* This is a broad, complementary process in the coordinative-control complex. Legitimation is a *sanctioning-evaluative* process, in which the actions of any social level are judged with reference to the *sacred core of values* in the total system, for which the institutional level is major representative and interpreter.

5) *Power.* According to the rather unique formulation by Parsons, and yet in line with the general orientation of structural-functionalism, power can be simultaneously viewed as a basic process of social systems and as a product of their operation. In the present context, power is primarily regarded as the generalized process by which the various resources of a social system are organized for achieving system goals. Thus,

power includes all the previously discussed functional mechanisms, which may be conceptualized as various legitimized patternings of power. A variable residue of force, coercion, threats, and unique manipulative practices is of course inherent in power. But *at the institutional level* this residue is taken to be small, by definition.

## A Structural-Functional Schema of Social Change: Analytical Phases

From these conceptual materials, we can derive at least two fundamental propositions concerning social change.

1) *Analytic stages in social change as a process.* In view of the earlier definition of social change ("significant variations from processual and developmental patterns of operation" of social systems), the description and explanation of change require an *historical* dimension so as to encompass the full course of processes of change. A structural-functional orientation toward change therefore posits a tentative three-phase sequence (10, pp. 289–302):

a) *Sources of innovative values or behavior.* In terms of the preceding framework, these sources are most likely to be technical and/or managerial levels of organization, or external sources (that is, derived from interaction with other systems). By its very nature, the institutional level is uncongenial to innovative roles *for itself.* This is of course in sharp contrast to theories of elites and leaders as initiators of change (52, pp. 1689–1694; 40, chapter 3; 71, chapter 11); but it is important to note that the statement asserts only that institutional levels do not participate *in the earliest stages* of innovation.

b) *The filtering process, or control of contributed innovations.* Because of the great significance of all four functional problems and the hierarchical system of social levels, innovations have little intrinsic meaning. They must be recognized, tried, and evaluated — a set of tasks which innovators themselves are largely unprepared to perform. In the social system, the major responsibility for such judgments is vested in the institutional level and its representative groups.

c) *Derivative structures and functional reverberations.* When innovations receive the sanction of control groups, attempts are inevitably made by subgroups at the managerial and technical levels to accommodate these innovations to any of the structural or functional components of the social system that seem to be significantly affected (in the form of pressures, threats, or extended opportunities) by the innovative practices (50, pp. 265–280; 49, chapters 12, 19). Thus, for example, the adoption of the wet rice system by the Tanala was followed by understandable adaptations in family structure, property, warfare and defense, and formal political organization (33, pp. 349–356).

2) The crucial stage is therefore phase (b), since phase (a) provides *possibilities* of significant change and phase (c) comprises the implemen-

tation of critical decisions (positive and negative) that are made during phase (b). In other words, phases (a) and (c) provide *necessary* components of social change, while phase (b) involves both *necessary* and *sufficient* conditions for given sequences of social change.

Two corollary propositions may be suggested at this point:

a) The process of social change reaches a significant point when the institutional level is ineffective in controlling the cumulation of variations and the strains of inconsistencies derived from such variations. This may be called *change by institutional default*. For example, modern metropolitan areas represent case studies of extensive and relatively uncontrolled change processes in which technical innovations (communication and transportation), changes in housing and space demands, and various permissible "inventions" in land subdivision and building have created severe challenges for institutional or policy-making groups. With negligible exceptions, these problems have not been successfully resolved in American urban regions because responsible leadership has failed to establish workable controls. Of course, this failure is essentially in line with the thinking of most urbanites. But the constantly evolving set of consequences is a transformation of urban living. One result is a sharpened segregation of status categories and associated styles of life. Another effect of institutional default is what Odum called "achievement lag," that is, an intensified insistence on realizing goals (gracious living, more land, spiritual progress, and other abstract ideals) for which the current technical-organizational facilities are unsuited. Change by institutional default is therefore experienced as "social problems," persistence of generally shared frustrations, and the temporary appearance of aimlessness that superficially resembles *stasis*.

b) The process of social change reaches a significant point when the institutional level undergoes significant variations in personnel and/or motivation in applying the functional control mechanisms. In this case, the institutional level has redefined its functional responsibility to include facilitation of proposed changes, with or without ulterior motives. This may be called *change by institutional acquiescence or facilitation*. A contemporary example of the effects of personnel change on the institutional level is the general shift to "liberal" interpretations in United States Supreme Court decisions. This may be traced to the New Deal period, but succeeding appointments (both Republican and Democratic) have largely altered the social philosophy of the Court. On the other hand, we may point to a motivational or valuational shift in an institutional elite in the case of the Japanese leadership less than 100 years ago. The Meiji Restoration adopted a formal political change (the revised role of the Emperor) and the technological bases of Western industrialism, but this was carried out by the prevailing leadership, which was thereby confirmed in its position in Japanese society.

### Toward a Theoretical-Research Repertory: Translating a Conceptual Scheme into Testable Propositions

The pursuit of these propositions requires considerable specification so that the theoretical import of this approach may be converted into researchable problems. Furthermore, it is important to underscore the interrelation of these research problems (and associated hypotheses) for an adequate theoretical system of social change. Consequently, each phase in the process of change will be translated into a series of hypotheses drawn from the initial framework and designed to explain the basic contribution of that phase to the overall process of social change.

#### Sources of innovative values or behavior

Hypotheses for this stage must deal with the conditions associated with structural and/or functional *opportunities* for variation, as well as the *motivations* for variation that can be attributed to structural and/or functional features of social systems. A representative set of such hypotheses might well include the following:

1) The greater the specialization of roles for discharging the four functional needs of social systems, the greater the opportunity for variation and innovation among technical and managerial persons in each functional division (adaptation, goal-attainment, pattern-maintenance, and integration) (57, pp. 62–66; 22, pp. 147–174, pp. 283–303). Thus, sacred societies (in which religious, political, economic, and socialization roles are concentrated in kinship groups) provide less evidence of innovation than that found in "civil," complex societies. The period of greatest experimentation in classical Greece — in government, art and literature, and religious cultism — followed the "reforms" of the sixth and seventh centuries B.C., which loosened the power of kinship, and permitted greater scope for military and economic enterprise. Similarly, innovations of a technical and organizational nature in industrial and commercial firms have increased in volume as an accompaniment of the shift from the small, partnership type to the complex corporate hierarchies of the present, with their internal specialization of production, personnel training, public relations, research and development, legal affairs, and political influence.

2) Other things being equal, adaptive and goal-attainment functions provide more opportunity for variation than the pattern-maintenance and integrative functions. As Merton, following Weber, has shown, once the impetus to innovation had been provided by the religious changes of the seventeenth century in England, the surge of scientific inventions in ensuing years was largely responsive to felt needs in industry and navigation. Of course, it is extremely difficult to compare — in a strict quantitative manner — economic and political innovations, on the one hand,

and artistic, educational, and familial innovations, on the other hand, during this period. However, it seems likely that seventeenth-century England was marked more by political and economic ferment than by changes in other spheres of activity.

3) The opportunity for adaptive and goal-attainment variations is directly related to complexity of societal types, with significant differences between folk and advanced secular types (49, chapters 14, 20; 59, chapter 12). For example, we would expect greater innovation and experimentation in technological aspects, forms of exchange and distribution, and in mechanisms of power and authority in complex, urbanized societies than in preliterate or "underdeveloped" societies. Not only are adaptive and goal-attainment functions more clearly specialized in complex societies; they are also assigned a special importance which, in practice, encourages "improvements."

The preceding hypotheses assume both constancy of motivation and some continuity of relations among the four functional needs. Since these are sometimes unwarranted assumptions, the following hypotheses may be tentatively offered:

4) The opportunity for variation is directly associated with significant shifts in the proportional effort (resources, time, personnel, verbalization, imagery, and so on) devoted by the social system to the four functional problems (29, chapter 32). As an illustration, Bales' study of small experimental groups seems to suggest that interaction focuses initially on appropriate ideas and a task-orientation (adaptive), then on organization of the group process to implement these ideas (goal-attainment). This is followed by indications of both hostile and amiable attitudes towards participants and by processes of composing these differences (tension-management); and subsequently by periods of common appreciation of the varied individual contributions toward solving the assigned task (integrative phase) (55, chapter 4). In a general way, but with considerably less precision in determining these "phases," American history reflects gross shifts in focus. The early republic was concerned with carving out and taming half the continental expanse, while a series of *policy* issues (the United States Bank, political rivalry, slavery, and so on) marked the period 1820–1860. The Civil War and Reconstruction reflected imperfect solutions to societal integration. By the '90's the adaptive emphasis became dominant again and soon questions of internal power struggles and then major foreign policy matters became insistent. After World War I, adaptive problems shifted somewhat to emphasis on socialization and broad educational problems (witness the growing importance of advertising, public relations, mass communications, and the seemingly incessant wrangles over educational philosophy and practice), while intermittent concern for national morale can be noted during the Great Depression and World War II.

a) One such pattern of shifts, analyzed by Sorokin, Toynbee, and

Parsons, involves a developmental, cyclical alternation of dominant societal concerns. Parsons and Bales (55, chapter 5) identify a "phase movement" pattern, for example, in which adaptation gives way to goal-attainment, then to pattern-maintenance and tension-management, to integration, again to adaptation, and so on. This of course assumes a relatively autonomous system. In any case, variant behavior is hypothesized to alter in intensity according to changing dominance of the four functions. An independent indication of functional dominance seems to be most imperative to prevent this from becoming a circular statement.

b) Significant shifts in the dominance of functional problems are (or can be) related to contacts with or pressures from other social systems and/or physical catastrophes, such as floods, earthquakes, drought, fires (24; 67, chapter 28).

5) Opportunity and motivation for innovation are directly related to the amount of interpersonal and intergroup conflict within each of the four functional areas, whatever the underlying reasons for such conflict (3, chapters 10, 14). Thus, innovations in industrial technology in Western nations have coincided with periods of heightened conflict between technical and managerial-institutional levels — though innovations can also be shown to be a source of such conflicts, as for example, the effects of commercial expansion on political divisions between aristocratic families and the new merchant families of classical Athens.

6) The opportunity and motivation for innovation within one or more functional areas are directly related to the amount of intergroup competition for dominance on the institutional level. For example, municipal inventions of the medieval period were a result of controversy between the previously dominant institutional leadership (clerical and noble-military) and the rising "technical" level of merchants (58). Similarly, "progressive education" is a set of innovations created by representatives of rising lower-middle-class and acculturating lower-class groups in opposition to the curriculum and philosophy of an aristocratically oriented (but socially "upper-middle class") elite (43). The adoption of "progressive" measures was dependent on prior change in the thinking and personnel of school boards (the institutional level) and superintendents (upper managerial level).

7) The opportunity and motivation for innovation are inversely related to *perceived* levels of efficiency in meeting specific functional needs. This of course involves the general problem of the relation between deviation and dysfunction. However, the concept of dysfunction needs greater empirical orientation, as suggested in the following subsidiary hypotheses:

a) The level of innovation or deviation within a given functional area is directly related to the *perceived* failure of existing practices in meeting that functional problem. In general, the effective motivation for innovation in this situation is more likely to be found among the "producers" of the "service" than the "consumers," though there is varying communication between consumers and producers. A tentative explanation for this locus of motivation may be the greater awareness of the availability of workable alternatives among technical and managerial units, and perhaps the seductive possibility that responsible (and approvable) variations can enhance status without directly challenging the position of the institutional level.

Martin Luther's famous assault on abuses in the Catholic church was an ideological innovation, not intended as a revolutionary thrust, from the "managerial" level. The same dependence on technical or managerial levels for innovation may be found in the military realm, particularly in the case of such originally contested innovations as the airplane, the tank, the aircraft carrier, and the atomic submarine. Finally, in the twilight zone between material and ideational inventions, mention might be made of the modern city-planning movement, which was (and is) largely an amalgam of notions and theories from architects, engineers, and a representative sprinkling of academic disciplines in close touch with local government (for example, economics and political science).

b) The level or amount of innovation within a given functional area is directly related to the perceived degree of overemphasis (in terms of allocated time, personnel, and resources) on otherwise legitimate objectives. Perception of overemphasis may occur at any of the organizational levels, but two foci of innovation responsive to this perception may be suggested.

(i) Technical units, by virtue of their specialized nature and subordinate position, are more likely to interpret the operations of managerial and institutional levels as "overemphasis" than *vice versa*. In a pattern-maintenance function such as formal education, for example, administrative (managerial) policies are often viewed by teachers (technical level) as beyond the bounds of necessity or wasteful of time more properly applied to more legitimate tasks. Innovative (deviant) responses are well-known to teachers: ignoring certain regulations or interpreting them to minimize paper work, political maneuvering by informal groupings of teachers, suggestions for shifting work to an available functionary, appointment of a special committee to "study the matter." Note that we are not required to evaluate the *utility* of innovations.

(ii) But a second source of innovation derives from technical (and managerial) units *outside* the area of perceived overemphasis. Because of the interrelated nature of the four functional problems, overemphasis in one area is sooner or later translated into indirect or direct interference with the operation of other subsystems. For example, much of the complex legal and administrative apparatus of the federal government during the past generation may be interpreted as necessary innovative reactions to the *perceived* autonomy or unbridled "imperialism" of an otherwise technically proficient and desirable economic system. Similarly, we may point to the perceived overemphasis on recreation and economic success asserted by many religious groups and the various non-religious attempts by such groups to attract and retain members, such as sponsored recreation, professionally conducted fund-raising, and baby-sitting facilities.

c) Finally, the level of innovation is directly related to perceived threats to the traditional operation of all organizational levels within a functional area that stem from changes introduced by other subsystems or by external systems. An excellent series of examples is surely the numerous and temporarily ingenious mechanisms by which judicially approved desegregation of public schools in the United States has been resisted in a number of Southern states by such tactics as pupil placement, tuition grants, privately operated grade schools, and even discontinuation of public schools. For this type of innovative situation, both experience and deductions from the general theoretical framework indicate that sources of innovation are likely to be found on several levels, including the institutional. This is of course a partial exception to the general hypothesis concerning the relative rarity of innovation among institutional groups. But it may be suggested that such "exceptions" occur when there is a high level of *consensus* (and therefore common perception of threat) among the various organization levels. Though evidence in these comparatively rare cases is understandably scanty, a plausible hypothesis can be advanced. We would expect that *initial innovations* derive from technical and managerial levels, while groups at the institutional level tend to innovate in response to perceived threats at a later period, in modification of earlier innovations, rather than as competitors or independent innovators.

None of these hypotheses seeks to identify highly specific categories of persons as predominant sources of deviation or innovation. The structural-functional framework thus far is restricted to concern with structural conditions favorable to innovation and to motivational patterns that enable broad categories of system members to perceive and utilize these structural opportunities. It is obvious that personality variables should also play some significant role in the operation and variability of social systems. In particular, personality variables should enable us to understand *why some but not all* persons in the preceding "innovative situations" respond in innovative or deviant ways. Some valuable clues may be found in the work of McClelland (41), Hagen (27), and Barnett (3). In the meanwhile, let us turn to the second phase.

## Control and Facilitation of Innovation

The basic propositions for this phase, as discussed previously, are: (1) that the control phase is the key to the overall process of social change, since the reception and derivative effects of innovation are largely determined during this stage; and (2) that the operation of the institutional levels is crucial to the facilitation or suppression of innovative behavior. Consequently, hypotheses directly concerned with the major factors in the structure and functioning of groups at the institutional level — as these contribute to promoting or arresting change — are extremely significant for a theory of social change.

1) Control or containment of innovations within any functional area — or within the system as a whole — is directly associated with success in pattern-maintenance and tension-management. In other words, the extent to which the institutional level can provide rewarding motivations to support existing practices and forms of relationships helps determine the diffusion and import of alternative (innovative) forms. Thus, it is suggested that the crucial function of institutional groups, as far as potential change is concerned, is neither goal-attainment nor integration, but "proper" socialization and motivation. Change is therefore indirectly but significantly fostered by prolonged deficiencies in performing the latter function.

2) Control or support of innovations by institutional groups is likewise related to characteristic patterns of interaction with subordinate levels. More specifically:

a) Control or promotion of innovation is associated with differentials in the bureaucratization (specificity of hierarchically-ordered responsibilities and control) of subsystems. In general, the more diffuse and the more flexible the system of interaction, the greater the opportunity for diffusion of innovations and the greater the likelihood that these will be ignored by personnel at the institutional level.

b) Closely related is the hypothesis that perception of innovations by institutional groups is conditioned by existing patterns of formal and informal communication (with respect to policy, orders, suggestions, grievances) with subordinate levels. Temporarily disregarding the personnel composition of the institutional level, we may suggest that one-way communication (from the top downward) reduces *perception* of innovation, and also serves to reduce potential diffusion of available innovations. Conversely, two-way communication may be expected to increase not only the likelihood of perception by the institutional level (and therefore opportunity for control) but also opportunities for the lower levels to influence superordinate levels to accept or approve innovations.

c) The response of institutional groups to innovation or deviation is associated with the selective pattern of control techniques adopted by such groups as a consequence both of (i) a previously preferred or legitimized range of techniques, and (ii) the relative security and prestige of current occupants of institutional roles. Institutional groups which rely on the more *direct* control mechanisms (for example, force or threat of force, personal influence over subordinates, prompt reward for prescribed actions or punishment for disapproved actions) tend to be uncomfortable and uncertain in their superordinate positions and therefore are more likely to feel uncongenial to innovation — unless it is under their own auspices. On the other hand, use of more *indirect* mechanisms of control (persuasion, manipulation, "divide and rule," political interchanges, and self-confirmatory compromises) may well indicate greater assurance and flexibility in assessing the responsibilities of the institutional level. In this case, innovations are more likely to be judged for their functional consequences (for a subsystem or the overall system). Of course, the probability of *correct* (pragmatically speaking) functional evaluations of innovations is a problem of great difficulty, part of which will be treated later.

3) Previous hypotheses have assumed a relatively invariant set of abilities, motivations, and socially relevant characteristics among members of institutional groups. However, historical data and the work of such theorists as Mosca (46), Pareto (52), Mannheim (39), Toynbee (71), Mills (44), and Dahl (19) strongly suggest not only recurrent changes in the composition of these groups — variously known as elites, power elites, top leaders, or influentials — but consequent changes in receptivity to innovation. Several specific applications of this theme seem to present possibilities of clarifying situations of potential change that remain unexplained by the previous hypotheses.

a) Changes in the criteria of recruitment into institutional elites help account for otherwise unpredictable reactions to innovations. Drawing upon clues contributed by Pareto (52) and Mannheim (39, pp. 86–96), we may analytically separate these criteria into two categories: one emphasizes ascribed qualities (such as race, family, inherited property), parochial interests, tradition, and direct controls; the other emphasizes previous achievement in some specialized endeavor, cosmopolitan interests, and the value of discussion, manipulation, and experimentation. Consequently, the latter would be more receptive to innovation than the former.

b) The relative *permeability* of institutional elites is likewise related to their general attitudes toward innovation. Those elites that restrict replacements to specific social categories, such as occupational or religious groups, without reference to internal differences in the above-mentioned qualities of members of such categories, tend to resist the diffusion of innovation, while elites with more varied social composition (other things being equal) are more exposed to divergent perspectives and thus view innovation with less hostility.

c) This of course raises the familiar problem of co-optation, the relatively voluntary process of absorbing socially and politically subordinate persons into the policy-determining level as a means of avoiding threats to its stability (62, pp. 217–226, pp. 259–261). In particular, what is the likelihood that innovative persons from technical and managerial levels will be co-opted by institutional groups and, more important, retain an innovative perspective?

Theoretical answers to this crucial problem have been few and rather inadequate, principally because relevant data have not been gathered. Since one function of hypotheses is to suggest some definite pattern or regularity, however incorrect later investigation may prove it to be, the following hypothetical statements may be of some value:

(i) Co-optation of managerial and/or technical levels by institutional elites is more likely in social systems that are characterized by comparatively specialized subsystems of power. "Democratic," "representative" systems (in government, economics, family affairs, and the like) carry on a structural dialogue between institutional and subordinate levels that limits the essentially sacred, arbitrary nature of institutional groups. For example, the traditional patriarchal family in Europe and America was marked by concentrated authority, as were the merchant guilds of latter-day feudalism. Co-optation was extremely difficult, for the existence of a serious challenge to incumbent policy-makers in either case was unthinkable. However, in the liberated middle-class family, both subtle and obvious forms of co-optation may be found in the wife's and the children's (managerial and technical levels) decisive influence on purchase and use of automobiles, family budget revisions, choice of vacation locales, family recreation patterns, and selection of proper mates for marriageable sons or daughters.

Furthermore, as Mosca (46, p. 244, p. 460) somewhat overextends a reasonably acceptable compound of fact and inference, in the long run there is a tendency for *all* "ruling minorities" to be recruited in terms of generally desired qualities that are appropriate to the needs of a given historical era. By implication, co-optation is a realistic necessity of social survival, regardless of differences in ideology and formal structure.

(ii) Co-optation is, from a structural-functional standpoint, a process associated with unique functional emphases characteristic of certain types of institutional groups. In general, it may be suggested that conditions which compel institutional groups to emphasize goal-attainment likewise create greater *access* of already innovative persons to the institutional level. Essentially, groups with prominent adaptive and goal-attainment functions tend to give more attention to the latter aspect during crisis situations — either when persistent failures accumulate or when new opportunities for success present themselves (the *windfall* situation). Crisis normally places an additional premium on *achievement,* to which the institutional level is particularly attuned, not only for the future of the system, but also to sustain the prestige of institutional personnel. Consequently, in view of the structural limitation on innovation among persons at the institutional level (previously discussed), it becomes necessary to seek fresh assistance from subordinate levels. Failure to do so is not unknown (for example, Hitler and the Romanovs),[1] but co-optation in one form or another is widely practiced in industrial organization, political parties at many levels, and sometimes in academic settings.

Parenthetically, it is quite probable that the general lack of co-optation (and, comparatively, of change) in religious, familial, and legal realms stems from a characteristic emphasis on *integrative* and *pattern-maintenance* functions. Indeed, under these conditions, change seems to require "social movements," which normally base their appeal on a goal-attainment theme, bolstered by charismatic persons who promise higher fulfillment of "neglected" values. Charisma, in this context, may be simply defined as an effectively personal attempt at innovative goal-attainment.

### An Empirical Typology of Social Change Situations

The range of hypotheses presented for the innovative and control-coordinative phases of social change gives some indication of the *complexity* that inevitably accompanies processes of social change. One aspect of this complexity implicit in our discussion thus far concerns the *alternative empirical courses* (direction, rate, and amount of resistance) that potentially and actually develop in social change phenomena. For convenience, then, let us construct an empirically relevant typology of social change situations that may be conceived as products of phases (a) and (b). This typology may well be based on four interrelated variables or dimensions:

1) The relative autonomy or vulnerability to external influences of the social system.

2) The *source* of innovation — internal or external.

[1] For example, the breakdown of Nazi Germany can in part be attributed to Hitler's refusal to accept competent military advice from professional officers. Many of his decisions from 1941 to 1945 were based on improvisation and an essential distrust of his General Staff. See H. R. Trevor-Roper (72, pp. 7–11, pp. 28–30, pp. 233–236); and Walter Ansel (2, pp. 76–86, chapter 10). Likewise, the Romanov Tsars during the period 1870 to 1914 steadily weakened their positions by failing to adopt rather mild political reforms which would have given more responsibility and a sense of identification with the government to various strata. In particular, the shackling of the powers of the Duma opened the way for subsequent revolutions. See Hugh Seton-Watson (63, pp. 48–49, chapters 2, 5, 8, epilogue); and Richard Charques (16, chapters 1, 7, 10).

3) Dominant response patterns of the institutional level — rigidity, passive acquiescence, active facilitation.

4) Short term effects of (2) and (3): strain, inconsistency, and limited change; relatively orderly change; rapid and disorderly change.

Out of the numerous logical combinations of these dimensions, however, four types seem to be most frequently encountered:

1) Gradual, orderly change in social systems marked by relative isolation and stable institutional groups.

2) Structured strains in social systems with rigid containment or suppression of innovation by dominant institutional levels.

3) Externally imposed innovations in social systems whose institutional groups are unable to channel or control the consequences of innovation.

4) Planned, internally based change in social systems characterized by unchallenged institutional groups operating on the societal level and either developing their own innovations or sponsoring specialized, technical units designed for solicited innovations.

### Derivative Consequences

From either a theoretical or empirical standpoint, it is abundantly clear that the development and legitimation of innovations are followed by a variable amount of secondary or "unanticipated" effects — both cultural and social organizational — on implicated social systems. One portion of the efforts of sociological and anthropological theorists in the past has been devoted to providing a generalized explanation of these consequences, with uncomfortably mixed results. This is of course an exceedingly difficult problem, one for which monistic determinisms of any sort cannot adequately supply a solution. However, once again the data of ancient and recent history, and a structural-functional framework, can be interpreted to give promise to several theoretical points.

a) Following the approved, institutionally sanctioned practice of some innovation, or the satisfactory but unsanctioned dissemination of an innovation, there is some alteration in the relative efforts given to the four functional problems, either in the overall system or in a significant subsystem. In short, the process of change encourages revised functional emphases, which are expressed in new skills and "knowledge," new or expanded roles and groups, and a new or heightened attraction of persons with appropriate characteristics. Innovation therefore furnishes opportunities for previously unused or unrewarded skills and thus increases potentialities for new organizational forms. Thus, the military, political, and economic changes of the tenth through the fourteenth centuries in Western Europe opened the way for merchant organizations and urban changes (that is, a shift from integrative to adaptive and goal-attainment emphases), just as the changes embedded in the failure of the Weimar Republic soon eventuated in the Nazi movement and the dominance of the lower-middle class in the German bureaucracy — a shift from adaptive to goal-attainment and integrative emphases (25, pp. 517–541).

b) Though there are undoubtedly pockets of autonomy in every social system, the fact that at least some integration exists among the component groups of society and among the functional problems the society has to solve insures that an approved innovation in one activity will have effects on one or more other functionally significant activities. The *typical direction* of these adaptations has long been a moot question in sociological theory — perhaps, from the present framework, a misleading and fruitless question. In general, however, complex societies may exhibit a certain priority in adaptive and goal-attainment functions, with derivative changes in pattern-maintenance (family, education) and integrative functions (law, religion). For simpler societies that retain cultural-geographic isolation, it is even more difficult to detect regularities of this sort. We can venture a plausible guess: by the debatable evidence of differential complexity, both religion and kinship provide greater opportunities for initial or "trigger" innovations, with derivative effects on economic systems, "power structure," and "science."

c) Intimately connected to (b) is the widespread phenomenon of relatively uneven processes of derivative change, which demonstrates that societies cannot be perfectly integrated in practice, or that some segment recurrently diminishes coordinative or integrative relations when the process of change attains an advanced state. But the presence of "lag" or differential rates of change is unquestionable. Two crucial theoretical problems arise at this point, for which the structural-functional schema may furnish useful clues.

First, what conditions contribute to uneven change? Though other explanations have been presented by Veblen (73), Ogburn (50, Part III), and Odum (49), the differential emphasis on functional problems — found in all social systems as a matter of practicality — is inevitably expressed in differential application of resources toward adjusting other areas to legitimized innovation. In addition, there is normally some competition among institutional groups representing the major specialized activities of complex social systems. Finally, uneven change results from the varied maneuvers of institutional groups engaged in contests for a *societal level* of functioning.

The second problem concerns the "normal" consequences of uneven change. In the most general terms, uneven change both produces and reflects a period of transition (9; 10, pp. 297–299), in which the most visible signs are a range of social problems and a continued incapacity to diminish the personal and social inefficiencies that accompany such problems. More specifically, periods of transition are marked by: (1) significantly reduced satisfaction of one or more societal functions; (2) uncertainty in the operation of institutional, managerial, and perhaps the technical levels; (3) one or more attempts to provide integration by direct mechanisms (force, fear, hysteria, witch-hunting, tightened controls, and the like) operated by institutional and managerial levels; (4) a derivative motivation for change (rather than for specific innovations) among technical and some managerial groups; and (5) a series of variably spaced "social movements" which do not seek fundamental, radical innovations, but rather innovations — in personnel and in responsibilities of institutional and managerial levels — that permit the consolidation and effective operation of previously sanctioned innovations. For example, the agrarian movements in the United States from 1870 to 1924 or so were basically devoted to obtaining greater political representation and more equitable economic returns ("parity") from a society in which desired technological change and organizational developments seemed to favor the urban segments of the nation.

Thus, in the structural-functional approach, change and tension (dysfunction) are reciprocally intertwined. Innovations initially arise in "normal" and/or disturbed functioning of social systems. When accepted, these in turn create further tensions, traceable to uneven derivative adjustments. And these tensions — expressed in social problems — incite further, presumably stabilizing changes.

d) A highly significant consequence of the preceding processes is, eventually, a corresponding change in the system(s) of stratification (8, pp. 124–125, pp. 130–131). This appears to be a complex and partly invisible or latent set of interrelations. The following simplified analysis is therefore presented provisionally, with the hope that its theoretical components provide a base for inevitable improvements.

Regardless of source or motivation, innovations devised in the first phase create new or greatly revised social roles for some members of a system. These roles may be associated either with a *shift* in functional emphasis (the scientific or research administrator is a recent and somewhat poignant example of such a shift) or with the attempt to discharge some consistently evaluated function (for example, pattern maintenance and the "progressive teacher" role). In either case, new roles and their occupants come to be evaluated in terms of (1) relative efficiency in providing solutions to a major functional problem, and (2) the organizational level at which the role is performed. According to prevailing general patterns of evaluation, new roles (and their occupants) likewise acquire special rewards, privileges, opportunities, and levels of prestige. Change processes, then, spawn roles that confer status, while in stable periods given status levels selectively entail certain role obligations or role-sets (42).

However, new roles and statuses also create new interactional possibilities, most significantly with traditional status groups. The result is some degree of status inconsistency (5; 30), which to some participants and observers seems to mean diminished stratification. Over longer periods, however, status inconsistency seems to reflect the changing relations among the four functional problems and the concomitant variations in the hierarchical and power position of competing institutional groups. Changes is social class systems can be charted, therefore, in terms of the weight assigned to ethnic background, family name and inheritance (pattern-maintenance), religion (integration), occupational type and earned income (adaptation), political influence and opinion leadership (goal-attainment).

e) A final and admittedly broad category of derivative consequences is *cultural,* comprising a range of demonstrable adaptations to change in the form of value systems, shared attitudes and opinions, and common aspirations — as these are expressed in philosophies, theologies, literature, recreation, and the arts. Essentially, derivative cultural changes perform two important tasks for participants in social systems. On the one hand, they provide a practical response to the altered "balance" of functional problems, as *rationales,* apologies, or sanctifiers. Alternatively, they serve as coherent protests (direct or indirect) to such changes. The relation between these types of cultural adaptation and Mannheim's (38) analysis of "ideologies" and "utopias" is immediately apparent. But the problem of demonstrating unambiguous relations between adaptive cultural productions and functionally differentiated social segments remains a formidable one for the sociology of knowledge and an overall theory of the process of social change (42, chapter 12; 17; 21).

## Conclusion

The analysis and understanding of social change are probably the most crucial task of sociology, both in its relation to other social sciences (12) and in its overall contribution to modern society and its problems. Consequently, whatever label is applied, any theoretical scheme that seeks to provide a detailed examination of the basic mechanisms of social change merits some attention and the leaven of criticism. I believe a modified structural-functional scheme constitutes the most promising available means of analyzing change. With the kinds of modification and explication suggested throughout this chapter, it is perhaps time to stop the oft-repeated but unexamined criticisms of structural-functionalism — in particular, the untenable assertion that functionalism contains a static model inapplicable to conflict, external factors, or change. Instead of a priori judgments, I suggest that sociologists put functional concepts and hypotheses to the test of use; only then can needed improvements be made.

What, briefly, are the potential contributions of this approach?

First, social change may be theoretically linked with its alleged "opposite" — order, stability — as extremes of the same continuum: the operation of social systems. Change, therefore, cannot be viewed as either inevitable or impossible.

Second, social change may be approached, not as a morass of seemingly vagrant processes, but as a product (along with stability) of the *variable capacity of social systems for generating and channeling innovative processes.* This compels us to approach change and order as probabilistic alternatives, as contingent effects of interrelated system components in their "historical" operation. And this in turn requires a renewed concern for usable classifications of social systems, in contrast to the traditional attraction for dichotomous societal types.

Third, the postulates and hypotheses discussed previously, despite their limitations, enable us to identify different types of change situations and, ultimately, to relate these types to a typology of social systems. In this way, the general explanatory value of our approach can be adjusted to the empirical variety of historical and contemporary social changes without yielding to the twin dangers of fragmentation or the reactive arbitrariness of Procrustean generalization.

Finally, this approach — and any alternative, coherent theoretical orientation — requires us to move from the comfortable level of *formulation* to the exciting but often disquieting level of *demonstration*. With some such scheme, sociologists can develop a growing fund of comparable, theoretically informed case studies of social change — in communities and societies — and for any historical period for which reasonably adequate data exist.

## BIBLIOGRAPHY

1. Aberle, David, *et al.* "The Functional Prerequisites of a Society," *Ethics*, Vol. 60 (1950), pp. 100–111.

2. Ansel, Walter. *Hitler Confronts England.* Durham, N.C.: Duke University Press, 1960.

3. Barnett, Homer G. *Innovation: The Basis of Cultural Change.* New York: McGraw-Hill Book Co., 1953.

4. Becker, Howard. *Through Values to Social Interpretation.* Durham, N.C.: Duke University Press, 1950.

5. Benoit-Smullyan, Emile. "Status, Status Types, and Status Interrelations," *American Sociological Review*, Vol. 9 (1944), pp. 151–161.

6. Bertalanffy, Ludwig von. *Problems of Life.* New York, N.Y.: John Wiley and Sons, 1952.

7. Bertalanffy, Ludwig von. "General System Theory," in Richard W. Taylor

(ed.), *Life, Language, Law: Essays in Honor of Arthur F. Bentley.* Yellow Springs, Ohio: Antioch Press, 1957.

8. Boskoff, Alvin. "Negro Class Structure and the Technicways," *Social Forces,* Vol. 28 (1950), pp. 124–131.

9. Boskoff, Alvin. "Postponement of Social Decision in Transitional Society," *Social Forces,* Vol. 31 (1953), pp. 229–234.

10. Boskoff, Alvin. "Social Change: Major Problems in the Emergence of Theoretical and Research Foci," in Howard Becker and Alvin Boskoff (eds.), *Modern Sociological Theory.* New York: Dryden Press, 1957.

11. Boskoff, Alvin. "Social Indecision: A Dysfunctional Focus of Transitional Society," *Social Forces,* Vol. 37 (1959), pp. 305–311.

12. Boskoff, Alvin. "Recent Theories of Social Change," in Werner J. Cahnman and Alvin Boskoff (eds.), *Reader in Sociology and History.* New York, N.Y.: The Free Press of Glencoe. (In press)

13. Blumer, Herbert. *An Appraisal of Thomas and Znaniecki's The Polish Peasant in Europe and America.* New York: Social Science Research Council, 1939, Bulletin 44.

14. Bredemeier, Harry C. "The Methodology of Functionalism," *American Sociological Review,* Vol. 20 (1955), pp. 173–180.

15. Cancian, Francesca. "Functional Analysis of Change," *American Sociological Review,* Vol. 25 (1960), pp. 818–827.

16. Charques, Richard. *The Twilight of Imperial Russia.* London: Phoenix House, 1958.

17. Child, Arthur. "The Theoretical Possibility of the Sociology of Knowledge," *Ethics,* Vol. 51 (1941), pp. 392–418.

18. Cottrell, Fred. *Energy and Society.* New York: McGraw-Hill Book Co., 1955.

19. Dahl, Robert A. *Who Governs?* New Haven: Yale University Press, 1961.

20. Dahrendorf, Ralf. "Out of Utopia," *American Journal of Sociology,* Vol. 64 (1958), pp. 115–127.

21. DeGré, Gerald L. *Society and Ideology.* New York: Columbia University Press, 1943.

22. Durkheim, Emile. *The Division of Labor in Society.* Glencoe, Ill.: The Free Press, 1947.

23. Eggan, Fred. *Social Organization of the Western Pueblos.* Chicago: University of Chicago Press, 1951.

24. Firey, Walter. "The Responsiveness of Interaction Patterns to Emergency," *Social Forces,* Vol. 21 (1942), pp. 17–21.

25. Gerth, Hans H. "The Nazi Party: Its Leadership and Composition," *American Journal of Sociology,* Vol. 45 (1940), pp. 517–541.

26. Gouldner, Alvin W. "Reciprocity and Autonomy in Functional Theory," in Llewellyn Gross (ed.), *Symposium on Sociological Theory.* Evanston, Ill.: Row, Peterson and Co., 1959.

27. Hagen, Everett E. *On the Theory of Social Change.* Homewood, Ill.: Dorsey Press, 1962.

28. Hempel, Carl G. "The Logic of Functional Analysis," in Llewellyn Gross (ed.), *Symposium on Sociological Theory.* Evanston, Ill.: Row, Peterson and Co., 1959.

29. Herskovits, Melville J. *Man and His Works.* New York: Alfred J. Knopf, 1947.

30. Lenski, Gerhard E. "Status Crystallization: A Non-Vertical Dimension of Social Status," *American Sociological Review,* Vol. 19 (1954), pp. 405–413.

31. Levy, Marion J. *The Structure of Society.* Princeton, N.J.: Princeton University Press, 1952.

32. Lillie, Ralph Stagner. *General Biology and Philosophy of Organism.* Chicago: University of Chicago Press, 1945.

33. Linton, Ralph. *The Study of Man.* New York: D. Appleton-Century, 1936.

34. Lockwood, David. "Some Remarks on 'The Social System'," *British Journal of Sociology,* Vol. 7 (1956), pp. 134–146.

35. Lowie, Robert H. *The History of Ethnological Theory.* New York: Rinehart and Company, 1937.

36. MacIver, Robert M. *Society.* New York: Farrar and Rinehart, 1937.

37. MacIver, Robert M. *Social Causation.* Boston: Ginn and Company, 1942.

38. Mannheim, Karl. *Ideology and Utopia: An Introduction to the Sociology of Knowledge.* London: Kegan Paul, Trench and Trubner, 1936.

39. Mannheim, Karl. *Man and Society in an Age of Reconstruction.* New York: Harcourt, Brace, 1940.

40. Martindale, Don. *Social Life and Cultural Change.* Princeton, N.J.: D. Van Nostrand Company, 1962.

41. McClelland, David C. *The Achieving Society.* Princeton, N.J.: Van Nostrand, 1961.

42. Merton, Robert K. *Social Theory and Social Structure.* Glencoe, Ill.: The Free Press, 1957.

43. Mills, C. Wright. "A Sociological Account of Some Aspects of Pragmatism." Ph.D. dissertation, University of Wisconsin, Madison, 1942.

44. Mills, C. Wright. *The Power Elite.* New York: Oxford University Press, 1956.

45. Moore, Wilbert E. "A Reconsideration of Theories of Social Change," *American Sociological Review,* Vol. 25 (1960), pp. 810–818.

46. Mosca, Gaetano. *The Ruling Class.* New York: McGraw-Hill Book Co., 1939.

47. Nagel, Ernest. "A Formalization of Functionalism," in *Logic Without Metaphysics.* Glencoe, Ill.: The Free Press, 1956.

48. Nisbet, Robert A. "Social Structure and Social Change," *Research Studies*

*of the State College of Washington.* Pullman, Wash.: Vol. 20 (1952), pp. 70–76.

49. Odum, Howard W. *Understanding Society.* New York: The MacMillan Co., 1947.

50. Ogburn, William F. *Social Change.* New York: B. W. Huebsch, 1922.

51. Ogburn, William F., and Meyer F. Nimkoff. *Technology and the Changing American Family.* Boston: Houghton Mifflin, 1955.

52. Pareto, Vilfredo. *Mind and Society,* 4 vols. New York: Harcourt, Brace, 1935, Vol. 4.

53. Parsons, Talcott. *Essays in Sociological Theory Pure and Applied.* Glencoe, Ill.: The Free Press, 1949.

54. Parsons, Talcott. *The Social System.* Glencoe, Ill.: The Free Press, 1951.

55. Parsons, Talcott, Robert F. Bales, and Edward A. Shils. *Working Papers in the Theory of Action.* Glencoe, Ill.: The Free Press, 1953.

56. Parsons, Talcott. "The Role of General Theory in Sociological Analysis," *Alpha Kappa Deltan,* Vol. 29 (1959), pp. 12–38.

57. Parsons, Talcott. *Structure and Process in Modern Societies.* New York: The Free Press of Glencoe, 1960.

58. Pirenne, Henri. *Medieval Cities.* Princeton, N.J.: Princeton University Press, 1925.

59. Redfield, Robert. *The Folk Culture of Yucatan.* Chicago: University of Chicago Press, 1941.

60. Redfield, Robert. *The Primitive World and its Transformations.* Ithaca, N.Y.: Cornell University Press, 1953.

61. Rex, John. *Key Problems of Sociological Theory.* London: Routledge and Kegan Paul, 1961.

62. Selznick, Philip. *TVA and the Grass Roots.* Berkeley, Calif.: University of California Press, 1949.

63. Seton-Watson, Hugh. *The Decline of Imperial Russia.* New York: Frederick A. Praeger, 1952.

64. Smelser, Neil J. *Social Change in the Industrial Revolution.* London: Routledge and Kegan Paul, 1959.

65. Sorokin, Pitirim A. *Contemporary Sociological Theories.* New York: Harper & Bros., 1928.

66. Sorokin, Pitirim A. *Social and Cultural Dynamics,* 4 Vols. New York: American Book Co., 1937–1941.

67. Sorokin, Pitirim A. *Society, Culture, and Personality.* New York: Harper & Bros., 1947.

68. Spiethoff, Arthur. "Pure Theory and Economic Gestalt Theory: Ideal Types and Real Types," in Frederic C. Lane and Jelle C. Riemersma (eds.), *Enterprise and Secular Change.* Homewood, Ill.: Richard D. Irwin, 1953.

69. Steward, Julian. *Theory of Culture Change.* Urbana, Ill.: University of Illinois Press, 1955.

70. Tarde, Gabriel. *The Laws of Imitation.* New York: Henry Holt, 1903.

71. Toynbee, Arnold J. *A Study of History.* Abridged by D. C. Somervell. New York: Oxford University Press, 1947.

72. Trevor-Roper, H. R. *The Last Days of Hitler.* New York: The Macmillan Co., 1947.

73. Veblen, Thorstein. *The Theory of the Leisure Class.* New York: The Modern Library, 1934.

74. Vogt, Evon Z. "On the Concepts of Structure and Process in Cultural Anthropology," *American Anthropologist,* Vol. 62 (1960), pp. 18–33.

75. Weber, Alfred. *Fundamentals of Culture-Sociology.* New York: Columbia University (mimeographed), 1939.

76. Weber, Max. *The Methodology of the Social Sciences.* Glencoe, Ill.: The Free Press, 1949.

77. Wilson, Godfrey, and Monica Wilson. *The Analysis of Social Change.* Cambridge: Cambridge University Press, 1945.

78. Znaniecki, Florian. *The Method of Sociology.* New York: Rinehart, 1934.

79. Znaniecki, Florian. *Cultural Sciences.* Urbana, Ill.: University of Illinois Press, 1952.

# 13

*David Lockwood*

# Social Integration and

# System Integration

The term "social change" will be taken to mean a change in the institutional structure of a social system; more particularly, a transformation of the core institutional order of a society such that we can speak of a change in type of society. I do not believe that it is necessary to reach agreement on what is meant by the "core institutional order" of a society or on how a typology of societies is to be differentiated before there can be meaningful discussion of how the process of change takes place. That is, unless there is some a priori commitment to a "dominant factor" theory of social change; in which case the wrangle about whether change has "really" taken place can be endless.

The main purpose of this chapter is to discuss some of the implications of recent criticisms of functionalism, especially those which have a bearing on how social change is internally generated in a society. The thesis is that, in concentrating their fire on a special, albeit prominent, version of functionalism ("normative functionalism"), critics have become over-involved with what may be called the problems of "social integration." As a result, they have tended to ignore what is just as relevant to their central interests in conflict and social change, namely, the problem of "system integration." And here the perspective of general functionalism would still seem to be the most useful instrument.

# I

In a recent article, Kingsley Davis (6) has proposed such a catholic definition of functionalism as to make it virtually indistinguishable from the most basic presuppositions of contemporary sociology. This is all very comforting. But if by functionalism nothing more were meant than seeing society as a system of interdependent parts, and an aversion to "reductionism," then most of those who have been engaged in criticism of functionalism would be proselytized overnight. How many would accept the attendant ideas, such as that of "functional requisites," is more debatable, and would probably depend on how they were interpreted. Again, exactly what elements are included as "parts" of a social system, and the exact implications of the idea of "interdependence" itself, are obviously areas of potential disagreement (10).

But, omitting these considerations, surely the "general" functionalist standpoint which Davis has restated must be distinguished from its more specific and controversial form. Davis avoids mentioning precisely those characteristics which are now widely associated with, though not logically entailed by, a functionalist orientation: first, the emphatic role attributed to "common value elements" in the integration of social action; and second, the unwarranted assumption that the study of social stability must precede the analysis of social change. Both these predispositions, but especially the first, typify what we wish to speak of from now on as normative functionalism.[1]

Before going on to examine the position to which we are led by the critics of normative functionalism, one further distinction is relevant to the subsequent argument. It is the wholly artificial one between "social integration" and "system integration." Whereas the problem of social integration focuses attention upon the orderly or conflictful relationships between the *actors,* the problem of system integration focuses on the orderly or conflictful relationships between the *parts,* of a social system.

It may be said at once that the connection between these two aspects of integration is neatly made by normative functionalism. The logic is simple. Since the only systematically differentiated parts of a society are its institutional patterns, the only source of social disorder arising from system disorder is that which takes the form of role conflict stemming from incompatible institutional patterns. If, however, it is held that such institutional patterns do not exhaust the generally relevant "parts"

---

[1] Gouldner quite properly points out that this tendency has amounted to what is in fact "implicit factor-theorizing": "Although the methodological position of the earlier functionalists commonly affirmed an amorphous interdependence of parts within a social system, it does not follow that the specific empirical analysis in which they engaged actually utilized this principle. In particular, the classic contributions, from Comte to Parsons, have gone out of their way to stress the significance of 'shared value elements' in maintaining the equilibrium of social systems" (10, p. 265).

of a social system, then this particular articulation of system and social integration is only one way of relating the phenomena of "deviance" and "conflict" to the operation of the system as a functioning entity. To this point we shall return later. For the moment, what needs stressing is that the critics of normative functionalism have devoted their critique entirely to the way in which this theory handles the problem of social integration; and particularly to the ambiguities of the concept of "institution."

## II

The leading exponent of the general functionalist school, Robert K. Merton, has already drawn attention to the static connotation of the term institution: "It is not enough," he writes, "to refer to the 'institutions' as though they were all uniformly supported by all groups and strata in the society. Unless systematic consideration is given to the *degree* of support of particular 'institutions' by *specific* groups we shall overlook the important place of power in society" (15, p. 122). The major criticism of normative functionalism which has frequently been made is that it treats institutions primarily as moral entities, without rigorously exploring the interplay between norms and power that is universally present in major institutional contexts. This weakness has been seized upon by such writers as Dahrendorf (5) and Rex (19). Their basic theses are sufficiently similar to be treated jointly. For the sake of convenience, their ideas may be called "conflict theory."

The conflict theorists have pointed out first that norms and power must be considered as general alternative modes of "institutionalizing" social relationships. To quote Rex:

> We have also to recognise that some of the ends which the actors in our system pursue may be random ends from the point of view of the system or actually in conflict with it. If there is an actual conflict of ends, the behaviour of actors towards one another may not be determined by shared norms but by the success which each has in compelling the other to act in accordance with his interests. Power then becomes a crucial variable in the study of social systems (19, p. 112).

Second, potential conflicts of interest are seen as endemic in all social systems which "institutionalize" power relationships,[2] because power

[2] Briefly, to define authority as institutionalized power is to beg exactly the question that Merton raises, if the line between authority and power is drawn in terms of the presence or absence of a claim to legitimacy, not in terms of the sentiments of those (principally) over whom authority is exercised. Perhaps the most general consideration which makes the "de-institutionalization" of authority an ever-present possibility is the fact that, whereas the legitimacy of authority tends to take the form of general principles, acts of authority are always specific; and they are always more specific than derived rules of authority, no matter how well developed the latter. Thus, the "exploitable" ambiguity surrounding the derivation and interpre-

(authority) over others is the most general form of "scarce resource" and one that is inherent in society itself. "The distribution of authority in associations," writes Dahrendorf, "is the ultimate 'cause' of the formation of conflict groups" (5, p. 172). Thus, if potential conflicts of interest between those who exercise authority and those over whom authority is exercised are a "normal" feature of social organization, the de-institutionalization of power, and the use of power to maintain institutions, are ever present possibilities. In any realistic and dynamic view of institutionalization, the role of power, both in the generation and control of conflict, is of prime concern.

At first sight, it would seem that the image of society constructed by normative functionalism has given rise to counter-arguments which bring us round full circle to the polemical starting point of modern sociology, namely, the debate on social contract. But fortunately both normative functionalists and conflict theorists are not prepared to recognize as a real issue the Greenian dichotomy of "Will" versus "Force" (11). The themes of norms-consensus-order, and power-alienation-conflict are not regarded as viable sociological alternatives.[3]

It is, therefore, a little surprising to find that both Dahrendorf and Rex consider it necessary to develop their antitheses to normative functionalism in a *systematic* form. These take the shape, respectively, of a "coercion theory of society" and a "conflict model of society".[4] For this strategy they give reasons which are even more surprising. The first is that they both feel their "models" or "frames of reference" are specially suited to certain problem areas in sociology, particularly to the study of industrial societies (5, pp. 161–164; 19, p. 112, p. 114). And, second, Dahrendorf feels that the unification of the "integration theory" (normative function-

---

tation of the legitimacy of specific acts means that authority is never given, but is always contingent upon its exercise. It is precisely with such conflicts arising within the interstices of institutionalized power that "conflict theory" is concerned; and not simply with the more unusual approximations to "unstructured" power conflicts.

[3] At any rate, in formal terms. For instance, Parsons: "I do not think it is useful to postulate a deep dichotomy between theories which give importance to beliefs and values on the one hand, to allegedly 'realistic' interests, e.g., economic, on the other. Beliefs and values are actualized, partially and imperfectly, in realistic situations of social interaction and the outcomes are always codetermined by the values and realistic exigencies; conversely what on concrete levels are called 'interests' are by no means independent of the values which have been institutionalized in the relevant groups" (18, p. 173). See also Dahrendorf (5, p. 159, p. 163) and Rex (19, p. 112). But while there is formal agreement on this point, both the normative functionalists and the conflict theorists fail to explore in any rigorous way the interrelationship of "normative" and "realistic" elements of social systems.

[4] Both authors state their propositions in summary form (5, pp. 236–240; 19, pp. 129–131, p. 195, pp. 236–240). Their premises are very similar: "Every society displays at every point dissensus and conflict; social conflict is ubiquitous" (5, p. 162); "Instead of being organised around a consensus of values, social systems may be thought of as involving conflict situations at central points" (19, p. 129). The major disagreement between the two would seem to be how far, *in fact,* lines of social conflict overlap. See Rex (19, pp. 117–118).

alism) and the "coercion theory" is unlikely and probably impossible (5, p. 164).

Neither of these reasons is very compelling. You cannot assert that society is unthinkable as either a purely moral or a purely coercive entity, and then suggest that a vocabulary built around one or the other of these unthinkable premises is necessary because some societies are manifestly more orderly or conflictful than others. To be sure, the degree to which power enters into social relationships is a factor indispensable for the understanding of both the "imperfection" of consensus and the propensity to conflict. But even in situations where power is very evident and conflict endemic, it is doubtful whether the phenomena of conflict can be adequately grasped without incorporating into conflict theory many of the concepts and propositions concerning the dynamic properties of value systems (or ideologies) which have been developed, or taken over, by normative functionalism. For, given the power structure, the nature of the value system is of signal importance for the genesis, intensity, and direction of potential conflict. Particularly crucial is the way in which it structures the levels of aspiration of different social strata. It may, of its own accord, create aspirations which generate demands for change, or add fuel to the fire of conflicting material interests. It may be sufficiently open and ambiguous to be exploited simultaneously by different conflict groups; or, contrariwise, be capable of absorbing counter-ideologies within itself. Or, sudden change in the relative material positions of different groups may result in widespread conflict as a consequence of what Durkheim calls "moral de-classification." It could, therefore, be argued that even the analysis of that facet of social integration to which Dahrendorf and Rex consider their theories to be especially relevant — namely, social conflict — requires nothing less than a systematic extension of their framework to take explicitly into account the variable properties of value systems that have been the focus of normative functionalism.[5] To the extent that this is done, their conflict theory ceases to be a "special" approach. That status is reserved for the unmodified version of normative functionalism.

Finally, both normative functionalism and conflict theory quite obviously utilize many sociological concepts (which are the property of neither the one perspective nor the other for the solution of their respective problems). Witness only Dahrendorf's (5, pp. 213–218) extensive use of the concept of "multiple group relationships" to account for the variability of class conflict in a way that is not at all dissimilar from the way it is used, for example, by Williams (24, pp. 560–561). Surely it is in the active use of precisely such common concepts and propositions, rather

<hr />

[5] To take an actual example, compare the explicit use of the idea of the "exploitability" of the common value system by Parsons (17, p. 293, p. 355) in accounting for the intensification of "deviance" with the implicit reference to such an idea by Rex (19, p. 125) in discussing class conflict.

than in procuring an agreed definition of "institution" or "society," that the desired unification of which Dahrendorf is so sceptical is constantly being achieved. In actual fact, the divergence between what he calls "integration theory" and "coercion theory" is much more evident in defining problems than in solving them.

Why, then, the concentration on the development of alternative conceptual schemes in which the ideas of power and conflict play a central role? Partly because the recognition given by normative functionalism to the arguments put forward along these lines has so far amounted to nothing more than lip service. More fundamentally, perhaps, it is because, in seeing equilibrium analysis combined in normative functionalism with a focus on shared value elements, Dahrendorf and Rex, with their manifest interest in social change, have as a consequence sought the key to this problem in the area of power and conflict. If this is so, how far do the conflict theorists take us in the analysis of social change?

Dahrendorf and Rex assert that social change is a result of the shifting balance of power between conflict groups (5, pp. 231–236; 19, p. 196). Now, while social change is very frequently associated with conflict, the reverse does not necessarily hold. Conflict may be both endemic and intense in a social system without causing any basic structural change. Why does some conflict result in change while other conflict does not? Conflict theory would have to answer that this is decided by the variable factors affecting the power balance between groups. Here we reach the analytical limits of conflict theory. As a reaction to normative functionalism it is entirely confined to the problem of social integration. What is missing is the system integration focus of general functionalism, which, by contrast with normative functionalism, involves no prior commitment to the study of system stability.[6]

This is exceedingly interesting because both Dahrendorf and Rex arrive at their respective positions through a generalization of Marx. Yet it is precisely Marx who clearly differentiates social and system integration. The propensity to class antagonism (social integration aspect) is generally a function of the character of production relationships (e.g., possibilities of intra-class identification and communication). But the dynamics of class antagonisms are clearly related to the progressively

---

[6] I may refer here once more to the excellent essay by Gouldner (10) and especially to his idea of the "functional autonomy" of parts. This concept provides an obvious link between social and system integration. He explicitly points out that "the concept of the differential functional autonomy of parts directs attention to the need to distinguish between parts having a greater or lesser vested interest in system maintenance," and that "not only efforts to change the system, but also those directed at *maintaining* it are likely to entail conflict and resistance" as a result of differential functional autonomy. What I find a little ambiguous, however, is his use of the term "parts" of a system: at one stage they seem to mean structural aspects (e.g., ecological conditions); at another, actual groups (the French bourgeoisie). The "parts" which may become functionally autonomous are surely *groups;* the "parts" whose interplay conditions their functional autonomy are the *structural* elements of the system. I hope this will become clear in the subsequent argument.

growing "contradictions" of the economic system. One might almost say that the "conflict" which in Marxian theory is decisive for change is not the *power* conflict arising from the relationships in the productive system, but the *system* conflict arising from "contradictions" between "property institutions" and the "forces of production." Though definitely linked, these two aspects of integration are not only analytically separable, but also, because of the time element involved, factually distinguishable. Thus it is perfectly possible, according to this theory, to say that at any particular point of time a society has a high degree of social integration (e.g., relative absence of class conflict) and yet has a low degree of system integration (mounting excess productive capacity).

Further interest attaches to the fact that the idea of structural contradictions is central to the general functionalist view of change:

> The key concept bridging the gap between statics and dynamics in functional theory is that of strain, tension, contradiction, or discrepancy between the component elements of social and cultural structure. Such strains may be dysfunctional for the social system in its then existing form; they may also be instrumental in leading to changes in that system. When social mechanisms for controlling them are operating effectively, these strains are kept within such bounds as to limit change of social structure (15, p. 122).

The vital question is, of course: what are the "component elements" of social systems which give rise to strain, tension, or contradiction? General functionalism, as I understand it, does not attempt to formulate an answer to this question (10, pp. 244–248). It is, by contrast, in normative functionalism that institutional patterns emerge as the only generally identified and systematically differentiated components of a social system between which there can be conflict and resultant strain. Since social systems are differentiated only along the institutional axis, there can be no place for the kind of contradictions which Marx envisaged, contradictions which are obviously relevant to the problem focus of conflict theory. We may ask, therefore, does the Marxian view contain the elements of a more general sociological formulation?

## III

Criticism of the Marxian interpretation of society and social change has focused on the meaning and importance attributed to the "material mode of production." Sometimes, this has been simply and erroneously interpreted as technology. Yet it is quite obvious that in the Marxian schema technological change is not regarded as the prime mover, but as a force which operates interdependently with the productive relations of the society, that is, the prevailing organization of property and labor. The inclusion of productive relationships in the concept "mode of production" lays the theory open to the criticism that the degree of differentiation and independence of such relationships from other social structures in the same society varies very considerably; and that in particular, the saliency of the economic system under capitalism is not at all characteristic of most historical societies in which the mode of political organization heavily conditioned the structure and potential change of productive relationships.[7] Marxian theory has not, for fairly obvious reasons, been overmuch concerned to rebut such criticisms of its basic sociological assumptions. Given its premises about the general long-run decisiveness of the economic order for social change, it has quite logically confined its discussion of system integration to the *internal* dynamics of the mode of production itself — to the economic theory of the contradiction between "forces of production" (technological potential) and the "relations of production" (property institutions).[8]

While this narrowing down of the problem of system integration is highly questionable, the idea of a contradiction between the material conditions of production and the productive institutions of the economic system has a more general relevance that should not be ignored.

First, contradiction implies that the material means of production (e.g., industrial technology) favor a set of potential social relationships (socialist ownership) which constitutes a threat to the existing social relationships institutionalized in the property system (private ownership). Now, whatever reservations one may have about the specific linkage of industrial production with socialist property relationships, there is nothing metaphysical about the general notion of social relationships being somehow implicit in a given set of material conditions. Material conditions most obviously include the technological means of control over the physical and social environment and the skills associated with these means. They include not only the material means of production, but also what Weber frequently refers to as the material means of organization and violence. Such material conditions must surely be included as a variable in any calculus of system integration, since it is clear that they may facilitate the development of "deviant" social relationships which run counter to the dominant institutional patterns of the system. Michels' study of oligarchical tendencies is only the classic example.

Second, according to Marx, the actualization of these potential counter-relationships is determined by the success with which those with vested interests in the existing order are able to resolve the functional incompatibility between the material means of production and the property framework. In the capitalist case, this incompatibility arises from the inability of private property institutions to accommodate the productive capacity of the industrial system. The focal point of strain is "overproduction." The argument, of course, goes further than this. The theory of the "crisis mechanism" not only postulates dysfunctionality but attempts

[7] See especially, Weber (22, pp. 739–43).
[8] See, for example, Baran (1) and Sweezy (20). For the difficulty of locating the "crisis mechanism" of feudalism, see Dobb (7).

to demonstrate how the internal contradictions of the mode of production are endogenously intensified to the point of system breakdown by the inherent development of productive forces. This mechanism, most fully elaborated in the case of capitalist societies, is the conveyor belt which moves a society from one stage of its historical evolution to the next. But in order to use the idea of a functional incompatibility between the dominant institutional order of a social system and its material base, it is not necessary to assume that the system must inevitably break down or that it must inevitably be succeeded by another system of a given type.[9]

We now have a view of system integration, particularly relevant to conflict theory, which may be summed up as follows:

1) One generally conceivable source of tension and possible change in a social system is that which arises from a "lack of fit" between its core institutional order and its material substructure.

2) The material substructure in such a case facilitates the development of social relationships which, if actualized, would directly threaten the existing institutional order.

3) The system will be characterized by a typical form of "strain" arising from the functional incompatibility between its institutional order and material base.

4) The actualization of the latent social relationships of the system will depend on the success with which groups having vested interests in the maintenance of the institutional order are able to cope with the dysfunctional tendency of the system in the face of particular exigencies.

5) If these exigencies lead to an intensification of the functional incompatibility of the system, and if compensating measures by vested interest groups lead (unintentionally) to a further actualization of the potential social relationships of the system, a vicious circle of social disintegration and change of the institutional order is under way. If, on the other hand, compensating measures are effective, the institutional order will remain intact, but the focal point of strain will continue to be evident so long as the functional incompatibility of the system persists.

These propositions do not limit the analysis of system integration to the productive system of a society. Nor do they imply a differentiation of types of societies primarily in terms of their modes of production. Such problems cannot be settled a priori. Consequently, the "dominant" or "core" institutional orders may vary from one type of society to another; and the identification of such institutional orders would seem to be first and foremost a way of defining what is meant by saying that a society has changed.[10] There are, however, certain problems which arise

---

[9] See the instructive remarks of Coulborn (4, pp. 254–269).

[10] Thus differences of opinion about the endurance of Western feudal society depend very largely on whether the military, the political, or the economic aspect of this institutional complex is singled out as the "core" order. See Hintze (13).

when the concepts of "dominant" institutional order and material base are applied to social systems. It may make sense to apply such a distinction to some particular subsystem of a society or to some particular type of corporate group; is it equally relevant, in the case of a society, to regard, for example, the productive system as a "material base" from the point of view of the "dominant" political system, even though the productive system manifestly includes institutional elements? Insofar as the predominant concern is with the way in which the material preconditions of a certain type of political action are, or are not, to be found in a given economic order, there would appear to be good reason for answering this question in the affirmative.[11] Such an answer would, of course, in no way prejudice the further explanation of how such a *given* economic order came about; the problem of the "causes" of the type of system instability under consideration is, anyway, a quite separate issue. It should also be noted that the degree of institutional differentiation of economic and political structures varies very considerably. In cases where the relations of production and the relations of political power are not institutionally very distinct, and especially where the relations of production are institutionalized to a considerable extent around political goals, it would seem reasonable to regard the economic order much more directly as a "material base" of the "dominant" political institutions. A brief reference to Weber's discussion of patrimonialism may serve to illustrate these points as well as the propositions previously advanced.

Although Weber's concept of patrimonialism, and especially that of patrimonial bureaucracy, refers primarily to a type of political structure, it is clear from his remarks that this structure might well be regarded as the "core" institutional order of the society and as a major point of reference for societal change. Moreover, Weber's analysis of the material preconditions of bureaucratization clearly indicates the nature of the functional problems facing societies of the patrimonial bureaucratic type. These center on the relationship between the institution of bureaucracy and the material substructure of a subsistence economy. After setting out the general rule that: "A certain measure of a developed money economy is the normal precondition for the unchanged and continued existence, if not for the establishment, of pure bureaucratic administration," Weber goes on to note that historical cases of "distinctly developed and quantitatively large bureaucracies" may be found which "to a very great extent, partly even predominantly, have rested upon compensation of the officials in kind." This he explains by arguing that "even though the full development of a money economy is not an indispensable precon-

---

11 What else does Weber imply when he writes: "Der Zerfall des Reichs war die notwendige politische Folge des allmaehlichen Schwindens des Verkehrs und der Zunahme der Naturalwirtschaft. Er bedeutete im wesentlichen nur den Wegfall jenes Verwaltungsapparats und damit des geldwirtschaftlichen politischen Ueberbaus, der dem naturalwirtschaftlichen oekonomischen Unterbau nicht mehr angepasst war" (21, p. 308).

dition for bureacratization, bureaucracy as a permanent structure is knit to the one presupposition of a constant income for maintaining it," and that "a stable system of *taxation* is the precondition for the permanent existence of bureaucratic administration." But again: "For well-known and general reasons, only a fully developed money economy offers a secure basis for such a taxation system" (23, pp. 205-209).

The strategic functional problem, then, is one of maintaining a taxation system that can effectively meet the material needs of a bureaucracy in the context of a subsistence, or near-subsistence, economy. The centralizing goal of bureaucratic institutions is constantly liable to sabotage by the potential social relationship structure of the subsistence economy which favors the decentralization and "feudalization" of power relationships.[12] As Weber himself says: "According to all historical experience, without a money economy the bureaucratic structure can hardly avoid undergoing substantial internal changes, or indeed, turning into another type of structure" (23, p. 205). The relationship between bureaucracy and taxation is a highly interdependent one. The efficiency of the bureaucracy depends upon the effectiveness of its taxation system; and the effectiveness of the taxation system depends on the efficiency of the bureaucratic apparatus. Thus, for whatever reason, any increase in the bureaucratic load or decrease in taxation capacity may generate a vicious circle of decentralization of power. Indeed, it might be argued that the "taxation" crisis of patrimonial bureaucracy is essentially analogous to the "production" crisis of capitalism. At any rate, the focal point of strain in this type of society is taxation capacity relative to bureaucratic needs.

This strategic functional problem sets the stage for the characteristic conflicts of interest that arise between the bureaucratic center, the officialdom, landed magnates, and peasantry. The points of tension are those which represent an actualization of the potential for "feudalization": the tendency of officials to "appropriate" the economic and political resources of the office; the struggle of large landowners to gain immunity from taxation and/or usurp fiscal and political functions; and the local relationships of economic and political dependency into which the peasantry are forced in seeking protection against the tax burden of the bureaucratic center. These "centrifugal" tendencies may be seen as both a cause and a consequence of the possible failure of mechanisms for maintaining effective taxation capacity and central control. The outcome of such struggles, and the success with which the functional problem is solved by the bureaucratic center, is, of course, decided in each historical case by the particular circumstances facing the patrimonial bureaucracy. These may vary very considerably; but whether they make for stability

[12] The logic of this is succinctly argued by Bloch (3, p. 68) and Hartman (12, p. 19).

or breakdown of bureaucratic institutions, all societies of this type may be studied from the point of view of their common contradiction.[13]

Another example of a not too dissimilar kind is that of the functional tensions arising from the relationship between the totalitarian political system and the industrial economy of the Soviet Union. It is noteworthy in this connection that many who would deny the relevance of the idea of "internal contradictions" to capitalist societies have only too readily exaggerated the incompatibility of industrialism and the institutions of a one-party state. Be this as it may, it would seem that the type of contradiction envisaged here is one which those having an interest in the dominant political institution have thus far successfully controlled, but which nevertheless is likely to remain as a focal point of strain and potential change. It arises from the tendency of an industrial mode of production to create latent interest groups of a class character. This tendency must be "dysfunctional" for a totalitarian political system, one precondition of which is a "classless" society, i.e., an absence of bases of potential social organization outside the party bureaucracy.

Such a contradiction could manifest itself either by such latent interest groups striving for an autonomous corporate existence (which seems unlikely given the nature of party control) or by their subversion of the party organization from within. Of such groups, associated with industrialization, the least potentially threatening is that of worker opposition. Using Weber's typology of class formation, worker protest hardly advanced beyond the stage of "mass reactions of a class character" (labor turnover and so on) in the early phase of Soviet industrialization; and, while disruptive to the economy, it was not allowed to develop into a more politically dangerous "societal" action. More of a threat from this point of view, however — and this is the element of truth in Burnham's otherwise extravagant thesis of a "managerial revolution" — is the so-called "Soviet bourgeoisie": the functionally important quasi-group of predominantly industrial bureaucrats which has emerged as a result of rapid industrialization (9).

The focal point of strain for the totalitarian political system is not simply that this latent class tends to develop vested interests in its position and privileges, but that it has an organizational capacity and cohesiveness that could form the basis of a political opposition. And, given the nature of the political system, such an interest group would be most

13 On the particular conditions favoring the stability of patrimonial bureaucracy in Egypt and China, see Weber (22, pp. 706–709 ff.). The most famous instance of breakdown, that of the later Roman Empire, is a case where the "defense mechanisms" introduced by the bureaucracy (aptly described by Lot as the "regime of castes") intensified the trend towards subsistence economy and actualized the potential for "feudal" relationships. See Weber (21); Lot (14, pp. 62–153); Bloch (2); and for the Byzantine case, Ostrogorsky (16). The general problem of "feudalizing" tendencies in patrimonial bureaucratic societies is discussed in Coulborn (4). On the major lines of conflict in such societies, see Eisenstadt (8).

likely to take the form initially of cliques within the party bureaucracy. Therefore, the strategic functional problem of the dominant institutional order, from this point of view, is that of maintaining the control of the party bureaucracy over the industrial bureaucracy, and more especially of securing the party against infiltration by vested interest groups of the managerial elite (which includes insulating the latter from any wider support in the society). Most fundamentally, the party must develop means by which it can systematically "de-classify" the lines of stratification and interest-group formation that have their basis in the industrial substructure. At the same time, however, (and here arises the point of system tension) such de-classification must not undermine the conditions of industrial efficiency.

## IV

The foregoing examples have been all too sketchy, but perhaps they may serve the purpose of illustrating the viewpoint advanced in the main body of the chapter. It has not been the intention to claim that this perspective is the only possible way to approach the problem of social change, still less to imply that there is anything other than a polemical advantage to be gained by focusing on system integration *as opposed* to social integration. What has been suggested, however, may be summed up as follows:

1) The propensity to social change arising from the functional incompatibility between an institutional order and its material base has been ignored by normative functionalists because of their concentration on the moral aspects of social integration.

2) It has been equally ignored by conflict theorists, who, in concentrating on the weakness of the normative functionalist approach to social integration, have failed to relate their interest in social change to the problem of system integration.

## BIBLIOGRAPHY

1. Baran, Paul A. *The Political Economy of Growth*. New York: Monthly Review, 1957.

2. Bloch, Marc. "The Rise of Dependent Cultivation and Seigniorial Institutions," in J. H. Clapham and Eileen Power (eds.), *The Cambridge Economic History*, Vol. 1. Cambridge: Cambridge University Press, 1942.

3. Bloch, Marc. *Feudal Society*, translated by L. A. Manyion. London: Routledge and Kegan Paul, 1961.

4. Coulborn, R. *Feudalism in History*. Princeton, N.J.: Princeton University Press, 1956.

5. Dahrendorf, Ralf. *Class and Class Conflict in Industrial Society*. Stanford: Stanford University Press, 1959.

6. Davis, Kingsley. "The Myth of Functional Analysis as a Special Method in Sociology and Anthropology," *American Sociological Review*, Vol. 24, No. 6 (December 1959).

7. Dobb, M. H. (ed.), *The Transition from Feudalism to Capitalism: A Symposium*. Patna, India: People's Book House, 1957.

8. Eisenstadt, S. N. "Political Struggle in Bureaucratic Societies," *World Politics*, Vol. 9, No. 1 (October 1956).

9. Feldmesser, Robert A. "Equality and Inequality under Khrushchev," *Problems of Communism*, Vol. 9, No. 2 (March–April 1960).

10. Gouldner, Alvin W. "Reciprocity and Autonomy in Functional Theory," in Llewellyn Gross (ed.), *Symposium on Sociological Theory*. New York: Harper and Bros., 1959.

11. Green, T. H. *Principles of Political Obligation*. London: Longmans, 1906.

12. Hartman, Ludo Moritz. *The Early Medieval State*. London: The Historical Association, 1960.

13. Hintze, Otto. "Wesen und Verbreitung des Feudalismus," *Staat and Verfassung*. Leipzig: Koehler and Amelang, 1941.

14. Lot, Ferdinand. *La Fin du Monde Antique et le Debut du Moyen Age*. Paris: Michel, 1951.

15. Merton, Robert K. *Social Theory and Social Structure*. Glencoe, Ill.: The Free Press, 1957.

16. Ostrogorsky, Georg. "Agrarian Conditions in the Byzantine Empire in the Middle Ages," in J. H. Clapham and Eileen Power (eds.), *The Cambridge Economic History*, Vol. I. Cambridge: Cambridge University Press, 1942.

17. Parsons, Talcott. *The Social System*. London: Routledge, 1952.

18. Parsons, Talcott. *Structure and Process in Modern Society*. Glencoe, Ill.: The Free Press, 1960.

19. Rex, John. *Key Problems of Sociological Theory*. London: Humanities Press, 1961.

20. Sweezy, Paul M. *The Theory of Capitalist Development*. New York: Monthly Review, 1942.

21. Weber, Max. "Die Sozialen Gruende des Untergangs der antiken Kultur," in *Gesammelte Aufsaetze zur Sozial- und Wirtschaftsgeschichte*. Tuebingen: Mohr (Paul Siebeck), 1924.

22. Weber, Max. *Wirtschaft und Gesellschaft*. Tuebingen: Mohr (Paul Siebeck), 1947.

23. Weber, Max. *From Max Weber: Essays in Sociology*, translated and edited by H. H. Gerth and C. Wright Mills. London: Oxford University Press, 1948.

24. Williams, Robin M., Jr. *American Society, A Sociological Interpretation*. New York: Alfred A. Knopf, 1960.

# 14

*H. David Kirk*

# Toward a Taxonomy of

# Social Discontinuities

## I. Introduction

Human beings are creatures of habit. Habits are formed and reinforced in social contexts. Habituated modes of conduct, directed and
sanctioned by group norms, give social life an aura of continuity. Indeed,
some minimum of continuity must be there or social life, and with it
the inculcation and learning of habits, would be unthinkable. Yet, to
live in the modern world is to experience the ubiquity of social *discontinuity*:

> Revolts, revolutions, uprisings, rebellions, agitations, civil wars, *coups d'etat*:
> these are the very fabric of history. They are part of human existence. Not
> an accident but a constant, not disruption but movement produced in the
> unhurried stream of history (1, p. vii).

In this paper I address myself less to drastic change than to the impact
change has on social systems, relations, and patterns of action. *Social
change* and *social discontinuity* are cognate concepts referring to closely
related events. But as used in this paper they are not interchangeable. All
drastic change. Thus, for example, it is possible to show that the dis-
discontinuous events in human affairs are demonstrably derived from
drastic change. Thus, for example, it is possible to show that the discontinuities in the experiences and relations between Americans of African and Caucasian ancestries developed gradually in the course of the
slave trade and the increasing legitimation of slavery. While they may

384

not have arisen from some *sudden* upheaval, the discontinuities in life conditions of the majority of black people in North America have much in common with those discontinuities suffered by people whose homes are suddenly inundated by floods or whose city is decimated by earthquake.

Much that has shown itself as of lasting interest and utility in sociology and related disciplines has emerged from an awareness of disparities, of disruptions, of conflicts in social life, in short from an awareness of social discontinuities. Marx's *false consciousness*, Durkheim's *anomie*, Toennies' *Gesellschaft*, Weber's *Protestant Ethic*, and Michel's *Iron Law of Oligarchy*, are but a few outstanding points of reference to systematic thought about social discontinuities.

My paper seeks to move toward a taxonomic model in which the interrelationship of different types of social discontinuity can be demonstrated and which will thereby aid in the cumulation of findings and the integration of frames of reference. My other aim is really complementary to the first one. Sociologists are only slowly moving toward the recognition that classroom instruction is a poor preparation for science and that our students must learn in contexts of social experience, by being immersed in, and handling, the stuff of social action. But while such phenomenological approaches may foster the *Verstehen* or discernment of the world as our partial conceptual map suggests it, we need also a further and equally important development for the training of our students and thus for the development of our science. We need a taxonomy of social phenomena, a model for ordering and classifying what we already know *but a model open enough to show lacunae, to direct us to questions, to activate in us and in our students the sociological imagination.*

## II. The Emergence of a Key Concept: "Role Handicap"

In this part of the paper, I want to speak personally because it was in the context of personal experiences that I came to ask what seemed burning questions about human society, and which, when I had learned to formulate them with increasing specificity, yielded not only answers but some unexpected theoretical dividends.

I came to North America in the late nineteen thirties, as a young refugee from Nazi Germany. That cauldron of prejudice and discrimination had sensitized me to the injustices of less brutal if more "normalized" patterns of minority treatment on this continent. In California I saw Americans of Japanese ancestry and their alien parents treated as enemies. Later on, as a college student in Harlem I noted the routine ravages of ghetto life. With this background, I looked to sociology for answers to the question of how inclusive human community might be fostered in a heterogeneous and schismatic world. In 1948, when I began graduate studies at Cornell University, I took that question with me, hoping to participate in empirical research in which some answers relevant to my question might be found. After a brief involvement in the department's intergroup relations studies I turned my attention elsewhere. Some years earlier, Professors Morris Opler and Alexander Leighton had been community analysts at Manzanar and Poston relocation centers respectively. They had assembled at Cornell large numbers of records from the day-to-day administration and researches conducted in these camps during World War II. It occurred to me that these archives reporting a minority group's plight could be examined to reveal how the breakdown of the inclusive community affected the political loyalties of the victims. Thus began a research adventure that has not yet ended. In its first phase, my attention was drawn to change-induced social discontinuities, the generic nature of which I did not discern until they recurred several years later, in a very different research context.

The following information is to help the reader understand the statistical data which alerted me to a connection between social change and impediments to role enactment. In 1942, more than 111,000 persons of Japanese ancestry were forcibly evacuated from California, Oregon, and Washington. They were sent to "relocation centers" farther inland. These centers, under the administration of the War Relocation Authority, were relatively makeshift assembly camps, intended as points from which the evacuated people could be relocated in other parts of the United States. The circumstances of wartime fear of a Japanese invasion of the West Coast and the longstanding pattern of anti-Oriental agitation there, combined to delay speedy relocation and to make the bleak, isolated desert and mountain camps into places of detention.

While the Japanese on the West Coast had had some warning of the impending storm, the danger signals had been ambiguous. Some groups pressed for their immediate removal after the attack on Pearl Harbor; other groups urged them to stay. Few among the Japanese-American minority had financial resources outside of small businesses, farms, or jobs. They were largely dependent on a Caucasian market. But a small minority left voluntarily. Most stayed on; some planted new crops. No evidence ever existed that they posed a threat to the safety of the United States.

In late March 1942, the first large group of Japanese residents and American citizens of Japanese ancestry was moved from Los Angeles to the Manzanar Reception Center in Owens Valley, California. The majority of the immigrant generation, *Issei*, were middle-aged or old. To be torn out of their life seemed to most of them, to amount to economic extinction in America. In the rush of events preceding evacuation they frequently sold farms, equipment, and household goods at great loss, or abandoned them.

The first impact of camp life was tremendous, but since the camps were initially regarded as way stations to a more settled life elsewhere, the shock was absorbed. In spite of adverse physical and psychological conditions of camp life many of the young citizens, *Nisei*, at first insisted that a better life was in store for them. But insidious racist propaganda led to demands by chauvinistic newspapers and organizations for further restrictions against the evacuees. Thus, work furloughs away from the camps were ended and the evacuees were restricted to a limited camp area which was surrounded by wire fence and guarded by soldiers. Conditions approximated internment and were alike for the alien parents and the citizen young.

Two well-meant but badly calculated administrative acts further aggravated the grievances of the interned people. The first of these acts called for the establishment of community councils for whose offices only Nisei would be eligible. This was meant as compensation for the ineffectiveness of their citizenship. It was a vain hope. In some centers, notably at Manzanar, plans for community government were being sabotaged. Feelings ran high. Not until May, 1943, when the official policy was altered to include Issei in the community councils, did some of the camps, which had refused to do so previously, set up such governments under charter. The main effect of the crisis was that the Issei, who had gradually been gaining in power and prestige among the young under the impact of total experience in center life, came to take a central position. Some Nisei had been forced into unconditional support of administrative policies, however unreasonable they might be, while others had similarly been made subject to the controls of the traditional Japanese family. These events set the stage for the second and decisive crisis in the camps.

As a result of Director Dillon Myer's hope for a speedier resettlement of the evacuees, a plan for leave clearance proceedings was made. This plan was joined to another one for voluntary enlistment of the Nisei. The enlistment policy was announced by the Secretary of War on January 28, 1943. Specially instructed officers visited the camps, addressed the evacuees, and sought to answer their questions. All evacuees of seventeen years and over were asked to register. Two types of questionnaire were set before them. One was for male citizens of Japanese ancestry, the other for female citizens and for aliens of both sexes. The first one was headed "Selective Service System," the other "War Relocation Authority Application for Leave Clearance." The questionnaires were similar — there were some thirty items dealing with personal and family history and status. It was a complicated and lengthy document, but really troublesome were questions 27 and 28, which for male and female citizens read respectively:

Male Citizens:
No. 27: Are you willing to serve in the armed forces of the United States on combat duty, wherever ordered?

No. 28: Will you swear unqualified allegiance to the United States of America and faithfully defend the United States from any and all attack by foreign or domestic forces, and forswear any form of allegiance or obedience to the Japanese Emperor, or any other foreign government, power, or organization?

Female citizens and aliens of both sexes:

No. 27: If the opportunity presents itself and you are found qualified, would you be willing to volunteer for the Army Nurse Corps or the WAAC?

No. 28: Will you swear unqualified allegiance to the United States of America and forswear any form of allegiance to the Japanese Emperor, or any other foreign government, power, or organization (11, p. 99)?

The position of the Issei had been difficult throughout. It became intolerable when they were asked to swear loyalty to the United States from whose citizenship they were barred by United States law. Under these circumstances most of them thought it necessary to do nothing that would invalidate their citizenship obligations toward Japan. At the same time they wished to assure the American authorities of their harmless intentions. One of them put it this way:

No Issei would disobey the laws of the United States. They've always been law-abiding. In that sense they can be called loyal to the United States. On the other hand, none of them are disloyal to Japan. *You can't use the word "loyalty" or "disloyalty" for Issei because it just doesn't apply to them* (13, p. 101, emphasis added).

When this situation came to be understood in Washington, an inoffensive question was substituted. The new question read:

Will you swear to abide by the laws of the United States and take no action which would in any way interfere with the war effort of the United States?

Now the vast majority of them proceeded to answer in the affirmative. But the damage had been done. Many Nisei had joined their parents in saying "no." When their elders were given the opportunity to change their answers, the Nisei were left with non-affirmative replies. From figures published by the Statistics Section of the Relocation Planning Division of the War Relocation Authority (12, p. 165) we obtain a picture of the final registration results for all the centers combined, and for Manzanar separately. Of the total number of aliens who registered, barely two percent said "no," whereas of the total number of citizens who registered, twelve percent said "no" to question 28. At Manzanar the ratio was even more extreme; one percent of the aliens and twenty-two percent of the citizens gave non-affirmative replies.

The plan was to segregate the disloyal from the loyal elements. But the results of the leave clearance registration were soon understood to be a poor indicator of the evacuees' true attitudes. The citizens who had given non-affirmative replies to question 28 were therefore to be given a chance to change their minds. For this purpose, hearing boards were established in the camps.

At Manzanar two such boards met sumultaneously. Morris E. Opler, Community Analyst at Manzanar, attended as many of the hearings as he could, shuttling back and forth between the two boards. His hearing records of 479 cases, somewhat more than half of all the cases being reviewed at Manzanar, represent a close approximation to a random sample.

The reader will recall that I had approached the records of Japanese-American relocation with the question how the breakdown of inclusive community — the community of United States citizenship, with rights and obligations defined by the United States Constitution — affected the political loyalties of the victims. Morris Opler's procedure had been to note whether an evacuee being interviewed had ever resided in Japan or whether the evacuee had never been abroad.

It occurred to me to compare the responses made by these two groups of Nisei who in other respects were believed to be similar. I decided to make that comparison on the assumption that Nisei who had never been abroad, and so could have attended schools only in the United States, might in their answers to the hearing board reveal a greater degree of acculturation to American political institutions than those who had lived in Japan for any length of time. I had reasoned that the more committed a Nisei was to American institutions, the greater would be the sense of deprivation brought forth by the effective loss of citizenship rights in the relocation camps. Opler's records provided an opportunity to assess degrees of relative deprivation, for he had noted the reasons given by the young internees to explain their refusal to swear unqualified loyalty to the United States.

Table 1 shows nine categories of reasons given by Manzanar Nisei to explain their refusal to swear unqualified loyalty. The first column (from left to right) lists all nine categories for refusing unqualified loyalty. The second column shows my summary label for a particular group of reasons. The third column shows the numbers and percentages of Manzanar Nisei in each of the reply categories whose hearings were recorded by Morris Opler.

Table 2 shows the summary response patterns for Nisei without foreign residence, and those with foreign residence. The Nisei in both residence categories had all retained non-affirmative replies to question 28. On superficial inspection they might thus seem to have responded quite similarly to the deprivation of citizenship rights. But as Table 2 shows, those Nisei who had never left the United States were far more likely than the others to give *protest* reasons for their refusal to swear unqualified loyalty. Thus, the citizen internees whom I had judged likely to

**TABLE 1**

Citizen Evacuees at Manzanar Maintaining Non-Affirmative
Replies to Question 28: By Reasons Given to Hearing Boards.

| ALL CATEGORIES OF REASONS GIVEN | SUMMARY LABELS | ALL MANZANAR NISEI HEARING BOARD RECORDS COLLECTED BY MORRIS OPLER | |
|---|---|---|---|
| | | Number | Percent |
| Fear of forced relocation<br>Family decision<br>Marriage or engagement to<br>  another person saying "no" | "FAMILY<br>ATTACHMENT" | 192 | 42.2 |
| Abridgement of citizenship<br>Race discrimination<br>Property loss (no future in<br>  the U.S.)<br>Generally angry at evacuation | "PROTEST" | 75 | 16.5 |
| Wanting to live in Japan<br>Loyalty divided or for Japan | "POSITIVE<br>TOWARD JAPAN" | 99 | 21.8 |
| Uncertain or ambivalent reply<br>No information or report<br>  incomplete | "RESIDUAL" | 89 | 19.6 |
| All Cases | | 455* | 100% |

*Twenty-four of Opler's 479 hearing records referred to aliens. Their records have been omitted from this table as our analysis concerns the responses of U.S. citizens only.

be most deeply committed to American institutions were shown also most likely to protest the loss of effective citizenship rights.

**TABLE 2**

Citizen Evacuees at Manzanar Maintaining Non-Affirmative
Replies to Question 28: By Residence and Summary Reasons
Given to Hearing Boards.

| TYPE OF REASON GIVEN FOR RETAINING NON-AFFIRMATIVE REPLY: | RESIDENCE ONLY IN U.S. (Interpreted as high commitment to American institutions) | | SOME RESIDENCE IN JAPAN (Interpreted as lower commitment to American institutions) | |
|---|---|---|---|---|
| | Number | Percent | Number | Percent |
| "FAMILY ATTACHMENT" | 90 | 41.4 | 102 | 42.8 |
| "PROTEST" | 64 | 29.6 | 11 | 4.6 |
| "POSITIVE TOWARD JAPAN" | 20 | 9.2 | 79 | 33.2 |
| "RESIDUAL" | 43 | 19.8 | 46 | 19.3 |
| ALL CASES | 217 | 100% | 238 | 100% |

$p < .001$

Such Nisei probably knew that the Fifth and Fourteenth Amendments to the United States Constitution specifically guarantee that no person shall be "deprived of .... liberty, or property, without due process of law." They and their families had in fact been deprived of liberty and property by executive order, without due process of law. The rights which American schools had taught them to expect on the basis of their birth in the United States had proved worth little or nothing when most needed. Given their sense of relative deprivation, when pressed to declare unqualified allegiance to the national community that had failed them, they were more inclined than their fellows with lesser expectations to protest.

In trying to understand this peculiar "loyalty of disloyalty" on the part of a sizeable minority of Nisei, I thought that it could be regarded as *a paradoxical response to an intolerably handicapping social disconti-nuity*. Much later on, in the course of a very different research problem, I stumbled on similarly paradoxical data and once again, the partici-pants responded in peculiar ways. At that point, I began to think that the phenomena I had discerned in two very different researches might have implications for the systematic analysis of social discontinuities. But I am getting ahead of my story. Now I must inform the reader of the second phase in my research adventure and of the theoretical insight it yielded.

I turn again, to personal experiences as these relate to my work. About the time when my studies of Japanese-American relocation were completed my wife and I were planning to adopt a baby. During the summer of 1950 I tried to find literature that might identify the main parameters of substitute parenthood. I did not find this literature help-ful, so I tried to think about adoption within a sociological perspective. It occurred to me that bonds of kinship — elemental human community — derive in this family type from social (including legal) contrivance rather than from institutionally sanctioned processes of nature. I thus began to think of the circumstances involved in adoption as an oppor-tunity for in-depth pursuit of my old question, namely how human solidarity could be fostered within groups formed in secular contexts, and made up of heterogeneous memberships.

Several structurally different family types are typically lumped to-gether under the rubric "adoption." Because I was interested in adop-tion as a special case of contrived formation of community with hetero-geneous membership, I chose to study the adoption type where members had not been kin to each other prior to legal adoption. I shall refer to this type of adoption as "extra-familial," in contrast with "familial" adoption frequently following divorce and remarriage.

The first of my adoption researches (5) was intended to identify the principal cultural values and sentiments surrounding adoptive families, specifically aspects of public opinion concerning illegitimacy, sterility, and other structural features salient to extra-familial adoption. My initial question had been what might be the latent as well as manifest cultural values that could be expected to impinge on members of adoptive families in the context of their relations with outsiders and among themselves. I learned that however supportive the overt attitudes toward adoption in the communities studied, there were also beliefs and values sharply at variance with the supportive ones. Originally, I had assumed that any latent invidious judgements of adoptive family relations could be correlated with suspicions of the developmental potential attributed to illegitimately born children. I was surprised to find myself mistaken. I discovered instead a very different antecedent variable positively related to invidious valuation of adoption. Persons who saw parenthood inevitably as a link between child bearing and rearing were also typically less ready to think of adoption as a full equivalent of natural parents' rearing their own children. I perceived a strong biologistic bias throughout the community study interviews in people's definition of parenthood. Correspondingly, non-fecund adoptive parents, especially adoptive mothers, were regarded as less "naturally" competent than their biological peers for the conduct of parental duties. Parts of this study, originally conducted in upstate New York were later carried out among French and English Canadians in the Province of Quebec, and very similar results were obtained.

The second in the series of adoption researches (7) sought to determine how the cultural values and sentiments surrounding adoptive families actually impinged on them. The plan was to send mail questionnaires to a large number of adopters sampled from the records of social agencies. In preparatory interviews, adopters typically denied that they or their children experienced other than cordial attitudes or behavior from others. My wife's experience and mine had been somewhat different; it had seemed to us that some of the questions and statements of other people suggested less positive support than we would have liked. In the context of this paper I cannot show how the technical research problem was solved, but can only indicate a rather serendipitous result obtained in the final questionnaire which was answered by 1,533 adoptive parents resident in New York, Quebec, Ontario, Ohio, and California. One page in that questionnaire had asked respondents to indicate which in a list of questions or remarks had been directed to them by outsiders. After that page they were asked to note other experiences or issues not covered by the questionnaire. Most of the page was left blank for the adopters to "blow off steam." And so they did: it was frequently filled with anecdotes, with problem statements, and with advices to the researcher. When the content of the entries was analyzed for constituent themes it was clear that the writers were principally responding to the preceding page which had listed types of questions posed and statements made by outsiders. And what the writers seemed to be doing in their very varied responses to the open-ended question was to try to define the nature of their adoptive parent roles. This they did in two main themes; in one they seemed to say that adoption was essentially not different from the experience of natural parenthood; in the other theme the writers noted differences. The "rejection-of-difference" theme was far more prevalent in the 1,533 questionnaires than the "acknowledgement-of-difference" theme.

While the public opinion study had shown that adoption was typically defined as "different" in the culture, the mail questionnaire study had suggested that adopters typically hesitate to acknowledge that cultural reality. What was the reason? Searching for answers in social rather than psychic structure it occurred to me to put down systematically what I knew from personal experience and from interviews with other adopters of specific differences between culturally given role expectations and actual encounters with the situation of adoptive parenthood. I was able to list seventeen different circumstances which contrast biological and adoptive parenthood. To illustrate this comparison I have chosen three instances from the stage of entry into the parental role.

THE SITUATION OF BIOLOGICAL PARENTHOOD WHICH TYPICALLY SERVES THE HUSBAND-WIFE DYAD AS THE FRAME OF REFERENCE FOR ROLE EXPECTATIONS:

1. Preparation for biological parent roles is *gradual*—the period of pregnancy provides the couple with a known timetable which moves them imperceptibly toward progressive commitment to their coming parent roles.

2. Fecund couples are ultimately *independent* in the procurement of their child. However much they may utilize the technological services of medicine, surgery, and hospital, they know that procurement is possible without any of these services. Essentially they are not in need of a middle man.

THE SITUATION CONFRONTING THE NON-FECUND COUPLE DESIRING FAMILY LIFE AND DECIDING TO ADOPT:

1. Preparation for adoptive parenthood tends to be *abrupt*, with no clear-cut timetable by which they can shape their feelings and thoughts about their hoped-for parenthood.

2. Adopting couples are ultimately *dependent* on the services of a middle man, whether professional or lay; social worker, physician, lawyer, minister, or black marketeer. (Note that relative dependence may be increased in the more legitimated agency adoptions, partly because in them no direct transaction occurs between procreative parents and adopters, but also because adopters frequently are not clear about an adoption agency's criteria for evaluating applicants.)

3. With the child's coming, parents are fully expected to do everything in their power to make him one of their group, to integrate him into their midst. Only after he has become fully a member need they give any thought to his participation in groups outside the family circle.

3. For over two decades, adopters have been advised that they must tell the adopted child about his adoption. Although this professional prescription has been surrounded by assurances that it will not be a problem if started early in the child's life, this very aspect of the prescription makes it especially problematic. It means that adopters are confronted by conflicting role obligations — the first calls on them to integrate the child fully before he is allowed to find other membership and reference groups; the second prescription perversely expects the adopters to give their child simultaneously a second reference group which not only conflicts with the first but which is invisible and which the adoptive parent typically does not really wish to discuss.

Until very recently, complete womanhood almost universally meant marriage and, as my work suggests, fecund motherhood. In such a cultural climate the discrepancies between role expectation and role reality experienced by non-fecund adopters reflect social discontinuity. As I mentioned earlier, the adopters who had given me information typically defined their parent roles as essentially identical with natural parenthood. It now occurred to me that this "rejection-of-difference" orientation represents a paradoxical type of adaptive response to the experience of role-inhibiting social discontinuity. At this point I recalled the similarly paradoxical "loyalty of disloyalty" of some Nisei evacuees at Manzanar and discerned what appeared to be a generic characteristic of social discontinuity, whether directly derived from social change or not. I saw that the change-induced, role-inhibiting discontinuities involved in wars, revolutions, and economic depressions, have characteristics similar to those of normalized situations such as can be found in the institutionalized inequities of slavery. What was needed at this point was a descriptive label to help in identifying and classifying types of role-inhibiting discontinuities. Eventual *"role handicap"* turned out to be heuristic: as a key concept it helped me to construct a typological model of social discontinuity.

### III. Prototype of a Taxonomic Model

In their attempt at reconciling Marx, Weber, and Freud in a "psychology of social institutions," Gerth and Mills proposed a model (3, p. 32) in which the constituent units of *social structure* are linked to those of *character structure* by *role*. This diagrammatic presentation suggested a way of ordering different types of social discontinuity. If the Gerth-Mills model's mediating concept was *role*, then *role handicap* might similarly serve to mediate social discontinuities at the level of social structure and of social identity or character. Although no reference to the earlier model appears in Mills' subsequent book *The Sociological Imagination*, his concepts of *personal troubles* and *public issues* suggest the beginning of a typology of social discontinuity (9, pp. 8–9).

> *Troubles* occur within the character of the individual and within the range of his immediate relations with others; they have to do with his self and with those limited areas of social life of which he is directly and personally aware. . . . A trouble is a private matter: values cherished by an individual are felt by him to be threatened.
>
> *Issues* have to do with matters that transcend these local environments of the individual and the range of his inner life. They have to do with the organization of many such milieux into the institutions of an historical society as a whole. . . . An issue is a public matter: some value cherished by publics is felt to be threatened. . . . An issue often involves a crisis in institutional arrangements, and often too it involves what Marxists call 'contradictions' or 'antagonisms.'

In skeletal form my modification of the Gerth-Mills model is shown in the following diagram:

How did this simplistic paradigm come to serve as a frame of reference for the identification and classification of different types of social discontinuity? I do not want to give the impression that the sequence of ideas I am discussing here represents the sequence of events, the course of discovery. I am trying to present the questions and the events in such an order that they make sense to others, and equally important, that they aid the reader in seeing the rationale behind the linkages of observations and of concepts which I am proposing. Let me return to certain observations I had made during the study of discontinuities in the role patterning of adoptive parenthood. The reader may recall that I had found seventeen (of which in this paper I showed three) role-inhibiting circumstances typically experienced by non-fecund adopters. At one point in the analysis of my research data I noticed that all the observed instances of role handicap experienced by adopters could be dichotomized. One of these subdivisions I labelled *"symbolic"* to indicate the principally ideational character of its role handicap constituents. The other subdivision I called *"instrumental"* to signify the principally manipulative focus of culture to which its instances of role handicap refer. Codification of the descriptive categories of role handicap, themselves *derived from empirical investigations,* is shown in Tables 3 and 4.

**TABLE 3**

Codification of Descriptive Categories of
Symbolic Role Handicap

| DESCRIPTIVE CATEGORIES OF SYMBOLIC ROLE HANDICAP | SUMMARY LABELS |
|---|---|
| *Symbolic role handicap occurs:* | |
| when roles are not clearly defined in the cultural script; | |
| when there is a lack of appropriate role models; | AMBIGUITY |
| when there is a lack of cultural symbols or of rituals that reinforce role learning; | |
| when the norms prescribing or proscribing role behaviors are internally inconsistent; | |
| when the sanctions controlling role behavior are inappropriate or inconsistent. | DILEMMA |

Having thus a set of summary labels to identify role-handicapping discontinuities I want to specify further in what sense such discontinuities can be thought of as capable of obstructing social action. This attempt at clarification is made in Table 5.

This organization of role handicap types into a typology of role-handicapping discontinuities now informed my search for *corresponding* types of social discontinuity at system and at personality levels of analysis. As will be seen presently, such types of social discontinuity are at least implicit in the work of other investigators. Before proceeding to the relevance of their ideas for developing a taxonomic model of social discontinuities I must raise the problematic question of validation of "im-

## TABLE 4

Codification of Descriptive Categories of
Instrumental Role Handicap

| DESCRIPTIVE CATEGORIES OF INSTRUMENTAL ROLE HANDICAP | SUMMARY LABELS |
|---|---|

*Instrumental role handicap occurs:*

when there is a lack of material or social resources needed for role enactment;

when there is discrimination, i.e. a lack of equity, in the distribution of the material resources, including goods and services, needed for role enactment; } SCARCITY

when the actors lack the authority for mobilizing needed goods and services;

when actors do not have sufficient freedom to seek alternatives to standard but blocked means for role enactment. } RESTRICTION

## TABLE 5

Typology of Role-Handicapping
Social Discontinuities

| SYMBOLIC DISCONTINUITIES HANDICAP ROLES WHEN: | INSTRUMENTAL DISCONTINUITIES HANDICAP ROLES WHEN: |
|---|---|
| *ambiguities* in the universe of discourse confound the meanings of the social acts related to particular roles; | *scarcity,* either absolute or relative, frustrates the actor's desire to enact a role; |
| *dilemmas* paralyze the actor's motivation toward role enactment. | *restrictions,* organizational or political, limit the actor's freedom or authority to enact a role. |

ported" concepts. How should one assess the validity of idea constructs in contexts other than those for which they were intended by their authors? If concepts proposed by other investigators were to be transformed into types of social discontinuity to correspond to the role handicap types I had noted, how could one tell whether these derived types truly *corresponded* to given role handicap types?

*One test of the validity of a derived type was to ask whether its definition describes the discontinuity in question as functionally equivalent to the role handicap type to which it is believed to correspond. A second test concerns the life history of the concept from which a particular type of social discontinuity can be logically derived. My question was whether the idea constructs I have borrowed are anchored in systematically observed social reality or whether such constructs are the brain-children principally of recollection, reading, and speculation-based analysis.*

This latter question bares my bias in favor of classification and codification supported by systematically observed data, as against more speculative paradigms. Kaplan notes that "observational terms localize problems and marshal the data; constructs and theoretical terms propound solutions and lead on to the next problematic encounter (4, p. 60)." Rather than serving as heuristic devices, the constructs and theoretical terms of the *ideal type* kind of paradigm, so dear to sociologists, have too frequently led to the scientific sin of reification.

> .... Reification is more than a metaphysical sin, it is a logical one. It is the mistake of treating a notational device as though it were a substantive term, what I have called a construct as though it were observational, a theoretical term as though it were a construct or indirect observable (4, p. 61).

I have long suspected a causal connection between a professional tendency to reify sociological concepts and the demonstrable fact that our discipline bears little resemblance to a *cumulative* science.

But to return to the problem of validating proposed linkages between types of discontinuity at the level of social system, role, and personality: I believe that the types proposed here in the main meet the standard of the first test. The descriptive definitions of their effects in social system and personality organization appear to correspond more or less closely to certain discontinuities known to have handicapping effects at the role level. Whether my critical readers will agree with this assessment I do not know, but I *do* know that types of discontinuity at the social system and personality levels clearly fail to pass the second test of validity.

The types of social system discontinuity to which I shall make reference are based on Parsons' system maintenance AGIL scheme. My types of social discontinuity at the level of personality or identity are based on Foote and Cottrell's specification of G. H. Mead's "I" and "me" aspects of the social self.

Parsons' four types of system maintenance prerequisites appear to be based less on observed and recorded notations of social reality than on educated and reasoned induction. At least I have found no indication in Parsons' work or that of his principal associates to suggest otherwise. Foote and Cottrell explicitly acknowledge that their typology is similarly inductive:

> Instead of attempting . . . to . . . elaborate a general concept of the origins of interpersonal competence, our main strategy of definition will be analytical, to name its parts, as manifested in observ*able* behavior. These we take to be: (1) health, (2) intelligence, (3) empathy, (4) autonomy,

(5) judgement, and (6) creativity. The final number and order of these components, as well as the names assigned to them, are the *result of reflection*, as well as extensive reference to previous literature and current discussion (2, p. 41, emphasis added.)

My proposed types of social discontinuity at system and personality levels are thus derivatives from types which, however inspired and however persuasive, are not empirically anchored. In spite of their failure to meet the second test of validity I am making use of these derived types because the conceptual articulation they appear to have with my empirically-based role handicap typology, suggests that they too reflect much of social reality. But because of the limitations noted here I regard the resulting typology (Tables 10 and 12) as representing at most an approximation, a prototype, of a taxonomic model of social discontinuities.

Table 6 summarizes Parsons' AGIL scheme of identifying what he believes are generic requirements for any social system to persist as a going concern.

**TABLE 6**

Types of "System Needs" Pointing to
Functional Components of Social Systems

| SYMBOLIC COMPONENTS | INSTRUMENTAL COMPONENTS |
|---|---|
| *PATTERN MAINTENANCE:* i.e. arrangements for assuring the continuation of social life through the inculcation and renewal of cultural patterns in a universe of discourse and value. | *ADAPTATION:* i.e. arrangements for making available the natural and social goods demanded in social life. |
| *INTEGRATION:* i.e. mechanisms for assuring the loyalty of members and thus the cohesion of the structure. | *GOAL ATTAINMENT:* i.e. mechanisms for mobilizing human and non-human resources toward the attainment of collective interests. |

In Table 7 I have "translated" the AGIL types to yield a typology of social discontinuities at the level of social systems.

With this listing of discontinuities at the social structure level let us now move to the level of personality or identity. What are the potential discontinuities there? A possible cue lies in the work of the philosopher G. H. Mead. In his celebrated *Mind, Self, and Society* (8, pp. 173–200) he conceived of the social self as partially constituted by what he termed the "I" and the "me." The latter aspect of the self arises in contact with the attitudes of others, which in the process of socialization one has made one's own attitudes. The "I" refers to that aspect of selfhood which

**TABLE 7**

Types of Social Discontinuity
at the Level of Social Systems

| Symbolic Discontinuities | Instrumental Discontinuities |
|---|---|
| *CHAOS* results when the arrangements meant to assure pattern maintenance are disrupted in circumstances of disaster or made obsolete in circumstances of riot and revolution. | *MALADAPTATION* exists when, as in circumstances of disaster, needed resources become scarce or non-existent, and when, as in circumstances of legitimated inequity, access to needed resources is institutionally restricted. |
| *ANOMIE* obtains when in the process of secularization there occurs such a degree of social disorganization as to void most claims of loyalty and thus threaten the cohesion of the system. | *GOAL-THWARTING* occurs when, as in oppressive conditions of 'total institutions' or of tyrannical regimes, opportunities for mobilizing needed physical and social resources are systematically circumscribed. |

reacts to the "me," which acts in the world on the basis of social values residing in the "me." Foote and Cottrell note that the "me" refers "to the vested and organized experience of the community as incorporated within personal conduct; the "I" to the active, assertive, and emergent features of human behavior, not reducible to standard roles in conventional situations (2, p. 58)." Once again the symbolic-instrumental dichotomy appears to be applicable, with the "me" as the more or less *symbolic* and the "I" as the relatively *instrumental* components of the social self.

As has already been indicated, Foote and Cottrell sought to translate these dichotomized aspects of social identity into notions of observable behavior. This they did with their typology of "interpersonal competence." They also noted that this typology could be dichotomized:

. . . . Looking at the elements of competence, three correspond roughly to the "me" phase and three to the "I" phase:

| Me: Intelligence | I: Health |
|---|---|
| Empathy | Autonomy |
| Judgement | Creativity |

(2, p. 58)

Thus intelligence, empathy, and judgement can be conceived of as components of the *symbolic* part of the social self while health, autonomy, and creativity represent the *instrumental* part.

But to demonstrate the applicability of the Foote-Cottrell typology to our quest for a typology of social discontinuities at the level of the social self or identity, it is necessary first to list the authors' descriptive definitions of their six elements of "interpersonal competence," and then to see whether these definitional statements can readily be translated into types of social discontinuity. Table 8 lists my abbreviated versions of the authors' definitions in their own words.

**TABLE 8**

Types of Interpersonal Competence
as Functional Components of Social Identity

| SYMBOLIC COMPONENTS | INSTRUMENTAL COMPONENTS |
|---|---|
| *INTELLIGENCE:* i.e. the "scope of perception among events; the capacity to abstract and symbolize experience, to manipulate the symbols into meaningful generalizations, and to be articulate in communication." (2, p. 53) | *HEALTH:* i.e. "achieving the maximum of sensory acuity, strength, energy, coordination, dexterity, endurance, recuperative power, and immunity of which a particular organism is capable." (2, p. 52) |
| *JUDGEMENT:* i.e. "the ability to estimate and evaluate the meaning and consequences to one's self of alternative lines of conduct. It means the ability to adjudicate among values." (2, p. 56) | *AUTONOMY:* i.e. "the capacity for recognizing real threats to self and of mobilizing realistic defenses when so threatened. Autonomy also implies readiness to give and receive evaluations of self and others." (2, p. 55) |
| *EMPATHY:* i.e. "those responses basic to taking the role of the other and hence to social interaction and the communicative processes upon which rests social integration." (2, p. 54) | *CREATIVITY:* i.e. "the capacity for innovations in behavior or real reconstruction of any aspect of the social environment. It also means the ability to invent or improvise new roles or alternative lines of action in problematic situations, and to evoke such behavior in others." (2, p. 57) |

In Table 9 I have transposed four of the Foote-Cottrell types of interpersonal competence into four corresponding types of social discontinuity. Again the reader has to judge whether the descriptive protocol provided satisfies the first requirement of concept validation, i.e. whether it demonstrates the functional equivalence of the provisionally linked types of discontinuity.

It remains for me to explain why two of the six types of interpersonal competence were omitted. *Empathy* and *Creativity* were excluded because both refer to aspects of behavior that are called out especially when, as in circumstances resembling "the passing of traditional society"

**TABLE 9**

Types of Social Discontinuity
at the Level of Social Identity

| SYMBOLIC DISCONTINUITIES | INSTRUMENTAL DISCONTINUITIES |
|---|---|
| *BEWILDERMENT* results when *ambiguities* in the cultural script obscure the meanings of social action, and so limit the development or the exercise of *intelligence,* i.e. the awareness of events, and the capacity to symbolize, generalize, and communicate experiences. | *DISABILITY* results when absolute or relative *scarcity* derived from disasters or inequitable distribution of resources affects the *health* of actors so as to limit the degree of sensory acuity, strength, energy, coordination, dexterity, endurance, recuperative power, and immunity of which a particular organism is capable. |
| *DEMORALIZATION* results when *dilemmas* derived from incongruities in the norms and from inconsistent sanctions obstruct the growth or the exercise of *judgement,* i.e. the ability to evaluate the consequences of alternative lines of conduct and to adjudicate among values. | *DEPENDENCY* results when organizational or political *restrictions* constrain one's *autonomy,* i.e. the capacity for recognizing real threats and for mobilizing realistic defenses. |

or "an age of social reconstruction," role definitions are in flux and patterns of social control are increasingly honored in the breach. It is then that Daniel Lerner's "empathic" and Karl Mannheim's "reflective" types of person gain special social utility, for empathy and thoughtfulness are adaptive in the sense that they help in maximizing the capacity for *intelligence* and for *judgment* which the ravages of social change will have impeded in less sensitive persons. Similarly, conditions of emergency call out any latent *creativity* for innovative social behavior, capable of maximizing conditions of *health* and *autonomy,* when less successful humans tend to become *disabled* and *dependent.* Such considerations led me to eliminate *empathy* and *creativity* from the typology of discontinuities at the level of social identity. In another publication I shall show how these two types of interpersonal competence become trigger mechanisms for the reconstruction of social environments during and after the impact of social discontinuity.

Now we are ready to summarize our typologies of social discontinuity. Tables 10 and 11 present the prototypical taxonomic model for symbolic and instrumental discontinuities respectively. In these tables I show only the summary labels of codification, omitting the detailed descriptive definitions that appeared in previous tables. These final tables will therefore not serve the critical inspection they require unless the details of preceding tables have been understood and can now be used for reference.

### TABLE 10

Prototype of a Taxonomic Model
of Symbolic Discontinuities

| | | |
|---|---|---|
| Symbolic Discontinuities at the *Identity* Level | BEWILDERMENT *vs. "intelligence"* | DEMORALIZATION *vs. "judgement"* |
| Symbolic Discontinuities at the *Role* Level | AMBIGUITY *vs. role clarity and reinforcement* | DILEMMAS *vs. congruity of norms and sanctions* |
| Symbolic Discontinuities at the *System* Level | CHAOS *vs. pattern maintenance* | ANOMIE *vs. integration* |

### TABLE 11

Prototype of a Taxonomic Model
of Instrumental Discontinuities

| | | |
|---|---|---|
| Instrumental Discontinuities at the *Identity* Level | DISABILITY *vs. "health"* | DEPENDENCY *vs. "autonomy"* |
| Instrumental Discontinuities at the *Role* Level | SCARCITY *vs. sufficiency of resources for role enactment* | RESTRICTION *vs. freedom and authority to explore alternatives to blocked role enactment avenues* |
| Instrumental Discontinuities at the *System* Level | MALADAPTATION *vs. adaptation* | GOAL THWARTING *vs. goal attainment* |

### IV. Caveat Emptor

In concluding this paper I must warn my reader against a potential misunderstanding which seems built into this paper by the nature of my analytic procedure. In Part II, I showed how with the emergence of the idea of *role handicap* I was alerted to a wider range of social discontinuities. But because of the context of my empirical researches I saw the system and personality linkages to role handicap very much in the light of *public issues* and *private troubles,* in other words as human predicaments at different levels of analysis. Now, as a final statement of the meaning of *social discontinuity,* this would be a serious distortion. Only a dyed-in-the-wool functionalist who orients his sociological journey entirely by a dynamic equilibrium map (are there still such single-minded devotees?) could think of social discontinuity as *necessarily* pathological. In so far as the special sequence of my analysis has given that impression it has been misleading, and I wish nothing more than to rectify the misunderstanding. To do so is really very simple.

Social discontinuity may benefit some members, groups, or strata in a society while victimizing others. Or the same group may appear to gain from the altered state of affairs in the short run, but not fare so well over the long haul. Thus every social discontinuity may have potentials for *eufunctional* as well as for *dysfunctional* consequences. How can this view be stated more precisely and systematically? Let me pretend for a moment that this is not the end, but the beginning, of my paper. Instead of introducing the concept of *role handicap* I could have begun with its antonym: "*role support.*" This concept appeared in an American social psychology text (10), six years after my first formulation of *role handicap* appeared in a sociological journal (6, pp. 316–26). The Newcomb, Turner, and Converse volume has this to say:

> Role support . . . has to do with the rewards of behavioral interaction . . . A small child's attraction to its mother is largely the outgrowth of interaction during which he receives help, physical comfort, consolation, and so on. Individuals who find that they play well together at tennis or in musical performance, or who merely enjoy conversational bantering, are providing role support for each other. These last illustrations are forms of reciprocal role support; that is, the interacting persons provide very similar forms of reward for each other. The interacting mother and small child, on the other hand, who reward each other in quite different ways, provide an instance of asymmetrical role support (10, p. 301).

If types of *role handicap* served me previously in identifying links to *predicaments* at social structure and personality levels, then types of *role support* should correspondingly alert us to types of potential benefit at different analytic levels.

The reader's patience may by now be exhausted. Certainly the editors will not allow me more space. But perhaps when you, good reader, have recovered from the strains of the current exercise you will put your mind to further work and your pen to paper, so as to refine and expand this first step toward a taxonomy of social discontinuity.

## BIBLIOGRAPHY

1. Ellul, J. *Autopsy of Revolution.* New York: Alfred A. Knopf, 1971.
2. Foote, N., and L. A. Cottrell, Jr. *Identity and Interpersonal Competence.* Chicago: University of Chicago Press, 1955.
3. Gerth, H., and C. W. Mills. *Character and Social Structure.* New York: Harcourt, Brace & Co., 1953.

4. Kaplan, A. *The Conduct of Inquiry.* San Francisco, California: Chandler Publishing Company, 1964.

5. Kirk, H. D. "Community Sentiments in Relation to Child Adoption." Unpublished Ph.D. Thesis, Cornell University, 1953.

6. Kirk, H. D. "A Dilemma of Adoptive Parenthood: Incongruous Role Obligations," *Marriage and Family Living,* Vol. XXI, No. 4, (1959).

7. Kirk, H. D. *Shared Fate.* New York: The Free Press, Collier-Macmillan, 1964.

8. Mead, G. H. *Mind, Self, and Society.* Chicago: University of Chicago Press, 1934.

9. Mills, C. W. *The Sociological Imagination.* New York: Oxford University Press, 1959.

10. Newcomb, T. M., R. H. Turner, and P. E. Converse. *Social Psychology.* New York: Holt, Rinehart and Winston, Inc., 1965.

11. Spicer, E. H. *Impounded People.* War Relocation Authority. Washington, D.C.: U.S. Government Printing Office, 1946.

12. Statistics Section, Relocation Planning Division, War Relocation Authority, United States Department of the Interior. *The Evacuated People — A Quantitative Description.* Washington, D. C.: U.S. Government Printing Office, 1946.

13. Thomas, D. S., and R. S. Nishimoto. *The Spoilage.* Berkeley, California: University of California Press, 1946.

# 15

*James M. Beshers*

# Mathematical Models of

# Social Change

We shall explore the mathematical representation of theories of social change in two steps. First, we shall examine the assumptions of the classical theories of social change.

A critique of these assumptions will provide the substantive basis for our formalization efforts.

Second, we shall consider the mathematical formulation of these assumptions. Several models that illustrate an increasing complexity of assumptions will be presented. A variety of mathematical approaches will be suggested in this way.[1]

Three criteria can be brought to bear on all model construction:

(1) Deductive criteria — does the model in fact yield unambiguous predictions? (2) Substantive criteria — does the model represent a reasonable substantive argument in the light of past theory and research in the area? and (3) Testability criteria — do there exist research procedures, or is it possible to indicate the nature of appropriate research procedures, such that the predictions of the model may be empirically tested? Our discussion will center on (1) and (2), with (2) receiving the heaviest emphasis. We wish to establish that models currently available and under development can express the substance of classic theories of social change.

[1] See Kaplan (13, pp. 1294–1313); some useful definitions are given in Beshers (3).

## Classical Theory

Three closely related classic problems in the theory of social change deserve our immediate attention. These are: (1) the distinction between social statics and social dynamics; (2) the notion of "equilibrium"; and (3) the notion of dialectical social change.

The distinction between statics and dynamics has been made in all the social sciences. This distinction can serve a useful purpose, but it has more typically served to obscure theoretical questions. Several issues arise. Let us agree on the setting for our problem in order that these issues be carefully distinguished.

We are studying a social unit — group, organization, community, society. We observe events in the passage of time. We discover regularities in these events. Certain patterns of events recur. Thus we might define social statics as the study of recurrent events — essentially a descriptive endeavor. In parallel one would then have two choices — social dynamics could be defined as the descriptive study of non-recurrent events, or social dynamics could be defined as the analysis of patterns of occurrence of events. The latter approach is more useful.

Another definition arises if we focus our attention upon certain events that exhibit great regularity over long periods of time, then seemingly shift or become irregular, but stabilize later in a new pattern of regularity. The study of the first and last situations is then defined as social statics whereas the study of the intermediate situation is called social dynamics. We may call this case "transition" theory.

A third definition, closely related to the second, is arrived at if we suppose that the occurrence of the events under study is the result of the interplay of several mechanisms. One may then classify mechanisms into those that tend to preserve a particular pattern of regularities, and those that tend to alter it. The study of the former mechanisms is called social statics whereas the study of the latter mechanisms is called social dynamics. This approach relies on the mechanical analogy of centrifugal and centripetal forces. We may call this a "balance of forces" approach.

A main difficulty that runs through all these definitions is that the causal, or analytic, aspect of the problem tends to become confused with the descriptive aspects. From the point of view of causal analysis the occurrence of any event, new or repeated, is supposed to be due to certain relationships with other types of events. It is the regularity of relationships among events in time that causal inquiry seeks to establish, not the simple descriptive recurrence of certain types of events.

Thus if an effective causal analysis has been carried out, the case "no change" should be predicted from the same laws from which the case "change" is predicted. The same causal analysis leads to both predictions as possibilities arising from the relationships among events; Kurt Lewin properly underscores this point (15). The descriptive classification of events into "change" and "no change" cannot serve as an explanation of these events, and must not lead to the belief that two entirely different sets of causal mechanisms are operating in the two cases.

With these strictures in mind the second and third definitions may serve as a basis for theories of social change. However, one must be aware that most of the writing on both topics is of a metaphorical rather than an analytic character. The mechanisms of the balance of forces approach must be spelled out specifically — preferably mathematically.

The notion of equilibrium is often used to describe either the "transition" or the "balance of forces" definitions of social statics given above. Here again, we must be cautious to differentiate between a descriptive equilibrium that may be implied by the transition definition and an analytic or explanatory basis for equilibrium that is implied by the "balance of forces" definition. In effect, this view suggests that the descriptive aspects of transition theory may be explained by the balance of forces approach. Description yields data, analysis provides explanation.

The dialectical theory of social change contains many of the elements in our previous discussions. Hegel, Marx, and Weber viewed social change as the resultant of conflict or contradiction among mechanisms in the system. Absence of change was also a resultant of these mechanisms. The time span, however, was viewed as broken into discrete units, or epochs, within which the mechanisms resulted in slight change but between which there was a complete change of mechanisms themselves (relativism of social laws). It is important to note that directionality may be implied in the sequence of epochs, as by Hegel and Marx, or that cyclical possibilities could occur, as by Weber and Sorokin. In either case we note the dissimilarity with the linear theories of evolution — with the assumptions of a continuous directionality of social change.

Especially from Weber we learn the essentially paradoxical nature of social change. The charismatic leader breaks tradition, yet becomes the inspiration of a new traditional bureaucracy (17, pp. 196–251). The compulsive psychological elements of modern capitalism stem in part from the other-worldly, antimaterialistic doctrines of Calvin (18). Such complex possibilities must not be dismissed out of hand as being too difficult to formalize, and therefore irrelevant to mathematical model construction. On the other hand, let us not expect the simpler mathematical models to do justice to such complex reasoning.

### Mathematical Models

Let us select a substantive problem in social change to illustrate mathematical methods. The classic problem of social mobility lends itself to our purposes. For simplicity consider mobility between generations in a two-class system, class $C_1$ and class $C_2$.

We shall employ several models to analyze this problem. All of them, however, will be of the stochastic process type — probability models for describing and analyzing processes (14, p. 177). First we establish the mathematical concepts and give them substantive interpretation. We say that our system always has two "states," $C_1$ and $C_2$. We say that our system has "elements" that are in either of the states, say, fathers and sons. We choose a finite time interval to describe the process — the generation.

We now describe the process as it passes through two successive time units, $t$ and $t + 1$. We form a matrix with two rows and two columns. The two rows represent $C_1$ and $C_2$ at time $t$. The two columns represent $C_1$ and $C_2$ at time $t + 1$. The entries in the matrix are probabilities that describe the change of state of elements between the two time periods. Thus $p_{11} \equiv$ the probability of an element being in state $C_1$ at time $t + 1$ given that the element was in state $C_1$ at time $t$. The matrix so defined is a "transition" matrix. Note that the row probabilities add up to unity.

**t + 1**

$$
\begin{array}{c|c|c|}
 & C_1 & C_2 \\
\hline
C_1 & P_{11} & P_{12} \\
\hline
C_2 & P_{21} & P_{22} \\
\hline
\end{array}
\qquad
\begin{array}{l}
P_{11} + P_{12} = 1 \\[2mm]
P_{21} + P_{22} = 1
\end{array}
$$

t

Besides the transition matrix we need a distribution vector that describes the *number* of elements in each state at each time. Let the vector be designated $m(t)$ with elements $(m_1(t), m_2(t))$ such that $m_1(t)$ is the number of elements in $C_1$ at time $t$ while $m_2(t)$ is the number of elements in $C_2$ at time $t$. Let us suppose that there are 100 males in our society and that they exactly reproduce themselves in each succeeding generation. For an initial distribution at $t$ let us take 50–50, $m_1(t) = 50$, $m_2(t) = 50$.

In applications we must specify the transition probabilities. They may be estimated directly from empirical data or supplied by theoretical considerations.

Let us probe another possibility. We wish to write down a theory from which we can deduce the whole history of the process — that is to say, the distribution vector m $(t)$ for any time period $t$. Several different assumptions yield several different models from which deductions can be obtained.

The first assumption we consider is that there is no historic effect, that the probability of a person being in $C_1$ at $t + 1$ is independent of whether he was in $C_1$ or $C_2$ at time $t$. Thus we reduce the problem of the distribution of persons by classes to the problem of flipping a coin — with heads equivalent to $C_1$ and tails equivalent to $C_2$. We note that the coin may be biased; so long as the bias is consistent throughout history, the assumptions of the binomial distribution are still met in this case.

The situation can be represented by a tree diagram of a branching process. We enumerate the possible paths that can be taken and then assign probabilities to each. For our problem two branches occur at each time interval, one to $C_1$ and one to $C_2$.

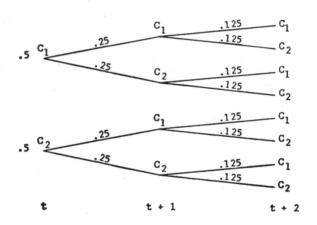

$$
\begin{array}{c}
\phantom{C_1} \\
\phantom{C_2}
\end{array}
\mathbf{t+1}
$$

$$
\begin{array}{cc}
 & \begin{array}{cc} C_1 & C_2 \end{array} \\
\begin{array}{c} C_1 \\ C_2 \end{array} & \left( \begin{array}{cc} .5 & .5 \\ .5 & .5 \end{array} \right)
\end{array}
$$

Suppose there is an even chance of ending in either class. Then the probability of a $C_1$ father having a $C_1$ son = the probability of a $C_1$ father having a $C_2$ son = the probability of a $C_2$ father having a $C_1$ son = the probability of a $C_2$ father having a $C_2$ son = .25. The analysis can be carried forward and we see that the expected distribution of persons by classes at any time is 50–50.

In terms of our previous notation: $p_{11} = p_1 \cdot p_1$, $p_{12} = p_1 \cdot p_2$, $p_{21} = p_2 \cdot p_1$, and $p_{22} = p_2 \cdot p_2$. The distribution vector $m\,(t) = (m_1\,(t),\, m_2\,(t)) = (50, 50)$ for all $t$.

The assumption of independence does not reflect a complex social theory, but it does represent a serious theoretical alternative that merits test in empirical situations. Independence is one way to define a "classless" society mathematically. It implies that class membership has no influence on mobility.

The next assumption is that history has an effect, but each time period only affects the succeeding time period. For time periods that are not adjacent there is no historical effect assumed. This assumption defines a Markov process.[2]

Our illustration is a special case, a first-order Markov chain. We assume that the same historical effect links each pair of adjacent time periods. Thus the transition probabilities for any pair of adjacent time intervals also hold for all pairs of adjacent time intervals. We need only study the long run effects of a single transition matrix.

For the case of the Markov chain we can represent several aspects of classical social theory. First let us choose several different values for the probabilities. Here are three cases:

$$\begin{pmatrix} 1 & 0 \\ 0 & 1 \end{pmatrix} \qquad \begin{pmatrix} .8 & .2 \\ .4 & .6 \end{pmatrix} \qquad \begin{pmatrix} .5 & .5 \\ .5 & .5 \end{pmatrix}$$

$$(1) \qquad\qquad (2) \qquad\qquad (3)$$

Case (1) would be called a caste system; Case (2) an "open" class system; and Case (3) is equivalent to the case of independence discussed above.

The long run effects of Case (3) have already been noted. If we examine Case (1) however, we see that the long run also implies a 50–50 distribution. Thus we see that the fact of a 50–50 distribution does not allow us to infer mobility rates of the social system. Quite often in sociology it is noted that an event is compatible with one hypothesis when in fact the event is compatible with a large number of hypotheses. Mathematics can help us successfully resolve such theoretical issues.

The long-run effects of Case (2) bring new complications. In a two-class system with both upward and downward mobility permitted, the long-run distribution of persons is in proportion to the ratio of the two

[2] Markov chains have been used in sociology in the following works: Blumen, Kogan, and McCarthy (7); Cohen (9, pp. 69–81); Prais (16, pp. 56–66); Anderson (1); and Goodman (12, pp. 57–78).

"change" probabilities, $p_{12}/p_{21}$. In Case (2) this ratio is one-half, and therefore, a ratio of 1 to 2 is implied, or approximately 67 to 33 in $C_1$ and $C_2$ respectively. Clearly $C_1$ will be largest, as it will initially receive twice as many as it gives up.

But Case (2) also has another interpretation. We note that the father-son mobility will never be "classless." But the possibility still exists that the grandfather-grandson mobility will be "classless" or some even more greatly attenuated ancestor-descendant relationship may be "classless." For Case (2) the grandfather-grandson, or two-step mobility relationship, is given by:

$$\begin{pmatrix} .72 & .28 \\ .56 & .44 \end{pmatrix}$$

and the four-step mobility relationship is given by:

$$\begin{pmatrix} .68 & .32 \\ .65 & .35 \end{pmatrix}$$

We note that the four-step chance to become a $C_1$ starting from $C_1$ is almost equal to the four-step chance to become a $C_1$ starting from $C_2$, i.e., ending up in $C_1$ is almost independent of four-step origin. In this sense our system is four-step classless. Note that the two rows of the four-step transition matrix are similar to the long-run distribution. As the number of steps increases the multi-step transition matrix will converge to (.67, .33) in each row. If each of the four probabilities in the transition matrix is not zero, then the method given here correctly deduces the long-run result.

We may complete the discussion with Case (4):

$$\begin{pmatrix} 1 & 0 \\ .4 & .6 \end{pmatrix}$$

Clearly in the long run everyone will be in $C_1$. Thus we discover another interpretation for a "classless" society — a society with only one class.[3] The rate at which this takes place can be computed, but we shall not pursue the matter here.

We have studied the situation in which a single transition matrix governs the entire history of the process. This case is sometimes called a "stationary" stochastic process. Now we turn our attention to the case in which the transition matrix itself becomes a variable dependent on time, the "non-stationary" case. We will continue, however, to use the Markov assumption that the historical effects extend only to adjacent time periods.

In order to trace out the history of the non-stationary process a definite mathematical formula or rule must be provided that permits us to calculate each transition matrix from the transition matrix and distribution vector of the preceding time period. An example of such a model is provided by Beshers and Reiter (6). The transition probabilities are made dependent upon the distribution of "power" among the classes. Power itself is distributed according to certain fixed parameters and according to the varying numbers of persons in each class.

At each time period we compute the number of persons in each class from a transition matrix, then we compute a new transition matrix from the number of persons obtained. Since this model assumes that the social mobility rates are determined by the balance of power, this model has classic substantive interpretation.

Another example of such non-stationary Markov processes lies in the field of contagion or epidemic models (2). Instead of two social classes changing in a generation we have two health categories, say, measles or not measles, and a week for a time unit. We may study the distribution of the number with measles over time as a result of the distribution of contacts among persons in the population. We want to know the probability of contacts between those who have not yet had measles and those who are currently infectious. Thus our system depends upon the number of persons in particular categories — specifically, the rate of infection, the transition probabilities, will vary according to the numbers of persons in the categories. We are assuming that the number with measles is the number infectious in this model. More realistic models have been constructed.

The contagion model can be interpreted in general as a diffusion model — diffusion of artifacts or diffusion of behavior throughout a population. This type of model of social change is under investigation by Coleman and his students. Sociometric measures must be used to supply empirical contact data in this approach (10, pp. 253–270). Another approach to

---

[3] The two concepts of "classlessness" presented in this chapter are completely different; no particular definition of this concept is adhered to. What I am trying to show is that the mathematics can be employed for any definition. In one case there are two "classes," but they do not serve to constrain mobility — any classical theorist would say that classes that do not have mobility effects are in fact not "social classes" and that a society with such classes as in fact a classless society. The issue turns on whether classes are defined by status symbols or by social mechanisms.

diffusion models can be made using the notion of social structure. The rate of diffusion of behavior among social "classes" may depend upon the amount of contact between the members of the various classes. The rates of intermarriage may serve to index such contact, or more general behavioral measures of the "social distance" between classes can be constructed. The probabilities of contact can be studied under the Markov assumptions (4, chapter 7 and appendix), also Beshers (5).

The non-stationary Markov processes we have been discussing all require a specification of the formula by which the new transition probabilities are calculated. This formula can be regarded as an extended "memory" of the system. As a memory, however, it is quite static in that the parameters are constant over time. Such systems are determined by their initial conditions, with no variability allowed for "experience."

One might well ask if a "learning" mechanism could be developed. Selective "recall," transitions to novel "response" patterns, or "insight" are all suggestive of the kind of mechanism that might be desirable. In effect, this raises the question of a cumulative culture — is Pareto correct in asserting that no essential change occurs in cultural history, or is Cassirer's view of the evolution of symbolic manipulation in culture more adequate?

Questions of this sort can be approached in several ways. Let us return to the basic branching process. The elements are traveling along the various paths. Now, let us regard the presence of an element on a path as the result of a "decision." We assume the existence of a "criterion" for selection of the path. Suppose further that during the journey down the path there is some "test" of the criterion — in the crudest case, a reward or punishment. The result of the test can influence the selection of path at the next "trial" of the experiment.

There are several different possibilities within this general situation. First, the probabilities underlying the "test" can be manipulated in various ways. If these probabilities are held constant during the experiment, then one might predict the "response" pattern on the basis of Markov chain theory as presented above. This is the basis for the Estes-Bush-Mosteller approach to psychological learning theory (8).

Second, we may regard the "test" as an introduction of new information into the system. Thus the criteria for decision may be fixed, but the alternative selected may depend upon the availability of "new" information during the process.

This case may be illustrated as a non-stationary process in which the formula for computing the new transition matrix contains fixed parameters. The formula is re-estimated from a sequential sampling of "new" information. In effect the formula is re-estimated by a least square procedure in which the parameters determining the general nature of the formula are fixed, but the new data also have an effect on the precise definition of the formula.

Third, we may have both "new" information and "new" decision criteria during the process. This is the possibility of "insight." In effect, the formula by which the transition probabilities are computed has fewer constants, or parameters, than in the previous case. Depending upon the relative weight assigned to new information as against past information, the change of the parameters themselves may be slow or rapid. If great weight is given to new information then a continuous "memory decay" takes place.

These last two types of models are not easily constructed. Yet great effort is being invested in this area and results pertinent to theories of social change can be expected from this effort (11). The more subtle theories of social change may hope to find mathematical representation in these developments.

Let us now indicate some problems not readily handled by mathematical methods. Generally speaking, the dialectical theories mentioned earlier cause the greatest trouble. The difficulties in formalizing such theories stem from two features.

First, the transitions from epoch to epoch in classical social theory often imply the emergence of entirely new relationships among variables. This view may be entirely realistic, but it provides little guidance for theory construction. Just how one is to deduce the form of this system is not suggested, save that certain variables, say, the economic or the technological, are assumed to have over-riding significance. The sequentially revised models mentioned above have some applicabilities, but if the change in system is radical then much time will pass before a suitably revised model is constructed.

Second, the emergence of new variables themselves creates difficulties. This is not a hypothetical question. Take the case of occupation. Any system of variables that includes occupation, either as a dependent or independent variable, has to contend with the fact that entirely new occupations have developed in the last 150 years. Only the grossest of classifications of occupations can be used to compare the new system with the old. Such gross classifications may, in fact, obscure essential features of the new system of variables.

Some other special problems can be noted in passing. Often short-run fluctuations are of interest, in contrast to long-run equilibrium analyses. Computer methods can be devised for this situation but it is not simple.

Cyclical equilibrium processes can be studied fairly easily. One can study the period of the cycles on a statistical basis, or one can investigate the mechanisms that bring about the cyclical behavior. In the latter case the mechanism must be explicit if formalization of the theory is to be undertaken. Note that we do not have to deal with the emergence of new relationships or new variables that can occur in certain transition problems discussed above.

## Summary

In summary, the study of social change can be aided by various mathematical methods. These methods make possible unambiguous deductions as to the course of social change. Quite a number of these methods are currently available, others are under development.

With these new methods the theory of social change can undergo a metamorphosis from being the most vague of social theories to being among the more precise social theories. Greater precision of theoretical statement makes possible more refined empirical testing.

## BIBLIOGRAPHY

1. Anderson, T. W. "Probability Models for Analyzing Time Changes in Attitudes," in Paul F. Lazarsfeld (ed.), *Mathematical Thinking in the Social Sciences*. Glencoe, Ill.: The Free Press, 1954.

2. Bartlett, M. S. *Stochastic Population Models in Ecology and Epidemiology*. New York: John Wiley & Sons, 1960.

3. Beshers, James M. "Models and Theory Construction," *American Sociological Review*, Vol. 22 (February 1957), pp. 32–38.

4. Beshers, James M. *Urban Social Structure*. New York: The Free Press, 1962.

5. Beshers, James M. "Urban Social Structure as a Single Hierarchy," *Social Forces*, Vol. 41 (March 1963), pp. 233–239.

6. Beshers, James M., and Stanley Reiter. "Social Status and Social Change," *Behavioral Science*, Vol. 8 (January 1963), pp. 1–13.

7. Blumen, I., M. Kogan, and P. J. McCarthy. "The Industrial Mobility of Labor as a Probability Process," *Cornell Studies in Industrial and Labor Relations*, Vol. 7 (1955).

8. Bush, Robert R. "Mathematical Learning Theories," in R. Duncan Luce (ed.), *Developments in Mathematical Psychology*. Glencoe, Ill.: The Free Press, 1960.

9. Cohen, B. P. "A Probability Model for Conformity," *Sociometry*, Vol. 21 (March 1958) pp. 69–81.

10. Coleman, James S., Elihu Katz, and Herbert Menzel. "The Diffusion of an Innovation Among Physicians," *Sociometry*, Vol. 20 (1957), pp. 253–270.

11. Ferguson, Charles E., and Ralph W. Pfouts. "Learning and Expectations in Dynamic Duopoly Behavior," *Behavioral Science*, Vol. 7 (April 1962), pp. 223–237.

12. Goodman, Leo A. "Statistical Methods for Analyzing Processes of Change," *American Journal of Sociology*, Vol. 67 (July 1962), pp. 57–78.

13. Kaplan, Abraham. "Sociology Learns the Language of Mathematics," in

James R. Newman (ed.), *The World of Mathematics.* New York: Simon and Schuster, 1956.

14. Kemeny, John G., Laurie J. Snell, and Gerald L. Thompson. *Introduction to Finite Mathematics.* Englewood Cliffs, N.J.: Prentice-Hall, Inc., 1956.

15. Lewin, Kurt. "On Aristotelian and Galilean Modes of Inquiry," in Kurt Lewin (ed.), *A Dynamic Theory of Personality.* New York: McGraw-Hill Book Co., 1935.

16. Prais, S. J. "Measuring Social Mobility," *Journal of the Royal Statistical Society,* Vol. 118 (1955), pp. 56–66.

17. Weber, Max. "Bureaucracy and the Sociology of Charismatic Authority," in Hans Gerth and C. Wright Mills (eds.), *From Max Weber.* New York: Oxford University Press, 1946.

18. Weber, Max. *The Protestant Ethic and the Spirit of Capitalism.* New York: Charles Scribner's Sons, 1958.

# SECTION FIVE

psycho-social models of change

# Introduction

Established definitions of the terms "social" and "psychological" have been breaking down in recent years. Almost anyone who reads this book will be able to remember some occasion, an examination perhaps, when he or she was called upon to provide a demarcation for these "levels" of scientific explanation. Yet it should be kept in mind that Auguste Comte saw no necessity for distinguishing between two such levels in his hierarchical system of classification of the sciences, and his disciple, Durkheim, found a reluctant place for "social psychology" in his own, very similar classification of scientific levels, only toward the end of his life. Perhaps the distinction of "levels," like many other spurious demarcations in human knowledge, has been no more than the resultant of traditional disciplinary boundaries and of the clash of academic vested interests. When social change (or personality change) becomes the focus of attention, rigid distinctions of such levels melt in one's gaze. Perhaps the very idea of "static" systems of society or of the personality is bound up with overt or covert attempts to maintain such distinctions. How otherwise could something as "unnatural" as a static system be conceived? Under the demanding discipline which requires one to account for changing situations, the traditional "levels" give way to a variety of interlocking systems, neither entirely "social" nor entirely "psychological" in the established usage of these words.

This is rather reminiscent of the *Angelology* of Duns Scotus, in which the weighty question posed in the *Liber Sententiarium* of Petrus Lombardus (Bishop of Paris) concerning the number of angels who could dance on the head of a pin was tempered by consideration of whether angels might interpenetrate. (To the best of our recollection, the question of angelic "saturation points" went beyond even the brilliant and prophetic imagery of John the Scott.) Later on, with Descartes, the question of angels became "immaterial" in more than one sense of the word. Materiality and extension were "self-evidently" co-terminous, and angels (if indeed they existed) were again forced to jostle cheek by jowl (if indeed they had cheeks or jowls), just as they were by the unimaginative Bishop of Paris. Our readers should not jump to the unwarranted conclusion, at this point, that we prefer the outpourings of the Scottish spirit to distillations of the French; we believe simply, that an interpenetration of fields of forces (or, for that matter, of angels), is vastly superior to cramped vortex motions in Descartes' "pushy" world. Many conceptual angels dance on the pinhead of human thought and action — and they interpenetrate!

Our authors in this section view the traditional boundaries of learning with healthy and peremptory disdain. For Levinson, an "idea system" interpenetrates with personalities and with social structures. Warshay draws a broad rainbow of perspectives across our vision, iridescent with sportive hues and shades. Zablocki is concerned with the interplay of motive and political manipulation. The Lauers straddle the fields of history and social psychology. Finally, Barnett, who earns his bread in the workshops of anthropology, strides magisterially through the thickets of both psychology and logic, leaving a path which can be followed in safety, if not with ease. It may all be very puzzling to university administrators and their kind, but none of our contributors can be chided for "narrowness of perspective," and those who lament the passing of Renaissance man should both pause and take courage.

Levinson's points are brought out very concisely in a series of propositions, which he embroiders in the body of his chapter. To paraphrase these propositions here would be pointless, but he presents leads for further research to which attention may fruitfully be brought. His first proposition emphasizes the importance of autocracy and democracy for the characterization of idea systems. It follows that the transformation of an authoritarian personality into an egalitarian one (or vice versa), or of an autocratic social structure into a democratic one (or vice versa), becomes a question of some importance for the study of social and personality change. The conditions under which such changes could occur are implied by Levinson. They have to do with the number and variety of ideological alternatives available in the socio-cultural matrix, in their legitimation, in the sanctions supporting the legitimized ideologies and discouraging non-legitimized ones, and, perhaps, in other elements as well. A model that could formally relate these elements and give them relative weight would be of the greatest importance in the study of ideology. Another question raised by Levinson that whets one's appetite for further researches concerns the feedback (if any) that exists to the social-cultural matrix from the personalities of strategically placed persons in the structure. For example, could the accession to leadership of an egalitarian person in an autocratic society increase the availability (or, perhaps, the production) of ideological alternatives? Thus, Levinson's discussion, though basically theoretical, is fecund in the empirically testable questions it raises, and this enhances its importance.

Zablocki's contribution provides a thoroughly Macchiavellian contrast with Levinson's foregoing concerns about democracy. Perhaps the difference of ten years between the times at which these pieces were written, as much as any personal differences of interest and style of the two authors, accounts for their distinct "atmospheres." By "crisis" Zablocki means much the same sort of thing as Zollschan terms "urgency." The chapter adds a useful dimension to motivationally oriented models of social processes by examining how crises can be manipulated for the advantage of those who hold power. Zablocki's pessimism concerning the possibility of testing motivational models is not shared by the editors. We hope the author will belie his own pessimism by providing some of the strategies and measures so badly needed for conducting adequate tests in this vital area of concern.

Out of the welter of "all possible character types," Warshay isolates what must surely be not only the "best" but also the most novel — the person of broad perspective. When we become thoroughly introduced to this character we discover (not, perhaps, with too much surprise) that he is a symbolic interactionist with interests ranging all the way from demography to the "perception habits" of experimental psychology. But he takes other forms as well. That such a person is better able to bring change about than others is highly probable (although, as Warshay demonstrates, this occurs only under specifiable conditions). "Aye, there's the rub," for the question then arises as to whether such a person is likely to be in a *structural position* to influence change. Here the answer is, generally speaking, negative, although exceptions to this rule are, again, subject to enumeration and specification. Although much more work is freely acknowledged by Warshay to be necessary before the relationship between perspective breadth and social change are fully disentangled, the delicate whimsicality of his characters, both broad-perspectived and narrow (as well as the predicament of his "house fly with its twenty-four hour cycle"), cannot but broaden the perspective of any whose eyes light on this essay.

While Warshay is concerned with his "wide-eyed" protagonist as an agent of change, Barnett's actor accepts, or rejects, innovations impinging upon him from outside. In common with the other scholars represented in his Section, Barnett proclaims that there is "no antithesis between a psychological and a sociological treatment" of his problem. Levinson's relatively organized conception of an idea system interpenetrates with individuals and social structures. Barnett, however, is concerned with the partial and differential interpenetration of systems of meanings and understandings, that is, with communications. Every "message" or stimulus, as it were, has the qualities of a *"multiple entendre,"* and every perceiver may receive the message in its entirety, selectively, in distorted form, or not at all. With great originality and logical acuity, Barnett develops a paradigm in which the acceptance-rejection possibilities in any given confrontation of a person with a message may be systematically and exhaustively explored. He reports on a test of its empirical applicability.

The chapter by Robert and Jeanette Lauer combines the viewpoints, respectively, of a social psychologist and a historian to an examination of the effects of the tempo of social change upon the amount of stress evinced by exposed individuals. This delightfully written contribution reveals, despite its lucidity of style and presentation or, perhaps, because of these, the difficulties inherent in making comparisons of data obtained from two such widely differing perspectives. The clarity and candour with which these problems are exposed adds greatly to the value of the piece. The chapter forms a natural transition to Section Six (concerned with historical perspectives), which immediately follows the group of chapters here discussed.

# 16

*Daniel J. Levinson*

# Idea Systems in the Individual

# and in Society*

Ideas have long been recognized as a moving force in the lives of nations and of individuals. Many of the sciences and humanities are concerned with the nature of man's thought, with his ideational productions, and with the causes and consequences of man's conceptions of himself and the world he lives in. The inquiries have been conceptualized in various forms: the sociology of knowledge; the psychology of attitudes; analyses of ideology, public opinion, cultural values and value-orientations, political and religious movements, themes in intellectual history, and the like.

The starting point for all such analyses, the phenomenal stuff on which they work, I should like to call the "idea system." By this I mean the total manifold of concrete ideas by means of which an individual or social group defines its reality and guides its affairs. For certain purposes it is useful to distinguish various types of idea systems according to the sector of the social world, or of human experience, with which they deal. Thus, there are idea systems concerning religion, politics, education, international relations, and so on.

* An early version of this paper was presented in 1954 at the Founders Day Institute of Boston University. The present version, developed after a period of gestation, follows the same line of reasoning but incorporates some recent trends in my own thinking and in the literature. For useful suggestions and criticisms I am indebted to Professors Gordon W. Allport, Alex Inkeles, and Robert W. White. Work on this study was facilitated by research grants M–687 and M–1000 from the National Institute of Mental Health, U.S. Public Health Service, and by a grant from the Foundations Fund for Research in Psychiatry.

For purposes of analysis, the idea system can be regarded as an aspect of the individual or as an aspect of a collective unit (community, class, nation). Every collectivity develops a limited number of viewpoints or rationales that justify and make meaningful its social structure, traditions, and modes of operation. Its idea systems are contained in "collective documents" such as constitutions, official statements of policy, folklore, newspapers, and other mass media. They are presented to children and to new members of adult groups by a variety of formal and informal indoctrination agencies. The collectivity provides, as it were, an ideological environment for its members — an environment that facilitates certain ideational learnings and impedes others. The collectivity, like the individual, must have ideational rationales that help in maintaining its integration and in meeting its day-to-day problems.

Every individual forms his own idea systems, utilizing passively or creatively the viewpoints available in his social environment. His idea systems have a particular content; they also reflect his modes of thinking, his character traits, his unconscious fantasies, and the like. A general theory of idea systems must take account of their functions for, and their impact upon, the individual as well as the collectivity.

The distinction between the concrete idea system and the analytically derived characteristics such as attitudes or values is an important one, for two main reasons. First, it serves to emphasize that terms such as "values" or "ideology" are analytic constructs selectively imposed by the social scientist for theoretical purposes. Since no one analytic device can ever take account of the full complexity of the phenomena being investigated, and since our theories are still of such limited power, we ought to be alert to new variables and new modes of analysis. Second, the distinction between ideational phenomena and analytic constructs is a reminder that seemingly disparate analyses of ideology, of social attitudes, public opinion, cultural values, and intellectual history, all deal with the same order of phenomena. The various modes of analysis should certainly not be combined or reduced to a single master plan. In these days of attempted synthesis in the social sciences, the distinctiveness of the single disciplines has also to be acknowledged. However, if we cannot have full synthesis we can at least strive for a kind of coordinated autonomy.

This chapter seeks to bring together, in a single framework, modes of analysis derived from sociology and from dynamic psychology. Its guiding concepts are *ideology, personality,* and *social structure.*

In ideological analysis, the idea system is characterized with regard to the type of social structure it supports and rationalizes. Thus, when we say that a man has a "fundamentalist Protestant" religious ideology, we mean that his idea system regarding religion is most consistent with, and gives the greatest support to, a fundamentalist Protestant form of religious organization. Again, various concrete idea systems concerning international relations can be classified according to the types of foreign policy they envisage. Ideology is a "type" concept; for example, "fundamentalist Protestantism" is a construct that will be approximated but seldom fully exemplified in any particular case.

Ideological analysis takes into account the scope and organization of the idea system. In this respect it differs from the mode of analysis used in many current studies which focus on a single, narrowly defined "attitude" or "opinion" concerning a specific social issue. Analysis in terms of broad ideological patterns would seem of greater value from a sociopsychological point of view. By viewing the individual's idea system as corresponding roughly to a currently available ideology, we are in a good position to "move outward," to coordinate the study of individuals with the study of social structures. At the same time, having thus characterized the idea system in terms of its relation to the external social world, we are in a better position to "move inward" and to analyze it in terms of its relation to the intra-psychic world. That is, we can consider the personal meanings, motives, and modes of functioning expressed in a given ideological pattern. This mode of analysis, which I should like to call *personological*, takes as its starting point the assumption that an idea system has expressive, adaptive, and defensive functions for its adherents — in short, that the idea system is an aspect of personality.

Ideology and personality thus constitute two distinct but interrelated analytic frameworks that can be applied to a common phenomenal reality, the idea systems of individuals or collectivities. Ideological analysis tells us about the kind of social world its adherents want to live in. Personological analysis tells us about the kind of person who prefers one rather than another social world. The influence of deeper-lying aspects of personality upon ideological preference will be considered below.

This chapter offers a theoretical approach to the analysis of ideology and of its interrelations with personality and social structure. We begin with a particular set of ideological orientations — "autocratic" and "democratic" — and relate these to a corresponding set of personality constellations — "authoritarian" and "equalitarian," respectively. Following this, we present a more general formulation of ideology viewed as an aspect of personality. Finally, relations among ideology, personality, and social structure are considered. The major elements of the theoretical argument will be stated as a series of theses or propositions.

## Autocratic Ideology and Authoritarian Personality

**Proposition I. The concepts of autocracy and democracy are widely applicable and of fundamental importance in the analysis of ideology.**

Autocratic orientations may be characterized briefly as follows. They emphasize, and seek to maximize, status and power differences in social life. They involve a hierarchical conception of society — "a place for everyone and everyone in his place." Status considerations permeate social interaction. There is great emphasis on authority. It is regarded as both natural and right that social power be concentrated in the hands of a few authorities or elites. An authority (higher-status) figure has the right, indeed the obligation, to dominate those in a subordinate position, in whom obedience and respect are the cardinal virtues. In more structural terms, an autocratic group is characterized by a unilateral, downward flow of power, the low-status roles having little opportunity to initiate or control in matters of group policy. This conception of social structure is applicable to small, face-to-face groups, to single institutions and organizations, to massive social structures within a nation, and to international relations.

It is more difficult to characterize the democratic orientations, whose ideal of societal patterning tends to be more open-ended, more predicated on "variousness" and change. In general, they are inclined to minimize control, to conceive of authority as temporarily delegated rather than permanently established, and to minimize the existing differentials in power and formal status. They may take an extreme libertarian or even anarchistic form in which all direct forms of authority and control are opposed, or they may attempt various forms of synthesis of the often conflicting demands of individual self-determination and collective integration. Clearly, to be democratic one need not in principle oppose the institutionalizing of authority nor the requirement of some degree of individual conformity as such. Democrats seek, however, to minimize these requirements, to replace "arbitrary" with "rational" authority (12), and to eliminate conformity based primarily on fear and on self-deception.

The autocratic-democratic distinction is a generic one in numerous analyses of the history and present characteristics of Western civilization. Thus, in describing the evolution of the Western intellectual climate since the Middle Ages, Crane Brinton (7) finds as perhaps the dominant trend the development of the democratic spirit, nourished first by humanism, Protestantism, and rationalism, and modified in various forms in the nineteenth and twentieth centuries. There is always a congeries of democratic orientations, for democratism is in principle individualistic, change-seeking, inductive rather of multanimity than of unanimity. Nor can any single democratic variant rightfully claim to be the ultimate or final realization of democratic ideals. In Parrington's (28) analysis, a dialectic between democratic and autocratic modes of thought is seen as fundamental in American intellectual history. Lionel Trilling (33), from a slightly different vantage point, writes of the "liberal imagination" on the assumption that liberalism constitutes a single, though diversely motivated and manifested, approach to life. A distinction between democratic and autocratic approaches underlies Fromm's (11) treatment of European history, Almond's (4) discussion of American foreign policy, the analyses of industrial firms by Gouldner (16), Argyris (6), MacGregor (24), and others, and various treatments of "modern" as contrasted with "traditional" approaches to the penal, educational, and mental hospital systems (e.g., Ohlin, [27]; Goffman, [14]; Greenblatt, Levinson and Williams, [15]).

**Proposition II. Consistency: Individuals are relatively (though by no means entirely) consistent from one ideological domain to another in their tendency to think autocratically or democratically.**

For example, persons who hold an autocratic ideology regarding the family will, according to this hypothesis, tend also to be autocratic in their views on intergroup relations, religion, education, and the like.

There are various lines of empirical study along which this hypothesis can be investigated. One may, for example, analyze the writings of various individuals who have played an important part in history. Thus, in our own country, we find variegated forms of democratism expressed in the ideas of such men as Roger Williams, Benjamin Franklin, Whitman, and Thoreau. Conversely, we find contrasting, autocratic conceptions variously expressed by Increase Mather, Alexander Hamilton, and Henry Clay, and more recently by a number of political and military figures well known for their extreme nationalism, anti-intellectualism, and propensity to limit civil liberties. C. H. Pritchett (29) has shown that our Supreme Court justices during the late 'forties can be divided into fairly clear-cut "liberal" and "conservative" factions in accord with their stand on a series of civil liberties cases. It would be of interest to determine whether this consistency extended to other ideological domains. There are, of course, national leaders who have shown conflict over, and attempted compromise between, autocratic and democratic modes of thought. They are in accord with the above hypothesis as long as their "intermediate" position between the two extremes is maintained in various ideological domains.

For more general theoretical purposes, however, it is important to determine whether the "consistency" hypothesis holds among ordinary individuals in various walks of life, and to test it in a more rigorous manner. Evidence of this kind is given by research reported in *The Authoritarian Personality* (1) and other related studies. I can attempt only the briefest summary here. It should be noted that the subjects for these studies are primarily of the urban middle class, and that the specific ideological content and techniques of measurement may have to be modified in other groupings. It should also be noted, however, that similar results have been obtained on highly diversified groupings in several regions of this country and in several other countries.

There appears to be a significant though imperfect relationship among the following ideological orientations. That is to say, an individual's tendency to support or to oppose an autocratic position in one ideological domain corresponds roughly to his position in the others.

a) In the domain of *intergroup relations,* autocracy is represented by *ethnocentric* ideology (1). Ethnocentrism, in our definition, "is based on a pervasive and rigid ingroup-outgroup distinction; it involves stereotyped negative imagery and hostile attitudes regarding outgroups, stereotyped positive imagery and submissive attitudes regarding ingroups, and a hierarchical view of group interaction in which ingroups are rightly dominant, outgroups subordinate." This conception of ethnocentrism as an ideology encompasses a variety of tendencies usually considered in isolation. It includes anti-minority prejudice, anti-intellectualism, illiberalism regarding civil rights, and that form of nationalism in which other nations are regarded as inferior and threatening and one's own nation is glorified (23).

b) Autocratic ideologies regarding the *family* most often take a relatively traditional, patriarchal form (even though the actual family structure may in some respects be matriarchal) (22). The husband is regarded as formal head of the household, and the wife is ultimately more responsible to him than he to her. Automatic acceptance of parental standards and discipline are of primary importance in the conception of a "good" child. The requirements of various roles, particularly the lower-status ones, tend to be concretely specified and conformity to them demanded. The conceptions of masculinity and femininity are disparate to the point of dichotomy; males and females are conceived of as made out of different stuff, and a double standard of sexual morality and social responsibility is held. The democratic family orientations are more variable. Concerning child-rearing, they may involve an easy-going informality, an anxious permissiveness in which difficulty in accepting the authority functions of the parental role may be discerned, or an attempted synthesis of the control-inducing and the individuality-supporting functions of parents. Similarly, concerning husband-wife relations and masculinity-femininity generally, the democratic orientations may attempt totally to equate or partially to differentiate the roles and personal characteristics of men and women.

c) In the case of *religion,* the autocratic ideologies tend to be either fundamentalistic (especially in rural and in lower-class urban settings) or "conventionalistic" — the somewhat diluted fundamentalism often found in middle and upper class urban settings (5; 21). The approaches conceived of here as more democratic are those which, broadly speaking, are more humanistic. These viewpoints tend to be associated with democratic viewpoints in other spheres. They ordinarily conceive of God in abstract terms or not at all; they emphasize the ethical more than the supernatural aspects of religion, and they view religion in individualized terms rather than as a matter of institutional allegiance and adherence to tradition (2).

d) Finally, the autocratic orientations take the form of traditionalism or *"custodialism"* in such diverse institutional settings as *mental hospitals, prisons, schools,* and *wartime relocation centers* (e.g., Leighton, 20). In each of these settings there is a massive membership — patients, criminals, pupils, or "enemy aliens" — who are in some sense being "treated" and cared for by employed personnel. The autocratically-minded personnel tend to conceive of the institution in hierarchical terms, to be mainly concerned in their work with maintaining order and efficiency, and to relate to the "inmates" in a stereotyped, essentially anxious and suspicious manner. The more democratic personnel, on the other hand, seek to minimize rules, to equalize the rights of all concerned, and to deal with the members on an individualized basis. Various forms of this approach have guided the development of rehabilitation-oriented policies in prisons and mental hospitals, and of the modern educational system.

I have briefly described prototypic autocratic and democratic positions in several ideological domains. I have suggested that the several autocratic viewpoints constitute a broad ideological syndrome in the sense that they tend to co-exist in the same individuals. And I have described a corresponding but contrasting democratic syndrome. Having stated a proposition in its most general form, let me add a few qualifications.

First, the world is not to be divided simply into democrats and autocrats. These terms refer not to simple categories but to opposing extremes of a continuum on which there are numerous intermediate positions. Moreover, the continuum is internally complex; at each point it contains a series of qualitatively distinctive variants. Although the distinction between autocratic and democratic viewpoints is of fundamental importance, the qualitative differences among democrats and among autocrats are also significant and worthy of investigation.

Second, I wish to emphasize both that the correlations among the several constellations are *significant* and that they are *imperfect*. At their best, the correlation values reach .8, at their worst perhaps .3. Few are the individuals who are ideologically all of a piece; and small wonder, in view of the internal contradictions and complexities of both individual personality and social milieu. Let us avoid, then, all spuriously homogenized conceptions, whether of individual ideology, of individual personality, or of sociocultural matrix. We shall consider presently conditions that make for more or less ideological consistency in the individual.

Third, the constructs of democratic and autocratic outlook regarding any institutional sphere are theoretical prototypes and are only approximated in any concrete individual case. This is particularly true of individuals assessed as "democratic" by our measures or by other, reasonably meaningful criteria. Ask a number of persons whether they have prejudices and, as several studies have shown, those who are relatively the most open-minded will answer most often in the affirmative. To be relatively low in prejudice and to be ready to oppose it in oneself and others, is not necessarily to lack prejudice. In attempting, however crudely, to measure a given democratic-autocratic continuum, we must keep in mind the range of possibilities to be found in the particular cultural setting. In our society, where the cultural diversity is so great and the ambivalence about it even greater, not many of us can get through childhood without forming some stereotypes about our own and other groups, some anxieties about our own identities, and some tendencies to project onto various groups what we cannot integrate in ourselves. However, some persons try harder than others to outgrow these early difficulties.

**Proposition III. The individual's readiness to hold an autocratic or a democratic ideology in one domain, and his relative consistency across domains, depends in large part on generalized, enduring personality characteristics.**

*Authoritarian personality* constellations make for receptivity to autocratic ideology, while *equalitarian personality* is associated with democratic ideology.

Authoritarianism and equalitarianism are conceived of as opposite poles of a broad continuum along which personalities differ. Each polar extreme is to be thought of not as a homogeneous entity but rather as a complex syndrome of dynamically interrelated characteristics. Each syndrome is defined broadly to allow for numerous individual and subtype variations, and enough component variables can be measured so that individuals can be crudely assessed with respect to their qualitative patterning and their quantitative position along this continuum. Although empirically derived, both syndromes are theoretical models or prototypes seldom found in their pure forms, at least in our society.

The numerous features of each constellation can be given only the briefest summary here. (The interested reader is referred to the work of Stagner [32], Fromm [11], Reich [30], Maslow [25], Dicks [8], and the collaborative research of Adorno, Frenkel-Brunswik, Levinson, and Sanford [1]). At one level, authoritarianism includes the values and conceptions of social symbols noted earlier in the generalized formulation of autocratic orientations (Proposition I): for example, a preference for hierarchical status structures and for strict conformity to established modes, and a conception of the "alien" as threatening to ingroup integrity. In addition, authoritarianism comprises other characteristics which underlie, and are reinforced by, the autocratic values and conceptions. These include: unconscious fear of weakness and immorality in oneself and the wish for a powerful, protecting-controlling authority; extreme self-deception concerning one's own impulses and feelings; a tendency to displace aggression from its early-childhood familial objects to others conceived of as immoral or weak; rigidity and intolerance of ambiguity in cognitive functioning and in the handling of inner conflicts; punitiveness as a favored way of dealing with value-violations; and others.

It is not necessary to continue the listing of specific characteristics. What we need, and what we do not yet have, is a well substantiated, theoretical formulation of the fundamental underpinnings of authoritarianism. Let me suggest the following as a tentative start in this direction: (a) Much of the early-childhood fantasy life of authoritarian personalities has become ego-alien and has continued in an extremely primitive form. Comparatively, the fantasy life has been unable to develop, to enrich the individual's conception of himself and his capacity for imaginative understanding of self and others. (b) The super-ego — the intrapsychic moral agency established in early childhood — has also remained strong but ego-alien. It continues as a source of threat to the ego-organization, imposing the absolutistic demands of childhood morality which the ego either accedes to (as in the case of compulsive conformity) or rebels wildly against (as in criminality and other anti-social rebellion). (c) As a corollary of the first two: the ego has been largely unable to fulfill its synthesizing functions, that is, to achieve a meaningful identity, a mature conscience, a capacity for genuinely loving relationships to self and others, and a freeing of the imagination and intellect for constructive, complex pursuits.

The various equalitarian syndromes merit fuller analysis than they have yet received. In their values, equalitarian individuals show an opposition to rigid hierarchy and a preference for self-expression, self-understanding, and affectional mutuality in human relationships. In comparison with authoritarians they tend, on the average, to be more insightful, flexible, autonomous, unvindictive, love-oriented and change-seeking. They have, by and large, come farther in the direction of moral integrity and personal maturity. Yet it would be an oversimplification to identify equalitarianism with maturity or mental health or total freedom from irrationality. The differences between the two constellations are in part quantitative; one might say that equalitarians are in many ways like authoritarians, only less so. In a more important sense, however, their values, conceptions, modes of ego functioning, and forms of irrationality differ qualitatively. For example, in contrast to authoritarians, relatively equalitarian persons may tend unrealistically to idealize the disadvantaged and to reject the legitimate authority.

There is considerable evidence that the authoritarian-equalitarian continuum of personality is associated to a significant degree with autocratic-democratic continua in the various ideological domains mentioned earlier in Proposition II. Measures of personal authoritarianism have been shown to correlate appreciably with measures of autocratic ideology regarding intergroup relations, the family, religion, education, the mental hospital, and other institutional structures. We thus have empirical support for the proposition that individual ideology has internal as well as external sources. What a man believes about the external world depends, in part at least, on what he *is* within himself.

The qualifications stated earlier with regard to ideological consistency hold also with regard to ideology-personality consistency. Authoritarianism and equalitarianism are not homogeneous entities or simple categories into which people can be neatly placed. Although we can for certain purposes speak of a single (quantitative) continuum and construct theoretical prototypes at each extreme, we must keep in mind that few individuals actually exemplify a given prototype in its entirety. Individual personality, like individual ideology, is seldom made of a single cloth. This is particularly true of relatively equalitarian persons, in whom opposing tendencies are more the rule than the exception. Moreover, the correlations between general authoritarianism and the several ideological orientations, though moderately high (of the order, .5 to .8), are by no means perfect or invariant. Ideological inconsistency in the individual is partly a reflection of deeper-lying contradictions of personality; but it is also due in part to contradictory ideological demands and opportunities in the social milieu. Finally, the depth of the psychic roots of ideology — the degree to which an ideology expresses, and has functions for, other aspects of personality — undoubtedly varies from individual to individual and from one ideological domain to another within a given individual (see Proposition VI, below).

### Formation of Ideology in the Individual: The Influence of Social Structure and of Personality

Our discussion has thus far centered on one particular set of ideological orientations, seen in relation to a corresponding set of broader personality constellations. However, the study of autocratic ideology and authoritarian personality is derived from, and has implications for, a more general theory of ideology and its relation both to personality and to social structure. This theory is broadly outlined in the remaining propositions.

**Proposition IV. The socio-cultural matrix of the adult plays an important part in establishing and maintaining his ideology.**

Every social milieu presents, explicitly or implicitly, directly or indirectly, a patterned set of general values and specific norms that defines the rights and obligations of the individuals within it. These values and norms legitimize certain kinds of behavior. They set limits on what may be regarded as acceptable behavior; beyond these limits behavior will be considered "eccentric," "criminal," or "subversive." An ideology is, in socio-cultural perspective, a *rationale* that serves to justify, interpret, and integrate the structurally-given norms.

The stability of any social order depends not merely on the inducing of behavioral conformity to its normative requirements, but also on the

inducing of some degree of ideological conformity. That is to say, societal stability requires that the most common (*modal*) ideologies held
by its individual members shall be congruent with, and thus serve to
maintain, the norms of the existing social structure. The greater the
prevalence of structure-congruent ideology, the greater the likelihood of
structure-supporting behavior. While societies differ in the degree of
ideological diversity they produce and tolerate, every society has, as part
of its apparatus of social control (stability-maintenance), numerous
means of encouraging individual ideology-formation in "appropriate"
directions and of hindering development in other ideological directions.

The following are but a few of the ways in which the social order
exerts an influence on individual ideology. It limits the number and
variety of ideological alternatives available to its members. It legitimizes
only those alternatives which are reasonably congruent with the existing
social structure and policy. Through an intricate system of sanctions,
it supports the holding of legitimized viewpoints and punishes ideological
deviance. The societal elite groups, which are likely to be identified with
the prevailing system, can exert great conformity-inducing influence as
a result of their prestige, their control over the indoctrination and communication media, and their politico-economic power. In every society
there are greater or lesser limitations on the range of available experiences. Very often, individuals are systematically prevented from having
experiences that might lead them to question the dominant ideologies;
for example, the idea that Negroes are uneducable is reinforced in the
deep rural South by a system that hinders the Negroes' intellectual development at every turn.

Many social scientists have been so impressed with the number and
pervasiveness of the mechanisms of ideological control, and with their
system-stabilizing value, that they have made rather generous assumptions about the degree of ideological uniformity achieved among the
members of any given society. They have tended also to assume that
such uniformities as do exist are brought about directly by social pressures of the kind listed above and they have given little consideration to
the part played by personality factors in this process. My position, to
be developed below, is that (a) the degree of ideological diversity in
most social systems is greater than most social scientists have recognized,
and (b) personality influences ideology-formation in all societies, whether
the ideological diversity among their members is small or great.

**Proposition V. The formation of ideology in the individual involves
numerous aspects of personality and is not a matter of simple imitation
or pure reason.**

Two conceptions of the process of individual ideology-formation
are rejected by this proposition. The *imitation* theories are represented
in caricature by Will Rogers' facetious expression, "All I know is what I

read in the newspaper." According to these viewpoints, people acquire their opinions and values by absorbing, in a more or less automatic fashion, those ideas which their environment presents most often and with the greatest pressure. It is only a moderate distortion to call them "sponge" theories, for they conceive of the individual as a passive material that soaks up whatever ideological liquids the environment provides. These theories have been historically useful in emphasizing the importance of learning and of the social environment in ideology-formation. They have been simplistic and dreadfully limiting, however, in their neglect of the complexities in the external "stimulus field" and in their failure to grasp the varied psychological processes involved in the selection, organization, and creation of ideas. In particular, they have overlooked the role of reason and the more complex conceptual-imaginative processes, as well as the myriad ways in which man's intellectual operations are influenced by non-rational and irrational processes. More on this shortly.

In the more *rationalistic* theories, "self-interest" becomes a primary basis for the formation of ideology. It is assumed that an individual's general orientation, or his stand on a particular issue, will be determined primarily by a more or less rational appraisal of his personal interest or the interests of the groups to which he belongs. This approach has been especially prominent in economics and political science, where the conceptions of "economic man" and "political man," each hedonistically and rationally pursuing his practical goals, have until recently prevailed. It has had value in pointing up the social functions of ideology and the role of social forces in the formation and change of ideology.

There are, however, several major inadequacies in this approach. First, it cannot account for those cases — too numerous to be lightly passed over — in which an individual's (or group's) ideology is not in accord with his immediate interests, and indeed may be antithetical to them. A few contemporary examples: anti-Semitism in Jews, the acceptance of chauvinistic ideologies against their own group interest by Negroes and women, the existence of extremely conservative, pro-business political ideology among workers, and the phenomenon of the upper-class radical. Second, it is often difficult to say what is the "true" interest of a given group. Every group has multiple aims and interests, some of which may limit or preclude the realization of others. Again, since each individual belongs to, and is identified with, a variety of groups whose interests are not likely fully to coincide, his ideology cannot serve all of them equally well but must reflect his personal attempts at compromise or synthesis. Given the existence of multiple groupings in society, of multiple group-memberships and group-allegiances in the individual, and of individuality in the synthesis of one's social outlook, it is almost inevitable that there should be alternative interpretations within any large group concerning its true interests and the best way to implement them. Those white employers who would hire Negroes (without discrimination), and equally those who would not, believe that their policy preferences best serve the economic interests of industry.

Clearly, imitation, reason, and group interest often play an important part in the formation and maintenance of ideology by the individual. However, none in itself, nor the three in combination, provide an adequate basis for the understanding of individual ideology. The first requirement, in my opinion, is a conception of individual personality within which ideology can be seen as an intrinsic, functional component. Seen in *personological* perspective, as an aspect of personality, ideology can be related to other cognitive-affective-conative processes (including the appraisal of reality-interests and the readiness to accept various kinds of conformity demands). This approach will, I believe, facilitate the effective meshing of psychology with the various social sciences.

Various theories of personality are available as starting points for a personological approach to ideology. My own preference is to start from psychoanalytic theory while utilizing concepts from other theories as well. For related though different approaches, see Flugel (10), Murray and Morgan (26), and Smith, Bruner, and White (31). The formation of ideology may be regarded as an *external function* of the ego, that is, as one of the means by which the person structures social reality, defines his place within it, and guides his search for meaning and gratification. Other external ego functions include the choice of an occupation, the development of a characteristic "style," of preferred modes of thinking and relating to others.

Like the other external ego functions, ideology-formation is related to the ways in which the ego carries out its *internal functions* — that is, to the ego's ways of coping with, and attempting to synthesize, the demands of ego, id, and super-ego. These internal activities, the "psychodynamics" of personality, include among other things: the individual's unconscious fantasies; his unconscious moral conceptions and the wishes against which they are directed; the characteristic ways in which these tendencies are transformed or deflected in his more conscious thought, feeling, and behavioral striving; his conception of self and his ways of maintaining or changing that conception in the face of changing pressures from within and from the external world. I am proposing, then, that *the ways in which the ego carries out its internal functions will heavily influence, though not entirely determine, the individual's selection, creation, and synthesis of idea systems.*

This general formulation implies a postulate of *receptivity:* the individual will be most receptive to those ideologies that have the greatest functional value in meeting the requirements of the personality as a system. He will prefer those ways of dealing with external religious, political, or other social issues that best mesh in with his preferred ways of dealing with internal issues of impulse control, maintenance of self-esteem, fulfillment of esthetic urges, and the like. We would make, also, a postulate of *immanence:* many of the personality characteristics that have influenced the individual's ideology-formation are directly reflected (immanent) in his idea system. It is possible through psychological analysis of the idea system to derive many of the personality features that have helped to establish and maintain it. As Lowell observed, "Truth is said to lie at the bottom of a well for the very reason, perhaps, that whoever looks down in search of her sees his own image at the bottom, and is persuaded not only that he has seen the goddess, but that she is far better-looking than he had imagined."

In summary, I have suggested that ideology is an aspect of personality and that central and enduring personality characteristics are often expressed directly or indirectly within it. The non-ideological aspects of personality influence ideological choice: they hinder the acceptance of "unappealing" (dynamically incongruent) orientations, and they facilitate the acceptance or creation of others that are personally meaningful.

However, there are important variations from one individual to another, and from one ideological domain to another within a given individual, in the degree to which psychodynamics influence the choice and the specific content of ideology. Clearly, no single set of ideas ever engages all of the personality. Ideological choice is affected from within not by the "total personality," but primarily by the particular facets of personality that are engaged at a given period of time. Moreover, inner compulsions and rigidities are seldom so strong that they permit acceptance of, and total involvement in, only one viewpoint. Most individuals have multiple ideological potentials and are capable of some measure of ideological change. Such change may come about not only through new knowledge and external circumstances but also as a result of inner changes in ideology-relevant aspects of personality. While acknowledging the importance and durability of the personality structure established by the age of five or six, we must still allow for important new developments and partial restructurings after that time and throughout life.

Relatively fundamental personality changes may occur at various ages through maturation and intense growth-inducing experiences. Also, changes in defensive equilibrium (e.g., from submission to rebellion, or from projective to introjective defenses against anxiety) and in involvement in social issues may alter the person's ideological receptivities. Adolescents, for example, commonly exhibit marked instability in their relationships, interests, and ideological preferences; their awkward, shifting attempts to find a meaningful and satisfying *modus vivendi* in the external world are closely and reciprocally related to equally difficult attempts to master anxieties and to outgrow infantile dilemmas in the intra-psychic world. After adolescence, however, both ideologies and personalities tend to become more stable, more resistant to change. The very limited effects of most efforts to induce ideological change in adults give evidence of this. When marked ideological change does occur in adults, it is ordinarily precipitated by equally marked change in external setting (e.g., depression, war, prosperity, drastic social-structural changes, tragic or euphoric personal experiences), *and* in internal equilibrium.

Finally, in emphasizing the intimate relation between internal dynamics and ideology, we must keep in mind that this is a two-way process. Ideology is not a "mere epiphenomenon" or superstructure, caused but having no causal force of its own, a simple instrument of the fundamental substructure. Ideas play their causal, dynamic role in individual personality as in social structure. They may promote change or they may serve to maintain the status quo; individual personalities, like societal orders, vary in this regard. To the extent that his ideology is personally congenial, it has significant equilibrium-maintaining functions for the individual: it helps to consolidate his ego defenses, to maintain control over fears and conflictful wishes, and to impel him in lines of activity that are morally appropriate and emotionally gratifying. This is true equally of the liberal and the conservative, the scientist and the artist, the businessman and the religionist. However, an individual's ideology may not be entirely congenial to him; the fit between ideology and dynamics is seldom perfect. A partially incongruent ideology perpetuates and perhaps intensifies inner conflicts and anxieties.

In addition, ideological change often has important system consequences. New ideological trends in a society, which emerge in part out of its social structure, have a serious impact on that structure. The same is true for ideological change in the individual. Although the gradual acceptance of a new ideology depends in part upon the individual's dynamics when the change began, it may very well have major re-equilibrating effects on the dynamics. For example, the availability of a chauvinistic nationalistic ideology during a period of international crisis may lead, in some of those who accept it, to the active use of projective, aggression-releasing defenses that might, in another ideological climate, be more controlled. Again, the new worker in a mental hospital is likely to be worried about the possibility of aggressive, homosexual, or otherwise threatening behavior from patients. The "humanistic" ideology available in some modern hospitals (13) may permit him not only to relate more constructively with patients but also to gain greater insight into, and control over, the inner sources of his anxieties regarding his own aggression and homosexuality. He must have some readiness to accept a humanistic ideology — something that depends in part on his personality when he comes into the hospital — but as he assimilates it, this ideology can have significant intra-psychic effects.

To sum up: I have argued against the sponge theories which regard ideology-formation as a process of mechanical absorption, and against the rationalistic theories in which ideology is conceived of solely as a tool serving group interests. In supporting a personological approach to the study of ideology in the individual, I have cautioned also against "mirage" theories according to which ideology is seen primarily as a psychic by-product, a result of inner defense maneuvers, with no (conceptualized) relation to social reality, and with no effects on the inner man. A more complete approach must take into account the interplay between the intra-psychic influences — rational as well as non-rational and irrational — the socio-cultural opportunities and demands, and the ideology itself.

**Proposition VI. The degree to which an individual's ideology is congruent with, and embedded in, other aspects of personality depends on both intra-personal and external socio-cultural conditions.**

In taking a personological approach, I have tried to indicate the value of studying individual ideology in relation to other aspects of personality. There is, of course, considerable variation in the degree to which ideology is immixed in the total personality. Allport (3) has proposed a distinction between "functional" prejudice and "conformity" prejudice, the latter referring to ideas which are passively accepted from the cultural environs and which have only the most shallow personal roots. Given this distinction, it becomes important to understand the conditions which maximize the role of personal characteristics in determining the choice and contents of ideology. Here are two hypotheses:

a) The greater the *effective range of ideological alternatives,* the greater the role of personality as a determinant of choice. Personality is likely to be of particular importance in modern, continually changing societies, where the number of ideological alternatives available is greater than in non-literate societies, and where the effectiveness of the conformity-inducing pressures is somewhat reduced. The greater the richness and complexity of the external stimulus field, the more will internal organizing forces operate in determining the individual's adaptation. This postulate has found considerable support in laboratory investigations of relatively simple cognitive processes. It promises to be equally valuable, though more difficult to apply, in more macrocosmic studies of complex cognitive-motivational processes taking place in a societal stimulus field.

b) The greater the degree of *personal involvement* in a given ideological domain, the greater the part played by personality in ideology-formation. Conversely, the less salient the issues involved, the less one cares about the problems in question, the more likely one is to accept or reject ideas on the basis of immediate external pressures. When a personally congenial ideology is not readily available to an individual, and he cannot create one for himself, he may nominally accept an uncongenial ideology, but without commitment or involvement. However, he is likely to be characterized by apathy or anomie and to have a strong potential for change to a new and more functional ideology.

## Ideological Unity and Diversity in the Collective Unit: The Influence of Personality and of Social Structure

**Proposition VII.** Within a total society, the degree of ideological diversity among the members is related to the degree of diversity in individual personality and to certain characteristics of the social structure.

a) Let us first consider personality-ideology relations in *monolithic* societies where the social order remains relatively constant over several generations and a high degree of ideological uniformity has apparently been achieved. I have in mind certain cohesive, encysted subcultures within modern nations, and various non-literate societies prior to foreign invasion, undisturbed by international pressures or internal technological changes. They are characterized — if we can believe the ethnographers — by a rigidly codified system of norms, effective systems of indoctrination and sanctions, a modal ideology that supports the overall structure, and minimal ideological deviance.

The monolithic society, if it is to be stable, requires uniformity in personality as a psychological substratum, a foundation for the maintenance of ideological and behavioral conformity (17). Personality is as important an element as ideology in the dynamics of social control. If its personality-forming devices, particularly the child-rearing system, are effective, the monolithic society may achieve a high degree of personality standardization. In this case, there will be a modal personality congruent with the modal ideology. This does not mean complete psychological uniformity; it does involve the widespread occurrence of those personality characteristics that make the dominant ideology seem reasonable and generally appealing.

However, it is conceivable that a society may induce ideological conformity on a large scale, without a corresponding modal personality. In this hypothetical case, many individuals accept the prevailing outlook although they do not have the personality to go with it. These individuals, already alluded to in Proposition VI, have a "conformity-based" ideology that has few functional roots in personality. As long as they continue to hold the required views, their system-incongruent personalities may be unnoticed. However, they have a strong potential for ideological change and are therefore of great strategic importance in social change. Under changed personal or social circumstances, they may play a key role in innovating structural change or in furthering change once it is begun by others. Conditions of social unrest contain numerous possibilities of institutional restructuring; which of the possibilities are implemented, and the degree of leadership and support for each, will depend in no small part on the psychological potentials — of which many may until then have been dormant — available for activation.

b) Most of the modern industrial nations are *pluralistic* societies in which individual differences seem to be relatively great with regard to both ideology and other aspects of personality. There are a number of major competing ideologies in almost all social domains — politics, religion, education, international relations, and the like. In addition, the variations in personality are sufficient to make things extremely difficult for the students of national character and culture-personality relations. The Soviet Russian regime, even after applying the most elaborate conformity-inducing pressures for over 30 years, has not been able to achieve anything approaching ideological uniformity (19). And the American South, despite its traditional, institutionalized subordination of Negroes, is showing an ideological diversity concerning educational desegregation that strongly contradicts a simple social-deterministic point of view.

The overall psychological diversity in these societies is, of course, related to their structural complexity and continual change. Continual technological change in industrial societies makes some degree of structural change inescapable. Moreover, ideological innovation is encouraged and to varying degrees legitimized by widely-held assumptions concerning the increasing perfectability of man and his institutions, and by the value for diversity as a good in itself. However, the ideological differences among individuals in each society are, according to the present hypothesis, associated with corresponding variations in individual personality. Thus, as Dicks' (9) research suggests, the Soviet government's difficulty in achieving ideological uniformity is due in large part to the uncontrolled and perhaps uncontrollable diversity in personality. And in the American South, I would expect the greatest uniformity of anti-Negro ideology in those states that have the most firmly established authoritarian modal personality.

**Proposition VIII.** Within a single social organization or institution, the existence of a structure-congruent modal ideology depends in part on the existence of a corresponding modal personality.

The referent here is not a total society, but rather a specific organized group (such as a social club, a political party, or the staff of a hospital or school) in which appreciable consensus of outlook prevails. The achievement and maintenance of ideological unity depend in part on the effectiveness of the group structure. They also require certain psychological conditions within the individual members. Let me suggest two.

a) The members will have joined the group voluntarily, as a matter more of personal choice than of external compulsion. The more weighty the internal determinants of choice, the greater the psychological homogeneity of the membership.

b) The members will have had, prior to joining, personality characteristics congruent with the dominant ideology, and perhaps certain explicit or implicit ideological tendencies which are further developed and articulated in the group setting. The group presents to its members various opportunities and demands for the formation of certain view-points; but the degree to which these external availabilities are "consumed" by individual members is strongly influenced by the psycho-ideological characteristics they bring to the group situation. A necessary though by no means sufficient condition for group unity is that the entering members have personality characteristics and ideological readinesses appropriate to the existing group aims.

While individual psychological characteristics provide an initial basis on which the group process develops, the member's participation in the group may then become a basis for significant changes in these characteristics. As I have already noted in Proposition V, the causal connections among personality, ideology, and system pressures are multilateral. With group support, an individual may be enabled actively to utilize an ideology that he would otherwise have been too timid to accept. Since most individuals have multiple ideological potentialities, group memberships are often of crucial importance in determining which potentials are actualized. Group participation helps the individual to articulate, legitimize, and find meaning in a given viewpoint; and it provides the ego-supports and external facilitations of which some minimum is necessary for the active maintenance of conviction. Finally, experiences in the group setting may affect deeper-lying personality characteristics. For example, going to a morally and intellectually "narrow" college is likely not only to prevent a broadening of the student's intellectual horizons but also to affect the way in which he deals with the central inner problems of adolescent development. To perhaps a lesser but still significant degree, group participation during the adult years will determine which of the individual's psychodynamic potentials are more fully realized and which are hindered or left dormant.

## Summary and Conclusions

The study of idea systems has been a major concern of psychology, social science, and the humanities. This concern is represented in the considerable work on ideology and public opinion, on the sociology of knowledge and communication, on culture as a system of values and orientations, on intellectual history and the role of ideas in massive social change. There has, however, been relatively little communication or intellectual exchange among the various disciplines. This chapter presents an initial step toward the coordination of psychological and socio-cultural approaches to the study of idea systems. Its theses are conveyed through a series of propositions:

I. The concepts of autocracy and democracy are widely applicable and of fundamental importance in the analysis of ideology.

II. Consistency: Individuals are relatively (though by no means entirely) consistent, from one ideological domain to another, in their tendency to think autocratically or democratically.

III. The individual's readiness to hold an autocratic or a democratic ideology in one domain, and his relative consistency across domains, depend in large part on generalized, enduring personality characteristics. Authoritarian personality constellations make for receptivity to autocratic ideology, while equalitarian personality is associated with democratic ideology.

IV. The socio-cultural matrix of the adult plays an important part in establishing and maintaining his ideology.

V. The formation of ideology in the individual involves numerous aspects of personality and is not a matter of simple imitation or pure reason.

VI. The degree to which an individual's ideology is congruent with, and embedded in, other aspects of personality, depends on both inner psychological and external socio-cultural conditions.

VII. Within a total society, the degree of ideological diversity among the members is related to the degree of diversity in individual personality and to certain characteristics of the social structure.

VIII. Within a single social organization or institution, the existence of a structure-congruent modal ideology depends in part on the existence of a corresponding modal personality.

Idea systems are at once individual and collective phenomena. They are aspects of individual personality and of socio-cultural milieu. They are to be seen *both* as superficial effects of more fundamental psychological and sociological processes, and as primary causal agents in individual and societal stability or change. This chapter has pointed to the need for a theoretical framework encompassing these several perspectives. Such an approach would take account of man's docility and of his creativity. It would comprehend man as a "social product," a "culture carrier," shaped and standardized to varying degrees by social, cultural, and ecological forces over which he has little control. It would also comprehend man's individuality, his capacity for re-interpreting himself and his world, and for influencing his own destiny. Finally, it would seek to grasp both the conformity- and the individuality-inducing features of societal patterning. Applied to collective policy, it might provide increasingly adequate answers to an old utopian problem: What forms of social organization (economic, familial, political, and the like) are best contrived to produce and sustain individuals who can make maximal use of the cultural past and yet be able as well to transcend the limitations of growing up within a single cultural form?

BIBLIOGRAPHY

1. Adorno, T. W., Else Frenkel-Brunswik, D. J. Levinson, and R. N. Sanford. *The Authoritarian Personality*. New York: Harper and Bros., 1950.

2. Allport, G. W. *The Individual and His Religion.* New York: The Macmillan Co., 1950.

3. Allport, G. W. *The Nature of Prejudice.* Cambridge, Mass.: Addison-Wesley Publishing Co., 1954.

4. Almond, G. A. *The American People and Foreign Policy.* New York: Harcourt, Brace, 1950.

5. Alven, W. C. "An Investigation of Patterns of Protestant Religious Ideology." Unpublished doctoral dissertation, Western Reserve University Library, 1950.

6. Argyris, C. *Personality and Organization.* New York: Harper and Bros., 1957.

7. Brinton, C. *Ideas and Men.* Englewood Cliffs, N.J.: Prentice-Hall, Inc., 1950.

8. Dicks, H. V. "Personality Traits and National Socialist Ideology," *Human Relations,* Vol. 3 (1950), pp. 111–154.

9. Dicks, H. V. "Observations on Contemporary Russian Behavior," *Human Relations,* Vol. 5 (1952), pp. 111–175.

10. Flugel, V. C. *Man, Morals, and Society.* New York: International Universities Press, 1945.

11. Fromm, E. *Escape from Freedom.* New York: Farrar and Rinehart, 1941.

12. Fromm, E. *Man for Himself.* New York: Rinehart, 1947.

13. Gilbert, Doris C., and D. J. Levinson. "Ideology, Personality, and Institutional Policy in the Mental Hospital," *Journal of Abnormal and Social Psychology,* Vol. 53 (1956), pp. 263–271.

14. Goffman, E. "Characteristics of Total Institutions," *Symposium on Preventive and Social Psychiatry.* Washington, D.C.: Walter Reed Army Institute of Research, 1958.

15. Greenblatt, M., D. J. Levinson, and R. H. Williams (eds.). *The Patient and the Mental Hospital.* Glencoe, Ill.: The Free Press, 1957.

16. Gouldner, A. W. *Patterns of Industrial Bureaucracy.* Glencoe, Ill.: The Free Press, 1954.

17. Inkeles, A., and D. J. Levinson. "National Character: The Study of Modal Personality and Sociocultural Systems," in G. Lindzey (ed.), *Handbook of Social Psychology.* Cambridge, Mass.: Addison-Wesley Publishing Co., 1954.

18. Inkeles, A., Eugenia Hanfmann, and Helen Beier. "Modal Personality and Adjustment to the Soviet Political System," *Human Relations,* Vol. 11 (1958), pp. 3–22.

19. Inkeles, A., and R. A. Bauer. *The Soviet Citizen.* Cambridge, Mass.: Harvard University Press, 1959.

20. Leighton, A. H. *The Governing of Men.* Princeton, N.J.: Princeton University Press, 1945.

21. Levinson, D. J., and P. Lichtenberg. *Authoritarian Personality and Re-*

*ligious Ideology*. Boston, Mass.: Center for Socio-psychological Research, Massachusetts Mental Health Center, 1950 (mimeo).

22. Levinson, D. J., and Phyllis E. Hoffman. "Traditional Family Ideology and its Relation to Personality," *Journal of Personality*, Vol. 23 (1955), pp. 251–273.

23. Levinson, D. J. "Authoritarian Personality and Foreign Policy," *Conflict Resolution*, Vol. 1 (1957), pp. 39–47.

24. McGregor, D. M. *The Human Side of Enterprise*. New York: McGraw-Hill Book Co., 1960.

25. Maslow, A. H. "The Authoritarian Character Structure," *Journal of Social Psychology*, Vol. 18 (1943), pp. 401–411.

26. Murray, H. A., and Christine Morgan. "A Clinical Study of Sentiments," I and II. *Genetic Psychology Monographs*, Vol. 32 (1945), pp. 3–311.

27. Ohlin, L. E. *Sociology of the Field of Corrections*. New York: Russell Sage Foundation, 1956.

28. Parrington, V. L. *Main Currents in American Thought*. New York: Harcourt, Brace, 1927.

29. Pritchett, C. H. *Civil Liberties and the Vinson Court*. Chicago: Chicago University Press, 1954.

30. Reich, W. *The Mass Psychology of Fascism*. New York: Orgone Institute Press, 1946.

31. Smith, M. B., J. S. Bruner, and R. W. White. *Opinions and Personality*. New York: John Wiley & Sons, 1956.

32. Stagner, R. "Fascist Attitudes: Their Determining Conditions," *Journal of Social Psychology*, Vol. 7 (1936), pp. 438–454.

33. Trilling, L. *The Liberal Imagination*. New York: Viking Press, 1950.

34. Weber, M. *The Theory of Social and Economic Organization*, edited by T. Parsons. New York: Oxford University Press, 1947.

# 17

*Benjamin Zablocki*

# The Use of Crisis as a Mechanism
# of Social Control

*The preservation of a constitution may not only be due to the fact that a state is far removed from the menace of any danger: it may also, on occasion, be due to the very opposite. When danger is imminent, men are alarmed, and they therefore keep a firmer grip on their constitutions. All those who are concerned for the constitution should therefore foster alarms, which will put men on their guard, and will make them keep an unwearied watch like sentinels on night duty.*

*Aristotle*

As individuals, in our own everyday lives, we generally try to avoid crises. Crisis involves risk, and risk necessarily involves the possibility of regret, and regret is painful. It might seem that the same reasoning would apply to social collectivities. But many observers have reported evidence that groups sometimes do purposely seek out crisis situations and seem thereby to become more closely integrated (15, p. 88f.; 2, p. 622f.). One possibility is that the collectivity as a whole may seek out a crisis situation. Another is that some members will seek out a crisis as a means of establishing, maintaining, or strengthening control over the rest of the group. It is the latter possibility which will be discussed in this paper.

Judicious use of crises has always been a mechanism for securing authority of a ruler over his subjects. Until recently, war served this purpose. In our own times, however, the risks of warfare among nations have become unendurably great, but without any concomitant reduction in the desires of governments to maintain themselves in power. We may ask what other social crises are capable of substituting for war in their capacity for maintaining civic order. Further, how can crisis itself, apparently unexpected, unpredictable, and uncontrollable by nature, enter into the stock of tools of government, even of bureaucracy?

A recent satirical work suggests that it may not be very easy to find such a functional equivalent to war:

> It may be, for instance, that gross pollution of the environment can eventually replace the possibility of mass destruction by nuclear weapons as the principal apparent threat to the survival of the species. Poisoning of the air, and of the principal sources of food and water supply, is already well advanced, and at first glance would seem promising in this respect; it constitutes a threat that can be dealt with only through social organization and political power. (11, p. 66f.)

In any case, we should not only consider grand crises, those that threaten the very existence of a society. For many purposes, little crises, limited crises, may serve the ruler (or the decision-making group) better. Certainly, if we are to consider the control function of crises within the family, the committee, the legislature, the scientific discipline, and the community, as well as at the level of the nation-state, we must be willing to widen our perspective to include situations less potentially devastating than war or ecological disaster.

### Definitions

Crisis has not been a well defined concept in social scientific writings. Before beginning our analysis, we must therefore, accomplish three preliminary tasks. Firstly, we must formulate a definition of crisis in terms of well defined and understood concepts. Secondly, we must distinguish between the concept of crisis and various related concepts such as catastrophe, disaster and predicament. Finally, we shall have to put forth a typology of crises based on distinctions suggested by our definition.

We need a human population to experience the crisis. The collision of two asteroids in space is not a crisis. The population may have only one member. If it has more than one member, then the members will have different orientations toward the crisis. Within a society, any given crisis may affect some members of the society but not others. For instance, a sudden shift in public opinion regarding tuna consumption caused by the discovery of dangerous levels of mercury in tuna fish will constitute a crisis for certain fishermen, canneries, and the various industries responsible for dumping mercury in the ocean. Let us define the population as only those individuals and groups whose interests are affected by the events under consideration. We need not assume that the interests of the population are identical, or even that they are affected by the events in the same direction. Let us refer to the relevant population in crisis as a *community of interest*. A community of interest may be a single individual or it may be the entire population of the world.

Perhaps less obviously, we also need a decision maker or group of decision makers. Here, we depart to some extent from common usage in the insistence that a sociologically useful concept of crisis must always involve the possibility of choice and the act of choosing. For the time being, let us leave open the question of whether the decision-making group may be identical with the community of interest, may be a sub-group of it, or may lie outside its boundaries. Certainly, in some cases, there may be more than one decision making group within the community of interest, the decision itself may be divided among several groups, or there may be conflict within the group itself. But, to begin with, let us assume that the act of decision making is a single indivisible action taken by a single group which behaves as a unitary actor. A community of interest cannot experience crisis if there is no ability to choose. This ability to choose, however, may rest in the hands of decision makers outside of the community.

Let us assume further that decisions have to be made in the face of uncertainty. Using conventional decision theory terminology, we have a set of possible *states of nature* and a set of possible *strategies*. For the sake of convenience, we will also speak of a set of *utilities* associated with the juxtaposition of each strategy with each possible state of nature. We need not, however, require that utilities, as such, really exist or that they be measurable.[1] Again, following decision theory convention, we will speak not of a set of utilities but (rather pessimistically) of the set of *losses* of utility. If, by some chance, the occurrence of a particular state of nature, given the choice of a particular strategy, results in a gain of utility, we will represent this as a negative loss.

A simple example will illustrate how these concepts are used. You get up one morning and look out of the window. There is a possibility of rain. The two possible states of nature are that it will rain or that it will not. You have to make a decision between two strategies, whether to take a raincoat or not. The combination of each of the two possible strategies with each of the two possible states of nature generates four possible *outcomes*. The worst outcome is that you don't take a raincoat but it does rain. The best outcome is that you don't take a raincoat and it doesn't rain.

Regardless of the strategy you choose, nature may give you cause to regret it. If you take your raincoat and it doesn't rain, you will regret

[1] Technically speaking, we must assume that units of utility can be measured on an interval scale in order to derive the concept of risk. However, since we are not going to be using risk as a quantity, but merely specifying differences between high and low risk situations, the explanation in terms of utilities can be regarded as a purely heuristic device.

it because you would have been better off (experienced less loss) if only you had not taken the raincoat. If you don't take the raincoat, you will experience regret if it does rain by similar reasoning. In general, we can define *regret* as the actual loss incurred minus the minimum loss possible, given a particular state of nature and the various strategies that might have been chosen. Now we can associate with each strategy a *risk*. The risk of adopting a particular strategy is the average regret over all possible states of nature given that strategy. If the decision maker is in possession of a priori probabilities for the various states of nature, a more technically correct definition of risk would be the expected regret rather than the average regret, but this need not concern us here.

It will be useful to distinguish losses that can be tolerated from losses that cannot be tolerated. For any given situation, let us assume that there exists a *tolerance level*. All outcomes having losses less than or equal to this tolerance level can be called *satisfactory* outcomes. Satisfactory for whom? An important special case occurs in the situation in which the losses are experienced by the community of interest but the tolerance level is set by a distinct group of decision makers. If the decision making body is a legislature, an outcome may be deemed satisfactory to a legislator if the loss incurred by the electorate does not generate sufficient discontent to remove him from office. *Hope* can be defined as the probability of obtaining a satisfactory outcome.

Now we are almost ready to define crisis. Crisis depends on the degree of risk present in the situation, on the degree of hope, and on time. We are going to define crisis as a situation in which the decision making group may find itself prior to making a decision. But first let us define four related situations depicted in Figure 1.

**FIGURE 1**

*Pre-Decision Situations of the Decision-Making Group*

|  |  | HOPE | |
|---|---|---|---|
|  |  | High | Low |
| **RISK** | High | predicament | bind |
|  | Low | contentment | malaise |

When will a group of decision makers be content? Our first thought might be to say that they will be content whenever there are reasonably high hopes of a satisfactory outcome. But a prisoner, forced as his punishment to play Russian roulette, has an 83⅓ percent chance of a satisfactory outcome, and only a 16⅔ percent chance of dying. The situation is too risky to be described as one of *contentment*. If the prisoner is offered the Russian roulette game as an alternative to spending twenty years in prison, he may say that he is *content* with the odds and will accept the game. To be content with an alternative is sometimes used to mean that the alternative is the most acceptable of those available. This should not be confused with our definition of contentment as the state of the decision maker upon perceiving the entire range of alternatives as one of low risk and high hopes.

An interesting and often neglected decision making situation is *malaise:* the state of low risk and low hope. This may be illustrated in the case of a hypothetical ghetto inhabitant on welfare. Let us suppose that he needs a minimum income of $300 per month in order to provide his family with a decent standard of living. Welfare gives him $240 a month as long as he is unemployed. If he seeks employment, the most that he can hope to take home, after payroll deductions and the expenses of working, is $280 per month. Welfare will always be there as a crutch, thus eliminating risk from the situation. Jobs paying decent wages are not available, thus eliminating hope. The situation is one of malaise.

When risk is high, the decision-making group is faced with either a *predicament* or a *bind.* If there is little or no chance of a satisfactory outcome, the situation is a bind. The prisoner, in our previous example, having to choose between twenty years in prison or playing Russian roulette, is faced with a predicament. If, however, the rules of Russian roulette are reversed so that the gun has five bullets and one blank instead of one bullet and five blanks, the situation may be called a bind. The distinctions, of course, depend on quite arbitrary decisions as to what constitutes low or high risk or hope.

So far we have neglected the important factor of time. Faced with a difficult choice to make, the decision maker may elect to wait. Of course, the decision to wait may be treated merely as one of the possible strategies available. In fact, this is how the decision to wait is generally treated within the discipline of decision theory. But, in the world of real events, the factor of timing is often so important that it is best treated as constituting a separate dimension in itself.

Whenever postponement is a possibility, we may consider both risk and hope as functions of time. If either hope is decreasing as a function of time, or risk is increasing, or both, we have the additional factor of *time pressure.* Time pressure may also enter the situation (as in the 24-second rule in basketball or in an election) simply because the decision has to be made within a certain time limit. If we let $R = $ risk; $H = $ hope; $t = $ time; and $T = $ the decision deadline, then the conditions for the existence of time pressure can be stated as follows:

$$dR/dt > 0 \quad or \quad dH/dt < 0 \quad or \quad t \to T.$$

Let us now define *crisis* as predicament + time pressure and *catastrophe* as bind + time pressure.

With this definition of catastrophe, we are quite arbitrarily departing from common usage. Catastrophe is often used synonymously with disaster to denote the occurrence of an unfortunate event. We are going to use the word *disaster* to indicate an event and catastrophe to indicate a decision state.

We are now in a position to distinguish among four types of crises:

    (1) The crisis of diminishing hope
    (2) The crisis of increasing risk
    (3) The fixed time crisis
    (4) The sudden death crisis

Crises of diminishing hope or of increasing risk do not necessarily involve a time deadline. The time pressure is a result of the deteriorating situation. Each postponement results in a worsening set of available strategies. The American involvement in Vietnam can be viewed as a (largely unsuccessful) attempt to inject a time pressure element into the North Vietnamese military predicament. Firstly, an attempt was made to create a crisis of diminishing hope; later (with the bombing of North Vietnam and the invasion of Cambodia) a crisis of increasing risk.

The fixed time crisis is one in which a predicament must be resolved at or before a given point in time known to the decision maker. An American election is a fixed time crisis. A sudden death crisis is similar to a fixed time crisis except that the time deadline is not known to the decision maker. Sometimes, the time deadline is under the control of another (rival) decision maker. After the setting up of the American blockade, the Cuban missile crisis immediately became a sudden death crisis for the Americans. For the Russians, on the other hand, it had become a crisis of diminishing hope. By seizing the initiative, the Americans had lost control of the timing dimension, since the next move was then up to the Russians. The Americans had, however, created on their own terms a crisis for the Russians since the longer the Russians delayed in deciding whether or not to defy the blockade, there was a corresponding decrease in their chances of succeeding.

### The Functions of Crisis

We have defined crisis as a rather undesirable decision-making state. Nevertheless, crisis serves certain important social functions. In this section, we shall discuss some of these functions, firstly for society as a whole, and then as control mechanisms for leaders.

On the simplest level, crises serve to punctuate the flow of social time. Our earliest civilizations seem to have arisen in response to periodic crisis-producing events such as the annual flooding of the Nile River delta. We have said that crisis cannot occur where there is no decision making, but perhaps the converse is also true — that the faculties of decisionmaking cannot evolve except in environments where the periodic return of critical events creates a felt social need for men who are good at coping with such events.

History and literature abound with examples of how long periods of contentment, unpunctuated with occasional crises, can lead to the decay of the decision making function. Perhaps, less obviously, unpunctuated catastrophe can bring about the same result. Bruno Bettelheim's experiences in a Nazi concentration camp have led him to emphasize this point:

> [The making of decisions and their] expression in action — is energy consuming. So if it leads to no benefit for the individual, it seems, offhand, to his advantage to save his energy; that is, as long as he is unaware of any need to maintain a "consciousness of freedom." As indicated, the two commonest situations in which a person may find it pointless to make decisions are an extremely oppressive situation where his decisions must not be acted on lest they endanger his life, or where all important decisions are made by others in what seem like his best interests (by the parents for the child; by religion or the government for the adult).
>
> Unfortunately decision making is a function which, like some nerves or muscles, tends to atrophy when it lies fallow. Or in terms of psychoanalytic theory, decision making is not just an ego function; on the contrary, it is the function that creates the ego and, once created, keeps it going and growing. (3, p. 69 f.)

Elections are important punctuating events in the political life of the community. These come in two varieties: American style, in which variable crises are fitted to a fixed election timetable; and European style, in which variable elections are fitted to the pattern of crisis occurrence. American style elections tend to provoke fixed time crises by the very fact of their existence. For instance, the presidential election of 1972 provoked a truce signing crisis for the North Vietnamese (and, to a lesser extent, for the Americans). Knowing that the election must, by law, be held on November 7, and knowing that a cease-fire in Vietnam prior to the election would be helpful to the incumbent, we can surmise that North Vietnam concluded that it could strike a better deal before the election than after it. Mr. Nixon may have kept the possibility of a pre-election truce alive as an option to draw upon if the polls showed that the election was going to be close. The existence of an election on a specified date transformed what would have otherwise been the uniform flow of time into disjointed pre-election and post-election periods. In doing so, it transformed a difficult predicament into an urgent crisis. For better or worse, a set of opportunities for both sides would disappear on election day, *and both sides knew that they would disappear, and knew that the other knew it.*

European style elections occur whenever the ruling party cannot obtain a vote of confidence. This usually occurs because of a crisis situation in political affairs. European style elections give the ruling party an important option whereby it may transform crises of diminishing hope or of increasing risk into fixed time crises. This is useful because there are often powerful groups surrounding any crisis whose interests involve prolonging the crisis as much as possible. An election, or even the threat of an election, can serve to mobilize opinion into action in cases in which the solution to the crisis is clear but is being avoided because of the pain which the correct solution necessarily involves.

Another function of crisis for society as a whole is the strengthening of solidarity. This is often observed to be a result not of the crisis situation itself but of the successful resolution of a crisis. The confidence of a population in its leadership depends less upon the quality of that leadership's performance of its everyday responsibilities than upon its handling of occasional crises.

Studies of human behavior during disasters have indicated that merely the common perception of risk or reduction of hope often generate increased solidarity. A National Research Council study reported:

> The net result of most disasters is a dramatic increase in social solidarity among the affected populace during the emergency and immediate post-emergency periods. The sharing of a common threat to survival and the common suffering engendered by the disaster tend to produce a breakdown of social distinctions and a great outpouring of love, generosity, and altruism. During the first days and weeks following a major communitywide disaster, people tend to act toward one another spontaneously, sympathetically, and sentimentally, on the basis of common human needs rather than in terms of pre-disaster differences in social and economic status. (2, p. 624)

After President Kennedy was assassinated and the event and its aftermath were fully covered on national television, the following effects upon the population as a whole were reported:

(1) allayed anxiety
(2) relieved grief
(3) reduced guilt feelings
(4) induced a sense of participation and a sense of involvement in the political system
(5) gave reassurance of institutional continuity
(6) strengthened social norms
(7) in sum, the effects were reintegrative, making a single public of the American people. (5, p. 227)

As indicated in our initial quotation from Aristotle, times of crisis do more than merely strengthen bonds among individuals. They also evoke a common felt need for clear, traditionally agreed upon decision rules — a strengthening of the constitution.

Time punctuation and the increase of solidarity are important functions not only for the society as a whole, but also for the leadership of society. They are control functions as well as integrative functions. Other functions of crisis may be thought of more exclusively as deliberate mechanisms of social control. We will discuss the following five: generating the upward flow of information, focusing sentiment on social change, fostering organized insecurity, redirecting hostility, and restricting excess freedom.

Any group with decision-making authority needs to keep itself informed as to the moods and attitudes of the population for which it makes decisions. In a free society, this can be accomplished by public opinion sampling and referenda. However, to the degree to which a decision making group maintains its authority through coercive means, significant numbers of the population will respond by withholding accurate information. Crisis can then be used as a means of obtaining information under these circumstances.

The Hundred Flowers period in the China of 1956 and the more recent Czechoslovakian summer of freedom can be viewed in this manner. Without implying that such a strategy was ever consciously employed (regarding which we have no evidence)[2] let us see how the above events resemble a strategy for generating upward information flow.

In both cases, the events can be grouped into three periods: pre-thaw, thaw, and post-thaw. In the pre-thaw period, the dominant decision making group was faced with an unknown but potentially serious degree of revolutionary discontent. The dissatisfied segment of the population was prevented from engaging in a set of desired activities by the imposition of conditions of high risk. During the period of thaw, the risk attached to these activities was drastically reduced. Many people engaged in these previously high risk activities. The dominant decision making group observed and noted these activities and, on the basis of its observations, was able to construct plausible indices as to range, depth, and organization of the pre-thaw discontent. The hope of still greater thaw was naturally engendered. Instead, an abrupt return to the pre-thaw conditions of high risk was imposed. The dominant decision making group now had the information it needed. However, as a necessary by-product of this information gathering, a crisis of diminishing hope had been created.

This is, of course, a very risky strategy. The crisis of diminishing hope can very easily turn into a revolution of rising expectations. It is useful in situations where the dominant decision making group has overwhelming power at its disposal and where the discontent elements within the society are not yet well enough organized to constitute any real revolutionary threat. It is a good way to nip a revolution in the bud.

Crisis can also serve as a focusing mechanism for social change.

---

[2] The methodological problem of determining motivation is a major stumbling-block in the way of developing a testable theory of crisis utilization.

Certain kinds of planned change might not be possible at all if it were not for the intervention of crisis. The movement of a complex society from a state of war to a state of peace is often an example of this kind of resistance to change.[3] Sometimes, this can be accomplished through a manufactured crisis. In other situations, the leading decision makers must wait until a crisis comes along. Thomas Bailey discusses an example of the latter situation in connection with America's entrance into World War II:

> Franklin Roosevelt repeatedly deceived the American people during the period before Pearl Harbor. . . . He was like the physician who must tell the patient lies for the patient's own good. . . . The country was overwhelmingly non-interventionist to the very day of Pearl Harbor, and an overt attempt to lead the people into war would have resulted in certain failure and an almost certain ousting of Roosevelt in 1940, with a consequent defeat of his ultimate aims (17, p. 3).

The value of crisis in promoting social change is that it functions to align a community of interest along a single dimension. Crises caused by disasters such as floods or earthquakes illustrate this phenomenon. For the duration of the crisis, nobody is concerned with anything other than its successful resolution. While political crises are rarely that dire, a similar, if less total, uni-dimensional ordering can be observed.

What has this to do with social change? James Coleman (6) has observed that conflicts within communities polarized around a single issue tend to be a great deal more severe than conflicts within communities in which a great many issues cross-cut the population into a great number of overlapping groups. The explanation for this is that only in the latter case can the traditional, democratic mechanisms of horsetrading and compromise be utilized. This has been taken to imply the superiority of multi-issue over single issue communities and, indeed, for most purposes, a slow peaceful democratic marketplace is certainly to be preferred to a single issue battlefield. But in situations which call for a radical social change — a discontinuous leap — the processes of compromise may actually be dysfunctional. If we assume that people will tend to avoid risk and will compromise when they can, the fostering of crisis may, in some circumstances, be the only method available for bringing about discontinuous change.

It is interesting to look at manifestations of collective behavior in this light. The formation of a rioting group or mob may be looked at as a rational strategy on the part of the participants to temporarily extinguish all goal orientation except along a single commonly shared dimension. It may do so in order to respond decisively to a crisis situation demanding a strategy in the direction of discontinuous change even though a

---

[3] Nieburg treats this matter at greater length (13).

large majority of the participants may have secondary interests in opposition to the direction of this change.[4]

Thomas Kuhn's study of scientific change (10, Chapter VII) has stressed the degree to which major changes in scientific understanding occur in the form of discontinuous leaps, very often in response to crisis situations. Certainly, one would not be justified in assuming that identical processes of change occur in scientific disciplines and in societies. In the former, attacks on established authority are (at least theoretically) accorded the highest honor. In the latter they generally evoke mistrust and resentment, and often repression. Nevertheless, crisis in society may be seen as an important force behind many major social changes.

Throughout our discussion thus far, there has been an undercurrent of Machiavellianism. The three functions of crisis that we have left to discuss can be described in no other way than as completely and overtly Machiavellian. Let us assume now the existence of a single dominant decision making group with no other interest but to maintain and strengthen its authority within the society. How may such a group make use of crisis?

In George Orwell's novel, 1984, the rulers of each nation maintained their authority by keeping their subjects in a state of perpetual insecurity. While this fictional account is extreme, even by totalitarian standards, it is true that the complexity of modern society creates an opportunity for mystification by social managers similar to that used by theocratic priests in ancient times. Karl Mannheim provides a useful insight into this phenomenon:

> When the rationalized mechanism of social life collapses in times of crisis, the individual cannot repair it by his own insight. Instead, his own impotence reduces him to a state of terrified helplessness. In the social crisis he allows the exertion and the energy needed for intelligent decision to run to waste. Just as nature was unintelligible to primitive man, and his deepest feelings of anxiety arose from the incalculability of the forces of nature, so for modern industrialized man the incalculability of the forces at work in the social system under which he lives, with its economic crises, inflation, and so on, has become a source of equally pervading fears. (12, p. 59)

Here, we come to consider the situation in which crisis is not an exceptional situation but the normal state of affairs. If any of us hired a business manager or a secretary and then found our affairs in a continual state of crisis, the employee would soon be fired. As long as we feel that we understand our affairs better than our employee understands them, we shall demand that he maintain us in a state of contentment or, at the very least, malaise. The greater the elements of habitual risk

---

[4] Cf. Turner and Killian (16, p. 416 ff).

and time pressure that enter into our business, the more dissatisfied we shall be.

Exactly the opposite situation occurs when we feel more ignorant than those who are charged with the responsibility of conducting our business for us. The greater the level of risk and time pressure involved in a decision, the greater will be our dread of losing the services of our wise decision maker and of being thrown upon our own resources. This is precisely the strategy employed by Uriah Heep, in Charles Dickens's *David Copperfield*, to gain control of a business organization.

The leadership of such a society has a vested interest in mismanagement as long as this steers clear of outright bind or catastrophe. A government that maintains a well-organized state at a slightly higher level of prosperity than any alternative government could, will be honored. But a government that maintains a disorganized state at a slightly lower level of misery than any alternative could, will be feared and respected. Karl Mannheim discusses the psychological effects of living in such a society.

> Finally long-term calculation also ceases, at least among those social groups most strongly affected by the partial dissolution of society. The panic reaches its height when the individual comes to realize that his insecurity is not simply a personal one, but is common to masses of his fellows, and when it becomes clear to him that there is no longer any social authority to set unquestioned standards and determine his behaviour. . . .
>
> During a period of unorganized insecurity, the normal person, owing to the lack of an immediate and real gratification for his strivings in the field of work and social acknowledgment tends to become a "gesture-adult," existing on substitute goals and being satisfied with gestures and symbols. . . .
>
> In such a society those who are leaders enjoy the possibility of raising hatred on one day and appeasing it on the next. Society becomes a structure where one presses a button and the expected reaction occurs. One day the detestation of a neighboring country may be preached, on the next you decide to live in friendship with it for ten years. In the phase of unorganized, as compared with that of organized insecurity, quite a different psychology characterizes the individual. In the former phase the psychological reaction of the people was important, the psychology of the masses governed everything. In the latter it seems as if the masses have abandoned their individual psychic life, at least as far as public affairs are concerned, and are ready to turn into robots. (12, pp. 130, 132, 137)

A government that maintains itself in power through the use of organized insecurity must provide a channel for the hatreds and resentments that are certain to arise in a population so governed. Ted Gurr (9, p. 309) discusses a peculiar phenomenon of interest here:

> Over a sixty-year period, Nebraska politicians were rather consistently voted out of office when rainfall was less than normal, whereas whatever party was in power was very likely to continue in power when rainfall was greater than normal.

This is the obverse of the situation which we have been discussing. Although in times of great insecurity the population may be unwilling to remove the leaders responsible for this insecurity, at other times leaders who clearly bear no responsibility for a particular misfortune may be removed just out of spite.

If the strategy of maintaining power through organized insecurity is to work, a way must be found to deflect spite reactions from the leaders who are their natural objects onto substitute objects. The most frequently used mechanism for this type of hostility redirection is the technique of scapegoating. Scapegoating has been defined by Veltfort and Lee as follows:

> Scapegoating is a phenomenon wherein some of the aggressive energies of a person or group are focused upon another individual, group, or object; the amount of aggression released is greater than that usually released by similar provocation; the fixing of blame and the release of aggression are either partially or wholly unwarranted. (16, p. 120)

Modern instances of scapegoating as public policy (such as Hitler's persecution of the Jews) are too well known to require much comment. However, it should be noted that the technique of scapegoating requires the creation of alternate crises to which the attention of the population can be diverted and their hostility rechanneled.

One last function of crisis remains to be discussed, perhaps the most insidious. This is the function of restricting excess freedom. Suppose a government succeeds in bringing about a state of prosperity. It could be argued that this in itself could create social control problems since, as Durkheim (*Suicide*) has stated, prosperity "... opens up the abyss of an endless search for the impossible." But if prosperity is the result of social planning, the situation is even worse. It is not possible to have prosperity without increasing individual freedom. Prosperity implies lowered risks. Lowered risks imply increased range of opportunities, which in turn imply further lowered risks. But the greater the range of low risk opportunities available to an individual, the greater the probability that he will deviate from doing his part in the plan which brought prosperity in the first place.

We have argued that crisis is an ineradicable part of social life whether times are good or bad. Moreover, to the stock of naturally occurring crises, we have seen that it is often to the interest of ruling groups to add deliberately planned crises. If this be the case, we should expect to find that the state of crisis itself (independent of particular subject matter) will be found in institutionalized forms and occurring at periodic intervals.

### The Institutionalization of Crisis

In order to use crisis as a technique of social control, two basic problems must be solved:

(1) ways must be found to trigger crises when needed;

(2) ways must be found to control the scope, duration and intensity of both accidental and deliberate crises as they occur.

We will speak of the crisis technique as being institutionalized to the extent that these problems have been solved. Of course, by this definition, there has never been a society in which the technique of crisis has been fully institutionalized.

Most studies of political or macro-social crises have concentrated on explaining the patterns of decision making during crises or the social changes caused by crises. For studies of the technique itself, we must turn to social-psychological treatments of small-group processes. In general, control mechanisms are more obvious, and thus easier to study, in the primary group than in more complex societies, but we must be on guard against making overly facile generalizations on the basis of small group observations.

*The Four-Stage Group Process*

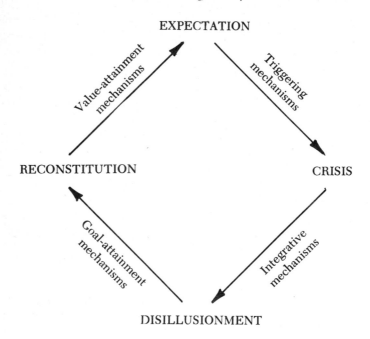

FIGURE 2

W. R. Bion has observed a cyclical four-stage process occurring with great regularity in the small non-directive group (4). The group starts out in the stage of expectation. Hopes are high, perceived risks are low. This corresponds to what we have defined as the state of contentment with an additional element of excitement caused by the fact that hopes are not merely high but are steadily getting higher. When the group attempts to act in order to realize its collective hopes, perception of risk undergoes a drastic change. The group members become acutely aware of their own individuality, the possibilities of separation from the group, and the personal risks involved in the subordination of the individual will to the group will. As perceived risk increases, collective hope plummets, and the group as a whole moves to the stage of crisis. In order to reduce personal risk, the crisis is eventually resolved by a mutually agreed upon, drastic curtailment of hopes. The group enters a kind of malaise which Bion calls disillusionment. Eventually, the group pulls itself together and begins to work toward the achievement of some modestly realistic goals necessary for the group's survival. This is the reconstitution stage. The common feeling and common sense of purpose engendered by the reconstitution help to set off a new flight of hopes which brings the group back, full circle, to the stage of expectation.

To the degree that the leader of the group is conscious of the four-stage process, he can exercise considerable control over it and hence, over the group itself. The leader's role can also be conceptualized in four steps. Firstly, during the expectation stage, he is responsible for triggering the crisis and doing so at just the right time. Secondly, during the crisis itself, he is chiefly concerned with integration functions — holding the group together. Thirdly, under the guidance of a good leader, the disillusionment following a crisis need not be a negative state. It can be, quite literally, a disillusionment in which the group gives up its utopian illusions in exchange for a solidly realistic awareness of the group's potentialities. If the group survives the disillusionment stage, the leader's role becomes the quite practical one of mobilizing collective resources toward the achievement of specific collective goals. The successful attainment of these goals provides the group with a new sense of collective identity with which it enters the fourth stage of reconstitution.

At the fourth stage of reconstitution, we can see how the intrinsic momentum of the hope function and the risk function contribute to making crisis a basic feature of group life. If the group, upon attaining its goals, were to reach a stable state of contentment, the four-stage cycle would be broken. But the very success in attaining goals fosters the illusion, on the wings of rising hope, that values might be attained through similar collective effort. This is one feature of small-group dynamics which does have many parallels on the macro-social level. Slaying a monarch gives rise to a quest for liberty; abolishing Jim Crow laws — to a quest for equality; attaining high production rates — to a quest for prosperity; ending a war — to a quest for peace. But values, unlike goals, are neither tangible nor finite and are thus not realistic candidates for attainment. Properly handled, however, the expectation stage can serve to generate a value consensus in the group which is sufficiently concrete to provide an ordering of priorities for the next round of goal attainment.

Society as a whole seems to exhibit some of the features of the four-stage process. Certainly, what might be called the momentum law of hope and risk applies to societies as well as groups. This is best seen in the dynamics of the business cycle, where both depressions and booms tend to get more extreme than economic indicators alone would predict. But in order to use the four-stage process as a model for studying societal crisis patterns we must introduce two new factors: the factor of divisiveness within the decision making group itself, and the factor of accidental crises caused by events external to the system.

In his discussion of the Cuban missile crisis, Graham Allison (1, p. 253 f.) argues the following:

> Difficulties arise when the thing to be explained is not the behavior of an individual but rather the behavior of a large organization or even a government. Nations can be reified, but at considerable cost in understanding. By personifying nations, one glides over critical characteristics of behavior where an organization is the main mover — for example, the fact that organizational action requires the coordination of large numbers of individuals. . . . Thinking about a nation as if it were a person neglects considerable differences among individual leaders of a government whose positions and power lead them to quite different perceptions and preferences. Thus where the actor is a national government, a conception of action for objectives must be modified.
>
> We should ask not what goals account for a nation's choice of an action, but rather what factors determine an outcome.

Although Allison is primarily concerned with the problem of decision making under crisis circumstances, his words of caution can be taken to apply even more strongly to an analysis of the use of crisis as a control technique. This technique, as we have seen, requires the ability to make rapid adjustments in the level of social risk and in the timing of events. In a modern government, however, these abilities tend to be diffused over many office holders. What to some may look like an opportunity to tighten the reins of social control through crisis, to others will appear as an opportunity for personal advancement, either through demonstrating efficacy at problem solving or demonstrating the incompetence of those currently in the most responsible positions. We must conclude that the technique of crisis will be useful to a government office holder only to the extent that his own position in the government is secure. This hypothesis might be tested empirically by observing the degree to which the technique has been employed by first term as opposed to second term presidents, assuming the latter to be more secure in office.[5]

In trying to observe the extent to which the technique of crisis is used (if at all) by governments, it is extremely difficult to distinguish between purposive crises and those caused by events outside the government's control. The latter "accidental" crises may also be viewed in the light of our discussion of the crisis technique. In these cases, the government in question does not have control over its intensity and duration and, most important, over its effect on the population.

It is interesting to examine two recent attempts to utilize the crisis technique (in very different ways) by American presidents. In 1961, John F. Kennedy attempted, unsuccessfully, to fabricate a fixed time crisis out of his first hundred days in office. This strategy had previously been employed successfully by Franklin Roosevelt, but under different circumstances.[6] Despite Kennedy's charisma, the strategy did not work. This supports our contention that triggering is a crucial problem which must be solved by anyone who wishes to utilize the crisis technique.

By way of contrast, Richard Nixon has often appeared to do nothing in the face of serious world crises. Public opinion would gradually mobilize around demands for decisive action. Waiting for the right moment, Nixon could then follow a radical and risky strategy and still appear to be a conservative, acting only because he could no longer resist the pressure of public opinion and the crush of events. In this way, Nixon was able to negotiate such difficult events as the dollar devaluation crisis of 1971 and the wage and price controls crisis of 1971-1972 without tarnishing his image of having abilities to assuage national fears.

Of the many strategies that have been employed to cope with and utilize crisis, three general types may be identified. These are: externalization, symbolization, and transcendence. The first of these we have already discussed in its most common manifestation, that of scapegoating. Externalization can be defined as any technique for deflecting interest and concern from the true crisis at hand to some other crisis or event.

Symbolization is a specific form of externalization, but one which is important enough to deserve separate treatment. It involves the deflection of concern from the world of real events to the world of symbolic events. Religion has been the primary cultural vehicle for the symbolization of crisis concerns. The ritual enactment of the Catholic mass is a symbolized crisis for the community, as confession is for the indi-

[5] By similar reasoning, one could also study the phenomenon among European prime ministers ranked by the strength of their parliamentary majorities.

[6] An economic crisis — the great depression — already existed. It was therefore not a question of moving from contentment or malaise to crisis but merely from one crisis to another, or perhaps from catastrophe to crisis.

vidual. In many primitive societies where sacred and secular power have gone hand in hand, we see examples of religion serving this symbolization function for the political sphere.

Finally, we come to the strategy of transcendence. Transcendence involves facing up fully to the implications of the crisis, accepting fully the burdens of its responsibility up to the point that a cathartic emergence of collective identity occurs. Winston Churchill's handling of the 1940 war crisis for England is an example of the strategy of transcendence. This strategy, quite obviously, above all others requires a high degree of charisma in the decision making group or individual.

Both symbolization and transcendence run the danger of becoming routinized if used extensively. This is the moral of the story of the boy who cried wolf. Religions tend to get routinized as well, to the point where it is probably only a small minority of Catholics today who experience anything of the terror and glory of the original celebrations of the mass. The routinization of crisis is a major problem for anyone who wishes to use crisis as a technique of social control.

Another major problem is to prevent any particular crisis from turning into a crisis of confidence. It is clear that for some statesmen the technique of crisis has backfired resulting in the removal of those men from office. Berelson and Steiner (2, p. 623) argue that crisis can serve either to bolster or to destroy the people's confidence in their leadership:

> Crisis hastens and intensifies the going trend in social relations: if the community is integrated, crisis will increase the integration; if the community is poorly integrated, crisis will disrupt it.
>
> This can be seen both in the large and in the small: in the nation-state (e.g., a depression) and within the family (e.g., the addition of a child dissolving some families but increasing the solidarity of others).

## Summary

The argument of this paper may be summarized as follows:

(1) Crisis is an important but neglected mechanism of social control.

(2) A crisis may be defined as any state of high risk and high hopes in which decisions must be reached under time pressure.

(3) To the degree to which a ruler can manipulate the perceived risks of a population and the timing of events, he can strengthen his authority over that population through the technique of crisis.

(4) At the level of the primary group, there exists a kind of natural institutionalization of crisis as one stage in a cyclical four-stage process, and there are hints that this process may also occur at the macro-social level.

(5) The fact that governments behave more like large bureaucratic organizations than unitary rational decision makers severely limits the use of the crisis technique on the macro-social level.

(6) At the primary group level, and to a lesser extent at the macro-

social level, crisis may be effectively institutionalized through externalization, symbolization, and transcendence, subject to the constraints of routinization and loss of confidence. There is also always the threat of hastening a long-term trend in the direction of social disintegration.

The arguments presented in this paper involve questions of motivation and thus cannot easily be tested empirically. Parallel work on the theory of revolutionary cycles (18) demonstrates some of the methodological problems inherent in studying the effects of conscious strategies of social control. Perhaps the most promising approach is to work out the dynamics of the crisis technique more thoroughly on the primary group level before attempting to formulate verifiable propositions at the macro-social level.

## BIBLIOGRAPHY

1. Allison, G. *Essence of Decision: Explaining the Cuban Missile Crisis.* Boston: Little, Brown, and Co., 1971.
2. Berelson, B., and G. Steiner. *Human Behavior: An Inventory of Scientific Findings.* New York: Harcourt, Brace & World, 1964.
3. Bettelheim, B. *The Informed Heart.* Glencoe, Illinois: The Free Press, 1960.
4. Bion, W. *Experiences in Groups.* New York: Basic Books, 1959.
5. Broom, L. and P. Selznick. *Sociology.* New York: Harper & Row, 1968.
6. Coleman, J. *Community Conflict.* Glencoe, Illinois: The Free Press, 1957.
7. Davies, J. *When Men Revolt and Why.* Glencoe, Illinois: The Free Press, 1971.
8. Durkheim, E. *Suicide.* Glencoe, Illinois: The Free Press, 1951.
9. Gurr, T. *Why Men Rebel.* Princeton: Princeton University Press, 1970.
10. Kuhn, T. *The Structure of Scientific Revolutions.* Chicago: University of Chicago Press, 1962.
11. Lewin, L. *Report from Iron Mountain: On the Possibility and Desirability of Peace.* New York: The Dial Press, 1967.
12. Mannheim, K. *Man and Society in an Age of Reconstruction.* New York: Harcourt, Brace & Co., 1954.
13. Nieburg, H. *Political Violence.* New York: St. Martin's Press, 1969.
14. North, R., H. Koch, Jr., and D. Zinnes. "The Integrative Functions of Conflict," *Journal of Conflict Resolution,* Vol. 4 (1960), pp. 355-374.
15. Simmel, G. *Conflict and The Web of Group Affiliations.* Glencoe, Illinois: The Free Press, 1955.
16. Veltfort, H., and G. Lee. "The Cocoanut Grove Fire: A Study in Scapegoating," in Ralph Turner and Lewis Killian (eds.), *Collective Behavior.* Englewood Cliffs, N. J.: Prentice Hall, 1972.
17. Waller, G. *Pearl Harbor: Roosevelt and the Coming of the War.* Boston: D. C. Heath & Co., 1953.
18. Willer, D., and G. Zollschan. "Prolegomenon to a Theory of Revolutions," in George Zollschan & Walter Hirsch (eds.), *Explorations in Social Change.* Boston: Houghton Mifflin Co., 1964.
19. Zablocki, B. *The Joyful Community.* Baltimore: Penguin Books, 1971.

# 18

*Leon H. Warshay*

# Breadth of Perspective, Social Type, and the Dialectic of Change

In introducing *breadth of perspective* as of relevance to social change, I present in this chapter a character type which only infrequently is in an effective position to influence social change directly. This is the person with broad perspective, that is, capable of redefining situations in radically different ways by alternately changing means, goals, and values and by not being satisfied with any given formulation for long. The "broad" person is seen as often "inorganically" related to society; as tending toward the informal and categorical (or "lightly-patterned") sphere of social life; as being at best only a temporary participant in legitimate seats of power and influence. His or her role in social change is a complex one and tends to be tangential.

It would seem that the person with a greater diversity of perspective would be better able to bring about change. Analysis of the problem, however, not only raises the question as to whether this is true (for our broad actor may, after all, value the status quo or value something else that requires the status quo), but the following questions as well:

1) Is the broad (or narrow) person likely to be in the *position* to influence, even to recognize, change?

2) If not, under what circumstances is he or she likely to enter such a position?

3) If relatively "sealed off" from said position, under what circumstances may he or she actively influence change from the outside?

4) Given a relatively powerless and isolated position, what kind of relationship to change does he/she then have?

5) What relation does his/her entrance into, or absence from, the legitimate centers of decision-making have to social change?

6) What other mechanisms and relationships embrace perspective breadth and social change?

The relationships are complex. They involve questions and issues having to do with the nature of perspective, of change, and of personal and societal processes that serve as context for perspective and change. Before discussing these processes, a preliminary outline of breadth of perspective and of social change will be presented.

### Breadth of Perspective: Preliminary Outline

Breadth of perspective is a relatively stable "capacity" of the actor to think of *alternate* kinds of solutions to problem situations presented to him/her (62, p. 245). In fact, it is the capacity to see *new* problems in *old* situations (rather than only in situations "presented to him" as such), by changing the focus or context, by seeing new goals, new means, and new contingencies as relevant (or as conceivably relevant), that is being delineated here. It is more than mere volunteering of countless solutions that hover around the same theme — the latter a sign more of verbal fluency than of breadth: Turner's (101, pp. 319-321) use of perspective in the plural is closer to this chapter's usage as he sees each perspective as a standpoint from which to observe and interpret the world.

This concept refers, therefore, to the broadness or scope of perspective, to the relative richness of meanings and ideas that people bring to situations that enable varied, concurrent definitions and names for the "same" situation. The concept does *not*, therefore, deal with: (i) the single overt response *actually* made; (ii) the *probability* of any response being made; (iii) the *consequences* of an overt (or covert) response; or (iv) the *efficiency* of an overt (or covert) response. On the contrary, perspective breadth refers to the covert rather than the overt, to possibility rather than probability, to more than one of these, and to range rather than consequence. In brief, it is the range and variety of angles or standpoints of the several possible alternate "solutions" that the actor is able to think of that is of interest.

An additional point needs to be made, that of self-propulsion, that is, the broader the actor's perspective, the more of a self-stimulator, self-organizer, and self-initiator he (she) can become. Not only does he excel at manufacturing alternate solutions to a problem but he also manufactures alternate problems without being asked to do so. He often does this for no apparent or compelling reason, in areas that he does not necessarily value; is often, in fact, irreverent. All humans do this but some more than others; perspective breadth is therefore a *variable* in that some "have" more of it than others. In an earlier, more eloquent moment, the writer wrote (109, p. 172):

> The person with broad perspective is not necessarily . . . the successful problem-solver in immediate situations; breadth of perspective is not analogous to social intelligence or even to intelligence in general. He is one who learns ideas, meanings, and values — but not for immediate use; they might be useful some time in the future, or perhaps never. He . . . [is] not . . . practical in the usual sense and is not, therefore, rewarded by others in the usual way. The tests and criteria for selecting the successful do not usually fit him very well nor is he likely to have much value for them.
>
> He has a variety of potential responses in his arsenal and these are often inconsistent. He is often, as Strauss (94, p. 28) says, a problem to himself and, therefore, a puzzle to others.

Plato might have sympathized with the attempt to define the role of aristocratic ruler as that of propeller, initiator or beginner. The ruler, however, would remain master over what he had begun, the actual carrying out of the activity being the responsibility of the ruled. Hannah Arendt writes that the Greek verb *archein* means to begin, that is, to lead, whereas *prattein* means to act, to achieve and finish. Plato thus, opened up a gulf between knowing and doing "which according to Greek understanding were interconnected" (4, p. 199).

This gulf has seldom been appreciated in the past. The same seems true in the current political world — Helen Fuller drawing from Jesse Unruh, California Democratic leader, the idea that "The man who succeeds in politics . . . is a self-starter who follows through on whatever he begins: 'To have one of those qualities is good — with both you are sure to be a comer'" (36, p. 65).

The doer is the more valued of the two, judging from current leadership emphases in educational institutions, corporations, and the military; it is the executor of predetermined goals — whether he be called functional leader, empathic leader, employee-centered supervisor, executive, manager, or bureaucrat — who is at a premium. Even a "humanist" of the John Ciardi stripe spoke deprecatingly of the writer who "is out for release, not for containment . . . is a self-expresser, not a maker" (18, p. 12). Traits of responsibility, decision, and effectiveness — of acting quickly and with dispatch on the basis of necessarily incomplete and imperfect information — are demanded; but these are not likely to characterize broad perspective.

The broad-perspectived is a more "sticky" type, usually holding back and, while he may sometimes play the role of agitator as well as in rare moments of grace be seen as a respected and/or effective manipulator, refraining from finishing or achieving the enterprise. Inwardly, he (she) is often characterized by wide associations, fleeting images, dissonance, obsessions, and even conflict; overtly, by occasional hesitancy, immobility, lack of confidence, impatience, and/or compulsiveness. In many cases, to be discussed further below, he gravitates toward the serene, the subtle, the ambiguous, and the untimely.

This person functions best when there is the time and room to think, rehearse, change viewpoints and sides, and change even goals, means, values, and the like, without the continual necessity of *public appraisal, justification,* or *validation.* Bolt argued for the freedom of the good Hollywood screen writer from having to meet continual quizzing by directors and producers. There is the danger that if "the discussion is intense and serious, he [the writer] will enter in wholeheartedly and be convinced, and leave the conference having undertaken to do things he feels, vaguely but passionately, he ought not to do" (10, p. 15).

Up to relatively recently, little or no attempt has been made to study this phenomenon in a conscious and systematic manner,[1] not even in studies of problem-solving in general, or of thinking, memory, self-concept, creativity, flexibility, empathy, and so on. It is only in the past decade that any empirical work, not to mention theoretical development, has been attempted.[2]

The student of social change may be interested in this mechanism, the possible relevance of the range of solutions and ideas and of the tendency to see new problems, in relation to anticipating, fomenting, carrying through, opposing, or forestalling social change. It might be that the person with breadth is better able to initiate social change though not necessarily able to guide or control it once it has begun.

## Social Change: Preliminary Outline

Before attempting to place social change and breadth of perspective within the same intellectual context, it is necessary to delineate social change. One useful method would be to ask a number of questions that not only might aid in understanding change but that will also suggest some possible or likely relationships between change and perspective. Some issues to be raised are: what is changing; change versus variation; short-term/long-term change; the form of change; its rapidity, its constancy, its causes and consequences, and probably embracing the above, its significance. (The question of what change itself *is,* apart from what one might infer from the answers to the above issues, is being conspicu-

---

[1] Combs (20) is a possible exception.

[2] For more full delineation of the concept, see the following sources: 109, pp. 149–151 and especially 107, pp. 5–15. For discussion of problems of measurement, there is the writer's unpublished paper delivered at a professional meeting (108, pp. 2–4), copies available upon request.

ously omitted, partly because that is the crux of this paper. Apart from a hasty, explicit definition of change as something that is both new and important to the observer, or to social definition, it is well to point out that this varies with breadth of perspective.)

## What Is Changing

Social organization is assumed to be changing, and is of relevance here, rather than people, behavior, or process. The past trend has been perhaps, because of the influence of contextualism, pragmatism, and general semantics, to emphasize process. Criticism of "structure" as static, however, has frequently led to the reification of process, one consequence being the formulation of abstract laws of change regardless of what it is that is changing (as if looking for Lewis Carroll's "grin without the cat"). Work, however, by such diverse writers as Spencer, Marx, Gumplowicz, Tarde, Simmel, Cooley, and Park have indicated fruitful ways of dealing with both structure and process in the same conceptual formulation without contradiction or the need for theoretical patchwork; more recent examples would be Sorokin, Anselm Strauss, and Walter Buckley. In this chapter, the emphasis is upon change in structures such as social relationships, groups, institutions, classes, communities.

## Change versus Variation and Short-term versus Long-term Change

No clear answer to this problem appears except as each student of change decides for himself (herself) what is *significant* change. To argue, for example, that the daily, weekly, and even yearly activities of people are merely variation or fluctuation with no significance for change may seem reasonable. That over four million Americans enter marriage each year and one and a half million leave it can be similarly interpreted since all this motion may still leave monogamy essentially unscathed. The molecules may move but the mass remains stationary.

Further, the time-span of an activity may be involved — though hardly relevant in itself — a 24-hour cycle (probably significant to the house fly), a yearly cycle or change, the course of a career or a marriage, the life of an industry, the life of a civilization, the creation and evolution of life, and other "long-term" and/or discontinuous changes in matter (cf. 66, Chs. 2-3). The significance of any of the above would depend partly upon the perspective of the observer — be he (she) passerby, participant, or student of change.

## Differential Rates of Change

Related to the previous paragraph is variation in rates of change: (i) between different parts of the same group, institution, society, civilization; (ii) between different groups, institutions, and so on; and/or (iii) *changes of rate* over time within and between groups, civilizations, and other social forms. Also related to the previous paragraph is the evolution-revolution dichotomy and its implications for different spheres of social life — economic, political, familial, religious, mass society, and the host of others that are differentially affected.

### Form of Change

The above considerations suggests the question of the form of change (cf. 66, Ch. 2). Given the above reluctance to posit abstracted change laws and curves, and the reasons for the reluctance, this question becomes less crucial unless one pay attention to the *mechanisms* involved in the forms of change. It seems less important, therefore, whether one expects a *linear* shape (from a biblical "fall from high perch" to some kind of "progress" assumption as in the work of St. Simon, Comte, Spencer, Marx, Darwin, Morgan, Taylor, Fiske, Ogburn, Boulding) or a *cyclical,* or even a *fluctuating* one (such as the works of Machiavelli, Vico, Ferguson, Gumplowicz, Pareto, Spengler, Toynbee, Sorokin), unless one examines mechanisms such as natural selection, external conflict, challenge and response, the principle of "limits," differentiation and integration, or internal contradictions leading to a dialectical process. The above mechanisms may be difficult for those with narrow perspectives to anticipate. Even more difficult might be *variations* on the linear and cyclical models such as (1) linear *civilization* and *cyclical* culture (for example, A. Weber, Ogburn, MacIver) and (2) the "vicious cycle," capable of either linear or cyclical form, alternately, as in the case of Thomas' "definition of the situation" (99), Myrdal's principle of "cumulation" (67, p. 1066), and Merton's "self-fulfilling prophecy" (64, Ch. 13). Calling for the greatest degree of perspective, perhaps, is Chapin's "synchronous culture cycles" of differing orders and degrees of "generality" (17, pp. 207–214), suggesting that much of this is a matter of scale. What appears to be an entire cycle from a small scale is part of a beginning or end of a larger cycle from the view of a larger scale. Further, what appears to be linear (or cyclical) from a narrow time perspective may be but one portion of a huge cycle (or linear series of cycles), or even part of a "changeless state," from a broader time perspective.

Analysis of the rapidity and perhaps the direction of social change issues as well as the causes and consequences depends on the scholar's theoretical and methodological scheme which determines what he deems significant change. Three issues that are not being raised directly are (i) the distinction among cause, mechanism, and condition, (ii) the prospect of some change as a restraint upon further change (cf. 58, Chs. 1-4, 14), and (iii) the measurement of change (cf. 1, Ch. 9; 12, pp. 99–107; 66, Ch. 4).

In relating perspective to change, a crucial variable is the answer that various participants, or potential participants, in the drama give to the above questions. It may or may not matter whether some have a uni-lineal or a cyclical view of change; it is more likely to be important — in asking the perspective question — which variation, fluctuation, or time span is considered significant. The relation of perspective breadth to the anticipating, as well as the answering, of the above, is one indication of what the present discussion is about.

### Perspective and Change: Four Ideal-Type Relationships

At the beginning of this chapter, the varying role of degree of breadth of perspective to social change was briefly indicated. Figure 1 presents the broad limits of the relationship in simple form.

**FIGURE 1**

|  | CHANGE LIKELY | CHANGE UNLIKELY |
|---|:---:|:---:|
| Person with Broad Perspective | a | b |
| Person with Narrow Perspective | c | d |

Box "a" above presents the relationship between perspective breadth and social changes that would occur first to many; that is, it is the broad person with alternate perspectives, foci, goals, and so on who is most likely to think of new social values and arrangements — be he (she) reformer, agitator, radical, innovator, utopian, schemer, creative person, or whatever; he can at least *recognize* that changes are on the way and can prepare to guide and/or stimulate these further. A continually changing urban-industrial society with a sufficiently pronounced produc-tive capacity, and perhaps a consumption emphasis, is likely to stress the role of broad knowledge and of education in bringing about change, if only in its sermons.

Box "b" suggests the less obvious relationship between breadth and change, that is, the broad-perspectived person who can prevent change because he (she) is better able to anticipate it. He may be one in a position of power and/or prestige, perhaps at a major communication network junction, this question being obviously relevant to the earlier raised problem of the broad person's relative access to positions of influ-ence. If he (she) has also a conservative orientation — in the classic Edmund Burke sense — then he is able to foresee the many possible changes and their pitfalls (he interprets "short-term" trends or fluctua-tions as "significant" potentially for the long-run) and move to forestall them even if he should eventually fail, as in the example of gaslight in-terests opposing the introduction of electric lighting. Often an "en-lightened conservative" will prevent change by solving a limited set of problems which, left to themselves, would lead to other problems and, perhaps, to more momentous change.

This is not to imply that perspective breadth always leads to more "correct" or "efficient" decisions, even when its possessor is located in a strategic position. As will be shown below, short- and long-term success depend also on the remaining elements of the "social equation."

In Box "c," change occurs because of *narrowness* of perspective; change is "inorganic," in the sense that it is an accidental, unanticipated, and often unwanted development. The actor unwittingly causes it to happen:

(i) In the case of the *planner* or *reformer* with narrow perspective, it is the unforeseen outcome of a purposely carried out change — such as the drop in the English birthrate following institution of child-labor legislation in the first half of the nineteenth century; this appears to be the fate of many new proposals, programs, doctrines, and philosophies.

(ii) In the case of the narrow *non-actionist,* much of what he (she) defines as merely variation or fluctuation turns out to be significant change (as in the case of "cultural drift") — but he was not broad enough to anticipate, or recognize, it. Change, when it in fact does come, is therefore the more likely to be violent.

Lastly, Box "d" presents the perhaps curious, and at least intriguing, phenomenon of change not occurring until and unless people envision it. Change is therefore slow, or left at the post, because elites, people in key positions, or significant numbers of the population at large, are too narrow to perceive, much less appreciate, the potentialities in a *possible* situation; they do not see that they are "at the flood." A new world would be theirs, were they but to grasp it.

What often happens is that, in the case of the narrow, both "c" and "d" are occurring, i.e., they do not get what they want, and what they do not want or anticipate, they get.

### Personal Considerations: The Relevant Behavioral Process

#### Habit in Relation to Perspective and Change

The crucial question therefore appears to be: Under what circumstances are people likely to anticipate a trend as *significant* change rather than merely as variation or fluctuation (and vice versa) and/or as a long-term rather than short-term trend (and vice versa)? Also relevant to this chapter is the following question: What difference does variation in breadth of perspective make to the above? A preliminary answer appears to be that the person with narrow perspective tends to see "new" situations in "old" terms whereas the broad person is more likely to see both old and new situations in new terms. But this is oversimplification.

Everyone's world contains ambiguity, whether in the classic folk village or in the modern metropolis. Social life, however, must go on as if most social forms and social "others" will continue to be stable and, therefore, more "predictable," even where the basis for interaction becomes "superficial" and less "relevant" (this is referred to below as "categorical association"). Even the most rapidly changing society provides the setting that rewards the person *without* extremely broad, though not with very narrow, perspective, for, to survive and be effective, one must ignore much change or variation, or perhaps never notice it (89, pp. 413–415).

Dewey (22:23) points to the tendency of humans to treat each new situation as if it were similar to the old, that is, to respond habitually until and unless habit is persistently blocked. Firemen are more likely to treat a fire in routine fashion when they believe they have the skills and equipment with which to cope with the fire (50, pp. 42–43). Experimental support was given this idea by research such as Luchins' classic water-jars studies of rigidity, the *"einstellung* effect" where subjects continued to apply techniques to new problems that were relevant to older ones, except where forewarned (57); Bruner and Postman (14) showed experimentally people's tendency to reject an "incongruous" physical pattern and to fall back upon already existing perception habits. Shibutani wrote that "although reference group behavior is generally studied in situations where choices are possible (that is, to the investigators), the actor himself is often unaware that there are alternatives" (88, p. 565).

The person with narrow perspective is therefore less likely even to recognize the existence of a new situation, let alone see it in complex, or contingent, terms and even less likely to anticipate its arrival. Often, he (she) is inclined to dogmatism (80). On the other hand, the broader-perspectived person is likely not only to see the new in the old (62, p. 245) but also to seek out the new and the different *actively*.

People tend to avoid, or resist defining as such, situations containing stress and threat. Camilla Anderson emphasized the very tendency of people to maneuver themselves into comfortable, habitual, and familiar situations "and thus avoid the anxiety that would otherwise be their lot" (3, p. 236); Rue Bucher, in her analysis of people's reaction to disaster (a plane crash), pointed to their immediate tendency to seek, and content themselves with, familiar explanations that enable them to rest "because their world was still in order" (15, p. 468). Also, emotional shock or trauma (such as death of husband) tends to narrow one's perspective as indicated in some of the writer's previous research on perspective (109, pp. 159–160).

The above is less true of broad people, who, for whatever reason, more often maneuver themselves into the threatening or stressful. Often, uncertainty and anxiety are built into their way of life without socially patterned devices for meeting these stresses; hence there is room, if not necessity, for innovation.

To many, this is indeed a moral world where what "ought" to be "will"; not all of these are children. The Millerites in nineteenth-century America continued to believe, even after their prophecy had failed, as did many other religious sects, including the more recent cases of the

Lake City believers (28). Bettelheim (8) reported that inmates of a Nazi concentration camp at first believed that outsiders were doing their utmost to free them, that the world would not sit by and let them suffer.

Much orderly and regular change is precluded by narrow perspective, and moral blindness make this the more true. To the degree that people, or people in crucial places, are ignorant and/or committed to particular values and situations, change does not occur, except in fits and starts, as in the case of Boxes "c" and "d," above (See Figure 1).

### Later Stages of Habit and Thought

What happens, finally, when the situation is actually *defined* as "new" by the actor, that is, he admits, to himself at least, that there is a structural difference in the situation (whether it be a three-car accident, a complex murder trial, a business upturn, or a new civilizational direction)? The person with broader perspective had already so defined it earlier, perhaps, had created it, certainly saw more in it, and perhaps, no longer is excited by it — compared with the narrower person. It is at this point that he (she) is ready to bring about, or to assist others to bring about, change.

If the new situation is not very stressful, threatening, or urgent, but simply unfamiliar and puzzling, there is the tendency to *interaction*. (Interaction is also a likely response in a *stressful* situation when that situation is preceded by forewarning [33].) People seek to talk the situation over with others, exchange hypotheses and facts. The formation of politics, and perhaps of social movements, is likely, except for the "isolate" for whom mass participation might substitute. Bucher wrote that

> [w]hen the disaster cannot be assimilated to a conventional frame of reference, the cause of it becomes a prolonged and serious issue. People continue to puzzle over what kind of disaster it was, why it happened, and under what conditions it may happen again (15, p. 468).

Experimental evidence tends to support the proposition that people are most suggestible in situations that they have defined as "ambiguous" (cf. 87; 85; 55; 19). Sherif and Harvey (86) demonstrated further that ambiguous situations make for decrease in norm-governed behavior and an increase in unpatterned behavior (see the below discussion of "categorical" association).

The narrower person is very capable of instituting, or at least engaging in, change (Box "c," Figure 1, above). However, his thoughts and actions are not likely to be very creative or far-reaching, nor is the change likely to be very clear or gratifying to him.

For the broad person, on the other hand, the problem is at a higher level, perhaps related by him (her) to areas that narrower people do not see as relevant or problematic; he may have similar confusion about change, but on a different level. And having gone through such excitement or turmoil before, he is perhaps better prepared for others so doing (as in Box "b," Figure 1, above) and may therefore be better able to prevent the incipient change if he wishes. If he is not in a position to do so, on the other hand, then heavy thinking and perhaps creativity and fantasy will have to substitute.

When the situation is seen as *threatening* and perhaps *urgent,* the first reaction appears to be rigidity, in both thought and action. Resignation is a frequent response to a "hopeless" situation (31). Without redefinition by others, a person is likely to be "frozen in his/her tracks"; with redefinition by others, such as "keynoting" (103, p. 47) and/or a "generalized belief" such as hysteria, wish fulfillment, or hostility (90, p. 83), little or no intelligent calculation is likely to follow — and one may become susceptible to confident leads and calls to action, perhaps even to participate in such leadership. "Isolates" from most social circles appear initially to be more susceptible to such calls than are the more socially integrated (48). With prolonged threat, increasing flexibility and permissiveness, even imagination and creativity are likely, and therefore, an increase in the degree and relevance of breadth.

Support for the first generalization just elaborated is given by accounts of response to sudden disaster, such as paralysis during the Halifax explosion of 1918 (76, p. 36), the narrowing of focus during a tornado in a Southwestern state (49, p. 42), and panic at the Iroquois Theater fire in Chicago in 1903 (104, pp. 197–207). Crowd behavior other than panic is likely, such as mobs, riots, and crazes. Experimental evidence in less momentous circumstances also supports the above: Cowen (21) gave the Luchins water-jars problems to subjects and found that increasing stress increased rigidity; Pally (72) achieved the same by increasing threat; Mintz induced panic, or "non-adaptive group behavior," by introducing "competitive stress" (65).

Then, as further stated above, the *prolongation* of stress, threat, and the like tends to make for change, both in the personal and in the social order. Vinacke paraphrased O. H. Mowrer as suggesting that anxiety "has an adaptive function in preparing the individual for threatening situations . . . [stimulating him to] adopt new and acceptable modes of behavior" (106, p. 285). Symonds (96, p. 156) saw the tension state associated with anxiety as interfering with efficient response to current demands of the external world and, while it tends to lead to personal discomfort and even disorganization, yet may also stimulate the inner mental processes — especially in the direction of fantasy; Hagen (42, pp. 141–143), on the other hand, gives aid and comfort to a frequently expressed tendency among men of letters to point out the advantages of personal difficulties, in that he sees anxiety as a more facile and direct motivator of innovation. Allport, Bruner, and Jandorf (2) studied the responses to deprivation, frustration, and persecution in Nazi Germany, from the subjects who reconstructed their feelings, finding not only that there had been resignation, regression, security-striving, and conformity (findings compatible with those of Bettelheim [8]) but also eventual adoption of temporary frames of reference, increased planning, and increased problem-solving.

Similarly, the broad-perspectived person sometimes finds himself (herself) in a position cut off from the usual sources of societal reward and satisfaction; though bombarded by stimuli, he cannot respond in any satisfying, effective, or far-reaching manner. He then develops his thinking processes further, at the expense of other things.

## Conclusion

The foregoing attempted to delineate the main kinds of relationships between breadth of perspective and social change, on the one hand, and the thinking and feeling human being, on the other. It not only sought to outline the structural elements of perspective and change but also raised the question of the cognitive and emotive processes that the various participants in the drama undergo. We have now to turn to a further, and perhaps broader, analysis of the larger context within which this occurs — society.

## Societal Consideration: Social Engagement, Alienation, and Detachment

Social change is also societal, that is, change in society or of some major portion thereof — institutions, classes, communities, groups. The person with narrow or broad perspective, on the other hand, is a psychological organism — he (she) has personality or personal organization and/or values, motives, perceptions, identities, anxieties, and other organizing and disorganizing characteristics; he is partly the product of past socialization and is behaving within a present social situation. It therefore appears incumbent upon the writer, at this point, to develop the social and/or societal context within which perspective breadth and social change are related.

A number of generalizations will now be made and treated in turn:

(i) The broad-perspectived person is not usually "organically" related to society and does not usually find himself (herself) in positions of authority or prestige that enable him (her) either to bring about orderly change (Box "a," Figure 1, above) or to forestall it (Box "b").

(ii) He often finds his comfortable relation to society, therefore, to be informal and, in many cases, "categorical" (to be described below).

(iii) Therefore, he appears to fit some of the "social types" and "character types" developed by Thomas, Park, Riesman, Fromm, Jung, Stern, and others.

(iv) He usually, therefore, finds himself either withdrawing "inwardly," ranging from mild "privatization" to psychosis, or

(v) He may turn "outward," but outside traditional or formal organization into sectarianism, social agitation, and the like.

(vi) When the broad-perspectived person is located in a position of authority and influence, he can then become more effective socially, if only temporarily, because he is then organically related to society.

(i) Inorganic Relation to Society

The man with broad perspective is less likely to "flow" organically in relation to his society. This is used both in the sense of his personal history and his contemporary relation to society.

In the first sense, the broad man is less likely to have grown to become what his family and community wanted and is therefore the result of much unanticipated socialization. He has probably had more "habit blockage" than most, and more ambiguity, stress, and threat during growth. His alienation thus is not only an orientation that differs from that of the previous generation (cf. 60; 29) but is the product of a broader combination of circumstances.

In the second sense he is not as likely to become the "child of his time," to have a basic personality that fits his society. The broad man is less likely to have been satisfied or successful with what will below be called the main *traditional, formal,* or at times even the *informal,* relationships of society, nor is he as likely to influence change through them. Instead, he appears satisfied, or compelled, to function through what will below be called *categorical* associations (and, at times, the informal as well). If he is to influence social change under normal conditions, he will gradually do so, if at all, largely through categorical and informal associations, by either his writing or personal influence.

(ii) "Categorical" Relation to Society

In the usual course of events, the person with broad perspective is unlikely to be found influencing change in the *traditional* (unplanned, publicly legitimatized and honored relationships that develop over a long time) and *formal* (planned, publicly legitimatized relationships set up for a specific purpose) centers of power and influence. He is not likely to be a leader or important functionary in any of the major institutions nor is he to be found in the ranks of celebrities attuned to a mass audience. Instead, there is the tendency to confine his traditional and formal associations to the minimum necesssary and to gravitate toward informal and categorical relationships.

By *informal* association is meant a relatively unplanned and not necessarily publicly legitimatized association, as a sewing circle or friendship group; it may be legitimatized within a narrow circle only. The influence of any of its members upon social change is likely to be minute, and indirect at best, except when the members begin to coalesce into something on the order of a social movement.

By *categorical* association, the writer refers to social association that is only "lightly patterned" (one interacts with others in terms of the barest social identities). Such association is unplanned, unorganized, and sometimes not even privately legitimatized and, of the four relationships, is the only one at all not likely to be "shared" with others. It is thus social in the barest sense in that interaction with others is in terms of categories such as age, sex, race, clothes, and/or manner; these usually present superficial and often, inaccurate and irrelevant bases for social intercourse and accustoms one to living with and manipulating ambiguity.

The above four forms of association broaden the primary-secondary group distinction (or several of its other versions: gemeinschaft-gesellschaft, mechanical-organic, folk-urban, sacred-secular, multibonded-unibonded, nonsegmented-segmented) by presenting four types of secondary associations (traditional, formal, informal, categorical) and two types of primary relations (traditional, informal). Examples of the four secondary associations in modern socety are: the consanguine family (traditional-secondary), bureaucratic organization (formal-secondary), calling a new acquaintance by the first name (informal-secondary), and the casual crowd (categorical-secondary). Examples of the two primary relationships are: the patriarchal, conjugal family (traditional-primary) and the friendship group (informal-primary) (See Figure 2). This

|  | SECONDARY ASSOCIATIONS | PRIMARY RELATIONS |
|---|---|---|
| Organized | | |
| Traditional | Consanguine family<br>Mores about relations<br>   between the sexes,<br>   races, ages | Patriarchal conjugal<br>   family |
| Formal | Bureaucratic organization<br>Partnership | ——————— |
| Informal | Work group<br>Calling a new acquaintance<br>   by first name | Companionate family<br>Friendship group |
| Unorganized | | |
| Categorical | Mass<br>Urban casual crowd<br>Public | ——————— |

**FIGURE 2**

broadens especially the concept of secondary association — of particular relevance to modern social life — and ties it further to the conceptually more clear primary relationship by seeing "traditional" and "informal" association as common to each.[3]

Yet the latter two relationships (informal and categorical) abound in modern life with its rapid urbanization and changing identities (filling the gaps left by the first two relationships, traditional and formal), and they are characteristic of many who have a broad perspective. The danger is, however, that where the broad person has not succeeded in establishing satisfactory informal contacts in society and since he tends to restrict his traditional and formal associations as well, categorical ties are all that remain. The problem with categorical associations is that, when exclusive, they tend to narrow perspective through "desocialization," as the following discussion concerning isolation and privatization will attest. While he might then be seen by some as a lower-class type because of his outward life style, he would certainly not exhibit the unimaginativeness, suggestibility, concreteness of thought, intolerance of the different, or the orientation toward the present that seems to be true of the industrial lower class (56, p. 115) and also of the village peasant (87, pp. 74–75, 505–508). Nor is he ever likely to become "massified" since his breadth would be incompatible with the shallowness and passivity of the mass.

Social change issuing from traditional or formal centers without broad perspective is more likely to be unintended, misdirected, and/or sudden and violent. A significant question therefore occurs here: In areas of non-legitimate power, under what set of circumstances does it promote, or prevent, change? This point will be discussed further below.

(iii) Social Type and Character

Though he (she) is clearly socialized, since broad perspective implies a well-developed set of ideas, values, goals, and means, there still is an aspect of isolation and privatization, as used by Lang and Lang (54, pp. 101–103), about the man of broad perspective. He will sometimes avoid the public arena and may be said to be more *enculturated* than *socialized* (he has a good sense of the culture but not of the social skills).

In the extreme case, perspective is acquired at a cost, following the path of turning inward in the face of stress, threat, rejection, or disappointment. A number of "character" analyses appear to point to the heightened creativity, insight, imagination, fantasy, or obsession that often results. Personality or character typologies such as Jung's introvert, Stern's subjective, Rorschach's introversive, Kretschmer's schizothymic,

---

[3] Gregory Stone (92, p. 94) has developed a four-type classification — human (universal) relations, structural (titled) relations, interpersonal (names and nicknames) relations, and masses (anonymous) — which strongly resembles the traditional-formal-informal-categorical scheme; the main differences from Stone are this writer's explicit emphasis on the traditional character of the first type and his relating of the scheme to the primary-secondary dimension.

Gross' deep-narrow, and Jaensch's disintegrate seem to emphasize several similar characteristics; for example, inwardly directed interest and experience, responsiveness to inner stimulation, less immediate adaptation to reality, greater creative ability, and more theoretical persevering (59, pp. 17–23).

Moreover, many of the social types and social characters would appear relevant, though privatization would hardly be characteristic of some. Included here might be Park's and Stonequist's marginal man and Becker's in-between adjusted or marginal, representing broad withdrawn types, and Thomas' bohemian, Rank's neurotic, and Merton's retreatist as examples of the more narrow. Less withdrawn and more successful might be Becker's liberated, Thomas' creative man, Rank's artist, Fromm's productive, Merton's innovator and rebel, Riesman's autonomous, Foote and Cottrell's autonomous, the humanistic scholar of Hutchins, Barr, and Adler, and the conservative of Kirk, Rossiter and/or Viereck.[4]

The next two sections will compare the "inward posture" of the more recluse broad type, largely outside the institutional structure, with the "outward posture" of the more effective broad-perspectived person who may become part of the structure.

(iv) The Inward Posture

The social science literature is amply endowed with analysis of socialization, its degrees, and the courses it might take. Whether in the philosophic vein of a Dewey (22) or Mead (62) or in the more empirical studies of isolation (for example, feral man, solitary confinement, schizophrenia in urban "transition areas"), the ideas behind concepts such as "autistic," "unsocialized," and "desocialized" indicate the general processes that are assumed to be involved in an "inward posture."

The broad-perspectived person who gravitates toward the "lightly patterned" social life (probably because he is less comfortable in the general swim and because the latter is not very comfortable with him, finds himself in dire straits. If genuine isolation sets in, or even *privatization* (defined by Lang and Lang [54, p. 83, 264–265], as a breaking off from social ties, especially primary, affective ones and the increased concern with one's own needs), one is very likely to remain ineffective with reference to social change and is also in danger of perspective eventually atrophying (89, pp. 409–424; 7, pp. 281–285).

An extreme case of withdrawal with pathological overtones, though not one of narrow perspective, is the *obsessive-compulsive*. Fenichel (27, pp. 46–51, 296–300) wrote that the obsessive is one who takes flight in the purely cognitive, at the expense of emotion; who, rather than using thought as part of a total act, falls back instead upon continual, repeti-

---

[4] Park (73; 74), Stonequist (93), Becker (6, pp. 217–219, 221–224), Thomas (98, pp. 159–161), Rank (77, pp. 263–268), Merton (64, pp. 207–209, 195–203, 209–211), Fromm (35, pp. 82–85, 90–106), Riesman (78, Part III), Foote and Cottrell (30), Kirk (51), Rossiter (81), and Viereck (105).

tive rehearsal of ideas. He seeks flight from the flesh and blood of realistic grappling with his problems into the shadowy world of words and concepts into fantasy. There is regression, according to Freud, into an earlier state of magical belief that the name, the word, the symbol is all one needs for the control of situations. It is the *omnipotence* of words, expressing itself for the normal person in obscenities, swearing, poetry, and logical exercises which for the obsessive becomes the major orientation. Parenthetically, this on the societal level is Toennies' conception of the *Gesellschaft* resident.

The obsessive may retain some broad perspective. Broad perspective may have been a necessary condition for the obsessive state; whatever other personal "defects" may be present, these by themselves may not be sufficient to make a person of *narrow* perspective an obsessive-compulsive. In other words, the narrow person can eventually develop many maladies, but obsessive-compulsive neurosis may very well not be one of these (See Figure 3).

|  | Obsessive Neurosis | No Obsessive Neurosis |
|---|---|---|
| Broad Perspective | Possible | Possible |
| Narrow Perspective | Impossible | Possible |

**FIGURE 3**

### (v) The Outward Posture

Lang and Lang present an alternative to privatization: instead of responding with apathy and withdrawal from the ambiguous and the anxious, one may seek a "positive solution" (54, pp. 264–265). Accepting some higher authority, mortal or not, one then becomes an agent of extreme change by identifying with and attempting to follow causes and social movements particularly of the "value-oriented" type (103, Ch. 14; 90, Ch. 10). Cantril, Fromm, Gilbert, Hoffer, and Toch discuss similar search after the dramatic, secure, and sweeping positive solution, as does the literature on the "sect" and, to a degree, Lipset's analysis of political "extremism" (56, Ch. 5).[5]

Blumer's second kind of *agitator* fits here, not the one who is excitable, restless, and aggressive and who infects people already disturbed and unsettled; but the one who, more calm, quiet, and dignified, raises doubts in the minds of people who take the status quo for granted. Foreseeing a possible future that his listeners do not, he is "likely to be a man

[5] Some citations are: Cantril (16), Fromm (34), Gilbert (37), Hoffer (44), Toch (100). For a representative analytic literature on the sect, see Gillin (39), Niebuhr (69; 70), E. Faris (26), Becker (6, Ch. 23), Kornhauser (52), Simmel (89). Weber's charismatic leader fits here as well.

sparing in his words, but capable of saying very caustic, incisive, and biting statements which get 'under the skin' of people and force them to view things in a new light" (9, pp. 204-205).

Among other outward postures might be social and spatial mobility, and other kinds of moving of the broad, sensitized person into new positions. Examples of this would be migrants, emerging family types, new occupations, and the entrance of women, minority groups, and other outsiders (cf. 42) into the arts and professions and therefore, into better position to influence social change.

Before moving to examine the broad-perspectived man (woman) who is more securely ensconced in society, it is interesting to note that four of Seeman's (84) five senses of *alienation* fit the types and processes discussed above. Powerlessness and value isolation, for example, fit "categorical association," meaninglessness fits the "agitator," and normlessness and the above three fit one or another of the social types and social characters. It is only self-estrangement, in the Marxian-Frommian sense, that may have no clear application here.

(vi) Organic Relation to Society

When broad perspective is found in high places, "intelligent" manipulation of social change is more likely, either to bring it about (Box "a," Figure 1, above) or to forestall it (Box "b"). While continual occupancy of legitimate centers of decision-making is not usually conducive to broadening perspective further, or even to maintaining its intensity, there is at least the means for its translation into effective action.

One example of this is the leader, whether *formal* or *traditional*, who finds himself in new and changing situations which present continuing and persistent challenges to his outlook thus, keeping him aware of new definitions, foci, goals, and so on. He tends to have a self organized broadly around the "near and familiar," one whose major activities and commitments are likely to have been *publicly recognized* and *validated;* he is also likely to be industrious, indefatigable, and, within socially tolerable limits, practical and opportunistic (61). Franklin D. Roosevelt, probably comparatively broad when he assumed the presidency, engaged in continual, pragmatic reformulation in peace and war. But whereas he found himself periodically challenged to think and act radically during turbulent times, he otherwise relaxed by "riding the waves" during the relatively tranquil times. An Edison or a Ford appears to have been a similar type in a similar time. These three examples fit an *innovation* (see 5; 42; 79) and *invention-accumulation* (cf. 97; 71; 38; 43) model and perhaps indicate something about the decisionmaking centers of industrial, if not post-industrial, societies.

On the other hand, there is the leader who, like the agitator referred to earlier, has long tried to cajole a sleeping potential followership and then suddenly finds himself in power. This leader has a self organized around the "strange and distant," many of his activities and commitments having been *privately recognized* and *validated*. Before his rise to respectability, this leader's viewpoint is likely to have been more widely accepted than was publicly recognized or conceded, a condition akin to Floyd H. Allport's "pluralistic ignorance" (47, pp. 174–175) having existed. The example of Winston Churchill may be cited here, as may that of Charles de Gaulle, although more pure examples would be preferred. Such a person has very broad perspective and in an emergency, finds himself catapulted into a position of authority; when the emergency is at an end, he is likely to be removed, as Churchill was in 1945 and de Gaulle in 1946 and 1969.

The more desperate the followers, the more likely they are to turn to the second type of leader. However, both *imply change* since one or the other is permitted to lead only where the more commonly found leader whether *traditional, formal,* or *informal,* has been socially defined as inadequate to the new situation. Where followers see a clearly new, and perhaps threatening, situation, they are more ready to turn to the previously humored, distrusted, and/or despised person for leadership; if the latter should then also be broad, then a more smooth and organic process of change, or its prevention, is likely. Sanford's work is relevant here when he distinguished between the "functional" leader, corresponding somewhat to the above, and the "nice guy" leader. The former arises in "a life-or-death situation [where] the follower's need for warm approval is likely to be less important than his need to survive" (83, p. 339). The previous experience of the latter (the "nice guy" leader), on the other hand, is "dangerous because it easily induces habits of sheer mechanized action, blindness, tendencies to perform slavishly, instead of thinking, instead of facing a problem freely" (110, p. 62).

The functional leader could be called in when radical *adaptation* to the "new" appears needed, but released when *integrative* functions become paramount (75, Ch. 2). When society is falling apart, he may be called in but, as the physician in cases of illness, he is less appreciated when society is "on the mend." [6] Present times call for some less haphazard method of bringing the broad perspective into positions of power and influence; perhaps Margaret Mead's "evolutionary clusters" idea is worth a try (63, Pt. III).

Most leaders, whether involved in politics or not, and in upper or in middle executive levels (and whether or not they really are "nice guys"), would appear to be in situations which do not call for, and would often not tolerate, very broad perspective; they often make decisions without quite verbalizing or knowing much of what went into their making. Yet they could not be very narrow-perspectived either, since having to

---

[6] Hogbin presents an interesting analysis of "disintegration and reintegration" in primitive society that is of some relevance to this chapter (45, pp. 46–54).

participate in diverse activity, mental variety is also assured. However, having to act makes a formulation that is radical, creative, and/or fantastic a luxury and a severe handicap: the active leader cannot normally have much tolerance for "inefficiency." Hence, whereas "followers" may be found to be distributed across the entire range from narrow to broad perspective, leaders might be expected to fall closer to the middle of the range, probably slightly above it (See Figure 4.)[7]

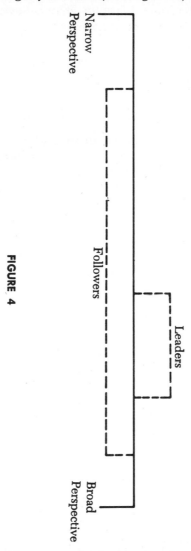

FIGURE 4

[7] Gouldner's (40, p. 33) statement that leaders generally are a bit more intelligent than the average of their followers may be relevant here even though intelligence and perspective breadth are not synonymous; Krout's statement that great men range between extremes of dull normal and genius (40, p. 34) can perhaps be explained by the "extreme" being recognized and/or utilized only during crises.

When the broad-perspectived finds himself in a position of legitimate power, and especially where this fits the logic of the times (more in the case of Churchill or de Gaulle than of F. D. R.), vast social changes, fluctuations, or resistances to change are likely. That the broad person can never be too comfortable when "organically" related to society may be seen by the relatively short and precarious tenure in office of a Churchill. Only in this uneasy manner does he become a child of his time and have a limited time to use up some "idiosyncrasy credit."

Perspective therefore appears to be in continual danger of narrowing at the poles of a *social contact* continuum, with isolation at one end and continual habitation of legitimate power and influence centers at the other (See Figure 5).

## Sequential Analysis of Perspective and Change

It may prove useful at this point, though admittedly premature theoretically and skeletal in form, to treat the relation of perspective to change sequentially, thus putting together many of the ideas discussed earlier. The analysis assumes a dialectic framework with cyclic modifications, and it begins from a rather static *traditional* social setting, though a beginning could have been made from any of several points.

Firstly, the existence of a traditional society is assumed, either in totality or in part, implying heavy reliance upon custom, particularly in the economic realm and in other areas defined as vital. Change is usually absent or is unnoticed by a populace with generally narrow perspective.

Then, an important change, caused internally or from without, occurs and is so perceived by a few but not noticed by the majority. The change can be either a misfortune or even sudden good fortune, but only a minority even suspects its implications. For some of the few, "categorical association" and some loosening of the norms arises, tending to isolate those not already in and around central, legitimate power positions. A breach in tradition comes into existence.

Should this process continue, more people or their children or other associates gain broader perspective and the fact, or possibility, of change becomes publicly recognized and legitimatized. This is accompanied by rapid development of new social types both of the inward and outward "posture" and of new subcultures not necessarily ethnically-based. A potential exists for crowd formation, the rise of publics, rumor spread, fashion, and perhaps the rise of new sects. People may still ask the "wrong" questions but there is "the new" in the very asking, as the great degree of "variation" and "fluctuation" is seen by some as possibly implying "significant," and perhaps long-term, change. The broad person may then be utilized either to create and guide change or to prevent it. Not only do *categorical* associations (and normlessness and feelings

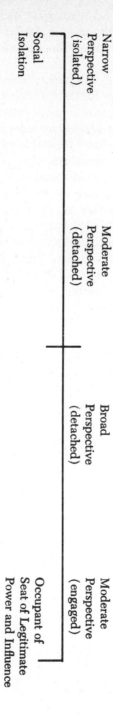

**FIGURE 5**

of powerlessness and meaninglessness) increase but also tendencies arise toward filling the newly-created "structural gaps" with *formal* and *informal* organization; that is, since *traditional* organization no longer "suffices."

In time, diversity and complexity increase and there is continuous change, with all it implies for the increased ambiguity and stress in social life. With a general increase in perspective breadth, there is the anticipation of future change and increased planning, and some discomfort at the idea of blind change — whether or not one favors change. Reformism, radicalism, conservatism, and reaction all take to the arena, often in turn; propaganda and social movements are likely to be added, if they have not indeed already made their appearance, to forms of elementary collective behavior discussed earlier. While perspective exists and is used, much of the more radical, and isolated, perspective breadth is omitted, coming to the fore at infrequent intervals largely via sudden and violent mechanisms. The society is becoming an "active" (24) or "self-guiding" (13) one, though its potential for "development" or "modernization" may be limited by following the military dictatorship model rather than either the capitalist or socialist models (46, Ch. 12).

If all goes well, a heightened period of change, creativity, florescence, and disorganization, alternating with attempts at reorganization, ensues. This is typified by strong secularity, relativism, perhaps a new conception of "freedom,"[8] and a greater turning toward abstractions, toward the "just possible." It is at this point that the *very broad* person, not just the moderately broad, is most "needed," that is, the person who can reorient his definitions of reality in radically new, and often amoral ways. His utilization or the lack of it helps determine the next condition of society.

Gradually, however, tendencies toward traditionalization, orthodoxy, integration, reaction, or at least a strong moderation emphasis begin to supersede the other three relationships (formal, informal, and categorical); this may occur in the society generally or in selected portions.[9]

---

[8] The concept of freedom as "absence of restriction" — i.e., defined negatively — becomes the "presence of more possibilities and opportunities" — i.e., defined "positively." This represents movement from a society with few restrictions but few opportunities to a more complex one with more restrictive organization but more choice and from relatively narrow persons to those with a richer mental life.

[9] Weber saw charisma as destined to routinization and rationalization, even tradition eventually descending to bureaucratic routine. Kroeber's historical studies suggested to him that all periods of florescence end in either disorganization or traditionalization (53, pp. 773–777) and Sorokin's "idealistic" middle point of the cycle of societal change eventually "descends" to the less creative sensate or ideational polar extremes (91). It is only fair to state, however, that more optimistic formulations exist, usually of a more positivistic nature. Apart from a St. Simon or a Comte, one may point to a Barnett "piecemeal" view of change as inherent in the interactive process (5) or to Ogburn's "exponential" pattern that results from an ever enlarging and self-generating "culture base" (71).

Perspective breadth is less likely to be sought; narrower, more effective, leader types and character structures develop and prosper, the broad person gravitating more and more to the periphery and/or to an appreciative subculture.

Eventually, however, tradition and, perhaps, the still existing formal and informal organization begin to be beset by stresses, and changes and categoricalization begin to increase. The process, an essentially *dialectic* one with reference to the four relationships, begins again, but more rapidly this time and from a new base (a rising cycle).

A more concrete example of this sequential process, one more easily examined within the present intellectual apparatus, is the development of new areas of social contact. As examples, we shall take social contact within a new geographic setting, as in a frontier town; or in the interstices of tradition and formal organization, as in the nineteenth century capital-labor conflict for instance, in the more recent examples of school integration, and in the rise of the urban fringe (11, pp. 121–123). Under all these conditions, categorical contacts are plentiful, in the absence of more organized relationships. In time, both formal and informal arrangements arise, as the development of law enforcement agencies, labor and race legislation, industrial pacts and understandings, and eventual informal understandings with one's neighbors indicate. Increasingly, these will tend to take the character of *tradition*, with the informal likely to do so sooner than the formal. With traditionalization, a relationship more organic to society, and embodying social respect and even honor, has been built within each of these areas of contact. Then, however, tradition (or either of the other two) eventually starts to break down and people again begin to interact more and more in ambiguous or lightly-patterned situations, that is, categorical associations, and the process begins anew. Here is the best opportunity for the gravitation of broad perspective to traditional and/or formal centers of power (if the breakdown is the beginning of a new social arrangement) or to the creation of new power positions as indicated above.

The foregoing has been an attempt, first, to outline, then to illustrate, application of the conceptual tools of this chapter to a sequential analysis of perspective and change. This is one way to organize the contribution of the chapter. The conclusion that follows is a second.

### Conclusion

One good way to begin the conclusion is not only to rephrase the quoted two paragraphs in the early portion of this chapter (pages 3–4), but to adapt them so as to relate perspective breadth to social change:

> The person with broad perspective is not necessarily the successful translator of his breadth into the bringing about or the preventing of social change; breadth of perspective is not easily translatable into the process of

social change, or even into orderly social process in general. He is one who has ideas, meanings, and values — but not easily channeled into the traditional or formal social process; they might be so channeled at some time in the future, or perhaps never. He is not organic to society in the usual sense and is not, therefore, utilized by others in the usual way. The groups and institutions that affect and control social change do not usually fit or select him very well nor is he likely to gravitate toward them.

He has a variety of potential reformulations of social life in his arsenal and these are often inconsistent. He is often a problem to himself and, therefore, a puzzle to others.

In capsule form, the following generalizations appear to reflect the above discussion:

(i) Both broad and narrow perspective may, under differing circumstances, either bring about or prevent change.

(ii) Perspective breadth is seen as affecting the likelihood of the actor's recognizing and distinguishing between "significant" change and mere "fluctuation," and between long-term and short-term change.

(iii) Perspective thus helps to account for why "the new" does or does not catch hold, as well as it does for why it is created or prevented.

(iv) The person with broad perspective is usually not found in the position to influence change, though this is less true in advanced societies and genuinely developing societies.

(v) Advanced and genuinely developing societies, more inclined to social change, are also more likely both to create and to appreciate, to value and to utilize, breadth.

(vi) Even in advanced and developing societies, however, the broad person is not likely to be called upon by the legitimate power centers (unless, of course, he or she is already part of such centers), nor to gravitate toward them, until the situation is defined by the powers that be as one of crisis.

(vii) Part of the reason for this is that the broad person's outlook is often less utilitarian, conscious, disciplined, or circumspect.

(viii) Much of the time, therefore, the broad person is either left out of the swim of things (in the area of the lightly-patterned) or seeks substitute power centers, often helping to create them.

(ix) While tending toward the societal periphery, then, broad perspective is found all along the line from isolation to influence — and in many social "postures" and character types — affecting change differently at each point.

(x) Therefore, unless and until broad perspective is utilized, the portending signs for significant social change are likely to be missed, thus making the change all the more likely to be unanticipated, sudden, violent, and misdirected or unwanted when it comes.

(xi) In accounting for the relationship between perspective and change, therefore, the nature of existing societal relationships and of the personal experiences of its members become of crucial importance, with elements of isolation, inorganic ties, categorical association, and mental distress and confusion figuring prominently in the outcome.

Social change is affected by breadth of perspective and is also un-affected, directly at least. It both creates the broad person and is also, at odd times and often tangentially, created by him (her) or at least is recognized, and sometimes prevented, by him. In tranquil times, society tends both to ignore and tolerate him and is likely only to seek him out in times of crisis when even he may be too late. At times, he will not wait and thus helps bring change about, whether from within the institutional structure or from without. At other moments, he may not exist at all, and neither will social change — except violently, whence the broad person will also be created. *Formal* organization excludes him, *informal* organization tolerates him, and *tradition* is blind to him; he is most likely to be ensconced in the *categorical,* or lightly-patterned. Hence, or hence not, social change.

In conclusion, the specific relationships between breadth of perspec-tive and social change are imprecisely known and stated. But the nature of these relationships in both promulgating and preventing change is perhaps better understood when one notes the inorganic relation be-tween the broad-perspectived person and society and the conditions under which this individual leaves the area of the lightly-patterned in order to participate, however briefly and anxiously, in the legitimate mechanisms of the social process.

## BIBLIOGRAPHY

1. Allen, Francis R. *Socio-Cultural Dynamics.* New York: Macmillan and Co., 1971.

2. Allport, Gordon W., Jerome S. Bruner, and E. M. Jandorf. "Personality under Social Catastrophe," *Character and Personality* 10 (1941), pp. 1–22.

3. Anderson, Camilla M. "The Self Image." *Mental Hygiene* 36 (1952), pp. 227–244.

4. Arendt, Hannah. *The Human Condition.* Garden City, N.Y.: Doubleday Anchor Books, 1959. (First published 1958)

5. Barnett, Homer G. *Innovation.* New York: McGraw-Hill Book Co., 1953.

6. Becker, Howard P. *Man in Reciprocity.* New York: Frederick A. Praeger, 1956.

7. Berger, Brigitte. *Societies in Change.* New York: Basic Books, 1971.

8. Bettelheim, Bruno. "Individual and Mass Behavior in Extreme Situations," *Journal of Abnormal and Social Psychology,* Vol. 38 (1943), pp. 417–452.

9. Blumer, Herbert. "Social Movements," in A. M. Lee (ed.), *New Outline of the Principles of Sociology,* revised ed. New York: Barnes & Noble, 1946.

10. Bolt, Robert. "The Playright in Films," *Saturday Review* (Dec. 29, 1962), pp. 15–16.

11. Boskoff, Alvin. *The Sociology of Urban Regions*, 2nd ed. New York: Appleton-Century Crofts, 1970.

12. Boulding, Kenneth. *A Primer on Social Dynamics*. New York: Free Press, 1970.

13. Breed, Warren. *The Self-Guiding Society*. New York: Free Press, 1971.

14. Bruner, Jerome S., and Leo Postman. "On the Perception of Incongruity." *Journal of Personality*, Vol. 18 (1949), pp. 206–223.

15. Bucher, Rue. "Blame and Hostility in Disaster." *American Journal of Sociology*, Vol. 62 (1957), pp. 467–475.

16. Cantril, Hadley. *The Psychology of Social Movements*. New York: John Wiley & Sons, 1941.

17. Chapin, F. Stuart. *Cultural Change*. Dubuque, Iowa: William C. Brown Co., 1928. (First published by The Century Co.)

18. Ciardi, John. "On Writing and Bad Writing." *Saturday Review* (Dec. 15, 1962), pp. 10–12.

19. Coffin, Thomas E. "Some Conditions of Suggestions and Suggestibility." *Psychological Monographs*, Vol. 53, No. 4 (1941).

20. Combs, Arthur W. "Intelligence from a Perceptual Point of View," in E. L. and R. E. Hartley (eds.), *Outside Readings in Psychology*. New York: Crowell-Collier Publishing Co., 1957. (First published 1951.)

21. Cowen, Emory L., "The Influence of Varying Degrees of Psychological Stress on Problem-Solving Rigidity." *Journal of Abnormal and Social Psychology*, Vol. 47 (1952), pp. 512–519.

22. Dewey, John. *Human Nature and Conduct*. New York: Henry Holt, 1922.

23. Dewey, John. *How We Think*. Boston: D. C. Heath & Co., 1933.

24. Etzioni, Amitai. *The Active Society*. New York: Free Press, 1968.

25. Evans, Robert R. (ed.). *Readings in Collective Behavior*. Chicago: Rand McNally & Co., 1969.

26. Faris, Ellsworth. "The Sect and the Sectarian." *American Journal of Sociology*, Vol. 60 (1955), pp. 75–89.

27. Fenichel, Otto. *The Psychoanalytic Theory of Neurosis*. New York: W. W. Norton, 1945.

28. Festinger, Leon, Henry W. Riecken, and Stanley Schachter. *When Prophecy Fails*. Minneapolis: University of Minnesota Press, 1956.

29. Feuer, Lewis S. *The Conflict of Generations*. New York: Basic Books, 1969.

30. Foote, Nelson N., and Leonard S. Cottrell, Jr. *Identity and Interpersonal Competence*. Chicago: University of Chicago Press, 1955.

31. Forman, Robert E. "Resignation as a Collective Behavior Response," *American Journal of Sociology*, Vol. 69 (1963), pp. 285–290.

32. Foy, Eddie, and Alvin F. Harlow. "The Iroquois Theatre Fire," in R. H. Turner and L. M. Killian (eds.), *Collective Behavior*. Englewood Cliffs, N. J.: Prentice-Hall, Inc., 1957.

33. Fritz, Charles E., and Eli S. Marks. "The NORC Studies of Human Behavior in Disaster," in R. R. Evans (ed.), *Readings in Collective Behavior*. Chicago: Rand McNally & Co., 1969.

34. Fromm, Erich. *Escape from Freedom*. New York: Farrar & Rinehart, 1941.

35. Fromm, Erich. *Man for Himself*. New York: Rinehart & Co., 1947.

36. Fuller, Helen. "The Man to See in California." *Harper's Magazine*, Vol. 226 (1963), pp. 64–72.

37. Gilbert, G. M. *The Psychology of Dictatorship*. New York: Ronald Press, 1950.

38. Gilfillan, S. C., *The Sociology of Invention*. Chicago: Follett Publishing Co., 1935.

39. Gillin, John L. "A Contribution to the Sociology of Sects." *American Journal of Sociology*, Vol. 16 (1910), pp. 236–252.

40. Gouldner, Alvin W. (ed.). *Studies in Leadership*. New York: Harper & Bros., 1950.

41. Gusfield, Joseph R. (ed.). *Protest, Reform, and Revolt: A Reader in Social Movements*. New York: John Wiley & Sons, 1970.

42. Hagen, Everett E. *On the Theory of Social Change*. Homewood, Ill.: The Dorsey Press, 1962.

43. Hart, Hornell N. *The Technique of Social Progress*. New York: Holt, Rinehart, & Winston, 1931.

44. Hoffer, Eric. *The True Believer*. New York: Harper & Bros., 1951.

45. Hogbin, H. Ian. *Social Change*. London: C. A. Watts & Co., 1958.

46. Horowitz, Irving L. *Three Worlds of Development*, 2nd ed. New York: Oxford University Press, 1972.

47. Katz, Daniel, and Richard L. Schanck. *Social Psychology*. New York: John Wiley & Sons, 1938.

48. Kerchoff, Allan C., Kurt W. Back, and Normal Miller. "Sociometric Patterns in Hysterical Contagion," in R. R. Evans (ed.), *Readings in Collective Behavior*. Chicago: Rand McNally & Co., 1969.

49. Killian, Lewis M. Unpublished material summarized in R. H. Turner and L. M. Killian (eds.), *Collective Behavior*. Englewood Cliffs, N. J.: Prentice-Hall, Inc., 1957.

50. Killian, Lewis M., and James R. Griffin. Unpublished material summarized in R. H. Turner and L. M. Killian (eds.), *Collective Behavior*. Englewood Cliffs, N. J.: Prentice-Hall, Inc., 1957.

51. Kirk, Russell. *The Conservative Mind*. Chicago: H. Regnery Co., 1953.

52. Kornhauser, William. "Social Bases of Political Commitment," in A. M. Rose (ed.), *Human Behavior and Social Processes*. Boston: Houghton Mifflin, 1962.

53. Kroeber, Alfred L. *Configurations of Culture Growth*. Berkeley and Los Angeles: University of California Press, 1944.

54. Lang, Kurt, and Gladys E. Lang. *Collective Dynamics*. New York: Thomas Y. Crowell, Co., 1961.

55. Lewis, Helen B. "Studies in the Principles of Judgments and Attitudes: IV. The Operation of 'Prestige Suggestion.'" *Journal of Social Psychology,* Vol. 14 (1941), pp. 229–256.

56. Lipset, Seymour M. *Political Man.* Garden City, N. Y.: Doubleday & Co., 1960.

57. Luchins, Abraham S. "Mechanization in Problem Solving: The Effect of *Einstellung.*" *Psychological Monographs,* (1942), No. 248.

58. MacIver, Robert M. *Social Causation.* New York: Harper, 1942.

59. Mackinnon, Donald W. "The Structure of Personality," in J. McV. Hunt (ed.), *Personality and the Behavior Disorders* (2 vols.), Vol. 1. New York: Ronald Press, 1944.

60. Mannheim, Karl. "The Problem of Generations." In K. Mannheim, *Essays on the Sociology of Knowledge.* New York: Oxford University Press, 1952.

61. McClelland, David C. *The Achieving Society.* Princeton: Van Nostrand, 1961.

62. Mead, George H. *Mind, Self, and Society.* C. W. Morris (ed.). Chicago: University of Chicago Press, 1934.

63. Mead, Margaret. *Continuities in Cultural Evolution.* New Haven: Yale University Press, 1964.

64. Merton, Robert K. *Social Theory and Social Structure,* 3rd ed. New York: The Free Press, 1968.

65. Mintz, Alexander. "Non-Adaptive Group Behavior." *Journal of Abnormal and Social Psychology,* Vol. 46 (1951), pp. 150–159.

66. Moore, Wilbert E. *Social Change.* Englewood Cliffs, N. J.: Prentice-Hall, Inc., 1963.

67. Myrdal, Gunnar, with the assistance of Richard Sterner and Arnold Rose. *An American Dilemma.* New York: Harper & Row, 1944.

68. Nettl, J. P., and Roland Robertson. *International Systems and the Modernization of Societies.* New York: Basic Books, 1968.

69. Niebuhr, H. Richard. "Sects." *Encyclopedia of the Social Sciences.* Vol. 13 (1937).

70. Niebuhr, H. Richard. *Social Sources of Denominationalism.* New York: Living Age Books, 1957.

71. Ogburn, William F. *Social Change.* New York: B. W. Huebsch, Inc., 1922.

72. Pally, S. "Cognitive Rigidity as a Function of Threat." *Journal of Personality,* Vol. 23 (1955), pp. 346–355.

73. Park, Robert E. "Human Migration and the Marginal Man." *American Journal of Sociology,* Vol. 33 (1928), pp. 881–893.

74. Park, Robert E. "Cultural Conflict and the Marginal Man," in E. V. Stonequist, *The Marginal Man.* New York: Charles Scribner's Sons, 1937, Introduction.

75. Parsons, Talcott. *Societies.* Englewood Cliffs, N. J.: Prentice-Hall, Inc., 1966.

76. Prince, S. H. *Catastrophe and Social Change.* New York: Columbia University Press, 1921.

77. Rank, Otto. *Will Therapy and Truth and Reality,* translated by J. Taft. New York: Alfred A. Knopf, 1945.

78. Riesman, David, Nathan Glazer, and Reuel Denney. *The Lonely Crowd.* New Haven: Yale University Press, 1950.

79. Rogers, Everett M. *Diffusion of Innovations.* New York: Free Press of Glencoe, 1962.

80. Rokeach, Milton. *The Open and Closed Mind.* New York: Basic Books, 1960.

81. Rossiter, Clinton. *Conservatism in America.* New York: Alfred A. Knopf, 1955.

82. Ryan, Bryce F. *Social and Cultural Change.* New York: Ronald Press, 1969.

83. Sanford, Fillmore H. "The Follower's Role in Leadership Phenomena," in G. E. Swanson, T. M. Newcomb, and E. L. Hartley (eds.), *Readings in Social Psychology,* revised ed. New York: Henry Holt, 1952.

84. Seeman, Melvin. "On the Meaning of Alienation." *American Sociological Review,* Vol. 24 (1959), pp. 783–791.

85. Sherif, Muzafer. *The Psychology of Social Norms.* New York: Harper & Bros., 1936.

86. Sherif, Muzafer, and O. J. Harvey. "A Study of Ego Functioning: Elimination of Stable Anchorages in Individual and Group Situations." *Sociometry,* Vol. 15 (1952), pp. 272–305.

87. Sherif, Muzafer, and Carolyn W. Sherif. *Social Psychology.* New York: Harper & Row, 1969.

88. Shibutani, Tamotsu. "Reference Groups as Perspectives." *American Journal of Sociology* 60 (1955): 562–569.

89. Simmel, Georg. *The Sociology of Georg Simmel,* K. H. Wolff (ed.). Glencoe, Ill.: Free Press, 1950.

90. Smelser, Neil J. *Theory of Collective Behavior.* New York: The Free Press of Glencoe, 1963.

91. Sorokin, Pitirim A. *Social and Cultural Dynamics,* (4 vols.). New York: American Book Co., 1937–1941.

92. Stone, Gregory P. "Appearance and the Self," in A. M. Rose (ed.), *Human Behavior and Social Processes.* Boston: Houghton Mifflin, 1962.

93. Stonequist, Everett V. *The Marginal Man.* New York: Charles Scribner's Sons, 1937.

94. Strauss, Anselm L. "Identification." Unpublished manuscript (revised to become *Mirrors and Masks.* Glencoe, Ill.: The Free Press, 1959).

95. Strauss, Anselm L. *Mead on Social Psychology.* Chicago: University of Chicago Press, 1964.

96. Symonds, Percival. *The Dynamics of Human Adjustment.* New York: D. Appleton-Century Co., 1946.

97. Tarde, Gabriel. *The Laws of Imitation,* translated by Elsie C. Parsons. New York: Holt, Rinehart & Winston, 1903.

98. Thomas, William I. *Social Behavior and Personality.* E. H. Volkart (ed.). New York: Social Science Research Council, 1951.

99. Thomas, William I., and Florian Znaniecki. *The Polish Peasant in Europe and America,* 5 vols. Boston: Badger Publishing Co., 1918–1920.

100. Toch, Hans. *The Social Psychology of Social Movements.* Indianapolis: Bobbs-Merrill Co., 1965.

101. Turner, Ralph H. "Role-Taking, Role Standpoint, and Reference-Group Behavior." *American Journal of Sociology* 61 (1956): 316–328.

102. Turner, Ralph H., and Lewis M. Killian. *Collective Behavior.* Englewood Cliffs, N. J.: Prentice-Hall, Inc., 1957.

103. Turner, Ralph H., and Lewis M. Killian. *Collective Behavior,* 2nd ed. Englewood Cliffs, N. J.: Prentice-Hall, Inc., 1972.

104. Veltfort, Helene R., and George E. Lee. "The Cocoanut Grove Fire," in R. H. Turner and L. M. Killian (eds.). *Collective Behavior,* 2nd ed. Englewood Cliffs, N. J.: Prentice-Hall, Inc., 1972.

105. Viereck, Peter R. E. *Conservatism.* Princeton, N. J.: Van Nostrand, 1956.

106. Vinacke, W. Edgar. *The Psychology of Thinking.* New York: McGraw-Hill Book Co., 1952.

107. Warshay, Leon H. "Breadth of Perspective, Culture Contact, and Self." Doctoral dissertation, University of Minnesota Libraries, Minneapolis, 1959.

108. Warshay, Leon H. "Breadth of Perspective: Further Thoughts." Unpublished paper presented at Midwest Sociological Society meetings, Omaha, April 28, 1961. (Dittoed)

109. Warshay, Leon H. "Breadth of Perspective," in A. M. Rose (ed.), *Human Behavior and Social Processes.* Boston: Houghton Mifflin and Co., 1962.

110. Wertheimer, Max. *Productive Thinking.* New York: Harper & Bros., 1945.

# 19

*H. G. Barnett*

# The Acceptance and Rejection

# of Change

Several years ago I proposed a scheme for systematizing reactions to innovations. It conceptualized positive and negative responses to new things, behaviors, and ideas as processes; that is, as controlled and limited sets of interrelations between variables in a closed system of events. Under this interpretation a process is a generalization from particulars and can be expressed as a formula. Its specific manifestations are regarded as action complexes, or mechanisms, with definite beginning and end points which will repeat themselves when the appropriate initiating conditions recur. In the present instance these action systems are psychological, that is, they are mental operations activated by sensory stimuli. Consequently, the acceptance or rejection of an innovation is essentially, and sometimes solely, an internal reaction which cannot be directly observed but can be inferred or postulated and which often becomes manifest in verbal or other behaviors.

Whether or not an acceptance or rejection becomes manifest is an important question because it bears directly upon our main concern, which is with social change. It is, however, another problem with its own set of variables which can be investigated in addition to, but not in place of, those conditioning the psychological reactions to innovation. This aspect of the problem is set aside in the interests of clarity and in order to focus attention upon what is believed to be the source and genesis of social change.

The same must be said with respect to an intimately related question, namely, how can an individual reaction to an innovation become a social fact? In brief, the answer is that it can and does become a group characteristic when the acceptance or rejection process is duplicated in $n$ individuals, the $n$ depending upon one's understanding of how many and what persons constitute a group. In other words, and contrary to common supposition, there is no antithesis between a psychological and a sociological treatment of this problem. One does not need to appeal to a transcendent or a reduction mechanism to get from one of these alleged "levels" of analysis and interpretation to the other. The social "leap" occurs when one individual does what another does, and imitation is one manifestation of the acceptance process.

The acceptance-rejection process, as here proposed, is an explanatory concept and cannot claim to be anything more. It has been abstracted from external events which are accessible and which therefore can be verified by repeated observations. As in all conceptualizations, however, the observable data have been interpreted and organized in a particular way, that way being determined by the objective of comprehending change systematically. The demands of the system must be specified before an attempt is made to demonstrate its applicability.

In a presentation such as this it is necessary at the outset to identify clearly the referents of the discussion because one set of symbols must be employed to designate other symbols, as well as concepts and things. The statement, "Women are inferior to men," for example, can be simply a particular assortment of black lines on the white paper of this page, as it would be to an illiterate person. It can be a sentence, that is, a grammatical phenomenon with a subject, a copula, and a predicate in that restricted order. It can be a communication, a piece of information in which inferiority is attributed to women by comparison with men. It can be a proposition, a statement which is either true or false and which presumably can be demonstrated. Finally, it can be a description in writing of an existing situation in which women are actually treated as the inferiors of men. Unless otherwise noted, the illustrative statements in the following discussion fall in this last category; that is, they are intended to be descriptions of situations with physical referents.

### Structuralization

Let us suppose that this headline appears in a reputable newspaper: "Scientists to Experiment on Condemned Criminals." Let us suppose further that it is intended to report an actual situation; it is not a verbal innovation, a plea, an announcement of a subject for debate, or a description of what scientists do. Even assuming that no reader questions the truth of the report, it is almost certain that individual reactions to the situation it describes will differ. One reason for this is that no sensory field is ever completely or unalterably structured in one way only (1, pp. 442–445). Its content, limits, and other properties may be more or less determined by the manner in which it is presented or approached; but by the same token, every experience is divisible, extensible, and partial. All of us are blind men groping around elephants, but many times the ears and tails we feel are not even connected. Indeed, they may be parts of other animals. Those who advocate an innovation, and those who report or describe it to others, exercise some control over the apperception of it by others, but never entirely so. Moreover, their structuring of it is subject to significant variation. The complex of events which inspired the hypothetical headline above could be reported quite differently: "Lifers to Become Guinea Pigs," "Incorrigibles May Redeem Selves," "Cure For Murder is Sought," "Drastic Therapy Legalized," or, most improbably, "Lobotomists Tackle Recidivism." Often there is no such intermediation, and one individual will apprehend a change in a way which its advocate or some other person would regard as grotesque or as nothing new at all. It may very well be perceived not as a unit, but as a chaotic assemblage of discrete and unrelated events, or as an undifferentiated mass in the background of more interesting things. It cannot be denied that there are newspaper accounts which produce this effect, and also that newspaper reporters are not the only people who fail to "make sense" or make the "wrong" kind of sense out of a "complicated" situation.

Utilizing letters of the alphabet, we can symbolize the latent possibilities in a stimulus field thus: P Q R S . . . . . X Y Z. If the field is an innovation, it is possible for a given observer to attend to it selectively, regardless of the way in which it is presented. One reader of the news reported under the first headline above may be so concerned about the criminals, whom we shall call Y, that he gives little or no attention to other components of the situation. His preoccupation may be so preclusive that he skims over, or does not read, the particulars about the scientists, the X component, nor those pertaining to the types of experiments to be conducted. For him the saliency of Y suppresses attention to X. Another reader may be concerned exclusively about the involvement of scientists in this kind of research, and so opposed to it that he does not care either about the subjects or the nature of the proposed experiments. For him just who the Y's are is unimportant; they could be criminals or any other people. For both readers, X and Y are independent.

There is a third possibility. It is realized when an observer attends to more than one component in his perceptual field. In terms of the symbols used above, both X and Y register with him. If they do, there must be some recognized connection between them; otherwise they will divide and divert his attention. He may supply the connection himself or he may accept the one given by someone else such as a newspaper reporter. In conceptual terms these connections are called relationships. They are extremely important in both innovation and the acceptance process; yet we have only a limited and imperfect terminology with which to communicate about them. They are significant because they reflect and govern our comprehension of the modes and dimensions by and through which we conceive our experiences to be linked. We have names for some of them: temporal, spatial, causal, predicative, affective, filial, genetic, subordinate, correlative, and so forth (1, pp. 411–432). Each of these has an indefinite number of named and unnamed nuances and inflections, and there are many more which we intuit and act upon without being able to verbalize them.

In our language, relationships often take the form of verbs and prepositions; but they can be expressed by other grammatical devices as well. Nouns, pronouns, and adjectives which name a state or a property of something usually denote the referents between which a relationship is asserted. Thus in "Man is sinful," man is X, sinful is Y, and is, the relationship asserted to obtain between them. In "Scientists to Experiment on Condemned Criminals," the scientists are X, the condemned criminals Y, and the rest of the sentence defines the relationship between them. The lack of precision with which relationships are stated in instances such as the last example is due in part to the grammatical requirements of our language — or any other language. Conventional speech forms have their own structural demands and these seldom conform to the conceptual framework of other systems. In addition, the relationships between persons and things are seldom simple, although a single strand in a complex set can be selected as the most important one.

This leads to the statement of an important assumption which is implicit in the foregoing, namely, that every innovation can be structured to conform to the pattern of X R Y; meaning that, however it might be stated linguistically, any given sectioning of a stimulus field is specific and polarized such that it consists of two and *only* two components with one and *only* one relation per section existing between them. This does not forbid multiple sectioning; in fact, this frequently happens. Moreover, a shift from one sectional axis, plane, or perspective of the field to another can occur instantaneously, as it does in the fluctuations of ambiguous figures (1, p. 437, pp. 445–447).

### Contact

The absence of rigidity in a stimulus field must be considered in conjunction with other factors in order to comprehend the diversity of reactions to new things and proposals (1, pp. 204–207). One of the most fundamental is the requirement that an innovation, or a part of it, make psychological contact with some antecedent experience of its potential acceptor or rejector. This factor is so intimately connected with structuralization that the one does not occur without the other. Structuralization operates selectively upon the inventory of past experiences of the acceptor-rejector, and the particular experience which it evokes, let us say, A, reacts upon its instigator to stabilize or to modify it. New experiences do not simply imprint themselves on a blank mental field; they must revive a component of the memory record if they evoke a reaction. If the words "incorrigibles" or "recidivism" are alien to the vocabulary of a reader, and if their referents in the newspaper story are puzzling, contradictory, or ambiguous, he is likely to turn to something else or to seek clarification from other sources. On the other hand, it is not essential that both the X and the Y components of an innovation evoke the recall of something familiar. Some readers may not know what "incorrigibles" or "lifers" (X's) are and get no illumination from a newspaper description of them, but may still have a basis for reacting through their familiarity with the concepts of redemption or guinea pigs (Y's). In this case we can say that X has failed to evoke an A out of the past experience of a reader but that Y has made contact with something else which can be labeled B. Failing that, the encounter has been sterile; both X and Y are psychologically inert.

Frequently an innovation directly recalls a past experience through the intermediation of an identical part of each. Identity in this sense means absolutely co-existent; X *is* A (or Y *is* B), not as members of a class or by definition, but because they are presumed to be simultaneously and co-extensively present. One and the same set of scientists X are to experiment on criminals Y as they do in training or performing surgery on rats B. We may symbolize identities of this kind by X O A, or alternatively as Y O B, signifying that it does not matter whether the contacting element is designated as X or as A, or, alternatively, as Y or B. Both sets, X O A and Y O B, cannot, in any given instance, have this property. If they could there would be no innovation.

It is important to bear in mind that identities have limits. Scientists may be regarded as an indiscriminate set in one context, such as Y, but not so in another context such as B; similarly for kidnappers and murderers as criminals, and guinea pigs and rats as experimental animals. Total and undeviating identity is a function of other constants.

A less direct means of establishing contact between the new and the old is by appeal to definition, consensus, or conventional dictate; X is A or Y is B by assertion or by tacit agreement. If our reader of headlines does not know what a "recidivist" is, he might resort to a dictionary or derive his own definition of it from such information as is provided in the text of the news story. Or he might guess what it is, which amounts to his projecting some familiar conception into the context of the account. The possibilities for structuring the stimulus data — sometimes called "distortion" — are evident here just as they are with identities. Except for logical definitions, which only partially relate to the world of sense experience, all definitions have elastic limits, and the identities among natural phenomena are always subject to redefinition.

Another way to bridge the gap between the new and the old is by means of their respective and overlapping analyses. This possibility requires that X and A or Y and B have some property in common. There must be something about individual X which recalls individual A, something which puts them in the category or class of scientists, for example; or some characteristic of a scientist which permits him to be equated with, let us say, a biologist or a psychologist. Alternatively, a conceptual analysis of the guinea pigs and rats with which these scientists work can be made, leading to their equation.

Equation by analysis is an extremely common reaction to new experiences as well as to a vast number which are not considered to be new. Very often it is not recognized because it is accomplished almost instantaneously and without awareness. Summarizing the results of some of his experiments on perception, Bartlett concluded that:

> the experiments show that the common method of an observer, in the absence of special conditions, which may be either objective or a matter of temperament and training, is to respond to whatever is presented as unitary. Nevertheless, there is no perceptual situation in which some detail does not stand out and influence what is perceived more than the rest. With structurally simply material, such dominant detail may be: gaps; odd and disconnected features; simple spatial references — above, below, right, left; light and shade. With structurally complex material it may be plan of construction; disposition of figures which are themselves given scant notice; general topic and representational significance. Thus, although perceiving is rarely analytical or piece-meal in its method, yet it *is* a kind of analysis, since always there are some features of the perceptual situation which take a lead over the others. These dominant details are a kind of nucleus about which the rest cluster. They set the stage for remembering (2, pp. 31–32).

It will be noted that equation by analysis is an expedient for locating identity in diversity. It is an indispensable operation because we live in such a constantly changing environment that it is doubtful whether any two of our experiences are absolutely identical, yet we must treat many of them as if they were. The discrepancies may be so microscopic that they elude all but the closest examination. Or they may be gross and easily located, their neglect being due to pragmatic considerations, to bias, to disinterest, or to a variety of other controls. In any event, there is some loss of fidelity in equating things, acts, and concepts, and considerable individual variation in the toleration of it. It is difficult to escape the conclusion that falsification is inevitable with the lapse of time, that there is always some difference between the mental record and the experiences which later impinge upon and activate it. When recall occurs and a present stimulus set is recognized, it is due to only a partial overlap, a common denominator, and not to complete correspondence. This would appear to be true even when a definition provides a bridge between old and new, because even though it translates a new experience into familiar terms, the latter must still be judged to be familiar.

While it is true that memory is fallible and that sense data are often unwittingly altered to make them fit a familiar pattern, it is not true that the lack of complete correspondence between X and A or between Y and B always goes unnoticed by the person who analyzes and equates them. On the contrary, he is often aware that his equations are only approximations, especially when they are challenged by other people or when a close inspection is necessary in order to establish them. In these instances X and A or Y and B are understood to be similar but not identical, their differences being considered to be immaterial for present purposes. In other words, they are enough alike that one can function in a given context of the other, but they may not be universally interchangeable.

Equation can be achieved, not only by the analysis of X and A (or Y and B), but by incorporating in each some referent to which both have the same relationship (1, pp. 189–202). Factitious as this may seem to be, it frequently happens under the pressure of bias, demands, training, or special interest. When it occurs, the saliency of the common referent obscures and belittles the differences between X and A (or Y and B). Psychologists and biologists may be equated, not because both are regarded as scientists but because both are associated with the same project, such as experimenting on criminals, the character and purpose of that research being the predominant concern of their classifier. In other words, he may not care whether psychologists are scientists or whether they have any other property in common with biologists, the relevant consideration is that both are going to experiment with human beings.

We can symbolize equations arrived at by identification, definition, analysis, or incorporation by $X = A$ and $Y = B$. Care must be exercised not to view them as truisms. $X = A$ is not a tautology but a conclusion or an assertion, a fact which this alphabetic means of expression is intended to emphasize. Yet when words are substituted for these letters confusion begins to creep in. "Psychologists = biologists" preserves the significance of their equation, but "scientists = scientists" can easily obscure it. What the latter equation signifies is that a specific group of persons denoted by the term "scientists" is judged to be the same as a second specific group designated by the same term. Furthermore, each group is a unit and, as such, is equated with the other despite the fact that they carry labels which are linguistic devices for characterizing pluralities of individuals.

It is assumed that it is impossble for an X or a Y to contact directly or spontaneously an A or a B which is totally unlike it in the estimation of the acceptor-rejector. Speaking more generally, some degree of similarity between experiences is essential for a present one to recall a previous one. Nevertheless, dissimilar concepts, things, and behaviors do at times confront each other. They may be juxtaposed by accident, or upon the suggestion of someone who thinks that they are similar or the same.

Just as often, however, their apposition is the result of an analysis which begins with a question about their similarity. Thus, a reader of the headline "Scientists to Experiment on Condemned Criminals" may wonder what kinds of scientists could be involved. He may mentally try out a list of the kinds with which he is familiar, including chemists and physicists, but in the end exclude chemists and physicists as possibilities in this context. He may also reflect upon what kinds of criminals are to be subjected to experimentation and reach the decision that even though children may commit crimes they cannot be included in the class of condemned criminals. Conclusions reached in these ways can be expressed symbolically as $X \neq A$ and $Y \neq B$.

### Assimilation

The union of a new with a familiar experience may terminate with identification, definition, analysis, or incorporation; but if it does, the acceptance-rejection process is incomplete. That is tantamount to rejection because the new, even though it has gained an entree, has not been located and fixed in the cognitive network of the potential acceptor. This is the outcome when he loses interest or patience in trying to determine what X or Y is, or when he is distracted by something else. Most often, however, it happens because the A or the B image, concept, or impression evoked by X or Y is vague, fluctuating, evanescent, or isolated from other past experiences; in short, because no part of the innovation has meaning. Any new thing or idea must be fitted into the context of the known in some fashion if it is even to be recognized; it is what it is understood to be only with reference to the associations of its familiar counterpart. Every new experience presents an observer with this problem of relating present to past experience; and whether he is aware of it or not he must find a solution to it if the new is to have meaning for him. Bartlett describes the situation thus:

> Because this task factor is always present, it is fitting to speak of every human cognitive reaction — perceiving, imaging, remembering, thinking and reasoning — as an *effort after meaning*. Certain of the tendencies which the subject brings with him into the situation with which he is called upon to deal are utilized so as to make his reaction the 'easiest,' or the least disagreeable, or the quickest and least obstructed that is at the time possible. When we try to discover how this is done we find that always it is by an effort to connect what is given with something else. Thus, the immediately present 'stands for' something not immediately present, and 'meaning,' in a psychological sense, has its origin. As we have seen, in certain cases of great structural simplicity, or of structural regularity, or of extreme familiarity, the immediate data are at once fitted to, or matched with, a perceptual pattern which appears to be pre-existent so far as the particular perceptual act is concerned. This pre-formed setting, scheme,

or pattern is utilized in a completely unreflecting, unanalytical, and unwitting manner. Because it is utilized the immediate perceptual data have meaning, can be dealt with, and are assimilated (2, pp. 44–45).

In terms of the symbolism adopted here this paragraph can be condensed to read: when $X = A$, X can be assimilated to some context B, this context being the idea of anything associated with A in the past experience of an acceptor-rejector; or alternatively, when $Y = B$, Y can be assimilated to context A, which is a familiar associate of B. One significant interpolation is necessary in order to fulfill a requirement of the acceptance-rejection process, namely, that some specific relationship exist between components A and B to make it possible for assimilation to occur. The recall of one component is contingent upon the activation of the other, and the relationship between them is the vector which makes their interaction possible. Together with their relationship they constitute a unit which can be analyzed, but at the instant of its activation it is an undifferentiated whole. It is a redintegrated section or slice of past experience, and on that account it has the character of a prototype (1, pp. 207–210).

The relationships which link A and B have the same characteristics and scope as do those already described as connecting elements for the X and Y components of the innovation which evokes A and/or B. In some instances they are identical, but this is by no means always so. In fact, differences between them are often the basis for the acceptance or rejection of something new. It is therefore important to indicate whether they are the same or different in any given case. Subscripts will serve this purpose. Thus $X_1 = A_1$, $X_2 = A_2$, $Y_1 = B_1$, and $Y_2 = B_2$ signify that the relationships are identical in equated experiences, while $X_2 = A_1$ and $Y_2 = B_1$ mean they are different. If the components and their relationships are both different, then $X_2 \neq A_1$ and $Y_2 \neq B_1$.

When A is activated by X, it can arouse B on the axis of their relationship, and since X is equivalent to A it can stand in the same relationship to B as does A. This means that it can be substituted for A in the context of B in the same manner and to the same degree to which A is related to B. In other words, B assimilates X. The assimilation can be preclusive in that X can displace A completely in the context of B. If lobotomists X are fully equated with psychologists A, who train rats B, they can take over that function entirely from the psychologists. On the other hand, A can share its relation to B, making X its alternative: either psychologists or lobotomists may experiment with rats. The same assimilative mechanism can bring Y into relationship with A through the activation of B: if condemned criminals Y can be equated with guinea pigs B, then biologists A can mate them as they do guinea pigs, either abandoning their experiments with guinea pigs in favor of the criminals or carrying on comparable research with both categories of subjects.

It is evident that X can be assimilated only if there is a context B into which it can be fitted. It should be made explicit, however, that the necessary condition for this is that A have its relationship to B, so to speak, attached to it. The satisfaction of this requirement can be indicated by writing A with its subscribed number 1 in this fashion: $A_1$. The same requirement holds for the assimilation of Y. That can happen only if Y can be connected with A through the intermediation of B and its attached relation, a condition symbolized as $B_1$.

Assimilation occurs when one or both components of an innovation X Y are so pronounced and demanding in the estimation of an acceptor-rejector that they contend with or assert their superiority over their familiar counterparts A and B. Sometimes it is believed by the acceptor-rejector that they *are* A and/or B; that is, he completely identifies them with what they bring to mind: lobotomists *are* psychologists. In other instances, and for a variety of reasons, the X and/or Y of an innovation appeal to an acceptor-rejector because they make at least as good if not a better fit in the framework of the prototype than do A or B or both. Also, as noted earlier, he may take a partial and selective view of the relative significance of the X and Y components of an innovation. The structuralizing capacity of his prototype may be such that X dominates his attention to the exclusion of Y and X's relationship to it. In common parlance, he "lifts X out of context," or "fails to take all of the facts into account." Stated in terms of our symbols, $X = A_1$. Alternatively, Y may command his attention exclusively, in which case $Y = B_1$. Both X and Y can be taken into account, and they frequently are. In that case the relationship between them, and between A and B, are important considerations, as is noted in the third paragraph above.

### Projection

In assimilation a relatively unfamiliar stimulus is absorbed into a familiar framework. The opposite effect is also possible. It is realized when, in the estimation of an acceptor-rejector, one (or both) component(s) of his prototype A B has a pre-emptive character about it (them) vis-à-vis the innovation counterparts X and Y. Components mentally contend with or displace their counterparts by what might be called a mechanism of projection, meaning simply that the acceptor-rejector can visualize them in place of their equivalent X and/or Y, or that he believes that they *are* X and/or Y: Christian Scientists A = scientists X; therefore they can experiment with condemned criminals Y along with, or to the exclusion of, other scientists. Or, the parents B of condemned criminals Y are equally criminal and so should be subjected to experiments by scientists X instead of, or along with, their offspring.

As with assimilation, projection may be selective and partial. In some instances this means that the prototype of the acceptor-rejector is not actually such because its A and B components must be completely disassociated. They may have been connected to begin with, but more often they are not components of the same system. Moreover, they are not firmly embedded in any system. We can represent this condition by $X_2 = A$ and $Y_2 = B$, to signify that A is projected into the context of Y in the same relationship that X has to Y, and that B is projected into the context of X in the same relationship that Y has to X. If the acceptor-rejector does not admit to the equality of X and A, then $X_2 \neq A$, and if Y and B are not alike in his estimation, then $Y_2 \neq B$.

If A and B do constitute a prototype, that is, are members of one related system, projection is still possible, or impossible, depending upon the acceptor-rejector's conception of equivalence. In either case, the relationship between A and B is a factor contributing to his decision. If he regards the compared components and their relations as equivalent, we can characterize his reaction as $Y_1 = B_1$, $X_2 = A_2$, $Y_2 = B_2$, or $X_1 = A_1$. Contrariwise, if the components *and* their attached relations are judged to be different, then $X_2 \neq A_1$ and/or $Y_2 \neq B_1$.

Projection can occur with or without an awareness of it. All of us resort to it when we see or hear something which to our private way of thinking is incomplete. Incompleteness in this sense "raises questions" and we fill in the blanks with whatever A's and B's we have at our command from past experience, sometimes tentatively, sometimes confidently, without a moment's reflection. This mechanism also represents an "effort after meaning." One reader of "Scientists to Perform Experiments on Condemned Criminals" may spontaneously and directly project "physiologists" A into the $X_2$ position occupied by the ambiguous term "scientists," and may perhaps in the same way assume that "murderers" B are the "condemned criminals" $Y_2$ intended by the report, and project accordingly. Other readers may wonder, that is, vacillate with tentative projections of physicians, physical therapists, psychiatrists, etc., into the $X_2$ position; with kidnappers, embezzlers, traitors, etc., into the $Y_2$ position; and with surgery, shock treatment, survival tests, etc., interpolated as the action which relates the scientists to the criminals.

Assimilation and projection are extremely common occurrences, not only with respect to innovations but to everyday experiences. They have been demonstrated experimentally and they can be identified in the daily course of our lives. The conditions which contribute to the one as opposed to the other, or to their partial as distinct from their complete manifestations, are complex and it is not possible to enlarge upon them here. Suffice it to say that the variations upon the interactions between an innovation and the prototype which it evokes are governed by the interplay of many variables deriving from the background of the acceptor-rejector as well as the circumstances which confront him at the moment he makes his decision.

## Values

This leads to one further matter which requires discussion before we can deal with the acceptance-rejection process as such. This is the bearing which individual values have upon it. From what has been said so far it is easy to assume that a familiar practice, custom, ideal, behavior, or concept, and the prototype which represents it, is approved by the person who thinks of it upon his encounter with an innovation. The mere statement of the problem in this way is sufficient to dispose of the assumption. Nevertheless, the treatment of contacts between innovations and the prototypes which they call to mind in terms of equality and inequality may give the impression that this settles the question of acceptability, and it is now necessary to explain why it does not. The reason is that the decision in favor of or in opposition to an innovation is made in consequence of an interaction between the values placed on familiar patterns and the similarity, or the lack of it, which these patterns have with the innovation. Thus $Y = B_1$ signifies acceptability only if the acceptor-rejector places a positive value on B. If he approves of B, then more of it (or a very similar alternative to it), Y, is agreeable to him — discounting considerations which may moderate or adversely affect this conclusion but which are external to this key issue. If, on the other hand, he objects to B, he is likely to object to something as similar to it as Y. If he sanctions experimental research on rats B by psychologists A, and if he thinks criminals Y make subjects as good or better than rats, he is led to the conclusion that psychologists should be permitted to conduct the same type of research on criminals as they do on rats. He has a basis for rejecting the suggestion if he is averse to experiments on rats in the first place, even though he might agree that criminals could be used as subjects just as well or perhaps better than rats. This same pattern holds for other equations, as $X = A_1$, $X_2 = A$, $Y_2 = B$, $Y_2 = B_1$, and $Y_1 = B_1$.

The issues are not so clearly defined when there are significant differences between X and A or between Y and B; that is, when $X_2 \neq A$, $Y_2 \neq B$, $X \neq A_1$, $Y \neq B_1$, $X_2 \neq A_1$, and $Y_2 \neq B_1$. In these instances the value placed upon the prototype by the acceptor-rejector may or may not dispose him to accept the particular innovation represented by X Y. He will not, for example, accept just any change from something which he dislikes. He may be opposed to capital punishment $B_1$ and be no less averse to a proposal to brand Y criminals A as an alternative form of punishment. On the other hand, he may favor the stigmatizing of criminals because it accomplishes something which their execution does not. Differences are thus a minimal basis for rejecting an innovation as a substitute for, or as an alternative to, an existing mode which is already personally rejected. The issue is likewise indecisive when a prevailing mode or some personal standard of thought or behavior has a positive value. A proposal to replace it with something different may be rejected because of the difference, but not necessarily so. An advocate of capital punishment may nonetheless be receptive to an alternative or to a substitutive form of punishment, such as exile or ostracism, which he regards as different but more effective, humane, or economical; but he may reject it because it lacks something which capital punishment has and which he regards as essential.

It seems that the only definitive acceptance-rejection situation is one based upon an equivalence. That circumstance reduces the ambiguity inherent in the perception of any unfamiliar configuration; and when such reduction operates in conjunction with a positive or a negative evaluation of its familiar equivalent the issue of acceptance is most clearly defined. It also appears that this manner of dealing with something new is a typical maneuver. That is, an acceptor-rejector tends to base his position on similarities rather than on dissimilarities. Thus, if an opponent of capital punishment is confronted with the alternative of a law which would permit criminals to go free but would make it illegal for anyone to associate with or assist them in any way, his reaction to it is more likely to depend upon his attitude toward something with which he is familiar that resembles it, such as exile, than upon the difference between it and capital punishment.

An innovation may be accepted or rejected in part only, or with reservations, because differential values are attached to components of the prototype with which it is compared. This must mean that the innovation and the prototype are analyzed in order to yield or exhibit their parts. Thus a rejector of experimentation on criminals may be such because to him the only permissible subjects for experimentation are dumb animals. He may at the same time be ambivalent about just which scientists should be involved. On the other hand, he may accept experiments on criminals if he can specify their nature and scope; or he may insist that clergymen and not scientists should attempt to treat criminals as they do other unfortunate individuals. These specifications and reservations amount to a subdivision or an amalgamation of classes of persons, procedures, and things which have saliency because of the values the acceptor-rejector feels compelled to assign to aspects of his experience. Their referents can be selective: some criminals, experiments, and scientists are admissible but not others. Their referents can also be most specific, even to the point of being individualized: the self, *this* criminal, or *that* scientist may be the only acceptable or unacceptable case among those encompassed by an innovation. At the other extreme are value emphases on categories of A's or B's or relationships that are total, exhaustive, and mutually exclusive: all or no scientists, or all or no criminals, always or never certain relationships, etc. These are variations upon the acceptance-rejection process which logicians deal with under the headings of quantity, quality, exclusion, and the distribution of terms in their traditional analysis of categorical propositions. As will be indicated shortly, their treatment of the validity of inference is directly relevant to this process.

When no aspect of an innovation is more salient than another to a given acceptor-rejector he reacts to it in its entirety in terms of its equivalence or non-equivalence with some prototype and the value he assigns to the latter. For him it is all or nothing. This reaction is typical of a special but significant case of the general scheme. In it the prototype is not a record of an observation with external referents; it is a statement of a principle, a law, an ethic, or a moral postulate. It is therefore a value declaration in itself and in its entirety, and upon it an acceptor-rejector frequently takes his stand. He does this as in the other cases, that is, by either agreeing or disagreeing with it and then transferring his evaluation to the innovation which it either resembles or does not. Thus some people will assert in effect that any tampering with human life is presumptuous, if not immoral, and that experimentation with criminals is tampering with human life. Others will either disavow the dictate, or the equation, or both. These are syllogistic arguments, and as might be expected, often resorted to by partisans and opponents of innovations.

### Acceptance and Rejection Possibilities

The chart on page 360 represents an attempt to incorporate most of the variables discussed in a general statement. It has been generated by a systematic permutation of these variables; consequently, it is a paradigm with 81 inflections on the acceptance-rejection process. In it each cell symbolizes the acceptance-rejection possibilities inherent in a given situation. The box of letter symbols in the left half of each numbered cell brings together the various combinations of elements in terms already defined. The conclusions which they embody can be determined by following the "rules" indicated by the foregoing discussion or by reference to their condensation in the chart explanation on page 361. The arrows to the right of the boxes do this graphically. Those in solid line which are directed to the left indicate projection possibilities; those to the right, assimilation. Arrows in solid line curving to the left and downward signify that B can replace Y in the context of X; those curving to the left and upward, that A can substitute for X in the context of Y; those curving to the right and downward, that Y can replace B in the context of A; and those curving to the right and upward, that X can replace A in the context of B. The dotted arrows mean an operation cannot take place because of an inequality between paired components. The absence of arrows signifies that the substitution which their presence would suggest is impossible because there is no relationship to provide a link with the context. *In all cases the indicated operations presume that a positive value is attached to the involved parts of the prototype.* If the prototype or a part of it is not valued, some of the solid lines will become dotted and some of the dotted ones solid in accordance with the preceding discussion of the acceptability of differences.

It should be emphasized that the chart does not assert that there are 81 acceptance and rejection possibilities. On the contrary, each curved line represents such a possibility. There are eight of these (four solid and four dotted), but they occur in varied combinations resulting from varied patterns of equivalences and differences between an innovation and some past experience with which it is compared. Each cell therefore represents a *situation* with a greater or lesser number of possibilities. Furthermore, not all of the potentials of a given situation are necessarily realized. Cell 41, for example, has the potential for four positive reactions but only one, two, or three of them may be activated in any particular individual's response to the situation it defines. , In brief, each cell is unique in the pattern of opportunities for interaction which it provides, not by the number which are actually perceived and given effect.

A full exposition of the chart is not intended, but a few features of it may be pointed out. Row 1 and Column 1 are the zones with the fewest possibilities, the reasons being the failure, or rejection, of contacts between familiar and unfamiliar components and the lack of a relationship between them. Cell 1 represents a situation in which nothing can happen because its components are unrelated, independent, or identical, however one might wish to describe a situation which does not initiate a response. The rest of the cells in Row 1 and Column 1 embody deductive reasoning wherein there are only three terms. In them there is a major and a minor premise, which means that one term of the general scheme is either identical with another of the four, or it is completely disassociated from it. X O A, for example, signifies either that X and A are completely independent or that they are identical. Thus, by assimilation (Cell 3) it does not matter what else X scientists Y are or do, they are equal to all biologists $B_1$ as far as experimentation with rats A is concerned; and by projection (Cell 4) it does not matter what else A biologists B are or do, inasmuch as they are equal to scientists $Y_2$ they can experiment with condemned criminals X. In the terminology of logical analysis (3, p. 82) this is called a syllogism of the "first figure" wherein the subject of the major premise, i.e., the B of the prototype or the Y of the innovation, is the predicate of the minor premise, which is Y = B. A reversed up-for-down reading of the content (scientists, biologists, etc.) assigned to X, Y, A, and B components in this example would put it in Cells 19 and 28. Cells 7, 8, 55, and 64 accommodate syllogisms of the "second figure" wherein the middle term is the predicate of both premises. Thus to refer to Cell 7: all experimentation with human lives A is interference with God's will $B_1$; no scientist Y may act in a manner which constitutes interference with God's will; therefore no scientist may experiment with human lives. Acceptance of this conclusion presumes a positive evaluation of both premises. Which of these several ways of stating the syllogism is adopted is a matter of cognitive structuring by the acceptor-rejector; subject and predicate designations depend upon the focal point of his attention; pro-

|  | YOB | Y₁=B₁ OR Y₂=B₂ | Y=B₁ | Y₂=B | Y₂=B₁ | Y₁=B₁ OR Y₂≠B₂ | Y≠B₁ | Y₂≠B | Y₁≠B₁ |
|---|---|---|---|---|---|---|---|---|---|
| **XOA** | 1 — YOB / XOA | 2 — Y₁=B₁ OR Y₂=B₂ / XOA | 3 — Y=B₁ / XOA | 4 — Y₂=B / XOA | 5 — Y₂=B₁ / XOA | 6 — Y₁≠B₁ OR Y₂≠B₂ / XOA | 7 — Y≠B₁ / XOA | 8 — Y₂≠B / XOA | 9 — Y₁≠B₁ / XOA |
| **X₁=A₁ OR X₂=A₂** | 10 — YOB / X₁=A₁ | 11 — Y₁=B₁ / X=A₁ | 12 — Y=B₁ / X=A₁ | 13 — Y₂=B / X₂=A₂ | 14 — Y₂=B₁ / X₁=A₁ | 15 — Y₁≠B₁ / X₁=A₁ | 16 — Y≠B₁ / X₁=A₁ | 17 — Y₂≠B / X₁=A₁ | 18 — Y₂=B₁ / X₁=A₁ |
| **X=A₁** | 19 — YOB / X=A₁ | 20 — Y₁=B₁ / X=A₁ | 21 — Y=B₁ / X=A₁ | 22 — Y₂=B / X=A₂ | 23 — Y₂=B₁ / X=A₁ | 24 — Y₁≠B₁ / X=A₁ | 25 — Y=B₁ / X=A₁ | 26 — Y₂≠B / X=A₁ | 27 — Y₂=B₁ / X=A₁ |
| **X₂=A** | 28 — YOB / X₂=A | 29 — Y₁=B₂ / X₂=A | 30 — Y=B₁ / X₂=A | 31 — Y₂=B / X₂=A | 32 — Y₂=B₁ / X₂=A | 33 — Y₂=B₂ / X₂=A | 34 — Y≠B₁ / X₂=A | 35 — Y₂=B / X₂=A | 36 — Y₂=B₁ / X₂=A |
| **X₂≠A** | 37 — YOB / X₂≠A | 38 — Y₁=B₂ / X₂=A | 39 — Y=B₁ / X₂=A | 40 — Y₂=B / X₂=A | 41 — Y₂=B₁ / X₂=A | 42 — Y₁≠B₂ / X₂=A | 43 — Y≠B₁ / X₂=A | 44 — Y₂≠B / X₂=A | 45 — Y₂=B₁ / X₂=A |
| **X₁≠A₁ OR X₂≠A₂** | 46 — YOB / X₁≠A₁ | 47 — Y₁=B₁ / X₂≠A | 48 — Y=B₁ / X₂≠A | 49 — Y₂=B / X₂≠A | 50 — Y₂=B₁ / X₁≠A₁ | 51 — Y₁≠B₂ / X₂≠A₁ | 52 — Y≠B₁ / X₂≠A₁ | 53 — Y₂≠B / X₂≠A₂ | 54 — Y₂=B₁ / X₂≠A₂ |
| **X≠A₁** | 55 — YOB / X≠A₁ | 56 — Y₁=B₁ / X≠A₁ | 57 — Y=B₁ / X≠A₁ | 58 — Y₂=B / X₂≠A₁ | 59 — Y₂=B₁ / X≠A₁ | 60 — Y₁≠B₁ / X≠A₁ | 61 — Y≠B₁ / X≠A₁ | 62 — Y≠B / X≠A₁ | 63 — Y₂≠B₁ / X₂≠A₁ |
| **X₂≠A** | 64 — YOB / X₂≠A | 65 — Y₂=B₂ / X₂≠A | 66 — Y=B₁ / X₂≠A | 67 — Y₂=B / X₂≠A | 68 — Y₂=B₁ / X₂≠A | 69 — Y₁≠B₁ / X₂≠A | 70 — Y≠B₁ / X₂≠A | 71 — Y₂≠B / X₂≠A | 72 — Y₁≠B₁ / X₂≠A |
| **X₂≠A₁** | 73 — YOB / X₂≠A₁ | 74 — Y₂=B₂ / X₂≠A | 75 — Y=B₁ / X₂≠A | 76 — Y₂=B / X₂≠A₁ | 77 — Y₂=B₁ / X₂≠A₁ | 78 — Y₁≠B₁ / X₂≠A | 79 — Y≠B₁ / X₂≠A₁ | 80 — Y₂≠B / X₂≠A₁ | 81 — Y₂=B₁ / X₂≠A₁ |

ACCEPTANCE AND REJECTION POSSIBILITIES

Explanation of the Chart

X O A     Signifies that X and A are identical or independent. They are also isolated unless Y or B respectively bear some relation to them.

$X_1 = A_1$     and $X_2 = A_2$ signify that X is equivalent to A and that their relationships to Y and B are the same.

$X = A_1$     Signifies that X is equal to A and that Y and the relationship of X to it are ignored. Only assimilation is possible.

$X_2 = A$     Signifies the opposite of $X = A_1$. Only projection is possible.

$X_2 = A_1$     Signifies that X equals A and that their relationships are different. Both assimilation and projection are possible.

$X_1 \neq A_1$     and $X_2 \neq A_2$ signify that X is not equivalent to A, but that their relationships to Y and B are the same.

$X \neq A_1$     Signifies that X and A are not equal. Projection is ruled out, and assimilation is impossible because of the inequality of X and A.

$X_2 \neq A$     Signifies opposite of $X \neq A_1$. Assimilation is ruled out, and projection is impossible because X does not equal A.

$X_2 \neq A_1$     Signifies that X is not equivalent to A and that their relationships to Y and B are different.

The combinations of Y and B symbols have parallel meanings.

jection and assimilation depend upon his frame of reference; and these have their own determinants. The cells just discussed also characterize situations in which internal conflict is produced by the identity of one component and the non-equivalence of the other two. They symbolize what are sometimes called conflicts in space, time, activities, and other needs and demands. In Cell 7, for example, employers are likely to agree that idleness Y is not an acceptable substitute for labor $B_1$ as a source of income A. Cell 41 takes all four components of an innovation into account and indicates that it is acceptable; Cell 77 does the same but indicates a basis for either acceptance or rejection because of the internal conflict produced by equivalence and non-equivalence of paired components. Cells in the last row and column appear to be relatively sterile but are such only when the prototype or its parts are valued over parts of the innovation. They are so apparently unproductive because either a component or its relation may come in conflict with its paired component and its relationship.

### Application

Recently an opportunity arose to test the applicability of this formulation systematically as a part of an investigation into "the nature, function, and control of resistance to education by television" in a population residing in the combined urban-suburban area in which the University of Oregon is located.[1] The inquiry was undertaken over a three-year period by an interdisciplinary research unit at the University of Oregon. The major part of it was conducted by recognized survey techniques using structured interviews and has resulted in several preliminary papers.[2] That part of it which is relevant here consisted of 178 unstructured interviews with individuals who were known or suspected of being "low consumers" of television output, including educational television. The interviews lasted from one-half to four and one-half hours, with an average of around two. They were free-ranging with unobtrusive steering by the interviewer to keep television the topic of the discussion.

The investigation concentrated its efforts upon a definition of the acceptance-rejection situation rather than upon the characteristics of the respondents. It sought to identify the psychological components of

[1] This research was supported by a grant from the U.S. Office of Education under the provisions of Title VII, National Defense Education Act of 1958 (P.L. 85–864).

[2] These have been mimeographed under the auspices of the Institute for Community Studies of the University of Oregon under the project title of *Studies in Resistances to Cultural Innovation.* They include "Preliminary Report Number One" by Marshall Goldstein, Walter R. Martin, and John R. Shepherd (no date); "A Study of Some Aspects of KOAC-TV Programming and Its Audience," by John R Shepherd, issued May 3, 1961; "A Sequence of Proposed Research Designs Relating Program Structure to Resistance to ETV," by John R. Shepherd and Thomas M. Scheidel, issued September 1, 1961; and "Problems in the Measurement of Educational Television Consumption," by Martin Meissner, issued November 1, 1961.

decisions in favor of or in opposition to television and gave only peripheral attention to the sociological characteristics of the decision-makers. It endeavored to elicit undirected responses to some form of the general question, "Why do you or do you not like television?" and accepted them, without interpretation, as the data to be analyzed. Inferences from the responses, from the contexts in which they were offered, and from other information forthcoming during the interviews were not incorporated in the analysis. They were recorded and constitute a body of information that is reserved for another treatment of the problem.

It is evident that this approach was designed to get people to state, in their own words, their reasons for liking or not liking television. It was adopted with full awareness that such responses are notoriously difficult to treat objectively and systematically. They can be untrustworthy, irrelevant, thoughtless, superficial, placatory, and many other things which vitiate their utility as indicators or measures of motivation. The inescapable question they raise is when or whether the reasons given are the "real" ones; there appears to be no way of answering it to the satisfaction of those who have seriously concerned themselves with it. Nevertheless it must be admitted that people do think in terms of reasons for their actions and that the reasons therefore constitute a significant dimension in human relations. This being so their analysis and interpretation may be regarded as an important problem and the question becomes one of how to deal with it (4).

The view adopted here is that reasons are more or less satisfying ways of structuring situations, whether familiar or unfamiliar. They are not simply expressions of approval or disapproval. Rather they are cognitive organizations of a field of experience which are reinforced by a positive, a negative, or a null affect. Since they are verbalizations, and since language is an imperfect means of representing many structural possibilities, it is not surprising that the reasons given for adopting a position are frequently at variance with how a person apperceives an experience, and consequently why his public reasons are often not his "real" reasons for doing something. He is and must be inarticulate about most of his cognitive organizations because he has no words to describe them. Moreover, he is not encouraged to find accurate expressions for his sense data. In the interest of common understanding he has been conditioned to justify the positions he adopts by resort to certain conventionalized organizational patterns which amount to a system of folk logic with premiums attached to its use, the premiums of being generally understood, supported, followed, and defended.

The 178 interviews produced many more than that number of reasons for liking or not liking television. This was not only because each respondent gave his own verbalization of his conceptualization of television — which accounts for the 178 — but because many of them multiplied their reasons. This is not to say, however, that each reason represents a different structuring of the phenomenological field the focal point of which is television. Rather, it means that they are more or less articulate statements about it, that "it" being a universe with many and diverse facets which are nonetheless amenable to classification. There is no single way to effect this classification, but it is suggested that it can be done in terms of the preceding analysis. In other words, the many specific reasons for accepting or rejecting television, including educational television, can be construed to be exhibits of one or another of the 81 situations constituting the paradigm on page 360.

Adopting this approach, it can be said that there are three categories of responses to the question, "Why do you or do you not like television?" They may be characterized as the two-, the three-, and the four-component structuring of the constellation of things, persons, and events called to mind by that question. The two-component structure is represented by Cell 1 of the paradigm wherein "television," Y or X, registers, either positively or negatively, as A or B, but as such is psychologically isolated and inert. This is practically a null category as far as commercial television is concerned, because among the respondents in this inquiry there was no one who had not heard of it and who therefore did not have some associations which gave it meaning for him. It is, however, a significant category with respect to educational television because there were many respondents who in one manner of speaking or another attested to the fact that such television presentations as a Shakespearean play or a laboratory demonstration of a chemical reaction had little or no meaning to them. They expressed their reactions in such terms as, "That's over my head," "It's too deep for me," "That's long-haired stuff." For such people, A and B do not constitute a prototype. The evoked A (or B) is fragmentary, diffuse, incomplete, unstable, or vacillating; or it is incapable of activating a clear or consistent B (or A): Elizabethan English strikes them as being ridiculous, precious, or contrived; and "an electrically charged atom or group of atoms" is just so many words which might as well be said in another language — as they are in equally unintelligible Italian operas.

The remainder of the cells in Row 1 and in Column 1 are three-component structurings of television, half of them acceptable, half not, if we continue to assume that a positive value is placed on A B. A large number of responses fall into this category, which as we have seen is the one comprising syllogisms. It is understandable that many reactions conform to this pattern because not only is it a common way to justify a position, it is also the one which is readily summoned by a question such as, "Why do you or do you not like television?" The same circumstances account for the fact that complete expressions of syllogisms occur only rarely. In part, this is because the question itself supplies the conclusion. Thus, to take an example exhibiting the pattern of Cell 3, *with a negative value placed on B:* "I (A) do not like violence and immorality ($B_1$), and there is too much of it on television (Y)." It is unnecessary and would seem pedantic to add "that is why I do not like television." Incompleteness also occurs because elliptical statements of this kind frequently occur in ordinary speech. Logicians call them *enthymemes*. They are characterized by the omission of one of the premises or the conclusion on the assumption that the listener takes the missing part for granted.[3] Thus, to illustrate with another negatively valued B in Cell 3 again: "I (A) cannot afford to waste time (B₁), and watching television (Y) is a waste of time," is an enthymeme with the conclusion omitted. But another respondent gave the same reason in a manner which conforms to Cell 55: "People (A₁) who watch television are wasting their time (B)." He tacitly assumed the negative minor premise "I (X) am not one of those people" (X ≠ A₁). To take another example, one respondent said that she did not like a certain professor or his manner of presenting Shakespearean plays on television because he tried to act the parts of the characters in the play instead of lecturing about them as did a former college professor of hers. In this reasoning we have a case conforming to Cell 9 in which the television plays X were regarded as identical with those A studied in a college class, but both the television professor Y and his treatment (relationship 2) of the plays were considered to be significantly different from the admired former professor B and his manner of presenting (relationship 1) the plays; that is, Y₂ ≠ B₁. Had the television professor's personal qualifications Y been acceptable to this respondent by comparison with her college professor B, but his role playing (relationship 2) still distasteful, her rejection of the programs would be described by the arrow directed to the left in Cell 5, but it would be dotted, not solid.

A few respondents categorically dismissed commercial television with a peremptory statement that *all* of it is undesirable. They used such terms as "trash," "horrible," "childish," "moronic," and even "vidiotic" to characterize its productions. They were in effect, and sometimes explicitly, equating television content X with that of books and magazines A₁, which they regard as sensational, inartistic, lurid, hackneyed, and blatant B. In so doing they were asserting that the Y component of Cell 19 is inconsequential or non-existent, for if *all* commercial television X is said to be trash, there can be no Y remainder.

There were a number of cases conforming to the three-component pattern which seemingly are not syllogisms, but are such in fact with their

[3] "The following are familiar illustrations of enthymemes: *This medicine cured my daughter's cough; therefore this medicine will cure mine.* The inference is valid on the tacit admission of the major premise: *Whatever is a cure for my daughter's cough is a cure for mine.* An enthymeme in which the major premise is unexpressed is of the *first order. All drunkards are short-lived; therefore John won't live long.* Here the missing premise is the minor: *John is a drunkard.* Enthymemes suppressing the minor premise are of the *second order. Usury is immoral, and this is usury.* The conclusion *This is immoral* is here left unexpressed. Such an enthymeme is of the *third order*" (3, p. 78).

minor premises expressing a denial of equality, as in Cells 7, 8, 9, 55, 64, and 73. They arise when mutually exclusive choices between X and A or between Y and B must be made. Thus, some respondents said that they could not view regular educational television programs because they were presented at the identical time when the respondents must do something else, such as work, prepare meals, take care of their children, have coffee with their neighbors, go fishing — or sleep. There were others who said that they could not afford a television set or a subscription to a cable service. Further inquiry revealed that what they meant was that they preferred to spend that part of their budget which they could have used for a set or service on such things as clothing, food, books, or recreational activities.

Four-component structurings of television and its offerings are often expressed in elliptical responses comparable to enthymemes. Thus, when one respondent was asked a question about television he replied, "I like television because you can see the people who are doing the talking." His unexpressed prototypes, as was soon verified, were the plays, newscasts, and speeches presented by radio. Thus, television $X_1$ was equated with radio $A_1$, and the audio-visual presentations $Y_1$ associated with television were equated with comparable presentations $B_1$ on radio, and a lesser value was placed on the latter. This situation is represented by the assimilation possibilities (the arrows directed to the right) in Cell 11. If the respondent had preferred radio to television in spite of their resemblances he would have rejected the substitution and his decision would be indicated by dotted instead of solid-line arrows to the right in the same cell. If the differences between the two media and their outputs had impressed him, and had he valued radio, Cell 51 would represent his rejection of assimilation. If he had preferred the programs on television but not that medium as contrasted with radio, Cell 47 would represent his partial acceptance by selective assimilation, not projection.

Many of the four-component responses were such only by implication, but the implications were clear. Thus it was evident that many respondents equated education $X_1$ with work $A_1$, and in effect said that the place for the latter was not in the home but in an office, shop, or school. Others made it plain that education is for children, not for adults, and that educational television was therefore not for them; or that educational television is for specialists, such as accountants, teachers, and engineers, therefore not for them. In all these instances there is an equation of two of the components and rejection of an equation of the other two, the results being selective assimilation as represented by the dotted and solid arrows curving down and up to the right in Cells 47 and 15.

Before leaving these illustrations it should be pointed out that something can substitute for "nothing," and vice versa (1, pp. 222–223). This becomes an entirely reasonable statement when it is realized that what is commonly called "doing nothing" is only a figure of speech. We never do absolutely nothing, but at times we do things which are not highly valued. Consequently televiewing can take the place of relaxing, conversing, dawdling, or drowsing. Furthermore, since we are dealing with ideas, educational television can take the place of an unrealized hope of getting an education in school, and many acceptors of it are explicit in acknowledging this substitution.

The foregoing illustrations could be multiplied, but to do so would become tedious. The examples above are intended only to indicate the flexibility of the model. It is believed that all the responses obtained in the course of the television interviews have a place within its framework.

The television research began with the notion that it was to be an inquiry into the reception of an innovation, i.e, educational television. For a time the question of whether educational television was in fact an innovation or not was a troublesome one, for it was evident that many respondents were familiar with it in some fashion, and therefore, with regard to them at least, our inquiry was more comparable to one which seeks to find out why some men prefer Camel to Chesterfield cigarettes. As it turned out this was not a significant question because with the analysis here employed it does not matter how familiar a person is with something toward which he takes a receptive or a non-receptive position. He in any case proceeds in accordance with one or another of the variations on the acceptance-rejection process.

## BIBLIOGRAPHY

1. Barnett, H. G. *Innovation, The Basis of Cultural Change.* New York: Mc-Graw-Hill Book Co., 1953.

2. Bartlett, Frederick C. *Remembering. A Study in Experimental and Social Psychology.* New York: Cambridge University Press, 1950.

3. Cohen, Morris R., and Ernest Nagel. *An Introduction to Logic and Scientific Method.* New York: Harcourt, Brace & Co., 1934.

4. Sills, David. *A Sociologist Looks at Motivation.* (Bureau of Applied Social Research, Reprint #298.) New York: Columbia University Press, no date.

# 20

*Robert H. Lauer*

*and Jeanette C. Lauer*

# The Experience of Change:

# Tempo and Stress

The Mexican villager who sent away travelers by saying, "May you go with God, and may nothing new happen to you" (16, p. 107), expressed a point of view about change that is not uncommon. Social scientists as well as Mexican villagers have sometimes assumed that change, the new, is stressful for humans. But the relation between change and stress should be a matter of investigation rather than an assumption. In this chapter, therefore, we will try to clarify the relationship between change and stress. By examining certain empirical materials, we will suggest that stress is not an inherent part of change. Contrary to the villager (and those who have agreed with him), we will argue that it is the rate and kind of change that is related to stress rather than change *per se*.

One point should be clear at the outset, however. We are not assuming that stress is always disjunctive for the individual or dysfunctional for social systems. On the contrary, we would argue that some kinds of stress facilitate individual growth, and, indeed, are necessary to that growth. Even at the animal level, an environment which is biologically adequate but "psychologically restricted" has been found to suppress problem-solving ability (21, pp. 335–341). At the human level, a host of voices ranging from the poet to the scientist, testify to the value of struggle and stress for human growth. For example, the Roman emperor,

Marcus Aurelius, a stoic, spoke of the flexibility of the understanding, which so operated that "a hindrance to a given duty becomes a help, an obstacle in a given path a furtherance" (2, p. 29). The historian Herbert Butterfield argues that a clear lesson of history "is the fact that men of spiritual resources may not only redeem catastrophe, but turn it into a grand creative moment" (9, p. 101). Bruno Bettelheim, the psychologist, recalled the delinquent boy who said, "You can't live if there's nothing to push against" (7, p. 92). To cite another example, the psychologist and personality theorist, Gordon Allport, denied that man always seeks to reduce tension. Growth only occurs by "risk-taking and variation," so that we may speak of "growth motives" which "maintain tension in the interest of distant and often unattainable goals" (1, pp. 65–68). It is precisely this maintaining of tension rather than an attempt to reduce it, pointed out Allport, that distinguishes adult human growth from animal and infant growth.

On the other hand, it is well known that stress can lead to both physical and emotional illness (29). Stress may manifest itself in anxiety (3, p. 7), in emotional tension and the inhibition of normal modes of behavior (25, p. 13), or in loneliness and nervousness (34, pp. 51–58). The focus of this chapter is on the stress that leads to these disjunctive reactions: we are inquiring into the relationship between change and that stress which is debilitating to human growth. Is that relationship an inherent one? Is change necessarily a two-edged sword that not only cuts away the impediments to progress but also slashes into the psyche of man? Is change always an "ordeal," or a "crisis," or a "foreign and unwanted agent?"[1]

### Change and Stress: A Hypothesis

As we shall show below, there is empirical evidence both to support and reject an affirmative answer to the above questions. Before examining that evidence, we will present a hypothesis designed to make sense of the contradictory positions. Essentially, we will argue that stress is not related to change *per se*, but to the rate and kind of change. A rapid rate of change tends to generate stress, and the relationship between rate and stress level will be modified by the intervening variable of kind of change. Specifically, the effects of the rate will be modified by whether the change is perceived to be controlled and whether it is seen as desirable; to the extent that people perceive the change as under control and as heading in a direction that they have chosen or willingly accept, stress will be diminished (though not negated).

In general, we expect that the more rapid the change the greater the stress. How can the relationship be explained? We suggest that rapid

---

[1] These labels have been applied to social change by, respectively, Eric Hoffer (22), Robert Nisbet (38, p. 282), and Richard LaPiere (27, p. 39).

change imposes severe social psychological demands upon people, a point noted by others. For example, Kirk has argued that drastic shifts in life circumstances may generate a contradiction between the expectations of actors and the reality they face, resulting in "role handicap" (26, pp. 258–280). Lifton found that rapid societal change may result in "historical dislocation," a sense of the inadequacy of traditional patterns and of the discontinuity of the self with the past (30, pp. 160–175). Individuals then confront an identity crisis and the necessity for establishing new self-concepts.

Our own argument is more complex than the above two. As Shibutani has pointed out, in order to understand a man's behavior we must know "(1) his definition of the situation, (2) the kind of creature he believes himself to be, and (3) the audience before which he tries to maintain his self-respect" (45, p. 279). The definition of the situation, the self-concept and the reference group, then, are the social psychological bases for behavior; they are the social psychological matrix out of which man acts, whether or not he consciously attends to a decision to act. That is, there are situations in which man behaves mechanically, without conscious thought to what he is doing; in other situations, he is confronted with the necessity for evaluation and decision. But in either kind of situation, he must orient himself in order to act, and his orientation rests upon these three social psychological bases.

Man's orientation has both a historical and a personal dimension. The individual's history is enmeshed in social history. Kirk illustrates personal disorientation that is independent of social disorientation. In either case, however, the social psychological bases for action can be undermined by rapid change.

But why should rapid change affect adversely these social psychological bases? Firstly, the definition of the situation, the self-concept, and the reference group enable us to construct a "reality" in which to act. "What people generally call 'reality' is a working orientation over which there is a high degree of consensus" (45, p. 118). The reality to which we respond is a social reality. Secondly, human life is an ongoing interaction between the existential situation and the social psychological bases by which man orients himself in order to act. This is similar to Blumer's conception of society "as a diversified social process in which people were engaged in forming joint actions to deal with situations confronting them" (8, p. 541). The fitting together of developing lines of action involves continual change — social reality is a process. Thus, change *per se* does not involve debilitating stress; on the contrary, change is normal.

Thirdly, while a moderate rate of change may provide sufficient tension between the existential situation and the social psychological bases of action for individual growth, a very rapid rate of change presents a quite different situation. If either life circumstances or the social context changes drastically or very swiftly, the individual confronts a situation that demands far more than mere adjustment. He confronts a situation in which the social psychological bases of his behavior have been rendered inadequate or even inappropriate. He is left in a disoriented state which is a state of stress. He is required to act, but the bases upon which he orients himself for action are no longer adequate. Tension between the cognitive and contextual facets of the individual's existence can be a stimulant for growth; a large cleavage or contradiction between the two leaves the individual disoriented and in stress.

The stress will be diminished if the individual perceives some degree of control over his changing social context or defines the changes as desirable or acceptable. To sense some degree of control or to accept the direction of change is to possess some orientation to personal and social history. But the sense of control and the desirability of the direction are precarious under conditions of rapid change; the stress is therefore diminished but not negated.

This suggests that a generalized level of stress results from rapid change. Most previous studies have examined stress as a situational phenomenon. For example, the notions of "exigencies," "articulation," and "action" deal with situated disparities between desired or expected goals and their achievement (56, pp. 89–97). The lack of achievement can lead to certain psychic consequences such as alienation (55, pp. 152–174). Without minimizing the importance of stressful situations (such as sudden and unanticipated changes in life circumstances or the problems involved in goal striving), we would posit a high level of stress deriving from broad and rapid societal change. As a simplified example, consider the stress of the Catholic priest in the 1960s. The number of men leaving the priesthood as well as the books and articles written by disillusioned priests indicates a high stress level. At that time, of course, the institution of religion was in flux along with other institutions of the society. In fact, rapid and sometimes radical changes were occurring in many facets of the Church, including its organization and ideology. Priests themselves were questioning traditional ways. To the extent that one's peers are an important reference group, this meant that for many priests a significant reference group was in flux. Moreover, the self-concept of the priest was problematic; one priest told us, "At times I'm not even sure what it means to be a priest anymore." Finally, definitions of situations were problematic; for example, what was the meaning of a situation in which a priest faced a group of parishioners who no longer accepted his judgment as final authority?

This is a speculative example, deduced from a general knowledge of the age and acquaintanceship with some priests. It serves, however, to illustrate our point that rapid change tends to undermine the social psychological bases for behavior. It also illustrates the point that the stress of the priest was more than situational; it was a function of broad changes that rendered the prior social psychological bases of action inadequate. The priest could no longer orient himself for action by a stable reference group, or a firmly held self-concept, or consensual definitions of situations. It was not merely the frustration of thwarted goal striving or the agony of traumatic changes in life circumstances of an individual that induced stress in the priest; rather, it was the broad, rapid changes that undercut his social psychological bases for action.

The stressful effects of those changes were maximized by the lack of control over them. The priest could control neither the changes in his Church nor those in the larger society. Some priests, for example, resented the changes in the liturgy, but could do nothing to prevent them. Some felt strongly that the war in Vietnam was immoral, but felt as helpless as the rest of us to alter the situation. We may understand the mitigating effects of control and desirability, as argued above, by speculating about them in this context. Had the priest perceived some control over the changes, his self-concept would have been enhanced even though he did not consider the changes desirable — at least he would not have been an impotent creature battered about by massive forces that were beyond him. With some degree of control, definitions of situations would not be as problematic; even the certainty of a less than desirable situation is better than a totally uncertain situation. Finally, had the changes been perceived as desirable, the priest would have defined his existence in gratifying terms; he might recognize that his self-concept was in flux, but the direction of the change would be defined as good.

To return to our argument, given a high level of stress under conditions of rapid change, what are the consequences for behavior? As we shall show below, the stress may be manifested in a variety of ways. We shall show, for example, that people in Jacksonian America manifested their stress in pervasive fears and a conspiracy mentality; in personal pathologies; in social movements and new organizations designed to regain control of their existence; and in widespread violence. Is there any way of linking these various modes of response to the changes that elicited them? Since there is neither historical nor experimental data to suggest directions, we can only speculate within the theoretical framework we have established. Generally, we would expect the responses to be related to the three social psychological bases identified earlier. Firstly, however, we would suggest three broad types of responses: adaptive, escapist, and activist. The first involves mere adaptation to the stress — somehow managing to "live with it." This would include the fear response; the individual lives with the stress and continual fear is both the result and the evidence of that stress. The second, the escapist response, is manifest in personal pathologies; the individual can neither adapt to the stress nor act so as to reduce it, and so escapes into alcoholism or mental illness. Finally, the activist mode of response includes social movements, organization, and violence. In this response, the individual strives to alter himself or his context in order to attenuate, or at least cope with, his stress. We include violence here because we view it as an effort to enhance the self-concept; if I am nothing else of which I can be certain, I can at least establish myself as a strong person through violence, and can at the same time demonstrate some degree of control over my existence.

Now how do the three bases of behavior relate to these modes of response? We would expect that whether an adaptive, escapist, or activist response is chosen would depend upon the degree of disruption of the social psychological bases. Maximal disruption would tend to lead to the escapist response; minimal disruption would tend towards the adaptive response, while moderate disruption would tend to elicit an activist response. All three modes are possible within the context of the same broad changes since those changes will have differential impact upon different segments of the society. Technological changes, for example, may have far greater impact upon the self-concept of a blue-collar worker than upon an athlete. In fact, the same changes may have contradictory consequences; changes in factory technology may increase the power (and thereby enhance the self-concept) of the manager at the same time that it intensifies the sense of powerlessness (and thereby diminishes the self-concept) of the worker.

This very general analysis leaves many unanswered questions. But an attempt to be more detailed and precise would carry us too far into the field of theorizing. Our own preference is for a dialectical development of theory and research; we must first try to firmly establish the relationships between rate of change, control over change, desirability of change, and experienced stress. Results of such research may then be used to define theory and give directives for further work.

Since we are breaking new ground rather than working in well-tilled soil, the remainder of this chapter will briefly note some evidence regarding change and stress, and then we will examine Jacksonian America as a case study in the light of our thesis. In Jacksonian America there were broad and rapid social changes which led to high stress levels. These changes existed in both an objective and perceptual sense. Our primary purpose is to show that a time of rapid change was associated with high stress. We shall, therefore, point to the evidence of rapid change and then detail the evidence for a high level of stress. Finally, we will note some hints in the historical materials that are congruent with our analysis of the cause of stress in times of rapid change.

## Change and Stress: Empirical Evidence

Those who want to argue that change is inevitably stressful for humans would find considerable evidence. Some of the evidence is indirect, such as the pervasive tendency to resist change which has been documented by numerous researchers. It could be argued that resistance to change is a defense mechanism against the stress of change. If the shift from picking peas to picking string beans can generate anxiety (22, p. 1), how much more stress will be generated by the introduction of railroads, or the automobile, or alternating current? Would it not be expected that people would resist such changes in an effort to avoid the stress they bring?

Technological changes seem particularly to fit into this idea of stress in change. A number of reasons have been suggested to explain this: technological change disrupts habitual patterns; technological change precludes the use of parental models for behavior, and may additionally involve conflict with parents or with the values of parents; and technological change demands the learning of new behavioral patterns in adulthood, patterns which diverge from those which were learned and rewarded in childhood (32, p. 269). All of these consequences are assumed to generate stress. Nor do we doubt the possibility of such psychological stress, even to the extent of those stone age Australians who suffered "a mental and moral void which foreshadowed the collapse and destruction of all Yir Yoront culture" under the shattering impact of technical change (44, pp. 85–86).

But are such debilitating consequences inevitable? In the context of his study of the Industrial Revolution, Neil Smelser has outlined a theory of change that incorporates psychic disturbances as an integral part of the developmental sequence (46, pp. 15–16, 32–42). Smelser tried to analyze a particular type of long-term change — structural differentiation, a type which he said is particularly characteristic of the developing social system. He described seven sequential steps in this process of differentiation and applied them to the Industrial Revolution in England. The seven steps are:

(1) Dissatisfaction deriving from the failure to satisfactorily achieve goals, and the awareness of the potential for change.

(2) Psychic disturbances, which take the form of varied emotional reactions and aspirations which are inappropriate in terms of resolving the problems.

(3) A more rational use of the energy expended in step 2 in an effort to "realize the implications of the existing value system."

(4) A brain-storming stage, in which ideas are generated in profusion without anyone being responsible for their implementation or consequences.

(5) An effort to specify the particular ideas and institutional patterns to be implemented.

(6) The implementation of change by individuals or groups, with their performance being sanctioned in accord with the value system.

(7) The "routinization" of acceptable changes.

For our purposes, it is step 2 which is of particular interest, for it posits psychic disturbance as an integral part of the process of structural change. Smelser supports this by reference to various kinds of hostility, anxiety, and fantasy in the behavior of industrial workers. Among the weavers, for example, hostility was evidenced in various political activities, in the writing and circulation of controversial pamphlets, and in rioting and the destruction of powerlooms. There were also "hints of alternating gloom and euphoria (anxiety and fantasy)" (46, p. 133). But none of these, says Smelser, were rationally appropriate for solving the problem that had occasioned them — the technological advance that threatened the weavers' position in the industrializing nation.

Such psychic disturbances were common among those experiencing the turmoil of industrialization. Between 1770 and 1840, the factory operatives also destroyed machines, went out on strikes, and began to show signs of the "familiar elements of disturbance — anxiety, gloom, and the glorification of the past . . ." (p. 236). Others, of course, have detailed the agony of the workers; there is little question that the experience of English workers involved great stress.

To show, however, that change *can* be stressful is not to show that it is *necessarily* stressful. To show that the industrial workers of England suffered debilitating stress is not to prove that such stress is an integral part of the process of change. We do not deny that stress is one possible outcome of change; what we do deny is that it is an integral part of the process of change.

If it is easy to gather evidence to support the stress of change, it is equally easy to marshal support for the position that change is desirable and welcomed by people. "The Tiv have liked change. For as long as they can remember, they have introduced new ways of government, new forms of decoration, new techniques, copied from neighboring tribes" (32, p. 122). However, the changes effected were not radical in the sense of being fundamental changes in the social structure.

On the other hand, the Japanese have a tradition of borrowing from others and changing their society, of accepting radical changes. The nineteenth-century Meiji restoration marked the beginning of the process of modernizing Japan within the course of a few generations. The change was deliberate. A group of the Samurai initiated and carried through the transformation of the nation. While the Japanese experience was unique in many ways, it was by no means a lone instance of people choosing to effect massive change.

The Japanese changed their society from a feudal to a modern, industrial system. What of an even greater transformation, that from the Stone Age into the modern era? Would people define this as desirable? Or would Stone Age people, like those mentioned above, find the transition devastating to their culture and their psyches? The tale of the

Australians is a tragic one. But another group of Stone Age people, the Manus, have had quite a different experience. Their exposure to Western culture in 1928 led to rapid modernization of the society. The Manus began the task of creating democratic government, a money economy, and they built schools and medical clinics. Far from being a debilitating experience, an overall evaluation of the developments on Manus Island is that "rapid change is not only possible, but may actually be very desirable," and that it may be better for people to make large-scale and rapid change rather than slow, partial changes (33, pp. 445-446).

Another instructive example is provided by the rapidly changing West African societies. As West African nations have begun to break into the modern era, there have been significant alterations in family relationships, the development of new means for attaining traditional goals, and the formulation of new goals. Young couples have set up independent households. Migrants to the towns begin to find security in ethnic associations rather than in their descent groups. Workers have organized to secure better conditions for themselves.

Have these changes intensified the stress of the people? A survey was conducted in 1961 in Western Nigeria to ascertain the extent of psychiatric disorders. A comparison of the results with the population of North America is somewhat complex, but generally speaking the changes experienced by the Nigerians do not "result in any great increase in individual tension, and ... contemporary Yoruba society manages to assuage this tension with a high degree of success, so that the health of the majority is not significantly impaired" (31, p. 248).

It would seem apparent, then, that for every case of psychic stress associated with change, we could find a case of change that is desired, and therefore gratifying. Furthermore, within societies there is some evidence that those experiencing change may find their experience more gratifying than those whose situation is stable. In his study of six Middle Eastern nations, Lerner found a general relationship between reported happiness and modernity; modern and transitional men tended to perceive themselves as happier than did traditional men (28, p. 102). The notion of the peasant or traditional community as one of *gemeinschaft* seems, at least in the contemporary world, to be largely a myth. People throughout the world may not find great appeal in the American or Soviet patterns; but neither do they cling to their traditional patterns. It would hardly be an exaggeration to say that the bulk of mankind today eagerly pursues change of one kind or another. Clearly, we cannot accept the notion that stress is inherent in all change.

Among the characteristics of modern man, according to Inkeles, are the willingness to have new experiences, an open attitude towards change, a present or future orientation rather than past orientation, and the conviction that man's action can shape the course of events (24, pp.

138–150). More and more of the world's peoples are becoming modern in this sense. If there was a point in history when most men would shrink from change, we have long since passed it.

Thus far we have shown that change may either be stressful or gratifying, that men may react violently to it or seek it with passion. What is it that distinguishes these two different reactions? Our hypothesis is that it is not change *per se* that generates stress, but that the rate and type of change is responsible for stress. With respect to the former, we expect stress to increase as the rate of change, or the perceived rate of change, increases. Sorokin anticipated this when he argued that periods of societal transition are characterized by increased mental disorders and suicide (48, p. 206). However, Sorokin based his argument upon a premise that we would not accept: "We well know that the indispensable prerequisite of a sound and integrated mind is the presence of social stability and unchallenged general norms" (48, p. 207).

More recently, Toffler has coined the phrase "future shock" to describe the psychic disruption that results from experiencing too much change in too short a time. There is historical evidence to support this view. Although, as we have noted, the Japanese have traditionally changed their society, and have valued change, the very rapid tempo of the Meiji era produced considerable stress. The 1868 "revolution" saved the Japanese from Western domination, but only at the cost of great psychic stress. The generation that experienced the brunt of the hectic rate of change suffered "extraordinary mental agonies" (40, p. 3). The biographies and writings of Japanese youth of the period talk of "mental agony," "melancholia and mental turmoil," "mental sickness," etc. (40, p. 18). According to one observer, such emotional disturbance was widespread among students during the 1870s and 1880s. Thus, even a people who valued activism and change found themselves writhing in the agony of an intensely high rate of change.

Further empirical evidence of the relationship between rate of change and experienced stress is provided by a study of the health records of military personnel. In this study, the change involved was in the life situation of individuals rather than in the society as a whole. It was found that "a cluster-year of life-changes was seen to occur immediately prior to an illness or to a clustering of illnesses" (41, p. 366). As used in the study, life-changes included such phenomena as death of a wife, divorce, marital problems, a new line of work, a child getting married, personal successes, new religious patterns and so on. When the rate of change, as measured by how many of the above changes in a specified period of time there were, physical or mental illness tended to follow. The various changes were weighted, with death of wife being the most heavily weighted and minor infraction of civilian law the least. The greater the total score of "life-change units" in a year, the greater the probability of a major health change the following year.

We would go a step further, and argue that not only is the rate of change as objectively measured related to change, but that the perceived rate of change is also crucial in the experience of stress. To explore this possibility, we gave an attitude questionnaire to 115 subjects (students and personnel at a military base). The questionnaire employed the short form of the Taylor manifest anxiety scale as a measure of stress, and ten statements designed to measure perception of change.[2] The statements dealt with such matters as the "pace of life," the accumulation of information confronting the subject, the demands of new situations for which the subject is unprepared by experience, perception of the rate of geographical mobility, etc. Subjects indicated their degree of agreement or disagreement with each of the statements. Scores from the anxiety scale and perceived rate of change statements were divided into three categories — low, medium, and high. Results are shown in Table 1. As may be seen, there is a strong and direct relationship between perceived rate of change and anxiety score, supporting our hypothesis.

### TABLE 1*

PERCEIVED RATE OF CHANGE

|  |  | Low | Medium | High |  |
|---|---|---|---|---|---|
|  | Low | 29 | 15 | 0 | 44 |
| Anxiety | Medium | 16 | 25 | 4 | 45 |
| Score | High | 0 | 17 | 9 | 26 |
|  |  | 45 | 57 | 13 | 115 |

*Low, medium, and high anxiety scores were, respectively, 0-5, 6-10, and 11-18 on the Taylor scale. "Perceived rate of change" was scored by summing answers to the ten questions; the scores were then divided into three groups of equal range.

### Change and Stress: A Case Study

Thus, we find support for a relationship between the rate of societal change and stress, rate of change of life circumstances and stress, and perceived rate of change in the social environment and stress. We would further argue that the evidence in the last section that seemed to support the inherent stress in change was actually drawn from cases of rapid change (at least relative to prior periods), and that cases of rapid change

[2] We noted above that stress may manifest itself in anxiety. In fact, some researchers have used stress to refer to that situation that generates anxiety. We are not arguing that anxiety is a measure of the total content of stress, however, but only that it is a useful indicator of stress. And among the measures of anxiety, the Manifest Anxiety Scale has been shown to yield impressive results. For a description of the scale and the short form which we have used, see Taylor (50) and Bendig (4).

which seemed minimally stressful were those involving perceived control or desirability of the change. We will now examine a particular socio-historical context more intensively in the light of our hypothesis.

Firstly, however, we would like to be clear about what we are claiming and not claiming for this study. The use of historical materials presents certain problems. One that merits comment here is the conceptual problem: to what extent is the content of variables such as stress and rate of change equivalent in the historical study on the one hand and experimental and survey data on the other hand? We are not claiming equivalency; we are not arguing that the stress we find in historical data is equivalent to that measured by the Taylor Manifest Anxiety Scale. Rather, the Taylor scale is a measure of stress, and the historical data provide other indicators of stress.

Furthermore, our concepts are relativistic. That is, we are not at this point positing any absolute rate of change that will generate stress; rather, we expect that an intensified rate, relative to the past, will increase the level of stress. Thus, whether Jacksonian Americans would have scored as high on our scale of perceived rate of change as those in our sample is beside the point (at least at the present level of knowledge); Jacksonian Americans and later historians agree that the rate of change increased greatly over that which obtained in prior times and this higher rate generated considerable stress.

The great value of the historical study lies in the potential for establishing a general pattern of behavior. We are convinced that the relationship between rate of change and stress is neither culturally nor temporally specific. Historical data are required to support this expectation. The case study, therefore, not only can provide support for the hypothesized relationships, but also can indicate the extent to which the relationships may be generalized. The limitations of historical data demand that our concepts be somewhat loosely defined. But we are not claiming precision; we are only claiming that we have found evidence to pursue more intensively what may be a general relationship.

Turning, then, to our case study, we find that nineteenth century America, between the War of 1812 and the Civil War, was a society in rapid flux. We would, therefore, expect it to be a society whose members experienced considerable stress.

Although historians have disagreed about many facets of Jacksonian America, "there is a general consensus that changes occurring in the United States after the War of 1812 significantly altered American society (17, p. 1). The changes, then, were not changes on the surface but fundamental alterations of the social order. Moreover, the changes were rapid, the result of the interaction of many forces: economic and political egalitarianism, spatial and social mobility, industrialization and urbanization, secularization, and immigration. Domestic and craft shop manufacturers gave way to factories. Skilled workers found themselves less in demand,

and the number of unskilled workers was greatly increased by immigrants. The 1840s and 1850s were decades of the greatest relative growth of cities in the country's history. The total value of manufactured goods increased fourfold from 1840 to 1860. In sum, the nation in the 1840s and 1850s experienced the full impact of "a radical departure from the agrarian past" (36, p. 121).

The resulting social context was one of extraordinary flux. The citizenry bore the brunt of new and radical changes in the economic, demographic, political, technological, and ideological spheres. Nothing seemed immune to the eroding power of time. Traditional leadership elites were displaced, institutional forms were torn down and reconstructed, and values withered before the onslaught of new ideologies. The instability and anxiety generated in this situation led people to make a variety of responses which were designed to make sense of the disorder and secure a modicum of security and meaning. Bureaucratization, social movements, even violence and repression were employed in the quest for stability and security.[3] All too often, however, these efforts only intensified the problem; men confronted a disordered world with tools that only fed the disorder and insured its continuation.

As we might expect, those who lived in the era perceived the fluid nature of their social context. To some of them, society seemed to be "in a state of chaos" (36, p. 22). James Fenimore Cooper has one of his characters say: "The whole country is in such a constant state of mutation, that I can only liken it to the game of children, in which, as one quits his corner another runs into it, and he that finds no corner to get into, is the laughing-stock of the others."[4] Tocqueville even opined that opposition to the Bank of the United States was rooted in the incessant change in the society, so that "the sight of that stable point jars, and the people want to see if they can shake it, like everything else" (52, p. 178).

Such a breathless pace of change should, according to our hypothesis, generate considerable stress. Indeed, Jacksonian America exhibited many of the symptoms of intense stress and nagging anxiety: pervasive fears that sometimes bordered on paranoia; strenuous efforts to order and make sense out of social life; deeply felt needs for a sense of community; irrational reactions to real and imagined threats; personal pathologies, etc. Taylor has characterized the 1830s as the "age of anxiety" (51, p. 96); it would not seem to be overstating the case to label the entire period in those terms.

---

[3] When we use the terms "order" and "stability" we are not implying that they are antonyms for change. Rather, these terms refer to perceptions of the people we are studying. From their point of view, the solution to the stress of their fluid existence was the establishment of "order" and "stability." To establish "order" is not to stifle change, but to regain control of change.

[4] The quote is provided by Meyers (35, p. 75).

The anxiety of the age seems to have led to the development of conflicting ideologies. In the 1830s the newly emerged, egalitarian ideology was confronted by a resurgence of the aristocratic ideal in the North, an ideal whose features resembled the popular version of plantation society. Why did an elitist, static ideal become so attractive during the time when American democracy and the idea of egalitarianism were spreading rapidly? It would appear that at least some Americans had serious doubts about the democratic tendencies: "Such praise of the gentleman planter ... seems to have masked a whole complex of fears and anxieties about the consequences of changes then taking place in American life" (51, pp. 97–98).

Thus, pervasive fears, our first indication of high stress, characterized the nation, and those fears focused on any number of developments (13, pp. 256–267). The period was one of increasing concern and ambiguity regarding sex norms and the female role. The pens of both journalists and clergymen recorded the frightening increase in prostitution, the growing number of divorces, and the sensual corruption of the urban areas. Many Americans devoured such fabrications as "The Mormon Seraglio," written by an excommunicated Mormon, John C. Bennett, which claimed that Mormons kept secret orders of prostitutes for the benefit of various officials of the Church. Similar fantasies were constructed about Catholic priests, who were sometimes portrayed as "lecherous" men who seduced female parishioners and gave vent to their lust in nunneries.

Americans not only feared various developments in the society, but feared each other as well. For example, Easterners tended to fear the West because they felt that the West threatened to drain their section economically, socially, and politically. They often portrayed the West as totally destitute of moral and spiritual qualities. Such conditions posed both a problem and a challenge to the Eastern religious establishment and set in motion the American home mission movement. This movement was designed to stabilize society through the establishment of orthodox institutions in the West. Thus, the leaders of the religious movements considered themselves "as much civilizing and Americanizing agents as soul winners" (47, p. 40).

Americans in the Jacksonian era, then, seemed haunted by a free-floating anxiety that found indiscriminate expression in numerous, diverse fears. It is not surprising, as Taylor points out, that there was "something like an epidemic of catastrophic fiction which swept the country in the eighteen thirties," nor that from both clergymen and public speakers came a message of the need for inner strength in the face of continuing crisis (51, pp. 99–100). Both in writing and in words, Americans were warned that they hung precariously at the edge of an abyss of doom. The turmoil of the age, according to many voices, demanded nothing less than the same kind of self-control and decisiveness that characterized the generation of George Washington.

In some cases, fear took the form of a conspiracy mentality, an irrational fear bordering on paranoia of various groups. Many Americans developed intense suspicion and anxiety about certain groups in the society. These groups may have posed real or imaginary threats to certain facets of the society, but in either case the response was an overreaction.

Roman Catholics, Mormons, and Masons were viewed as evil groups determined to overthrow American society. In spite of the differences between the three groups, each was stereotyped as "the Great American Enemy, whose traits formed an inverted image of the ideals of popular democracy and the cult of the common man" (12, p. 116). Literature designed to show the threat posed by the groups clearly reflects an anxiety that is incongruous with any real threat and even with any real conflict of interests.

The secrecy with which certain rituals were cloaked in each of the three groups helped feed the anxiety and confirm the suspicion of conspiracy. Those who advocated egalitarianism and an open, democratic society could not tolerate the existence of groups which demanded total commitment of their members to the group and its partially secret ways. The anxiety that attended the existence of such groups was further heightened by the tales of former members of the groups. We have already noted the revelations of John Bennett; other former Mormons, including females, told similar stories of sexual exploitation. Former Masons insisted that they were risking their very lives by revealing the secrets of the order. Former Catholics sought desperately to arouse Americans to see the threat to their freedom posed by the Papists, and reminded their hearers of the unbounded abuse they suffered from the Church because of their efforts.

The anxiety regarding Catholics was compounded by the immigrants; a people who were not only Catholic but also foreign seemed doubly threatening. For example, the anti-Catholic activists of the 1830s did not take root in Boston as they did in many other parts of the nation. An effort to publish an anti-Catholic paper in Boston in 1829 did not succeed. But the decades following saw an increasing number of Irish immigrants settle in Boston and the concomitant growth of fear. A mayor of Boston declared that the Irish would always be a "distinct and hostile" group. And while Bostonians willingly employed Irish girls as servants, they developed a distrust of them, and sometimes thought of them as spies for the Pope "who revealed their [that is, the Protestant Bostonians'] secrets regularly to priests at confession" (18, p. 186). Thus, the conspiracy mentality took hold in Boston also, and Catholics were viewed as subversives who wanted to seize control of the nation and subjugate it to the Pope. Violence against Catholics and Catholic property increased. Temperance leaders saw the Irish as impediment to their work; they announced their determination to battle with Catholicism in their effort to gain men's freedom. There was a proliferation of literature that severely castigated the Catholics and called upon Protestants and native Americans to rise up and suppress the threat.

The conspiracy mentality in the South focused on the slaves. According to Freehling, the residents of Charleston, South Carolina, "knew firsthand the anxiety of slave conspiracy and incessantly guarded against it (15, p. 17). This anxiety mingled with that generated by other issues to create situations of explosive tension. Freehling argues that the nullification controversy can be understood in these terms. This controversy arose over the passage of the 1832 tariff bill by the Congress. In November of that year, a convention met in Columbia, South Carolina, and declared both the tariff acts of 1828 and 1832 to be "null, void, and no law." South Carolina citizens were instructed to pay no duties under the laws, and the government was put on notice that any effort to force obedience to the laws within South Carolina would be sufficient grounds for secession. Between 1816 and 1833, then, South Carolina had shifted from a secure place within the Union to the brink of separation.

According to Freehling, this change was the result of more than a mere political controversy. The planters of South Carolina, who comprised the social and political elite of the state, had witnessed the near destruction of their world. Severe economic depression in the 1820s had caused acute financial distress among up-country planters and the emergence of antislavery agitators in the North had brought intense psychological tension to low-country planters.

Freehling pictures the low-country aristocracy as an idle, brooding elite who were obsessed by fear of slave insurrection and thus reacted hysterically to the relatively harmless abolitionist crusade of the 1820s. Their exaggerated fears probably reflected a deep sense of guilt regarding the institution of slavery. They tried to reduce this guilt by propagating the myth of the benevolent plantation where "dutiful, carefree Sambos" worked without threat of punishment, and where "master and slave lived together in rich comradeship and intuitive understanding" (15, p. 65). But the gap between myth and reality became more and more glaring, intensified by the nation's liberal political ideals, the spread of evangelical Christianity over the South, and the necessities of slave discipline.

Although the up-country was freer of slavery tensions, it was "sufficiently disturbed by fear and guilt to appreciate the anxieties at tidewater" (p. 86). Bound by common anxieties and united by social and marriage ties, the up-country and low-country planters presented a cohesive political leadership which responded militantly when its security was threatened.

The nullification controversy was the culmination of a series of events in which the national government was increasingly viewed as an antagonist. Nullification provided the means to undo the onerous economic burden of protective tariffs, and thus end sectional exploitation which South Carolinians feared would lead to the abolition of slavery. The entire South Carolinian world appeared threatened, and leading nullifiers apparently were willing to risk civil war in order to maintain their social world.

Nullification ended in defeat, but in the ensuing years the fight against anti-slavery forces intensified; slavery apologists responded to continued threats against their "peculiar institution" by claiming that slavery was a positive good, a blessing rather than a curse. The legislature enacted a more rigorous slave code; and a severe repression of civil liberties was instituted — "the most thoroughgoing repression of free thought, free speech, and a free press ever witnessed in an American community" (15, p. 333).

Apprehension about slave rebellion was realistic. But the point is that there was an overreaction to that threat, to the influence of abolitionists, and to a number of other controversial issues not directly related to slavery. Furthermore, Americans everywhere exhibited fear. Depending upon a person's social and geographical location, a host of enemies were present to create fear: slaves, Catholics, Masons, Mormons, Irish, the central government, etc. Some Americans expressed anxiety about "the people," the common man who had seemingly ascended into a dominant position with the election of Jackson. An elite lady, commenting on the activities of inauguration day, expressed a fear that "the People" of America "will be found, as they have been found in all ages and countries where they get the Power in their hands, that of all tyrants, they are the most ferocious, cruel and despotic" (17, p. 120).

Philip Hone, a prominent New York City business and political figure, also expressed a fear of the common man. In addition, he wrote with evident anxiety about "unworthy immigrants," the tendency to make Jackson into a godlike figure, the dangers of unionism, etc. A list of the threats about which he wrote "is a scarifying catalog of phantoms, and one must conclude that many a night Hone went to bed frightened" (17, p. 166).

While the objects of anxiety were diverse, the pervasiveness of anxiety was evident. Americans of the Jacksonian era were a frightened people. They were embedded in a social milieu abounding with enemies. The land of opportunity was also a land of subtle dangers, a land envied by and sought by those who would seize it and remake it into their own image. Conspiracies were everywhere; vigilance and counterattack were the orders of the day.

A second indication of high stress was the existence of a variety of personal pathologies. The well-known observations of Tocqueville convey the picture of the American as a driven, compulsive creature. Although Americans lived in the best of circumstances, wrote Tocqueville, "a cloud habitually hung on their brow, and they seemed serious and almost sad even in their pleasures" (52, p. 536). Tocqueville went on to say that Americans pursued affluence with "feverish ardor," yet always seemed "tormented by the shadowy suspicion that they may not have chosen the shortest route to get it." Americans seized new things with passion, then quickly discarded them as even newer "delights" appeared within reach. Americans began all sorts of ventures, then abandoned them just at the moment when it seemed their efforts had come to fruition. Americans were always in a hurry, continually goaded on by the knowledge of the brevity of their earthly existence. And the thought that the shortness of life might cause one to miss some of the pleasures available "fills him with distress, fear, and regret and keeps his mind continually in agitation, so that he is always changing his plans and his abode."

Other observers noted the extreme restlessness of Americans. One man pointed out that Americans were distinguished by "a restlessness, a striving and driving onward," for they want "to perform within a year what others do within a much longer period" (39, p. 22). Another spoke of the "disease of locomotion" which led children to separate themselves from their families. And another felt that a "national feature" of Americans was leaving one's childhood home "without any visible effort or symptom of regret" (39, p. 22).

This restless, driven character was also expressed in drinking habits, which a variety of observers labelled as excessive. This was not the conclusion of a few prudes, but of a number of contemporary observers. Frederick Marryat, an English novelist, visited America in 1837–1839 and asked the question, "Why do they get so confoundedly drunk?" Another English visitor, J. S. Buckingham, offered the opinion that the American love of alcohol was leading the country to ruin. An American librarian, Christopher Baldwin, reported that members of the Worcester Temperance Society "drank very freely of cyder . . . of the very worst sort" (39, p. 24). And John Woods, a traveler to frontier Illinois, observed that one of the failings of frontier character was "drunkeness; and they are extremely quarrelsome when intoxicated" (54, p. 174).

The extent of other kinds of personal pathologies, such as mental illness, is difficult to assess. Tocqueville says that he was told that "madness" was more common in America than anywhere else. In any case, it is clear that personal pathologies were observed by a number of contemporaries, and, even allowing for some literary hyperbole, were sufficiently widespread to justify their inclusion as indicators of stress during the era.

A third indication of high stress involved social organization. Social movements and new organizations proliferated. In the midst of great material progress, Americans evidenced a hunger for some kind of security that was more than material, and for immersion in some kind of cause that transcended their own self-interests. Thus, various "movements of counter-subversion were symptomatic of a profound need for community and consensus, and for personal dedication in a higher cause" (12, p. 121).

This indication of stress, of course, overlaps with the first one, because many of the movements and organizations were fed by the conspiracy mentality: "In a rootless environment shaken by bewildering social change the nativist found unity and meaning by conspiring against imaginary conspiracies" (13, p. 267). For others, participation in movements and organizations was an effort to bring order into existence or meaning into life. As one young recruit put it: "My life, what has it been? the panting of a soul after eternity — the feeling that there was nothing here to fill the aching void, to provide enjoyment and occupation such as my spirit panted for" (14, p. 35). His groping soul found rest in the Anti-Slavery movement.

In the religious sphere, the revival was the means of searching both for community and for national identity. In large measure, it was "the hunger of the lonely spirit and of the whole society which brought the crowds of simple citizens to [revivals] . . ." (37, p. 17). A significant point here is that for a number of decades the entire nation "was periodically swept by tidal waves of conversions, notably in 1830–1832, 1842–1843, and finally in 1857–1858 . . . never again were Americans susceptible to revival on a national scale" (6, p. 243). One region, western New York, was so inundated by wave after wave of revival that it became known as the "burned-over district." The revivals were intensely emotional affairs; the "indifferent, cautious, or merely less than supremely zealous person seemed to the ultraist a very poor specimen of humanity" (11, p. 205). Anti-intellectualism flourished along with these revivals, and there were even cases of treating insane persons as gurus who would show the way to higher levels of spiritual experience.

Movements of social reform were apparently motivated as much by a thirst for control as for the well-being of those in whose name they were undertaken. For example, the members of the New York Society for the Prevention of Pauperism during the years 1817–1823 were pious, fairly well-to-do, upper-middle-class merchants and professional men who "were anxious to preserve an orderly society and . . . hoped to do this by indoctrinating the poor with sound moral values" (20, p. 16). These reformers, like many before and after them, believed that pauperism stemmed from immorality. Their task, therefore, was to quicken the moral sense of the poor through education and instruction in religion.

Not only the poor, but other deviant and dependent Americans became the object of concern. It was as though the nation suddenly became aware of such people in its midst and immediately set out creating programs and constructing institutions for them. But without denying that some degree of altruism and compassion was associated with these efforts, the primary purpose was "a vigorous attempt to promote the stability of the society at a moment when traditional ideas and practices appeared outmoded, constricted, and ineffective. The almshouse and the asylum all represented an effort to insure the cohesion of the community in new and changing circumstances" (43, p. xviii).

Among those who opted for the organizational response were the varied professions. Physicians, lawyers, and clergymen were part of stable professions in the latter half of the eighteenth century; their professions were organized in a communal type of structure with a high level of discipline. But this stability was eroded as tendencies toward vocational specialization, individual advancement, and sectarianism increased in the nineteenth century. The changes outstripped both the institutional and the social psychological capacities for dealing with them.

For example, among physicians the structure and discipline of the eighteenth century was reflected in detailed fee tables which protected the patient from exploitation and the doctor from competition. But that highly regulated and communal structure broke down in the nineteenth century; physicians became concerned with personal advancement, quarreled among themselves, and encountered increasing hostility from the larger society. In New York, efforts to provide the organization necessary for stabilizing the profession were weakened by individual physicians' attempts to get ahead. In their efforts to "restrain individualism" without resorting to coercion, the physicians tried "to create some self-regulating conscience that would bind the medical community" (10, pp. 57–58). This conscience was found in an ideology that emphasized the needs of the group — the medical profession — and gave those needs priority over the needs of individuals. The ideology was institutionalized in the New York Academy of Medicine. Thus, the response of physicians to professional disorder was the creation of an organization that institutionalized a stabilizing ideology.

Problems of disorder and organizational efforts to deal with the disorder also characterized the legal and clerical professions. In all three, according to Calhoun, there was a move toward bureaucratic impersonality which provided professional stasis at the cost of individual initiative (10, pp. 192–193).

A fourth and final indication of stress which may be detected was that of violence. This, too, overlaps with the others. It took place, for example, in the context of conflict based on the conspiracy mentality and in the course of efforts by movements. But it also occurred independently of these, and needs to be treated in its own right.

Among the violence associated with movements was the sharp increase in violent conflict that accompanied the struggle over slavery. It was believed that abolitionists provoked slave insurrections, race riots, and tensions which led to other hostilities. The growing threat of the abolitionists, resulting from widespread use of the mail and the press for propagandizing, drew a response from anti-abolitionist forces in the form of mob action.

There were two types of anti-abolitionist mobs, those arising spontaneously and those developing out of definite plans. The former were larger, more likely to get out of control, and composed of greater numbers of lower class individuals. The latter can best be viewed "as an attempt by an aggrieved class to protect its social dominance and to reinforce its traditional values" (42, p. 150). They were composed of "leading citizens" who sought to secure their world against the danger posed by abolitionists. Again, it should be noted that the violence of the reaction seems disproportionate to the threat, so that many Americans were "puzzled" by the "sudden outbreak of mobs, the growing propensity . . . to 'take the law into their own hands'" (42, p. 9).

But violence occurred far more often than those instances where it erupted in the clash of groups with opposing ideologies. European visitors were appalled by the ubiquity of violence and the apparent readiness of the American to resort to brutal means. Among the sights and events that shocked visitors were: the apathy or glee with which a crowd of respectable people could watch a Negro being burned alive; the indiscriminate pelting of Negroes with stones; the enthusiasm with which hangings were attended (again, by so-called respectable people); the trivial reasons (opening a coach window) that elicited violent reaction (killing); the brutal form which the violence took — gouging out eyes and biting off noses or ears as well as stabbings and shootings (See 39, pp. 14–15). The tendency to shoot or stab, most marked in the West and South, was so great that one visitor warned: "Should a stranger jostle an American by accident he runs extreme risk of being shot or stabbed" (39, p. 33).

Violence, then, pervaded American life. The frontier was characterized by primitivism, with problems solved by muscle rather than reason, with brawls, gangs, and mobs a commonplace, and with vigilante groups providing an alternative to law. But the violence was not confined to the rough frontier, just as it was not confined to the confrontation of groups with contradictory ideologies. If one is to judge by Jacksonian days, violence is indeed as "American as cherry pie."

Thus far, we have argued that stress is the consequence of a rapid tempo of change. And we have provided a case study in which the change was convulsive and the stress was evident. Every facet of life in America was in a state of flux in the first part of the nineteenth century. The psychic consequences may be seen in the pervasive fears, the development of a conspiracy mentality, the personal pathologies, the movements and organizations designed to restore order and secure meaning, and the frequent and intense violence in the society.

But obviously not every American showed stress. Not every American was haunted by irrational fear. In fact, some displayed quite opposite characteristics — unbounded optimism and delicious anticipation of the future. As a number of historians have noted, optimism and despair were two contradictory themes that existed in precarious tension. The question is, why did these two diverse responses exist? Why do some people endure debilitating stress while others seem to revel in the swiftness of change?

We suggest that the reason lies in what we have called the quality of change. The effects of rate are diminished when the change is perceived either to be desirable or to be under control. In the context of a study of technological change among primitive peoples, Spicer pointed out that "people resist changes that appear to threaten basic securities; they resist proposed changes they do not understand; they resist being forced to change" (49, p. 18). It seems to us that these conditions apply to any people. In other words, those Jacksonian Americans who did not experience the stress so evident among others, or who experienced it more moderately, perceived the changes either to be under control or to be desirable, or both.

Unquestionably, many did desire the change. As Hurst points out, they "valued change more than stability and valued stability most often where it helped to create change because imagination could scarcely conceive that it could be other than for the better . . ." (23, p. 24). For many Americans, imbued with the idea of unlimited potential for the individual, the future would necessarily be better than the past. But others echoed the feeling of the Reverend Ludovicus Weld: "I have . . . felt like a stranger in a strange land" (14, p. 28). And it was these latter whose stress was manifested in the ways described above. Donald sums up the nature of the abolitionists, for example, by describing them and their efforts as "the anguished protest of an aggrieved class against a world they never made" (14, p. 36). Those who felt they had lost control, those who looked upon the always changing society and saw directions that were distasteful, were driven by their anxiety to somehow cope with "a world they never made."

## Conclusion

Our historical data have clearly supported the relationship between rapid change and high stress. But what of our social psychological analysis of that relationship? We can expect little more than hints from such data, but those hints are also clearly there. Consider the behavior of early nineteenth century physicians. As we have seen, that behavior became problematic with the breakdown of the communal type profession. How should the physician act with respect to the non-medical aspects of the doctor-patient relationship? How should that relationship be defined? Peers were inadequate as a reference group; there was neither cohesion nor consensual norms among physicians. The physician's role, and thereby his self-concept, was ambiguous. With a problematic self-concept, a reference group filled with internal contradictions, and no firm set of social meanings by which to define his relationship with his patient, the physician lacked a basis for orienting himself towards action. Interaction with patients was demanded, but the social psychological bases for guiding that interaction had been eroded by rapid change.

There is other evidence. We have seen personal accounts that reveal a struggle of the author with his identity. We have seen movements that reflect a hunger for meaning and for some measure of control; we get a feeling that for many Americans social reality was amorphous at best and chaotic at worst. Indeed, how can a man find meaning to his existence when he is continually required to function in a "world he never made"? The social psychological bases of behavior assume that a considerable amount of that behavior can be taken for granted. Human behavior is "subject to habitualization," which provides "a stable background in which human activity may proceed with a minimum of decision-making most of the time" (5, p. 53). But, as the Handlins point out, the "inabiilty to take anything for granted" characterized nineteenth century America, and this inability "lay beneath many of the tensions and disorders of American life" (19, p. 108).

In sum, self-concepts, reference groups, and definitions of the situation all become inappropriate or problematic in times of rapid change. We feel that other studies will support this thesis. For example, a most important reference group for the young in Japan has been the adult generation. But during the rapid changes in Meiji Japan, there developed "marked differences of outlook between generations . . . there was a widely shared feeling that — despite filial traditions — the knowledge and responses of the adult generation were unsuited to a time of unprecedented reform" (40, p. 6). When men are required to act without adequate social psychological bases, considerable stress results; we have already noted the high stress in Meiji Japan among the young.

The historical data, combined with the other evidence we have presented, convince us that we are dealing with a general relationship. We have provided a variety of evidence that supports the correlation between high rates of change and high levels of stress. We have found some support for the notion that stress levels may be moderated by perceived control of or desire for the direction of the change. We have found some encouragement for further exploration of the social psychological analysis that explains the relationships. Certain questions remain and provide directives for both additional historical and new experimental research. What is the relationship between change as measured objectively and perceived rate of change and level of stress? To what extent does perceived control of change or desirability of the change moderate stress? What are optimal rates of change and levels of stress? Are the optimal figures absolute, or are they relative to a prior time? Since it seems unlikely that the rate of change will diminish (at least, without conscious, planned efforts), such questions take on an urgency for all those concerned with a humane existence.

## BIBLIOGRAPHY

1. Allport, Gordon W. *Becoming: Basic Considerations for a Psychology of Personality.* New Haven: Yale University Press, 1955.

2. Aurelius, Marcus. *Meditations,* translated by A. S. K. Farquharson. London: J. M. Dent & Sons Ltd., 1961.

3. Basowitz, Harold, Harold Persky, Sheldon J. Korchin and Roy R. Grinker. *Anxiety and Stress.* New York: McGraw-Hill, 1955.

4. Bendig, A. W. "The Development of a Short Form of the Manifest Anxiety Scale." *Journal of Consulting Psychology,* Vol. 20 (1956), p. 384.

5. Berger, Peter L. and Thomas Luckmann. *The Social Construction of Reality.* Garden City: Anchor Books, 1967.

6. Berthoff, Rowland. *An Unsettled People: Social Order and Disorder in American History.* New York: Harper & Row, 1971.

7. Bettelheim, Bruno. "The Problem of Generations," in Erik H. Erikson (ed.), *The Challenge of Youth.* Garden City: Anchor Books, 1965.

8. Blumer, Herbert. "Sociological Implications of the Thought of George Herbert Mead." *American Journal of Sociology,* Vol. 71 (1966), pp. 535–544.

9. Butterfield, Herbert. *Christianity and History.* London: Fontana Books, 1949.

10. Calhoun, Daniel H. *Professional Lives in America: Structure and Aspiration: 1750–1850.* Cambridge, Mass.: Harvard University Press, 1965.

11. Cross, Whitney R. *The Burned-Over District.* New York: Harper & Row, 1950.

12. Davis, David Brion. "Some Ideological Functions of Prejudice in Ante-Bellum America," *American Quarterly,* Vol. 15 (1963), pp. 115–125.

13. Davis, David Brion. "Some Themes of Counter-Subversion: An Analysis of Anti-Masonic, Anti-Catholic, and Anti-Mormon Literature," in Frank Otto Gatell (ed.), *Essays on Jacksonian America.* New York: Holt, Rinehart and Winston, Inc., 1970.

14. Donald, David. *Lincoln Reconsidered.* New York: Harper & Row, 1965.

15. Freehling, William W. *Prelude to Civil War.* New York: Harper & Row, 1965.

16. Gardner, John. *Self-Renewal: The Individual and the Innovative Society.* New York: Harper & Row, 1963.

17. Gatell, Frank Otto, and John M. McFaul (eds.). *Jacksonian America: 1815–1840*. Englewood Cliffs: Prentice-Hall, Inc., 1970.

18. Handlin, Oscar. *Boston's Immigrants*. New York: Atheneum, 1969.

19. Handlin, Oscar and Mary Handlin. *The Dimensions of Liberty*. Cambridge, Mass.: Harvard University Press, 1961.

20. Heale, M. J. "The New York Society for the Prevention of Pauperism, 1817–1823." *New York Historical Quarterly*, Vol. 55 (1971), pp. 153–176.

21. Hebb, D. O. "The Mammal and His Environment," in Eleanor E. Maccoby, Theodore M. Newcomb, and Eugene L. Hartley (eds.), *Readings in Social Psychology*. New York: Holt, Rinehart and Winston, 1958.

22. Hoffer, Eric. *The Ordeal of Change*. New York: Harper & Row, 1952.

23. Hurst, James Willard. *Law and the Conditions of Freedom in the Nineteenth Century United States*. Madison: University of Wisconsin Press, 1964.

24. Inkeles, Alex. "The Modernization of Man," in M. Weiner (ed.), *Modernization: The Dynamics of Growth*. New York: Basic Books, 1966.

25. Janis, Irving L. *Psychological Stress*. New York: John Wiley & Sons, 1958.

26. Kirk, H. David. "The Impact of Drastic Change on Social Relations: A Model for the Identification and Specification of Stress," in George K. Zollschan and Walter Hirsch (eds.), *Explorations in Social Change*. Boston: Houghton Mifflin, 1964.

27. LaPiere, Richard T. *Social Change*. New York: McGraw-Hill, 1965.

28. Lerner, Daniel. *The Passing of Traditional Society*. New York: Free Press, 1958.

29. Levine, Sol, and Norman A. Scotch (eds.). *Social Stress*. Chicago: Aldine Publishing Co., 1970.

30. Lifton, Robert J. "Individual Patterns in Historical Change: Imagery of Japanese Youth," in S. N. Eisenstadt (ed.), *Comparative Perspectives on Social Change*. Boston: Little, Brown & Company, 1968.

31. Lloyd, P. C. *Africa in Social Change*. Middlesex, England: Penguin Books, 1969.

32. Mead, Margaret (ed.). *Cultural Patterns and Technical Change*. New York: Mentor Books, 1955.

33. Mead, Margaret. *New Lives For Old: Cultural Transformation — Manus, 1928–1953*. New York: William Morrow and Company, 1966.

34. Mechanic, David, and Edmund H. Volkart. "Stress, Illness Behavior, and the Sick Role," *American Sociological Review*, Vol. 26 (1961), pp. 51–58.

35. Meyers, Marvin. *The Jacksonian Persuasion*. Stanford: Stanford University Press, 1957.

36. Miller, Douglas T. *Jacksonian Aristocracy*. New York: Oxford University Press, 1967.

37. Miller, Perry. *The Life of the Mind in America*. New York: Harcourt, Brace and World, Inc., 1965.

38. Nisbet, Robert A. *Social Change and History*. New York: Oxford University Press, 1969.

39. Pessen, Edward. *Jacksonian America: Society, Personality, and Politics.* Homewood: The Dorsey Press, 1969.

40. Pyle, Kenneth B. *The New Generation in Meiji Japan.* Stanford: Stanford University Press, 1969.

41. Rahe, Richard, Joseph D. McKean, Jr., and Ranson J. Arthur. "A Longitudinal Study of Life-Change and Illness Patterns." *Journal of Psychomatic Research,* Vol. 10 (1967), pp. 355–366.

42. Richards, Leonard L. *Gentlemen of Property and Standing: Anti-Abolition Mobs in Jacksonian America.* New York: Oxford University Press, 1970.

43. Rothman, David J. *The Discovery of the Asylum: Social Order and Disorder in the New Republic.* Boston: Little, Brown and Company, 1971.

44. Sharp, Lauriston. "Steel Axes for Stone Age Australians," in Edward H. Spicer (ed.), *Human Problems in Technological Change.* New York: Russell Sage Foundation, 1952.

45. Shibutani, Tamotsu. *Society and Personality.* Englewood Cliffs: Prentice-Hall, Inc., 1961.

46. Smelser, Neil J. *Social Change in the Industrial Revolution.* Chicago: The University of Chicago Press, 1959.

47. Smith, Timothy. *Revivalism and Social Reform.* New York: Harper & Row, 1965.

48. Sorokin, Pitirim A. *The Crisis of our Age.* New York: E. P. Dutton & Co., Inc., 1942.

49. Spicer, Edward H. *Human Problems in Technological Change.* New York: Russell Sage Foundation, 1952.

50. Taylor, Janet A. "A Personality Scale of Manifest Anxiety," *Journal of Abnormal and Social Psychology,* Vol. 48 (1953), pp. 285–290.

51. Taylor, William R. *Cavalier and Yankee.* New York: Harper & Row, 1967.

52. Tocqueville, Alexis de. *Democracy in America,* translated by George Lawrence. Garden City: Anchor Books, 1969.

53. Toffler, Alvin. *Future Shock.* New York: Random House, 1970.

54. Woods, John. *Two Years Residence on the English Prairie of Illinois.* Chicago: R. R. Donnelley and Sons, Co., 1822.

55. Zollschan, George K., and Philip Gibeau, "Concerning Alienation: A System of Categories for the Exploration of Rational and Irrational Behavior," in George K. Zollschan and Walter Hirsch (eds.), *Exploration in Social Change,* Boston: Houghton Mifflin Company, 1964.

56. Zollschan, George K. and Walter Hirsch (eds.), *Explorations in Social Change.* Boston: Houghton Mifflin Company, 1964.

# SECTION SIX

## broad historical perspectives
## on change

# Introduction

A few years before his death Albert Einstein remarked ruefully that when he was a young man he could easily keep up with developments in the entire field of physics, but at the end of his career he could not even assimilate what was going on in the area of his special competence. In spite of the relatively recent birth of sociology its practitioners are also faced with the specter of specialization: several generations ago even great scholars like Max Weber were castigated for their inadequate grasp of specialized historical materials. One possible solution to the problem is interdisciplinary team work — an approach which however raises additional questions relating to creative scholarship. Yet even at this stage of development of the social sciences there are men willing and able to sacrifice the safety of specialization for a greater though riskier task. In this section, we present authors who may be said to stand with one foot in the realm of the traditional *Geisteswissenschaften*, and the other in the realm of contemporary social science. We need not review here the controversies about the differences between history and sociology; suffice it to say our authors do not believe history is "just one damned thing after another," nor that contemporary social changes can be adequately conceptualized and described without a knowledge of past events.

Future students of the history of sociology (and some present ones as well) will not find it difficult to show that "it is no accident" that a veritable Sorokin revival is taking place at this time. The "dialogue" between Schneider and Sorokin which initiates this Section is ample evidence of the viability of Sorokin's contribution to the study of large-scale sociological change. Like all "grand theorists," Sorokin has to pay the price for the grandeur of his enterprise, and although Schneider does not insist on exacting the last ounce of flesh, neither is he willing to let Sorokin get away with logical inconsistencies or doubtful empirical documentation.

Schneider sees Sorokin's major contribution in his use of the dialectical mode of analysis, but at the same time he seeks to show that more explicit and rigorous use can be made of this method. (Our readers will note the ubiquity of the dialectical approach throughout this volume.) Schneider is critical of Sorokin's triad of the major cultural systems, including his tendency to fall back upon the invocation of what in pre-social science days would have been called the *zeitgeist*. Among the many problems raised by Schneider we may single out one which has an important bearing on the analysis of social systems at the "micro" as well as the "macro" level — the relation between the degree of integration of a system and its ability to withstand disruptive influences from without. Here, as in several other instances, Schneider proposes an alternative hypothesis to Sorokin's "self-evident" axioms.

Sorokin, in his characteristic "inner-directed" and vigorous manner stands up to Schneider's criticisms, and we leave the reader to decide who has the better of the intellectual combat. Let us simply add our own adage to that with which Sorokin is pleased to call his "yarns": "Si monumentum requiris, circumspice!" (Poppendieck's chapter in Section 8 applies Sorokin's concepts to the contemporary scene. Unfortunately his passing away does not allow for another confrontation, but we should like to think that he would have been pleased by the continued relevance of his analysis of the death rattle of sensate culture and the birth pangs of a new super-system.)

Martindale's analysis can be conceived of as an exercise in the sociology of knowledge. He starts out with two sets of "perspectives": the individualist-collectivist and the humanistic-scientific, which serve as the matrix within which sociology develops, along with other systems of thought. In so doing he takes account of both the "immanent" changes within the discipline and of the "existential conditions" which impinge upon the growth and decline and permutations of various combinations of the perspectives. He then proceeds to close the circle by showing how subtypes within the matrix of perspectives have developed from the impact of the preceding interactions.

Martindale's procedure tends to be more empirically oriented than Sorokin's in several respects, and avoids some of the question-begging aspects which Schneider criticizes in Sorokin's approach. Thus, Martindale adduces specific reasons for his assertion that "sociology arose under conditions which virtually guaranteed that it would be a form of scientism," rather than falling back upon a generalized "sensate factor." Similarly, in discussing contemporary sociological frames of reference he shows that the reaction against "scientific collectivism" may take the alternate forms of either existentialism, with its individualistic orientation, or of "humanistic collectivism." Whether or not one accepts Martindale's formulation, it is evident that he has gone far beyond the facile proposition that there are "two cultures" which are either at war or exist in blissful ignorance of each other. If nothing else, he makes plain that there is a "third culture" with some claim to recognition, along with the natural sciences and the humanities. (In several respects this chapter has anticipated the current *Kulturkampf* about the "true" methods and goals of sociology. Zollschan and Brym's analysis of the possibilities of a scientific sociology in Section 2 is highly relevant to this discussion).

Hoselitz jumps across disciplinary fences to investigate the role of social values in economic growth. He considers the Weberian dichotomy of traditional and rational systems, and the assumption of a unilinear historical change from the former to the latter as inadequate for a description of the multiform behavior patterns actually or potentially existing. Consequently he adds another continuum, borrowed from F.C.S. Northrop, with western "theoretical" and oriental "aesthetic" belief systems at its poles. He then proceeds to use the resulting fourfold table as an instrument for the delineation of the conditions under which various combinations of value systems may produce maximum economic performance. Hoselitz invokes a "feedback" mechanism; that is, he considers the impact which economic behavior has on the prevailing value system and vice versa. He is concerned with the fact that value systems and technology do not change at the same rate, and with the differences in values and attitudes among various segments of the population.

# 21

*Louis Schneider*

# Toward Assessment of Sorokin's
# View of Change

Pitirim A. Sorokin's *Social and Cultural Dynamics* is certainly one of the most interesting, as it is one of the most elaborate, efforts of a contemporary sociologist to analyze socio-cultural change. But it is not an easy effort to assess. It is spread over nearly 3,000 pages. It contains material of very varying value, ranging through both doubtful and suggestive statistical data and exhibiting both a determined effort to fit cultural materials into a certain framework, come what may, and inordinately acute and illuminating observations on philosophic, scientific, and religious positions that have been held from antiquity on. Sorokin himself refers (23, vol. 1, p. 84; vol. 4, p. 65, p. 755) to an interesting work by Wilhelm Ostwald[1] in which the latter distinguishes between classical and romantic types of scientists, the main point of differentiation between the two, from which in Ostwald's view others follow, being speed of reaction. The classical type is slow and the romantic fast. The great speed of reaction of the romantic type occasions much breadth of interest, abundance of ideas, and high productivity. The romantic is also less likely than the classical type to tidy up ideas very carefully and present them solely in finished form. Ostwald contends that a greatly effective stimulator of science in the field of sociology can scarcely be conceived as other than a romantic type, while a romantic type of mathematician is precluded, although there were still such mathematicians in the nineteenth century. Whether Ostwald is right on this last

[1] The reference is to (16, esp. pp. 371–378).

point or not, Sorokin certainly appears to incline toward the romantic side. The consequence is that the would-be critic, unless he has a range comparable with Sorokin's and the space of a sizable monograph at his disposal, confronted as he is with a tremendous quantity of material, sometimes superb in quality and sometimes exasperatingly defective, soon finds himself utterly frustrated unless he chooses to confine himself to a decidedly limited number of things.

The decision to be very selective in the present effort at assessment of Sorokin's work has perforce been made. At the same time, no attempt to assess the contribution of the work as a whole to the theory of socio-cultural change can afford to bypass its central features. The best solution I can offer is to treat Sorokin's work in rather broad terms as presenting two main aspects: a perspective on change which, following Sorokin's own usage, will be designated as dialectical; and a view of culture and the movement of western history set out in the well-known language Sorokin employs: the language of "Sensate," "Ideational," and "Idealistic" culture forms. If a great deal is necessarily bypassed by treating the work in this way, at least the procedure allows a clear statement of the theme of this chapter, which is basically quite simple. The theme is that Sorokin's main contribution to the analysis of change lies in his employment of a dialectical approach to change, that this approach has significant foundations in the history of social science and is susceptible of further development, and that this approach, finally, can be seen as largely independent of the merits or shortcomings of Sorokin's contentions with regard to the triad of cultural forms which he sees as central in the socio-cultural realm. Some scepticism about the latter contentions will be expressed.

Two other things should be said at this point. First, much of the peculiar character of the present chapter is to be explained by the circumstance that it is conceived as an item in a kind of debate with Sorokin, while at the same time it is addressed to a wider audience. Thus, for example, a brief summary of the main theme of the *Dynamics* follows. Sorokin hardly needs instruction in the content of his own major work. Readers, on the other hand, may be unfamiliar with it in varying degrees and may find a résumé helpful in following the subsequent argument. Also, it will be noted that the chapter has been entitled "Toward Assessment." A "definitive" evaluation of Sorokin's work is not even remotely thought of for present purposes, if this is not already sufficiently clear. It will be enough if the chapter in some degree sharpens a few of the questions that must be asked about his theory of socio-cultural change. Procedurally, the chapter goes on from the summary of Sorokin's argument to a discussion of dialectic and change and then to some observations on Sorokin's culture forms and a few final words toward assessment.

### The Argument of the *Dynamics*

A culture, for Sorokin, is above all a system of meanings organized about and to an appreciable extent (not wholly) derivable from premises about the character of ultimate reality. What Sorokin calls logico-meaningful method is in his view accordingly necessary for the comprehension of culture, and the method is designed to probe for "the central principle (the 'reason') which permeates all the components" of a culture, "gives sense and significance to them, and in this way makes cosmos of a chaos of unintegrated fragments" (23, vol. 1, p. 32).[2] Actually existing empirical cultures will never show perfect integration. The central principle(s) will *not* be all-pervasive. Empirical cultures are, rather, likely to represent some degree of fusion of or compromise on premises not completely reconcilable. However, it does appear that there are two main empirical cultural forms that show considerable integration or consistency, and one compromising or intermediate or synthetic form that shows sufficient stability (although it is less stable than the other two) to be fairly readily discernible as at least an incident in the alternations of the other two main forms in the course of Western history since the Greeks. The two main forms are Sensate and Ideational culture; the intermediate form is Idealistic.

A major premise of Sensate culture — indeed, it is fair to say, *the* major premise — is that "reality" is what can be perceived by the sense organs and that there is no reality beyond this. In Ideational culture, on the other hand, reality is taken as non-Sensate and non-material, as a form of transcendent or everlasting Being. While Sensate culture is concentrated upon this world and its goods and engaged in striving in and with this world, for Ideational culture this world is snare and delusion, and the man cognizant of true reality will disdain it. Sensate culture (at least in its Active form) typically seeks to solve a variety of problems presented by and in this world by onslaught on the world itself and modification thereof, as it might try to solve a public health problem by improving sanitation. Ideational culture seeks to solve a variety of problems less by onslaught on the world than by addressing the human agent who faces the world, as it might try to solve a public health problem by fortifying the inner man in a conviction that health is in any case ultimately vanity and a this-worldly good with which one should not have excessive concern. The intermediate Idealistic culture by definition compromises on or fuses or synthesizes the distinctive outlooks of the other two. In detail, Sorokin discriminates seven types, but he is ordinarily preoccupied with the three main ones.[3]

---

[2] The quoted words are italicized in the original.

[3] Within Ideationalism, Active is distinguished from Ascetic Ideationalism. The latter is bent upon maximizing spiritual ends and minimizing carnal ones and seeking detachment from this world. The former, while sympathetic with ascetic impulse,

The culture forms or types are recurrent in history. Hence a characterization such as Sensate will be applied to the early centuries of Greek culture *and* to the period roughly between Alexander the Great and the fourth century A.D. *and* to the West from about the beginning of the thirteenth century until the present. The three main types follow one another in what Sorokin regards as a rather reliable sequence, such that Sensate will be followed by Ideational and the latter by Idealistic culture forms and so on. Since early Greek times, western culture has completed two cycles of this sequence and is ostensibly in the Sensate and perhaps already even incipiently Ideational phase of a third. (We are at present destined to live in a time of Sensate decline, amid wars and rumors of wars and numerous other untoward circumstances, but Sorokin's "pessimism" is only interim, for he believes he already discerns the outlines of a new Ideational culture to be the possession of western man.) A very large portion of the *Dynamics* is devoted to tracing fluctuations in a variety of fields, from the arts to forms of social relationships, in the double sequence in western history of Sensate-Ideational-Idealistic. The "portions" or "sectors" (art, religion, science, etc.) of the cultures developmentally traced are in at least rough accord with one another, "integrated" and informed by dominant outlooks (as Sensate outlooks). They are also more or less temporally aligned with one another.

All cultural forms are in endless flux. And they change by what Sorokin regards as a kind of inner destiny. Thus, integrated cultural systems "change according to the course of life which is predetermined for them by their very nature." Or as regards a single system, Sorokin asserts that "at a certain point in its history (slightly accelerated or retarded by . . . external circumstances) the cultural system must undergo its inwardly ordained change." And again he avers that "a cultural system has its own logic of functioning, change, and destiny, which is a result not only

seeks to change the world of culture and society by moving it toward the demands of the spirit; it is bent on the salvation of others as well as the self and must operate in the world. Within Sensate culture, Active Sensate, Passive Sensate, and Cynical Sensate forms exist. The first transforms the outer world and is exemplified by the outlooks and actions of the great executives, conquerors, and empire-builders. The second takes the world as a set of given instrumentalities for the enhancement of sensual pleasures. The last encourages hypocritical conformity and quick "adjustment" in any direction that will "pay off." The intermediate Idealistic form gives a sixth type. And Sorokin adduces a Pseudo-Ideational form. For the Pseudo-Ideational culture mentality, which is "unintegrated," needs and ends are predominantly physical and reality is largely felt as Sensate. The mode of satisfaction of needs is "neither an active modification of the milieu to any appreciable degree, nor a free modification of self, nor a search for pleasure, nor successful hypocrisy." Representatives of this culture mentality are imposed upon by an external agency which they cannot resist. Slaves working under cruel conditions and harshly dominated persons in general exemplify this mentality or cultural form (see 23, vol. 1, p. 76).

(and regularly not so much) of the external conditions, but of its own nature" (23, vol. 1, p. 50, p. 51, p. 53). This view is often reiterated. It is in virtue of the principle of immanent change that "each of the three integrated forms, or phases, of the Ideational, Idealistic and Sensate supersystems cannot help changing; rising, growing, existing full-blooded for some time, and then declining" (23, vol. 4, p. 737).[4] Sorokin relies on the notion of the immanent necessity of change and on the notion of limited possibilities to account for change and recurrence. As regards limited possibilities, he believes that there are only five basic answers to the question of the nature of true reality — that it is supersensory; that it is sensory; that it is supersensory-sensory; that it is unknown and unknowable; that it is phenomenally known and transcendentally unknowable (23, vol. 4, p. 738). Cultural systems must change, but as they change they are confronted only with limited possibilities soon enough exhausted. Hence change as it goes on must involve recurrence.

It is also true that cultural systems are internally constrained by a principle of limit. A certain kind of truth, by way of example, will stand only so much stress and development. It becomes richer and more productive up to a point and produces good sounds, as it were, up to that point, but beyond that it becomes decreasingly productive and emits bad or feeble sounds or none at all. Cultures are indissolubly wedded to systems of "ultimate" truth. Again they appear as phenomena that develop from premises about true or ultimate reality. The cognitive character of culture could hardly be contended for more emphatically. Each of the three main systems of truth (the first three of the above five) is in the end "partly true and partly false, partly adequate and partly inadequate," and the same kind of assertion is applicable to the culture associated with it. As a cultural system rises and becomes powerful and monopolistic, "its false part tends to grow, while its valid part tends to decrease." Indeed, the system becomes more and more "inadequate," and inadequacy, although undoubtedly intended in a philosophical sense, is clearly also intended in an "institutional" sense, for Sorokin writes that, with inadequacy, the system "becomes less and less capable of serving as an instrument of adaptation, as an experience for real satisfaction of the needs of its bearers; and as a foundation for their social and cultural life" (23, vol. 4, pp. 742–743). The time comes when the false outweigh the true parts of the system. The dominant system, as it were compulsively exaggerating, and thereby in an ultimate view distorting, the portion of truth of which it has hold, immanently prepares its own demise and clears the path for one of the rival systems. "All the forms of truth are subject to . . . 'dialectical destiny' and are hardly exempt from a self-preparation of their own decline in the course of their development" (23, vol. 2, pp. 121–122).

---

[4] Italicized in original.

### Dialectic and Change

It is not by accident that the above summary has been ended with a quotation relating to "dialectic." I hold to the view that it is in connection with dialectical notions that Sorokin makes his largest contribution to the theory of change — at the very least in a *sociological* perspective. There is one other line of thought with regard to change (aside from the whole matter of the Sensate-Ideational-Idealistic forms and recurrences) which is arguably quite important in Sorokin's work, namely, his treatment of the relations of vehicles, agents, and meanings, but even this is in part handled dialectically, as will appear below.[5] The object of the present section is to stress Sorokin's own dialectical bent and to suggest, by reference, at least, to some of the more obvious sources, that this bent has been and continues to be an important one in the history of both social and specifically sociological thought. Also, I want to stress that dialectical insight is in principle subject to further development. And the dialectical stress is not an *incidental* part of Sorokin's work. As the above has, it may be hoped, already made clear to some extent and as should become clearer shortly, dialectical argument is a very significant aspect of what Sorokin has to say.

Certain understandings are needed with regard to what is done in the present section. Dialectic is taken in a rather "de-philosophized," even, if the reader will, in a "naive" sense and with an admitted "social science" bias.[6] It is taken as a set of insights with regard to how change takes place, although it is not necessary to argue that *all* change must have dialectical form. It is taken, in particular, as a set of insights, then, with respect to the *manner* of socio-cultural change. It is taken heuristically or, in a loose sense of the term, experimentally, and most certainly not as a set of revealed truths. It is *not* taken as something that can perform all the functions of a rounded sociological theory of change. That would be quite impossible. Indeed, the severance I suggest between dialectical thought in Sorokin and the latter's conception of the Ideational, Sensate, and Idealistic would seriously affect the structure of the *Dynamics* as a

---

[5] On vehicles, agents, and meanings, not only the *Dynamics* should be consulted but also other work of Sorokin's, particularly the brief but very able presentation in (21, pp. 51–63).

[6] In other words, there is much of the historic philosophical background of the whole notion of dialectic which is given no room in the conception here set out. This is quite deliberately done, but it does not mean that I would necessarily contend that various philosophical problems not touched upon here, but often touched upon in connection with some past presentations of dialectic, are either useless or reducible to sociological propositions or insights. Thus, in the past the notion of dialectic has at times been associated with critical stances toward existing schemes of society and culture. Whether these stances were justifiable or not, I would regard any effort to *dissolve* ethical standpoints by tracing them to such social foundations as they may have as a particularly unfortunate form of "sociologism."

sociological theory of culture (or as a "philosophy of history"); I have no doubt whatever that he will be inclined to resist the severance precisely on this ground, if on no other. Dialectic, as here understood, definitely cannot perform a variety of significant functions. But it can perform some others, and, if it is indeed susceptible of further development in heuristic use, I suggest that it may in time become a very useful instrument, conceivably even of greater help in the formulation of more or less rounded sociological theories than appears likely at first blush. Finally, the meaning here attached to the notion of dialectic need not be formally announced as a prelude to the argument, but may be allowed to "unfold" in due course.

As it happens, in Sorokin the dialectical outlook may be said to develop in three phases. This is only a rough view of the matter, but it seems to me useful in following the trend of his thought. The first phase perhaps has no necessary connection with dialectic, but it is unmistakably present and significant in Sorokin's work and it could very easily be one important source of motivation for adopting a dialectical outlook, even if it does not "determine" such an outlook. It may be called a phase of *general vision of change*. (The other phases may be called *dialectical bent or bias* and *stress on dialectically relevant mechanisms*.) In the phase of general vision of change, Sorokin's view is indeed a broad, general one, as it is also a very old one. It ultimately comes to an insistence that the things of this sensory realm are transitory. This sometimes appears tinged with a suggestion of near-melancholy and it evidently gives Sorokin a special sympathy with Ideational outlooks that point toward "the eternal" and away from the circumstances of this evanescent world. The insistence undoubtedly antedates the Buddha, who, however, provides a very clear statement of it and already affords it in such fashion as to shadow forth the second phase just mentioned. Thus, the Buddha is represented in an eloquent rendering of his life as saying to his favored disciple Ananda, as that life draws to an end: "But now, Ananda, was I not wont to declare to you that in the very nature of things we must separate ourselves from all things that are near and dear to us, and leave them? For how, Ananda, can it be otherwise? Everything whatsoever that is born, brought into being, and organized, carries within itself the inherent need for dissolution. How therefore can such things not be dissolved? Ananda, it must be so" (2, p. 44).

The Buddha thus not only expresses a view of the transitoriness of the things of this sensory realm, including humans, but refers to "inherent dissolution." In all Sorokin's central theses about change, amid all his elaborations, it is certainly not difficult to discern his general vision by the light of which all systems to be found in this world are involved in endless change, renewal, and decay; but he also has given marked stress to immanent or "inherent" dissolution of systems. One of the indicators and components of dialectical thought as here understood is a pronounced readiness to exploit the possibilities of "immanentalist" views of change. Further, in dialectical perspective, change works by processes such that we can see that the seed of death is in the thrust of life and the price of success is failure. (The "poetry" here involved does not inhibit the possible conversion of statements such as these into sociologically significant propositions.) Sorokin would agree that in the inner development of a system the very component that originally guarantees the system viability or success may become the source of its downfall or destruction (and sometimes he would undoubtedly say *must* rather than *may*, for, as in the case of a culture's system of truth, he would insist that its hold of a portion of truth would bring it "success" but the further development of the very component guaranteeing success would bring "failure" or downfall). He concurs with Marx in the view that "the capitalist system bears within itself the seeds of its own destruction," perhaps less because he has various specifically Marxian leanings than because he thinks this kind of assertion is safely made about any system. And he notes also his agreement with the claim of "the dialectic logic" that "every concept contains in itself its own negation, that in its full form any concept is a *coincidentia oppositorum* . . . that a thesis passes into its antithesis and this into a synthesis which as a new thesis contains again its antithesis and passes into it" (21, p. 327, fn. 3, p. 704).

This kind of statement makes it easy to infer that the Sensate-Ideational-Idealistic triad was originally conceived as a form of thesis-antithesis-synthesis. But such observations are of limited utility, and it will be more helpful to adduce some of the detail of dialectical process Sorokin offers when he deals with somewhat less ambitiously large entities and phenomena, or at least with other phenomena even if they may be said to be equally "large." In the following illustrative matter from Sorokin's work it will be quite evident that he is well launched beyond his general vision of change and into the phase of dialectical bent or bias. The third phase of stress on dialectically relevant mechanisms is also, at the very least, adumbrated in some of the following. What is meant by the third phase is simply this: it is possible to stop at a still rather vaguely "poetic" or "general" level in the course of dialectical thought; but to take dialectical hints and insights seriously for purposes of sociological analysis is to go on beyond this level and examine in rigorous detail how a dialectical movement takes place. Thus, I argue in the first illustration from Sorokin that follows that in effect he approaches the phase of stress on dialectically relevant mechanisms by indicating that the immanent movement from Ascetic Ideational to Active Ideational culture discernibly operates in a *variety* of ways. In the third phase, the hard work of "locking in" dialectical mechanisms is done (insofar as it *can* be done, so that the *probability* of "escape" from dialectical effect becomes low, other things being equal) through careful and comprehensive specification of how the dialectical movement occurs.

What follows represents a selection from Sorokin's work and does not offer an exhaustive view of instances of his dialectical perspective on change.

1) Sorokin contends that "it is the tragic and immanent destiny of the Ascetic Ideational culture system to turn into the Active Ideational." As the followers of an Ascetic Ideational way increase and an organization arises, organizational necessities impose "the world," and, with organization, there comes movement toward the Active Ideational.[7] For success in the world, some of the ways of the world must be adopted, and these are bound to compromise or endanger the original ascetic ideals: "When we read about the activities of St. Paul, the great organizer of Christianity, we notice at once how he had to busy himself with worldly matters and how the empirical world caught him more and more in its web . . . most of the matters in which his flock involved him, from riots and politics to property and wealth, were of this world" (23, vol. 1, pp. 135–136). This is *one* way, one mechanism, whereby Ascetic Ideationalism turns into its "opposite," the Active variant. If it had no worldly "success," this transformation would not occur. What appears to be a somewhat different mechanism comes from the circumstance that saints can and often do become objects of veneration that draw crowds, stimulate markets and trade, and create prosperity, so that thereby asceticism is again jeopardized or destroyed (23, vol. 3, pp. 223–224). The contrast need not be over-strained, but there is evidently a difference between a situation in which there is a threat to the asceticism of men who themselves become directly involved in organizational circumstance and one in which the total quantum of asceticism is reduced by unforeseen consequences of saintliness even if the saints themselves remain intact. A third mechanism is suggested by the view that large numbers of followers cannot in any case attain or long remain at the Ascetic Ideational level (23, vol. 1, p. 135). Success of a church or religion brings increase of adherents, but the increase guarantees that that to which there is adherence will change significantly.[8] Sorokin is clearly probing for a "full" specification of the meaning of his proposition about Ascetic and Ideational culture. Yet just here he offers little that would suggest specific dialectically relevant mechanisms. Do masses flatly reject prophets? Are kindly leaders perhaps indulgent of ignorance, lack of understanding, and inveterate magical bias until there is a certain fatal cumulation

[7] Cf. the stimulating discussion by Thomas F. O'Dea (15).

[8] This theme has been developed in the specific sphere of religion by Gustav Mensching. See (13, pp. 132–160). Mensching argues (p. 155): "We must . . . take into consideration an inner dialectic of universal religion. On the one hand, universal religion, as its name indicates, aspires to make good its universal claim through the greatest possible expansion and thereby through incorporation of the masses. But on the other hand this expansion is possible only at the price of the depth and distinctiveness of the high religion — and in turn this outcome produces criticism and protest from the side of pure high religion."

of consequences? The dialectical bias has to pay its way by presentation and analysis of dialectically relevant mechanisms. (Even these simple questions may be allowed to indicate that the bias is "sensitizing" and susceptible of elaboration through examination of specific mechanisms.) Sorokin is, I believe, already effectively aware of this necessity, although he gives it no formal stress.[9] (But questions of empirical accuracy arise here also. Do masses simply "degenerate" a religion or does a religion perhaps serve in some degree to "raise them up?")

2) In further illustration of his dialectical bent, Sorokin *generalizes* the assertion about the involvement of failure in the success of religion or church. He claims that like phenomena are at work far beyond the sphere of religion alone. Thus: "Quantitative success of almost any system of meanings is bought at the cost of its identity, purity, and adequacy." Or: "Qualitatively, the greatest religious, philosophical, ethical, scientific, or artistic systems are at their best and purest when their followers are limited to a small group of faithful, competent, and understanding apostles. When they are diffused among vast millions, their purity, verity, adequacy is lost, disfigured, and vulgarized." And again Sorokin writes of "the tragedy of vulgarization and decisive disfiguring of any complex and great and sublime system of cultural values when it infiltrates and roots itself among the large masses." He adds: "Such a success is invariably bought at the cost of . . . simplification and distortion" (23, vol. 4, p. 82, p. 84, p. 259, fn. 83). Sorokin does not push these rather general observations into the area of dialectically relevant mechanisms, nor does he care to make the obvious point that democratic concern might well seek ways to blunt the effects he observes and thereby come upon close acquaintance with relevant mechanisms, but it would be easy enough to outline a few such mechanisms and it is not unreasonable to suppose that analysis of the workings of mass culture will in time yield a large number of them. (There does still remain a question of empirical accuracy. "Dialectic" must not beguile us into inaccurate or incomplete views. Sorokin is, one may suggest, too inclined to see only "bad" effects from popularization.)

3) Even before widespread adoption of a religion, doctrine, art form, or the like has occurred, there are at work processes that subtly change the cultural phenomena of doctrine or form or the like, in Sorokin's view. There is a "tragedy of culture" which shades into the tragedy of popularization and is connected with the latter in that popularization may greatly enhance it, but it is not the same as the tragedy of popularization. Sorokin's position here may be put as follows. "Pure" cultural phenomena, to have effect in the world, need some kind of initial "embodiment" (and socialization or diffusion). The embodiment is vehicular, i.e., in the form of what Sorokin calls "vehicles." Language functions as

---

[9] (23, vol. 3, pp. 221–224) seems to me to reinforce this assertion.

a vehicle when, say, the inventor of an idea gives it its first embodiment in words (and its first socialization and diffusion to another) by expounding it to a friend. "Pure" cultural meanings are constantly influenced by the vehicles used to carry them. Language as a vehicle has its inadequacies and human agents have their imperfections, and cultural systems in their "pure" form are subject to the inadequacies and imperfections. One may say that culture is, paradoxically, "imperfectly" realized because the vehicles it must have to be other than pure, to be involved in empirical human existence, change it and decrease its original purity. In this connection, it has constantly to be kept in view that not only does culture influence vehicles but vehicles influence culture. An elevated conception of a deity may suggest an originally symbolically conceived artistic representation of that deity, but the representation may quickly become an idol worshipped for itself and, so treated, influence the initial lofty conception retroactively. This suggests the process when it is perhaps already far advanced in vulgarization, but it may serve to clarify Sorokin's basic notion. "Defeat" of pure culture may occur just at that point of "success" where it finds a vehicle, or at the point where the vehicle begins to influence that which it conveys.

Sorokin, also, refers to Simmel in this general connection and apparently takes the phrase "tragedy of culture" from a paper by the latter (20, pp. 236–267). Simmel's paper is concerned with the "alienation" between man or personality and "objectified spirit." He examines this alienation in some detail and is especially concerned with what he regards as the circumstance that the realm of cultural objects has "its own logic of development." He gives the case of a writer's having proposed a riddle with a specific solution when another solution should be found, fully as apt and meaningful as the writer's own. The latter becomes just as "correct" as the writer's and exists as "ideal objectivity." "As soon as our work," Simmel says, "stands out, it has not only objective existence and a life of its own, which have detached themselves from ourselves, but it contains in this self-sufficiency strengths and weaknesses, components and significances, for which we are not accountable and by which we ourselves are often surprised." There thus arises opposition between man and his cultural world, and, interestingly, Simmel remarks that the "fetish-character" which Marx attributed to economic objects is but "a specially modified case of this general fate of the content of our culture" (20, pp. 259–260). Whatever the precise value of these observations of Sorokin's and Simmel's, they foreshadow the significant dialectical play whereby something generates or develops into its own "opposite" — in the specific sphere of the relation between intention and outcome, for the former often is oriented in one direction but leads to an outcome that points in a very different direction. Human intention for the cultural sphere is one thing, but that sphere has some tendency to confront man as a world he never made even if its origins in his own strivings are undeniable.

4) The third set of phenomena just referred to, then, suggests discrepancy between initial intentions and final outcomes.[10] This in turn suggests the dialectical play referred to, involving the creation of outcomes "opposite" to those intended.[11] In regard to Mandeville's paradox whereby public virtue arises out of private vice, Weber writes pertinently of "that power 'which constantly seeks the bad and constantly creates the good," (29, p. 33). Sorokin is interested in much the same thing, although he might wish to say that when, for example, he indicates how Ideationalism, despite its indifference to wealth, brings wealth into being or increases it, he is talking about a power which "constantly seeks the good and constantly creates the bad." Sorokin notes: "Like any other variable or process, Ideational and Sensate cultures generate in the course of their existence a series of characteristic consequences that follow inevitably from their individual natures. Some of these consequences may operate in the direction of weakening and destroying the culture that generates them." And he adds that "thus, in the field of economic conditions, some of the consequences of Ideational culture may, in spite of its negativistic attitude to 'prosperity,' work toward an accumulation of wealth, careful and successful organization of economic activity, and therefore toward 'prosperity'" (23, vol. 3, p. 222).[12]

The entire basic phenomenon of discrepancy between intention and outcome, between purpose and consequence, which Robert K. Merton has suggested in his phrase "the unanticipated consequences of purposive social action" (14, pp. 894–904), is of really major interest for Sorokin insofar as he is constantly concerned to note how actions undertaken in the terms of the norms and premises of one cultural system immanently generate effects that encourage movement to an "opposite" or radically different cultural system. The focus in this shifts somewhat from the matter of how success involves failure — but, clearly, only somewhat — toward the matter of how an "opposite" of a strategic element in a system arises from within the system itself. This kind of concern is also an old one on the part of social theorists. Mandeville has been mentioned in passing. Adam Smith's awareness of the discrepancy between individual intentions on the line of making profits and the general prosperity of the community that he claims comes out of the myriad individual efforts to make gain (under circumstances of order, justice, and restraint of

[10] That it suggests this to Sorokin himself is clearly indicated in the footnote in (23, vol. 4, p. 43).

[11] I mark the dialectical process (or processes) here involved without prejudice to the question of just what its (or their) status in relation to others might be found to be after intensive analysis.

[12] The treatment in (23, vol. 3, pp. 221–224) is one indication of Sorokin's interest in dialectical or dialectically relevant mechanisms.

tendency to eliminate competition) is one of the best known intellectual achievements of any social scientist. The eighteenth century was apparently quite rich in this particular cognizance of discrepancy between intention and outcome. Vico gave the discrepancy a significant twist in connection with his entire notion of "a rational civil theology of divine providence," for providence so acts that "out of the passions of men each bent on his private advantage, for the sake of which they would live like wild beasts in the wilderness, it has made the civil orders by which they may live in human society" (26, p. 56; see also pp. 3–4, p. 21, p. 210, p. 382).[13] For Turgot, also, men's "blind passions" were unwitting instrumentalities that functioned to bring about excellent ends.[14]

Sorokin's cognizance of the intention-outcome discrepancy clearly puts him in the line of a very significant tradition. Certainly, the whole notion of this discrepancy has long since been secularized: its present-day neutrality or independence in relation to theologically tinged thinking is quite plain in social science; but this does not remove the provenience of the notion in older social science. Neither in the history of social thought *nor* in Sorokin's views on socio-cultural change has the notion been an incidental one.

On broader fronts of dialectical thought, stress on dialectical modes of change again antedates Sorokin's *Dynamics* (and also postdates it). Thus, the fourth volume of the *Dynamics,* in which the theory of change is most extensively presented, is replete with references to Ibn Khaldun (the index shows eleven references), Pareto (thirteen references), and Toynbee (forty-five references). Ibn Khaldun shares Sorokin's very general vision of the impermanence of the things of this realm: "It should be known that the world of the elements and all it contains comes into being and decays." Indeed, "duration belongs to God alone." As if for good measure, Ibn Khaldun adds: "This entire world is trifling and futile. It ends in death and annihilation" (7, vol. 1, p. 278, p. 301, p. 386). But, as is well known, what is in effect clearly a dialectical view of change goes along with this. Dynasties come and go. They dissolve and rebuild in a repeated cycle from hardy desert virtues and solidarity to the decay of virtue, the development of luxurious ways of life, and financial troubles. Among other things, the dilemma of wealth for Protestant sects that Wesley and Weber recognized is foreshadowed. Conquest brings

[13] Fisch has noted that Vico's notion of a rational civil theology of divine providence may be compared with Wundt's idea of the heterogony of ends, Mandeville's private vices-public virtues, Smith's invisible hand, and Hegel's cunning of reason. He has even suggested that Vico may have been thinking of Mandeville when he averred that the public virtue of the Romans was but a good use that providence made of their "grievous, ugly and cruel private vices." See Fisch's "Introduction" to (28, pp. 54–55) and his "Introduction" to (27, p. xxxii.)

[14] The reference is to an often quoted passage in Turgot's *Oeuvres.* The passage is translated in Karl Löwith (9, p. 103). For an indication that Turgot here only states a rather general eighteenth-century theme, see F. E. Manuel (10, pp. 46–47).

wealth, but wealth breeds luxury and luxury corrupts the virtues of hardiness that enabled conquest in the first place, much as the old "Protestant" virtues of thrift, frugality, and industry were later represented to bring about a wealth that reacted disintegratingly on the virtues that produced it. That which enabled conquest in the end turns on itself when its consequences are fully developed, and a kind of dialectical suicide takes place. The flower destroys the seed from which it came. Ibn Khaldun is so keen on dialectical process and suggests it so variously that one is almost tempted to attribute to him a specific awareness of the need to go on for purposes of close analysis to the examination of dialectical or dialectically relevant mechanisms.

For Pareto, it will suffice to recall that in the circulation of elites one notable process is that whereby, once lions are in power, it becomes evident that leonine virtues are not adequate for the running of a government, and clever foxes, full of chicane, must be returned to various offices as they begin a new infiltration (changing the distribution of residues in the ruling group) that finally occasions a new lion revolt. The governmental system changes out of itself and by internal processes a governmental form constantly generates its own "opposite" (17, vol. 4).

The dialectical mode of thought is certainly not uncongenial to Toynbee. Immanent development is given its measure of stress by him also. "In demonstrating that the broken-down civilizations have not met their death from an assassin's hand . . . we have been led . . . to return a verdict of suicide." And Toynbee quotes Meredith: "In tragic life . . . no villain need be. . . . We are betrayed by what is false within." The theme of the failure of success is a very important one for Toynbee. He contends that the successful creator is handicapped by his success, and remarks that if this is true, "so that the chances are always against 'the favorite' and in favor of 'the dark horse,' " when it comes to writing a new chapter in creativity, "then it is plain that we have run to earth a very potent cause of the breakdown of civilizations." Toynbee goes on at once to note that this nemesis of creativity would operate in two ways: "On the one hand it would seriously diminish the number of candidates for playing the creator's role in the face of any given challenge, since it would tend to rule out those who responded successfully to the last challenge and these . . . were potential creators before their very success in turning promise into achievement threatened to sterilize their creativity in the act of demonstrating it." And in the second place, the past creators, by virtue of their past achievement, have come to hold "key positions where their senile impotence to create is aggravated by their lasting potency *ex officio* to thwart and hinder." (Toynbee holds that this nemesis of creativity can be averted.) This specification of two kinds of possibilities also suggests possible ease of transition to the notion of working out dialectically relevant mechanisms. Another instance of the "law" that success leads to failure (or that nothing fails like success) is found in those "fumbling and irresolute" animal adaptations which, just because they are indecisive, leave open possibilities of change and adjustment which are closed off for organisms that have worked out "perfect" and detailed solutions to particular problems in evolutionary course — and of course the "law" has its human applications of main interest to Toynbee (24, Vol. 4, p. 120, p. 259, p. 260, pp. 423 ff.)[15] For Toynbee, as for others, so very bare and partial an indication must suffice.

The dialectical approach to change as here taken exploits the possibilities of understanding change immanently. It is willing to take assertions such as "the seed of death is in the thrust of life," "the price of success is failure," or "the flower destroys the seed whence it came," and explore the prospects of developing these into sociologically relevant propositions that go carefully into the detail of what is initially intimated by rather "poetic" assertions. It involves interest, therefore, in dialectically relevant mechanisms. It is further concerned with the possibilities of understanding change suggested by notions that may be crudely rendered as follows: the very "factor" that brings strength or viability or success to a system will also bring its downfall; "elements" at work in a system are likely to engender their own "opposites" (the intention-outcome discrepancy being a special case of this); in a process of realization (as of realization of culture in the sense that it gets launched into the world through receiving vehicular expression), realization is baffled as soon as it occurs.

Sorokin's thought has been richly dialectical when dialectic is thus understood. It would also appear that this kind of thought is susceptible of further development. It postdates Sorokin's work as surely as it antedates it. Further development need not be understood as mere further illustration, which obviously would hardly be development at all, but as movement into detailed analysis of dialectically relevant mechanisms, which may also be enriched through exploration of the relations of such mechanisms to phenomena such as feedback.[16] Again, although I

[15] The points involved here have been interestingly developed by Elman R. Service, in (19, chapter 5). Service holds that "the more specialized and adapted a form in a given evolutionary stage, the smaller is its potential for passing to the next stage," and that "the evolution of species takes place *because* of adaptation; the evolution of the total system of life takes place in *spite* of adaptation." Service applies this view to socio-cultural development and accordingly writes of "the privilege of backwardness." Being unstabilized and relatively amorphous and uncommitted in ways in which more advanced countries are stabilized and specifically formed and committed, the backward country may move ahead more quickly at crucial junctures. The privilege of backwardness is inevitably reminiscent of Thorstein Veblen's idea of "the penalty of taking the lead." Cf. Veblen (25) and Dowd (3, chapters 15 and 16) for pertinent efforts to apply Veblen's ideas.

[16] Reference has been made above to the "Protestant" virtues of thrift, frugality, and industry as creating wealth that reacted disintegratingly on the virtues themselves. This is "suggestive" in regard to feedback, but my intention is not to vulgarize this now too often loosely used term.

acknowledge freely that a dialectical bent renders no rounded sociological theory, I would suggest tentatively that it may in time be more helpful for a rounded or full-scale theory, even of the "grand" type that Sorokin seeks to afford, than at first appears. Presumably no adequate view of socio-cultural change will ever develop that does not pay attention to "structures" or "forms" or the like that are in process of change. And here dialectic as it has been taken in this chapter seems not to be of much help. Yet a medical analogy, if I may be permitted it, may suggest a slightly brighter prospect. Ambitious analysts of socio-cultural change may evoke the picture of physicians who have begun to show a shrewd eye for symptoms and pathological process, who are not as yet ready to say just what the symptoms are symptoms *of* and are therefore not prepared to set out definite disease entities, but whose incipient understanding of process already gives promise that disease entities will in time be well discriminated.

If this analogy may be continued for a moment, Sorokin has already proposed "disease entities," mainly in the form of his Sensate, Ideational, and Idealistic cultures. Whether or not these are useful for purposes of sociological analysis — and this is the focus of my concern with them — it seems evident that Sorokin's illuminating work on dialectical process has no necessary relation to them, in the simple sense that one may be quite willing to explore the possibilities of a dialectical approach to change while perhaps casting about for very different "entities" from those Sorokin proposes and being measurably skeptical about the latter. It will be clear by now that I am proposing that, despite inevitable limitations, Sorokin's application of dialectic is a very considerable contribution to sociological thought. I am less sure about the contribution made by his main "entities:" [17] It is as well to turn to what I indicated, in beginning, as the second aspect of Sorokin's work.

## The Culture Forms

This section takes the form of some reservations bearing on the value, for purposes of describing and analyzing culture, of Sorokin's cultural terms or units. In one way or another, Sorokin himself concedes a good many of the difficulties that will be indicated in the following. He evidently concedes them, however, in the conviction that his basic terms or units — Ideational, Sensate, Idealistic — remain illuminating and useful. Of course, much depends on what meaning one assigns to "illuminating and useful" or like phrases. It should be clear that I am not contending in what follows that Sorokin's cultural theory is lacking in all merit.

[17] The circumstance that I am rather skeptical of Sorokin's main culture "entities" of course does not mean that I would be equally skeptical of other "entities" that have been proposed in the social sciences or in sociology in particular (and, indeed, by Sorokin himself).

This is far from true. Many of his sets of data are undoubtedly of real help in piecing out his general characterizations of culture, and his essential triad (Sensate-Ideational-Idealistic) describes many phenomena quite aptly. But no one, even today, I submit, can read, let us say, Comte's *Positive Philosophy* or his *Positive Polity* without acknowledging that the categories Comte applies to Western history "describe many phenomena aptly" (as they also fail to describe numerous other phenomena aptly). It is a measure of the standards one is tempted to bring to bear on Sorokin's work that one wants more than this from him — something closer to a rather rigorous sociological theory of culture.[18] In a mood of impatience because of a feeling that he does not offer this, one might get out of humor with him and echo Manuel, who refers to Vico's adoption of Varro's scheme of three ages of gods, heroes, and men and writes of this "rather hackneyed triad," already old in Vico's day, and "worn even thinner by a long line of philosophers of the rise, maturity, breakdown, and distintegration of nations, states, societies, civilizations" (10, p. 151). In other moods, one can certainly be more admiring. But even then reservations must be made. The following notes set out some of them under three headings.

1) The first heading may be designated as "facts and data." The task Sorokin confronts in the *Dynamics* (as well as the task of any critic) would have been considerably eased had Sorokin always had "hard" data at his disposal. I have asserted that many of his sets of data are helpful to him, as indeed they are. But there are also many occasions when he has genuine and perhaps insuperable difficulties with them. It should be pointed out that some of the easiest and most obvious criticisms of Sorokin can be levelled at the quality of his data. He tends to make the task rather easy himself by frequent acknowledgement of difficulties. (This is a merit of his work complemented by that other high merit of the relative clarity of his exposition — which involves the great advantage that his mistakes are relatively easy to discover.) But the difficulties remain, and they touch on essential themes of Sorokin's with sufficient frequency to cause him embarrassment. Comprehensive criticism of his data would be beyond the limits both of this chapter and of my competence, but I may allude to a few typical problems.

Sorokin's data on art may be cited as exemplifying some of his problems. These data are often unique, and good checks on them are gen-

---

[18] It is possible to see in the *Dynamics* elements of three kinds — "sociological" in a rather limited sense, "culture-analytical," and "philosophical" (as bearing on philosophy of history). A philosophy of history is clearly not the same as a sociology in a contemporary sense. But I am here presuming that sociological and culture-analytical enterprise can be conceived as very close to one another and that it makes sense to speak of "a sociological theory of culture." An example of the distinguished sterility that may emerge from a learned effort to fence off carefully from one another the three elements in the *Dynamics* just mentioned is afforded by Anton Hilckman, in (6, pp. 405–420).

erally not available, to the best of my knowledge. Something of the pressure the difficulties these data put upon Sorokin may be inferred from his evidently rather less than joyous comment, with respect to the materials he uses to exhibit fluctuations in Western European art, that these materials "may be unreliable but they are more reliable than any data presented up to the present time, so far as the general course of art fluctuation in the countries studied is concerned" (23, vol. 1, p. 375).[19] When discussing medieval literature from the fifth to the tenth centuries, a literature which he regards as strongly Ideational, Sorokin remarks in a footnote that "there is no doubt that on the lower levels of literature there existed a great many pagan and partly heroic, partly Sensate, and even indecent songs, poems, stories, tales. But ... these levels are beyond the scope of this work" (23, vol. 1, p. 612). Should they be beyond the *scope* of the work? Evidently one hardly proves that the most important or characteristic literature of the Middle Ages is the Ideational literature Sorokin stresses without seriously considering how important the more vulgar literature may have been. The art historian, Hauser, remarks that "even in epochs in which the most influential work is founded on a single class, and from which only the art of this class has come down to us, it ought to be asked whether the artistic products of other groups may have been buried or lost," and he adds that "in the Middle Ages the creations of secular art must have been, at any rate, more significant in relation to ecclesiastical art than the works that have survived would lead us to expect" (5, vol. 2, pp. 179–180). If fuller evidence than Sorokin affords were in fact afforded, medieval art might well appear less "monolithic" and less Ideational than he represents it to be. If we assume that there are close affinities between Sensate culture and achievement motivation, a not unreasonable assumption, there are some interesting discrepancies between Sorokin's work on Greek culture and work that has recently been presented by McClelland (12, pp. 108–129). The detail cannot be reviewed here, but it may be noted that in a period of Greek history (about 900 to 500 B.C.) which Sorokin regards as dominated by Ideational art, McClelland's materials suggest rather the existence of an art which reflects achievement motivation, which in turn may be broadly construed as involving strong preoccupation with this world and drive toward mastery thereof.[20]

If the example of discrepancy just given (assuming that it is indeed allowed to constitute an example of discrepancy) does nothing else, it reinforces the point that Sorokin's data often need checks that are still to be made and may well never be made. Again, there should not be misunderstanding. I do not really doubt that there are occasions when Sorokin's categories apply well to his data and when the data themselves

---

[19] Italicized in original.

[20] See McClelland's review (12, p. 124–127) of Aronson's work on Greek vases.

are meaningful. But there are occasions when one must be more dubious. It is very likely that there are points where errors balance out or cancel one another, but there are also chances of systematic bias. In the absence of a careful and comprehensive evaluation of Sorokin's various data, one is constrained to say that the difficulties with his data and the uncertainties bearing on them that are now discernible make it the harder to assess the overall organizing or explanatory power of his basic cultural terms.

2) A second heading may be designated as "the relation of premises and norms and behavior." There is considerable evidence in the *Dynamics* of struggle on Sorokin's part with the problem of the relation of ideas and norms to behavior or conduct. It has been noted in the summary how strong a stress he puts on cognitive premises in the determination of the character of a culture. Yet he makes constant qualifications in the sense of indicating that conduct will not follow the pure line of premises (even if premises are themselves pure and unmixed in the first place). Again he admits a great deal that a critic might say in this matter. But the question is where the admissions leave his final stand. Let us mark some illustrative statements. "Historically, there has probably never existed in pure form in a single individual, group, or culture, any one of the unmixed types of culture mentality. . . . Even the most ascetic, the most austere, mystic cannot help changing his empirical milieu or satisfying to some extent his bodily needs. Otherwise he would die. . . . Sometimes even those of Sensate mentality modify themselves, and not their milieu; satisfy their spiritual, instead of their material needs." Again: "All the earmarks of the mentality of a given culture may appear to be Ascetic Ideational, and yet it is thinkable that the external aspect of such a culture may be a shocking contrast to such a mentality: materialistic, comfortable, luxurious, ostentatious, mercenary." And we are warned that "we must not postulate without a test, that mentality and actual behavior of human beings are always clearly integrated and logically consistent" and that "a man may agree with and extol the Christian principle of loving one's neighbor as oneself, and yet in his actual behavior be the most egotistic of individuals" (23, vol. 1, pp. 77–78, p. 101; vol. 3, p. 221, p. 510).

Thus there is, after all, a considerable margin of indeterminacy, a considerable number of degrees of freedom (or, if one will, a considerable number of variables not specified and perhaps not even recognized) in the relationship at least between *Sorokin's* over-arching, ultimate cultural premises and behavior or conduct. The more "free" conduct is from determination or constraint by the premises the more one may question their significance for various purposes of analysis.[21] (They *could* finally appear as philosophical irrelevancies or near-irrelevancies so far as a great deal

[21] Bidney writes that "normative idealists tend to define culture in terms of social ideals and to exclude the actual practices as not constitutive of culture," and accordingly marks a "normativistic fallacy." See Bidney (1, p. 32).

of conduct is concerned.) How *much* freedom is there? One feels almost guilty about asking such a question, which is so easy to ask, since it would be so hard to answer in any case and since Sorokin's own relevant data and lines of argument are far from strong enough to bear its burden.

Sorokin concedes that the existence of like rudimentary biological needs for participants in all cultures will lessen behavior contrasts, and he states: "The members of the Ideational and Sensate societies must eat, drink, have shelter, sleep, work, reproduce their kind, defend themselves against agencies and forces menacing their existence" (23, vol. 3, p. 511). He has already been quoted as saying that even the most ascetic or austere mystic must satisfy his bodily needs to some extent. To this extent, minimally, the Sensate-Ideational contrast is irrelevant to conduct. It is theoretically possible, in Sorokin's scheme of analysis, that in contrasting cultures one might begin with a sharp differentiation (on the basis of ultimate premises and norms) of some as Sensate and others as Ideational and yet come around to the final view that, by the criteria of conduct, there is nothing of importance to distinguish the one set of cultures from the other.[22] The matter of degrees of freedom referred to above is again relevant. There can be no question of a rigorous specification of the factors that might bring about practical identity of conduct in the cultures with the different premises, but three roughly distinguishable sources of the outcome of conduct resemblance, in effect suggested by Sorokin himself, may be noted. The constraint toward likeness across cultures exercised by like biological needs may be put together with constraints exercised by strictly "social" interaction.[23] Even if one begins with a sharp differentiation of Sensate and Ideational cultures, in Sorokin's view there are likely to appear in empirical cultures all sorts of "admixtures" and "impurities," intrusions of alien premises and norms that would mitigate the effect of the initial differentiation. This is a second source (although it may be fed from the first) of elements bring-

[22] I indicate this as a possibility. It is true that Sorokin's general bias would be toward seeing effective pervasion of a culture by ultimate premises. But I take it that this is an empirical issue. If so, the possibility indicated remains open. It has also been noted above that Sorokin himself makes statements such as: "All the earmarks of the mentality of a given culture may appear to be Ascetic Ideational, and yet . . . the external aspect of such a culture may be a shocking contrast to such a mentality. . . ." Sorokin's own argument in regard to relationships of culture and conduct will be considered below.

[23] It is commonplace to make distinctions between "biological," "social," and "cultural" spheres. Sorokin distinguishes social from cultural (23, vol. 3, p. 3). Franz Zwilgmeyer is particularly aware of the distinction between the social and cultural (see his article [30]). Kroeber makes one of numerous statements that might be cited which suggests limits on cultural elaboration exercised by social and biological factors: "Since human culture cannot be wholly concerned with values, having also to adapt to social (interpersonal) relations and to reality (survival situations), the totality of a culture can scarcely be considered outright as a sort of expanded style" (8, p. 152).

ing different cultures about to likeness of conduct in their carriers. Finally (and without comment on the relation of this source to the others), there would be gaps or lack of carry-over or absence of permeation from one "portion" of a culture to another, such that premises and norms that would otherwise have a differentiating effect on conduct would "skip" or "miss" and thereby leave conduct unaffected.

Sorokin often seems to me to allow this third source of conduct-convergence through lack of permeation of otherwise differentiating premises and norms, by implication if not directly. The notion of this third source is closely related to one or more of the various senses in which he uses the term "integration." It may be remarked, incidentally, that a careful analysis of this term as Sorokin employs it would be most interesting. Such analysis would surely reveal that some of the propositions that appear in intimate connection with the term are quite vulnerable. Thus, Sorokin claims that "the greater and better" the integration of social and cultural systems, the greater their length of life, among other things. His criteria for integration at this point in his argument are: amount of causal and meaningful interdependence of the components of a system, so that the system whose components are highly integrated causally and in terms of meanings is in this regard highly integrated; second, the "solidary" character of relationships among the members of a system, a criterion which may be roughly understood by noting that at an extreme of non-integration there would not even be quite impersonal or contractual contacts among the human members of a socio-cultural system (although this extreme might raise problems of definition: would there still be a "system" in the extreme case? — but this and other questions may be left aside); third, as Sorokin puts it, "consistency between the components of the system." Highly integrated systems of philosophy, religion, art, or law will definitely tend to outlast less highly integrated systems. "The same," says Sorokin, "is true of the social systems. Unintegrated armies have always been beaten by integrated ones. Unintegrated states have always been short-lived compared with the integrated ones. A poorly integrated family, or business organization, or any 'eclectic social organization' has . . . as a rule, more quickly and frequently . . . come to an end. . . ." The argument has a suspiciously "abstract" flavor and does not carry conviction. Taking Sorokin's criteria for integration, one could equally well argue that the more highly integrated social and cultural systems are the more liable to shortness of life and to destruction. In case of a threat or danger from outside or inside such systems, that threat or danger will sweep through the entirety of the systems the more quickly and the more devastatingly the more integrated the systems are — precisely because of high conductivity (see also 4, p. 253). Lower conductivity would increase the chances of localizing danger or "infection." What might be regarded as a possibly significant qualification, to the effect that integration should not be identified with "plasticity" or "rigidity," is too vague to be of much help. A variety of considerations might lead one to the tentative view that on the whole an "Idealistic," compromising, fusing sort of structure (of organizations if not of culture-meanings, and perhaps of the latter also) might be most viable.[24]

To revert to the general matter of the factors that baffle or stultify the differentiating effect on conduct of different (Sensate and Ideational) premises with which one may start, it seems that these factors may come to a great deal. At least this can be said, even if it is hardly a precise statement. Moreover, on the whole, little is known about these several sources of de-differentiation. It is possible to get beyond a few wholly rudimentary statements (of the type that even ascetics must eat to live), but it is not clear that it is now possible to get *far* beyond them. Yet Sorokin, because of the character or structure of his system, is in effect responsible for handling the exceedingly difficult problems of analysis all this suggests. His theory of culture becomes very hard or impossible to work out in rigorous fashion. His often fine sense for the character of systems at large (both social systems, in the very broadest meaning, and non-social systems) affords him good insights, but these remain rather "Platonic" in that he cannot carry them forward into a precise handling of the interaction of ultimate premises and norms and the de-differentiating factors that have been noted. Evidently, too, the sheer theoretical possibilities of conduct-convergence despite initial premise-norm differentiation may be quite embarrassing to his outlook. And, given the complexity of the process whereby one may have to get around to strong conduct resemblance after initial premise-norm differentiation, it may be asked whether other ways of handling the relevant problems than those Sorokin proposes may not be better. If strong conduct resemblance is taken as a consequent, it may be variously interpreted, may have more than one antecedent. Simply as a possibility, one might suggest that there is much more central tendency (*Idealistic* bias) across cultures than Sorokin's scheme allows and that it might be feasible to derive a large part of conduct resemblance more or less directly from this, instead of through a cumbersome and most-difficult-to-handle set of factors mitigating an otherwise supposedly expectable conduct-differentiation.[25] (Even if it be granted — as I think it must — that problems of culture analysis, at least on occasion, have to be handled in rather cumbersome fashion, this is plainly no guarantee of rigor. Conflicting "themes" may have to be posited and treated, but the power of analysis in treating them

---

[24] The material from Sorokin quoted in the above paragraph is contained in (23, vol. 4, p. 610, pp. 613–614).

[25] I am well aware that this statement regarding alternative possibilities of explanation might be extended and refined and particularly regret that this cannot be done here, for the whole matter of alternative possibilities of explanation for various phenomena Sorokin seeks to explain seems to me to be extremely important.

has not been conspicuously high. I have here treated the whole matter of "emanationism" insufficiently. Conduct for Sorokin too often appears as sheer, direct emanation from cultural premises while men's *interests* and the *situations* they face and *already existent social structures* seem like merely incidental and perhaps even theoretically annoying "interferences.")

It is only fair to note that Sorokin seeks to face up to the problem indicated. He presents a brief treatment of the "relationship between types of culture and types of personality and behavior" in the fifteenth chapter of the third volume of the *Dynamics*. Here he contends that there will be a *closer* relationship between the character of a dominant culture and the "mentality" of its carriers than between the character of culture and the conduct of its carriers. But he adds that "though the relationship between the dominant culture and the behavior of its bearers is not always close, nevertheless, it does exist," and further affirms: "In application to the various types of culture, this means that the bearers of the Ideational and Sensate cultures differ from one another not only in their mentality (ideas, opinions, convictions, beliefs, tastes, moral and aesthetic standards, etc.) but also in their behavior and personality" (23, vol. 3, p. 512).[26] Sorokin's data, however, for so important a point are meager and quite crude. Thus, for example, he puts a good bit of stress on a table of geometric means for participation in religion by contrast with participation in business, the data being derived from materials on historical personages, from 900 B.C. to 1849 A.D., included in the *Encyclopedia Britannica*. Religion and business are two of ten fields of activity covered (geometric means for participation in each field being converted into percentages, the total for all fields coming to 100 per cent). Others include statesmanship, literature, scholarship, and fine arts. No specific data are given for fields other than religion and business. Sorokin remarks that activity in these other fields "may, by their nature, be either Ideational or Sensate" (23, vol. 3, p. 527). Very plainly, it would be important to know something about the character of conduct in these other fields, more particularly since religion and business, taken together, appear to constitute less than 25 per cent of total activity in more than 40 per cent of 55 fifty-year periods, on the face of Sorokin's materials.[27] Moreover, there is no measure of the character of conduct in religion and business; there is only an indication of amount of participation in each, which is perhaps suggestive, but far from conclusive for what Sorokin wishes to show. The trends from one time period to another indicated by these data in detail also raise very ticklish questions. On the basis of data such as these, Sorokin cannot get far, granted that they may have

[26] The two statements quoted are italicized in the original.

[27] See the table in (23, vol. 3, p. 527). Sorokin comments that what activity in the fields of statesmanship, literature, etc., was like in any specific case "we cannot know without further details. . . ." The admission is significant.

been the best data available to him. If the relationship between dominant culture, as Sorokin understands it, and behavior is in principle susceptible of some sort of determination by measurement and can be adequately treated only through measurement, much better measurements will have to become available before the relationship can be convincingly set forth.[28]

Sorokin clearly wishes to vindicate the notion that ideas (and norms) are not mere epiphenomena, but have genuine independent efficacy in shaping conduct, even conduct close to the level of biological needs (23, vol. 3, p. 529). He breaks a lance for human rationality. One might sympathize with his endeavor to do this. (Also, by the way, one may grant him whatever he might want granted in favor of the notion of the independent efficacy of ideas and norms and yet wish to stress *different* ideas and norms from those he sees as crucial.) At the same time it is quite evident that the analysis of ideas and norms in relation to conduct presents great complexities. Sorokin is most certainly aware of this, but he often presents solutions to a variety of pertinent problems that are not compelling. Thus, he contends that the existence of magic and supersensory religion among primitive and prehistoric peoples argues the presence of "a variety of the Ideational conception of causality" and then avers that these peoples "have also a Sensate form of causality applied to many daily experiences where the connection between the phenomena is explained sensately and 'experimentally' as a result of the 'natural' properties of the variables involved" (23, vol. 2, p. 389). This is a particularly interesting assertion because it suggests that one may have to infer "ideas" themselves from conduct. (If there is little explicit primitive formulation of "experimental" notions and yet appreciable adherence to such notions implicit in conduct, the matter of deciding on the character of primitive "thought" becomes the more complex.) Is it satisfactory to conclude from Sorokin's observations about primitives' ideas that they have, say, a "mixed" form of culture mentality? This would be to take two sets of "ideas" with equal seriousness, which may or may not be warranted. Sorokin's brief treatment of culturally variant conceptions of number (23, vol. 2, pp. 433–437) bears on number symbolism or a kind of number poetry among the Chinese and others. Sorokin himself suggests something similar can be found in Western culture. How large a role did the variant conception of number play in China? Is it a variant conception of *number*, anyway, or a superadded kind of play with numbers of which some signs can also be found in the West? If the Chinese in important parts of their numerical "behavior" act much as we do — if, for example, in the simplest terms, they demonstrate behaviorally that they fully accept such notions as the notion that two and two

[28] Taken individually and together Sorokin's indices bearing on culture and behavior or conduct exhibit considerable insensitivity and may at the very most be said to be "suggestive."

make four; and it is hard to see how they could do otherwise, on pain of certain unhappy results — we may well allow their behavior to influence our own views as to what their very *"ideas"* of number are. Certain kinds of variant verbalizations, even certain kinds of variant styles, may well conceal a common substance. The philosopher Woodbridge somewhere has a remark to the effect that when a man of the eighteenth century referred to the woman he loved as "a handmaiden of the Lord" he "meant" she was "a darn fine girl." The "Sensate" and the "Ideational" cannot always be allowed to go on their own most obvious appearances and persuade us that they do not need further interpretation.

It is pertinent to note that no effort is made in the *Dynamics* to develop anything like a systematic psychological theory. Psychological observations are made *ad hoc* in the course of Sorokin's major work.[29] It may at least be suggested that an effort to develop something on the order of a socio-psychological theory might have given Sorokin considerable help with some of the problems above indicated. I do not pursue the matter further. But this particular omission, whatever its effect for Sorokin's work may have been, suggests a few others worth noting.

3) Under a final heading of "undeveloped themes," I wish merely to indicate several points that Sorokin has evidently left in incomplete form and the elaboration of which might have brought greater conviction on the part of his reader of the organizing or explanatory power of his basic cultural terms. The points indicated may be taken as a short listing of examples of undeveloped themes.

While in very broad terms Sorokin contends that the "portions" or "sectors" of the cultures he treats are in accord with one another, "integrated" and informed by dominant outlooks (as Sensate outlooks), this is indeed only a loose way of rendering his notion on the matter. He contends that in Sensate cultures and periods, art, by way of example, understood as a value area, is "separated" from other value areas, but so are other value areas separated from one another. Religion, morals,

[29] When Sorokin is annoyed with psychoanalysis, as he often is, he is likely to refer to its image of man as one that represents the latter as a "bag" filled with libido, lust, and aggression. Sorokin's own "man," as he appears in the *Dynamics,* seems to be largely an imprint or reflex of Sensate or Ideational or Idealistic culture — a "bag" filled with the appropriate premises and values. He seems to have no motors, no insides that work on the materials given him by his cultural environment. This should not be taken to mean that Sorokin never has anything of interest or cogency to say on psychological matters. (Note, for example, his useful discussions of fundamental and conditioned, normative, and purposive motivation in [21, pp. 45–46, pp. 96–97]). In recent years, he has shown an interest in creativity that was already foreshadowed in the *Dynamics* (see 23, vol. 4, pp. 747 ff.), and has observed: "No one is entirely passive. Every person selects, combines, and sometimes even creates, and to that extent he is an active agent in the social process" (22, p. 93). It remains true that in the *Dynamics* there is no interaction worth noting of psychic and socio-cultural stuff in the sense of systematic psychological treatment.

science, philosophy, and so on, are united in Ideational culture, but apart and even in conflict, in Sensate culture. Sorokin does say that the Sensate culture is also "an integrated culture," but it is "integrated around the principle of diversity, and the mutual independence of its main values and compartments" (23, vol. 1, p. 672).[30] He adds of Sensate culture that "it is not an absolute 'patriarchal monarchy' with one 'we' of its values, but a federal republic based upon the principle of the separation and division of its main states" (23, vol. 1, pp. 672–673, p. 677). Problems are thus raised about the character of the connections between "sectors" of culture on which Sorokin does not satisfy us. His entire treatment suggests unequivocally that there is "unity" in Sensate culture in that its painting is like its architecture, its literature like its music, and so on. These and other fields share Sensate characteristics: preoccupation with the world of sense instead of the transcendent world, with Becoming rather than with Being, with the immediate rather than with the eternal, and others. Whence *this* unity? and just how shall it be described? Perhaps Sensate culture gets a distinctive kind of unity from some form of consensus that its diverse "sectors" shall be allowed autonomy—and perhaps this is what Sorokin means by his analogy with a "federal republic." This, however, would be unity at one level only. It might help account for, or at least point to, "unity in diversity," unity despite independence and even unity based on independence. But there remains to be explained the unity that comes from the culture-content resemblance of the various "sectors" to one another. Perhaps the "government" holds together on the basis of an agreement that the "states" shall be allowed to go very much on their own, but why do the states turn out to be so like another (in Sensate culture)? The whole matter is left unexplored, to the possible impoverishment of Sorokin's differentiation of his two fundamental terms and of his theory of culture.

A second point is that Sorokin does not systematically collate all the elements in his work that bear on the like or common and the unlike or uncommon in various cultures, to reach a thoroughly reasoned judgment about the extent and importance of resemblances and differences. Undoubtedly, this would have been a herculean task; I suggest nevertheless that it might have aided his basic cultural analysis greatly. It has already been noted that he acknowledges minimum like biological needs across societies (so that, by way of example, there always has to be some provision for acquisition of food and the rudiments of an economy, and a culture must ordinarily stop short of prohibiting all sexual intercourse). He contends that forms and categories of thought are profoundly shaped by cultures and will differ appreciably as the latter do. But he does not contend this without reservation. He seems to stop short of a relativism that would take the extreme form of the contention that there is no truth except "truth" so conditioned culturally that it is not truth at all. He both

[30] Italicized in original.

allows a measure of independence of the rest of culture to some branches of scientific thought and appears not unwilling in principle to concede the substantial independence of other culture of the formal laws of logic and mathematics (23, vol. 2, chapter 12, esp. p. 466). In his study of "ethico-juridical mentality in criminal law" (23, vol. 2, chapter 15) he finds in the criminal codes of five leading European countries some 16 types of criminal actions which he calls "absolute crimes," criminal and punishable in all the codes analyzed. Sorokin is thereby prompted to think in terms of something like an approximation to "moral consensus" (23, vol. 2, pp. 577–578), which further investigation might well show to be more extensive. These and other elements of the like or common are not taken up in a rigorous overall accounting, balancing the like or common against the dissimilar across cultures, with particular reference to Sensate and Ideational forms. Again, I recognize that the job involved would have been very considerable, and resources for doing it were even less when Sorokin wrote the *Dynamics* than they are now. It is still unfortunate that the job could not be done.

Finally, Sorokin never develops his original seven-fold typology in any detail. He operates, as has been noted, mainly with his three grand types. There are various points in his work where it appears likely that a further development and refinement of his entire typology would have been helpful. He inclines to think we are now in transition from a Sensate to an Ideational form. Granted that his theory allows for differences between Sensate-turning-to-Ideational, on the one hand, and Idealistic, on the other, there also seem to be considerable resemblances between these two. In this case, as in others, his sheer description shows a crudity that might have been mitigated by a conscientious elaboration of subtypes and careful assignment of subtypes to various portions of the social structure, including social strata. I recognize again that this is to ask for a good deal, which it may simply have been impossible to offer.

The reservations suggested will indicate why I am not convinced that Sorokin has "cut" the socio-cultural universe in a theoretically very useful way — to be sure, judging by high standards. His "blocks" or "wedges" (or, if one will, his "disease entities") would, minimally, appear susceptible of very much refinement.[31] I remain unconvinced, in particu-

---

[31] It may be argued that in this section I have tried to judge Sorokin's work by standards that should not be applied to it. Here, after all, one may say, in the form of the *Dynamics,* is another imposing culture theory and philosophy of history, to be regarded critically, yet, in a sense, not too critically. One may expect knowledge and sagacity from a Vico, a Hegel, a Comte, a Sorokin, but not an authentic and resounding scientific triumph in a strict sense. If one applies certain strict criteria, one is adopting a rather unimaginative and perhaps even humorless attitude. An organism that may be expected to have certain notable frailties (even if along with sturdy qualities) need not be stretched on a rack. I am not at all averse to taking Sorokin's work in the "tolerant" way suggested. But clearly it would not follow that the theory of culture forms he offers would then fare better: one would merely expect less of it.

lar, that he has locked in the whole historical process with his view that there are only five basic answers to the problem of the nature of true reality and that these must recur. If we grant that these five answers are "basic" and recur, it is still quite possible (as has already been intimated) that each, first developed, then exhausted and rendered effete in turn, and in turn paradoxically generative of one of its own siblings, might have considerable irrelevance to the concerns, character, and conduct of the majority of mankind.

### Final Remarks toward Assessment

I may summarize and extend slightly by some additional remarks the view of Sorokin's work that has been proposed.

I have indicated that I regard Sorokin's dialectical approach to change as very valuable and that it appears to me to have further potential for illuminating change. Nevertheless, it remains an *orientation* to change, a set of shrewd notions of how change takes place that still needs a great deal of checking and should be frankly recognized as "experimental." It does not in itself constitute a theory of change. When to it are added, as Sorokin does add, the scheme of Sensate-Ideational-Idealistic culture forms and the hypothesis of few and recurrent basic views of truth inseparable from and informing whole cultures, and the whole scheme is given historical application, then something on the order of a theory of change with empirical reference is undoubtedly offered. But I have tried to show there is reason for much skepticism about such additions and applications. If there is justification for this view of the matter, is the outcome not quite disappointing? But it may be proposed, once more, that one should not expect too much from exceedingly ambitious and difficult enterprises in the understanding of entire cultures and all history.

For the near future, at any rate (and pending a time when perhaps further patient dialectical — and other — work may give us more aid), we may not be able to achieve a great deal more in the field of qualitative macro-culture analysis helped out by statistical data than has been achieved by a work of the type of, say, Kroeber's *Configurations of Culture Growth*. Kroeber's work is based on much learning and is carried through with characteristic care. While the patience and caution and immense common sense manifested in it are wholly admirable, the results *are* rather modest. Kroeber's conclusions about the clustering of cultural achievement in particular times and places and some of his leading concepts, such as the concept of pattern saturation, are, with the best will in the world, less than overwhelming. Sorokin does try to do more. He is much more adventurous — and is bound to make many more mistakes. The matter might be let go at that, but one other point should be suggested. It is often the mark of a man of stature that he takes chances and ventures on matters from which others would shrink. Sorokin is at one with many of the leading figures in the history of the social sciences (or, for that matter, in other disciplines) in displaying an audacity that simultaneously gets him into trouble and ensures that he is likely to be worth listening to even when he is in trouble.[32] His struggles with a large variety of problems, such as, say, the problems of the relation of ideas to conduct, may yet yield more, however subject to criticism they may be, than I am inclined to think at present. Nevertheless, and at least for the present, I, for one, remain convinced that his largest contribution is in the immense suggestiveness of his dialectical outlook on change.

Since I have stressed that Sorokin makes errors, it is only appropriate to add that this effort at assessment has been so conceived and deliberately limited that it has not been possible to give recognition to some of his outstanding virtues. It has not been possible to do justice to the circumstances that he is most extensively and brilliantly informed about numerous aspects of the history of social thought;[33] that he often presents issues on the borderlands between sociology and philosophy in a fresh, sharp, distinctive way;[34] that his specifications of significant terms can be extraordinarily apt;[35] that he is capable of powerful cultural portraiture;[36] that, more broadly, the *Dynamics* abounds in insights some small portion of which many a social scientist would be happy to claim as his own. Judged by the standards set by rather similar enterprises, his *Dynamics* is a tremendous achievement.[37]

[32] It is worth recalling that Robert E. Park, in a review of the first three volumes of the *Dynamics* (18, pp. 824–832), remarked that his teacher, Windelband, had observed that "in the realm of philosophy it was not those who were right who contributed most, but those who had been wrong."

[33] See (23, vol. 4, chapter 8) on theories of rhythm and phases in socio-cultural change.

[34] See (23, vol. 2, chapters 6 and 7) on realism, conceptualism, and nominalism, and on universalism and singularism.

[35] Note, e.g., the descriptions of "fideism" in (23, vol. 2, passim).

[36] See (23, vol. 1, chapter 12) on music.

[37] *1974 Note.* Were Sorokin still alive I would have asked editors and publisher for the chance to offer a much revised and somewhat expanded version of this chapter. But, alas, Sorokin is no longer with us and obviously could not respond to a refurbished endeavor on my part. I can, however, refer the interested reader to two pertinent later articles that I have written: "Pitirim A. Sorokin: Social Science in the Grand Manner," *Social Science Quarterly*, June, 1968, pp. 142–151; "Dialectic in Sociology," *American Sociological Review*, August, 1971, pp. 667–678.

# BIBLIOGRAPHY

1. Bidney, David. *Theoretical Anthropology.* New York: Columbia University Press, 1953.

2. de Silva-Vigier, Anil. *The Life of the Buddha.* Great Britain: Phaidon Publishers, 1955.

3. Dowd, Douglas F., ed. *Thorstein Veblen: A Critical Reappraisal.* Ithaca, N.Y.: Cornell University Press, 1958.

4. Gouldner, Alvin W. "Reciprocity and Autonomy in Functional Theory," in Llewellyn Gross (ed.), *Symposium on Sociological Theory.* Evanston, Ill.: Row, Peterson & Co., 1959.

5. Hauser, Arnold. *The Social History of Art,* 2 vols. New York: Alfred A. Knopf, 1951, Vol. 2.

6. Hilckman, Anton. "Geschichtsphilosophie-Kulturwissenschaft-Soziologie," *Saeculum,* Vol. 12 (1961), pp. 405–420.

7. Khaldun, Ibn. *The Muqaddimah,* 3 vols., translated by Franz Rosenthal. New York: Pantheon, 1958.

8. Kroeber, Alfred L. *Style and Civilizations.* Ithaca, N. Y.: Cornell University Press, 1957.

9. Löwith, Karl. *Meaning in History.* Chicago: University of Chicago Press, 1949.

10. Manuel, Frank E. *The Eighteenth Century Confronts the Gods.* Cambridge, Harvard University Press, 1959.

11. Manuel, Frank E. *The Prophets of Paris.* Cambridge: Harvard University Press, 1962.

12. McClelland, David C. *The Achieving Society.* New York: D. Van Nostrand, 1961.

13. Mensching, Gustav. *Soziologie der Religion.* Bonn: Ludwig Röhrscheid, 1947.

14. Merton, Robert K. "The Unanticipated Consequences of Purposive Social Action," *American Sociological Review,* Vol. 1 (December 1936), pp. 894–904.

15. O'Dea, Thomas F. "Five Dilemmas in the Institutionalization of Religion," *Journal for the Scientific Study of Religion,* Vol. 1 (October 1961), pp. 30–39.

16. Ostwald, Wilhelm. *Grosse Männer,* 5th ed. Leipzig: Akademische Verlagsgesellschaft, 1919.

17. Pareto, Vilfredo. *The Mind and Society,* 4 vols., translated by Andrew Bongiorno and Arthur Livingston. New York: Harcourt, Brace, 1935, Vol. 4.

18. Park, Robert E. "Review of *Social and Cultural Dynamics,* Vols. 1–3," *American Journal of Sociology,* Vol. 43 (1938), pp. 824–832.

19. Sahlins, Marshall D., and Elman R. Service (eds.), *Evolution and Culture.* Ann Arbor: University of Michigan Press, 1960.

20. Simmel, Georg. "Der Begriff und die Tragödie der Kultur," *Philosophische Kultur*. Potsdam: Gustav Kiepenheuer, 1923, pp. 236–267.

21. Sorokin, Pitirim A. *Society, Culture, and Personality*. New York: Harper and Bros., 1947.

22. Sorokin, Pitirim A. *The Ways and Power of Love*. Boston: Beacon Press, 1954.

23. Sorokin, Pitirim A. *Social and Cultural Dynamics*, 4 vols. Totowa, N. J.: Bedminster Press, 1962.

24. Toynbee, Arnold J. *A Study of History*, 12 vols. London: Oxford University Press, 1939.

25. Veblen, Thorstein. *Imperial Germany and the Industrial Revolution*. New York: Viking Press, 1939.

26. Vico, Giambattista. *The New Science of Giambattista Vico*, translated from 3rd ed. by Thomas G. Bergin and Max H. Fisch. Ithaca, N. Y.: Cornell University Press, 1948.

27. Vico, Giambattista. *The New Science of Giambattista Vico*, revised and abridged, Thomas G. Bergin and Max H. Fisch. Garden City, N. Y.: Doubleday Anchor, 1961, p. xxxvii.

28. Vico, Giambattista. *The Autobiography of Giambattista Vico*, translated by Max H. Fisch and Thomas Bergin. Ithaca, N. Y.: Cornell University Press, 1944, 1963.

29. Weber, Max. *Gesammelte Aufsätze zur Wisschenschaftslehre*, 2nd ed. Tübingen: J. C. B. Mohr (Paul Siebeck), 1951.

30. Zwilgmeyer, Franz. "Kultur," in Werner Ziegenfuss (ed.) *Handbuch der Soziologie*. Stuttgart: Ferdinand Enke Verlag, 1956, Pt. IV, Chapter 3.

# 22

Pitirim  A.  Sorokin

# Comments on Schneider's

# Observations and Criticisms

### Preliminaries

I find Professor Schneider's dissection and criticism of my views of socio-cultural change most thoughtful, competent, and admirable in many respects. Since his analysis deals with the basic problems in this field the importance of his observations and criticisms goes beyond virtues and vices of my views: his insightful remarks become relevant for all investigators of socio-cultural change. In this sense his paper is a real contribution to our knowledge of the how and why of change. So much for my general reaction to his paper.

As to Schneider's *diagnosis of myself as a Romantic type of a scholar* (in terms of W. Ostwald's typology), *the diagnosis appears to me essentially correct.* Perhaps it would be still more accurate to say that predominant Romantic characteristics are mixed up with some Classic features such as: re-issuings and translations of my works without any change some 30 years after their initial publications; the term "classic" applied to my *Social Mobility, Contemporary Sociological Theories, Source Book in Rural Sociology,* and the *Dynamics* by a number of fellow-sociologists, and so on. In Ostwald's typology these features are assigned to the Classic rather than to the Romantic type.

*Roughly accurate is also* Schneider's summary of the main themes of the *Dynamics.* However his outline needs a few corrections. They will be made farther on when I shall deal with his criticisms of the Ideational,

583

Sensate, and Idealistic supersystems of culture. After these preliminary remarks, we can pass to the main themes and criticisms of Schneider's chapter.

### Dialectic Method and Dialectic Models of Socio-cultural Change

The section dealing with Dialectic is one of the most important parts of Schneider's essay. He is not only the first to discover an important role played by dialectical method in my theories of change[1] but — what is more important — he forcefully brings the fruitfulness of this method to the attention of American sociologists who, with a few exceptions, have largely neglected it. I completely agree with most of his observations concerning this method. First, he is quite right in stating that this method had a long, venerable, and cognitively fruitful history.

Indeed, we find its skillful and extensive use in the early texts of Taoism, Hinduism, and Buddhism[2] by the Greek pre-Socratic thinkers like Heraclitus, by Plato, Aristotle, Plotinus, and other Neoplatonists.[3] In the period of the first seven centuries of our era, it finds a magnificent development by the great Mahayana Buddhist logicians: Nagarjuna, Asanga, Vasubandhu, partly Gotama, Dignaga, and Dharmakirti.[4] In about the same period and later on, dialectical logic is well used by Damascius and by some of the Church Fathers, such as Clement of Alexandria, Origen, Tertullian, St. Augustine, Pseudo-Dionysius, Erigena, and others up to Nicolas of Cusa.[5] Subsequently in various forms, including Kant's "dialectic of a radical negation of dialectic," this method and logic have been skillfully applied by many eminent philosophers, natural and social scientists such as Fichte, Hegel, Proudhon, K. Marx, and Lenin,[6] to mention but a few names.

This sketch shows that the dialectic method has been fruitful not only in philosophy but also in the social and humanistic sciences because, largely through its use, many of these thinkers made their significant contributions to our knowledge of psycho-social and cultural phenomena generally and of cosmic and socio-cultural change specifically. Schneider is quite correct in his statement that the dialectic method can perform a number of important cognitive functions and that "it is susceptible of further development in heuristic use . . . and may in time become a very useful instrument, conceivably even of a greater help in the formulation of more or less rounded sociological theories than appears likely at first blush."

[1] His paper well supplements the essays of some 25 eminent scholars dealing with my various theories in P. Allen's volume (1) and E. Tiryakian's volume (35).

[2] See a brief sketch of a history of dialectical logic in P. Sorokin (24, pp. 364 ff.).

[3] See an outline of dialectics of Plato and Plotinus in G. Gurvitch (6, pp. 30–44).

[4] See on this the excellent work of Th. Stcherbatsky (33), also (32); see also R. G. H. Siu (15).

[5] See on the dialectics of Damascius and Pseudo-Dionysius, Gurvitch (6, pp. 44–49).

[6] See on their dialectics, Gurvitch (6, pp. 50–156).

As a matter of fact, his prognosis is already being realized by the natural as well as by the social sciences. Surprisingly, for many a too-narrow empirical sociologist who still regards the dialectical method as sterile speculation, the recent decades have been marked by a strong resurgence of dialectic method in the social as well as in the natural sciences. A galaxy of eminent physicists and mathematicians such as Niels Bohr, Louis de Broglie, F. Gonseth, J. L. Destouches, G. Bachelard, W. Heisenberg, and others have introduced it, in the form of "a dialectic complimentarity," into microphysics, nuclear physics, the mathematics of the infinitely great and the infinitely small, and so on for reconciliation of the opposite theories in these fields.[7] Likewise in recent years we observe an increasing number of works devoted to the dialectic in philosophy and the social sciences and a still more rapidly increasing use of this method in research of social, cultural, and psychological phenomena. As representative examples of such works, besides the works of some of the Marxians, the recent monographs of M. Merleau-Ponti, J. P. Sartre, and G. Gurvitch can be mentioned here.[8]

These concise comments show a complete agreement between Schneider's and my views concerning the cognitive functions of the dialectical method in a study of natural and socio-cultural processes.

Turning now to Schneider's comments on my use of dialectic, I find his interpretations essentially correct and insightful. Their only shortcoming is that he concentrates his analysis almost entirely on one — the "immanentist" — variety of dialectical method[9] and passes by without examination other forms of this method used in my works.

Whatever the reasons for this oversight, it may be responsible for Schneider's "severance" of my dialectical method from my conception of the Ideational, Sensate, and Idealistic supersystems of culture. This severance, as he correctly expects, I find unwarranted. In other words, in the construction of my Integral system of sociology and in my analysis of culture as systems, supersystems, and congeries I continue to use the dialectic method in its different forms (tempered and tested by empirical verification and combined with "postulational-deductive" and inductive methods).

[7] Instead of giving the titles of the respective works of these and other eminent scientists I simply refer to the international review, *Dialectica*, established in 1947, where the scientists of diverse exact sciences endeavor to find through dialectic method a solution of various (conceptual and experimental) difficulties confronting them in their research.

[8] Cf. M. Merleau-Ponti (10); J. P. Sartre (13); G. Gurvitch calls his system of sociology "dialectique empirico-réaliste." He developed it in a number of his works. His *Dialectique et Sociologie* gives a summary of his views of cultural and psychological phenomena. Resurgence and refinements of dialectic method and of the philosophy of dialectic materialism among the Marxians can be observed by reading *Voprosy Filosofii*, the main philosophical and partly sociological journal of the U.S.S.R. Almost in each copy of this journal several studies devoted to dialectics are published.

[9] Schneider himself quite skillfully uses this variety of dialectic in his study of "the Role of the Category of Ignorance in Sociological Theory," in (14, pp. 492–508).

## Dialectic and Ideational-Sensate-Idealistic Supersystems

To show this, I shall remind the reader of two things concerning dialectic method. First, as Gurvitch correctly states, "The dialectical method is first of all the method of adequate cognition of the *real* social and historical" totalities (or unified systems in contrast to congeries). Second, that it involves at least five different operational procedures: (1) dialectic complementarity; (2) mutual dialectic implication; (3) dialectic ambiguity; (4) dialectic polarization; (5) dialectic reciprocity of perspective.[10] At least four of these dialectic procedures have been used in construction of my Integral system of philosophy, sociology, and personality structure;[11] of my conception of the superorganic as the form of being different from the inorganic and the organic forms of reality; of three-dimensional (social, cultural, and personal) aspects of the superorganic; and especially for construction of my theory of social, cultural, and personal systems (including Ideational-Sensate-Idealistic supersystems) and congeries.[12]

Without a use of dialectic procedures of complimentarity, mutual dialectic implication, dialectic polarization, and dialectic reciprocity of perspective, it is hardly possible to define and study adequately social or cultural systems as *Ganzheiten* (quite different from congeries); their three-componential structures, their three-dimensional aspects, their meaningful causal unity, their triple interdependence of parts upon the whole, upon each other, and of the whole upon the parts, and other basic characteristics.[13] Anyone who carefully examines either the *Dynamics*

[10] Gurvitch (6, pp. 27 ff., pp. 184 ff.). Gurvitch correctly states that a study of the movements of the real social and historical totalities is a common characteristic of all diverse forms of dialectic.

[11] See for my Integral system of philosophy (27); also (30); for my system of sociology cf. (29); for my theory of personality structure cf. (24); also (38).

[12] May I be permitted to state that already in (17) and then in (18), I introduced and delineated the concept of social and cultural *systems* vs. mechanistic, nominalistic, atomistic, and organismic conceptions of society and culture. In (19) and then in (29), the conceptions of *social systems* vs. unorganized and semi-organized groups and *cultural systems* vs. congeries were fully developed and built in their concrete, empirical, historical manifestations and forms. At the present the concept of social or cultural system has become quite popular but most of such concepts are still permeated by nominalistic and atomistic fallacies that rob such "systems" of their unity and other inalienable characteristics of the real systems as *Ganzheiten* quite different from a nominalistic group of interacting individuals or congeries of cultural phenomena unrelated to each other either meaningfully or causally.

[13] When definition and analysis of social or cultural system is attempted without use of the mentioned dialectic operational procedures, the invariable result is either a mere nomenclature of various interactional or even singularistic activities of individuals like: "knowing, feeling, achieving, norming, ranking" and so on, which completely miss a social or cultural system as *Ganzheiten*, as unified reality different from these activities; or a semi-nominal and semi-atomistic pseudo-unity of actors and roles without delineation of the play they are supposedly playing together. Charles Loomis's books (8; 9) give an example of such a nomenclature and T. Parsons (11) supplies an example of semi-nominalistic pseudo-social system.

or *Society, Culture and Personality* and who is versed in the mentioned operational procedures of dialectic method can easily see my use of these procedures throughout my Integral system of philosophy, sociology, and psychology. This explains my rejection of Schneider's severance of my dialectic from my theory of social and cultural systems and congeries, including the Ideational, Idealistic, and Sensate supersystems. Contrary to his statement that in a study of socio-cultural structures and forms "The dialectic seems not to be of such help," I think that without a skillful use of the dialectic in its various forms no adequate theory of the socio-cultural structures and forms is possible.

We can now pass to examination of Schneider's criticisms of the Ideational, Idealistic, and Sensate supersystems of culture.

## Corrections

But before answering the criticisms I have to make two corrections in Schneider's outline of the main themes of the *Dynamics* and *Society, Culture and Personality*. First, my conception of culture or of the superorganic socio-cultural world is not "derivable from premises about the character of ultimate reality" and not "indissolubly wedded to systems of ultimate truth." These statements of Schneider are accurate only in regard to the Ideational, Sensate, and Idealistic supersystems of culture, as the specific and vastest forms of its integration. In my conception the whole realm of the superorganic or socio-cultural reality represents an incomparably vaster universe than these supersystems. This reality is basically different from the inorganic and the organic forms of being. In contradistinction to the inorganic phenomena that have only one physico-chemical component, and to the organic phenomena that have two components — physical and vital (life) — the socio-cultural or superorganic phenomena have the "immaterial" component of — conscious, rational, and superrational — *meaning* (or meaningful value and norm) superimposed upon the physical and vital components. This component of "meaning" is decisive in determining whether a phenomenon is socio-cultural. All phenomena that have the component of meaning are cultural phenomena. Such phenomena are found only in the world of mindful human beings who meaningfully interact with one another and create, operate, accumulate, objectify, and "materialize" their meanings in and through an endless number of physical and biological media ("vehicles"). To sum up: the totality of the "immaterial" meaning-values-norms, not objectified as yet through the material vehicles but known to some members of mankind; the totality of already objectified meanings-values-norms with all their physical and biological vehicles and energies; finally, the totality of interacting mindful individuals and groups — past and present — these inseparable totalities make up the total man-made socio-cultural world, superimposed on physical and biological realms of the total reality of the universe.[14] This definition of culture shows that the total cultural reality is neither "derivable" from, nor "wedded" to, the Ideational-Sensate-Idealistic forms of its integration.

In a systematic and detailed way this superorganic universe is studied in my works in its main structural and dynamic, as well as in its social, cultural, and personal aspects; in its ideological, behavioral, and material forms, as well as in its social and cultural systems basically different from unorganized collectivities and cultural congeries.

It is precisely my study of cultural systems which attracted my attention to the reality of the Ideational, Sensate, and Idealistic supersystems. The point is that in the *total* culture of any population or even of an individual, there exist a multitude of cultural congeries and of causal-meaningful (logically or aesthetically) consistent systems. These range from the smallest systems of meanings like "A is B," or "Two and two make four," to ever vaster ones. The "two by two is four" is a little cultural system; the multiplication table is a larger system; arithmetic is a still larger system; all mathematics (arithmetic, algebra, geometry, calculus, etc.) is yet a vaster system; the entire field of science is a still more embracing system. Similarly, we find a wide range of systems, beginning with the smallest and ending with the vastest, in other fields of cultural phenomena.

Since in the total culture of any population there are millions of various cultural systems and congeries, a study of all the millions of small systems (and congeries) would give, at best, only a knowledge of diverse, infinitesimal fragments of the total cultural universe. It never can give an essential knowledge of the basic structural and dynamic properties of this superorganic reality. As any nomothetic (generalizing) science, sociology endeavors to overcome this bewildering diversity of the millions and millions of systems and congeries in two different ways of its cognition: first, by concentrating our attention on the generic static and dynamic properties of *all* socio-cultural phenomena; second, by particular and intensive study of the *main* social and cultural systems. Cognition of the generic properties and relationship of *all* socio-cultural phenomena gives us a knowledge of their basic properties, relationships, and uniformities. Cognition of the main socio-cultural systems delivers to us a substantial knowledge of "the main continents" or "galaxies" of the superorganic universe and — through that — the knowledge of its total structure, of the relationships and configurations of these continents to each other, of the main processes and uniformities in the life history of each of these main systems and — through that — of the whole cultural world. Even more, as an adequate cognition of each of the main systems is impossible without a cognition of the subsystems of which each main system is made up, a thorough knowledge of all the main systems and

---

[14] P. T. de Chardin aptly calls the superorganic reality by the term of "noosphere" in difference from the "biosphere" and physical classes of reality. Cf. his (4).

especially of the vastest supersystems (if a given total culture reaches this highest form of integration) provides us with macro-sociological as well as with micro-sociological knowledge of the total superorganic universe.[15]

Exactly these two ways — a study of the *generic* characteristics of *all* socio-cultural phenomena as well as an investigation of the structural and dynamic properties of the main social and cultural systems and, among them, of the vastest — Ideational, Sensate and Idealistic supersystems (supplemented by a study of the unorganized social groups and cultural congeries) have been used in my works for obtaining a basic knowledge of the superorganic or socio-cultural universe.

These remarks explain why in the *Dynamics*, side by side with a study of the basic properties of the generic socio-cultural phenomena, of cultural systems and congeries, I concentrated on a study of the Ideational, Sensate, and Idealistic supersystems. As mentioned, my investigation of these supersystems has led me to a systematic study of the systems of science, philosophy, religion, fine arts, ethics, law, and the vast derivative systems of applied technology, economics, and politics with their sub-subsystems and congeries. In this way the *Dynamics* represents a nomothetic, macro- and micro-sociological investigation of the many-dimensional superorganic universe in its cultural aspect.

These remarks show why my conception of culture is not "derivable . . ." and is "not indissolubly wedded to systems of ultimate truth." The *Dynamics* clearly states that only a few total cultures of a few societies and periods reach the highest possible integration into the Ideational, Sensate, and Idealistic supersystems. Even in such *Hochkulturen* these supersystems unify only their significant part, and not their total culture. In other words, these supersystems are neither coextensive nor equivalent with the total human culture.

Finally, one more correction. Schneider, like many other commentators on the *Dynamics*, states that "the three main types (of culture) follow one another in what Sorokin regards as a rather reliable sequence, such that Sensate will be followed by Ideational and the latter by Idealistic culture forms and so on," and that the present disintegrating Sensate culture will be replaced by a new Ideational culture. This statement is incorrect. "I nowhere claimed that such an order of succession is a universal uniformity . . . I do not think the sequence observed in the history of the Greco-Roman and the Western cultures is universal or uniform for all societies and at all times." These remarks, and those in several other places of the *Dynamics* make my position clear. I do not have any sufficient logical ground on which to contend that the observed

---

[15] A detailed descriptive cognition of some of the unique, concrete fragments — persons, groups, events, etc. — of this superorganic universe is given to us by the ideographic disciplines of history, anthropology, and other ideographic sciences. See on this P. Sorokin (28, pp. 235–254).

order is invariable. Neither is there a sufficient empirical evidence for such a claim. Neither have I claimed that the dying Sensate order of our time would be necessarily followed by a new Ideational order (19, vol. iv, pp. 770–773).

After these corrections we can turn to an examination of Schneider's thoughtful criticisms of the supersystem of culture.

### Reply to Schneider's Criticisms of the Concept of Supersystems

#### 1. Argument of "Hackneyed Triad"

Schneider's first criticism suggests that my triad of the Ideational-Sensate-Idealistic supersystems is "a rather hackneyed triad, already old in Vico's day." The criticism is partly correct: even before Varro and Vico a number of known and unknown thinkers of ancient Egypt, India, China, Persia, Greece, and Rome formulated several cyclical and rhythmical theories somewhat resembling my triad. The *Dynamics* gives an extensive survey of these theories; it indicates the points of resemblance between these theories and my "triad."[16] However, from the fact that atomic theory was formulated long ago, even before Demokritos and Leukippos, and has been reiterated since many times in subsequent centuries, it does not follow that the atomic theories of the contemporary physicists are "hackneyed stuff." From the fact that many of the basic concepts and principles of physical and biological sciences such as "number," "time," "space," "causality," "emanation and undulatory theories of light," vitalism, mechanism, abiogenesis, struggle for existence, determinism, indeterminism, geocentric, heliocentric, and other cosmogonies[17] were conceived centuries before our era, the conclusion does not follow that the respective theories of today's physicists, chemists, astrophysicists, and biologists are "hackneyed stuff . . . worn even thinner by a long line" of the scientists who have dealt with these problems. The same argument still more applies to philosophy and the psychosocial sciences: these disciplines are still busy mainly with the problems and theories formulated two or three millenia ago.

When one compares today's and the early theories of each of the main problems of physical, biological, psychological, and philosophical disciplines, one cannot fail to notice that the contemporary theories, though remotely resembling their ancient predecessors, nevertheless are quite different from their great-grandfathers. The same is true in regard to many a predecessor of my theory of the Ideational-Sensate-Idealistic supersystems. Using the term of the detective stories, one can say that their remote resemblance is largely coincidental. These remarks are sufficient to dismiss the argument of "a hackneyed triad."

[16] See (19, vol. 2, chapters 10, 11, 12; vol. 4, chapters 7, 8, 9, 10, 11. See also G. C. Cairne (3).
[17] See on the genesis and fluctuation of these theories in (19, vol. 2, chapters 11, 12); cf also (20).

## 2. Defective Quality of My Data

The next and more important criticism consists of the indication of the defective quality of some of my data. As an example of such questionable data, Schneider mentions my data on art, particularly on literature. Again in a small degree his criticism is correct: in comparison with the *ideally* complete, precise, and thoroughly verified data, my data are, of course, deficient. I myself repeatedly stress their shortcomings and inadequacies in almost each chapter of the *Dynamics*. But Schneider knows well that the ideally perfect data may exist only in the Platonic world of ideal forms and (unless they concern elementary platitudes) they are unobtainable for a mortal investigator of real, everchanging, and many-dimensional empirical phenomena. For this reason defectiveness of my data should be decided not by comparison with the ideal *but with the obtainable empirical data used by other sociologists and scholars working on similar problems.* If and when the only such possible, fair, and real comparison is made, I am ready to reiterate my statement that my data "are more reliable and complete than any data presented up to the present time, so far as the general course of art fluctuation in the countries studied is concerned." The same contention I am ready to make in regard to my data concerning the forms and fluctuation of materialism, idealism, nominalism, realism, rationalism, mysticism, temporalism, eternalism, movement of scientific discoveries and inventions, oscillation of main ethical theories, changes in the codes of law, movement of wars, internal disturbances, fluctuation of theocratic and secular governments, of governmental regimentation, and of all the other socio-cultural processes studied in the *Dynamics*.

The main reasons for this contention are as follows:

a) Even the best sociological works dealing with the long-term fluctuations or formulating some uniformities in the relationship of the studied socio-cultural variables give for empirical verification of their hypotheses only a few illustrative cases (for example, Max Weber's empirical corroboration of his theory of Protestantism-Capitalism, or Marx's opposite theory in this field, or A. Toynbee's unduly generalized Hellenic model of civilization in the first six volumes of his *Study of History,* or Durkheim's generalization that "the intensity of punishment is proportional to the degree of absolutism and unlimitedness of the central government" (5, pp. 65 ff.), or they use so-called "representative samples" (whose representativeness ordinarily remains unproved and questionable). In contrast to these doubtful procedures, I give, instead of a few cases or samples, *the complete known series* or *the total known universe of the relevant empirical facts;* not just samples, but *all known* scientific discoveries and inventions; *all* Greco-Roman and Western philosophers, mentioned in the fullest histories of philosophy; *all* historical persons mentioned in the *Encyclopaedia Britannica; all* ethical thinkers; almost *all* European pictures and sculptures (more than 100,-

000) known to the most complete histories of European painting and sculpture; almost *all* the French, the German, and the Russian codes of criminal law beginning with the Barbaric codes of the fifth-sixth centuries and ending with the Soviet, the Nazi, the Fascist codes; *all* Greco-Roman and Western wars and internal disturbances recorded in historical annals; and so on. It is needless to say that a study and measurement of a *complete universe* or of the *total class* of the phenomena investigated gives a more adequate knowledge of the movement of these phenomena in time and space than a study and measurement of *a mere fraction* or *a mere sample* of these facts. Even the best sampling techniques, when applied to a study of long-term fluctuations of many-dimensional, somewhat abstract and discrete phenomena, are liable to yield but fragmentary, inadequate results, since they are based on cases selected in an unsystematic or biased manner.

b) To reduce the elements of subjectivity and incompetence in the collection of the relevant empirical data for verification of my hypotheses, I intentionally eliminated myself from this collection in all quantitative series of the *Dynamics* and arranged this enormous spadework done by *the internationally known specialists in the field of each series, without telling them for what purposes or hypothesis each of the factual series was needed.*[18] This simple procedure more efficiently eliminated the element of subjectivity and at the same time secured a more competent collection of the relevant empirical data than could be done by myself or by ordinary research assistants (graduate students and the like) who are not eminent specialists in these fields.[19]

c) Contrary to Schneider's statement that my data "are often unique, and good checks on them are generally unavailable," *I give a complete possibility of verification of every detail of my procedures and summary tables.* In many long appendices to each volume of the *Dynamics,* there are given detailed lists of all the wars, revolutions, philosophers, ethical thinkers, scientists, painters, sculptors, and so on, with all the details of quantitative evaluation of each person or event. In this way any competent scholar is given a complete opportunity to check each detail of factual accuracy of my quantification procedures, of all the summary tables, and all the main conclusions and generalizations.

[18] Professor N. S. Timasheff, who was one of the collectors of the series of all the known internal disturbances in the history of Greece, Rome, and the Western countries, testifies to this fact in his essay in (34).

[19] The danger of subjective biases and incompetence in collection of the empirical facts studied (for substantive and verificatory purposes) is not eliminated by the modern "data collecting and processing technique," neither by the techniques of sampling or item analysis or paired comparison and others. In many empirical studies using "the modern techniques" this phase of research is often entrusted to incidental and hardly competent agents without an effective control of the competence of their operations. The material presented by them to the researcher-scholar is frequently "processed" without a sufficient test of its accuracy, completeness, and so on. As a result many an empirical research is vitiated already at this early phase and yields therefore doubtful conclusions based on defective data.

d) A further precautionary measure in my quantification of the many-dimensional, qualitative-quantitative phenomena has been my preferential use, whenever possible, of the *simplest quantitative procedures involving either none or the minimum of arbitrary assumptions, ranking, scaling, complex formulae, and other intricate manipulations with figures and facts.* The scientific reason for this preference is almost axiomatic: the less arbitrary assumptions, ranking, scaling, estimates, and other arbitrary manipulations a measurement or quantification contains, the more roughly reliable and correct the results of the quantification are likely to be.[20] This explains why most of my tables give just the actual number and percentage of the counted — and countable — items obtained through simple arithmetic computation.[21] Side by side with these tables there are also tables involving several assumptions, estimates, ranking, and other arbitrary operations in quantification of their not completely scalar data. The tables giving the movement of the internal disturbances from 600 B.C. to A.D. 1925 are a conspicuous example of such tables. But just because, for their construction, several arbitrary assumptions were made, such tables appear to me less reliable than the simple "arithmetic" tables free from most of the arbitrary manipulations.

e) As an additional measure for securing a comparative reliability, completeness, and adequacy of my quantitative data and of my conclusions derived from them, I regularly checked these conclusions by logical (including dialectical) analysis and supplemented them by a qualitative description and interpretation of additional points not shown by the quantitative indexes.

f) Perhaps as a further evidence of a comparative accuracy of my data I can mention the fact that, when some of my pioneering studies like the movement of wars in Greco-Roman and Western populations from 600 B.C. to A.D. 1925 were repeated along somewhat similar lines by Quincy Wright and B. Urlanis, their results happened to be in essential agreement with my results, indexes, and curves of war movement.[22] If this agreement happened in regard to the time-series of wars in which several arbitrary assumptions were made, I am reasonably certain that

[20] A more developed criticism of these assumptions, ranking, and other arbitrary manipulations with figures is given in (25).

[21] This straightforward arithmetic counting seemingly is responsible for several criticisms of my "statistical methods" by the devotees of the complex, statistical manipulations infected by a legion of the arbitrary assumptions, subjective scalings, and other simulacra of "refined and precise" statistical procedures with impressively looking pseudo-mathematical formulae having in fact no relationship to real mathematics and sound statistical operations. Cf. for substantiation of this statement (25, chapters 7, 8, and also 4, 5, 6).

[22] See (19, vol. 3, chapters 9, 10, 11; 40; 37). Despite Urlanis' criticism of some of my procedures and assumptions — which criticism reproduces mainly my own warnings of the deficiency and inadequacies of the available data and of the assumptions made in my study — nevertheless his main indexes and curves of the movement of wars of the seventeenth, eighteenth, nineteenth, and twentieth centuries are in essential agreement with my indexes and curves.

my tables and curves obtained through a mere arithmetic computation of the items counted will be still better confirmed by future competent studies of the same phenomena along similar lines.[23]

The totality of considerations (a), (b), (c), (d), (e), (f), explain why I do not agree in this point with Professor Schneider and why I do not hesitate to contend that, though from the ideal standpoint, my data "may be unreliable but they are more reliable than any data presented up to the present time, so far as the general course of art fluctuation (and also of fluctuation of other variables) in the countries studied is concerned."

After these considerations we can turn to Schneider's case of an alleged deficiency of my data. I myself state that it is probable that during the early Medieval period "on the lower levels of literature there existed many pagan, partly Sensate and even indecent songs, poems, and tales." "But," I add, "these levels are beyond the scope of this work." Schneider seems to have failed to pay attention to this addition. In the *Dynamics* I study *not "the lower levels"* of science or philosophy or religion or fine arts or other cultural congeries and primitive systems of the Greco-Roman and the Western total cultures, but precisely their highest levels — the levels that give individuality and creative originality to these (or other) cultures: their greatest and highest systems and supersystems. And these "highest levels" are studied throughout the whole existence of these cultures. If therefore my study shows that the grand literature, grand sculpture-architecture-philosophy-science-religion-ethics-law-politics-economics of these cultures were in some periods predominantly Ideational, while in other periods they became predominantly Idealistic or Sensate; if, in addition, my study shows that in these transformations all these great systems of these cultures have been changing "in togetherness," in mutual interdependence — then the demonstration of these metamorphoses clearly testifies that, on their highest levels, these cultures have indeed undergone respective Ideational or Idealistic or Sensate transformation and that, on this high level, their main cultural systems have indeed been integrated into respective dominant supersystems. The existence of all sorts of cultural congeries and "vulgar" systems on the lower levels of these cultures in no way damages or cancels the accuracy of my data and the validity of my conclusions concerning the high levels or the dominant grand systems and supersystems of these cultures.

---

[23] The comparative accuracy of my data has been confirmed even by vitriolic critics of my *Dynamics*. "In general, Mr. Sorokin appears to have been most conscientious about his facts" (2, p. 252). On the other hand, several eminent historians like M. I. Rostovtzeff, and sociologists like L. von Wiese found "the factual framework of the *Dynamics* so solidly built that its essentials are unlikely to be changed by future investigators; they certainly will correct here and there some sidewalks and secondary streets of the city of the *Dynamics* but its main features are likely to remain unchanged" (12). "In comparison with Sorokin's great work, the works of Comte, Spencer, Pareto and Spengler appear to be arbitrary and fanciful" (39). See also (36).

Furthermore, in contrast to the Danilevsky-Spengler-Toynbee theories of complete integration of their *Hochkulturen*[24] or "Civilizations," I persistently contended that *the total culture* of any group or even of any individual is hardly ever completely integrated, that it always represents a co-existence of various, sometimes even contradictory, congeries and systems; that in each of *the total Hochkulturen* there exists, side by side with the dominant supersystem, the other supersystems as minor structures. For this additional reason, the existence of a vulgar Sensate literature on lower levels of cultures which on their higher levels have been dominated by grand Ideational literature in no way damages my data or contradicts my conclusions concerning the fluctuation of Ideational, Idealistic, and Sensate literature on the higher levels of the cultures studied. This argument alone is sufficient to negate Schneider's criticism.

Several additional reasons and empirical evidence notably reinforce my argument. First, we should not exaggerate the contrasts between the cultures of the higher and the lower levels of the same total culture, or between the cultures of the higher and lower classes and groups of the same society. Despite ever present differences of higher and lower levels of the same total culture, or the differences of cultures of different strata and groups of the same society, the dominant forms of the culture of the higher levels or of the dominant classes, as a rule, greatly influence and mold the culture of the lower levels or strata. With the exception of the periods of disintegration of the culture of the higher levels or of the dominant, upper classes, in normal periods the culture of the lower levels or classes largely imitates that of the upper levels or classes (see 19, vol. 4, chapter 5; 29, pp. 568 ff.). During a vigorous domination of Ideational (or Sensate, or Idealistic) culture on the higher levels or in the dominant classes, a simplified version of Ideational (or respectively Sensate, or Idealistic) culture usually becomes dominant also on the lower levels of the same total culture or in the culture of the lower classes of the same society. For this reason the scarcity of Sensate literature in the early Mediaeval Ideational period may be due not only and not so much to the hypothetical factor of such a Sensate literature "being buried and lost," but also and mainly to the factor of an insignificant production, diffusion, and use of such a literature in a culture dominated on its higher levels, or in its dominant classes, by an Ideational supersystem. The validity of this last hypothesis is supported by the fact that in the periods of domination of a given culture by the Sensate supersystem, a vast production of Sensate culture on its lower levels and classes does not become "buried and lost": it leaves abundant evidence of its wide

---

[24] See my criticism of their theories of complete integration of the total *Hochkulturen* and of similar theories of the German "holystic morphologists" and of other "total integralists" in my (23, chapters 3, 4, 5; 21, chapter 43; 19, vol. 4, chapter 3; 30).

diffusion, popularity, and use; many samples of it enter and are preserved in the annals of history; many forms of it survive in its "vehicles" and in the historical traditions of subsequent generations. This means that the very hypothesis of Schneider and Hauser about the Sensate literature of the early Middle Ages "being buried and lost" is quite doubtful: it is supported by practically no empirical evidence. Neither is an explanation offered for why Sensate literature of the lower levels or classes at some periods becomes "buried and lost" leaving few, if any, traces of its existence, and why at other periods it leaves a vast body of evidence of its vigorous life and does not become "buried and lost." To take other examples from the data, tables, and curves of the *Dynamics:* glancing at the tables of the movement of scientific discoveries and inventions, we see that in Greece their number and curve decline after the fourth century B.C., in Rome after the first century A.D., and in Europe they remain at exceedingly low level throughout the period from A.D. 700 to 1200.[25] Can these (and many other) declines and scarcities of scientific discoveries and inventions in these periods be explained by the hypothesis of "being buried and lost"? Hardly; at least I do not know any competent historian of science and technology who advances this sort of explanation. Generally accepted explanations account for the declines and scarcity by the fact that in such periods actually only a few discoveries and inventions were made.

Or glancing at the tables of movement of idealistic and materialistic philosophies in the history of the West, we see that in the period of A.D. 580 to 1280 there is a zero index for all kinds of materialistic philosophy: the annals of history of philosophy do not register any single materialistic philosophy having emerged, diffused, and socialized during this period.[26] Again can this disappearance of materialistic philosophy in the total philosophical thought and culture of Europe of this period be accounted for by the hypothesis of "being buried and lost"? If someone would try to account for it by this hypothesis then he has to explain the still more formidable problem of why materialistic philosophies have not been buried and lost but on the contrary have prospered and become dominant at other periods of the Western or Greco-Roman cultures. I am reasonably certain that neither of these two questions can be satisfactorily answered by the hypothesis of "being buried and lost." With these remarks I can wind up my reply to this criticism of Schneider.[27]

[25] See the detailed tables and curves in ( 19, vol. 2, chapter 3 ).
[26] See for the tables and details ( 19, vol. 2, chapter 4 ).
[27] I pass by without comments Schneider's reference to D. C. McClelland's work because his "achievement motivation" is too generally defined without differentiation of Ideational or Sensate or Idealistic "achievement motivations." McClelland's interpretation of some parts of Greek art for the period 900–600 B.C. can hardly be interpreted as Sensate art. Even if they are interpreted in this sense, they represent only a fragment not representative of the total Greek art of these centuries. As a minor part of this art, it does not contradict the theory of the domination of Ideational art of the upper levels as well as of the total Greek art culture of this period.

### 3. Influence of the Ideological Systems and Supersystems on Behavior

Schneider's next criticism is still more serious than the preceding ones. Boiled down, it aims to show that I have not given sufficient evidence that the Ideational-Sensate-Idealistic supersystems of culture exert tangible influences upon the overt behavior of individuals living in such cultures: "By the criteria of conduct, there is nothing of importance to distinguish the one set of cultures from the other." Therefore if the overt behavior of persons living in predominantly Ideational culture does not differ tangibly from that of the persons living in predominantly Sensate culture, then these supersystems and their premises "could finally appear as philosophical irrelevancies or near-irrelevancies so far as a great deal of conduct is concerned."

This main criticism implies two other shortcomings of my theory of culture: first, that it seemingly excludes the conduct-phenomena from my conception of culture, which "exclusion would on the whole be quite unacceptable"; and second, that "no effort is made in the *Dynamics* to develop anything like a systematic psychological theory."

"Not guilty" is my plea in regard to both these charges.

a) That I do not exclude behavior-phenomena from my conception of culture follows from my very definition of the superorganic in its cultural as well as in its social and personal aspects: "All empirically rooted socio-cultural phenomena are made up of three components: 1. meanings-values-norms; 2. physical and biological vehicles objectifying them; 3. *mindful human beings (and groups) that create, operate, and use them in the process of their interaction*" (19, vol. 4, pp. 46 ff.). Conduct or behavior phenomena are discussed throughout all volumes of the *Dynamics,* and Chapter 15 of Volume Three: "Relationship Between Types of Culture and Types of Personality and Behavior" is specially devoted to this problem. Furthermore, behavior or conduct phenomena enter my very definition of culture in its differentiated forms as "Ideological, *Behavioral* and Material Cultures of Individuals and Groups." Here is my definition of these forms: "1. the totality of meanings, values, norms possessed by interacting individuals and groups make up their 'ideological' culture; 2. the totality of their meaningful *actions-reactions* through which the pure meanings, norms, and values are objectified, conveyed, and socialized make up their *behavioral* culture; 3. the totality of all the other vehicles, the material, biophysical things and energies through which their ideological culture is manifested, externalized, and socialized make up their 'material' culture. Thus the total empirical culture of a person or group is made up of these three levels of culture: ideological, behavioral, and material" (29, p. 313). Subsequently, in several chapters of this work, each of these forms of culture, including the behavioral one, and their relationships to each other are analyzed in considerable detail. For these reasons I find this charge of Schneider unwarranted.

b) Unwarranted also is his charge that I failed to develop a systematic psychological theory (of human personality and behavior). It is true that, though in various parts of the *Dynamics* such a theory is given, it is not summed up in a systematic form in special chapters. However, in my *Society, Culture and Personality*, in my *The Ways and Power of Love*, a systematic theory of the mental structure of human personality and of human behavior is clearly outlined and in several important points investigated in considerable detail. The gist of my theory of man, personality-structure, and behavior can be summed up as follows. I find the prevalent theories in this field grossly defective and offer my "integral" version, considerably different from these prevalent (unduly Sensate) theories. The prevalent Sensate theories view man mainly as an animal organism of the *homo sapiens* species. They tend to interpret his nature and behavior predominantly in mechanistic, materialistic, reflexological, and other "physicalistic" terms.

"The depth psychology" of these theories "either flattens the mental structure of personality to the level of the unconscious or subconscious, with a sort of epiphenomenal and vague 'ego' and 'superego,' or just depicts it as a "two-story building" — the unconscious (subconscious) and the conscious (rational). They see mainly the lowest forms of man's energies (the unconscious and subconscious) and are blind to man's rational and supraconscious genius." Among other blunders they "merge into the category of the 'unconscious' or 'subconscious' (E. von Hartmann, P. Janet, S. Freud, and others) two radically different energies of man: *the biologically unconscious* that lies below the level of the conscious state of mind and *the supraconscious* ("genius," "creative plan," Greek *nous*, Pneuma, 'Creative self,' 'Tao,' 'jnana,' 'prajna,' etc.) that lies above the level of any rational thought or energy."

In contrast to this "physicalistic," "animalistic" conception of man the Integral theory of man views *homo sapiens* not only or mainly as an animal organism, but especially as a mindful rational thinker and doer and as a supersensory and super-rational creator (genius). It is in the rational and the supra-conscious levels of man that the answer may be found to the ancient question: "What is man, that thou shouldst magnify him?" In contrast to the shallow "depth psychology" of personality structure, the Integral "height psychology" (as it is aptly called by Björn Sjövall, using Franz Kafka's dictum: *"des Menschen Tiefe ist seine Höhe,"* — "the deepest in man is his highest"[28] distinguishes in the total human personality and behavior "four different forms of energies — four mental levels and activities: (1) *the biologically unconscious;* (2) *the biologically conscious;* (3) *the socio-culturally conscious;* and (4) *the supraconscious.*"

1) Man is an animal and all the hereditary anatomical properties,

[28] See (16, pp. 48 ff., also 38).

physiological processes, reflexological, instinctive and unconscious excitations and inhibitions, drives and activities of the human organism necessary for animal life and survival make up the biologically unconscious matrix of human personality. Activities and processes determined by anatomical and physiological constitution of our organism, like breathing, eating, drinking, micturition, defecation, sleeping, rest after fatigue, sexual conjugation, avoidance of pain, cooperating with and fighting other human beings in the struggle for existence, reflexological crying, laughing, yelling, or growling and so on — such are the main biological drives, needs, and activities. This biological part of a human individual manifests, and is conditioned, by the biophysical properties of the organism and of the total cosmos. Being unconscious, this part of the personality's psyche does not have a conscious experience of "ego" or "I." Strictly automatic reflexes and activities of breathing, heart-beating, or digestion proceed without any consciousness of ego. This unconscious part of our mental apparatus and the reflexological-instinctive activities of the human personality are something much more complex and manifold than Freud's unconscious 'id,' 'libido' and complexes. . . .

2) Next to the unconscious energies and activities come the bioconscious ones associated with a set of biological egos and roles in personality. When a person becomes aware of his biological tension and the tension enters the field of consciousness (e.g., "I am hungry," "I have pain in my arm," etc.), the biological energy becomes bioconscious and leads to bioconscious activities on the part of the corresponding biological ego ("hungry ego," "sex ego," "thirsty ego," "urinating ego," "physically painful ego," and so on). Side by side with these short-term replacements of one biological ego by another in the course of each day, there is an irreversible long-time succession of the biological age — egos of the individual: the egos of a child, adolescent, mature man, old man. It is determined by biological forces and is accompanied by a legion of anatomical, physiological, and psychological changes in the individual, in his behavior, his relationships with others, and his position in his social groups.

3) Above this bioconscious stratum lie the *conscious socio-cultural energies, activities, egos, and roles.* They are generated by the conscious, meaningful interaction of mindful persons in their collective living, experience, and learning. Through their collective experience, they are accumulated and transmitted from person to person, group to group, generation to generation. In the process of this interaction, they are patterned into scientific, philosophical, religious, ethical, artistic, political, and technological forms of socio-cultural thought, norms, values, activities, and institutions. *A person possesses as many socio-cultural egos, roles, and activities as there are socio-cultural groups with which, voluntarily or not, he is connected.* Most of us have our *family ego* and activities, our *national, occupational, recreational, religious, political* egos and activities and the *lesser egos* and activities of the societies, clubs,

associations to which we belong. Each of these egos is a reflection of the meanings, values-norms of the particular group it represents. The activities and the role of each of our socio-cultural egos are defined by their respective social group. . . . Each of the groups seeks to impress upon a person its own image, in the form of a particular ego; each attempts to mold the individual after its own pattern; each prescribes to him a detailed course of his conduct; each demands a portion of his time and energy, a pound of flesh and a part of his soul or conscious mind. This explains the proposition that *each of us has as many conscious socio-cultural egos as there are organized groups with which we are in contact. The totality of these egos occupy almost the whole field of our conscious mentality, and the totality of these roles and activities fill a major part of our time, activities, and life. . . . If the groups to which a given individual belongs are in a solidary relationship with one another, if they all urge the individual to think, feel, and act in the same or concordant way, push him towards the same or concordant goals and prescribe to him the same or concordant duties, rights, then the different egos of the individual which reflect these groups will also be in harmony with one another, unified into a single, large harmonious ego.* (On this socio-cultural level) *he will be blessed with peace of mind and consistency in his conduct. . . . If on the other hand the groups to which an individual belongs are in conflict; if they urge him to contradictory ideas, values, convictions, duties and actions, then the individual's respective egos will be mutually antagonistic.* The individual will be a house divided against himself and split by inner conflicts. His conduct will be irresolute, inconsistent, and contradictory, as will also be his thoughts and utterances. The conscious, socio-cultural part of our mentality and behavior is directly connected with the socio-cultural human world.

4) Finally, there is a still higher level in the mental structure of man, a still higher form of energies and activities realized in varying degrees by different persons — namely, the *supraconscious* level of energies and activities. These constitute the fourth and highest stratum of man's personality, energies and activities. . . . At its purest and best, the supraconscious manifests itself in the greatest discoveries and creative achievements of men of genius in all fields of creative activity: science, philosophy, fine arts, religion, technological inventions, law, ethics, politics, and economics. These men of genius unanimously testify to the fact that their discoveries and creations have been inspired and started by the supraconscious flash of enlightenment — quite different from sensory observation and rational logico-mathematical thought — and then developed and tested by the sensory and rational methods of cognition and creativity.[29]

[29] The outline and quotations are taken mainly from my (24, chapter 5). For a developed form of this theory of personality structure see (24, chapters 5, 6, and 7),

This sketch of my Integral theory of personality structure and behavior shows that contrary to Schneider's statement, I have a systematic psychological theory in this field, fairly well developed and verified by a substantial body of empirical evidence.

Now, having in the background the outlines of my theory of the Ideological Behavioral and Material forms of culture of individuals and groups and the Integral ("Height-psychology") theory of personality structure and behavior, we can turn to a concise examination of Schneider's main criticism that I have not given sufficient evidence that the Ideational-Sensate-Idealistic supersystems exert a tangible influence upon the overt behavior of individuals and groups living in such cultures. If by sufficient evidence he means perfectly apodictic or unquestionably certain evidence, then his criticism is largely correct. But again in all empirical sciences and particularly in psychosocial disciplines there are very few, if any, theories and propositions that are apodictically certain. Instead of this ideal — hardly ever realized — standard of sufficiency of evidence, we must take the obtainable, comparative standard of adequacy of empirical corroboration as it is given by almost all psychological and sociological theories in this field. Measured by such a standard my main propositions concerning the influence of the cultural supersystems upon the mentality and overt behavior of individuals living and acting in the atmosphere of predominantly Ideational-Sensate-Idealistic cultures have a fairly substantial logical and empirical corroboration. These main propositions (developed in the *Dynamics*, in *Society, Culture and Personality*, and the *Ways and Power of Love*) are summed up as follows:

1. In accordance with my theory of personality structure and behavior the *actual overt behavior of a person is a resultant of the bio-physical-unconscious, the biologically-conscious, the socio-culturally conscious, and for especially creative men of genius, of the superconscious forces, incorporated in the individual himself, and of his — physical, biological, social, and cultural — worlds in which he is born, reared, lives, and acts.* Each of these factors generates and determines a set *of specific activities of an individual and no one of them can be regarded as the generator and determiner of the total behavior of a human being.*

2) This means that only a part of the total behavior of an individual is tangibly influenced — generated, molded, and patterned — by his culture, particularly by his cultural systems and supersystems and by the totality of social groups of which he has been and is a voluntary or involuntary member.

3) Each of the above five factors may generate in and "urge" the individual to the activities mutually antagonistic to each other (for instance, the biological sex drive may urge him to commit a sex act while

---

also (21, chapters 17, 18, 19, and 35). For a detailed analysis of the supraconscious and for an empirical evidence of its difference from sensory perception and rational thought, cf. also (19, vol. 4, chapter 16).

his religious-ethical "ego" may oppose it). Therefore the activities generated by each of the mentioned five factors may be — and often are — in conflict with each other.

4) In accordance with the theory of the Ideological, Behavioral, and Material cultures of an individual, his total Ideological culture contains many ideas, values, norms, which are not realized in his behavioral or material cultures. One may know a great deal about Communism or Buddhism or Shintoism or homosexuality without practicing their teachings in his behavior or objectifying these "ideologies" in any material vehicles of his total "material culture."

5) "There has hardly ever been any single individual whose total sum of meanings, values and norms (the total ideological culture) has been either completely integrated or completely contradictory. . . . There has hardly been an individual whose ideological culture has been either fully and closely integrated with his behavioral and material cultures, or entirely unintegrated with these. . . . Therefore the total (ideological, behavioral and material) culture of a person either in each or on all three levels is never completely integrated, nor completely unintegrated and contradictory."

6) "A human being is neither perfectly logical and rational, nor entirely nonlogical, illogical, nonrational and irrational. He is partly both."

7) "The degree and amount of integration of all three forms of culture in their meaningful-causal connections fluctuate from person to person, from group to group."[30]

From these general propositions, as their detailed form, follow the propositions formulated in the *Dynamics*, namely:

8) "The dominant type of culture tangibly molds the type of mentality (the Ideological culture) of human beings who are born and live in it. . . . Other conditions being equal, the mentality of a person will be predominantly Ideational if he has had a contact only with the Ideational culture." The same is true with regard to the Sensate, Idealistic, or Mixed type of culture.

9) "It is quite another matter with the problem of the relationship between the dominant type of culture and the actual behavior or conduct of the persons who are a part of it. . . . The relationship between the character of the dominant culture and the conduct of the persons who live in it either cannot be very close or cannot be as close as the correlation between the dominant culture and the mentality (Ideological culture) of these persons."

10) "Though the relationship between the dominant culture and the behavior of its bearers is not always close, nevertheless, it does exist. . . . The bearers of Ideational and Sensate cultures differ from one another not only in their mentality (Ideological culture) but also in their

---

[30] (21, pp. 325 ff.) contains the development and substantiation of these generalizations.

behavior and personality. All in all, the conduct and personality of the Ideational man would be more Ideational than that of the Sensate man, and vice versa. . . . The difference between the bearers of the Ideational and Sensate cultures is less great with respect to conduct and personality (their Behavioral and Material cultures) than to mentality (their Ideological cultures); nevertheless, the difference exists and is quite readily perceptible" (19, vol. 4, pp. 509 ff.).

Schneiders' criticism concerns mainly Propositions Nos. 9 and 10 in the sense that I have not given a sufficient evidence of their validity. Therefore my whole theory of the Ideational, Sensate, Idealistic, and Mixed types of culture may amount merely to a sort of "philosophical irrelevancies or near-irrelevancies so far as a great deal of conduct is concerned."

As I mentioned already I cannot agree with him on this point. First, he does not give practically any — logical or empirical — corroboration of his challenge: it remains a purely dogmatic statement. Second, his main argument consists essentially of an unduly exaggerated reiteration of my own statements that the predominant types of culture determine the overt behavior of their bearers much less than their mentality (Ideological culture). Even his considerations of the main factors of this lesser determination of the conduct of persons and groups by the predominant types of culture correctly outline my own factors of: an incomplete integration of ideological-behavioral-material cultures in individuals due to the frequent mutual conflicts of various biologically unconscious and conscious parts in their personality structure; the socio-cultural factor of affiliation of most of the individuals with different and often mutually contradictory social groups — the affiliation producing, in an individual, conflicts and inconsistencies among his socio-cultural egos and the activities required by each of them; and the conflicts between the demands of the biological, the socio-cultural, and the supra-conscious forces in the human personality. As can be seen from the above sketch of my theory of personality structure and of the ideological, behavioral, and material cultures of a person, there is no disagreement between Schneider's considerations and my fairly fully developed theories in this field. For this reason, Schneider's considerations of this point become irrelevant as an evidence against the Propositions Nos. 9 and 10. Third, in the *Dynamics* and in my subsequent works I give, if not apodictic then, at least, a comparatively substantial body of empirical evidence corroborating the Propositions Nos. 9 and 10. In the first place, insofar as the *Dynamics* has demonstrated the existence of Ideational-Sensate-Idealistic types of mentality (Ideological supersystems) and the existence of vast Ideational-Sensate-Idealistic systems of truths, philosophy, religion, fine arts, ethics, law, even politics and economics, and so far as it has demonstrated an interdependent change in togetherness of these systems and supersystems in time in the total cultures of Greece, Rome, and the West (and more cursorily in several other cultures), the very demonstration of these cardinal facts (which none of the critics has been able to disprove) represents a most substantial empirical corroboration of Propositions Nos. 9 and 10 as well as other propositions sketched above. Why? *Because all these empirically rooted Ideational-Idealistic-Sensate systems and supersystems of "fine arts, systems of truth (science, philosophy, religion) moral systems, systems of law; forms of political, social, and economic organizations; and so on are not only the phenomena of mentality (Ideological culture) but also the phenomena of behavior in the most overt, 'behavioristic' sense.* Their creation, existence and functioning in any culture presupposes an incessant stream of actions and reactions — that is, of behavior — on the part of the members of the culture. The creation of the Parthenon or the Chartres Cathedral (as well as that of the Empire State or the Wall Street buildings) involved the capital and labor (that is an enormous amount of activities) of thousands of persons for a notable length of time. The creation and functioning of any institution, be it the Roman Catholic See or the New York Stock Exchange, are carried on through incessant activities, i.e., through certain forms of behavior, of a few or of many human individuals. Since these activities assume one (behavioral and material) form in an Ideational and a quite different form in a Sensate society in all the socio-cultural compartments, this means that a very large part of the conduct of the members of an Ideational culture assumes Ideational forms, while that of the members of a Sensate society take on Sensate forms" (19, vol. 4 pp. 511 ff.) It is not a phenomenon of mentality only, but also of behavior that members of Medieval society build a multitude of cathedrals, churches, and abbeys as their greatest buildings outlining the skyline of their cities and villages, while the members of Sensate society build the Empire State, Radio City, and other commercial and secular buildings towering above all churches and cathedrals lost among these secular giants. It is not merely a phenomenon of ideological culture but no less a very solid and massive manifestation of behavioral and material culture that in the dominant Ideational culture its artists paint, sculptors sculpt, musicians compose their masterpieces almost entirely on religious topics, while in Sensate society they do so on perfectly Sensate themes. The same is true of literature and drama. The same is to be said of the Ideational-Sensate-Idealistic codes of law and ethics (with the behavior of their judges and violators, with the court buildings and systems of punishment), of the theocratic and secular governments, of respective systems of philosophy and theology, of their economic systems, of prevalency of respective familistic, contractual and coercive forms of social relationships, even of their modes of wars and revolutions. The *Dynamics* has fairly conclusively demonstrated the existence and fluctuation of Ideational-Sensate-Idealistic forms in practically all compartments of culture and organized social systems in the Greco-Roman and the

Western social worlds. Millions and millions of these "materialized and congealed objectifications" of Ideational-Idealistic-Sensate ideological systems represent uncontestable, massive empirical evidence of quite a tangible and unquestionable influence of these ideological systems upon the behavior and "material culture" of these populations. "To the extent that the *Dynamics* has shown that Ideational, Idealistic, Sensate and Mixed cultures have their own forms of mentality in all the main fields of cultures and social relationships; to the extent that any phenomenon of this culture mentality is at the same time a phenomenon of overt behavior (of the respective populations) — to these limits the conduct and behavior of the members of any such culture is quite tangibly conditioned by it, and stands in a consistent and clear association with it."[31]

This massive evidence, underestimated by Schneider, fairly convincingly repudiates his charge.[32]

As to the additional statistical evidence given in the *Dynamics* for a supplementary corroboration of the discussed Propositions Nos. 9 and 10, there are the tables of the Ideational-Sensate-Mixed types of personality of the Roman Catholic Popes from the year 42 to 1937; of the types of French-Russian-Austrian-English kings from 800 to 1917; of the percentages among all the historical persons listed in the *Encyclopaedia Britannica* of the persons who became historical through their religious (Ideational) or their business (Sensate) activities and achievements at the specified periods from 900 B.C. to A.D. 1849. Each of these tables alone would indeed be insufficient evidence for confirmation of Propositions Nos. 9 and 10, but taken together they significantly reinforce my main evidence to an extent to which a significant coefficient of correlation may be taken for a proof of a validity of a proposition.[33] So much for this criticism.

[31] See (19, vol. 4, p. 514). See there a development and specification of this influence upon the forms and patterns of respective behavioral actions, stimulation or inhibitions of certain forms of actions in conformity with the nature of each of these cultures; influences on the frequency of commission or non-commission of the favored and prohibited activities, and so on.

[32] This sort of evidence anyone can observe daily by visiting and studying the ideological, behavioral, and material cultures of, say, a monastic community and that of a night club; or of the Dukhobor, the Mennonite, the Hutterite village communities and those of secularized farmers; of a typical Catholic or of a Southern Baptist college and the non-denominational, secular college. Even in the case of the colleges a number of differences in the courses, in the attendance of religious services, and in dozens of other behavioral and especially material cultural traits can be easily observed.

[33] Since writing the *Dynamics* two additional statistical series showing the number of the saints sanctified by the Christian church (before its splitting into different denominations and after its split) by the Roman Catholic and the Russian Orthodox churches from the first to twentieth century, and the statistics of the number of the Christian and Roman Catholic Popes sanctified at various periods of existence of the Papacy from 32 A.D. to 1823 reinforce the testimony of the mentioned three tables. Taken together, all five statistical series corroborate the main evidence discussed. For these additional two statistical series see my (22, chapters 37 and 38; 31, pp. 80–82).

I do not have space to examine carefully other, somewhat casual, critical remarks of Schneider concerning the Ideational and Sensate meanings of such concept as causality and number. I can only state that the distinction of these forms is not invented by me but is pointed out and carefully analyzed by the most competent historians of these concepts. All I did was to apply to their forms the terms Ideational and Sensate, which accurately fit these forms. Yes, in many operations the Chinese count "Four plus four makes eight," and "Eight is a bigger number than three," but in a number of operations when they attach a "mystic" meaning to a certain number then, as my quotation from Granet testifies, "Number three becomes greater than the number eight," because "Three means 'unanimity' while eight means only a 'majority.'" Precisely when an ideational meaning is attached to this or that number — and such "numerological" attachment has been prevalent in the predominantly Ideational cultures and periods and sometimes its survivals are found even in a Sensate culture (like the unlucky number thirteen in our Sensate culture, a replica of Hesiod's "calendar of the lucky and unlucky days": the sixth day in each month unpropitious for the birth of a female, the thirteenth, for sowing; the fourth day for good marriage, etc.) — many small numbers become in their value larger than quantitatively bigger numbers, and vice versa. The numbers with the ideational meaning attached to them influence the behavior of their believers in different ways than purely quantitative numbers affect Sensate behavior. This Ideational meaning sometimes makes three greater in its mystic power than eight or 100 and for that reason more desirable than many quantitatively bigger numbers.[34] To these remarks I add the observation that Schneider does not give any evidence for his contention. To sum up: even the Ideational or Sensate conception of numbers exerts a tangible influence on the behavior of their partisans and sometimes Ideationally makes a greater number of what, from a purely quantitative Sensate standpoint, is a smaller number, and vice versa.

With a slight modification these remarks can be applied to Schneider's statements concerning the psychology and behavior of the pre-literate peoples and the Ideational and Sensate concepts of causality.[35]

Finally, acknowledging the subtlety of Schneider's analysis of my concept of "integration," I cannot accept his replacement of my proposition by his two propositions. My proposition states that "other conditions being equal, the highest amount of self-determination belongs to those

[34] See the details in (19, vol. 2, pp. 433–437; vol. 4, chapters 9, 10, 11. In these chapters many examples of "mystic interpretations" of numbers like 3, 7, 12, and others are given. The to us more familiar Jewish cabala contains many samples of an Ideationally-esoteric interpretation of numbers.

[35] See for the definitions of Ideational and Sensate causality and also of time and space, for fluctuation of these two forms in history of the Greek, the Roman, and Western thought, and for their behavioral effects in (19, vol. 2, chapter 11; vol. 4, chapters 9, 10, 11; also 20, passim).

social and cultural systems which are most perfectly integrated, causally and meaningfully." Additionally I warn not to mix "integration" or lack of it with "plasticity," "rigidity," and similar meanings. Schneider finds this proposition doubtful and replaces it by two propositions: (1) "the more highly integrated social and cultural systems are the more liable to shortness of life and destruction"; and (2) "on the whole an 'Idealistic,' compromising, fusing sort of structure might be more viable."

As to his second proposition, with a proviso that his "compromising and fusing" do not undermine the integration of the system, it does not necessarily contradict my generalization; a well-integrated system may be plastic and elastic. As to his first proposition, since he does not give any proof of it except an abstract consideration of a faster sweeping of danger or threat throughout the whole integrated system, instead of a long argument I simply say that, despite his proposition, I still (and I suspect he also does) prefer to drive a well-integrated automobile to a poorly constructed or dilapidated jalopy; I still believe that other conditions being equal, a well-organized army or a football team will defeat a poorly-trained and unintegrated army or team. And I do not criticize our military authorities for installation of a radar system immediately able to inform the defense authorities and the whole nation about the enemy's missiles and bombers. I think that fast communication to the whole nation of the danger helps but does not hurt the nation's defense or survival. Likewise the longevity, survival, and self-determination of well-integrated scientific, philosophical, religious, or artistic systems on the whole has been much greater than those of the eclectic "too much compromising and fusing" congeries. Since Schneider does not give any other evidence, and since the *Dynamics* furnishes a considerable number of cases corroborating my proposition, I can refer the reader to my work (19, vol. 4, pp. 604–620) and with these remarks can end my reply to this section of Schneider's criticism.

## 4. Shortcomings of the "Undeveloped Themes"

In this section Schneider points at a series of themes touched in my works but left without a sufficient analysis and development. His charge is correct to the extent that my analysis of these problems neither gives an adequate knowledge of, nor makes unnecessary further research for a better understanding of these themes. Acknowledging this shortcoming, at the same time I think that my analysis of the themes gives at least a rough approximation to such an understanding. As a thorough discussion of these problems here is impossible, I may be excused for the sketchiness of my answers to the critical remarks of Schneider.

a) His first question is, what really unites various Sensate systems or "value areas" into one Integrated Sensate culture (supersystem) since these "value areas," according to my own statements, are separated from one another. "Whence this unity? And just how shall it be described?" My answer in black and white is: they are united into a Sensate *Ganzheit* by the identity of their ultimate premise that the true reality (and value) is sensory and by empirical grounding of this premise in the material vehicles and behavior of a respective population.

This premise in its manifold differentiations unifies, and is articulated by, all Senate "value areas"; Sensate arts, science, philosophy, religion, ethics, law, economics, politics in their ideological, behavioral, and material forms. From this premise also follow similar, predominantly utilitarian, hedonistic, and sensate value systems, motivations, social tasks, "ethos and pathos" permeating and animating all the systems or "value areas" of Sensate culture; like Sensate art they all endeavor to serve mainly the Sensate "life, liberty, and pursuit of happiness." For this purpose Sensate science studies only the sensory empirical reality, Sensate philosophy philosophizes about mainly empirical forms of Becoming, Sensate ethics prescribes utilitarian and hedonistic rules of conduct aimed at "the maximum of Sensate happiness for the maximum of human beings"; likewise Sensate codes of law, Sensate economics and politics aim to realize the same objectives, if not for all human beings then, at least, for the respective "power elite" that controls legislation, economics, and politics. From the same premise issue the Sensate "unity in diversity" or "*ex pluribus unum,*" relativity, and the incessant change of Sensate values and norms of conduct and many other characteristics of Sensate culture analyzed in great detail in the *Dynamics.*

b) Schneider's second charge is that I do not give a systematic classification of the resemblances and differences of Ideational-Sensate-Idealistic and other cultures. My answer is: in my system of general sociology that deals with the *generic* characteristics of *all* superorganic phenomena, of *all* organized social systems, unorganized social groups and nominal social plurels, and with generic traits common to *all* integrated cultural systems and unintegrated congeries and in my general and differential theory of personality structure, *the generic resemblances of all varieties of socio-cultural phenomena in their structural and dynamic aspects are listed, classified, and analyzed.*[36] In still greater detail are classified and analyzed the differences of main social systems and of their strata (in my systematic theory of social differentiation and stratification),[37] of main cultural systems,[38] and particularly of Sensate-Ideational-Idealistic systems and supersystems.[39] For this substantial reason I do not think that this charge is correct.

c) If this charge means that I did not give a systematic theory of the factors of these multitudinal resemblances and differences — their reasons or sources — then the charge is partly correct, but only partly,

---

[36] See for that (21, chapters 3, 4, 5, 8, 9, 17–34).
[37] See for this (21, chapters 10–17).
[38] See (21, chapters 17, 18, 35–39, 44, and 45).
[39] See (21, chapters 40–43), and then all volumes of the *Dynamics,* passim.

because in my theory of the *generic* "resemblances" and "differences" in personality structures, in social and cultural systems, the main reasons for their similarities and dissimilarities are indicated. In shortest form "the resemblances" in personality structure and behavior, in various social and cultural systems, including the Ideational-Sensate-Idealistic supersystems, are due to the common biological and psychosocial properties of human nature or of the species *homo sapiens.*

Biologically all members of this species (with the exception of a few biologically defective individuals) have basically similar anatomical structure, physiological processes, neurological mechanisms of unconditioned reflexes, and other biological properties, needs, and "drives." Psychosocially, likewise, they are equipped with essentially similar "mechanisms" of sensations-perceptions-reproductive imagination, feelings, emotions, volition, conditioned reflexes and associations, elements of rational thought and potential creativity. In the terms of my theory of personality structure, almost all human beings have many basic resemblances in the "biologically-unconscious," the "biologically-conscious," "the socio-culturally conscious," and, to a lesser degree, even in the "supra-conscious" parts of their total psyche. These biological and psychosocial basic similarities largely account for the *generic* similarities of all social and cultural systems, including the Ideational-Sensate-Idealistic supersystems built upon these similarities. Then, once created, these cultural and social systems of interacting human beings often increase these basic similarities by adding to them many similarities created and imposed by the culture and social systems themselves.

On the other hand, side by side with these similarities there exist many biological and psychosocial dissimilarities of individuals and groups: biological differences of sex, age, race, inherited constitution, health, nervous system, reflexes, needs, and others; and psychological differences in their intellectual, affective, emotional, volitional and creative equipment; plus the differences in the cosmic, biological, and psychosocial environment of their rearing and living. These differences make up the first basis for emergence of many differences of various cultural systems and supersystems.

These initial similarities and differences are continuously modified and transformed by the incessant process of interaction of the person and groups in social living together, by their changing environment, and by the factor of the manifold possibilities of solution of their problems. These factors generate several additional differences and resemblances superimposed upon the inherent bio-psychological ones.

Such in black and white are the sources of similarities and differences of various cultures, including the Ideational-Sensate-Idealistic ones. In each of these cultures, members satisfy their basic biological needs and each culture has complex systems of scientific, economic, political, legal, religious rules and institutions that regulate the activities and relationships of their populations involved in the satisfaction of these needs. In each of these cultures their members manifest and, in accordance with the nature of the culture, satisfy their quest for knowledge, wisdom, goodness, beauty, and other "super-biological" values by creating their systems and congeries of science, philosophy, religion, ethics, law, fine arts, political, economic, and other "value areas." A long series of essentially the same activities, cultural systems, institutions, and "value areas" are found practically in *all human societies and cultures,* beginning with the paleolithic and ending with the contemporary ones.

On the other hand, on account of biological and psychosocial differences, and different environments of individuals and groups, and of the manifold possibility of achievement of these tasks in different ways, each and all of these activities, systems, and institutions have assumed *concretely different forms and contents,* including the differences of Ideational-Sensate-Idealistic-Eclectic cultures. They are similar in having their systems and congeries of science, philosophy, religion, fine arts, ethics, politics, and economics, but the concrete Ideological, Behavioral, and Material forms and contents of these systems are different. Such is the gist of my answer — extensively developed and documented in my works — to this question.

d) This answer leads us to the pointed question of Schneider: if each of these cultures has its own system and criteria of truth (or of beauty or goodness), then does this mean there are only perfectly relative truths and no universal, perennial, or absolute Truth (and ethical and aesthetic standards) whatsoever? No. First of all, as Schneider himself correctly observes, there is a large "area of consensus" among the Ideational-Sensate-Idealistic systems of truth, of aesthetic, ethical, legal, even political and economic systems. Even beyond this "area of consensus" there is "an area of mutual complementarity" of these systems. Only in part are these systems mutually incompatible and contradictory. While this "incompatible and mutually contradictory" area embodies perfectly relative, local, temporary, evanescent, "small" truths, "small" ethical and legal norms, aesthetic, economic, and political values, the cognitive-aesthetic-ethical-legal-political-economic and other systems that lie in the "areas of consensus and mutual complimentarity" are much closer and truer approximations to the universal and perennial values-standards-norms which in their turn are a still truer approximation to the Absolute Truth, Absolute Beauty, Absolute Goodness.[40] In other terms, each of the Ideational-Idealistic-Sensate cultures creates and contains the values that approach

---

[40] In the terms of St. Thomas Aquinas the "area of mutual contradiction" somewhat corresponds to what he calls "human law" (relative, changeable, temporary); the areas of "mutual complementarity and consensus" correspond to what he calls "natural law" and my Absolute Truth-Beauty-Goodness is congenial to his "divine law" of to the Platonic ideal forms and values. In the terms of the Integral system of socio-cultural time the area of contradictions lies in *tempus,* the area of consensus and complimentarity in *aevum,* the absolute values in *aeternitas.* Cf. on this my (20, chapter 4).

the universal and perennial values side by side with the temporary, local values and plain pseudo-values. None of these cultures embodies "the whole truth and nothing but the Truth" or immortal values. Exactly for this reason when each of these cultures realizes its limited fund of the real values, it is bound to decline and be replaced by another form of culture pregnant with its own fund of the real values.[41]

Such is my answer to this question of Schneider.

Leaving his minor remarks without a reply,[42] in conclusion I thank Professor Schneider for his most thoughtful observations and criticisms of my "yarns" and the editors of this volume for their willingness to publish my *"Reply."* I can finish it by quoting the old adage: *Feci quod potui faciant meliora potentes.*

## BIBLIOGRAPHY

1. Allen, Philip. *Pitirim A. Sorokin in Review.* Durham, N.C.: Duke University Press, 1963.

2. Brinton, C. "Socio-Astrology," *The Southern Review* (Autumn 1937), p. 252.

3. Cairne, G. C. *History of Cyclical Theories.* New York: Philosophical Library, 1963.

4. de Chardin, P. T. *The Phenomenon of Man.* New York: Harper & Bros., 1959.

5. Durkheim, E. "Deux lois de l'evolution penale," *L'Annee sociologique,* Series 1, Vol. IV, pp. 65 ff.

6. Gurvitch, G. *Dialectique et Sociologie.* Paris: Flammarion, 1962.

7. Kroeber, A. *Configurations of Culture Growth, Style and Civilizations.* Berkeley: University of California Press, 1947.

8. Loomis, Charles. *Social Systems.* New York: Van Nostrand, 1960.

9. Loomis, Charles. *Modern Social Theories.* New York: Van Nostrand, 1961.

10. Merleau-Ponti, M. *Les aventures de la dialectique.* Paris: Flammarion, 1955.

11. Parsons, Talcott. *The Social System.* Homewood, Ill.: The Free Press, 1951.

12. Rostovtzeff, M. I. Personal letter to P. A. Sorokin, dated Dec. 1, 1937, in which Rostovtzeff gives his evaluation of the *Dynamics.*

[41] This answer is connected with my Integral system of philosophy — in its ontological and epistemological parts. Cf. an outline of my Integral philosophy, ontology, and theory of cognition and creation in (26) and in (27). See also (30).

[42] There are many similarities between A. Kroeber's theories of culture developed in (7) and my theories. My analysis and appraisal of Kroeber's theories are given in (23, chapters 9 and 13).

13. Sartre, Jean Paul. *Critique de la reason dialéctique,* Tome I. Paris: Gallimard, 1960. "Theorie des Ensembles pratiques."

14. Schneider, Louis. "The Role of the Category of Ignorance in Sociological Theory," *American Sociological Review,* Vol. 27 (August 1962), pp. 492–508.

15. Siu, R. G. H. *The Tao of Science.* New York: John Wiley & Sons, 1957.

16. Sjöval, Björn. *Hojdpsykologi.* Stockholm: Svenska Kyrkans, 1959.

17. Sorokin, Pitirim A. *Sistema Soziologii,* 2 vols. St. Petersburg: isdatelstvo Kolos, 1920.

18. Sorokin, Pitirim A. *Contemporary Sociological Theories.* New York: Harper and Bros., 1928.

19. Sorokin, Pitirim A. *Social and Cultural Dynamics.* New York: American Book Co., 1937.

20. Sorokin, Pitirim A. *Sociocultural Causality, Space, Time.* Durham, N.C.: Duke University Press, 1943.

21. Sorokin, Pitirim A. *Society, Culture and Personality.* New York: Cooper Square Publishers, 1947.

22. Sorokin, Pitirim A. *Altruistic Love: A Study of American Good Neighbors and Christian Saints.* Boston: Beacon Press.

23. Sorokin, Pitirim A. *Social Philosophies of an Age of Crisis.* Boston: Beacon Press, 1951.

24. Sorokin, Pitirim A. *The Ways and Power of Love.* Boston: Beacon Press, 1954.

25. Sorokin, Pitirim A. *Fads and Foibles in Modern Sociology and Related Sciences.* Chicago: H. Regnery, 1956.

26. Sorokin, Pitirim A. "This is My Faith," in S. G. Cole (ed.), *This is My Faith.* New York: Harper and Bros., 1956.

27. Sorokin, Pitirim A. "Integralism is My Philosophy," in Whit Burnett (ed.), *This is My Philosophy.* New York: Harper and Bros., 1957.

28. Sorokin, Pitirim A. "Theses on the Role of Historical Method in the Social Sciences," *Transactions of the Fifth World Congress of Sociology.* Washington, D.C.: International Sociological Association, 1962, Vol. 1.

29. Sorokin, Pitirim A. *Society, Culture and Personality.* New York: Cooper Square Publishers, 1963.

30. Sorokin, Pitirim A. "Reply to My Critics," in Philip Allen (ed.), *Pitirim A. Sorokin in Review.* Durham, N.C.: Duke University Press, 1963.

31. Sorokin, Pitirim A., and W. Lunden. *Power and Morality.* Boston: Porter Sargent, 1959.

32. Stcherbatsky, Th. *The Central Conceptions of Buddhism.* London: Royal Asiatic Society, 1923.

33. Stcherbatsky, Th. *Buddhist Logic,* 2 vols. Leningrad: U.S.S.R. Academy of Science, 1932.

34. Timasheff, N. S. "Sorokin on Law, Revolution, War and Social Calami-

ties," in Philip Allen (ed.), *Pitirim A. Sorokin in Review.* Durham, N.C.: Duke University Press, 1963.

35. Tiryakian, E. *Sociological Theory, Values and Sociocultural Change,* Essays in Honor of P. A. Sorokin. New York: The Free Press of Glencoe, 1963.

36. Toynbee, Arnold J. "Professor Sorokin's Philosophy of History," in Philip Allen (ed.), *Pitirim A. Sorokin in Review.* Durham, N.C.: Duke University Press, 1963.

37. Urlanis, B. *Voiny i narodonaseleniye Evrope.* Moscow: Isd. Soz. Ekon. Literatury, 1960.

38. Vexliard, A. "Psychological Theories of P. Sorokin," in Philip Allen (ed.), *Pitirim A. Sorokin in Review.* Durham, N.C.: Duke University Press, 1963.

39. von Wiese, L. "Ideenkultur und Sinnenkultur," in *Archiv für Rechts und Sozial Philosophie,* Band XXXI, Heft 3.

40. Wright, Q. *A Study of War,* 2 vols. Chicago: University of Chicago Press, 1942.

# 23

*Don Martindale*

# The Roles of Humanism and

# Scientism in the Evolution

# of Sociology

In the curriculum of the modern university the courses fall into three clear divisions: the humanities, the sciences, and the social sciences. Even persons who have not attended closely to the development of Western intellectuality are well aware of the fact that the humanities are the oldest, and the social sciences are the youngest of the trilogy. Moreover, one can quickly assure himself that the social sciences are insurgent between the humanities and science, borrowing from each and somewhat in tension with each. Many a hard-headed physical scientist of the old school will exclaim, if pressed, that the social sciences "are not even sciences." And many a traditional humanist is so sure that social concerns belong properly in the humanities as to find the very idea of a social science "revolting." The social scientists, for their part, often smugly consider themselves as the true synthesizers of the thought and experience of modern man, as the bearers of the discipline which fused the humanistic and scientific poles of Western thought. Auguste Comte thought sociology was the queen of the sciences, and C. Wright Mills observed:

It is *not* true, as Ernest Jones asserted, that "Man's chief enemy and danger is his own unruly nature and the dark forces pent up within him." On the contrary: "Man's chief danger" today lies in the unruly forces of contemporary society itself, with its alienating methods of production, its enveloping techniques of political domination, its international anarchy — in a word, its pervasive transformations of the very "nature" of man and the conditions and aims of his life.

It is now the social scientist's foremost political and intellectual task — for here the two coincide — to make clear the elements of contemporary uneasiness and indifference. It is the central demand made upon him by other cultural workmen — by physical scientists and artists, by the intellectual community in general. It is because of this task and these demands, I believe, that the social sciences are becoming the common denominator of our cultural period, and the sociological imagination our most needed quality of mind (18; p. 13).

In this forthright statement sociology is the true synthesis of the intellectual currents of the West, and only in the hands of sociologists may its affairs be trusted. "To be aware of the idea of social structure and to use it with sensibility is to be capable of tracing . . . linkages among a great variety of *milieux*. To be able to do that is to possess the sociological imagination" (18, pp. 10–11).

The rise of sociology as a discipline which sought to substantiate claims such as those of C. Wright Mills to be the representative outlook of contemporary man is intimately bound up with its relation to the intellectual currents and the substantive issues of Western man. Humanism and science — the two main streams of Western thought — summarize the alternative ways by which Western man solves the problems of his social and natural world. The two most comprehensive substantive problems which Western man must solve are those of the individual and those of the collective (society). No orientations to the problems of existence are more fundamental than those which take the individual as primary (individualism) and those which take the collective as primary (collectivism). It is not misleading to take these two methodological orientations (the humanistic and the scientific) and substantive theoretical alternatives (individualism and collectivism) as the primary compass points of Western thought.

If we pass quickly in review the main methodological orientations of Western thought and the major substantive theoretical alternatives, it is possible to employ the resultant sketch to map the evolution of sociology. The primary forces playing upon sociology arise out of the experience of Western man.

### Humanism as the Pioneering Outlook of Western Man

The distinctive communities of the Middle Ages were agrarian and religious in character: peasant villages, feudal manors, and monasteries (15, pp. 409–415). Though they have roots in the Middle Ages, the first

Main Compass Points of Western Thought

| Perspectives | | Substantive Alternatives | |
| --- | --- | --- | --- |
| | | Individualism | Collectivism |
| | Humanistic | Humanistic Individualism | Humanistic Collectivism |
| | Scientific | Scientific Individualism | Scientific Collectivism |

of the distinctive communities of the contemporary world were cities
(15, pp. 415–418). Humanism, the pioneering outlook of Western man,
was born in the city. Early civic humanism can be most simply defined
as a secularized, man-centered outlook and methodology developed for
the needs of civic man in contrast to the God-centered outlook and salvation technology of the members of typical medieval communities.

The most highly valued types of men of the Middle Ages were chivalrous knights and ascetic monks. The most meaningful life was one devoted to God's work, whether this consisted of vigils, fasting, ascetic
privations, prayer, or engaging in military activities in the name of the
faith. The most sanctified of all modes of deportment were those of the
monastic recluse. The technology of the religiously significant life centered in withdrawal from sensual pleasure, fasting, privations, and prayer
— especially in contemplation of the holy.

In the rising cities the modes of deportment associated with chivalrous
adventurers or contemplative ascetics were retrograde. In the streets
of the city, knights and monks rubbed shoulders with new commercial
and industrial types: plutocrats rich from international trade and able
by their new wealth to deck themselves out with fineries from afar in a
manner that outshone the poor knight and poorer monk. Moreover, in
the streets there appeared a variety of others: traders from afar speaking
strange tongues, craftsmen, former serfs enjoying the freedom of the city.
While knight and monk lost comparative status with the rise of the new
commercial types, they lost it also with the rise of the new freemen from
the base of society. In these cities a new thriving secularity was evident.
The silent watches and vigils of the knightly novitiate or the silence of
the monastic chamber had no place. The religious structures serving the city were propelled to a new grandeur. In the cities the magnificent Gothic cathedrals were being subscribed and constructed. The
humble monasteries were withdrawing to a vine-draped countryside as
the tides of life surged away from them.

The overpowering sense of the evil of the secular world which had sent

Christianity into the monastery in the days of the decay of the Roman cities was replaced by a new optimistic sense of abundant life. In the cities Western man even began to re-tool his religion to correspond to the new secular optimism that fired his aspirations. In the cities men were individualized, cast upon their own resources, and compelled to employ their own talents to construct the institutions they needed:

> In the Middle Ages both sides of human consciousness — that which was turned within and that which was turned without — lay dreaming or half awake beneath a common veil. The veil was woven of faith, illusion, and childish prepossession, through which the world and history were seen clad in strange hues. Man was conscious of himself only as a member of a race, people, party, family, or corporation — only through some general category. In Italy this veil first melted into air; an *objective* treatment and consideration of the State and of all the things of this world became possible. The *subjective* side at the same time asserted itself with corresponding emphasis; man became a spiritual individual, and recognized himself as such. In the same way the Greek had once distinguished himself from the barbarian, and the Arab had felt himself an individual at a time when other Asiatics knew themselves only as members of a race (1, p. 81).

In the twelfth century, in response to the need for guidance in their new civic communities, the humanists had begun to examine the classics of antiquity. It was not the slightest intention of the persons engaged in this enterprise to deify the past: quite the contrary. They recognized in the literature produced in the ancient *polis* the writings of people with experience in many points similar to their own. In the course of their interest in the exploitation of classical sources, they pioneered an elaborate array of new skills: they acquired the classical languages and began to insist on the study of the classical texts in the original; they developed philological techniques; they began to elaborate the standards of historical criticism in a manner not seen since the days of the classical Greeks.

The humanists belonged to the civic types responsible for developing the institutions of the city: corresponding secretaries, the tutors in important political and merchant families, advisors of princes, and, at times, even the princes and popes themselves, rich merchants with strong voices in the councils of the cities, and professors in the newly forming universities (1, pp. 128–136). While a single coherent philosophy cannot be assigned to the humanists as a whole, they were characterized by their optimistic theory of human nature, the employment of scholarship as a device for the solution of contemporary problems, the evaluation of classical learning as a source of guidance in social and intellectual affairs, and the development of alternatives to medieval theological explanations of the world (2, pp. 47–133, pp. 223–254).

By the twelfth century the traditional powers of the medieval world had become fully aware of the new spirit that was breaking away from their control. At the University of Paris in 1210, 1215, and again in 1231, professors and students were excommunicated for having disobeyed orders of the Church by reading Aristotle (21, pp. 460–461). In the cities the new social and intellectual ferment so completely eluded traditional structures as to lead to the formation of a wide variety of voluntary associations. Some of the new formations were eventually taken over by the Church, and made into new official monastic movements like the "Four Orders," the Dominicans, Franciscans, Carmelites, and Austin Friars (12, p. 727). But other semi-religious social movements such as the Beguines and Beghards of the Low Countries, the Humiliati of Italy, and the Poor Men of Leon were not blessed with Church approval.

Representatives of the new mendicant orders pressed their way into the newly forming universities and took up the battle against the new intellectual ferment. It was quickly perceived that one could not destroy the new intellectual currents. The task was to turn them to the religious advantage of the Church. If masters and students were going to read Aristotle at the risk of excommunication, the task was to take over Aristotle and purge the texts. The reconciliation of Aristotle with Christian theology was urged by great Franciscan scholars such as Robert Grosseteste, and by even more prominent Dominicans such as Albert the Great (1200–1280) and Thomas Aquinas (1225–1274). In the thirteenth century the Benedictine orders won the day and clamped an official scholasticism down on the universities.

With this development, the humanists were forced to minor positions in the universities and to purely private circles, where at times, like Ficino, they established private academies, and at times promoted the cause of Platonism against the official scholasticism and Aristotelianism that were becoming dominant in the universities (2, pp. 4–6, pp. 185–186). By the fifteenth century in private circles of the Italian cities, the tide turned again. Humanism broke through the spell of official scholasticism and achieved a kind of classic fullness.

### The Emergence of Western Science

In the same civic world where humanism had formed, Western science emerged. Humanism arose in circles of cultivated social and political strata; science arose in the circles of artists and craftsmen. Humanism pioneered a new mode of deportment in the social and political world, while science pioneered a new method of procedure toward the world of physical things.

The peculiarities of science are found in its fusion of a rational conception of knowledge with a systematic experimentalism toward the world of facts. From the ancient world the West inherited the rational proof and the dream of systematically transforming all thought into a comprehensive rational unity (14, pp. 6–10). Social developments in the ancient *polis* had cast its citizen-intellectuals on their own conceptual resources without the opportunity for recourse to institutional devices to settle differences of opinion. Under these circumstances, the philosophers of ancient Greece began to analyze the thought process in the attempt to establish rules which would automatically guarantee the truth without the need to appeal to any agency outside the thought process itself. The unique place of Socrates among the Greek philosophers was bound up with the self-consciousness he brought to this search for an autonomous thought process. The great monuments to the search for the rational proof were Euclidean geometry and Aristotelian logic.

However, the rational proof and the dream of the rational integration of all knowledge born in Greek philosophy was restricted from any extensive application to the world of fact by the social situation of the ancient philosopher. The ancient philosopher was a citizen-soldier (15, pp. 353–355) in a society where the status of work was determined by slavery. Wherever slavery appears, the conduct of practical activities tends to be technologically unprogressive. While the ancient world supplied the rational proof to science, it could not supply the progressive technology which science also needed.

Contrary to those historians of science who see no contribution at all to science from the Middle Ages and the Renaissance, they supplied it with the technology that science required. The decline of slavery in the Middle Ages freed technology from its bondage to that unprogressive system. The new progressiveness has been skillfully phrased recently by Lynn White, Jr. The heavy-wheeled plow which was invented and developed to cultivate the heavy soils of northern Europe in turn sustained developments critical to the emergence of the modern world:

> The increased returns from the labour of the northern peasant raised his standard of living and consequently his ability to buy manufactured goods. It provided surplus food which, from the tenth century on, permitted rapid urbanization. In the new cities there arose a class of skilled artisans and merchants, the burghers who speedily got control of their communities and created a novel and characteristic way of life. . . . In this new environment germinated the dominant feature of the modern world: power technology (26, p. 78).

It was of crucial importance for the rise of science that when the medieval cities arose, they grew out of and continued to evolve on the basis of the free technologies of the medieval world:

> The later Middle Ages, that is, roughly from A.D. 1000 to the close of the fifteenth century, is the period of decisive development in the history of the effort to use the forces of nature mechanically for human purposes. What had been, up to that time, an empirical grouping, was converted with increasing rapidity into a conscious and widespread programme designed

to harness and direct the energies observable around us. The labour-saving power technology which has been one of the distinctive characteristics of the Occident in modern times depends not only upon a medieval mutation of men's attitudes towards the exploitation of nature but also, to a great extent, upon specific medieval achievements (26, p. 79).

Under a slave economy, the capitalist owns both slaves, as a kind of human cattle, and the tools with which they work. It is usually to the advantage of the slave to work as little as possible to keep the level of demands on himself reduced. He has no incentive either to preserve the tools with which he works or to improve them. He is far more inclined to express his resentment for his condition by sabotage of his tools. However, men working for themselves and in possession of their own equipment consider their tools as a virtual extension of their personalities. Moreover, any improvement they make in their tools or in the use of non-human forms of energy eases the burden of their labors and increases the supply of the material things which enhance their styles of life. The conditions of a free economy, thus, may promote an attitude of systematic instrumentalism toward tools and the material conditions and things of life. Pragmatic instrumentalism has appeared frequently among pre-literate peoples. The technology of the Eskimo, for example, is dominated by a hardheaded pragmatic instrumentalism:

> The physical environment of the Eskimo is so forbidding and its peculiarities so extreme that a human group, finding itself in this environment, would perish unless it achieved a very special adjustment to environmental conditions. This is precisely what has happened in the case of the Eskimo. By means of a large number of special devices they have managed to make the inhospitable Arctic their home, and so well have they solved this difficult problem that occasional visitors from the outside world, such as white traders or ardent anthropologists, have been known to accept the Eskimo mode of life rather than, in usual fashion, impose theirs upon the Eskimo (9, p. 74).

Boas' studies of Eskimo technology showed that there were times in the past when the Eskimo's fascination with tools and implements led to surprisingly delicate elaborations which adapted them to tasks of a refinement that could not possibly have had survival value. Needles, for example, were developed for tasks of such refinement that they could only have had aesthetic use. Such periods of empirical tool and implement refinement are invariably followed by a reaction in the direction of practical efficiency once again. In the end pragmatic instrumentalism always dominated the Eskimo's orientation to nature.

However, pragmatic instrumentalism in man's orientation to his tools and to nature is not, per se, science. Science presupposes a rational ideal of knowledge conjoined to a method of establishing "truths" in the world of fact comparable to the role played by logic and mathematics in establishing truths in the world of ideas. The rational proof in the world of ideas was recovered from antiquity by the humanists. The breakthrough from the pragmatic instrumentalism of the medieval rural and urban worlds to the rational ideal of knowledge was the work of the Renaissance craftsman-artist.

When the artist is a slave, as he often was in antiquity, he can hardly be expected to pioneer a new orientation in thought binding on his times. The free artist of the Western city, on the other hand, operating with a free technology, was in quite a different position. The artist worked in a world of material things and tools. His competence was related, in the first instance, to his knowledge of and control over them. When in addition the artist was expected to create new patterns with his materials and tools, he had only one recourse. It was necessary to experiment. The Renaissance artist ever and again had recourse to experimentalism and to explore the possibilities of materials. He often found himself in a position where he had to invent new instruments for his researches. Systematic instrumentalism was being transformed into a general procedure as fundamental for the investigation and establishment of "truths" in the empirical world as logic and mathematics were in the world of thought.

In the medieval and Renaissance cities, where systematic instrumentalism was emerging as a basic method for the investigation of nature, the humanists had recovered the rational proof from antiquity. In the instant these two configurations (rational proof and empirical experimentalism) were linked, science was born. Their conjoint operation in the minds of the Renaissance artists is evident in the notebooks of Leonardo da Vinci. Leonardo went to considerable lengths to recover mathematical treatises from antiquity. In the world of thought, he argued, mathematics provides certainty:

> He who blames the supreme certainty of mathematics feeds on confusion, and will never impose silence upon the contradictions of the sophistical sciences, which occasion perpetual clamour (5, p. 83).

To anyone who wished to understand the world, he advised: "O students study mathematics and do not build without foundations" (5, p. 82). But, at the same time Leonardo recognized that some knowledge has a non-mathematical origin in the world of fact. "All our knowledge originates in our sensibilities" (5, p. 67). However, the world of fact, knowledge of which is gained by experience, also has an order. By means of experiment, experience can be made to yield up its certainties:

> Experience is never at fault; it is only your judgment that is in error in promising itself such results from experience as are not caused by our experiments (5, p. 64).

When one undertook to experiment with nature, he was convinced that it was advisable to proceed by the most direct and least complicated route possible. "When you wish to produce a result by means of an instrument, do not allow yourself to complicate it by introducing many subsidiary parts, but follow the briefest way possible" (5, p. 64). And once one has ascertained natural causes, the need for further experiment ceases. "There is no result in nature without a cause; understand the cause and you will have no need of the experiment" (5, p. 64). In short, nature presents a lawful world.

### Contrasts between Humanism and Science

Humanism arose in educated and politically responsible circles of the medieval and Renaissance cities; science arose in artistic and industrial circles. Humanism arose as a new secular orientation toward social and intellectual affairs; science arose as a new orientation toward instruments, material things, and the physical world.

The methodological differences between humanism and science are of considerable interest, since they supplied the major disciplines of the university. Humanism developed a series of techniques for exploring ancient literature and contemporary experience for guidance in current affairs. It elaborated the techniques of philological criticism and historical research. Science, on the other hand, developed systematic experimentalism into a general procedure for the investigation of nature.

The sharpest of differences, however, appear in the objectives of humanism and science. Humanism was a man-centered (secular), normative orientation intended to justify as well as implement the new kinds of individuality and community represented by the citizen and the medieval city. Humanism was inspired by an optimistic view in contrast to the pessimistic medieval view of human nature. Humanism saw the fullness of man's powers in terms of his achievements in secular contexts. Science, on the other hand, arose as a non-normative method for investigating nature. Its objectives were not to establish a particular state of natural or social affairs but to acquire the most exact knowledge of nature possible and to increase to the maximum man's ability to control the material world (15, pp. 424–458).

The elements of the fundamental polarity in Western thought, humanism, and science, arose in the city, the first distinctive community of Western men. However, the initial polarity was between humanism and theology. In the sixteenth century the new community represented by the nation-state (15, pp. 418–421) had begun to replace the city as the primary community of Western man. Humanism gravitated to the new national communities, where it became foundational to seventeenth- and eighteenth-century rationalism (15, pp. 440–443). At this time the old tensions between humanism and theology began to break down. Theology was beginning to cast its lot with the humanities. Science began to display its unparalleled powers to increase men's objective knowledge of nature. It was found to be invaluable in the new military and economic contexts associated with the rise of the nation. With this development the basic polarity of Western thought achieved its classic form.

## Individualism and Collectivism in Western Thought

There are no more basic problems to men attempting to account for themselves and for their social world than the comparative significance to be assigned to the individual and to the collective. In the medieval monastic communities there was even a hermitic (individualistic) and cenobitic (communal) theory of monastic life. The major contrast between the forms of Eastern and Western monasticism was in the hermitic character of the former — a property which transposed Eastern monastic establishments into *laissez-faire* communities of competitive religious virtuosos. In Western monasticism, stemming from St. Benedict, on the other hand, cenobitic patterns prevailed and individual ascetic virtuosity was always subordinated to the collective requirements of the monastery as a whole under the abbot. Eastern monasticism, in short, rested on the theory and practice of ascetic individualism; Western monasticism rested on the theory and practice of collective asceticism.

The individualistic or collectivistic orientations emerge in every community. When these perspectives are raised to the level of systematic philosophies of the importance of the individual and of the group, they formulate a very fundamental ideological contrast. Individualism is an ideology which maintains that the person is the highest of all values and the vindication of a society is to be found in its assistance in the maximum unfolding of the individual's potential. Collectivism is an ideology which maintains that the highest of all values is the society (and the peace and harmony it guarantees). While individuals are important, they are second to the community, for without the community the individual is insignificant.

Individualism leads naturally to the assumption that society and institutions are instrumental — institutions are made for people, not people for institutions. Collectivism leads naturally to the position that internal peace is the highest of all values, without which only chaos ensues. Hence, collectivism maintains that people must order their behavior to the priority of the community.

As shown by the hermitic and cenobitic theories of monasticism, there is an individualism and collectivism in the monastic community as well as in any other type of community, be it a rural community, a city, or a nation-state. As these ideologies have developed in Western thought, the individualistic position has been most closely linked with liberalism; the collectivistic position has been most closely linked with conservatism.

However, because liberalism and conservatism are not consistently linked with individualism and collectivism, this terminology is avoided in the present chapter.

While individualism and collectivism represent alternate categories of life in every community, and while they are never completely absent as alternative perspectives, they are very often present in quite different proportions. Without attempting to account for minor cycles in the alteration of individualism and collectivism in the course of the development of a community, it can be noted that individualism tends to be strong in the periods of the formation of a community. Collectivism, on the other hand, tends to dominate the period of a community's maturity. The reasons for this are not far to seek.

At the time people are in the process of creating a new community, they are forced to solve problems which are quite new. This is what it means to create a new community. Since there are no established patterns to go by, individuals must be free to create new ones. At such times the average age of the community's leaders tends to be lowered. The outstanding individual is followed because of his creativity, without regard for external qualifications (such as derivations from an old or an outstanding family). It is the time of the charismatic leader. Every community tends to remember from its formative period an array of charismatic leaders whom it may apotheosize as cultural heroes.

On the other hand, once the new community has been formed and its institutions stabilized, there is a tendency to discourage individualism, which can, at this time, appear only as a disruptive principle. The age of a community's leaders is often raised, for people prefer the stable older men and not the young hotheads. Anti-individualistic, collectivistic ideologies enjoy greater popularity during the maturity of a community.

The rhythm of an early individualism followed by a mature collectivism is discernible first in the Western city and later in the nation-state. In the formative period of the Western city (in the eleventh and twelfth centuries), a new spirit of individualism was apparent in the works of the first wave of humanistic intellectuals. A new, impudent note of social criticism was manifest in the songs of the jongleurs. In the same period the universities were beginning to take shape out of voluntary associations (guilds) of scholars and teachers. Famous teachers wandered from place to place with remarkable independence, and were often followed by their students. By the end of the twelfth century most of the institutions of the city had been established, and the process of perfecting them into an urban synthesis was under way. At this very time, the counterattack on the individualism which had been released in the city was launched by the mendicant friars, particularly the Dominicans and Franciscans. The counterattack was successful. The method of Abelard, who had been a spokesman for the newly powerful secular clergy, and the method of dissolving all issues into a conflict between equally impressive authorities and freeing thought for a new formulation, was transformed into the procedure of scholasticism for disposing of the objections of the opposition. Aristotle, for the reading of whom scholars and masters at Paris had once been excommunicated, was fused with medieval theology and lifted into the position of a dogmatic authority.

Without tracing the cycles more closely, in the early city the humanistic individualism of the eleventh and twelfth centuries was followed by the scholastic collectivism of the thirteenth and fourteenth. Unfortunately, the analysis of the individualistic and collectivistic aspects of the civic humanism of the fifteenth- and sixteenth-century city has never been carried out.

Again in the formative period of the nation-state, when it was fusing into an integrated community (in the seventeenth and eighteenth centuries), the wave of philosophy from Descartes to Kant reflects a powerful upsurge of individualism. Even Descartes' formula, which is frequently taken as the starting point of modern philosophy, *cogito ergo sum*, expressed the assumption that the one indubitable reality is the individual. The indisputable reality (unquestioned assumption) of the collectivistic medieval world was *God is*, but in Descartes' world one starts with the individual. All other realities, including God, were to be established by a chain of logical reasoning beginning with the first reality of individual thought.

However, once the revolutions of the nineteenth century had brought the modern nation-state into existence, collectivistic philosophies (Hegelianism, Absolute Idealism) became popular. Within the nation-state the individualistic ideologies of the seventeenth and eighteenth centuries were thrust into the background by the comparative dominance of collectivistic ideologies in the nineteenth and twentieth centuries.

## Some Important Subdivisions in the Modern Individualistic and Collectivistic Ideologies

Recent individualism and collectivism have been subdivided in further ways. Individualism has taken two major forms, depending on whether the forms of rationalism were or were not made central. One may agree that the individual is the most significant of all realities without considering men to be primarily distinguished by their reason or rationality. It is possible to distinguish rationalistic and non-rationalistic forms of individualism even at an early period. In the cities, for example, a form of theological collectivism, scholasticism, (Aquinas) attempted to press the forms of ancient rationalism to the support of scholasticism. In reaction to this attempt, many humanists fused their humanistic individualism with a non-rational (mystical or emotional conception of the individual (Ficino). On the other hand, eighteenth- and nineteenth-century rationalism detached rationalism from scholastic contexts, and found the essence of the individual in his rational faculties (Voltaire). On the other hand, various forms of nineteenth-century romantic individualism found the essence of the individual to be in his feeling and his emotional life, (Victor Hugo) not in his rationality. Western individualism has alternated between rational and non-rational forms.

Collectivism, too, has significant subtypes. Collectivism is identified by its establishment of the primacy of the community over the individual. However, the collective has different implications, depending on whether it is under the control of the upper or lower classes. In the nineteenth century a basic division appeared in the contrast between Hegelianism and Marxism. The Hegelians were spokesmen for middle- and upper-class collectivism; Marxism, together with other forms of so-called scientific socialism, was spokesman for a collectivism for the lower classes.

It is possible to diagram some of the major positions in recent Western thought in terms of their humanistic and scientific components and their positions with respect to one or another of the individualistic or collectivistic ideologies.

*Some Major Intellectual Positions in Terms of Their Humanistic-Scientific and Individualistic-Collectivistic Components*

| M e t h o d o l o g i c a l | P e r s p e c t i v e s | | SUBSTANTIVE ISSUES | | | |
|---|---|---|---|---|---|---|
| | | | INDIVIDUALISM | | COLLECTIVISM | |
| | | | *Rationalistic* | *Non-Rationalistic* | *Left Wing* | *Right Wing* |
| | | Humanism | 17th- & 18th- Century Rationalism | Phenomenology Existentialism | Radical Roman- ticism | Neo- Thomism |
| | | Science | *Laissez-faire,* Neo-Kantianism Utilitarianism | | Marxism, Scientific Socialism | Hegelian- ism, Absolute Idealism |

## Early Sociology: Science or Scientism

From the time of Francis Bacon there were sporadic suggestions for the application of science to social phenomena. However, a number of factors in Western thought and social experience prevented this for a time. In the first place, sometimes a possible line of intellectual development is frustrated by the prior occupancy of the field. The scientific analysis of social phenomena was prevented in the city from the twelfth to the sixteenth century by the fact that the interpretation of social phenomena was virtually monopolized by the theologians (the Roman Catholics in Southern Europe and, somewhat later, the Protestant theologians in Northern Europe) and the humanists. Comparable to the division of the sphere of thought between the humanists and the scholastics in the early period (twelfth and thirteenth centuries) was the division of the sphere of social thought between the northern humanists and such Protestant leaders as Luther and Calvin in the later period (fifteenth and sixteenth centuries).

Meanwhile, also operating against the application of science to social affairs was the adaptation of science to the study of physical things. Science had developed as a form of non-evaluative instrumental knowledge. Human social experience, on the other hand, was traditionally a sphere for evaluation. To extend science to social phenomena meant, literally, that one had to treat men "like things." This was a notion for which humanists and theologians (both Roman Catholics and Protestants) had an almost instinctive repugnance. Hence, one could expect a science of social phenomena to be seriously proposed only if science had proved, beyond any question, its value for the study of the physical world, while the humanistic and theological interpretations of social affairs had been brought into serious question. Both contingencies came to pass.

The religious and nationalistic wars of the sixteenth and seventeenth centuries shook European man, and left many persons for a time determined to avoid all forms of religious excess. Meanwhile, the primary arena of social development was shifting to the nation-states. The religious wars powerfully promoted their formation. In the newly forming nations, a reconstituted humanism was taking shape in which rationalism (which had been torn loose from its anchorage in scholasticism) was conjoined to humanistic values. However, the thought of the enlightenment gradually evolved the social criticism that provided the rationalizations for the revolutions which rocked eighteenth-century society.

The French Revolution terminated in the Terror, and then in the dictatorship of Napoleon. The whole of European society was shaken, first by the example of the Revolution, and then by the force of French arms. When the storm of revolution had passed, responsible groups in European society were sick to death of revolution and everything it signified. Above all, there was a profound repugnance on the part of many people for those ideas which had justified revolution and provided its program.

However, the reaction to the excesses of revolution occurred in a world which revolution had brought into being. Medieval institutions had been swept away. The new mass societies of the contemporary world had made their appearance. In the nations of Western Europe and in the United States, the middle classes had been thrust into a central position. At the same time, the continuing revolutionary ferment which had brought the middle classes to power was setting in motion the laboring classes of the rising nation-states. Once the friend of the middle classes, revolution had become their enemy, for if revolution had given birth to middle-class democracy, it had also spawned socialism.

The Western world was at last ripe for an attempt to employ science for the analysis of social phenomena. The theological interpretation of social events and the humanistic program for them had both been cast into disrepute. However, if science was to take over the ancient role of theology and humanism, it would be expected to do more than analyze in a spirit of complete neutrality. Nevertheless, in the instant that science undertakes the task of *justifying* one social arrangement rather than another, it ceases simply to be science. Whenever science becomes normative and assumes tasks that exceed empirical explanation, it is, perhaps, best described as *scientism*. Sociology arose under conditions which virtually guaranteed that it would be a form of scientism.[1]

However, the fact that sociology arose under conditions which tended to subordinate it to ideological requirements of special social groups does not eliminate the possibility of a scientific sociology. Whenever it abandons normative objectives and devotes itself purely to the task of investigating and explaining social phenomena, sociology is on the road to science. It was a foregone conclusion that whatever ideological elements were present in early sociology would eventually come into conflict with scientific requirements.

### From Positivistic Organicism to Functionalism

The three persons conventionally viewed as the founders of sociology — Comte in France, Spencer in England, and Ward in the United States — were spokesmen for nineteenth-century middle-class groups in their respective nations. France in the early nineteenth century was fresh from the throes of revolution. The nation had glided into the hands of the new middle classes. But as an earthquake that sends out minor tremors after the main shock waves, the revolutionary ferment continued. Comte turned his face against the scientific socialism he had flirted with as a young man (as a disciple of Saint-Simon). In England the country had come into the hands of the middle classes by more peaceable means. Spencer opposed the forces of radical democracy and socialism which represented English parallels of the French scientific socialists. In America the Revolution had also placed the nation in the hands of the middle classes. Coming from the middle-class stratum of the American Midwest,

---

[1] The term "scientism" is here being applied to all attempts to settle questions of value by means of scientific methods. This usage should be distinguished from that of F. A. Hayek who employs the term to refer to the "slavish imitation of the method and language of science." Hayek continues: "'scientism' or the 'scientistic' prejudice . . . describe . . . an attitude decidedly unscientific in the true sense of the word, since it involves a mechanical and uncritical application of habits of thought to fields different from those in which they have been formed" (10, pp. 15–16).

Ward was spokesman for those groups pressing the federal government for assistance in opening the West. Inasmuch as Spencer was opposed to government interference in social affairs while Ward urged it, the mistake has occasionally been made of supposing that they were intrinsically opposed: quite the contrary. In Spencer's nineteenth-century England, social reform meant a movement in the direction of radical democracy and socialism. But in the American Midwest the efforts to secure government assistance meant the promotion of the interests of the same groups that Spencer wished to protect with his policies. When it was suggested that Ward's program was identical with socialism, Ward was — quite correctly — thoroughly shocked. Comte, Ward, and Spencer were all spokesmen for the middle classes of their own countries. Differences were related to the peculiar problems of the middle classes in each country.

In any case, Comte, Spencer, and Ward subscribed to an organismic theory of society and attempted to found it on a scientific methodology. They were quite aware that they were recombining the traditions of Western thought in an essentially new manner. They conceived sociology as the great intellectual synthesis of the West. They proposed to take materials from the humanistic disciplines — above all, from history, the discipline which had come more than any other to combine humanistic perspectives. At the same time they all proposed to analyze historical (and ethnographic) materials by means of the methods of the physical sciences.

The more fully Comte developed his system, the clearer it became that a specific normative intent lay at the foundation of his thought. He proposed to establish a new religion of humanity in a society under the guidance of sociologist-priests. The secular affairs of society were to be placed in the hands of businessmen who would possess so much power that they would no longer be greedy. Women would be returned to the home. Some 20,000 sociologist-priests, Comte thought, would be required for the administration of social affairs in Europe alone. He generously suggested his own services as chief high priest with his headquarters in Paris. Historically, Comte's idea was most clearly approximated by the Indian caste system, whose stability he praised. He evidently conceived of sociologists as the Brahmins of his sociocracy (4).

Not all adherents of the Positivistic Organismic position expressed its normative presuppositions with so much clarity. However, a strong normative orientation remains characteristic of a large number of Positivistic Organicists even into the period of its decay. According to Lundberg, science operates as a kind of mental hygiene: "The mere possession of scientific knowledge and scientific habits of thought regarding the natural universe relieves us of a world of fears, rages, and unpleasant dissipations of energy" (13, p. 2). The lines between normative theory and empirical theory are erased in the instant one speaks of "scientific solutions of social problems." This Lundberg does in a forthright manner:

> It is not true . . . that scientific solutions of social problems face a peculiar situation in that large numbers of people do not want such solutions and would be under no compulsion to accept them. Scientific solutions, in the long run, carry with them their own compulsions for acceptance. The demonstrated superiority of scientific methods has been, in the last analysis, the major reason why they have triumphed. Also, once scientific criteria are accepted in a community as the final arbiters, no one challenges their decisiveness (13, p. 8).

This formulation of Lundberg represents scientism in relatively pure form. His position rests on the notion of the self-evident superiority of the value of the community over individuals:

> There can be no doubt at all that the authority of a properly *constituted state* is preferable to what seems to be the alternative, namely, private and self-constituted legislatures, police, and courts, as they occur today among all kinds of organizations, seeking to impose their private wishes upon the larger public (13, p. 54).

Lundberg's sociologist is not far removed from Comte's sociologist-priest:

> When people are in trouble, they will look for a savior. . . . They are likely to surround themselves with seers, poets, playwrights, and others alleged to possess . . . powers of "seeing." The idea is a sound one. The only reform needed is a substitution of scientists for these soothsayers and soothseers (13, p. 54).

Toward the end of the nineteenth century competitors of Positivistic Organicism began to appear on the scene. Nevertheless this first school of sociological theory retained much of its original prestige and only began to disintegrate into its component parts (positivism and organicism) in the interwar period (14, pp. 110–121). It is quite possible that the world-wide depression of the 1930's which shook people's confidence in the self-evident superiority of the modern nation-state played a role in the decline of Positivistic Organicism. However, after World War II the Functionalistic school of sociological theory rapidly took shape, combining an organismic theory of society with a revised positivism of method, once again making it the true heir of Positivistic Organicism (14, pp. 446–450).

Beyond any question the dean of contemporary Functionalism is Talcott Parsons. Hence, if there are still elements of scientism in Functionalism, his work offers the most authentic of all sources for their study. In 1961 Talcott Parsons, Edward Shils, Kaspar D. Naegele, and Jesse R. Pitts joined their talents to bring out the most ambitious selection of readings in sociological theory ever attempted. The result appeared in two large volumes, together with long introductions by the editors. In all, several hundred fragments of early sociological writings were cut and pasted into a framework provided primarily by Parsons' Functionalistic theory.

Rarely has a monument of such proportions been erected to a scholar while still alive, for the big two-volume assemblage of elements from early sociology is organized into the form of an anticipation of Parsons. Moreover, his theories are stated to be the great climactic synthesis of sociology. The reason why 1935 is the break-off point for the assemblage of readings in sociological theory seems to be explained by the conviction of the editors that since 1935 Parsons' Functionalism is the only theory that counts. In Shils' apotheosis of the dean of Functionalism, these points are explicitly stated:

> *The Structure of Social Action* was the turning point. It was this work that brought the greatest of the partial traditions into a measure of unity. It precipitated the sociological outlook that had been implicit in the most interesting of the empirical inquiries; it made explicit the affinities and complementarity of the sociological traditions that had arisen out of utilitarianism, idealism, and positivism. It redirected sociology into its classical path, and in doing so, it began the slow process of bringing into the open the latent dispositions that had underlain the growth of sociological curiosity. Abstract and complicated though its argument was, *The Structure of Social Action* laid out the main lines of the concrete sociological outlook that has come forward in academic study and in the public appreciation of sociology since its appearance (22, pp. 1406–1407).

Shils too frequently and too emphatically emphasizes the fact that Functionalistic sociology intentionally eliminates the lines between normative and empirical explanation to permit the possibility that this is unintentional:

> Sociology has come into its present estate because its own development bears a rough correspondence to the development of the consciousness of mankind, its moral progress (22, p. 1410).

A few pages later Shils formulates the relation between the sociologist and his objects of study as priest-like:

> Sociology is not a purely cognitive undertaking. It is also a moral relationship between the human beings studied and the student of the human being (22, p. 1413).

And finally Shils blurs the lines between sociology and the reality it studies:

> Sociological theory is not just a theory like any other theory; it is a social relationship between the theorist and the subject matter of his theory. It is a relationship formed by the sense of affinity.

The sociological theory that grows from the theory of action is simply a more forward part of a widespread consensual collectivity (14, p. 1420).

In a word, morally and ethically sociology is itself the best that contemporary society has to offer.

Once this extraordinary position has been put forward, Shils henceforth speaks of the sociological position that he shares with Parsons as *Consensual* Sociology. He describes its operation as follows:

> The content of a human life flows outward into other minds and lives through the medium of sociology. The "larger mind" is extended and deepened through the program of the sociology that moves in the direction of the theory of action. . . . The consensual impetus to sociological inquiry is . . . something new in the world, and a positive addition to the moral progress of the race (14, p. 1430).

All sociology which does not accept the "consensual" position is described by Shils as oppositional sociology. Those who accept oppositional sociology, he argues, are often "former or quasi-Marxists — who, without giving their allegiance to Marxism, wish nonetheless to retain its original disposition" (14, p. 1422). Such sociology, he insists, has an "alienated outlook" and the analyses of its members have "an overtone to the effect that those in authority have acted wrongly, out of incompetence, blindness, or disregard of the good. . . . The result is an outlook that radically distrusts the inherited order of society" (14, p. 1422). Having hung the stigma of "Marxists" on all who disagree with Functionalism, Shils summarizes his view that "consensual sociology is alone capable of satisfying the requirements of an adequate theory and a proper relationship to policy" (14, p. 1440).

## The Scientific Impulse in Sociology

In its first theoretical school, Positivistic Organicism, sociology attempted to synthesize a scientific method for the study of social phenomena with a collectivistic theory of society. The humanistic individualism of the Enlightenment had lost prestige by its association with the Revolutions which ushered in the mass democracies. Besides, the rationalistic impulse of the Enlightenment had been borne in large measure by the advisers to and critics of the Enlightened Despots, who proposed to reform the monarchies, not replace them with democracies. In the nineteenth-century world, the point of gravity had shifted to the middle classes, who had never been the primary bearers of the humanistic outlook. Moreover, the intellectual program of the middle classes in the post-revolutionary period was the reverse of their program in the pre-revolutionary world. They now had the task of conserving and justifying a social and political order that had been taken over into their own hands, whereas in the pre-revolutionary period, their objective had been to eliminate the remnants of medievalism and other obstacles in their path.

At the time of its origin, thus, Positivistic Organicism was structurally parallel to Hegelianism. As a matter of fact, when Hegel's work was called to Comte's attention, Comte saw the essential similarity between their positions. To Comte, Hegel's Absolute Idealism was merely a more metaphysical form of his own position (14, p. 156). In his youth Comte had dallied with the brilliant scientific socialism of Saint-Simon, but soon reacted powerfully against it, though he did not hesitate to appropriate large blocks of Saint-Simon's ideas. There is little question that in Comte's own mind sociology was a conservative answer to scientific socialism, as it still is for Shils and Parsons.

Positivistic Organicism numbers powerful figures among its adherents: Comte, Spencer, Ward, in the early period; Tönnies, Pareto, and Durkheim, later; and Sorokin, Lundberg, and Redfield in the modern period. When contemporary functionalism thus conceives of itself as the legitimate heir of the whole of sociology, it must be admitted that it is at least the heir of the single, most pervasive of the early positions. And when some contemporary functionalists automatically identify anyone who disagrees with them as a "Marxist," they are repeating a drama as old as Comte's denunciation of Saint-Simon and the reaction of some Hegelians to the Marxists.

However, there was no reason why the scientific impulse in sociology should be exhausted by the combination of Positivism and Right-Wing Collectivism in the manner of Positivistic Organicism and Functionalism. From an analytic point of view, the most obvious second school of scientific sociology to develop should have been a form of positivistic, left-wing collectivism. In view of Comte's self-conscious opposition to Saint-Simon and the scientific socialists, this would seem doubly probable. When Marxian sociology eventually developed, this possibility was finally realized. However, it was a late rather than an early development.

The slowness of a positivistic form of left-wing collectivism to develop must be sought in social conditions. Schools of thought do not develop among the sociological theorists simply because they are abstractly possible in the panorama of intellectual positions. Positivistic Organicism had developed because it was needed by the middle classes, in whose hands the modern nation-state had formed. Left-wing collectivism, on the other hand, was put forth to satisfy the needs of the modern proletariat. In the nineteenth century at the time sociology arose, it was practically impossible for a sociology representing a positivistic form of left-wing collectivism to make its way alongside Positivistic Organicism and be heard in the same forums. While the middle classes were sponsoring the development of the social sciences in the colleges and universities, the lower classes were in no position to place their versions of social science in competitive position with them. Only in the twentieth century have academic versions of the sociological counterpart of scientific socialism appeared. Moreover, it is more frequent in Europe than in America.

It was quite possible, however, that various forms of sociological theory representing combinations of positivism and individualism should appear. As noted earlier, in any given community a differentiation appears between the collectivists and the individualists. Once the nation-state had begun to assume its modern form and find its point of gravity in the middle classes, a new differentiation could be expected among the middle classes between collectivists and individualists. Two schools of sociological theory combining scientific positivism and individualism (a non-rational and rational form) eventually made their appearance: Conflict Theory and Neo-Kantian Formalism.

Conflict Theory developed first. A number of persons in different countries such as Bagehot in England, Gumplowicz and Ratzenhofer in Austria, and Small in America were thoroughly convinced that a science of social phenomena was not only possible, but necessary. If anything, they found themselves opposed to the Positivistic Organicists on the grounds that they were too lax in their positivism. However, they found themselves far more dissatisfied with the organismic theory of society. This theory, they believed, obscured the fluid dynamism that everywhere came into view whenever one actually looked at social life. To the conflict theorists society is not an organism; it is a process. Its events consist of endlessly varied encounters between people as individuals and in groups. Each is in hot struggle to advance its own peculiar interests (14, pp. 127–211).

However, Conflict Theory was no return to the optimistic individualism of the Enlightenment. It had no faith in human reason, and had serious doubts about the doctrine of progress sponsored by Positivistic Organicism. Peace was a kind of treaty marking an interval between the wars and contests of groups. Most individuals, according to its view of things, are weak and sheep-like. It is only in groups that the fundamental combativeness of the individual is able to manifest itself in full force. *Conflict Theory, thus, was a positivistic form of non-rational individualism.*

Although there was a sharp impact of realism about Conflict Theory, it presented some anomalies. It was a form of individualism hardly calculated to appeal to the ordinary individual, who was conceived of as sheep-like (as by Gumplowicz for example), but inwardly aggressive. Society was visualized as a series of major and minor arenas of conflict. Both pictures are rather unappealing. The case was different with Sociological Formalism.

In the course of the continuing differentiation of individualistic perspectives within the nation-state, it was perhaps a foregone conclusion that the pessimistic formulas of the Conflict Theorists would satisfy few. Toward the end of the nineteenth century a neo-Kantian revival took place not only in Western philosophy, but also in a number of other humanistic disciplines. It carried with it strong impulses toward rationalism and optimism. Sociological Formalism reflected this movement in sociology. The movement in sociology sustained an optimistic outlook toward the individual — an outlook far more attractive to most people than was Conflict Theory. The rationality of the individual had not received equivalent emphasis since the eighteenth century. At the same time, this rationalistic revival occurred in a framework of science rather than of humanism.

Social life was conceived by the neo-Kantian Formalists as distinguishable into form and content. Sociology was visualized as a discipline, like geometry, and concerned with the forms of social life in separation from their content. Such forms, moreover, were conceived as in some respect directly accessible to man's reason. Sociological Formalism seemed to offer the prospect of integrating the whole of social life in terms of forms of varying degrees of comprehensiveness. For a time, it appeared that Formalism would sweep the entire field.

## The Humanistic Counterattack on Sociology

As has been observed, from the time of Comte to the contemporary Functionalists, there have been strong normative elements in sociology which in any strict construction have no scientific standing. The Humanists who were skilled in analyzing value suppositions at an early date brought the value premises of the new science of society under critical review. In 1887 Isabel Hapgood brought out a volume of Tolstoy's essays, which were at the time circulating in Russia in manuscript form. In one of them Tolstoy analyzed the evaluative elements of the sociology of Comte and Spencer.

The justification of all persons who have freed themselves from toil is now founded on experimental, positive science. The scientific theory is as follows:

"For the study of the laws of life of human societies, there exists but one indubitable method — the positive, experimental, critical method.

"Only sociology, founded on biology, founded on all the positive sciences, can give us the laws of humanity. Humanity, or human communities, are the organisms already prepared, or still in process of formation, and which are subservient to all the laws of the evolution of organisms.

"One of the chief of these laws is the variation of destination among the portions of the organs. Some people command, others obey. If some live in superabundance, and others in want, this arises not from the Will of God, but because the empire is a form of manifestation of personality, but because in societies, as in organisms, division of labor becomes indispensable for life as a whole. Some people perform the muscular labor in societies; others, the mental labor" (24, p. 169).

Tolstoy formulated the central argument of the Positivistic Organicists:

> The theory is as follows: All mankind is an undying organism; men are the particles of that organism, and each one of them has his own special task for the service of others. In the same manner, the cells united in an organism share among them the labor of the fight for existence of the whole organism; they magnify the power of one capacity, and weaken another, and unite in one organ, in order the better to supply the requirements of the whole organism. And exactly in the same manner as with gregarious animals — ants or bees — the separate individuals divide the labor among them. The queen lays the egg, the drone fructifies it; the bee works his whole life long. And precisely this thing takes place in mankind and in human societies. And therefore, in order to find the law of life for man, it is necessary to study the laws of life and the development of organisms (24, p. 175).

It is on this new doctrine, Tolstoy observes, "that the justification for men's idleness and cruelty is now founded" (24, p. 176).

> From this view of science, it appears that all previous knowledge was deceitful, and that the whole story of humanity, in the sense of self-knowledge, has been divided into three, actually into two, periods: the theological and metaphysical period, extending from the beginning of the world to Comte, and the present period — that of the only true science, positive science — beginning with Comte (24, p. 178).

This whole edifice, Tolstoy argues, rests on an error — that of conceiving humanity as an organism. "In humanity itself all actual signs of organism — the center of feeling or consciousness — are lacking" (24, p. 178).

Comte's work, Tolstoy observes, had two parts: his positive philosophy and his positive politics. Both had evaluative aspects. However,

> Only the first part was adopted by the learned world — that part which justified, on new premises, the existent evil of human societies; but the second part, treating of the moral obligations of altruism, arising from the recognition of mankind as an organism, was regarded as not only of no importance, but as trivial and unscientific (24, p. 179).

Tolstoy's argument was sound. There were evaluative elements in both aspects of Comte's sociology.

Some 15 years, at least, after Tolstoy had written these lines, he summed up his estimate of the sociology deriving from Comte and Spencer in an essay on "The Restoration of Hell." In it Beelzebub, the chief of the devils, received reports on the state of the contemporary world from various of his cohorts. To distract men from spiritual things, one reports:

> "I have devised for them . . . sociology, which consists in studying how former people lived badly. So instead of trying to live better themselves according to the teaching of Jesus, they think they need only study the lives of former people, and that from that they will be able to deduce general laws of life, and that to live well they need only conform their life to the laws they thus devise. . . .

> "And as soon as those who are considered the promoters of science become persuaded of their infallibility, they naturally proclaim as indubitable truth things that are not only unnecessary but often absurd, and having proclaimed them they cannot repudiate them" (25, pp. 326–327).

Tolstoy's comments on Comte's and Spencer's Positivistic Organicism may illustrate how devastating the humanistic critique of the ideological elements of early sociology could become. But it was perhaps to be expected that the humanities should also mount a methodological counterattack on sociology. After all, Comte had proposed taking over bodily the materials of history. However, Comte brushed aside the assumptions on which the study of history had traditionally rested — that it was a manifestation of men's ideas, thoughts, and feelings, in short, of the human spirit. In accord with his positivism, history was reduced by Comte to the overt happenings in human behavior. The existence of the human spirit behind them was denied (4, vol. 1, p. 9). Sociology analyzed such occurrences with the methods of natural science and the notions of succession, co-existence, and cause, thereby establishing the general laws of social evolution (4, vol. 4, p. 17). Comte's arguments were reinforced by John Stuart Mill, who also hoped to improve the state of the social sciences by application of the methods of natural science. Mill thought it possible to deduce the successive states of consciousness from the physiological functions of the brain. This was the first step, Mill believed, in establishing the natural laws of activity of human pluralities (16, pp. 529–532).

Comte, Mill, Henry Thomas Buckle, and others not only developed a collectivistic view of society and man which was radically in opposition to the traditional humanistic and individualistic conception, but which brushed aside the methods by which the humanists had studied man and society. Sociology might claim to be the queen of the sciences, but history was the queen of the humanities. If a counterattack on sociology were to proceed out of the humanities, it was most plausibly to be expected from history. When this counterattack came, as it did, it would be expected to be from a historicism different from its eighteenth-century rationalistic forms, for the rationalistic humanism of the eighteenth century had seriously suffered from its identification with revolution. Moreover, the rationalistic impulse in Western thought was being pre-empted by science. Rationalism, thus, was twice damaged in the view of many humanists: first by its identification with the cause of revolution, then by its role in the social sciences, where it seemed to many persons to be bringing about a wholesale destruction of spiritual values.

A major attempt to combat positivism by means of a reconstructed historicism was made by Johann Droysen, who in 1852 developed a course at the University of Berlin on the "Methodology and Encyclopedia of the Historical Sciences," which sought to study history on historical foundations (11, p. 31). Droysen drew a sharp distinction between the methodology of the natural and historical sciences (8, pp. 307–342), and argued (7) that the spheres of history and science are quite distinct: history deals with the sphere of moral judgment which eludes statistical and causal study. However, statistical and causal methods are appropriate to the study of *things*.

The scholar who more than any other came to synthesize the counterattack by a reconstituted historicism was Wilhelm Dilthey. Without tracing the steps by which he arrived at his final position, it may be noted that Dilthey took history, not sociology, to be the most fundamental of all disciplines. Positivism, in Dilthey's opinion, was not new. Comte's positivism was merely the culmination in modern times of the materialistic explanation of events running through d'Alembert and Hobbes to Comte (6, p. 357). The peculiarities of the materialistic philosophy of history are its attempts to explain mental and spiritual events in terms of categories originally developed to explain things.

However, if we cut beneath such gross materialism as that of Comte and Mill, which would explain spiritual events by categories appropriate to things, we must still recognize that their materialism is an outlook (*Weltanschauung*), a form of analysis, and an activity of mind. History is more fundamental than sociology or any science because its subject matter is not one or another of the products of mind (of which Positivism is only one), but because *its subject matter is life itself*. Yet this does not mean that Rationalism or Idealism are more fundamental than Positivism. They, too, are world views, the ultimate source of which is life.

> The ultimate root of any world view is life itself. Life is present all over the globe in innumerable particular lives, and is lived and re-lived by every individual. Being but an instant of time present, it eludes strict observation. But in retrospect and in its objective manifestations Life is better capable of being fully grasped and meaningfully interpreted than life according to our personal knowledge and in its countless forms today, and thus it reveals everywhere the same identical traits and common features (6, p. 21).

History, to Dilthey, was the most fundamental of all disciplines, because its subject matter is the mind. History is meaningful, because it is the product of the forms of the mind. The ultimate category of mind is meaning, and history is the study of the manner in which the mind objectifies itself according to its own principles.

Thus it may be seen that Dilthey shares with the eighteenth-century rationalists the conception (humanistic) of a universal human nature manifesting itself according to its own principles. However, since Dilthey has treated rationalism as merely one of the products of the human mind, and reason as only one of its capacities, he was not in the position to derive the forms of human life as manifest in history from man's reason or from the categories of the mind in the manner of Kant or any other of the rationalists. Rather, Dilthey followed a suggestion contained in Schopenhauer and in his one-time associates at Basel, Burckhardt and Nietzsche. Poetry may be more revealing than logic as a source of insight into the forms which come to serve as the receptacles for systems of ideas in which human life ultimately objectifies itself.

In the Basel *Introduction* (1867) Dilthey declared that poets had taught him to understand the world.

> The systems of Schelling, Hegel, and Schleiermacher were but logical and metaphysical translations of a *Lebens- und Weltansicht* of a Lessing, a Schiller, and a Herder. The poet is the interpreter of a state of mind, which permeates a generation and crystallizes it into a system. A system lives or dies, not according to reasons of logic, but by virtue of the duration of that state of mind which has originated it (11, p. 75).

If history is to yield its richness for the study of man, some method other than that of the physical sciences is essential. Moreover, such analysis cannot proceed simply on the basis of logical forms, which are appropriate to only one of the basic aspects of life (its cognitive aspect). In addition, life has affective (emotional) and conative (moral) dimensions. Depending on which one of these basic properties of experience is uppermost, the mind objectifies itself in different ways. These objectifications, in turn, become the vehicles of world views which define immediate experience and give them form. There are three fundamental world outlooks: objective idealism, the idealism of liberty, and naturalistic realism. The third of these is contained in the view of Comte and Spencer. "The Naturalistic concept of 'type' not only renders historiography schematic, but reduces it to sociology" (11, p. 97).

Dilthey's methodological attack on sociology led him to offer typology as the peculiar method of the spiritual (historical) sciences.

## The Humanistic Impulse in Sociology

The foregoing sketch of some of the forms of the humanistic counterattack on sociology was not intended to set up a particular sequence of influences. An essay is not the vehicle for such an enterprise. Tolstoy's and Dilthey's reactions to sociology were selected, not because they brought about changes in sociology, but because they typify some of the forms of the humanistic reaction to sociology's value commitments and positivistic method. Tolstoy's critique of sociological collectivism and the philistine support of the status quo by the Positivistic Organicists may dramatize the fact that so far as sociologists remained sensitive to the humanistic critique of their theories they would find reason for a shift to more individualistic orientations. On the other hand, Dilthey's vigorous criticism of the positivistic analysis of social phenomena and his development of typology as an alternative method for the analysis of socio-historical events, could well force some sociologists to re-examine their methods.

As time has gone by a number of forms of humanistic individualism and collectivism have appeared. These, however, developed in very different degrees and at different times. Forms of humanistic individualism developed first and most completely; forms of humanistic collectivism have developed only recently and rather sporadically.

It could, perhaps, be assumed — if abstract possibilities were the primary consideration — that humanistic collectivism would have developed in sociology before humanistic individualism. After all, the oldest school of sociological theory was Positivistic Organicism. The organicism of the early sociologists so strongly sustained the need of the new middle classes to justify the status quo (which had recently come into their hands) that a non-positivistic organicism would seem to have been a logical product the moment the application of physical science methods to social events was questioned. However, until such time as sociology was firmly established, the reaction to the physical science bias of early sociology tended rather to take the form of rejection of sociology altogether rather than of the establishment of a new school of sociology. It was only after sociology became indubitably established and had made its way into the universities as one of the basic academic disciplines that it became desirable formally to establish a kind of right-wing humanistic collectivism which still described itself as a sociological theory. When, eventually, the attempt was made in Roman Catholic circles to establish sociology on a basis of Neo-Thomism, this possibility was realized. Perhaps the main stream of what is, at times, called Roman Catholic sociology fits this category.

The conditions for the development of a humanistic form of left-wing collectivism which still described itself as a form of sociology are even more difficult to realize. For this to occur, the given individual would have to reject both right-wing collectivism (Positivistic Organicism and Functionalism) and science; otherwise the thinker would fall into the camp of Marxism or of other scientific socialists.

This seems to be the precise description of the form of sociological theory which was being embraced by C. Wright Mills at the time of his death. In his impressive major works, *Character and Social Structure* (with Hans Gerth), *White Collar,* and *The Power Elite,* Mills conducted his theorizing within the framework of Social Behaviorism (14, pp. 430–433). However, in his later works Mills increasingly subscribed to a collectivistic position which was combined with a forthright anti-empiricism. In an essay for Llewellyn Gross' *Symposium,* Mills stated:

> Now I do not like to do empirical work if I can possibly avoid it. . . . Besides, and more seriously, in the social sciences there is so much to do by way of initial "structuring" . . . that "empirical research" is bound to be thin and uninteresting.
>
> In our situation, empirical work as such is for beginning students and for those who aren't able to handle the complexities of big problems; it is also for highly formal men who do not care what they study so long as it appears to be orderly. All these types have a right to do as they please or as they must; they have no right to impose in the name of science such narrow limits on others. Anyway, you ought not to let them bother you (17, p. 35).

Later in the same year, Mills generalized his opposition to physical science.

> The cultural meaning of physical science — the major older common denominator — is becoming doubtful. As an intellectual style, physical science is coming to be thought by many as somehow inadequate. The adequacy of scientific styles of thought and feeling, imagination and sensibility, has of course from their beginnings been subject to religious doubt and theological controversy, but our scientific grandfathers and fathers beat down such religious doubts. The current doubts are secular, humanistic — and often quite confused. Recent development in physical science — with its technological climax in the H-bomb and the means of carrying it about the earth — have not been experienced as a solution to any problems widely known and deeply pondered by larger intellectual communities and cultural workmen have come to feel that "science" is a false and pretentious Messiah, or at the very least a highly ambiguous element in modern civilization (18, pp. 15–16).

Mills' powerful impetus in the direction of left-wing collectivism was made fully manifest in his passionate propaganda tract in defense of the Cuban revolution and in his apotheosis of its leader in *Listen, Yankee.*

> My major aim in this book is to present the voice of the Cuban revolutionary, as clearly and as emphatically as I can, and I have taken up this aim because of its absurd absence from the news of Cuba available in the United States today. You will not find here The Whole Truth about Cuba, nor "an objective appraisal of the Cuban revolution." I do not believe it is possible for anyone to carry out such an appraisal today, nor do I believe that anyone — Cuban or North American — can yet know "the whole

truth about Cuba." That truth, whatever it turns out to be, is still being created, and every week it changes. The true story of the Cuban revolution, in all its meaning, will have to wait until some Cuban, who has been part of it all, finds out the universal voice of his revolution (19, p. 8).

At no time does the slightest hint of criticism of Fidel Castro ever creep into Mills' account. Castro looms through the pages of *Listen, Yankee,* as an apotheosized superman.

> When men seize an opportunity, they make history; this man has. And he is. He is the most directly radical and democratic force in Cuba. He has always appealed, at every juncture, to public opinion, on the TV and also in person. Before any problem is solved, Fidel spends long hours on the TV. In the last eighteen months the power in Cuba has rested upon the people. He explains and he educates, and after he speaks almost every doubt has gone away. Never before has such a force of public opinion prevailed for so long and so intimately with power. So close, for example, that even a weak rumor sends Fidel to the TV to refute it or to affirm it, to explain what it is all about. So long as Fidel is there, we are going to be all right. His speeches actually create the revolutionary consciousness — and the work gets done. It is fantastic to see how, as it goes along, the revolutionary process transforms one layer after another of the population. And always, there is Fidel's anti-bureaucratic personality and way of going about things, of getting things done, without red tape and without delay and in a thoroughly practical and immediate way (19, pp. 122–123).

In his last book, *The Marxists,* Mills divided the most vital of the intellectual currents of modern times into Marxism and liberalism. They are, he argued, animated by common ideals.

> Both Marxism and liberalism embody the ideals of Greece and Rome and Jerusalem: the humanism of the Renaissance, the rationalism of the eighteenth-century enlightenment (20, pp. 13–14).

Of these alternatives, Mills emphatically preferred Marxism.

> What is most valuable in classic liberalism is most cogently and most fruitfully incorporated in classic Marxism. Much of the failure to confront Marxism in all its variety is in fact a way of not taking seriously the ideals of liberalism itself, for despite the distortions and vulgarizations of Marx's ideas, and despite his own errors, ambiguities, and inadequacies, Karl Marx remains the thinker who has articulated most clearly — and most perilously — the basic ideals which liberalism shares. Hence, to confront Marx and Marxism is to confront this moral tradition (20, p. 14).

A few pages earlier, Mills had formulated the reasons for his preference for Marxism over current social science.

> The social scientists study the details of small-scale *milieux;* Marx studied such details, too, but always within the structure of a total society. The

social scientists, knowing little history, study at most short-run trends; Marx, using historical materials with superb mastery, takes as his unit of study entire epochs. The values of the social scientists generally lead them to accept their society pretty much as it is; the values of Marx led him to condemn his society — root, stock, and branch (20, pp. 10–11).

These passages from Mills, to be sure, contain a fuzzy bundle of half-truths. It is not true, for example, that classic liberalism and Marxism share the same values: classic liberalism is individualistic; Marxism is collectivistic. It is not true that all social scientists study only the details of small-scale *milieux* and have no mastery of historical materials: some do, some do not. Marx's mastery of historical materials — far from being "superb" — has been seriously questioned by some scholars. The ambiguous statement that both Marxism and liberalism embody the ideals of Greece, Rome, and Jerusalem, humanism and rationalism, fails to discriminate the very different aspects of Western thought which are distributed among these positions. Finally, Mills has himself emphatically rejected the linkage between his left-wing collectivism and science — a link which Marxism resoundingly affirmed.

The important point for the present context is this: Mills cast his lot simultaneously with left-wing collectivism and against the linkage between it and science. In his last years, there has been some seething ferment around Mills. If this ferment should condense into a new school of sociology with C. Wright Mills as its charismatic founder, its distinctiveness will be seen to lie in its unique combination of humanism and left-wing collectivism.

Far more important (in terms of numbers of adherents and richness and variety of works) than either right-wing, humanistic collectivism (Neo-Thomistic sociology), or left-wing, humanistic collectivism (the position of C. Wright Mills), are the sociological forms of humanistic individualism represented by Social Behaviorism and Phenomenological Sociology.

Social Behaviorism, the powerful school of sociological theory which acts as the great counterweight in American sociology to Functionalism, represented a reaction both to collectivism (of both right- and left-wing varieties) and to what it conceived to be the excessively rigid positivism which stood in the way of an adaptation of physical methods to the unique properties of social life. All three branches of Social Behaviorism (Pluralistic Behaviorism, stemming from Tarde, Le Bon, Giddings, and Ross; Social-Action Theory, stemming from Max Weber, Robert MacIver, John R. Commons, and Thorstein Veblen; and Symbolic Interactionism, stemming from William James, Cooley, George Herbert Mead, and W. I. Thomas) represented positions in sociology which combined humanistically modified methods with an individualistic approach to social events. Social Behaviorism, thus, is the nearest approach to eighteenth-century rationalism that sociology offers (14, pp. 285–440). It should be noted, however, that the Social Behaviorists actually tried to find a common ground between the methodological perspectives of humanism and science. It thus represented what might be described as either a humanized positivism or scientific humanism. Social-Action Theory, for example in its methodological perspectives, attempted to press to scientific account the typological procedures which Dilthey had offered as an alternative to scientific methods.

Finally a non-rationalistic form of humanistic individualism took shape as a departure from Neo-Kantian Formalism (14, pp. 267 ff.). On analogy with a procedure of Kant, who had treated science as the empirical study of experience but had drawn a distinction between mind-given forms and empirical content, the neo-Kantian Formalists in sociology drew a distinction between the form and content of social life. The content was studied by other social sciences, but sociology was argued to be similar to geometry. It was said to be a study of pure social forms in separation from their content.

However, if one examined the Kantian view carefully, it quickly became apparent that although both form and content were said to be objects of scientific study, they were assigned very different properties. Since forms are present from the moment experience occurs, and since they are present as possibilities before experience occurs, it is not necessary to employ experimental methods to discover social forms. In fact, experiment is of no help in studying forms, since they are present from the beginning of experience. It should only be necessary to examine experience carefully though introspectively to discover social forms. There was a potential crisis for scientific methodology buried in Neo-Kantian sociology, for the most significant of all methods would seem to point toward introspection.

Long before Neo-Kantian sociology came face to face with its methodological problems, other developments had been occurring in Western thought which were to offer a possible solution to the Sociological Formalists. The ferment in the methodology of the humanists of the nineteenth century (in part illustrated by Dilthey above) was forcing them to look to alternatives to science for the analysis of social phenomena. Dilthey, it was noted above, had thought that poetry could be more valuable in the understanding of the operations of the human mind than logic. A primary product of the search during the nineteenth and early twentieth centuries for a non-logical (non-rational in this sense) procedure for analyzing the events of human experience was phenomenology. In its most rudimentary sense, phenomenology may be described as a new method of controlled or directed introspection that was believed by its proponents to be more fundamental than either logical analysis or empirical-scientific procedures.

Once it became completely clear that the methodological status being assigned to social forms was potentially quite different from that of social content, phenomenology offered itself as a natural method. Phenomenological sociology, pioneered by Alfred Vierkandt, was developed with particular brilliance for the analysis of various social and cultural forms by Max Scheler (14, pp. 267–281).

## Existentialism and Sociology

With phenomenology, sociology had already entered the edifice of Existentialism. However, a fully developed Existentialist sociology is only now under way. This is no place to consider these problems in detail, but it is useful to sketch some of the major elements of Existentialism and indicate the direction of their possible influence on sociology.

It has been argued that the essence of Existentialism is found in a profound sense of alienation from their society and their traditions by Western men. However, Marxism, too, has argued that modern workers are alienated by the methods of production and the operation of those forces which separate them from ownership of the instruments of production. It has been argued that the essence of Existentialism is found in the formation of an outlook resting on a profound sense of dread. Some Existentialists (Kierkegaard, Heidegger) fulfill this definition, but some others (Ortega y Gasset and Jaspers) seem basically to have had Apollonian dispositions. It has been argued that the essence of Existentialism is a powerful subjective religious sense (Kierkegaard and Jaspers qualify on this standard), but some persons accepting the label of Existentialism have been quite irreligious (Sartre and Ortega y Gasset for certain, Heidegger perhaps). Hence it has finally been argued that Existentialism has no coherent position and is, in fact, indefinable (Walter Kaufmann).

However, there are a number of things shared by those to whom the label of Existentialism has been applied. None of the Existentialists is collectivistic. A powerful anti-collectivism runs through them all in two respects: they radically reject the collectivistic philosophies of both right and left wing; they are powerfully opposed to collectivistic trends in contemporary society. Whatever else may be true of it, Existentialism is, first, a powerful individualistic reaction in an age of collectivism.

In its individualism, Existentialism finds a deep echo from ancient traditions of the West, from the civic humanism of the earlier period, and from the tradition in its period of maturity from Descartes to Kant, reaching a kind of culmination in eighteenth-century Rationalism. However, Existentialism represents an individualistic reaction in an age of collectivism in a world disillusioned with the individualistic rationalism of its classic period. The rationalistic traditions had operated like dissolving acid on the traditional faiths of Western man. When the traditional faiths declined, they left in their place only the unstable compound: faith in Reason. But Reason rationalized the Revolution which ushered in the mass world — a world that powerfully thrust Reason aside.

The new individualism that arose in the collectivistic world was disillusioned with the rationalistic formulas of the earlier age. It had no confidence in the products of reason. All "systems" cast up by the thought process in the course of experience were now conceived ultimately as mere "rationalizations" of a more fundamental psychic reality. The new individualism thus rejected the rationalism that had served as so powerful a tool for the individualism of the seventeenth and eighteenth centuries. This means, however, that the new individualism was automatically pressed into the situation where it had to develop a new analysis of experience. It explored not logic, but the non-logical areas of individual activity for a method of personal orientation. When personal experience is examined, it presents no clear, logical distinctions and organized sequences of thought, but an amazing complex of ambiguities, doubts, anxieties, and uncertainties. When thought intervenes in personal experience it often imposes a set of categories as if from the outside, categories which force the ill-fitting densities of experience into a condition of half-fittedness. Hence, the exponents of the new individualism looked to areas thrust into the background by men who had thought that the essence of man was his reason: to poetry, to art, to the experience of the religious mystic, to mythology. And when phenomenology attempted to gather these many impulses into a single procedure for a new analysis of experience, the Existentialists were powerfully influenced by them.

Finally, it may be noted, there was good reason why the new individualism might not wish to arm itself with science. For one thing, the rationalistic impulse in Western thought was in considerable measure taken over by science. But more importantly, the great collectivistic movements in modern times had taken over science as a powerful instrument. Science had been used with great efficiency by the large business and industrial combinations of modern industry, by the big states and powerful armies. Science was the great implement of collectivism!

There was a time when the peculiar ingredients of Existentialism would have been quite impossible to assemble in the West. However, a series of powerful individualistic figures responding both to the social trends and to the traditions of the West gradually pulled these ingredients into its eventual synthesis. Perhaps most noteworthy were Schopenhauer, Kierkegaard, Burckhardt, Nietzsche, Dilthey, and Edmund Husserl. Near the turn of the century several of these influences were woven into systematic interpretations of modern man and his times. Among the persons playing a major role in bringing about the Existential synthesis are Bergson, Ortega Y Gasset, Heidegger, Jaspers, Berdyaev, and Sartre.

It is not unfair to conceive the social doctrines of the Existentialists as constituting an Existentialist Sociology. An able young writer, Edward A. Tiryakian, accurately summed up the general social doctrines of the Existentialists as follows:

From Kierkegaard's *The Present Age* to Jaspers' *Man in the Modern Age,* the existentialists' evaluation of the individual-and-society relationship remains strikingly the same. What stands out in particular is their rejection and condemnation of modern society as an impersonal environment antithetical and inimical to the development of authentic selfhood. While some thinkers stress the importance and the positive aspects of the inter-subjective relations, there is none who looks with favor at society itself. Everything societal is considered either an unauthentic, unreal abstraction, or a sort of technological Chronos devouring the personality by means of an implacable, devastating levelling process (23, p. 144).

Tiryakian maintains that there is a need for a reunion of sociology and philosophy, and proposes bringing about this union by a fusion of *sociologism* and *existentialism* on the ground that the contemporary predicament of the individual and of society is their common concern. "Basically both are reactions to the disorganization of the modern world" (23, p. 151). It should be noted that, even in the unlikely event that one were able to unite Existentialism and what is called sociologism, one could still not claim to have united philosophy and sociology. Existentialism is only one — though a vigorous one — of the traditions in contemporary philosophy. What Tiryakian calls sociologism is only one of the traditions (again, though, a vigorous one) of the recent forms of theory. By *Sociologism* Tiryakian means Positivistic Organicism and Functionalism. Durkheim is his favorite illustration.

Tiryakian accurately sums up the difference between Existentialism and this type of sociology in the following passages:

Durkheim stressed the reality of society as a psychic entity, a collective consciousness produced by the association and interaction of individuals. Gabriel Marcel warns against the notion that elements A and B, endowed respectively with consciousness C' and C' ' may form a whole having a synthetic consciousness C' ' ' (23, p. 151).

Durkheim saw no fundamental conflict between the individual and society. . . . Heidegger regards the social self as the unauthentic part of human-being, but Durkheim considered it that which gives us true humanity, because it makes us civilized (23, p. 152).

In Durkheim's thought . . . the end of moral action is the collectivity. . . . In contrast to Durkheim, the existential perspective on morality is . . . ambiguous and ambivalent. . . . For Nietzsche, the utility of social morality is no proof of its validity. . . . Kierkegaard also took an ambiguous position on morality. The ethical, for him, is a higher realm of existence than the aesthetic (23, p. 152).

Unlike Kierkegaard, Durkheim did not perceive any opposition between morality and religion (23, pp. 153–154).

Durkheim believed emphatically that society pervades the individual: he cannot, without contradicting his nature, liberate himself from the limits imposed upon him by his participation in the social world. . . . The authentic selfhood of the person is to be found only through participation in a collectivity, in social reality. This view is antipodal to that of existentialism. . . . Beginning with Kierkegaard all existentialist thinkers have been aware of and disturbed by the levelling process of civilization. The existential perspective sees this process as a threat to the individual, robbing him of authentic, unique existence. The levelling process effects equality by obliterating individual differences. Kierkegaard, Nietzsche, Marcel, Heidegger, and Jaspers, holding social equality to be tantamount to mass mediocrity, make a common front in decrying both the process and the advocates of egalitarianism (23, p. 155).

After detailing the contrasts between existentialism and the form of sociology he describes as sociologism, Tiryakian proposes that they be fused in a single perspective. The first step in such synthesis is to conceive Existentialism and sociology, simply, as alternate responses to the same problem.

If sociologism and existentialism have a common source in their awareness that the modern world is in a state of moral crisis, are they irrevocably apart because of their contrasting evaluation and approach to the relation of the individual and society? Stated in somewhat broader terms, are sociology and philosophy to remain in a state of "cold war" (23, pp. 162–163)?

By an extraordinarily simple re-interpretation, Tiryakian seeks to reduce sociologism and Existentialism to complementary rather than contrasting perspectives.

We propose that Durkheim's fundamental concern was really to study objectively a *subjective* reality, not, as is sometimes assumed by existentialists among others, an *objective* reality (23, p. 163).

And by one blow Tiryakian claims to have cut the Gordian knot, to have synthesized sociologism and existentialism and reunited sociology and philosophy.

It would surely be a triumph of dialectical reasoning if, in this manner and at one blow, one were able to synthesize scientific, right-wing collectivism with humanistic, non-rational individualism. However, it is not true that a common moral crisis produced sociologism and Existentialism and that these are merely different evaluations of the same crisis. Decisives to act come first: moral crises may or may not ensue. Nor does one wipe away the collectivistic theories of Durkheim or any other Positivistic Organicist by such a device as discovering that Durkheim was simply trying to treat a subjective reality objectively. One has merely equivocated on the meaning of individuality by reducing it to subjectivity.

There is an Existentialist sociology or at least an Existentialist interpretation of social phenomena, but any such fusion of contradictory positions such as those of the Existentialists and the Functionalists is out of the question. One is reminded of the old story of the two Russians who found themselves on a train, one going to Minsk, the other to Pinsk, and broke into hot argument, since they were in opposite directions. Peace was restored only when one suggested — "it must be the dialectic."

*Sociological Theories in Terms of Their Humanistic-Scientific and Individualistic-Collectivistic Components*

| M P<br>e e<br>t r<br>h s<br>o p<br>d e<br>o c<br>l t<br>o i<br>g v<br>i e<br>c s<br>a<br>l | | SUBSTANTIVE ALTERNATIVES | | | |
|---|---|---|---|---|---|
| | | INDIVIDUALISM | | COLLECTIVISM | |
| | | Rationalism | Non-Rationalism | Left Wing | Right Wing |
| | Humanism | Social Behaviorism | Phenomenological Formalism Existential Sociology | The Sociology of C. Wright Mills | Main Stream of Catholic Sociology |
| | Science | Neo-Kantian Branch of Sociological Formalism | Conflict Theory | Marxian Sociology | Positivistic Organicism Functionalism |

## Summary

The most fundamental of all perspectives in Western thought are those of humanism and science. Humanism arose as a man-oriented secular outlook in the dawn period of the Western cities, when offspring of medievalism were cast as orphans into a new world and forced to exploit the resources of their own natures to solve the unprecedented problems of their existence. Humanism arose in politically-responsible (elitist) circles: the advisors or princes, the tutors in eminent households, diplomatists, secretaries, and university professors. In the attempt to solve their problems, the humanists searched through the literature of the past, developing philological methods and techniques of historical research. They left a permanent heritage in the humanistic disciplines of the present day. Later, when the city began to crystallize and the rising nation-state took up the curve of development, the humanistic skills and techniques were transferred to the sphere of the nation-state. Perhaps their highest and fullest expression was achieved in seventeenth- and eighteenth-century Rationalism. However, another phenomenon accompanied this transition. In the course of the shift from the city to the nation-state, the old polarity of humanism and theology of the city was lost, and theology was shifted into the sphere of the humanities.

Western science, which fused the rational proof discovered and worked up by man in the classical polis with systematic experimentalism — the world of things — was also born in the Western city. It emerged in quite different circles from humanism, and had, originally, a different intent. It proceeded out of the circles of craftsmen and artists. It was intended, not to solve problems of man's social experience, but to discover new things about the world of physical things. Science powerfully implemented the free technology which formed its medieval birth matrix, and in whatever sphere it was released it worked revolutions.

The primary substantive issues of human social life are formed by the relation between the individual and the collective (society). In every society, including the Western city and later the nation-state, individualistic and collectivistic theories have developed. Individualistic theories see the highest human values in the most harmonious and smooth-running society possible.

In the period of the Western city, individualistic theories were most frequently advocated by the humanists, while collectivistic theories were most often advocated by the theologians (of both Roman Catholic and Protestant persuasion, though more frequently by the former).

In this early period there were only the most sporadic suggestions for lifting science from the world of physical things and applying it to human affairs.

When the curve of development shifted to the nation-state, the early division between humanism and theology was wiped away, and humanism and theology often found themselves making common cause against the forces of a new world. Moreover, a re-division in the forms of individualism and collectivism was carried through and the lines between rationalistic and non-rationalistic individualism and left- and right-wing collectivism were crystallized.

Perhaps the single most dramatic intellectual event of the nineteenth and twentieth centuries has been the rise of the social sciences with their attempt to transplant techniques which proved so powerful in dealing with the physical world to the social world. While the social sciences held out the promise of fusing the scientific and humanistic poles of Western thought, they have carried with them the danger (from some points of view) of permanently transforming the ratio between individuality and collectivity and carrying through an unprecedented curtailment of the sphere of individual freedom. Against the forces moving in this direction, Existentialism has represented an insurgent protest. Its essence is found in a new anti-rational and anti-scientific individualism.

Some of the major ways in which sociology has evolved under the strains of these diverging forces have been traced. Sociology is a dynamic development opened by the establishment of Positivistic Organicism, dividing into many contrasting and, in part, complementary forms, and continuing in the present with the emergence of an Existentialist sociology, on the one hand, and forms of left-wing, humanistic collectivism on the other.

## BIBLIOGRAPHY

1. Burckhardt, Jacob. *The Civilization of the Renaissance.* New York: Oxford University Press, 1945.

2. Cassirer, Ernst, Paul Oskar Kristeller, and John Herman Randall, Jr. *The Renaissance Philosophy of Man.* Chicago: University of Chicago Press, 1958.

3. Comte, Auguste. *Cours de Philosophie Positive.* Paris: Au Siege de la societe positiviste, 4 vols., 1892.

4. Comte, Auguste. *Systeme de politique positive* or *Traite de la Sociologie instituant la Religion de l'Humanite,* 4 vols., translated by John Henry Bridges as *System of Positive Polity.* London: Longmans, Green, 1875–1877.

5. Da Vinci, Leonardo. *The Notebooks of Leonardo Da Vinci,* edited by Edward MacCurdy. New York: Braziller, 1956.

6. Dilthey, Wilhelm. *Dilthey's Philosophy of Existence,* translated by William Kluback and Martin Weinbaum. New York: Bookman, 1914.

7. Droysen, Gustav. *Grundrissder Historik,* translated by E. B. Andrews as *Outline of the Principles of History.* Boston: Ginn & Co., 1893.

8. Droysen, Johann Gustav. "Zur Characteristik der europaischen Krisis," in Felix Gilbert (ed.·), *Politische Schriften.* Munich, 1933, pp. 307–342.

9. Goldenweiser, Alexander. *Anthropology.* New York: F. S. Crofts, 1937.

10. Hayek, F. A. *The Counter-revolution of Science.* Glencoe, Ill.: The Free Press, 1952.

11. Kluback, William. *Wilhelm Dilthey's Philosophy of History.* New York: Columbia University Press, 1956.

12. Little, A. G. "The Mendicant Orders," in *The Cambridge Medieval History,* 8 vols. New York: The Macmillan Co., 1929, Vol. 6.

13. Lundberg, George Andrew. *Can Science Save Us?* New York: Longmans, Green, 1947.

14. Martindale, Don. *The Nature and Types of Sociological Theory.* Boston: Houghton Mifflin, 1960.

15. Martindale, Don. *Social Life and Cultural Change.* Princeton: Van Nostrand, 1962.

16. Mill, John Stuart. *A System of Logic.* New York: Longmans, Green, 1949.

17. Mills, C. Wright. "On Intellectual Craftsmanship," in Llewellyn Gross (ed.), *Symposium in Sociological Theory.* Evanston, Ill.: Row, Peterson & Co., 1959.

18. Mills, C. Wright. *The Sociological Imagination.* New York: Oxford University Press, 1959.

19. Mills, C. Wright. *Listen, Yankee.* New York: Ballantine Books, 1960.

20. Mills, C. Wright. *The Marxists.* New York: Dell Publishing Co., 1962.

21. Munro, W. G., and George Sellery. *Medieval Civilization.* New York: Century Co., 1910.

22. Shils, Edward A. "Epilogue: The Calling of Sociology," in Talcott Parsons, Edward Shils, Kaspar D. Naegele, and Jesse R. Pitts (eds.), *Theories of Society,* 2 vols. New York: Free Press of Glencoe, 1961, Vol. 2, pp. 1403–1449.

23. Tiryakian, Edward A. *Sociologism and Existentialism.* Englewood Cliffs, N.J.: Prentice-Hall, Inc., 1962.

24. Tolstoy, Leo. *What to Do?* translated by Isabel F. Hapgood. New York: Thomas Y. Crowell, 1887.

25. Tolstoy, Leo. *On Life,* translated by Aylmer Maude. London: Humphrey Milford, 1934.

26. White, Lynn, Jr. *Medieval Technology and Social Change.* Oxford: Clarendon Press, 1962.

# 24

*Bert F. Hoselitz*

# Economic Development and Change

# in Social Values and Thought Patterns

## I

In the last few years the study of economic development has gradually been pushed into wider and wider social, political, and cultural dimensions. Whereas in the early post-war phase of the concentration of social scientists upon problems of economic growth, communication between economists and other social scientists was quite limited, contacts have increased and the various participants in the discussion have given increased recognition to the fact that those coming from other disciplines in the social sciences have a genuine contribution to make to a general understanding of economic growth. When in 1951 a group of scholars representing the various social science disciplines met at Chicago to discuss, under the auspices of the Norman Wait Harris Memorial Foundation in International Relations, the problem of the progress of underdeveloped areas, one economist at the meeting clearly expressed his discouragement with the potential contribution of anthropologists to the problem of economic growth, by saying: "You are only interested in simple tribes like the Hopi; but you have nothing to say about the improvement of the lot of millions of downtrodden peasants in India and other parts of Asia, about the failure by Middle Easterners and Latin Americans to react constructively to more modern ways of production." To this one of the anthropologists answered that, he, in turn, was bewildered by the concentration on abstract models which economists were so fond of, and their failure to concern themselves with living people and their values and thoughts, rather than with bloodless mathematical formulas describing collective behavior of a kind no human society had ever experienced.

I am citing this exchange — and I will leave the two very distinguished participants in it anonymous — in order to show that a dozen years ago many social scientists still lived in secluded compartments and had little regard for each other's contributions to the understanding of economic growth. It was as a response to this contrast that the Research Center in Economic Development and Cultural Change was founded at the University of Chicago, and it was one of the chief purposes of its past activities in the 11 years of its existence to bring about a closer and better understanding of the contributions of the various social sciences to the problems of economic growth and development.

I present these remarks to explain why an economist has the temerity to attempt a paper on the role of societal values in economic development. This task is made a great deal easier by the development of interdisciplinary contacts and communications in the last few years. The model builders in economics have gradually come to recognize that in addition to economic changes, actual economic growth will only take place if social relations, cultural behavior, and patterns of values in developing nations are altered. The anthropologists have come to see that the cake of culture is not so hard that it cannot be broken, and have begun to study with increasing interest and frequency situations of change, of "modernization," and of acculturation. There is still a great area of ignorance and a good deal of mutual lack of understanding between persons representing different disciplines in the social sciences. But this mistrust and lack of communication is declining and we may look forward to a time when more general theories of economic development, not tied to a rigorous model composed of a few relatively easily measurable variables, will become the leading theoretical formulations in the study of economic growth. But even in broader-based theories the concept and analysis of social values is likely to form one of the most difficult and intractable variables. Hence, all I can do, here, is to present some very general and preliminary ideas on this topic, and I wish to express the hope at this point that further research and investigation will provide us with greater insights and more certain facts to cope more adequately with the problems in this difficult field.

## II

In the analysis of social values, as in so many other fields of studying the process of economic growth, a convenient starting point is the delineation of widely distinct ideal types representing, on the one hand, the economically highly advanced and, on the other, the underdeveloped, societies. Another way of handling this problem consists of attempting to answer briefly the question of what differences may be found in the value and belief systems of Western and non-Western societies which may have decisive significance for the comparative rates of economic development in the two sets of societies. There are some societies which would fall outside this twofold classification. On the one hand some non-Western societies, e.g., Japan, have shown clear abilities for economic growth, and some Western societies, e.g., Portugal or certain Latin American countries, have exhibited an inability to pass beyond a very modest level of economic advancement. But, on the whole, the great division in the world today between economically advanced and under-developed countries coincides almost completely with the contrast between the Western and the non-Western nations, and it may be opportune to ask somewhat more insistently what are the value and belief patterns in the two sets of societies.

On one level this difference appears to have been extensively discussed already by Max Weber and some other writers who followed him in the study of the sociology of religion. Weber has shown, on the one hand, how Protestant (especially Calvinist) and other dissenting religious doctrines were instrumental in aiding in the growth of an economic ethic which was extremely favorable to economic advancement, notably under conditions of private enterprise and initiative. He has shown, on the other hand, how the religious doctrines of Eastern creeds, in particular, Buddhism, Hinduism, and Confucianism, failed to produce such an ethic and how, in spite of the often encountered greed and urge for gain displayed in market transactions in Asian countries, these motives were expressions not of a rationalized economic ethic, but of personal traits or magical beliefs (1, pp. 117–211).

The chief distinction in Max Weber's analysis is the difference between societies in which economic activity is subject throughout to rational calculation and those in which economic action is principally traditional. In fact, Weber extends the application of the principle of rationalism in modern societies to other sectors of social action, e.g., the political and, in some aspects, the integrative spheres of social action, to maintain the argument that he sees the overall process of economic growth as dependent upon an increasing imposition of rationalist modes of behavior and hence a growth of rationally determined systems of social values. For we must interpret his distinction between *Zweckrationalitaet* (instrumental rationality) and *Wertrationalitaet* (value rationality or purposive rationality) in this sense (14, p. 184 ff.).

But to many students of economic development this distinction has not been wholly satisfactory and has left unanswered several doubts, particularly since the contrast between rationalism and traditionalism, which forms the basis of Weber's distinction, constitutes only a partially closed system. For although one extreme of the dichotomy, that of rationalism, is extensively elaborated, the other extreme, the discussion of tradition and traditionalism, is left largely unexplored. Though Weber has not remained completely unconcerned with the content of traditional action, many of the finer distinctions between different types and roles of tradition are barely sketched in and often not discussed in any detail. In particular, Weber did not deal in any explicit fashion with the role of tradition in economically advanced societies, though it cannot be denied that, especially on the level of values, tradition plays an important role in these societies also. And once rational decision-making in a profit-oriented economy becomes widely generalized, it is impossible to deny that a good deal of social action in the adaptive sector of social behavior, i.e., in the realm of economic activity, becomes subject to many traditional norms and traditionally determined behavior patterns.

An example may make this clear. As I pointed out earlier, the main impact of the Protestant ethic has been the development of an economic spirit, which, in the words of Weber, created an "attitude which seeks profit rationally and systematically" (13, p. 64). Yet Weber admits elsewhere in his work that entrepreneurs in other societies also seek profit, in fact that "the people of Asia are notorious all over the world for their unlimited and unequalled greed . . . but the point is that this 'acquisitive drive' is pursued by all the tricks of the trade and with the aid of that cure-all: magic" (1, p. 207).[1]

How can we distinguish these two attitudes, the profit motivation based on greed and that based on a permeating rationality of the economic system? Weber himself tries to contrast rational and "traditionally" inspired entrepreneurship in a distinction he presents in *The Protestant Ethic*. He shows there that many of the men operating under the putting-out system were animated by traditions, "the traditional manner of life, the traditional rate of profit, the traditional amount of work, the traditional manner of regulating the relationships with labour, and the essentially traditional circle of customers and the manner of attracting new ones" (13, p. 67). In the business behavior encountered in Asian countries, this distinction is even clearer, though based on a different set of attitudes than those described by Weber for the putting-out system. Some of the relations of the businessman to others in these societies may also be regarded as based on tradition, but what matters most is his relation to the profitability of his enterprise and his calculation of its returns. The characteristic of the Western entrepreneur, both the modern capitalistic businessman and the merchant in the putting-out system, is that he considers the returns from his enterprise in terms of its appraisal in the long run and of its general position within the entire community in which he exercises his economic activity. The modern businessman is concerned with a particular transaction not as an end in itself, but as one of the many links in a large chain of events, the total impact of which

[1] The original passage may be found in Max Weber (15, p. 337).

is designed to yield a certain total profit. The bazaar-entrepreneur of Asia or the Middle East has a completely different attitude. For him each single transaction is an end in itself, and a calculation of his over-all returns is either not undertaken at all, or is only the incidental result of adding the profits made on each transaction by itself. In other words, when the modern entrepreneur is developing a plan for his enterprise, he estimates the prospective volume of trade, the various costs involved in performing the productive, merchandising, and service functions of his enterprise in this context, and he estimates a total return of his en-terprise based upon these calculations. He may be in error on many points; he may estimate wrongly the demand for his output, the cost of its production, or the effect of the impact of his competitors. But though he may suffer losses, or unexpected profits, his rationalism is ex-hibited by his looking at his activity from the viewpoint of the system as a whole and the place of his activity within the system.

The bazaar-entrepreneur has no such concerns. He is interested in the profitability of a given transaction and disregards the long-run impact of his business activity and the general rate of return he may make. If he thinks that a given transaction may involve a loss, he will usually forgo concluding it, even if the loss in this transaction may produce sizeable profits in the long run. If he has publicly announced a price for a good or a service and finds that, in a given case, he would lose or have to forgo the expected profit by performing the service or selling the good at the published price, he will find some excuse for not having to fulfill the transaction. In brief, he will not act on the basis of an evaluation of his position in a social and economic system as a whole, nor on a calculation of his returns in the long run; he will be concerned with each transaction as a separate entity, and will disregard the long-run consequences and the "systematic" integration of each transaction in his economic activity as a whole.[2]

But if we make this distinction between the "rationally" inclined busi-nessman in the advanced economies of the Western countries and the "traditionally" inclined businessman in the Orient, we find that the latter is operating on different principles even from those of the individual operating in a putting-out system. For the latter has a wider horizon than the merchant or producer in the Oriental bazaar. He may not develop the aggressiveness and the full-scale rationality of the modern capitalist business leader in charge of a large enterprise. But his outlook, though beset with a number of traditionally inspired attitudes, is influenced by a recognition of his activity as an outcome of the overall functioning of a total system. Rather than interpreting each transaction as a separate

[2] This evaluation of the principles of bazaar-entrepreneurship is based mostly on my personal experience in the bazaars and similar markets of Middle Eastern, African, and South Asian countries. But see also the discussion of bazaar-entrepreneurship by Clifford Geertz in (2, p. 390 ff.).

action unrelated to others and forming a self-contained entity, the merchant or manufacturer in a putting-out system regards his function as flowing out of the system as a whole. Hence though it lacks certain aspects of rationality it presents a very different type of traditional attitude than that of the greed-ridden bazaar-entrepreneur.

This discussion suggests that the more extensive exploration of traditionalism and its various forms of appearance may yield some further insights into differences in changes of attitudes and values in the process of economic growth in various societies. A more extensive discussion of this problem would be out of place here, particularly since I have attempted to indicate some of its dimensions in a paper published not very long ago (5, pp. 83 ff.). The views expressed in that essay constitute only a beginning in the fuller analysis of the differential impact of value systems on economic development, and more specifically on the question of what differences in Western and non-Western value systems appear to be crucial in the development of those economic motives and forms of economic behavior which are likely to initiate and support self-sustained economic growth.

An attempt to work out a general solution of this problem meets with great difficulties, because of the wide variety in cultural values and beliefs in different non-Western societies. One of the great advantages of the dichotomy between rationalism and traditionalism was the fact that it brought many widely diverse cultures into a relatively tight framework of analysis, in which emphasis was placed on the examination of a rather small, though crucial, set of variables which were considered the major determinants of the social system and the values of the system as a whole. Upon this general dichotomy between rationalism and tradition, Weber's followers have built somewhat more complex schemes, but apart from pointing more precisely to the selection of relevant variables, they have not extended the theory in an important manner. In other words, the general state of theoretical discussion of values affecting social change and economic growth is still founded upon some dichotomy such as that of the traditionalism and rationalism of Max Weber, or the folk-urban continuum by Robert Redfield, or other relatively simple dichotomies (9, pp. 293–308).[3]

## III

One of the principal shortcomings of the Weberian analysis, and other theories of social change based upon it, is the implicit assumption of unilinearity, that is, the assumption that the destruction of tradition will lead gradually or abruptly to its replacement by rationalism. An example

---

[3] The theme has been discussed by Redfield in many other places and has been taken up in somewhat different form by several of his students. A full account of the literature based on the folk-urban dichotomy would fill a sizeable book.

of how Weber conceived of this change was touched upon earlier in this chapter when I showed how he considered the transformation within Western capitalism from the predominance of the tradition-oriented putting-out system to the rationalism-oriented factory system. The crucial phase in this process was considered to be the breakdown of traditional modes of belief and behavior influenced by this belief, and their change into rational ones under the impact of a new economic ethic. Yet it is reasonable to assume that the process of culture change is not unilinear, but multilinear, i.e., that the destruction of a simple traditional belief system does not always lead to the same outcome, but may produce quite different results. In the earlier discussion of two tradition-oriented patterns of business behavior, the one characteristic of the Western putting-out system and the other designated as bazaar-entrepreneurship, I have already shown that different varieties of belief and attitude systems, which all may be lumped together under the general designation "traditional," do exist. Hence the processes of change in these contrasting situations begin from quite different starting points, would show considerable variations, and it is now appropriate to stipulate that the outcomes of these processes of change may vary considerably.

In order to examine one possible set of alternatives in greater detail I shall attempt to discuss the variation in the Western and the non-Western pattern of change from traditional to rational forms of social values and attitudes. This analysis is assisted greatly by the work of F. S. C. Northrop, who upheld the view that, in addition to the Weberian dichotomy between traditional and rational action, we should consider also the difference between East and West. Northrop himself refers to the two related dichotomies in the following passage:

> Cultures with differing political, economic, aesthetic and religious ideals or values are grounded in differing philosophical conceptions of the nature of man and of the universe. These diverse philosophical conceptions fall into two groups: those which differ because they refer to different factors in the nature of things, and those which conflict because they are affirming contradictory things of the same factor. The philosophy of the Orient with its attention upon things in their aesthetic immediacy in contrast with the philosophy of the West with its emphasis upon the theoretically designated and inferred factor in things exemplifies the first group; the medieval and modern worlds or traditional communistic and democratic economic and political theory are instances of the second (7, p. 437).

What Northrop calls the difference between medieval and modern values is the contrast between traditional and rational action which we have traced back to Weber and his disciples. The other contrast between aesthetic and conceptual patterns of thinking, on the other hand, forms the new dimension which is added by Northrop's analysis. I shall not attempt here to discuss at length the meaning and significance of this difference, since Northrop's own work largely turns around this problem as a central theme. In very few words this point can be summarized as follows:

In the Western world, and as an outflow of Western philosophical tradition which emerged gradually in the Christian philosophy of the early Middle Ages, patterns of reasoning were evolved which tended to stress abstract, general, theoretical thought. Though these patterns of thought are most clearly displayed in the scientific and philosophical writings of Western authors, this thought has become so widely current that it penetrates all thinking, it affects attitudes toward and interpretations of things, and therefore it may be regarded as an underlying principle of all Occidental intellectual performance.

In the Orient a different basic value attitude is discernible which is in stark contrast to the theoretical orientation of the West. Northrop calls it the aesthetic orientation, but this concept requires explanation. Unlike Western thought, which contains a substantial ingredient of theoretical reasoning, Eastern aesthetic thought is directly empirical, and immediately self-expressive. Northrop uses as an example a comparison between the complex grammar in Western scientific exposition and Chinese writing in which each idea is expressed by a picture showing the general sense impression of an object in its original, primitive form with direct immediacy. The same contrast can be traced through Chinese and Western painting: the latter with its insistence upon providing the illusion of three-dimensional space, the rules of perspective, and emphasis on appropriate effects of lighting and color, and the former with its naive and direct expression of an immediately aesthetic principle characteristic of the object depicted. It finally can be studied by contrasting Western and Eastern philosophy, and through it Western and Eastern systems of beliefs.[4]

In this last area the contrast between aesthetic and theoretical approaches becomes more explicit, for here we deal with the actual methodological explanation of basic thoughts and ultimately determinative approaches to thought. It may be argued that no valid set of philosophical propositions is meaningful in purely theoretical or in purely aesthetic terms. In other words, a purely theoretical philosophy would rely on complete a priori reasoning without need to verify its findings by appeal to empirical validation. Some aspects of Hegelian philosophy come closest to this ideal, but the deficiency of this purely theoretical aspect of Hegelianism has quite appropriately been criticized often, most convincingly perhaps by Karl R. Popper.[5] In fact, Marx's argument of having placed Hegel's philosophy back on its feet is based on Marx's

---

[4] For a more extensive discussion of the "intuitive aesthetic character" of Eastern values, see Northrop (7, pp. 315 ff.).

[5] See the brief remarks in K. R. Popper (8, vol. 2, p. 26, pp. 38–39) on Hegel's philosophy of nature and on Hegel's doctrine of identity.

conviction that the empty "idealism," i.e., the purely theoretical approach, of Hegel is inadequate as a system of propositions designed to form the fundament of a structure for empirical scientific inquiry.

But if a purely theoretical philosophy, i.e., a philosophy which allows no appeal to empirical verification, is of no utility, a purely aesthetic philosophy also is of no value, for it makes impossible virtually by definition the elaboration of theoretical generalizations. But, in truth, neither Western nor Eastern philosophies are purely aesthetic or purely theoretical; they contain both elements mixed, though each of the two elements is present in different proportions. In Eastern belief systems and ways of thinking aesthetic tendencies prevail, whereas in the West theoretical tendencies prevail. Thus we may reinterpret Northrop's system as delineating a continuum with purely theoretical and purely aesthetic patterns at either end, with a series of intermediate stages, each representing a mixture of both extreme elements in different proportions. We may then attempt to represent the two dichotomies, one derived from Weber and the other from Northrop, in a diagram which in turn is based upon a fourfold table.[6]

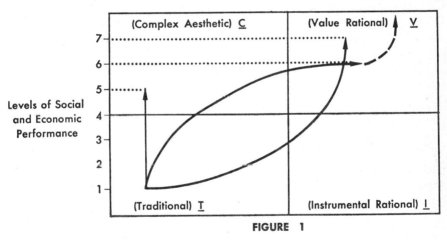

**FIGURE 1**

Degree of Change in Theoretical Orientation

The diagram is very simple; it is a rectangle in which each of the four sections represents a social system with one predominating value and thought system. In other words, societies which are dominated by a purely traditional value system would cluster around the lower left-hand corner, societies which respond to instrumental rational values in the

[6] I am indebted to Mr. H. Berringer of Northwestern University for having brought to my attention the possibility of combining Weber's and Northrop's analysis and of having devised originally a table from which the diagram is derived.

lower right-hand corner, and societies following purposive rationality as a predominant value in the upper right-hand corner. In Weber's system a movement was assumed which proceeded from Area T to Area I and from there to Area V in a more or less direct path. The line labeled A represents such a possible path of development and change of social values. The introduction of Northrop's dichotomy of aesthetic and theoretical orientations produces a fourth area in the diagram, which has been labeled "complex aesthetic" (C). We now can draw two more lines, B and C, the former of which ends in the same sector as A, but rather than passing through Area I, passes through Area C, and the latter of which only goes from Area T to Area C. At the same time, we can indicate what prevailing forces will determine the shape of the line tracing the change in values associated with progressive economic and social change. The path followed will depend, on the one hand, on the rate of economic and social change, but, on the other, on the rate of change from an aesthetic to a theoretical orientation. In the case of Lines A and B this change in philosophical orientation is clearly shown. It is strongest in the case of Line A, less so in the case of line B. These lines, especially Line A, represent schematically the change in social values in Europe from the pre-industrial to the industrial stage. But the more characteristic development of Eastern countries is represented by Lines B and C. In the second case a set of rational values does not become internalized, but the underlying attitude and thought patterns remain within a system of aesthetically determined values. In the first case a system of rationality is ultimately reached, but only after a long process of development, and after an intermediate period during which aesthetic thought patterns predominate.

One further comment on the level of economic development, which can be reached by different processes of change, might be made. Comparison of Lines A, B, and C in Figure 1 shows that the first (assuming only the solid portion of the lines) reaches the highest level, the second attains a somewhat lower level, and the third the lowest altitude. If we measure the degree of social and economic performance by some indicator or index on the vertical axis, the three lines, as drawn in the diagram, tend to show that different levels of economic development may be reached, depending upon whether a society can attain a position of internalization of a system of socially rational values, or whether its value system remains in the sphere of complex aesthetic values.

In other words, the diagram exhibits the proposition that different systems of social values may have different effects on the level of economic performance which can be achieved, and that the path by which value systems undergo change may have some impact on this result. This is shown by the solid portion of Line B which ends at a lower level of economic performance than Line A. On the other hand, it could be maintained that once a society has reached a system of socially rational values, the attainment of the highest levels of economic performance is not impossible and this is represented by the dotted portion of Line B. All these propositions, which are graphically represented in Figure 1, are, however, purely a prioristic and speculative. Whether they are accurate will depend on closer examination of value systems and their interaction with economic performance, and the more precise identification of the various components making up traditional, rational, and aesthetic systems of values.

At this point it may be useful to state more explicitly the mutual interdependence of the three main variables represented in Figure 1. On the horizontal axis the mixture between aesthetic and theoretical approaches is indicated according to some index. This means that any point further to the right in Figure 1 represents a situation in which the theoretical ingredient is greater and the aesthetic ingredient smaller in a society's system of thought. This means that if we wish to find a position along the horizontal axis for the thought systems of Oriental societies, especially at the time before their original cultural systems became subjected to a great extent to foreign influence, we would have to locate it on the left side of the diagram. Then as Oriental cultures adopted increasingly theoretical orientations from their contact with the Western world, their position shifted farther to the right. But the shift from left to right at a given level of scientific knowledge does not imply economic, social, or scientific progress. It merely shows a gradual change in the composition of thought patterns dominant in a society.

For example, a perusal of Joseph Needham's discussion of the origin of scientific thought in China would, I believe, show quite clearly how strong the aesthetic approach in early Chinese science was.[7] Yet it is well known that China experienced a more rapid and far-reaching scientific and technical progress than the Western world before the twelfth or the thirteenth century. The invention of such important objects and processes as gunpowder, porcelain, printing, and various more efficient methods of smelting and refining metals occurred much earlier in China than in the West. These facts are too well known to require extended discussion. In fact, it may be maintained that the inventions which can be accomplished on the basis of intensive practical experiments may be as readily, and perhaps more easily, possible in a civilization with predominantly aesthetic thought patterns rather than in one with principally theoretical thought patterns.

To this might be added that not all Oriental societies exhibited the same mixture of aesthetic and theoretical thought patterns in their original state. Though my acquaintance with scientific or pseudo-scientific thought in ancient Indian natural philosophy is limited, I have the

---

[7] See Joseph Needham (6, vol. 2, pp. 220–231 esp.), depicting the origin of scientifically relevant ideographic characters; but see also the subsequent presentation of the growth of basic scientific conceptions in China.

impression that it comprehended a somewhat larger element of theoretical orientation than Chinese philosophical thought of the Han or pre-Han period. Some supporting evidence for this may perhaps be derived from a study of the ideological and philosophical contrasts which arose as a consequence of the introduction of Buddhism in China. But a comparative study of either Indian or Chinese thought patterns with those of early medieval Europe shows that, in spite of the fact that scientific insights and technical performance of Europe in the eleventh and twelfth centuries were in no way superior, and in fact quite inferior, to the corresponding attainments in Asia, the Asian thought processes displayed a much less intensive theoretical orientation than the European ones. In fact the philosophy of early medieval Europe shows a strong deficiency in adequately confronting aesthetic approaches.[8] It might perhaps even be argued that the slowness of technical and material progress in early medieval Europe was not unrelated to the predominantly abstract a prioristic thought patterns of the tenth and eleventh centuries.

Hence, one of the variables related to different value systems represented in Figure 1 are systems of thought. The other variable related to them in the diagram is the level of economic and social complexity. Little needs to be said about this relation, for it will be quite commonly accepted that with an increase of some magnitude in economic and social complexity the system and hierarchy of socially relevant values change. Thus the diagram may be interpreted as presenting, in a very general way, the interrelation of values, economic performance, and patterns of thought, without any indication as to which of these variables are independent and which are dependent. We are concerned with a complex process of change often of long duration (i.e., lasting over decades and even centuries), and assigning the role of independence under all circumstances to any one of the three variables would constitute a highly one-sided interpretation. The transformation of value systems depends upon economic and socio-structural as well as "philosophical" variables, and changes in all these latter variables are partly dependent upon variations in social values.

The consequence of this mutual interdependence of several broadly defined factors is that each of the four boxes in Figure 1 represents a separate economic and cultural system exhibiting a particular combination of thought patterns, economic performance, and social values. But this conclusion raises the further question of what process of change takes place when a social system moves from one of the boxes to another. The three curves, labeled A, B, and C in Figure 1, show the path along which a society may move, and in view of the preceding propositions

---

[8] On the differences between the philosophical attitudes in India and China, see Needham (6, pp. 419 ff.), where the influence of Buddhism on Chinese science and scientific thought is discussed. On the development of western theory-oriented thinking see the very excellent exposition in R. W. Southern, (12, chapter 4, esp.).

presented, the crucial point on the path is that where a society passes from one box to the next one.

Now it should be stated that though in the diagram the lines between the boxes establish sharp boundaries, in actual fact each of the boundaries is a fairly fuzzy area. In other words, we may consider the passage from one box into the next as a historical process which may often take place during a long period of time. We may also consider it as a process in which the transition in values, economic performance, and thought patterns does not affect all social classes and sub-groups at the same time and that there are certain members of the society which perform the transition to new values, new thought patterns, and new forms of economic action faster and others slower. Hence the boundary areas between the systems represented by the four boxes should be interpreted as forming situations in which some members of a population adopt different attitudes and accept different values than others. I will discuss these points in somewhat more detail later in this chapter.

In view of what has been said so far it appears desirable to say, before concluding, a few more words on three topics which are raised by the analysis presented in the preceding paragraphs. First, some further explanation of the complex aesthetic sector of the diagram has to be given; second, a few comments should be made on the relationship between the diagram and my comments on it and Northrop's anticipation of the "proper" integration between Eastern and Western value systems in the form of what he calls "epistemic correlations."[9] Finally a few words may be in order on a problem which is also raised by the attempt to introduce thoughts derived from Northrop, i.e., the interrelation between systems of thought and philosophical speculation and systems of values. As we shall see, there is some interrelation between the first two topics, whereas the third covers a more general and independent set of propositions.

The stipulation of a complex aesthetic sector provides a fourth alternative to Weber's unilineal tripartite classification of tradition, instrumental rationality, and rationality in social values or purposive rationality. A brief examination of this fourth alternative shows that it is the result of economic and social progress, on the one hand, and the refusal to move away from the predominance of an aesthetic orientation, on the other. In other words, it is a system in which often complex and sometimes highly productive economic units or large complex social groups have become accepted and institutionalized, but in which individuals react and think in terms of immediate, strictly isolated issues and events rather than in response to an integrated system of abstract analysis of these

---

[9] See Northrop (7, pp. 440 ff., esp. pp. 442–443). Perhaps the briefest definition of this term given by Northrop himself is: "The aesthetic, intuitive, purely empirically given component in man and nature is related to the theoretically designated and indirect verified component . . . by the two-termed relation of epistemic correlation."

events or to a generalized schema of expectations. The differences which were outlined earlier between modern rationalized capitalist entrepreneurship, on the one hand, and bazaar-entrepreneurship, on the other, clearly show the basic mode of operation of a privately-owned economic unit in a complex aesthetic system of values. Though the typical bazaar-entrepreneur controls a small or at best medium-scale business, the principle of decision-making manifested by his behavior can also be applied to large-scale plants. This may be one of the reasons why, in spite of much lower unit costs of labor and some other services, total operating costs in many modern Asian firms are higher than in Western enterprises of comparable size. It may also be the reason why certain new fields of industrial development in Asia and other non-Western countries depend upon foreign investment or are left to the initiative of public agencies, though there are no legal impediments for the full display of private entrepreneurship.

This development is the outcome of a combined impact of the maintenance of complex aesthetic values and a growth in overall productive and general economic efficiency. But the decisive step is only taken when a society gradually passes beyond the aesthetic system of thought and achieves some compromise with the theoretical system of thought, i.e., when it moves to the right in Figure I. In more concrete language, once a society has, in terms of economic performance, reached a relatively high level of output, it finds itself in what I have called the complex aesthetic sector. As its system of values and thought gradually adopts characteristics of the theory-oriented Western societies, it is moving from the complex aesthetic to the value rational sector. This movement corresponds to what Northrop calls epistemic correlation, except that he disregards the level of economic performance at which this association between Eastern and Western systems of thought and values is attained. To Northrop the attainment of an epistemic correlation is due to adjustments in philosophy and rules of scientific inquiry, whereas if explicit attention is given to the conditions of economic growth, this correspondence between differentially derived systems of thought and values leads to the reflection that it is normally the result of social and economic progress on the one hand and the refusal or inability to abandon abruptly the predominance of a value orientation and adopt the other.

A study of the economic structures prevalent in social systems characterized by this correspondence of value and thought systems would show that some of the planned Asian economies have begun to incorporate more or less well integrated systems of epistemic correlation of thought. In practice this correlation is shown by the adoption of a multitude of theoretically derived strategies of economic planning, associated with frequent dismal failures in the execution of these plans owing to the imperfect penetration with theoretical attitudes of those who are called upon to execute the plans. An analysis of the experience of Communist

Chinese planning during the last few years yields results which could be interpreted in this fashion. A similar result would emerge from a study of the theoretical and concrete issues involved in the execution of development plans in other Asian countries. The dominance of an epistemic correlation in its initial, and as yet very imperfectly integrated, stage results in the fact that in spite of official efforts to impose rational plans, their implementation meets with very unequal success. Conflicts arise because each project is judged in its own terms, rather than as a fitting part of a whole, and these conflicts often lead to failures in execution, for the participants in a conflict situation tend to interpret each issue as an indivisible whole, circumscribed within its own dimension, rather than as part of a total system in which its function and place can be at least roughly estimated.

This discussion could be expanded from the analysis of economic performance to that of political behavior. The results in this sector of social action would differ from those arising in the economic sector, but here also a wide contrast may be expected between the interpretation of issues on the part of some, especially Western-educated leaders and that of the large mass of followers. This, in turn, will influence the practical exercise of political activity, the kind of propaganda employed, and the type of party organization preferred. This is not the place to enter into a full discussion of these consequences, but they would clearly be brought to light by an examination of the recent history of political movements in newly independent countries of Asia, especially in India, Burma, and Indonesia, where an effort for, or at least a semblance of, democratic political action was made. In these countries political developments, consisting either of widespread acquiescence to sudden changes in political objectives, frequent violent demonstrations, abrupt changes in leadership, and other forms took place, which can most easily be explained by the failure of epistemic correlation of values and thought patterns to have taken place on any other level than that of a small leadership group of intellectuals and members of a political and economic elite.

This discussion suggests that in the nations of Southern and Southeastern Asia, and possibly elsewhere, there exists a contrast of thought processes between persons on different levels of education, political power, and economic roles. The intellectual, political, and economic elites are sufficiently Westernized to understand, and to have integrated to a considerable degree, thought and even values based upon the Western theoretical approach. In other words, these persons have achieved, to a fair degree, the internalization of thought and value patterns exhibiting the epistemic correlation described in Northrop's work. But the large masses in these countries, though touched upon externally by the theoretical approach of the West — if in no other form, at least through contact with the former colonial administrations, businessmen, or planters, who came from Europe — have remained fully within the aesthetic thought and value patterns of their cultures. And it should be added that even the intellectuals and members of other elites, in spite of their adoption of theoretical approaches on the level of thought and scientific enquiry, have adopted them much less on the level of socially relevant values. This intermediate position of many members of the elites in Asian countries has been observed numerous times, and has been well described by Edward Shils in his various essays on the Indian intellectuals.[10] Though Shils maintains that the frequently asserted uprootedness and the suspense between two cultures of the Indian intellectual is based on a romantic and wrong conception of his role, he shows in the sphere in which explicit thought processes predominate, that influence of and commitment to European theoretical patterns is widespread, and that the impact of what we have designated as an aesthetic orientation predominates in the personal relations of these individuals, in their contacts with their families and friends, and in the general acceptance of social value systems. Anyone who, like this writer, has maintained close personal contacts with Indian intellectuals must have observed that many of them lead what might almost be described a Jekyll-and-Hyde existences, i.e., that in some contexts they act in a manner based almost exclusively on theoretical thought patterns, and in others, especially those relating to the ordinary performance of daily living and close personal relations, they revert to behavior ultimately inspired by aesthetically determined attitudes.

These views could be elaborated further. As a first step they may be regarded as providing some examples for the proposition made earlier in the chapter that the passage of a society from one box in Figure 1 to another takes place through a "fuzzy" zone in which different social groups or classes have contrasting and often contradictory values and economic attitudes. India and China may be assumed to be in such an intermediate position at this time. The impact of theoretical orientations in the thought patterns of these nations tends to increase the influence of rational approaches to various forms of behavior and to subject the intellectuals especially to a growing internalization of rational attitudes. In both India and China this differentiation in values and thought patterns and even in economic attitudes is apparently quite pronounced and is surely one of the reasons why some have observed a wide cultural gap between urban and rural areas in these countries; in other words, why they have regarded urban areas as social and cultural "exclaves" of the nations in which they are located.[11]

A more complete understanding of this problem of transition from one socio-cultural system associated with a particular level of economic performance and a peculiar mixture of thought patterns to an-

---

[10] See, for example, Edward Shils (10), and M. K. Halder and Robin Ghosh (3).
[11] I have discussed this problem in greater detail in (4, chapter 7).

other may perhaps be provided by a discussion of the economic and social history of Japan in the last 200 years. For in the pre-Tokugawa period, Japan, due to the far-flung adoption of cultural, intellectual, and even socio-economic traits from China, may be said to have been in an economic and cultural situation which would have placed it in Area T in the diagram presented earlier. During the Tokugawa period it gradually moved from Area T into Area C, and in the period since the Meiji restoration, from Area C into Area V. An extensive elaboration of this process would require too much space, but consultation of the more enlightened descriptions of Japanese social and economic history during the last 400 years shows that during the Tokugawa period, especially from about 1600 to 1800, there occured a substantial growth of the Japanese economy without a profound change in values. The social structure also changed; the actual or putative kinship groups which had formed the village, through which production was organized, and which were quite common at the beginning of the Tokugawa period, had come to survive only in highly isolated outlying villages. The use of technology, e.g., various improved fertilizers in agriculture, the growth of a middle sector, the great rise of urban populations, the establishment of a fairly widespread market system in which merchants, craftsmen, and middlemen of various kinds could be found, were developments which all took place in the period of Tokugawa rule, even though the basic traditional cultural and social values, though under stress and strain, fundamentally remained unchanged.

T. C. Smith has presented a good deal of support for this interpretation of social and economic, as well as cultural, developments in Tokugawa Japan. He explains that the stability of the system depended upon the loyalty and discipline of the peasants (who formed the vast majority of the population of Japan at that period), upon the "traditional language of loyalty and obligation," upon "old values," and upon the fact that while the Tokugawa regime "created conditions favorable to change; cities grew, communications improved, industry spread from town to countryside . . . government did its best to isolate the village from the effects of these and other changes." Traditional values in the villages and even among many of the more recent migrants to urban areas survived into the early Meiji period and the new masters of Japan in that period still attempted to use tradition, on behalf of change, and "the primacy of values of loyalty and obedience did not collapse; they were continuously reinforced by stronger, more efficient measures of indoctrination and thought control by the state."

Yet even though in the period after the restoration of the Meiji emperor the support of traditional values was used, the new developments in the economy and the political situation of Japan required the gradual transition to more rationally inspired patterns of thought. Smith describes this by pointing to the fact that "rational thought, which an educational system dedicated to the advancement of science and technology was bound to promote," grew and affected not only economic but also political and social relations. In fact the whole development of Japan in the period from the end of the nineteenth century to the outbreak of the Pacific war may be interpreted as a period in which the growing demand for the wider spread of rational values conflicted with the attempt to base the power of the dominant political elite on reinforcement of certain traditions, especially those relating to loyalty and obedience. In this situation, as Smith points out, "the groups in control of the state had no choice but to sustain orthodoxy. . . . There was no way to go ahead; but that way lay a further weakening of tradition which, the weaker it became, was the more needed to give stability and command effort. . . . The ultimate price the nation paid was to be led without enthusiasm into a war that could not be won."[12]

From this we may note that in the period roughly before 1870, the advance of the economy and the growing complexity of the social stratification system were associated with little change in values, but that with the new industrialization pattern and the development of new and much more far-reaching objectives in foreign policy, new thought patterns and with them gradually new values, based on more rational orientations, became the rule. It is in this sense that the historical development of Japan may be considered to .have passed from the more simple and traditionally-oriented system of social order to the more complex and rationally-oriented one. I cannot produce a set of clear-cut explanations for the causes of this development. The regularization of political control, the successful enforcement of internal peace, and the strong and persistent leadership of a small conscientious elite in the early Tokugawa period may have been among the major causal factors responsible for the economic advancement of Japan. Similarly, the growing involvement in world affairs, the recognition of the need for rapid industrial development, improved armament, and modernization of production and administrative processes, again by a small, conscientious, and strongly devoted elite interested primarily in the advancement of their own country, may have been among the causal conditions bringing about a trend towards rationalization of thought patterns and the rapid adoption of intellectual, scientific, technological, and other characteristics of the Western world. The result is that at the present time even the last surviving traditional, chiefly aesthetically-oriented values tend to disappear completely in Japan and its overall attitudes and approaches to problems are almost undistinguishable from those of the Western world.

These reflections lead us to the final point, the relationship between values and thought patterns, and changes in each. In the work of Northrop there is no sharp distinction made between the two, and though

[12] The discussion in this and the preceding paragraphs is based on the excellent book of Thomas C. Smith (11, pp. 203–206).

sociologists following Weber have usually talked only of values, they believe that values influence patterns of thought. In societies with cultures in which change is slow, or in which strong traditions have developed which pass on the major framework of an existing value structure from generation to generation, there is a close correlation between values and thought patterns, and instituted aesthetic or theoretical thought systems will be closely associated with social values, since both are acquired through the same socialization processes. In other words, as children grow up in a society with well-established cultural traditions, they acquire in the course of their upbringing manifold parts of a system of cultural values and thought processes which already are integrated through tradition and the long-standing operation of various forms of mutual social adjustment.

But the situation is different in a society in which the socialization process and that of formal education are separated, as is true now for an increasing number of persons in Asia and Africa. This separation brings about conflicts in the underlying assumptions and understandings of persons who go through each of these processes by itself; conflict is likely to be stronger in those societies in which socialization requires close association with persons who are neglected or even treated as inferior in more formal schooling. It is not necessary to go into this point further, since its consequences are easily intelligible. It is a very rough description of what happens in Asian countries today, where the general process of socialization takes place in the homes of the people and is strongly associated with deeply tradition-bound women, and where education takes place in schools with a curriculum and a course content derived from a foreign culture. The persons who have only brief and relatively superficial contact with formal schooling are little touched by this experience and have therefore maintained value patterns and thought patterns basically derived from the aesthetic attitude. But those who have spent much time in schools, particularly those who have attended school in Western countries, and who upon returning home have been placed in jobs in which their knowledge acquired abroad is considered necessary, are in a serious dilemma. Their values were acquired through socialization in their homes subject to a prevalence of Eastern aesthetic inclinations, whereas their thought patterns were shaped powerfully by the theoretical orientations of the West.

One of the as yet unsolved problems is the question of how these two parts of the "educational" process influence one another. It is often maintained that the more advanced theoretical inclinations of Western-trained persons in Asia gradually bring about acceptance of these Western "values." It is also said that since the persons with the more strongly pronounced theoretical orientation occupy high positions of political or economic power, their "values" tend to exert an influence on those on lower levels in their societies. All these conclusions may be true, but they may also be merely comfortable arguments without empirical support of those who favor political, economic, and intellectual "modernization." It is possible to cite quite a few historical cases in which an intellectual or even political elite had to accept the value system of the population at large if it wanted to maintain its position in the societies of which it was part.[13] In short, in nations in which the socialization and the formal education processes are subject to principles derived from different value orientations and different ingrained thought patterns, the two systems of thought and values lead to different adjustments in persons, depending in part on the varying degree of exposure to the two kinds of influences, and hence tend to produce a range of persons subject to a variety of combinations of value and thought patterns derived from two conflicting origins. Some do incorporate the epistemic correlation which Northrop considers to be required for the whole society, if East and West are ultimately to meet. But in the present period, the basic value orientations of many Asians conflict with their thought patterns to a considerable extent and the mutual impact of these conflicting attitudes is still in doubt. For although, as already pointed out, the general assumption is made that the Western-educated elite will bring about a change in the general values, this is by no means certain, and the interrelation between values acquired in early youth and thought patterns acquired principally through formal educational experience requires a good deal more research. Only when we have looked more intensively and carefully into this interrelation in the changing societies of Asia and Africa will we have a more certain view on the role of values in social and economic change.

## BIBLIOGRAPHY

1. Bendix, Reinhard. *Max Weber, An Intellectual Portrait*. Garden City, N.Y.: Doubleday & Co., 1960.

2. Geertz, Clifford. "Social Change and Economic Modernization in Two Indonesian Towns," in Everett E. Hagen (ed.), *On the Theory of Social Change*. Homewood, Ill.: The Dorsey Press, 1962.

3. Halder, M. K., and Robin Ghosh. *Problems of Economic Growth*. Delhi: Congress for Cultural Freedom, 1960.

4. Hoselitz, Bert F. *Sociological Aspects of Economic Growth*. Glencoe, Ill.: The Free Press, 1960.

5. Hoselitz, Bert F. "Tradition and Economic Growth," in Ralph Braibanti and J. S. Spengler (eds.), *Tradition, Values and Socio-Economic Development*. Durham, N.C.: Duke University Press, 1961.

[13] A good example is provided by the political changes in Burma in the last few years in which the more "modernized" and the more "traditional" factions held each other in balance.

6. Needham, Joseph. *Science and Civilization in China.* Cambridge: Cambridge University Press, 1956.

7. Northrop, F.S.C. *The Meeting of East and West.* New York: The Macmillan Co., 1960.

8. Popper, K. R. *The Open Society and Its Enemies.* London: George Routledge and Sons, 1947.

9. Redfield, Robert. "The Folk Society," *American Journal of Sociology,* Vol. 52, No. 4 (1947), pp. 292–308.

10. Shils, Edward. "The Culture of the Indian Intellectual," *The Sewanee Review,* Vol. 67 (April and July), pp. 239–261, pp. 401–421.

11. Smith, Thomas C. *The Agrarian Origins of Modern Japan.* Stanford: Stanford University Press, 1959.

12. Southern, R. W. *The Making of the Middle Ages.* New Haven: Yale University Press, 1961.

13. Weber, Max. *The Protestant Ethic and the Spirit of Capitalism,* translated by Talcott Parsons. London: Allen & Unwin, 1930.

14. Weber, Max. *The Theory of Social and Economic Organization.* New York: Oxford University Press, 1947.

15. Weber, Max. *The Religion of India.* Glencoe, Ill.: The Free Press, 1958.

# SECTION SEVEN

cultural change, cultural contact,
and social movements

# Introduction

When J. A. and Olive Banks wrote a chapter for *Explorations in Social Change* in 1964, "Women's Lib" had not been invented yet. What has happened since attests to the rapidity of current socio-cultural change, and to the dangers and pitfalls of extrapolation of current phenomena by social analysts. In their explanation of the ups and downs of feminism the Banks are in the happy position of being immune to accusations of sexism.

The desire for political and cultural autonomy and dominance has been among the most powerful forces for change in recent human history (unless we follow the theorists espousing extreme formulations of historical or cultural determinism). The Banks address themselves to the questions of how British feminism differed from other social movements, and why it "petered out" in a relatively short time.

As to the first question, they show that "sex consciousness" paralleled class consciousness to some degree, but lacked the systematic blueprint for utopia found among most socio-political movements of the nineteenth century. With reference to the second question, the authors search for "structural" origins of women's dissatisfaction with their lot, and in the context challenge certain assumptions made by the Parsonian school regarding women's role in child rearing. They also raise the problem of why female dissatisfaction "withered away" in view of the continued existence of the double standard. The Banks are concerned with several of the most problematic aspects of social movements, namely, those regarding the mobilization of values and motivations of collective action. We need to refer here only to the concept of false consciousness, or to Ferdinand Lassalle's complaint about "the damned wantlessness of the poor." The other side of the coin is represented by the fanaticism of the "true believers," whose involvement in collective action is reduced by some observers to a kind of irrationality or other manifestation of pathological needs. Finally, we should mention some of the most challenging statements made by the authors, namely that "the most significant change in the position of women during the last hundred years" was connected with the fall of the birth rate, and that this was not at all an explicit goal of the feminist movement. Apparently, Lysistrata had few adherents among the suffragettes.

In 1971, the crude birth rate was at its lowest point in the history of the United States, and yet the cry for "zero population growth" has been raised among some of the advocates of environmentalism (another social movement which has grown phenomenally, to the extent that the political establishment has found it necessary to co-opt it). Evidently, the social context has changed radically, and the "end of ideology" which was predicted after World War II would seem to be as premature as the news of Mark Twain's death.

Another example of the extraordinary speed of change is the growth of communes. In 1964, one could count the number of communes outside Israel on the fingers of two hands. Since then, literally thousands of them have sprung up in the western world, of all conceivable (and inconceivable) structures and ideologies. The Israeli kibbutzim have for three generations been among the most viable, and the question can be raised to what extent their experience can be transferred to other societies. But this is not the major concern of Eric Cohen's chapter. Together with the late Yonina Talmon-Garber he has followed the changes in the kibbutzim for several decades. One of the basic concepts used is that of the *Bund,* first conceived after World War I, a concept which seems particularly applicable to the structure and spirit permeating much of the current communal effloration. On a more general level relevant to other organizations ranging from religious institutions to labor unions, Cohen deals with the problem of the flesh and the spirit: Does the very success of the institution sound the deathknell of its original ideals and goals?

In his analysis of the political operations of a dual elite (the British and the Nigerian) in Nigeria, Ronald Cohen tests a set of hypotheses previously applied to the study of the Soviet industrial system. These hypotheses are based on a "conflict" model, which would seem to be the most meaningful kind in view of the fact that the Nigerian definition of the goals and methods of political rule differ substantially from that of the colonial administrators. Cohen shows that in spite of this the system has been viable, partly because of the adroit use of informal arrangements which often deviated from the traditional formal norms of both cultures. The ability of the British to "muddle through" has often been commented upon; one might add that the success of their Commonwealth depended in equal measure on the same ability among the relevant counterparts among the "lesser breeds." In the case described by Cohen the existing conflicts, far from producing disorganization and anomie, were "utilized" by the society to meet new exigencies with a high degree of flexibility. The native emirates learned to adopt mechanisms for their own transformation, thus obviating the "need for revolution." Other societies have been less successful in this respect; for a systematic treatment of the reasons for this we refer the reader to the chapter on revolution by Wolf in Section 1.

In spite of the great increase in international travel, except for scientists, artists, and some businessmen, most Americans are only dimly aware of the existence of other nations, even during war time. As Evan points out in the introduction of his chapter, social scientists too, have neglected the role of multi-national corporations and international professional associations. Both are facets of a new "internationale," of a system *in statu nascendi*. As a start he posits a linear model of such a system. Espousing Durkeim's notions on the integration of social systems he thus follows in the footsteps of one of the founding fathers.

# 25

*J. A. Banks*

*Olive Banks*

# Feminism and Social Change —

# A Case Study of a Social Movement

Sociologists have, on the whole, been remarkably uninterested in feminism and it is rare, even in books about social movements generally, to find the subject dealt with in any depth. Yet, changes in the status of women have occurred in all countries where there are sociologists, and feminist organizations have been, and often still continue to be, associated with the movement towards emancipation which those changes in status are usually held to connote. Feminist literature, moreover, can hardly be said to be lacking in quantity and the social historian or historically-minded sociologist who is concerned with relating social ideologies and organized social movements to contemporary shifts in the balance of social, economic, and political power, cannot be excused on this ground for failure to consider the subject. The contrast between the attention paid to feminism and to other social movements, such as socialism or trade unionism, is sufficiently striking for a plea to be entered here that there is good cause for an inquiry to be directed towards this subject.

Since, in the view of the present writers, feminism has so much to offer to both sociologists and social historians on matters of considerable theoretical importance, it is of some interest to consider why it has been for so long neglected. McGregor has suggested that the reason, or part of the reason, might be in the nature of feminism itself: "It is not a subject on which men and women easily find their way to rational views" (17, p. 48). This is true, but it would seem to apply equally to other social movements. The long debate over socialism has hardly been notorious for its level-headed reasoning. A similar objection would also seem to apply to McGregor's alternative suggestion — "a formidable obstacle to serious investigation is the vast, repellent literature raised by the hagiographers of the 'women's movement'" (17, p. 49). All partisan literature includes a fair share of the repellent which will be particularly obnoxious to those who are not themselves parties to the controversy. It seems more likely that a fundamental reason for the neglect of the feminist movement by historians, at any rate, is the belief that the emancipation of women has been of little historical importance. This attitude of the mind is the product of a number of influences not least of which is the fairly widespread acceptance of a Marxist or quasi-Marxist interpretation of history which sees all struggles for power in economic terms. Nor does feminism fit easily into the traditions of political or constitutional historiography which tends to concern itself, if it concerns itself with women at all, only with the struggle for the suffrage, a spectacular but comparatively minor aspect of the feminist endeavor. It might not indeed be too fanciful to ascribe the neglect of feminism on the part of historians to their more general neglect of genuine *social* history.

Sociologists, it is true, have been far more concerned than historians with the position of women in society but they too have ignored its possible relationship with organized feminism. This seems to be because they have approached the subject, in the main, as part of the study of the family. They have tended, therefore, to see women primarily as wives and particularly as mothers. Other roles which women may from time to time fill are regarded, somewhat askance, as liable to be in conflict with what Parsons has called "root functions" — "which must be found wherever there is a family or kinship system at all" (18, p. 8). There has been accordingly a kind of reproductive determinism underlying the structural-functional approach which is analogous to the economic determinism of the Marxist writers, and which has led it to overlook feminism and organized feminist movements as impotent to achieve changes in role and status where these are conceived to be incompatible with woman's "root" roles in the family. It must also be admitted that the structural-functionalists, who have been responsible in recent times for a good deal of work on the family, have been notoriously uninterested in the more general problems of social change. They have been more interested in the history of sociology than in the sociology of history, and with a few exceptions, they have preferred to gather data from contemporary society or to rely on the work of historians, rather than to conduct their own researches into the past. These two dominant trends in their approach have predisposed them to ignore a movement which has few adherents even today. Nevertheless, the protagonists of an alternative sociology which would give pride of place to the study of changes in ideology, social systems, and personality have so far not proceeded much beyond the kind of alternative to structural-functionalism which is presented by conflict theory, with its emphasis on clashes of material interests. In their turn, they have dismissed feminism, ruling it out of account almost, by the very way in which a social movement has been defined. For example, its main criterion, it has been said by a textbook writers on the subject, "is that it aims to bring about fundamental changes in the social order, especially in the basic institutions of property and labor relationships" (13, p. 6). There is a sense, of course, in which the feminist movement could be included under this definition, but Heberle does not mention it, although he lists proletarian, fascist, peasants', and farmers' movements as examples. The efforts of women to change their status vis-à-vis men does not fit easily into the categories of analysis customarily employed by historians and sociologists; to argue a case for the study of feminism is in fact to assert the validity of a different set of categories.

Indeed, perhaps one of the most valuable contributions to sociology which can be performed through an investigation of feminism and its correlate, the emancipation of women, is the correction it offers to some of the stereotyped thinking about social movements which arises from equating them with socialism. Thus, one of the easiest traps into which the sociologist or the social historian may fall is that of assuming all social movements to display the same kind of thoroughly articulated ideology which characterizes socialist movements. There is, that is to say, good ground for accepting Sombart's argument that the writings of Utopian socialists, Marxists, and revolutionary syndicalists — "the spiritual precipitate of the modern social movement" — attempt to realize in the world of thought what the organized socialist movement undertakes to realize in the world of reality; but it by no means follows from this that all social movements will necessarily possess 'not only an economic and social-political program but almost a whole *Weltanschauung*" (24, p. 1, p. 15, p. 25). Feminism, to be sure, has its *Vindication of the Rights of Women* (Wollstonecraft: 1792) and its *Appeal of One Half of the Human Race, Women* (Thompson: 1825) to put alongside the *New View of Society* (Owen: 1813) and the *Manifesto of the Communist Party* (Marx and Engels: 1848), but the literature of the "cause" is on the whole poor in messianic and utopian content when compared with the flood of socialist aspirations for a new world order. It tends, moreover, to be concerned with particular abuses and it becomes indignant about wrongs for the organized movement to put right, rather than with fashioning the blueprints of a new society for it to achieve. There is in this respect, superficially at least, a closer relationship between ideology and achievement than obtains with socialism. At the same time, it should not be assumed that feminist writers are solely concerned with practical reforms. They too have ideals to sustain them. The point is that emancipation for them means more often than not emancipation from the restrictions of the existing order, without a very clear idea of some other order which will take its place; equality means equality with men, irrespective of the economic, social, and political systems which exist. This is not to suggest that feminist thinkers cannot be revolutionary in their ideas, but where widespread and radical changes are advocated these are primarily in the relationship between the sexes, in morality, and in the family. Alternatively, feminism and socialism are seen as part and parcel of the same social movement.

There is one quite obvious reason why this should be. Unlike the advocates for class warfare who are always subject to the danger of confusing the role of the capitalist with the person of the individual businessman and who are easily led into the position of seeking the abolition of the former through the liquidation of the latter, it is far more difficult for feminists to preach sex warfare with the intention of exterminating men. However much it was believed by an extreme wing of the English movement, for example, that sexual desire was a sign of the moral inferiority of men and that women were happier and better if they remained spinsters, parthenogenesis was never seriously advocated as a practical possibility within the foreseeable future, whatever was thought to be the rapidity of evolutionary development or the advance of biological technology (2, pp. 111–113). Socialists might dream of a world without a boss class, but a world without men was not part of the feminist concept of the millenium. On the contrary, the ideal was one of comradeship between the sexes — a new woman matched with a new man — and for this there was no need to counsel revolutionary upheaval. Feminists believed that all they needed concern themselves with was the development of a general recognition that the widespread material advance of their time required fresh intellectual, emotional, and moral attitudes to what had been the traditional roles of the sexes. The old division of labor could be seen as no longer making sense (22, chapter 6).

The fact that the ideological expression of feminism has normally stopped short of that kind of revolutionary chiliasm which is a marked feature of many types of socialist propaganda, is related to another aspect of difference between social movements which is often overlooked. There is in feminism little tendency towards what the Dutch refer to as *verzuiling* — the forming of columns or blocs. Applied primarily to the contemporary religious scene in Holland it is, nevertheless, capable of generalization to all kinds of social ideology and organization. The main point is that *verzuiling* permeates every aspect of life. For example, in Holland "alongside the central organizations such as the party and the trade union, there was a strong socialist youth movement, a socialist people's school, press and radio, socialist sports leagues and holiday camps, publishing and scientific institutions" (6, p. 43). People of the same faith, people with the same dream of a better world order, can through this proliferation of organizations prepare themselves regularly for it and in the meantime more easily sustain the period of waiting. *Verzuiling* is thus to be seen as a form of isolation within an existing society, the consequence of techniques employed to build up solidarity among the committed by concentrating upon their ideological similarity and emphasizing their lack of genuine dependence upon the "enemy." It is significant that among feminists, the clearest signs of *verzuiling* tendencies were demonstrated by those who rejected men outright — a section of the movement in Great Britain which has been accused of homosexuality (5, p. 142), and this section apart, the most striking feature of feminism was indeed its attack on sex segregation. A world denied to women, in the universities and in the professions, was a citadel to be stormed. There can be little doubt that most feminists saw the Victorian society of their day as composed of two vertical strata — *verzuiling* carried to the extreme — and the movement was in consequence organized deliberately to break down barriers rather than to build them up. Within the feminism of the Women's Liberation Movement, however, the tendency toward *verzuiling* is perhaps stronger. In the United States, and particularly amongst the so-called 'consciousness training' groups there has been a strong emphasis on the idea of feminine self-discovery. To this end there have been demands for a female social science, female political systems and female language and culture (27).

Of course, it goes without saying that from the point of view of developing a satisfactory sociological theory of the part played by social movements in social change, it is insufficient merely to point out where stereotyped thinking persists and to show empirically that various types of social movement occur. It is also necessary to develop an explanation for the variations. Underlying the assertion that separatism was not appropriate for tackling the situation in which feminists found themselves, is the hypothesis that the way in which a social movement is organized depends on the problems it has to solve. Both ideology and organization are in their different ways responses to the issues people have to face. A satisfactory theory of social movements must show how such responses occur.

A challenge and response theme of this kind, however, is not the only one to be considered. Even if it can be shown that an ideology and an organized social movement are the results of dissatisfactions with an existing order, no matter how those dissatisfactions arise, it should not be too lightly assumed that any changes which afterwards occur in the circumstances of the dissatisfied must necessarily have been produced in response to their demands. There is always the possibility that ideologies and organized movements are in this respect epiphenomena. The sociology of social movements, accordingly, requires that empirical evidence be provided for the alleged translation of ideology into effort and for the asserted consequences of that effort, whether it is held that such consequences were intended or not. In the present context this means that the organized movement for reform of the position of women in society be distinguished from those changes in their position with which it is customary to associate the term "emancipation" and that other possible explanations of emancipation can be considered alongside the exertions of the feminists. It cannot be denied that this demand implies a much larger program of research than is usually thought necessary in this area, but at the same time, even a slight familiarity with the literature on social change shows that it has been for the most part hastily executed (1, pp. 61–65). The alternative to superficiality is either to embark on more ambitious long-term projects or to limit the field to aspects of the problems which are manageable in size. Thus, the authors have studied the relationship between the feminist movement and the decline of family size in Britain in the late nineteenth century, demonstrating that the advent of the smaller family, with all its consequences for the position of women, was not only unrelated to feminist propaganda but was not even perceived by them as a desired goal, before the actual change in family size had occurred. This study, it is true, was developed as part of a larger inquiry into the genesis of family planning and was not conceived with the present issue in mind, and for that reason, it can be of limited relevance only. Nevertheless, in the absence of meticulous sociological studies of feminism it may be referred to as an example of the kind of work which might be undertaken, and the present chapter read as a sketch of the lines on which a more detailed account of the relationship between feminism and the emancipation of women, or between a social movement and the processes of social change, for that matter, might proceed. While it is hoped that it will have a general applicability, for reasons of convenience the empirical evidence has been taken largely from British experience. American data on some comparable points may be found in 10, pp. 227–302.

"At its inception the feminist movement was essentially a middle-class movement. Nor could it have been otherwise. Power machinery was no respecter of sex. It drove women and children into factories where the privilege of sharing the right to work with their menfolk was the privilege of basic subsistence. Only among those exempt from the choice between wage work and starvation did the social status of women emerge as a challenge to self-regard" (12, p. 315). An interpretation such as this is commonplace. Feminism is usually regarded as a protest movement of middle-class women, a part of the general rise to importance of the middle classes as a consequence of what, for the sake of brevity, may be called the capitalist industrial revolution. Yet, although the evidence superficially supports this point of view, it cannot be accepted at its face value. Of course, it is true that the feminist movement was led by middle-class men and women, but this was also true of most other movements in the nineteenth century. More important is the fact that feminism never seemed to appeal to the working classes. This is not to suggest that organized working-class opinion has necessarily beeen anti-feminist. It has, rather, been indifferent to the claims of women as such, in spite of support given to the feminists by prominent individuals within the labor movement, such as Keir Hardie (9, p. 134), and in spite of occasional working-class support for certain of the feminist goals, such as the Trade Union Congress resolution in favor of equal pay in 1885 (26, p. 52).

It is also true that, for their part, feminists have not been interested *as feminists* in those hardships suffered by working-class women solely as a consequence of their class position — hardships, that is to say, which they have shared along with working-class men. Nor did the feminists, in their organized movement, ally themselves with working-class protest movements or with left-wing political parties. Even when, from time to time, the feminists were associated with radicals of the Liberal Party, it was an alliance of expediency rather than of principle, and many of the well-known feminists were Conservative in politics (25, pp. 264–285). At the same time, it would be a serious mistake to assume that feminists have been concerned only with issues affecting middle-class women. They were ready and eager to take up cases of every type of exploitation of women by men, some of which applied almost exclusively to women of the working or, at the most, of the lower-middle classes. A most interesting example of this — and one which is extremely revealing of the nature of feminism — is the agitation conducted for the repeal of the Contagious Diseases Acts of 1864–69. These Acts required, in 17 garrison towns of Great Britain, that women suspected of being prostitutes should be registered and supervised by the police, should be periodically medically examined, and should, if found suffering from venereal disease, be compulsorily detained in special hospitals. It is hardly likely that these Acts affected any of the women who were active in the feminist organizations which existed while they were on the statute book, and it is clear that the leaders of the organized protest movement had no personal interest in the outcome. They saw the Acts moreover as genuine examples of double-standard legislation. As Strachey has put it, in the opinion of Josephine Butler and her colleagues the evils and misfortunes suffered by prostitutes arose from the fact not that they were prostitutes as such, but that they were women. "It was actually because of their sex that they were outcasts, not because of their behaviour. The men who did as they did, and who shared their vice and their degradation, were not dealt with in the same manner, nor held in the same disgust. The double moral standard allowed to men what it forbade to women, and it was from this root that the worst of the evil grew" (25, pp. 189–190). The fight for repeal was, accordingly, conducted in terms of a struggle between the sexes in which class issues were largely irrelevant.

It is, however, when we come to look more closely at those changes in the social structure which helped to produce feminism that we see how misleading it can be to think of it as an exclusively middle-class phenomenon. The industrial revolution, it is true, "transferred an increasing number of productive activities from the home to the factory and thereby relieved women of many household burdens." It is also true that in some degree "it excluded the women of the middle-class from the economic process and made their lives idle and futile" (16, p. 163). But it would be an error to think of feminism on that account as the middle-class woman's answer to idleness and boredom. Of really much greater importance was the change in her role and status as housewife which had resulted from the separation of home from work. From being a partner, although certainly never an equal partner with her husband, when the family was organized as a production unit, she had rapidly become dependent in the course of the late eighteenth and of the nineteenth centuries upon some other person's earning capacity for the income she spent as the family representative. What the organized feminist movement was concerned with in consequence was the plight of single, widowed, divorced, and married women who were exploited as a result of this dependency. It should be obvious that the new methods of production which, by enlarging the scope and scale of industry, had taken it out of the middle-class home into the factory had had precisely the same effect on the working class. The family system of domestic production gave way, first to the employment of the whole family in the factory and later to the partial, although never wholly complete, removal of the married, working-class woman from the industrial scene. The situation in her case was, however, complicated because the position of working-class women as members of the working class appears to have often overshadowed their position as women. As employees or potential employees, they more often had interests in common with the men of their own class in conflict with their employers than they had interests in common with the women of other classes. As a result we can find examples of members of the working classes and their sympathizers asking for the protection of working-class women in industry or for their removal from it altogether, rather than, as did the feminists, demanding equal rights for women in industry. Yet this interpretation should not be pressed too far. The spokesmen of the organized working class for most of the nineteenth century were men and may well have expressed only their own point of view. We do not always know how working-class women responded to the various attempts made to protect them. There is, indeed, some evidence that on occasions they reacted to such protection precisely as their middle-class counterparts might have done and even joined with the feminists to help voice their disapproval. Ray Strachey cites two examples of this, both in 1887, when the effort to restrict women's employment in the interest of their health was actually resisted by the women involved, and with the support of middle-class feminists the proposed legislation was abandoned (25, pp. 236–238). It is quite possible, therefore, that there was more support for feminist goals among working-class women than the attitude of the organized working-class movement would lead us to suppose, and it is to be regretted that newspapers and other sources of local protest on the part of such women, as women, have not been subjected to the same intensive scrutiny as has been employed for the study of class conflict. All we can conclude is that middle-class women were more acutely aware of the problem which arose from their role as consumers in a world dominated by men as producers than were working-class women; but at the same time all women had interests in common as a result of the industrial revolution which the organized feminist movement sought to realize.

Yet it is unsatisfactory to attempt to understand the nature of feminism by looking only at the effect of industrialization on the role of the house-wife. Alongside the recognition of particular disabilities, such as the restriction of employment opportunities for women, and the desire for certain legal reforms (as, for example, the right of a married woman to her own earnings), was a general consciousness amongst feminists of, as they put it themselves, the rights of woman and her wrongs. There was within the organized movement, and particularly in its leadership, a sense of sex consciousness which paralleled the developing class consciousness of the labor movement at the same time. This consciousness of great exploitation by men led the movement far beyond the formulation of specific remedies for particular wrongs into the more radical claim for equality between men and women, in every sphere, from the vote to the standards of sexual morality. It was this essentially ideological position which drew the various "causes" together and made what might other-wise have been a series of pressure groups into a single movement, just as socialism united and gave direction to the various aspects of the working-class struggle for social and economic improvement in the conditions of life.

What significance such an ideology has is not so clear. Was it entirely created and sustained to provide a rationale to justify the demand for the reform of particular wrongs — a rationale to match the cry of "woman's place is in the home" with which these reforms were resisted? Or had it an independent source in a general surge towards legal, polit-ical, economic, and social equality which is characteristic of all social movements in the nineteenth and twentieth centuries? Either view of feminism is plausible. The evidence of the rise and fall of feminism, however, seems rather to support the first hypothesis. Each successive campaign, from that of the 1850s and 1860s to improve the education of girls, to the final tumultuous fight for the vote, ended successfully for the feminists; those who took part in the struggle could look back as at a war in which they were at long last victorious.

For a quarter of a century or more, feminism as an active social movement was dead. This is not to suggest that the ideology of feminism had become reality. Old attitudes persisted in spite of changes which freed women from the legal domination of husbands and fathers. In the occupational sphere, too, in spite of near-equal educational opportunities and the opening up of professional emloyment, women have been limited in the main to occupations of lower skill, status and prestige. Yet, until the recent eruption of the new feminism, in the shape of the Women's Liberation Movement, the great majority of women appear to have considered that emancipation had gone far enough. It would seem that an ideology cannot win the backing to sustain a social movement unless it can enter upon a series of reforms urgently desired by those to whom it sets out to appeal.

It remains to consider briefly how far the changes in the position of women over the past hundred years have in fact been the achievement of the feminists and how far they have been brought about by social and economic changes independent of feminist agencies. This, the role of social movements in producing social changes, is an important theoretical issue in the study of social movements and it is, perhaps, the greatest methodological difficulty in disentangling cause and effect in any historical process which has made it so consistently neglected. Given the requisite research, it is, however, possible to make some approach to this problem, although its full solution depends upon a detailed comparative study of feminism and other social movements. Certainly it would be fairly straightforward to discover those feminist campaigns which have been unsuccessful, or only partially successful. The opening of the professions to women is such an example, for while there are few professions which are either legally or customarily barred to women altogether, in most, women enter only in small numbers and rarely rise to the top.

It is also possible to discover changes of great significance for the status of women which owe nothing to feminist influence. In some cases, and these are the most straightforward methodologically, the feminists have not even tried to bring about such a change; in others, although the movement has campaigned long and constantly, the change itself has been brought about in other ways. The nineteenth century fall in the birth rate in Britain, is one very striking example of a change which does not seem to have occurred to the feminists as either necessary or desirable before the new trend in family size had already established itself (2, pp. 9–10). On the other hand, although the feminists were very anxious about the limited opportunities for women, the great expansion of non-manual work which provided so many jobs for girls and women was a consequence not of the efforts of the feminists but of the technological and social diversification of industrialism and its demand for cheap labor (17, pp. 54–55). The same is true of the tremendous expansion in the proportion of married women at work at the present time. Although of obvious significance for the position of women in society, and although to some extent in line with feminist ideology, it has been brought about entirely by demographic and industrial changes.

There are other aspects of feminism which still remain so little investigated that we can do no more than guess at their relationship with social change. How far, for example, are the changes in sexual morality over the past hundred years a consequence of feminist propaganda? We know so little about this that it is not even clear whether the result of feminine influence, where it has occurred, has been in the direction of a tightening or a loosening of the allegiance to Puritan morality. In spite of the allegations of its opponents that feminism was equivalent to free love, there is more evidence that the organized movement as a whole interpreted a single standard of morality in terms of male chastity rather than female licence (2, pp. 109–111).

This is not to suggest that the feminist movement was without effect, but rather that its effect was both more subtle and more complicated than might be supposed. It was the feminists and their allies, for example, who persuaded the House of Commons to change the law with respect to married women's property and the custody of children. It was also mainly, if not predominantly, feminist influence which abolished state-regulated prostitution in Britain. Further research might well reveal many more such examples.

What we do not know, and what we as sociologists need to know, is the kind of reform a social movement can achieve, and the kind of reform which is outside its scope and power. The evidence we have is severely limited, but there is sufficient to make it worthwhile to suggest some generalizations which should serve as useful pointers in future research. In the first place, it would seem that feminism has not succeeded in making great or wide-sweeping changes in the status of women. Reforms that we can genuinely attribute to feminist efforts have been small in scope, even if of considerable importance to those affected by them. A typical example is the law relating to married women's property or earnings. This has been of enormous benefit to divorced and separated wives without making any *fundamental* difference to women's subordinate role in society. Even in the United States where women own about two-thirds of all wealth, "it must also be conceded that they neither control nor manage the organizations maintaining and producing that wealth" (10, p. 278). Moreover, studies of married women at work in Britain invariably indicate not only that they subordinate the job to the needs of their family but also that their earnings are spent on home and children, rather than on themselves (15, pp. 120–122). The same may be said of the opening of the universities to women, the repeal of the Contagious Diseases Acts, or any other of the successful campaigns waged by the feminists. The most significant change in the position of women during the past hundred years, the fall in the birth rate, was not produced by feminism at all.

It seems likely, therefore, that the role of the feminist movement has been a two-fold one. Firstly, it has acted as a pressure group, representing certain classes of women and providing them with relief from particular disabilities. Its work for the middle-class spinster is perhaps the example that springs most to mind, for it was this particular issue that lay behind the campaign for improved education for girls and the opening of employment opportunities for women. This was not, however, its exclusive concern, and the same year saw the struggle to give deserted wives some share in the custody of their children, and the campaign for the repeal of the Contagious Diseases Acts. Moreover, as is the case with all pressure groups, it has operated most effectively when the reform has been a simple and straightforward one; a change in the law or in the rules governing some particular organization.

Secondly, the feminist ideology has provided justification for these reforms by challenging the traditional attitude towards women in society. This was done by arguing that the old view of women as inferior, dependent, and subordinate was no longer relevant to contemporary problems. By a series of propaganda devices the feminists sought to show the consequences of women's dependent and subordinate role in the situation of spinster or prostitute, or tried to prove, by achievements in previously masculine spheres, that women were capable of equality with men. We have already suggested that in its fullest expression this ideology was never realized in practice and was indeed probably not shared by even the bulk of those who called themselves feminists, but this is not to argue that the ideology was not immensely important, if only to give direction and courage to the leaders of the movement and misgivings to its enemies. The ideological aspect of feminism is also apparent in the rise of the new women's movement. Although, like the nineteenth century feminism with which this paper is chiefly concerned, it has its practical side, it is also characterised by a fundamental questioning of traditional attitudes to women. In its more radical expression this becomes not just a question of women's subordinate role in the occupational sphere or in the family, but a challenge to marriage itself. "If women are to effect a significant amelioration in their condition," Germaine Greer argues, "it seems obvious that they must refuse to marry" (11, p. 319). Such statements, although possibly more frequent today, have their parallel in the nineteenth century advocacy of free love, just as the anti-man propaganda of Ti-Grace Atkinson can be paralleled in the writings of an earlier militant, Christabel Pankhurst (2, p. 112).

What general, if tentative, conclusions emerge from this necessarily sketchy treatment of a movement which still remains to be more thoroughly investigated? Our main assertion has been that feminism constitutes a genuine movement, rather than a series of pressure groups, because it possesses a unifying ideology which is shared by the separate "wings" of the movement, even though this ideology is limited and does not take the *Weltanschauung* form, typical of messianic and utopian movements generally. The methodological point of importance here is that such an ideology, if it is to be regarded as characterizing a social movement, must not be simply inferred by later sociologists and historians from the activities of the individuals who are members of the various organizations associated with it. It must be consciously formulated as an ideology by those who have committed themselves to the movement's goals and activities. They must have deliberately created it, that is to say, in order to foster and sustain the solidarity of the adherents to the movement, both positively and directly, by giving them a slogan to work with — in this instance, "equality in all things with men" — and negatively and indirectly, by providing an antidote to the counter-ideology of those who opposed the movement's particular aims — "woman's place is in the home" (2, pp. 33–67). It is possible, indeed, that ideologies are necessary to social movements because people are unable to nerve themselves for the task of carrying out what may become a long and bitter struggle with others for the reform of "abuses" as they see them, unless they are able to couch their demands in the form of deductions from more general ethical principles, perhaps even from a *Weltanschauung* or a whole cosmography, although the study of feminism suggests that such refinements are not essential. Moreover, the fact that such ideologies are related in this way to particular "abuses," accounts for another characteristic feature, namely, that no matter how fantastic they may become in the hands of some of their propounders, they are never pure fantasy. The core of feminist thinking, for example, was intimately concerned with the real situation in which women found themselves, that of inequality in all their relations with men, and this persistent inequality lies behind the new feminism of the Women's Liberation Movement. In this respect it is relevant to consider the parallel situation of the working classes with which the socialist ideology has been concerned. We may then ask whether the predominant aspect of a social system which provides the *sine qua non* for the emergence of movements of social protest is the existence of latent conflict between those with authority and those without, between the legitimate makers of decisions and those who are constrained to submit to them. Of course, it may be that not every social movement is necessarily built up around inequalities between social roles and around the potential conflicts between individuals which these role inequalities imply. Some purely religious movements may obtain the allegiance of their adherents primarily from the uncertainties of man's place in nature, rather than from the certainties of his place in society, but even here, the sociologist must proceed with caution. The messianic movements of the Middle Ages, for all their fantastic eschatology and their leadership possessed of megalomania, obtained their impetus from the desperation of "the surplus population living on the margin of society" (4, p. 314); while those of contemporary Melanesia are impelled by the native's consciousness of a discrepancy between his possessions and those of the white man who "perversely" denies him cargo (27, p. 246). Whether an explanation of social movements which confines itself to the sociologically relevant is likely to be ignoring a theoretically important issue is not a question which can be answered one way or the other, given the current state of knowledge of such movements. For our present purpose it seems not unreasonable to claim that one powerful source of the drive behind them is to be found in the persistence of conflicts in society.

Yet, the subordinate position of women existed long before a feminist movement came into being to campaign about it, and it continued during those years when the movement was in abeyance. Clearly it is not enough that potential conflicts should exist for an organized social movement to occur. Some further condition is necessary, and it is with the nature of this condition that the sociology of social movements should be most concerned. What the study of feminism may contribute most to theory in this regard is the demonstration that this condition cannot be equated with the actual making manifest of conflict or inequality. Mary Wollstonecraft, William Thompson, and many others (2, pp. 136–137) developed a feminist ideology many years before organized movements for reform agitated Victorian complacency, and feminists occasionally emerge today to protest at the continued inequality of the sexes. Nor is it satisfactory to attempt to avoid the issue by tracing a thread of continuity from the *Vindication* or the *Appeal* to the articles in the *English-Woman's Review* and the *Victoria Magazine*. The pages of these feminist journals indicate, on the contrary, that the ideological output of the second half of the nineteenth century was built around the problems women of that time had to face; where their authors repeated what had been written before them by the so-called precursors of the movement, it was not because they were familiar with their works — the evidence on this point is obscure — but because the same fundamental fact of inequality had impressed them all. If we take the trouble we can trace the course of socialist ideology from Plato to the present day, but we miss the significance of the exercise if we think of the historical continuity as being itself one of the causes of socialism. What still has to be accounted for is how it comes about at a given period of time that a large number of people become sufficiently intolerant of their own circumstances to seize upon slogans such as "from each according to his ability, to each according to his needs," and to apply them to themselves in such a degree that they become moved to attend and organize meetings, devise petitions, and enter generally into the struggle with the "enemy." The sociology of social movements still needs to determine whether deviants such as Wollstonecraft and Thompson, and perhaps even the leaders of a movement which has obtained some popular support, are deviants in some basic personality sense. It also needs to consider means whereby the expression "a large number of people" may be given a more precise, numerical magnitude. We can do no more at the present time than to notice such tasks in passing. More immediately manageable is the consideration of theoretical positions, taken generally from sociology, which may be employed to account for the spread of awareness through a subject group that its situation is open to improvement through a challenge being offered to those who take advantage of it.

The Marxist conception of class consciousness seems obviously pertinent here. Marx, it will be recalled, not only emphasized that society was divided into conflicting classes, he also asserted that class consciousness on the part of the eventually victorious class was inevitable once certain conditions were fulfilled, these conditions being the development of easy communication between individuals in the same class position and their continuous record of failure in struggles with the ruling class over economic rewards (3, p. 30). There could be no successful revolution without class consciousness and no class consciousness without both the dissemination of ideas and programs of action amongst the working class and a realization of their position through unsuccessful attempts to improve their economic situation. The non-Marxist sociologist may treat these hypotheses for what they are, and regardless of whether they are validated by the evidence of trade union and socialist organizations of the nineteenth and twentieth centuries, consider in the present context whether they are applicable to feminism. This approach does violence, of course, to the Marxist interpretation of capitalism which conceives of the emancipation of women as the inevitable outcome of the replacement of the domestic economy by large-scale industry (7, pp. 210–219, p. 282). Hence, it would probably explain the organized struggle of the feminists as part of the wider class struggle, or dismiss it as a sign of inner contradictions in the position of the bourgeoisie; but in the absence of convincing demonstration that feminism can be explained in this way, we have no alternative as sociologists other than to use it in our own way. This means that we should consider whether the evidence of feminism supports the view that sex consciousness appeared, not because a few feminists were articulate about it, but because a number of women became involved in unsuccessful struggles with men over economic issues, such as the right to determine how their own earnings were to be spent, and because as members of a literate and mobile section of the community they regularly came into contact with women involved in a similar conflict to their own. The Marxist conception of class consciousness, modified in this way to refer to the growth of self-consciousness on the part of any social group, seems especially fruitful in the present instance, since it would go far to explain why the great bulk of the feminists were likely to be members of the middle rather than of the working classes, and why women employed in factories alongside men were more likely to become involved in class rather than in sex warfare. At the same time, it also seems unnecessarily restrictive in its emphasis on struggles over economic rewards; for the long struggle of the feminists to put an end to the double standard of sexual morality was undoubtedly of considerable significance in the development of sex consciousness on the part of the women of the day, and that struggle had only a very tenuous relationship with economics. While it is true that Victorian men often took advantage of the weak economic position of women to exploit them sexually, the advantages they gained were not economic. The Marxist conception needs to be broadened to allow for different kinds of exploitation which can give rise to conflicts of interest other than those which center upon the extortion of surplus labor, if it is to be of use to the sociologist who wishes to develop a general theory of social movements.

The general Marxist formulation, as applied to feminism, may be said to be found wanting in another respect. As applied to trade unionism and to political socialism, it can still make some pretension to maintaining the inevitability of revolution on the grounds that these are movements still involved in struggle and the conditions for a change of system are not yet ripe. But feminism largely withered away without a revolutionary upheaval and a dictatorship of the second sex. Group consciousness, in this instance, faded before the full promise of the movement had been realized. How can this be? The obvious answer would seem to lie in the essentially pressure-group type of allegiance given to a social movement by the great bulk of its members. If this is always the case, as we have attempted to show through this brief account of feminism, that widespread adherence to the ideals of a movement occurs only where and when the shoe pinches, it would follow that as this pressure is reduced, a more general apathy will return. Erstwhile active members of the movement lose interest, the older ones die, and the younger generation, from whom the newest recruits might be expected to come, will not have the same urgent need to take part in the campaigns which so preoccupied their elders. The real problem for the sociologist is that of ascertaining the factors responsible for those changes in the circumstances of broad categories of people — in this instance, of single, widowed, divorced, and married women — which create dissatisfaction with their lot sufficient to drive them to look for leaders to voice their discontent, or on the other hand, which so lessen their sense of being the victims of exploitation that they cease to feel the urge to combine.

In this connection we need to examine the dramatic resurgence of feminism originating largely from the publication in 1963 of Betty Friedan's *The Feminine Mystique* (8) and the subsequent foundation of the National Organization of Women which has campaigned for the reform of women's occupational chances. Subsequently the Women's Liberation Movement took up a much more radical, and indeed, revolutionary position under the influence of left wing ideologies. We may well ask why this should have happened now, when only a few years ago the feminist movement as an active and lively force for change appeared to be dead. Alice Rossi (21, p. 534) has argued that one important factor has been the changed composition of the female labour force which provided the impetus to the formation of the new women's rights organization in the mid 1960s. For these women the impetus was provided by daily experiences of economic discrimination in their working lives. The more radical wing of the movement, however, can only be seen as part of the resurgence of left-wing and revolutionary thinking, particularly in the universities. Concern with the inequalities in society, whether of the black American or the working classes, led a number of women to a new appreciation of their own position. As part of this new thinking has come an attempt at a new understanding of the relationship between feminism and Marxism. In particular, this has taken the form of an emphasis on the necessity not only for radical changes in the position of women, but to make this possible for revolutionary changes in society itself. While such a position was not altogether absent from nineteenth century feminism, it seems to be a more central feature of the modern movement.

It is here that a reference to Smelser's attempt to develop a structural-functional type of explanation in working-class history seems not only relevant but imperative and not least because among other qualities, it claims to avoid the shortcomings of the Marxist concept of exploitation and hence, of class conflict, as an explanatory principle. From Smelser's point of view, "it is less embarrassing analytically to interpret cases of outright conflict between the classes as disturbed reactions to specific, structural pressures rather than as manifestations of a permanent state of war between them" (23, p. 394). To the extent that this position is valid it would follow that feminism should be seen as a reaction to structural pressures operating on the family and the explanation for the rise and decline of the feminist movement should be sought for in the sequence of events by which these structural pressures were relieved and a new family system became institutionalized. There is, to be sure, little reference to feminism in Smelser's work. This is mainly because it is a study of the Lancashire cotton industry between 1770 and 1840 and stops before the organized movement of feminists began. It is also, partly because it is confined to the separation of home from work as it applied to the working-class textile family. Hence the only feminist writing referred to, William Thompson's *Appeal* (1825), is classified along with Owenism and early Co-operation generally, as among examples of what Smelser regards as "unjustified" negative, emotional reactions to pressures on the family economy and as "unrealistic aspirations on the part of various elements in the population," produced as a response to the dissatisfactions which these pressures had created (23, p. 170). Thompson's plea for the ending of the inequality between sexes is seen, that is to say, as an attempt to minimize conventional differences between the sexes through "a massive de-differentiation of roles," a feature of the movements of this time (23, pp. 254–257). Early feminist ideology, from this point of view, at least in its implied application to the problems of working-class women, is to be regarded as no more than a "symptom of disturbance."

Smelser's hypothesis for the explanation of structural changes in social systems asserts that in "growing and developing social systems" seven definite steps of change which follow each other in sequence are discernible. "Symptoms of disturbance" occur early on, occupying only the second step of the sequence, which is said to begin with "dissatisfactions with the goal-achievements of the social system . . . and a sense of opportunity for change in terms of the potential availability of facilities." The disturbances produced by these dissatisfactions are thereupon " 'handled' by mechanisms of social control and 'channelled' into mobilization of resources." This leaves Smelser with four more steps to cope progressively with the conversion of these resources into "more and more specific proposals to innovate. Favourable innovations are rewarded by extraordinary sanctions and then gradually routinised" (23, p. 15). The organized feminist movement, and the feminist ideology of the second half of the nineteenth century, can be interpreted in terms of this approach, provided that the symptoms of disturbance are read as a reaction, not to the problems which faced working-class mothers employed in the textile factories, but to those which faced the unemployed women of all classes who depended on the goodwill of others for their livelihood. As we have seen, the real drive behind feminism came from those single, widowed, divorced, and married women who were exploited in various ways as a result of this dependency. The organized feminist movement may accordingly be interpreted as finding its place on step five of Smelser's sequence — "positive attempts to reach specification of the new ideas and institutional patterns which will become objects of commitments" (23, p. 15) — soon to become routinized into the form of new types of employment for women, in hospitals and in offices, accompanied by the legal right to determine for themselves what might be done with their earnings. Indeed, the decline of feminism would appear to be reasonably well accounted for by this hypothesis since it is to be expected that some of the support for the organized movement would die away by step seven, once these aims had been achieved. Similarly, the reactivation of feminism in its new guise can be seen as a response to women's changing occupational role in the 1950s and 1960s. A new set of disturbances, centered around the efforts of employers to get women out of the home and into the workplace, has sparked off a modern seven-stage sequence which has rapidly passed through its first five stages and has entered its sixth.

There are, it must be admitted, certain discrepancies between this account and the strict Parsonian line taken by Smelser. For example, the outcry "Woman's place is in the home," is regarded by him as a realistic reaction to the legislation which forbade the employment of children; it is placed in step six of his sequence, on the ground that the separation of adult from child at work "gave commanding importance to formal education and to the role of women in the socialization of children *in the home*" (23, p. 299). It is, however, not difficult to show that the slogan, "Woman's place is in the home," was far more characteristic of the anti-feminist ideology of the 1850s and later, than it was of the factory agitation of the earlier period. It was applied, moreover, not to mothers who were employed in the factories, but to single women who were never likely to get married while monogamy lasted, because of the preponderance of women of marriageable age. In terms of the realities of their situation, it was an "unjustified negative, emotional reaction" to the development of the nuclear family amongst both middle and working classes — a family which had no place for unmarried aunts and sisters if they were unproductive in the industrial sense of income earning — and the later steps of the sequence should be more correctly interpreted as the process whereby the contemporary nuclear family became the institutionalized form for an industrial society. Clearly, whether an ideology is to be classified as positive rather than negative, as realistic rather than fantastic, and hence placed on steps four or six of a sequence rather than on step two, depends on a prior decision about the nature of the new institutionalized forms which are "consolidated as permanent features of the institutionalized family" and which constitute the seventh and last step in the sequence of structural change experienced by the household (23, p. 164). It is pertinent to consider, therefore, what there is about the structural-functional approach which led Smelser to conclude his sequence in the 1840s. As he has presented the argument, he has implied not only that the new family system of the Lancashire cotton workers was one in which the function of socialization was performed in the home, but also that the women came out of the factories to perform it, whereas in point of fact all evidence suggests that the employment of wives and mothers in textiles continued right through the nineteenth century (14, pp. 1–18). In addition, the new family system which has appeared under industrialization has been one in which accommodation has been made to permit women to combine the two roles of wage-earner and housewife.

It can hardly be doubted that the root of the difficulty is to be found in the tendency towards reproductive determinism which characterizes the structural-functional approach to the family. This may perhaps be best seen in Parson's treatment of the modern household, where he differentiates between sex roles along "instrumental-expressive" lines and justifies the differentiation on the ground that "the bearing and early nursing of children establish a strong presumptive primacy of the relation of mother to the small child and this in turn establishes a presumption that the man, who is exempted from these biological functions, should specialize in the alternative instrumental direction" (18, pp. 22–23). Feminist ideology, from this point of view, is unrealistic as applied to equality between the sexes, because it must either deny the essentially biological difference between them, or refuse to admit that the allocation of roles is, as a matter of fact, determined by the consequences which flow from these differences. It is, of course, notorious that this latter argument was precisely the one which the organized movement sought to combat, asserting that some women would never become mothers, and that others would be obliged to combine the role of mother with that of income-earner, and that *for these women* it was absurd to deny them occupational opportunities on the ground that they ought to be in the home. In effect, what the feminists asserted was that the simple Victorian identification of role differentiation within the household with biological differentiation between the sexes was nothing more than ideology, a negative reaction to the everyday demonstration that women were quite obviously filling instrumental roles on behalf of the family. It is, indeed, open to inquiry whether one of the successes of feminist agitation might not have been the acceptance by the twentieth century of the position that the rigid differentiation of sex roles within the household along "expressive-instrumental" lines is an anachronism. As compared with the Victorian era it is now accepted that women may adequately fill a number of roles on behalf of the household, some expressive and some instrumental, and that for those which may be performed only within the home — those concerned with the "maintenance of integrative relations between the numbers, and regulation of the patterns and tension levels of its component units," which is Parsons' way of describing expressive roles (18, p. 47) — men have comparable roles to perform which were below the dignity of their grandfathers. Husbands, that is to say, now provide "solid, reliable help" to their wives in homemaking (15, p. 126) and fathers are expected to participate to a large extent in the early socialization of the child, so that the residual tasks of actual childbearing and breast feeding have been relegated to a very minor place in the functions performed.

It should be understood that we have called the Parsonian approach "reproductively determinist" not merely because it takes sheer reproduction to be a "root" function which differentiates social roles along sex lines, but also because it would account for the differences between the roles performed by men and women in the occupational sphere on the same basis. "The distribution of women in the labor force," he has asserted, "clearly confirms this general view of the balance of the sex roles. Thus, on higher levels, typical feminine occupations are those of teacher, social worker, nurse, private secretary and entertainer. Such roles tend to have a prominent expressive component, and often to be "supportive" to masculine roles. Within the occupational organization they are analogous to the wife-mother role in the family" (23, p. 15, n. 13). It can hardly be denied that in general, women are employed in "supportive" occupations and that in this respect the feminist dream of equality has not been realized. Yet, we suggest this is not because the demand was unrealistic in the light of the biological function of women in the family, but because the whole trend of industrialization has been in the direction of the increasingly hierarchical organization of roles within the economy. Women worked as "assistants to their husbands and fathers" before the Industrial Revolution (20, p. 2); their subsidiary role was perpetuated afterwards in the factories and in the offices. But whereas previously their menfolk had been able to make authoritative decisions on behalf of the family enterprise, only amongst the power elite is it now possible for them to determine their own economic destinies. For men of the middle ranks of society, industrialism has replaced the uncertainties of market fluctuations and climatic conditions by the specified certainties of subsidiary roles in the large bureaucracies and has inserted a host of new supervisory and managerial roles between the manual workers and their employers. A large number of modern occupations filled predominantly by men, that is to say, are not merely subordinate and supportive to others. They are concerned with the internal affairs of the enterprise, with coordinating the activities of the manual and clerical labor force employed, and with handling tensions between subordinates. They are, in the language of the Parsonian calculus, primarily "expressive." Hence, it may be questioned whether industrialism might not have been responsible for weakening the traditional association between biological differentiation and the differentiation of roles along "expressive-instrumental" lines by requiring more and more men to fill expressive roles. Indeed, it is a matter of further research to ascertain whether this, rather than the efforts of the feminists, has been the reason why men have come increasingly to perform expressive roles within the household.

This brings us back to the central problem of this chapter, to the circumstances which activate a social movement. Neither the Marxist interpretation of history, understood in a very broad sense, nor the Parsonian interpretation of social equilibrium, also understood broadly, provides a very satisfying explanation for the rise and decline of feminism, although both in their separate ways illuminate aspects of it. We can hardly escape the conclusion, therefore, that what the sociology of social movements most lacks at this time is not general theory but empirical research conducted in the light of some middle-range hypotheses, developed perhaps through submitting general theory to the kind of empirical challenge we have attempted here. In particular, there is a need for systematic studies of movements in decline and vigorous examination of those changes in their social environment which are conceived to be responsible for fluctuations in their fortunes. This is why we have sought to argue the case for the treatment of feminism as a critical instance in this field. The accumulation of historical and contemporary data on the position of women and on women's organizations in a great variety of countries is one of the most obvious next steps for sociologist interested in social change.

## BIBLIOGRAPHY

1. Banks, J. A. "Social Implications of Technological Change, Some Reflections on Historical and Social Research on the Impact of Technological Change on the Local Community, the Enterprise and the Family," in *Les Implications Sociales du Progres Technique*. Paris: Conseil International des Sciences Sociales, 1962.

2. Banks, J. A., and Olive Banks. *Feminism and Family Planning*. Liverpool: Liverpool University Press, 1963.

3. Bendix, Reinhard, and Seymour Martin Lipset. "Karl Marx' Theory of Social Classes" in R. Bendix and S. M. Lipset (eds.), *Class Status and Power, A Reader in Social Stratification*. London: Routledge and Kegan Paul, 1954.

4. Cohn, Norman. *The Pursuit of the Millenium*. London: Mercury Books, 1962.

5. Dangerfield, George. *The Strange Death of Liberal England*. London: Constable, 1936.

6. van Doorn, J. A. A. "Verzuiling·een eigentijds systeem van social contrloe," *Sociologische Gids*, Vol. 3 (1956), pp. 41–49.

7. Engels, Friedrich. "The Origin of the Family, Private Property and the State," in Karl Marx and Frederick Engels, *Selected Works in Two Volumes*. Moscow: Foreign Languages Publishing House, 1949.

8. Friedan, Betty. *The Feminine Mystique*. New York: Norton, 1963.

9. Fulford, Roger. *Votes for Women, The Story of a Struggle*. London: Faber and Faber, 1957.

10. Green, Arnold W., and Eleanor Melnick. "What has Happened to the Feminist Movement?" in Alvin W. Gouldner (ed.), *Studies in Leadership*. New York: Harper and Bros., 1950.

11. Greer, Germaine. *The Female Eunuch*. New York: McGraw-Hill, 1971.

12. Hamilton, Henry. *History of the Homeland: The Story of the British Background*. Primers for the Age of Plenty, No. 4. London: Allen and Unwin, 1947.

13. Heberle, Rudolf. *Social Movements: An Introduction to Political Sociology*. New York: Appleton-Century-Crofts, 1951.

14. Hewitt, Margaret. *Wives and Mothers in Victorian Industry.* London: Rockliff, 1958.

15. Jephcott, Pearl. *Married Women Working.* London: Allen and Unwin, 1962.

16. Klein, Viola. "The Emancipation of Women: Its Motives and Achievements," in *Ideas and Beliefs of the Victorians.* London: Sylvan Press, 1949. (B.B.C. Publication of a series of talks on the "Third Programme.")

17. McGregor, O. R. "The Social Position of Women in England, 1850–1914: A Bibliography." *The British Journal of Sociology,* Vol. 6 (1955), pp. 48–60.

18. Parsons, Talcott. "The American Family: Its Relations to Personality and to the Social Structure," in Talcott Parsons and R. F. Bales et al. (eds.), *Family, Socialization and Interaction Process.* Glencoe, Ill.: The Free Press, 1955.

19. Parsons, Talcott. "Family Structure and the Socialization of the Child." In Talcott Parsons and R. F. Bales et al (eds.), *Family, Socialization and Interaction Process.* Glencoe, Ill.: The Free Press, 1955.

20. Pinchbeck, Ivy. *Women Workers and the Industrial Revolution.* London: Routledge and Kegan Paul, 1930.

21. Rossi, Alice S. "Women — Terms of Liberation." *Dissent,* November–December, 1970.

22. Schreiner, Olive. *Women and Labour.* London: R. Fisher Unwin, 1911.

23. Smelser, Neil J. *Social Change in the Industrial Revolution.* London: Routledge and Kegan Paul, 1959.

24. Sombart, Werner. *Sozialismus und soziale Bewegung.* Jena: Gustav Fischer, 1908.

25. Strachey, Ray. *The Cause, A Short History of the Women's Movement in Britain.* London: Bell and Sons, 1928.

26. Trade Union Congress. *Women in the Trade Union Movement,* issued on the occasion of the 25th Annual Conference of unions catering for women workers, May 1955.

27. Ware, Celestine. *Woman Power: The Movement for Women's Liberation.* New York. Tower Publications, 1970.

28. Worsley, Peter. *The Trumpet Shall Sound, a Study of 'Cargo' Cults in Melanesia.* London: MacGibbon and Kee, 1957.

# 26

*Erik Cohen*

# The Structural Transformation

# of the Kibbutz[1]

## Introduction

The collective movement in Israel is now more than 60 years old. From the days when a small group of people established the first "Kvutza" (collective) at Um Jumi (later to become Degania Alef) to the present day, the kibbutz movement has come a long way indeed. In 1969, there were 231 kibbutzim with about 84,670 inhabitants, about half of them full members. The kibbutz is by now famous throughout the world and

[1] This essay should have been written by the late Yonina Talmon-Garber, to sum up many years of work on the collective movement. But her premature death prevented her from writing in a comprehensive form the many single findings and insights of her work. So it happened that, though Mrs. Talmon always talked in terms of a structural typology of kibbutzim and its internal dynamics, she never put her ideas on this central theme of the sociological study of the kibbutz into written form (except in a summary fashion in [25]; this summary has been reprinted in [32]). It is a sad task for me, and one which I approach with much reluctance, to make up for that deficiency.

As I worked so closely with Yonina Talmon it is hard to point out exactly which ideas are hers and which are my own. I shall try, however, to indicate, wherever possible, where I am using Mrs. Talmon's ideas in my analysis.

The ideas presented in this paper were largely developed on the basis of the Research Project on Social Structure and Social Change in Collective Settlements, conducted at the Department of Sociology, Hebrew University, from 1954-1968; the study was directed by the late Yonina Talmon-Garber, and, in its later stages, by the author. I am indebted to Professor D. Katz, Dr. H. Meier-Cronemeyer and Dr. M. Rosner for their useful comments.

has been much studied, though only seldom copied.[2] It is one of the most prospering sectors of the Israeli economy, its agriculture ultramodern, though industry is gradually dominating its economy and beginning to provide the main source of its income. Among its members figure politicians, scientists, artists, managers of large public enterprises, etc. Nevertheless, at present, it experiences a deep internal crisis, caused, in part, by its very success. How has all this come about? What was the underlying process of transformation and what are the sources of the contemporary situation? We shall not attempt to give an exhaustive answer to this problem. But we shall try to uncover the basic sociological dynamics of the process of structural transformation of the kibbutz and indicate some of the factors at the root of the present crisis.[3]

Structural typologies of social development are among the most common tools of macrosociological analysis. Beginning with F. Toennies' conceptualization of social evolution in terms of "Gemeinschaft" and "Gesellschaft" (36), through the more refined typologies of Becker (1), Redfield (23), and many others, modern sociologists have attempted to provide a general paradigm of overall social change and transformation.[4]

Particularly relevant for our purpose is the attempt of the German sociologist, H. Schmalenbach to amend the basic Gemeinschaft-Gesellschaft typology by the addition of a new type, the Bund.[5] Schmalenbach's much neglected concept can be applied to many of the social and religious movements which, nourished by the discontent of contemporary life, strive to renew and rejuvenate society through a complete abandonment of its established institutions and through a radical or revolutionary transformation of its values and ways of life. Schmalenbach conceived of the Bund as a voluntary, and essentially transient, type of social structure. It is characterized by intensive emotional bonds between the members, and a strong attachment to the ideals which inspire them. The members of this Bund live in a state of heightened emotionality. The Bund is formed by similarly minded adults, who join each other by free choice and as a consequence of personal decision; they do not possess any common primordial attributes prior to joining the Bund. The Bund is, then, essentially a universalistic structure. In this respect it differs fundamentally from Toennies' "Gemeinschaft."

Schmalenbach's contribution makes possible the introduction of a

[2] There exist several bibliographies of publications on the Kibbutz: those by Horigan (18), Cohen (6), and Schur (30) are the most comprehensive ones.

[3] The theme of the contemporary crisis in the kibbutz is taken up in a more philosophical form in another paper by the author (7).

[4] For one of the best analytical discussions of these typologies see (24, Ch. VL).

[5] Schmalenbach's seminal essay was originally published in German (28); parts were translated into English under the title "The Sociological Category of Communion" (22, pp. 331–347).

radical change into the historical model of Toennies: the Gemeinschaft-Gesellschaft model is a linearly-evolutionary one, leading from a social past rooted in blood and soil to an ever more rationalized, uprooted, and individualistic future society. The addition of the Bund leads to a change of the model. Schmalenbach talked of the possibility of the Bund emerging from both the Gemeinschaft and the Gesellschaft as well as turning into each of these. For our purpose, however, it is important to point out that his analysis leads to an essentially cyclical model of social development. The full cycle could be presented schematically as Gemeinschaft turning into Gesellschaft, Gesellschaft being rejuvenated through the appearance of the Bund, the Bund striking roots and becoming through institutionalization a new Gemeinschaft, which again turns into Gesellschaft, etc. The fateful unilinearity of Toennies' conception is thus substituted by a cyclical model which emphasizes oscillation between institutionalization and rejuvenation. We shall see in the following that such a model serves well for the analysis of the structural transformations of the kibbutz.

The concept of the Bund was further refined by E. Shils (29, p. 138), who, on the basis of differentiation between ideological and personal primary groups, claimed that it is possible to differentiate, accordingly, two types of Bund — the ideological and the personal Bund. This insight provided another very useful lead for our own analysis.

The general conceptual scheme outlined here was applied by Yonina Talmon, at the early stages of our investigation, to the study of the social dynamics of the kibbutz. Mrs. Talmon dealt with these dynamics on two separate levels: phylogenetically the kibbutz movement as a whole undergoes a historical process of transformation from the Bund to the Commune (her term for the Gemeinschaft); orthogenetically each individual kibbutz undergoes such a transformation, irrespectively of the particular point in time when it was founded — though those kibbutzim which were founded at a relatively advanced point in the development of the movement will never exemplify fully the characteristics of the Bund and will pass quickly this stage of development. The transition from Bund to Commune is irreversible. Mrs. Talmon, however, conceived of the transition in terms of a multilateral scheme, and defined several constructed types of Communes into which a Bund may pass.

My own approach to the structural dynamics of the kibbutz is based on Mrs. Talmon's scheme but I attempt to amplify and amend it in two ways: firstly, I have further refined the typology and brought it in tune with reality through the addition of several new subtypes, discovered in the process of our analysis. Secondly, I have tried to bring the analysis up to date by conceptualizing some of the recent transformations in the largest and most mature kibbutzim in terms of a transition to a new structural type, the Association (my term for "Gesellschaft"). I have also tried to indicate the first stirrings towards a movement of internal rejuvenation in terms of the rebirth of the Bund through the strivings of some second-generation members of these mature kibbutzim.

### The Underlying Variable: Mode of Integration

Figure 1 presents in the most concise as well as comprehensive form the various structural types of our typology as well as the dynamic interrelationships between them. The terms in bold-faced type represent the basic types; the others represent the constructed subtypes. This typology has been derived by way of abstraction from a variety of concrete findings as well as from several partial typologies which had been developed in the course of our study, embracing such aspects as types of institutionalization (4), family structure (33), structure of the sphere of work (5), etc. Our study lasted for about 14 years; during

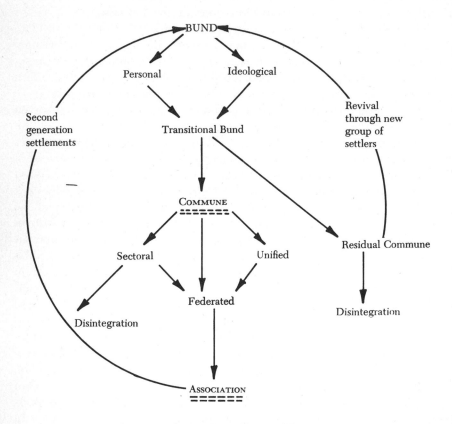

FIGURE 1: The Paradigm of Structural Types

that time structural types were provisionally conceptualized and then again reconceptualized under the impact of new findings and of a fuller view of the interrelationships between the various spheres of life on the kibbutz. The typology here presented represents only the last stage of this process of constant reformulation. It is thus possible that it will be further refined as additional data accumulate and as the kibbutz undergoes new historical changes.[6]

Our types are of necessity composed of a wide variety of characteristics. Though most of these are empirically derived, I do not claim that every kibbutz which can be categorized under one of the types will necessarily exhibit *all* the traits characteristic of that type. However, the various characteristics of a type usually cluster together and will appear whenever there are no strong local historical, geographical, or social conditions which work to the contrary. Whenever such conditions become a common factor influencing significantly a number of kibbutzim, an additional constructed type had been added to the typology.

Though empirically derived, our types are not unsystematic congeries of empirical traits. The various features of each type are logically interrelated. The focal theoretical variable of our typology is the characteristic manner in which each of the various types achieves social integration.

The concept of "mode of integration"[7] refers to the fundamental principle through which a community coheres and forms a unified whole. In each of the three main types of kibbutzim, the Bund, Commune and Association, a different mode of integration predominates:

(1) The integration of the Bund focuses on the *level of values.* The members of the Bund adhere to a common set of intensely lived "ultimate values" which give a transcendent though vaguely-defined meaning to every act of their daily life and to every aspect of their social relationships. The social integration of the Bund derives from the intensive and common attachment to values on part of all the members. The close personal ties between the members derive from that universalistic common attachment. Integration through common attachment to values will be most pronounced in the "ideological Bund," though the "personal Bund" is also essentially integrated in the same way; only the values, and the consequences of the value-attachment, are different: whereas in the "ideological Bund" the value emphasis is on the tasks of the kibbutz in the world beyond the community (e.g., pioneering for the broader Zionist movement), in the "personal Bund" the value emphasis is turned principally to the community itself — to the ideals of human relationships the members are expected to live up to.

[6] For comparative purposes, see an early statement of the typology in (33, pp. 123–127 and 25).

[7] I use this concept as defined by Holzner (17).

(2) The integration of the Commune focuses on the *level of social relations*. The members of the Commune are closely attached to more or less well-defined subgroups within the broader community. These particularistic attachments are permitted and valued for their own sake as well as accepted as a means through which the individual is integrated into the broader social framework. Integration of the community is achieved through the interlacing of the subgroups through increasingly formalized processes of arbitration and mutual adaptation between the subgroups. Some degree of allegiance of the members to the ultimate values is still essential for the smooth functioning of the Commune, though this allegiance is now much less intensive than it had been in the Bund.

(3) The integration of the Association focuses on the *level of formal institutions*. These institutions, of which there is a wide variety in the large and complex modern kibbutz, allocate to the individual members their tasks and roles on the one hand and services and rewards on the other, and thus function as the principal means of regulation of life in the Association. The set of formal institutions is supported on the one hand by a degree of value consensus through which the institutions and their principal functionaries are legitimized, and on the other by the complex of primary relations and social groupings which still continue to exist in the Association, though they cease to be the principal mechanism of integration.

### The Structural Types: The Bund

The Bund, like the kibbutz movement in general, is the result of the interplay of a variety of factors: firstly, it was a reaction of young Jews against traditional, stagnant Jewish society in the Diaspora (12); as such it constituted the extreme form of revolutionary Zionism. Secondly, it was a revolutionary reaction of idealistic Jewish youths against the social malaise of Western bourgeois, capitalistic, urban society; in this respect it was one of the varieties of the European youth movement of the twenties, akin in ideas and spirit to such movements as the German *Wandervogel*, which inspired Schmalenbach to formulate the concept of the Bund in the first place.[8] Finally, it was a tool for the realization of broader Jewish national aims in Palestine, a form of life deemed most suitable for the difficult and often hostile natural and social conditions with which he pioneers had to struggle in the early period of Jewish settlement in Palestine.

The values of the early kibbutz had, then, two chief points of reference: on the one hand they were inward-directed, towards the improvement

---

[8] On the Jewish youth movement in Germany see (21); for a comparison of Jewish and non-Jewish youth movements in Germany see (20).

of man and society through the whole-hearted acceptance of a set of humanistic and socialist ideals; on the other hand they were outward-directed, towards the broader society, through the acceptance of the precepts of pioneering Zionism which allotted the kibbutz the role of the spear-head of Jewish settlement in Palestine. The kibbutz was conceived at one and the same time as an end in itself, as well as a means towards broader societal ends; it was an ideological creation, but unlike other utopian movements it was also expected to fulfill national tasks and, hence, had to adapt itself effectively to changing conditions. This fact prevented its early petrification and endowed it with a dynamism absent from the other utopian movements (3).

The relative emphasis on the internal versus the external point of reference of the kibbutz values led to important ideological differences between the various federations of kibbutzim, which in turn caused significant variations in the social structure between the settlements associated with each Federation. On one end of the continuum is the federation with which the earliest-established kibbutzim were associated, the Chever Hakvutzot, which gave primary emphasis to humanistic values, such as personal freedom and self-accomplishment, and hence advocated small, loosely organized settlements (called kvutzot, from Hebrew "Kvutza," a group). From this federation stem the best examples of the "personal" Bund. On the opposite end of the continuum is Hakibbutz Hameuchad, the movement which gave primary emphasis to the values of pioneering Zionism and considered the settlements primarily as tools for national goals. Hence it advocated the creation of large kibbutzim (19), endowed from the start with a higher degree of formal organization than that typical of the early settlements of the other movements.[9] From this movement stem the best examples of the "ideological" Bund. Socialist values, which attempt to harmonize personal ideals with ideals of social service, were most emphasized by the Hashomer Hatzair movement, which takes an intermediate position between the two other federations. The small Religious Kibbutz Federation came closest to the Chever Hakvutzot in the secular aspects of its ideology, but in addition to them also kept to the precepts of the orthodox Jewish religion; some of its leaders even tried to derive the collective principles of life from their religious convictions.

The ideal type of the Bund was most closely realized by some of the earliest established kibbutzim for a relatively long period of time. These settlements were founded in the wake of an intensive Jewish social and ideological awakening in the Diaspora. They had to struggle against highly adverse conditions in Palestine, with very meagre resources, while enjoying only limited support from Jewish national institutions.

[9] For a sociological analysis of the development of Hakibbutz Hameuchad see (39, Ch. III and VI).

Only a very strong commitment to the cause helped them to persist in their efforts. The kibbutzim which had been founded in later periods, and especially after the establishment of the State of Israel, resembled the ideal type of the Bund less completely. The intensity of their communal experience was somewhat muted by the institutionalized process of establishing new kibbutzim by powerful and well-organized institutions. The value-commitment of their members was no longer as absolute as that of the founders of the first collectives. They underwent a structural transformation more quickly. The pace of structural transformation also seems to have been generally quicker in the "ideological" Bunds than in the "personal" ones. Whereas the "personal" Bund tends to change into a more or less stable Commune, there are already strong pressures within the "ideological" Bund towards an early transformation into an Association. The reason for this difference is that the "ideological" Bund puts a greater premium on objective, instrumental achievements, and hence is more amenable to quick growth and formal institutionalization than the "personal" Bund, where direct and spontaneous person-to-person relationships are more highly valued. Since in our investigation we dealt with movements such as Chever Hakevutzot and Hashomer Hatzair where the "personal" Bund predominated in the early stages, we shall deal primarily with this variant of the Bund.

As mentioned before, the integration of the Bund is based, primarily, on the common and intensive commitment of its members to a set of ultimate values. However, though the commitment is intensive, the precise social meaning of the values for various concrete situations is still vague. The Bund is not an institutionalized form of life and hence no precise social norms, referring to expected behavior in concrete situations, have yet been formulated. Moreover, in the "personal" Bund there is a particularly strong opposition against any attempt at such a formulation. Social order is expected to derive from mutual understanding, not from rules of conduct.

This fact in itself would suffice to produce a very intensive activity in the Bund around matters of public concern. Such activity has in fact been even more intensified, and sometimes became extremely hectic, owing to a fundamental characteristic of the ideological orientation of the members of the early Bund: they were convinced that they participated in a social experiment which, to their mind, might be crucial for the future of Jewish society in Palestine, or even prototypical for a new, communal world order in the future. Hence every aspect of life, every decision on the way in which things were managed, became endowed with an existential, almost transcendent importance. Every detail of life was seen "sub specie aeternitatis," and otherwise prosaic problems had to be dealt with in most fundamental terms. All areas of life were judged directly from the point of view of the ultimate values. Since no specific norms were yet institutionalized, no segregation of subspheres which would enjoy relative isolation from the basic precepts had yet taken place. There existed no secondary sets of values, no functional independence, no relative autonomy. In this respect, the Bund comes close to the early stages of formation of a religious sect, the life of which is completely and rationally permeated by a set of basic religious precepts (37, p. 331–343). In religious-sociological terms it might be said that life in the prototypical Bund had been endowed with a "sacred" quality; there was nothing merely instrumental, merely secular. Everything had a broader, symbolic meaning. Therefore, no special "sacred" period is set aside from the ordinary flow of time for ceremonies or festivities, except those directly concerned with the expression of the solidarity of the collective (for example, the commemoration of the day the settlement was established). The Bund abolished most traditional distinctions in the reckoning of time, kept neither the sabbath nor most other Jewish religious festivals.[16] In the celebration of those festivals which it still kept, national or natural themes were emphasized, while the religious themes were completely disregarded.

In the Bund, the collective assembly was the only political authority. It ruled the community and decided on matters large and small. In the early Bund, each member could convene the assembly at will to discuss a grievance. The collective had no officials or functionaries. Gradually, however, several such roles, initially with very limited authority and ill-defined responsibilities, appeared: the "work-coordinator," a technical role concerned with the allocation of workers to jobs; the secretary, a role which later split into the roles of the internal secretary, concerned mainly with social and personal matters within the community, and of the external secretary, dealing with relationships of the kibbutz with institutions and other communities; and the "production-manager," concerned with the over-all coordination of production. At first, such public roles had to be performed in the member's spare time. Time for such work was allocated later.

In the economic sphere, work in the Bund was organized by production and service branches. The economy was diversified and the branches were small. However, heterogeneity did not imply occupational specialization: members were not yet permanently attached to any branch, but rotated freely between branches, according to their shifting needs. The branches had initially no formal leaders; only with time did the role of the branch-manager emerge, initially as a role concerned mostly with the technical ties of the branch with the kibbutz, such as care for the supply of manpower and materials, despatch of products, etc. This role was also performed in the member's free time, after he worked a full workday in the branch like any other worker.

---

[16] The Protestant sects also disregarded feasts and festivals and reduced their number radically.

Social life in the Bund focused on the collective. The dining hall, the communal green and the public shower were the most common meeting places. The importance of the family was reduced to a minimum — in the secular kibbutz movement, marriage was informal and expressions of conjugal love and of solidarity of the married couple were shunned. Children were delegated to the children's home, where they received all the personal services as well as education. Relations with the parents were very restricted (34). The whole community formed one undifferentiated body, and ideally there were no factions or social subdivisions within it.

Integration of its members around a set of strongly felt ultimate values is the basic strength of the Bund. However, such a form of social integration is essentially an unstable one. There is a fundamental conflict or dilemma inherent in the social structure of the Bund, between the pressure to conform and thus to preserve collective solidarity as against the liberty of each member to interpret freely the basic precepts of kibbutz life. Members of the Bund are asked to achieve full agreement on any issue facing the collectivity. Still, there exists no well-defined institutional mechanism through which such an agreement could be achieved. Hence, public life in the early Bund tended to be hectic. The constant and intensive social interaction, concerning matters large and small, required a great mental and physical effort from all the members. With time they tired,, and discussion on principles sometimes degenerated into personal conflicts. This led to breakdowns in relations and often also to the desertion of the kibbutz by dissatisfied members. The intensity of the discussion was not necessarily related to the functional importance of the matter on hand or to the personal interest of the participants. Rather, it had to do with the symbolic significance of sometimes small matters for the overall design of a utopian society. This very fact also endowed acts of personal behavior with exceptional importance: hence, the demand to lead an "exemplary" life, without clear and unequivocal norms of conduct and without formal sanctions, often created strong inner tension in the individual, who constantly forced himself to live up to the model of exemplary behavior held forth by his group. Though I possess no precise data, I suspect that there were several cases of "altruistic" suicide (14) in the kibbutz, due to overly intensive concern of the members with the demand to comply with all too highly set standards of personal conduct, strongly supported by informal but all-pervasive public opinion. These cases of suicide might serve as the most extreme indications of the sometimes severe psychological pressure under which the individual in the Bund had to labor.

As long as the kibbutz is still small, socially homogeneous, functionally undifferentiated and enjoying a measure of external support from the kibbutz Federation to which it belongs, or from the national institutions, it is generally within its powers to overcome its internal strains. As conditions change, however, its stability becomes jeopardized by its internal conflicts. The mode of integration typical of the Bund, common adherence to a set of ultimate values, does not suffice any more to prevent change or even disintegration.

### The Structural Types: The Transitional Bund

Virtually every Bund experienced a period of crisis some time after its establishment. Internal dissent, disenchantment, and lack of sufficient economic and organizational support on part of the national institutions actually led to the disintegration of several kibbutzim established in the early stages of the collective movement. In the later stages, most such disintegrating settlements have been physically salvaged through the efforts of the national institutions and the kibbutz federation. Only very few places were completely abandoned. However, many such settlements remained socially unstable for prolonged periods of time, as we shall see in our discussion of the Residual Commune. Nevertheless, most Bunds succeeded in overcoming the initial crisis and in making the transition to the Commune. The period of transition might last a considerable time, and hence we often find an intermediary type of kibbutz which is not any more a Bund, neither yet a Commune. We called it the "Transitional Bund."

The tension caused in the original Bund by the lack of criteria for an agreed upon translation of ultimate values into concrete norms for daily behavior, aggravates as the kibbutz matures. In the early stages of its existence the members are immersed in a state of "primaeval experience," an enthusiasm of pioneering and creation which enables them to overcome, or overlook, the difficulties of daily life. As time goes on this primaeval enthusiasm gradually ebbs and a more prosaic, practical approach to the many problems of life in a young, small, and remote agricultural settlement becomes necessary. The point of crisis is usually reached when a new group of settlers is sent to the kibbutz to complement it.[11] This group of newcomers is often similar to the founders in ideological outlook, but younger and comes from a different country of origin. This introduces a degree of strangeness between the two groups. However, the main difficulty stems from the differential perspective of the two groups towards the kibbutz: the newcomers did not partake in the "primaeval experience," and though they might be as enthusiastic about collective life as the founders, their initial collective experience is usually not as intensive and profound as that of the founders had been.

Moreover, a degree of differentiation is liable to take place with the

---

[11] Such groups, sent by the federation to which the kibbutz pertains, are called in Hebrew "Hashlama" (complement) and hence we shall refer to them in the following as "complements."

coming of the new members. Whereas until now all members had approximately the same knowledge and experience in the management of collective affairs and were rotated among all roles as a matter of principle, now a difference in the level of knowledge and experience appears: the newcomers are much less knowledgeable and experienced in kibbutz affairs than the founders. For a time, at least, the more skilled and responsible jobs have to be performed by the founders. The question as to when and to what degree responsibilities will be shared with the newcomers often becomes one of the chief points of conflict between the two groups.

The kibbutz at this stage is still permeated by a spirit of overall unity, and hence considerable effort is spent to integrate the newcomers completely into the original Bund. If this effort succeeds, the kibbutz is likely to preserve for an additional period its Bund-like qualities. However, it will not remain unchanged indefinitely since other factors act for transition. The most important of these is, perhaps, the life-cycle of the members. At foundation, most members are young and still single. As families are created and children born, a new focus of interest and identification emerges — the nuclear family. The original Bund used to be hostile to the nuclear family group and tended to restrict its functions and its social importance to the minimum. The members viewed the family from the perspective of their own youth experience: as members of a youth movement, they rebelled against their own parents and started a new and revolutionary way of life. However, as the new families expand and children grow up, a gradual shift of perspective takes place in the outlook of at least part of the members. In the Transitional Bund there is, typically, an open conflict between the emergent family solidarity and the efforts of the collective to safeguard the total allegiance of its members. This conflict is one of the chief sources of tension in this type of settlement; it achieves resolution only with the redefinition of the role of the family in the fully-fledged Commune.

The demographic change is usually accompanied by a crisis in the economic and organizational structure of the kibbutz. At foundation, the kibbutz usually enjoys financial support from the colonizing institutions. Such support enables it to overcome the hardship inherent in settlement in a new and often hostile region. It is initially not utterly dependent for its livelihood upon the market value of its products, and hence able to devote itself to some social experimentation. This includes, among else, the attempt to realize directly some of its values in the sphere of work: for example, the rejection of functional authority or specialization as means for the realization of the values of equality and full personal development. Such rigorous application of these values in the sphere of work is not necessarily conducive to high productive efficiency.

As the kibbutz matures, external financial support is gradually phased out. The kibbutz is expected to become economically viable as quickly as possible. Viability has to be proved in terms of income, in an essentially capitalistic, competitive economy. Since the kibbutz is often located on an economically disadvantageous site, only extreme efficiency in production will ensure viability. Pressures for specialization, mechanization, rational organization, and definition of authority are thus created. Such pressures often coincide with the period of social crisis in the Bund mentioned above. The strain upon the system is thereby considerably increased and many kibbutzim find themselves on the verge not only of social, but also of economic and organizational breakdown. In more recent times, many Transitional Bunds had to receive extensive support, financial and organizational, from their federation, or from the Settlement Department of the Jewish Agency, to enable them to survive the crisis.

As the Transitional Bund strives to overcome its difficulties it passes through a process which we shall call the "struggle of institutionalization." In this process day-to-day conduct in the economic sphere — and gradually also that in other institutional spheres — becomes separated from the ultimate values of collective life, through a series of new normative arrangements, often against the wishes of the more orthodox members of the community.

Under pressure for efficiency and increased production, old branches expand and become mechanized and new ones are added. Work becomes more specialized and more and more members have to acquire some basic training and experience in order to be able to perform the more skilled jobs. Hence, rotation of members among jobs gradually decreases and most members become permanently attached to their branches. As work in the branch becomes more complex, a greater need for coordination arises. Hence, an increase in the branch-manager's authority takes place. Concomitantly, there is more need for overall organization. The administrational and organizational structure of the kibbutz becomes strengthened, and the importance and authority of central functionaries increases. These functionaries feel most strongly the tensions resulting from the conflict between the concept of an absolutely egalitarian, nondifferentiated society and the need for functional authority and specialization. They often pay the price of their organizational success in terms of loss of solidary ties with their fellow members. As in the case of the nuclear family, so too in the sphere of work, reintegration is achieved only in the Commune where functional authority achieves a degree of legitimation.

However, it would be wrong to consider the struggle of institutionalization as a simple, unilinear translation of ultimate but vague values into concrete, unequivocal norms. The vagueness of the ultimate values permits a multiplicity of interpretations and the normative translation of these values implies a decision as to their "correct" meaning. The struggle of institutionalization, though caused by the tension between direct allegiance to ultimate values and the exigencies of existence, actually brings to the fore some of the fundamental dilemmas in the value system itself. I shall illustrate this problem through the analysis of the implications of one central value, that of equality, for one sphere of life, that of consumption, in which the dilemma is particularly acute.[12]

The value of equality was one of the chief foci of social integration in the original Bund. Its practical implications, however, were often vague. In the sphere of consumption, it was at first applied as meaning "to each according to his needs." Since there were very few goods to be distributed at this early stage, and since the strong future-orientation of the members diminished the saliency of consumption, the system at first worked well. A member would approach the communal clothing store, for example, and ask for an item of clothing; he would be given the object *bona fide,* provided that it was available. Even so, there was some informal social control; the members' "needs" were rudimentary and similar and hence, he would not, or could not ask for any fancy goods (which in any case were not available). If he did, he would be ridiculed or admonished by his peers.

However, as conditions changed with the entrance of new complements of members, the emergence of families and of children and the growing present-orientation of the members, the sphere of consumption gained in importance. More and more disputes occurred with the manager of the clothing store about who "really" needs what, and social tensions increased. The struggle of institutionalization started with the growing pressure to define the idea of equality in consumption. However, there were two equally valid definitions: "essential equality" would recognize the inherent differences between members, implying differential needs; equality would be then achieved through the equal *relative* satisfaction of differential needs: whoever needs more, gets more. "Mechanical equality" would allocate to everyone an equal share of goods, notwithstanding the "real" needs. The original method of distribution embodied the concept of essential equality. Since this concept is not amenable to institutionalization, pressure was building up towards a more mechanical concept of equality. The community decided upon what the needs of a member "really" were and formalized them concretely in terms of a "norm of distribution," which specified how much of the various goods a member should receive during a given period of time ("norm of time") or how many articles (e.g., shirts or underwear) a member is entitled to possess at any given moment of time ("norm of quantity").

This new arrangement led to the achievement of a degree of stability in the Transitional Bund and in the early Commune. However, it curtailed the members' opportunity to satisfy individual needs and preferences in consumption. As the kibbutz prospered and the level of con-

---

[12] E. Rosenfeld (27) presents an interesting and detailed account of the struggle of institutionalization in the sphere of consumption.

sumption rose, new pressures for freedom of choice and expression of personal taste in consumption built up. The system of "norms" could not respond to such pressures: hence, new mechanisms of distribution such as a "personal budget" or a system of "points" had to be introduced. These mechanisms provided again, some leeway to personal choice, albeit within financial limits. Thereby, an element inherent in the conception of "essential equality," the adaptation of consumption to personal needs and preferences, was again introduced into the distributive mechanism. The pendulum, therefore, moved again away from mechanical equality and in the direction of qualified "essential equality." The demand, voiced in some quarters, to permit complete freedom of consumption in an ever increasing number of areas as the kibbutz becomes affluent, points in the same direction.

This example shows very clearly the possibility of alternative interpretations of an ultimate value and the way in which emphasis moves with changing conditions from one interpretation to another, without ever doing full justice to every possible legitimate interpretation of that value. I think that this pendulum-like movement in the interpretation of values forms the basic characteristic of the ideological dynamics in the kibbutz.

### The Structural Types: The Residual Commune

Before turning to the description of the Commune, a few words should be said on the Residual Commune, a type of settlement lacking integration and stability, which results from an unsuccessful transition from the Bund to the fully developed Commune. The Residual Commune has lost its integration around a set of intensely felt ultimate values, but at the same time has not achieved a new and stable integration through a well-developed network of social ties, characteristic of the Commune. It is a small kibbutz, the growth of which had been arrested and hence failed to "take off."

The Residual Commune is not larger or even smaller than the Bund. However, it is not socially homogeneous, but composed of a series of residua of groups which passed through the settlement at various periods of time. The typical process through which such a situation arises is the following: a few years after a Bund has been founded, a serious internal crisis of transition induces many of its founders to leave the settlement. Among those who leave are often individuals who have been the pillars of the community. The settlement, therefore, remains without leaders. The new complement sent to reinforce the settlement finds nothing to hang on to and usually disintegrates quickly. The kibbutz federation at this moment often starts a losing game. As the danger arises that the young kibbutz will completely disintegrate, the federation is forced to send additional reinforcements. As these successive waves of reinforcements disintegrate in their turn, the typical social structure of the Residual Commune emerges: each group of members sent to the kibbutz — the founders included — leaves behind a tiny residuum. The community thus becomes a patchwork of small, separate, ill-integrated subgroups. Such a social framework cannot provide the necessary support for the absorption of newcomers and often not even for the retention of those already living in it. Plagued by social as well as functional problems, the Residual Commune shows a strong tendency to disintegrate completely.

The phenomenon of the Residual Commune became relatively frequent in the period immediately following the establishment of the state, when the kibbutz movement as a whole suffered its major internal crisis and when the kibbutz federations were yet unable to deal effectively with the challenge presented by the new circumstances. The federations learned gradually that they cannot resolve the problem of the instability of the Residual Communes through the dispatchment of more and more reinforcements, since they thereby only dissipated their meager resources. They initiated a new strategy: several settlements were left to disband almost completely and were then settled anew by a large nucleus, thereby virtually recreating a Bund. Other such settlements have been "adopted" by larger and more mature kibbutzim, who nurtured them out of their difficulties (35). Many of the younger, relatively small kibbutzim of our days are not Bunds any more, but such Residual Communes which achieved a degree of stability through the joint efforts of the kibbutz federations and of the colonizing institutions. A special term has been coined to designate these settlements: "Hakibbutz Haza'ir" ("the tiny kibbutz"). After achieving a degree of stability the tiny kibbutz finally starts on a belated transition to the Commune.

### The Structural Types: The Commune

Most kibbutzim, particularly in the earlier periods, successfully accomplished the transition to the Commune. The Commune represents a new point of stability, in which the focus of integration is transferred from the level of ultimate values to the network of social ties between the members of the community. The overall solidarity of the collective, characteristic of the original Bund, is permanently weakened during the struggle of institutionalization in the Transitional Bund. Various kinds of subgroups appear in the community. Efforts to realise the ultimate values completely and directly in every sphere of daily life are also weakened. Social differentiation and institutionalization introduce a sober, profane quality into kibbutz life. The original enthusiasm disappears, but so do also the incessant internal struggles. Members settle down to business. Vaguely defined general ideological and national goals of the kibbutz movement are translated into concrete, localised terms: the economic and social independence and development of the individual community gains precedence over all other concerns. Success of the movement as a whole is often judged in terms of the economic prosperity of the kibbutz.

The newly won, partial autonomy of various institutional spheres from overall ideological regulation makes possible the efficient solution of functional problems in the spheres of work, organization, consumption, education etc. It is interesting to note, however, that at the same time that life in the kibbutz has lost its "sacred" quality, there is renewed interest in purely symbolic activities, and a concomitant gradual revival of rituals and celebrations — particularly, the reintroduction of religious marriage ceremonies and the observation of Jewish religious festivals. The content of the latter is often adapted to serve the symbolic needs of the kibbutz. Such symbolic activities reinforce overall social cohesion and allegiance to basic values, which might be weakened through total preoccupation in daily, routine activities.

The personal motivations of the members to live in the kibbutz also change: if previously they chose kibbutz life out of a deep attachment to the collective ideal and the task of the kibbutz as the spearhead of a future society, they now shift to more mundane, concrete considerations. Chief among these are job-satisfaction, attachment to the community as such and particularly, social involvement with their peers. The nuclear family serves as an important integrating mechanism: since most members are married, they are attached to the kibbutz not only through their personal social ties but also through the various social ties of the other members of the nuclear family. The young, unattached member of the Bund could easily leave everything and give up kibbutz life if his initial enthusiasm turned into disenchantment. The middle-aged member of the Commune, who had lived in the kibbutz for most of his adult life, in addition to his ideological commitment is involved with it through a multiplicity of ties.

Social ties, not idealistic allegiance, thus become the chief focus of integration of the Commune, the force which holds its members together and motivates them to work for the common good. Different types of subgroups, with varying degrees of cohesion, emerge in the kibbutz. According to the nature of such subgroup we differentiate three subtypes of Communes: [13]

*The Unified Commune* exemplifies most fully the mode of integration typical of the Commune: its integration rests almost completely on the network of personal relations among its members. This is less true of the other subtypes. The Unified Commune is socially homogeneous, lacking a clear-cut division into several clearly differentiated subgroups. However, it has also lost the strong, overall cohesion of the early Bund. The social

---

[13] The subtypes have been defined by Mrs. Talmon in (25). In the following discussion I have drawn heavily upon her work.

ties typically form a network of interrelated and intertwined small sub-groups. The pivotal points of this network are the nuclear families and the penumbra of other kinship ties which become the more numerous as the settlement matures and gains a three-generation depth. Other types of small groups which appear in the Unified Commune are groups of common origin, age groups, solidary work-groups, neighborhood groups, groups of members with common cultural interests, etc. Though the family predominates among these various subgroups, none of them is either strong enough or comprehensive enough to divide the community along clear-cut lines. Integration is, then, achieved through the intersection of subgroups, and the appearance of a complex, dense, all-embracing network of relationships much in the way typical of the Gemeinschaft.

The Unified Commune often originated from a slowly growing Bund, which made the transition without serious social upheavals. However, though this subtype of Commune is closest to the Bund, the social dynamics of the Unified Commune differ considerably from those of the Bund. Since the community is homogeneous and grew without major perturbations, it often develops a body of local customs, almost a tradition, supported by considerable consensus, which guides daily life. There is little dissent and social life is ordinarily quiet. As a result, the Unified Commune develops a tendency to apathy — members withdraw into their narrow circles of kin and acquaintances and take only a limited interest in matters of importance to the community as a whole. They tend to delegate authority to decide on such matters to the elected public bodies and officials, the secretary, the production manager, or the secretariat, since there is ordinarily no basic conflict of interest between the groups in the community. The officials are the representatives of the common consensus. The Unified Commune may, as a result, develop a group of official role-bearers who, though not expressly an "elite" in the ordinary sense of the term, nevertheless bear considerable responsibility and hence possess a high degree of authority in many matters of public concern.

In the sphere of work, the Unified Commune is characterized by a considerable degree of autonomy of the various branches of production, the members of which usually work together for long periods of time and characteristically form a cohesive primary group (15). Though work in the Unified Commune is more formally organized than in the Bund, the mechanisms of control are still rather loose and most of the actual coordination of production is carried out through informal, personal contacts between the various role-bearers. The extent and manner of development of various branches depends largely on the personal ability and zeal of its workers. The overall economic development of the Unified Commune is, hence, chiefly the result of the various forces operative in its individual branches. As yet, there exists but little overall planning and rational direction.

Social life centers on the family group. In the mature Unified Commune, the network of kinship ties is often of considerable scope. Large kinship groups often form corporate groups. The dominance of family ties over other types of social relations may occasionally lead to a situation in which the community is dominated by a coalition of several such groups which are powerful enough to impose their will upon the collective in most matters of importance regarding the daily life of the members. Such groups sometimes act in unison in matters of direct personal concern to the members or to their offspring, such as the distribution of important articles of consumption, allocation of work-places or opportunities for higher education for the children. The corporate kinship groups may act in such matters as pressure groups, using their influence in communal institutions, presenting a common front in the communal assembly, etc. Sometimes severe, though covert, conflicts between such groups might disturb the usually placid atmosphere of the Unified Commune. This may lead to a family-based factionalism, which is essentially foreign to the non-familistic spirit of the kibbutz ideology.

*The Federated Commune.* This subtype of the Commune is composed of several large, clearly distinct subgroups, each of which provides a primary focus of identification to its member. The individual member is integrated into his community through attachment to his subgroup. Overall integration is achieved through the interplay between the subgroups, though the Federated Commune relies less on direct, personal relations than the Unified Commune and more on formalized institutional relationships.

Whereas in the Unified Commune the complements of new members are gradually absorbed by the community, and lose their distinctiveness, in the Federated Commune they keep their separate identities. It is difficult to state the precise reasons for these differing paths of social development. It seems that two main factors are operative here: the differences in origin and in cultural background between the subsequent groups of settlers, and the period of time which elapses between the entrance of each group into the kibbutz. If new members come from different countries and cultural backgrounds and arrive after lengths of time so that there exists a considerable difference in the age of members of the various groups, the probability of mutual assimilation diminishes considerably. When the second generation grows up in the kibbutz it often, though not necessarily always, forms a separate subgroup in the community. The main criteria of differentiation between subgroups in the Federated Commune are, then, one or several of the following: country of origin, cultural background, length of stay in the community, age and generation. The larger the number of criteria which differentiate the subgroups from each other, and the greater the differences in each criterion, the sharper the social segregation between the subgroups and the stronger the impact of the segregation upon all spheres of social life. For example, in those Federated Communes where the differences between the criteria were many and considerable, the social cohesion of workgroups in the branches is affected: the branches tend then either to be composed only of members of the same subgroup, or several solidary cliques, composed of members of various subgroups, appear in the branch (15).

The subgroups provide the chief framework of the day-to-day life of the Federated Commune. The majority of the friends and acquaintances of a member are found in his subgroup. Many of his neighbours also belong to his subgroup, since dwelling units are allocated to members in accordance with their length of stay in the kibbutz. Most matters of communal interest are discussed first within the subgroup before they are dealt with formally by the communal assembly or by another public institution of the kibbutz. The subgroup resembles to some degree the original Bund, but its social life and the commitment of the members are less intensive. Still, the subgroup serves as a mediating framework between the individual member and the collective — the member's ties to the subgroup are the chief social mechanism which safeguards his attachment to the community. The family, which used to be all-important in the Unified Commune, loses some of its importance in the Federated Commune; it becomes secondary to the subgroup (25, p. 15).

Relations between members of different subgroups are cooler and more formal than those within the subgroups. A good deal of competition between subgroups is quite common; this may focus on spheres such as public offices, norms for the allocation of goods (particularly dwellings and furniture, which are mostly allocated by length of stay in the kibbutz) and allocation of jobs in the branches. Sometimes serious crises may break out on such matters and a considerable amount of tension may be generated. However, the subgroups do not ordinarily fight with each other, and there is no thorough-going "class-conflict" between them.[14]

Since the Federated Commune is more heterogeneous than the Unified one, there exist fewer points of overall agreement between its members. The members of the subgroups perceive the possibility of conflict on various issues and are hence more aware of matters of public importance, particularly those which might concern them individually, than are members of the Unified Commune. There is less apathy on part of the rank and file and less readiness to leave matters to the functionaries to de-

14 For an opposite view see (26).

cide. Instead, their authority tends to become more formally defined, and their behavior more tightly controlled.

In the sphere of work there is also more centralization. The branches lose part of their independence vis-à-vis the central institution. The process of production, for instance, is centrally controlled. Overall rational planning of investments and of the development of the economy is gradually introduced.

Whereas in the Unified Commune there is a tendency towards "traditionalization" — institutionalization of various customs — in the Federated Commune there is a tendency towards increasing formalization — institutionalization through explicit and fixed rules and regulations. The Federated Commune is more bureaucratized, centralized, and rationalized than the Unified Commune. Many of its basic characteristics point already towards the transition to the Association.

*The Sectorial Commune.* Before we discuss the emergence of the Association as a social type of kibbutzim, short consideration should be given to a deviant type of the Commune, the Sectorial Commune.[15] Like the Federated Commune, this subtype is also divided into a few subunits, which we call sectors. The sectors differ from the subgroups of the Federated Commune in the nature of their cohesion. In the Federated Commune the focus of cohesion is *internal,* the emotional attachment of the members is the basis of their subgroup. The focus of cohesion of the sectors is *external,* the sectors are formed through mutual opposition of groups of members. But they do not enjoy a high degree of internal cohesion. The sectors are essentially power or pressure groups, contending with each other over the distribution of resources and rewards in the community. The allegiance of the members to their sector does not derive principally from their emotional attachment to it, but from the necessity to ally themselves with people of similar interests in opposition to those whose interests are different. The Sectorial Commune is, then, involved in continuous social conflict often accompanied by a disregard of the basic norms of kibbutz life.

The Sectorial Commune is not only a deviant type of the Commune from the point of view of kibbutz values — in its "pure" form, it is not a viable community. The Sectorial Commune is too ridden with dissent and socially disjointed to be able to mobilize much support for institutional arrangements intended to regulate its social life and help it to overcome its difficulties. Without such support, formal arrangements malfunction. A certain amount of anomie is hence endemic to this subtype of the Commune. In extreme cases, the Sectorial Commune will collapse since the kibbutz does not possess the mechanisms necessary

---

[15] This subtype was called by Mrs. Talmon the Split or Factional Commune (25, p. 13).

to contain and regulate the perpetual internal struggle. Such extreme cases, however, are rare. Most concrete examples of the Sectorial Commune which came up in our study only approximated the theoretical case here described. Still, a few of these reached the verge of collapse at some points in their past. They were generally saved from total collapse by the emergence of a group of rather authoritative leaders, usually central functionaries of the kibbutz, who entered the social and institutional vacuum and imposed their will upon the community in an effort to save it. These leaders tended to concentrate in their hands the control over the most important social, political and economic processes and decisions and thereby endowed the kibbutz with a measure of order and continuity in the performance of essential tasks, which would otherwise be completely lacking. This group of functionaries usually belonged to the dominant sector in the community. Its members enjoyed personal authority in the community. The ability to control people and processes has been the principal reward for their efforts. In some cases the functionaries may also have enjoyed a few personal material benefits from such control, but these are at best of secondary importance. Nevertheless, in the kibbutz situation personal authority and authoritarian control over people are considered highly illegitimate forms of behavior, and though these functionaries managed to hold the community together by their actions, they nevertheless generated a considerable amount of antagonism, particularly on the part of the opposing sector. However, the functionaries held on to their offices, often for considerable periods of time and in spite of opposition, owing to the fact that most members were unwilling to accept any kind of public office. The majority was apathetic towards community-wide issues and mainly concerned with their personal advantages and problems.

The tendency toward individualistic self-concern has spread even into family life (25, p. 15). Attendance at the collective assembly is ordinarily low, except when issues of personal interest to the members are on the agenda. Cohesion of work-groups is low. Work tasks are accomplished primarily through the application of close personal control by the branch manager and other office bearers on the workers. The organization of work is deficient and work often inefficient. Members' attention is given predominantly to the sphere of consumption while their commitment to collective goals is generally low.

The Sectorial Commune emerged as a result of weakening of social ties within the various contingents of members constituting the kibbutz accompanied by a rise of antagonism between those contingents. Historically, such conditions were created by the aftermath of the schism in one of the kibbutz federations, Hakibbutz Hameuchad, in 1951. After the schism — the causes of which were ideological and political — groups of dissenting members left the kibbutzim of Hakibbutz Hameuchad and joined the former Chever Hakvutzot federation which now became

Ichud Hakevutzot Ve'Hakibbutzim. The schism shift was a traumatic experience: in some cases several groups of dissenting members were sent by their new federation to establish a new kibbutz. In others, a group of dissenters joined an old, established kibbutz of the Chever Hakvutzot, which had been in need of reinforcement. Most such settlements suffered serious social convulsions. Most members who switched federations were not enthusiastic youngsters looking for new experiences, but middle-aged disenchanted individuals, who were forced to change their kibbutz affiliation for political reasons. The conditions of life in the new settlements were mostly much below the standards which the members had enjoyed previously. Hence, the primary concern of many has been to achieve improvements in their individual standard of living. They were less interested in the common good of the new collective. People who knew each other from before united and formed "sectors" which acted as power groups. The clash between the sectors was produced through their conflicting interests, particularly in the sphere of distribution of commodities and other rewards.

Most Sectorial Communes seem to have been created through the historic accident of the schism in one of the kibbutz federations. Others might have emerged through different social processes though such cases seem to be rare.

Obviously, the various subtypes of Communes which we have described, do not appear in reality in their "ideal-typical" form. Many kibbutzim represent combinations of traits characteristic of two or even all three subtypes. Moreover, transition from one type to the other is common. Though, in principle, such transition can take place from each of the types into all the others, the most common process is the transition from the Unified, or Sectorial, Commune into the Federated Commune. As a Unified Commune matures, a new group of settlers, or more often the emergent second generation, may introduce internal, social differentiation into the community and transform it into a Federated Commune. As a Sectorial Commune matures and overcomes its crisis, internal cohesion of the various sectors increases and relations between them become less strained, so that the kibbutz gradually becomes a Federated Commune. All the large, mature Communes tend, therefore, to become federated. Only very few pass into maturity preserving the essential traits of a Unified Commune. None can remain indefinitely as a Sectorial Commune. Developmentally, as well as structurally, the Federated Commune forms the type of transition to the Association.

## The Structural Types: The Association

The Commune represents a point of equilibrium in the social development of the kibbutz movement. Indeed, Mrs. Talmon, working on the data of a large-scale comparative study conducted in the middle fifties, conceptualized the process of social change in the kibbutz merely as a transition from the Bund to the Commune. She had not detected in her data any indication of a further major step in the process of structural change.

However, since the middle fifties considerable changes have taken place in the kibbutz (particularly in the large, mature and developed Communes) as well as in the position of the kibbutz itself in Israeli society. These changes had important repercussions on the social structure of the kibbutz. It is necessary to introduce a new ideal type, the Association, which will present in a coherent, theoretical form the emergent social characteristics of the mature kibbutz of our days. It has to be emphasized that no systematic study has yet been conducted of the kibbutzim which approximate the type of the Association. Hence, my analysis of the forces of transition to the Association as well as of its structural characteristics will of necessity be somewhat sketchy.

The transition from the Commune to the Association differed in some important respects from the process of transition from the Bund to the Commune. The latter has to do primarily with the internal crisis of the kibbutz in the early stages of its growth and the pangs of adaptation to its immediate environment. This process of transition takes place on an individual basis, each kibbutz undergoing it, in a more or less similar manner, as a step in its own development. The transition from Commune to Association is also connected with far-going internal changes in the kibbutz, particularly with its enormous economic and organizational success (7). However, the economic and organizational changes which took place in the kibbutz reflect in themselves a major change in the relationship between the kibbutz and the national society.

The first kibbutzim were established to serve as spearheads of development in a socially and economically largely backward country. The kibbutz considered itself as performing a pioneering role in the development of a new society. With the establishment of the state the pioneering functions of the kibbutz were greatly reduced and confined mostly to the outlying regions of the country. The mature, older Communes lost much of their society-wide importance and prestige; they turned to their own affairs and became primarily preoccupied with their economic advancement. This change, however, coincided with major developments on the national scene. Since the establishment of the state, and especially in the last 10 or 15 years, Israel underwent a rapid process of economic development and modernization, during which the country became industrialized with an increasingly large number of the population becoming urbanized. The mature kibbutzim came to participate actively in this process of development and modernization, and in some areas, such as the industrialization of agriculture, served as its spearhead. The kibbutz itself thus became industrialized and its way of life partly urbanized.[16] The functional interdependence between the kibbutz and the broader society grew considerably and its ideological separation from other sectors of that society decreased in importance. The individual settlements became economically and culturally involved with their regions as well as with national institutions and frameworks to an unprecedented degree.

One can only speculate on what would have happened to the kibbutz if Israeli society reached an advanced stage of development much before the transition from Bund to Commune was completed in most kibbutzim, so that the still highly solidary and ideologically oriented Bunds had to face a modern, complex society. In my opinion, the kibbutz would either crack up under the impact of external forces penetrating most spheres of life of the yet tender collectives; or, alternatively, it would seal itself off hermetically from outward influences and come to resemble other utopian communities in the Western world. The stabilizing effect of the transition to the Commune, made the further transition to the Association feasible. The mature kibbutzim led the way and assisted the younger and less developed ones to come to terms with the new conditions. Our discussion will follow the developments in mature kibbutzim. But we have to keep in mind that almost all contemporary kibbutzim are affected by the external factors which are at work in the transition to the Association and tend to show some traits of the Association.

The Association, unlike the Bund or the Commune, is to a large extent an "urbanized" community, in the cultural sense of the term. Not only is its economy geared to the general forces of the market but its whole way of life is increasingly influenced by standards and values which derive from the broader society.[17] This reorientation can be seen in several spheres of life: members of the large, mature kibbutz tend increasingly to look upon Jewish, middle-class, urban society as a reference group in matters of living standards or even of life styles. As the kibbutz became more affluent it could strive realistically to emulate urban living standards. In the process, the attempt to create a distinctive kibbutz "style of life" fell into oblivion. The same process can be seen even more clearly in the sphere of cultural activity and the arts. During the early stages the kibbutz put great emphasis upon a distinctive kibbutz style in the creative arts and in music, upon the organic interdependence of the artist and his community. In recent years, as artistic creativity in the kibbutz proliferated and the artists became increasingly professionalized, their primary reference group became

[16] The first to draw attention to this point was Weinryb (38).

[17] For a description of a similar process of transition from local to general cultural standards in American society, see M. Stein's reanalysis of the Lynds' studies of Middletown (31, p. 60 ff.).

other artists and artistic movements outside the kibbutz.[18] The direct communication between the artist and his community became of secondary importance, particularly as the artistic taste of the members themselves underwent differentiation. Whereas previously the kibbutz would publicly exhibit the work of a member because the members liked it, now it is exhibited because the artist is esteemed *outside* the kibbutz.

This process can also be followed in the area of occupational and professional activities of the members; as more and more members receive a special professional education, the focus of their interest at work changes subtly: though contribution towards the success of the branch or enterprise remains the primary goal of most members, the evaluation of individual performance by other members is increasingly based on general professional criteria. The reference group of the professionalized worker becomes other professionals outside the kibbutz. This means, in terms of our value analysis, that the performance of roles in various institutional spheres is now made subject to values and norms which often hail from other value-systems and are only remotely   related to the original values of the kibbutz. The values of the broader society, then, penetrated into the kibbutz and introduced a degree of value-pluralism which reflects the pluralism existent in the broader society.

Our argument leads to the conclusion that the social boundaries between the kibbutz, particularly the large mature ones, and the surrounding society have been considerably weakened under the impact of internal as well as external forces.[19] The boundaries have not been abolished completely — the large kibbutz of today continues to be a corporate entity maintained by the contributions of members, but the breadth of common ties has been narrowed considerably and the effort of the members to develop the kibbutz economically or even culturally contributes to the further narrowing of these ties.

The processes of interpenetration and dependence are particularly strong in the economic sphere where they are chiefly a consequence of the enormous increase in the scale of production and differentiation of economic activities which took place in the last few years. The branches of production and services grew considerably and became internally differentiated. A large number of workers with special skills are necessary to maintain these highly developed branches. A process of professionalization set in, accompanied by the provision of specialized training outside the kibbutz in courses provided by the kibbutz movements or in national educational institutions. High premium was set on efficiency, profitability of production, and the ability of the kibbutz

---

18 On this point see the interesting discussion in (2, p. 82).

19 On the concept of social boundaries and the problems of their relative strength or weakness, see (11).

economy to compete on the national and sometimes even international markets. The kibbutz, always innovation-prone, underwent a "scientific revolution." The most advanced agricultural techniques were introduced into the branches and agriculture became gradually industrialized.

The original kibbutz was an agricultural settlement. The modern kibbutz introduced industrial enterprises at the beginning, as a means to process its agricultural products. Later, industry was intended chiefly to absorb the manpower unsuitable for agricultural work, particularly the aging members. Ultimately, industrial development became an economic goal in its own right, until it reached such proportions as to vie with agriculture as the primary source of the income.

Efficiency and profitability now became primary criteria for economic decisions to the detriment of all other considerations, such as the ideological or the traditional agricultural ones, which were previously profoundly influential. Henceforth, the kibbutz will engage in those pursuits which promise the highest rate of return. Such considerations lead it to move even further away from agriculture into secondary and even tertiary processes of production. As industry comes to dominate the economic life of the kibbutz, commercialized personal services such as guest-houses within the community and commercial outlets for products, located in the big cities, gain increasing importance as a major source of income.

As specialization and mechanization of productive processes increased, the individual settlement is often unable to provide the investments and managerial resources for large scale enterprises. The remedy in such cases is often sought in outside economic alliances: large-scale regional cooperation, economic ventures common to a number of kibbutzim or to a kibbutz and a private investor, sub contracting parts of the production process to other enterprises, and so on. The most important form of outside involvement is regional cooperation in which kibbutzim of the same region or several adjoining regions establish a series of regional enterprises. These are predominantly of two types: processing plants for agricultural products and mechanical services to agriculture (9). The boundaries of the individual kibbutz as a productive unit are gradually blurred as outside involvement grows.

There is a growing tendency towards regional and interregional economic integration between kibbutzim. As regional cooperation in the economic sphere advances, regional frameworks in other spheres have been established. Of particular importance are regional frameworks of adult education, some of which have recently become regional colleges. The forces which led to such development were similar to those which started economic regional cooperation in the first place: the demand for an increasingly higher level of education which the individual kibbutz could not provide. These developments culminated in the proposal to establish a "kibbutz-university" on the national scale, which is at present being seriously considered.

The rising level of professionalism and the general education of members of the Association in conjunction with greater personal freedom of occupational choice leads to another phenomenon: the highly skilled professional who lives on the kibbutz but works in the city as a university teacher, high-level governmental employee, or is independently employed (for example, freelance graphic designer). Though few people as yet engage in the free trades, their appearance is an important indication of the economic "opening up" of the Association.

The growth and increasing complexity of the economy, accompanied by similar but not quite as far-reaching changes in other areas of kibbutz life, has led to considerable changes in the organizational structure of the kibbutz.

The individual kibbutz more and more resembles a corporation with the central functionaries serving as executives for a series of semi-independent but coordinated enterprises within and outside the kibbutz. The decision-making process has been rationalized: basic decisions on investments, planning, and coordination are preserved for the central decision-making bodies of the kibbutz. The various branches and industrial enterprises achieved a considerable degree of autonomy within the limits of basic decisions. Changes are also taking place in the branches themselves: the branch manager and most of the members who work steadily in the branch are now mostly professionals, semiprofessionals or skilled workers. Many of the unskilled jobs are relegated to hired workers or other workers who are not full members of the community. In many cases, mechanization or automation does away with many or all unskilled functions. The highly specialized nature of most economic or organizational decisions prevents the rank and file members from participating meaningfully in the decision-making processes outside their sphere of competence. Several kibbutzim of the Association type established a new political institution: an intermediate public body between the secretariat or other committees and the general assembly, called a "council." Many members of the council are current or ex-functionaries of communal institutions and understand the problems and the language of management. The general assembly is, in such kibbutzim, relegated to the ratification of basic decisions and meets relatively infrequently. In order to close or narrow the communication gap with the assembly, the Association introduces modern techniques of mass-communication for the explanation of complex matters in relatively simple language. Though this enables the rank and file to gain a degree of participation in important decisions, the formation of their opinion becomes dependent upon the way information is presented to them, and hence is subject to manipulation. Moreover, the general tendency of the rank and file is to move away from economic and organizational matters and concern itself mainly with social and personal matters.

Effective power over decisions lies more and more with the trained manager and professional. Even though the functionaries continue to be elected by the general assembly, the assembly's choice becomes narrowed by educational requirements. Only those with prior training and experiences are in fact eligible for the top jobs. The principle of rotation is still adhered to, but the circle of potential top functionaries becomes fairly limited.

A large part of the membership continue even in the Association to perform important and meaningful economic tasks as managers, professionals, or skilled workers. However, in spite of increasing mechanization and automation, there remains a group of members who perform only routine, uninteresting tasks. They often find compensation in increased leisure time activities, which include adult education programs and many varieties of creative activities such as acting, painting, dancing, participation in home study groups and so on. The over all tendency in the Association is, hence, towards increased differentiation of interests and activities, with some of the members being chiefly work-oriented and others leisure-oriented. Still, not all the members are deeply involved with either work or some creative leisure activity — there is a growing margin of passive and alienated members.

The increasing demographic complexity and social heterogeneity in the Association leads to a growing differentiation of needs and tastes; coupled with the growing influence of the Association, this differentiation leads to important changes in the pattern of consumption.

Consumption remains one of the chief areas of concern of the members of the Association, but its focus changes. Previously the controversy focused on items of daily material consumption, such as clothing and furnishings. With prosperity, the supply of such items became ever more plentiful and variety increased. Simultaneously, however, tastes and levels of aspiration changed. The member of the Association demanded increased freedom of choice, not only *within* each of the principal areas of personal consumption (safeguarded, for example, by the personal budget arrangements, which appropriated limited sums of money for clothing, shoes, books, etc.), but also in the allocation of his appropriations *between* these areas. Several large kibbutzim were therefore forced to adopt the "comprehensive budget," which consists of an allocation of a lump sum of money to members without limitation as to the areas in which it might be used. Though such sums are still relatively small, and though the amount allocated is not dependent upon the tasks performed by the member in the kibbutz, such arrangements come very close to the payment of an actual yearly salary to the members. They may, indeed, use the resources allocated to them to their best advantage, but a large part of the sphere of personal consumption thereby becomes almost completely de-institutionalized, the collective virtually losing control over its members.

The personal budget, even the comprehensive one, still covers only a small part of the members' total consumption. Not only are food and all personal services within the kibbutz excluded from the budget, but so are living facilities, education outside the kibbutz and foreign travel. As goods of personal consumption become abundant, the focus of interest in the sphere of consumption shifts to these other areas. Members demand improved personal services within the community. They press for larger dwelling units with more rooms and better amenities. The distribution of such amenities is usually well regulated in the mature kibbutz. The case of foreign travel and higher education is different. Only a small percentage of members can as yet be sent to travel abroad. Though some order of priority has usually been established, the matter still causes considerable tension and controversy, since many of the younger members resent having to wait a long time for their turn to travel. The demand for higher education grew enormously in recent years. This demand points to an increasingly individualistic tendency in the modern kibbutz. Second-generation members, in particular, tend to pursue their personal interests in higher studies and are often not inclined to adapt their studies to the needs of their community. Since the kibbutz did not develop any clear guidelines to regulate the provision of higher education outside the kibbutz, this matter is also the subject of considerable controversy and dissatisfaction. The inability of young people to get the kind of education they aspire to is probably the chief major factor in the decision of those who leave the kibbutz.

The processes of social and economic changes heretofore described have important repercussions upon the structure of social ties in the Association. Though these repercussions have not been systematically studied, it appears that there are two interrelated tendencies involved: the loosening up of the federated structure which ordinarily preceded the Association, and the emergence of a complex, shifting, pluralistic or even individualistic pattern of social relations, on the one hand; and the increasing social involvement of the members outside their proper settlement, on the other.

The criteria of origin, age and seniority which provided the basis for the differentiation of subgroups within the first generation in the Federated Commune, lose much of their importance as most of first generation members become older and the kibbutz grows numerically. Even the generational criterion becomes less cutting: whereas earlier the second generation tended to be a homogeneous, cohesive subgroup, age groups now form within the second generation. The arrival of the third generation provides the kibbutz with a continuous, three-generational structure in which all ages are represented. This smoothes the edges of generational and age differentials as a basis for social differentiation.

On the other hand, new criteria for the formation of groups, in accordance with the professional orientation or the personal interests of members, arise: these "functional" groups cut across the old subgroup boundaries within the kibbutz. However, these new group formations seem to be of a less permanent, less cohesive, as well as less comprehensive character than the subgroups which preceded them. They are mostly restricted to a certain sphere of interest or type of activity. It seems that the characteristic patterns of social relations in the Association are loose networks, rather than distinct, cohesive groups. The element of individual choice of personal relations grows in importance. Concomitantly, the member is less completely integrated into the social setup of the Association than he was in the Commune.

The Federated Commune, not unlike the Bund, is a closed society: only few of the significant social ties of the members stretch beyond the confines of their community. Such ties are mostly of a political nature: relations with the kibbutz federation, the political party with which the federation is associated, or with the youth movement of the federation in the cities. The Association, however, opens up socially. Professional or cultural interest groups are formed on the regional level. Members participate in professional, cultural or scientific activities and associations on the regional level. Here, they can find people who speak their language and share their interests, which are often too specialized to find much response within the confines of their own relatively small community. Since they tend to choose their friends and acquaintances in accordance with their tastes, members may entertain close social ties with people living in cities and other localities who are not necessarily close to the kibbutz and its ideology. As the initial rejection of relatives outside the kibbutz gradually dies out and new ties of kinship between the kibbutz and the outside society are formed through intermarriages, relations with kin become an important focus of outside attachments (39, p. 281). As in any other highly differentiated and highly specialized society, the social allegiances to the members of the Association tend to change from local to functional ones: many associate less with members of their own community and more with people with whom they have common interests and inclinations, wherever these may live. Such a process of realignment of social ties is well known from modern urban societies. The fact that we find the same process in the contemporary kibbutz attests to the extent to which the Association is diametrically opposed to the Bund, which emphasized undifferentiated internal solidarity and the rejection of the surrounding society.[20]

Owing to the complexity of the institutional structure of the Associa-

---

[20] For the connection between internal differentiation and weakening of boundaries of social systems, see (11, p. 111).

tion as well as to the loosening of the network of social ties between the members, integration ceases to rest primarily on the network of social relations. The focus of integration, instead, moves to the formal institutional structure. The chief mechanism through which a member becomes attached to his community now becomes the set of formally defined rights and obligations of membership, roles and relationships. The member is expected to fulfill his duty toward the community. In exchange, he and his offspring receive a broad array of communal services. Still, the distribution of rewards, particularly of material ones, remains even in the Association dissociated from the individuals' contribution to the community. There are still no formal sanctions which could be applied in case a member does not comply with the rules. Social control is, then, still predominantly informal, though it is guided by the formal rules of the community, fed by the media of mass-communication emanating from the formal institutions and often directed by public functionaries.

Life in the Association lacks many of the original attractions of kibbutz life, such as the intensive communal experience of the Bund or the cosy togetherness of the Commune. But as life in the kibbutz becomes less attractive socially, it provides more opportunities for personal development and self-fulfilment than ever before, both in the professional sphere and in the sphere of leisure activities. Though the member does not receive any personal material rewards for his work, he still contributes to the general affluence and thus indirectly enjoys the fruits of his efforts. Indeed, the level of consumption and services in the Association quickly approximates, and sometimes even surpasses, those enjoyed by the urban middle class. The member of the Association, hence, sacrifices much less than before in terms of personal comfort and opportunities, and many of the factors which would previously attract him to the city lose some of their appeal. The Association can provide most of the advantages of urban living, while sparing the member many of its disadvantages. Under these conditions the kibbutz becomes increasingly an alternative form of life in a modern and industrialized society.

Though the modern Association in general functions adequately, its emerging institutional structure finds it hard to resolve some of the problems called forth by its very size and complexity. The most important problem is the growing marginality of part of the membership: as the processes of specialization and increasing complexity proceed, the differences between members who participate actively in the economic, organizational, political, social and cultural life of the community and those who do not become even more pronounced. Thus, almost no one can any longer participate in *all* spheres and many do participate in *some*, to the neglect of others. But a group of members gradually emerges who participate in almost no sphere of activity. The growing individualization of the Association and concomitant lack of concern with participation enables these members to live on the kibbutz without really constituting an integral part of the community. Closely connected with this problem is that of anomie. We have already mentioned the decline of informal social control in the loosely-knit Association. However, the increased formalization of social control is unable to prevent really serious deviation, since the kibbutz, as a voluntary community, does not possess a set of legitimate informal sanctions to be applied to those cases in which informal controls prove ineffective. Nor is there a system of differentiated rewards which would compensate members for extra efforts or for extra time spent for the common cause. Hence, the performance of functions depends, even in the Association, on the personal motivation of members. Important changes in motivation have taken place, and the devotion to a common cause has largely receded into the background and been substituted by the aspiration to achieve individual professional success and to derive a broad spectrum of intrinsic job-satisfactions provided by interesting and creative tasks in production. Though such motivations are supported by the institutional system and though members are encouraged to strive for professional achievement, on which their standing in the community largely depends, there still exists no means to *force* them to succeed. Hence, if a member is not positively motivated to work, he can easily carve out a corner for himself in the complex structure of the large Association where he can subsist indefinitely without contributing any real efforts to the common cause. Conversely, those members who are most active and contribute most to the common good are also often able to arrange special rewards for themselves such as increased personal use of common facilities (for example, cars) which are, strictly speaking, illegitimate by kibbutz standards.

Finally, and again closely related to the above points, the Association obviously runs the danger of losing its ideological compass. Value-change was a characteristic of the kibbutz throughout its history. But the problem now is that the members of the Association might gradually abandon even the basic ideological assumption of the kibbutz movement, which up till now provided a common bond among them, as well as a most important dividing line between them and the rest of Israeli society. The members might then turn each to his private conception of life and society, and thereby blur or even abolish one of the last boundaries which separate the kibbutz as a corporate entity from its surroundings. Such a state of things has not yet developed, but the probability of such a development increases progressively.

Our analysis so far points to a basic dilemma of the contemporary kibbutz, which can be felt to various extents in every kibbutz settlement but is most prominent in the large Association: the very economic and organizational success of the kibbutz led to a thorough-going transformation of its social structure, of its way of life, and of the relationships between members. As an ongoing enterprise, the modern kibbutz is a success. But it is not the realization of the original utopia. Moreover, it is not at all clear whether the basic institutional arrangements of the kibbutz are capable to contain the tendency of continuous growth and expansion. We have seen some indications of emergent problems and strains which the Association finds extremely hard to resolve.

Most members of the generation of founders accept this transition to the Association as perhaps unfortunate but necessary; the alternative would be an ossified, underdeveloped, small community, out of touch with modern reality, resembling some of the religious utopian communities of the Western world. Members of the kibbutz-born second generation often find themselves in a dilemma in this respect. They were brought up on the utopian ideals of the early days. But the only kibbutz they really know is often the modern Association. Most react to the dilemma by a selective interpretation of the basic precepts of kibbutz life.[21] But there are variations. On one extreme are those who tend towards the introduction of additional changes and innovations into the kibbutz, which would make it resemble even further the modern, urban society.[22] On the other extreme are those second generation members who, though they were raised on the modern, large and complex kibbutz, still hanker after the days of its inception. They revolt against the encroaching urbanization and the increasing complexity and anonymity of the contemporary kibbutz. These youths react to the modern kibbutz in two diametrically opposed ways: for some, the kibbutz has already lost its distinctive value and so they quit and move to the cities, mostly in search of higher education. Others seek to experience anew the spirit of excitement of pioneering, like that of the early days. In the late fifties and early sixties, when no new kibbutzim were established, some of these quit the kibbutz, and settled in moshavim or new towns which were being established in the newly developing regions of the country. Several new moshavim were based on nuclei of second-generation youths from the kibbutz. Such youths were also prominent in the nucleus of first settlers in Arad, a new town in the Judean Desert. Other second-generation members found the excitement of a fresh start when they were sent by their federation to help out small, new kibbutzim, which suffered from serious social and economic problems and tended to become Residual Communes. However, only few second-generation members stayed on beyond the one-year period of service to the Federation (35). The members of the parent settlement

---

[21] For a fuller discussion of the dilemmas which the second generation faces see (10).

[22] For example, at a recent convention of second-generation members of one of the movements it was proposed to remunerate the principal economic functionaries for their work, thereby abolishing the principle of separation between work and consumption; the proposal was, however, rejected.

are usually opposed to the idea that second-generation members settle in the new kibbutzim or even establish kibbutzim of their own. They see the chief task of the new generation to continue the life work of their parents in the kibbutzim in which they were born.

Indeed, until recently no new kibbutzim had been established by second-generation members, though the idea was often discussed and had been attractive to many of them. Only in the last few years have a few such kibbutzim emerged. After the Six Day War, particularly, second-generation youths participated in the establishment of new kibbutzim in the occupied areas, such as the Golan Heights, for instance. The new kibbutz settlements are located in underdeveloped and outlying areas, and their atmosphere resembles to an extent that of the early kibbutz. This development could thus be considered as a re-emergence of the Bund, but this did not grow out, as the original Bund had, as a revolt against the bourgeois society of the Diaspora, but as a reaction to the way of life in the large and complex, urbanized contemporary kibbutz. It seems then, that with this development the structural transformation of the kibbutz completed a full cycle: it started with the Bund, moved to the Commune and later to the Association; while lately a few new Bunds are established by or through the active participation of second-generation members. One should not, however, expect that the return to the Bund among second-generation youths will take major proportions in the near future. It will stay confined to a select few, in the same way in which the pioneering Zionism of the generation of founders of the kibbutz movement embraced only a small fraction of the Jewish society in the Diaspora. The very re-emergence of the Bund among the second generation, however, attests both to the underlying dilemma as well as to the continuing vitality of the kibbutz movement.

## Prospects for the Future

In this paper I used a historical-typological approach in order to trace the major social transformation of the kibbutz and to analyze the dynamic forces, both internal and external to the kibbutz movement, which brought about these transformations. The analysis enables us now to identify the sources of the spiritual crisis experienced by the contemporary kibbutz, and exemplified most clearly by the Association type. We find that the kibbutz has become more vigorous than ever before through the processes of industrialization, modernization, and urbanization. Nowadays, it forms an integral and important sector of Israeli society. However, these developments also changed profoundly the nature of the institutional arrangements and social relations in the kibbutz and thus put into question its ability to preserve its unique social characteristics. The large and mature kibbutz may easily become just another form of modern urban

life, distinguished from other such forms merely by some peculiar arrangements and institutions, but losing most of its historically distinguishing
characteristics as a revolutionary communal and corporate entity. The
crisis of the contemporary kibbutz does not result from weakness or
disorganization, as did the crisis which characterizes the Transitional
Bund. Rather, it is a crisis called forth by material success which has
not been paralleled by the establishment and internalization of new
spiritual goals. The crisis in the kibbutz is in this respect strikingly similar
to the general crisis of contemporary Western society. The question,
then is: What are the alternatives for the future of the kibbutz? More
specifically, are there any alternatives for the kibbutz which do not
exist for the rest of modern society?

In the past, questions of this sort were often discussed in terms of the
"viability" of the kibbutz.[23]   Such an indiscriminate approach to the
problem is obviously beside the point. In the course of our discussion we
have dwelt upon some forms of kibbutz life, like the "Residual Commune," which suffer from serious functional problems and, if these are
not rectified, are probably doomed to extinction. These, however, are
extreme and exceptional cases. There is no question whatever that in
the future the viability and growth of the kibbutz is secure. The loss of
distinctiveness and uniqueness in the way of life is sufficiently com-
pensated for by material well-being, professional opportunities and possibilities for self-fulfillment. Granting, then, that the kibbutz will continue
to exist, the question is often asked whether it will preserve its "essential"
characteristics. The answer to this question depends upon one's conception of what these "essential" characteristics actually are. One has to
remember that the kibbutz is not a religious movement and did not
intend to realize on earth a "sacred" community, reflecting a transcendental order of things. Though the values of the early kibbutz had a
"sacred" quality, they were essentially secular values. Hence, neither the
values nor the arrangements based on them are immutable. There exist
no fixed, accepted criteria by which to judge the success or failure of the
kibbutz in a transcendental sense. Whatever the conception of the
kibbutz maintained by the "Founding Fathers" might have been, it is
perfectly legitimate, within the framework of a secular conception of
values, for members of successive generations to alter its values, goals
and institutional arrangements. The only legitimate question about the
future of the kibbutz, then, is the one relating to the kinds of alternatives which one could conceive of for its future development and the
probabilities attached to each of them.

The concrete problem at hand is whether the transition to the Association will continue in the future or whether a reaction against this devel-

---

[28] See, e.g., the discussion between S. Diamond (13) and B. Halpern (16) on this
point.

opment will set in and curb or reverse it. The forces which push towards the Association are unquestionably very strong and impinge upon the kibbutz movement as such, and not only upon the large and mature kibbutzim, though in the latter these forces are particularly strongly felt. Nevertheless, several forces are already at work in the kibbutz movement which act to attenuate the present trend, though it is doubtful whether they will be strong enough to reverse it.

First, the present trend towards increasing social differentiation and interpenetration with the surrounding society, two of the chief characteristics of the Association, could be attenuated in the future. As the kibbutz depends less and less on the influx of new members from the outside and grows more and more through natural increase, the kibbutz-born members are becoming the predominant, and might even later become the only, group of origin in the community. This is an element of homogeneity which endows the kibbutz with bonds of common descent and separates it from the surrounding society. As such, this demographic trend works against the "Eclipse of Community" tendency, characteristic of the transition to the Association.[24] Still, we have to keep in mind that the kibbutz participates increasingly in the marrage market of the broader society and hence, many of the spouses of second-generation members of any kibbutz will not be kibbutz-born.

Secondly, the kibbutz is characterized by a considerable degree of self-consciousness and self-criticism and by an uncanny ability to adapt its social arrangements to changing circumstances, so as to keep them in tune with those values of the basic ideology which are still meaningful to its members. The young second-generation members who long for the experience of the original Bund, are by no means the only ones who dislike the atmosphere created by the transition to the Association. Many thoughtful old-timers and many leaders of the movement are aware of the fact that the very material success of the kibbutz might undermine the realization of some of their most cherished values. Though the problem is the subject of frequent discussions and much controversy, the effective measures taken to countervail the trend towards individualization and the weakening of social ties are as yet few. Among the most effective is the establishment of "Members' Social Centers" (Mo'adon Le'chaverim) as a means to provide a novel and attractive focus of social interaction. Another is the establishment of community radio stations, which have been attempted in at least one of the largest kibbutzim. Other measures were taken on the regional or even national level: as mentioned, the kibbutzim are in the process of establishing a series of regional colleges and it has also been proposed to establish a nationwide "University of the Kibbutz." These institutions enable members to receive highly specialized professional training as well as

---

[24] I am indebted to Mr. Y. Shatil on this point.

general education of a high quality within frameworks controlled by the kibbutz movement. Such institutions serve, then, to counter the tendency towards increased interpenetration with the general society. The educational programs of such institutions also take into account the special needs and problems of the kibbutz and thereby serve to ameliorate the impact of professionalization and diversification of interests on community life.

Another series of measures intends to smooth out the raw edges left by the tendencies towards increased specialization and formalization, particularly in the spheres of work and of public activities. The growing emphasis upon the human relations approach, particularly in industry, and the constant effort to improve communication between the institutions and the rank and file members attest to efforts to overcome some of the obstacles to good relations and to full participation of members in increasingly more complex processes. In this connection, the rising interest in organization and development and similar techniques should be noted. Some of these countervailing mechanisms, however, are not without dangers of their own: after all, "social engineering" of various kinds has been applied in the modern Association-like society, to manipulate people as well as to counter tendencies to passivity, social atomism and alienation. There is no guarantee that they will not be used in this way in the kibbutz as well, though we have to keep in mind that there is no fundamental opposition of interests between the leadership and the general membership of the kibbutz and that leaders are still rotated at a relatively high, though declining, rate (8).

Whatever the usefulness of these various measures discussed earlier, they are, to my mind, mainly palliatives which do not cut to the heart of the matter. If the kibbutz is really set to achieve a reversal of present trends, it will probably have to decide in the future on some very radical changes in the allocation of its resources, both material and human. In the past, the necessity to achieve economic consolidation and prosperity led the kibbutz to give primary emphasis to the instrumental sphere. The large and mature kibbutzim have already achieved considerable affluence. Therefore, some of the settlements at least could allow themselves even to forego a degree of technological or economic advance in order to realize more fully some social and humanistic values. A trend in this direction can already be discerned among some of the leaders. If it prevails, an interesting change of emphasis might occur in the kibbutz. If the fifties were an epoch of rapid technological change and the sixties an epoch of economic and organizational consolidation, the seventies might become an epoch of social renaissance of kibbutz-life. Almost paradoxically, such a development would seem to coincide with a parallel trend in modern, post-industrial society — a trend which often points to the kibbutz as to a model of the "good life."

# BIBLIOGRAPHY

1. Becker, H. "Sacred and Secular Societies: Retrospect and Prospect," in: H. Becker (ed.) *Through Values to Social Science*, pp. 248–280. Durham, N.C.: Duke University Press, 1950.

2. *Bein Tze'irim (Among the Young)* (in Hebrew) Tel Aviv: Am Oved, 1969.

3. Buber, M. "Epilogue — An Experiment that Did Not Fail," in M. Buber, *Paths In Utopia*. Pp. 139–149. Boston: Beacon Press, 1950.

4. Cohen, E. "Patterns of Institutionalization in the Sphere of Work in the Kibbutz." *Niv Hakvutsa*, 7, (3), 1958, pp. 519–530 (in Hebrew).

5. Cohen, E. "Changes in the Social Structure of the Sphere of Work in the Kibbutz." *Riv'on Lekalkala (The Economic Quarterly)*, 10, 1963 (in Hebrew).

6. Cohen, E. *Bibliography of the Kibbutz*, Tel Aviv: Giv'at Haviva, 1964.

7. Cohen, E. "Progress and Communality: Value Dilemmas in the Collective Movement." *International Review of Community Development*, No. 15–16, 1966, pp. 3–18.

8. Cohen, E. and E. Leshem. "Public Participation in Collective Settlements," *International Review of Community Development*, No. 19/20, 1968, pp. 251–270.

9. Cohen, E., and E. Leshem. *Survey of Regional Cooperation in Three Regions of Collective Settlements.* Publications on Problems of Regional Development, No. 2, Rehovot: Settlement Study Center, 1969.

10. Cohen, E. and M. Rosner. "Relations Between Generations in the Israeli Kibbutz." *Journal of Contemporary History*, 5(1), 1970, pp. 73–86.

11. Cohen, Y. A. "Social Boundary Systems." *Current Anthropology* 10 (1) 1969, pp. 103–126.

12. Diamond, S. "Kibbutz and Shtetl: The History of an Idea." *Social Problems* 5(2), 1957, pp. 71–99.

13. Diamond, S. "The Kibbutz: Utopia in Crisis." *Dissent*, 4, 1957, pp. 132–140.

14. Durkheim, E. *Suicide.* Glencoe, Illinois: Free Press, 1951.

15. Etzioni, A. "Solidaric Work Groups in Collective Settlements." *Human Organization*, 16(3), 1957, pp. 2–7.

16. Halpern, B. "Comments on Science and Socialism." *Dissent*, 4, 1957, pp. 140–146.

17. Holzner, B. "The Concept of 'Integration' in Sociological Theory." *The Sociological Quarterly*, 8(1), 1967, pp. 51–62.

18. Horigan, F. D. *The Israeli Kibbutz.* Psychiatric Abstract Series No. 9, National Institute of Health, Public Health Service, U.S. Dept. of Health, Education and Welfare, 1962. (mimeo.)

19. Lavi, Ch. "Hakvutza Hagdolah" (The Large Kvutzah) in Sh. Gadon (ed.) *Netivei Hakvutza VeHakibbutz* (The Path of the Kvutzah and the Kibbutz), Am Oved, Tel Aviv, 1958, pp. 351–356 (in Hebrew).

20. Meier-Cronemeyer, H. "Die Politik der Unpolitischen," *Koelner Zeitschrift fuer Soziologie und Sozial-Psychologie*, 7, 1965, pp. 833–854.

21. Meier-Cronemeyer, H. "Juedische Jugendbewegung." *Germania Judaica* 8, 1969.

22. Parsons, T., et al. (eds.). *Theories of Society*. New York: Free Press, 1961.

23. Redfield, R. *The Folk Culture of Yucatan.* Chicago, Illinois: University of Chicago Press, 1941.

24. Reissman, L. *The Urban Process*. New York: Free Press, 1964.

25. *Research Report,* No. 3, 1959-1963, Dept. of Sociology, Hebrew University, Jerusalem, 1964.

26. Rosenfeld, E. "Social Stratification in a Classless Society," *American Sociological Review*, 16, 1951, pp. 766–774.

27. Rosenfeld, E. "Institutional Change in the Kibbutz," *Social Problems*, 5(2), 1957, pp. 118–136.

28. Schmalenbach, H. "Die soziologische Kategorie des Bundes," *Die Dioskuren*, 1, 1922.

29. Shils, E. "Primordial, Personal, Sacred and Civic Ties," *British Journal of Sociology*, 8, 1957.

30. Shur, S. H. *Kibbutz Bibliography* . The Van Leer Foundation, Jerusalem, Dept. for Higher Education, Kibbutz Artzi, Tel Aviv, and Social Research Center on the Kibbutz, Giv'at Haviva, 1971.

31. Stein, M. *The Eclipse of Community*. New York: Harper and Row, 1960.

32. Talmon-Garber, Y. *Family and Community in the Kibbutz*. Cambridge, Mass.: Harvard University Press, 1972.

33. Talmon-Garber, Y. "Social Structure and Family Size," *Human Relations*, 12(2), 1959, pp. 121–145.

34. Talmon-Garber, Y. "The Family in a Revolutionary Movement: The Case of the Kibbutz in Israel," in: M. Nimkoff (ed.); *Comparative Family Systems*, pp. 259–286. Boston: Houghton Mifflin and Co., 1965.

35. Talmon-Garber, Y., and E. Cohen. "Collective Settlements in the Negev," in Y. Ben David (ed.): *Agricultural Planning and Village Community in Israel*, UNESCO, Paris, 1964, pp. 69–82.

36. Toennies, F. *Gemeinschaft und Gesellschaft*. 8th Ed., Leipzig: 1935.

37. Troeltsch, E. *The Social Teachings of the Christian Churches*. New York: Harper and Row, 1960.

38. Weinryb, B. D. "The Impact of Urbanization in Israel," *Middle East Journal*, 11(1), 1957, pp. 23–36.

39. Weintraub, B., M. Lissak, and Y. Azmon. *Moshava, Kibbutz and Moshav*. Ithaca, N.Y.: Cornell University Press, 1960.

# 27

*Ronald Cohen*

# Conflict and Change in a

# Northern Nigerian Emirate[1]

## I

Up until recently much of the descriptive work of the ethnographer, especially in dealing with African societies, has been carried out by placing a great deal of reliance on the assumption, often implicit, that action follows from institutionalized patterns. Because many of the institutions in the African societies are unfamiliar and exotic, it has always been a primary responsibility of the anthropologist to discover what these are, and to describe them in a systematic fashion. This is often an arduous task which requires detailed observation and long, hard hours of analysis. By the time it is completed, however, the anthropologist is often oriented to the social behavior he has observed in terms of the institutions he has outlined.

Several factors have conspired to turn the attention of anthropologists in other directions. Studies of African peoples are now much more common, and the overall structural types of the segmentary and non-segmentary societies are widely understood. This has allowed us to concentrate more attention on the details of social life within these now familiar types of social structures. Furthermore, the rapid social change taking

[1] Revised version of a paper entitled, "The Analysis of Conflict in Hierarchical Systems," in *Anthropologica* n.s., 4, 1, 1962, pp. 87–120; based upon a paper presented at the Annual Meeting of the Canadian Political Science Association, Kingston, Ontario, June 1960.

place in Africa is pointing our attention more towards the behavior of persons in new situations, rather than at the varieties and interrelations of traditional institutions. Finally, at the theoretical level, a number of workers in both anthropology and sociology have been discussing the limitations of the social system model in which man lives in a group with a tradition such that the rules are functional and the entire system is a nicely balanced, self-supporting, integrated whole.[2] Social life in this model revolves around the internalizing of norms so that the individual can take his place in the system and play out the part tradition has ordained for him. Activity not functionally directed is labeled deviant, dysfunctional, or disequilibrating, and often put forward or selected as a major cause of social change. However, as Buckley (2) has pointed out, this carries with it a danger that we may negatively evaluate change, since the model stresses stability and persistence in its analytic perspective. Because change is separated from the integrated model as a kind of irritant which forces the system to adjust, it is difficult to use it in a rapidly altering situation where change is a primary characteristic of the social situation under observation. What is needed then is a theoretical perspective which attempts to order the changing situation *while it is changing.*

To begin such an approach, it is necessary to assume that the institutionalized social structure is only one among many facets of social reality which determines the course of social life.[3] This leads us to a more complex, but perhaps more realistic, view of social process, in which man is seen as an actor who acts and reacts in relation to a multitude of pressures and stimuli. These are internal and external to himself in origin; traditional and novel in time depth; interpersonal, supernatural, material in substance. In this chapter we shall deal with only one facet of these stimuli — that of the exigencies or pressures, and the reaction to these, which result from a hierarchical political organization.

The situation chosen is one in which there are conflicts among the standards governing behavior. This forces us to pay attention to the adjustive responses of the actors instead of looking out for the "functional" or "integrative" qualities of the cultural norms which pertain to behavior. If an actor in a given context is institutionally enjoined to behave in a certain way, and not to behave in this manner — all at the same time — then a description and analysis of the rules governing behavior cannot give us any adequate predictive conclusions about the resultant action. What is obviously necessary is an analysis of the resultant behavior itself.

The analysis to follow has been organized with the aid of a theoreti-

[2] See for example, Dahrendorf (5), Epstein (6), and Leach (10).

[3] Compare this with Radcliffe-Brown's assumption that "the social life of the community is here defined as the functioning of the social structure" (14, p. 180). A more extreme example of this approach can be seen in Levi-Strauss' statement that social anthropology consists "exclusively of the study of rules" (11, p. 538).

cal schema first put forward by Frank (8) as a method for the description and analysis of conflicting standards. He developed the theory as a result of his interest in the Russian industrial system, but suggests that it is more widely applicable. The following discussion therefore has a two-fold purpose: first, to present material on the Kanuri political system using a new approach, and second, to test the applicability of Frank's theory to an entirely different cultural context.

## The Theory

Frank (8) feels that if three conditions are present in a social situation, it is possible to predict a series of behaviors which are of necessity associated with them. These conditions are (1) conflicting standards, (2) ambiguous goals, and (3) selective enforcement.

Conflicting standards are rules or prescriptions for conduct which are enforceable through formal or informal sanctions. Their distinctive feature is that they pertain to rules or prescriptions which cannot be satisfied simultaneously, since compliance with one involves the failure to meet another equally enforceable standard.

Goal ambiguity refers to the state of affairs in which it is difficult for members in the system, or indeed for any observer viewing the system in part or as a whole, to ascertain clearly the desired ends towards which everyone should be striving. Thus the social structure cannot in any empirical sense be made to resemble a simple means-ends scheme.

Selective enforcement is the process by which the model is put into operation. It postulates a differential enforcement over time of the total gamut of enforceable standards so that not all standards must be conformed with to the same extent.

Frank puts it this way:

Multiple and at least in part conflicting standards are set by superiors for subordinates. More than one hierarchical channel of communication is maintained. Conflict may arise among standards set within each hierarchy as well as among those set by different hierarchies. Subordinates are free to decide which of the conflicting standards to meet, if any. However, subordinates are responsible to superiors for their performance with respect to all standards; and subordinates may be held accountable for failure to meet any standard. The relative importance of standards is neither well, nor completely defined, nor is it entirely undefined. The priority among standards is ambiguous. Subordinates make their assessment of priority to guide their decision-making and task performance. Each subordinate appeals to those standards which are most in accord with his incentives and the circumstances of the moment and to those which are most likely to be invoked by superiors in evaluating his performance. Superiors in turn make their assessment of priority to guide their necessarily selective evaluation of subordinates' performance and enforcement of standards. The entire process is continuous: superiors modify the set of standards to comply with their changing objectives; subordinates adapt their decisions to changing standards and to changing circumstances; superiors enforce standards in accordance with changing priority (8, p. 11).

The author of the theory goes on to suggest that if the above conditions are present, then the following behavior can be observed:

A. Member Behavior

The more the system relies on conflicting standards organization, the more the members will:

1) Fail to meet all standards and exhibit differences in selection of the standards they do meet.

2) Change the selection, over time, of the standards they do meet.

3) Simulate or feign meeting of standards.

4) Provide themselves with safety factors for contingencies.

5) Have recourse to (and become) intermediary dealers in information, influence, and any other organizational resource which enhances a particular member's ability to meet standards by eliminating some of the conflict (for him) among standards.

B. System Organization

The obstacle to formal rationality entailed by conflicting standards suggests that:[4]

6) The more conflicting standards there are the more the system will be oriented toward substantive rationality.

The system will also exhibit:

7) Changing standards for members.

8) Ready adaptation to changes of environment by system members at the system-environment boundary.

9) Widespread member initiative as a possibility (but not a necessity). Where this is not expressed in a standard, Frank suggests that a "let sleeping dogs lie" policy can be expected.

10) Widespread information about standards and system goals among members.

11) Strong incentive to, and evidence of, member use of information and attempted compliance with standards.

[4] Frank uses the Weberian terms *formal rationality* and *substantive rationality* to mean roughly what anthropologists imply by the terms *ideal* and *real*, respectively. For our purposes here, formal rationality refers to a means-end schema in which stipulated ends are achieved through a set of stipulated means and these rules are the only ones used by actors to achieve their agreed-upon ends. Substantive rationality refers, here, to a system in which actors are oriented to situations rather than to ends or means. They achieve ends through their understanding and reaction to a situation, and whether or not this situation has within it formally recognized and culturally acceptable means is immaterial, or at least less important than the fact that the actor is reacting to his perception of the situation and its constituent social, cultural, and psychological ingredients. In other words, a shift from formal to substantive rationality is a shift from an emphasis on rules to one in which there is an emphasis on the social situation itself.

## C. System Change

The flexibility of a conflicting standards system, particularly changing standards and initiative (Hypotheses 7 and 9, respectively), should:

12) Permit substantial change or variability within the given systematic structure.

13) Render a conflicting standards system continuously receptive and responsive to external pressure for systemic change; and, *ceteris paribus*, to change by small steps, rather than (pressure having built up on the outside and finally breaking through) by a few big steps or by evolution rather than revolution.

The possibility of institutionalizing initiative (Hypothesis 9):

14) May result in internally (as well as externally) generated system change.[5]


## II

Turning now from theory to data, it is necessary first to indicate the context in which the conflict takes place. It is then established that the three premises of the theoretical model are present in this context. Finally data are presented to illustrate the presence or absence of the theoretically predicted behavior said to be associated with the premises.


### The Context[6]

The Kanuri of Bornu province of northeastern Nigeria have been organized as a Muslim emirate in the Chad basin for many centuries. Their language classification by Greenberg (9), early Arabic sources, and the scattered work of a few interested scholars, supports the notion of their continuity in the region, with possible origins somewhere to the northeast of their present habitat. The pre-colonial emirate kept up continual trade and cultural contacts with the Maghreb during its long history as an organized state.

The Kanuri number about one and one-half million with a population density of 50 to 60 per square mile. There is no pressure on farmland, which can be extended simply by clearing new bush areas farther away from the population settlements. The majority of the people are farmers who carry on three analytically separable economic activities. These consist of (1) farming (primarily millet and guinea corn, supplemented

---

[5] These hypotheses have been taken, for the most part, verbatim from Frank (8, p. 13).

[6] The field data were collected in Bornu Province, Nigeria, between January 1956, and August 1957, with the financial assistance of the Ford Foundation Area Training Fellowship Program. The author would like to express his thanks to Professor C. W. M. Hart, under whose guidance field research among the Kanuri was planned and carried out. Professor A. G. Frank has read and commented on previous drafts of this chapter. The writer would like to express his appreciation to Professor Frank for many useful hints and suggestions.

by maize, beans, squash, cucumbers, and groundnuts), (2) cash crop-
ping (mostly groundnuts), and (3) a dry season non-farming activity
connected with the market. Market activities are in turn divided into
craft work, sales of agricultural products, and a complex middleman
trade between markets. There is much variation in the dependence of
each household upon farming as compared to market activity, although
some farming is carried on by almost everyone except a few full-time
specialists.

In pre-colonial Bornu the Kanuri were ruled by a monarch, the Shehu,
and his nobles. These latter were given fiefs. Taxes were levied, and
men conscripted for wars which involved punishing or subduing vassal
states, and/or taking slaves to be used for agricultural labor and servants.
There were courts and an independent or specialized judiciary, although
all political leaders served in a judicial capacity as well. Stability was
maintained through the tight control exerted on the society by the Shehu
and his followers. All followers who were titled fief-holders, except one
— the Galidima was almost a vassal lord of his own sub-state — had to
remain in the capital under the eye of the monarch, while the fiefs were
run for them by subordinates. Internal political instability resulted from
the competition for kingly office which followed the death of the Shehu.
Segments of the royal lineage and their followers became factions in the
state and vied with one another for the supreme power. Stability en-
sued when a faction emerged whose members were able to organize a
strong central government under their royal leader.

The society has been stratified for a long time, with status differences
based on tribal membership, occupation, birth, age, wealth, and, to
some extent, urban residence identifications. The people recognize two
major class divisions — the upper or ruling class (*kantuoma*) and the
broad base of the peasant class (*tala*) under the autocratic hegemony
of the rulers. This is complicated by the recognition that there is a
royal group within the nobility, and that the low status of slaves may
vary and cross-cut other rankings through achievement and appointment
to high office. In analytical terms, the stratification system is a highly
complicated resultant of the interplay of status determinants. Rosman
(15) uses eight separate categories of social status in his work on
Kanuri acculturation. Cohen has used status gradients and their interrelationships to explain social differentiation, upward mobility, and class
structure (3).

Today, the Shehu (King or Emir) of Bornu lives in his capital city of
Maiduguri. There is a courtly life with titled nobles, including *Ajia*
(District Heads) who live in their own District capitals as sub-rulers of
21 segments of the emirate under the Shehu. District heads, in turn,
have under their jurisdiction a group of contiguous Village Area units
headed by *Lawan* (Village Heads). Under these latter are Hamlet
Heads (*Bulama*), in charge of small settlements of contiguous com-

pounds. Peasants call themselves the peasants of such and such a *Lawan*. Today the Native Administration departments have their personnel stationed throughout the district. Along with the district head and his chief followers, they form an urban upper class living in the districts throughout the state.

At the interpersonal level of village and city life, social relations are governed by the organization of households. These vary enormously in size, although the usual peasant household is often not more than four to eight people. However the households of very wealthy men, or more especially, politically important men, can be as large as 50 or 60. These units are regarded *as if* they were kinship organizations and indeed, for peasants, they often are nuclear, polygynous, or patrilocal extended family groupings. However in a large number of cases totally unrelated persons live in the compound as the subordinate of the compound head. Marriage is polygynous for all classes and the usual Muslim custom of allowing up to four wives is followed, although political leaders often have a small number of concubines, as well as male slaves. Divorce is common and household units break up continuously, either through divorce or through the death of the household head which can provoke competition and conflict among his heirs. The household is regarded as the basic social unit in the society and relations to the household are modeled on the father-son relationship for all males in the organization. It is this relationship, that of household head to household (male) member that provides the model for proper superior/subordinate relations in the political system. Traditionally, the superior gives the subordinate economic security, social status, and a role in the community, and may even provide the subordinate with a wife in return for disciplined loyalty and obedience.

For purposes of clarity and expression, and because most of the conditions described here are still present in Bornu society, this chapter was written in the present tense, although the data were gathered during 1955-57 when the country was not yet an independent state.

## III

### Establishment of the Theoretical Premises

In order to establish that "goal ambiguity," "conflicting standards," and "selective enforcement" do occur in Kanuri society, it is necessary to take a detailed look at behavior in the system. Although these processes are present at all levels of Kanuri social organization, documentation of this contention would carry us well beyond the limits of one chapter. Therefore, our attempt to establish the relevance of the premises of the theory to Kanuri society will concentrate on the role of the district head. The same purpose would have been served just as well, however, by focusing on the role of district officer, Native Administration official, village area head, or indeed of the Shehu (Emir) himself.

## The District Head

The appointment of district heads is officially made by the Shehu in consultation with his Waziri (chief minister) and Council. In practice, it is agreed upon by both the Native officials and the British administrative personnel present in the area. This means that a district head owes his appointment to both these sources. Furthermore, the deposition or re-stationing of a district head can be traced to complaints coming from either of these central agencies.

Traditionally, the district head collected taxes, and raised militia for his superior from his fief. Taxation was a form of tribute in kind given to superiors for the privilege of holding office. The subordinate raised enough to support himself and his dependents, as well as to pass on a surplus to those above him in the hierarchy to whom he owed security of tenure. During 1956–57, although direct evidence was scarce, tribute was referred to as normal by the population at large, by junior Native Administration officials, and among several close associates of district heads, throughout the emirate. Periodic gifts of horses, foodstuffs, and cash were the items most often referred to by informants as the kinds of tribute normally sent by district heads to powerful Kanuri leaders above them in the hierarchy. One high-placed Kanuri official at the capital told the writer that all district heads are "corrupt" (he used the English word). However, during the same interview, this official received and accepted a presentation of several goats and sheep, and two bags of millet sent to him by a district head.

The office of district head is a pivotal one in the political structure of the Emirate. Although others at the district level, such as the Native Administration departmental personnel, and the village area heads are also responsible for carrying out various aspects of emirate governmental action, the district head is the person to whom all attention at the capital turns if something goes wrong. This is reflected in the dependence that local Native Administration officials have upon his cooperation. Thus a young agricultural extension worker found that he could not obtain any participation in his departmental program in the district until the district head sent word to the village area heads concerned, to the effect that they must arrange for a certain number of household heads to take part in the program. When programs fail, officials at the center, aware of the widespread power exerted by the district head in his own domain, tend therefore to suspect him of either active or passive disobedience to the central organization of the state.

Difficulties in the system are reflected in the rate of turnover of district heads per district. Figures from four of the 21 districts of the emirate indicate that in the six decades of colonial rule, the range of district head tenure is between five and nine years in any one district, for two-thirds of the cases, even though tenure is potentially for life. Of the 38 persons who held the post of district head in each of the four districts during the colonial period, three retired, five died, 14 were dismissed, and 16 were transferred to other districts. In other words, 79 per cent of all turn-over was due to dismissals or transfers. The figures are probably higher for the emirate as a whole when it is realized that retirement is often "suggested" by the senior British officials, as a means of replacing a district head.

Dismissals from the position of district head are always due to some continued infringement of rules, and follow a series of warnings by the colonial and Native Administration officials at the center. Thus between 1929 and 1932, a district head was warned continually to stop using fol-lowers as village area heads instead of the officially recognized ones. These followers were raising their own taxes and levying court fines for adjudication. Finally, the British officials recommended to the Shehu and his Council that this particular district head be dismissed, and the Bornu annual report of 1932 stated that the Shehu-in-Council had de-posed the district head in question. During 1956–57 the writer observed the series of warnings by British district officers delivered to one district head because of tax irregularities. He was warned that a recommenda-tion for his dismissal might have to go to the Shehu-in-Council if the irregularity continued. Letters from the area since that time indicate that he was sent to a low-salary district — a "punishment station."

District head salaries are a function of the tax receipts and population size of their districts, standardized at some date and adjusted from time to time. Districts are ranked in the minds of district heads and their subordinates, as well as by a large part of the population, as "better" or "worse" in relation to one another. Transfer from a high-paying district to a low-salary one is seen as a punishment, while movement to a higher-salaried district headship is seen as a reward. British officials agree with this interpretation and feel the same way about district head transfers. Thus the high turnover of district heads due to transfers and dismissals is associated with action by superiors in terms of rewards and punishments in relation to standards of district head performance.

### Orientation and Goal Ambiguity

It is now a commonplace in the acculturation literature to think of culture contact as involving some ambiguity or ambivalence, and writers like Fallers (7) and Mair (12) have emphasized this point for the African chief. The term "orientation" is used here to refer to a syndrome of goals derived from one cultural tradition. Bornu displays two major orientations, derived from differing cultural backgrounds. The British conceived of political behavior as involving a very high degree of public responsibility, personal integrity, and slow but steady progress in economic and social development. Consequently, they looked forward to decreasing corruption, introduction or extension of Western schooling, higher productivity, democratic government, and all the paraphernalia required by Western-European socio-cultural values. In contrast, the Kanuri think of their political organization in feudal and Muslim terms. The social order is regarded as the result of divine will; and attempts to change it, although conceivable, are not morally defensible. Thus, the opposition party in modern Bornu is regarded not merely as a result of the new contact situation but also as an heretical group whose aims are said to be the perversion of the moral universe of traditional society. Kanuri concepts of social interaction, from the Shehu down to the lowly peasant, are feudal; loyalty and obedience are exchanged for various economic and political functions performed by the superior. District heads, like other political functionaries in Bornu, occupy roles which combine these diverse British and Kanuri orientations.

Possibly less obvious, and we suggest insufficiently emphasized in the above-cited literature on the African chief, is the ambiguity of orientation and the conflict among standards *within* each of the cultural traditions. The British administration was committed to the "peace, order and good government" of the area. The exact meaning of this phrase is open to various interpretations. On the one hand, much was said officially and privately about "progress" and "economic and political development," while *slow*, steady, but *well considered,* progress was held to be better than rapid growth. Initiative and innovation were often approved officially, and privately condemned. Or again, while colonial officials publicly accepted eventual self-rule, many of them privately admitted that the Nigerian (including the Kanuri) was unable to govern himself.

Kanuri leaders are committed to the political and economic development of the area, but they value their traditional political system and their religion and hope to keep these unchanged now that self-government has been achieved. Although most political leaders fervently wanted an end to colonial rule, they did not intend to abandon the political structure of colonialism. Many young Western-educated Kanuri, as well as high-placed officials, said that self-government will not mean an end of district officers, residents, *et al.* It will mean, merely, that these jobs would be filled by the Kanuri themselves.

These ambiguities within and between orientations (and many others not mentioned here) mean that the Bornu political organization cannot be seen in terms of a single means-end schema in which the entire system is committed to a simple set of formally-stated ends or goals. The orientations are not clear-cut; the inconsistencies tend to make the objectives of the political structure vague and indistinct. Thus "progress" is often discussed by both British and Kanuri leaders in terms which sound as if it should be negatively valued, while at other times it is obviously positively valued.

District heads, being Kanuri, are variably committed to Kanuri value orientations. However, they are also committed to maintaining their roles and minimizing the danger of dismissal or transfer to a district of less prestige. This means that all district heads are aware, again to a greater or lesser extent, of the ambiguities in objectives present in Bornu politics. In day-to-day terms, these ambiguities are translated into action through the conflicting standards under which district heads operate, particularly in their relations with the capital.

### Conflicting Standards

There are three agencies at the capital which exert pressure on the district head in his rural district. These are the Native Administration, the colonial administrators, and the colonial government technical departments. At the top of the Native Administration is the Shehu, the traditional head of state, and his council. This council, under the chairmanship of the Waziri, forms a cabinet, with the Waziri as chief minister and with each cabinet member serving as the nominal head of one of the Native Administration civil service departments in the emirate.

The differences in orientation between British and Kanuri culture are reflected in the conflicting standards of performance which govern the behavior of the district head. Perhaps the most common of these is the clash between British colonial and Kanuri feudal standards of tax collection. The British regard the district head as a salaried agent of government who performs a public service by collecting taxes. Many members of the Kanuri hierarchy at the capital see him as a feudal fief-holder who collects tribute and passes surpluses to his superiors in the organization. Since delivery of taxes to anything but the Native Administration treasury is illegal under colonial law, the payment of tribute to the Shehu and other members of the royal family, as well as to other high-ranking officials, is conducted in secrecy. But failure to meet either of these tax standards could lead to punishment.

Much conflict in standards of performance emerges for the district head because of the colonial orientation towards Western democracy. Thus, he is pressured to introduce and support "democratic" elections and local councils which violate traditional standards of autocratic political behavior. Similarly, some of the British disapprove of chiefs, rather than the Muslim judges, adjudicating legal cases, even though adjudication is part of the chief's traditional power. The British pressure the district head to reduce his large group of followers, fearing he may have to embezzle tax funds to maintain this group. These and many more standards of performance are promoted and enforced by the British. If the district head submits to these demands, he weakens his traditional role, thus making his job of political control more difficult.

Consistent with the British orientation, colonial officials demand that the district head maintain his tax receipts at a constant or rising level. The British do not officially recognize subordinates of the district head as active members of the revenue collection system; and yet to be able to collect taxes at all, he must support these men and their families and give many of them horses. These men ride out annually over the district in several groups to collect *Jangali*, the cattle nomad tax which accounts for approximately two-thirds of all emirate tax revenues. If the district head succumbs to British demands to reduce his following, the efficiency and numbers of his tax collectors, hence his total receipts, decline.

To add to the incongruity, the British expect district heads to put on large displays periodically. If the Queen or any senior colonial official from outside the province visits the area, district heads are called to the capital to take part in a large *durbar*, (a horse show, and parade). Competition among district heads for prestige demands that they spend a good deal more on these events than the allowance allotted for such exhibitions. The British thus discourage large followings on the one hand, and demand them as part of the local scene on the other, without, however, affording the district head the necessary support for this traditional institution.

As noted earlier, conflict among standards is not confined to differences between the colonial and native administrative demands; conflict is similarly common among standards set *within* each of the administrations — as well as, indeed, with some of the minor administrative organs. Conflicting standards often arise from the partial separation of the various departments of the colonial government. For instance, technical service officers try to enforce their own program objectives in public works, education, or agricultural improvements, while at the same time the administrative officers demand that the necessary resources be devoted to meeting other objectives. Thus, if the education officer wants more children in the district school during the several months of the tax-collecting period, the district head has to deflect some of his followers from tax work to rounding up children to meet the demand.[7]

In the Native Administration, constant transfers, dismissals, arrests, and retirements produce changes in the personnel of superior/subordinate relations. Village area heads, although formally subordinate to their local district head, often have ties to other district heads in the Emirate.[8] In

---

[7] In parts of Bornu the district head must force parents to give up their children for Western schooling because of the unpopularity of the schools, especially for girls. To do so, the district head's followers ride out over the district and obtain a few children by methods that are most aptly described as capture.

[8] The British set up this conflict at the beginning of the colonial era by appointing district heads from the capital on the advice of the Shehu, and appointing village

one district, five village area heads were strongly loyal to a previous district head, and the present office-holder enforced his authority with great difficulty. He could not easily get rid of these five, since their real superior belonged to a very powerful faction in the state that could bring pressure to bear on him. On the other hand, he could not allow the five complete freedom since he is officially responsible for the affairs of the district. Somewhat the same thing occurs at the capital. The district head carefully cultivates personal relationships (through gift-giving and tribute) with high-placed officials at the center. He hopes these will protect him against other leaders in the Native Administration and/or the British. However, rapid turnover of personnel counteracts this process, leaving the district head constantly searching for supporters in the capital.

Social and cultural change has also introduced conflicting standards into the district head's role in the Native Administration. This is easily exemplified in the literacy campaign strongly supported by high-placed officials at the center. The district head knows he must support literacy campaigns and uses the Native Administration propaganda when doing so. This propaganda, originally inspired by the British, tells of the benefits to be gained from learning to read. The peasant is told that literacy will allow him to check on district heads and village area heads who give tax receipt slips indicating a smaller amount than the actual tax collected. But peasants believe that this practice is widespread among chiefs. Thus, the district head must persuade peasants to learn to read so they can undermine his customary tax collection procedures.

Another conflict in standards occurs when Native Administration personnel come to the district. Each district has its complement of young semi-educated civil service personnel from the various departments of the Native Administration. Traditionally, a fief-holder controlled his fief completely; everyone in the area was *ipso facto* his political subordinate. The Native Administration personnel, however, are less easily turned into subordinates. They have departmental responsibilities as well as traditional links of loyalty and respect for the positions of the district head. Thus a district head may find his attempt to win the affections of nomad cattle-herders in the area is being subverted by the ardor of a young Native Administration member from the Veterinary Department who is condemning many of the cattle in the area and forcing herders to give up some of their stock for quarantine.

Not all pressures exerted upon the district head originate from his superiors in the political organization. The district head is a local potentate and must act like one. He lives in a much larger compound than other people in the district, and supports a large number of dependents

---

area heads on the basis of some hereditary claim to local leadership. Traditionally, district heads appointed their own village heads; thus making sure of a loyal political machine in their fiefs.

and their families. He must maintain his own band of praise-singers and his own group of Koranic *malams* (teacher-priests). Periodically he feeds the local Native Administration personnel and gives out money to wandering players who come into his town to entertain the populace and to sing his praises. His dependents, many of whom he supplies with horses, must have dress costumes for ceremonial occasions and gifts from him at times of *rites de passage* in their families and at annual religious festivals. All of these things must be done and "done well" if the district head is to be judged by himself and others as a successful chief. Common people, Native Administration personnel in the bush, and district heads often discussed or made allusions to the relative merits of one district head's chiefly attributes as opposed to another's. Since widely-known cultural values define what is meant by "good" district head behavior, the person in this role constantly feels pressure, both from his own values and the demands of those under him, for proper chiefly activity.

In sum, it should be realized that the salary given the district head by the Native Administration is never sufficient to allow him to maintain his social role. He must give gifts to many above and below himself in the political structure; he must support a large following; and he must live in a style which befits his high-ranking position in the state. As a result, he must constantly devise means of support which lie outside the formal rules of the political organization, reliance on which makes him vulnerable to criticism at all times.

### Selective Enforcement

Although many of the standards of performance to which a district head must accede conflict with one another, all standards are not equally enforced. Personnel changes in both the Native Administration and the colonial government produce changing emphases among the district heads' superiors. One district officer may be interested in roads, while his predecessor pressed for an improvement in the tax collection system. Others might keep aloof from innovation and simply carry on what they think are the current policies of the agency. Furthermore, as time passes, both the Native Administration and the colonial government recruit their staff from approximately the same age range, and from slowly changing worlds. The young colonial servant of today, and his Native Administration counterpart even more so, have somewhat divergent views from those of their respective forbears at the turn of the century.

It should also be realized that Bornu Emirate is only a part of a much larger political unit. The government of Northern Nigeria and the Federation of Nigeria have been moving towards self-government for some time. With this development, new bodies of African legislators, cabinet members, and high-level bureaucrats are all vying for the furtherance of their pet schemes. In such a rapidly changing situation it is often difficult to maintain consistency among all directives coming into the province. This means that the district head experiences unequal pressures from the capital, not only as a result of the personnel priorities of superiors, but also because of the demands on these superiors themselves.

## IV

### Kanuri Political Organization: The Test of the Hypotheses

Having established that goal ambiguity, conflicting standards, and selective enforcement occur in Bornu political organization, it is now possible to test whether or not the limitations they impose on individual behavior and the social consequences they produce are those hypothesized by the theory. Since the hypotheses are given in full above, they are referred to below by number. It should be noted that, for the sake of clarity in presentation of the data, the original order has not been adhered to in the test. Several of the hypotheses have been found to allude to similar behaviors, and have been treated together.

### Hypotheses 1 and 2 (Selection and Change of Standards that Are Met)

One of the most obvious responses among district heads to Bornu political organization is the widespread practice of simply not living up to all standards of performance. All district heads attempt to collect enough taxes to keep their superiors happy. Some accomplish this objective by maintaining large groups of horsemen, some by working in close collaboration with village area heads, and some work out close ties with Fulani headmen[9] and agree on cattle counts below the actual number but in excess of the district head's treasury commitments. Others use all these methods. One district head decided to reduce the number of his followers and thus lower his own expenditures. He also hoped that by complying with administration demands on the size of his following, he would avoid pressure from this source and be congratulated for complying with official demands. Instead his tax receipts fell drastically, which brought threats of dismissal from his superiors. The following year he reversed his decision and worried about tax collections rather than the size of his following. Some district heads station followers in each of the district towns in order to ensure some measure of control when they have no long-term superior/subordinate relations with the village area heads of the district. This is illegal, and several district heads do not

---

[9] Under the authority of their local headmen, Fulani pastoralists move through Kanuri territory annually in small bands for transhumance purposes.

use their followers in this way. Nevertheless, no one can possibly meet all standards in such situations, and breakage of certain rules has become almost a commonplace occurrence. Consequently, all district heads mulct some tax money or they could not possibly afford to maintain their social positions or the organizations necessary for tax collection. For the same reason, all district heads adjudicate cases, levy court fines, and accept tribute from the people of their districts.

### Hypothesis 3 (Simulation of Standards)

One of the most widespread kinds of behavior among district heads, and indeed among many of the Native Administration officials, is feigning or simulating British standards of performance. Whenever the author met district heads or other top Kanuri officials for the first time, attitudes towards standards of performance and goals were universally fairly accurate reflections of the official colonial government policy in the area. Besides the dangers implicit in not simulating British standards, it should be noted that in traditional Kanuri society it is considered bad manners to disagree with superiors. Thus when a district head speaks, listening persons keep repeating *nam, nam* (yes, yes) to show their assent and unanimity. When the district head is in the presence of his superiors in the political organization, he behaves in the same way.

Another example of this simulation of standards occurs in the district council meetings. In order to maintain their autocratic leadership and yet comply with the British standards of parliamentary procedure, some district heads rehearse the meeting before the British official who is to witness it arrives in the district. Others run a second meeting after the official leaves, re-arranging a few of the decisions, and ordering out of, or into, existence other matters which have been democratically accepted or declined at the formal meeting. This helps maintain the district head's status as an autocratic leader and gives traditional force to unaltered decisions of the "democratic" council.

### Hypothesis 4 (Safety Factors)

District heads also tend to provide themselves with safety factors for unforeseen emergencies. Excuses like sickness are often used. Thus one district head often had a "fever" on occasions on which he anticipated some threats from his superiors. At a ceremony, another district head announced to a district officer that it was now time for him and the other Kanuri present to go into another courtyard and say their prayers. The district officer politely excused himself and a part of the ceremony which involved the giving of money to the district head continued without the district officer present.[10]

[10] I am indebted to Professor A. Rosman for this information.

The operation of safety factors can also be seen in the contacts that many district heads maintain among the wealthy traders. These relations are due partly to the traders' desire to be friendly with a political leader who often borrows money from them. However, another aspect of these links is their possible usefulness to a district head if he is dismissed or retired from his political position. Several ex-district heads in the capital are making a profitable living from trade. One of these remarked on several occasions that most of his present suppliers of goods and credit are men whom he had known and befriended during his years as a district head.

One of the most interesting safety factors is that of factional membership. District heads not only cultivate office-holders in the capital but also maintain traditional links with segments of the royal lineage. Groups of district heads, like other high-status nobles of the realm, inherit relationships to one or another of the living male heirs to the throne. Tribute in cash and kind is delivered by district heads (not all) to their royal faction whether or not this person holds a Native Administration office. It is believed that the royal person argues for, and helps protect, his faction members in the higher councils of the emirate. Although the evidence is far from clear on this point, it may be that the linkage of some district heads to their royal factions is maintained as a safety factor resulting from inability to obtain protection and permanent or stable factional links with other high-ranking officials at the capital, because of the high turnover of these latter personnel.

### Hypotheses 10 and 5 (Information and Dealers in Information)

One of the important ways in which a district head alleviates the tensions inherent in conflicting standards and ambiguous goals is to have as many sources of information as possible. Indeed, information in Bornu is a valuable commodity. District heads lavish hospitality on messengers, native police, and Native Administration officials from the city who pass through the district. Touring British officials are listened to intently so that currently stressed goals and standards may be discerned. One district head knew English but kept this knowledge to himself, that he might appear ignorant and catch stray pieces of information from local and touring Europeans. Each district head keeps a compound in the city with a *Wakil* (chief follower) heading up a group of his subordinates. A major task of these followers is to maintain a steady flow of information on town affairs to the district head out in the bush. One district head kept a follower continually travelling back and forth from city to bush. This man visited town houses of other district heads, the Shehu's court, the Shehu's Council, and houses of rich traders, picking up information for his superior about the state of politics in the emirate. Almost everybody in Bornu seems to be in the information business; and all peasants know that every follower of a district head is an informal seeker of information for his superior. Very often persons who are not district head clients but have aspirations in that direction, or who are hoping for some other favor from him, try to win his affections by bringing information of a political nature to him.

The results of all this are twofold. First, most news travels quickly throughout the emirate. Indeed, the transfer or dismissal of a district head is usually known before the event occurs, because of leaks in and around high places in the Native and Colonial Administrations. A Kanuri messenger working for the Colonial Administration is a man cultivated by many of the richest and most successful district heads, especially if he has some knowledge of English. Second, gossip and rumor about the goals and enforcement of standards of political behavior in the state can be heard at almost every level of society. As much of the information is false as it is true, and a successful district head tries always to check and recheck a piece of information before relying on it. This widespread interest in political news and the endless search by district heads for information gives to Bornu political life a strong quality of intrigue. However, underlying this surface quality is the lack of adequate information in the system, and the end result of this fact is that the district head with the most reliable sources of information is able to predict more accurately what standards are most likely to be enforced.

### Hypotheses 11 (Incentive to Use Information and Comply with Standards)

Related to the widespread scarcity of information and its use by district heads is the strong incentive to obtain and use good information. This varies from one district head to another. Some may have very good sources of information already, and are only mildly interested in additional knowledge from new sources. Others felt the lack of information about policy enforcement by superiors so strongly that, after very little acquaintance with the anthropologist, they would move the conversation towards a discussion of goals and standards and future enforcement by this or that agency at the capital. In these situations it was difficult to tell who was conducting the interview, the anthropologist or the district head. One district head asked a district officer, who had threatened him with transfer, to "Tell me what to do, and I will do it," when the officer hinted that punishments might ensue because of the lowered tax revenues in the area. The district officer replied that it would be wise for the district head to go out and tour his district on horseback as well as sending out his followers. A few days later the district head left on the proposed tour.

## Hypothesis 9 (Sleeping Dogs and Initiative)

One of the most widespread consequences of conflicting standards and scarce information is the general acceptance by everyone in the Bornu political system of a policy of "let sleeping dogs lie." British officials know that local troubles require reports to their own superiors in the regional capital, followed by multitudes of questions, and often some sort of inspection and increased supervision of the local scene. A senior official explained his own aversion to trouble by saying that "agitators" were everywhere. Any irregularity could therefore, he claimed, reach "international proportions" and would undoubtedly be distorted if given any publicity. On the other hand, no trouble can always be alluded to as "steady progress" in reports. Furthermore, colonial officials and senior officers in particular are often held responsible (officially or unofficially) for any sizable disorder within their jurisdictional area. Thus a recently retiring officer in Bornu was described by one local district officer as having "left somewhat under a cloud" because of the political riots which broke out just before his last days in a senior position. Native Administration officials, including the district head, all recognize that any trouble may bring an investigation by the colonial administrators who, although reluctant to start anything really serious, will enforce their standards when matters are brought to their attention. This always opens the possibility that more trouble will result. In 1956 a Native Administration treasury official, angry over organizational matters, suddenly took the Bornu treasury records to the Colonial Administration. Before very long an investigation was ordered which was followed by a long series of dismissals, arrests, and jail sentences which reached into every department of the Native Administration. The British attitude to this kind of apprehension was summed up by one British official who claimed that all Kanuri are "corrupt," i.e., that they do not believe in British standards of political responsibility in public office. Since there are so few educated Africans it would be folly, he said, to be investigating all the time since "corrupt" officials would only be replaced by less well-trained ones who were also "corrupt." Nonetheless, initiative by district heads towards the realization of the policy objectives of the central government is formally encouraged. Speeches by visiting officials, and the official literature of the Northern Nigerian government constantly stress the district head's role as a progressive leader. He is regarded as the link between the past and the future, as a man who has a place of traditional leadership and who should also lead the way towards higher living standards, modern democracy, and the spread of Western education. On the other hand, as a result of goal ambiguity and conflicting standards (some of which are not even officially recognized), initiative is dangerous unless it is carried out under the aegis of extremely good information. Generally speaking, only highly acculturated district heads can afford the luxury of initiative towards official goals. Only those persons who can discriminate which goals can be achieved without any danger from the relinquishing of other goals are safe. One district head has previously been headmaster of the European School in the capital; he knew much about both Kanuri and Western culture. Consequently, he knew that his project to improve the water supply in the district, which he had cleared with the proper authorities, was unassailable by anyone. Most district heads do not have so clear an understanding of what they can and cannot do; as we have seen, information is scarce, goals and standards often difficult to pin down and/or reconcile with one another.

Furthermore, like officials everywhere, the colonial government personnel, especially the older ones in the more senior positions, resent disturbances. Initiative can very often be confused with disturbance or at least the unsettling of the status quo. Thus, several young officials complained to the writer that they had been squelched in development schemes because they had not consulted higher-ups first before going ahead with their plans. Higher-ups were angry at such initiative since the junior members of the political organization were subordinates, and the higher-ups would be responsible if anything went wrong.

### Hypotheses 7, 12, and 14 (Changing Standards and Internal Variability)

Changes in colonial government staff are frequent. District officers and technical staff are often moved from one part of Northern Nigeria to another every time they start an 18-month tour of duty. Indeed, in several instances colonial officials were re-stationed within one tour. Previous writers have commented on this practice so that we can safely assume that it has been a characteristic of Nigerian administration for a long time (13). It is beyond the scope of this present chapter to discuss the pros and cons of this mobility; for our purposes it is sufficient to mention its presence and note one of its major effects — the variation in standards and their emphases resulting from the continuous movement of colonial personnel.

In Bornu a young energetic official can easily institute innovations by simply proclaiming his goals widely and making sure that none of his superiors disapprove of his actions. Because district heads are used to changing standards and selective enforcement, they are generally receptive to new pressures from the top of the political structure. More emphasis on schools, roads, or taxation can easily be instituted. Some of these trends, once begun, are not terminated even when pressures ease off due to the transfer of the official originally responsible for the innovations. New roads built under pressure from one particular official must be maintained, as are schools and medical dispensaries.

It is becoming more and more common among district officers to narrow down the broad general range of their duties and specialize in only one or two branches of administrative work. Thus, one district officer in Bornu specialized in local government, another in fiscal policy and revenue collection, and so on. Furthermore, young assistant district officers often attempt to initiate changes in various sectors of the emirate government under their jurisdiction.

One young district officer started a race track up in a bush district as his pet project. The local district head approved of the idea, probably because it kept the officer busy. As a distraction for touring officials from the capital and for local entertainment, the race track has become a local institution. This same district head institutes formal, and public, Friday services in the local mosque no matter what district he is stationed in, and no matter what the previous practices in the area have been. On the other hand, others merely continue to stress those areas of the administration program about which their superiors on the local scene are enthusiastic. One district officer carried on the policy of his superior concerning the alleviation of cruelty to animals. Because of the constant shifts in personnel, it is not always a simple matter for the district head to know far ahead just what part of the administration goals will be stressed, since the emphasis can quite easily change with the personnel.

In the technical departments one education officer may spend more of his time at the provincial capital looking after matters there; others spend much time going around the province. Both tasks are performed by all officials, but stress on one or the other area of work varies. This means that with changing personnel, the district head must expect changes in the amount of pressure applied locally by the technical officers. When an officer spends more time in the capital, power is delegated to the Native Administration officials and much of the departmental pressure felt by the district head comes from the Native Administration. If the officer tours out in the districts a great deal, then his personal policy preferences become more important pressures.

In the Native Administration, center officials tend to exhibit constant and often unpredictable job turnover. Only three of the dozen or so chief councilors of the emirate retained their positions during the period 1956–57, and letters from the area since then indicate that the rate of personnel shifts and depositions has remained much the same. Illicit practices, which come to light periodically, can bring a quick series of removals, and even a jail sentence, to what seem to be a random assortment of positions throughout the Native Administration.

### Hypotheses 8 and 13 (Adaptability to Externally-initiated Change)

As a result of the high amount of conflict in the Bornu political organization, social and cultural change has an ever-ready route into the society. It has already been noted that goals as well as enforcement of standards may change over time.

A major change was the very introduction of the British rule itself, and the Kanuri political system's adaptation to that externally induced change. The colonial era has served to complicate the traditional obligations of district heads to members of the hierarchy. That the district head should pay heed to the wishes of officials at the center such as the Shehu, the Council members, and other high-placed persons in the Native Administration departments is easily understood, since these persons are engaged in tasks that require the cooperation of the district head and these responsibilities are backed up by the colonial officials. It is somewhat surprising, however, to find other nobles who, like top Native Administration personnel, also receive gifts but have no officially recognized high office in the contemporary political organization. Thus the writer, having promised his kerosene refrigerator to a district head at the end of the field trip, was asked to deliver it to a member of the Bornu royal family who has no Native Administration position whatsoever. This is explained by the fact that the district head involved has a client relationship which he inherited from his father with this particular segment of the royal lineage. That is to say, this district head feels that he is a part of the faction in the state as whole which is allied to a particular heir to the throne. He also feels that this royal person is still a power in the state and will help protect him against other factions and authorities in the political organization. To a certain extent this is true. When this district head is to be disciplined for some misdemeanor, the head of his faction pleads his case before the Shehu and as many Council members as he can contact. Thus the older traditional factions and their leaders still perform some political functions in the emirate, in addition to the officially recognized Kanuri hierarchy above the district head at the capital. Lack of support by all these people, or at least a majority of the most powerful among them, leads to easy punishments when district heads are accused of breaking the rules. On the other hand, informants feel that delivery of gifts to faction leaders, as well as to high-placed Native Administration officials, ensures the district head of some support by traditionally powerful persons as well as the official hierarchy recognized and supported by the colonial government.

Externally originated change still finds ready reception in Bornu today. A Kanuri agricultural officer, after traveling to Israel and Pakistan, has decided that Bornu, especially its southern portions, can support a citrus-growing industry. By utilizing the British-inspired goal of economic development and his own authority, as well as his friendship links with both British and Kanuri leaders, he has been able to introduce citrus growing into the Bornu economy. That is to say, Kanuri leaders, whether they be district heads or other officials, can usually find some goal or standard which gives jural support to the acceptance of innovations brought in from the outside world. It should be noted at this point that all the top Kanuri leaders spoken to during the field trip are to a variable degree committed to the goal of economic development. Many of them feel that the two biggest blocks to this end are (a) the poverty of the area, and (b) the conservatism of the senior British officials. They are not at all worried over the traditionalism of the people. This is due to their own stated understanding that innovation is not excessively difficult in a system in which people react to pressures more often than to rules.

### Hypothesis 6 (Substantive Rationality)

The discussion of Bornu political organization indicates that jural rules are hardly the primary guides for individual conduct, or the sources of social integration in the system. In Frank's Weberian terms, the Kanuri do not place substantial reliance on formal rationality. District heads who do, usually get into some kind of trouble, and are either punished or eliminated. One district head is reported to have behaved as if there were no conflicts in the system. He ruled his district autocratically, extorted large amounts of excess taxes from its inhabitants, and even tried to buy up the surplus millet at low harvest prices to sell later in the year. He was soon apprehended and transferred out of the district. He is said by those who have worked under him to be contemptuous of modern times, and to prefer traditional pre-colonial rules of political behavior. Most district heads know that they must accommodate to the real system rather than any idealization of it, and in so doing the sets of jural rules (derived from Kanuri and British orientations) governing their political roles become merely a backdrop against which a real system political action is played out. In this "real" system it is pressures and information that form the basis for active political response and initiative. Thus in more theoretical parlance the structural features of the political system in terms of its formal rules are less important than its constituent interpersonal and hierarchical relations.

## V

### Conclusion

This chapter has dealt with organization of political activity among the Kanuri of Northern Nigeria by approaching the behavior of one political role, that of the district head, as if this person's actions were responses to a series of conflicts. In so doing, we have demonstrated that conflicts do in fact exist in the situation, and that the activity of persons occupying political roles is predictable within the limits outlined in a theory of conflict derived from a study of Russian industry.

Concerning the theory itself, Frank's schema has come from empirical data, but it is in itself a deductive system in which certain behaviors follow logically from the basic premises. In using it, we have found that several of the predicted behavioral correlates associated with the premises actually deal with the same events. Thus, Hypotheses 10 and 5, dealing with information and dealers in information, refer to the same area of political behavior in the district head's role. Similarly, and perhaps more importantly, all hypotheses dealing with change focus on the same mechanism: the response to, and desire to comply with, known pressures from higher-ups, rather than any idealization of the traditional rules. This is due to Frank's (8, p. 13) deductive separation of the hypotheses into levels of "member behavior" and "system" consequences, when in fact the only material available for study is the response by members of the hierarchy to conflicts among standards. Recently Berliner (1, p. 102) has commented that anthropology has no detailed theories of self-generating internal change such as the economists have in their conceptualization of the dynamics of the business cycle. A close look at the way in which change has been treated in this chapter shows that the change mechanism being discussed is indeed "internal" and "self-generating." Because actors in the hierarchy are more concerned with compliance to superiors than they are with the essentials of tradition, there is a ready avenue for change to enter the society, from within or without, at all times.

This brings up another point of theoretical interest. What do the terms "internal" and "external" actually mean in the context of this analysis? The author has had a number of long discussions with Professor Frank over this point and we find it difficult to resolve the problem. As it is used here, the term "internal" really refers to the political hierarchy itself as a distinct and analytically separate phenomenon in comparison to other systems of social action and cultural traditions in which it is embedded in everyday life. In other words, this chapter suggests by its method of analysis that the boundaries of different systems of social action within social and cultural systems of much greater complexity should not be considered coincident to one another in the culture contact situation. The political hierarchy dealt with in this work included both British and Kanuri officials. At the time of fieldwork research (1955–57) and even more so today, after the achievement of Nigerian independence, all these leaders were part of the same political structure. It is within this system of political action that change can be said to be internal. In other words, as I have pointed out elsewhere (4), the comprehensive inclusion of all facets of a society and its cultural traditions within a unifying set of boundary conditions can lead to an oversimplified view of any social situation, especially when we are interested in change and the forces that bring it about. Thus we should think about the boundaries of much more limited sets of activities, such as the economic system, or the moral order, or the political system, or even sub-sections of these, and make no assumptions about the congruency of any of these systems and their boundaries.

It is also of note in view of the contemporary interest in evolution that this method of presenting and analyzing data approaches in many major respects a genetic model of evolution. This model depends basically on two conditions. First, the evolving phenomenon must be shown to be variable in terms of its constituent units, and second, there must be analytically distinct selective factors which operate on the variation within the phenomenon to produce a constantly adapting and thus an evolving history of development. Although there are more or less stable orientations of tradition present in Bornu, conflicts in the political organization produce a variability of response by the actors upon which selective pressures exerted by superiors in the political hierarchy may operate to bring about innovations and changes that are incremental in their nature, i.e., evolutionary rather than revolutionary.

The rate of change has not been established in this study, but it is possible to make some theoretical statements about the rate on the basis of this analysis. Factors which promote change, such as the ones isolated here, when intensified should hasten the rate of change. Thus we can hypothesize that the greater the intensity of conditions which promote the conflicts described here, then the greater will be the rate of change. In the Bornu situation the conditions most likely to produce conflicts are the differences in orientation of superiors and subordinates, the differences in interests and goals of superiors, and the rate of turnover amongst superiors. These will be summarized in Hypothesis 9 below.

Summing up the discussion of the theory we can now re-state it in light of its submission to the Kanuri material.

If it is established that there are present in any hierarchical social situation differences in cultural orientation which create goal ambiguity, and/or goal ambiguities are present for any other reason, as well as conflicting standards, and selective enforcement of these standards, then the following may be predicted to occur:

1) Members (of the hierarchy) fail to meet all standards, exhibit differences in selection, and change the selection, over time, of standards they do meet.
2) Members simulate or feign the meeting of standards.
3) Members provide themselves with safety factors for contingencies.
4) Information is a scarce and positively valued commodity in the hierarchy, and members are motivated to use any and all methods to obtain information on enforcement policies. This may or may not become institutionalized so that professional information seekers may or may not be present. If not, then the social organization takes on an atmosphere of intrigue.
5) Widespread member initiative is possible; but unless it is incor-

porated into standards, individuals will "let sleeping dogs lie." That is to say, the failure to comply with some standards is widely known within the hierarchy, and members are prone to overlook this fact for the sake of making the organization work on a day-to-day basis.

6) Standards change continually, thus re-orienting and possibly changing the organizational form of social life.

7) Conflicting standards generate innovations and selective enforcement provides for their acceptance.

8) Conflicting standards and selective enforcement make for ready adaptation to changing circumstances.

9) The rate of change in a hierarchy is a function of:
   (a) The differences in orientation of superiors and subordinates,
   (b) The differences in interests and goals of superiors to one another,
   (c) The rate of turnover among superiors.

The greater any of these factors are, the more rapid will be the rate of change.

One final conclusion of a practical nature emerges from this analysis, especially from Hypothesis 8 above. Many observers of the modern Nigerian scene attribute a conservative, anti-progressive character to the emirates of Northern Nigeria. If our analysis is correct, these emirates have within themselves well-developed mechanisms for their own transformation. That is to say, it is predictable that, given a continuation of conflicting standards, and selective enforcement, along with changing and more modern goals emanating from the top of the political hierarchy (which is a very likely occurrence, given the increasing amount of Western education amongst top officials), these societies will incorporate and accept modern developments. This means that it will not be necessary to change and modernize the northern emirates by a drastic revolutionary measure, but merely by continued and constant pressure, to which, as has been shown, they are definitely responsive.

## BIBLIOGRAPHY

1. Berliner, J. S. "The Feet of the Natives are Large: An Essay on Anthropology by an Economist," *Current Anthropology* Vol. 2, No. 5 (1961), pp. 90–103.

2. Buckley, W. "Social Stratification and the Functional Theory of Social Differentiation," *American Sociological Review*, Vol. 23, No. 4 (1958), pp. 369–375.

3. Cohen, R. "The Structure of Kanuri Society." Ph.D. thesis. University of Wisconsin, University Microfilms, Inc., Ann Arbor, mic 60–986.

4. Cohen, R. Comment on "The Feet of the Natives are Large: An Essay

on Anthropology by an Economist," J. S. Berliner. *Current Anthropology*, Vol. 2, No. 5 (1961).

5. Dahrendorf, R. "Out of Utopia: Towards a Reorientation of Sociological Theory," *American Journal of Sociology*, Vol. 64, No. 2 (1959), pp. 115–127.

6. Epstein, A. L. *Politics in an Urban African Community*. Manchester: University of Manchester Press, 1957.

7. Fallers, L. "The Predicament of the Modern African Chief," *American Anthropologist*, Vol. 57, No. 2 (1955), pp. 290–305.

8. Frank, A. G. "Goal Ambiguity and Conflicting Standards: An Approach to The Study of Organization," *Human Organization*, Vol. 17, No. 4 (1959), pp. 8–13.

9. Greenberg, J. H. "Studies in African Linguistic Classification; VIII. Further Remarks on Method: Revisions and Corrections," *Southwestern Journal of Anthropology*, Vol. 10 (1954), pp. 405–415.

10. Leach, E. R. *Political Systems of Highland Burma: A Study of Kachin Social Structure*. London: G. Bell and Sons Ltd., 1954.

11. Levi-Strauss, C. "Social Structure," in A. L. Kroeber (ed.), *Anthropology Today*. Chicago: University of Chicago Press.

12. Mair, L. P. "African Chiefs Today," *Africa* Vol. 28, No. 3 (1958), pp. 195–206.

13. Perham, M. *Native Administration in Nigeria*. London: Oxford University Press, 1937.

14. Radcliffe-Brown, A. L. *Structure and Function in Primitive Society*. London: Cohen and West Ltd., 1952.

15. Rosman, A. "Social Structure and Acculturation Among the Kanuri of Bornu Province, Northern Nigeria," *Transactions of the New York Academy of Sciences*, Ser. II, Vol. 21, No. 7 (1958), pp. 620–630.

# 28

*William M. Evan*

# Transnational Mechanisms

# of Social Change[1]

Discerning societal changes that are incipient and latent before they emerge full-blown and come to the attention of journalists, politicians and the public at large, is presumably one of the tests of the counter-intuitive and predictive power of social science theory and research. This is a manifestly hazardous enterprise because it may involve an extrapolation of trends which may in fact not occur.

Additional complications which the effort at social prediction must consider are the inadequacies of available theory and data. Current theories of social change are anemic and the body of societal data because of the perilous state of time series of social indicators of various institutions, is so sparse as to impede data-based speculations and inductions. Another hazard in predicting social change is drawing a clear line between a positive and a normative theory of social change. Marx's theory of social change is an instance of the admixture of description and prescription, prediction and advocacy.

Perhaps the best example of Marx's blend of prediction and advocacy is that class interests dominate national, religious and other values comprising the superstructure of a society. Hence, he not only predicted but also called for the internationalization of the proletariat. To assist this ineluctable social process he participated in the founding, in 1864, of the First International — the International Working Men's Association. Implicit in

[1] Revised version of a paper presented at the Seventh World Congress of Sociology, Varna, Bulgaria, September 14-19, 1970.

Marx's theory and political action is that the bourgeoisie, under a developing system of capitalism, is itself becoming internationalized, notwithstanding the rifts that occur as the bourgeoisie extends its hegemony via a global system of imperialism. To counter this trend, the proletariat must and will unite, according to Marx, in its historic mission to replace capitalism with communism.

As a theory of social process Marx was in error in underestimating the political impact of various components of the superstructure; as a blueprint for revolution his followers would claim that it already has been successful in many countries and in due course, will pave the way for communism in many other countries. From the vantage point of the twentieth century, paradoxically, several revisions of Marx's theory of internationalization along class lines are required. First the objects, basis, and rate of internationalization are different from those Marx envisioned. Instead of the proletariat becoming internationalized, professionals of various kinds appear to be undergoing internationalization. Not only have trade unions not become distinctively internationalized, but as industrialization of a society increases, the proportion of manual workers who comprise the overwhelming majority of the trade union membership declines. On the other hand, the proportion of professionals in the labor force increases as industrialization increases. An ever increasing proportion of professionals, particularly from highly industrialized societies, are becoming involved in the activities of international professional associations. Moreover, instead of Marx's "bourgeoisie" extending its sway the world over, there has been a transformation of the corporation — a social invention Marx hardly appreciated — from a national enterprise to a multinational enterprise.

These observable trends toward internationalization are *organizational* and *occupational* in nature and are not propelled by the motive power of social classes. The furtherance of the occupational and organizational interests of the multinational firm and the international professional association may eventually have systemic implications for social change but, in all likelihood, in a manner different from Marx's vision. Instead, an evolutionary "unconscious patterning" (47), not unlike the law merchant activities which extended over several centuries and gave rise to the capitalist system, may be at work generating a new global economy and a new international system. It is the general assumption of this paper that the multinational enterprise and the international professional association are two noteworthy transnational mechanisms (26) of social change that deserve the systematic research attention of students of organization theory, international relations, and social change. They may be unintentionally generating new "internationals" unanticipated by Marx or his followers.

## Alternative Models of Integration of the International System

It is indeed interesting that the term "international organization," as used by most political scientists and other scholars in the field of international relations, refers to the interaction of nation-states (20; 31). Haas, acknowledging the ambiguity of the term, states that, "a loose definition of international organization . . . would say that it consists of intergovernmental institutions, members of which perceive each other to be basic units of the world polity" (20, p. 505). The widespread assumption underlying this usage is that the international system is composed of various relationships among sovereign actors. In order to improve the prospects for peace between nations, it is necessary to generate normative integration — a commitment to a common set of values and norms — through the mechanism of a universal intergovernmental organization. With the aid of multilateral agreements, a complex of intergovernmental organizations is created which builds commitment among nation-states to a body of international law designed to increase the forces for international order. With an increase in the level of normative integration, the international system evolves in the direction of a world community of peaceful, sovereign states. In effect, the model implicit in this conception of the international system, diagrammed in Figure 1, involves a direct, linear process of normative integration increasing as a function of interaction of nation-states within the framework of intergovernmental organizations.

This model guided the formation of the League of Nations and to some extent, that of the United Nations as well. The failure of the League of Nations to evoke compliance on the part of its sovereign members undermined its authority as well as its capability of generating normative integration. Without abridging national sovereignty, membership in an intergovernmental organization is neither a necessary nor a sufficient condition for the development of normative integration. Nor is normative integration a sufficient condition for significantly transforming the international system. Other modes of integration notably economic, organizational, and occupational which create new patterns of interdependence, are essential if the international system is to undergo a major transformation (16).

The failure of the League of Nations was not lost on some of its former members in Western Europe. After World War II, they began to explore problems of economic integration via regional organizations which would impose limitations on national sovereignty. The Economic and Steel Community, founded in 1952, was conceived as a supranational organization which paved the way for the more inclusive European Economic Community in 1958 (19; 48). Among the Communist countries of Eastern Europe and the Soviet Union a similar movement toward economic integration was initiated, which gave rise in 1949 to the Council on

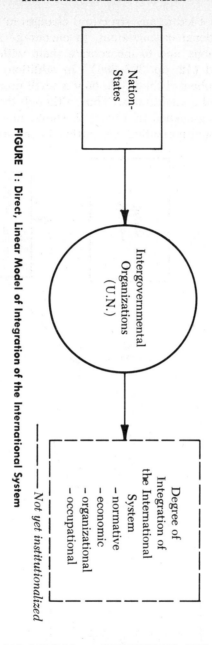

**FIGURE 1: Direct, Linear Model of Integration of the International System**

Mutual Economic Aid (CEMA or COMECON) (17). Similiar regional organizations have since emerged in Latin America (the Latin American Free Trade Area and the Central American Common Market), Africa and elsewhere (34).

The U. N. Charter recognizes regional organizations and seeks to bring them into closer relations with the United Nations (Articles 32-54). Yet, this has thus far not led to any structural changes in the U. N. to foster the growth of regional organizations, to encourage interactions among regional organizations, and to incorporate them within its structure, as has been proposed (12; pp. 396–398). In addition, of the 135 nation-states that are members of the U. N., only a small proportion are actively involved in regional organizations. Thus, although the model underlying regionalism, as diagrammed in Figure 2, shows much promise of generating economic and normative integration in the international system,

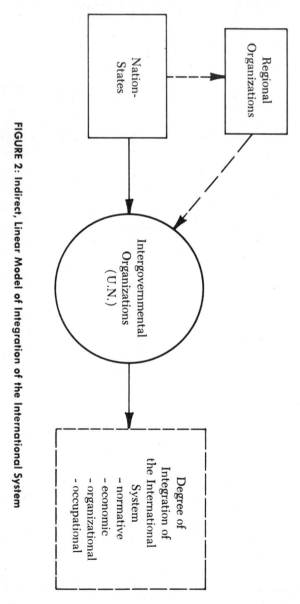

**FIGURE 2:** Indirect, Linear Model of Integration of the International System

it is probably premature to assess its effectiveness in this regard. However, it is doubtful whether in the absence of an infrastructure of multinational, non-governmental organizations of a profit and non-profit variety, adequate system linkages can be forged among nation-states, regional organizations and intergovernmental organizations. This conjecture about the potential role of multinational non-governmental organizations suggests a complex non-linear model of integration of the international system to which I now turn.

With few exceptions, social scientists engaged in the sociology of organizations, the sociology of occupations, and in the study of international relations have ignored the international, non-governmental organization, in general, and the international professional association, in particular (61; 12; 51; 15; 4, pp. 240–243; 29). By contrast, researchers in international business and international economics have recently begun to speculate about and inquire into the multinational corporations (41; 42; 58; 14, 28; 6; 7; 45; 36). Under the circumstances, it should come as no surprise that the functions of these organizations in the international system have not yet been systematically studied, much less clarified. Our basic assumption is that because these types of organizations are simultaneously sub-national, cross-national and multinational in character, they already provide or may provide in the future many significant linkages between nation-states, regional organizations, and intergovernmental organizations, thus contributing to the process of *normative, economic, organizational* and *occupational* integration of the international system.

Instead of conceptualizing the international system with the aid of a direct or an indirect linear model of integration, as shown in Figures 1 and 2, a complex, non-linear model with a variety of feedback loops is presented in Figure 3. Nation-states, particularly those that are highly industrialized, give rise to multinational corporations, that is, enterprises that develop production, research, and distribution facilities in various countries of the world. Nation-states also spawn a multitude of non-governmental organizations, a high proportion of which consists of professional associations which become federated at the international level. Some of these non-governmental, non-profit organizations are accorded official consultative status under the U. N. Charter (Article 71).

Each type of organization has mutual interactions with regional organizations. Although there are as yet, few linkages between the multinational corporation and the international professional association, they are likely to develop in the future as these organizations discover their intersecting interests in common third parties such as nation-states, regional organizations, and various inter-governmental organizations. Collectively, and cumulatively, international non-governmental organizations, multinational corporations, and regional organizations interact with one another and with nation-states and inter-governmental organizations in such a manner as to increase the degree of integration of the interna-

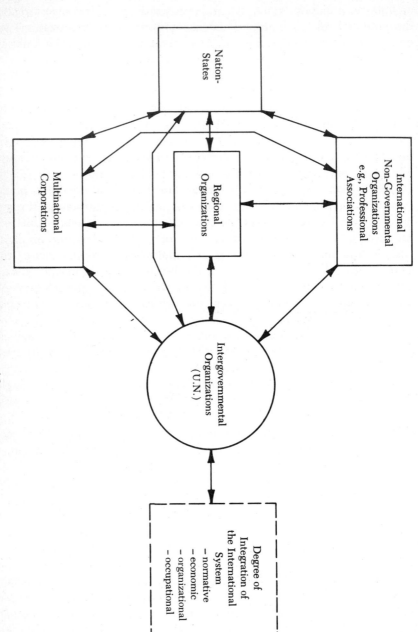

FIGURE 3: Nonlinear Model of Integration of the International System

tional system along four dimensions: normative, economic, organizational, and occupational.

With the aid of our non-linear model of integration of the international system, we shall now consider in turn the growth and system linkages of multinational corporations and international professional associations.

## Growth and System Linkages

### Multinational Corporations

Although the term "multinational corporation" has become current only in the past two decades, the phenomenon of international business operations is, of course, not new. "The first wave of foreign investment by manufacturing companies began in the closing decades of the nineteenth century, and continued, gathering strength, up to 1914. Much of it was American, not only in Canada . . . but also in Europe. . . . A few European companies were also beginning to expand abroad. Lever set up his first soap factory outside Britain in 1899, and Alfred Nobel was establishing armament factories all over Europe" (32, p. 259). In the interwar years, direct foreign investment scarcely grew. It was in the 1950s that the second great wave of business investment began. "Between 1950 and 1967 the United States' capital stake in European manufacturing industry increased more than ten times, to a figure of $9,800,000,000 in the latter year" (32, p. 259). Other major industrial countries such as Britain, France, West Germany, Canada and Japan have also participated in the burgeoning growth of the multinational corporation. It is anticipated by some students of international business that the involvement of the Soviet Union and other Communist countries in multinational corporations will increase in the coming decade.

One of the factors that stimulated the exponential growth of multinational corporations in the past decade is the emergence of the European Economic Community (45; p. 11; 25, p. 103). It is now recognized that American corporations have taken more advantage of the economic opportunities created by this regional organization than European corporations themselves, so much so that it has prompted Servan-Schreiber to deplore this trend and exhort his fellow Europeans to ward off the invasion of American enterprise (49).

Notwithstanding the rate of growth of multinational corporations, data on this type of firm, particularly of an organizational nature, are hard to come by. For the first time in its history, the Union of International Associations included a section on multinational corporations in the 12th edition of its *Yearbook on International Organizations* (57, pp. 1189–1214). In a preliminary survey, the *Yearbook* reports 7,045 parent companies in 14 European countries and the U.S.A. with affiliates in one or more countries. Omitted from this survey are data on Japan, Canada,

**TABLE 1**

*Country of Corporate Headquarters of Multinational*
*Firms by Number of Countries in which Affiliates are Located**

| Country of HQ | No. of Countries in which Affiliates Located | | | | | | | Total | % |
|---|---|---|---|---|---|---|---|---|---|
| | 10-12 | 13-15 | 16-20 | 21-25 | 26-30 | 31-40 | 41+ | | |
| Denmark | 3 | — | — | — | — | — | 1 | 4 | 1 |
| Netherlands | 8 | 2 | 4 | 2 | 2 | — | 1 | 19 | 3 |
| U.K. | 47 | 31 | 43 | 14 | 10 | 5 | 3 | 153 | 26 |
| U.S.A. | 92 | 59 | 40 | 37 | 18 | 14 | 9 | 269 | 46 |
| Germany (FR) | 18 | 10 | 9 | 1 | 2 | 2 | — | 42 | 7 |
| Italy | — | 2 | 2 | 4 | 1 | 1 | — | 10 | 2 |
| Sweden | 10 | 4 | 3 | 2 | 5 | 2 | — | 26 | 4 |
| Switzerland | 8 | 3 | 3 | 2 | — | 2 | — | 18 | 3 |
| France | 19 | 6 | 8 | 5 | 2 | — | — | 40 | 7 |
| Belgium | 3 | 2 | 1 | — | — | — | — | 6 | 1 |
| Norway | — | — | 1 | — | — | — | — | 1 | ** |
| Austria | — | 2 | — | — | — | — | — | 2 | ** |

*Source: Union of International Associations, *Yearbook of International Organizations*, 12th edition, Brussels, Belgium, 1969, Table 3, p. 1203.

**Less than .5 percent.

communist countries, and others, presumably because they were unobtainable. A subset of these corporations with affiliates in ten or more countries, totalling 590, is listed by name which suggested an analysis, presented in Table 1, of the nationality of the corporate headquarters of these organizations. Of these relatively large multinational corporations, 46 percent are American, 26 percent are British, 7 percent are German, and 7 percent are French, with the remainder distributed among eight European countries. Underlying this uneven distribution of parent companies among countries is a differential in economic development. This is borne out by a statistically significant rank order correlation coefficient of .39 (Kendall tau) between the number of multinational firms in a country and its GNP per capita, shown in Table 2.

Although no consensus has yet been reached as to the definition of a multinational corporation, it is evident from the foregoing discussion that we are dealing with a relatively large firm with extensive resources in many countries. "A multinational company does more than import and export from its . . . . home plant. It may do research in Germany, engineering design in Japan, and then manufacture in Taiwan, Italy, and Mexico to supply a hundred national markets, including the . . . [home] market in which its headquarters may be located" (46, p. 337). To per-

**TABLE 2**

*Rank Order Correlation of Number of Multinational Firms of a Country and its GNP per Capita**

| COUNTRY OF HQ | NUMBER OF MULTI-NATIONAL FIRMS | RANK ORDER | GNP/CAPITA (000 U.S. DOLLARS) | RANK ORDER |
|---|---|---|---|---|
| U.S.A. | 2816 | 1 | 8.8 | 1 |
| United Kingdom | 1651 | 2 | 1.9 | 8.5 |
| Germany (FR) | 801 | 3 | 2.0 | 6.5 |
| France | 471 | 4 | 2.1 | 5 |
| Switzerland | 349 | 5 | 2.5 | 3 |
| Netherlands | 222 | 6 | 1.7 | 10 |
| Sweden | 219 | 7 | 2.7 | 2 |
| Belgium | 197 | 8 | 1.9 | 8.5 |
| Italy | 101 | 9 | 1.2 | 12 |
| Denmark | 82 | 10 | 2.3 | 4 |
| Norway | 78 | 11 | 2.0 | 6.5 |
| Austria | 38 | 12 | 1.4 | 11 |
| Spain | 9 | 13 | 0.8 | 13 |

$\tau = .39$, significant at .03

*Source: Union of International Associations, *Yearbook of International Organizations,* 12th ed., Brussels, Belgium, 1969, p. 1189.

form such highly complex operations in a multitude of differing environments it is necessary to transfer products, capital, managers and other technical personnel, as well as technology. The extensive transfer of the factors of production points to some of the effects functional as well as dysfunctional, of the multinational corporation on various components of the international system.

The most proximate effect is on the host countries in which affiliates are located. By employing nationals in various capacities, from unskilled laborers to professional and managerial personnel, the parent company creates many new employment and career opportunities in the host country. While no overall figure is available as regards the number of people employed in various countries by the 7,045 multinational corporations reported in the *Yearbook*, one estimate for approximately 3,000 American parent companies is 5,000,000 foreign employees, a staggering number which exceeds the size of the labor force of many countries. And for 1,000 Swedish companies operating in 70 countries, the estimate is 200,000 foreign employees (28, p. 88).

Invariably, employees in host countries are the recipients of new bodies of knowledge and skills essential to man the technology transferred by the parent company (45, pp. 48–60). As one researcher on the transfer of technology observes:

> Repeatedly, multinational companies operate training programs for host country nationals on a scale which is equivalent to adding a large technical high school in the country. They train nationals as operators, functional executives, and eventually as top managers. Trained people who leave such companies often seed domestic organizations with competent personnel and so diffuse know-how elsewhere in the economy (38, p. 152).

Apart from such beneficial effects on a segment of the host country's labor force and, in turn, on the standard of living of employees, the inflow of foreign capital potentially stimulates economic development. On the other hand, the outflow of capital from the home country of the parent corporation may have dysfunctions for the labor force in question. Trade union officials in the U. S. point to a net loss of 400,000 jobs over five years due to capital and technology transfers by multinational firms (1; 5). To counteract the threat posed by the internationalization of the corporation, trade unions are developing strategies for multinational union organization and collective bargaining (10).

As regards reciprocal effects, from the host country on the parent company, several are noteworthy. First it grants the company legal protection of incorporation. Secondly, it subjects the company to taxation which may be of economic as well as political importance to the host government. Thirdly, as a condition for admission in the first place, particularly in a developing country, the parent company may be required to enter into a joint venture with the host government as a partner.

Less proximate effects of the multinational firm may be discerned in the changing relations between nation-states. By virtue of the fact that these firms operate production facilities in various countries, they stimulate trade among nation-states. To the extent that they have recourse to vertical integration, international trade includes the transfer of products among affiliates of multinational firms.

> . . . trade is no longer simply the result of national middlemen in one country interacting with importers in another. International firms have taken over, and there is every indication that international business is now the dominant factor in determining changes in the pattern of world exports as well as capital flows. . . . The movement of goods across national boundaries becomes foreign trade and exports even though the goods are only being transferred from one unit of the firm to another unit of the same firm. . . . A large and growing share of world exports and changes in them are . . . accounted for by internal product movements of the international company (43, pp. 6, 7, 13).

Moreover, because such firms often have similar operations in more than one country, there is a tendency, over time, to standardize technology (7, pp. 74–75; 28, pp. 84–86). There is also a tendency to standardize various policies, including wage scales. At least one international economist has suggested that such companies are exerting an influence in the direction of wage equalization, thus in the long run contributing to a reduction of one source of income inequality between nations (28, pp. 34–35, 188).

Yet another impact of these firms on the relationships between nation-states, is the recent emergence of what Perlmutter has called the "trans-ideological venture" (37). To modernize their industrial plant, communist countries have encouraged their state-owned enterprises to enter into co-production contracts with western firms. Such contracts usually provide for the cooperative manufacture of finished industrial products. A western firm, as a rule, contributes a technologically sophisticated component which an eastern firm uses to produce a finished product salable in highly competitive markets (21). Several examples of East-West ventures are as follows:

> (a) IKEA, a Swedish furniture chain, supplies to associates in Poland machinery and designs under its technical control for the semimanufacture of furniture, which is then shipped to Sweden for finishing by IKEA.
>
> (b) The U. S. based Simmons Machine Tool Corporation has agreed with Czechoslovakia's Skoda to have the latter produce a line of specialized heavy equipment under the Simmons-Skoda trademark. The U. S. firm has exclusive sales rights in the Western Hemisphere, but there are no other territorial limitations for either side.
>
> (c) Krupp of Essen, Germany, and the Csoepel machine tool factory of Hungary have jointly developed digitally controlled short lathes based

on German designs and drawings, which are to be exported to Germany and other markets (37, pp. 39–40).

The benefits derived from such ventures are mutual. According to one scholar:

> To the Western firm, they represent an opportunity to expand its market, while reducing to a minimum the drain on the limited hard currency funds of the East European partner. To the state enterprise in the East, a joint venture provides a practical opportunity to broaden its technological horizon, to study advanced management practices and to learn the contemporary marketing techniques of the commercial world (21, p. 53).

Whether such co-production contracts will become regularized, whether they will diffuse to such regional organizations as the European Common Market and the Council on Mutual Economic Aid and, in turn, have the effect of attenuating conflicts between communist and non-communist countries, only time will tell.

Operating within and between sovereign states exposes the multinational firm to various hazards, chief of which, of course, is nationalization by a host country. Other hazards do not affect all multinational firms alike. If the home government, as in the case of the U. S., restricts expansion of enterprises through horizontal integration, such firms can be subject to anti-trust law violations. Another restriction on the operations of multinational firms occurs when a home government, in exercising its rights of extra-territoriality, intervenes in the operations of a subsidiary in a host country. A case in point is when the U. S., committed to a policy of preventing the proliferation of nuclear weapons, prohibits IBM's subsidiary in France from selling the French Government a particular type of computer needed for the production of nuclear bombs (28, p. 43).

Such risks and restrictions, stemming from the fact that the multinational company is a citizen of several sovereign states, have prompted some scholars to speculate about a new legal status for this type of organization. Instead of being subject to various sovereignties, they advocate that it be chartered, taxed and controlled by an international organization, perhaps an agency of the U.N. (40, p. 224; 41, p. 154).

If such a transformation in legal status were ever wrought, the U.N. and the international system obviously would be the primary beneficiaries. The U.N. would have a greatly expanded source of income from many thousands of companies to finance adequately its own activities as well as the urgent development programs of many poor member states, thus substantially strengthening the economic, organizational and normative levels of integration of the international system.

In short, the multinationalization of the corporation has brought into being a new "transnational actor" which intentionally or unintentionally affects nation-states and relations among nation-states (59; 60).

As Wells puts it:

Multinational business enterprises are clearly important transnational actors. They move large amounts of resources across international boundaries. Some of them have organizations that centralize decision-making processes so that these resources can be used to fulfill objectives that may be at variance with those of a particular country in which a subsidiary is located. These firms have at their disposal many tools for frustrating governmental policies, but the policies that they frustrate may be those of the host government or those of the home government.

Some multinational enterprises may seem to form alliances with governments. Yet, as they grow and begin to take a more global view, these alliances may prove to be no more lasting than those of nation-states. . . .

The fact that some of these organizations are operating in a coordinated fashion or that they even seem to have the potential for doing so makes them appear to governments as a challenge to their control. The result is a feeling of frustration on the part of governmental officials that results in occasional lashing out at foreign investment. . . . The desire of the government to retain control leads to attacks on enterprises that appear to challenge its sovereignty (60, p. 113).

## International Professional Associations

Although it antedates the multinational corporation, the international professional association is also essentially a twentieth century phenomenon. What is more, like the multinational corporation, its growth rate in the past two decades has been impressive (50). It is by far the most numerous and probably the most influential type of organization in the class usually referred to as international, non-governmental organizations or INGOs. In a study of INGOs, Smoker found that the rate of formation between 1870 and 1960 has increased exponentially, except for two slumps associated with World Wars I and II (51, pp. 640–641). This finding very likely applies to international professional associations as well.

From the perspective of the sociology of occupations we are dealing with a group of occupations which are either full-fledged professions or in the process of professionalization (13, pp. 100–101). In either case, professional associations are formed in order to contribute to the fund of technical and systematic knowledge underlying an occupation, to promote an orientation of service to society rather than self-interest, and to increase autonomy in professional practice. Some professions have ancient origins, such as medicine, law, the ministry, and teaching; others have come into being as a result of the emergence of industrialization and the rise of modern science and technology. In the transformation of an occupation in accordance with the two primary characteristics of a profession, that is, the possession of a body of abstract knowledge and the commitment to an ideal of service, Wilensky suggests that it entails the following sequence of stages: (1) full-time performance of the occupational function; (2) establishment of a school that is not connected with a university; (3) establishment of a university school; (4) formation of a local professional association; (5) formation of a national professional association; (6) enactment of a licensing law; and (7) development of a formal code of ethics (62). Even if this sequence of stages is neither invariant nor exhaustive, we would expect, as a rule, that international professional associations would emerge following the formation of national professional associations. Thus, in the case of the engineering profession, local professional associations were established in various parts of England and Scotland during the latter part of the eighteenth century. In 1818 the first national professional association, the Institution of Civil Engineers, was established in England. Similar organizations came into existence in the United States in 1852 and in Canada in 1887. Almost a century later, several regional associations of engineering were founded, such as the European Federation of National Associations of Engineers and several highly specialized international associations, such as the World Power Conference. It was not until 1951 that an omnibus international association, referred to by Galtung as a super-INGO (15) was formed, under the aegis of UNESCO, known as the Union of International Engineering Organizations (13).

In the development of modern science, it is also possible to identify a sequence of .stages of professionalization which, however, differs in some respects from that of engineering. Already at the stage of the formation of local professional associations there is an active interest in facilitating the dissemination of knowledge and the collaboration among scientists across national boundaries. With the advent of modern science, learned societies and academies were founded, such as the Royal Society of London in 1662, the Academie des Sciences in 1666, and several decades later, the Berlin Academy of Sciences and the Academy of St. Petersburg. In an address commemorating the 300th anniversary of Isaac Newton, the renowned Russian physicist, Kapitza, refers to Newton's active role in the affairs of the Royal Society. He observes that the Royal Society "in contrast to all academies, has still the character of a non-state society . . . Since the very beginning of its existence, the Royal Society has maintained contact with many foreign scientists. Sometimes foreigners were elected as Foreign Members of the Society, including our scientists Euler, Kruzenshtern, Struve, Chebyshev, Mechnikov, Pavlov, Timiryazev, Golitsyn . . . Since Newton's times, the Royal Society has maintained a lively contact with scientific societies the world over." (18, p. 139).

Until the eighteenth century, the scientific community was relatively small and communication was facilitated by the use of common languages such as Latin and French and a common core of knowledge since there were still few fields of specialization. With the growth of the scientific community and the multiplication of specialities in the nineteenth century, national and international associations arose. One of the oldest international scientific organization, the International Meteorological Committee, was founded in 1872. Numerous international associations were subsequently founded so that by the end of World War I there was a felt need for a new association to coordinate the multitude of scientific organizations, thus giving rise in 1919 to a super-INGO called the International Council of Scientific Associations (35, pp. 11–16).

For a more precise assessment of the growth of different types of international professional associations, we turn again to the invaluable *Yearbook* of the Union of International Associations. Over the years this organization has struggled with the problem of classifying INGOs. In its 12th edition, nineteen categories of organizations are presented from which I have selected the following six that appear to include a great variety of professional associations: social sciences; law, administration; professions, employers; economics; finance; technology, science; health, medicine (57, p. 13). Examining various editions of the *Yearbook* yielded data, shown in Table 3, on the number of associations reported in each of these six categories for a sixty-year period, from 1909–1969.

The first noteworthy finding is that as of 1969 there were 757 international professional associations which constitute 50 percent of the population of 1,515 active INGOs for that year. In all likelihood, this percentage underestimates the total number of INGOs that are in fact engaged in professional activities. A re-classification of the population of associations in the *Yearbook* would probably yield a higher percentage. Secondly, over a sixty-year period these associations have increased about ten-fold; and during the last twenty years they have increased about 169 percent. The average annual percentage increase in the past two decades is about 9 percent, a striking growth rate which approximates that of the multinational corporation.

The findings in Table 3 leave unanswered at least four important questions concerning the growth of international professional associations: (1) How many national professional associations and individual members are involved in these 757 INGOs? (2) How many nation-states indirectly participate in these associations? (3) How widely dispersed is nation-state participation geographically as well as ideologically? (4) What are the annual budgets of these associations?

A partial answer to the third question concerning the distribution of participation in these associations was gleaned from some data reported by the Union of International Associations. In Table 4, data on the nationality of the principal officials, such as, the president and secretary general, of the 757 associations are tabulated. Examining the total column of the number of officials for each of the 44 countries listed suggests a rather uneven distribution. France tops the list with 202 officials and four countries (Guatemala, Peru, Malaysia, and UAR) have but one

**TABLE 3**

*Growth of International Professional Organizations\**

| CATEGORY | 1909–1910 | 1951–1952 | 1956–1957 | 1966–1967 | 1968–1969 | % INCREASE 1909–1969 | % INCREASE 1951–1969 | AVERAGE ANNUAL % INCREASE SINCE: 1909 | 1951 |
|---|---|---|---|---|---|---|---|---|---|
| Social Science | 10 | 35 | 57 | 80 | 90 | 800 | 157 | 13.33 | 8.26 |
| Law, Administration | 13 | 30 | 28 | 48 | 54 | 315 | 80 | 5.25 | 4.21 |
| Professions, Employers | 2 | 34 | 67 | 93 | 105 | 5150 | 208 | 85.83 | 10.99 |
| Economics, Finance | 3 | 14 | 15 | 35 | 40 | 1233 | 185 | 20.55 | 9.77 |
| Technology | 8 | 35 | 36 | 83 | 102 | 1175 | 191 | 19.58 | 10.07 |
| Science | 21 | 56 | 69 | 137 | 152 | 623 | 171 | 10.38 | 9.02 |
| Health, Medicine | 16 | 77 | 100 | 173 | 214 | 1237 | 178 | 20.62 | 9.96 |
| TOTAL | 73 | 281 | 372 | 649 | 757 | 936 | 169 | 15.61 | 8.91 |

*Source: Union of International Associations, *Yearbook of International Organizations*, Brussels, Belgium; 1st, 4th, 6th, 11th and 12th editions.

*Nationality of Principal Officials of International Professional Associations*\*\*\*

| Country | Social Sciences # | % | Law, Administration # | % | Professions, Employers # | % | Economics, Finance # | % | Technology # | % | Science # | % | Health Medicine # | % | Total by Country # | % |
|---|---|---|---|---|---|---|---|---|---|---|---|---|---|---|---|---|
| *Africa* | | | | | | | | | | | | | | | | |
| Ghana | — | — | — | — | — | — | — | — | — | — | 2 | 1 | — | — | 2 | * |
| Nigeria | — | — | 1 | 1 | — | — | — | — | — | — | — | — | 1 | * | 2 | * |
| UAR | — | — | 1 | 1 | — | — | — | — | — | — | — | — | — | — | 1 | * |
| Others | — | — | 1 | 1 | 2 | 1 | — | — | 1 | 1 | 2 | 1 | — | — | 6 | 1 |
| *America* | | | | | | | | | | | | | | | | |
| Argentina | 3 | 2 | — | — | — | — | — | — | 1 | 1 | 1 | * | 3 | 1 | 8 | 1 |
| Brazil | 2 | 1 | 1 | 1 | — | — | — | — | — | — | 1 | * | 2 | 1 | 6 | 1 |
| Canada | — | — | 1 | 1 | 4 | 3 | — | — | 1 | 1 | 6 | 2 | 6 | 2 | 18 | 2 |
| Chile | — | — | — | — | — | — | — | — | 1 | 1 | — | — | 2 | 1 | 3 | * |
| Columbia | — | — | 2 | 2 | — | — | — | — | 1 | 1 | — | — | 1 | * | 4 | * |
| Guatemala | 1 | 1 | — | — | — | — | — | — | — | — | — | — | — | — | 1 | * |
| Mexico | 3 | 2 | — | — | 1 | 1 | 1 | 2 | 3 | 2 | — | — | 1 | * | 9 | 1 |
| Peru | — | — | 1 | 1 | — | — | — | — | — | — | — | — | — | — | 1 | * |
| USA | 22 | 16 | 12 | 14 | 7 | 4 | 10 | 19 | 5 | 4 | 36 | 15 | 41 | 14 | 133 | 12 |
| Uruguay | — | — | — | — | 2 | 1 | — | — | 1 | 1 | — | — | 4 | 1 | 7 | 1 |
| Venezuela | — | — | — | — | 1 | 1 | — | — | — | — | — | — | 1 | * | 2 | * |
| Others | — | — | 1 | 1 | 1 | 1 | — | — | — | — | — | — | 1 | * | 3 | * |
| *Asia* | | | | | | | | | | | | | | | | |
| India | — | — | 1 | 1 | 1 | 1 | — | — | 3 | 2 | 7 | 3 | 1 | * | 13 | 1 |
| Israel | 1 | 1 | — | — | — | — | — | — | — | — | 1 | * | 3 | 1 | 5 | * |
| Japan | 2 | 2 | 2 | 2 | — | — | — | — | 2 | 1 | 5 | 2 | 7 | 2 | 18 | 2 |
| Malaysia | — | — | — | — | — | — | — | — | — | — | — | — | 1 | * | 1 | * |
| Philippines | — | — | 2 | 2 | — | — | — | — | — | — | — | — | 2 | 1 | 4 | * |
| Others | — | — | 1 | 1 | — | — | — | — | — | — | 2 | 1 | 1 | * | 4 | * |

**TABLE 4 (contd.)**

| Country | Social Sciences | | Law, Administration | | Professions, Employers | | Economics, Finance | | Technology | | Science | | Health Medicine | | Country Total By | |
|---|---|---|---|---|---|---|---|---|---|---|---|---|---|---|---|---|
| | # | % | # | % | # | % | # | % | # | % | # | % | # | % | # | % |
| *Australasia* | | | | | | | | | | | | | | | | |
| Australia | — | — | — | — | — | — | — | — | 1 | 1 | 2 | 1 | 2 | 1 | 5 | * |
| New Zealand | 1 | 1 | — | — | — | — | — | — | — | — | 1 | * | — | — | 2 | * |
| *Europe* | | | | | | | | | | | | | | | | |
| Austria | 1 | 1 | 1 | 1 | 3 | 2 | — | — | 1 | 1 | 3 | 1 | 3 | 1 | 12 | 1 |
| Belgium | 16 | 12 | 10 | 12 | 22 | 14 | 11 | 20 | 11 | 8 | 14 | 6 | 22 | 7 | 106 | 9 |
| Czechoslovakia | 1 | 1 | — | — | — | — | — | — | — | — | 1 | * | — | — | 2 | * |
| Denmark | 5 | 4 | 1 | 1 | 4 | 3 | — | — | 2 | 1 | 8 | 3 | 10 | 3 | 30 | 3 |
| Finland | — | — | — | — | 1 | 1 | — | — | — | — | 1 | * | — | — | 2 | * |
| France | 21 | 16 | 15 | 18 | 38 | 24 | 10 | 19 | 31 | 23 | 31 | 13 | 56 | 19 | 202 | 18 |
| Germany | 6 | 4 | 5 | 6 | 6 | 4 | 2 | 4 | 12 | 9 | 9 | 4 | 10 | 3 | 50 | 4 |
| Greece | 1 | 1 | 1 | 1 | 1 | 1 | — | — | — | — | — | — | — | — | 3 | * |
| Hungary | — | — | — | — | — | — | — | — | 1 | 1 | 1 | * | 1 | * | 3 | * |
| Ireland | 2 | 1 | — | — | — | — | — | — | — | — | — | — | — | — | 2 | * |
| Italy | 9 | 8 | 3 | 4 | 10 | 6 | 1 | 2 | 4 | 3 | 6 | 2 | 20 | 6 | 53 | 5 |
| Luxembourg | — | — | 2 | 2 | — | — | — | — | — | — | — | — | — | — | 2 | * |
| Netherlands | 13 | 10 | 2 | 2 | 9 | 6 | 7 | 13 | 9 | 7 | 20 | 8 | 14 | 5 | 74 | 7 |
| Norway | — | — | — | — | 1 | 1 | 1 | 2 | 2 | 1 | 5 | 2 | 4 | 1 | 13 | 1 |
| Poland | 2 | 1 | — | — | — | — | — | — | 1 | 1 | 1 | * | — | — | 4 | * |
| Portugal | — | — | — | — | — | — | 1 | 2 | — | — | — | — | 2 | 1 | 3 | * |
| Rumania | 1 | 1 | — | — | — | — | — | — | 1 | 1 | 1 | * | 1 | * | 4 | * |
| Spain | 1 | 1 | 2 | 1 | 1 | 1 | 2 | 4 | 3 | 2 | 1 | * | 5 | 2 | 11 | 1 |
| Sweden | 3 | 2 | 1 | 1 | 9 | 6 | 4 | 7 | 14 | 10 | 5 | 2 | 8 | 3 | 31 | 3 |
| Switzerland | 10 | 7 | 5 | 6 | 13 | 8 | 4 | 7 | 22 | 16 | 31 | 13 | 28 | 9 | 105 | 9 |
| United Kingdom | 4 | 3 | 13 | 15 | 22 | 14 | — | — | 1 | 1 | 4 | 2 | 37 | 12 | 138 | 12 |
| U.S.S.R. | 1 | 1 | — | — | — | — | — | — | — | — | 2 | 1 | — | — | 6 | 1 |
| Yugoslavia | 1 | 1 | 1 | 1 | — | — | — | — | — | — | 1 | * | — | — | 3 | * |
| Others | 1 | 1 | — | — | 1 | 1 | — | — | — | — | — | — | — | — | 4 | * |

## TABLE 5

*Rank Order Correlation of Number of Multinational Firms by
Nationality of Corporate Headquarters and Number of Principal Officials
of International Professional Associations by Nationality*\*

| Country | Number of Multinational Firms | Rank Order | Number of Principal Officials of International Professional Associations | Rank Order |
|---|---|---|---|---|
| U.S.A. | 2816 | 1 | 133 | 3 |
| United Kingdom | 1651 | 2 | 138 | 2 |
| Germany (FR) | 801 | 3 | 50 | 8 |
| France | 471 | 4 | 202 | 1 |
| Switzerland | 349 | 5 | 105 | 5 |
| Netherlands | 222 | 6 | 74 | 6 |
| Sweden | 219 | 7 | 31 | 9 |
| Belgium | 197 | 8 | 106 | 4 |
| Italy | 101 | 9 | 53 | 7 |
| Denmark | 82 | 10 | 30 | 10 |
| Norway | 78 | 11 | 13 | 11 |
| Austria | 38 | 12 | 12 | 12 |
| Spain | 9 | 13 | 11 | 13 |

$\tau = .69$, significant at .0005

\*Source: Union of International Associations, *Yearbook of International Organizations*, 12th ed., Brussels, Belgium, 1969, p. 1189; *International Associations*, 19 (May 1967), pp. 354–355.

official each. Thirteen of the 44 countries with a range of 202 to 11 officials are arrayed in Table 5. Also included in Table 5 is a rank order for the same countries according to the number of multinational firms, which information is reproduced from Table 2. The resulting rank-order correlation coefficient of .69 (Kendall Tau) between the number of multinational firms in a country and the number of principal officials of international professional associations is significant at .0005. It suggests that this dimension of participation in international professional associations is in part a function of economic development, since as the development of a country increases, so does the proportion of professionals in the labor force. Some evidence in support of this interpretation is provided by partialling out the effect of economic development (as reflected in GNP/capita), on the rank-order correlation coefficient. When this is done, the original Kendall Tau of .69 is reduced to .55.

Given the number and growth rate of international professional associations, what effect are they having on the process of integration of the international system? In the absence of relevant systematic research, I shall approximate an answer to this question with the aid of the non-linear model of integration of the international system, presented in Figure 3. This entails mapping the interaction patterns of these organizations with other components of the international system. To do this, we shall first consider some of the activities of these organizations.

The principal functions of these assocations are to convene congresses and other special meetings, publish conference proceedings and research reports, facilitate an exchange of visits, stimulate collaborative research, etc. In organizing a congress, the international professional association depends upon the cooperation and assistance of its member organizations in various countries. Of the estimated 3,000-4,000 international congresses of INGOs held annually (22, p. 144), involving at least one million people, probably one-half are convened by international professional associations. It is, therefore, no wonder that the problems of planning and managing congresses have themselves become the subject of international congresses (56).

On the occasion of the Fifth World Congress of Sociology in 1962, Lazarsfeld and Leeds pointed out that congresses perform three important interrelated functions: they afford an opportunity for personal contacts, stimulate joint research projects, and sensitize participants to theoreical perspectives of members from different countries (30).

That personal contacts, in turn, increase sensitivity to foreign perspectives was recently noted by Marshall, a former president of the International Sociological Association:

> When representatives of countries in which the Marxist-Leninist philosophy prevails began to attend international Congresses and meetings in Western Europe, and when, under the auspices of Unesco, similar meetings were held in one or other of the countries of Eastern Europe, there was naturally, some tension in the air, and mutual suspicion, tempered by curiosity and a genuine desire to understand. Friendly debate took place in its early stages, more as an exchange of views between two sides than as the free intercourse of independent minds. But by the early 1960's things had changed, the experience of attending fully representative international meetings had become a familiar one, and many of the participants were now old friends. Ideological differences still make themselves felt, of course, and they are sometimes stimulating and sometimes frustrating, but a big step forward has been made towards finding a common ground of scientific discourse on which all can meet without distinction of national origin or political allegiance. It remains to be seen whether, or within what space of time, this idea can be fully realized (55, p. 11).

The various functions performed by international professional associations tend to increase the bonds between the parent international organization, as it were, and the affiliated national organizations, that is, the national professional associations in the various nation-states. By eliciting participation of national professional associations from various nation-states, the international professional association unintentionally creates a network of relationships between nation-states. This is especially true for those associations that are relatively free of ideology. Thus, for example, Kriesberg found that in health and science INGOs, in which consensus is presumably high, participation of professional associations from the U.S. and the U.S.S.R. is higher than in INGOs in which consensus is low, such as those dealing with international relations, art and religion (29, p. 471).

There are also other links with nation-states, one of which is of considerable moment to the international professional association. The nation-state is the source of incorporation of this type of association; and depending on how liberal its incorporation law is, it affects the legal status of the association and more specifically, such rights as owning property, holding funds, entering into contracts, transferring funds from one country to another, and the freedom of its representatives to travel over the world (44). Another link with the nation-state, which is quite different, involves rendering expert professional guidance, as in the case of the International Statistical Institute which has helped nations with their censuses to insure high professional standards and comparable classifications (27, p. 235); and a variety of medical associations such as the International Union Against Tuberculosis, have aided nation-states in the combatting of diseases (61, p. 171).

Compared with the links between the international professional association and the nation-state, those with regional organizations are probably fewer. The European Economic Community has accorded consultative status to various INGOs, some of which would fall into the category of professional associations (48, pp. 392–395). In all likelihood, *regional* professional associations, such as the European Federation of National Associations of Engineers, develop closer ties with the European Economic Community than do *international* professional associations. This may also be true in other regional communities, e.g., the Latin American Free Trade Area and their corresponding professional associations, e.g., the Pan-American Federation of Engineering Societies.

As regards the bonds between the international professional association and the multinational firm, they seem somewhat tenuous. Several international professional associations such as the international arbitration tribunals of the International Chamber of Commerce and Inter-American Commercial Arbitration Commission, perform a direct service to multinational corporations by helping them resolve conflicts outside the framework of judiciaries of nation-states (3, pp. 134–178).

In view of the fact that there is a high overlap in membership of engineers and scientists in international professional associations and multinational firms and that both organizations struggle with the ambiguities of operating across national boundaries, one would expect a variety of types of interactions to develop among these organizations. It can reasonably be predicted that when each type of organization becomes fully cognizant of the other's existence — and the Union of International Associations already is, witness the addition of a section of multinational corporations in its *Yearbook* — new patterns of interaction will emerge which may significantly increase the level of organizational and possibly also normative integration of the international system.

By far the most highly developed interaction patterns are observable between international professional associations and inter-governmental organizations or IGO's as they are customarily abbreviated. This is to be expected since some INGOs have for a long time sought to influence the decisions of IGOs. The fact that INGOs are accorded consultative status to the Economic and Social Council of the U. N. and to its many specialized agencies, such as the International Labor Organization, the World Health Organization, and UNESCO, has encouraged the growth of INGOs — so much so that it has been asserted that "Every IGO . . . has at least one counterpart in the INGO world" (44, p. 8).

The reciprocal effects between these two types of organizations have been extensive. Some international professional associations have been instrumental in the formation of some IGOs, and, in turn, some IGOs have created some international professional associations.

According to an official of the International Labor Organization:

> . . . medical specialists from different countries gradually formed contacts, and so there came into being the International Committee on Industrial Medicine which before the War Organized International Congresses on Industrial Diseases, the first in Milan in 1908 . . .
>
> The year 1900 saw the foundation at Paris of the International Association for . . . [Labor Legislation], with headquarters at Basle, which represented the first attempt to make an international collection of legislative measures relating to industry, and which arranged for the holding of meetings where problems of hygiene and pathology were discussed resulting in the drawing up of Conventions, such as the Berne Convention relative to the prohibition of the use of phosphorus in the making of watches (1908).
>
> Such tentative suggestions and efforts paved the way for the post-war creation of the International Labour Organization. . . . (61, pp. 171–172).

The unique role of UNESCO in creating and reorganizing various international associations in the social sciences and in establishing two super-INGOs, the International Social Science Council and the International Committee for Social Science Documentation, is well known (55). Less well known, and of considerable importance, is the fact that UNESCO provides subsidies to various international professional associations to supplement their meager budgets.

In short, there is already in being an elaborate network of relationships between international professional associations and various components of the international system.

## Conclusion

Two types of international organizations — the multinational enterprise and the international professional association — have thus far largely eluded the ken of awareness of students of organization theory and social change. The field of international relations has likewise not done justice to these types of organizations. Many scholars in this field evidently assume that these types of organizations, though operating in the interstices of nation-states, have little consequence for the future development of the international system (22, p. 143). In subscribing to this view they may be overlooking the potential of these organizations for cumulatively and unanticipatedly transforming the international system. This conception of the international system is not unique to international relations specialists. Some futurologists, like Kahn and Wiener, in their broadgauged analysis of various possible structural modifications of the international system within the next three decades, likewise ignore such nongovernmental, international organizations as the multinational firm and the international professional association (24, pp. 359–385).

Yet the dynamism of the international system of the future may derive from a force for integration intimated in Durkheim's famous preface to the second edition of *The Division of labor*, entitled, "Some Notes on Occupational Groups."

> . . . as advances are made in history, the organization which has territorial groups as its base steadily becomes effaced . . . These geographical divisions are, for the most part, artificial and no longer awaken in us profound sentiments. The provincial spirit has disappeared never to return; the patriotism of the parish has become an archaism that cannot be restored at will . . . the State is too remote from individuals; its relations with them too external and intermittent to penetrate deeply into individual consciences and socialize them within. Where the State is the only environment in which men can live communal lives, they inevitably lose contact, become detached. . . . A nation can be maintained only if, between the State and the individual, there is intercalated a whole series of *secondary groups* near enough to the individuals to attract them strongly in their sphere of action and drag them, in this way, into the general torrent of social life. We have just shown how occupational groups are suited to fill this role, and that is their destiny. (11, pp. 27–28).

Broadly conceived, the multinational corporation and the international professional association may be collectively performing the solidary functions at the international level which Durkheim envisioned for "occupational groups" within the nation. To those social scientists who discern an intellectual challenge in the study of these organizations, the task that lies ahead is at least fourfold:

A) developing a model, akin to the non-linear model of integration diagrammed in Figure 3, which copes with the complexity of the linkages among the components of the international system;

B) operationalizing various dimensions of integration of the international system, such as the four identified in the model presented in Figure 3;

C) designing an information system on various components of the international system, including multinational corporations and international professional associations, of the kind recently described and proposed by Judge (23, pp. 47–64); and

D) providing for longitudinal data collection on (1) the various system linkages, such as those postulated in our non-linear model of integration and (2) the various dimensions of integration of the international system.

By studying the interaction patterns of these organizations to ascertain whether they are in fact creating networks of people transcending the nation-state and generating new levels of normative, economic, organizational and occupational integration, social scientists can discover whether Durkheim's anticipations are valid for the international system.

## BIBLIOGRAPHY

1. Adám, Gyorgy. "New Trends in International Business: Worldwide Sourcing and Dedomiciling." Paper presented at International Conference on Multinational Corporations at Queens University of Belfast, May, 1971. (mimeo)

2. Aiken, Michael, and Jerald Hage. "Organizational Interdependence and Intra-Organizational Structure." *American Sociological Review*, Vol. 33 (December 1968), pp. 912–929.

3. American Management Association. *Resolving Business Disputes.* New York: American Management Association, 1965.

4. Angell, Robert C. "The Growth of Transnational Participation," in Louis Kriesberg (ed.), *Social Processes in International Relations: A Reader.* New York: John Wiley & Sons, 1968.

5. Anonymous. "Why Unions Fear the Multinationals." *Business Week,* December 19, 1970, pp. 95–98.

6. Behrman, Jack N. "Multinational Corporations, Transnational Interest and National Sovereignty," *Columbia Journal of World Business,* Vol. 4 (March-April 1969), pp. 15–21.

7. Behrman, Jack N. *Some Patterns in the Rise of the Multinational Enterprise.* Chapel Hill: University of North Carolina Graduate School of Business Administration, 1969.

8. Boddewyn, J., and R. Nath. "Comparative Management Studies: An

Assessment." *Management International Review*, Vol. 10 (January 1970), pp. 9–11.

9. Brams, Steven J. "The Search for Structural Order in the International System: Some Models and Preliminary Results." *International Studies Quarterly*, Vol. 13 (September 1969), pp. 254–280.

10. Casserini, Karl. "The Challenge of Multi-National Corporations and Regional Economic Integration to the Trade Unions, Their Structure and Their International Activities," in Hans Günter (ed.), *Transnational Industrial Relations*. London: The Macmillan Co., 1972.

11. Durkheim, Emile. *The Division of Labor in Society*, translated by George Simpson. Glencoe, Ill.: The Free Press, 1960.

12. Evan, William M. "Transnational Forums for Peace," in Quincy Wright, William M. Evan, and Morton Deutsch (eds.), *Preventing World War III: Some Proposals*. New York: Simon and Schuster, 1962.

13. Evan, William M. "The Engineering Profession: A Cross-Cultural Analysis," in Robert Perrucci and Joel E. Gerstl (eds.), *The Engineers and the Social System*. New York: John Wiley & Sons, 1969.

14. Fouraker, Laurence E., and John M. Stopford. "Organizational Structure and the Multinational Strategy." *Administrative Science Quarterly*, Vol. 13 (June 1968), pp. 47–64.

15. Galtung, Johan. "On the Future of the International System." *Journal of Peace Research*, Vol. 4, No. 4 (1967), pp. 305–333.

16. Galtung, Johan. "A Structural Theory of Integration." *Journal of Peace Research*, Vol. 5, No. 4 (1968), pp. 375–395.

17. Grzybowski, Kazimierz. *The Socialist Commonwealth of Nations: Organizations and Institutions*. New Haven: Yale University Press, 1964.

18. Haas, Ernst B. *The Uniting of Europe*. Stanford: Stanford University Press, 1958.

19. Haas, Michael. "A Functional Approach to International Organization." *Journal of Politics*, Vol. 27 (August 1965), pp. 498–517.

20. Herman, Leon M. "CIMECON Reform Depends on Trade with World Markets." *Columbia Journal of World Business*, Vol. 4 (1969), pp. 51–58.

21. Judge, A. J. N. "Evaluation of International Organizations." *International Associations*, Vol. 21 (March 1969), pp. 141–147.

22. Judge, A. J. N. "Information Systems and Inter-organizational Space." *Annals of the American Academy of Political and Social Science*, Vol. 393 (January 1971), pp. 47–64.

23. Kahn, Herman, and Anthony J. Wiener, *The Year 2000*. New York: The Macmillan Co., 1967.

24. Kaufmann, O. "Diverging Structural Patterns in the Development of American and European Firms." *Management International Review*, Vol. 10 (January 1970), pp. 101–107.

25. Keohane, Robert O., and Joseph S. Nye, Jr. (eds.). *Transnational Relations and World Politics*. Cambridge, Mass.: Harvard University Press, 1972.

26. Keyfitz, Nathan. "Government Statistics." *International Encyclopedia of the Social Sciences*, Vol. 6, pp. 230–240. New York: The Macmillan Co. and The Free Press, 1968.

27. Kindleberger, Charles P. *American Business Abroad.* New Haven: Yale University Press, 1969.

28. Kriesberg, Louis. "U.S. and U.S.S.R. Participation in International Non-Governmental Organizations," in Louis Kriesberg (ed.), *Social Processes in International Relations: A Reader.* New York: John Wiley & Sons, 1968.

29. Lazarsfeld, Paul F., and Ruth Leeds. "International Sociology as a Sociological Problem." *American Sociological Review,* Vol. 27 (October 1962), pp. 732–741.

30. Luard, Evan (ed.). *The Evolution of International Organizations.* New York: Frederick A. Praeger, 1966.

31. Miles, Caroline M. "The International Corporation." *International Affairs,* Vol. 45 (April 1969), pp. 259–268.

32. Miles, Edward. "Organizations and Integration in International Systems." *International Studies Quarterly,* Vol. 12 (June 1968), pp. 196–224.

33. Nye, J. S. "Comparing Common Markets: A Revised Neo-Functionalist Model." *International Organization,* Vol. 24 (Autumn 1970), pp. 796–835.

34. Organization for Economic Cooperation and Development. *International Scientific Organizations.* Paris: Organization for Economic Cooperation and Development, 1964.

35. Perlmutter, Howard V. "The Tortuous Evolution of the Multinational Corporation." *Columbia Journal of World Business,* Vol. 4 (September-October 1969), pp. 9–18.

36. Perlmutter, Howard V. "Emerging East-West Ventures: The Transideological Enterprise." *Columbia Journal of World Business,* Vol. 4 (September-October 1969), pp. 39–50.

37. Quinn, James Brian. "Technology Transfer by Multinational Companies." *Harvard Business Review,* Vol. 47 (November-December 1969), pp. 147–161.

38. Robinson, Richard D. "Joint Ventures of Transnational Business?" *Industrial Management Review,* Vol. 6 (Fall 1964), pp. 59–65.

39. Robinson, Richard D. *International Business Policy.* New York: Holt, Rinehart, and Winston, 1964.

40. Robinson, Richard D. *International Management.* New York: Holt, Rinehart, and Winston, 1967.

41. Robinson, Richard D. "Ownership Across National Frontiers." *Industrial Management Review.* Vol. 11 (Fall 1969), pp. 41–61.

42. Robock, Stephen H., and Kenneth Simmonds. "International Business: How Big is It — The Missing Measurements." *Columbia Journal of World Business,* Vol. 5 (May-June 1970), pp. 6–19.

43. Rodgers, Raymond Spencer. *Facilitation Problems of International Associations.* Brussels: Union of International Associations, 1960.

44. Rolfe, Sidney E. *The International Corporation.* Paris: International Chamber of Commerce, 1969.

45. Rutenberg, David P. "Organizational Archetypes of a Multi-National Company," *Management Science,* Vol. 16 (February 1970), pp. B-337-349.

46. Sapir, Edward. "The Unconscious Patterning of Behavior in Society," in E. S. Dummer (ed.), *The Unconscious: A Symposium*. New York: Knopf, 1927.

47. Schokking, J. J., and Nels Anderson. "Observations on the European Integration Process." *Journal of Conflict Resolution*, Vol. 4 (December 1960), pp. 385–410.

48. Servan-Schreiber, J. J. *The American Challenge*. New York: Atheneum, 1968.

49. Skjelsbaek, Kjell. "The Growth of International Non-Governmental Organizations in the Twentieth Century," in Robert O. Keohane and Joseph S. Nye, Jr. (eds.), *Transnational Relations and World Politics*. Cambridge, Mass.: Harvard University Press, 1972.

50. Smoker, Paul. "A Preliminary Empirical Study of an International Integrative Subsystem." *International Associations*, Vol. 17 (November 1965), pp. 638–646.

51. Smoker, Paul. "Nation-State Escalation and International Integration," in Louis Kriesberg (ed.), *Social Processes in International Relations: A Reader*. New York: John Wiley & Sons, 1968.

52. Thompson, James D. *Organizations in Action*. New York: McGraw-Hill, 1967.

53. Turk, Herman. "Interorganizational Networks in Urban Society: Initial Perspectives and Comparative Research." *American Sociological Review*, Vol. 35 (February 1970), pp. 1–19.

54. UNESCO. *International Organizations in the Social Sciences*. Paris: UNESCO, 1966.

55. Union of International Associations. *International Congress Organizations: Theory and Practice*. Brussels: Union of International Associations, 1961.

56. Union of International Associations. *Yearbook of International Organizations*. Brussels: Union of International Associations, 1969.

57. Vernon, Raymond. "Multinational Enterprise and National Sovereignty." *Harvard Business Review*, Vol. 45 (March-April 1967), pp. 156–172.

58. Vernon, Raymond. "Multinational Business and National Economic Goals," in Robert O. Keohane and Joseph S. Nye, Jr. (eds.), *Transnational Relations and World Politics*. Cambridge, Mass.: Harvard University Press, 1972.

59. Wells, Louis T. "The Multinational Business Enterprise: What Kind of International Organization?" in Robert O. Keohane and Joseph S. Nye, Jr. (eds.), *Transnational Relations and World Politics*. Cambridge, Mass.: Harvard University Press, 1972.

60. White, Lyman C. *International Non-Governmental Organizations*. New Brunswick, N.J.: Rutgers University Press, 1951.

61. Wilensky, Harold L. "The Professionalization of Everyone?" *American Journal of Sociology*, Vol. 70 (September 1964), pp. 137–158.

# SECTION EIGHT

the dynamics of organizations,
professions, and foundations

# Introduction

The studies presented in this Section deal with the problematics faced by various kinds of associations, and the way in which the particular problem realm of each associational structure affects its development within a wider context. Sociology has travelled a long distance since Tönnies first enunciated a distinction between communities and associations premised (as is often forgotten today) on two types of Nietzschean *Wille*. Whether it has travelled in the right direction is open to question. Max Weber's work on imperatively coordinated associations and, in particular, on the analysis of bureaucracy, had the effect of diverting attention from motivational to more strictly structural considerations. In so doing, and also because of the high level of structural generality on which Weber's discussions were conducted, the sociological theory of associations came to concentrate on the internal dynamics of structural transformation. It is only quite recently that the study of associations as "systems within systems" has gathered momentum.

The small group of studies presented in this section adumbrate the most recent trend. Marcus, in reviewing the spectrum of extant organizational theories, opts for a conception of organizations based on their relations with enveloping external structures as well as on the interrelation of organizational sub-units. Gold's chapter places the professionalization of urban planning within the context of industrial urbanization. It then procedes to relate this process wth problems inherent to the new profession as well as with considerations concerning its "fit" with pre-

801

existing political structures. Colvard shows how philanthrophic foundations are both examples of social change and instruments of it.

In his overview of theories of organization, Marcus opts for a model
of competition and cooperation and foresees the integration of sociological and economic perspectives in a framework in which organizational
evolution will become predictable. Interestingly enough, this chapter can
be read equally well as a study in the professionalization of organizational analysis. In the diversity of theoretical schools which luxuriated
before the advent of a Kuhnian paradigm, vested interests become
established. The discussion of these vested interests lends itself quite
readily to analysis by aid of the organizational model Marcus favours.
The essay pulls together most of the strands of organization theory which
are normally separated in the different literatures of sociology, psychology, and economics.

Gold's study illustrates the twin problems of professionalization and of
the interplay between occupational categories and groups and the associational structures in which they operate. This is done by focusing on a
single case: urban planning. The editors find it notable how well professionalization fits into the framework of the theory of institutionalization
proposed in Sections Two and Three of this book. Professions arise in
response to recognized problems (articulated exigencies) and, in emerging, bring in their wake second order exigencies peculiar both to the
technologies they carry and to the structural set-up in which they operate.
Gold's lucid argument clearly differentiates phases of the professionalization process and, in so doing, reveals many of the gaps which further
research must close.

Colvard analyzes the manner in which philanthropic foundations attempt to maintain their social legitimacy while at the same time fulfilling
their functions as tax shelters for those who wish to go down in history
as "benefactors" rather than "malefactors of great wealth" (an expression used by Theodore Roosevelt to castigate the men who accused him
of being a traitor to his class). Accomplishing this successfully requires
that the foundations avoid being hung upon the horns of several
dilemmas: they must show that the money they are spending could not
be spent more equitably and intelligently by public agencies, yet they
must avoid "controversial" causes which can be attacked as not being
"in the public interest." Several foundations have been under double
jeopardy; they have been accused on the one hand of subsidizing social
research in safely established areas on the part of individuals and
organizations which already get the lion's share of support; on the other
hand, they have been accused of subverting established social norms by
supporting empirical research, such as Kinsey's study of sexual behavior.
Furthermore, Colvard points out, in attempting to implement the goals
of improving the work of scientific and educational institutions, the
foundations necessarily are limited by their clients' legitimate assertions

of autonomy from outside constraints, thus losing the freedom of action necessary for accomplishing their purpose. In a sense, the foundations are committed to sowing the seeds of their own destruction; but since no organization can be expected to engage in such enterprise whole-heartedly, we must expect them to build defense mechanisms to maintain their own autonomy and continued existence.

# 29

*Philip M. Marcus*

# Organizational change: A Review and

# Synthesis of the Literature*

### Introduction

In a previous paper, published over a decade ago, I discussed the importance of certain variables needed to investigate some aspects of organizational change(50). Specifically, using the example of American trade unions, I tried to show how trends toward centralization and oligarchy created opposing forces which contributed to representative government and decentralized decision-making. Some of the variables discussed were environmental, such as the role of government, industrial and labor force composition, density and degree of similarity of labor unions in a geographical and work area. Other variables considered included internal organizational properties such as density of union locals, degree of membership homogeneity, age of the organization, communication patterns (for example, frequency of newspaper publication and conventions), and nature of executive board representation. My argument focused upon the erosion of Michels' Iron Law of Oligarchy as countervening pressures emerged to insure membership prerogatives.

In the past decade, organizational change has received much attention and the body of literature has swelled from a wide variety of sources. Those active in social movements have realized that their goals can be

* I am indebted to Robert Banks, Thomas Conner, Nancy Hammond, Richard Hill, Dora Marcus, Harry Perlstadt, and Werner von der Ohe for many helpful comments and critical reading of earlier drafts of this paper.

attained only by organizing their own efforts as well as understanding governmental, industrial and other private bureaucracies. The poverty program, civil rights groups, women's liberation, student movements, welfare rights and anti-war activists were only a few of the many groups attempting to modify social policy by changing organizations which delivered the goods and services. As a result, many social scientists were drawn into the fray either by their own ideological or theoretical commitments, or by the opportunity to provide concrete service as advisors and consultants.

This paper brings together literature from four diverse perspectives, examining the contribution of each toward a theory of organizational change. This literature, at present, is widely scattered, often feeding upon itself and seldom integrated. The reader should be warned that the literaature discussed varies in quality from idle speculations which have spawned many investigations of dubious quality and distinction, to sophisticated theoretical and empirical studies. Indeed, a number of the papers discussed are not directly concerned with change but have implications for it. Thus, one contribution of this paper is to indicate how some organizational literature can be modified slightly to provide insights into change processes. In the concluson, I will sketch a change model which seems promising to integrate existing theories and suggest new avenues of research.

### Evolutionists and Neo-Evolutionists

An evolutionary theory of organizational change examines the natural unfolding of social processes. Most of the writers in this category would probably deny such an assumption in their work. They might contend that, unlike the traditional social evolutionists, the modern approach does not assume certain set stages or unilinearity of development. However, I would classify Weber, Michels, Troeltsch and Merton as obvious examples of theorists who assume certain specified directions of change are virtually inevitable and guided by historical forces, Iron Laws, or other social processes. Lipset, Blau, and Gouldner, in their early work, reflect a revisionist school which attempts to modify and specify conditions under which changes occur.

Most contemporary sociologists have accepted the Weberian assumptions (73, pp. 363–373) that bureaucracy emerges when an existing social structure cannot provide a demand for goods and services. Specifically, when a founding charismatic leader leaves office, a succession crisis occurs, because the leader has pursued vague and abstract goals, has been devoted to a mission, and has not attended to the mundane allocation of resources and the effective production of goods and services. After a period of competition among lieutenants, a bureaucratic organization emerges with rules, an impersonal hierarchy of authority, and a rational division of labor for the allocation of duties. Weber envisioned a movement toward the ideal type of bureaucracy, with each characteristic he delineated becoming more entrenched and elaborated: for example, hierarchy of authority, impersonality, rules, division of labor, and so on (73, pp. 324–340).

Concurrent with the Weberian theory of organizational evolution, Michels was developing his *Iron Law of Oligarchy* (55). Studying a German workers' political party, Michels postulated that pressures upon leaders induced them to utilize non-democratic means to retain their offices. Participation of members begins to decrease under these conditions, and a small group of officials determines policy and sets goals without regular accountability through elections. In many instances, an organization begins to engage in practices which are virtually antithetical to its membership's interest because established community power groups demand programmatic and ideological concessions from the leadership. Thus, concludes Michels, even in those organizations whose initial set of goals is to increase the impact of its members upon society, the nature of the leadership system engenders the development of an unresponsive oligarchy.

Michels had a great impact on the work of social scientists as they desperately sought to find exceptions to his postulates. Their conclusions, nevertheless, tended to support the *Iron Law*. They studied many different kinds of organizations, but oligarchy predominated in groups as diverse as labor unions, industrial corporations, voluntary associations, political parties, and even symphony orchestras (74; 22; 1; 32).

A third major evolutionary model of organizational change was developed from the study of religious institutions. Perhaps Troeltsch's typology of sect and church is most widely known, although Becker and Yinger have contributed substantial theoretical amplifications to the original distinction, (72, pp. 331–382; 4, pp. 252–255; 75, pp. 16–50). According to Troeltsch, a sect is associated with the lower classes and stresses radicalism and literal obedience by a small, discontinuous and voluntary membership. The church, on the other hand, interacts with the secular world and adapts to changes within it. Recently, other writers have depicted in great detail the transition of religious groups toward bureaucratic structures.[1] Some have focused upon the changing characterstics of the members who modify structural processes, while others have considered the difficulty of attaining goals without a professional and centralized staff (76, pp. 926–948; 29).

Another theorist who illustrates the evolutionary model of organiza-

---

[1] An excellent historical study of Protestant church development using an evolutionary approach is found in Niebuhr (57). A study of emerging church bureaucratization is in Harrison (29). For a discussion of measures of religious organizational change, see Demerath, III (18, pp. 391–409).

tional change, Robert Merton, examined changes in behavior and personality which are related to the bureaucratic structure (54, pp. 195–207). In order to hold a job, says Merton, disciplined employees must focus upon means to the virtual exclusion of ends, and sentiments become transferred to the details of behavior. Structural sources of over-conformity include the seniority system, pensions and an *esprit de corps* that leads to a defense of entrenched interests. Consequently, this interplay between personality and structure displaces goals rather than attains them, and thereby changes an organization's direction and impact on the larger society.

Social scientists have utilized these four examples of the evolutionary model of organizational change when elaborating, amplifying, and specifying conditions that lead toward an inevitable structural differentiation and bureaucratization. In the late 1940s, a group of revisionists emerged whose underlying motivations seemed to be a desire to forestall the evils of modern organization and cleanse it of dysfunctions. Many of the "say-it-isn't-so" group were heavily influenced by the Nazi and Stalinist eras, which clearly demonstrated the horrors possible with a bureaucratic behemoth. Lipset, Gouldner, and Blau, each heavily influenced by Merton in the late 1940s, did case studies that did not follow the expected pattern of development. Their arguments rested heavily on an assumption that case studies which provide exceptions to the general patterns allow the specification of concrete social mechanisms which have undesirable effects, and permit social intervention to preclude negative consequences. Gouldner, for example, has suggested that we focus more on the positive aspects of human behavior which provide alternative paths away from dismal conclusions; that is, we should seek an *Iron Law of Democracy* as well as an *Iron Law of Oligarchy* (24, pp. 496–507).

Lipset's reformulation of Michels' theory is based on his study of the Typographers' Union (ITU), an organization that has maintained a competing two-party political system (41, pp. 387–436; 39). Lipset analyzed the factors contributing to oligarchy, such as the need for an administrative staff to handle a large number of members, the pressures from industry and government to coordinate and control locals, the control of communication, monopoly over the acquisition of political skills and union jobs, and the relative ability of leaders to return to the jobs they held before election. In the ITU, however, a set of countervening situations modified these oligarchical tendencies. Lipset found, for example, that the industry was decentralized, members had a high level of education and social status, the occupational community was small and homogeneous and permitted intensive social interaction, and work loads and deviant work schedules allowed for the dissemination of information as well as involvement in organizational affairs. Thus, Lipset and his colleagues provide us with a dynamic alternative of change in which the orderly processes of democratically held elections substitute for the inevitable oligarchy (39, pp. 393–418).

Gouldner's study of the gypsum plant is a case study of the succession crisis (23). According to Gouldner, the appointment of a new plant manager, followed by the replacement of a few middle managers, induced anxiety in the firm's hierarchy. Rules were promulgated to mend broken communication lines, set minimum standards of performance, and supplement close, personal supervision with remote universalistic control. Gouldner contrasts the reactions of surface workers to those of miners in the same company who retained their traditional belief systems and particularistic relationships in spite of attempts to bureaucratize their jobs. The emergence of a rigid, controlling, and centralized organization was limited among the miners by the prevalence of small, homogeneous groups whose boundaries were hard to permeate with bureaucratic techniques. Thus, Gouldner, like Lipset, focused on the social and interpersonal relations that tend to stabilize structures rather than contribute to the emergence of bureaucratization.[2]

Blau's study of two government agencies is an intensive analysis of the functioning of small informal groups in large organizations (9). "The central thesis of [the] study is that bureaucratic structures continually create conditions that modify these structures" (9, p. 12). Thus, if Weber and Michels saw the inevitable march toward bureaucratic rigidity and oligarchy, if Schumpeter foresees only limited and controlled innovation under bureaucratic socialism, Blau contends that the seeds of new social forms lie within the organizations themselves.[3] For example, Blau shows how anxiety on the job, created by conflict with clients or supervisors, leads to social relationships which create norms, and, ultimately, rules and organizational practices become modified. Thus, Merton's conception of goal displacement becomes a limiting case for those whose low integration in the work group precludes anxiety reduction. Goal succession, that is, attaining one objective and moving along to another, derives from social relationships on the job which mediate the organizational structure.[4] Social status distributions, an emergent group property, affect not only performance, social relations, and personal anxiety, but, more important for our considerations, the willingness to change procedures and undertake new responsibilities.

While Lipset, Gouldner, and Blau drew attention to conditions that inhibit the unfolding of bureaucratic forms, another series of studies, centered on the concept of goals, provided insights into organizational change when the socially approved ends were thwarted. In essence, this set of studies focused upon the impotency of organizations in the face of

[2] A related study of managerial succession is Guest (25, pp. 47–54).

[3] This thesis is also argued by Marcus (50, pp. 749–777).

[4] Blau devotes a large segment to social change and this discussion abstracts but a small part which directly bears on the Merton hypothesis (9, pp. 183–219).

entrenched internal or environmental obstructions. For example, Lipset's study of the Cooperative Commonwealth Federation (CCF) in Saskatchewan showed that a socialist party obtaining office could not initiate social change due to obstructions created by the entrenched officials; that is, mere promulgation of policy was insufficient to assure execution (38).

Selznick's study of the TVA also depicted the inability of an organization to have its desired impact upon the environment (66). In this case, however, it was not the internal organizational structure that inhibited change, but rather the community officials who represented powerful local vested interests. The coöptation of these officials helped to decrease local opposition to the TVA, but in the process some of its programs were modified, and even increased conflict with other change-oriented liberal government agencies. In short, just as internal social processes and structures can deter organizations from their goals, so the external environment also makes demands and inhibits change. The evolution of an organization, then, is not unidirectional and there is little evidence to conclude that desired or undesired outcomes would be forthcoming. Indeed, to complicate matters further, Katz and Eisenstadt found that change often occurred in the direction of debureaucratization, or less formalism (35, pp. 113–133; 20, pp. 302–320).

What happens when organizations striving to acquire new goals attain them? In his study of the National Foundation for Infantile Paralysis, Sills found that the discovery of the Salk vaccine forced the organization to re-evaluate its objectives on a broader scale, that is, fight all childhood diseases (68). While some volunteers, and even officials, left the organization because they did not accept these new goals, other persons were induced to join and contribute. Acceptance by the local community and former commitments to the original goals supported the Foundation in its transition period. On the other hand, both Gusfield and Messinger's studies showed how declining organizations were compelled to modify goals and redirect energies toward a different audience (26, pp. 221–232; pp. 3–10). While these are not pure examples of goal succession, they do illustrate a sequential development and acquisition of new objectives.

In general, most literature using an evolutionary model has sought principles of change which affect the total organization which was considered to be a monolithic structure. The revisionists, or neo-evolutionists, have focused upon segments of the organization which preclude or encourage the attainment of formal goals. Few of these researchers conceptualize conflict or competition among sub-units other than as dysfunction, contributing to goal displacement rather than goal succession. And, finally, most evolutionists, and their offspring, are implicitly horrified by large-scale organizations, their potentially centralized authority structure and ability to command resources. While the studies of the revisionists clearly demonstrate the role of differentiation in subverting adminstrative practices and goals, most neo-evolutionists have neglected the systematic exploration of problems of integration. As a result, there has been a neglect of the theoretical examination of differentiation and competition among sub-units within an organization, and diversity among organizations within a community. Slogans still prevail in the absence of either theory or research.

### The Interventionists and Planned Change

During the 1930s and 1940s while most sociologists looked with horror upon the apparent emergence of bureaucratization, oligarchy, and rigid organizational stagnation, the followers of Elton Mayo and Kurt Lewin sought social-psychological mechanisms which could induce changes, decrease anomie and increase productivity of small groups. Many laboratory and field surveys were conducted utilizing a series of simplistic assumptions on different analytic levels.[5] For example, a few assumptions included the perception that modern man was anomic, the group was superior to the individual in decision-making, egalitarian supervision was more desirable than authoritarian or laissez-faire, and structural and social variables were inherently constraining upon the creativity and motivation of self-generated people. In effect, then, the followers of Mayo and Lewin took the organizational leviathan as a given, and attempted to change perceptions and attitudes toward it. They assumed that modifications of behavior would follow changes in perception and contribute, ultimately, to new and desirable structural forms.

The most obvious example of the interventionist approach is the famous Coch and French experiment, whose conclusion was that resistance to technological change was inversely related to participation in group decision-making (15, pp. 319–341). The authors concluded, "It is possible for management to modify greatly or to remove completely group resistance to changes in methods of work or the ensuing piece rates. This change can be accomplished by the use of group meetings in which management effectively communicates the need for change and stimulated group participation in planning the changes" (15, p. 341). Clearly, management can introduce major changes that could encourage resistance among those affected, but good communication or that which persuades, to individuals in groups that exert pressure for conformity will produce favorable attitudes toward the innovation. In other words, all conflicts of interest between echelons can be reduced by "effective communication" or some simple parameters of the topics open for group

5 It is impossible to review all of the studies; good summaries of the change literature by devotees include Shepard (67, pp. 1115–1143), Leavitt (36, pp. 1144–1170), and Bennis, Benne, and Chin (6). A most restrained and judicious evaluation can be found in Perrow (60, pp. 61–144).

discussion. The weakness of this assumption is that no one asked the subjects whether or not they wanted the new machine.[6]

As a result of these experiments, organizational interventionists, or planners, invaded management schools, colleges of education, and social work training centers with their designs for restructuring social relations.[7] Using a variety of techniques from T-groups (sensitivity, encounter, or confrontation groups) to systematic surveys and problem-solving exercises, these interventionists sought tension release, power redistribution, conflict resolution, and the development of new values. But irrespective of their techniques, targets of change, or over-all goals, the locus of investigation was the person, especially those at the lower echelons of the organization.[8]

Likert's model of organizational change is an attempt to summarize one active group of social researchers using an interventionist model. He utilizes over two decades of survey research which employ a relatively consistent set of concepts and measures (37). Although many of the studies do not substantiate the specific hypotheses, Likert selects findings to piece together a change model based on interpersonal competence and supervisory styles of leadership.[9] Implicitly assuming a monolithic structure, Likert contends that top management, being sincerely interested in subordinates' welfare, should hold group meetings to create an atmosphere of trust and mutual respect. Subordinates' participation in problem-solving and decision-making would stimulate loyalty and increase job satisfaction. The delegation of responsibility and autonomy will improve communication vertically and enhance a superior's ability to innovate programs for review by subordinates. Peers will exert pressure upon each other for compliance to group standards by allocating rewards and punishment. Thus, the decrease in close supervision will build cohesive groups with high consensus. The ultimate outcome, says Likert, will be an increase in production and a decrease in waste, absenteeism, and turnover. If top management behaves appropriately, each successively lower echelon will do likewise. Although Likert's work relies heavily on studies of lower participants in a wide variety of organizations, he gives little consideration to functional differentiation across the hierarchy, for instance, whether the foreman in industry is considered the same as a vice-president of GM irrespective of job structure.

---

[6] Werner von der Ohe tells me that over 50 percent of these studies were financed by the Navy, Air Force, and Army.

[7] A summary of these change models can be found in Bennis (7, pp. 125–165).

[8] The most exhaustive critique of the methods employed by interventionists is Back (2). He concludes that the techniques and ideological foundations are virtually untenable in the face of evidence.

[9] Good summary evaluations of the Likert school can be found in Perrow (60) and Dubin (19).

The inevitable movement of an organization following Likert's prescriptions is toward a participative group. Likert argues that organizations start at different points on a continuum from *Exploitive Authoritative* to *Benevolent Authoritative* toward *Consultative* and then *Participative Group*. Operating characteristics of organizations are subsumed under seven general concepts:

1. Motivational forces (satisfaction, attitudes)
2. Communication (amount, direction, accuracy)
3. Interaction-influence (amount, cooperation)
4. Decision-making (level, group or individually made)
5. Goal-setting (where and how done, forces of resistance)
6. Control processes (level, measurement, informal or formal)
7. Performance (productivity, absence, quality, waste)

In all, Likert lists over 40 variables within these seven concepts as illustrative of the measures required for the classification of an organization. Presumably, almost all variables will cluster together (at least Likert's discussion does not indicate their independence). For instance, high satisfaction will be positively related to high communication and favorable attitudes toward peers and company policy. Although Likert would never conceptualize his work this way, his approach is closely related to Eisenstadt's abstract formulations of debureaucratization (20). The major difference between the two, other than the level of analysis, is Likert's interventionist strategy for modifying personal attitudes and behavior; Eisenstadt, by contrast, focuses on role change resulting from environmental impingements.

Seashore and Bowers conducted an extensive field experiment to test four of the central propositions in the Likert Model (64). The site was a factory employing over 800 persons; three departments were selected for experimental purposes and two were used as controls. Questionnaires and interviews were used to gather the data, measurements being obtained before, during, and after the change efforts. The independent variables included: 1) Increase in emphasis on work group (as opposed to individual) as a functioning unit of the organization; 2) Increase in amount of supportive behavior by supervisors and peers; 3) Increase in participation by employees in decision-making processes; and 4) Increase in amount of interaction and influence among work group members. The four dependent variables were: 1) Increase in employee satisfaction; 2) Increase in productivity rate; 3) Decrease in waste rate; and 4) Decrease in absence rate (64, p. 19). Satisfaction and productivity rates did increase, as predicted by the independent variables; however, changes in waste and absence rates were ambiguous.[10]

[10] A perceptive analysis of this work, detailing general problems of field experiments, is provided by Seashore (65, pp. 164–170). Another good discussion and review of the literature is Barnes (3, pp. 57–112).

Certainly, the Seashore and Bowers data are encouraging to a Likert devotee. However, before one markets his balm, a few questions of generalizability must be answered.[11] For example, little mention is made about changes in environmental conditions which might have led to the results. Market patterns, labor force conditions, company mergers, etc., all could have differential effects upon the group studied. Variations in reassignment of personnel, technological innovation, and spatial distribution of workers are other possible contaminating factors. No attempt is made to show consistent results across hierarchical lines. Likert's conception of organizational change implies a top-down managerial strategy, while the Seashore-Bowers' model employs the utilization of change agents who manipulate variables at the lower echelons.

Floyd Mann, a close associate of Likert, studied organizational change as related to technological innovation (46; 47). His major thesis that management focuses upon technological matters to the exclusion of social relations makes basic assumptions about the negative aspects of organizational change. Thus, the entire focus of electric power plant workers dwells upon reducing resistance and managing personal anxiety to automation. Supervisory roles are depicted as transmitters of information and mitigators of tension. Continuous measurement and feedback monitor disruptions during five stages of movement:

1. The state of the organization before the change.
2. The recognition of a need for change.
3. Planning for change.
4. Taking the action steps to make the change.
5. Stabilizing the change (47, p. 3).

In each stage there is an implicit assumption that top management's prerogatives are to initiate and control change; lower echelons are put in a reactive capacity even though they may recognize problems and bring them to the attention of superiors. In short, Mann focuses on conscious and deliberate change initiations which may have unintended consequences. Once again, as in most interventionist literature, upper echelons are depicted as retaining a monopoly on rational behavior whose good intentions are misunderstood by the emotional subordinates.

Mann's thesis is not supported by his own study of the electric power plant. For example, throughout the comparison between the workers in the automated and traditional power plants, subordinates in the former reported more satisfaction with most aspects of their jobs, more sense of responsibility and optimism, and more eagerness to learn new skills. These workers also reported more tension than those in the traditional plant. But one can hardly interpret this tension negatively because it

[11] Seashore and Bowers discuss a few of these research limitations (64, pp. 101-106).

very likely reflects the increased sense of responsibility, job upgrading, and realistic assessment of potential major problems which coincided with employment in the new plant. Unless this is a most unusual group of workers in the automated plant, and Mann and Hoffman have no pre-measures, then one concludes that organizational change liberates and enhances participants' psyches, and little intervention is necessary to provide solicitude for imagined personal reactions. Resistance to change may be a function of one's perception of the ability to influence the decision, and the degree of investment in both the current state as well as the new outcome. For many people, a job is merely to provide income for non-work activities, and their resistance to technological innovation would be nil. In short, as Mann and Hoffman's data show, technological innovation may be adequate to increase productivity, modify interpersonal relations and psychic states toward a positive ideological goal. The need for change agents, or organizational developers (as Bennis euphemistically labels them), may be purely a function of the hard-sell practitioners themselves (2, pp. 159–173).

Katz and Kahn offer one of the most sophisticated presentations of an organizational theory from the interventionist perspective (34, pp. 390–451). Based heavily on Miller's open-systems theory, Katz and Kahn examine the nature of inputs, throughputs and outputs. This conceptualization immediately enlarges the scope of the traditional interventionist theories because the organization is no longer considered an isolated, self-contained organism. Maintenance inputs, including values, socialization patterns, and social goals, support the organization and link it to the environment as much as do production inputs such as goods and services.

But Katz and Kahn are concerned primarily with roles that delimit specific forms of behavior and derive from task requirements. People are located in sets of ongoing relationships among unique points in organizational space (the office); the specific set of activities for each office constitutes the role. Expectations of appropriate behavior are sent from one role to another, are perceived, and are reacted to in a feedback loop. Thus, the role episode is completed when the sender himself perceives and reacts to the response he initiated (34, p. 182). One might assume that slight changes in the episodes are virtually continuous due to variations in personalities, organizational and technological operations, as well as environmental concerns.

When Katz and Kahn discuss organizational change, they virtually neglect their entire theoretical perspective in favor of a review of social-psychological approaches to changing personality, social relationships, or attitudes toward slightly modified organizational structures (34, pp. 390–451). Their basic unit of analysis, role, is never seriously considered when treating change; they conclude that only "direct manipulation of organizational variables" is sufficiently powerful to sustain change. Katz and Kahn base their arguments upon the work of Morse and Reimer and Trist and Rice, but specific variables are never isolated and related to the larger theoretical open-systems theory. For example, the locus of decision-making in the hierarchy was a crucial variable in the Morse and Reimer study, and even though the experimental results are ambiguous, Katz and Kahn use them but pay little attention to their possible effect upon the social-psychological aspects of organizations. What were some of the resistances to the Autonomy Program in the Morse and Reimer study? Why did only 25 percent of the subjects report increased group cooperation, and under 20 percent report increased friendliness? Like their predecessors, Likert and Mann, Katz and Kahn selectively weave through data in the face of obvious facts: most anticipated experimental changes did not materialize, and the authors reluctantly admit that increased hierarchical pressure is an effective power to increase productivity (34, p. 432).

One is forced to conclude from the literature that interventionists have been unable to isolate significant variables to change major segments of an organization, that is, the amount of variance accounted for in their research is apparently negligible.[12] Indeed, Katz and Kahn and Likert, three of the foremost interventionists, have no theory of organizational change; they rely on outsiders who enter to manipulate variables, and the dynamics of interacting sub-units are never considered.

The contributions of the interventionists to organizational research should not, however, be disregarded. They have convinced both administrators and funding agencies to devote resources to organizational phenomena in addition to traditional managerial concerns of technology and formal structure. Refined research techniques have been developed for utilization by social scientists.[13] Catering to practical problems, interventionists have eased the access to research sites, and administrators in industry, government, education, welfare, and others almost eagerly accept their investigations.[14]

[12] This harsh generalization is warranted by the amount of research over a 25 year period which has produced very little consistent theoretical or scientific advancement. When the history of the interventionist phase of organizational theory is written, most devotees will be considered as part of a larger social movement which, concurrent with shifting manpower distributions from manufacturing to service sectors, tried to exploit managerial anxiety. Back (2, pp. 3-27) reaches similar conclusions about T-groups and sensitivity training. See also Bendix (5, pp. 319-340). The reader must realize that all interventionists have not been covered by this brief review. All of the individualistic or psychological theorists have been omitted because of lack of space. Many of these theories are extremely sophisticated and promising. For examples of very different approaches, see Jaques (33) and March and Simon (48, pp. 173–210).

[13] One must not forget that Likert and his colleagues have built the Institute for Social Research into the foremost non-federal social survey center in the world.

[14] Contrast this relatively happy situation with Blau's problems locating a research site in the late 1940's (II, pp. 28–31).

## Environmentalists

Although Katz and Kahn provided an abstract consideration of an organization's environment in their open-systems model, most interventionists have eschewed any consideration of the larger social framework. This was one of the first criticisms leveled at the Hawthorne studies over 40 years ago, and with a few notable exceptions the Lewin-Mayo descendants have continued to avoid the issue. Even Katz and Kahn, as we have seen, give only a courteous nod toward environmental concepts when discussing change.

Bendix, using historical data, has shown the intricate relationship between social ideologies and managerial techniques for authority and control (5). He implies an almost pendulum model of organizational change in which the two polarities are: 1) hierarchy based upon consensus legitimation ("I am only doing what you subordinates want when I initiate action") and, 2) hierarchy based upon interdependent functional differentiation ("I have special qualities and that is why I can initiate action for you.") Bendix described changes in managerial ideologies in England, Russia, and the United States over the past 200 years as Smith, Malthus, Marx, Darwin, and other major (and minor) thinkers changed basic conceptions of man and social organization. Concurrently, organizational authority relationships changed to reflect the decline of a large agricultural labor force, the emergence of urbanization, and the industrialization of the society. Human Relations' approaches to supervisory-subordinate relationships, according to Bendix, are merely reflections of these larger social developments (5, pp. 287–319).

Without question, the ideologies of Social Darwinism and the similarities between religious and business values greatly supported superordinate directives in the late nineteenth century. Unionism in the United States made little progress until after 1890, as managers had successfully argued that they possessed special abilities to help the workers attain increased rewards for work. But economic depressions, formations of managerial organizations, increasing separation of ownership and control, and repeated violations of Christian morality tended to undermine managerial claims for legitimacy. The emergence of a specialized staff increased managers' dependencies and clearly indicated that elites' claims to supremacy were shallow, their substance predicated on assumptions that no longer pertained to the modern organization. Indeed, the superior became one who possessed certain social skills to plan, coordinate work, and motivate subordinates. Special training groups emerged to help supervisors (at all levels of management) control their anxiety and learn of their impact on others during interaction. Social scientists eagerly rushed in to provide the latest findings on the psychological or social characteristics that affect personal and social control. Thus, Bendix documented the social historical processes that interventionists assume are purely a function of attitudinal change.

Stinchcombe's brief analysis of the changing roles of participants in emerging organizations supplements that of Bendix who focused on established businesses (69, pp. 142–169). Stinchcombe's discussion assumes organizational instability due to the liabilities of learning new roles, the acquisition of resources, and methods and criteria for their allocation (69, pp. 148–149).

Stinchcombe's analysis explores some of the environmental conditions which precipitate the origins of organizations (69, pp. 146–148):

"People found organizations when

a) they find or learn about alternative better ways of doing things that are not easily done with existing arrangements;

b) they believe that the future will be such that the organization will continue to be effective enough to pay for the trouble of building it and for the resources invested;

c) they or some social group with which they are strongly identified will receive some of the benefits of the better way of doing things;

d) they can lay hold of the resources of wealth, power, and legitimacy needed to build the organization; and

e) they can defeat, or at least avoid being defeated by, their opponents, especially those whose interests are vested in the old regime" (69, p. 146).

Each aspect listed by Stinchcombe assumes the existence of certain commodities, resources, or social situations. For example, *a*, learning about alternatives, presupposes a communication system providing information and a social support system tolerating deviance; both *b* and *c* assume appropriate social values to sustain the existence of administrative mechanisms for the allocation of organizational products.[15] Stinchcombe himself discusses the importance of literacy, urbanization rates, a money economy, political stability, and past experience in sustaining a developing organization (69, pp. 150–153).[16]

The instability of confronting emerging organizations demands strong commitments from participants, and, hence, a social value system supporting personal output may be considered a prerequisite for change. While most theorists have emphasized the demand (or need) aspects

---

[15] Stinchcombe does not entirely neglect these points, but apparently does not consider them as important as the usual demand variables.

[16] *Ceteris paribus*, organizational density greatly affected the success or failure of a new union. For example, many unions copied constitutions and organizational structures from those already existing. Staff trained in one union were lured to work in the new one, and the mobiles could take with them their technology, i.e., knowledge and experience. Stinchcombe also contends that the period when the organization was formed is of crucial importance in understanding structural developments (69, pp. 155–160).

for organizational change, few have examined the social resources that must be present if internal or external modifications are to occur.[17] To be sure, Weber emphasized the role of values in capitalistic development, and recently, psychologists such as McClelland and Atkinson have operationalized some of Weber's concepts as Need for Achievement (N-Ach), while the economist Hagen studied motivation and economic growth (52; 28). But virtually no theorist or investigator of organizational change has examined the importance of any of these related concepts.[18]

For some reason Stinchcombe devotes very little discussion to the role of government in affecting organizational change. This neglect is curious, but not uncommon, when one realizes that local and national political structures provide both the normative, and often, the physical, resources for development. Obvious examples include the hostility of the U.S. government to corporations during the early nineteenth century and to unions prior to World War I. Union growth during the 1930s was directly linked to government support and laws enacted in the late 1940s and 1950s greatly affected internal structural changes (50, pp. 754–757). Government policies have not only set boundaries for organizational development, but have often initiated programs or new structural forms that support and cooperate with existing organizations while competing with others. For example, the structure of the poverty program was predicated upon the assumption that many people were unattended by existing organizational arrangements. The aluminum industry, virtually founded by government funds during World War II, was sold at a nominal price to private concerns for further development.

In sum, organizational operations are affected by government policies that shape the competitive environment through enactments encouraging or limiting entry into a market, tariffs, taxation that affects product development (i.e., internal specialization), patents and copyrights which determine diffusion rates and directions, reward allocations (for example, grievance procedures, hiring of minority groups and women, child labor laws), licensing of personnel, and educational subsidies for training novitiates and specialists (such as grants to medical and engineering schools, draft deferments). In general, most Western governments have become increasingly involved in organizations concerned with social dependency problems, for example, those of health, welfare,

---

[17] Two decades ago, Boulding suggested we examine "supply" as well as "demand" in organizational analysis (12). To my knowledge, virtually no work has been done on this important point. Competition among organizational sub-units for internal and external resources might be a profitable way to begin such a study of supply initiating change.

[18] The works of McClelland and Hagen are reviewed carefully in Swanson (70, 41–45). Related comments on commitment can also be found in Moore (56, pp. 37–44).

social control, and education (61). In countries undergoing rapid modernization, government is often the prime financial support, and hence, major environmental constraint upon organizational change. The inability to conceptualize government-organizational relationships will plague studies of organizational change for some time to come.[19]

Other environmental theories of change treat the organization as an organism responding to outside pressures. Some writers, like Emery and Trist, and Terreberry, have described the environment with relatively little concern for changes in the internal structure of organizations (21, pp. 21–32; 71, pp. 590–613). Emery and Trist provide four basic types of organizational environments based on the distribution of goals and noxiants (goods and bads) (21, p. 24). When goals and noxiants are relatively unchanging and randomly distributed, Trist and Emery call the environment placid and randomized; when goals and noxiants hang together in certain ways, the environment is called placid and clustered. The third type of environment, disturbed-reactive, is similar to an ultra-stable system or oligopolistic market, that is, there is more than one similar organization in a field and they are compelled to be cognizant of each other. Finally, Trist and Emery depict the turbulent field in which relevant uncertainty increases. Presumably, and the authors do not specify this situation, goals and noxiants are in constant flux. Internal organizational structures are mentioned briefly as Trist and Emery suggest that, in placid, clustered environments, organizations tend to increase in size and become hierarchically controlled and centralized.

Terreberry, adhering to the Trist and Emery model, argues for the increasing turbulence of the organizational field in which "complexity and rapidity of change in external interconnectedness give rise to increasingly unpredictable change in transactional interdependencies" (71, p. 598). Two hypotheses conclude the analysis: 1) "Organizational change is largely externally induced"; 2) "System adaptability is a function of ability to learn and to perform according to changing environmental contingencies" (71, pp. 610–612). One might question whether or not turbulence and dependence upon the environment have increased, given the additional number of techniques to cope with external conditions. However, Terreberry's contribution does call attention to the importance of changes in the kind or quantity of output that increase the probability of survival. One need not assume, as Terreberry does, that

---

[19] These general comments obviously exclude studies by economists who focus intensively upon the legal impact on industrial structure. For example, see Caves (14, pp. 55–115) and Scherer (62, pp. 412–542). But few sociologists have explored the relationship between law and complex organization variables. Notable exceptions are Blau (9), Selznick (66), and Lipset (40, pp. 1–50). Even the group of sociologists calling themselves institutionalists neglect the impact of government and law. For example, two recent books by Perrow cover in great depth organizational variables but nary a word on these two constraints (59; 60).

the organization obtains a knowledge and awareness of external contingencies in order to survive in the turbulent environments. Many organizations, their antennae rotating vigorously, still receive snowy pictures for purposes of learning and creating new strategies. One function of marketing and public relations is to structure a market, an environment, in which output is acceptable. Government and professional organizations are especially prone to *create* demands when they wish to dispose of inputs. As mentioned earlier, the supply of organizational dynamics must be considered equally with the demand for outputs.

Hage and Aiken, integrating both theoretical concerns and empirical data, postulate two basic types of organizations, dynamic and static (27, pp. 65–69). The former is characterized by relatively rapid program change, great complexity, decentralization, low formalization, and low stratification; the static type relies heavily upon task specialization and hierarchical centralization with formalized rules and procedures. The causes of change are found in the environment, according to Hage and Aiken, as movement toward equilibrium produces static organizations in dynamic environments (27, pp. 71–82). There is an implication that dynamic environments increase over-all knowledge to which organizations respond with additional complexity, thereby inducing other intra-organizational modifications (27, pp. 74–76). Four stages of organizational change ensue (27, pp. 93–106):

1) Evaluation, "when organizational decision makers determine that either the organization is not accomplishing its present goals — or amend the goals . . .";
2) Initiation, "when the decision makers . . . have decided to add a new program or activity . . ." which starts a chain reaction and often triggers other organizational problems;
3) Implementation, which frequently brings about disequilibrium and conflict as participants compete in the reallocation of resources;
4) Routinization, when criteria are imposed by elites to determine whether or not to sustain the new program or continue searching for other programs.

Hage and Aiken postulate that criteria of quality are associated with program retention while those of quantity (and measures of efficiency) are likely to lead to rejection (27, p. 105).

Hage and Aiken's contribution is primarily the specification of variables and an attempt to formulate testable hypotheses about directions of change at different stages of the process. Their stages are related to those of other theorists of change, but for our purpose are useful because of the emphasis upon environment and organizational variables, in contrast to Mann and Neff, for example, who focus primarily upon psychological phenomena (27, pp. 112–116). The empirical evidence is sometimes ambiguous; for instance, one measure of formalization, job codification, is negatively related to the rate of program change, while another, rule observation, has no association (27, p. 45). Similarly, one measure of job satisfaction was positively related to rate of program change, while satisfaction with fellow workers had a low negative association (−.17). Hage and Aiken suggest that job satisfaction is a precondition for program change, but it might be argued that change itself leads to satisfaction because of the challenging novelty and release from boring routine (27, pp. 53–54).[20] It is not clear why a satisfied group of workers, or decision makers, would induce change if the first stage, evaluation, did not show an undesirable (or satisfactory) set of job circumstances. Similarly, Hage and Aiken cite both Marx and Michels to substantiate the rationale underlying the expected relationship between high stratification and *low rate of program change*. However, both Marx and Michels may be interpreted differently when they argue that elites (or oligarchs) continue to select policies, and to introduce programs, in order to increase their own benefits. Marx is explicit about the introduction of technology, rearrangement of work, decrease of labor profits, and expansion of markets in order to maintain a competitive advantage; Michels, as described above, focuses upon goal displacement and compromises with the environment (and increasing oligarchy) to retain office. Clearly, these are program changes in an objective sense. One cannot designate only the desirable change as "change."

A few theorists of organizational change conceptualize the environments which affect internal structural arrangements. Litwak and his associates have focused primarily upon different types of authority structures, communication patterns, and the nature of tasks, that are linked to variations in primary groups (42; 43; 44; 45). Essentially, Litwak argues there are different types of organizations, each of which requires control over primary groups if goals are to be attained for both clients and organizations.[21] For example, parents and peer groups must provide social support to school children and enforce teacher directives if learning is to occur. In some cases, the target population may be a deviant group and require special techniques to handle their hostility to an organization; juvenile gangs, immigrants, or reluctant customers are obvious examples.

Litwak and Meyer postulate a set of mechanisms which are appropriate to different kinds of organizations to handle their respective clients (43,

[20] Interestingly, Hage and Aiken approvingly cite Mann and Hoffman and other University of Michigan studies to support the argument that satisfaction is conducive to change. The Mann and Hoffman data do not support this conclusion, as noted above.

[21] Litwak's argument here and in the following discussion is actually more complicated than presented in this brief review. For example, he sometimes discusses more than the three types of organizations, considering mixtures of structures (42, pp. 177–184). This review also omits a discussion of principles of communication utilized by coordinating mechanisms (43, pp. 42–45). In general, Litwak does not discuss change except in the technology paper (44).

pp. 49–52). For example, some organizations employ the mass media, while others use voluntary associations or detached experts. Each mechanism of coordination is appropriate to the internal structure of an organization as well as the type of primary group from which compliance is sought. Thus, a Human Relations type of organizational structure would provide few constraints upon its coordinating mechanism and, according to Litwak and Meyer, would be relatively ineffective if it employed the mass media or a formal authority (for example, truant officer) to work with a set of deviant primary groups (43, p. 53).

Although not explicitly stated, change would occur when an organization moves toward a balanced situation after conflict resulted from inappropriate combinations. For example, change can be expected if there is no balance between the bureaucratic structure and the coordinating mechanisms, or between the latter and the type of primary group to be handled. Feedback from the imbalance would cause change, but Litwak does not indicate its direction. Presumably, neither the primary group nor the bureaucratic structure will modify its nature and the coordinating mechanism is most vulnerable to pressure. Such interesting speculation entices the researcher to specify the relative impact of both primary groups and bureaucratic structure in modifying the mechanism.[22]

More recently, Litwak explored the theoretical impact of technological innovations upon the relationship between primary groups and bureaucratic structures (44). While limitations of space preclude a discussion of the paper here, the implications are patent. Technology is depicted as both increasing and decreasing the need for expertise when innovations both increase and decrease complexity of tasks. Primary groups fill the interstitial areas between technology and experts. The model of change, Litwak suggests, is one of technology replacing experts who have supplanted the primary group. But, as each innovation opens new areas for additional modifications in the other two areas, continual balances and adjustments become necessary. Technological innovation, expertise, and primary group may well be the three major concepts Litwak would use to develop a model for indicating the selection of coordinating mechanisms with environmental influences. Indeed, replacing phlebotomy with pharmacology has changed the structure of

[22] Because Litwak and Meyer provide a number of alternative mechanisms, interesting empirical questions are raised: for example, which alternative will be selected, and what are the internal pressures in different directions? If professional organizations are a mixture of hierarchic authority structures, and combine both routinized and flexible procedures, almost any coordinating mechanism would be utilized. Obviously, this is not so. Perhaps the Litwak-Meyer scheme must be modified to indicate specific organizational units that contact primary groups rather than characterize organizations as a whole. Thus, sub-units would vary in their selection of mechanisms to match the type of group they confront. It would also be important to distinguish among primary groups along dimensions other than predilections for compliance.

community hospitals and the relationships between doctors and patients.

Litwak's most recent contribution has been an examination of coordination among formal organizations (45). Beginning with a set of assumptions about the need for pursuit of multiple goals requiring autonomy and delegated functions, Litwak asks how coordination of specialized tasks can be developed without a centralized authority structure (45, pp. 137–144). Partial interdependence is the minimum condition for linkage, with formal procedures effective for standardized tasks, and informal ones for non-standardized events (45, p. 154). The number of interactions among organizations, awareness of others, and hierarchical structure are three additional variables affecting coordination. Litwak then sets forth a series of hypotheses about the degree of formality of the linkages, the adjudicative processes, and the communicative mechanisms. Finally, the degree of autonomy for each organization is placed on a continuum from informal, non-binding agreements among friends to rules specifying changes (for example, cost of living clauses, governmental regulatory bodies).

Again, without explicitly stating a theory of change, Litwak has constructed a set of variables which feed back and modify organizational structures (45, p. 178). He distinguished linkage networks along a continuum: few and small organizations would be at one end with no third party intervention, and many large organizations would have some constraints upon their operations. Almost every example Litwak provides is a change mechanism; this makes the reader aware of the diversity of change sources, as well as providing a preliminary classification of agents and the conditions under which they function. For example, under conditions of high organizational awareness (of other organizations in the network) where few or small organizations have high standardization of tasks, one would expect little change as directories or rules regulate inputs of clients and criteria for employment. One would assume such organizations would be most vulnerable to shifts in the environmental demand, or competitors with a marginally differentiated product. In other organizations where feedback would not be binding, new constraints will merge in the form of knowledge about recent developments in technology, resource allocation, staffing, and evaluation criteria. Rapid and extensive pressure for change would come in small organizations with low standardization, where agreements among friends add to each organization's problem-solving repertoire and coalitions of these informal primary groups demand modification of programs. Because of the multiplicity of such groups, as well as their continual realignment over different issues, stability within the organization as a whole becomes a most unusual occurrence.[23]

[23] Elsewhere I have argued that in organizations such as these, employees will form horizontal coalitions to introduce stability and a predictable structure. See Marcus (51).

In sum, Litwak's contribution has been to link the Weberian rationalistic model of organization with the interventionists who focus mainly upon small, primary group interactions. Using a few explicit assumptions derived from balance theory, Litwak has expanded our knowledge of linkages and their strains toward consistency, between an organization and its environmental components. Throughout his discussion, refinements have been introduced to account for variations in tasks, hierarchy and communication structures. Few studies of organizational change can afford to neglect this important body of hypotheses.

## Competition and Conflict

It would be most remiss to omit in this review a brief discussion of literature reflecting the contributions of economists to the study of organizational change. To be sure, few sociologists have examined or utilized this literature, and the empirical sociological research is sparse. Most sociologists have shown a marked preference for elaborating the interface with psychology rather than systematically reformulating the well-established theories and evidence marshalled by "the dismal science." Perhaps one explanation for this neglect lies in an ideological preference for social harmony as stated clearly by George Homans almost two decades ago (31, pp. 48–58). Certainly, as indicated above, the interventionists and other Lewin-Mayo followers have zealously sought the reduction of resistance and conflict and the virtual elimination of competition as a source of motivation for goal attainment. Even the evolutionists modified their Darwinian origins by neglecting the dynamic of natural selection through competition for scarce resources.[24]

The most consistent set of organizational-change hypotheses developed by economists was derived from theories of imperfect competition. By the 1930s, most economists realized that in many industries, a few sellers dominated the market, set prices, indirectly controlled quality and determined performance standards. Traditional economic theory required modification to include oligopolies, or a theory of large-scale organizational behavior.

Richard Caves argued that a number of factors affect market concentration, including product differentiation, barriers to entry, role of government, demand elasticity, etc. (14, pp. 18–32). When product differentiation is great, competition among sellers tends to be increased as buyers distinguish among outputs. Small organizations compete relatively

---

[24] Surely, the reader who has come this far will realize this outrageous oversimplification is not without exception. For example, see the work of Lipset, whose very definition of democracy posits two contending political parties (39: 41). Recently, an increasing number of sociologists have called for a greater emphasis on conflict and competition. Few, however, have deigned to provide empirical or systematic studies of organizations. Instead, they rely on a case history or observational set of insights, which almost invariably precluded systematic generalizations for heuristic evaluation. However, promising theoretical statements can be found in Caplow (13) and Dahrendorf (17).

effectively when their output is dissimilar to that of large producers. Obviously, this argument assumes that great investment is not required in either personnel or capital goods, or that legal constraints do not preclude acquisition of land or other productive requisites. Thus, one would not expect much competition among community hospitals, and their changing structures would stem from other sources, such as competition within their sub-units.

Market conduct is the behavior of organizations as they react to rivals' attempts to gain favored positions (14, p. 37). If prices do not meet costs, and if all organizations react by raising prices, then profit ensues; or if one lowers prices, then, presumably, profit would increase because a larger share of the market would be captured (14, p. 41). The latter assumes, however, that others do not also lower prices, for that would merely maintain the relative positions of the sellers. Hence, volume would probably rise only slightly, and total profit would probably fall sharply (14, pp. 41–42). Economists refer to this situation as a *kinked demand curve.*

For the sociologist, conceptualizing price and profit in a broad sense, these economic propositions have great implications. For example, using the illustration of hospitals, one would expect relatively little change in an organizational structure which produces lowered costs to the patient (for example, fees, waiting time, deference to M.D.'s, compliance to directives) if other hospitals were to engage in similar behavior. According to this theory, over-all profits to the medical profession would drop because patients would depreciate the value of the service, take it for granted, be less willing to pay other social costs, such as supporting medical research or providing high prestige to the occupation. In the long run, this line of reasoning contends that only low ability personnel would be attracted to the field and over-all service would be impaired.

In order to obviate these unhappy consequences of decreasing profits, oligopolists coordinate their efforts. Prices are determined by agreements among sellers, or leadership by the largest or most powerful organizations determine costs to buyers (14, pp. 42–45). A sociological example of the former would be informal professional standards which require deference levels (being called, "Doctor," dress codes, etc.), as well as the more obvious fee schedules. Price leadership develops through informal channels, by observation and emulation, in addition to direct social influence. Continuing the hospital example, patients are placed in awe when told of the latest equipment or services. The diffusion of rooming-in facilities determined for many women, especially primiparae, which obstetrical units to use.[25] As with many similar products, marginal

---

[25] Diffusion of pharmaceuticals is apparently related to prestige of initial adopters according to Coleman, Menzel, and Katz (16, pp. 253-270). Even interventionists in organizational change manifest forms of price leadership. Warren Bennis says that $300 per day is his regular consulting fee, although upon special occasions he will donate time and advise for less (7, pp. 41–42).

differentiation supports the sellers' demands for higher prices, and also acts as return on participants' investments. ("I work at the hospital that does the best episiotomies in town!").[26]

Organizations can use coercive measures to compete effectively (14, pp. 49–52). In general, coercion either eliminates existing rivals or raises barriers to entry for potential rivals. In either case, a greater concentration of sellers occurs as defeated competitors are compelled to change markets or become suppliers to the enlarged oligopoly. Thus, competition itself, and coercive measures in particular, lead to continued differentiation among organizations and the establishment of symbiotic exchange relationships (10, p. 220). The next stage of the relationship is dominating the exchanges between the two organizations. Money, goods and services and symbolic affect are but four commodities of potential exchange.

This brief discussion of oligopoly theory draws our attention to a new set of variables, entirely different from those traditionally employed by sociologists studying organizational change. Instead of focusing on coordination and control of sub-units, on balance among parts and functional integration, on goals and social values, we would turn our attention to competition for resources, commodities utilized in exchange, the participants and boundaries of the market place, strategies employed for obtaining resource allocation, and constraints on tactics and coalition formation.

The potential utility of the economic model is illustrated by Hirschman's discussion of declining organizations; it stands as a notable exception to the economist's general inability to conceptualize failure (30). Noting that little attention has been paid to repairable lapses of economic actors, Hirschman argues that one cannot continually assume unchanging levels of rationality, or losses "of maximizing aptitude or energy with supply and demand factors being unchanged" (30, pp. 1–2). Traditional economists do not consider recovery important, as the unfit supposedly do not survive competition. This assumes *exit* — customers (sociologists might read "members" if a voluntary association is the referent) no longer demand output and they switch to a competitor. Organizational officials, presumably, modify their behavior to correct faults.

However, when demand is not met, there often arises *voice*, a protest about the output. Both exit and voice are feedback, but the latter still uses the output, and thus permits resource reallocation before great stress is placed on the organization. Voice, then, if employed properly, permits the utilization of organizational slack to compensate for the inability to optimize continually.

---

[26] The functions of prestige for organizations, especially hospitals, are discussed by Perrow (58, pp. 335–341).

Hirschman provided a theoretical model of conditions under which exit and voice occur. Assuming costs constant, and the demand inelastic, drops in quality lead to recuperation of the organization, and hence, no exit. But with constant cost and elastic demand, no recuperation will occur when quality drops, because the organization will be on a downhill spiral, that is, continued exit. Thus, for competition to be a corrective mechanism, an organization requires both alert and inert customers: the former provide feedback, while the latter sustain operations during the period of readjustment (30, p. 24). Although this may seem an ideal state, leading toward balance, the process is not static. Those customers (members) who exit first, says Hirschman, withdrawing their inputs, will be those with the most resources; there is no reason to believe that modifications to cut costs and regain one's position in the market will induce persons with quality inputs to return.

Voice occurs most frequently among those who have the most investment in the organization or under conditions of monopoly (30, p. 34). Officials must have time to respond, to evaluate whether or not changes are necessary to retain those with most resources. Obviously, under conditions of monopoly, no changes are necessary. However, voice does not always lead to exit, even with inelastic demand. For example, exit will not occur when those engaged in voice think the quality will rise again, or the costs of exit are very great (compared to the costs of voice).

The optimal mix, according to Hirschman, would be to make an organization responsive to voice and participants to invest loyalty (in addition to other resources). While exit would remain an alternative when voice fails, Hirschman prescribes the use of voice to curtail exit (30, pp. 120–126). Thus, a continual readjustment process between voice and exit will maximize operations because both are change mechanisms providing feedback for responsive behavior.

Implicitly, Hirschman's contribution helps integrate traditional economic theory with the views of some of the interventionists discussed above. While few of the latter would consider competition or exit a viable alternative to cooperation, voice, and loyalty, there is little doubt that monopolistic control and inelastic demand does lead toward sloth and decay. What is required, then, is a model of organizational change which includes the possibility for interactions among subparts in the same way that total organizations behave. The latter is generally handled well by traditional oligopoly theory, but it lacks precision for use in the non-industrial sector. Therefore, reconceptualization becomes necessary prior to empirical investigations.

## Conclusions

In this section I will suggest a perspective for future studies of organizational change. This is a humbling task because of the great diversity of existing theories, the often contradictory material, and worst of all, a desert of empirical research. Almost 20 years ago, Blau called for diachronic, or longitudinal, studies of organizations; our review located very few (9, pp. 6–13). Such studies are expensive and time consuming but initial attempts could be made to study formal charters and organizational structures which are relatively easily accessible.[27]

Let us assume, then, along with the economists and ecologists, that competition and cooperation are two of the basic dynamics of organizational life. Resources are limited and strategies must be employed to obtain essential commodities. Resources are of three kinds: goods, services, and affects. The latter are symbolic, and developed through human interaction. Examples include values, legitimation, norms, goals, sentiments, prestige, etc.

The more similar the organizations, the greater the competition for resources. Organizations may be similar in their demands upon the environment, in their internal structures (the way they process the resources) or in their outputs. The greater the competition for resources, the greater the attempt to differentiate the intake procedures, the processing mechanism or the outputs. In this first stage, all organizations are engaged in the process of differentiation and only marginal gains can be made in the competitive struggle because mechanisms of diffusion tend to mitigate superior advantages. Some mechanisms of diffusion, disseminating skills and techniques, include professional norms which require communication across organizational boundaries. They also include pressures from coalitions dependent upon the output which regulate the degree of advantage one organization may gain, and the visibility of practices which may be emulated by those of inferior position. An example of the latter is the recent adoption of computer facilities as each organization assumed that efficient administration required automatic data processing units.

In a second stage, competition among organizations leads to a pattern of dominance in the allocation of resources. Some organizations determine the resources available to others, or the ability to market outputs. The hierarchy of dominance decreases competition within the field because, in order to survive, some must withdraw and elaborately differentiate themselves. They make demands upon an entirely different market, modifying their internal structures and often supplying their outputs to former competitors. In this manner, some former competitors form coalitions and cooperate to obtain resources. Obviously, coalitions can be formed only when organizational resources are additive, when environmental resources gained can be distributed among the members of the coalition, and when gains derived are greater than costs.

Competition, then, leads to differentiation among organizations, and,

---

[27] An attempt using this technique is in Marcus (49).

internally, an increased division of labor. Specialization of participants is encouraged by the division of labor and sub-units compete for the allocation of resources within each organization. Just as dissimilar organizations cooperate in coalitions, so dissimilar sub-units form symbiotic relationships whereby exchanges occur for mutual survival and enhancement.

The third stage of organizational evolution is an internal division of labor leading to changes in the market for allocation of resources. At first, a central unit in the organization allocates most of the resources, but with increases in size and division of labor, distribution becomes increasingly problematical. Coalitions of sub-units may force the central unit to reallocate resources; or a coalition of sub-units may create a special mechanism to obtain additional resources or reduce costs for the deprived sub-units. In any case, the internal coalitions try to enhance their competitive position over other sub-units. Decentralization, sometimes an affectual resource, may also enhance a sub-unit's competitive advantage if additional demands are not made upon it by the dominant unit. With the resources allocated to it, each decentralized sub-unit can use a variety of strategies to obtain additional resources for exchange in the total internal, organizational marketplace. Thus, Litwak's discussion of technological innovation and mechanisms of control over primary groups (both internal and external) become strategies for gaining resources and competitive advantages over similar sub-units (43; 44). One would expect slightly dissimilar techniques of communication mechanisms to be employed (to gain compliance over primary groups) the more similar the structures of the sub-units, the types of primary groups involved, the specializations of the employees. However, when similar techniques of communication mechanisms are employed, then marginal differentiation of structure will occur to obtain a competitive advantage. Forming coalitions with university interventionists is but another strategy to survive in the competition for internal, organizational resources.[28]

In general, organizational sub-units will increase in total resources controlled until they too have difficulty allocating goods, services or affects. Horizontal coalitions may be expected to arise when resources cannot be obtained by subordinates, for instance, when a supervisor cannot provide guidance, or when the allocation of resources does not coincide with the outcomes of a competitive struggle among subordinates. Teachers joined unions when principals could no longer provide job information or reward superior abilities (51).

Competition among equal sub-units may decrease the ability of the total organization to survive. Resources often become demanded at many different points at the same time; allocation mechanisms are often in-

---

[28] One reason why interventionists continually obtain ambiguous results is that they conceive of an organization as a monolithic whole, failing to recognize the competing subgroups' marginal differentiation as a prerequisite for survival.

adequate to distribute commodities. Some sub-unit demands made upon the environment may go beyond its regenerative capacity, thereby disrupting exchange relationships and threatening the total set of resources supplied to the organization. It is at such times that organizations die unless external coalitions form to preserve their existence; for example, suppliers may have no other place to market outputs, or clients may have no other source of service. If an organization dies, sub-units will also die or merge into a similar surviving organization. Sometimes, sub-units will reallocate resources and form their own organization. The overall process of reorganization, reshaping the competitive processes among sub-units, is called mutation. Sills' study is an excellent example of this process (68).

Rigidities within organizations may stem from two sources: 1) when outside competition is dominated either by the organization itself or controlled by the market in which it operates; 2) when coalitions of sub-units within the organization are unable to acquire additional resources to differentiate their structures or outputs. However, it is unlikely that both these conditions, internal and external, can occur simultaneously. Hence, organizational change is an expected state, contrary to the dire predictions of many social critics who focus almost entirely upon rigid and static structures.

This brief statement, then, suggests that some existing organizational change literature can be reformulated into a model of competition and cooperation, wherein change results from a pressure to obtain resources for survival. The division of labor results, not from pressures to simplify the allocative mechanism of the whole organization, but rather to differentiate the subparts for overall competitive advantage. However, the subparts compete among themselves for resources, thereby contributing to the organization but also threatening its ability to coordinate and integrate specialized functions. Hopefully, a thorough development of this model will permit the integration of sociological and economic hypotheses into a theory which both explains and predicts organizational evolution.

## BIBLIOGRAPHY

1. Arian, Edward. *Bach, Beethoven and Bureaucracy.* University, Ala.: University of Alabama Press, 1971.
2. Back, Kurt W. *Beyond Words.* New York: Russell Sage Foundation, 1972.
3. Barnes, Louis B. "Organizational Change and Field Experiment Methods," in V. Vroom (ed.), *Methods of Organizational Research.* Pittsburgh: University of Pittsburgh Press, 1967.
4. Becker, Howard. "Four Types of Religious Organizations," in A. Etzioni (ed.), *Complex Organizations* (first edition). New York: Holt, Rinehart and Winston, 1961.

5. Bendix, R. *Work and Authority in Industry*. New York: Harper and Row, 1956.

6. Bennis, Warren G., K. D. Benne, and R. Chin (eds.). *The Planning of Change*. New York: Holt, Rinehart and Winston, 1962.

7. Bennis, Warren G. "A New Role for the Behavioral Science: Effecting Organizational Change," *Administrative Science Quarterly*, Vol. 8 (1963), pp. 125–165.

8. Bennis, Warren. *Organizational Development: Its Nature, Origins and Prospects*. Reading, Pa.: Addison-Wesley, 1967.

9. Blau, Peter M. *The Dynamics of Bureaucracy*. Chicago, Ill.: University of Chicago Press, 1955.

10. Blau, Peter M., and W. Richard Scott. *Formal Organizations*. San Francisco: Chandler Publishing Co., 1962.

11. Blau, Peter M. "The Research Process in the Study of the Dynamics of Bureaucracy," in P. E. Hammond (ed.), *Sociologists at Work*. Garden City, N.Y.: Anchor Books, 1967.

12. Boulding, Kenneth. *The Organizational Revolution*. New York: Harper and Bros., 1953.

13. Caplow, Theodore. *Two Against One*. Englewood Cliffs, N.J.: Prentice-Hall, 1968.

14. Caves, Richard. *American Industry: Structure, Conduct, Performance* (second edition). Englewood Cliffs, N.J.: Prentice-Hall, Inc., 1967.

15. Coch, Lester, and John R. P. French, Jr. "Overcoming Resistance to Change," in D. Cartwright and A. Zander (eds.), *Group Dynamics* (second edition). Evanston, Ill.: Row Peterson, 1960.

16. Coleman, James S., Herbert Menzel, and Elihu Katz. "The Diffusion of an Innovation Among Physicians," *Sociometry*, Vol. 20, pp. 253–270.

17. Dahrendorf, Ralf. *Class and Class Conflict in Industrial Society*. Stanford, Calif.: Stanford University Press, 1959.

18. Demerath, N. J., III. "Trends and Anti-Trends in Religious Change," in E. B. Sheldon and W. E. Moore (eds.), *Indicators of Social Change*. New York: Russell Sage Foundation, 1968.

19. Dubin, R., G. Homans, F. Mann, and Delbert C. Miller. *Leadership and productivity*. San Francisco: Chandler Publishing Co., 1965.

20. Eisenstadt, S. N. "Bureaucracy and Debureaucratization," *Administrative Science Quarterly*, Vol. 4 (1959), pp. 302–320.

21. Emery, F. E., and E. L. Trist. "The Causal Texture of Organizational Environments," *Human Relations*, Vol. 18 (1965), pp. 21–32.

22. Garceau, Oliver. *The Political Life of the American Medical Association*. Cambridge, Mass.: Harvard University Press, 1941.

23. Gouldner, Alvin W. *Patterns of Industrial Bureaucracy*. New York: The Free Press of Glencoe, 1954.

24. Gouldner, Alvin W. "Metaphysical Pathos and the Theory of Bureaucracy," *American Political Science Review*, Vol. 49 (1955), pp. 496–507.

25. Guest, Robert H. "Managerial Succession in Complex Organizations," *American Journal of Sociology*, Vol. 68 (1962), pp. 47–56.

26. Gusfield, Joseph R. "Social Structure and Moral Reform: A Study of the Women's Christian Temperance Union," *American Journal of Sociology,* Vol. 61 (1955), pp. 221–232.

27. Hage, Jerald, and Michael Aiken. *Social Change in Complex Organizations.* New York: Random House, 1970.

28. Hagen, Everett. *On the Theory of Social Change.* Homewood, Ill.: Dorsey Press, 1962.

29. Harrison, Paul M. *Authority and Power in the Free Church Tradition.* Princeton, N.J.: Princeton University Press, 1959.

30. Hirschman, Albert O. *Exit, Voice and Loyalty.* Cambridge, Mass.: Harvard University Press, 1970.

31. Homans, George C. "Industrial Harmony as a Goal," in A. Kornhauser, R. Dubin and A. M. Ross (eds.), *Industrial Conflict.* New York: McGraw-Hill Book Co., 1954.

32. Howe, I., and B. J. Widick. *The UAW and Walter Reuther.* New York: Random House, 1949.

33. Jaques, E. *The Changing Culture of a Factory.* London: Tavistock Publications, 1951.

34. Katz, Daniel, and Robert L. Kahn. *The Social Psychology of Organizations.* New York: John Wiley and Sons, 1966.

35. Katz, Elihu, and S. N. Eisenstadt. "Some Sociological Observations on the Response of Israeli Organizations to New Immigrants." *Administrative Science Quarterly,* Vol. 5 (1960), pp. 113–133.

36. Leavitt, Harold J. "Applied Organizational Change in Industry: Structural, Technological and Humanistic Approaches," in J. G. March (ed.), *Handbook of Organizations.* Chicago: Rand McNally, 1965.

37. Likert, Rensis. *New Patterns of Management.* New York: McGraw-Hill Book Co., 1961.

38. Lipset, Seymour Martin. *Agrarian Socialism.* Berkeley and Los Angeles: University of California Press, 1950.

39. Lipset, Seymour Martin, Martin Trow and James Coleman. *Union Democracy.* Glencoe, Ill.: The Free Press, 1956.

40. Lipset, Seymour Martin. "The Law and Trade Union Democracy," *Virginia Law Review,* Vol. 47 (1961), pp. 1–50.

41. Lipset, Seymour Martin. *Political Man.* Garden City, New York: Anchor Books, 1962.

42. Litwak, Eugene. "Models of Bureaucracy Which Permit Conflict," *American Journal of Sociology,* Vol. 67 (1961), pp. 177–184.

43. Litwak, Eugene, and H. J. Meyer. "A Balance Theory of Coordination Between Bureaucratic Organizations and Community Primary Groups," *Administrative Science Quarterly,* Vol. 11 (1966), pp. 31–58.

44. Litwak, Eugene. "Technological Innovation and Theoretical Functions of Primary Groups and Bureaucratic Structures," *American Journal of Sociology,* Vol. 73 (1968), pp. 468–481.

45. Litwak, Eugene. "Towards the Theory and Practice of Coordination Between Formal Organizations," in W. R. Rosengren and M. Lefton

(eds.), *Organizations and Clients*. Columbus, Ohio: Charles E. Merrill Publishing Co., 1970.

46. Mann, Floyd C., and L. Richard Hoffman. *Automation and the Worker*. New York: Henry Holt and Co., 1960.

47. Mann, Floyd, and Franklin W. Neff. *Managing Major Change in Organization*. Ann Arbor, Mich.: Foundation for Research on Human Behavior, 1961.

48. March, J. G., and H. A. Simon. *Organizations*. New York: Wiley and Sons, 1958.

49. Marcus, Philip M. "Trade Union Structure: Study in Formal Organization." Ph.D. dissertation, University of Chicago, 1962.

50. Marcus, Philip M. "Organizational Change: The Case of American Trade Unions," in George K. Zollschan and Walter Hirsch (eds.), *Explorations in Social Change*. Boston: Houghton Mifflin Co., 1964.

51. Marcus, Philip M. "Teachers as Professionals," in E. Friedson (ed.), *The Professions and Their Prospects*. Beverly Hills, Calif.: Sage Publications, forthcoming.

52. McClelland, David C. *The Achieving Society*. New York: Van Nostrand Reinholt Co., 1961.

53. Messinger, Sheldon L. "Organizational Transformation: A Case Study of a Declining Social Movement," *American Sociological Review*, Vol. 20 (1955), pp. 3–10.

54. Merton, Robert K. *Social Theory and Social Structure* (second edition). Glencoe, Ill.: The Free Press, 1957.

55. Michels, Robert. *Political Parties*. Glencoe, Ill.: The Free Press, 1949.

56. Moore, Wilbert E. *The Impact of Industry*. Englewood Cliffs, N.J.: Prentice-Hall, 1965.

57. Niebuhr, H. Richard. *The Social Sources of Denominationalism*. New York: Living Age Books, 1957.

58. Perrow, Charles. "Organizational Prestige: Some Functions and Dysfunctions," *American Journal of Sociology*, Vol. 66 (1961), pp. 335–341.

59. Perrow, Charles. *Organizational Analysis: A Sociological View*. Belmont, Calif.: Wadsworth Publishing Co., 1970.

60. Perrow, Charles. *Complex Organizations*. Glenview, Ill.: Scott Foresman, 1972.

61. Rothman, David J. *The Discovery of the Asylum*. Boston: Little, Brown and Co., 1971.

62. Scherer, Frederic M. *Industrial Market Structure and Economic Performance*. Chicago: Rand McNally and Co., 1971.

63. Schumpeter, Joseph A. *Capitalism, Socialism, and Democracy*. New York: Harper, 1950.

64. Seashore, Stanley E., and David G. Bowers. *Changing the Structure and Functioning in an Organization: Report of a Field Experiment*. Ann Arbor, Mich.: Institute for Social Research, University of Michigan, 1963.

65. Seashore, Stanley E. "Field Experiments with Formal Organizations," *Human Organization*, Vol. 23 (1964), pp. 164–170.

66. Selznick, Philip. *TVA and the Grass Roots.* Berkeley and Los Angeles: University of California Press, 1949.

67. Shepard, Herbert A. "Changing Interpersonal and Intergroup Relationships in Organizations," in J. G. March (ed.), *Handbook of Organizations.* Chicago: Rand McNally, 1965.

68. Sills, David L. *The Volunteers.* Glencoe, Ill.: The Free Press, 1957.

69. Stinchcombe, Arthur L. "Social Structure and Organizations," in J. G. March (ed.), *Handbook of Organizations.* Chicago: Rand McNally, 1965.

70. Swanson, Guy E. *Social Change.* Glenview, Ill.: Scott, Foresman and Co., 1971.

71. Terreberry, Shirley. "The Evolution of Organizational Environments," *Administrative Science Quarterly,* Vol. 12 (1968), pp. 590–613.

72. Troeltsch, E. *The Social Teachings of the Christian Churches,* Vol. I. New York: Macmillan and Co., 1932.

73. Weber, Max. *The Theory of Social and Economic Organization.* Glencoe, Ill.: The Free Press, 1947.

74. Wilensky, Harold L. *Intellectuals in Labor Unions.* Glencoe, Illinois: The Free Press, 1956.

75. Yinger, J. Milton. *Religion in the Struggle for Power.* Durham, N.C.: Duke University Press, 1946.

76. Zygmunt, Joseph F. "Prophetic Failure: The Case of Jehovah's Witnesses," *American Journal of Sociology,* Vol. 75 (1970), pp. 926–948.

# 30

*Harry Gold*

# The Dynamics of Professionalization:

# The Case of Urban Planning

One of the dominant responses to the many social problems in modern, urban-industrial societies has been the emergence of a wide variety of new occupations which have, as their major goal, the application of human skills and resources to the solution or amelioration of these problems. This chapter is an exploration of the process of professionalization of one of these new occupations: that of city planning, or "urban" planning, as the field is more and more coming to be called. More specifically, two major questions will be explored: 1) what are the forces promoting and impeding the process of professionalization within the occupation of urban planning; and 2) how does the representative, professional association of urban planners (The American Institute of Planners) respond or adapt to these forces through its policies and programs?[1] By examining the recent history of this occupation and the social context in which it emerged, its internal composition and organization and its external relationships with other social institutions and occupations, we will attempt to identify some of the ways in which urban planning has deviated from or conformed to the natural history of well-established professions such as law, medicine, or architecture. An attempt will also be made to develop a model of professionalization which better fits some

[1] This analysis is limited to the organized profession of urban planning, as represented by the membership of the American Institute of Planners. No effort has been made to assess the entirety of social planning in its broadest or most general sense, as in the tradition of Karl Mannheim and others.

of the newly emerging urban service professions such as urban planning, since these largely bureaucratized occupations do not necessarily have all of the same characteristics or potentialities for professionalization as have the already well-established professions.

Urban planning is but one of the many occupations which are emerging, expanding, and becoming increasingly more visible in the United States. It is also clear that many such occupations are becoming more professionalized. Indeed, increased professionalization may be viewed as an inevitable result of urbanization and industrialization, and as part of a general tendency for almost all occupations to seek some sort of professional status. The motives behind this trend are obvious. The well-established professions stand at the apex of the occupational prestige structure, their members receive higher incomes than most workers and they exert greater power by occupying a high proportion of governing posts in modern society (15, pp. 8–9). As a result, more and more white collar and technical occupations strive by various means to emulate the traditional professions. In absolute terms, many of them do succeed in raising their prestige and income.

While professional status is widely sought and represents a significant aspect of rapidly changing occupational structures in modern societies, it has also been noted that very few of the wide variety of existing occupations seeking professional status actually have or will become fully professionalized (61, p. 142). The traditional view of the professions sees them as tightly organized, autonomous and independent, highly specialized, high in prestige, and monopolistic in their controls over their respective fields of practice (6, p. 287; 42, p. 38; 36, pp. 55–56). In fact, one of the most important characteristics referred to by many students of the professions is the existence of a professional association having a high degree of control over the use of the techniques of the profession in actual practice, often by law. Much of the authority that the well-established professions enjoy is derived from their high position of prestige in the institutional structure of the larger society (51, p. 496; 13).

Yet, a glance at some of the newer, less well-established occupations, such as urban planning, would suggest that as a result of rapid social and technological change, it may be more accurate to view such occupations as operating in the context of increasingly more complex organizational environments over which they have only very limited control (12). While the motive conducive to professionalization may be powerful, the desire is not enough to insure that such status can or will be achieved. As Goode has noted, the struggle by almost all occupations for the benefits of professional status may be viewed as a zero-sum game, in which the relative position of some occupations inevitably moves down on the power-prestige scale as the position of other occupations moves up. Each occupation that rises does so at the expense of others which it surpasses, and when many occupations are rising, their net gain in terms of power and prestige is low, relative to one another (15, p. 8). Thus, the striving toward greater professionalization may be viewed in part as a competitive game, in which the occupations aspiring to professional status are engaged in a competition for relatively higher positions of prestige and power in the occupational structure.

The discussion so far raises the question of what the processes are by which an occupation normally becomes an established profession. Many studies of the professionalization process have attempted to answer this question through the use of the "natural history" approach (26, pp. 132–136). This concept refers to a sequence of changes or set of stages that pertains to a particular class of phenomena. When the concept is applied to the professions, it implies that any occupations undergoing professionalization would follow a given sequence of changes. Wilensky has gone furthest in systematizing the major sequence of events which characterize the natural history of professionalization. His summary of some selected events in the history of eighteen occupations of varying professional status lends some support to the notion that there is a recognizable pattern associated with the professionalization process. Highlights of his summary are as follows: 1) Practitioners, from other occupations at this early stage, begin performing the necessary tasks on a full-time basis; 2) The early recruits press for establishment of a training school, preferably connected with a university. This leads to an upgrading of training standards and requirements; 3) Those pushing for prescribed training and the first ones to complete it combine to form a professional association; 4) There will be persistent political agitation in order to win the support of law for the protection of the job territory and its sustaining code of ethics. Where the area of competence is not clearly exclusive, legal protection of title will be the aim — where the definition of the area of competence is clearer, then mere performance of the act by someone outside the profession will be declared a crime; 5) Eventually, rules to eliminate the unqualified and unscrupulous, rules to reduce internal competition, and rules to protect the clients and emphasize the service ideal will be embodied in a formal code of ethics (61, pp. 142–146).

The above sequence is by no means invariant. Wilensky, himself, suggests that there may also be factors unique to specific occupations acting to promote or impede professionalization which have not been conceptually identified in his model (59; 61). The fact that occupations do vary widely in their rate of professionalization and in the degree of professional status they eventually are able to acquire (largely due to the particular and unique aspect of each occupational group), does suggest that there remains a need for more case studies and comparative studies of occupations that have recently become professionalized or are still in the process. For example, occupations vary widely in the degree to which they are specialized, in the complexities of the tasks performed, in the nature of the work environment, in the teamwork involved or the amount of competition from rival occupational groups, in the nature of practitioner-client or practitioner-employer relationships, in the confidentiality of the work, in the kind of life and death risks involved, and so on. Each of these conditions is crucial to the way an occupation defines its role and relates itself to the society in which it functions.

Urban planning belongs to a class of occupations which can be characterized as relatively small in numbers, heterogeneous in composition, bureaucratic in setting, and highly generalized or diversified in role and function. For this class of occupations, it is hypothesized here that full social control over their respective fields of practice may not be a realistically attainable goal. Failure to recognize the constraints involved leads many occupations to create a social "myth" to support continued activity in this direction, no matter how unsuccessful the results may be. On the other hand, recognition of internal or external barriers to full jurisdictional control over a field of practice, such as represented by licensure, registration, or certification, may lead an occupational group to the abandonment of full legal control over the practice of the occupation as an unattainable goal. Under this circumstance, the organized occupational body may attempt to substitute more realistic and attainable goals as secondary alternatives.

For the occupation of urban planning, the kinds of internal and external social controls illustrated in steps four and five of Wilensky's summary of the natural history of professionalization reviewed above have been difficult, if not impossible, to achieve. It is further hypothesized that once aspirant professional groups such as urban planning reach apparently unremovable barriers to their acquisition of suitable, jurisdictional controls over their fields of practice, they shift their goals to the pursuit of greater prestige for their professional associations and their members. For such occupations, there may be a number of alternatives short of full legal control to which they may realistically aspire. In the long run, these may eventually increase the amount of informal social control that a professional body is able to exercise over its own membership.

Some of the particular circumstances and conditions under which formal social control goals have been abandoned by the organized urban planning profession, along with some of the alternative prestige oriented goals and policies which have been substituted, will be reviewed and assessed in the analysis to follow.

### The Emergence and Early Development of Urban Planning

It is very difficult to establish the theoretical relationship between a very broad and general social process such as urbanization and major institutional responses such as the emergence of new organizational structures and occupations. The emergence of urban planning as a profession can be best understood in the context of a series of at least three historically related and intertwined developments: 1) the emergence of planning as a social movement; 2) the emergence of planning as a legitimate and continuing function of local government; and 3) the emergence of urban planners as a distinct occupational skill group which attempts to apply in practice a specified body of knowledge and technique, and which occupies a more or less specific set of role positions in the structure of local government (21).

We shall begin our discussion by reviewing the emergence of urban planning in the United States in its own concrete socio-historical context. Planning cities is not a new development, of course, and there are examples of planned cities that go back several thousand years in history. Even in the United States planned cities were a part of its early history. William Penn laid out a planned street system for Philadelphia in 1682, an important plan was prepared for Manhattan Island in 1811, and the original plan for Washington, D. C., was prepared in 1802. Nevertheless, these were fragmentary, isolated efforts and did not in themselves generate a full-scale social movement.

The origins of city planning as a modern social movement can most accurately be traced back to the demands for social reform in both England and the United States near the middle of the nineteenth century. These demands were a response to some of the conditions associated with the industrial revolution, which brought extremely large numbers of people to the cities and helped create urban slums and blight, overcongestion and a variety of related health and sanitation problems. The concentration of large numbers of people in relatively small land areas made itself felt in intolerable living conditions and repeated epidemics of major proportions.

As early as 1834, a sanitary report from New York City called attention to bad housing as a cause of disease. A second report, submitted in 1842, was even more detailed and insistent in pointing out the relation between the two. For example, these reports pointed out that buildings with no sanitary facilities beyond the privy and the gutter were being crowded together in such a way as to leave many dwellings virtually without light and air. The first tangible result of these studies and of agitation for improvement was the creation of a city health department in 1866 and the passage of the first tenement law in 1867. Not until 1879 was a law passed prohibiting the buildings of rooms without windows (53, pp. 6–7).

Nor were these conditions confined to New York City. None of the large cities in the United States had made adequate public provisions for disposal of sewage until late in the nineteenth century, and as late as 1900 Philadelphia and St. Louis had twice as much street mileage as sewer mileage. In the same year, Baltimore, New Orleans and other cities were still relying on open gutters for drainage. Frequently, cities were prompted to construct sewer systems only by social catastrophe. Memphis, for example, did not take this step until after the city had been practically depopulated by a yellow-fever epidemic in 1879 (53, pp. 7–8).

A more indirect and somewhat separate attack on the emerging problem of urban overcrowding and congestion was the recreation movement of the latter part of the nineteenth century, which concerned itself with the development of large urban parks, the preservation of scenic resources in and around the larger cities, and the development of playgrounds in the more congested urban areas. Under the direction of leading figures of this movement, the city of New York laid out Central Park in 1857, and before 1900, park plans had been prepared for other large cities around the country. Many of these early parks were landscape developments designed largely to preserve natural scenery and provide passive relaxation. But the participants of this movement also saw the need for more active recreation, and they generated demands for a more comprehensive park system which would supplement the larger parks with readily accessible neighborhood recreation areas. In 1893, a study of Boston's park requirements led to legislation creating the Metropolitan Park Commission. This and similar programs in other cities set new patterns for comprehensive park planning (53, pp. 7–8).

But the fact that fragmentary and isolated efforts being made in a wide variety of American cities to ameliorate problems of urban congestion, poor housing, inadequate facilities for transportation, sanitation, and a host of other need services were inadequate, it began to be recognized around the turn of the century that there would have to be more comprehensive approaches to solve these problems. There was a growing realization among those interested in all these matters that they were interrelated. It has been suggested that it was in this recognition of relationships, along with a growing awareness of the necessity of mapping long-range programs and of anticipating future developments, as contrasted with piecemeal corrective measures, that the mainspring of modern urban planning can be found (53, p. 10).

In England, these same concerns gave rise to the town planning or garden city movement. This movement, led by men such as Patrick Geddes, called for the creation of new, self-sufficient and self-contained garden cities and suburbs decentralized from the existing metropolitan centers. This movement was based for the most part on utopian concepts which envisaged a return to the less complex organization and physical appearance of smaller, pre-industrial communities of the past (33, pp. 139–152). The garden city movement was influential in the development of numerous, experimental communities in England, Europe, and the United States in the early part of the twentieth century, but was not particularly influential in the later development of urban planning in the United States (11, p. 27). That the American experience has been a distinct departure from the earlier examples of planned cities and from the garden city movement has been explained as follows:

> The problem of modern city planning is one of planning new cities only to a minor degree. It is primarily a problem of replanning cities already built; also the planning movement in the United States has followed lines which set it apart rather sharply from recent European experience. This is particularly true with respect to administrative organization for planning (53, pp. 5–6).

Another important aspect of the early phases of the modern city planning movement in the United States, was a growing concern on the part of certain civic improvement organizations with improving the appearance of their communities. Beginning in the last part of the nineteenth century and lasting roughly until World War I, this phase has been identified by Perloff as the "City Beautiful" movement (44, p. 55). Probably inspired by the English town planning movement, the major emphasis was on the aesthetic appearance of the city, as reflected in civic centers, parks, streets, and landscapes. It has been reported that much of the inspiration for this movement was drawn from the Chicago World's Fair of 1893. Returning visitors, impressed by the architectural splendor of the exhibits, stimulated popular interest in civic aesthetics, while the Fair itself helped activate the "City Beautiful," which effectively epitomized the spirit of the movement (44, p. 55).

Real estate boards, private builders, and bankers were among the private civic groups which had a major influence on this phase of the planning movement, and while they may have viewed the ugliness, crowding, and lack of public facilities as among the worst features of urbanization, they were also probably seeking symbols of their own status and achievement through the creation of urban "monuments" which would enhance the physical image of their own cities (44, pp. 9–11).

Except for a few notable exceptions, the plans advocated and prepared by the earlier protagonists of planning received no official or legal status and were usually never implemented. Most of them have been characterized as little more than broad outlines of future possibilities designed to arouse public enthusiasm (53, pp. 13–14). Also, the actual producers of the plans, usually architects or landscape architects hired by the private civic groups on a consultant basis, usually had no official affiliation with the municipalities which their plans involved.

The next phase of the planning movement, which dated roughly from the Burnham plan for the city of Chicago of 1909 to the late 1920s, began to focus on the efficient functioning of cities and the rational coordination of municipal services. Perloff has labeled this phase of the planning movement the "City Practical" (45, pp. 55–56). It provides   set of goals which could be more easily incorporated into the ongoing process of city government, such as zoning and subdivision controls, public works, and other activities that could be justified on the basis of engineering and financial considerations. Also, the preservation and increase of property values associated with sound zoning practices were most certainly predominant factors in the early promotion of zoning as a necessary function of local government.

Among factors equally important in explaining the emergence of zoning and other aspects of this phase of the planning movement were technological changes then taking place. One of these was the evolution of structural steel for building, which brought about a concern for the need to set some limits on the height and density of urban buildings (21, p. 152). Another was changes in the means of transportation which led to mixed and incompatible land uses, as well as new kinds of traffic congestion in the central areas of the big cities. During the 1920s, the rapid acceptance and use of the automobile increased the importance of the control of traffic and the development of efficient street plans as major goals of the "practical" phase of the planning movement. In the 1920s, the economic boom also greatly increased the construction of housing on a mass basis and this also increased the concern for building, safety, and environmental standards as a response to some of the more problem-creating aspects of the building boom.

The 1930s saw the planning movement continuing cumulatively to broaden the scope of its goals and activities into a more comprehensive attack on urban problems. The disorganizing effects of the depression were instrumental in focusing increased attention on economic and social problems, such as slums, poverty, inadequate housing, disease, and other social problems that had been glossed over in many of the architectural or engineering oriented activities of the planning movement during the 1920s. The 1930s were also characterized by an increased interest by the planning movement in questions of the administration and organization of planning as an integral part of local government (53, pp. 42–44). Closely related to the growing concern with administration was the increasing preoccupation with intergovernmental relations. There was also a growing interest in planning for a wider variety of geographic and governmental units, such as counties, metropolitan areas, regions and states, leaving the boundaries of the units for which planning was done open to almost all possibilities. It was probably this trend which led to the use of the more generic term "urban" planning to describe the movement in favor of the more restrictive concept of "city" planning, although these terms now tend to be used interchangeably (11, p. 32). In fact, city planning, urban planning, regional planning, town planning, comprehensive planning, physical planning, and land use planning are now among the various labels used intermittently by the agencies and professionals involved in planning for the orderly growth and development of urban communities.

As implied earlier, the initial activities of the planning movement in the United States were largely carried out by civic improvement associations promoted and financed largely by a small handful of philanthropic and civic-minded individuals who had begun to turn their attention to the aesthetic and physical problems of the urban community. A subsequent organizational development was the emergence of private or lay city planning committees which eventually replaced the efforts of the initial civic improvement groups. These committees were also unofficial and they were led mainly by business and professional groups, interested in protecting and increasing property values in their communities through street improvements, zoning, and so on. These unofficial committees laid the groundwork for the public acceptance of planning and led to the establishment of official, city planning commissions which ultimately replaced the earlier private organizations.

In 1907, some decades after the emergence of city planning as a social movement, the first official planning commission in the United States was created in Hartford, Connecticut. The major functions of the first planning commissions included the preparation of zoning ordinances and long-range "master" plans for community development. Initially, the planning commissions had little or no formal authority, and they functioned primarily as separate advisory boards to the executive and legislative branches of local government, to be consulted largely at the discretion of the mayor or city council. In theory, the planning commissions were supposed to represent a broad cross section of community interests, but in practice they were usually heavily over-represented by realtors, architects, engineers, and lawyers. This was often justified on the grounds that appropriate technical knowledge or professional training contributed the most desirable qualification for membership on a planning commission (57, p. 105). Such disproportionate representation continues to the present, now more of a carry-over of an earlier pattern rather than a functionally sound prerequisite. At any rate, the particular occupational composition of the earlier planning commissions was crucial in spelling out their activities and technical focus to and beyond the time that a distinct planning occupational skill group with its own alleged body of knowledge and techniques actually emerged.

The breadth and limitations of the technical scope of planning in its early days as a new function for local government can best be illustrated by a summary of the contents of the major plans of that period. An extended survey of plans prepared in the late 1920s reported that they typically included and were restricted to the following range of topics:

A commonly used classification divides a comprehensive city plan into six main elements: zoning, streets, transit, transportation (rail, water, and air), public recreation, and civic art or civic appearance. Taken together, street planning, land subdivision regulations, and zoning are counted on to motivate the types of land development and housing which the city plan aims to secure, so that in many plans housing does not appear as a separate element (24, p. 109).

During the depression era of the 1930s, there was some cutback in expenditure for many local, physical improvement programs with which city planners were closely identified, and this was a minor setback in the development of city planning programs and agencies at the local level. Instead, Federal agencies such as the WPA, NRA, FHA, and the newly created National Planning Board were created and made funds available for dealing with a wide range of economic and social problems of human welfare on a national scale.

Despite some of the advances in its technical scope and its acceptance as a legitimate function of local government, it can be reasonably concluded that on the whole urban planning has not made any significantly visible impact on the urban scene in the United States previous to World War II. Planning activities were few, planning commissions had little or no power to effect changes in the structure and processes of urban areas, and the movement itself was little more than a handful of individuals attempting to advance the cause of planning. Their success was limited to the preparation of master plans, which were usually ignored, discarded, or filed away for some indefinite or vaguely defined future use.

Since the end of the war, however, the picture has changed markedly. The postwar population explosion, the boom in housing and transportation, the rapidly growing suburbs, the declining central cities, the increased social and geographic mobility of the population and the resulting demands for higher standards in all phases of urban living led to the dramatic postwar expansion of the planning field. Many of the current controversies and debates revolving around planning efforts in areas such as urban renewal and slum clearance, mass transportation, suburban housing and development policies, recreation facilities and other public facilities grow out of the fact that urban planning has begun to be recognized as a visible agent of change on the current urban scene.

### The City Planning Agency: The Work Setting of Urban Planners [2]

The position of responsibility, authority, and prestige that a well-estab-

[2] These conclusions as well as those in the following sections are drawn largely from a study conducted by the author between 1961 and 1965. The study was based in part on direct observations from the vantage point of the national office of the AIP, where the author served temporarily in the capacity of "Special Administrator for Professional Affairs," and in part on a content analysis of various AIP records and documents which were made available for purposes of the above study. For methodological notes, a complete list of supporting documents, correspondence, and memoranda, and a more detailed analysis of the major components of urban planning as an occupational system, see (11). Also, for purposes of this more current analysis, the author has reviewed the AIP *Proceedings of the Annual Conference* (distributed yearly to its members) for the years 1965 through 1970. For an extremely insightful self-analysis of the current "state" of the planning profession by some of its most influential members, see (8). This is a collection of papers from a symposium held to commemorate the 50th anniversary of the founding of the AIP.

lished profession may have in the institutional structure of the community is not an advantage that such an occupation can ordinarily grant itself. Instead, this usually comes about through public recognition of the value of the function that a given occupation serves. Informal recognition may include the esteem with which individual practitioners are regarded, praise for outstanding contributions, trust in the competency of the practitioner, and so on. These informal kinds of recognition, however, are difficult to measure. In addition, certain members of a given profession may be held in higher regard than others.

On the other hand, there are certain kinds of formal recognition which can be identified more precisely. For example, the formalization and classification of positions that members of a profession occupy in the institutional structure of the community serves as one valid measure of professional status. For urban planners, such recognition and acceptance can be measured in part by the classification of urban planning as a professionally distinct occupational category at various levels of local government where job descriptions and titles resembling those recommended by the AIP have become commonplace (11, p. 60).

In more general terms, the current acceptance of planning in the United States as a necessary and desirable function of local government is illustrated by the fact that since the early 1960s over 96 percent of all cities with populations over 10,000 have official planning commissions or boards. But the growth of planning as a salaried staff function, or the function of paid consultants, has been somewhat slower and less uniform. Before federal planning grants became available to local communities of 50,000 or less in the mid-1960s, less than half of the cities with populations over 10,000 recently reported expenditures for planning consultants' services, and only one-third of them employed any full or part-time professional staff (11, p. 44). With cutbacks in short lived federal grants for local planning programs in the early 1970s, planning has remained primarily a big city activity with only the few largest cities employing as many or more than 50 full time professional city planners; cities under 50,000 rarely employ more than two or three full time professional planners (11, p. 44). Planning differs from many other professions in that its clientele are municipalities and other governmental units, rather than individuals. Thus, in any given community the ratio of urban planners to the total population is extremely small (The American Institute of Planners has less than 5,000 members nationally). The extremely small size of the planning profession and its relatively sparse distribution over a major portion of the United States serves as a barrier to further professional status by making urban planning work rather invisible to the public, even though planning has gained some acceptance as a legitimate function of local government. Also, the power exerted by the planning profession, at least in numbers, falls far short of the older, well-established professions, which generally hold a disproportionate share of seats in state and national legislative bodies, boards of directors, advisory commissions, and so on, and which largely shape any legislation relating to their respective professional activities.

Before considering further the professional status of planning in terms of its established position in the public agencies, it is necessary to consider the role and technical scope of the planning function in local government. This is so broad and varied that at times it seems to defy description. Webster, for example, has suggested that the scope of urban planning is almost as broad as the entire range of municipal activities (57, p. 137). A summary of the scope and methods of urban planning by the faculty of the MIT School of City and Regional Planning, suggests that the determination of planning objectives is the most important part of the planning process, and these have been summarized as follows:

> *Economic:* efficiency of land use and circulation patterns; preservation or enhancement of economic base. *Social:* adequate provision for human needs; work, home, play; maximum choice of living environment; congenial social contacts; educational and cultural opportunities within easy reach. *Physical:* sound land use planning (types, quantities); proper distribution and density of population; efficient circulation and services; preservation of scenic and historic areas and other amenities (11, p. 48).

The range of techniques required to achieve the above goals includes two- and three-dimensional physical design, social and economic analysis, research techniques and survey methods, and the varied techniques of law and public administration. A published statement by the AIP suggests that the practice of urban planning has as its central focus "the planning of unified development as expressed through the determination of the comprehensive arrangement of land uses and land occupancy and the regulation thereof" (11, pp. 48–49). Finally, urban planning has continued to extend its range from its already broad technical base by borrowing from a wide variety of newer techniques, which themselves have been expanding at a rapidly accelerating pace in other fields: mathematics and systems analysis, electronic data processing, aerial photography, photogrammetry, social work, community development, or community organization (8).

It follows from the discussion so far, that the boundaries of the professional skills areas claimed by urban planners lack a high degree of "functional specificity." The failure to provide a clearer notion of where the boundaries of the profession are is at least partly due to the elaborate and complex division of labor associated with the planning function in local government. In the larger communities, a staff of many persons with many different specializations is usually required and these specialized skills are often organized into as few as six or more than twenty, functionally separate divisions within the planning agency.

There appears to be a tendency among all newly emerging skill groups that work within a complex organizational setting to define their own functions rather broadly so as not to unduly limit their own growth potential and planners are no exception. Thus, the range of technical competence claimed by urban planners is as broad as the entire range of even the most extensively developed local planning programs. What the planning agency does is, in effect, what the professional urban planner claims as his legitimate job territory.

Until about 1950, planning offices were primarily staffed by engineers, draftsmen, and architects. The nucleus of the planning agency staff was the "planning engineer." More recently, economists, sociologists, social workers, statisticians, geographers, and administrators have been employed by planning agencies in increasing numbers and they too, have interpreted agency goals from their own occupational frame of reference. Thus, the claims of various occupations represented on the planning staff tend to resemble their own previously existing job territories, as follows:

A planner with a civil engineering background tends to emphasize drainage, sewer and water extensions, street-widening, elimination of grade crossing and streetcar track removal; a planner with an architectural background tends to emphasize civic centers, monumental buildings, harmonious exteriors and quality of design; a planner with a landscape architectural background emphasizes scenic parks, recreation site planning, tree planting and scenic vistas; a planner with a background in geography tends to emphasize topography, climate, weather, water resources, soil conditions and land forms; a planner with a background in sociology tends to emphasize family and communal relationships, social interaction, physical influences on group and individual behavior and the social effects of planned as against unplanned environment; the planner with a background in public administration tends to emphasize the management functions of the chief executive, capital budget programming, smoother relations with the planning commission, and the city council chain of command and the interdepartmental relationships; the planner with the background in law tends to ... (57, p. 115).

The overlapping and conflicting claims to technical competency between groups with competing occupational orientations has limited the degree to which those identifying themselves as professional urban planners have been able to carve out an exclusive job territory in local government and to maintain effective social control over their selected areas of professional practice. Competition between many of the occupational groups listed above is particularly complicated by the fact that the boundaries of their service areas are so overlapping and blurred. This is largely because the problems which these groups deal with in the planning field are themselves overlapping and highly interdependent in their causes, consequences, and treatment. An important result has been many intense, jurisdictional disputes and conflicting claims to exclusive technical competency between the rival professions working in the same general problem areas.

Another factor that blurs the image of urban planners as occupying a functionally, specific area of technical competence is that in the complex organizational setting of the planning agency, its members are ranked in a hierarchy of status and responsibility. Those members of the planning profession at the top of this hierarchy serve administrative, policy making, and public relations functions; they no longer perform staff duties of a strictly technical nature. As planners move upward in their careers from the relatively routinized, technical positions at the bottom of the agency hierarchy, they often find their previous technical training and experience does not qualify them for the more complex administrative roles they must play at the higher levels. On the other hand, the smaller agencies that hire professional planning administrators without sufficient technical training or experience, often find they are not technically competent to supervise and direct the day to day work of the planning staff. Thus, the skills appropriate to each of the various status levels of the planning agency are sufficiently distinct to create difficulties in assigning personnel and in guaranteeing sufficiently stable, predictable, or secure and satisfying careers in planning to its professional recruits.

Although many professional planners occupy the higher technical or administrative positions of the planning agency, the formal authority structure of local government places them under the controls of a previously existing power structure. This usually consists of the mayor or city manager, the city council, and the lay city plan commission. The barriers to professionalization that are implied here grow out of the view among many leading planners that at its highest levels, planning is essentially a policy formulating or decision-making process, which often brings it into direct conflict with the authority structure. Most of the technical decisions which are made in planning, in contrast to those common in many other professions, are by their nature closely tied to and affected by public policy. For example, zoning decisions affecting land use, population projections based on controlled density standards and long-range transportation, facility, and capital budget programming are all part of the professional planner's technical work role. It is impossible, however, to perform these tasks without regard to public policy. What often occurs is that the professional planners come into direct conflict with the political authority structure over matters which cannot clearly be differentiated according to a technical-policy dichotomy. In such cases, the professional planners often view the "politicians" as major sources of obstructionism in blocking the achievement of program goals which they have recommended. Part of the frustration that results is also due to the fact that the large scale and complex community wide changes that are so often a part of the urban planners' objectives may take a good many years before they get underway or show results. Thus, public rejection of their proposals, or sharp opposition by elected or appointed officials after years of effort, can be especially discouraging to the public policy oriented planner.

To conclude this section, some of the major forces promoting the process of professionalization of urban planning in the context of the local agency include the institutionalization of the planning function in local government, the growing financial support of local planning activities by various levels of government and the classification by officers of public agencies of urban planning as a separate and distinct occupation of growing professional status. But some of the barriers to full professionalization of urban planning include its relatively small size, its heterogeneous recruitment base, its overly broad, obscure, and rapidly changing technical focus, its relative invisibility, its complex bureaucratic setting, its complex hierarchy and division of labor, its competition with rival professional groups and with the political power structure, and, more generally, its inability to regulate or control its own stated area of practice. How the representative professional association responds to these barriers will be the focus of the following section.

### The Professional Association: The American Institute of Planners

One essential characteristic of a profession is that its members are formally organized as a professional association. Such an association is necessary because it is the major instrument for formulating the policies and goals of the profession and developing the procedures for their implementation. In the broadest sense, the professional association may be described as a *categoric* unit of social organization. According to Hawley, a categoric unit is one made up of members occupying a single status category who unite in a collective attempt to meet common external threats; or, to put it another way, to maintain the status quo (17, p. 218). Professional groups which are well established do tend to be protective or conservative in their basic functions. But paradoxically, there may be situations where these functions can best be served by the active promotion of change. This is especially true for occupations which have just emerged and are not yet well established. Therefore, when aspiring professional groups emulate the more protective and conservative patterns of professions such as medicine, law, or architecture, such behavior may in fact serve as a barrier to their further professional development. This dilemma will be considered more fully later on.

The American Institute of Planners (originally called The American City Planning Institute) was formed in 1917 by approximately two dozen planning consultants, trained initially in other fields, who had begun to conceive of themselves primarily as city planners. One of the stated functions of this new organization was to be that of providing a "forum for consideration of technical details of the new science of city planning" (11, p. 35). This event, more than any other, signaled the initial recognition of city planners as a distinct occupational skill group laying claim to professional status, as distinct from the existing occupational groups from which they stemmed.

In its earliest days, the AIP maintained its headquarters at Cambridge, Massachusetts, where it was dominated by planning educators at Harvard and MIT. Because of its limited membership and resources, the organization did not maintain a permanent, full-time staff until the mid 1950s, and its formal activities were limited mainly to publication of a professional journal, holding annual meetings, and processing membership applications. But with a growing membership and increased interest in and support of planning activities by the Federal Government in the post World War II period, the AIP followed the pattern of many similar associations and moved its national headquarters to Washington, D. C., in 1958. It reorganized and expanded its staff and began to develop a much broader range of policies and programs, in response to both vastly increased internal demands for increased professional status and some external opportunities for further growth and recognition. Since that time, these policies and programs have been in a continuous state of flux, reflecting both the opportunities and the barriers to the advancement of the professional status of the organization and its members.

There are two major kinds of goals which are representative of any ascendent, organized professional group considered throughout this discussion. They include: 1) enhancing the prestige of the organization and its members; and 2) acquiring a high degree of social control over its professional field of practice. These goals may be seen as highly interrelated in the sense that more prestige may give a group a higher degree of social control, and vice versa. Also, both of these goals may be viewed as functional for both the profession and the larger society. Goode suggests that the professions hold power in the community as a result of both their prestige and the legal and social controls they exert. Each profession demands highly educated members, and this is given crucial importance by the larger society (13, p. 195). It is the values of the larger society which give rise to the power of the professional community, although Goode also suggests that no such power would be given if there were not a formal body to demand it and be responsible for its utilization. As a consequence of the rewards given by the larger society, the professional group can demand higher talents in its recruits and require that they go through a considerable adult socialization process (13, p. 196).

As suggested earlier, many aspirant professional groups fall short of acquiring as much prestige or social control in comparison with the well-established professions. This is true for the occupation of urban planning in its current stage of development, particularly in the area of social control. Here, the AIP has not yet acquired legal protection of title or practice. Challenges by rival occupations have led to many jurisdictional disputes between planners and other professions working in the same general problem areas, and these challenges have been perceived by many planners to be among the greatest immediate threats to the existence and growth of their profession. Many of the AIP's resources and energies have been focused on trying to develop suitable alternatives for dealing with this particular problem. The alternative which has been given the most attention is legal registration of the urban planning profession.

Theoretically, it would be expected that legal licensure of some sort would be a natural and logical goal in the professionalization process. Until the past decade, this was considered a desirable goal for the planning profession as reflected in past policies of the AIP. Now, however, it is not even certain whether the profession actually does desire such controls. One of the more interesting developments in this particular area is the fact that the leadership of the profession has recently adopted a position which is opposed to or at least does not actively seek legal registration or certification, in a clear reversal of earlier policy. In some instances, efforts in this direction were dropped because of a lack of clear support among the members of the group for various reasons, including a lack of agreement as to what specific areas were to be covered and whether practice and title or title only would be covered. There was also lack of agreement over how to measure and evaluate qualifications, and other reasons directly related to the overly broad and obscure role definitions among the members.

Given the current composition and nature of the profession, it does not appear likely that the group will soon be able to achieve complete legal control over its stated field of practice, no matter what future policy might be. Past attempts by planners to introduce registration bills into legislation in various states have failed, largely due to organized opposition of the larger and more influential state engineering and architectural societies, which have achieved more effective representation in these legislative bodies. New Jersey is the only state to date where a registration bill regulating the practice of urban planning and the use of a planning title has actually become law. Even here, the law does not grant the planning profession the power to regulate the field of practice covered by the legislation. While the law exempts all licensed engineers, land surveyors, and registered architects from the necessity of registering to practice urban planning, it requires the members of AIP who are not also licensed members of the above rival professions to meet the additional registration requirements. In other words, the burden of formally qualifying for the legal right to practice urban planning in New Jersey has been imposed on members of the AIP, while their rivals are not subject to such restrictions or qualifications! Needless to say, this is not the kind of legal status sought by the AIP! It was these rival groups, not the AIP, who submitted the legislation that was eventually passed into law, partly in retaliation for AIP efforts in this direction.

The potential impact of the retaliatory actions of the larger, better established and more powerful, rival professions is now becoming more recognized by the leadership of the AIP, as making effective legal control and self-regulation an extremely difficult, if not impossible, task. To some extent, the negative experience in New Jersey and other states, plus the threats of further retaliatory actions by rival professions, has dampened the enthusiasm for seeking legal registration in several other states where local chapters of the AIP had been actively considering some form of registration. This has led the AIP to shift its emphasis away from legal registration as a goal toward achieving a higher level of prestige for the organization and its members as the only realistically achievable alternative. Some of the recent AIP policies and programs designed to achieve this end are described below. These are now considered by the AIP leadership as the most feasible way that more informal and more indirect kinds of control over the conditions of urban planning practice can ever eventually become a real possibility.

### Professional Ethics

In addition to the lack of legal control over the professional activities of non-members, the AIP has had difficulty in establishing what it considers to be adequate internal control over the behavior of its own members. Thus, the AIP has produced a *Code of Professional Conduct*, which attempts to prescribe appropriate behavior on the part of its members. The Code consists of those professional relationships between planners and the public, clients, colleagues, employers, and other professions. The AIP takes the position that the existence of such a code of ethics is by itself a valid indicator of high professional status for the occupation.

In a well-established profession, the need to regulate the conduct of individual practitioners is minimal, since each member usually has been socialized to maintain professional norms. A formal code of ethics can achieve its purpose only when a large majority of the members of the profession adhere to such a code voluntarily and as an integral aspect of their own self identity. As an instrument of control, the enforcement of such a code can, at best, regulate the behavior of those who are already committed to the norms of the profession. It cannot control the behavior of those who are not formally affiliated. In cases where professional status is dependent on membership in the professional society, the limited internal controls inherent in a formal code may in fact be quite effective. But in cases where professional status does not require membership in the professional society as a real imperative, enforcement of a code may be quite ineffective, because the nonconforming practitioner who wishes to avoid the internal controls of the professional society can sever his formal affiliation!

In the AIP, the Code of Professional Conduct as a source of internal control has all the limitations suggested above. In addition, the code has been subject to other kinds of criticism. It has been pointed out, for example, that most of its provisions pertain to conditions of private consulting practice, such as competitive bidding, advertising, etc., which directly affect only a small portion of the planning profession (less than 20 percent of the AIP membership is in private consulting practice). It only provides negligible guidelines for appropriate professional conduct within the framework of the public agency, where most members are employed. Many of its provisions are generalized to the point of obscurity. Equally important, the procedures for the internal enforcement of the code of ethics have been found to be inadequate and efforts to take action against alleged violators of the code have to date been largely unsuccessful. The Code of Professional Conduct has been subject to continuing evaluation and major revisions in its provisions and procedures for enforcement have been underway. But, however effective the AIP may be in regulating its own members, there still exist large numbers of people employed in the planning field who are not members, and therefore are not bound to the provisions of the official AIP code of ethics.

### Professional Education

The AIP has no direct control over the various educational programs in planning, but it has played an indirect role in promoting professional graduate education. It has prepared a number of reports which make recommendations for the content of curricula, spell out current educational trends and their implications for the planning profession, and support efforts to establish new planning programs in universities which have not already done so. It has established criteria for the recognition of planning schools for AIP membership standards. While these criteria fall short of actual accreditation, they have some influence on planning education, especially in suggesting standards to be adopted by the newer educational programs. Approximately 60 percent of the existing planning schools have been recognized by the AIP and several more were actively seeking recognition or were altering their programs to meet AIP recognition standards as of the end of the 1960s. Also, most of the privately sponsored fellowship programs for recruiting and training planners have been limited to planning schools which have been formally recognized by the AIP.

The AIP seeks in a variety of ways to improve the techniques of practice and the body of knowledge on which they are based outside as well as inside the planning schools. It has actively sought to develop an index and abstracting service to meet the growing problems of handling planning data and information, which is exploding in volume. It has promoted the development of more comprehensive urban research, especially in connection with federal legislation in urban related fields such as housing and urban renewal. It has also sponsored programs of continuing education for practitioners and assisted in the development of educational programs for training "sub-professionals" at community colleges. Along with the National Science Foundation, the AIP has co-sponsored an inter-university program of courses on computer applications to urban analysis. This program, along with the others listed above, illustrates the rapid changes in the technological base of the profession and the efforts of the AIP to keep itself and its members abreast of these changes.

### Membership Standards

One important alternative to external controls such as legal registration is internal control over membership standards within the AIP. In the past, the basic criterion for membership was job experience. While some levels of educational achievement were accepted as equivalent to planning experience, professional degrees were not in themselves the major criterion. More recently, the AIP Board of Governors has decided to shift its emphasis so that full membership would no longer be based primarily on experience but rather on "a demonstrated understanding and ability to apply a basic core of knowledge of the field as defined by the AIP." Further, "The requirements of an AIP recognized planning degree is considered to be the basic professional qualification. A formal examination should be the alternate route to membership to those without the graduate planning degree" (11, p. 131).

One of the major difficulties in carrying out these recommendations has been the lack of agreement upon a suitable examination and procedures for its implementation and administration. But most important here is the fact that professional education itself has been upgraded in importance, and that as entry into the profession becomes increasingly more difficult for those who do not have this qualification, the membership in the AIP is expected to become increasingly more homogeneous and technically distinct. This is looked upon by the AIP leadership as a source of increased prestige and recognition for the organization and its members.

### Inter-Professional Relations

As a major alternative to registration as a means of protecting its field of practice from excessive competition with rival professional groups, the

AIP has taken the view that it is necessary to move toward greater understanding with other professional bodies with similar and often rival interests. In 1959, it initiated a formalized and active program of interprofessional cooperation and coordination with other relevant professional societies. It established joint committees with the Institute of Traffic Engineers, The American Society of Civil Engineers, the American Institute of Architects and the American Bar Association. In more recent years, efforts to establish better relations with professional social workers have proceeded amicably as both groups have recognized their interdependent and overlapping concerns.

But the least successful efforts at cooperation and understanding have been with the various civil engineering groups that work in planning and related fields, as evidenced by the many jurisdictional disputes and battles over legal registration discussed earlier. There have been numerous efforts to work out joint statements spelling out the responsibilities of the various "design" professions and to work out formal guides for collaboration, but without positive results. Statements acceptable to one professional group have been rejected by the others, thus leading to a virtual stalemate in this area. While there is a growing concern at the national leadership level of these groups that there needs to be greater cooperation between them, the failure to ratify formal guides for reciprocal recognition and collaboration has sprung from the competition and poor working relations that continue to exist between planners and engineers at the local and state levels across the country. In response, the AIP has produced a series of documents intended to "educate" rival professions as to the legitimacy of the urban planning profession's jurisdictional claims.

In addition to professional societies, the AIP maintains joint committees and/or staff relationships with at least fifty other organizations having interests in the urban field. All of these interorganizational contacts, whatever their immediate purposes, can be viewed as efforts by the AIP to gain recognition and prestige for itself and its members among those groups it considers relevant for this purpose.

## Lobbying and Public Relations

In addition to the activities already mentioned, the AIP attempts to maintain a more broad and generally favorable public image as a bona fide body of "experts" in the planning area. This is done primarily through exhibits provided for civic affairs and meetings of other organizations, by providing speakers for these affairs, by serving as "expert witness" at legislative hearings at the local, state, and federal levels. They also develop and publish a series of policy statements on various subjects, such as urban renewal, housing, urban mass transit, state planning, etc. In these, the AIP presents a strong image of itself as a skill group working for the "public interest."[3]

While the AIP does not ordinarily address itself to the public at large, there have been a number of instances in which the planning profession has come under widespread public attack, to which the AIP has publically responded. For example, Jane Jacobs sharply criticized the planning profession in her popular book, *The Death and Decline of American Cities*, which opens with the sentence, "This book is an attack on current city planning and rebuilding" (28, p. 1). The AIP answered these harsh criticisms by organizing letter writing campaigns to popular publications which reported Mrs. Jacobs' views, by inviting her to debate planners at various meetings and forums, and in speeches by AIP leaders at various public meetings, conventions and conferences. Finally, the AIP publishes for wide distribution a series of brief statements which attempt to explain and describe its own history, internal organization and goals to a broad audience of lay and professional groups alike.

### Present and Future Prospects for Professionalization

The natural history approach to the study of the well-established professions would suggest that emergent professions such as planning would continue to develop along similar lines. Yet, this chapter does not support the conclusion that urban planning will necessarily become fully professionalized in the foreseeable future. While planning is relatively new, it is not the recent origins of the occupation that is offered as an explanation. Instead, it is suggested that there may be emerging a class of occupations similar to planning in significant characteristics that will become partially professionalized in the conventional sense, but which will not take on all of the attributes of the well-established professions. Such occupations include those that are largely dependent on other disciplines for the development of crucial knowledge and techniques. Such occupations include those that are grounded mainly in human-relations skills or on programs of reform such as social work and teaching, as well as many of the newer administrative occupations (city management, hospital administration) which may be based on knowledge or a vocabulary with which almost everyone claims some familiarity and competency. Goode's analysis of librarianship would suggest that it also belongs in this category (15). Planning has been described here as a "generalized" profession. Whereas the generalist orientation appears directly in the occupational self-definitions, it is most significantly

---

[3] Leaders of the planning profession had long lobbied for the creation of a cabinet level department of urban affairs at the federal level, as represented by the creation of HUD. But they have been rather disappointed at many of the resultant programs, especially in the housing and urban renewal areas, over which they collectively have had little or no influence in designing or implementing. See (8, Part 1).

reflected in the technical base of the profession. Here, it has been shown that planning borrows its knowledge and techniques from an impressively wide variety of previously existing disciplines and skill areas. It has been suggested that there may be an optimal base for professional practice — neither too vague nor too precise, too broad nor too narrow — and to exceed these limits in either direction constitutes one of the major barriers of professionalization (59). Given such a knowledge and skill base for urban planning, it may be that there is a poor foundation for any claims to exclusive jurisdiction in *any* of the skill areas represented. Perhaps the old cliché, "jack-of-all-trades, master of none," which some planners facetiously apply to themselves, fits the occupation of urban planning better than might be seriously admitted. Carr-Saunders has also much earlier stated the problems of the more generalized occupations this way:

> Where the technique is specialized, the rise of a profession is unescapable. Where it is generalized, its coming must wait upon the growth of a sense of a common responsibility in order that the loose bond, created by the possession of a common but ill-defined technique, may be drawn more tightly (6, p. 287).

It may be that as new programs and institutional arrangements develop in response to increasingly more complex urban problems, there will be more room and opportunities created for professionals to function as generalists, but within the existing maze of established agencies and departments of urban government, the resistance to such change is still great.

Another characteristic common to some newly emerging professions which are not expected to assume a full degree of control over their respective job territories is that their movement toward autonomy is blocked by pre-existing power structures which often include better established professional groups as well as lay governing boards, political officials, and legislative bodies. In a broader sense, any profession which operates primarily in a bureaucratic setting faces similar limitations in the amount of autonomy they are able to exercise in the practice of their respective fields. Even the older, well-established professions such as law and medicine also now work more and more in complex organizational settings, where these same limitations might also apply. However, there are significant differences in the amount of autonomy exercised by those professions which have achieved high professional status *before* they began to function extensively in bureaucratic settings, such as medicine and law, and those which have emerged primarily *within* bureaucratic organizations, such as city planning.

In the structure of bureaucratic organizations, the professions occupy an intermediate and indeterminant status somewhere between the routinized technical positions at the bottom of the organizational hierarchy, which require minimum skills and training, and the managers and policy makers of the organizations which they serve. At most, the professionals share a limited amount of power with the directors of the organizations. This causes no serious conflicts for those professions which define their roles in purely technical terms, but in the case of many of the newly emerging "urban service" professions the nature of the tasks they perform suggest that they include many individuals who are directly concerned with the kinds of policies formulated at the top of the organizational decision-making structure. Thus, one finds in many bureaucratic service organizations what Wilensky calls the "program" professionals. These are the problem-solving professionals whose commitments to particular programs and policies are as great as their commitments to the techniques and procedures of their professional field (61, p. 158). Program professionals play an indispensable role in service organizations with rapidly changing and expanding functions, and they are in growing demand at strategic points in the urban service structure. Perhaps it would be more accurate to speak of some of these professionals as organizational innovators — that is, as individuals whose major role is to create new organizational machinery for getting a wide variety of specialized urban tasks done efficiently and effectively; at least, to better coordinate existing programs.

But it is unlikely that the innovator role in bureaucracy can ever be fully professionalized in the traditional sense, or that such innovators can be trained routinely as a matter of course in professional schools. The program professional is to some extent a maverick to his own technical profession, and in many cases he may have no strong commitments to its formal associations. This may be a matter of embarrassment to the professional association when such individuals have made prominently acknowledged contributions to the larger society (the AIP has unilaterally named Lewis Mumford as an honorary member, although he himself has never chosen to affiliate with this organization).

In the earliest stages of professionalization, a newly formed professional group takes on the social movement characteristics of its members, and so there is a great deal of organizational support for experimentation and innovation. These may be important sources of prestige and recognition for the occupations, especially if they are successful. This is to say that new occupational groups attempting to get themselves established have a stake in producing a visible impact in their field of specialization. In the case of urban planning, the activities of the earliest practitioners in getting planning programs established as legitimate functions of local government actually did advance the status and prestige of the newly emerging city planning profession.

But for professions which have already found some niche in the occupational hierarchy, innovation becomes less important as a source of status, and in fact may then be viewed by the professional society with caution or suspicion. In well-established professions, there have been many instances where innovators have been viewed with alarm as radicals, charlatans or quacks and expelled from membership in their formal associations. When it reaches the stage where the innovator must become a maverick to his own technical profession, it may be said that the professional society has reached the stage where its self-conserving and protective functions have become dominant, at the expense of other important considerations. It is, however, impossible to determine with any degree of precision the point at which an occupation ceases to be "innovative" and becomes "conservative." The main point here, however, is that in the advanced stages of professionalization, "professionalism" in the traditional sense, and "innovation" are two processes that may be partially incompatible, both for the professional society and for the individual practitioners who attempt to reconcile the two roles.

Failure to reduce this source of role strain may produce several outcomes. First, many program professionals may retreat from the complex problems and find it difficult to maintain program professional orientation. For example, they may retreat either to a strictly technical orientation, which stresses the procedural rather than the policy aspects of their work, or they may retreat to a form of provincialism which allows them to become a compliant part of the local power structure. The innovating program professional may also retreat to a "careerist" orientation, which stresses security, gradual job advancement, and the symbols of professional status, rather than either the technical or policy aspects of the work (60). All these forms of retreatism are probably motives for the legalistic kinds of protectionism discussed earlier, but more important, they serve as barriers to the maintenance of innovator and policy oriented roles for occupations such as urban planning. In the fluid and rapidly changing social context in which these kinds of occupations function, such retreatism must be viewed as among the pathologies or disfunctions of professionalization, rather than one of its healthy and essential characteristics.

We close this discussion with some suggestions for further explorations into the nature and scope of the planning profession, and of the planning function in local government. More needs to be known about the impact of planned change on the structure and shape of modern urban communities and the degree to which professional planners actually have participated in or guided the formulation of policies which have brought such change about. For example, Hawley has found that success in urban renewal is related to the type of power configuration in the local community (17; 18). But little is known of the relative impact of the various segments of the local power structure, such as public officials, business groups, or professional urban planners, in the local decision-making processes.[4]

It has been suggested here that planning is a relatively invisible profession, but not enough is really known about the public image of the planning profession or how this image has changed as the effects of planning programs have become increasingly more visible. There is some preliminary indication of negative public reaction to at least some of the results of urban planning, but these reactions and their sources need to be more systematically explored (3; 4; 10; 54). Also, the prestige ranking assigned to professional urban planners has not been adequately measured. It is interesting to note, in this respect, that urban planning as a distinct occupation has never appeared on any of the various occupational prestige scales used by sociologists in stratification research!

Finally, no adequate set of criteria has yet seemed to have emerged for measuring the success or failure of planning practices and procedures, or for rating the skills and efficacy of individual practitioners of urban planning. Although this is probably not one of the most significant characteristics of professionalization, it is extremely doubtful that any occupational group could long make valid claims to professional competency in a climate of repeated failure to achieve the goals expected from the rendering of its professional services. In a situation where these goals have not been specifically stated or where they are so broad in scope that they cannot be readily evaluated, as in the case of urban planning, the rating of professional performance is an extremely formidable task. But in the short run, the lack of specific performance criteria may be beneficial for an ascending occupational group because its claims to professional competency, while they cannot always be adequately defended, also cannot be successfully challenged. It can be speculated in this respect that some ascending professions that function in complex organizational settings and which have very broadly defined goals, are able to advance their prestige higher and more rapidly in their emergent stages than those which are more functionally specific. In planning, this may be due to the previously discussed tendency of the profession to become identified and equated with the planning agency. But these are also tentative observations which need to be further explored.

---

[4] Most studies of decision-making processes in local communities focus on broad segments of the community (public officials, business elites, etc.) or on individuals occupying key community positions. Rarely do they isolate the various technical professions employed by municipalities for more concrete analysis (3; 17; 48; 50; 54). One exception is Rabinovitz, who tentatively begins to make explicit the power exercised by urban planners in several local communities (47).

# BIBLIOGRAPHY

1. Adams, Frederick J. *Urban Planning Education in the United States.* Cincinnati, Ohio: Alfred Bettman Foundation, 1954.

2. Beckman, Norman. "The Planner as a Bureaucrat," *JAIP*, November, 1964, Vol. 30.

3. Bellush Jewel, and Housnecht, Murray. *Urban Renewal: People, Politics and Planning.* Garden City, N.Y.: Doubleday, 1967.

4. Boskoff, Alvin. *The Sociology of Urban Regions.* New York: Appleton-Century-Crofts, 2nd Edition, 1970, Part V.

5. Carr-Saunders, A. M. "Metropolitan Conditions and Traditional Professional Relationships," in Fisher, R. M. (ed.). *The Metropolis in Modern Life.* Garden City, N.Y.: Doubleday and Co., 1955.

6. Carr-Saunders, A. M., and Wilson, P. A. *The Professions.* Clarendon, Texas: Clarendon Press, 1933.

7. Doebele, Mary R. "Abstracts of City Planning Theses," *JAIP*, February, 1962, and February, 1963.

8. Erber, Ernest (ed.). *Urban Planning in Transition.* New York: Grossman, 1970.

9. Frieden, Bernard J. "The Journal's Editorial Policy," *JAIP*, February, 1963.

10. Gans, Herbert J. *People and Plans.* New York: Basic Books, 1963.

11. Gold, Harry. "The Professionalization of Urban Planning," Ph.D. Dissertation, University of Michigan, 1965.

12. Gold, Harry. "The Professionalization of Problem Solving," in H. Gold and F. Scarpitti, *Combatting Social Problems: Techniques of Intervention,* New York: Holt, Rinehart and Winston, 1967.

13. Goode, William J. "Community within a Community: The Professions," *ASR*, April, 1957.

14. Goode, William J. "Encroachment, Charlatanism, and the Emerging Professions: Psychology, Medicine and Sociology," *ASR*, December, 1960.

15. Goode, William J. "The Librarian: from Occupation to Profession?" in P. H. Ennis, and H. W. Winger, *Seven Questions about the Profession of Librarianship.* Chicago: University of Chicago Press, 1962.

16. Erber, Ernest. "The Relationship of Science to the Practicing Professions," *JAIP*, November, 1958.

17. Hawley, Amos H. *Urban Society.* New York: Ronald Press, 1971.

18. Hawley, Amos H. "Community Power and Urban Renewal Success," *AJS*, January, 1963.

19. Heikoff, Joseph M. "Urban Planning and the Professional Planner," *JAIP*, August, 1960.

20. Howard, John T. "The Planner in a Democratic Society," *JAIP*, 1955.

21. Howard, John T., in Harvey S. Perloff. *Planning the Urban Community.* Pittsburgh: University of Pittsburgh Press, 1961.

22. Howard, John T. "Planning is a Profession," *JAIP*, 1954.

23. Hubbard, H. V., and Menhinick, H. K. "City Planning as a Professional Career," *JAIP*, 1942.

24. Hubbard, H. V., and Hubbard, T. K. *Our Cities Today and Tomorrow.* Cambridge, Mass.: Harvard University Press, 1969.

25. Hubbard, H. V. "The Profession of City Planning," *JAIP*, 1937.

26. Hughes, Everett C. *Men and Their Work.* New York, N.Y.: Free Press, 1958.

27. Hughes, Everett C. "The Professions," *Daedalus,* 1963, pp. 655–68.

28. Jacobs, Jane. *The Death and Decline of American Cities.* New York: Random House, 1961.

29. Lee, James E. "Planning and Professionalism," *JAIP*, February, 1960.

30. Lee, James E. "The Role of the Planner in the Present: A Problem of Identification," *JAIP*, August 1958.

31. Long, Norton E. "Planning and Politics in Urban Development," *JAIP*, November, 1959.

32. MacIver, Robert. "Social Significance of Professional Ethics," *Annals of the American Academy of Political and Social Sciences,* 1922.

33. Mairest, Phillip. *Pioneer of Sociology.* London: Lund Humphries, 1957.

34. Marshall, T. H. "The Recent History of Professionalism in Relation to Social Structure and Social Policy," *Canadian Journal of Economics and Political Science* (August, 1939).

35. Marvick, D. *Career Perspectives in a Bureaucratic Setting.* Ann Arbor: University of Michigan Press, 1954.

36. Maude, A., and Lewis, R. *Professional People.* Kennesaw, Ga.: Phoenix House, 1952.

37. Merton, Robert K. "The Functions of the Professional Association," *American Journal of Nursing,* January, 1958.

38. Merton, Robert K., et al. *The Student Physician.* Cambridge, Mass.: Harvard University Press, 1957.

39. Moynihan, Daniel P. *Toward a National Urban Policy.* New York: Basic Books, 1970.

40. *Occupational Licensing Legislation in the States.* Chicago: The Council of State Governments, June, 1952.

41. Parsons, Talcott. *The Social System.* New York: Free Press, 1951, pp. 428–479.

42. Parsons, Talcott. *Essays in Sociological Theory.* New York: Free Press, 1954, 2nd ed.

43. Parsons, Talcott. "Social Change and Medical Organization in the United States: A Sociological Perspective," *The Annals of the American Academy of Political Social Sciences* (March, 1963).

44. Perloff, Harvey S. *Education for Planning: City, State, Regional.* Baltimore, Md.: Johns Hopkins Press, 1957.

45. Perloff, Harvey S. (ed.). *Planning and the Urban Community.* Pittsburgh, Penn.: University of Pittsburgh Press, 1961.

46. Perrow, Charles. "The Analysis of Goals in Complex Organizations," *ASR* (December, 1961).

47. Rabinovitz, Francine F. *City Politics and Planning.* New York: Atherton Press, 1969.

48. Rose, Arnold. *Power Structure.* New York: Oxford University Press, 1967.

49. Seeley, John R. "What is Planning? Definition and Strategy," *JAIP,* May, 1962.

50. Shank, Alan. *Political Power and the Urban Crises.* Boston, Mass.: Holbrook Press, 1969, Part 2.

51. Stone, Robert C. "The Sociology of Bureaucracy and Professions," in Rocek, Joseph S. *Contemporary Sociology.* New York: Philosophical Library, 1958.

52. Strauss, G. "Professionalism and Occupational Associations," *Industrial Relations,* May, 1963.

53. Walker, Robert A. *The Planning Function in Urban Government.* Chicago: University of Chicago Press, 1950.

54. Walton, John. "Differential Patterns of Community Power Structure," in Walton, J. and Carns, D. E.(eds.). *Cities in Change.* Boston, Mass.: Allyn and Bacon, 1973.

55. Wardwell, Walter L. "Social Integration, Bureaucratization, and the Professions," *Social Forces,* May, 1955.

56. Weber, Melvin M. "Comprehensive Planning and Social Responsibility: Toward an AIP Consensus on the Professional Roles and Purposes," *JAIP,* November, 1963.

57. Webster, Donald H. *Urban Planning and Municipal Public Policy.* New York: Harper & Bros., 1958.

58. Wheaton, William L. C. "Operations Research for Metropolitan Planning," *JAIP,* November, 1963.

59. Wilensky, Harold L. "The Dynamics of Professionalism: The Case of Hospital Administration," *Hospital Administration,* Spring, 1962.

60. Wilensky, Harold L. *Intellectuals in Labor Unions.* New York: Free Press, 1956.

61. Wilensky, Harold L. "The Professionalization of Everyone?" *AJS,* September, 1964.

62. Wilensky, Harold L., and Lebeaux, Charles N. *Industrial Society and Social Welfare.* New York: Russell Sage Foundation, 1958.

# 31

*Richard Colvard*

# Risk Capital Philanthropy: The

# Ideological Defense of Innovation

Many of the large philanthropic foundations established in ever increasing numbers in this country since the turn of the century (7, p. xiii; 11) are both examples and instruments of social change. Collectively, they represent a new type of institution, evolved from an ancient model; individually, they are ongoing organizations committed to continual educational and social innovation.

As organizations, unlike many others interested in reform, these foundations' formal aim is to withdraw — to go on to something else — once the particular cause or idea they have supported (within a given field or location) has either gained considerable support from other sources or apparently proved abortive. Again, because they both represent and command considerable wealth, they have been perpetually deemed as having more potential power than many other organizations with analogous aims. For these and other reasons they have been constrained through the years to develop a circuitous style of operation aimed at what might be termed "innovation by indirection." Except as prominent advocates — and symbols — of the deliberate investment of surplus wealth in efforts at social improvement, their influence is exerted more through the giving of a wide variety of grants to other organizations than through the direct carrying out of operations themselves.

It is the distinctive and complex ideology which the large grant-making foundations have gradually developed — to explain their existence as institutions and justify their engaging-disengaging role as professional foster parents of innovation — in which we are most interested here, and which we shall analyze as the "risk capital concept" in American philanthropy. Like "academic freedom," "free enterprise," and other ideologies intended in part to win public acceptance of considerable organizational autonomy, the risk capital concept is a cultural precipitate: in this case, a combination of ideas both drawn from many elements of the culture of Western civilization and variously interpreted by many groups in the American foundation environment. The three sources — both of support for and resistance to the risk capital concept — to be dealt with here are: a) Anglo-American law, especially that bearing on private wealth applied to philanthropy; b) political-economic theory, particularly American interpretations of the ancient ideas of self-help and voluntary enterprise; and c) the idea of progress, especially as amalgamated — in education and science — into the pragmatic theme of "progress through knowledge."

The guiding theses — to put them more specifically — are: 1) that the need to frame policies and programs justifiable to the courts, to the government and allied economic groups capable of affecting legislation — and also to the colleges and universities which have become their major "client" organizations — has been a major incentive to the development of the risk capital concept; 2) that the same mixture of encouragement and constraint has enabled the foundations to acquire considerable freedom of expression and action, but has also led them to engage primarily in efforts not only more indirect than those open to other institutions and reform organizations but less venturesome than the risk capital concept implies. The larger implication eventually developed is that, in the judgment of history, the risk capital ideology itself may be deemed a more important innovation than those stimulated by actual foundation grants. That is to say, the specific *structural* changes in medical education or university administration, for example, stimulated by foundation grants may prove less significant in time than the general *cultural* change represented 1) in the creation of a politically defensible rationale for continual research and reform, and 2) in the incorporation of that rationale in the ideological armory of government, industry, science, and education — as well as large-scale philanthropy. For the idea of systematically and continually putting surplus wealth to public purposes — of, so to speak, vaccinating the social system with weakened forms of the lively virus of change — has probably helped induce in American society an ability to tolerate the "creative destruction" endemic to both capitalism and science.

### The Risk Capital Ideal

The risk — or venture — capital concept has been succinctly described in a historical passage by Andrews, who has done much to bring it into prominence in the foundation world:

Early in the twentieth century the foundation idea began to take deep root in American soil, but with this significant difference. Substantial endowments were set up, often in perpetuity, as in England; but frequently with wide latitude in their use. . . . The new doctrine asserted that the funds of foundations were largely the venture capital of philanthropy, best spent when invested in enterprises requiring risk and foresight, not likely to be supported either by government or the private individual. The usual purpose was not relief or even cure; it was research, prevention, and discovery. The very word "foundation" acquired in America connotations of freedom of action (5, p. 12).

And Keppel, a widely influential foundation executive of an earlier era, once elaborated it:

Though strictly limited in its scope, the foundation is nevertheless a factor of the first importance, for it has certain great assets. It is free to choose its objective, it can give when others withhold, it can give quickly, and if it keeps its funds free from obligations against future income, it can continue to give. Foundation support for any enterprise should be significant for its timeliness rather than for its amount, it should reveal imagination and courage. Incidentally, it needs nearly as much imagination and more courage . . . to stop support when the area of diminishing returns is reached. But only by so doing, can it continue to be creatively useful (62, pp. 593–594).

Support of the research of Goddard, Banting, Lawrence, Myrdal, and Kinsey; direct involvement in the eradication of hookworm in the South and the establishment of improved public health facilities and medical research and education in many parts of the world; sponsorship of such long-range efforts as the development of more liberal curricula in teacher education; acceleration of — to mention just two — the adult education and mental health movements: these and many other foundation activities are frequently mentioned as important examples of the carry-over into practice of this commitment to work on the frontiers of knowledge and preventive — not palliative — action (see e.g., Embree [40, pp. 31–32]; Bremner [20, p. 136]; 20; 99; 33).

But many critics both inside and outside the foundations have, with varying degrees of persuasiveness, persistently pointed out through the years that such examples are commitment-confirming exceptions to the more general tendency to support the politically "safe" field and the professionally "sound" project or person (1, pp. 227–228; 68, pp. 11–12; 3, p. 54; 40, p. 32; 103, p. 140, p. 214, p. 216; 67; 9; 36; 37; 66; 80; 48).

Differing value judgments aside, the evidence bearing on both of these contentions is simply not clear. The existent statistics, for example, improving but chronically incomplete and imperfectly categorized, do not often detail individual recipients and specific proposals or otherwise provide a means of adequately dealing with the question of what might be "sound" and who might be most apt to break out of conventional patterns of thinking. On the matter of fields, such historical figures as are available do make it fairly clear that, although the purely palliative "welfare" types of programs have been pretty regularly avoided, the bulk of grants through the years have been concentrated in what we would consider the ordinarily politically "safe" fields of education and health (11, table 8, p. xvii). The most recent year for which fairly comprehensive figures are available is 1971. Grants that year (of over $10,000 from the foundations included in the grants index of *Foundation News*, 43) totaled $1.06 billion. Education got $343 million, or 32 percent, nearly half (47 percent) of it for higher education (cf. 31). Welfare activities of various kinds were granted $174 million, or 16 percent. Health fields received $156 million, or 16 percent, 61 percent of it for hospitals. Science, international activities, and humanities each received about 10 percent of the $1.06 billion — $111, $106, and $103 million respectively. Within the sciences, 52 percent of the funds went to the life sciences, 36 percent to social science, and 10 percent for physical science. Comparable percentages in 1957, e.g., were 41, 28, and 31; both the life sciences and the social sciences got increased support (cf. 7, table 8, p. xxviii). The remainder, some $73 million, or 7 percent of the $1.06 billion, went for various programs in the field of religion.

Given limited space as well as incomplete data, it is impossible to examine all the reasons why many would agree with Andrews that: "in their first half-century many foundations have chosen by preference non-controversial projects, but on occasions . . . have shown great courage and initiative . . ." (3, p. 54). Personality differences, the varying interests and influences of donors and officers, the generally conservative backgrounds of board members (68, pp. 32–46; 6; 68; 104; 80; 15), the natural scarcity of truly venturesome ideas in most fields, the definite limits to foundation assets in relation to costs and needs,[1] and a host of other factors are probably all important pieces of the puzzle. But much of the overall pattern, particularly the continuing support of education, may well be understood as a reflection of the foundations' efforts to arrive at a new way of working within a contradictory cultural heritage — a heritage whose internally conflicting legal, political-economic, and educational-scientific elements we will now take up in turn.

---

[1] Using reports mostly for 1956, 1957, or 1958, Andrews (7, xiv-xv) estimated the total market value of 5,113 reporting foundations (including Ford at over $3 billion and nine others at over $100 million each) as $11,518,019,000. Roughly comparable measures ca. 1969 showed $25.2 billion in assets for 5,454 foundations, whose grants totaled $1.5 billion (11, pp. x-xi). The approximately $625 million a year Andrews (8, p. 161) estimated as available for grants in a normal year made up about 8 per cent of the total for all fiscal forms of private philanthropy.

## Private Wealth and Public Purposes

Although the formalization of philanthropy can be dated back at least to the Pharaohs, highly organized grant-making guided by a risk capital ideal is almost entirely an innovation of this century and this society (54, p. 575). Legal support for the idea that philanthropic funds should be kept free to be spent in creatively constructive ways came in part as a long-developing reaction against early unsatisfactory experiences with charitable trusts. The latter often had narrow, specific purposes and were established in perpetuity, both trustees and courts being obliged to carry out the donor's wishes even when purposes and beneficiaries became obsolete (47, pp. 15–27). Establishment in perpetuity is still common, as are charitable trusts. But the philanthropic organizations of the sort established by Carnegie and Rockefeller deliberately coupled greater breadth of purpose with more administrative flexibility. Their trustees, to cite Andrews again, "spent less time in conserving money than in exploring new and enterprising ways of spending it" (5, pp. 11–12).[2]

### Legal Supports

The frequently discussed doctrine of *cy pres* (18, p. 190), a method of attempting to counter "dead hand" obsolescence by approximating the donor's originally stated purpose, is one indicator of the increasing legal acceptance gradually obtained. But it is less significant, because weak and seldom applied (54, pp. 584–585), than the eventual general granting of broad powers to the corporate form of organization (94, p. 23) and the establishment of permissive tax laws. Of the latter development Chambers observed not long ago:

> Under long traditions of Anglo-American law, the State not only permits voluntary . . . charitable . . . associations to exist and operate with a high degree of autonomy . . . it also habitually encourages and aids them by various means, one of the most common of which is exemption from taxation (30, p. 44–45).

And, as an even more recent and summary statement has it: "the law largely gets out of the way of individuals who want to transfer their assets to foundations in deference to the private property concept" (94, p. 23).

### Legal Constraints

By 1950 it was being argued (19, p. 484) that the freedom of foundations to operate as they pleased had become virtually complete. But

---

2 But cf. the comprehensive, somewhat less sanguine, overview by Curti (35, pp. 146–156; also 48, 69).

this was and still is a considerable exaggeration for the foundations of the sort with which we are concerned here, for there are definite elements of constraint as well as of support in the legal heritage affecting foundation ideology and operation. It has unquestionably remained true, for example, that federal and state regulations are often vaguely worded and weakly enforced.[3] But even the oblique language of the Internal Revenue Code can affect foundation deliberations in variously constraining ways.

One Code provision, for example, ordinarily (cf. 7, xvii) proscribes the unreasonable accumulation of income. As one recent statement explains:

> Federal laws regulating foundations require, among other things, that foundations must not accumulate out of income an amount that is "unreasonable in amount or duration." This is aimed at getting foundations to make their grants as soon as is practical after receiving their income and at preventing a foundation manager from using the charitable organization to build control of the business or businesses (72, p. 15).

While enforcement of this provision can presumably keep a foundation on a general philanthropic track, it may actually discourage the building of the main line, or even of spur lines, into new territories.

To mention two varying cases in point: one foundation was ruled as having forfeited its tax-exempt status for 1951 and 1952 because it had not spent more of its income during that period; the foundation's argument was that a new director had been taking time to develop plans for effective giving (72, p. 15). Another was led several years later, partly because of an unanticipated growth of assets and thus of income, to give huge grants for teachers' salaries, hospitals, and medical schools — an action highly praised by some but condemned by others as essentially palliative (70, pp. 141–142, pp. 117–137, pp. 166–171).

Another Code provision[4] restricts the claiming of tax-exemption where propagandizing or "otherwise attempting to influence legislation" constitutes a "substantial part" of the foundation's activity. But foundations not only find it difficult to avoid what some might consider propagandizing when supporting one kind of field or problem instead of another, but also sometimes find it necessary to get assurance of legislative clearance before certain kinds of demonstration projects, for example, can get started (27, pp. 147–160). By working through special advisory committees or even through grantee organizations themselves, program

---

[3] See e.g., 93, 45, 55; also the 1965 *Treasury Department Report* (90); cf. the Federal Tax Reform Act of 1969 (81) and 100.

[4] For an interesting general discussion of "legal and taxation factors," see Andrews (4, pp. 254–261); subsequent quotations are from sections of the Code reproduced there (4, pp. 272–293). For a picture of bolder, earlier days, e.g., of the General Education Board and the allied Southern Education Board, see Fosdick and Pringle (42, p. 7, pp. 19–20, pp. 25–126).

promotion and legislative clearance can sometimes be obtained indirectly. But even these tactics can bring criticism, e.g., that the foundations exert undue influence or abdicate social responsibility for acts of groups they support financially (105; 41, pp. 14–30; cf. 51).

Use of more direct tactics, however, can be even more suspect. As its director recently described the dilemma long confronting one of the few large foundations choosing to function as an operating rather than a grant-making organization in a controversial social science field:

> I have an old friend in Boston, an old professor, who says, "——, if you fail; if you don't do something controversial, you'll all be dispossessed like the monasteries in the sixteenth century." . . . [But] we foundations operate on a very thin legal basis. . . . There are many ways you can get harassed. . . . We testified before . . . [a] Congressional committee and had our tax-exemption removed for a year because they said that we were propagandizing. . . .
> [But] if you're not trying to influence legislation what are you trying to do? You're trying to do it at another level . . . trying to influence thinking (Interview with author; November, 1961).

For grant-making foundations, the most frequent result of the legal constraints of the sort just described has been the reinforcement of an attitude of circumspection about fields to enter and projects and organizations to support. As a spokesman for one of the larger foundations of this sort reported a few years ago, "Tax considerations have restricted us somewhat . . . we've not been able to go the route we would have preferred in some cases. But they haven't seriously impeded our activities — we're just being extra careful" (49, p. 1). In a specific case involving a grant for civic planning, the route chosen (35, p. 156), as the overall figures on grants cited earlier showed to be typical, was one leading through a campus.

That it is a university — rather than either a social work agency or a militant reform organization — with which the foundation has been most frequently compared through the years,[5] is thus partly a matter of foundation preference, partly one of legal constraint. In their efforts to break away from the traditional palliative model of philanthropy, the foundations have worked through universities and colleges partly because such organizations already have a degree of legal — and popular — support which the foundations are still only gradually acquiring (51). And as will be explained further below, in thus seeking acceptance for their new mode of giving they have become less private and more public, both more responsive and responsible to the organizations in which they have sought, and given, support.

[5] Two of the best statements are those several decades ago by Keppel (60, pp. 9–12) and by Hollis (53, pp. 23–26).

## Self-Help and Voluntary Enterprise

A society's legal traditions and innovations reflect its broader cultural heritage, including the political and economic theories held by groups creating (or influencing) actual legislation. If the legitimation of risk capital activity has been importantly dependent on interpretations made by the courts, it has been as much or more dependent on interpretations — and investigations — made by the Congresses. And if the major legal theme in foundation ideology has been that of the legitimacy of putting private wealth to public purposes, the major political-economic theme has been that of the importance of preserving the "American way" of limited government — of self-help and voluntary enterprise.

### Political-Economic Supports

In our society, the idea of tax-exemption already mentioned is itself significantly based on a theory of the delegation of societal functions and a separation of powers:

> The theory underlying the whole [of the legal tradition supporting tax-exemption] is that to a considerable extent the voluntary institutions "relieve the burdens of government," that is, they perform functions which, if not so performed, might be considered mandatory or at least desirable for the state itself to perform. That the state delegates, in a manner of speaking, a variety of public functions to non-governmental agencies, which it encourages, assists within limits, and sparingly regulates and supervises (26, p. 45).

And, relying on this theory and related ideas, e.g., from Carnegie's "Gospel of Wealth" (24) which stressed the obligation of the rich to help the poor help themselves, many of the foundations' spokesmen have come to argue that their support helps individuals and organizations (sometimes including government agencies) do important research and experimentation they could not otherwise afford. Others go even further, arguing — and with considerable success, e.g., with the Cox Committee (96) — that foundations sponsor such work in ways state or national governments either don't attempt adequately, if at all; can't attempt effectively; or shouldn't attempt, because this would mean an ineffective expansion of the sphere of government. A related theme — frequently expressed, and as frequently criticized — is that risk capital philanthropy and economic free enterprise have a similar value (see, e.g., 57, chapter 1; 32, pp. 107–108; cf. 44).

In general, Marts' contention (55, p. 149) that "the endowed foundation stands out, beyond question, as one of the great bulwarks of the American way," finds support in a lot of the foundation literature; as do Kiger's conclusions that:

(1) American foundations are the result of the capitalistic system which, contrary to its European counterpart, allowed neither church nor state a monopoly on philanthropic activity.

(2) They were motivated by a concern for the secular well-being of mankind (65, p. 25).

Although religious themes — as Moe, for example, has shown (75, p. 143) — have traditionally influenced both the legal thought and the political-economic theorizing affecting philanthropy, the values of individual initiative and decentralization of power have become more integral components of this philanthropic ideology.[6]

## Political-Economic Constraints

As was the case with legal themes and the courts, however, Congressional and public acceptance of these "American way" arguments, although substantial, has always been far from complete. From the efforts to get a federal charter for the Rockefeller Foundation, held up in Congress from 1910 to 1913, through the current rapid growth of foundations of many kinds, risk capital ideology and action have generated criticism from both left and right (59, pp. 22–24; cf. 36; 37; 77; 80).

During the trust-busting era before World War I (95), and again in the Depression (68; 32), for example, critics argued that the foundations retained the most illiberal features of *laissez faire* economics. Then in the fifties, while being hailed by some (e.g., 57) as representing capitalism at its most responsible best, they were twice investigated by Congress as agencies subverting not only capitalism but democracy itself. The latter investigations repeated the pattern: the first (97) resulted in what was essentially a vote of confidence in the risk capital concept, the second produced a strongly condemnatory report (98; cf. 105). A third investigation still going on dealt more with the use and abuse of tax regulations, its central ideas being: (1) that foundation money is really public money because it has been derived from tax-exemption; (2) that more adequate government supervision is needed to make sure the money goes for valid charitable purposes — not to enhance further the power of large business firms (98; cf. 10).

Factors ranging from the suspicion of capitalism (32), and of wealth and power generally (20, p. 2, p. 119), to the maneuverings of presidential aspirants (73) have certainly been involved in all this through the years. But much of the general difficulty for foundations stems from the fact that the central political-economic elements of the risk capital concept are themselves extremely pliable; so pliable, in fact, as to be used to justify, on the one hand, support of scholarly studies based on the premise that capitalism "thrives upon a steady drumfire of criticism"

[6] See especially the succinct rationale in Belknap and Mandel (14, p. 28).

(96, p. 183), and, on the other, the support of efforts to teach school children that the profit motive, free competition, and the idea of "government as protector, not as provider" (38, p. 1), are the fundamental bulwarks of our way of life.

The net result of this sort of ideological flexibility is to multiply the possible bases of external acceptance and tolerance and also of criticism and control. For incomplete Congressional acceptance of the foundations' "American way" arguments contributed to the establishment and more extensive enforcement of the legal restrictions already mentioned. And, both in the past and the present, fear of legislative retaliation has accelerated the tendency of some foundations to avoid sponsoring controversial activities. To mention just one prominent case in point: the Fund for the Republic has been described by its director as a "completely disowned subsidiary" of the Ford Foundation (70, pp. 69–70). Significantly, perhaps, one of the early efforts supported by this Fund was a study of Congressional investigating committees (70, pp. 70–71; cf. 80; 51).

Lest we be misunderstood, the issue here is not that the Ford "Funds" or other foundations sometimes avoid controversy, for they have also been bold at times; neither is it simply that boldness and timidity are matters involving selective perception. Our contentions are, rather: (1) that, using the flexible self-help and voluntary enterprise components of the risk capital ideology, the foundations can incur criticism for almost any kind of grant; and (2) that foundation adoption of these "American way" arguments reflects not just the values of donors and trustees but the broader pluralistic political environment in which the foundations operate, and in which they have continually had to justify their existence and operation. Like the need to take legal stipulations into account, the need to develop and maintain a broader political-economic legitimacy has persistently limited the foundations' willingness and freedom to carry their risk capital commitment to all the sectors of society in which it might otherwise be possible to apply private wealth to public purposes.

Not at all incidentally, such constraint has been apparent even *within* some sections of what we would consider to be the generally "safe" fields of education and science — the foundations' record of approach-retreat-and-return in the social sciences being probably the best concrete case in point. The relative inability of social scientists to convince foundation officers and trustees of not only the objectivity but the relevance of their studies has also been involved.[7] But, as indicated earlier, the

---

[7] For a general discussion of factors limiting the development of the social sciences, see Young (107, pp. 325–335). We cannot resist citing these statements (interview with author, 1962) by one foundation official:

When it comes to social science: I got a letter once from [a prominent official of another foundation]. . . . He said, "I've kept my foundation out of that. It's too full of crackpots and I can't tell them apart."

Walsh Commission Report before World War I (when the Rockefeller Foundation was considering the industrial relations field); the "tainted money" criticism during the twenties and thirties (20, pp. 138–139); and the criticism of empirical social science made by the Reece Committee later on (98); all seemed to leave fairly clear marks on foundation programs.

Though even the data for the 1950's are imprecise and detailed comparisons with earlier eras very difficult to make with much accuracy, it is at least informative in this connection that the larger foundations' relative expenditures (including grants) for social science research, which had declined from 1939 to 1946 then increased again (6, Table 22, p. 270), dropped from 42 percent of expenditures for all types of scientific research in 1953 to 28 percent in 1957 — the years just after the Reece investigation.[8] Whatever forces were at work, probably a great many, it also seems pertinent here that Alpert's (2, p. 154) estimates of the annual rates of expenditures for social science research *performed* by various types of organizations in the United States in 1958 indicate that — of $215 million in such funds — private foundations spent $2 million or 0.9 percent, independent institutes and the like 1.4 percent, colleges and universities 16.3 percent, the federal government 17.7 percent, and industrial and commercial organizations 63.7 percent.

### Progress Through Knowledge

Whatever their record in the social sciences, and that is a history yet to be written, the foundations have, through the years, become significantly involved in supporting the research, experimentation, and teaching activities of persons in the interrelated social systems of science and higher education generally. And as this has happened, a third ideological component — itself a synthesis of elements from the idea of progress (21, pp. 278–349) and from what might be termed the scientific faith (cf. 17) and the pragmatic temper — has become another integral part of the risk capital ideology.

---

My criticism of social science is that . . . [it] is not enough interested in social engineering. In imitating the hard sciences the descriptive approach won't hold water . . . [I mean, the attitude that] "Well, if my next-door neighbor over here can spend the rest of his life describing the protein molecule, I'll do the same thing of society." But society won't let you do that. You have to be willing to do something. The shelves are full of descriptive studies nobody has read.

[8] For 77 larger foundations' expenditures (including grants) in 1953 and 1957, see Walton and Andrews (7, Table 13, xxxix). The interested reader should go to this source and to Andrews (6, pp. 270–273), being sure to note the bases of comparison, the qualifications, and the effects of large grants. Support for social science increased again in the 1960's. See 11 and 43.

## Educational-Scientific Supports

Taylor's argument (91, p. 6) that the freedom of private welfare enterprises should be protected because they have sponsored the research which has "set the pace of our social progress"; Rose's early (1923) assertion (cited in Fosdick 41, p. 141) that knowledge of the spirit and technique of modern science "affects the entire system of education and carries with it the shaping of a civilization"; and Kiger's explanation (65, pp. 118–119) that the pragmatic tendency to adopt better procedures "permeates the foundations and our capitalistic society alike"; all are good illustrations of the various elements of this third line of defense of foundation existence and freedom. The foundations' creative synthesis of these ideas,[9] however, is most remarkably illustrated in Fosdick's explanation of a turning-point in the career of the Rockefeller Foundation:

> The decision in the late 1920's . . . to concentrate the work of the Foundation on the extension of knowledge was based on a growing conviction that the margin between what men know and what they use is much too thin. . . . Unless research is constantly maintained, the stockpile of knowledge becomes much too low for safety. There is a sense in which the practical applications of knowledge are the dividends pure science declares from time to time (41, p. 140.)

By thus publicly linking their own efforts with the functions and traditions of prestigious and ostensibly "neutral" scientific professions and educational institutions, the grant-making foundations have helped enhance their legal and political-economic legitimacy, particularly in recent decades. In the Cox investigation (96) especially, for example, the record makes it clear that support for the risk capital concept from leading scientists and educators considerably increased the impact of the defense made by eminent foundation officials. Even more recently, an increasing number of industrial firms have adopted a similar "progress through knowledge" rationale in establishing their own "company" foundations (74, pp. 218–223). And similar lines of ideological argument are now increasingly visible in the writings of academic economists (86, pp. 571–583) and government officials (83, pp. 1–53; 39, p. 9), currently intrigued with the possibilities of spurring economic growth, both here and abroad, by accelerating investments in education, considered as a national resource.

[9] Akin to many of those in "educational meliorism," which Ballinger, in an important study (12, pp. 88–89), has traced, e.g., through Helvetius and Condorcet to Thomas Jefferson, Horace Mann, and John Dewey.

### Educational-Scientific Constraints

Such relative gains in legal and political-economic legitimacy have, nonetheless, come at a considerable cost in increased dependence on the educational and scientific organizations whose work the foundations have considerably stimulated and financed. This dependence, as we have argued in more detail elsewhere (28, pp. 167–184; 29, pp. 4–6), is reflected in the shift from the endowment to the limited-project method of grant-making, the increased use[10] of academic consultants, and the addition of layers of specialists to many foundation staffs. For involved in the adoption of these and other administration methods is a fundamental dependence — not always apparent to the man scrabbling for a particular grant — on the creativity and the technical knowledge and resources of the men actually conducting the work on the frontiers of research, experimentation, and the dissemination of new knowledge.

Some of the innovative work of interest to the foundations has been work done by these organizations themselves; more of it, plus a lot of important but routine intellectual activity, has been carried out in the colleges, universities, and research institutes they have supported. And these academic organizations (and the individual professions with which they are both cooperatively and competitively linked) not only have considerable contractual and moral control over the persons needed to man foundation programs and projects; they also provide library and laboratory facilities — necessary instruments of intellectual production which even the wealthiest foundations could not permanently provide, even if this were compatible with the risk capital commitment. And, because most professions and many colleges and universities seek with considerable vigor to protect and enhance their own legitimacy and autonomy, these major clients' control over the human and material resources which foundation grants must rent or buy is additionally bolstered by their better institutionalized (and somewhat rival) ideology of academic freedom (see, e.g., [42, pp. 150–171; 30]).

Thus in various cumulative ways — in publicly embracing the "progress through knowledge" rationale (which includes the idea of giving

---

[10] Even several decades ago, as Keppel pointed out (61, pp. 13–14):

At first foundations negotiated directly. Today there are advisory and supervisory groups of various kinds. For example, the first $2,000,000 given away by the Carnegie Corporation was given wholly on the basis of direct negotiations between the Corporation and the institution concerned. Seventeen years later, 68 per cent of the annual program was based upon consultation with some representative advisory body. In a single recent year, the records showed that our Corporation had been in consultation with no fewer than 68 national scholarly organizations of one kind or another.

credit[11] where it is due), in utilizing academically-oriented staff members and trustees, and in actually making grants to (and otherwise working with) educational-scientific clients, the foundations have acquired an increasing obligation not to undermine the internal or external conditions protecting the general academic freedom to teach and do research. As H. Rowan Gaither once described this obligation quite succinctly: "If a foundation steps over the invisible line and encroaches on a grantee's independence, the opportunity for service is transformed into a visible and grievous disservice" (46, p. 23).

The perpetual paradox for contemporary grant-making foundations is that the same vigorous advocacy of "progress through knowledge" which has helped gain legal and political-economic support for their existence as complementary educational institutions has increased their dependence, as organizations, on the very groups whose effectiveness they have sought to improve, both as a value in itself and in the larger interest of social innovation. As Ross put it so well several decades ago, "Human institutions and relations . . . glide insensibly into forms which would not be assumed of intention (84, p. 471)."

## Summary

As an important part of the effort to establish their collective legitimacy as a new type of institution and enhance their individual autonomy as self-perpetuating organizations sponsoring educational and social reform, the large grant-making philanthropic foundations of twentieth-century American society have synthesized from a contradictory cultural heritage a distinctive ideology — the risk capital concept. Because this concept has proved to be a fairly successful rationale for minimizing legal control, deflecting political-economic criticism, and engaging in only temporary relations with specific educational-scientific clients, the foundations have sometimes been able to conduct — and, more often, to sponsor — widely acclaimed ventures on the frontiers of research, education, and social action.

Incomplete *legal* acceptance, e.g., of arguments for tax-exemption and for freeing philanthropic funds from the "dead hand" of original donors, however, has persistently tended to lead the foundation along two intersecting paths somewhat off to one side of the risk capital route imprecisely indicated in their principal ideology. One path, difficult to trace with certainty, is the support, in many locations, of activities more conventional and palliative than innovative and preventive. The other, more clearly marked and often overlapping the main route — but only

[11] Cf. Macdonald (70, pp. 97–98), but also West (101, pp. 54–62); on the *incentive* to shift the burden of both evaluation and responsibility to grantees, see Colvard (29, p. 5) and Yarmolinsky (106, p. 83).

occasionally doing so in precipitous places — is a circuitous path skirting many college and university campuses. For the larger grant-making foundations have concentrated on working through prestigious and politically "neutral" educational and scientific organizations, and this has been a matter partly of preference, partly of constraint.

The latter tendency, to adopt the foster parent role of "innovation by indirection," has been intermittently accelerated through the years by active *political-economic* opposition, stemming both from the political pluralism of the broader society and the ideological pliability of the "American way" components of the risk capital concept. To many Congressional critics — from Walsh to Patman, for example — the existence and operation of large foundations has not been completely compatible with the self-help and voluntary enterprise traditions.

Again, the fiscal and ideological support the foundations have given to the "progress through knowledge" argument — that both industrial and social progress are now continually dependent on technical and educational innovation — has helped the foundations gain access to, and legitimizing support from, many of their major *educational-scientific* clients. But the scientific professions, for example, and the colleges and universities which train and employ their leaders, are the vital centers of this new institutionalization of innovation, and they are also organizations competitively interested in enhancing their own legitimacy and autonomy. To gain acceptance and freedom for themselves, the foundations have thus over time become considerably dependent on their ability to stimulate their academic clients' creative potential without jeopardizing these grantee groups' own acceptance and freedom.

The foundations' leaders have not always balanced these delicate tasks as wisely or well as either they or their critics would prefer. But they have had the sometimes bittersweet satisfaction of seeing many of their interests acquired by and their methods adopted and improved upon by federal agencies.[12] And much of their risk capital ideology has returned as a new stimulus to the idea of progress and other elements of the cultural heritage from whence it came.

### Broader Implications: Risk Capital and "Creative Destruction"

The foundations' contribution to the vitality of the American Dream[13] may prove to be their greatest achievement. For, as much of the overall analysis has probably made clear by now, the risk capital concept appears, to us at least, to be a striking example of the ideological affinity of capitalism[14] and science, and this affinity may help explain much of the

[12] See, e.g., Young ( 108, pp. 14–15), and Kidd (63, pp. 189–205).

[13] CF. the perceptive appraisal in Polak ( 82, pp. 300–331, pp. 363–365). We are indebted to Gideon Sjoberg for calling this interesting work to our attention.

[14] On the affinity of science and socialism see, e.g., Bernal ( 12, pp. 32–33, pp. 221–231).

history of American society in the years of its industrialization and urbanization.

For if the continuation of capitalism is dependent on continual obsolescence and innovation, the growth of science comes as much through the constant questioning and criticism (cf. 89, pp. 67–68) of old ideas as through the decisive proof of new ones. Science, that is to say, is a universal solvent of its own intellectual structure and substance as capitalism is of its industrial arrangements and products. Their individual organizations both appear to operate through what Schumpeter, in referring only to capitalism, aptly called a process of "creative destruction" (87, pp. 82–83); and, collectively — as institutions set in larger contexts — both must legitimize or market this inherently disruptive rationalizing process: the freedom it requires and the societal changes it brings, including the idea that change itself is the continuing condition of industrial-urban life.

It is difficult, as yet,[15] to know whether or to what extent the systematic investment of excess private profits in science, and education more generally, can actually yield knowledge and skill "dividends" capable of keeping the obsoleting-innovating process in motion while stimulating higher education and mobility. It does not, however, seem ridiculous to consider that, for better or for worse, such investments may have functioned to reconcile some American intellectuals (see 78, pp. 275–288) to some of the contradictions in capitalism, and also that the foundations' development and official advocacy of the risk capital concept may have functioned during persistent "times of troubles" to perpetuate public belief — not simply in foundations, but in capitalism, science, and the possibility of progress.[16]

To put these thoughts another way: both the theory and the practice of giving extensive private and public[17] support to education and science

15 See especially Jewkes *et al* (58, pp. 4–14), Sweezy (91), Morrison (76), and Vidich (92), which was apparently being written at the time the first version of this discussion was also in preparation.

16 As Chambers (25, p. 197) has noted in a valuable article, the "reaffirmation of this faith . . . in the midst of . . . an 'age of anxiety' was remarkable." For a broad view of such phenomena in general see Shils (88, pp. 60–83).

17 Cf. the evidence and argument in Alpert (2, pp. 152–157). The changes here in less than fifty years would probably seem incredible to the men in the Walsh Commission, who pointed out with concern that:

Two groups of the 'foundations' namely the Rockefeller and Carnegie foundations, together have funds yielding an annual revenue of at least $13,500,000, which is at least twice as great as the appropriations for the Federal Government for similar purposes, namely, education and social service (95, p. 81).

Forty-four years later, Kidd reported that for research in universities and associated research centers alone:

During the year ending June 30, 1960, the Federal Government will spend somewhat more than $650 million . . . (64, p. 4).

may be seen eventually as important factors in the relocation and perpetuation of the innovative industrial functions once much more dependent on the individual capitalist entrepreneur. For, in our own society at least, the creation of production techniques, the identification of new markets — and even the development of new ideological justifications for private enterprise — increasingly are activities involving professional research conducted with colleges and universities as well as within industrial firms themselves.[18]

If capitalism has indeed become both ideologically and operationally linked with science and higher education, and professionalism even more permanently "mated with progress,"[19] both the foundations and the federal government have helped with the matchmaking and the provision of dowries. These unions and their issues will probably receive considerable attention by sociologists and historians of the future; they deserve far more attention now than they have yet been given[20] by contemporary students of social and cultural change.

## BIBLIOGRAPHY

1. Allen, W. H. *Modern Philanthropy*. New York: Dodd, Mead & Co., Inc., 1912.

2. Alpert, Harry. "The Funding of Social Science Research," in Donald S. Ray (ed.), *Trends in Social Science*. New York: Philosophical Library, 1961.

3. Andrews, F. Emerson. "New Challenges for Our Foundations," *New York Times Magazine* (April 3, 1949), pp. 16–17, pp. 53–54.

4. Andrews, F. Emerson. *Corporation Giving*. New York: Russell Sage Foundation, 1952.

6. Andrews, F. Emerson. *Philanthropic Foundations*. New York: Russell Sage Foundation, 1956.

7. Andrews, F. Emerson. "Introduction," in Ann D. Walton and F. Emerson Andrews (eds.), *The Foundation Directory*, Ed. I. New York: Russell Sage Foundation, 1960.

[18] See e.g., (39); also Carlton (23, esp. pp. 440–443). Halsey argues very generally that "The mark of the educational institutions of a technological society is that they are in a special sense crucial to its maintenance and, to the institutionalization of technological research, and to its further development" (50, p. 119).

See Barzun, however, on philanthropy as an "enemy of intellect" (13, chapter 1, pp. 6, 7), and Jaspers (56, pp. 871–884) on the various meanings of science, and the various historical attitudes toward it. For example:

Science left to itself becomes homeless. The intellect is a whore, said Nicholas of Cusa, for it can prostitute itself to anything. Science is a whore, said Lenin, for it sells itself to any class interest.

[19] The terms are Whitehead's (102, pp. 294–295); see also his important discussion of the invention of the method of invention, in the same work.

[20] See, e.g., the report of the Princeton conference, containing many recommended research topics (85), and Curti (34).

8. Andrews, F. Emerson. "Growth and Present Status of American Foundations," *Proceedings of the American Philosophical Society*, Vol. 105 (1961), pp. 157–161.

9. Andrews, F. Emerson, ed. *Foundations: 20 Viewpoints.* New York: Russell Sage Foundation, 1965.

10. Andrews, F. Emerson. *Patman and Foundations: Review and Assessment.* New York: The Foundation Center, 1968.

11. Andrews, F. Emerson. "Introduction," in Marianna O. Lewis and Patricia Bowers, eds. *The Foundation Directory*, Edition 4. New York: Columbia University Press, 1971.

12. Ballinger, Stanley E. "The Idea of Social Progress Through Education in the French Enlightenment Period: Helvetius and Condorcet," *History of Education Journal*, Vol. 10 (1959), pp. 88–99.

13. Barzun, Jacques. *The House of Intellect.* New York: Harper & Bros., 1959.

14. Belknap, Chauncey, and Philip Mandel. *The Federal Income Tax Exemption of Charitable Organizations: Its History and Underlying Policy.* Report prepared for the Rockefeller Foundation, March 8, 1954. (mimeo)

15. Bennett, André M. "Links: Foundation Trustees and the Corporeal World," Ph.D. dissertation, State University of New York at Buffalo, 1973 (in process).

16. Bernal, J. D. *The Social Function of Science.* New York: The Macmillan Co., 1939.

17. Bernard, Jessie. "The Power of Science and the Science of Power." *American Sociological Review*, Vol. 14 (1949), pp. 575–584.

18. Beveridge, Lord. *Voluntary Action.* New York: The Macmillan Co., 1948.

19. Bittker, Boris I. "The Modern Philanthropic Foundation: A Critique and a Proposal," *Yale Law Journal*, Vol. 59 (1950), pp. 477–509.

20. Bremner, Robert H. *American Philanthropy.* Chicago: University of Chicago Press, 1960.

21. Bury, J. B. *The Idea of Progress.* London: The Macmillan Co., 1921.

22. Calkins, Robert D. "The Impact of Foundations on Higher Education," in *The Impact of Foundations on Higher Education.* Commission on Colleges and Universities, North Central Association of Colleges and Secondary Schools, 1954, pp. 1–13.

23. Carlton, Frank T. "Capitalism and Social Change," *Sociology and Social Research*, Vol. 28 (1944), pp. 440–451.

24. Carnegie, Andrew. *The Gospel of Wealth, and Other Timely Essays.* New York: The Century Co., 1900.

25. Chambers, Clarke A. "The Belief in Progress in Twentieth-Century America," *Journal of the History of Ideas*, Vol. 19 (1958), pp. 197–224.

26. Chambers, M. M. *Charters of Philanthropies.* New York: Carnegie Foundation for the Advancement of Teaching, 1948.

27. Colvard, Richard. "The Foundation and the Colleges: A Study of Organizations, Professions and Power in the Arkansas Experiment in Teacher Education." Unpublished Ph.D. dissertation, University of California, Berkeley, 1959.

28. Colvard, Richard. "Foundations and Professions: The Organizational Defense of Autonomy," *The Administrative Science Quarterly*, Vol. 6 (1961), pp. 167–184.

29. Colvard, Richard. "Foundations and Their Clients: Why the Project Method?" *The American Behavioral Scientist*, Vol. 5 (1962), pp. 4–6.

30. Colvard, Richard. "The Colleges and the 'Arkansas Purchase' Controversy," in Matthew B. Miles (ed.), *Innovation in Education*. New York: Teachers' College Bureau of Publications, 1963.

31. Colvard, Richard, and Bennett, André M. *Patterns of Concentration in Large Foundations' Grants to U.S. Colleges and Universities*. ACT Research Report No. 63, April, 1974. Iowa City: The American College Testing Program.

32. Coon, Horace. *Money to Burn*. New York: Longman's Green, 1938.

33. Cuninggim, Merrimon. *Private Money and Public Service*. New York: McGraw-Hill Book Co., 1972.

34. Curti, Merle. *The History of American Philanthropy as a Field of Research*. Mimeo. n.d., 17 pp. 1957 (?).

35. Curti, Merle. "Tradition and Innovation in American Philanthropy," *Proceedings of the American Philosophical Society*, Vol. 105 (1961), pp. 146–156.

36. Domhoff, G. William. *Who Rules America?* Englewood Cliffs, N.J.: Prentice-Hall, Inc., 1967.

37. Domhoff, G. William. *The Higher Circles*. New York: Random House, 1970.

38. Dugger, Ronnie. "Target: The Schools," *The Texas Observer* (December 18, 1959), p. 1, p. 3.

39. Editors of *Fortune. The Mighty Force of Research*. New York: McGraw-Hill Book Co., 1956.

40. Embree, Edwin R. "Timid Billions: Are the Foundations Doing Their Job?" *Harper's Magazine*, Vol. 198 (1949), pp. 28–37.

41. Fosdick, Raymond B. *The Story of the Rockefeller Foundation*. New York: Harper & Bros., 1952.

42. Fosdick, Raymond B., Henry F. Pringle, and Katherine D. Pringle. *Adventure in Giving*. New York: Harper & Row, 1962.

43. *Foundation News*, Vol. 13 (1972), pp. 4–6.

44. *Foundations, Private Giving and Public Policy:* Report and Recommendations of the Commission on Foundations and Private Philanthropy (Peter G. Peterson, Chairman). Chicago: University of Chicago Press, 1970.

45. Fremont-Smith, Marion R. *Foundations and Government: State and Federal Law and Supervision*. New York: Russell Sage Foundation, 1965.

46. Gaither, H. Rowan, Jr. "The President's Review," in *The Ford Foundation Annual Report, October 1, 1955 to September 30, 1956.* New York: The Ford Foundation, 1956.

47. Gordon, Milton M. "The Girard College Case: Resolution and Significance," *Social Problems,* Vol. 7 (1959), pp. 15–27.

48. Goulden, Joseph C. *The Money Givers.* New York: Random House, 1971.

49. Grimes, John A. "Tax Crackdown," *The Wall Street Journal* (December 9, 1958), p. 1, p. 4.

50. Halsey, A. H. "The Changing Functions of Universities in Advanced Industrial Societies," *Harvard Educational Review,* Vol. 30 (1960), pp. 118–127.

51. Heimann, Fritz, ed. *The Future of Foundations.* The American Assembly, Columbia University. Englewood Cliffs, N.J.: Prentice-Hall, Inc., 1973.

52. Heller, Walter W. "Economic Growth: Challenge and Opportunity." Address to the Loeb Awards Fourth Annual Presentation Luncheon, New York, May 18, 1961. Cited in Luther W. Stringham and Earl E. Huyck, "Measuring Returns from Investments in Human Resources," a paper presented at 56th Annual Meeting of the American Sociological Association, St. Louis, Mo., August 31, 1961.

53. Hollis, E. V. *Philanthropic Foundations and Higher Education.* New York: Columbia University Press, 1938.

54. Hollis, E. V. "Evolution of the Philanthropic Foundation," *The Educational Record,* Vol. 20 (1939), pp. 575–578.

55. Horowitz, I. L., and R. L. Horowitz. "Tax-Exempt Foundation: Their Effects on National Policy," *Science,* Vol. 168 (1970), pp. 220–228.

56. Jaspers, Karl. "Philosophy and Science," *Partisan Review,* Vol. 16 (1949), pp. 871–884.

57. Jenkins, Edward C. *Philanthropy in America.* New York: Association Press, 1950.

58. Jewkes, John, David Sawers, and Richard Stillerman. *The Sources of Invention.* London: The Macmillan Co., 1958.

59. Keele, Harold. "Government's Attitude Toward Foundations," in *Conference of Michigan Foundations.* Ann Arbor: Foster Foundation, 1954.

60. Keppel, Frederick P. *The Foundation: Its Place in American Life.* New York: The Macmillan Co., 1930.

61. Keppel, Frederick P. *Philanthropy and Learning.* New York: Columbia University Press, 1936.

62. Keppel, Frederick P. "The Responsibility of Endowments in the Promotion of Knowledge," *Proceedings of the American Philosophical Society,* Vol. 77 (1937), pp. 591–603.

63. Kidd, Charles V. *American Universities and Federal Research.* Cambridge: Belknap Press, 1959.

64. Kidd, Charles V. "New Government-University Relationships in Research," *Higher Education,* Vol. 16 (1960), pp. 3–6, pp. 18–19.

65. Kiger, Joseph C. *Operating Principles of the Larger Foundations.* New York: Russell Sage Foundation, 1954.

66. Lankford, John. *Congress and the Foundations In the Twentieth Century.* River Falls, Wis.: Wisconsin State University, 1964.

67. Lazarsfeld, Paul F., in collaboration with Sydney S. Spivack. "Observations on Organized Social Research in the United States: A Report to the International Social Science Council," 1961. (mimeo)

68. Lindeman, Eduard C. *Wealth and Culture.* New York: Harcourt, Brace and Co., 1936.

69. Lundberg, Ferdinand. *The Rich and the Super-Rich.* New York: Lyle Stuart, Inc., 1968.

70. Macdonald, Dwight. *The Ford Foundation: The Men and the Millions.* New York: Reynal, 1956.

71. Marts, Arnaud C. *Philanthropy's Role in Civilization.* New York: Harper & Bros., 1953.

72. Merry, Howard. "Charity and Business: More Foundations Get Involved in Dealings of Their Own Officers," *The Wall Street Journal* (July 10, 1961), p. 15.

73. Miller, H. H. "Investigating the Foundations," *The Reporter,* Vol. 9 (1953), pp. 37–40.

74. Millett, John D. "Higher Education," in Beardsley Ruml, with Theodore Geiger (ed.), *The Manual of Corporate Giving.* Washington, D.C.: National Planning Association, 1952.

75. Moe, Henry Allen. "Notes on the Origin of Philanthropy in Christendom," *Proceedings of The American Philosophical Society,* Vol. 105 (1961), pp. 141–144.

76. Morrison, Philip. "The Innovation Industry," *Monthly Review,* Vol. 11 (1959), pp. 103–110.

77. Nielsen, Waldemar A. *The Big Foundations.* New York: Columbia University Press, 1972.

78. Nomad, Max (pseud.) *Aspects of Revolt.* New York: Noonday Press (N212), 1959.

79. Polak, Fred L. *The Image of the Future,* II., Elise Boulding (ed.). New York: Oceana Publications, 1961.

80. Reeves, Thomas C. *Freedom and the Foundation: The Fund for the Republic in the Era of McCarthyism.* New York: Alfred A. Knopf, 1969.

81. Reeves, Thomas C., ed. *Foundations Under Fire.* Ithaca: Cornell University Press, 1970.

82. Rivlin, Alice M. *Research in the Economics of Higher Education: Progress and Problems,* 1961. (mimeo)

83. Ross, E. A. *Principles of Sociology.* New York: Century, 1930.

84. Russell Sage Foundation. *Report of the Princeton Conference on the History of Philanthropy in the United States.* New York: Russell Sage Foundation, 1956.

85. Schultz, Theodore W. "Capital Formation by Education," *The Journal of Political Economy,* Vol. 68 (1960), pp. 571–583.

86. Schumpeter, Joseph A. *Capitalism, Socialism, and Democracy*, 3rd ed. New York: Harper & Bros., 1950.

87. Shils, Edward A. "The Macrosociological Problem: Consensus and Dissensus in the Larger Society," in Donald S. Ray (ed.), *Trends in Social Science*. New York: Philosophical Library, 1961.

88. Sjoberg, Gideon, and Leonard D. Cain, Jr. "Negative Values and Social Action," *Alpha Kappa Deltan*, Vol. 29 (1959), pp. 63–70.

89. Sweezy, Paul M. "Theories of the New Capitalism," *Monthly Review*, Vol. 11 (1959), pp. 65–75.

90. *Tax Reform Act of 1969, Public Law 91-72*. Chicago: Commerce Clearing House, 1970.

91. Taylor, Eleanor K. *Public Accountability of Foundations and Charitable Trusts*. New York: Russell Sage Foundation, 1953.

92. *Treasury Department Report on Private Foundations*. Washington, D.C.: Government Printing Office, 1965.

93. Tunks, L. K. "Legal Basis for Foundations," in *The Impact of Foundations on Higher Education*. Commission on Colleges and Universities, North Central Association of Colleges and Secondary Schools, 1954, pp. 22–28.

94. U.S. Congress, Senate. *Industrial Relations: Final Report and Testimony Submitted to Congress by the (Walsh) Commission on Industrial Relations created by the Act of August 23, 1912*. 64th Congress, 1st session. Senate Document No. 415. Washington, D.C.: Government Printing Office, 1916, 11 Vols.

95. U.S. Congress. *Hearings Before the Select (Cox) Committee to Investigate Tax-Exempt Foundations and Comparable Organizations*. 82nd Congress, 2nd session. Washington, D.C.: Government Printing Office, 1953, pp. 1–792.

96. U.S. Congress. *Final Report of the Select (Cox) Committee to Investigate Tax-Exempt Foundations and Comparable Organizations* 82nd Congress, 2nd session. House Report No. 2514. Washington, D.C.: Government Printing Office, 1953, pp. 1–15.

97. U.S. Congress. *Hearings Before the Special (Reece) Committee to Investigate Tax-Exempt Foundations and Comparable Organizations*. 83rd Congress, 2nd session. Washington, D.C.: Government Printing Office, 1954. Part I, pp. 1–943; Part II, pp. 945–1241.

98. U.S. Congress, *Tax-Exempt Foundations and Charitable Trusts: Their Impact on our Economy*, Chairman's Report to the Select (Patman) Committee on Small Business, House of Representatives, 87th Congress, December 31, 1962. Washington, D.C.: Government Printing Office, 1963.

99. Vidich, Arthur. "The Higher Dialectic of Philanthropy," *Social Research*, Vol. 30 (1963), pp. 509–518.

100. Weaver, Warren, ed. *U. S. Philanthropic Foundations: Their History, Structure, Management and Record*. New York: Harper & Row, 1967.

101. West, S. S. "The Ideology of Academic Scientists," *IRE Transactions on Engineering Management*, EM–17 (1960), pp. 54–62.

102. Whitehead, Alfred N. *Science and the Modern World*. New York: The Macmillan Co., 1941.

103. Whyte, William H., Jr. "Where the Foundations Fall Down," *Fortune*, Vol. 52 (1956), pp. 140–141, pp. 211–212, p. 214, p. 216, pp. 219–220.

104. Williams, Laurens. *Foundations and the Tax Reform Act of 1969*. New York: The Foundation Center, 1970.

105. Wormser, Rene. *Foundations: Their Power and Influence*. New York: Devin-Adair, 1958.

106. Yarmolinsky, Adam. "How to Run a Small Foundation," *Harper's Magazine*, Vol. 222 (1961), pp. 80–84.

107. Young, Donald. "Limiting Factors in the Development of the Social Sciences," *Proceedings of the American Philosophical Society*, Vol. 92 (1948), pp. 325–335.

108. Young, Donald. "Philanthropic Foundations, Sociology, and Human Betterment." Paper presented at the Annual Meeting of the American Sociological Association, Washington, D.C., September 2, 1962.

109. Young, Donald A., and Wilbert E. Moore. *Trusteeship and Management of Foundations*. New York: Russell Sage Foundation, 1969.

# SECTION NINE

diagnoses of our time

# Introduction

As we and many of our collaborators have reiterated (we hope not ad nauseam), the prophecies and prognoses of things to come are fraught with dangers and pitfalls. The question has been raised, it seems to us legitimately, whether the experts, be they old-fashioned historians or newly fashionable futurologists, have a better batting average in this kind of game than the amateurs. There are counter-arguments: what is there to lose as long as nobody acts in accordance with these predictions, and, if the experts do not have the right, and indeed the responsibility to play the game, who does?

The temptation to proceed from a diagnosis of the present to the prognosis of the future is great. The authors in this last section have practiced considerable restraint by confining themselves in the main to an analysis of the present as it has been conditioned by the past, but they do offer occasional glimpses beyond.

Poppendieck considers her explicit task to be to use Sorokin's theory to answer the question: What is the potential of the counter-culture change? She characterizes the nature of the counter-culture, and she sets up the means for assessing the utility and validity of his theory for those who want to see if the shoe fits. As is the case for Schneider in Section Six, her admiration for the grandeur of Sorokin's scheme is tempered by the sobriety of her analysis.

The New Left has accused the older generation of academics of lacking social responsibility, ivory-tower retreatism, and the use of objectivity as a fig-leaf to cover their self-imposed impotence. There is a considerable kernel of truth in the indictment; Sorokin, before his rehabilitation by the sociological establishment, was considered a black sheep because of his outspoken views on the sensate culture.

Martindale is no "activist" but he unabashedly states his value position vis-à-vis the new imperialism of the great powers. His rapid tour of the historical roots of nationalism and its ramifications in contemporary American society is informed by his adherence to a "humanistic" view of sociology which he described in Section Six. Given the current state of "scientific" sociology it would be difficult to prove that the socio-cultural changes he touches on are causally related to nationalism in general or to the Viet Nam war specifically. He does offer a challenge to those who do not share his values to prove the contrary.

The strategic role of science as a determinant of social change needs no documentation. What is still largely unexplored is the degree to which science depends on political and social institutions for its optimum development. The assumption that democracy is the best matrix for the flourishing of science is no longer as obvious as it was during the pre-Sputnik period. In his chapter, Hirsch raises the question of the actual degree of freedom possessed by American scientists in order to clarify the basic problems relating to the autonomy of science in different social systems. If science is one of the major determinants of social change, are scientists aware of their role as potential "legislators of humanity," and if so, are they in a position to implement this role? The first question is raised for rhetorical purposes only in the present chapter. As to the second, Hirsch seeks to demonstrate that scientists operate typically within three major settings: the industrial, the political, and the academic. In the industrial and political settings, the scientist must necessarily "integrate" his role as scientist with the requirements of organizations whose basic goals are non-scientific. As a result, the scientist is "co-opted" by the political and economic decision-makers, reducing his decision-making power and the autonomy of the scientific establishment. Furthermore, the universities, traditional bastions of *Lehrfreiheit* (freedom to teach) and *Lernfreiheit* (freedom to learn), are coming increasingly under the hegemony of the political and economic realms. Whatever countervailing power scientists seek to muster is seriously limited by the splintering of the scientific roles and the lack of consensus as to social goals within the scientific establishment.

Rather than rewriting the chapter which originally appeared in *Explorations in Social Change,* Hirsch decided instead to add a postscript for the present volume. This will enable the reader to appreciate the changes which took place during the last decade and to judge whether the author's prognoses were more than random ruminations.

# 32

*Janet Poppendieck*

# Sorokin's Theories of Cultural Change:

# Implications for the Future of

# the Counter-Culture.

## Part I: Introduction

During the last few years, many young and a few middle-aged and older people in America have engaged in a departure from predominant societal norms and assumptions which some observers have labeled the counter-culture. The emergence of this dissenting minority within our society raises many questions for students of social change — questions about the origin, the internal structure and processes, and the future of the counter-culture. In this chapter the social theory of Pitirim Sorokin will be used to explore one of these questions: What is the potential of the counter-culture for changing the values of the larger society?

The counter-culture is difficult to define operationally, but clarity requires that some attempt be made to describe or at least identify this phenomenon. As a departure from societal norms, the counter-culture includes a whole series of new or resurrected behaviors, fashions, ways of living: long hair and beards, bright clothes, psychedelic drugs, communal experiments, organic foods, confrontation politics, interest in oriental religions, rock music, and so on. The list is indicative rather than exhaustive. The deeper level of counter-cultural values and assumptions is harder to define, but this study proceeds on the belief that this deeper level exists and is an essential part of the new culture. Many writers identify in the counter-culture an assertion of the primacy of human needs, rights, and emotions, over the technological dominance, competitiveness and alienation of modern life. Along these lines, Philip Slater in his polemical analysis of American culture, *In Pursuit of Loneliness,* differentiates the new culture from the old on the basis of the priorities of each:

> The old culture, when forced to choose, tends to give preference to property rights over personal rights, technological requirements over human needs, competition over cooperation, violence over sexuality, concentration over distribution, the producer over the consumer, means over ends, secrecy over openness, social forms over personal expression, striving over gratification, Oedipal love over communal love, and so on. The new counter-culture tends to reverse all of these priorities (6, p. 100).

The counter-culture also seems to be characterized by an emphasis on, or at least an openness to, subjective, non-rational, non-scientific knowledge as opposed to the dominant culture's emphasis on objective, calculable, empirical fact. The nature of counter-cultural values and assumptions will be explored more fully later in this chapter.

The selection of this strange constellation of ideas, values, social arrangements, life styles, and cultural objects for academic study is somewhat risky. Although most observers seem to agree that a substantial number of people have indeed chosen something other than the dominant American life style and that these deviants are to some extent inter-related — are not merely a collection of discrete, individual, non-conformists — there is little unanimity as to precisely what the counter-culture includes and even less agreement as to its significance. Theodore Roszak, in the preface to *The Making of a Counter Culture,* captured some of the difficulty of studying this phenomenon:

> I have colleagues in the academy who have come within an ace of convincing me that no such thing as "The Romantic Movement" or "The Renaissance" ever existed — not if one gets down to scrutinizing the microscopic phenomena of history. At that level, one tends only to see many different people doing many different things and thinking many different thoughts. How much more vulnerable such broad-gauged categorizations become when they are meant to corral elements of the stormy contemporary scene and hold them steady for comment! (5, p. xi).

Despite these difficulties, the question of the counter-culture's potential for influencing values and assumptions in the larger society seems to me to merit the attention of students of social change. If the counter-culture is only a passing fad, or if it is destined to influence the values and life styles of only a tiny minority of the nation's citizens, then it can safely be dismissed from consideration by planners, policy-makers, societal analysts, and others whose work is predicated upon assumptions about the future. It may be studied as an interesting cultural aberration, or even taken seriously as a measure of disaffection with the quality of life made available by the dominant culture, but it need not be taken into account as a source of significant change in major social institutions or in the relationships between persons and institutions. If, on the other hand, the counter-culture signals the nature and direction of a major process of cultural change, then those concerned about institutions and social relations in the dominant society would be well-advised to make some attempt to understand the values and perceptions underlying the counter-culture and the life styles and social arrangements which it fosters.

Empirical answers to questions about the counter-culture's permanence and influence must await the future. But we live with this new culture now and we cannot postpone our response to it until all of the data are in. It is at a point such as this that theory becomes especially useful. A number of contemporary observers have stated clear and direct answers to the question under consideration here,[1] but they have not brought to their analyses and predictions about the counter-culture any systematic theory of society or of social and cultural change. I have chosen the work of Pitirim Sorokin as a theoretical viewpoint from which to assess the counter-culture (despite the fact that Sorokin died several years too early to address himself directly to the questions raised by its emergence) because of the comprehensiveness of his theory and the extent to which it deals with societal values and cultural change. While many valid criticisms can be — and have been — raised regarding Sorokin's work, the extension of such criticism is not the primary purpose of this chapter; nor is the study intended as "theoretical proof" for an interpretation of observable reality. It seeks simply to use Sorokin's work as a basis for exploring the change-inducing capacity of the counter-culture. The reader is invited to apply his or her own critique to the theories discussed here and to adjust any conclusions which may be reached in order to take such criticisms into account.

### Part II: Summary of Sorokin's Theory of Culture[2]

Sorokin's exhaustive research into the history of culture yielded extensive theories of the nature of culture and the dynamics of cultural change. His theories of social and cultural change will be discussed and applied

[1] See for example Reich (4 p. 2): "This is the revolution of the new generation. Their protest and rebellion, their clothes, music, drugs, ways of thought, and liberated life style are not a passing fad. . . . The whole emerging pattern from ideals to campus demonstrations to beads and bell bottoms to the Woodstock Festival makes sense and is part of a consistent philosophy. It is both necessary and inevitable, and in time it will include not only youth, but all people in America."

[2] Statements of Sorokin's theory in parts II and III of this paper are based primarily on Volume IV of Sorokin's *Social and Cultural Dynamics* (10) with some references for clarification to Volumes I and III. The summary which follows is drawn primarily from chapters 1, 2, and 3 of Volume IV. Page references will be specified only for direct quotations.

in subsequent sections of the chapter, but before they can be fully appreciated, several important aspects of his theory of culture must be presented as background. Sorokin's writings are voluminous, and no brief summary can do justice to the complexity of his theory or the thoroughness with which he traces its ramifications and implications. Furthermore, any attempt to summarize so extensive a theoretical system must of necessity be highly abstract and generalized, lacking the interesting details and illustrations which give such liveliness to Sorokin's own work. It is hoped, however, that the reader will bear with a summary of his theory of culture in order to obtain some framework with which to approach the theories of change dealt within the remainder of this study.

Perhaps the key concept for understanding Sorokin's work is that of the *system*. A group of elements constitutes a system when all of the elements are interdependent, that is, when all of the parts are dependent upon each other and upon the whole, and the whole is dependent upon the parts. There are two forms of interdependence, "functional" or "causal" interdependence due to the "physiochemical or biological properties of the whole and of its parts" (10, Vol. IV, p. 4), as in a human body or a machine, and "logico-meaningful" interdependence due to the meanings or values assigned to the elements of the system and to the system as a whole, as in a mathematical proposition or a syllogism. A group of elements which does not meet the criterion of interdependence, Sorokin labels a "congeries," using the image of a dump to illustrate the meaning of this term. Either a system or a congeries can be composed of discrete elements, of smaller systems, or of both. Having established the important, theoretical difference between a system and a congeries, Sorokin makes clear that these are ideal types; most actual, cultural conglomerates fall somewhere in between along a continuum ranging from mere spatial proximity to complete logical integration.

The purely causal or functional systems which make up the natural world are of little concern to Sorokin. Beyond these, he distinguishes between *social* systems such as a family, a corporation, or a nation, which are defined by the human beings which compose them, and *cultural* systems which derive their basic identity not from the human beings who accept them but from the meanings or ideas which they embody. His primary concern in much of his work is with these cultural systems.

According to Sorokin, a cultural system is born in a process which he calls "mental integration" — the synthesis within the mind of an individual of a system of meanings. Such a system can be very simple, a value judgment, a perception of fact, or it can be a very complex system of ideas such as a new system of mathematics. This system of meanings remains the dominant element in a cultural system throughout its life.

In order to become part of the empirical world, however, a cultural system must undergo two additional stages of development. The second stage, called "empirical objectification," is the process by which a system of meanings acquires material "vehicles"; it occurs as soon as some effort is made to communicate a system of meanings to a person or group. The vehicles of a cultural system include the speech, written word, music, art, and so on, used to convey the system of meanings and any material objects which become associated with and important to that system.

When a natural object becomes a vehicle for a system of meanings, its original properties tend to recede in importance, while its symbolic properties come to the fore. A flag, for example, is seldom perceived as a piece of fabric attached to a pole. Conversely, objective vehicles also affect the systems of meaning which they convey. Some very complex systems of meanings cannot be accurately expressed through available vehicles and therefore become weakened and "infected by congeries" and other imperfections when they become grounded in the empirical world. Some vehicles, on the other hand, are themselves so attractive that they enhance the systems of meanings which they embody.

The final stage in the development of a cultural system is "socialization," the process by which an objectified system of meanings is accepted by human beings. As with material vehicles, systems of meanings both shape and are shaped by the human beings who adhere to them. Once a meaning system has acquired vehicles and human agents, it is a living, empirical system which can grow or decline, persist or die.

The "total culture" of any "cultural area" is composed of thousands, even millions, of systems, congeries, and discrete elements. The smallest such culture area is the individual person who accepts, makes use of, and is shaped by a multiplicity of cultural systems, some of which are integrated into larger systems and some of which are contradictory or unrelated to these larger, integrated systems. As the size of the culture area increases to larger social systems such as the family, or to geographical areas, the number of systems tends to increase, and the level of integration (or the proportion of cultural elements integrated into a single system) is likely to decrease.

Sorokin brings some order out of this chaos by grouping cultural systems into larger and larger systems until five "main cultural systems" or categories of culture are reached. These are language, fine arts, religion, science, and ethics (which includes as major sub-systems, law and morals). All five of these systems are to some extent present in any cultural area and in even the most primitive cultures. This does not mean that every culture has a highly developed and integrated system in each of these areas, but that every culture has some sort of language, some form of creative expression, some stance toward the supernatural, some knowledge of the world around it, and some standards of conduct. In addition, Sorokin identifies a number of mixed, derivative, and composite, cultural systems, such as philosophy and economics, which draw on elements from two or more of the major cultural categories.

Using this framework as a base, Sorokin searched the historical record for patterns which might explain the differences among cultures and changes in the nature of systems within continuous, cultural streams. Why is the fine arts system of twentieth century western culture, for example, so different from the fine arts system of eleventh century western culture? He concluded that cultural systems are influenced in their basic natures by the beliefs about reality which they embody. He identified three basic premises about the nature of reality which have, alternately, shaped the cultural systems of the world.

These three reality premises he identifies as the *Ideational, Sensate* and *Idealistic* (or *Integral*) "cultural mentalities" or cultural super-systems. In Ideational culture, reality is believed to be super-sensory, non-material, and everlasting; the day to day world of the senses is thought to be a mere illusion. In Sensate culture, reality is believed to be that which is perceived by the five senses and it is assumed to be in a constant state of flux or process. Idealistic or Integral culture proceeds from the belief that reality is many-sided — both super-sensory and sensory, spiritual and material, being and becoming. It represents a synthesis of the reality premises of the other two super-systems. In addition to these three highly integrated super-systems, there are also "mixed" culture mentalities which involve some blend of the Ideational and Sensate conceptions of reality without unifying them into a real synthesis.

Sorokin makes clear that these cultural super-systems are ideal types which have probably never existed in pure form in an individual, group, or nation. Nevertheless, each of these super-systems has had periods of dominance when it has influenced and integrated most of the systems of meaning and left its mark on most of the social systems and institutions of a culture area. Further descriptions of these cultural super-systems will appear in part IV of this chapter.

* * * * *

Although the material above is presented primarily as a basis for understanding the theories of cultural change dealt with in subsequent sections, even this introductory material has implications for understanding the counter-culture.

First, it suggests that since a system of meanings is the origin and dominant ingredient of a cultural system, the phenomena which comprise the counter-culture are truly *cultural* only to the extent that they embody systems of meaning. A mere congeries of long hair styles and strange clothing does not make a culture, but such styles can be the vehicles of a cultural system if they are the expression of a set of meanings. The styles associated with the counter-culture do in fact, seem to reflect a set of ideas: a belief that the styles of the dominant culture are restrictive and that they have been misused as a means to discriminate arbitrarily among persons; a preference for "naturalness" and for styles which require little or no planning and preparation; and a critique of the creation of artificial needs and desires by advertising.

An individual, however, does not become a part of the counter-culture or a given counter-cultural system simply by adopting its vehicles and outward manifestations, by growing long hair or abandoning commercial makeup, for example, but only if in so doing, he or she is expressing the meanings which those styles embody. If this theory is correct, then the spread of counter-cultural styles in the society cannot be taken as objective evidence of the spread of the counter-culture itself. On the other hand, the theory makes clear that once a material object becomes a part of a true cultural system, its objective properties give way to its symbolic values. When long hair became associated with a hippie life style and attitude toward society, it took on meaning as a cultural expression, and in many areas of the nation, any male currently sporting shoulder-length hair risks being identified as or associated with the counter-culture in the minds of those with whom he comes into contact. Thus, the adoption of counter-cultural styles by individuals in the larger society frequently indicates at least some sympathy for the values and meanings which they embody.

A second implication which can be drawn from the theory of culture presented above has to do with the validity of the term "counter-culture." Is this phenomenon a true culture and thus, a legitimate target for the application of theories of cultural change? If so, according to Sorokin, it should include all of the five main cultural systems. That is, there should be counter-cultural language, art, religion, science, and ethics, each complete with systems, congeries, discrete elements, ideas, vehicles and human agents. Without attempting to identify the nature of these cultural systems in terms of Sorokin's three culture mentalities or super-systems, a task which can be better handled in part IV, let us look briefly at the counter-culture to see if counter-cultural expressions exist in each of the five fields essential to Sorokin's definition of culture.

In the case of language, the evidence is easy to find. Something on the order of a whole new dialect of English seems to be spoken by many of the young people involved in the counter-culture. This counter-language not only uses new words such as "be-in" and assigns new meanings to old words such as, "grass," "pig," but also differs markedly in syntax, placing far less emphasis on correct grammar and completion of sentences than does the language of the dominant culture, but far more emphasis on the communication of feelings and emotion.

In the field of fine arts, counter-cultural expressions seem to abound: rock music is an example with its avowed intent to "turn the audience on," to create strong, emotional response and involvement as opposed to the lulling, background-music quality of much popular music of the pre-counter cultural era. Similar counter-cultural values are expressed in psychedelic painting, in light shows, and in poetry such as Ginsberg's *Howl.*

In religion, too, the evidence is fairly clear. The growth of the counter-culture has included a tremendous expansion of interest in and involvement with oriental religions, mystical experiences, and the occult; counter-cultural minorities such as the underground church can be found giving counter-cultural expression to western religious tradition as well.

In science, perhaps, the evidence of counter-cultural activity is less obvious, but it becomes clearer when we recall that Sorokin included within the category of science a culture's whole knowledge of itself and the world around it. Counter-cultural science, then, includes not only knowledge of organic farming and experimentation with hallucinogenic chemicals but also with a vast array of other sorts of new knowledge which adherents of the new culture have been developing and sharing with each other. There is, for instance, a search for deeper knowledge of the self (obtained through Yoga, meditation, drugs); a preoccupation with alternative life styles and patterns of human interaction (communal living, group marriages, non-authoritarian decision-making processes); the resurrection or re-creation of lost technologies (spinning, weaving, working with leather, clay, and the like); and, finally, all of the practical knowledge of how to survive — both in the straight world and in isolation from it.[3] In addition, the New Left radicals within the counter-culture have developed new interpretations of history and new analyses of society which also fall within Sorokin's definition of science.

The remaining basic cultural category, in Sorokin's system is ethics, a category with which the counter-culture is deeply concerned. While there are significant conflicts over ethics within the counter-culture, there are also fundamental agreements about the primacy of human life, the importance of liberation (freedom to express and develop one's real self), the dangers of the acquisition of material wealth, the destructiveness of authoritarian institutions and patterns of interaction, and the necessity of eliminating inconsistencies between ethical beliefs and life styles. Counter-cultural ethics differ from those of the dominant culture not only in content but also in style and urgency, placing moral demands above considerations of etiquette, good taste and law.

While the argument above would certainly not satisfy all definitions of culture, it does suggest that the phenomenon of the counter-culture has systems of meaning in all of Sorokin's five cultural categories and can

---

[3] Underground newspapers and publications like the *Whole Earth Catalogue,* for example, provide extensive information on how to "rip off" the necessities of life from the dominant culture (including information on free goods and services and suggestions for uses to which to put the trash so abundantly left behind by the larger society), instructions for building houses, identifying good and bad marijuana or growing your own, information on selecting land for rural communes, and advice on what to do if you are "busted."

therefore legitimately be referred to as a culture (however integrated or unintegrated it may be) within the framework of his theory. It goes almost without saying that this culture borrows most of its language, much of its art, science, ethics, and some of its religion from the larger western culture within which it is growing and can, therefore, also be identified as a sub-culture.

After establishing a basic theory of the nature of culture, Sorokin went on to investigate the nature of cultural change. His work deals extensively with both the *process* and the *content* of such change. Part III which follows will explore several of Sorokin's theories about the process of cultural change and apply them to the question of the contemporary counter culture's potential for changing the values of the larger society. Part IV will proceed in similar fashion, discussing theories regarding the content of cultural change.

### Part III: The Process of Cultural Change: Implications for the Counter-Culture [4]

Three elements in Sorokin's theories regarding the process of cultural change are particularly important in understanding the counter culture: (1) theories about the life and death of cultural systems; (2) theories about the diffusion of cultural systems; (3) the theory of immanent change of socio-cultural systems. Each of these will be treated in turn.

*Theories about the life and death of cultural systems.*

In order to survive in the empirical world, Sorokin states that a cultural system must maintain the identity of its system of meanings and continue to have some vehicles and human agents. As long as these three conditions are met, the system continues to live "no matter what changes may occur in the secondary — peripheral — elements of the meanings and in its vehicles and human agents" (10, Vol. IV, p. 65). A cultural system can grow in two ways: (1) quantitatively by increasing the number of its vehicles or human agents or both, and (2) qualitatively by improving its system of meanings, its vehicles, or its human agents. Improvement of the system of meanings can be either a further unfolding, making explicit that which has been implicit, or a purification through the elimination of contradiction, congeries, and extraneous elements. Similarly, an empirical, cultural system can decline in two ways: (1) quantitatively by decreasing its vehicles or human agents or both, or (2) qualitatively by the deterioration of the system of meanings, or by the weakening of the connections between the meanings and their vehicles and agents, or by a decline in the quality of the material vehicles

[4] The statements of Sorokin's theory in Part III are again based primarily upon *Social and Cultural Dynamics* (10), Volume IV. Section A is based on Chapter 2, B is drawn from Chapter 5, and C relies upon Chapter 12.

or human agents. Deterioration of the system of meanings can occur through the loss of parts of the system, the addition of congeries or other inimical elements and also, through the discovery of certain previously hidden contradictions. When a system declines to the point that its meanings become unrecognizable or it loses all of its vehicles or agents, it dies.

Sorokin's comments about the growth, decline, and possible death of cultural systems have direct implications for the question under consideration. Whatever the systems of meaning which lie within the counter-culture are, they must survive if they are to have any sizeable impact on the dominant culture. Sorokin makes clear that this three-fold task of maintaining human agents, vehicles and the identity of a system of meanings is not easy.

Several factors or forces can cause the loss of human agents in a cultural system. First, the system itself may not be powerful, useful or satisfying enough to hold the loyalty and enthusiasm of human beings. The former hippies and retired radicals whom one finds at the margin of the counter-culture suggest that at least some systems within the counter-culture might fail to survive for this reason. On the other hand, the satisfaction and enjoyment which many of the counter-culture's adherents evidently derive from the life styles it promotes would augur well for its continued existence. Sorokin does not suggest that a cultural system must maintain the same human agents with whom it begins life, but rather makes clear that most systems experience a succession or "turnover" of human adherents. Thus a cultural system such as the high school football game which is adopted in turn by generation after generation of high school students continues to live. Similarly, various counter-cultural systems may continue to be adopted by a portion of each college-age generation but this is not necessarily the case. While at least one observer, Theodore Roszak, suggests that young people have been adopting counter-cultural styles and attitudes at earlier and earlier ages (5, p. 40), it seems reasonable to expect that they will continue to do so only as long as the meanings embodied in the counter-culture continue to speak usefully and forcefully to their situation and experience. This suggests that those systems of meanings within the counter-culture which are basically negative, which do not move beyond criticism of the dominant culture, will continue to draw human adherents only so long as the problems of the dominant culture against which they are directed continue to be a part of the experience of the society. Those aspects of the new culture which have articulated not only a negative reaction to the current society but also a vision of the alternative are probably stronger because they are not as dependent upon the maintenance of the status quo in the dominant culture.

The characteristics of the system itself are not the only factors which influence its survival as a living system among human beings. A cultural system can be destroyed through the destruction of its human agents, or the penalties for adopting it can be made so great as to render it unattractive to most of its potential adherents. The destruction of the International Workers of the World offers an illustration from relatively recent American history. While the large-scale extermination of hippies and other adherents of the counter-culture does not appear to be an immediate probability, the hostility of elements within the larger culture is certainly obvious. A number of local governments, for example, have recently passed "anti-commune" laws prohibiting more than four un-related persons from living together. Communes or persons living in groups of more than four un-related persons were specifically excluded from the benefits of recent food stamp legislation. Similarly, some observers of the counter-culture accuse the media of a deliberate attempt to destroy counter-cultural phenomena by means of bizarre and adverse publicity. Finally, the attitudes and actions of police toward counter-cultural youth sometimes seem to verge on persecution. It remains to be seen whether counter-cultural systems thrive on martyrs and become stronger when persecuted — as have many religious systems which were counter-cultural in their earlier days.

Although the destruction of a cultural system through the loss of its vehicles is not very likely, Sorokin suggests several ways in which this might happen. In theory, at least, the vehicles of a cultural system can be destroyed. Its newspapers, for instance, can be banned and the books, records, tapes or posters which carry its message can be confiscated and destroyed. Because speech is also a cultural vehicle, however, the complete destruction of a cultural system's vehicles would require the destruction of effective verbal communication as well. This sort of extinction does not seem to threaten the contemporary counter-culture. Vehicles can also be the downfall of a cultural system, however, in situations where they are inadequate to express fully the systems of meanings. When this happens, the meanings tend to become corrupted by their vehicles and their original identity may be lost. Within the counter-culture, the emphasis on style and outward manifestations make this sort of damage a substantial possibility.

Finally, in order to survive, a cultural system must maintain the identity of its systems of meanings. Sorokin makes clear that the systems most likely to maintain themselves intact are those which are relatively free from internal contradictions and congeries, and those which are the most clearly defined. Vaguer and more flexible systems may, he suggests, have more apparent success in the short run in quantitatively expanding their vehicles and adherents. He asserts, however, that these best-sellers are seldom classics and that the systems of thought which withstand the test of history are those which are maintained in their original clarity and purity. This part of the theory does not, it seems to me, bode well for the survival of the counter-culture in its present form, as it is hardly clear and free from contradictions. Perhaps the most obvious example of division within the new culture is the difference between the ethical standpoints held by its radical activist stream and those of the "dropout" segments of the culture. Similarly, the counter-culture seems to be characterized by a rampant vagueness — its systems of meanings are nowhere clearly and consistently articulated and its boundaries are not easily defined.

In summary, threats to the survival of the new culture can come either from within the culture itself or from the environment of the dominant culture. While this environment is far from friendly, the greatest threats to the counter-culture at the present moment seem to lodge in that culture itself, in its lack of clarity, in the incompleteness of its vision and in its internal conflicts.

Even the long-term survival of the counter-culture, however, would not ensure it significant impact on the larger culture. This seems likely to require the expansion of the new culture or at least the diffusion of its values. Let us turn, therefore, to Sorokin's theories of cultural diffusion.

### Theories of cultural diffusion.

Sorokin wrote extensively about the spread of cultural phenomena in space, but much of his work deals specifically with the transfer of culture between geographically separated groups and is, therefore, of limited usefulness in understanding the spread of the counter-culture.[5] Due to limitations of space, only those aspects of his diffusion theory which seem to have direct implications for the question at hand will be presented.

Sorokin begins with the nearly obvious proposition that the diffusion of culture requires contact and communication between the diffusing and receiving cultures. The implications of this proposition for the counter-culture are also very nearly obvious: the counter-culture's chances of spreading within the larger culture depend in part upon the maintenance of contact and communication between the two cultures. As long as the current preponderance of youth within the counter-culture persists, opportunities for such contact are likely to exist in great number in families and schools. The current fascination of the new culture with media — music, underground newspapers, poster art, grafitti — also suggests a high level of such contact. If, however, the trends toward the establishment of isolated rural communes and the concentration of energies on internal growth and development should continue within the counter-culture, contact and communication between the two cultures may decrease. Similarly, repressive acts by the dominant culture which

---

[5] It is clear, however, that Sorokin is also concerned in part with the sort of spread among human agents within a geographic area which concerns us here; he refers to spread from "man to man, group to group, in social space" (10, Vol. IV, p. 202).

destroy the vehicles through which the counter-culture communicates, isolate its adherents, or force its institutions "underground," could produce a decrease in contact and communication.

Another basic proposition which flows directly from the one above is that those groups in a population which are exposed to a different culture earliest and most frequently, "tend to be the first importers and recipients of it" (10, Vol. IV, p. 227), while those whose contact is indirect or delayed, tend to "lag" in adopting new values or ways of living and may never do so. Generally, Sorokin noted that urban and upper-class persons are likely to be exposed to and adopt new cultural systems before rural and lower-class persons. Again, the implications in regard to the counter-culture are relatively obvious. First, this premise suggests that the spread of counter-cultural values should be expected first among those who have the most frequent and significant interchange with counter-cultural ideas. If counter-cultural assumptions and values do not, for example, begin to be adopted by teachers and college professors, their diffusion into the larger society will remain doubtful. Secondly, the theory implies that even a rather rapid diffusion of counter-cultural systems among the urban, middle-class, college-age youth of the nation, does not indicate the eventual penetration of these systems into the larger population.

Another portion of Sorokin's theory of cultural diffusion deals with the changes in culture which occur during the process of diffusion. Sorokin states that almost any single element, cultural congeries, or system of culture is in some way transformed by its entrance into another culture. The greater the difference between the culture of origin and the recipient culture, the greater the amount of change is likely to be. On a different dimension, the more complex and difficult a diffusing cultural system is, the more likely it is to be changed as it is adopted by new groups. If a system undergoes enough change it loses the identity of its systems of meanings and is, in effect, replaced.

The implications of this theory for the counter-culture depend upon an understanding of the extent of the counter-culture's difference from the dominant culture and its complexity. It is my supposition that the two American cultures share a common language and a common fund of experience to a sufficient extent to make the passage of some minor elements of the counter-culture into the dominant culture relatively easy. There clearly are, however, values and assumptions within the counter-culture which are so opposed to those which form the basis of the dominant culture that they cannot be assimilated. It requires more strenuous mental gymnastics than most of us can manage, for example, to maintain simultaneously both the dominant culture's emphasis on production and achievement for the future and the counter-culture's emphasis on relationships and experience in the present moment. If Sorokin's theory is correct, these values are not likely to be assimilated without undergoing substantial transformation. Similarly, there seem to be aspects of the counter-culture, such as its emphasis on honesty and openness in human relationships, which are very simple and speak directly to basic, human experience. Elements of this sort, according to Sorokin, might pass into the dominant culture with little if any change. More complex counter-cultural systems, however, including everything from difficult-to-prepare organic foods to sophisticated critiques of American military power, are likely to undergo substantial distortion if transferred to the larger culture.

From the foregoing propositions concerning the change of culture during diffusion, Sorokin derives several sub-propositions which are even more useful in understanding the counter-culture. A group of cultural elements in the process of diffusion may represent either a system or a congeries. The infiltrated culture, in the specific "field of infiltration," may also represent either a system or a congeries. Sorokin suggests that the status of each (as system or congeries) makes an "enormous difference" in the extent to which the infiltrating culture-group is changed in the process and in its ability to penetrate at all.

Sorokin deals specifically with only three of the four possible cases which might occur. If both the infiltrated and infiltrating culture groups are congeries, he suggests that there can be neither affinity nor disaffinity between the two groups and the extent of infiltration and the amount of change in the infiltrating congeries are completely fortuitous. Such infiltrating congeries may pass easily into the infiltrated cultural congeries, "but rarely will they have a widespread and successful rooting in the infiltrated culture" (10, Vol. IV, p. 266). If the specific field of the infiltrated culture is a system, and the infiltrating value is a congeries, the success of the infiltration and the extent of transformation are again accidental.

The third case is more interesting. If the infiltrated field and the infiltrating element are both systems, the extent to which penetration is possible and the degree of transformation occurs, depends upon the content of the two systems. In Sorokin's words:

> . . . if the two systems are congenial and have a mutual affinity the infiltrating system will have an easy and great success and will root itself in the new culture deeply and organically. If the two systems are antagonistic and mutually contradictory, the infiltrating system will meet an active resistance on the part of the other system, and unless it is backed by force or other supporting circumstances, it has little chance to penetrate the other culture. Only by overpowering the competitive system can it root itself in the new culture, and even then only after undergoing considerable transformation (10, Vol. IV, p. 267).

It seems fairly clear that neither the dominant culture nor the counter-culture is a mere congeries of elements and that neither is a perfectly integrated system. Both contain congeries — passing fads, anachronisms, styles or habits, or extraneous systems which are not really related to any of the basic systems of meanings of either culture. These, Sorokin suggests, may pass interchangeably between the two cultures, depending upon merely accidental circumstances, without affecting the basic values and assumptions of either. Thus, the participation of adherents of the counter-culture in some fad of the dominant culture would not signal their defection from the counter-culture.

On the other hand, both the dominant culture and the counter-culture contain logically integrated systems and in both cultures some of the individual systems are linked together, or integrated into larger systems. Deferring for the moment the question of their relative degrees of integration, let us pursue an important implication of Sorokin's comments about antagonistic and congenial systems — to the extent that counter-cultural systems do indeed run counter or stand in contradiction to their counterparts in the dominant culture, they cannot be integrated into that culture. They are in competition with it.

To what extent is this the case? It is at points like this that the lack of information about the counter-culture and the absence of generally accepted analyses of the dominant culture are most frustrating. Certainly, there are deep affinities between the new culture and the old. A considerable amount of the language, experience and many of the perceptions of the world are shared. But it has been the assumption of this study that there are also many points of real opposition — that on some issues at least, the counter-culture reverses the priorities of the dominant culture in something like the manner suggested by Slater in the selection cited in the introduction to this chapter (see p. 892 above). Although like other analyses of the counter-culture, this assertion falls into the realm of conjecture and opinion, it seems that the primary, unifying force within the counter-culture is precisely its self-conscious opposition to those aspects which it perceives as destructive and depersonalizing in the dominant culture.

If this is true, then Sorokin's theory implies that a synthesis of dominant culture systems and their counter-cultural partners, as they presently exist, is unlikely to occur. If the counter-culture is to increase its influence in the society as a whole, it must do so either by "converting" adherents of other systems of culture and thus gaining new human agents, or by undergoing such transformation that it loses its own identity. It cannot take root in a dominant culture to which it is, at heart, antagonistic.

According to Sorokin, however, this set of "either-or" categories is misleading, for he believes that it is precisely in the process of gaining new adherents that a cultural system is likely to lose its identity:

> With too great an increase in the agents, the given system of meanings finds a progressively increasing difficulty of adequate realization and articu-

lation. . . . Quantitative success of almost any system of meanings is bought at the cost of its identity, purity, and adequacy (10, Vol. IV, pp. 81, 82).

Furthermore, he suggests that the vagueness and contradictions which characterize the counter-culture make such expansion and concommitant loss of identity particularly likely:

> Vaguer and less definite systems are possible of interpretation by many in whatever way they like and, therefore, are bound to be accepted, because of their very vagueness and suppleness, by much larger groups (10, Vol. IV, p. 79).

Ironically, the vagueness which is so likely to result in the new culture's expansion is exactly the factor which reduces its chances of coming through such expansion intact.

This brings us again to the question of the counter-culture's potential for survival and ability to maintain the identity of its systems of meanings in its encounters with the larger culture. In order to shed further light on this problem, let us turn briefly to a third segment of Sorokin's theory of cultural change.

### The theory of immanent change.

The theory of immanent change is an essential part of Sorokin's overall theory of cultural dynamics. According to this theory, the basic cause of change in a socio-cultural system lies within that system itself, but change may be influenced by the milieu in which it takes place, just as it, in turn, influences that milieu. Change is a constant process in a living system. The system itself bears the seeds of its own change and thus molds its own "life career" or "destiny." The role of the environment (which is itself composed primarily of other immanently changing systems) "consists essentially in retardation or acceleration; facilitation or hindrance; reinforcement or weakening, of the realization of the immanent potentialities of the system" (10, Vol. IV, p. 619). The environment can crush a system or stop its development, but it cannot change the nature of its immanent potentialities. The relative influence of the system's own potentials and of the effects of the environment, however, are not constant. They vary for each individual system.

With this understanding of change as a base, Sorokin draws two conclusions which are particularly relevant to this study:

> (1) Other conditions being equal (including the milieu), in the social and cultural systems of the same kind, the greater and better is their integration, the greater is their self-determination (and autonomy from the environment) in molding their own destiny (10, Vol. IV, p. 610).
> (2) Other conditions being equal (including the identical environment and the perfection of integration), the greater the power of the system, the greater its autonomy from the social, biological, and cosmic environment, and the greater its self-control and self-direction (10, Vol. IV, p. 615).

Elaborating on the first of these premises, Sorokin suggests that "greater and better integration" means the extent of causal and meaningful interdependence among the system's components, the degree of solidarity in the relationships among its human agents, and the degree of consistency or compatibility of its vehicles. Thus cultural congeries have almost no self-determination. Their continued existence or their disintegration is brought about by forces in their environment. At the other end of the scale, perfectly integrated logical systems have a great deal of control over their own destinies. In between are the vast majority of actual cultural systems exhibiting a variety of levels of consistency and integration. The more a system is ridden by conflict and infested with extraneous elements, the less it is able to withstand the forces of the milieu. Thus, clearly defined systems in which once latent contradictions have been exposed and eliminated, have greater independence than vaguer systems. The poorly defined boundaries of vaguer systems admit unrelated elements and permit contradictions to continue unnoticed. This is true not only of logical inconsistencies and conflicts but also of conflicts among human adherents of systems. A system in which the human relationships among adherents are characterized by loyalty and commonness of purpose is likely to determine its own destiny more fully than a similar system in which the human agents are antagonistic toward each other.

Sorokin explains the second of the two premises stated above at some length, summarizing as follows:

> The greater the number of human agents of the system . . .; the better their biological, mental, moral, and social qualities; the greater the wisdom, knowledge, and value it incorporates . . .; the better it fits the social organization of its followers; the greater is its logico-causal integration . . .; the greater the sum total of means or vehicles for its unfolding, broadcasting, and maintenance at its disposal; the greater the power of the cultural system — the more independent it is from its environmental forces (10, Vol. IV, p. 618).

He stresses particularly the importance of the system of meanings, here called "value," which a cultural system incorporates, and the degree of integration, suggesting that the rest of the conditions listed above are to some extent derived from these two properties. Sorokin makes clear that he believes that some systems of meaning are inherently better, more truthful, stronger than others, and, with profound optimism, argues that the more adequately a system of meanings represents true reality, the greater its strength and independence.

At the theoretical level, these implications for the question under study are quite straightforward. The counter-culture's chances of surviving with its systems of meaning intact depend to a great extent upon its logical integration, the solidarity of its human agents, and its "power" as defined above, particularly, the inherent truthfulness of its system of meanings. The somewhat hostile environment of the dominant culture can crush the new culture or thwart the growth of some of its aspects and favor others, but it cannot change the basic nature of the counter-cultural systems once they have begun their lives in the empirical world.

At the level of practical application, however, this segment of Sorokin's theory presents almost overwhelming difficulties. We might be able to obtain accurate estimates of the number of human agents of the counter-culture, but we would have little basis for interpreting those numbers. We not only lack factual data on the "biological, mental, moral, and social qualities" of these human agents, but even if we obtain such information, there are no widely accepted scales against which we could measure our results.[6]

Perhaps, the greatest practical usefulness of this theoretical statement lies in pointing the direction in which survival and self-determination for the counter-culture lie. If we see the counter-culture decline in numbers, and if we see its human agents lose their physical and mental health in experimentation with drugs or in confrontations with police we will find the chances of its survival to be threatened. If we see the social systems and institutions which are bearers of the new culture lose their solidarity and disintegrate and if the conflicts within the culture grow and the ability of its adherents to find grounds for fundamental agreement decline, then we will know that its chances for surviving intact are disappearing. On the other hand, if the new culture continues to grow and consolidates itself by broadening the common ground and mutual loyalty shared by its sub-groups, eliminating some conflicts and learning to live with others, expanding its attempts to articulate and communicate its systems of meaning, developing viable social institutions and systems, then we will know that its chances of survival are growing.

With a similar tentativeness, we might use the theory of immanent change to reflect on the possible outcome of competition between the dominant and counter-cultures. While we may not be able to move much beyond the realm of opinion in assessing the comparative standing of the two cultures on any of the dimensions identified by Sorokin (for instance, which is the more fully integrated, which has the better quality of agents and vehicles, etc.), we may be able to discern something by comparing the directions in which each is moving. Is the dominant culture becoming more or less conflict ridden? Are its institutions growing, flourishing or declining?

Clearly, opinion rather than fact must play a major role in any such assessment or comparison, but perhaps this is as Sorokin intended, for at

[6] Some factual data about some segments of the counter-culture is available. For example, in his book on New Left activists, *Young Radicals*, Kenneth Keniston cites a substantial number of studies which show that student protesters tend to be drawn from among academically successful students (2, p. 306).

the heart of his concept of the power of a cultural system lies an inescapable value judgment: a judgment of the wisdom and truthfulness of the system of meanings incorporated in any cultural system. Thus, anyone who wants to use Sorokin's theory of change is forced finally to look at the changing system itself and to make an evaluation of its inherent worth.

Fortunately, Sorokin does not leave us with only our own opinions and value judgments as a basis for drawing conclusions. He has extensive opinions and judgments of his own on the nature of the system of meanings embodied in modern western culture, its wisdom and truthfulness, and the direction in which western culture is moving. These judgments are not discrete from his theories of cultural change but are derived directly from them; they represent his own attempts to apply his general theories to the specific culture and the events which he observed. These applications, along with some further background information on his understanding of the content of cultural change are the subject of Part IV of this chapter.

Before moving on to that section, however, it may be useful to attempt to synthesize the three segments of Sorokin's theory dealt with here. Taken together they suggest several conclusions.

1. While the environment is certainly hostile to the counter-culture the greatest threats to the culture's survival come from the conflicts within the counter-culture and its general lack of clarity.
2. To the extent that the counter-culture is really in opposition to the dominant culture, it cannot be expected both to maintain its identity and to be integrated into the larger culture.
3. The counter-culture's ability to maintain its identity and determine its own destiny depends upon its integration and its power (as defined above), particularly the inherent worth and truthfulness of its system of meanings.

If these conclusions are correct there seem to be two routes by which the counter-culture might be expected to influence the norms and values of the dominant culture. The first is by loss of identity. If the new culture were to remain vague, its boundaries undefined, a gathering place for all the disaffections bred by the dominant culture, it would, Sorokin suggests, expand. Its very vagueness would make it attractive to all sorts of people, and it would be interpreted by these new agents to suit their own needs. Conflicts among human agents would prevent agreement on fundamental meanings. In the process of diffusion, its systems would be changed into something which is not totally opposed to the dominant culture and would be integrated into that culture. The resulting hybrid would not preserve the original norms and systems of meaning of the counter-culture, but would represent some shift, however minimal, of the dominant culture toward the meanings and values now underlying the counter-culture.

If I understand Sorokin correctly, the other possible route lies in almost the opposite direction. If the systems of the counter-culture should experience what Sorokin labeled "qualitative growth" by the elimination of conflicts and congeries, if they become more clearly defined, then another future might lies in store for the new culture. Such a qualitative growth would have a refining or purifying effect. Extraneous elements would be expelled, the number of vehicles and adherents would probably decrease, temporarily at least, but the common ground and solidarity among the remaining human agents and the ability of the counter-cultural systems to maintain their identities intact would increase greatly. The differences between the dominant culture and the counter-culture would become clearer. The counter-culture would exist in the society as an alternative to the dominant culture.

As such as alternative, it might evoke changes in the dominant culture of several very different sorts: (1) threatened by competition for human agents, the dominant culture might respond repressively, increasing the penalties for involvement with the counter-culture; (2) in order to compete more successfully with its alternative, the dominant culture might itself adopt certain features of the counter-culture (for example, it might legalize marijuana); (3) enlivened by competition, the dominant culture might also undergo a process of "qualitative growth" in its systems, differentiating itself even more strongly from the counter-culture. Theoretically, at least, there is also the possibility that the refined, smaller but stronger counter-culture might survive intact through a period of competition and growth to become the dominant culture.

Sorokin's theories about the process of cultural change do not tell us what will happen. At best, they tell us what will not happen, and by process of elimination, indicate the possible alternatives. Sorokin, however, was not shy of predictions. Having derived his theories primarily from extensive study of actual historical processes, he did not hesitate to apply them to the cultural change going on around him or to use them as a basis for concrete predictions. Although this prophetic vein has met with some disfavor in academic circles, it is illuminating to apply Sorokin's theory to a contemporary problem. Let us turn, therefore, to his analysis of western culture and his predictions about its future. The section which follows will discuss these aspects of Sorokin's work after presenting some background on the three cultural "super-systems" mentioned earlier in Part II.

### Part IV: The Content of Cultural Change: Western Culture at the End of an Era

Sorokin's theories about the content of cultural change focus around the Ideational, Sensate, and Idealistic super-systems. He saw these super-systems or "culture mentalities" as the archetypes of culture, differentiated by their fundamental beliefs about the nature of reality. He saw the history of cultural change as the ongoing rise and decline of these three systems.

Ideational culture is built on the belief that reality is super-sensory, non-material, and unchanging. The needs and ends of Ideational culture are predominantly spiritual and in periods when the Ideational culture mentality is in ascendance, men minimize their physical needs and turn their efforts to the pursuit of the kingdom of heaven, Nirvana, or other spiritual ends. These goals are sought primarily through attempts to modify the self rather than through efforts to control or change the material environment. The art of Ideational culture is heavily symbolic, as is its language: theology becomes the "queen of the sciences" and religion dominates other attempts to understand the world. Ethical standards are derived from absolute values and constitute a fixed system.

The reality which is affirmed by Sensate culture is that which is perceived by the senses, and it is believed to be characterized by a state of flux or process. The needs and ends of Sensate culture are primarily physical, although Sorokin broadens the common understanding of physical needs to include needs for fame and power. The methods by which these ends are sought involve the manipulation of the environment — including other people. Sensate art tends either to reproduce reality precisely as it is perceived or to stimulate the senses. Sensate culture is marked by a strong interest in science — particularly in applied science or technology — and is usually a period of great creativity and productivity in the technological realm. Sensate language is precise, descriptive, technical. The ethics of this culture tend to be pragmatic and relativistic as absolute standards of truth, beauty, and goodness recede before more practical norms which can be empirically tested. Religion in Sensate culture tends to decline in importance and stagnate.

Sorokin is not entirely consistent in his descriptions of Idealistic culture. At times, he describes it as a synthesis of Ideational and Sensate cultures, built on the belief that reality is an "infinite manifold," both sensory and super-sensory, material and spiritual, eternal and changing. Similarly, its needs and ends are a synthesis of both spiritual and material goals, and they are sought through the transformation of both the self and the environment. At times, however, Sorokin introduces the concept of reason, suggesting that while Ideational culture emphasizes the "truth of faith" and Sensate culture the "truth of the senses," Idealistic culture is dominated by the "truth of reason." In some of his later works, Sorokin refers to this third major culture mentality as "Integral" culture and states that it is based upon a synthesis of all three of these truths. Sorokin's inconsistency in defining the third cultural super-system creates substantial difficulties in the application of this aspect of his theory. Despite this variation in his approach, however, Sorokin seems to see the Idealistic-Integral super-system as the basis for a particularly satisfying culture, marked by great creativity in the fine arts and in fields such as philosophy which combine spiritual and theoretical reflection with empirical observation.[7]

Sorokin asserts that none of these super-systems is based on a wholly true or fully adequate reality principle. Each contains some truth which provides the basis for the development of a satisfying culture, and some error, which "leads its human bearers away from the reality, gives them pseudo knowledge instead of real knowledge, and hinders their adaptation and the satisfaction of their physiological, social, and cultural needs" (10, Vol. IV, pp. 742–743). This internal inadequacy of cultural systems is, according to Sorokin, the (immanent) reason for their alternating rise and decline, the underlying basis of the patterns of cultural change in history. For as a system ascends, it builds not only on its truth but on its error as well, and the aspects of a culture built on error finally become its downfall. Sorokin describes this process in the life of a system as follows:

> Becoming monopolistic or dominant, it tends to drive out all the other systems of truth and reality, and with them the valid parts they contain. At the same time, like dictatorial human beings, becoming dominant, the system is likely to lose increasingly its validities and develop its falsities. The net result of such a trend is that as the domination of the system increases, it becomes more and more inadequate (10, Vol. IV, p. 743).

The system becomes increasingly unable to satisfy the needs of human beings until finally, "the false part of the system begins to overweigh its valid part" (10, Vol. IV, p. 743). When this happens, the society which is the bearer of such predominantly false and disintegrating culture must either redefine its basic reality premise or perish. Such periods of disintegration and transition are usually marked by extensive bloodshed and turmoil.

The process of redefinition is not an overnight miracle. It occurs gradually as individuals and small groups begin to defect from the inadequate, dying super-system and seek alternative values and meanings. Those new values and meanings consolidate into larger and larger systems, eventually yielding a new super-system (8, p. 305).

For Sorokin, these super-systems and change processes were not mere theoretical constructs; they were actual, historical occurrences. Starting with an Ideational period stretching from the ninth to the sixth century B.C., he traces the life history of what he calls "Greco-Roman-western

---

[7] The description of the Ideational and Sensate culture mentalities are based on *Social and Cultural Dynamics* (10), Volume I, pp. 66–101. The discussion of Idealistic culture is drawn from the same source but modified by material found in Volume IV, pp. 741–765 and in a later collection of Sorokin's lectures and essays, *The Basic Trends of Our Times* (7, pp. 22–23).

culture" in terms of these culture mentalities, pursuing this quest through to the twentieth century.[8] Despite his apparent fascination with history, Sorokin was motivated to undertake his search for patterns of cultural change by the turmoil and change in his own lifetime (10, Vol. I, preface). It is not surprising, therefore, that he devoted a substantial portion of his efforts to a diagnosis of the culture around him. With the above material as background, let us turn to his analysis of modern western culture and his predictions concerning its future, for the insights they may yield concerning the contemporary counter-culture.

Sorokin believed that we are living through the disintegration of Sensate culture. He saw in the wars and brutal conflicts of the twentieth century, the escalation of bloodshed which generally accompanies such a transitional period. Furthermore, in keeping with his general theories, he found the causes of disintegration to be within the Sensate reality system itself.

Although these reasons are multiple, they can be usefully grouped into two categories.[9] The first of these immanent sources of the decay of Sensate culture is competition for scarce material goods and values. Because the major premise of western culture is that the true reality is sensory, the value scale of our society is basically materialistic. Success is measured in terms of comfort, wealth, power, and fame, and the human agents of this culture are socialized from birth to value and strive for these goals. Unfortunately, however, these values are in limited supply; the individual can attain them only by competing for them. Thus, in Sorokin's words:

> This philosophy of sensate values produces primarily egoistic individuals and groups. . . . The relative scarcity of sensate values generates a relentless and often ferocious struggle. . . . In this sense it is essentially a culture of enmity and war rather than of love and peace (9, pp. 102, 103).

Such a culture produces conflict and competition among its human agents rather than solidarity and cannot help but fail to meet the needs and desires which it generates.

The second of the two immanent sources of the destruction of Sensate culture lies in the simultaneous decline of moral absolutes and moral concern on the one hand and growth of technological know-how and scientific understandings of man on the other. Sorokin describes the problems caused by an overdeveloped science coupled with an underdeveloped morality as follows:

> With the progressive fading of the medieval universalitic standards, the moral, religious, and social irresponsibility of Sensate science and technology

[8] For a brief summary of these patterns in Western culture, see *The Basic Trends of Our Times* (7, p. 23).

[9] For a fuller statement of Sorokin's diagnosis, see *The Reconstruction of Humanity* (9, pp. 101–126).

has grown apace. Inventors have produced not only gadgets beneficial to humanity but also those that have brought death and destruction, beginning with gunpowder and ending with atomic bombs, poisonous gases, and means of bacteriological warfare (9, p. 111).

He goes on to suggest that Sensate technology's disregard for human life is due in part to the incomplete understanding of man produced by the empirical world view — "all the physical, reflexological, biological, endoctrinological, psychoanalytic, economic, and similar desocializing and demoralizing interpretations of man and his sociocultural universe . . ." (9, p. 111). Although Sorokin recognizes the contributions of Sensate culture, he does not mourn its passage:

> Mankind should be grateful to the Sensate culture for its wonderful achievements. But now when it is in agony; when its product is poison gas rather than fresh air; when through its achievements it has given into man's hands terrific power over nature and the social and cultural world, without providing [him] with self-control, and power over his emotions and passions, sensate appetites and lusts — now, in the hands of such a man, with all its achievements of science and technology, it is becoming increasingly dangerous to mankind and to all its values (10, Vol. III, p. 539).

While Sorokin predicted that the passing of Sensate culture would be a period of turmoil, marked by confusion and conflict, he foresaw beyond these labor pains the birth of a new era, a birth which could be prevented only if a catastrophic war should destroy humanity. In *Social and Cultural Dynamics,* Sorokin indicated that the new culture would be Ideational in character, but his later works showed a growing conviction that the new order would be of the Idealistic or Integral type. In one of his last works, a book of essays and addresses published in the early 1960s (7), he made explicit predictions: if a catastrophic Third World War could be avoided, western culture would move into a period of Integral culture, potentially the greatest in its history. At the same time, eastern culture, passing from a decayed and disintegrated Ideational state would also move forward towards an Integral super-system.

In the West, the establishment of the Integral order would involve the de-emphasis of material values and the addition of rational and supersensory values. In the East, where Sensate realities and values have been neglected, the reverse would be necessary. The growing interaction between eastern and western cultures would facilitate the process of transition in both cultures by exposing each to the values of the other (7, pp. 70, 71).

Sorokin saw signs of the coming of western Integral culture in many fields. Among the signs he interpreted as such, for instance, is the refusal of an increasing number of scientists to cooperate in the use of science and technology for destructive ends. Again, the emergence of philosophical systems congenial to the Integral conception of reality such as

Existentialism, neo-Hegelianism and neo-mysticism could be seen in this manner. He also suggests that new religious movements and especially the increase in western interest in eastern religions show the trend toward an approaching Integral super-system. Further examples are the "growth of moral heroism, sublime altruism, and ennobled moral conduct . . . in the form of many organized movements for the abolition of war, bloody strife, misery, sickness, poverty, exploitation, and injustice . . ." (7, p. 45). The emergence of a symbolic and ennobling modern art are additional signs.

In the realm of social relations, Sorokin also noted an important change: the emergence of new forms of familistic (as opposed to contractual or compulsory) relationships and social institutions, characterized by mutual love and commonality of purpose — particularly the development of welfare provisions, mutual aid arrangements, and "the growth of various strictly familistic communities such as the Society of Brothers, the Hutteries (sic), the Mennonites, the Friends Communities . . . (7, p. 55). In all of these signs, Sorokin saw what he called the "first spring blades" of the coming Integral order (7, pp. 24, 60).

Sorokin's analysis of modern western culture and his predictions are certainly debatable and they have been the subject of considerable criticism. They do, however, provide a particularly interesting framework for the consideration of cultural innovations and alternatives such as the counter-culture. Without taking issue here with Sorokin's predictions, let us look at the counter-culture in the light of the views outlined above. If his theories and predictions bear any resemblance to reality, a whole new dimension is added to the debate about the culture's future. For, if the counter-culture is a part or a "forerunner" of an emerging, Integral culture, its chances of influencing the dominant culture are very great. If, however, it is only one of the many conflicts which beset the dying Sensate order, it is unlikely to have significant or lasting influence.

There are three kinds of evidence which suggest that the contemporary counter-culture might indeed be a step toward a new cultural synthesis of the type described by Sorokin. First, the counter-culture appears to be, in part at least, a reaction against precisely those elements of the dominant culture which Sorokin identified as the immanent sources of destruction of Sensate culture: competition for scarce material wealth and the life-destroying propensities of modern technology.

The rejection of both competition as a means and material wealth as a goal is strong in the counter-culture. It takes a variety of forms: attempts to reduce competition by the development of non-hierarchical, decision-making patterns in families and other intimate social systems, in educational experiments, and in political and action organization; interest in socialist theory and economics and in various cooperative utopian schemes; demands for redistribution of wealth within the United States and a sharing of the nation's ill-gotten gains with the Third World;

the development of communal living arrangements and various "subsistence" life styles (including nomadic wandering, homesteading, and "ripping-off" a minimal living from "the system" through food stamps, giveaways, and occasional, part-time jobs); the general rejection of the consumer mentality, of large-scale acquisition and the 9 A.M.–5 P.M. productivity required for conspicuous consumption.

Although most descriptions of the counter-culture and most attempts to identify its basic themes are somewhat in the nature of rumor, Philip Slater has provided us with what appears to be an insightful comparison of the old culture and the new. He deals directly with the question of competition for material goods:

> The core of the old culture is scarcity. Everything in it rests upon the assumption that the world does not contain the wherewithal to satisfy the needs of its human inhabitants. From this it follows that people must compete with one another for these scarce resources . . . (6, p. 103).

The counter-culture, he finds, does not share the scarcity mentality:

> The new culture is based on the assumption that important human needs are easily satisfied and that the resources for doing so are plentiful (6, pp. 103, 104).

According to Slater, the counter-culture seeks to reduce competition not only by eliminating artificial scarcities of goods, but also by reducing the level of involvement with material possessions:

> It argues that instead of throwing away one's body so that one can accumulate material artifacts, one should throw away the artifacts and enjoy one's body. . . . The new culture . . . embodies a sociological consciousness . . . [in which] lies the key insight that possessions actually generate scarcity. . . . To accumulate possessions is to deliver pieces of oneself to dead things (6, pp. 108, 109).

While it is fairly easy to trace the theme of opposition to competitive materialism in the counter-culture, it is perhaps even easier to find a reaction to the second stumbling block of Sensate society identified by Sorokin: destructive technology. Among the activist elements within the counter-culture, this takes the form of anti-war activity, opposition to the arms race and sometimes to the space adventure, defense of the environment from the onslaught of pollution and destruction and a general critique of American society as technologically dominated. In addition, the reaction against technology can be seen in the retreat to rural communes, in the preference for "naturalness" — organic foods, wooden and clay utensils, abandonment of makeup and elaborate hairstyles — and a variety of other attempts to simplify life and decrease dependence upon technology.

Many observers of the counter-culture have identified the destructiveness of modern technology as a major source of the counter-cultural phenomenon.  It is interesting to note that several have followed Sorokin's lead in linking it to the decay of moral and spiritual values.  Theodore Roszak, for example, refers to modern industrial societies as areas

> where two centuries of aggressive secular skepticism, after ruthlessly eroding the traditionally transcendent ends of life, has concomitantly given us a proficiency of technical means that now oscillates absurdly between the production of frivolous abundance and the production of genocidal munitions (5, p. 13).

Similarly, Charles Reich in *The Greening of America* suggests that the logic of the new culture "must be read from the fact that Americans have lost control of the machinery of their society, and only new values and a new culture can restore control" (4, pp. 2, 3).  He goes on to argue that:

> Technology demands of man a new mind — a higher, transcendent reason — if it is to be controlled and guided rather than to become an unthinking monster.  It demands a new individual responsibility for values, or it will dictate all values (4, p. 5).

Certainly, it can be argued that there are also elements within the counter-culture which affirm rather than oppose materialism and technology: a fascination with all sorts of trinkets, a fondness for elaborate sound systems and light shows; an emphasis on outward manifestations and styles, a willingness to experiment with chemically induced states of expanded consciousness.  To some extent, this represents a real ambivalence within the counter-culture — although if Sorokin is correct about the Integral nature of the coming age, this contradiction may find its resolution in a culture which uses technology and material abundance for people rather than against them.  It is also possible to interpret such inconsistencies within the counter-culture as simple, human frailty.  Most counter-culturists were socialized within the context of the values and institutions of the dominant society and have been exposed to those values and institutions for a considerably longer period of time than they have been subjected to the influence of counter-cultural alternatives.  It should come as no surprise, then, that individuals and groups within or associated with the counter-culture have not been ready to part with all aspects of the materialism they criticize.  Nor should we expect a culture which has arisen so recently and, with the help of the media, expanded so rapidly, to be free of "congeries" and other extraneous and incompatible elements.  It is a testimony to the seriousness of some adherents of the new culture that they have recognized the difficulty of changing one's behaviors and inclinations to conform with newly acquired values and have sought to build a variety of group efforts — collectives, consciousness-raising groups, growth centers — in which people can help each other along in the sometimes painful process of "personal revolution."

A second set of evidence suggesting that the counter-culture may be part of an emerging new super-system lies in the extent to which the process by which the counter-culture has emerged fits the pattern of transition which Sorokin predicted. In a book published in 1941, when Sorokin still believed that the new super-system would be Ideational, he described the transition as an increasing defection of human agents and vehicles from the dying Sensate culture to new values, a decline in the coherence and power of Sensate systems of meaning. He predicted that the best brains would increasingly go into fields other than science and business, that the ethics and standards of conduct in Sensate society would increasingly deteriorate, while on the other hand there would increasingly appear "partisans of the Absolute ethical norm" who would reject Sensate materialism and "flee the sensory world into a kind of new refuge, new monasteries, and new deserts" (8, pp. 298–302). In a more recent work, Sorokin suggested that the creation of the new order would begin in opposition to the "wars, revolutions, revolts, and crimes" produced by the disintegrating culture:

> Fortunately . . . the disintegration process often generates the emergence of mobilization of forces opposed to it. Weak and insignificant at the beginning, these forces slowly grow and then start not only to fight the disintegration but also to plan and then to build a new sociocultural order . . . (7, p. 24).

Some of the predictions bear haunting similarities to the emergence of the contemporary counter-culture. Although it takes more than a minor stretch of the imagination to see today's hippies and activists as ascetics, there is certainly an element of austerity and rejection of decayed Sensate materialism in their attempt to build new, less consumption-oriented life styles. While the counter-culture contains its share of relativistic norms, it has produced more than its share of "partisans of absolute norms" — conscientious objectors and draft resisters being prime examples. Within the counter-culture, if not within the dominant culture, the best brains increasingly tend to engage in pursuits other than business or traditional science.

Another similarity to the process described by Sorokin can be found in some of the changes within the counter-culture during its brief history. The earliest manifestations of counter-cultural activity tended to be negative — critiques and rejections of the dominant culture, struggles against war, racism, sexism, and pollution. The discussion and experimentation with positive alternatives came later. The same sort of progression seems to occur within the lives of many individuals who become part of the new culture. There is first a recognition that something is very wrong with the dominant society, which is followed by a search for new values and assumptions to replace the old discredited norms. This seems to parallel the process of defection and creation described by Sorokin.

Although these similarities are not conclusive, they are sufficient to suggest that insofar as the counter-culture embodies a defection from the values and assumptions of the dominant culture, it has the potential for developing into a nucleus within a new super-system. One caution should be added here, in fairness to both Sorokin and the reader. Sorokin makes clear that not all attempts to change or oppose the dying order are parts or sources of the coming super-system. Some such attempts, and he specifically includes efforts to bring about violent revolution, share in the basic values of the Sensate super-system. He suggests that these are "the vultures that appear when the social and cultural body is decomposing," and that their function in the transition is to "pull . . . to pieces" the dying system, "to clear the ground for a new life" (10, Vol. III, pp. 536, 537). Their schemes may echo, in distorted form, the coming culture, but their values, assumptions, and means are part of the passing age. Certainly there are within and around the counter-culture advocates of revolutionary violence who seem to fit this mold. It remains to be seen whether the counter-culture will grow primarily in the direction of such destructive violence or primarily in the creation of positive alternatives.

A third type of evidence that the counter-culture may represent what Sorokin called the first "spring blades" of the coming Integral order rests in the "Integral" or "Idealistic" nature of some forms of counter-cultural thought and activity. If the counter-culture is indeed Integral in nature, it should de-emphasize sensory values and truths without abandoning them; it should supplement them with rational and intuitive truths and values, and it should foster the growth of cooperative and familistic social institutions.

We may be witnessing these very developments. While the counter-culture has rejected competition for material goods and prestige, it has vigorously affirmed a number of other sensory values and pleasures, particularly sex, human relationships, sense-stimulating music, art, and dress. Unlike an ascetic, Ideational system, the counter-culture's rejection of material wealth does not imply a neglect of basic human needs, but a provision of necessities for all human beings. While the counter-culture has retained much of the useful information and empirical approach to the world fostered by the Sensate scientific world view, it has supplemented these with truths achieved through yoga, meditation, and intuition, and it has begun to search for truth in the realm of religion. In truly Integral fashion, it pursues its ends both through the transformation of the self and through the modification of the material and social environment. Finally, the social systems and institutions fostered by the counter-culture — communes, free schools, food cooperatives, free clinics, street theater troups, etc. — tend to be cooperative or familistic rather than contractual or compulsory in character.

Within the framework of Sorokin's predictions, then, I find substantial evidence to suggest that the counter-culture is in part at least a fore-runner of the new order which he foresaw. The aspects of the dominant culture which the counter-culture rejects are precisely those which Sorokin identified as sources of the decay and eventual downfall of western Sensate culture. The process by which the new culture has emerged parallels that defection and synthesis of new values which Sorokin described as characteristic of the development of a new culture during a transition period. Elements within the counter-culture bear a remarkable resemblance to the Integral culture mentality as Sorokin describes it.[10] If Sorokin's predictions and these interpretations are cor-rect, if the counter-culture is a forerunner of an emerging new super-system, then the question to which this paper is directed may be answered straightforwardly: under these circumstances the counter-culture would be one of the sources of the new order and as such would eventually have a profound influence on the values of the larger western society.

This conclusion differs substantially from those reached at the end of Part III after a consideration of Sorokin's theories concerning the process of cultural change (see pp. 909–10 above). Although this may appear to suggest a contradiction at the theory level, or a major inconsistency in application, it should be noted that Sorokin's process theories were in-tended to apply to cultural change in general, while his predictions applied to very special circumstances which occurred infrequently: the transitional period at the end of a cultural era. If indeed Sensate culture is close to a downfall or disintegration, made inevitable by the cumula-tive impact of fundamental inadequacies in its perception of reality, then any alternative culture has a far better chance of "winning the

---

[10] This is not intended to imply that Sorokin himself, had he remained alive long enough to watch the development of the couunter-culture, would necessarily have come to the same conclusions. Even if he had selected the same portions of his theory as relevant to an assessment of the counter-culture (and even if I have applied his ideas fairly and accurately), he might have perceived that culture rather differently than I. Since there is no generally agreed upon, definitive study of the counter-culture, I have relied upon my own observations and those of several writers whose approach to the new culture is basically sympathetic. Sorokin might have placed greater emphasis on those aspects of the counter-culture which partake of Sensate values and assumptions and might have seen the new culture as just one more variation on the themes of the dying order. But when I apply *his* theoretical categories to *my* perceptions of the counter-culture, it looks remarkably like emerging, Integral culture. Since Sorokin is not here to defend himself, the reader is invited to continue the exercise using his or her own perceptions of the new culture.

hearts and minds of the people" than it would if it were competing with a cultural system flourishing at mid-career. Similarly, if the counter-culture has indeed emerged in the context of such accumulated error, a new light is shed upon its negative cast, its heavy emphasis on critique and opposition. Sorokin suggests that the rejection of the destructive and error-based portions of the old culture is the impetus to the search for new values. He implies that any new system which failed to recognize and negate the error of the old culture would be doomed along with the dying order. Thus, negation becomes an essential step in the process by which new cultural systems arise at the end of an era and can be seen as a strength rather than a weakness of the counter-culture. Even the conflicts and contradictions within the counter-culture which seemed to indicate its probable demise when interpreted from the perspective of the theories discussed in part III, take on a more encouraging aspect if the counter-culture has emerged amid the turmoil of the end of a cultural era. They become a part of the experimentation and pluralism necessary in the search for new values and satisfying alternatives to the present order.

This study has proceeded almost entirely *within* the framework of Sorokin's theories, not because I accept all those theories as accurate or adequate, but simply because a look at the counter-culture from the vantage-point of Sorokin's work seemed a sufficient task, a useful first step, in itself. I hesitate, however, to leave the impression that Sorokin's ideas are valuable only if his theories are accepted wholesale and applied as a unit. In fact, the opposite is true. Not only do Sorokin's theories remain useful when applied critically, but some portions of his ideas can be used to examine and clarify the objections raised to other portions. Let me illustrate by explaining one of my own disagreements with his formulations.

In one of his later books, Sorokin suggests that, if an annihilating nuclear war can be avoided, three logical options exist for western culture: (1) the continuation in a slightly refreshed form of the decayed Sensate culture; (2) the death of the Sensate super-system followed by "the indefinitely long existence of an eclectic mixture of heterogeneous sociocultural odds and ends" (7, p. 71); or (3) the emergence of the new Integral order. He argues that the creativity of the western people is sufficient to ensure the triumph of a new integrated system over mere eclecticism and that the lessons of the past are sufficient grounds for dismissing the possibility that Sensate culture will continue. I am not convinced that the "lessons of the past" apply with much fidelity to modern western culture, so vastly different from its predecessors in its material forms and technological capabilities. The dying super-systems of the past did not have instantaneous communications, rapid transportation, or doomsday machines to extend their hegemony. Those who defected from the decaying cultures of history could withdraw from the dominant society and turn their attention to the creation of alternatives far more completely than can most modern defectors. Their new systems had some time to develop — to experience what Sorokin calls "qualitative growth," integration, the exposure and elimination of incompatible elements — before they were publicly discussed and dissected. Without modern media, they did not attract new adherents so rapidly, and thus, as Sorokin makes clear, were not as vulnerable to that destruction by disintegration, conflict, and the addition of extraneous and contradictory elements which generally accompanies the too-rapid expansion of a cultural system. I am not sure that the pace of modern life allows for the careful nurturing and slow synthesis which the building of a new super-system would seem to require. Thus, Sorokin's own theories give substance and clarity to my nagging doubt and inability fully to share his optimism about the future.

The value of Sorokin's thought, however, is certainly not confined to its ability to clarify our disagreements with it. In the long run, differences and disagreements are probably less important than an appreciation for the usefulness of Sorokin's categories and theories for thinking seriously about the changes occurring around us. His idea that cultures are built upon and take their character from their beliefs about the nature of reality is perhaps the most penetrating insight into the nature of culture which I have encountered. His ideas are helpful not only in organizing data from the past but also in understanding contemporary cultures and subcultures. Furthermore, his general description of the rise and decline of cultural systems and the inevitable multiplication of "error" and inadequacy as a cultural system grows, lends needed perspective to current critiques of modern western culture, particularly those which focus on the imbalance between moral, humanistic concern and technological capacity and activity. Sorokin makes clear that the growth of technology with its benefits as well as its potential for destruction and the decline of moral concern, are a single process, the logical outcome of a limited appreciation of the nature of reality. He is then able to move the discussion of the ills of western culture from the level of shrill, moralistic attack to the level of analysis and understanding — a level which seems far more likely than mere invective to provide the basis for the creation of alternatives and solutions.

## BIBLIOGRAPHY

1. Cowell, Frank R. *History, Civilization, and Culture: An Introduction to the Historical and Social Philosophy of Pitirim A. Sorokin.* Boston: Beacon: Beacon Press, 1952.
2. Keniston, Kenneth. *Young Radicals.* New York: Harcourt, Brace & World, Inc., 1968.

3. Ponsioen, J. A. *The Analysis of Social Change Reconsidered*. The Hague: Mouton, 1969.

4. Reich, Charles A. *The Greening of America*. New York: Bantam Books, 1970.

5. Roszak, Theodore. *The Making of a Counter Culture*. Garden City, New York: Doubleday Anchor, 1969.

6. Slater, Philip. *The Pursuit of Loneliness: American Culture at the Breaking Point*. Boston: Beacon Press, 1970.

7. Sorokin, Pitirim A. *The Basic Trends of Our Times*. New Haven, Connecticut: College and University Press, 1964.

8. Sorokin, Pitirim A. *The Crisis of Our Age*. New York: E. P. Dutton, 1941.

9. Sorokin, Pitirim A. *The Reconstruction of Humanity*. Boston: Beacon Press, 1948.

10. Sorokin, Pitirim A. *Social and Cultural Dynamics*. 4 Volumes. New York: American Book Company, 1937–1941. Reprinted, New York: Bedminster Press, 1962.

11. Tiryakian, Edward. *Sociological Theory, Values, and Sociocultural Change: Essays in Honor of Pitirim A. Sorokin*. New York: The Free Press of Glencoe, 1963.

# 33

*Don Martindale*

## The Crisis of Nationalism

Human social life consists of what individuals do in concert and social change consists of transformations in its forms. Institutions are more or less stabilized strategies of interpersonal action; the formation and destruction of institutions is an elementary manifestation of social change. The state as the institution which has managed to secure a monopoly of the use of power in a given territory, tends to be a major focal point in the institutional order. Students of social change have quite correctly paid much attention to the state. Communities are the grand strategies of the collective life of pluralities, hence, they are of special concern to all students interested in the comprehensive drift and thrust in human affairs. The contemporary nation is usually conceived as a community of sufficient integrity to sustain a state; the nation state has been bound up with all of the distinctive events of the contemporary world. No student of social change at present can afford to ignore nationalism (the complex of ideas, sentiments and institutions sustained by the citizens of nation-states) or the origin, career and crises of the nation state.

As nationalism began to crystalize into the most effective strategy of collective life in the western world in the seventeenth and eighteen centuries, it proved to be superior in survival power to alternative forms of collective integration. Pluralities which came within the sphere of an emerging nation were forced to accept an exploited role or develop national strategies of their own. In the original series of nations (England, France and Spain) the formation of the state preceded the reorganization of the community into national form, permitting the kings and monarchs to view the state virtually as private property. But a reorientation of interests and institutions was occurring around the new states. The revolutions that ushered in the modern period tore the states out of the hands of the kings and despots and made them the property of the nation as a whole — or at least, of broader groups than previously. In some measure, the competition between the original states had brought about the reintegration of interests and institutions represented by the nations.

As the original nation-states took shape, a secondary series began to take form (the United States, Germany, Russia and Italy). In the secondary series of nation-states, the formation of the nation largely preceded the establishment of a contemporary type state. The pattern of nation-state formation was coming to characterize the whole of Europe and North America.

National competition between the original nations set them on a career of exploitation of the material resources of the entire world. Waves of nation formation spread out from the western world to the farthest shores of human occupancy. In this third great wave of nation formation, cadres of the native elite typically took the lead both in forming states on the model of the western type and of reordering the community into national form.

The extension of the influence of the original nations in the world beyond their borders was powerfully facilitated by the applications of scientific technology to the solution of industrial, military and communications problems in the original states. Classical imperialism was the political domination of underdeveloped areas by the developed nations for material advantage.

## The Sunset of Nationalism

The very processes that put the western nations into competition for the resources of the world and resulted in domination of underdeveloped areas eventually brought classical imperialism to an end. There was no way, in the long run, to prevent the export of western technology to the rest of the world encouraging former colonized areas to exploit their territories for themselves. The imperialistic domination of underdeveloped areas, moreover, weakened their traditional institutions and communities, thus helping clear the way for reconstruction on the basis of new principles. Cadres from underdeveloped areas trained in western universities and placed in the service of the imperial powers were tempted, at times, to strike out on their own. Moreover, in the wars between the imperial powers, native forces were at times trained and employed, forming the core of a military force that could be enlisted into native, nationalistic aspirations. International competition, in short, inevitably brought in its train a world wide crystallization of new nations curtailing the early forms of imperialism.

While the early forms of imperialism were called into question, so too, were early forms of sovereignty (the monopoly of power of the state within the nation). While sovereignty is national, major modern wars are transnational and fought by power blocs. The result is that any nation can potentially start a major war, but no nation alone can bring one to an end. War ceases to be an institution under national control and it is no longer appropriate for the conduct of politics by other means. Competence has been separated from responsibility and war as a policy tends to be resorted to when national institutions fail. Under the circumstances, the super power blocs have pressed policies that run roughshod over the internal autonomy of smaller nations. Among the major social changes since World War II has been the appearance of a new style of imperialism.

### The New Imperialism

World War II rendered the old style of imperialism obsolete. It set in motion the final phase of the crystallization of the societies of the world into national form. Even minorities had begun to give their aspirations national form as illustrated by the Zionism of the Jews and the national aspirations of French Canadians. Japan's empire had been destroyed. The imperialistic systems of the British, French and Dutch were in process of speedy dismantlement. Under the circumstances, surely one of the ironies of the post World War II period to future students, will be the manner in which the victorious super powers continued to worship at the shrine of the dead gods of imperialism. But, as Nietzsche had observed, great events take time to be comprehended even after they have happened.

The implications of the Second World War on imperialism were not readily clear. For instance, at the end of the war, the economy of Soviet Russia was in ruins. Though the German forces had been destroyed and a major task of reconstruction faced the nation, Stalin and other Kremlin leaders were led by their paranoia to fill the vacuum of power created by the defeat of the Nazis and they attempted to seize as many areas of control as possible. The Kremlin leaders undertook to exploit occupied territories with a brutality which could be matched by the annals of the old-fashioned imperialists, to the extent of dismantling much of the industrial plant of occupied countries and carrying it back to Russia. The Kremlin leaders also set about to consolidate their world position as if they feared imminent attack by the United States and other western powers.

The leaders of the United States and other western powers, for their part, seemed to have been determined to prove that psychopathology in high places was no exclusive invention of the Kremlin. If the Soviet Union was determined to orient themselves to international affairs on the basis of paranoid fantasies, the western leaders seemed determined to respond with an odd combination of diffuse anxiety and megalomania.

The simple facts were: (1) the old style imperialism was dead and all attempts to perpetuate it could be expected to backfire to the ultimate disadvantage of the would-be imperialists; (2) Russia was in no position to mount a military threat against her former allies; (3) the new atomic weapons had permanently transformed the nature of warfare, rendering all forms of the arms race to develop and stockpile atomic weapons insane.

Instead of exercising rudimentary common sense, recognizing that Soviet Russia was in no position to engage in military adventures against the United States and could only hurt her international situation by imperialistic operations, the leaders of the United States chose to turn the Kremlin's machinations into realities by taking them seriously. The leaders of the United States undertook to play Soviet Russia's own game and to form a powerful anti-communist bloc of nations in NATO. When this occurred, the Russians in turn, organized the Warsaw Pact to counter-balance NATO.

The United States opened the post World War II arms race with an enormously expanded program of developing and stockpiling atomic weapons while simultaneously seeking to restrict their diffusion to the nations of the world. This was done despite the scientific consensus that atomic weapons employed on a global scale would impartially destroy aggressors, defenders and the innocent bystanders. Furthermore, all attempts to restrict the spread of atomic weapons were vain and the attempts by the United States to maintain a monopoly was a virtual guarantee of their rapid diffusion. If the strongest nation on earth was frantically equipping itself with atomic weapons, other nations had good cause to seek access to them as well.

In resting international behavior on the myth that the world was in imminent danger of a communist domination, the leaders of the United States could only confirm the Soviet Russians in their own myth, that the capitalistic nations were planning a global take-over. When, through the Marshal Plan and other forms of economic and military aid, the United States undertook to influence the internal policies of other nations, the Russians denounced the action of the United States as imperialistic; the leaders of the United States were in the habit of denouncing similar practices by the Russians as imperialistic. For once the leaders of neither nation appeared to be speaking with forked tongues. As the Russians and Americans sets out to arm themselves against one another and to win the world to their respective sides, the result was a self-fulfilling prophecy: they created the very threat to world peace each claimed to be arming to prevent.

Although Presidents Roosevelt and Truman had supported the United Nations Organization (the charter of which was ratified by the World

War II allies in 1945) it was weakened from the onset as a peace keeping organization by the reservation to the United States, Soviet Russia, Great Britain, France and Nationalist China of the power to veto any actions they wished and the right to form regional alliances outside the United Nations. Hence, when the Soviets imposed forms of government favorable to themselves on occupied countries and carried on a systematic campaign of agitation and subversion to advance their cause, the United States was drawn, however reluctantly at first, into a Cold War. The United States was not long in seeking to influence the internal policies of countries in its sphere in a manner very similar to the Soviet Russians. In 1947, in accord with the "Truman Doctrine," military and economic aid was sent to Greece and Turkey to assist them in putting down communist rebellion. The Greek army was in part trained by United States advisors and equipped with United States aid. The practice of sending military hardware and technical advisors to nations of the world was institutionalized in the Marshal Plan. In the first stage, billions of dollars were sent to the countries of Western Europe to assist them in rebuilding their economies, resisting "communist subversion" and forming their military forces into anti-Soviet systems.

In 1949 the Czechoslovakian government was destroyed by communist subversion and Berlin was blockaded, leaving the Allies to counter with an airlift. When the North Atlantic Treaty Organization (NATO) was organized in 1949 most of the western nations joined. The Soviet Union countered with an alliance among the communist powers in the Warsaw Pact. To a naive outsider it could well appear that the superpowers were equally at fault; however, to a patriotic American it was quite evident that only Soviet Russia was engaged in acts and gestures of aggression; the United States was engaged in acts of anticipatory defense. It was not long in becoming evident that the same game was to be played in the Far East.

In the Far East, Imperial Japan's conquests had badly disrupted Chinese society. After Pearl Harbor, Japan invaded South East Asia, eventually taking over the colonies of the European powers. The leaders of the United States had plenty of advance warning of the future course of events in the Far East during World War II. War material and technical assistance were generously supplied to the Chinese Nationalist Government under Chiang Kai-shek.

When Japan was defeated it left a vacuum of power in Asia. The smaller nations which had been partially or completely colonized under the imperial policies of the great nations (particularly Korea and the nations of South East Asia) were encouraged to make their bid for national autonomy. When the British, French and Dutch sought to reassert their imperialistic claims they were faced with native rebellion. Civil war broke out in China.

The leaders of the United States were fully aware of the fact that the

Nationalist Chinese regime was corrupt and was continually losing popular support while the communists were moved by revolutionary fervor and enjoyed the support of the peasantry. While the United States did not actively take sides in the Chinese Civil War, it continued to support Chiang Kai-shek's forces with weapons and supplies between 1945 and 1949. Chiang's forces suffered repeated defeats and were eventually forced to flee to Taiwan.

The advice of informed students was repeatedly set aside. The United States continued to support the nationalist regime despite its corruption and lack of popularity. When the communists triumphed and the People's Republic of China confirmed its sovereignty over the Chinese mainland, the United States still refused its recognition and continued to give millions of dollars of aid into the Nationalist Chinese cause. Such a policy, quite clearly, drove the People's Republic of China into the camp of Soviet Russia and for a time gave Russia a relatively free hand in Asia. The United States policy toward China appears to have had major consequences for the course of events in the smaller nations, beginning with Korea.

World War II ended with the United States in occupancy of Japan and sharing with Russia the occupancy of Korea which was divided at the 38th parallel. The Americans and Russians appear to have been determined to carry out parallel programs in the East to those in the West: the Russians promoted communism in the north; the Americans promoted capitalism in South Korea. The Russians helped train and equip an army in the north to take over the whole of Korea and incorporate it into the Soviet sphere. Though they received somewhat less cooperation, south Korean nationalists, for their part, dreamed of uniting the whole of Korea. Once war broke out, when South Korea faced defeat, the United States rushed back in. Truman and his advisors, however, were successful in converting the Korean conflict into a United Nations War with the United States primarily paying the bill. In part, as a direct product of General Douglas MacArthur's desire to turn the Korean conflict into a general war on the People's Republic of China, the communist Chinese were brought into the war on the North Korean side and the Korean conflict came dangerously close to escalating into a general Asian War.

It is surely one of the major ironies of the post World War II period, that the effect of the American stereotype of the danger of world communism was to drive mainland China into temporary alliance with Soviet Russia (who was her natural rival on the Asian mainland), to give Russia a free hand in North Korea and to bring China into the war against the United States to prevent the fall of North Korea to the American armies. If the policies of the United States had not so systematically alienated the communist Chinese, they would have been a natural ally of the United States and the Korean conflict could easily have been avoided altogether.

The Asian policy of the United States was put on a course paralleling that in western Europe. The South East Asian Treaty Organization (SEATO) was formed and massive American military aid and the employment of military advisors became standard operating procedure. The American involvement in Vietnam was an inevitable by-product of these policies.

The Cold War, thus, was by no means an exclusive American invention, though the American power elite had done its share in bringing it to full reality. If the Russians were seeking to interfere in the internal politics of nations within their sphere in considerable measure by use of terror, the Americans were trying to achieve the same by means of economic and military aid. However, each of the superpowers was quite prepared to employ the tactics of the other: the Soviets, for example, extended economic aid and technical assistance to communist China, to Egypt and other Arab countries in the Near East, to Cuba and to other underdeveloped countries. While it will be a long time before the full story is known, some evidence has suggested that the American Central Intelligence Agency (CIA) has organized sabotage, military cadres with revolutionary objectives and other types of subversive activities in various countries to pull them out of the communist camp.

By 1950 the United States has begun, under the mantle of military aid, to play a paternalistic role throughout much of the world. Its role was still benign when, in the 1960s, Senator Fulbright began to ask why the United States was called upon to play house mother to the world. By the 1960s, the United States and Soviet Russia had become engaged in a nuclear arms race and were being drawn ever further afield on neo-imperialistic adventures. The consequences of this competition included an unprogressive response by both of the superpowers to nationalism.

Nationalism tended to be respected as a principle in the area of its origin, that is, western Europe, where it has ceased to be progressive. National claims tended to be disregarded in the underdeveloped world where it was a progressive force (here a force is taken as progressive when it tends to create a larger peace group). At points of contact of the superpowers, nations were ruthlessly torn apart: Eastern and Western Germany; North and South Korea; North and South Vietnam. By bribery (economic and military aid) and by subversion, attempts were made to influence the domestic policies of nations. When the leaders of the United States undertook to give military aid and training and to sponsor a military coup of the Cuban exiles in what terminated in the disastrous Bay of Pigs invasion, some thoughtful observers began to wonder whether there was actually any ultimate difference in the international behavior of the superpowers.

The full implications for the United States of policies which contemplated influencing the domestic life and politics of other nations not only by economic aid, but by technical military advisors, subversion and, if need be, outright military intervention, became clear in Vietnam. On the basis of the hypothetical threat of international communism, the so-called "domino theory" was advanced (that if South Vietnam fell to communism the whole of South East Asia and ultimately, India, would fall like a row of dominos) to justfy continued interference with Vietnamese politics. On the basis of the same stereotype, the state department and foreign service had long since been purged of critics who might have debated this theory from inside the government. The operations of the McCarthy inquisitions and the House UnAmerican Activities Committee had long since dispersed the type of intellectual dissent which might have debated the theory outside the government. The domino theory was, thus, never subjected to a searching review.

Serious doubt has been raised in the *Pentagon Papers* (1) and the CBS Television Program *Sixty Minutes* as to the authenticity of the incidents by which Congress was persuaded to authorize the President to under- take direct military intervention in Vietnam. By failing to appreciate the manner in which the causes of communism and nationalism were not coextensive, the United States manipulated itself into the position where it was opposed to Vietnamese nationalism — for not only were the South Vietnamese communists opposed to the United States presence in their country, but the South Vietnamese nationalists were opposed to it as well. South Vietnamese nationalists formed a communal base from which both North and South Vietnamese guerillas could operate against American forces. Lacking a conventional enemy American mili- tary forces were drawn into a situation where atrocities such as that of My Lai could occur and wholesale use of napalm, herbicides and the transplantation of the whole populations were undertaken. The "en- emy" had in large measure become South Vietnamese society which had to be destroyed to eliminate the foundations for guerilla opera- tions.

The United States has repeatedly had recourse to the massive bomb- ing of North Vietnam, an impoverished, underdeveloped nation with a population of 21 million people, chiefly peasants, living in an area of 61 thousand square miles. Since 1965, the United States has dropped more than 7 million tons of bombs on South East Asian nations. After the American elections prior to which President Nixon's personal envoy assured the American people that "peace was at hand," President Nixon on December 18, 1972 personally ordered without consultation of Congress, the bombing of the Hanoi-Haiphong area of North Vietnam and engaged for the next ten days in the most massive sustained bomb- ing attack in the history of the world. More than 10 million pounds of explosives were dropped on the Hanoi-Haiphong area in a single day. This bombing attack elicited the repeated pleas of the Vatican to halt the war and stirred the moral revulsion of many nations of the world, some of whose leaders described the behavior of the United

States as comparable to the genocidal atrocities of the Nazis. American interference in the domestic policies of other nations which began as relatively mild paternalism thus led, on this occasion, to extremities which merits the New Yorker description of the United States as the "mad bomber of Asia."

Perhaps the total cost to the world of the neo-imperialistic policies of the great powers (Soviet Union, the United States and China) will never be computed. They placed the great powers in an arms race characterized by the invention of ever more sophisticated weapons systems and the stockpiling of atomic weapons in a manner which may some day appear to have been the prelude of the ultimate destruction of mankind. It led to the arming of the smaller nations of the underdeveloped world (in some measure with technologically displaced weapons outmoded by the rapid advances in weapons technology) in a manner that promoted countless coups, revolutions, minor wars and military confrontations.

There seems little doubt that both Soviet Russia and China were convinced that the United States was in Southeast Asia on a course which could engulf the world in World War III, for both Peking and Moscow were amenable to visits by President Nixon. However, it is also true that in both areas, there had been major crop failures and millions of Chinese and Russians faced possible starvation and the leaders of both countries were anxious to arrange deals for American wheat. At the same time, these visits to the capitals of the great communist powers gave the lie to the stereotype of the "threat of World Communism," the war in Vietnam continued, as it does at the present writing, to grind on. Some of the writers for the New Yorker magazine were moved to observe that whatever their ultimate meaning, Nixon's visits to the capitals of the communist powers had not been to secure peace, but to make the world safe for war.

## The Domestic Crises

Internal to the society where it occurs, nation formation is possible only with the breakdown of subcommunities of all sorts whatever their origin: feudal subsistence communities, peasant villages, towns and cities cannot be permitted to preserve their autonomy and exercise ultimate control over their members if the nation is to become a reality. In the conflict between local and national interests, the institutions that serve local interests eventually yield all or most of their powers to the large-scale organizations which operate translocally. Totalitarianism and the movement toward mass society represent the tendency for all local structures to weaken or vanish, such that masses of individuals stand in more or less unmediated confrontation with the large-scale structures that serve the nation. When the consolidation of power is primarily in the hands of big government, the result is conventionally designated as totalitarianism; when the consolidation of power is shared by big government and big business, the result is conventionally designated as mass society.

The parallelism of the two forms of massification, to be sure, does not eliminate important, qualitative, differences between the two systems: in the control of the masses, the communist and fascist countries have tended to rely on fear and censorship; in the control of the masses, the capitalist countries have tended to rely primarily on advertising and myth management. The second system of control tends to preserve much more open space for individuals and dissident groups.

In the following, attention will primarily be directed to the internal consequences of the continuing process of national integration in the capitalist countries, particularly in the United States.

## The Crisis of the Cities

The continuing process of national integration in the United States during and after World War II was the primary factor in the crisis of of the cities.

Wars, particularly for the victors, enormously strengthen national at the expense of local institutions. Wars create enormous demands for raw materials (reorienting the economy around the needs of the nation) and concentrate decision-making power in the hands of political, military and big business personnel. Wars take manpower from agriculture and industry while increasing the demand for production encouraging an accelerated application of scientific technology to all phases of production. Cold Wars tend to prolong war economies into times of peace, keeping the war-time elites in power and confirming the concentration of populations in metropolitan centers brought about by war needs. World War II confirmed the fact that society in the United States no longer consisted of rural villages and small towns, but at the same time it dramatized the crisis of the city.

Society in the United States had been dominated up to the Civil War period by the forms and mentality of the small town. North America was primarily settled by North European middle class urbanities and was never affected in a major way by peasant villages or plantation communities, but developed a world of small towns and cities. Though the industrial revolution in the post Civil War period had begun to concentrate masses of immigrants in the cities, pressing them into the service of mass industry, traditional Americans still viewed their society as a world of small towns. The larger cities with their masses of immigrants surviving as unskilled laborers, with their alien cultures and languages were experienced as alien. City bosses organized the urban masses into political machines and participated with business men in the plunder of urban economic opportunities in a manner which scandalized traditional Americans still reasoning in terms of town-meeting democracy and economy-minded civic consciousness. The pre-World War I exposés of urban corruption by the muckrakers dramatized the reactions of traditional Americans to developments in the great cities.

The center of gravity of American life was, however, shifting to the great cities. Efforts to clean up city government began to have results. A new and more responsible type of professional had begun to emerge and by the time the final, great thrust of the American population into the cities took place, most aspects of urban government, with the possible exception of the police force, had been much improved. Americans, it would appear, were ready with the end of World War II to accept the great city as their distinctive community.

There were many Americans who still clung to the traditional idea of the autonomous small town as the only proper place to live and raise a family. The masses of men whose life plans had been delayed by the Depression and World War II, who wished for nothing more than the chance to settle down and raise their families in peace, took advantage of the low costs involved and veterans' loans to buy or build in the suburbs (working in the city but assimilating urban life to the ideal image of the small town). The automobile, the state and federal highway programs and the low cost housing loan permitted the suburbs to grow at the expense of the central city. Mass transit facilities began to collapse for lack of sufficient patronage. Shopping centers in the suburbs began to draw patronage from the central city. The suburban populations required social services of all sorts: streets and highways, sewage systems, water systems, schools and so on. To build up their tax bases the suburbs created industrial parks and shopping centers. While the central cities had unused facilities they could not keep up, the suburbs were struggling with inadequate facilities. Urban ghetto areas were isolated from easy access to work opportunities. The government of major metropolitan areas was being fragmented into hundreds, sometimes even into thousands, of competing units.

It is difficult to discover a single aspect of metropolitan life that is not in deep trouble. The crisis of the cities is multidimensional.

### The Minority Crisis

The changing ratio of power and autonomy between the nation and its subcommunities manifest in the crisis of the cities and expressed in the ironic stereotype "the federal government gets the money, the city gets the problems," has been a major component in the changing form of minority problems, particularly those of Blacks, Chicanos and American Indians.

In the period of the rise of mass production, American industry concentrated in urban areas where it had access to raw materials, labor and markets. However, with the development of forms of power (particularly electric and diesel power) which permitted the dispersion of industry and forms of transportation (automotive) which freed industry from dependence on mass transportation facilities, many economies could be realized by dispersal. Automation and computerization increasingly released industry from dependence on masses of unskilled and semi-skilled laborers.

Meanwhile, the general forces that turned agriculture into an increasingly factory-like form and which pulled manpower into industrial centers also operated on minorities that had long retained a rural character: the Blacks, Chicanos and American Indians were also being drawn into metropolitan areas.

Originally, poor minorities drawn into the cities in response of American industrial needs had been able to mitigate their problems by forming ghetto communities. Ghetto communities were often able to develop protective institutions which eased the immediate pressures on poor minority group members. Ethnic businesses, insurance societies, burial societies, newspapers, historical societies and the like were able to provide members of ghetto communities with a wide variety of economic and professional experience to which they rarely had access to on the outside.

However, with the decreasing need of industry for unskilled labor and its removal to the suburbs, many work opportunities were lost to slum dwellers. The departure of middle and laboring class groups to the suburbs depopulated cushioning areas surrounding the slums, further weakening the city's tax base, encouraging still more departures of business and industry and leaving unused facilities which no longer paid for themselves. The deterioration of the mass transit facilities made it increasingly difficult for slum dwellers to commute to suburban relocated industries even when they still required unskilled or semiskilled labor. The ghetto community was less and less able to sustain a system of protective institutions and it ceased to be the lowest rung on the socio-economic ladder leading up and out of the slum. As ghettos turned into permanent dead ends periodic acts of violence erupted usually turning against ghetto institutions themselves. They usually left the ghetto permanently worsened.

The Civil Rights movement, the organization for national political action, became one of the few ways in which the new minorities could hope to improve their situation. Through protests, demonstrations, the pressing of strategic or symbolic cases and a variety of Civil Disobedience activities, the minority sought to obtain coverage in the mass media (particularly national television) and to win public support and favorable legislation. Once the basic techniques of the Civil Rights movement had been worked out for the Blacks, they became available to the Chicanos and American Indians.

## The Generation Crisis

In times of rapid social change the generations may find themselves in tension, not only on the basis of functionally different positions which are, nevertheless, organically related to one another by a shared body of suppositions, but also on the very bases of different, fundamental suppositions. Such a contrast in suppositions appears between the pre- and post-war generations of Americans. The decisive experiences of the pre-World War II generation were the Depression and the War. The post-war generation on the other hand, was oriented to the world on the basis of the suppositions of the affluent society.

The pre-war generation had passed the child labor legislation that has taken young people off the labor market and legitimized the labor unions which have since evolved from radical to establishment institutions. Compulsory education has kept the young in school for much longer periods in comparison with the older generation. Meanwhile, automation and computerization have eliminated the industrial need for masses of unskilled and semi-skilled labor. Young people are kept off the labor market for longer periods of time. The flexible entry of the young into the workaday world of the adults is thus delayed. Taken together with the democratization of the family this means, among other things, that their peer groups and the mass media have increased their influence over the young while parental influence has declined.

The generation gap has been widened because the entry of young people into the labor force is delayed and there are fewer occasions for young people to engage in a long apprenticeship; the adult worker gradually acquiring an array of adult skills and, incidentally, finding models of manhood among adults. More and more young people remain in the educational process for want of anything better to do. But education which is prolonged insulation from daily experience tends to be drained of significance. The young are inclined to turn their energy and imagination into control of an educational process they experience as alien.

The parental generation which, by contrast, looked on life from the standpoint of a generation that had been through the Depression and the War, had experienced prolonged, delayed gratification. The provision of material comfort and educational opportunity for their children had, under such circumstances, spiritual significance. Their children who had only known affluence found material comforts, which had never been in doubt, spiritually barren. Into this situation came the Vietnamese war.

The Vietnamese war was the liberal's own war, seriously getting underway in the Kennedy administration. The liberal economists of the Kennedy administration confidently assured Americans that they could have both guns and butter, the American economy was so powerful that it need not affect economic development at home. To the parental generation the Vietnamese war was interpreted in Cold War terms as an unavoidable necessity. While it was never popular, it was tolerated out of patriotic faith.

The actual burden of fighting the Vietnamese War fell on the young of the affluent generation. They were being asked to fight a war that was never popular. Initially, there were so many possibilities of exemptions, that upper class, professional and educated classes were largely escaping war service. This had the effect of intensifying discontent for the burden of war service was falling on Blacks and the Poor. As the war began to escalate and more and more young people from middle class and educated strata faced induction, the criticism of the war became more incisive.

One of the oldest lessons of politics was forgotten or ignored by American leaders: that it is almost impossible to fight an unpopular war in a democracy for long without corrupting the democracy. In an unpopular war the impulse to avoid war service is able to pass itself off as a higher form of morality. The draft dodger can pass himself off with the genuine conscientious objector, as a hero. Meanwhile, war heroism tends to be devalued and the volunteer for war service may come, in time, to view himself as a dupe. To treat the thousands upon thousands of young people who explored every conceivable avenue to avoid war service simply as cowards and draft dodgers, as many persons of the parental generation are inclined to do, is monstrously inappropriate. Without any question it often takes more courage to actively resist the war than simply to accept it and put in one's time, hoping for the best. The disruption to a young man's life by imprisonment or exile is often greater than would occur through war service. One could expect that the average war resister would experience a mixture of motives varying from fear to exaltation when he finally makes the tough decision to stand by his conscience despite its consequences. But this same emotional ambiguity would tend to haunt him during the course of his imprisonment and exile.

In any case, the Vietnamese war has been a major factor in the generation crisis for it has tended to be assimilated by the parental generation to the beliefs that sustained it during World War II while the modality of experience by both the Vietnamese veteran and the war resister have centered on a different register of suppositions.

## The Sex Crisis

As in the case of the generation crisis, the sex crisis was long in the making. Recent events have merely brought the problem to a new level of urgency. The institutional arrangements that gave sex its traditional meaning have been coming apart with the rise of the mass society.

In the course of the nineteenth century industrial revolution many household industries and occupations have been transferred to the school, the office, the hospital and the factory. In the long run, women have followed their former jobs as they moved outside the household. As women became independent, economic, agents the patriarchal family weakened. Meanwhile, the continuous erosion of local communities of all types, tore the family lose from the context of institutions which in traditional society had helped hold it in place. These changes accelerated in the twentieth century. With women's suffrage, the whole field of politics was opened to them. During World Wars I and II, the shortage of man-power permitted women to expand their economic opportunities outside the home and to exert pressure for equal pay for equal work. Wars also loosened *mores* tending to erase the double standard as was already apparent in the jazz age following World War I. Meanwhile, the welfare institutions of the thirties mitigated the disaster to the family of male abandonment and began to modify the stigma of illegitimacy. These developments in turn were a factor in the increase in the number of broken homes through abandonment and divorce.

One of the clearest indications of the accelerated change of sex mores after World War II was the new freedom of representation of a wide variety of sex phenomena in the mass media that only a short time before would have been treated as pornographic. As representations of sex became routine, the drive toward sensationalism quickly expanded to a variety of sexual abnormalities and representations in the mass media of rape, pederasty and homosexuality also quickly moved from the sphere of prohibited pornography to the status of routine entertainment.

The change in sexual mores could be seen in the greater ease of obtaining abortions, the decline of stigmatization because of adultery or pregnancy outside of marriage. The widespread usage of the "pill" and dissemination of the use of contraceptive devices of other sorts are further signs of the new attitudes of change. In addition, the new antibiotics took away some of the fear of venereal disease. All these developments permitted the translation of the new sex attitudes into action.

In a world marked by the rapid decay of the local community contexts that had sustained the traditional family system and marked by changing sex mores and a new permissiveness, the persistence of restrictions based on sex of special groups became intolerable. Women and homosexuals began to employ the techniques pioneered in the civil rights movement to remove sex-based obstacles to full social and economic status.

### The Economic Crisis

The Cold War perpetuated the war time economy into a peace time situation, facilitating the movement to hot war situations in the Korean and Vietnamese wars. For the first time in American history a peace time draft was sustained. Meanwhile the enormous costs of the new types of weapons systems, military and economic aid to allied and underdeveloped nations, and adventures in national egotism set off by Sputnik and leading to the enormously expensive, manned space program with the objective of placing men on the moon, displaced economic effort from internal domestic projects to politico-military ventures. As a result, while taxes grew continuously, the average citizen received less and less for his money.

Finally, rather than risk the public reaction that could be expected if the Vietnamese War were run on a pay-as-you-go basis, the American leaders resorted to deficit financing. This resulted in an intensification of inflationary pressures which had begun progressively to undermine the economic viability of all persons living on fixed incomes: the old, the retired, the pensioned. Maintaining wages and salaries on a parity with the rate of inflation was somewhat more possible for the worker and salaried employee, though these groups, too, tended gradually to fall behind.

The rate of unemployment has hovered between five and six percent. Moreover, if it were not for the numbers of men and women in educational institutions and the armed forces, the unemployment rate would easily be twice as high. Furthermore, the displacement of populations into institutions of higher learning, inevitably leads to excess B.A.'s, M.A.'s and Ph.D.'s that the job market cannot absorb. A shortage of workers simultaneously appears in the blue collar trades.

By ironic contrast, the economies of Japan and West Germany had become within the same period the most powerful in Europe and Asia respectively — testifying to the enormous advantage in the economic life of a nation if it is prevented from wasting its substance on relatively wasteful, military projects. Japan, for example, has been able to import oil and scrap metal from the United States and sell high grade steel back to the United States cheaper than it can be made at home. Japanese exports to the United States have been a major factor in America's unfavorable balance of trade, which in 1972 was the worst in American history.

### The Crisis of Confidence

In all societies, collective action presupposes that the decisions of some men become binding on others. If all men's ideas and opinions had equal weight one could expect as many plans of action as there are people in the group. In complex societies the decision process assumes the form of a pyramid of power in which a relatively few men at the top influence the many at the bottom. In times of war when the requirements for collective action become urgent, the pyramid of power narrows with a relatively few (a power elite) monopolizing power. In war time the position of the power elite is further enhanced by the restriction on the flow of information on crucial affairs of the state to the masses.

After a war the normal tendency in a democratic society is for the pyramid of power to broaden and, perhaps, develop a series of subpeaks for a greater diffusion of information about the affairs of the nation to the nation as a whole. In the United States this has meant that the war time powers of the presidency have been in part modified by the increase in power of Congress in peace time.

However, the Cold War after World War II perpetuated the monopoly of power by the elite and prolonged the policy of restricting information not only to the mass of Americans but even to Congress. The Post War period has been marked, not by a return of power to Congress, but by a continuous increase in the power of the American presidency as against all other branches of government. The American government in times of war is actually an elected dictatorship. The secrecy that surrounds the actions of the president and the power elite in directing the affairs of the nation in war time means that the public does not participate in decisions, it is managed from the top. The Cold War continued this process, tending to convert the management of opinion from the top into a permanent feature of American life. Among the primary implements of opinion management has been the hypothetical threat of international communism.

McCarthyism illustrates the operation of the official mythology concerning the threat of communism in leveling of all internal forms of dissent. The ranks of many government agencies were purged of independent minded persons. Moreover, individuals in a wide spectrum of professional groups from Hollywood, the Churches, the Universities and the ranks of a variety of professional organizations were harassed. Only when McCarthy's attack was directed toward the Army and the Republican Party were the means quickly found to turn off his attacks. Not the least of the effects of McCarthy's inquisitorial procedures was the consolidation of the power of the elite in peace time. Meanwhile, the same threat of international communism justified the preservation of an aura of secrecy around major military and political decisions while the Pentagon's enormous budgets were legitimized.

However, there are some untoward consequences of a system resting on opinion management so long as the nation pretends to be a democracy. When the official mythology is applied, as in the case of McCarthyism, to silence all forms of dissent, public policy ceases to be toughened by the requirement of running the gauntlet of critical review. Whenever sudden changes of policy are necessary, and sooner or later they always are, there may not be time to "prepare" the public at large for the change. As a result, there have been repeated occasions when the public (including the press) and Congress have been told one thing, when later events revealed that the facts were quite otherwise. Or again, the public discovers repeatedly that information was withheld from it though it was well known by the enemy.

The term "credibility gaps" has come to designate repeated revelations of the hiatus between what the public was told and the realities of the situation. Unfortunately, there has been a tendency to visualize "credibility gaps" as only occasional phenomena and as the product of the mendacity of particular individuals. However, "credibility gaps" are a structural aspect of the situation in which opinion of the masses is managed from the top.

National elections, under the circumstances where much of the information essential for the judgment of policy is withheld from the public, can hardly represent situations in which a serious review of candidates and programs is possible in the light of the relevant facts. National elections instead, represent the variably adept shuffling of public myths. This was evident in the 1972 presidential election.

The 1972 presidential election in the United States will probably be continued to be discussed long after the actual event took place. Already columnists, commentators and the candidates themselves are second-guessing as to what led to the "startling" result of an overwhelming victory for President Nixon accompanied by what could only be viewed as a sharp defeat for his party due to the lack of a "drag" effect of the presidential landslide. Furthermore, Nixon hardly campaigned in person at all and Senator George McGovern campaigned on a platform of shutting down the unpopular Vietnamese war. There seems little doubt that the relation of the two candidates to the myths and realities surrounding the war were decisive.

The average American is hard working, sober, civic minded and patriotically proud of his country which he loves to think of as the most powerful, prosperous and democratic in the world. Senator McGovern's message to the average American was that the entire Vietnamese war had been in vain: that the more than 100 billion dollars that had been spent on it, that the more than fifty thousand Americans who had been killed, that the more than 1,000 Americans in prisoner of war camps, that the several million North and South Vietnamese that had been killed or wounded — that all these things had been mistaken. By contrast, President Richard Nixon who hardly campaigned at all simply reasserted that he was about to bring "peace with honor." Just prior to the election Henry Kissinger went on national television to assert that "peace was at hand." In short, the American public was being offered by the two candidates the choice between a possible horrifying truth and a face saving myth. The startling event under the circumstances is not that Nixon was reelected by a landslide, but that George McGovern still received around four out of every ten votes cast. But at some level in their responses many Americans had acted as if they realized that in the presidential elections they had voted on the basis of a face saving myth and on the rest of the national and local ticket they voted according to their consciences and their interests.

In general, Nixon managed his credibility gaps with more public relations finesse than President Johnson. At times he has technically avoided credibility gap problems by declining to give any explanation at all. At other times he has employed abrupt changes of strategy to upset mounting dissent before it has an opportunity to gain momentum. Meanwhile the press has been brought under repeated attack and policies have been sponsored which members of the press feel seriously weaken the First Amendment.

These processes and developments have been components of an increasing disillusionment of Americans with their government. In the opinion of some observers they add up to a crisis of confidence. This crisis of confidence, in turn, seems to be a major factor in the widespread sense of alienation and identity crisis of many Americans. In addition to the crisis of confidence, the sense of alienation has been anchored in the decreasing control of individuals over their life fates, frustration as taxes rise ever higher while the quality of public service declines, a sense of desperation when inflation outruns income, the pressure for higher and higher academic degrees while the horizon of ultimate job opportunities retreats. These stresses are accompanied by an erosion of civil rights in the name of law and order even while crime and violence increase and continued deterioration of the situation of minorities.

### Extracommunity Pressures on Nationalism

The three and three-fourths billion people in the world today (representing about half the people who have ever lived) are pursuing national strategies of collective life. From the standpoint of a theory of social change which locates its primary problems in the type of community formation characterizing an epoch, the trends within and between nations are of central concern. In the present essay, the attempt has not been made to work up new evidence, but to review the evidence familiar to everyone and to estimate in very general terms, the internal and external trends in the nations. Internally, particularly in the older nations, the general evidence suggests that the breakdown of traditional community forms which was required to make the nation possible has reached such an advanced stage that they are entering the stage of collectivization that students have described as mass society and totalitarianism. Externally, we seem to be in the sunset period of nationalism and while more new nations have been in process of formation since World War II than at any previous period, the nation has been decaying as a viable community form in the area of its origin.

However, there are two additional problems of importance to the student of social change, which have not yet been examined: the relation of the contemporary nation to its biological bases and to the physical world. A community, including the national community, is a strategy of life pursued by a plurality. One of the relatively unexplored problems in the theory of social change is the relation between community types and their demographic bases. A peculiarity of the national community is that it is adapted to relatively large populations. But, even within the nation, increase of populations will have to be handled in a variety of ways if it is not to destroy the traditional institutional system. The nation may have to expand at the expense of neighboring nations; it may have to transform its economic and social system; it may have export excess populations; it may have to exercise internal control over its population size.

The attempts to expand into other areas or to transform its economic and social system may lead to wars for living space and raw materials. The third possibility of emigration may be limited by the willingness of other areas to receive immigrants. Efforts to control the size of its population may lead to internal transformations of institutions which themselves modify or destroy the traditional way of life. If all such expedients are ineffective, the increase of population may force sharing, dividing the national product up into smaller and smaller portions with the prospect of reaching, for major segments of the population, that bare subsistence level which Malthus foresaw.

Traditionally, the United States has met population pressure by increased productivity and still at present with around 6½ percent of the world's population the United States consumes around 40 percent of the world's resources. At the opposite extreme, some of the underdeveloped nations have subdivided their production to a starvation level such that at least one third of the people of the world at present are starving. In some nations of the world, millions of people are born, live and die on the streets like animals. Among the relatively unnoted problems of American society is a vast illegal flow of aliens from both developed and underdeveloped nations into the United States despite a 5 percent unemployment rate and a welfare system in acknowledged crisis.

Increasing attention has been drawn to instabilities in the relation of the nation state to its ecological basis. Contemporary scientific technologies have permitted an unprecedented manipulation of the physical environment. As a result the relation between human pluralities and the physical environment is out of balance. In a comparatively short time, fossil fuels will be exhausted. Natural resources have been plundered and usable supplies of many metals will virtually be exhausted by the end of the century. The soil resources of the world are being shamefully wasted; water resources are being abused to a point where even the oceans are threatened.

Some students have estimated that if the relation between the human population of the world and the physical environment is to be stabilized in order to make continuing human social life possible for an indefinite future in something like its present form, the world population would have to be reduced to around one fifth of its present size. Demographic and environmental forces are thought by many to be on a collision course that may well lead to world wide disasters before the end of the twentieth century.

If it is not possible for nation states to reach some sort of condition of stability with respect to demographic and ecological pressures relatively soon, it is quite possible that this form of human community will disappear to be replaced by some more efficient community form. The age of mankind may otherwise soon come to a rather abrupt end.

## BIBLIOGRAPHY

1. Sheehan, Neil, and E. W. Kenworthy, eds., *Pentagon Papers*, New York: Quadrangle, 1971.

# 34

*Walter Hirsch*

# Knowledge, Power, and Social

# Change: The Role of American

# Scientists

The fact that science and technology constitute one of the major variables in contemporary social change needs no scholarly documentation. Our present inquiry will focus on the degree to which American scientists and engineers are aware of their actual or potential role as "agents" of social change, and on their ability to exercise significant decision-making power, vis-à-vis other agents.[1] In what ways do scientists[2] in a democratic society play a part in determining the nature of their "product," i.e., knowledge, and the uses to which it is put?

The proposition that a "democratic," as distinguished from a "totalitarian," social structure is the most conducive for the optimal development of scientific institutions is no longer as self-evident as it appeared less than a generation ago (6, pp. 105–7; 19). The Comtean dream (or nightmare) of a scientific elite running a society is not seriously entertained by any significant segment of the scientific community, even in

[1] We shall by-pass the "great man" vs. "cultural forces" controversy whose ancient flames have been lately fanned by Leslie A. White (50) and others.

[2] For the sake of brevity the term "scientist" will include engineers, unless the differences between the two categories need to be pointed up. For some of these, cf. Kornhauser (24, pp. 149–154). For that matter many generalizations about scientists will be shown to be of little utility in the discussion to follow.

the watered-down form of technocracy. There seems little evidence to support Veblen's post-World War I prophecy that the engineers, having been "thrown into the position of responsible directors of the industrial system," became organized for the "common purpose" of eliminating the "lag, leak and friction" pervading industry and are now the "arbiters of the community's material welfare" (46, p. 440). During the period following World War II, when the prestige of the physical scientists, and even of the "pure" scientist, at least in the field of nuclear physics, had risen to unprecedented heights, they were loath to translate their newly-found influence into the kind of power which some of their predecessors had vainly sought (42).

The reasons and feelings associated with this disinclination range from a "realistic" interpretation of the nature of the power structure through various assessments of the valid role of the scientist to a feeling of resignation. A poignant example of the latter is contained in a letter which Albert Einstein sent to a group of Italian scientists:

> The man of science, as we can observe with our own eyes, suffers a truly tragic fate — striving in great sincerity for clarity and inner independence, he himself through his sheer superhuman effort has fashioned the tools which are being used to make him a slave and to destroy him also from within. He cannot escape being muzzled by those who have political power in their hands (35, p. 144).

But others, especially among those who were directly involved in the creation of the atom bomb, were and are compelled to take their stand in the political arena, in part because, as Robert Oppenheimer put it, "in some sort of crude sense which no vulgarity, no humor, no overstatement can quite extinguish, the physicists have known sin, and this is a knowledge which they cannot lose" (32, p. 69). And to the extent that we can speak of prevailing opinion among scientists, the new sense of responsibility and urgency in their ranks is expressed by the Report of the Committee on Human Welfare of the American Association for the Advancement of Science:

> With each advance in our knowledge of nature, science adds to the already immense power the social order exerts on human welfare. With each increment in power, the problem of directing its use toward beneficial ends becomes more complex, the consequences of failure more disastrous, and the time for decision more brief. . . . At a time when decisive economic, political, and social processes have become profoundly dependent on science, the discipline has failed to attain its appropriate place in the management of public affairs. . . . Recent events have lent substance to the conviction of our Committee . . . and we believe to that of scientists generally — that scientists have a serious and immediate responsibility to help mediate the effects of scientific progress on human welfare (4, p. 68, p. 71).

The application of science to military uses and the impact of new devices on national and international politics is one area to which we will devote our attention. Another major area, less dramatic in its implications, but probably more salient for the "average" scientist, concerns the disposition of his product by industry and the scientist's position in the marketplace. It is, of course, evident that these areas are intimately related, but for our purposes we will treat them separately. Later on we will consider the role of other institutional settings for scientific activity, notably the traditional one of the university, which is being increasingly drawn into the orbit of the military-industrial complex.[3]

## The Scientist in Industry

The industrial scientist's power position stems from his specialized knowledge and abilities. To what extent can he use his power to determine the goals to which his knowledge should be directed and the subsequent use to which it should be put? Even if he is engaged in "basic" research and has no personal concern about the "utility" of his product, he must find a sponsor willing and able to undertake the economic risks involved with the understanding that the research will eventually "pay off." He faces the dilemma which, according to Merton, is typical for intellectuals generally:

> If the intellectual is to play an effective role in putting his knowledge to work, it is increasingly necessary that he become a part of the bureaucratic power structure. This, however, often requires him to abdicate his privilege of exploring policy-possibilities which he regards as significant. If, on the other hand, he remains unattached in order to preserve full opportunity of choice, he characteristically has neither the resources to carry through his investigations on an appropriate scale nor any strong likelihood of having his findings accepted by policy-makers as a basis for action (27, p. 217).

It should be understood that the dilemma is more acute for some than for others. Not every scientist feels the need to exercise "policy-making" powers or the desire to have full control over the economic exploitation of his product. Thus one prominent aeronautical engineer and inventor, in discussing the putative powers afforded the scientist by the patent system, states that:

> . . . patent activities involve innovation, protection, and exploitation. Only exploitation has the possibility of directly producing returns of any considerable magnitude, and requires people who have the capabilities of the

[3] For an excellent treatment of the problems arising from this relationship, see Kidd (21). Our main reason for focusing on the scientists' position in the political and industrial areas is that it is easier to ascertain the decision-making powers there. As one sociologist has put it, "ideas are influential; they may alter the process of history, but for the sake of logical and sociological clarity it is preferable to deny them the attribute of power" (9, p. 732).

entrepreneur, the promoter, the businessman, the manager. . . . These people are not necessarily or even very often, the innovators or the patent negotiators who started a chain of events that culminate in successful exploitations.

. . . I have come to see clearly that rewards in our society go not to the people who make inventions but to the people who are able to exploit the knowledge and patent rights that have been created (11).

Rather than resenting this state of affairs, this scientist concludes that he is not bothered by it, since he's not interested in money but the "intellectual excitement" of research as is every "typical scientist or inventor." There exist few systematic data which would allow us to estimate the proportion of scientists who are typical in this sense,[4] but we do know that most people are not motivated by a single, overriding need, but rather by a hierarchy of needs which is rather fluid. In our society it seems that in many ways values are increasingly becoming "monetized"; thus the recognition of *professional* status depends to a great extent on the symbolic function of salary levels. Even though "money isn't everything," neither is the satisfaction of intellectual curiosity, and even if he's not "interested in money" the scientist is under pressure to maximize his income if he wants to exploit his status as a man of knowledge vis-à-vis other functionaries. One effect has been the success which industry has had in luring scientists away from academic and government employ, even though the economic incentive in many cases has turned out to be inadequate.

Let us consider further implications of the potential dilemma. As we have said, the scientist's power position entails two aspects: the ability to determine his research goals and working conditions; and the ability to dispose of his product in the market. To the extent that the conventional distinction between "pure" and "applied" research has any validity,[5] it is the "basic" scientist who should be most concerned with the former aspect. He typically works in a large firm, the kind which can afford the luxury of hiring him and of occasionally following up his hunches in the hope that they will pay off (29; 15). The available evidence leads to the conclusion that even in these firms economic considerations take priority, and that "typically, industrial scientists must be prepared to drop, or at least interrupt, projects in which they are professionally interested" (24, p. 69). The "applied" scientist has, of course, even less opportunity (and probably, it must be said, less motivation) for exercising his role as a searcher for knowledge. A study of six major industrial firms gives an indication of the degree and range of participation research scientists report having in major decisions affecting their work assignment:

[4] Some relevant empirical studies are Stein (45), who found that for his sample "scientific" incentives were lower than he had anticipated, and "administrative and monetary" rewards were higher; Opinion Research Corporation (31); West (48).

[5] The validity of the distinction is becoming increasingly questionable Cf. Kidd (22); Wolfle (49, pp. 210 ff.).

TABLE 1

|  | Often Participate | Sometimes | Rarely or Never | Total | N |
|---|---|---|---|---|---|
| All scientists and engineers | 41% | 32% | 27% | 100% | 622 |
| Research administrators | 56% | 28% | 15% | 100% | 90 |
| With Ph.D. degree | 52% | 26% | 22% | 100% | 186 |
| With M.S. or B.S. | 36% | 36% | 28% | 100% | 389 |
| Company with highest participation | 59% | 26% | 15% | 100% | 102 |
| Company with lowest participation | 28% | 37% | 35% | 100% | 102 |

Source: Kornhauser (24, p. 63).

The data indicate that holders of Ph.D. degrees have greater decision-making power than the rest, but not as much as the research administrators. The latter category represents a function typically found in large firms engaged in research and development ("R & D") and constitutes one of the major methods for integrating research into the organization. Does the research administrator operate mainly as a scientist or is he essentially an agent of management? Typically he would seem to be the latter, both in terms of the requirements of the job and of the capacities and motivations of the incumbents. "The dominant pattern in industry is not to select research administrators on the basis of scientific competence" (5, p. 31), and in one presumably typical company, "interviews show . . . that organizational incentives are more important for research supervisors and professional incentives for researchers" (24, p. 144). The recently created role of the research administrator tends to take the edge off the dilemma for those scientists whose commitments are to the organization rather than to their profession, but at the same time it tends to weaken the decision-making power of the "pure" scientist, since his communication to management is filtered through a "gatekeeper" whose orientations tend to make him take the side of management.

What other institutional devices exist by which the scientist can increase his power? According to the proponents of the patent system, one of its major functions is to provide for a continuous flow of scientific innovation by offering the incentives of economic rewards and public recognition to the innovator. Whether or not the patent system has been or is at present functional in these terms is a subject of considerable controversy.[6] Our specific concern is with the question of how patents can be utilized by the industral scientist to control the use of his product.

Management policies regarding patentable inventions vary. The em-

[6] For a review of the relevant literature and a test of the hypothesis which concludes that it cannot be accepted or rejected, see Machlup (26).

ployer may or may not pay bonuses, royalties, or other benefits to the inventor. Generally, "one condition of employment for engineers in most industrial plants . . . is the signing of a patent agreement in which the engineer guarantees to sign and execute all documents necessary to assign the employer the right to benefit from his invention" (47, p. 91). In the event that the inventor should retain his patent, "it seems safe to say that the average established corporation with its productive, financial, and marketing resources will be in a better position to make use of a patent . . . than will a private individual who lacks these resources" (10, p. 361). The majority of patents are held by large corporations (26), precisely those whose resources allow the greatest scope for the pure scientist in industry. Again we see another aspect of the dilemma: there is no positive relation between the scientist's chance to maximize his professional role and his ability to dispose freely of his product.

Undoubtedly, the fissioning process in such rapidly growing industries as electronics is indicative of some scientists' desire to participate more fully in the economic exploitation of their knowledge by combining the scientific and entrepreneurial functions. Non-economic motives are also involved, particularly the freedom from interference by non-professionals, for "in study after study, scientists and engineers in industry indicate that they think their special competence is not adequately utilized" (24, p. 139), and as Merton has demonstrated, the scientist has a legitimate need for recognition (28). The degree to which the scientist-entrepreneur is able to maximize both these roles and the extent and possible resolution of role conflicts are areas for intensive investigation.

One of the most important of the scientist's non-economic needs is that of communication with other scientists — a need frustrated by the firm's desire to maintain its competitive advantage, and, particularly since World War II, by the legislation affecting national security. The role of the latter has been sufficiently discussed in a variety of sources[7] for us to forego further documentation, especially since the differentiation between "military" and other aspects of research is becoming increasingly blurred. However, some general comments on problems involved in the freedom to communicate and some specific data recently made public warrant presentation here.

Even though most managers would probably agree with Charles F. Kettering's dictum that locking the laboratory door excludes more knowledge than it keeps in, the open-door policy is not generally maintained. Reliable data on industrial espionage are obviously unobtainable[8] but perhaps the most prevalent and efficient manner of conducting this operation consists simply of hiring one's competitor's "brains" away. Thus even if a process is patented the firm owning the patent may have no control

[7] For an incisive analysis of the causes and consequences of this phenomenon, see Shils (41).

[8] For one survey of prevailing attitudes and practices, see Furash (16).

over the knowledge possessed by the inventor. According to one legal authority, "the employee who departs with a trade secret is the most exasperating of all competitors," and in the United States there appear to be no effective sanctions for controlling this traffic in ideas (23). Here then is one possible way in which the scientist can dispose of his own knowledge (and incidentally that of his peers also) by selling it to the highest bidder. But again, unless he becomes an entrepreneur himself his freedom to dispose of the use of the product is out of his hands.

What of the scientist who has no such commercial ambitions but is simply motivated by the "natural" need to let others know what he has been doing? Very likely he will find that his professional papers cannot be published or will be censored before publication. A recent survey of company policies regarding publication of *basic* research findings shows the following:

**TABLE 2**

| RESEARCH FINDINGS PUBLISHED | NO. OF COMPANIES | PER CENT |
|---|---|---|
| Substantially all | 24 | 14 |
| Most | 46 | 26 |
| Some | 77 | 45 |
| None | 27 | 16 |
| Total | 174 | 100 |

Source: National Science Foundation (30, p. 7).

Permission to write a paper for publication and preparation for its release in final form may require approval and revision by numerous functionaries, including representatives of the governmental or other agency supporting the research under contract, R and D directors, patent attorneys, and officials from public relations, sales and marketing, and security departments of the firm (30, pp. 11 ff.). In some instances as many as 12 officials will have had a hand in the publication process. No comparable data are available for publications of *applied* research, but there is no reason to believe that greater freedom of communication exists in that area.

Finally let us consider the role of unions and professional organizations as a source of power for the scientist. Like other professionals, scientists have been reluctant to participate in the kind of collective organization and bargaining typical of "ordinary" labor unions and generally have remained aloof from formal affiliation with the labor movement (47, p. 37). At the same time, they have been unable to use the sanctions employed by other professions, such as law and medicine, because of the nature of their industrial employment. According to one observer the "popular model of the professional . . . has to be distorted almost out of recognition if it is to include the members of the engineering department of a large firm. . . . In fact, the professional model is at such variance with the state of affairs in industry that a discussion of professionalism would seem irrelevant . . . if it were not for the fact that a large proportion of scientists and engineers in industry think of themselves as professionals" (40, p. 308). Nevertheless, the exigencies of industrial employment have produced a number of organizational attempts to maximize both economic and professional power on a collective basis, resulting in such federations as the Engineers and Scientists of America (ESA) and the Engineers and Scientists Guild (ESG).[9] How successful have they been in meeting their goals?

In a recent study exploring this problem Walton states that historically "the growth and rationalization of the engineering functions have deprived the individual professional of most of his influence over the many aspects of the employment relationship. He lost a share in the control of the job: the nature of the work assignment, the methods and pace of the specific task assignment, working conditions, pay and status" (47, p. 371). After having surveyed the impact of unions on management policy Walton concludes that "engineers need an independent mechanism for being heard that is influential at the level where decisions are made affecting the multiform terms of engineering employment" (47, p. 384). The results of his study indicate that this "independent mechanism" is available for only a small proportion of professionals in industry, and that its impact on managerial decisions is generally weak. The professional unions occupy a marginal position: while reluctant to engage in strikes and to enlist the help of other labor unions, and while far from engaging in "featherbedding" practices they press for full utilization of their members' capacities, they nevertheless incur management's suspicion and enmity because it is felt that they ought to identify fully with management (47, p. 353, p. 357, pp. 368–369). Recruitment of new members is inhibited by managerial identification among young professionals — college graduates and placement officials are suspicious of firms which are unionized (47, p. 244). The "company union" pattern is pervasive, since national technical and professional societies typically "are led by men who are the employers of those whom they represent" (24, p. 93).

In summary, it seems clear that in order to maximize their *professional* power potential, scientists must enter the managerial ranks; once having done so, their professional goals tend to become subordinate to or transmogrified into organizational ones. The possible impact of this process on the role of scientists as "agents" of social change is elucidated by one scientist:

[9] For a list of these organizations, see "Compilation of Unions Representing Engineering and Technical Employees," Walton (47, pp. 388 ff.).

Today an unusually able scientist, figuratively speaking, is on the scrap-heap sometimes at the age of thirty or forty; he becomes director of research of a large unit, or head of a large department, or dean, or an important committeeman oscillating between his home town and Washington, D.C. Not that he ceases to be useful, but he is doing work that many others could do equally well or better; and he has to abandon work, usually more important in the long run, in which there is no substitute for him. . . . If an outstanding scientist succumbs to the higher salary and prestige of an "executive" position, his opportunities for high-level work do not increase with the number of those under him; they probably diminish very sharply (34, pp. 237–238).

## Scientists and Political Power

One knowledgeable observer recently made the assertion that "the plain fact is that science has become the major Establishment in the American political system: the only set of institutions for which tax funds are appropriated almost on faith . . ." (36, pp. 1099–1100). Apart from the questions of whether the appropriation of tax funds is a valid index for the power of an Establishment, and of whether faith does in fact precipitate the opening of the public purse for "science," our main concern will be with the degree to which the scientist *qua* scientist is able to dispose of his knowledge so as to influence decisions in the realm of politics.

Our discussion will in the main center on the circumstances attending the discovery and early utilization of atomic fission, since the historical record is becoming reasonably accessible.[10] (On the other hand, much of the current interaction of scientific and political variables is hidden in a miasma of classified information, e.g., the incidence of radioactive fallout, not to speak of problems of arms control and military strategy.)

The basic thesis which we shall attempt to elucidate and document subsequently runs as follows: scientists provided their professional knowledge and personal motivation to make atomic fission possible, but the use or disposition of their discovery did not remain in their hands. Rather than being decision-makers they were utilized to support decisions made by others while they (the scientists) may have been under the impression that the decision was theirs. In technical terms, they were co-opted by others who had the requisite power:[11] much of the glory —

[10] The most complete, and hopefully most objective source available at this time is Hewlett and Anderson, *The New World*. Whatever biases may inhere in the fact that this is the first volume of the official history of the Atomic Energy Commission is counterbalanced by the standing of the authors as professional historians and by their use of much hitherto classified information.

[11] "Co-optation is the process of absorbing new elements into the leadership of the policy-making structure of an organization as a means of averting threats to its stability or existence. . . . One means of winning consent is to co-opt elements . . . which in some way reflect the sentiment, or possess the confidence of the relevant public or mass" (39, p. 34).

and for some the "knowledge of sin" of which Oppenheimer speaks —
remained for the scientists.[12]

Certain historical facts are not in dispute here — the exciting story of
the realization that the atom could be split and that an atomic weapon
could be constructed, and the successful enlistment by Szilard and other
physicists of the prestige of Einstein and of the persuasive powers of
the banker Alexander Sachs to convince President Roosevelt that he
should set aside some funds to follow up the scientists' hunches. But
what has often been overlooked is that the establishment and successful
operation of the Manhattan Project required the enlistment and direction of forces which went far beyond the powers of the scientists. In the
words of Hewlett and Anderson "it had taken the exigencies of war and
all of [Secretary of War] Stimson's personal force and prestige to keep
funds flowing to the Manhattan gamble" (18, p. 346). On the other hand,
for those who believe that the decision to drop the atom bomb without
previous warning on Hiroshima was imposed by bloodthirsty warlords
on peace-loving scientists, the actual events may be disturbing.

In order to explore the future military and other uses of atomic energy
President Truman had appointed an Interim Committee, chaired by Stimson and having as members three scientists (Bush, Conant, and Karl
Compton), the Under Secretary of the Navy, the Assistant Secretary of
State, and Truman's personal representative (James F. Byrnes). In
order to help this Committee in its deliberations, Stimson set up a Scientific Advisory Panel, consisting of Arthur Compton, Lawrence, Oppenheimer, and Fermi — all of whom had been intimately involved in the
atom bomb project. Conant had asked for the establishment of this advisory panel since "the government needed full support from the scientific community. There should be no public bickering among experts"
(18, p. 345). An explicit statement of the functions of co-optation! When
Stimson met with this group the question of the best military use of the
atom bomb, about to be completed, was brought up. When it was suggested that a harmless demonstration of the bomb's destructive power
should be considered, "Oppenheimer could think of no demonstration
sufficiently spectacular to convince the Japanese that further resistance
was futile. . . . Besides, would the bomb cause any greater loss of life
than the fire raids that had burned out Tokyo?" Finally, "Conant suggested and Stimson agreed that the most desirable target would be a
vital war plant employing a large number of workers and closely surrounded by workers' houses" (18, p. 358). This decision was, of course,
implemented, after a number of desirable targets had been chosen from

---

[12] The glory had to be shared with engineers, the military, and businessmen. Thus
in the 1947 Congressional hearings on the creation of the Atomic Energy Commission,
Senator McKellar of Tennessee went on record that General Groves had "discovered
the secret of atomic fission" (Dupré and Lakoff, 13, p. 138).

which Kyoto was specifically excluded because of its significance as a religious center.

The scientist's role in this decision is cast in an ironic light in view of Stimson's feeling that "[General] Marshall and he had convinced the scientists that they were thinking like statesmen, not mere soldiers anxious to win the war at any cost" (18, p. 359). This conviction was not shared by other members of the "scientific community," notably the Chicago group spearheaded by James Franck and Leo Szilard, who were concerned about the implications of the military use of the atom. Their attempts to influence the Scientific Panel and President Truman directly were in vain.[13]

Our aim is not to find scapegoats for the unleashing of the destructive powers of the atom. Rather, we wish to pose the question whether the members of the Scientific Panel were chosen because it was felt that their views would most likely be in accord with those of the military and political leaders, while the potential critics were left "outside." We have no direct evidence that this involved Machiavellian skullduggery on the part of Stimson and his colleagues, but in the context of the available data the hypothesis of co-optation is inescapable. To be sure, the agitation among the Chicago scientists caused sincere concern to their official representatives. Compton had asked that the scientists at the Metallurgical Laboratory of the University of Chicago be polled on the use of the atom bomb, and the results showed a considerable range of opinion. In forwarding them to Washington, Compton stated that "his own sentiment was with the 46 per cent that leaned toward a military demonstration," to be followed by "a renewed opportunity to surrender before full use of the weapons." But "nothing could have seemed more irrelevant to Stimson . . . than further exposition of scientific opinion. Scientists had been given an opportunity to express themselves, and the current arguments added nothing to what had already been said. The responsible authorities had considered how best to use the bomb and had reached a decision" (18, pp. 399–400).

The next episode to be investigated concerns the future functions and control of the Atomic Energy Commission (AEC). One of the major issues revolved around the role to be played by the military authorities in directing its policies and operations. After the surrender of Japan the feeling became widespread among many scientists that now, having completed their job for the war effort, their opinions were no longer in demand. In fact, the first version of the relevant legislation (the so-called Royall-Marbury bill) had been drafted by two War Department lawyers without consultation with the established scientific authorities, and scientists were not to see a draft of the bill before its introduction in Congress (18, pp. 421–422). In its later version, as the May-Johnson

---

[13] For a detailed account of the entire episode, see Smith (43).

bill, the matter became subject to long Congressional and public controversy during which occurred the establishment of a vigorous scientific lobby in Washington, and organization of the Federation of American Scientists with its medium, the *Bulletin of the Atomic Scientists.*

There is no doubt that the scientists engaged in lobbying and airing their concern over military control of the AEC were using their newly acquired prestige with considerable effect, thus helping in the eventual defeat of the May-Johnson bill. It is of interest that the members of the Scientific Panel had *supported* the bill when it came up for hearings, thereby further deepening the rift between themselves and the scientists who up to now had no direct access to the political decision-makers. But now the latter group of scientists suddenly found new allies — men like Senators Vandenberg and McMahon who wished to reduce the power of the military, and members of the executive branch, including the President, who became aware that their powers and prerogatives were severely limited by the proposed legislation. "A new alliance of scientists and senators had joined the issue" (18, p. 445). Could the May-Johnson bill have been defeated without help from the "scientific community"? The answer appears to be a "yes" rather than a "no," in view of the deep split within the "community." On the other hand, it is most unlikely that the scientific opponents of military control could have gotten very far without powerful allies in Congress and the administration, who had their own good reasons for wanting to establish civilian control. Once more the co-optation process was in operation, though a new group of scientists was now "on tap," if not "on top."

Our analysis could be further extended to survey problems of international control, the decision to produce the hydrogen bomb, and the like. It is our impression that the pattern is essentially the same as we have described it. Granted that "all but one of the major departures in American foreign policy toward nuclear weapons were initially conceived by scientists: the Baruch plan, the hydrogen bomb, the development of tactical nuclear weapons, the ballistics missile, and a nuclear test ban. Only the doctrine of massive retaliation originated elsewhere" (17, p. 37). But — "the mood of the nation lent support to the group of scientists [favoring a strategy of mass retaliation]. The attitude within the government invited advice from that group and excluded the others" (13, p. 123). Many of the latter lost their standing as "wise men" and in the case of Oppenheimer were even branded renegades and traitors — an ironic and tragic fate for one of the chief architects of the atom bomb.

According to Gilpin, who has made a thorough study of the role of scientists in nuclear weapons policy, "failure to maximize the potential benefits of the scientists' entry into political life has been both the cause and the effect of a lack of coherent and realistic American policy toward nuclear weapons" (17, p. 38). He concludes that "scientists must be utilized in a more realistic manner." But how can this be done in view of Gilpin's finding that "it was the assumptions of a political character and not simply technical judgment that divided the scientists over the hydrogen bomb" and several other issues? He advances a number of possible solutions, including better education of scientists in political matters and of politicians in scientific ones, and "integrated" studies involving various types of expertise (17, pp. 324 ff.). Similarly, C. P. Snow has called for a bridging of the existing gap between scientific and political know-how (44), but his own historical example (the Lindeman-Tizard controversy over the employment of the best weapons and strategy during World War II) does little to convince one that scientific expertise will carry the day in the arena of political decisions where a Churchill represents *vox Dei.*

In what ways then can scientists bring their special knowledge to bear upon issues requiring objectivity but which are entangled in "assumptions of a political character"? The American Association for the Advancement of Science, the organization most representative of the "scientific community," at least in terms of the range and extent of its membership, has charged its Committee on Human Welfare with answering this question. The Committee split the issues into two major categories: (1) Those where scientists have particular, esoteric interests and knowledge, namely, those relating to the development of science itself, such as legislation affecting the National Science Foundation or the establishment of a Cabinet post for science and technology; and (2) those issues of broader impact where the scientist figures essentially as the "informed citizen" on a par with other groups, as in the case of nuclear weapons policy (4). Assuming for the moment the possibility of drawing a line between these two categories, we are left with the question of how scientists are to become members of the "power elite."

One political scientist has some pertinent observations in this context, apropos the first of the categories we mentioned, but even more so for the second. He points out that "a policy with which the scientists are to be influentially identified requires the scientists to have leaders who can act as their representatives in that bargaining with public officials and other groups which accompanies the policy-making process" (37, p. 859). His historical survey shows that in the past the spokesmen of "science" have often been self-nominated or in many instances, as in the case of "advisory committees," the co-optation process has been the rule. At any rate it is not realistic to refer to the "scientific community" in view of the "pluralistic, fragmented and internally competitive attributes" which scientists share with other groups. If it should be possible to set up reasonably democratic methods of representation for scientists it becomes plain that more than ever before "the leaders of the scientists are perforce politicians" (37, p. 863). This means that, in order to be effective, they must enter alliances with other power groups and must be in a position to enforce sanctions. The choices involved will revolutionize the traditional status of the scientist, whether conceived in terms of the simple technician or of the sage hovering above the fields where "ignorant armies clash by night."

## Knowledge, Power, and Social Entanglement

Fifteen years ago, Harold Lasswell characterized physical scientists as being "in a state of social entanglement without comprehension" (25, p. 141). It seems safe to state that the increase of "comprehension" has been substantially smaller than that of "entanglement" during the intervening years. However, the problems of "value-free" science, which had been mainly the concern of social scientists in relatively recent times, are increasingly coming to the forefront of the natural scientists' consciousness. While there is a relatively high degree of consensus among scientists as to their rights and responsibilities in an academic setting, their status in the industrial-military-political arena is far from having reached a state of crystallization among scientists themselves, not to speak of its legitimation in society generally.

Typically the contemporary scientist is operating at points of institutional intersections where new exigencies are created at an unprecedented pace. Thus on the top level of power and prestige a physicist may at the same time be a university professor, teaching courses in the more or less traditional manner, and doing and supervising research financed by university funds; a supervisor of research under contract arrangements between the university and an agency of the Department of Defense or an industrial firm which, in turn, may have sub-contracted its program; a researcher or consultant for a national laboratory such as Oak Ridge or Argonne, set up outside the framework of both the conventional university structure and the civil service of a federal department such as the Bureau of Standards; an owner or manager of a private firm engaged in research and production; a "private" consultant to several industrial firms; a member of the President's Scientific Advisory Board; an expert serving to screen applications and making recommendations for a variety of grants given by the National Science Foundation or a private foundation; a member of the board of directors of the American Association for the Advancement of Science and of the American Physical Society; an editor for a variety of professional journals; an author of textbooks affording royalties greater than all his other income; a writer of scientific articles for the mass media; and a teacher of a television program attracting a nationwide audience. The list of offices and titles could be easily extended, and is as long and resplendent as that of many a potentate cited in the *Almanach de Gotha* — and who today would not prefer the presidency of a professional society to an earldom?

What are the implications of such a variety of roles for the power position of the scientist? One possibility is that as the number of institutional intersections increases the degree of "leverage" available to the scientist increases concomitantly. What kinds of needs will be specified by those having such leverage at their command? Will the needs be individually or institutionally oriented, and which institutions will have priority? Consider a specific, and not at all hypothetical situation: suppose a physicist is able to negotiate a million dollar research grant from the Atomic Energy Commission for his department or institute. The desirable aspects of such funds are plain enough; but will he be able to foresee its impact on the existing balance of teaching and research on his department and the potential dangers to the "independence" of scientific investigation? The potential impact of the grant is greater than the often-expressed fears about "federal control of education," precisely because the controls are not "naked," and consequences often unanticipated.

Hence the strong possibility of an alternative effect of the increasing involvement of the scientist in a multiplicity of institutional arrangements — namely, the attenuation of his adherence to the ethos and institutions of science, an attenuation which functions as both cause and consequence of an increasingly successful co-optation by other institutions. As the scientist's "role set"[14] proliferates, whatever chance of common action among scientists may have existed is dispelled by the splintering of professional loyalties and responsibilities[15] — a contemporary version of what Benda called "the betrayal of the intellectuals." Benda was aware that the "true intellectual", whose values are not contaminated by the "realistic" needs of ordinary men, cannot exist in any society, except as an isolated case. But who can gainsay his prophecy that "the logical end of this realism is the organized slaughter of nations and classes" (8, pp. 154–162)?

The nefarious effect of totalitarian social systems on science has been delineated with considerable thoroughness (albeit not without important biases). Our present concern is with the paradoxical alternative possibility that in a democratic society the increased power of scientists in terms of their market position (i.e., demand for their services) may undermine the freedom of movement of the "scientific establishment." (An analogy with the history of organized labor in the United States may not be too far-fetched here.) By way of further illustration let us list a number of instances where freedom of movement is increasingly curtailed — instances which are particularly relevant to the scientist working in a university setting, where the degree of autonomy presumably is higher than in industrial or governmental employment:

1. Increasing dependence on large-scale government financing of university research, which may be dependent upon policy decisions regarding the priority to be given to certain weapons systems. Not only does

14 For discussion of this concept relevant to the present context see Merton (27, pp. 368–384).
15 For empirical data on the existence of role conflicts in specified organizational settings, see for example Evan (14).

this put emphasis on "applied" research, but scientists may be required to drop whatever they have been working on and shift to another line of inquiry.

2. Increased growth in the area of research *administration*, which tends to siphon off many able scientists whose *political* skills are then no longer available to support the interests of their former peers.

3. The prevalence of expensive machinery, which tends to inhibit gambling on experiments with a low probability of "pay-off" (38).

4. The creation of a "scientific proletariat" — researchers who are hired to meet the requirements of a specific grant, but do not become full-fledged members of the faculty and thus do not add anything to its political power vis-à-vis the administration (21, pp. 152–154).

5. Increasing specialization, which intensifies the difficulty of communication among scientists and thus tends to reduce the possibility of concerted political action.

What of the counter-forces which are available to maintain the relative autonomy of the scientific institution? There have been several recent instances of their mobilization. Thus a number of universities, including Harvard and Yale, refused to participate in the National Defense Education Act because of the "disclaimer affidavit" requiring recipients of loans or grants to swear that they do not believe in or belong to any organization that teaches the illegal overthrow of the government. Protests by scientists and organizations such as the American Association of University Professors, coupled with non-participation by universities, resulted in substantial modification if not complete repeal of the undesirable provisions by Congress.[16]

The amount of federal support for research accorded to different universities varies tremendously; during 1958–59, for example, Yale derived 16 per cent of its total income from federal support, and M.I.T. 58 per cent.[17] In the absence of systematically gathered data the hypothesis is plausible that institutions without federal tie-ins and with a sufficiently large private endowment or other sources of support are in a better position to maintain autonomy in research by their staff, and in the decisions affecting the training of their students. But does this necessarily mean that these "autonomous" universities are in a better position to influence decisions made on a political level? What are their channels of influence? Independence from governmental funds may leave freedom of action within the university, but it eliminates one possible channel of reciprocal interaction between the university and government.

The most logical device for exercising political pressures are the pro-

---

[16] For a detailed discussion of the protest against the disclaimer affidavit and its subsequent modification see (1, 2.).

[17] The data cited are taken from Hubbert (20). The author expresses strong misgivings about the effects of federally-supported research. The fact that even the definition of what constitutes "support" is highly problematical is indicated by the arguments and data adduced by DuBridge in challenging Hubbert, and by the latter's defense. See DuBridge (12).

fessional societies, but the heterogeneity of their membership and the lack of consensus regarding specific political action has kept their power position in a rather weak state, especially compared with that of the American Medical Association or the American Bar Association. There remains the possibility of a scientific organization devoted explicitly to political action, such as the Federation of American Scientists. It remains to be seen whether their kind of program will attract enough scientists to impose sanctions great enough to influence the power of the purse wielded by government and industry.

Granted that the ideal type of scientific establishment has never in fact existed, the choices facing scientists today require that we ask questions relevant to fundamental changes from a "traditional" to a "contemporary" stage in the development of the institution. Such an analysis has barely begun.[18] Social science has been indebted to natural science for over a century; it is to be hoped that some of the debt can be repaid so as to afford the natural scientist better insight into his social entanglements.

## BIBLIOGRAPHY

1. American Association of University Professors. "Repealing the Disclaimer Affidavit," *Bulletin of the AAUP*, Vol. 46, No. 1 (1960), pp. 55–61.

2. American Association of University Professors. "The Disclaimer Affidavit: A Valedictory," *Bulletin of the AAUP*, Vol. 48, No. 4 (1962), pp. 324–331.

3. American Behavioral Scientist. "Science, Scientists and Society," (December 1962).

4. American Association for the Advancement of Science, Committee on Human Welfare. Report, *Science*, Vol. 132 (1960), pp. 68–73.

5. Anthony, Robert A. *Management Control in Industrial Research Organizations*. Cambridge: Harvard Graduate School of Business Administration, 1952.

6. Barber, Bernard. "Sociology of Science," *Current Sociology*, UNESCO, Vol. 5, No. 2 (1956).

7. Barber, Bernard, and Walter Hirsch. *The Sociology of Science*. New York: The Free Press of Glencoe, 1962.

8. Benda, Julian. *The Betrayal of the Intellectuals*. Boston: Beacon Press, 1955.

9. Bierstedt, Robert. "An Analysis of Social Power," *American Sociological Review*, Vol. 15 (1950), pp. 730–738.

10. Dernburg, Thomas, and Norman Gherrity. "A Statistical Analysis of Patent Renewal Data for Three Countries," *The Patent, Trademark and Copyright Journal of Research and Education*, Vol. 5 (1961), pp. 340–361.

18 For a representative sample of the extant literature, see Barber and Hirsch (7); American Behavioral Scientist (3).

11. Draper, Charles S. "The Patent System From a Scientist's Point of View," *The Patent, Trademark and Copyright Journal of Research and Education*, Vol. 5 (1961), p. 72.

12. DuBridge, Lee S. "Letter," *Science*, Vol. 140 (1963), p. 573.

13. Dupré, J. Stefan, and S. A. Lakoff. *Science and the Nation.* Englewood Cliffs, N.J.: Prentice-Hall, Inc., 1962.

14. Evan, William M. "Role Strain and the Norms of Reciprocity in Research Organizations," *American Journal of Sociology*, Vol. 68 (1962), pp. 346–354.

15. Fisher, J. C. "Basic Research in Industry," *Science*, Vol. 139 (1950), pp. 1653–1657.

16. Furash, Edward E. "Industrial Espionage," *Harvard Business Review*, Vol. 37, No. 6 (1959), pp. 7 ff.

17. Gilpin, Robert. *American Scientists and Nuclear Weapons Policy.* Princeton, N.J.: Princeton University Press, 1962.

18. Hewlett, Richard G., and Oscar E. Anderson, Jr. *The New World, 1939–1946.* Philadelphia: University of Pennsylvania Press, 1962.

19. Hirsch, Walter. "The Autonomy of Science in Totalitarian Societies," *Social Forces*, Vol. 40 (1961), pp. 15–22.

20. Hubbert, M. King. "Are We Retrogressing in Science?" *Science*, Vol. 139 (1963), p. 887.

21. Kidd, Charles V. *American Universities and Federal Research.* Cambridge, Mass.: Belknap Press, 1959.

22. Kidd, Charles V. "Basic Research Description vs. Definition," *Science*, Vol. 129 (1959), pp. 368–371.

23. Klein, Herbert D. "The Technical Trade Secret Quadrangle," *Northwestern University Law Review*, Vol. 55 (1960), pp. 437–467.

24. Kornhauser, William. *Scientists in Industry.* Berkeley: University of California Press, 1962.

25. Lasswell, Harold D. *Power and Personality.* New York: W. W. Norton, 1948.

26. Machlup, Fritz. "Patents and Inventive Effort," *Science*, Vol. 133 (1961), pp. 1463–1466.

27. Merton, Robert K. *Social Theory and Social Structure.* Glencoe, Ill.: The Free Press, 1957.

28. Merton, Robert K. "Priorities in Scientific Discovery," *American Sociological Review*, Vol. 22 (1957), pp. 635–659.

29. National Science Foundation. *Funds for Research and Development in Industry.* Washington, D.C.: 1961.

30. National Science Foundation. *Publication of Basic Research Findings in Industry.* Washington, D.C.: 1961.

31. Opinion Research Corporation. *The Scientific Mind and the Management Mind.* Princeton, N.J.: 1959.

32. Oppenheimer, Robert J. "Physics in the Contemporary World," *Bulletin of the Atomic Scientists*, Vol. 4 (1948), pp. 69–72.

33. Orlans, Harold. *The Effects of Federal Programs on Higher Education.* Washington, D.C.: Brookings Institution, 1962.

34. Orowan, Egon. "Our Universities and Scientific Creativity," *Bulletin of the Atomic Scientists*, Vol. 15 (1959), pp. 237–238.

35. Piel, Gerald. *Science in the Cause of Man.* New York: Alfred Knopf, 1961.

36. Price, Don K. "The Scientific Establishment," *Science*, Vol. 136 (1962), pp. 1099–1106.

37. Sayre, Wallace S. "Scientists and American Science Policy," *Science*, Vol. 133 (1961), pp. 859–863.

38. Schwartz, Melvin. "The Conflict Between Productivity and Creativity in Modern Day Physics," *American Behavioral Scientist*, Vol. 6, No. 4 (1962), pp. 35–36.

39. Selznick, Philip. "Foundations of the Theory of Organization," *American Sociological Review*, Vol. 13 (1948), pp. 25–35.

40. Shepard, Herbert A. "Nine Dilemmas in Industrial Research," *Administrative Science Quarterly*, Vol. 1 (1956), pp. 295–309.

41. Shils, Edward A. *The Torment of Secrecy.* Glencoe, Ill.: Free Press, 1956.

42. Shils, Edward A. "Freedom and Influence: Observations on the Scientists' Movement," *Bulletin of the Atomic Scientists*, Vol. 13 (1957), pp. 13–18.

43. Smith, Alice Kimball. "Behind the Decision to Use the Atom Bomb," *Bulletin of the Atomic Scientists*, Vol. 14 (1958), pp. 288–312.

44. Snow, Charles P. *Science and Politics.* Cambridge: Harvard University Press, 1961.

45. Stein, Morris I. "Creativity and the Scientist," in Bernard Barber and Walter Hirsch (eds.), *The Sociology of Science.* New York: The Free Press, 1962.

46. Veblen, Thorstein. "The Engineers and the Price System," in Wesley Mitchell (ed.), *What Veblen Taught.* New York: Viking Press, 1936.

47. Walton, Richard E. *The Impact of the Professional Engineering Union.* Boston: Harvard University Graduate School of Business Administration, 1961.

48. West, S. Stewart. "The Ideology of American Scientists," *IRE Transactions of Engineering Management* (June 1960), pp. 54–62.

49. Wolfle, Dael (ed.), *Symposium on Basic Research.* Washington, D.C.: American Association for the Advancement of Science, 1959.

50. White, Leslie A. *The Science of Culture.* New York: Grove Press, 1949.

*Walter Hirsch*

Knowledge, Power and Social Change:

The Role of American Scientists

# Post-Script 1975

Those who have the temerity to predict the direction of major social trends leave themselves open to the chance of being brutally upended by history, unless, like professional oracles, they enshroud their prophecies in the veil of ambiguity. In the present chapter, we attempted to show the general direction of forces affecting the role of American scientists. Now, with superior hindsight we can evaluate the validity of the analysis and take account of the impact of major events and developments which occurred since the original account was written.

### Extrinsic and intrinsic factors

A convenient way of discussing the present state of scientific institutions is to distinguish between extrinsic and intrinsic aspects — though it is clear that in many respects there is some degree of interaction between the two. Among the factors which appear to be relatively independent of the actions of scientists were the escalation of the war in Viet Nam and the consequent economic and moral repercussions. Another important event is the preoccupation with environmental pollution, exhaustion of natural resources and related problems, such as the high rate of population increase. It is in this area that scientists are accorded high expertise and feel free to provide "inputs."[1]

[1] For a useful bibliography, see (15).

Another prominent trend which seems to have reached its zenith in 1971 is the counter-culture movement, which found its most massive support among the young and the intellectuals.[2] The aspect most relevant for the present discussion is the disenchantment with rationalism in general, and the neo-Luddite attack on science and technology.[3] However, the major thrust of the attack is directed not against the pursuit of knowledge and its applications, but against it misuse by the "power structure."

Finally, the series of events with the most direct impact on the scientific community involves the cut-back in federal spending in the military and space projects, and the contraction of federal funds for education in science and medical training. This has been offset to some degree by new programs in other areas, for example, cancer research, environmental protection, urban renewal, and most recently, energy, but this does not help the thousands of well-trained and established scientists and engineers who suddenly found themselves literally without work in many cases and for most, without the kind of work for which they had been trained. The unprecedented exponential growth of support for scientific research and development, which was a prominent feature of the post-World War II period has now reached a lower level, one which may be considered "normal." From the projections made by Derek Price and others (21) it has been obvious for some time that there had to be some upper limit to the Malthusian pattern of growth, but the nature of the "natural checks" was left largely unspecified. The great majority of scientists were either promoting, or at least content with the notion of a perennially open frontier. One immediate reaction was an admission of guilt: we erred in trying to attract more students into the discipline when we should have known that there was no market for their services by the time they had come through the academic mill with their degrees. Others maintain that there should be no panic in the face of every kink in the growth curve and that there is no top limit in the long run for the need for more practitioners in either basic or pure research.

Along with the quantitative changes there has been a shift of emphasis from support of basic to applied, or "mission-oriented" research. Even the National Science Foundation, which was created in 1950 for the furthering of basic research, has been enlisted in the pursuit of some tangible and immediate pay-off, and the potential recipients of funds have made the necessary adjustments. Thus, even the high energy physicists found it necessary to justify the expenditure of vast sums of public funds on their hardware by showing that in the long run there may be a practical use for the penetration of the secrets of sub-atomic

[2] Perhaps the outstanding *ideological* statement is (22). See also Poppendieck's chapter in this section.

[3] For representative work, see (6; 17).

structure (10, 16, 26). There is no dearth of evidence to document the fact that in many instances the economic tail is wagging the research dog. For example: a survey of a presumably representative sample of sociologists in 1965 revealed that 29 percent considered mental health their professional specialty (18) — a result probably not unrelated to the fact that the National Institute of Mental Health had vast sums available for sociological research, and that the survey was undertaken by NIMH. Such data tend to document the charge by critics that scientists are consciously or unconsciously serving as handmaidens of Mammon. Leaving aside the questions of the ethics involved and whether scientists are or should be different from other professions in this respect, we want to make it plain that the evidence is not sufficient for a vulgar-Marxist conclusion. Instead, some studies indicate at least a modicum of independence from readily available fundings (1; 13). In this connection it should also be mentioned that industrial concerns and other non-academic organizations, including the so-called non-profit "think tanks" have discovered that there is money in morally desirable concerns such as poverty, pollution control, urban renewal and so on (5).

Paradoxically, there is increasing concern both within the "establishment" and among those participants of the counter-culture who are not content with "dropping out" or abjuring the use of science and technology *in toto* for more immediate results of research. One element's "mission orientation" is the other element's "relevance." A related emphasis is the revival of the demand for prediction as a prerequisite for rational control. In its contemporary version this involves a broad spectrum ranging from futurology as a quasi-cult, to specific methodologies involving "systems" analysis; most of them depend heavily on the use of computers to handle large masses of data (2; 28). These enterprises also tend to be coupled with the practice, or at least the profession, of interdisciplinary cooperation, particularly, a call for the greater involvement of social scientists and humanists in the common enterprise. This neo-Comtean stance of the natural scientists and engineers could in theory enhance the status and power of the social scientists, but the latter are often heard to complain that even with the best of intentions it is difficult to arrive at a common universe of discourse.

### Politicalization

The demand for greater social responsibility of scientists, involving both increased activism in the political arena and "relatedness" of research is one of the chief characteristics of the radical left in academic institutions and the professional organizations. The notion of "value free" science is increasingly coming under attack; it does not lack its vigorous defenders, though it seems that their number is decreasing. To the extent that the general population is concerned with these matters it will also tend to support the demands for immediate pay-off, since the concept of "pure science" as an end-in-itself has hardly been a meaningful value for the silent majority. The phenotypical, if not genotypical, agreement among the three camps is a fascinating phenomenon worthy of further investigation; we shall be content with simply noting it and discussing some of its consequences.

### Reactions to extrinsic factors

We have already touched upon some of the ways in which various elements of the scientific community were affected by and responded to trends and events coming largely from outside the social system of science. What are some of the other ways in which they have reacted?

In the main, unemployed scientists and engineers have resorted to individualistic rather than collective solutions of their economic plight. Typically, they draw unemployment insurance and look for new jobs, with their aspirations declining as their savings are eaten up. The professional societies are slowly beginning to take concerted action for alleviating the misfortune of their colleagues and to try and exercise some control of the market for the next few years.[4] Attempts at unionization are being renewed, but it is doubtful whether they will be more successful than they have been in the past (15; 23; 24). Some university graduate departments are cutting down on new enrollments, but there is no general call for a reduction of scientists and engineers. In the first place, there is no consensus in the predictions about the demands of the market five or ten years from now (29; 30). Further, as mentioned earlier, the argument is made that one should not be panicked by the short run, extrinsic effects, but keep in mind the vision of science as the "endless frontier" which invites, and indeed demands, an unlimited supply of pioneers, followed by colonizers. Advocates of this point of view will, however, concede the need for the re-ordering of priorities within disciplines, or between pure and applied research. Some argue from a position based on intrinsic elements for example, that most of the secrets of the physical universe have been unlocked, that the exciting research has been mined out, and that the real frontiers lie in the area of applying this knowledge to the benefit of mankind. (Again a case of phenotypical congruence) (7; 27). It is of interest that these arguments come from some of the elder statesmen of science who are relatively immune from the vagaries of financial support to which their less eminent colleagues are exposed.

---

[4] The last two presidents of the American Chemical Society — generally considered among the most conservative scientific groups — were elected on a reform platform pledging remodeling of the society along "professional" lines. In practice this entails attempts to find jobs for unemployed chemists and a general amelioration of their economic position.

### Prestige and Power

How have the events and trends discussed above affected the prestige and power of American scientists and engineers? Have the successful expeditions to the moon offset their controversial role as both hand-maidens and critics of the military in the pursuit of a war which had become less and less popular? According to one poll, the percentage of respondents who "had faith in the scientific community," dropped from 56 in 1967 to 32 in 1972, though a similar evaporation occurred in the case of banks, business, the military and other institutions (12). Less than a decade ago it was asserted that "because of their relative newness in the higher government councils [scientists'] reputation is less tarnished by special pleading and self-serving" (3). At this point it would be very difficult to make a case for the moral superiority of scientists. In fact, the most vehement attacks on the ethics of current research comes from within their own ranks, that is, the radical left, but there is a large literature by outside observers documenting the fact that scientists have learned a great deal about the game of politics (9).

Less visible but perhaps more important is the fact that often there is so little consensus among the experts concerning the mere scientific "facts," and *a fortiori*, the policy-related advice given. The controversies about the cost/efficiency of pesticides, various types of detergents, or the best means for educating the culturally deprived are examples of a climate which tends to undermine the credibility of scientists. Political leaders still routinely invoke the need for scientific input, but one gets the impression that this may mean as little as asking for divine blessing at the beginning of each session of the Congress.

"It is becoming increasingly clear that scientists, like many other interest groups in Washington, sometimes win, and they sometimes lose; but unlike the others, they have a kept interest that has little to rely upon but the goodwill of the political community when vital matters are at stake." The same observer goes on to ask, "is public policy about to become the 'captive' of a scientific technological elite? The theory is intriguing, but the candidates for their role are too preoccupied with their work to fulfill the prophecy." (8) A more realistic appraisal would indicate that as scientists increasingly enter the arena of public policy, activism and "relatedness" of research, they become more aware of the problems and implications involved.[5] Ironically, as the scientists are gaining more insight, their position at the center of political power is rapidly deflating: Nixon has abolished the position of the President's Science Advisor, which in fact had steadily lost influence for several years, along with the committee which he headed (PSAC) and the Office of Science and Technology. Scientists no longer have the privileged position which

---

[5] For a good example, see (19), and for a more general treatment (4; 11).

they enjoyed starting with World War II and which continued with the Cold War, and the need for their cooperation by the executive branch is no longer apparent. It seems likely that only a state of panic such as that engendered by the launching of the Soviet sputnik will give them back their former glory. As this is being written, "science policy in the White House will now be made not by top-ranking scientists but by young Republican lawyers." (25).

In its relatively short history, science has been faced before with disillusionment brought about by the assumption of the omniscience, if not omnipotence of its practitioners. Perhaps it is not unreasonable to hope that, if history has anything at all to teach, scientists will be among the beneficiaries of her lessons.

## BIBLIOGRAPHY

1. Biderman, Albert D., and Elizabeth T. Crawford, "Paper Money: Trends of Research Sponsorship in American Sociological Journals," in *Social Sciences Information*, Vol. 9, No. 1 (197), pp. 51–77.

2. Boguslaw, Robert. *The New Utopians*, Englewood Cliffs, N.J.: Prentice-Hall, 1965.

3. Brooks, Harvey. "The Scientific Advisor," in Robert Gilpin and C. Wright, (eds.), *Scientists and National Policy*. New York: Columbia University Press, 1964, pp. 73–96.

4. Brooks, Harvey. "Can Science Survive the Modern Age?" *Science*, vol. 174 (1971), pp. 21–30.

5. Dickson, Paul. *Think Tanks*. New York: Atheneum, 1971.

6. Ellul, Jacques. *The Technological Society*. New York: Vintage Books, 1967.

7. Glass, Bentley. "Science: Endless Horizons or Golden Age," *Science*, vol. 171 (1971), pp. 23–29.

8. Greenberg, Daniel S. "The Myth of the Scientific Elite," *Public Interest*, No. 1 (1965), pp. 51–62.

9. Greenberg, Daniel S. *The Politics of Pure Science*. New York: The New American Library, 1967.

10. Greenberg, Daniel S. "Basic Research: The Political Tides are Shifting," *Science*, Vol. 152 (1966), pp. 1724–26.

11. Hirsch, Walter. *Scientists in American Society*. New York: Random House, 1968, Chapter 5.

12. Hooper, Bayard. "Can We Believe What the Young Tell Us?" *Social Education*, Vol. 36 (1972), pp. 265–70.

13. McCartney, James L. "The Financing of Sociological Research" in Edward A. Tyrakian (ed.), *The Phenomenon of Sociology*. New York: Appleton-Century-Crofts, 1971, pp. 384–97.

14. Menard, Henry W. *Science: Growth and Change*. Cambridge, Mass.: Harvard University Press, 1971.

15. Moore, John A. *Science for Society*. Washington, D.C.: A.A.A.S. Commission on Science Education, Revised Ed., 1971.

16. Mosley, Ann. "Change in Argonne National Laboratories: A Case Study," *Science*, Vol. 173 (1971), pp. 30–38.

17. Mumford, Lewis. *The Myth of the Machine*. New York: Harcourt, Brace, 1966.

18. National Institutes of Mental Health, Division of Manpower and Training Programs, *Sociologists and Anthropologists: Supply and Demand in Educational Institutions and their Settings*, 1969.

19. "The Obligations of Scientists as Counsellors," *Minerva*, Vol. 10 (1972), pp. 107–57.

20. Perl, Martin L. "The Scientific Advisory System: Some Observations." *Science*, Vol. 173 (1971), pp. 1211–16.

21. Price, Derek de Solla. *Science Since Babylon*. New Haven: Yale University Press, 1961.

22. Reich, Charles. *The Greening of America*. New York: Random House, 1970.

23. Shapley, Deborah. "Unionization: Scientists, Engineers Mull Over One Alternative," *Science*, Vol. 176 (1972), pp. 618–21.

24. Shapley, Deborah. "Professional Societies: Identity Crisis Threatens on Bread and Butter Issues." *Science*, Vol. 176 (1972), pp. 777–79.

25. Shapley, Deborah. "Science in Government: Outline of New Team Emerges." *Science*, Vol. 179 (1973), p. 455.

26. Spinrad, B. I. Letter to *Science*, Vol. 176 (1972), p. 7.

27. Stent, Gunther S. *The Coming of the Golden Age*. Garden City, New York: Natural History Press, 1969.

28. Toffler, Alvin (ed.). *The Futurists*. New York: Random House, 1972.

29. Ted R. Vaughan and Sjoberg Gideon. "The Politics of Projection: A Critique of Cartter's Analysis." *Science*, Vol. 177 (1972), pp. 142–147.

30. Wolfe, Dael and Charles V. Kidd. "The Future Market for Ph.D.'s. *Science*, Vol. 173 (1971), pp. 784–793.

# Contributors

*J. A. Banks and Olive Banks* are Professors of Sociology at the University of Leicester, England.

*Homer G. Barnett* is Professor Emeritus of Anthropology at the University of Oregon.

*James M. Beshers* is Professor of Sociology at Queens College, City University of New York, and at the Graduate School of the City University of New York.

*Alvin Boskoff* is Professor of Sociology at Emory University.

*Kenneth E. Boulding* is Professor of Economics at the University of Colorado.

*Robert J. Brym* is a Ph.D. Candidate in Sociology at the University of Toronto.

*Erik Cohen* is a Senior Lecturer in the Department of Sociology and Anthropology at the Hebrew University in Jerusalem, Israel.

*Ronald Cohen* is Professor of Anthropology and Political Science at Northwestern University.

*Richard Colvard* is a Professor in the Department of Sociology and Anthropology at Southern Oregon State College.

*James Dow* is Assistant Professor of Anthropology at Oakland University, Michigan.

*William M. Evan* is Professor of Sociology and Management at the Wharton School at the University of Pennsylvania.

*Walter Friedman* is Assistant Professor of Sociology at Spring Hill College, Alabama.

*Harry Gold* is Associate Professor of Sociology at Oakland University, Michigan.

*Walter Hirsch* is Professor of Sociology at Purdue University.

*Bert F. Hoselitz* is Professor of Economics and Social Science at the University of Chicago and Editor of *Economic Development and Cultural Change*.

*David Kirk* is Professor of Sociology at the University of Waterloo, Canada.

*Jeanette C. Lauer* is a Ph.D. Candidate in History at Washington University in St. Louis and Instructor of American History at Florissant Valley Community College, Missouri.

*Robert H. Lauer* is Associate Professor and Chairman of the Department of Social Science at Southern Illinois University at Edwardsville.

*Daniel J. Levinson* is Professor of Psychology in the Department of Psychiatry at Yale University School of Medicine.

*David Lockwood* is Professor of Sociology at the University of Essex in Wevenhoe Park, Essex, England and is a member of the British Social Science Research Council.

*Philip Marcus* is Professor of Sociology at Michigan State University.

*Don Martindale* is Professor of Sociology at the University of Minnesota.

*T. Dunbar Moodie* is Professor of Sociology at the University of Witwatersrand, South Africa.

*Michael Overington* is Assistant Professor of Sociology at St. Mary's University in Halifax, Nova Scotia.

*Janet Poppendieck* is a doctoral candidate at the Florence Heller Graduate School for Advanced Studies in Social Welfare at Brandeis University and is Coordinator of the National School Breakfast Campaign of the Food Research and Action Center, Inc., New York.

*Louis Schneider* is Professor of Sociology at the University of Texas.

*Pitirim A. Sorokin,* 1889-1968, was one of the major sociologists of our times.

*Irving Sosensky* is Professor of Philosophy at Purdue University.

*Leon Warshay* is Associate Professor of Sociology at Wayne State University.

*C. P. Wolf* is Senior Sociologist at the Institute for Water Resources, U.S. Army Corps of Engineers and is Co-Director of Earthrise, a non-profit corporation for future research, education, and design.

*Benjamin Zablocki* is Associate Professor of Sociology at Columbia University.

*George K. Zollschan* is Adjunct Associate Professor of Sociology at the State University of New York at Stony Brook.

# INDEX